Land Law:
Cases and Materials

Land Law:

Cases and Materials

by R. H. Maudsley

LL.D., B.C.L., M.A., Hon. LL.D. (U.S.D.), S.J.D.
of Lincoln's Inn, Barrister;
Professor of Law, University of San Diego Law School
and New York Law School
sometime Fellow and Law Tutor, Brasenose College, Oxford, and
Professor of Law in the University of London

and E. H. Burn

B.C.L., M.A.
Honorary Bencher of Lincoln's Inn;
Student and Tutor in Jurisprudence of Christ Church, Oxford;
Lecturer in the Law of Land in the Inns of Court

Fourth Edition

London
Butterworths
1980

England   Butterworth & Co (Publishers) Ltd
            88 Kingsway, LONDON WC2B 6AB

Australia   Butterworths Pty Ltd, SYDNEY, MELBOURNE, BRISBANE, ADELAIDE
            and PERTH

Canada   Butterworth & Co Ltd, TORONTO
            Butterworth & Co (Western Canada) Ltd, VANCOUVER

New Zealand Butterworths of New Zealand Ltd, WELLINGTON

Singapore   Butterworth & Co (Asia) Pte Ltd, SINGAPORE

South Africa Butterworth Publishers (Pty) Ltd, DURBAN

USA   Mason Publishing Co, ST PAUL, Minnesota
            Butterworth Legal Publishing, SEATTLE, Washington; BOSTON,
            Massachusetts; and AUSTIN, Texas
            D & S Publishers, CLEARWATER, Florida

ISBN Hardcover   0 406 62306 6
     Softcover   0 406 62307 4

Reprinted 1982
Reprinted 1983

Printed in Great Britain by
Thomson Litho Ltd., East Kilbride, Scotland.

Preface

Our object remains the same as it has been in the three previous editions: to provide the most important readings which cannot, in the nature of things, be included in text-books. The wealth of material available makes the decision as to inclusion and exclusion all the more difficult as the years go by. But the increasing complexity of the subject makes it all the more important for the student to have original material readily available. We have attempted to give a treatment to the chosen topics which is thorough enough to provide a serious student with an opportunity to learn the subject by studying what the statutes and the judges and selected writers have said. A superficial collection of snippets and dicta could cover a wider field in less space. We have tried to provide the minimum material necessary for a proper understanding of the subject. We have attempted to take advantage of various constructive suggestions made by critics of the previous editions; but managed to resist the temptation offered by one reviewer, to start again and write a different book. This edition, to our relief, and somewhat to our surprise, turned out to be two pages shorter than its predecessor.

The basic organisation remains as before. We have attempted to emphasize the matters which are of practical importance; and have continued the policy of the previous edition of dealing with registered and unregistered land side by side throughout the book, and of emphasizing the trust for sale at the expense of the strict settlement. We regret once again that it has proved impossible to provide space to deal with the Rent Acts, Agricultural Acts, and Landlord and Tenant Acts. We have on this occasion gathered together all the registration provisions and put them into Chapter 1; that is to say the Land Charges Act, the Local Land Charges Act, the Companies Act, the Agricultural Credits Act, and the Commons Registration Act. It was thought that it would be more helpful to have these provisions all in one place.

The chapters on Licences and Perpetuities have largely been rewritten; the former to comply, as best we can, with the pace of change in that field; and the latter to present the subject more in accordance with the views of one of the authors as expressed in The Modern Law of Perpetuities. Much new material on land registration needed to be included; much of this is controversial, and we have not been able to wait for the decision of the House of Lords in *Williams and Glyn's Bank Ltd v Boland.* Recent changes in matrimonial property law, particularly in the context of section 30 of the Law of Property Act 1925, have been included in Chapter 4. Chapter 3, on Limitation of Actions, required basic changes in the light of recent decisions; and includes the Limitation Amendment Act 1980.

Another hazard is that of brand new doctrine being laid down by the Court of Appeal while we are checking the page proofs. *Federated Homes Ltd v Mill Lodge Properties Ltd* [1980] 1 WLR 594, [1980] 1 All ER 371 has changed long-accepted doctrine relating to the methods of annexation of the benefit of a restrictive covenant to the land of the covenantee. It lays down the section 78 (1) of the Law of Property Act 1925 has the effect of making each covenant be taken with the covenantee and his successors in title (which includes the owners and occupiers for the time being) and the persons deriving title under him or them, and that this language is effective to annex to the covenantee's land all covenants which touch and concern the land. Thanks to super-human work by the printers and publishers, we were able to include the case at this stage, and to refer, in various places in the book, to some of its ramifications. The full effect of the decision may take some time to become clear. We ask readers to appreciate that we have been able only to deal with the case within the confines of a set of page proofs. We thought, however, that it was too important to overlook, even at this late stage.

We are grateful to the many friends who have given help and advice in connection with the preparation of this edition, especially Keith Davis, Esquire, Reader in Law in the University of Reading, who, as in the two previous editions, prepared the material on Planning Law; to the authors and publishers of material which we have been permitted to reproduce; to Marian Forney, research assistant at the University of San Diego, California, who gave much expert help in the proof reading; and finally to the staff of Butterworths for undertaking the compilation of the Tables and Statutes and for ready and expert help at all times.

1 April 1980
University of San Diego   R.H.M.
Christ Church, Oxford   E.H.B.

Contents

Table of Statutes

References in this Table to *'Stats'* are to Halsbury's Statutes of England (Third Edition) showing the volume and page at which the annotated text of the Act will be found. Page references printed in bold type indicate where the Act is set out in part or in full.

Table of Statutory Instruments

Page references printed in bold type indicate where a Statutory Instrument is set out in part or in full.

Table of Cases

In the following Table references are given to the English and Empire Digest showing where the case appears in that work. Cases which are set out in this work are indicated by page numbers in bold type.

PAGE

PAGE

PAGE

PAGE

C

PAGE

PAGE

E

PAGE

F

G

PAGE

H

PAGE

PAGE

I

PAGE

PAGE

O

P

PAGE

T

PAGE

U

V

PAGE

W

PAGE

PAGE

List of Abbreviations

Statutes and Rules

A.E.A.	Administration of Estates Act
A.J.A.	Administration of Justice Act
C.P.A.	Compulsory Purchase Act
F.A.	Finance Act
L.C.A.	Land Charges Act
L.L.C.A.	Local Land Charges Act
L.P.A.	Law of Property Act
L.P.(A.)A.	Law of Property (Amendment) Act
L.R.A.	Land Registration Act
L.R.R.	Land Registration Rules
P. & A.A.	Perpetuities & Accumulations Act
S.L.A.	Settled Land Act
T.A.	Trustee Act
T.C.P.A.	Town and Country Planning Act

Journals

Aust LJ	Australian Law Journal
CLJ	Cambridge Law Journal
CLP	Current Legal Problems
Conv	Conveyancer
Conv (NS)	Conveyancer (New Series)
Cornell LQ	Cornell Law Quarterly
HLR	Harvard Law Review
JPL	Journal of Planning and Environment Law
LGR	Local Government Reports
LJ News.	Law Journal Newspaper
LQR	Law Quarterly Review
LT	Law Times
Mich LR	Michigan Law Review
MLR	Modern Law Review
New LJ	New Law Journal
Sol Jo	Solicitor's Journal
U of WALR	University of Western Australia Law Review
Yale LJ	Yale Law Journal

Books

Cheshire	Cheshire: The Modern Law of Real Property (12th edn. 1976)
Comp Enc	Encyclopaedia of the Law of Compulsory Purchase and Compensation
Dawson & Pearce	Licences Relating to the Occupation or Use of Land (1979)
Farrand	Contract and Conveyance (2nd edn. 1973)
Fisher and Lightwood	Law of Mortgage (9th edn. 1977)
Gale	Law of Easements (14th edn. 1972)
H & M	Hanbury and Maudsley: Modern Equity (10th edn. 1976)
Heap	An Outline of Planning Law (7th edn. 1978)
Holdsworth	A History of English Law
Jackson	Law of Easements and Profits
Maudsley	Modern Law of Perpetuities (1979)
M & B (T)	Maudsley and Burn: Trusts and Trustees: Cases and Materials (2nd edn. 1978)
M & W	Megarry and Wade: The Law of Real Property (4th edn. 1975)
MM	Megarry: A Manual of the Law of Real Property (4th edn. 1969)

Morris & Leach	The Rule Against Perpetuities (2nd edn. 1962)
Pl Enc	Encyclopaedia of the Law of Town and Country Planning
Preston & Newsom	Restrictive Covenants Affecting Freehold Land (6th edn. 1976)
Ruoff	Concise Land Registration Practice (2nd edn. 1967)
Ruoff & Roper	The Law and Practice of Registered Conveyancing (4th edn. 1972)
Snell	Principles of Equity (27th edn. 1973)
Waldock	The Law of Mortgages (2nd edn. 1950)
W & C	Wolstenholme and Cherry: Conveyancing Statutes (13th edn. 1972)

Part One. Basic Concepts

1. Introductory Topics

I. Estates and Interests in Land

A. Introduction

i. FREEHOLD AND LEASEHOLD ESTATES

The theory of the common law is that all land is held of the King who is the supreme feudal lord. Subjects may hold directly of the King or of other subjects superior to themselves. Those who hold directly of the King are tenants in chief. Intermediate holders between the King and the tenants in actual possession are mesne lords.

A holder of land is entitled to a number of legal rights in respect of his landholding, and these legal rights are "crystallised into one thing[1]". This is the tenant's "estate". To ascertain his rights, it is necessary to decide what estate he owns and to know what rights and duties the law attaches to that type of estate.

Freehold estates, i.e. the estates held by freehold tenure, are those which were in use in the feudal system. In medieval times that system was the basis of the social, military and economic structure of the state; and the holding of freehold land was itself the basis of social position, wealth and power. It was essential for the security of the state and of the social structure that the ownership of freehold estates should be protected; and it is not surprising that the land law was the first of the fields of private law to be undertaken by the King's Court[2].

The freehold estates are the fee simple, fee tail, life estate and estate pur autre vie. They are freehold because they were recognised by the feudal order, because persons holding such estates in possession were recognised as standing upon a rung in the feudal ladder, because the remedies available in the King's Court were available to the owner of such an estate and gave a claimant specific recovery. Such estates are "real property" or "realty", and are contrasted with the term of years, a leasehold estate, whose owners were never on the feudal ladder; they could not protect themselves by the same actions as the freeholder: their estate as personal property, or "personalty", passed on intestacy with chattels. A convenient way of distinguishing between freeholds and leaseholds is to note that freeholds are always of indefinite duration, leaseholds for a fixed period or such as can be made certain. But this is just a label; it does not help to understand the basic gulf between the two, which was so obvious to the medieval lawyer.

Something will be said here of the freehold estates; leaseholds will be considered in a later chapter. But a further sub-division must be introduced here because of the treatment of estates by the 1925 legislation. This is the distinction between legal estates and equitable interests. Pursuant to the Legislature's insistence upon the legal estate being the basis of conveyancing with beneficial interests kept off the title, the 1925 legislation permits two estates only to exist as legal estates, one freehold and one leasehold, all other interests being capable of existing in equity only.

ii. CONVEYANCING

A knowledge of the estates and interests recognised at law and in equity is necessary to an understanding of Conveyancing; that is, the practice of creating and transferring estates and interests in land. The owner of an estate may transfer it to another, as on the sale of a house, or create a series of smaller interests out of it as on the creation of a settlement; or create other rights which are recognised at law or in

---

[1] Hargreaves, *Introduction to Land Law* (4th Edn. 1963), p. 46.
[2] Maitland, *Forms of Action at Common Law*, p. 20 et seq.

equity, but which are not estates in land, such as a licence or a restrictive covenant. Details of the practice of Conveyancing are beyond our present scope; but it is material to say here that there are two quite separate and distinctive methods of conveyancing in operation in England at the present day; that relating to unregistered land and that relating to registered land. The former is the development of techniques which reach back to medieval times. The system in essence is one whereby the estate owner proves his title to land by showing from deeds and documents in his possession that he derives his title lawfully from some person or persons who have been in peaceful possession for a long period of time. In the nature of things, the title to his estate can never be proved absolutely, for there may have been an interference with the rights of the true owner many years back. However, with the assistance of the Limitation Acts[3], proof of title during the last fifteen years is, for practical purposes, sufficient; and a purchaser is now required to trace the title back to a good root of title at least fifteen years old[4]. On completion of the purchase, the deeds are handed over to the purchaser, and he will make title in a similar manner when he decides to sell.

A much more satisfactory system of proof of title is that of registration of the title in a central registry. New countries and states commonly use such a system. The practical difficulties, however, of changing over from a system of unregistered conveyancing to one of registered conveyancing are great. The change involves the recording of all interests in land which need to be placed on the register and this is a huge undertaking. In England and Wales, a system of registration of title, introduced in 1862[5], was superseded by more comprehensive legislation in 1925[6]. It provides for registration of title following the first conveyance of land after the Act has been made applicable to the district in question; and subsequent conveyancing will be based on the title so registered. The system of registration is explained in Chapter 2.

The present decade is one of transition from unregistered to registered conveyancing, from the old to the modern. As yet, the registered system is not universally applicable, but compulsory registration of title now extends to areas comprising three quarters of the population of England and Wales. The Chief Land Registrar estimates that "currently a little over 50 per cent of all property transactions (that is, broadly, conveyances, transfers and long leases) in England and Wales relate to registered land and approximately 25 per cent lead to applications to bring the title on to the register for the first time'"[7]. It is still necessary to understand the unregistered system, and to distinguish between the doctrines applicable to the two. In the discussions which

---

[3] See p. 151, post.
[4] L.P.A. 1969, s. 23; p. 73, post.
[5] Land Registry Act 1862.
[6] L.R.A. 1925, p. 87, post.
[7] Report of Chief Land Registrar for 1978–1979, paras. 2, 3.

follow, the two systems will be compared wherever possible. There is no doubt where the emphasis of a present day student should be.

B. Legal Estates

i. THE FEE SIMPLE ABSOLUTE IN POSSESSION[8]

a. *Definition*

LAW OF PROPERTY ACT 1925

1. Legal estates and equitable interests. — (1) The only estates in land which are capable of subsisting or of being conveyed or created at law are —

   (*a*) An estate in fee simple absolute in possession;

   (*b*) A term of years absolute[9].

(2) The only interests or charges in or over land which are capable of subsisting or of being conveyed or created at law are —

   (*a*)   An easement[10], right, or privilege in or over land for an interest equivalent to an estate in fee simple absolute in possession or a term of years absolute;

   (*b*)   A rentcharge[11] in possession issuing out of or charged on land being either perpetual or for a term of years absolute;

   (*c*)   A charge by way of legal mortgage[12]; . . .

   (*d*)[13] . . . and any other similar charge on land which is not created by an instrument[14];

   (*e*)   Rights of entry exercisable over or in respect of a legal term of years absolute, or annexed, for any purpose, to a legal rent-charge.

(3) All other estates, interests, and charges in or over land take effect as equitable interests.

(4) The estates, interests, and charges which under this section are authorised to subsist or to be conveyed or created at law are (when subsisting or conveyed or created at law) in this Act referred to as "legal estates," and have the same incidents as legal estates subsisting at the commencement of this Act; and the owner of a legal estate is referred to as "an estate owner" and his legal estate is referred to as his estate.

(5) A legal estate may subsist concurrently with or subject to any other legal estate in the same land in like manner as it could have done before the commencement of this Act.

---

[8] Cheshire, pp. 148–162; M & W, pp. 52–57, 66–74, 137–140; MM, pp. 15, 21, 23, 68–72.

[9] See pp. 355 et seq., post.

[10] See pp. 502 et seq., post.

[11] See Law of Property (Entailed Interests) Act 1932, s. 2.

[12] See pp. 597 et seq., post.

[13] As amended by Finance Act 1963, s. 68, Sch. 14. Part VI, and Tithe Act 1936, s. 48, Sch. IX.

[14] E.g. tithe redemption annuity (which replaced tithe rentcharge in 1936. See M & W pp. 801–805). This was extinguished as from 2 October 1977. F.A. 1977 s. 56.

(6) A legal estate is not capable of subsisting or of being created in an undivided share in land[15] or of being held by an infant.

7. Saving of certain legal estates and statutory powers. — (1) A fee simple which, by virtue of the Lands Clauses Acts, the School Sites Acts, or any similar statute[16], is liable to be divested, is for the purposes of this Act a fee simple absolute, and remains liable to be divested as if this Act had not been passed, [and a fee simple subject to a legal or equitable right of entry or re-entry is for the purposes of this Act a fee simple absolute][17].

(2) A fee simple vested in a corporation which is liable to determine by reason of the dissolution of the corporation is, for the purposes of this Act, a fee simple absolute.

205. General Definitions. — (1) (xix) "Possession" includes receipt of rents and profits or the right to receive the same, if any.

In *District Bank Ltd v Webb* [1958] 1 WLR 148, [1958] 1 All ER 126[18] the question was whether an estoppel was raised against vendors by reason of a recital that they were "seised in unencumbered fee simple in possession upon trust for sale," when the property was subject to a lease. DANCKWERTS J held that the representation was not sufficiently unambiguous to create an estoppel; and added: "Secondly, the words 'in possession' are relied upon, but I do not think that 'in possession' means vacant possession. It seems to me that the meaning is 'fee simple in possession' as opposed to 'fee simple in reversion' and there again it seems to me impossible for the bank to rely upon such representation in the recital to cause the vendors to be bound by any estoppel."

---

[15] See pp. 218 et seq., post.

[16] Welsh Church (Burial Grounds) Act 1945, s. 1 (2). The Law Commission is examining these statutory provisions for reverter. Law Commission 13th Annual Report 1977-1978 (Law Com. No. 92, para. 2.33). See *Re Clayton's Deed Poll* [1979] 3 WLR 351, [1979] 2 All ER 1113, [1979] Conv 438 (F. R. Crane).

[17] The words in square brackets were added by L. P. (A.) A. 1926 Sch., and the intention of the Legislature appears to have been to include as legal estates certain holdings, common in the North of England, where a fee simple is purchased in return for a perpetual rentcharge upon the land. But the enactment is, in its terms, wider than this, and appears to include a grant to A in fee simple subject to a right of entry in the grantor on the happening of some event, such as, for example, A's marrying outside a certain religious persuasion. One would have expected a fee simple subject to such a condition to have been an equitable interest, and for such a grant to have created a settlement. Indeed S.L.A. 1925, s. 1 (1) (ii) *(b)* provides that a grant of a fee simple . . . subject to an executory limitation over on the happening of some event shall create a settlement; it would be strange if the distinction were to depend upon the difference between an executory gift over and the right of the grantor to re-enter and terminate for breach of condition. It is tempting to suggest that the words of the amendment are wider than the Legislature intended; how they will be construed is not known. Cheshire p. 150; M & W, pp. 137-139; MM, pp. 71-72.

[18] See also *Re Morgan* (1883) 24 ChD 114 at 166; and *Pearson v IRC* [1980] Ch 1, [1979] 3 All ER 7, which holds that, for the purposes of capital transfer tax, an interest in possession may exist even though subject to a provision for accumulation.

b. Creation[19]

LAW OF PROPERTY ACT 1925

60. Abolition of technicalities in regard to conveyances and deeds. —
(1) A conveyance of freehold land to any person without words of
limitation, or any equivalent expression, shall pass to the grantee the
fee simple or other the whole interest which the grantor had power
to convey in such land, unless a contrary intention appears in the
conveyance[20].

(2) A conveyance of freehold land to a corporation sole by his
corporate designation without the word "successors" shall pass to the
corporation the fee simple or other the whole interest which the
grantor had power to convey in such land, unless a contrary intention
appears in the conveyance.

(4) The foregoing provisions of this section apply only to conveyances and deeds executed after the commencement of this Act:

Provided that in a deed executed after the thirty-first day of
December, eighteen hundred and eighty-one[1], it is sufficient —

> (a) In the limitation of an estate in fee simple, to use the words "in
> fee simple," without the word "heirs";

205. General definitions. — (1) In this Act unless the context
otherwise requires, the following expressions have the meanings
hereby assigned to them respectively, that is to say:—

(ii) "Conveyance" includes a mortgage, charge, lease, assent,
vesting declaration, vesting instrument, disclaimer, release and every
other assurance of property or of an interest therein by any instrument, except a will. . . .

c. Alienability[2]

RE BROWN
[1954] Ch 39, [1953] 2 All ER 1342 (ChD, HARMAN J)

The testator devised freehold properties in trust for his wife for life,
and after her death, on his youngest son attaining 21, for all the sons
then living in equal shares as tenants in common. Clause 6 of the will
provided that if any son should allow his share to be vested in any
person other than one of the brothers, that share should be held on
discretionary trusts for the son and his wife and children. The question, on one son wishing to sell outside the family, was whether the
restriction upon alienation was good.

Held. No.

---

[19] Cheshire, pp. 152–154; M & W, pp. 52–57; MM, pp. 21–23.
[20] A similar rule applies to devises: Wills Act 1837, s. 28.
[1] The Conveyancing Act 1881 came into force on 1 January 1882.
[2] Cheshire, pp. 371–373; M & W, pp. 78–79; MM, pp. 31–32; (1917) 33 LQR 11 (E.
Jenks); (1917) 33 LQR 236, 342 (C. Sweet); (1954) 70 LQR 15 (R.E.M.). A life interest
may be made determinable upon the happening of various events, including
alienation. This is the basis of protective trusts; *Brandon v Robinson* (1811) 18
Ves. 429; *Rochford v Hackman* (1852) 9 Hare 475; H & M p. 218.

HARMAN J: This is a point on which it appears that the authorities give no certain guide, and the various editors of Jarman on Wills give it up, as textbook writers, therein more fortunate than judges, are entitled to do with the bland statement that the law is uncertain.

The point is a very narrow one, and it is whether a restriction on alienation appended to an absolute devise of real estate is good or no. The instinct of any equity lawyer is, to start with, to say that all restraints on absolute interests which tend to negative the rights attached to those interests are abhorred by the law and disallowed. That is a general rule cited by Jarman (8th edn., Vol. 2, p. 1477): "A power of alienation is necessarily and inseparably incidental to an estate in fee."

The view at the outset is that anything which seeks to deprive the feoffee (so to call him) of his rights is void, but there is no doubt that some degree of restriction may be put upon him . . .

As I have said, the instinct of any Chancery lawyer is to say that this is a restriction quite inconsistent with an absolute interest in real estate (or in proceeds of sale, for that matter) and that the restriction is not good. Mr. Thompson[3], however, has been able to persuade me that there is a great deal to be said for the view that a restriction of this sort may be good, if it do not amount to a total restriction. He starts with Coke upon Littleton (11th edn., Part 1, book 3, section 360), where the translation is as follows: "Also if a feoffment be made upon this condition, that the feoffee shall not alien the land to any, this condition is void because when a man is enfeoffed of lands or tenements, he hath power to alien them to any person by the law: For if such a condition should be good, then the condition should oust him of all the power which the law gives him, which should be against reason; and therefore such a condition is void." That is to say, it is repugnant to the gift. The passage following (section 361) is in these terms: "But if the condition be such that the feoffee shall not alien to such a one, naming his name, or to any of his heirs, or of the issues of such a one, etc. or the like, which conditions do not take away all power of alienation from the feoffee, etc., then such condition is good." That merely says that you may point out a certain person (or, I suppose, persons) and prohibit alienation to him or them: quaere as to how many persons may you extend that prohibition? According to two cases to which I shall refer in a moment, you may extend it to all the world except a certain class of people; but that seems to me to be a very curious way to read the doctrine of Coke, which, after all, merely says that you may exclude A or B from the world of people to whom it is permissible to alienate.

The earliest case to which I was referred is a decision of the Court of King's Bench, where the judgment was given by Lord Ellenborough CJ, *Doe* d *Gill v Pearson* ((1805) 6 East, 173). The gift in that case was of a piece of land to "my daughters . . . Ann and Hannah, their heirs and assigns for ever, as tenants in common, and not as joint tenants;

---

[3] Counsel for infants interested under the discretionary trusts.

upon this special proviso and condition, that in case my said daughters Ann and Hannah Collett, or either of them, shall have no lawful issue, that then and in such case they or she having no lawful issue as aforesaid shall have no power to dispose of her share in the said estates so above given to them except to her sister or sisters, or to their children." The exception was confined to sisters and the children of sisters, which is a narrow enough class, although one does not know exactly how many there were in the class. There were five daughters.... the whole court, the Court of King's Bench, decided apparently that the condition not to alienate except to a class consisting of four sisters and their children was good.

That case was considered in *Attwater v Attwater* ((1853) 18 Beav 330), where Sir John Romilly, MR refused to follow the Court of King's Bench, and merely said that, notwithstanding *Doe* d. *Gill v Pearson,* he held the opposite. The limitation in *Attwater v Attwater* was: "I bequeath to *Gay Thomas Attwater,* jun., eldest son of my niece, the family estate at *Charlton, Wilts.,* to become his property on attaining the age of 25 years, with an injunction never to sell it out of the family; but, if sold at all, it must be to one of his brothers hereafter named." He had three brothers. Sir John Romilly declined to hold that condition good; in his judgment he said: "It is obvious, that if the introduction of one person's name, as the only person to whom the property may be sold, renders such a proviso valid, a restraint on alienation may be created, as complete and perfect as if no person whatever was named; inasmuch as the name of the person who alone is permitted to purchase, might be so selected, as to render it reasonably certain that he would not buy the property, and that the property could not be aliened at all. It appears to me also, that this is the true construction of the words used by the testator; it is, in truth, an injunction never to sell the hereditaments devised at all. ... It is not, in my opinion, desirable to impose fresh fetters on the enjoyment of property, and it appears to me, that this proviso is distinctly at variance with the rules laid down by Lord Coke, and which have always been considered and treated as good law. I am of opinion, therefore, that this clause is merely inoperative."

That is a decision on a limitation exactly in pari materia to the one before me. I should feel no difficulty about following it, rather than *Doe* d *Gill v Pearson* ((1805) 6 East, 173), but for the fact that in *Re Macleay* ((1875) LR 20 Eq 186), the great authority of Sir George Jessel appears to be on the other side. In that case the devise was "to my brother J. on the condition that he never sells out of the family". The limitation was not, therefore, to named persons, it was "out of the family". Sir George Jessel said (ibid., p. 187): ... "It has been suggested, however, that it is void as being repugnant to the quality of the estate, that is to say, that you cannot restrict the right of an owner in fee of alienating in any way in which he may think fit. If that were the law, the condition would be plainly void. But, with the exception of one authority, a case decided by my immediate predecessor, I am not aware that the law has ever been laid down in that way." Sir George Jessel then discussed the point in Coke on Littleton, *Muschamp v Bluet* ((1617), J Bridg 132), *Attwater v Attwater* ((1853) 18 Beav 330), and *Jacobs v Brett* ((1875) LR 20 Eq 1). He decided (ibid., p. 189): "So that, according to the old books, Sheppard's Touchstone being to the same effect, the test is whether the condition takes away the whole power of alienation substantially: it is a question of substance, and not of mere form." . . . He came to the conclusion that the words were not sufficiently restrictive to be in substance an absolute bar. His reason was that "the family" was a larger term than "sister or sisters, or their children" and that the only restriction was to sell and not to dispose, which might include leases or mortgages. He came to the conclusion that the limitation in that case was a good one.

That decision, therefore, inclines to the view for which Mr. Thompson has argued. In *Re Rosher* ((1884) 26 ChD 801), however, Pearson J felt it necessary to make an elaborate attack upon Sir George Jessel's decision in *Re Macleay* ((1875) LR 20 Eq 186). Although the decision in *Re Rosher* was, as a matter of construction that the restriction was in effect an absolute one, Pearson J delivered a long judgment explaining why he could not agree that *Re Macleay* was well decided. The restriction in *Re Rosher* was that if the testator's "son, his heirs or devisees" wished to sell over a certain period, property worth £15,000 had to be offered to the testator's wife during her lifetime at a price of £3,000; and the judge held that that meant in effect that it could not be sold at all, because nobody would give away property worth £15,000 for £3,000. Although *Re Rosher*, qua its decision, is not of much help, it shows that in the view of Pearson J, *Re Macleay* was wrongly decided.

I need take the law no further. I have to choose one way or the other . . .

It is most pertinent to remember, as Mr. Armstrong[4] has also pointed out to me, that the class to whom it is permissible to alienate begins with three for any one share and that the prohibition goes on not only during the joint lives of all the brothers, but during the lives of the survivors and survivor of them, and therefore a period will be reached when there are two, and then only one, and at last no person to whom any alienation is allowed. If none it is plainly bad. If it is only one, that in substance, as in *Muschamp v Bluet* ((1617) J Bridg 132), is equivalent to none. If one be bad, are two good? It seems to me that a class of this sort, which is bound to be a diminishing class, brings it about, in substance, that this is a general prohibition on alienation. It would be an extraordinary thing if no-one could postulate of any one of these brothers that he would or would not during his lifetime be able to dispose of his own share; and that it must depend on whether he outlives two of his brothers. In my view, this is the kind of restriction which the law views, or should view, with dislike. It is exactly the same kind of condition as in *Attwater v Attwater* ((1853) 18 Beav 330),

---

[4] Counsel for the sons.

and I think that I should be at liberty to follow that decision were it necessary for me to do so, but I do not think that I need follow any case in this region, because the cases are inconsistent with one another, and I am entitled to take my own view. It is pertinent that a number of persons, as in this clause, is in essence different from a class consisting, for instance, as Sir George Jessel's did in *Re Macleay,* of members of the family, which he said was a large indeterminate class of people and might, of course, increase as time went on; whereas, if alienation be restricted to three or four or five persons such as brothers, the class is bound to diminish as death takes its toll of the members. I hold therefore, that the restriction in clause 6 of the will is an attempt to fetter the natural qualities of the interest given, and is accordingly void and can be disregarded[5].

ii.   THE TERM OF YEARS ABSOLUTE[6]

LAW OF PROPERTY ACT 1925

1.   **Legal estates and equitable interests.** — (1) p. 6, ante.

C.   **Equitable Interests**

LAW OF PROPERTY ACT 1925

1.   **Legal estates and equitable interests.** — (3) All other estates, interests, and charges in or over land take effect as equitable interests.

(7) Every power of appointment over, or power to convey or charge land or any interest therein, whether created by a statute or other instrument or implied by law, and whether created before or after the commencement of this Act (not being a power vested in a legal mortgagee or an estate owner in right of his estate and exercisable by him or by another person in his name and on his behalf), operates only in equity.

(8) Estates, interests, and charges in or over land which are not legal estates are in this Act referred to as "equitable interests," and powers which by this Act are to operate in equity only are in this Act referred to as "equitable powers."

4.   **Creation and disposition of equitable interests.** — (1) Interests in land validly created or arising after the commencement of this Act, which are not capable of subsisting as legal estates, shall take effect as equitable interests, and, save as otherwise expressly provided by statute, interests in land which under the Statute of Uses or otherwise could before the commencement of this Act have been created as legal interests, shall be capable of being created as equitable interests:

---

[5] Cf. *Caldy Manor Estate Ltd v Farrell* [1974] 1 WLR 1303, [1974] 3 All ER 753. A fee simple determinable (whether on alienation or for any other reason) is settled land under S.L.A. 1925, s. 1 (1) (ii) *(c)* and the land thus becomes alienable by the tenant for life (p. 249, post). Any term which would operate to restrict the tenant for life's freedom of alienation is void. (S.L.A. 1925, s. 106, p. 265, post).

[6] Chap. 8, p. 355, post.

Provided that, after the commencement of this Act (and save as hereinafter expressly enacted), an equitable interest in land shall only be capable of being validly created in any case in which an equivalent equitable interest in property real or personal could have been validly created before such commencement[7].

i. ENTAILED INTERESTS[8]

a. Creation[9]

LAW OF PROPERTY ACT 1925

60. Abolition of technicalities in regard to conveyances and deeds. — (4) The foregoing provisions of this section[10] apply only to conveyances and deeds executed after the commencement of this Act:

Provided that in a deed executed after the thirty-first day of December, eighteen hundred and eighty-one[11], it is sufficient —

(b) In the limitation of an estate tail, to use the words "in tail" without the words "heirs of the body"[12]; and

(c) In the limitation of an estate in tail male or in tail female, to use the words "in tail male" or "in tail female," as the case requires, without the words "heirs male of the body," or "heirs female of the body."

130. Creation of entailed interests in real and personal property. — (1) An interest in tail or in tail male or in tail female or in tail special (in this Act referred to as "an entailed interest") may be created by way of trust in any property, real or personal[13], but only by the like expressions as those by which before the commencement of this Act a similar estate tail could have been created by deed (not being an executory instrument) in freehold land, and with the like results, including the right to bar the entail either absolutely or so as to create an interest equivalent to a base fee, and accordingly all statutory provisions relating to estates tail in real property shall apply to entailed interests in personal property.

Personal estate so entailed (not being chattels settled as heirlooms) may be invested, applied, and otherwise dealt with as if the same were capital money or securities representing capital money arising under the Settled Land Act, 1925, from land settled on the like trusts.

---

[7] See the discussion in *National Provincial Bank Ltd v Ainsworth* [1965] AC 1175, [1965] 2 All ER 472, on the question of interests capable of existing as proprietary rights; p. 113, post; H & M p. 671.

[8] Cheshire, pp. 237–262; M & W, pp. 57–60, 82–99; MM, pp. 15, 24–26, 34–44.

[9] Cheshire, pp. 247–255; M & W, pp. 57–60; MM, pp. 24–26.

[10] See p. 8, ante.

[11] The Conveyancing Act 1881 came into force 1 January 1882.

[12] Note that the words "heirs of the body" remain sufficient. The technical common law required that an estate tail be created by the use of the word "heirs" plus words of procreation: "heirs of the body" was the most common formula. The Conveyancing Act 1881 provided the alternative.

[13] Before 1926 an estate tail could not be created in personalty; and not, therefore, in an interest under a trust for sale.

(2) Expressions contained in an instrument coming into operation after the commencement of this Act, which, in a will, or executory instrument coming into operation before such commencement, would have created an entailed interest in freehold land[14], but would not have been effectual for that purpose in a deed not being an executory instrument, shall (save as provided by the next succeeding section) operate in equity, in regard to property real or personal, to create absolute, fee simple or other interests corresponding to those which, if the property affected had been personal estate, would have been created therein by similar expressions before the commencement of this Act[15].

(3) Where personal estate (including the proceeds of sale of land directed to be sold and chattels directed to be held as heirlooms) is, after the commencement of this Act, directed to be enjoyed or held with, or upon trusts corresponding to trusts affecting, land in which, either before or after the commencement of this Act an entailed interest has been created, and is subsisting, such direction shall be deemed sufficient to create a corresponding entailed interest in such personal estate.

b.   Rule in Shelley's Case[16]

LAW OF PROPERTY ACT 1925

131.   Abolition of the rule in Shelley's case. — Where by any instrument coming into operation after the commencement of this Act an interest in any property is expressed to be given to the heir or heirs or issue or any particular heir or any class of the heirs or issue of any person in words which, but for this section would, under the rule of law known as the Rule in Shelley's case, have operated to give to that person an interest in fee simple or an entailed interest, such words shall operate in equity as words of purchase and not of limitation, and shall be construed and have effect accordingly, and in the case of an interest in any property expressed to be given to an heir or heirs or any particular heir or class of heirs, the same person or persons shall take as would in the case of freehold land have answered that description under the general law in force before the commencement of this Act.

---

[14] Before 1926 an entail could be created in a will or executory instrument without the use of the formal words required for creation of a fee tail by deed. In a will or executory instrument informal words were sufficient if the intention was clear. Cheshire, pp. 248–249; M & W, p. 59; MM, p. 26.

[15] For the effect of this provision see (1938) 6 CLJ 67 (S. J. Bailey); (1947) 9 CLJ 46 (R. E. Megarry); 185 (S. J. Bailey); 190 (J. H. C. Morris). Re Crossley [1955] Ch 627, [1955] 2 All ER 801: Cheshire, pp. 250–252; M & W, p. 59–60; MM, p. 26.

[16] Cheshire, pp. 253–255; M & W, pp. 60–65; MM, pp. 26-27. Challis, Law of Real Property (3rd edn., 1911), pp. 152–167. The rule still applies to an instrument coming into operation before 1926: Re Routledge [1942] Ch 457, [1942] 2 All ER 418 (testator died in 1874); Re Williams [1952] Ch 828, [1952] 2 All ER 502 (testator died in 1921).

c. Barring an Entail[17]

(i) Inter Vivos

FINES AND RECOVERIES ACT 1833

1. Meaning of certain words and expressions. — "estate" shall extend to an estate in equity as well as at law . . . ; "base fee" shall mean exclusively that estate in fee simple into which an estate tail is converted where the issue in tail are barred, but persons claiming estates by way of remainder or otherwise are not barred; . . .

15. Power, after the 31st Dec. 1833, to dispose of lands entailed, in fee simple or for a less estate, saving the rights of certain persons. — . . . After the thirty-first day of December one thousand eight hundred and thirty-three every actual tenant in tail, whether in possession, remainder, contingency or otherwise, shall have full power to dispose of for an estate in fee simple absolute or for any less estate the lands entailed, as against all persons claiming the lands entailed by force of any estate tail which shall be vested in or might be claimed by . . . the person making the disposition, at the time of his making the same, and also as against all persons . . . whose estates are to take effect after the determination or in defeasance of any estate tail[18]; saving always the rights of all persons in respect of estates prior to the estate tail in respect of which such disposition shall be made, and the rights of all other persons, except those against whom such disposition is by this Act authorized to be made[19].

19. Power, after 31st Dec. 1833, to enlarge base fees; saving the rights of certain persons. — . . . After the thirty-first day of December one thousand eight hundred and thirty-three, in every case in which an estate tail in any lands shall have been barred and converted into a base fee, either before or on or after that day, the person who, if such estate tail had not been barred, would have been actual tenant in tail of the same lands, shall have full power to dispose of such lands as against all persons, . . . whose estates are to take effect after the determination or in defeasance of the base fee into which the estate tail shall have been converted, so as to enlarge the base fee into a fee simple absolute; saving always the rights of all persons in respect of estates prior to the estate tail which shall have been converted into a base fee, and the rights of all other persons, except those against whom such disposition is by this Act authorized to be made[19].

---

[17] Cheshire, pp. 240–242; M & W, pp. 83–92, 95–96, 98–99; MM, pp. 35–39, 41–44.

[18] *Re St. Albans' Will Trust* [1963] Ch 365, [1962] 2 All ER 402; where a disentailing assurance was held good under this section when executed by the heir presumptive (contingent upon the Duke dying without issue) with the consent of the Protector of the Settlement, on the ground that he was a "tenant in tail in contingency". But it was held in *Re Midleton's Will Trusts* [1969] 1 Ch 600, [1967] 2 All ER 834 that such a person did not have a contingent interest, but a mere expectancy.

[19] If the tenant in tail is not in possession, the interests of the remaindermen are only affected if the entail is barred with the consent of the Protector of the Settlement: ss. 22, 34, infra.

22.   The owner of the first existing estate under a settlement prior to an estate tail under the same settlement, to be the protector of the settlement. — ... If, at the time when there shall be a tenant in tail of lands under a settlement, there shall be subsisting in the same lands or any of them, under the same settlement, any estate for years determinable on the dropping of a life or lives, or any greater estate (not being an estate for years), prior to the estate tail, then the person who shall be the owner of the prior estate, or the first of such prior estates if more than one then subsisting under the same settlement, or who would have been so if no absolute disposition thereof had been made, (the first of such prior estates, if more than one, being for all the purposes of this Act deemed the prior estate), shall be the protector of the settlement so far as regards the lands in which such prior estate shall be subsisting, and shall for all the purposes of this Act be deemed the owner of such prior estate[20].

34.   Where there is a protector, his consent requisite to enable an actual tenant in tail to create a larger estate than a base fee. — Provided always, . . . that if at the time when any person, actual tenant in tail of lands under a settlement, but not entitled to the remainder or reversion in fee immediately expectant on the determination of his estate tail, shall be desirous of making under this Act a disposition of the lands entailed, there shall be a protector of such settlement, then and in every such case the consent of such protector shall be requisite to enable such actual tenant in tail to dispose of the lands entailed to the full extent to which he is herein-before authorized to dispose of the same; but such actual tenant in tail may, without such consent, make a disposition under this Act of the lands entailed, which shall be good against all persons who, by force of any estate tail which shall be vested in or might be claimed by, or which but for some previous act or default would have been vested in or might have been claimed by, the person making the disposition at the time of his making the same, shall claim the lands entailed.

35.   Where a base fee, and a protector, his consent requisite to the exercising of a power of disposition. — Provided always, . . . that where an estate tail shall have been converted into a base fee, in such case, so long as there shall be a protector of the settlement by which the estate tail was created, the consent of such protector shall be requisite to enable the person who would have been tenant of the estate tail if the same had not been barred to exercise, as to the lands in respect of which there shall be such protector, the power of disposition herein-before contained.

---

[20] Section 32 allowed a settlor to appoint not more than three persons to act as protector of the settlement in lieu of the person described in s. 22. This power of appointing a special protector has been abolished for settlements made after 1925: L.P.A. 1925 7th Sch., repealing s. 32 Fines and Recoveries Act 1833.

If there is no protector under s. 22, the Court may be protector (s. 33); or the tenant in tail in remainder may disentail without consent (*Re Darnley's Will Trusts* [1970] 1 WLR 405, [1970] 1 All ER 319).

(ii) By Will

LAW OF PROPERTY ACT 1925

176. Power for tenant in tail in possession to dispose of property by specific devise or bequest. — (1) A tenant in tail of full age[1] shall have power to dispose by will, by means of a devise or bequest referring specifically[2] either to the property or to the instrument under which it was acquired or to entailed property generally —

  (*a*) of all property of which he is tenant in tail in possession at his death; and

  (*b*) of money (including the proceeds of property directed to be sold) subject to be invested in the purchase of property, of which if it had been so invested he would have been tenant in tail in possession at his death;

in like manner as if, after barring the entail, he had been tenant in fee-simple or absolute owner thereof for an equitable interest at his death, but, subject to and in default of any such disposition by will, such property shall devolve in the same manner as if this section had not been passed.

(2) This section applies to entailed interests authorised to be created by this Act as well as to estates tail created before the commencement of this Act, but does not extend to a tenant in tail who is by statute restrained from barring or defeating his estate tail, whether the land or property in respect whereof he is so restrained was purchased with money provided by Parliament in consideration of public services or not, or to a tenant in tail after possibility of issue extinct, and does not render any interest which is not disposed of by the will of the tenant in tail liable for his debts or other liabilities.

(3) In this section "tenant in tail" includes an owner of a base fee in possession who has power to enlarge the base fee into a fee-simple without the concurrence of any other person.

(4) This section only applies to wills executed after the commencement of this Act, or confirmed or republished by codicil executed after such commencement.

d. Descent

LAW OF PROPERTY ACT 1925

130. Creation of entailed interests in real and personal property. — (4) In default of and subject to the execution of a disentailing assurance or the exercise of the testamentary power conferred by this Act, an entailed interest (to the extent of the property affected) shall devolve as an equitable interest, from time to time, upon the persons who would have been successively entitled thereto as the heirs of the

---

[1] See Family Law Reform Act 1969, s. 1; p. 263, n. 20, post.
[2] See *Acheson v Russell* [1951] Ch 67, [1950] 2 All ER 572; where the section was held to apply to a will which said: "All other my estate and interest in the family property at" K.H. It was clear from the context that entailed interests were intended to be included: (1950) 66 LQR 449 (R. E. Megarry).

body (either generally or of a particular class) of the tenant in tail or other person, or as tenant by the curtesy, if the entailed interest had, before the commencement of this Act, been limited in respect of freehold land governed by the general law in force immediately before such commencement, and such law had remained unaffected.

ii.   LIFE INTERESTS

a.   Creation

A life interest may be created by the use of any words showing an intention to create a life interest[3]. As explained above[4], the rule now is that a conveyance executed after 1925 passes to the grantee the whole interest which the grantor had power to convey, unless a contrary intention appears in the conveyance. For conveyances executed before 1926, the rule was that, in a conveyance inter vivos[5], a life estate only was conveyed unless the correct technical words for the conveyance of a greater estate were used[6].

The significance of the grant of a life interest is much increased since the coming into operation of the Settled Land Act 1882, under which a tenant for life[7] enjoys powers which extend far beyond his beneficial life interest. The crucial question in a grant of land at the present day therefore is not whether a claimant may enjoy the land for his life, but whether he has the powers of a tenant for life under the Settled Land Act 1925[8].

b.   Waste[9]

A limited owner may not use land to the prejudice of those entitled in reversion or remainder. The remedy is by action for damages or an injunction. There are four forms of waste.

(i)   Permissive

In *Woodhouse v Walker* (1880) 5 QBD 404, a devise to a tenant for life provided that she should keep the premises in repair. She failed to do so, and after her death the remainderman brought an action against her executor under a statute of William IV[10] which gives an action against the executor of a deceased person in respect of wrongs committed by the testator to another in relation to his property. In upholding the action, LUSH J said at p. 406: "This action is brought to recover out of her personal estate the expenses he has so incurred. It is remarkable that no direct authority is to be found for a case which

---

[3] See also L.P.A. 1925, s. 149 (6), p. 20, n. 13, post, and p. 363, post.
[4] See p. 8, ante, L.P.A. 1925, s. 60 (1).
[5] Wills Act 1837, ss. 28, 34, reversed this rule with regard to wills.
[6] Litt 1; Co. Litt, 20a: Conveyancing Act 1881, s. 51; L.P.A. 1925, s. 60 (4) and pp. 8, 13, ante.
[7] Now defined by S.L.A. 1925, ss. 19, 20, p. 261, post.
[8] See pp. 264 et seq., post; *Bannister v Bannister*, [1948] 2 All ER 133; p. 459, post; *Binions v Evans*, [1972] Ch 359, [1972] 2 All ER 70, p. 455, post; *Dodsworth v Dodsworth* (1973) 228 Estates Gazette 1115, p. 492, post; *Ivory v Palmer* [1975] ICR 340; *Griffiths v Williams* (1977) 248 Estates Gazette 947, p. 494, post.
[9] Cheshire, pp. 267–271; M & W, pp. 103–109; MM, pp. 46–51.
[10] Civil Procedure Act 1833.

must, we should suppose, have frequently occurred, and that we have to go back to first principles in order to find a solution of the question raised.

Before the statutes of Marlbridge[11] (52 Hen 3) and of Gloucester (6 Edw 1, c. 5), an action for waste lay against a tenant in dower and tenant by the curtesy, but none against a tenant for life or years. The reason was, as stated by Coke in 2 Inst. 300, 'for that the law created their estates and interests, therefore the law gave against them a remedy: but tenant for life or years came in by demise and lease of the owner of the land, &c., and therefore he might in his demise have provided against the doing of waste by his lessee, and if he did not, it was his negligence and default.'

Here it is plainly implied that, where the grantor in his grant provides against the doing of waste, the grantee will be liable for waste in like manner as a tenant in dower or by curtesy was liable, and this is in perfect accordance with legal principle as expressed by the maxims, 'Qui sentit commodum, sentire debet et onus et transit terra cum onere' (Co. Litt. 231a: and see per Holroyd J, in *Burnett v Lynch* (1826) 5 B & C at p. 607). The first of these maxims has a very wide application in our law. See Broom's Maxims.

The statute of Marlbridge, c. 23, extended the common law liability by ordaining that 'fermors during their term shall not make waste, sale nor exile of house, woods or men, nor of anything belonging to the tenements that they have to ferm without special licence had by writing of covenant making mention that they may do it, which if they do and thereof be convict they shall yield full damage and shall be punished by amerciament grievously.'

The term 'fermors' here, says Coke, 2 Inst. 145, comprehended all who held by lease for life or lives, or for years by deed or without deed, and the words 'do or make waste' in legal understanding in this place (as well as in the statute of Gloucester) includes as well permissive waste which is 'waste by reason of omission or not doing, as for want of reparation, as waste by reason of commission, as to cut down timber trees or prostrate houses and the like: for he that suffereth a house to decay which he ought to repair doth the waste.'

The 'special licence' mentioned in the statute of Marlbridge is commonly expressed by the well-known phrase 'without impeachment of waste.'

The statute of Gloucester gives, as a more stringent remedy, a writ of waste under which the tenant was liable to forfeiture of the thing wasted and treble damages.

The right of action against a tenant for life belongs to the owner in fee of the immediate reversion.

In course of time an action on the case founded on the Statute of Westminster 2, came to be substituted for the writ of waste, as being a

---

[11] "I prefer Marlborough to Marlberge, to say nothing of Marlbridge which is an idiotism"; (F. W. Maitland in a letter to H. A. L. Fisher 7 July 1893, cited in *Letters of Frederick William Maitland*, ed. C. H. S. Fifoot, p. 122).

more simple and practical remedy, and the writ of waste having fallen into disuse was ultimately abolished by 3 & 4 Wm 4, c. 27, s. 36. But the rights and liabilities of the parties remained as before, the remedy only being changed: *Bacon v Smith* ((1841), 1 QB 345). It is not necessary in this case to enter into the question whether an action on the case for permissive waste can be maintained against a tenant for life or years, upon whom no express duty to repair is imposed by the instrument which creates the estate. The modern authorities, or rather the dicta upon this point, appear to be strangely in conflict with the ancient reading of the statutes[12]. See notes to *Greene v Cole* ((1682), 2 Wms Saund, 252).

We think it must be held, upon the principle before mentioned, that in this case the tenant for life was liable at common law, and that the plaintiff as immediate reversioner had a right of action, and probably might have obtained an injunction against her for the permitted waste, if he had made such an application in her lifetime. The right of action which at common law would have died with the person is continued by 3 & 4 Wm 4, c. 42, s. 2, against the executor.''

(ii) Voluntary

In *Dashwood v Magniac* [1891] 3 Ch 306, a testator gave to his widow an equitable life tenancy[13] in the West Wycombe estate, which was situated partly in Buckinghamshire and partly in Oxfordshire, the devise requiring her to keep the estate in repair and entitling her to fell timber (not being ornamental timber) necessary for such repairs.

The estate contained beech trees which were timber in Buckinghamshire, though not in Oxfordshire. The widow cut and sold a large number of these trees to furniture manufacturers in High Wycombe and the proceeds of the sale were treated as her income.

On the widow's death, the remainderman brought this action for (inter alia) voluntary waste. The defendants relied on a local usage which would permit a limited owner to cut beech trees (even though they were "timber") and to treat the proceeds as income; and on the fact that the testator had so treated the beech trees during his lifetime.

The Court of Appeal (LINDLEY and BOWEN LJJ, KAY LJ dissenting) affirmed CHITTY J in holding that, by reason of the local usage, the widow had not committed waste.

LINDLEY LJ said at p. 351: "Laying aside all custom, whether ancient or modern, this action would fail, for the tenant for life would have done nothing wrong; she cut beech in the ordinary course of good forestry, and, apart from custom, that was not waste.

---

[12] KAY J held in *Re Cartwright* (1889) 41 ChD 532, that, in the absence of express provisions, a tenant for life was not liable for permissive waste. *Warren v Keen* [1954] 1 QB 15, [1953] 2 All ER 1118 contains a dictum of DENNING LJ that a weekly tenant is not liable for permissive waste.

[13] The estate was given to her for 100 years if she should so long live. After 1 January 1926, such leases, if granted at a rent or a fine, became leases for 90 years. If no rent or fine is payable, an equitable life interest is given; L.P.A. 1925, s. 149 (6), p. 363, post.

As regards the beech woods in *Oxfordshire*, where beech trees are not timber, this is admitted to be true. But as regards the beech woods in *Buckinghamshire*, where beech is timber, the case is said to be different. The testator made no distinction between his estates in the one county and those in the other; he gave the rents and profits of both alike to Lady *Dashwood* for life, with power to cut timber for repairs; but yet it is contended that, although she was entitled to cut and sell beech trees in those parts of the estates which were in *Oxfordshire*, she was not entitled to do the same with beech trees on those parts of the estates which were in *Buckinghamshire*. Such a conclusion would, I think, startle the testator, and would be to defeat, and not carry out, his intentions as expressed in his will.

It is contended by the Appellants that, beech being timber by custom in *Buckinghamshire*, cutting it, even in the ordinary course of good forestry, is necessarily waste and actionable.

. . . if it is said that there cannot be a custom to commit waste, the answer is that there may be a usage which renders that not waste as between persons claiming under a particular instrument framed with reference to the usage which would be waste as between other persons . . . .

The ordinary law of waste is, therefore, I think, not applicable as between the persons claiming under the will with which we have to deal. In other words the cutting of beech woods according to the usage was not waste in the contemplation of this testator; and, it not being waste, the Plaintiffs cannot claim the proceeds of their sale. . . ."

KAY LJ (dissenting) said at p. 371: "The custom or usage relied on in the present case is one which would entirely alter the ordinary common law of waste as applicable to this estate, and would enable the tenant for years, who is made impeachable of waste, to commit waste, notwithstanding the infirmity of her estate in that respect. It seems to me that, to produce that effect, it must be at least proved that from time immemorial such a limited owner, though impeachable of waste, has been accustomed to exercise the right so claimed.

In this case there is not the slightest evidence that any limited owner who was impeachable of waste ever attempted to exercise any such right, and the usage for the owners of the fee simple, or for limited owners who were not impeachable of waste, to manage the woods in the way which is complained of, cannot, as it seems to me, possibly justify a limited owner, who is impeachable of waste, in doing the same[14]."

(iii) Ameliorating

In *Doherty v Allman* (1878) 3 App Cas 709, a tenant for a long term of years had covenanted in the lease to "uphold, support, maintain and keep the demised premises . . . in good order repair and condition" . . .

---

[14] Larch is not timber. A tenant for life does not therefore commit waste by felling a plantation of larch when ripe for felling; he is entitled to the proceeds of sale and is under no obligation to replace it at his own expense (*Re Harker's Will Trusts*, [1938] Ch 323, [1938] 1 All ER 145).

The premises which had been used as a corn store, and then for military purposes, fell into disrepair. The lessee decided to convert the store premises into dwelling houses, which would greatly increase their value. The question was whether he could be restrained on the grounds that he would be in breach of contract or would be committing waste.

The House of Lords (Lord CAIRNS LC, Lords O'HAGAN, BLACKBURN and GORDON) refused an injunction on either ground[15]. Lord O'HAGAN said at p. 724:

"Now we have, I think, established for the purposes of this decision the principles in this case by which we ought to abide. In the case of *Mollineux v Powell* ((1730) 3 P Wms 268, n.), which contains perhaps the clearest dictum we have upon the matter, two conditions as to the exercise of jurisdiction in cases of waste have been very clearly pointed out, and one at least of those conditions is expressly recognised afterwards in the Irish case of *Coppinger v Gubbins* ((1846) 3 Jo & Lat 411). Those conditions are that the waste with which a Court of Equity, or your Lordships acting as a Court of Equity, ought to interfere, should be not ameliorating waste, nor trivial waste. It must be waste of an injurious character — it must be waste of not only an injurious character, but of a substantially injurious character, and if either the waste be really ameliorating waste — that is a proceeding which results in benefit and not in injury — the Court of Equity, and your Lordships acting as a Court of Equity, ought not to interfere to prevent it. I think that is perfectly well established. On the other hand, if the waste be so small as to be indifferent to the one party or the other — if it be, as has been said by a great authority in our law, such a thing as twelvepence worth of waste, a Court of Equity, and your Lordships acting as a Court of Equity, ought not to interfere on account of the triviality of the matter. Now, in my view of the case, those principles decide the question so far as this portion of it is concerned; for it appears to me that we have here established to the full satisfaction of your Lordships, by a series of authorities to which I shall not refer, that the waste, to be of any sort of effect with a view to an injunction, must be a waste resulting in substantial damage."

(iv)   Equitable

LAW OF PROPERTY ACT 1925

135. Equitable waste. — An equitable interest for life without impeachment of waste does not confer upon the tenant for life any right to commit waste of the description known as equitable waste, unless an intention to confer such right expressly appears by the instrument creating such equitable interest.

---

[15] There is, however, technically an act of waste for which an action for damages would lie at law. But, no damage being suffered, no damages would be recoverable.

VANE *v* LORD BARNARD
(1716) 2 Vern. 738 (Earl COWPER LC)

The Defendant on the Marriage of the Plaintiff his eldest Son with the Daughter of *Morgan Randyll,* and 10,000*l* Portion settled (*inter alia*) *Raby Castle* on himself for Life, without Impeachment of Waste Remainder to his Son for Life, and to his first and other Sons in Tail Male.

The Defendant the Lord *Barnard* having taken some Displeasure against his Son, got *two Hundred* Workmen together, and of a sudden, in a few Days, stript the Castle of the Lead, Iron, Glass, Doors, and Boards, &c. to the value of 3,000*l.*

The Court upon filing the Bill, granted an Injunction to stay Committing of Waste, in pulling down the Castle; and now, upon the Hearing of the Cause, decreed, not only the Injunction to continue, but that the Castle should be repaired, and put into the same Condition it was in, in *August* 1714, and for that Purpose a Commission was to issue to ascertain what ought to be repaired, and a Master to see it done at the Expence and Charge of the Defendant the Lord *Barnard;* and decreed the Plaintiff his Costs.

In *Turner v Wright* (1860) 2 De GF & J 234, Lord CAMPBELL LC held that an owner in fee simple subject to an executory limitation over was liable for equitable waste. He said at p. 243: "Equitable waste is that which a prudent man would not do in the management of his own property. This Court may interfere where a man unconscientiously exercises a legal right to the prejudice of another — and an act may in some sense be regarded as unconscientious if it be contrary to the dictates of prudence and reason, although the actor, from his peculiar frame of mind, does the act without any malicious motive. The prevention of acts amounting to equitable waste may well be considered as in furtherance of the intention of the testator, who, no doubt, wished that the property should come to the devisee over in the condition in which he, the testator, left it at his death; the first taker having had the reasonable enjoyment of it, and having managed it as a man of ordinary prudence would manage such property were it absolutely his own."

iii.   DETERMINABLE INTERESTS AND INTERESTS SUBJECT
TO A CONDITION

There is a basic difference between determinable interests and interests subject to a condition. The former is a grant of something less than the interest specified; the latter is a grant of the interest subject to a liability to be cut down. To give land to trustees so long as it is used for Church purposes is a grant less than a fee simple. To give land to trustees in fee simple subject to a condition that the fee simple shall terminate if the land is not used for Church purposes is a fee simple subject to a condition. The difference is that between an eleven inch ruler and a foot ruler subject to the last inch being cut off. Whether or not a grant is one or the other is a matter of construction, and is thus reduced to a matter of words. There are many difficulties and fine distinctions, but these are unavoidable; the interests are similar, but different, and the line between the two must be drawn somewhere[16].

In *Re Bowen* [1893] 2 Ch 491, STIRLING J said at p. 495:

"The question which I have to decide, therefore, appears to me to reduce itself to one of the construction of the testator's will — *i.e.*, whether the testator has given the property to charity, in perpetuity, subject to an executory gift in favour of the residuary legatee, or whether he has given it for a limited period, leaving the undisposed of interest to fall into residue."

In *Re Sharp's Settlement Trusts* [1973] Ch 331, at p. 340, [1972] 3 All ER 151, PENNYCUICK V-C referred to: "the extremely artificial distinction between a 'determinable fee' and a 'fee simple on condition.' For explanation of these expressions see *Megarry and Wade, The Law of Real Property*, 3rd edn. (1966) p. 75 et seq. and in particular the statement at p. 77:

'The question is whether the words limit the utmost time of continuance of the estate, or whether they mark an event which, if it takes place in the course of that time, will defeat an estate already granted; in the first case the words take effect as a limitation, in the second as a condition. A limitation marks the bounds or compass of the estate, a condition defeats the estate before it attains its boundary.'

The distinction has been described in an Irish case as 'little short of disgraceful to our jurisprudence': see the quotation in *Megarry and Wade* at p. 78. I am bound to say that according to modern ideas this criticism appeals to me. However, the distinction is well established and must be accepted so far as it is comprehensible."

II. Registration and Notice

A. The Doctrine of the Bona Fide Purchaser of a Legal Estate for Value Without Notice[17]

The recognition of the use, and later of the trust[18], has given to English law a unique form of duality of ownership. The feoffees to uses, (later the trustees), own a legal estate which, like other forms of legal ownership, is valid against all the world. They obtain, however, no personal benefit from their legal ownership, for they must hold the land and all the income from it for the benefit of the beneficiaries.

The interest of the beneficiaries has its origin in the willingness of the Chancellor to give relief in a situation in which the owner of the

---

[16] For the differences between a determinable fee and a fee subject to a condition see Cheshire, pp. 362–370; M & W, pp. 74–82; MM, pp. 30–33.

[17] Cheshire, pp. 59–71; M & W, pp. 113–126; MM, pp. 57–60; H & M; pp. 21 et seq.; Snell, pp. 44–57, 109–110; Maitland, pp. 106–116.

[18] Holdsworth, vol. 4, pp. 407–480 and Simpson, *Introduction to the History of the Land Law* (1961), pp. 163–194.

legal estate had undertaken to hold his legal estate to the use of another. The conscience of the feoffee to uses was affected and the Chancellor compelled him to observe his obligation. So long as the original parties to the arrangement remained, the position is comparatively simple; but complications arise where the legal or equitable ownership changes. A change of legal ownership raises the question whether the use is enforceable against a person other than the original feoffee; a change of equitable ownership raises the question of the form of equitable ownership which the Chancellor will recognise. In general, equity followed the law and recognised in equity estates corresponding to those which were recognised at law. But that is another story; here, we are concerned with the question of enforcement of equitable interests against persons other than the original feoffee.

The use was based upon conscience. If a feoffee to uses transferred to a purchaser with notice, the purchaser was bound as being a party to the fraud; if he had no notice the use was "transferred" to him. A donee was bound, notice or no notice; for, without consideration being given, the original use was not changed. A use was however only binding on persons claiming through the original feoffee; and a disseisor therefore took free[19]. With the rise of the trust, however, this technicality disappeared; and an interest under a trust is now valid against all the world with the exception of a bona fide purchaser[20] of the legal estate for value[1] without notice actual, constructive or imputed[2].

It may be helpful to add three comments upon the application of this doctrine in modern law. First, in respect of rights and interests which are registrable as land charges under the Land Charges Act 1972[3], registration constitutes notice. Thus, a purchaser takes subject to registered land charges whether he knows about them or not; and,

---

[19] Simpson, op. cit., pp. 169–170.

[20] As to the meaning of "purchaser" see Cheshire, p. 243 n. 5; M & W, pp. 116–117; MM, pp. 57, 264.

[1] M & W, p. 116. "It means any consideration in money, money's worth ... or marriage. 'Money's worth' extends to all forms of non-monetary consideration in the sense used in the law of contract, but it also includes the satisfaction of an existing debt. 'Marriage', however, extends only to a future marriage: an ante-nuptial agreement ... is deemed to have been made for value as regards both the spouses and the issue of the marriage; but a promise made in respect of a past marriage ... is not."

[2] In the case of those interests and charges which are registrable under the L.C.A. 1972, registration constitutes notice: L.C.A. 1972, ss. 2, 4; pp. 29–45, post. For the meaning of imputed notice, see L.P.A. 1925, s. 199 (1) (ii) and p. 41, n. 9, post.

The doctrine of constructive notice applies differently with personalty. A transferee cannot disregard equitable interests of which he is aware or which present themselves to his notice. (*Nelson v Larholt* [1948] 1 KB 339, [1947] 2 All ER 751): but as there are no title deeds to chattels, there is no duty to examine the title. *Joseph v Lyons* (1884) 15 QBD 280 (pledgee under no obligation to search register of bills of sale, and not bound by a bill of sale assigning after-acquired property); H & M, p. 24.

Similarly with negotiable instruments; a holder may be "in due course" without having taken steps to examine the title of the transferor. (*London Joint Stock Bank v Simmons* [1892] AC 201.)

[3] See pp. 29–39, post. L.C.A. 1972 consolidates L.C.A. 1925 (apart from local land charges) and other enactments relating to the registration of land charges. It does not make any substantive alterations.

conversely, he takes free from unregistered (but registrable) land charges even if he knows about them[4]. Secondly, where there are successive beneficial interests in land, a settlement exists; the tenant for life has power to sell the fee simple, and the equitable interests are "overreached", that is, transferred from the land to the purchase money. Thus, the purchaser takes the land free of the equitable interests, although he knows that some exist; and, after the sale, the equitable interests exist in a fund of money whose value is equivalent to the land. A similar result is reached where land is held upon trust for sale. In other situations the doctrine may still apply. The pattern of the 1925 legislation was that all interests in land, other than the fee simple absolute in possession and the term of years absolute[5] should be either registrable or overreachable[6]. Situations have arisen to destroy the tidiness of this pattern, and in these cases the old doctrine will apply[7]. An understanding of the doctrine is essential to an appreciation of the relationship between law and equity.

Thirdly, the doctrine of the purchaser for value of the legal estate without notice is relevant only to *un*registered land. The concept of the duality of ownership, legal and equitable, developed in that context. Where a totally new system of registration of *title* to and of *certain interests* in land is introduced, wholly different concepts apply. It will be seen from Chapter 2 that such a system was made available in 1925, and is spreading throughout the country. The essence of a system of registration of title is that the Register controls and that any person dealing with the land will be safe in relying on the Register. The basic division is thus between estates and interests which appear on the Register and those which do not, rather than between legal estates and equitable interests[8]. But it will be seen that some modern cases do seem to allow this old distinction to penetrate the registered land system, and cause the greatest confusion in its administration[9].

---

[4] Pp. 41–45, post.

[5] L.P.A. 1925, s. 1, p. 6, ante.

[6] See RUSSELL LJ in *Shiloh Spinners Ltd v Harding* [1972] Ch 326, at 340–341, [1971] 2 All ER 307.

[7] I.e. (1) where an interest is not registrable, e.g. restrictive convenant entered into before 1926, L.C.A. 1972, s. 2 (5), Class D (ii); *Shiloh Spinners Ltd v Harding*, [1973] AC 691, [1973] 1 All ER 90 (equitable right of re-entry on breach of covenant), p. 34, post; *E. R. Ives Investment Ltd v High* [1967] 2 QB 379, [1967] 1 All ER 504 (estoppel licence), p. 485, post; *Poster v Slough Estates Ltd* [1969] 1 Ch 495, [1968] 3 All ER 257 (right of entry to remove fixtures).

(2) where an interest is not overreachable, e.g. *Caunce v Caunce* [1969] 1 WLR 286, [1969] 1 All ER 722, (1974) 38 Conv (NS) 226, (capital money paid to only one trustee), p. 230, post.

[8] *Parkash v Irani Finance Ltd* [1970] Ch 101 at 109, [1969] 1 All ER 930 at 933, where PLOWMAN J found a plaintiff's reliance on the doctrine "a little surprising, since one of the essential features of registration of title is to substitute a system of registration of rights for the doctrine of notice." See also CROSS J in *National Provincial Bank Ltd v Hastings Car Mart Ltd* [1964] Ch 9 at 16; *Miles v Bull* (No. 2) [1969] 3 All ER 1585.

[9] *Barclays Bank Ltd v Taylor* [1974] Ch 137, [1973] 1 All ER 752; p. 687, post; *Peffer v Rigg* [1977] 1 WLR 285, [1978] 3 All ER 745; p. 103, post; see also *Hodgson v Marks* [1971] Ch 892, [1971] 2 All ER 684; p. 118, post; *Williams and Glyn's Bank Ltd v Boland* [1979] Ch 312, [1979] 2 All ER 697; p. 122, post.

PILCHER *v* RAWLINS
(1872) 7 Ch App 259 (Lord HATHERLEY LC, JAMES and
MELLISH LJJ)

In 1851, the trustees of Jeremiah Pilcher's settlement advanced the
funds to Rawlins on the security of land including the 'Whitchurch'
property, which was conveyed by Rawlins to the trustees in a deed
which noticed the trusts.

In 1856 W.H. Pilcher, the surviving trustee of the settlement,
reconveyed the Whitchurch property to Rawlins, who repaid only part
of the loan. Rawlins, with W.H. Pilcher's connivance, mortgaged that
property to Stockwell and Lamb, showing only the title deeds prior to
the 1851 mortgage and thus appearing as unincumbered owner in fee
simple.

Stockwell and Lamb thus received the legal estate, not under the
title deeds which showed that Rawlins had a good title prior to 1851,
but through the 1851 mortgage and later reconveyance also. The
complete deeds thus disclosed the trusts. There was no way in which
Stockwell and Lamb could have discovered the missing deeds, or
learned of their contents. The question was whether the fact that the
title deeds disclosed the trusts constituted constructive notice.

Held. Stockwell and Lamb took free from the trusts as bona fide
purchasers of the legal estate for value without notice.

JAMES LJ: I propose simply to apply myself to the case of a
purchaser for valuable consideration, without notice, obtaining, upon
the occasion of his purchase, and by means of his purchase deed, some
legal estate, some legal right, some legal advantage; and, according to
my view of the established law of this Court, such a purchaser's plea of
a purchase for valuable consideration without notice is an absolute,
unqualified, unanswerable defence, and an unanswerable plea to the
jurisdiction of this Court. Such a purchaser, when he has once put in
that plea, may be interrogated and tested to any extent as to the
valuable consideration which he has given in order to shew the *bona
fides* or *mala fides* of his purchase, and also the presence or the absence
of notice; but when once he has gone through that ordeal, and has
satisfied the terms of the plea of purchase for valuable consideration
without notice, then, according to my judgment, this Court has no
jurisdiction whatever to do anything more than to let him depart in
possession of that legal estate, that legal right, that legal advantage
which he has obtained, whatever it may be. In such a case a purchaser
is entitled to hold that which, without breach of duty, he has had
conveyed to him.

In the case of *Carter v Carter* ((1857) 3 K & J 617), which was decided
by the present Lord Chancellor, and which was followed by the Master
of the Rolls in this case, and with which I am bound to say I am unable
to agree, an exception from that rule was, under the circumstances,
supposed to exist.

It is very clearly expressed in a few lines of the judgment in that
case: "But here the purchaser taking the conveyance under one will,

supposed by all parties to be really the last will of the testator, finds himself driven to rely upon another and a second will containing on the face of it all the trusts which the testator has created;" — and that circumstance is supposed to create the exception. To my mind there are to that supposition two short and conclusive answers — the one a matter of principle, and the other a matter of fact. My view of the principle is, that when once you have arrived at the conclusion that the purchaser is a purchaser for valuable consideration without notice, the Court has no right to ask him, and has no right to put him to contest the question, how he is going to defend himself, or what he is going to rely on. He may say, honestly and justly, "I am not going to tell you. I have got the deeds; I defend them, and you will never be able to make me produce them, and you will never be able to produce secondary evidence of them. I am not obliged to produce them at all; probably before you get half way through your action of ejectment you will find a *jus tertii* which you will not dispose of; the estate is in the hands of a legal tenant to whom I have let it, and no one can determine that tenancy without notice, and no one can give that notice but myself; I will not give that notice, and no Court has any power to compel me to give it, I have a right to rely, as every person defending his position has, on the weakness of the title of the person who is seeking to displace me," That seems to be exactly the position of such a purchaser as this. . . .

I am therefore of opinion that whatever may be the accident by which a purchaser has obtained a good legal title, and in respect of which he has paid his money and is in possession of the property, he is entitled to the benefit of that accident, just as a purchaser would be entitled to avail himself of the possession so acquired, without any reference to the rights of the persons who may be otherwise interested. . . .

The decision in the case of *Carter v Carter* ((1857) 3 K & J 617), which has been so much referred to, is a decision which I have considered for some years, and I have more than once thought it right to express my views of that case. I differ in some respects in my views from those of the Lord Chancellor with regard to that case, but I say that the right of a person without notice is absolute and unqualified, when once he has made it out. . . .

In *Wilkes v Spooner* [1911] 2 KB 473, Spooner, the lessee of two premises, No. 137 and No. 170, in High St., East Ham, assigned the lease of No. 170 to the plaintiff and covenanted, in effect, not to compete with the plaintiff's business of general butcher. Spooner then surrendered the lease of no. 137 to the landlord with a view to terminating the restrictive covenant. The landlord knew nothing of the covenant; he accepted the surrender and granted a new lease to Spooner's son, who did. The son opened a business in competition with the plaintiff, who sued to restrain this breach of the covenant. The Court of Appeal (VAUGHAN WILLIAMS, FLETCHER MOULTON and

FARWELL LJJ, reversing SCRUTTON J) held that the restrictive covenant was not binding. The landlord was a bona fide purchaser for value without notice; and the covenant, once destroyed, did not revive on the passing of the land to the son. VAUGHAN WILLIAMS LJ said at p. 483: "I think that this appeal must be allowed. This case has been very well argued, but really, when certain conclusions of fact are arrived at, there is very little left to argue. It cannot seriously be disputed that the proposition which I quoted from Ashburner's Principles of Equity, p. 75, is good law. It is as follows: 'A purchaser for valuable consideration without notice can give a good title to a purchaser from him with notice. The only exception is that a trustee who has sold property in breach of trust, or a person who has acquired property by fraud, cannot protect himself by purchasing it from a bona fide purchaser for value without notice.' The learned author cites as authorities for that proposition the cases *Sweet v Southcote* ((1786) 2 Bro CC 66), and *Barrow's Case* ((1880) 14 ChD 432)."

B.   Registration of Land Charges

i.   UNREGISTERED LAND[10]

a.   *Registration Constitutes Actual Notice*

LAW OF PROPERTY ACT 1925

198.   Registration under the Land Charges Act, 1925, to be notice. — (1) The registration of any instrument or matter in any register kept under the Land Charges Act 1972 or any local land charges register[11] shall be deemed to constitute actual notice of such instrument or matter, and of the fact of such registration, to all persons and for all purposes connected with the land affected, as from the date of registration or other prescribed date and so long as the registration continues in force.

(2) This section operates without prejudice to the provisions of this Act respecting the making of further advances by a mortgagee[12], and applies only to instruments and matters required or authorised to be registered in any such register[13].

LAW OF PROPERTY ACT 1969

24.   Contracts for purchase of land affected by land charge, etc. — (1) Where under a contract for the sale or other disposition of any estate or interest in land the title to which is not registered under the

---

[10] Cheshire, pp. 63–67, 100–103, 110–112, 737–749; M & W, pp. 121–126, 1035–1054; MM, pp. 75–77, 501–513; Barnsley, *Conveyancing Law and Practice* (1973), pp. 335–361; Report of the Committee on Land Charges, 1956 (Cmd. 9825); [1956] CLJ 216 (H. W. R. Wade); see Report of Committee on Positive Covenants Affecting Land (1965) Cmd. 2719, paras. 23–27, Law Commission Interim Report on Root of Title to Freehold Land (1967), para. 46 (1) and Law Commission Report on Land Charges Affecting Unregistered Land 1969 (Law Com. No. 18).

[11] As amended by L.L.C.A. 1975 s. 17 (2), Sch. 1.

[12] See p. 680, post.

[13] As amended by L.L.C.A. 1975 s. 17 (2), Sch. 1.

Land Registration Act 1925 ... any question arises whether the purchaser had knowledge, at the time of entering into the contract, of a registered land charge, that question shall be determined by reference to his actual knowledge and without regard to the provisions of section 198 of the Law of Property Act 1925 ...

b.   What Interests are Registrable

LAND CHARGES ACT 1972[14]

1.   The registers and the index. — (1) The registrar shall continue to keep at the registry[15] in the prescribed manner the following registers, namely —

    (*a*) a register of land charges;

    (*b*) a register of pending actions;

    (*c*) a register of writs and orders affecting land;

    (*d*) a register of deeds of arrangement affecting land;

    (*e*) a register of annuities[16],

and shall also continue to keep there an index whereby all entries made in any of those registers can readily be traced.

(6) Subject to the provisions of this Act, registration may be vacated pursuant to an order of the court[17].

---

[14] See also Land Charges Rules 1974 (S.I. 1974 No. 1286).

[15] In Plymouth, where over 5 million records are in computerized form. Report on H.M. Land Registry, 1978–79, para. 34. In 1975 the Land Registry received the John Player award given by the British Computer Society. See generally Ruoff, *Searching without Tears* (1974); H.M. Land Registry, *Computerised Land Charges Department* (1974); (1974), 118 Sol Jo 692; 48 ALJ 593 (T. B. F. Ruoff). In 1978–79, there were 271,249 new registrations, (including priority notices) rectifications and renewals of land charges, and 4,331,151 searches of the Register. Report on H.M. Land Registry 1978–79, para. 30.

[16] Sch. 1. No entries have been possible in this register since 1925.

[17] This is wider than the corresponding L.C.A. 1925, s. 10 (8): *Calgary and Edmonton Land Co Ltd v Dobinson* [1974] Ch 102 at 109, [1974] 1 All ER 484 per MEGARRY J. For recent examples see *Heywood v BDC Properties Ltd* [1963] 1 WLR 975, [1963] 2 All ER 1063; *Heywood v BDC Properties Ltd (No 2)* [1964] 1 WLR 971, [1964] 2 All ER 702; *Georgiades v Edward Wolfe & Co Ltd* [1965] Ch 487, [1964] 3 All ER 433; *Taylor v Taylor* [1968] 1 WLR 378, [1968] 1 All ER 843; *Rawlplug Co Ltd v Kamvale Properties Ltd* (1969) 20 P & CR 32; *Boobyer v Thornville Properties Ltd* (1968) 19 P & CR 768; *Re Longlands Farm* [1968] 3 All ER 552; *Thomas v Rose* [1968] 1 WLR 1797, [1968] 3 All ER 765 (all discussed in (1968) 118 New LJ 1167 (S. M. Cretney), who points out that a charge can be registered without any proof of its validity, the function of the Registry being purely ministerial; but the registration of such a charge might in practice make the land unsaleable); *Hooker v Wyle* [1974] 1 WLR 235, [1973] 3 All ER 707; *Jones v Morgan* (1973) 231 Estates Gazette 1167; *Mens v Wilson* (1973) 231 Estates Gazette 843; Cf. the position in registered land. L.R.A. 1925, ss. 56 (3), 82, p. 137, post. *Rawlplug Co Ltd v Kamvale Properties Ltd* supra; *Calgary and Edmonton Land Co Ltd v Discount Bank (Overseas) Ltd* [1971] 1 WLR 81, [1971] 1 All ER 551; *Clearbrook Property Holdings Ltd v Verrier* [1974] 1 WLR 243, [1973] 3 All ER 614; *Tiverton Estates Ltd v Wearwell Ltd* [1975] Ch 146, at 161, 171, [1974] 1 All ER 209; *Lester v Burgess* (1973) 26 P & CR 536 (a useful analysis of the jurisdiction by GOULDING J); *Price Bros (Somerford) Ltd v J. Kelly Homes (Stoke-on-Trent) Ltd* [1975] 1 WLR 1512, [1975] 3 All ER 369; *Calgary and Edmonton Land Co Ltd v Dobinson* supra.; *Norman v Hardy* [1974] 1 WLR 1048, [1974] 1 All ER 1170, (1974) 38 Conv (NS) 208 (F. R. Crane); *Northern Developments (Holdings) Ltd v UDT Securities Ltd* [1976] 1 WLR 1230, (1976) 41 Conv (NS) 173 (F. R. Crane).

(7) In this section "index" includes any device or combination of devices serving the purpose of an index.

2. **The register of land charges.** — (1) If a charge on or obligation affecting land falls into one of the classes described in this section, it may be registered in the register of land charges as a land charge of that class[18].

(2) A Class A land charge is —

    (*a*) a rent or annuity or principal money payable by instalments or otherwise, with or without interest, which is not a charge created by deed but is a charge upon land (other than a rate) created pursuant to the application of some person under the provisions of any Act of Parliament, for securing to any person either the money spent by him or the costs, charges and expenses incurred by him under such Act, or the money advanced by him for repaying the money spent or the costs, charges and expenses incurred by another person under the authority of an Act of Parliament[19]; or

    (*b*) a rent or annuity or principal money payable as mentioned in paragraph (*a*) above which is not a charge created by deed but is a charge upon land (other than a rate) created pursuant to the application of some person under any of the enactments mentioned in Schedule 2 to this Act[20].

(3) A Class B land charge is a charge on land (not being a local land charge)[1] of any of the kinds described in paragraph (*a*) of subsection (2) above, created otherwise than pursuant to the application of any person[2].

(4) A Class C land charge is any of the following (not being a local land charge)[3], namely —

    (i) a puisne mortgage[4];
    (ii) a limited owner's charge[5];
    (iii) a general equitable charge[6];
    (iv) an estate contract[7];

and for this purpose —

    (i) a puisne mortgage is a legal mortgage which is not protected by a deposit of documents relating to the legal estate affected;

---

[18] For the date of effective registration and priority notices, see L.C.A. 1972, s. 11; (1977) 74 LSG 136 (P. Freedman).
[19] E.g. a statutory charge under the Improvement of Land Act 1864.
[20] E.g. Landlord and Tenant Act 1927, s. 12, Sch. 1, para. 7 (charge in respect of improvements to business premises).
[1] As amended by L.L.C.A. 1975 s. 19, Sch. 2.
[2] E.g. a charge on property recovered or preserved for an assisted person arising under the Legal Aid Act 1974, s. 9.
[3] As amended by L.L.C.A. 1975 s. 17 (1) (*b*).
[4] P. 678, post.
[5] P. 259, post.
[6] This does not include mortgages of equitable interests which are treated separately; p. 678, post.
[7] P. 76, post.

(ii) a limited owner's charge is an equitable charge acquired by a
tenant for life or statutory owner under Part III of the
Finance Act 1975 or under any other statute by reason of the
discharge by him of any capital transfer tax[8] or other
liabilities and to which special priority is given by the statute;

(iii) a general equitable charge is any equitable charge which —

(a) is not secured by a deposit of documents relating to the
legal estate affected; and

(b) does not arise or affect an interest arising under a trust
for sale or a settlement; and

(c) is not a charge given by way of indemnity against rents
equitably apportioned or charged exclusively on land in
exoneration of other land and against the breach or non-
observance of covenants or conditions; and

(d) is not included in any other class of land charge;

(iv) an estate contract is a contract by an estate owner or by a
person entitled at the date of the contract to have a legal
estate conveyed to him to convey or create a legal estate,
including a contract conferring either expressly or by statutory implication a valid option to purchase[9] a right of pre-
emption[10] or any other like right.

(5) A Class D land charge is any of the following (not being a local
land charge)[3], namely —

(i) an Inland Revenue charge;

(ii) a restrictive covenant[11];

(iii) an equitable easement[12];

and for this purpose —

(i) an Inland Revenue charge is a charge on land, being a charge
acquired by the Board under Part III of the Finance Act
1975[8];

(ii) a restrictive covenant is a covenant or agreement (other than a
covenant or agreement between a lessor and a lessee) restrictive of the user of land and entered into on or after 1st January
1926;

(iii) an equitable easement is an easement, right or privilege over
or affecting land created or arising on or after 1st January
1926, and being merely an equitable interest.

---

[8] As amended by F.A. 1975 s. 52, Sch. 12 para. 18.
[9] *Beesly v Hallwood Estates Ltd* [1960] 1 WLR 549, [1960] 2 All ER 314; *Taylor Fashions Ltd v Liverpool Victoria Friendly Society* (1979) 251 Estates Gazette 159 (option to renew, contained in lease, held registrable as option to purchase).
[10] *Pritchard v Briggs* [1979] 3 WLR 868, [1980] 1 All ER 294; (1980) 39 CLJ 35 (C. Harpum), Barnsley, *Land Options* (1978), chap. 7.
[11] Pp. 412, 704, post.
[12] Pp. 519–520, post.

(6) A Class E land charge is an annuity created before 1st January 1926 and not registered in the register of annuities.

(7) A Class F land charge is a charge affecting any land by virtue of the Matrimonial Homes Act 1967[13].

(8) A charge or obligation created before 1st January 1926 can only be registered as a Class B land charge or a Class C land charge if it is acquired under a conveyance made on or after that date.

3. Registration of land charges. — (1) A land charge shall be registered in the name of the estate owner whose estate is intended to be affected[14].

(2) A land charge registered before 1st January 1926 under any enactment replaced by the Land Charges Act 1925 in the name of a person other than the estate owner may remain so registered until it is registered in the name of the estate owner in the prescribed manner.

(3) A puisne mortgage created before 1st January 1926 may be registered as a land charge before any transfer of the mortgage is made.

Report on H.M. Land Registry for the Year 1978–1979, para. 31.

31. The new registrations of land charges made during the year (excluding priority notices) were divided between the various classes as follows:

Class of land charge	Number of registrations	Percentage increase or decrease compared with 1977–78
A	9	− 55.00
B	689	+144.33
C(i) (puisne mortgages)	123,093	− 1.99
C(ii) (limited owners' charges)	152	− 25.85
C(iii) (general equitable charges)	3,147	− 2.47
C(iv) (estate contracts)	39,115	+ 28.33
D(i) (Inland Revenue charges)	85	+ 3.55
D(ii) (restrictive covenants)	73,656	+ 6.30
D(iii) (equitable easements)	1,914	− 2.20
F (matrimonial homes)	10,324	− 3.40

---

[13] Pp. 232–235, post.

[14] P. 39, post. Registration against the name of a person who has contracted to purchase land is not sufficient: *Barrett v Hilton Developments Ltd* [1975] Ch 237, [1974] 3 All ER 944, (1975) 39 Conv (NS) 65 (F. R. Crane). For the machinery of registration see *Oak Co-operative Building Society v Blackburn* [1968] Ch 730, [1968] 2 All ER 117. See also [1979] Conv 249 (A. M. Prichard).

In *Shiloh Spinners Ltd v Harding* [1973] AC 691, [1973] 1 All ER 90[15], the respondents were assignees of part of leasehold premises which was subject to covenants. The appellants had the right to re-enter and retake the premises in the event of breach. The respondents were aware of this all the time, and, in breach of covenant, they demolished the premises, and argued that the right of entry was void against them because it was not registered.

The House of Lords held that the right of entry was not registrable, and was enforceable against purchasers with notice. Lord WILBERFORCE said at p. 718:

"The right of entry, it is said, is unenforceable against the respondent, although he took with actual notice of it, because it was not registered as a charge under the Land Charges Act 1925. There is no doubt that if it was capable of registration under that Act, it is unenforceable if not registered: the appellants deny that it was so capable either (i) because it was a legal right, not an equitable right, or (ii) because, if equitable, it does not fall within any of the classes or descriptions of charges registration of which is required.

[His Lordship held that the right of entry was equitable and continued:]

So I pass, as did the Court of Appeal, to the Land Charges Act 1925. The original contention of the respondents was that the equitable right of entry was capable of registration under Class D (iii) of the Act. In the Court of Appeal an alternative contention was raised, apparently at the court's suggestion, that it might come within Class C (iv). In my opinion this is unmaintainable. Class C (iv) embraces:

'Any contract by an estate owner or by a person entitled at the date of the contract to have a legal estate conveyed to him to convey or create a legal estate, including a contract conferring either expressly or by statutory implication a valid option of purchase, a right of pre-emption or any other like right (in this Act referred to as "an estate contract").'

The only words capable of including a right of entry are 'any other like right,' but, in my opinion, no relevant likeness can be found. An option or right of pre-emption eventuates in a contract for sale at a price; this is inherent in 'purchase' and 'pre-emption'; the right of entry is penal in character and involves the revesting of the lease, in the event of default, in a previous owner. There is no similarity in law or fact between these situations[16].

Class D (iii) reads:

'A charge or obligation affecting land of any of the following kinds, namely:— . . . (iii) Any easement right or privilege over or affecting land created or arising after the commencement of this

---

[15] (1973) 32 CLJ 218 (P. B. Fairest).

[16] But a proviso in a lease requiring a lessee, who wishes to assign, first to offer a surrender of the lease to the lessor is an estate contract: *Greene v Church Comrs for England* [1974] Ch 467, [1974] 3 All ER 609. *Bocarde SA v S and M Hotels Ltd* (1979) 252 Estates Gazette 59.

Act, and being merely an equitable interest (in this Act referred to
as an "equitable easement").'

The argument for inclusion in this class falls into two parts. First it
is said that a right of entry falls fairly within the description, or at
least that, if the words do not appear to include it, they are sufficiently
open in meaning to admit it. Secondly it is said that the provisions of
the Law of Property Act as to 'overreaching'[17] compel the conclusion
that a right of entry must fall under some class or sub-class of the
Land Charges Act, and since this is the only one whose words can
admit it, they should be so interpreted as to do so. Thus the argument
depends for its success upon a combination of ambiguity, or openness
of Class D (iii) with compelling consideration brought about in the
overreaching provisions. In my opinion it fails under both limbs: Class
D (iii) cannot be interpreted so as to admit equitable rights of entry,
and no conclusive, compelling, or even clear conclusions can be drawn
from the overreaching provisions which can influence the interpretation of Class D (iii).

Dealing with Class D (iii), I reject at once the suggestion that any
help (by way of enlarging the content of this class) can be derived
either from the introductory words, for they limit themselves to the
'following kinds,' or from the words 'and being merely an equitable
interest,' for these are limiting, not enlarging, words. I leave out of
account the label at the end — though I should think it surprising if so
expert a draftsman had attached that particular label if the class
included a right of entry. To include a right of entry in the description
of 'equitable easement' offends a sense both of elegance and accuracy.
That leaves 'easement right or privilege over or affecting land.' If this
were the only place where the expression occurred in this legislation, I
should find it difficult to attribute to 'right' a meaning so different in
quality from easement and privilege as to include a right of entry. The
difference between a right to use or draw profit from another man's
land, and a right to take his land altogether away, is one of quality, not
of degree . . . . I do not further elaborate this point because a reading of
their judgments leaves little doubt that the Lords Justices would
themselves have read Class D (iii) as I can only read it but for the
influence of the overreaching argument.

So I turn to the latter. This, in my opinion, only becomes compelling
if one first accepts the conclusion that all equitable claims relating to
land are either registrable under the Land Charges Act, or capable of
being overreached under section 2 of the Law of Property Act; i.e., are
capable by use of the appropriate mechanism of being transferred to
the proceeds of sale of the land they affect. If this dilemma could be
made good, then there could be an argument for forcing, within the
limits of the possible, an equitable right of entry into one of the
registrable classes, since it is obviously not suitable for overreaching.
But the dilemma cannot be made good. What may be overreached is

[17] P. 189, post.

any 'equitable interest or power affecting that estate': yet 'equitable interest' (for powers do not enter into the debate) is a word of most uncertain content. The searcher after a definition has to be satisfied with section 1 (8) 'Estates, interests, and charges in or over land which are not legal estates are in this Act referred to as "equitable interests" ' — a tautology rather than a definition. There is certainly nothing exhaustive about the expression 'equitable interests' — just as certainly it has no clear boundaries. The debate whether such rights as equity, over the centuries, has conferred against the holder of the legal estate are truly proprietary in character, or merely rights in personam, or a hybrid between the two, may have lost some of its vitality in the statutory context but the question inevitably rises to mind whether the 'curtain' or 'overreaching' provisions of the 1925 legislation extend to what are still conveniently called 'equities' or 'mere equities,' such as rights to rectification, or to set aside a conveyance. There is good authority, which I do not presume to doubt, for a sharp distinction between the two — I instance Lord Upjohn in *National Provincial Bank Ltd v Hastings Car Mart Ltd* [1965] AC 1175 at 1238, [1965] 2 All ER 472 and *Snell's Principles of Equity,* 25th edn. (1960) p. 38. I am impressed by the decision in *E. R. Ives Investment Ltd v High* [1967] 2 QB 379, [1967] 1 All ER 504[18] in which the Court of Appeal held that a right by estoppel — producing an effect similar to an easement — was not registrable under Class D (iii). Lord Denning MR referred to the right as subsisting only in equity. Danckwerts LJ thought it was an equity created by estoppel or a proprietary estoppel: plainly this was not an equitable interest capable of being overreached, yet no member of the court considered that the right — so like an easement — could be brought within Class D (iii). The conclusion followed, and the court accepted it, that whether it was binding on a purchaser depended on notice. All this seems to show that there may well be rights, of an equitable character, outside the provisions as to registration and which are incapable of being overreached.

That equitable rights of entry should be among them is not in principle unacceptable. First, rights of entry, before 1925, were not considered to confer an interest in the land. They were described as bare possibilities (*Challis's Real Property,* 3rd edn. (1911), p. 76) so that it is not anomalous that equitable rights of entry should not be treated as equitable interests. Secondly, it is important that section 10 of the Land Charges Act 1925[19] should be given a plain and ordinary interpretation. It is a section which involves day to day operation by solicitors doing conveyancing work: they should be able to take decisions and advise their clients upon a straight-forward interpretation of the registration classes, not upon one depending upon a sophisticated, not to say disputable, analysis of other statutes. Thirdly, the consequence of equitable rights of entry not being

---

[18] P. 485, post.
[19] Now L.C.A. 1972, s. 2.

registrable is that they are subject to the doctrine of notice, preserved by section 199 of the Law of Property Act. This may not give complete protection, but neither is it demonstrable that it is likely to be less effective than the present system of registration against names. I am therefore of opinion that Class D (iii) should be given its plain prima facie meaning and that so read it does not comprise equitable rights of entry. It follows that non-registration does not make the appellants' right unenforceable in this case.

The consequence is that the appellants' claim to re-enter must succeed unless the respondent can and should be relieved in equity against the appellants' legal right."

Relief against forfeiture was refused[20].

---

c. *Effect of Registration*

LAND CHARGES ACT 1972

4. Effect of land charges and protection of purchasers[21]. — (5) A land charge of Class B and a land charge of Class C (other than an estate contract) created or arising on or after 1st January 1926 shall be void as against a purchaser of the land charged with it, or of any interest in such land, unless the land charge is registered in the appropriate register before the completion of the purchase.

(6) An estate contract and a land charge of Class D created or entered into on or after 1st January 1926 shall be void against a purchaser for money or money's worth[22] (or, in the case of an Inland Revenue charge, a purchaser within the meaning of Part III of the Finance Act 1975)[23] of a legal estate in the land charged with it, unless the land charge is registered in the appropriate register before the completion of the purchase.

(7) After the expiration of one year from the first conveyance occurring on or after 1st January 1926 of a land charge of Class B or Class C created before that date the person entitled to the land charge shall not be able to enforce or recover the land charge or any part of it as against a purchaser of the land charged with it, or of any interest in the land, unless the land charge is registered in the appropriate register before the completion of the purchase.

(8) A land charge of Class F shall be void as against a purchaser of the land charged with it, or of any interest in such land, unless the land charge is registered in the appropriate register before the completion of the purchase.

17. Interpretation. — (1) In this Act, unless the context otherwise requires, — "purchaser" means any person (including a mortgagee or

---

[20] P. 406, post.
[21] Sub-ss. (1)-(4) contain provisions relating to land charges Class A.
[22] *Midland Bank Trust Co Ltd v Green* [1979] 3 WLR 167, [1979] 3 All ER 28; p. 45, post.
[23] As amended by F.A. 1975 s. 52, Sch. 12.

lessee) who, for valuable consideration, takes any interest in land or in a charge on land, and "purchase" has a corresponding meaning.

d. Registers in Existence before 1926

LAND CHARGES ACT 1972

5. The register of pending actions. — (1) There may be registered in the register of pending actions —

(a) a pending land action[24];

(b) a petition in bankruptcy filed on or after 1st January 1926.

(7) A pending land action shall not bind a purchaser without express notice of it unless it is for the time being registered under this section.

(8) A petition in bankruptcy shall not bind a purchaser of a legal estate in good faith, for money or money's worth, without notice of an available act of bankruptcy, unless it is for the time being registered under this section.

(10) The court, if it thinks fit, may, upon the determination of the proceedings, or during the pendency of the proceedings if satisfied that they are not prosecuted in good faith, make an order vacating a registration under this section, and direct the party on whose behalf it was made to pay all or any of the costs and expenses occasioned by the registration and by its vacation[1].

6. The register of writs and orders affecting land. — (1) There may be registered in the register of writs and orders affecting land —

(a) any writ or order affecting land issued or made by any court for the purpose of enforcing a judgment or recognisance;[2]

(b) any order appointing a receiver or sequestrator of land;

(c) any receiving order in bankruptcy made on or after 1st January 1926, whether or not it is known to affect land.

(4) Except as provided by subsection (5) below and by section 36 (3) of the Administration of Justice Act 1956 and section 142 (3) of the County Courts Act 1959 (which make special provision as to receiving orders in respect of land of judgment debtors) every such writ and order as is mentioned in subsection (1) above, and every delivery in execution or other proceeding taken pursuant to any such writ or order, or in obedience to any such writ or order, shall be void as against a purchaser of the land unless the writ or order is for the time being registered under this section.

(5) A receiving order in bankruptcy shall be void as against a purchaser of a legal estate in good faith for money or money's worth,

---

[24] For definition, see L.C.A. 1972, s. 17 (1); *Calgary and Edmonton Land Co Ltd v Dobinson* [1974] Ch 102, [1974] 1 All ER 484; *Whittingham v Whittingham* [1979] Fam 9, [1978] 3 All ER 805; *Greenhi Builders Ltd v Allen* [1979] 1 WLR 156, [1978] 3 All ER 1163.

[1] *Calgary and Edmonton Land Co Ltd v Discount Bank (Overseas) Ltd* [1971] 1 WLR 81, [1971] 1 All ER 551; *Norman v Hardy* [1974] 1 WLR 1048, [1974] 1 All ER 1170; *Northern Developments (Holdings) Ltd v UDT Securities Ltd* [1976] 1 WLR 1230, [1977] 1 All ER 747; Cf. L.C.A. 1972 s. 1 (6), p. 30, ante.

[2] E.g. an order charging the land of a judgment debtor with the payment of the money due. Charging Orders Act 1979, p. 246, post.

without notice of an available act of bankruptcy, unless it is for the time being registered under this section.

(6) Where a petition in bankruptcy has been registered under section 5 above, the title of the trustee in bankruptcy shall be void as against a purchaser of a legal estate in good faith for money or money's worth without notice of an available act of bankruptcy claiming under a conveyance made after the date of registration, unless at the date of the conveyance either the registration of the petition is in force or a receiving order on the petition is registered under this section.

7. The register of deeds of arrangement affecting land. — (1) A deed of arrangement affecting land may be registered in the register of deeds of arrangement affecting land, in the name of the debtor, on the application of a trustee of the deed or a creditor assenting to or taking the benefit of the deed.

(2) Every deed of arrangement shall be void as against a purchaser of any land comprised in it or affected by it unless it is for the time being registered under this section.

8. Expiry and renewal of registrations. — A registration under section 5, section 6 or section 7 of this Act shall cease to have effect at the end of the period of five years from the date on which it is made, but may be renewed from time to time and, if so renewed, shall have effect for five years from the date of renewal.

e. Registration Against Estate Owners Prior to Root of Title

Since the system of registration of land charges provides for the registration of charges against the name of the estate owner, a purchaser can only search against those persons whom he knows to have been estate owners. He will find their names from the deeds. But if the number of years between 1926, when the Register of Land Charges began, and the date of the purchase is greater than 15 years, which is the statutory period of search[3], then it is possible that persons may have been estate owners since 1925 without the purchaser knowing about them. He would then be bound by land charges registered against their names without having any way of searching against them. This hazard began in 1956, 30 years (then the statutory period of search[4]) after registration began.

When, as will be seen[5], the statutory period of search was reduced in 1969 to 15 years, the purchaser's risk greatly increased, and some protection was needed.

LAW OF PROPERTY ACT 1969

25. Compensation in certain cases for loss due to undisclosed land charges. — (1) Where a purchaser of any estate or interest in land

---

[3] P. 5, ante, p. 73, post.
[4] L.P.A. 1925, s. 44 (1).
[5] L.P.A. 1969, s. 23, p. 73, post.

under a disposition to which this section applies has suffered loss by reason that the estate or interest is affected by a registered land charge, then if —

(a) the date of completion was after the commencement of this Act; and

(b) on that date the purchaser had no actual knowledge of the charge; and

(c) the charge was registered against the name of an owner of an estate in the land who was not as owner of any such estate a party to any transaction, or concerned in any event, comprised in the relevant title;

the purchaser shall be entitled to compensation for the loss.

(2) For the purposes of subsection (1) (b) above, the question whether any person had actual knowledge of a charge shall be determined without regard to the provisions of section 198 of the Law of Property Act 1925 (under which registration under the Land Charges Act 1925 or any enactment replaced by it is deemed to constitute actual notice)[6].

(9) This section applies to the following dispositions, that is to say —

(a) any sale or exchange and, subject to the following provisions of this subsection, any mortgage of an estate or interest in land;

(b) any grant of a lease for a term of years derived out of a lease-hold interest;

(c) any compulsory purchase, by whatever procedure, of land; and

(d) any conveyance of a fee simple in land under Part I of the Leasehold Reform Act 1967;

but does not apply to the grant of a term of years derived out of the freehold or the mortgage of such a term by the lessee; and references in this section to a purchaser shall be construed accordingly.

(10) In this section —

"relevant title" means —

(a) in relation to a disposition made under a contract, the title which the purchaser was, apart from any acceptance by him (by agreement or otherwise) of a shorter or an imperfect title, entitled to require; or

(b) in relation to any other disposition[7], the title which he would have been entitled to require if the disposition had been made under a contract to which section 44 (1) of the Law of Property Act 1925[8] applied and that contract had been made on the date of completion.

(11) For the purposes of this section any knowledge acquired in the course of a transaction by a person who is acting therein as counsel, or

---

[6] P. 29, ante.
[7] E.g. compulsory purchase or acquisition under Leasehold Reform Act 1967.
[8] P. 73, post.

as solicitor or other agent, for another shall be treated as the knowledge of that other.

f. Effect of Non-Registration. Actual and Constructive Notice

LAW OF PROPERTY ACT 1925

199. Restrictions on constructive notice. — (1) A purchaser shall not be prejudicially affected by notice of —

(i) any instrument or matter capable of registration under the provisions of the Land Charges Act, 1925, or any enactment which it replaces, which is void or not enforceable as against him under that Act or enactment, by reason of the non-registration thereof;

(ii) any other instrument or matter or any fact or thing unless —

(a) it is within his own knowledge, or would have come to his knowledge if such inquiries and inspections had been made as ought reasonably to have been made by him; or

(b) in the same transaction with respect to which a question of notice to the purchaser arises, it has come to the knowledge of his counsel, as such, or of his solicitor or other agent, as such, or would have come to the knowledge of his solicitor or other agent, as such, if such inquiries and inspections had been made as ought reasonably to have been made by the solicitor or other agent[9].

In *Hollington Brothers Ltd v Rhodes* [1951] 2 TLR 691, [1951] 2 All ER 578, the plaintiffs purported to take an unsealed 7 year underlease from the defendants at a rent of £612 a year. They went into possession and paid rent, but did not register the informal lease as a land charge. The defendants then sold the legal reversion to Daymar Estates Ltd "subject to and with the benefit of such tenancies as may affect the premises". On the same day Daymar Estates Ltd served half a year's notice to quit on the plaintiffs contending that Daymar Estates Ltd were not bound by the equitable lease but only by the legal tenancy from year to year. The plaintiffs agreed to take a new lease from Daymar Estates Ltd at a premium and an increased rent and sued the defendants for the difference between their old rent and the new payments.

HARMAN J held that there was no concluded agreement between the plaintiffs and the defendants, and so the plaintiffs failed. He then considered what the position would have been had there been a contract. He referred to the pre-1926 law and quoted FARWELL J in *Hunt v Luck* ([1901] 1 Ch 51):

"(1) A tenant's occupation is notice of all that tenant's rights, but not of his lessor's title or rights; (2) actual knowledge that the rents are

---

[9] Cheshire, p. 64; M & W, p. 124; MM, p. 60. This re-enacts Conveyancing Act 1882, s. 3. See also *Sharpe v Foy* (1868) 4 Ch App 35 and *Re Cousins* (1886) 31 ChD 671.

paid by the tenants to some person whose receipt is inconsistent with the title of the vendor is notice of that person's rights."

HARMAN J continued at p. 695: "After 1925, however, by virtue of section 10 of the Land Charges Act 1925[10], this contract came within Class C (iv) as a charge on or obligation affecting land, and therefore might be registered as a land charge in the Registry of Land Charges. Accordingly, by virtue of section 13 (2)[11], this being a land charge of Class C is void 'against a purchaser of the land charged therewith, or of any interest in such land, unless the land charge is registered in the appropriate register before the completion of the purchase.' Moreover, by section 199 of the Law of Property Act 1925, a purchaser is not to be prejudicially affected by notice of any instrument or matter capable of registration under the Land Charges Act 1925, which is void against him by reason of non-registration. This land charge was not registered, and accordingly it is said that it was void against Daymar Estates, Limited, notwithstanding their notice or knowledge, and, moreover, that there was no duty lying on the plaintiffs to register the contract in order to prevent this result. This has been held to be so by Wynn Parry J in *Wright v Dean,* ([1948] Ch 686, [1948] 2 All ER 415) where he said that it could not be urged that there was any such duty on the plaintiff. I propose to follow that decision, although I may observe in passing that there is in section 200 (4) of the Law of Property Act 1925, a reference to 'the obligation to register a land charge in respect of . . . any estate contract.'

The defendants' answer to this point was that in fact Daymar Estates, Limited, did not contract to obtain, and did not by the assignment get, any estate in the land expressed to override the plaintiffs' rights, and that consequently they took subject to those rights which are expressly mentioned, and that the land which they purchased was in fact only an interest in the land subject to the rights of the plaintiffs in it. This argument seemed to me attractive because it appears at first glance wrong that a purchaser, who knows perfectly well of rights subject to which he is expressed to take, should be able to ignore them. It was, moreover, pointed out that *Wright v Dean* was distinguishable in this respect because there the option which was overriden by the conveyance was not mentioned in it, nor did the purchaser take expressly subject to it. It seems to me, however, that this argument cannot prevail having regard to the words in section 13 (2) of the Land Charges Act, 1925 which I have quoted, coupled with the definition of 'land' in the Act. The fact is that it was the policy of the framers of the 1925 legislation to get rid of equitable rights of this sort unless registered. . . .

Finally, as under section 13 of the Land Charges Act 1925. . . . an unregistered estate contract is void, and under section 199 of the Law

---

[10] Now L.C.A. 1972, s. 2.
[11] Now L.C.A. 1972, s. 4 (6). An estate contract is void only against a purchaser for money or money's worth of the legal estate.

of Property Act 1925, the purchaser is not to be prejudicially affected by it, I do not see how that which is void and which is not to prejudice the purchaser can be validated by some equitable doctrine."

In *Smith v Jones* [1954] 1 WLR 1089, [1954] 2 All ER 823, the defendant Jones purchased, at an auction, a farm which the plaintiff, to Jones' knowledge, occupied as a tenant.

Disputes arose between the plaintiff and defendant as to the liability for certain repairs, and eventually the plaintiff brought this action claiming that his tenancy agreement should be rectified so as to make the defendant liable for structural repairs.

The defendant contended that, even if a case for rectification could be established against the original lessor, he, as a bona fide purchaser for value, was not bound by the equity to rectify. UPJOHN J held that there was no equity for rectification; and even if there had been, the defendant would have taken free of it. On the second point, he said at p. 1091:

"Lastly, Mr. Arnold for the plaintiff argued that as the plaintiff was in actual occupation as tenant, the defendant was affected with notice of all his rights and all his equities, including an equity to rectify. On the view I have formed of the facts and law as to rectification, this point does not strictly arise, but as it has been fully argued, I think that I ought to express my views thereon.

In *Barnhart v Greenshields* ((1853) 9 Moo PCC 18), when [sic] the law is clearly and compendiously stated, the judgment of the Privy Council was delivered by Mr. Pemberton Leigh, afterwards Lord Kingsdown, who said (ibid. at p. 32): 'With respect to the effect of possession merely, we take the law to be, that if there be a tenant in possession of land, a purchaser is bound by all the equities which the tenant could enforce against the vendor, and that the equity of the tenant extends not only to interests connected with his tenancy, as in *Taylor v Stibbert* ((1794) 2 Ves 437), but also to interests under collateral agreements, as in *Daniels v Davison* ((1809) 16 Ves 249), *Allen v Anthony* ((1816), 1 Mer 282), the principle being the same in both classes of cases; namely, that the possession of the tenant is notice that he has some interest in the land, and that a purchaser having notice of that fact, is bound, according to the ordinary rule, either to inquire what that interest is, or to give effect to it, whatever it may be.'

Then a little later on he cited the language of Lord Eldon in *Allen v Anthony* (ibid. at p. 284): 'It is so far settled as not to be disputed, that a person purchasing, where there is a tenant in possession, if he neglects to inquire into the title, must take, subject to such rights as the tenant may have.'

On the other hand, Mr. Arnold has not produced any case which goes so far as to say that an equity of rectification is an equity which is enforceable against a purchaser. In my judgment it would be extending the doctrine of notice and the obligation to make inquiry far too much if the doctrine was intended to cover an equity of rectification.

Of course the purchaser is bound by the rights of the tenant in occupation — that is quite clear. He is not entitled to assume — as was argued in the earlier cases, notably, I think, *Taylor v Stibbert* — that the tenant is in possession from year to year. He must look at the agreement and he is bound by the agreement, and if, as in *Daniels v Davison*, the tenant not only has a tenancy agreement but an option to purchase, he is also bound by that.

But, in my judgment, a purchaser is not only entitled but bound to assume, when he is looking at the agreement under which the tenant holds, that that agreement correctly states the relationship between the tenant and the landlord; and he is not bound to assume or to ask or make inquiry whether the tenant has any rights to rectify that contract.

Barnhart v Greenshields ((1853) 9 Moo PCC 18) was followed in the Court of Appeal by the well-known case of *Hunt v Luck* ([1902] 1 Ch 428), where the principle was again stated, but as Cozens-Hardy LJ pointed out in argument, and Vaughan Williams LJ pointed out at the beginning of his judgment, the real question for determination was the true construction of the Conveyancing Act 1882; Farwell J, who heard the case at first instance ([1901] 1 Ch 45), having dealt with the matter without reference to the statutory enactment. I have no doubt that that was because he treated the Act as merely declaratory of the existing law; but it is after all a matter of construction of the Act, although I have already expressed an opinion as though the matter rested solely upon decided cases.

The relevant section which re-enacts exactly, so far as relevant, the provisions of the Conveyancing Act 1882, is to be found in s. 199 (1) of the Law of Property Act 1925 [His Lordship read ss. (i) and (ii) (*a*) and continued]:

The question which I have to answer is this: What inspection and inquiries ought reasonably to have been made by the defendant of the tenant before the sale, so far as relevant to this question? I think the only relevant inquiry that he would have made would have been this: 'May I see your tenancy agreement? I want to see whether it corresponds with the copy agreement I have seen in the auction rooms.' That is the document which governed the rights of the parties.

He ought to have asked whether he had seen a correct copy, but he was under no obligation, in my view, to proceed further and say: 'Does that correctly represent your rights?' In fact, if he had asked that question, the answer honestly but erroneously given would have been 'Yes'. Still less was he bound to take the tenant step by step through the document and ask how the tenant interpreted its provisions. He could not be so bound, and it would be most unwise for any intending purchaser to do so.

In my judgment the defendant is entitled and bound to rely on the terms of the document, and the document speaks for itself. Accordingly, had I come to a contrary conclusion upon the claim for rectification, I should have found that this action was barred by the plea of bona fide purchaser of [*sic*] value without notice. In the circumstances, I must dismiss the action."

In *McCarthy and Stone Ltd v Julian S. Hodge & Co Ltd* [1971] 1 WLR 1547, [1971] 2 All ER 973, the plaintiffs, who were engaged in building work on the premises of Cityfield Properties Ltd, obtained on 17 February 1964 an option to purchase. On 14 March 1964, Cityfield Properties Ltd created an equitable mortgage by deposit of title deeds[12] with the defendant bank. On 13 April 1964, the bank registered the equitable mortgage under the Companies Act 1948. s. 95[13].

On 27 September 1965 the plaintiffs registered their option as an estate contract. On 21 June 1967, Cityfield Properties Ltd were in liquidation.

One question was whether the plaintiffs' estate contract had priority over the bank's equitable mortgage. FOSTER J held that it had. The Land Charges Act 1925, s. 13 (2) (now Land Charges Act 1972, s. 4 (6)) did not apply, because the bank was not a purchaser for value of a legal estate contract. On 21 June 1967, Cityfield Properties Ltd were in between the plaintiffs and the bank depended on the time of creation, in accordance with the equitable principle *Qui potior est tempore, potior est jure*. The option was created before the mortgage and therefore the bank took subject to it[14].

QUESTION

In 1961 a father granted to his son a 10 year option to purchase the farm of which the son was his tenant. The option was not registered as an estate contract under L.C.A. 1925. In 1967 the father, wishing to deprive the son of his option, conveyed the farm, then worth about £40,000, to the mother for £500. When the son found this out, he registered the option and purported to exercise it.

In proceedings for a declaration that the option was binding on the mother, OLIVER J held at first instance in *Midland Bank Trust Co Ltd v Green* [1978] 3 WLR 149, [1978] 3 All ER 555 that the mother was "a purchaser for money or money's worth" and therefore the unregistered option was void against her under L.C.A. 1925 s. 13(2) (now L.C.A. 1972, s. 4(6)). The Court of Appeal, by a majority of 2 to 1, [1979] 3 WLR 167, [1979] 3 All ER 28[15], reversing OLIVER J, held that the conveyance of the farm to the mother was at a gross undervalue and that she was not a purchaser for money or money's worth.

The Court of Appeal gave leave to appeal to the House of Lords. If you were an additional Lord of Appeal, what would you say?

---

[12] P. 604, post.

[13] P. 51, post.

[14] At p. 1555. See (1972A) C.L.J. 34, (P. B. Fairest), where the point is made that if the plaintiffs' interest had been a land charged in a different category within Class C (e.g. a puisne mortgage), the bank would not have been bound. An unregistered puisne mortgage is void against a purchaser for value of any interest in the land.

[15] [1979] Conv 441 (F. R. Crane); (1979) 96 LQR 8 (R. J. Smith).

ii.   REGISTERED LAND

The Land Charges Act 1972 is not applicable where the title to land is registered[1]. Interests or charges which are registrable against the name of the estate owner under the Land Charges Act 1972 in the case of unregistered land must be protected in the case of registered land by the entry of a notice or caution on the register of title to the land itself.

The principles of notice work differently in the two systems. An interest or charge which is not registrable under the Land Charges Act 1972 may be enforceable under the old doctrine of notice in the case of unregistered land; but in the case of registered land, it must either be protected by an entry on the register or take effect as an overriding interest[2]. There is theoretically no room in the registered system for a residual category of third party rights whose enforceability depends on the old doctrine of notice[3].

C. Other Registers

i.   LOCAL LAND CHARGES[4]

Registers are maintained under the Local Land Charges Act 1975 by all district councils in England and Wales, and also by London boroughs and the Common Council of the City of London[5]. Only those land charges which would not normally be disclosed by an inspection of the property or the title deeds have been made registrable. The register relates to both unregistered and registered land[6].

LAW OF PROPERTY ACT 1925
198.   Registration under the Land Charges Act, 1925, to be notice. — p. 29 ante.

LOCAL LAND CHARGES ACT 1975
1.   Local land charges — (1) A charge or other matter affecting land is a local land charge if it falls within any of the following descriptions and is not one of the matters set out in section 2 below:—

   (a) any charge acquired either before or after the commencement of this Act by a local authority, water authority or new town development corporation under the Public Health Acts 1936 and 1937, the Highways Act 1959, the Public Health Act 1961 or the Highways Act 1971, or any similar charge acquired by a local authority under any other Act, whether passed before or

---

[1] L.C.A. 1972, s. 14.
[2] L.R.A. 1925, s. 70 (1), p. 109, post. Rights such as those in p. 26, n. 7, ante may be protected by an entry under L.R.A. 1925, ss. 49 (1) (f), (notice), 54 (1), (caution), or 58 (1) (restriction), pp. 125–137, post. Ruoff and Roper, pp. 699 n. 25, 724 n. 4.
[3] P. 26, ante.
[4] L.L.C. Rules 1977 (S.I. 1977 No. 985); L.L.C.(A.) Rules 1978 (S.I. 1978 No. 1638); L.L.C.(A.) Rules 1979 (S.I. 1979 No. 1404). The Act came into force on 1 August 1977. See Garner, *Local Land Charges* (8th edn. 1978), and especially the useful table of all land charges arranged alphabetically, and the part of the register in which each is registrable (pp. 102–110).
[5] L.L.C.A. 1975, s. 3 (1). This includes the Inner Temple and the Middle Temple, s. 3 (4).
[6] See L.R.A. 1925, s. 70 (1) (i), p. 112, post.

after this Act, being a charge that is binding on successive owners of the land affected;

(b) any prohibition of or restriction on the use of land —
  (i) imposed by a local authority on or after 1st January 1926 (including any prohibition or restriction embodied in any condition attached to a consent, approval or licence granted by a local authority on or after that date), or
  (ii) enforceable by a local authority under any covenant or agreement made with them on or after that date,
  being a prohibition or restriction binding on successive owners of the land affected;

(c) any prohibition of or restriction on the use of land —
  (i) imposed by a Minister of the Crown or government department on or after the date of the commencement of this Act (including any prohibition or restriction embodied in any condition attached to a consent, approval or licence granted by such a Minister or department on or after that date), or
  (ii) enforceable by such a Minister or department under any covenant or agreement made with him or them on or after that date,
  being a prohibition or restriction binding on successive owners of the land affected;

(d) any positive obligation affecting land enforceable by a Minister of the Crown, government department or local authority under any covenant or agreement made with him or them on or after the date of the commencement of this Act and binding on successive owners of the land affected;

(e) any charge or other matter which is expressly made a local land charge by any statutory provision not contained in this section.

(2) For the purposes of subsection (1) (a) above, any sum which is recoverable from successive owners or occupiers of the land in respect of which the sum is recoverable shall be treated as a charge, whether the sum is expressed to be a charge on the land or not.

2. Matters which are not local land charges. — The following matters are not local land charges:—

(a) a prohibition or restriction enforceable under a covenant or agreement made between a lessor and a lessee;

(b) a positive obligation enforceable under a covenant or agreement made between a lessor and a lessee;

(c) a prohibition or restriction enforceable by a Minister of the Crown, government department or local authority under any covenant or agreement, being a prohibition or restriction binding on successive owners of the land affected by reason of the fact that the covenant or agreement is made for the benefit of land of the Minister, government department or local authority;

    (*d*) a prohibition or restriction embodied in any bye-laws;

    (*e*) a condition or limitation subject to which planning permission was granted at any time before the commencement of this Act or was or is (at any time) deemed to be granted under any statutory provision relating to town and country planning, whether by a Minister of the Crown, government department or local authority;

    (*f*) a prohibition or restriction embodied in a scheme under the Town and Country Planning Act 1932 or any enactment repealed by that Act;

    (*g*) a prohibition or restriction enforceable under a forestry dedication covenant entered into pursuant to section 5 of the Forestry Act 1967;

    (*h*) a prohibition or restriction affecting the whole of any of the following areas:—

      (i) England, Wales or England and Wales;

      (ii) England, or England and Wales, with the exception of, or of any part of, Greater London;

      (iii) Greater London.

5. Registration. — (1) Subject to subsection (6) below, where the originating authority as respects a local land charge are the registering authority, it shall be their duty to register it in the appropriate local land charges register.

(2) Subject to subsection (6) below, where the originating authority as respects a local land charge are not the registering authority, it shall be the duty of the originating authority to apply to the registering authority for its registration in the appropriate local land charges register and upon any such application being made it shall be the duty of the registering authority to register the charge accordingly.

(3) The registration in a local land charges register of a local land charge, or of any matter which when registered becomes a local land charge, shall be carried out by reference to the land affected or such part of it as is situated in the area for which the register is kept.

(4) In this Act, "the originating authority", as respects a local land charge, means the Minister of the Crown, government department, local authority or other person by whom the charge is brought into existence or by whom, on its coming into existence, the charge is enforceable; . . .

(5) The registration of a local land charge may be cancelled pursuant to an order of the court.

(6) Where a charge or other matter is registrable in a local land charges register and before the commencement of this Act was also registrable in a register kept under the Land Charges Act 1972, then, if before the commencement of this Act it was registered in a register kept under that Act, there shall be no duty to register it, or to apply for its registration, under this Act and section 10 below shall not apply in relation to it.

10. Compensation for non-registration or defective official search certificate. — (1) Failure to register a local land charge in the appropriate local land charges register shall not affect the enforceability of the charge but where a person has purchased any land affected by a local land charge, then —

>   (a) in a case where a material personal search[7] of the appropriate local land charges register was made in respect of the land in question before the relevant time, if at the time of the search the charge was in existence but not registered in that register; or

>   (b) in a case where a material official search[8] of the appropriate local land charges register was made in respect of the land in question before the relevant time, if the charge was in existence at the time of the search but (whether registered or not) was not shown by the official search certificate as registered in that register,

the purchaser shall (subject to section 11 (1) below[9]) be entitled to compensation for any loss suffered by him by reason that the charge was not registered in the appropriate local land charges register or, as the case may be, was not shown by the official search certificate as registered in that register.

(3) For the purposes of this section —

>   (a) a person purchases land where, for valuable consideration, he acquires any interest in land or the proceeds of sale of land, and this includes cases where he acquires as lessee or mortgagee and shall be treated as including cases where an interest is conveyed or assigned at his direction to another person;

>   (b) the relevant time —

>>   (i) where the acquisition of the interest in question was preceded by a contract for its acquisition, other than a qualified liability contract, is the time when that contract was made;

>>   (ii) in any other case, is the time when the purchaser acquired the interest in question or, if he acquired it under a disposition which took effect only when registered under the Land Registration Act 1925, the time when that disposition was made;

>   and for the purposes of sub-paragraph (i) above, a qualified liability contract is a contract containing a term the effect of which is to make the liability of the purchaser dependent upon, or avoidable by reference to, the outcome of a search for local land charges affecting the land to be purchased.

>   (c) a personal search is material if, but only if —

>>   (i) it is made after the commencement of this Act, and

---

[7] S. 8.
[8] S. 9.
[9] S. 11 (1) deals with the position of mortgagees in respect of a claim.

     (ii) it is made by or on behalf of the purchaser or, before the relevant time, the purchaser or his agent has knowledge of the result of it;

  (*d*) an official search is material if, but only if —

     (i) it is made after the commencement of this Act, and

     (ii) it is requisitioned by or on behalf of the purchaser or, before the relevant time, the purchaser or his agent has knowledge of the contents of the official search certificate.

(4) Any compensation for loss under this section shall be paid by the registering authority in whose area the land affected is situated; and where the purchaser has incurred expenditure for the purpose of obtaining compensation under this section, the amount of the compensation shall include the amount of the expenditure reasonably incurred by him for that purpose (so far as that expenditure would not otherwise fall to be treated as loss for which he is entitled to compensation under this section).

(7) In the case of an action to recover compensation under this section the cause of action shall be deemed for the purposes of the Limitation Act 1939[10] to accrue at the time when the local land charge comes to the notice of the purchaser; and for the purposes of this subsection the question when the charge came to his notice shall be determined without regard to the provisions of section 198 of the Law of Property Act 1925[11] (under which registration under certain enactments is deemed to constitute actual notice).

LOCAL LAND CHARGES RULES 1977

3.   Parts of the Register. — The register shall continue to be divided into parts, for the registration of different types of charge, as follows:

Part 1, for general financial charges;[12]

Part 2, for specific financial charges;

Part 3, for planning charges;

Part 4, for charges not registrable in another part of the register ("miscellaneous charges");[13]

Part 5, for charges falling within section 8(4) of the Agriculture (Miscellaneous Provisions) Act 1941 ("fenland ways maintenance charges");

Part 6, for charges falling within section 8(4) or 52(8) of the Land Compensation Act 1973 ("land compensation charges");

Part 7, for charges falling within section 1(4) or 9 of the New Towns Act 1965 ("new towns charges");

Part 8, for charges falling within section 33 of the Civil Aviation

---

[10] P. 155, post.

[12] P. 29, ante.

[12] L.L.C.A. 1975, s. 6.

[13] This includes a variety of prohibitions of and restrictions on the user or mode of user of land or buildings, other than planning charges.

Act 1949, section 21 of the Civil Aviation Act 1968 or section 16(2) of the Civil Aviation Act 1971 ("civil aviation charges");

Part 9, for charges falling within section 11(1) or 16(6) of the Opencast Coal Act 1958 ("opencast coal charges");

Part 10, for charges falling within section 54(6) of the Town and Country Planning Act 1971 ("listed buildings charges");

Part 11, for charges falling within section 2(4) of the Rights of Light Act 1959 ("light obstruction notices");[14]

Part 12, for charges falling within section 31(4) of the Land Drainage Act 1976 ("drainage scheme charges").

ii. COMPANIES

A register is maintained by the Registrar of Companies under the Companies Act 1948 of land charges created by a company for securing money[15].

LAND CHARGES ACT 1972

3. Registration of land charges. — (7) In the case of a land charge for securing money created by a company before 1st January 1970 or so created at any time as a floating charge, registration under any of the enactments mentioned in subsection (8) below shall be sufficient in place of registration under this Act, and shall have effect as if the land charge had been registered under this Act.

(8) The enactments referred to in subsection (7) above are section 93 of the Companies (Consolidation) Act 1908, section 79 of the Companies Act 1929 and section 95 of the Companies Act 1948.

COMPANIES ACT 1948

95. Registration of charges created by companies registered in England. — (1) Subject to the provisions of this Part of this Act, every charge created after the fixed date by a company registered in England and being a charge to which this section applies shall, so far as any security on the company's property or undertaking is conferred thereby, be void against the liquidator and any creditor of the company, unless the prescribed particulars of the charge together with the instrument, if any, by which the charge is created or evidenced, are delivered to or received by the registrar of companies for registration in manner required by this Act within twenty-one days after the date of its creation, but without prejudice to any contract or obligation for repayment of the money thereby secured, and when a charge becomes

---

[14] P. 587, post.

[15] Records are in the process of being microfilmed and moved from London to Crown Way, Maindy, Cardiff. They will also be visible at Companies House, City Road, London. (1976) 120 Sol Jo 326 (T. B. F. Ruoff). A limited company must also keep a register of charges at its registered office. Companies Act 1948 ss. 103–106. See generally *Gore-Brown on Companies* (43rd edn. 1977) 18-11-18-39; Palmer *Company Law* (22nd edn. 1976) ch. 44.

void under this section the money secured thereby shall immediately become payable[16].

(2) This section applies to the following charges:—

(a) a charge for the purpose of securing any issue of debentures;

(b) a charge on uncalled share capital of the company;

(c) a charge created or evidenced by an instrument which, if executed by an individual, would require registration as a bill of sale [16a];

(d) a charge on land, wherever situate, or any interest therein, but not including a charge for any rent or other periodical sum issuing out of land;

(e) a charge on book debts of the company;

(f) a floating charge on the undertaking or property of the company;

(g) a charge on calls made but not paid;

(h) a charge on a ship or any share in a ship;

(i) a charge on goodwill, on a patent or a licence under a patent, on a trademark or on a copyright or a licence under a copyright.

(7) The holding of debentures entitling the holder to a charge on land shall not for the purposes of this section be deemed to be an interest in land.

(10) In this Part of this Act —

(a) the expression "charge" includes mortgage;

(b) the expression "the fixed date" means in relation to the charges specified in paragraphs (a) to (f), both inclusive, of subsection (2) of this section, the first day of July, nineteen hundred and eight, and in relation to the charges specified in paragraphs (g) to (i), both inclusive, of the said subsection, the first day of November, nineteen hundred and twenty-nine.

iii. AGRICULTURAL CHARGES

AGRICULTURAL CREDITS ACT 1928[17]

5. Agricultural charges on farming stock and assets. — (1) It shall be lawful for a farmer as defined by this Act by instrument in writing to create in favour of a bank as so defined a charge (hereinafter referred to as an agricultural charge) on all or any of the farming stock and other agricultural assets belonging to him as security for sums advanced or to be advanced to him or paid or to be paid on his behalf under any guarantee by the bank and interest, commission and charges thereon.

---

[16] See *Re Molton Finance Ltd* [1968] Ch 325, [1967] 3 All ER 843; *Re Wallis and Simmonds (Builders) Ltd* [1974] 1 WLR 391, [1974] 1 All ER 561. See also s. 97 which provides for the registration of charges existing on property acquired by a company: *Capital Finance Co Ltd v Stokes* [1969] 1 Ch 261, [1968] 3 All ER 625.

[16a] *Borden (UK) Ltd v Scottish Timber Products Ltd* [1979] 3 WLR 672, [1979] 3 All ER 961.

[17] Agricultural Credits Regulations 1928 (S.R. & O. 1928 No. 667/L 25); Agricultural Credits Fees Order 1975 (S.I. 1975 No. 1314). In 1978–1979 there were 1,435 new regulations, and 9,861 searches. Report of Chief Land Registrar for 1978–79, para. 33.

9. Registration of agricultural charges. — (1) Every agricultural charge shall be registered under this Act within seven clear days after the execution thereof, and, if not so registered, shall be void as against any person other than the farmer:

Provided that the High Court on proof that omission to register within such time as aforesaid was accidental or due to inadvertence may extend the time for registration on such terms as the Court thinks fit.

(2) The Land Registrar shall keep at the Land Registry a register of agricultural charges in such form and containing such particulars as may be prescribed.

(8) Registration of an agricultural charge under this section shall be deemed to constitute actual notice of the charge, and of the fact of such registration, to all persons and for all purposes connected with the property comprised in the charge, as from the date of registration or other prescribed date, and so long as the registration continues in force:

Provided that, where an agricultural charge created in favour of a bank is expressly made for securing a current account or other further advances, the bank, in relation to the making of further advances under the charge, shall not be deemed to have notice of another agricultural charge by reason only that it is so registered if it was not so registered at the time when the first-mentioned charge was created or when the last search (if any) by or on behalf of the bank was made, whichever last happened.

iv. COMMONS AND TOWN AND VILLAGE GREENS[18]

COMMONS REGISTRATION ACT 1965

1.[19] Registration of commons and town or village greens and ownership of and rights over them. — (1) There shall be registered, in accordance with the provisions of this Act and subject to the exceptions mentioned therein[20], —

    (*a*) land in England or Wales which is common land or a town or village green;

    (*b*) rights of common over such land; and

---

[18] Cheshire, pp. 564–565; M & W, pp. 868–869; MM, p. 418; Harris and Ryan, *Outline of the Law Relating to Common Land and Public Access to the Countryside* (1967); Campbell, *Guide to the Law of Commons* (2nd edn. 1976); *Decisions of the Commons Commissioners* (1972). Decisions of the Commons Commissioners are reported in Current Law. There will be further legislation about the management and improvement of registered common land as well as its user by the public. The Department of the Environment issued a consultative document in 1978.

[19] Commons Registration (General) Regulations 1966 (S.I. 1966 No. 1471), as amended by S.I. 1968 No. 658 and S.I. 1970 No. 1996; S.I. 1970 No. 1996; S.I. 1972 No. 437. For the liability of a solicitor who failed to search the register, see *G and K Ladenbau (UK) Ltd v Crawley and De Reya* [1978] 1 WLR 266, [1978] 1 All ER 682.

[20] The Act does not apply to the New Forest, Epping Forest or to any land exempted by an order of the Secretary of State, s. 11. Commons Registration (Exempted Land) Regulations 1965 (S.I. 1965 No. 2001).

(c) persons claiming to be or found to be owners of such land or
becoming the owners thereof by virtue of this Act;
and no rights of common over land which is capable of being registered
under this Act shall be registered under the Land Registration Acts
1925 and 1936.

(2) After the end of such period, not being less than three years
from the commencement of this Act, as the Minister may by order
determine[1] —

(a) no land capable of being registered under this Act shall be
deemed to be common land or a town or village green unless it
is so registered; and

(b) no rights of common shall be exercisable over any such land
unless they are registered either under this Act or under the
Land Registration Acts 1925 and 1936[2].

2.   Registration authorities. — (1) The registration authority for
the purposes of this Act shall be —

(a) in relation to any land situated in any county the council of
of that county[3]; and

(b) in relation to any land situated in Greater London, the Greater
London Council; . . .

3.   The registers. — (1) For the purposes of registering such land as
is mentioned in section 1 (1) of this Act and rights of common over and
ownership of such land every registration authority shall maintain —

(a) a register of common land; and

(b) a register of town or village greens;
and regulations under this Act may require or authorise a registration
authority to note on those registers such other information as may be
prescribed.

(2) Any register maintained under this Act shall be open to inspection by the public at all reasonable times.

22.   Interpretation. — (1) In this Act, unless the context otherwise
requires, —
"common land" means —

(a) land subject to rights of common (as defined in this Act)
whether those rights are exercisable at all times or only during
limited periods;

(b) waste land of a manor not subject to rights of common[4];

---

[1] 31 July 1970. Commons Registration (Time Limits) Order 1966 (S.I. 1966 No. 1470),
as amended by Commons Registration (Time Limits) (Amendment) Order 1970 (S.I.
1970 No. 383). Applications for registration had to be made before 3 January 1970.
For registration where land becomes common land or a town or village green after 2
January 1970, see Commons Registration (New Land) Regulations 1969 (S.I. 1969
No. 1843).
[2] *Central Electricity Generating Board v Clwyd County Council* [1976] 1 WLR 151,
[1976] 1 All ER 251; *Re Turnworth Down, Dorset* [1978] Ch 251, [1977] 2 All ER 105.
[3] As amended by Local Government Act 1972, s. 272 (1), Sch. 30.
[4] *Re Britford Common* [1977] 1 WLR 39, [1977] 1 All ER 532; *Re Box Hill Common*
[1979] 2 WLR 177, [1979] 1 All ER 113.

but does not include a town or village green or any land which forms part of a highway;

"rights of common" includes cattlegates or beastgates (by whatever name known) and rights of sole or several vesture or herbage or of sole or several pasture, but does not include rights held for a term of years or from year to year;

"town or village green" means land which has been allotted by or under any Act for the exercise or recreation of the inhabitants of any locality or on which the inhabitants of any locality have a customary right to indulge in lawful sports and pastimes or on which the inhabitants of any locality have indulged in such sports and pastimes as of right for not less than twenty years[5].

10. Effect of registration. — The registration under this Act of any land as common land or as a town or village green, or of any rights of common over any such land, shall be conclusive evidence of the matters registered, as at the date of registration[6], except where the registration is provisional only.

Registration is final, if no objection to it was lodged before 1 August 1972[7]. If there are any such objections, registration is provisional, and only becomes final if it is confirmed after a hearing before a Commons Commissioner[8]. There are three full time and one part time Commissioners. In 1980 some 8,500 disputed registrations and 4,000 claims to ownership remained to be heard, and, given the present complement of Commissioners, this is expected to take another 4-5 years[9].

QUESTIONS

1. Why is no provision made for the registration of equitable beneficial interests?
2. Francis David Blackburn entered into a contract to sell a house to a purchaser who registered the contract as an estate contract against the name of Frank David Blackburn, which was the name in which Francis David Blackburn carried on business as an estate agent.

   Is the registration valid:

   (a) against a mortgagee who does not search?

---

[5] *Re The Rye, High Wycombe, Bucks* [1977] 1 WLR 1316, [1977] 3 All ER 521. 20 years means 20 years immediately preceding the passing of the Act (5 August 1965); *New Windsor Corpn v Mellor* [1975] Ch 380; [1975] 3 All ER 44.

[6] *New Windsor Corpn v Mellor* [1975] Ch 380 at 392, per Lord DENNING MR; *Cooke v Amey Gravel Co Ltd* [1972] 1 WLR 1310, [1972] 3 All ER 579 (provisional registration is of itself no evidence of the existence of the right registered).

[7] Commons Registration (Objections and Maps) Regulations 1968 (S.I. 1968 No. 989), as amended by S.I. 1970 No. 384.

[8] Commons Registration Act 1965, ss. 4-7. There is a right of appeal to the High Court on a point of law; s. 18. Commons Commissioners Regulations 1971 (S.I. 1971 No. 1727); S.I. 1973 No. 815.

[9] House of Commons, 20 February 1980.

(b) against a mortgagee who searches against the name of Francis David Blackburn and receives a nil certificate?

(c) against a mortgagee who searches against the name of Francis Davis Blackburn and receives a nil certificate?

See *Oak Co-Operative Building Society v Blackburn* [1967] Ch 1169, [1967] 2 All ER 340, revsd at [1968] Ch 730, [1968] 2 All ER 117; L.C.A. 1972, s. 10 (4); *Du Sautoy v Symes* [1967] Ch 1146, [1967] 1 All ER 25; (1968) 84 LQR 303 (PVB). *Diligent Finance Co Ltd v Alleyne* (1972) 23 P & CR 346; Ruoff, *Searching Without Tears* (1974), chaps. 9, 10, 11. As to errors in searches in respect of registered titles, see L.R.A. 1925, s. 83 (3), p. 139, post, and *Parkash v Irani Finance Ltd* [1970] Ch 101, [1969] 1 All ER 930.

Of what significance would be the fact that the erroneous entry or certificate was due to the negligence of a clerk in the Land Registry?

See *Ministry of Housing and Local Government v Sharp* [1970] 2 QB 223, [1970] 1 All ER 1009; *Coats Patons (Retail) Ltd v Birmingham Corpn* (1971) 69 LGR 356; L.C.A. 1972, s. 10.

3. Is a decision that an equitable right or interest is registrable likely to improve or reduce its prospects of being enforceable against third parties?

See *E. R. Ives Investment Ltd v High* [1967] 2 QB 379, [1967] 1 All ER 504, *Shiloh Spinners Ltd v Harding* [1973] AC 691, [1973] 1 All ER 90; H & M p. 671.

4. Consider how the registration of a non-existent land charge can prejudicially affect a land owner. Should the Land Registrar be required to find a prima facie case for registration before adding a charge to the register?

See per MEGARRY J in *Thomas v Rose* [1968] 1 WLR at 1805, and *Rawlplug Co Ltd v Kamvale Properties Ltd* (1969) 20 P & CR 32 at 39, (1968) 118 NLJ 1167; and per BRIGHTMAN J in *Jones v Morgan* (1973) 231 Estates Gazette 1167; p. 30, n. 17, ante.

Consider this in the context of the Matrimonial Homes Act 1967; see per MEGARRY J in *Miles v Bull* [1969] 1 QB 258 at 261; *Wroth v Tyler* [1974] Ch 30, [1973] 1 All ER 897.

5. Could/Should the Land Charges Act 1925 have established a better system of registration than that of registration against the name of the estate owner? Report of the Committee on Land Charges (the Roxburgh Committee) (1956) Cmd. 9825; Report on Land Charges Affecting Unregistered Land (1969) Law Com. No. 18; L.P.A. 1969, s. 25, p. 39, ante.

6. Consider —

(i) the moral and other difficulties which are met by allowing a purchaser with notice to ignore an equitable interest of which he is aware;

(ii) the legal difficulties of allowing the Register to be overridden by the doctrine of constructive notice;

(iii) the absurdity of putting a purchaser with his eyes shut in a better position than one with his eyes open.

D. Mere Equities[10]

A mere equity, (rescission for fraud, undue influence, rectification for mistake, the right to consolidation, or to reopen a forceclosure, and, perhaps, an equitable right of entry) as opposed to an equitable interest, is not binding on a bona fide purchaser of an equitable interest for value without notice.

Lord WESTBURY in *Phillips v Phillips* (1862) 4 De GF & J 208, when speaking of the occasions on which the ordinary rules of priority in point of time among claimants in equity would be disturbed by the doctrine of bona fide purchaser, said at p. 218:

"Thirdly, where there are circumstances that give rise to an equity as distinguished from an equitable estate — as for example, an equity to set aside a deed for fraud, or to correct it for mistake — and the purchaser under the instrument maintains the plea of purchaser for valuable consideration without notice, the court will not interfere."

III. Creation and Transfer of Estates and Interests

A. Legal Estates. Contract and Conveyance

i. CONTRACT

A contract usually precedes the conveyance which in unregistered land effects the transfer of the legal estate to a purchaser; and a contract also usually precedes a transfer in registered land. In practice such contracts are generally in standard form. The Law Society's Contract and Conditions of Sale (April 1973 Revision) and the National Conditions of Sale (19th edn. 1976) are both standard forms of contract containing a set of general conditions of sale[11]. They are usually employed with such alterations as the parties may make for the purpose of the particular transaction.

A contract for the sale or other disposition of land must comply with the general rules of the law of contract. Thus, it must be a final and complete agreement between the parties on its essential terms, i.e. the parties, the property, the consideration and the interest to be granted. It is usual to make a preliminary agreement "subject to contract", the effect of which is that, until a formal contract has been concluded, there is no contract and either party can withdraw from the negotiations with impunity[12].

Further, a valid contract for the sale or other disposition of land will only be enforceable by action, if there is a sufficient memorandum in

---

[10] [1955] CLJ 160–161 (H. W. R. Wade); (1955) 19 Conv (NS) 346 (F. R. Crane); H & M, p. 670, et seq.; Snell p. 39; Cheshire pp. 70–71; (1976) 40 Conv (NS) 209 (A. R. Everton).

[11] Wilkinson, *Standard Conditions of Sale of Land* (2nd edn. 1974). Aldridge, *Guide to National Conditions of Sale* (1979). See also *Conveyancing Lawyers' Conditions of Sale* (1978); (1979) 129 NLJ 286 (H. W. Wilkinson).

[12] See Law Commission Report on "Subject to Contract" Agreements (1975) Law Com. No. 75.

writing that complies with section 40 of the Law of Property Act 1925, or, failing that, if there is a sufficient act of part performance.

a.   Formalities[13]

LAW OF PROPERTY ACT 1925

40.   Contracts for sale, &c., of land to be in writing. — (1) No action may be brought upon any contract for the sale or other disposition of land or any interest in land, unless the agreement upon which such action is brought, or some memorandum or note thereof, is in writing, and signed by the party to be charged or by some other person thereunto by him lawfully authorised.

(2) This section applies to contracts whether made before or after the commencement of this Act and does not affect the law relating to part performance, or sales by the court.

46.   Forms of contracts and conditions of sale. — The Lord Chancellor may from time to time prescribe and publish forms of contracts and conditions of sale of land, and the forms so prescribed[14] shall, subject to any modification, or any stipulation or intention to the contrary, expressed in the correspondence, apply to contracts by correspondence, and may, but only by express reference thereto, be made to apply to any other cases for which the forms are made available.

b.   Subject to Contract

TIVERTON ESTATES LTD *v* WEARWELL LTD[15]
[1975] Ch 146, [1974] 1 All ER 209 (CA, Lord DENNING MR, STAMP and SCARMAN LJJ)

On 4 July 1973, Tiverton Estates Ltd, the registered proprietors of the lease of Empire House, Stepney, orally agreed to sell it to Wearwell Ltd for £190,000. On the same day, Wearwell Ltd's solicitors wrote to Tiverton Estates Ltd's solicitors: "We understand that you act for the vendor in respect of the proposed sale ... to our clients ... at £190,000 leasehold subject to contract."

On 9 July Tiverton Estates Ltd's solicitors replied: "We refer to your letter dated the 4 July, upon which we have taken our clients' instructions. We now send you draft contract for approval," On 19 July, Tiverton Estates Ltd decided not to go on with the sale. Wearwell Ltd lodged a caution to prevent dealings with the lease. Tiverton Estates Ltd asked for an order that the registration of the caution be vacated. The question was whether the letter of 9 July together with the draft contract was a sufficient memorandum of the

---

13 Cheshire, pp. 115–121; M & W, pp. 542–561; MM, pp. 292–297; Farrand, pp. 32–49; Cheshire and Fifoot, *Law of Contract.* (9th edn. 1976), pp. 184–189; Barnsley, *Conveyancing Law and Practice* (1973) pp. 82 et seq.; (1967) 31 Conv (NS) 182, 254 (H. W. Wilkinson).
14 S R & O 1925, No. 779.
15 (1974) 38 Conv (NS) 127 (F. R. Crane). See generally Emmet on Title (17 edn. 1978), pp. 49–53; Barnsley, pp. 101–104.

oral agreement of 4 July to satisfy section 40 of the Law of Property Act 1925.

Held. Vacation of the register ordered. There was no sufficient memorandum.

LORD DENNING MR. So I turn to the point of substance, which is this: is there any writing sufficient to satisfy the Statute of Frauds, now section 40 of the Law of Property Act 1925. . . .

During the argument before us, it became clear that there are two lines of authority to be considered. According to the one line, in order to satisfy the statute, the writing must contain, not only the terms of the contract, *but also* an express or implied recognition that a contract was actually entered into.

According to the other line, it is *not necessary* that the writing should acknowledge the *existence* of a contract. It is sufficient if the contract is by word of mouth and that the *terms* can be found set out in writing without any recognition whatsoever that any contract was ever made.

[1] *Sale of goods cases which require recognition of a contract*
This line of authority is derived from a problem which arose under section 17 of the Statute of Frauds which required a writing in the case of the sale of goods over £10. The seller would write a letter demanding payment. The purchaser would write denying liability on the ground that the goods were not up to contract and he had rejected them. . . .

It was essential that the writing should contain an admission of the existence of the contract and of all the terms of it. If it failed to do so, it was not sufficient to satisfy the statute. That is plain from the decision of this court in *Thirkell v Cambi* [1919] 2 KB 590. . . .

The requirement of writing [for contracts of sale of goods] was repealed on 4 June 1954, by the Law Reform (Enforcement of Contracts) Act 1954. But those cases on sale of goods are of good authority in relation to the sale of land. The words of sections 4 and 17 of the Statute of Frauds are so similar as to preclude any distinction between them. In *Re Hoyle* [1893] 1 Ch 84 at 99, Bowen LJ so treated them.

[2] *The "offer cases" requiring only the terms to be set down in writing*
This line of authority is derived from a problem which arose when one party made an offer in writing which was accepted by the other party by word of mouth or by conduct. It has always been held that the party who signed the offer was bound by it. The contract could be enforced against him, but he could not enforce it against the other. The first of this line was an obiter dictum in 1856 in *Warner v Willington* (1856) 3 Drew 523 at 532, which was approved in the next year by the Court of Common Pleas in *Smith v Neale* (1857) 2 CBNS 67 at 88 and established beyond doubt by a strong Court of Exchequer Chamber in *Reuss v Picksley* (1866) LR 1 Exch 342. In that case Willes J, giving the judgment of the court, said, at p. 351:

> ". . . The only question is, whether it is sufficient to satisfy the statute that the party charged should sign what he proposes as

an agreement, and that the other party should afterwards assent
without writing to the proposal? As to this it is clear, both on
reasoning and authority, that the proposal so signed and assented
to, does become a memorandum or note of an agreement within
section 4 of the statute."

Now, I can well understand the reason why the courts established
this doctrine about a written offer. Very often the offer was accepted
by conduct. A good instance is where a man gives a guarantee in
writing for the price of goods thereafter to be supplied to a buyer. Once
the seller supplies the goods, he can sue on the guarantee. In *Reuss v
Picksley,* the defendant made in writing an offer to the plaintiffs of an
agency for Russia for 10 years, if the plaintiffs would bear a part of the
expenses of an exhibition. The plaintiffs accepted the offer by conduct.
They sent goods to the exhibition at much expense. They thus accepted
a written offer. It would be most unfortunate if they could not thereafter sue upon it. It was held that they could. Seeing that the common
law knew nothing of the doctrine of part performance (see *Britain v
Rossiter* (1879) 11 QBD 123), these decisions — about the acceptance
of a written offer — were very necessary to meet the justice of the case.
They were bold decisions on the words of the statute, just as were the
decisions in equity on part performance: see *Britain v Rossiter* (1879)
11 QBD 123 at 129 approved in *Maddison v Alderson* (1883) 8 App Cas
467. That is perfectly plain from a comment made by Bowen LJ on the
offer cases. He said in *Re New Eberhardt Co, Ex parte Menzies* (1889)
43 ChD 118, at 129:

"... We are bound by *Reuss v Picksley,* and that no doubt pushed
the literal construction of the Statute of Frauds to a limit beyond
which it would perhaps be not easy to go;".

I would only add this. It is well settled that a written offer accepted
orally or by word of mouth is a contract in writing: see *Mercantile
Bank of Sydney v Taylor* [1893] AC 317 at 321 and *L'Estrange v F.
Graucob Ltd* [1934] 2 KB 394 at 405. So these cases come with the
words of the statute as an "agreement in writing."

[3]   *The "subject to contract" cases*

During the last three years the "offer cases" have been extended far
beyond the limit thus set by Bowen LJ. They have been stretched so as
to cover correspondence which is expressly stated to be "subject to
contract." This was done because the "offer cases" were thought to
support a wide principle which was stated in these words by Buckley
LJ in *Law v Jones* [1974] Ch 112 at 124 [1973] 2 All ER 437 at 444:

"... it is not, in my judgment, necessary that the note or
memorandum should acknowledge the existence of a contract. It is
not the fact of agreement but the terms agreed upon that must be
found recorded in writing."

In accordance with that principle, this court held that a solicitor's
letter setting out terms "subject to contract" was a sufficient writing
to satisfy the statute.

The court said that the words "subject to contract" are a suspensive
condition which can be waived by subsequent oral agreement between

the parties. They can be removed from the document by oral evidence: see *Griffiths v Young* [1970] Ch 675, [1970] 3 All ER 601, by Widgery LJ at p. 685; by Cross LJ at p. 686 and by Russell LJ at p. 687 and *Law v Jones*, at p. 126, by Buckley LJ.

This court acknowledged that a letter which denied the very existence of a contract would not satisfy the statute: see *Law v Jones*, [1974] Ch 112 at 125, [1973] 2 All ER 437 at 445, by Buckley LJ. But it held that the words "subject to contract" were not to be treated as a denial of the contract, but only as imposing a suspensive condition, the subsequent waiver of which could be established by oral evidence: see p. 128, by Orr LJ[16].

Law v Jones has sounded an alarm bell in the offices of every solicitor in the land. And no wonder. It is everyday practice for a solicitor, who is instructed in a sale of land, to start the correspondence with a letter "subject to contract" setting out the terms or enclosing a draft. He does it in the confidence that it protects his client. It means that the client is not bound by what has taken place in conversation. The reason is that, for over a hundred years, the courts have held that the effect of the words "subject to contract" is that the matter remains in negotiation until a formal contract is executed: see *Eccles v Bryant and Pollock* [1948] Ch 93, [1947] 2 All ER 865. But *Law v Jones* has taken away all protection from the client. The plaintiff can now assert an oral contract in conversation with the defendant *before* the solicitor wrote the letter and then rely on the letter as a writing to satisfy the statute, even though it was expressly "subject to contract": or, alternatively, the plaintiff can assert that *after* the solicitor wrote the letter, he met the defendant and in conversation orally agreed to waive the words "subject to contract." If this is right, it means that the client is exposed to the full blast of "frauds and perjuries" attendant on oral testimony. Even without fraud or perjury, he is exposed to honest difference of recollections leading to law suits, from which it was the very object of the statute to save him.

The decision in *Griffiths v Young* [1970] Ch 675, [1970] 3 All ER 601 can be justified on other grounds. It would appear that, after the initial oral contract, there was a new and separate oral contract on 3 May 1963, of which the letter of 3 May was a sufficient memorandum. Alternatively, the letter of 3 May was an offer in writing which was accepted by the giving of a guarantee.

The decision in *Law v Jones* cannot be, however, justified on other grounds. Was it correctly decided? I do not think it was. Russell LJ dissented from the majority. I find his reasoning convincing. Take an imaginary case where there is said to have been an oral contract between vendor and purchaser. The vendor writes: "This is to confirm our agreement today, whereby you agreed to buy Blackacre for £10,000."

---

[16] See the "explanatory observations" by BUCKLEY LJ with which ORR L.J. "entirely agreed", in *Daulia Ltd v Four Millbank Nominees Ltd* [1978] Ch 231, at 249, [1978] 2 All ER 557 at 569.

1. The purchaser writes back: "I know we discussed the purchase of Blackacre for £10,000: but we did not come to any agreement about it." Clearly that is no sufficient memorandum.

2. The purchaser writes back: "I agree that, in the course of negotiation, we had arrived at a figure of £10,000 for Blackacre, but the whole matter is still in the course of negotiation: we have not finally agreed." That would also be no sufficient memorandum. It cannot be distinguished from the first case.

3. The purchaser writes back: "I know that I agreed to buy Blackacre for £10,000, but I made it clear to you that it was subject to contract, and I repeat it now. It was all subject to contract." That, too, is no sufficient memorandum. It cannot be distinguished from the second case.

I cannot myself see any difference between a writing which — (i) denies there was any contract; (ii) does not admit there was any contract; (iii) says that the parties are in negotiation; or (iv) says that there was an agreement "subject to contract", for that comes to the same thing. The reason why none of those writings satisfies the statute is because none of them contains any recognition or admission of the existence of a contract.

[4]   *Is this court bound by Law v Jones?*

In my opinion . . . we are not bound to follow *Law v Jones* [1974] Ch 112, [1973] 2 All ER 437. The legal profession should be freed from the anxieties which beset them. It should be done at once without delay. I would, therefore, hold here and now that *Law v Jones* was wrongly decided and should be overruled. The writing here, being expressly "subject to contract," was not sufficient to satisfy the statute. There is no enforceable contract between the parties. There was no sufficient reason for entering a caution on the register. It should be vacated at once. . . .

[5]   *Other points*

Such is sufficient for the decision of this case. But I may say that there is another fatal objection to the alleged note or memorandum. It does not contain all the terms of the oral contract as sworn to by Mr. Nadir in his affidavit. The draft omits the term that: "within a short time of completion, the Tiverton company would move out, giving vacant possession of the parts of the premises occupied by his company." The draft adds a term that: "the prescribed rate of interest will be 12 per cent per annum." Those seem to me to be material terms which, being omitted from the note or memorandum, are fatal to its validity: see *Hawkins v Price* [1947] Ch 645, [1947] 1 All ER 689.

c.   *The Doctrine of Part Performance*[17]

In the absence of a note or memorandum as required by the Law of Property Act 1925, s. 40, equity will decree specific performance of an

---

[17] Cheshire, pp. 121-125; M & W, pp. 561-571; MM, pp. 297-301; H & M, pp. 34-39; Snell, pp. 586-588.

oral agreement if there are acts sufficient to satisfy the equitable doctrine of part performance.

In applying this doctrine, "the defendant is really 'charged' upon the equities resulting from the acts done in execution of the contract, and not (within the meaning of the statute) upon the contract itself[18]." When will this be done? Before *Steadman v Steadman*[19] the authorities indicated that the doctrine applied if "the acts in question be such as must be referred to some contract and may be referred to the alleged one: that they prove the existence of some contract and are consistent with the contract alleged[20]." Thus, in *Kingswood Estate Co Ltd v Anderson*[1] a widow vacated rent-controlled premises in favour of others provided by her landlord under an oral agreement that she would be permitted to remain there for the rest of her life. She was able to set up the oral agreement in answer to a claim for possession by the landlord. And in *Wakeham v Mackenzie*[2], Mr. Ball, a widower of 72, orally agreed with Mrs. Wakeham, a widow of 67, that if she would give up her council flat, move into his house and look after him and the home for no wages, he would leave his house and contents to her in his will. After he died without making provision for her, she was able to enforce the contract. In *Maddison v Alderson*[3], where a housekeeper continued in service in a similar situation, the House of Lords took the view that the housekeeper could not enforce the contract because "her mere continuance in Thomas Alderson's service . . . was not such an act as to be in itself evidence of a new contract, much less of a contract concerning her master's land[4]."

The acts of part performance commonly involve a change of possession; but not necessarily. In *Rawlinson v Ames*[5], the landlord of a flat made alterations to premises in accordance with the wishes of the defendant who had orally agreed to take a lease of the flat. Specific performance was granted. But it had been laid down that money payments could never be a sufficient act of part performance." "Payment of money" it was said, ... raises no equity except possibly a right to recover it back[6]."

The jurisdiction was extended in *Steadman v Steadman.*

---

[18] *Maddison v Alderson* (1883) 8 App Cas 467 at 475, per Lord SELBORNE LC.
[19] [1976] AC 536, [1974] 2 All ER 977, infra.
[20] Fry, *Specific Performance* (6th edn.) p. 278, quoted by STAMP J in *Wakeham v Mackenzie* [1968] 1 WLR 1175 at 1181, [1968] 2 All ER 783 at 787; *New Hart Builders Ltd v Brindley* [1975] Ch 342, [1975] 1 All ER 1007.
[1] [1963] 2 QB 169, [1962] 3 All ER 593.
[2] [1968] 1 WLR 1175, [1968] 2 All ER 783.
[3] (1883), 8 App Cas 467.
[4] At p. 480 per Lord SELBORNE LC.
[5] [1925] Ch 26.
[6] *Thursby v Eccles* (1900) 49 WR 281 at 282, per BIGHAM J, quoted by SWINFEN EADY LJ in *Chapronière v Lambert* [1917] 2 Ch 356 at 360.

STEADMAN *v* STEADMAN[7]
[1976] AC 536; [1974] 2 All ER 977 (HL Lords REID and MORRIS OF
BORTH-Y-GEST, Viscount DILHORNE, Lords SIMON OF GLAISDALE
and SALMON.)

An oral compromise was made between spouses of various claims by
the wife to a half share in the matrimonial home, and £194 arrears of
maintenance payments. The compromise was that; (i) the wife should
surrender her interest in the house for £1,500; (ii) the wife's
maintenance order should be discharged; (iii) the arrears should be
remitted if £100 was paid by 30 March; (iv) the maintenance order for
the daughter should continue.

The husband paid the £100, and on 2 March, in proceedings before
the justices, who were told of the compromise, orders were accordingly
made in respect of the maintenance payments.

The husband's solicitors prepared the deed of transfer of the wife's
interest in the house. She refused to sign it, and demanded £2,000 for
her interest in the house or further maintenance payments. In
proceedings under s. 17 of the Married Women's Property Act 1882,
the question was whether or not the wife was bound by the oral compromise. She relied on s. 40 of the Law of Property Act 1925.

Held. (Lord MORRIS OF BORTH-Y-GEST dissenting). There were
sufficient acts of part performance by the husband, and the compromise was enforceable.

LORD SALMON: During the last 300 years there has been a mass of
authority on this topic. Unfortunately many of the cases are irrecon-
cilable with each other and it is by no means easy to discover the
true answer to the question with which we are faced, namely, what
are the essential elements of part performance in relation to contracts
disposing of an interest in land. One rule, however, emerges clearly; a
parol contract relating to land cannot be enforced unless the acts relied
on as part performance, of themselves, establish a prima facie case
that they were done in the performance of a contract. Then, but only
then, may parol evidence of the contract be accepted. In order to
discover the significance of the alleged acts of part performance, the
circumstances in which they were performed must, I think, clearly be
relevant. What is perhaps not so clear is whether the acts are sufficient
to constitute part performance if they establish only that they were
done in the performance of some contract which might but equally well
might not be a contract disposing of an interest in land. There is
certainly powerful authority for the view that this is not enough but
that the acts relied on must of themselves show prima facie that they
were done in performance of a contract disposing of such an interest.

It is perhaps not very difficult to see the reason for this view. Acts
relied on as part performance which show that a parol contract of the
kind referred to in the statute was probably made and that it has

---

[7] (1974) 38 Conv (NS) 354 (F. R. Crane), 388–391; (1974) 90 LQR 433 (H. W. R. Wade);
[1974] CLJ 205 (C. T. Emery).

been partly performed by the party who seeks to enforce it, raises a substantially stronger equity in his favour than acts which are equally consistent with the existence and part performance of a contract having nothing to do with land. The object of the statute was to prevent a dishonest person from fraudulently inventing a parol contract under which someone was supposed to have disposed of an interest in land to him and then bringing perjured evidence in support of his claim under the spurious contract. An act which proves that probably a contract for the disposal of an interest in land had been concluded and that the person seeking to enforce it had done his part under it goes further to obviate the mischief at which the statute was aimed than an act which shows merely the existence of some contract which may equally well have nothing to do with land.

The celebrated but perhaps somewhat Delphic passage in the speech of the Earl of Selborne LC in *Maddison v Alderson* (1883) 8 App Cas 467 at 475 which has been cited by my noble and learned friend, Viscount Dilhorne, is not inconsistent with either view. I think, however, that it is plain from other passages in the Earl of Selborne's speech that he took the view, generally held in his time, that for an act of alleged part performance to preclude a defendant from relying on the statute it must be an act "indicative of a contract concerning land". . .

To my mind, Lord Blackburn clearly agreed with the Earl of Selborne LC that, to take a case out of the statute, the act of part performance must show the existence of a contract concerning land. Indeed, he went a good deal further. He said, at p. 489:

"... there are cases that for the purpose of enforcing a specific performance of a contract for the purchase of an interest in land, a delivery of possession of the land will take the case out of the statute.". . .

I respectfully consider that Lord Blackburn went too far in limiting part performance to a change of possession but, in my opinion, all the speeches in *Maddison v Alderson* laid down that acts which prima facie establish the existence of some contract no more likely to be concerned with land than with anything else cannot be sufficient part performance for the purpose of taking a case out of the statute. This expression of opinion may have been obiter because the House concluded that no contract of any kind had been established. Nevertheless, it is a highly persuasive authority and for the reasons I have already indicated, I am not prepared to reject it.

We have certainly been referred to no reported case, and I have found none, in which an act of part performance which did not point to the existence of a contract concerning land has been held sufficient to take the case out of the statute. *Kingswood Estate Co Ltd v Anderson* [1963] 2 QB 169, [1962] 3 All 593 did not explode the idea accepted in *Maddison v Alderson* and a host of other cases. It exploded only the idea which had been expressed in some of the older authorities that, in order to take a case out of the statute, the act of part performance had to show not only the existence of a contract concerning land but also the very terms of the contract upon which the party seeking to enforce it relied. In the *Kingswood Estate* case a widow had for 45 years resided in premises of which she had become the statutory tenant. Her landlords were anxious to obtain possession of these premises in order to redevelop them. They acquired other premises to which they asked her to move. Having regard to the value of these premises, the Rent Acts did not apply to them, and she would, therefore, have had no security of tenure except by agreement. She entered into a parol agreement with the landlords under which she agreed to move on the terms that she would be left in possession of the new premises for the rest of her life. After she had moved, the landlords served her with a notice to quit. She set up the parol agreement. The landlords relied on the statute, arguing, unsuccessfully, that although the facts established a contract between them and the tenant relating to land, they did not take the case out of the statute because they did not show that the contract was for a life tenancy; they were equally consistent with a weekly tenancy. In his judgment, Upjohn LJ at p. 189 cited a passage from *Fry on Specific Performance*, 6th edn., p. 278. . . . That passage in its context does not, in my view, mean more than that if the acts of part performance relate prima facie to some contract concerning land, then parol evidence may be given to show what the terms of that contract are. I think that Upjohn LJ would have been surprised if anything which he said in that case were to be construed as throwing any doubt on the long-established principle that the only acts which can take a case out of the statute are acts which establish prima facie that they were done in part performance of a contract concerning land — especially as the point did not arise for decision since it was there necessarily conceded that the acts relied on did raise such a prima facie case. . . . [8]

It has never been held, nor, so far as I can discover, ever before the present case, suggested, that acts alleged to be in part performance of a parol contract take the contract out of the statute unless they make plain the general nature of the contract. I can find no reason for departing from that principle.

This, however, by no means concludes the appeal. Although I accept the authorities which show that acts of part performance, if they are to take a parol contract out of the statute, must be acts from which the nature of the contract can be deduced, I do not accept the line of authority which, overruling Lord Hardwicke LC in *Lacon v Mertins* (1743) 3 Atk 1 and *Hill v Allen* (1748) 1 Ves Sen 83, laid down that payment can never constitute such an act because it is impossible to deduce from payment the nature of the contract in respect of which the payment is made. It is no doubt true that often it is impossible to deduce even the existence of any contract from payment. For example,

---

[8] See *Re Gonin* [1979] Ch 16 at 31, [1977] 2 All ER 720 at 736, where WALTON J followed this view, that the act must be referable to some contract concerning land.

a payment by a parent to his child or a husband to his wife is in general no evidence of a contract; indeed, the presumption is to the contrary. Nevertheless the circumstances surrounding a payment may be such that the payment becomes evidence not only of the existence of the contract under which it was made but also of the nature of that contract. What the payment proves in the light of its surrounding circumstances is not a matter of law but a matter of fact. There is no rule of law which excludes evidence of the relevant circumstances surrounding the payment — save parol evidence of the contract on behalf of the person seeking to enforce the contract under which the payment is alleged to have been made.

My Lords, let us assume evidence of the following facts: A is anxious to sell an attractive house at a reasonable price of, say, £20,000. Full particulars of the house are sent to B by A's estate agents. The estate agents tell B, truthfully, that there are several people anxious to buy the house for the price asked but that owing to present economic conditions they have not yet been able to complete the necessary financial arrangements. They are expecting to do so at any moment. The estate agent, at B's request, makes an immediate appointment for B to inspect the house and meet A. B keeps the appointment. No written contract of sale comes into existence. B's cheque in favour of A for £20,000 is specially cleared by A the day after the appointment. A then refuses to convey the house to B and there is good reason to suppose that he is unable to repay the £20,000. Can anyone doubt that this evidence, unexplained, establishes a strong prima facie case that A orally agreed with B to sell him the house for £20,000 and that B performed his part of the contract by paying A the purchase price? If B sues A for specific performance of the parol agreement and applies for an interlocutory injunction to restrain A from parting with the house pending the trial of the action, it is surely inconceivable that our law can be so defective that it would allow A to shelter behind the statute. Yet A could succeed in doing so if the authorities which hold that payment can never substitute part performance for the purpose of taking a contract out of the statute were correctly decided. In my opinion, they were not.

Suppose another set of facts. B sues A for specific performance of a parol contract for the sale of A's house to him for £X,000 and alleges that he has paid A the £X,000. B gives evidence of the payment. A pleads the statute. A would have no case to answer because there would be no evidence of any circumstances surrounding the payment to connect it with the parol agreement. Suppose, however, that B, who is unrepresented, says to the judge at the trial: "Of course I agreed with A to sell him my house for £X,000 and he has certainly paid me that sum which unfortunately, I cannot repay." A's admission would, in my view, be sufficient to connect the payment with the parol contract, establish part performance and deprive A of his defence under the statute. Once a party to a parol contract relating to land admits to any court the existence of the contract and that he has received a benefit under it which he is unable or unwilling to restore, the mischief aimed at by the statute disappears. It would be most unreasonable and unjust that, in such circumstances, he should be able to rely on the statute in order to break his word and evade performing his part under the contract. There is certainly no authority binding on this House which would enable him to do so.

In the present case, the payment of £100 by the husband to his wife who had divorced him — looked at without regard to its surrounding circumstances — would not be any evidence of any contract, let alone of a contract concerning land. If the proposition that payment in part or even in full can never be part performance is correct, which, in my view, it is not, then the circumstances surrounding the payment must be irrelevant. I think, however, that the Court of Appeal were bound to accept this proposition by the authorities referred to with approval by the Earl of Selborne in *Maddison v Alderson* (1883) 8 App Cas 467, 469. On this basis, the reasons given by Edmund Davies LJ for reluntantly dismissing the appeal appear to me to be impeccable. The proposition has, however, never yet been debated before this House. In *Maddison v Alderson* it was assumed, without argument, to be correct: in any event it was wholly unnecessary for the decision of that appeal. This House is, therefore, not bound to accept the proposition and, for my part, I am unable to do so. I believe that the analysis of the proposition which I have attempted demonstrates that the proposition is fundamentally unsound and would lead to grave injustice.

If, in the present case, the payment of the £100 is looked at in the light of its surrounding circumstances, it is, in my opinion, quite plain that that sum was paid in part performance of a parol contract concerning land. The correspondence prior to 2 March 1972, shows that the only outstanding differences between the husband and the wife were then (a) the amount which he was to pay to her for transferring to him the interest which she claimed in the former matrimonial home and (b) what was to be done about the amount of arrears of maintenance to the wife which were then outstanding.

The husband had applied for the whole of these arrears to be remitted, and for an order for the wife's maintenance to be discharged. She had agreed to the discharge of that order. It is plain that the parties had very nearly reached agreement under which the wife should accept a total of £1,250 in full discharge of both her claims. Her solicitors then wrote on 17 February 1972, "Our client feels that she cannot compromise her claims for less than £1,500." The husband's solicitors wrote on 21 February 1972, stating that he would pay the £1,500 providing it was accepted in full discharge of both claims and asking the wife's solicitors to confirm that this was finally agreed. Having had no answer to that letter, the solicitor wrote on 29 February "Perhaps we could meet you at the court to finalise the final terms of settlement and then explain them to the magistrates." The next day the wife's solicitors wrote to say that they did not propose to attend the court and that they found difficulty in advising their client that the £1,500 should cover the arrears of maintenance as well as the purchase of the wife's interest in the house.

On 2 March the husband's solicitor met the wife outside the magistrate's court. There is no suggestion that he put any pressure upon her or behaved otherwise than with complete propriety. He and the wife came into court and he told the magistrates that they had come to an agreement settling all differences between the wife and the husband as follows. 1. She was to transfer her interests in the house to the husband for £1,500. 2. The husband was to pay her £100 not later than 30 March 1972, in full discharge of the arrears of maintenance, the balance of such arrears to be remitted. 3. The order for her maintenance was to be discharged but he was to continue paying maintenance (as previously ordered) in respect of the child of the marriage. The clerk then asked the wife if she had indeed come to this agreement. She replied that she had. The magistrates made an order implementing the agreement so far as they were able to do so. They also adjourned the proceedings until 30 March with an intimation that if the husband did not then pay the £100, further proceedings might be taken against him. He did pay the wife that sum on 30 March.

It is plain from the registrar's finding that the wife admitted in open court the parol agreement which she had made. It was a composite indivisible agreement, the integral parts of which were that she was to receive £100 within one month and that she was to transfer her interest in the house for £1,500.

The wife's admission in open court plainly connected the payment of the £100 with the parol agreement relating to the disposition of an interest in land and showed that the payment was in part performance of that agreement. She has not repaid or ever offered to repay any part of the £100. This payment, in my opinion, bars the wife from relying on the statute and she is accordingly bound to perform her part of the agreement.

I had some doubt whether incurring the costs incidental to the preparation of the deed of transfer and the transmission of that deed to the wife's solicitors also constituted part performance. A deed could well be prepared and transmitted in contemplation of a concluded agreement so as to save time. This clearly could not constitute part performance. The unchallenged evidence, however, shows that the deed in fact was not prepared until after 2 March 1972, the date upon which the wife admitted before the magistrates that the parol agreement was made. According to established practice, such an agreement calls for the transferee to incur the expense of preparing the deed and forwarding it to the transferor for approval. I am, therefore, inclined to think that in the circumstances of this case the preparation and transmission of the deed of transfer also amounted to part performance of the parol agreement[9].

---

[9] See *Re Windle* [1975] 1 WLR 1628, [1975] 3 All ER 987 (instructions to solicitors to prepare transfer and the payment of their costs and disbursements held sufficient acts of part performance).

My Lords, for these reasons I would dismiss the appeal.

LORD MORRIS OF BORTH-Y-GEST (dissenting): Courts of equity did not set out to make the terms of an Act of Parliament virtually nugatory. What the courts did was to consider the alleged acts of part performance and to decide whether the reasonable explanation of them was that the parties must have made (or stated otherwise had made) some contract such as the contract alleged. As the whole area of the law of part performance relates to contracts "for the sale or other disposition of land or any interest in land," I would have thought that it followed that on a consideration of alleged acts of part performance it has to be decided whether their reasonable explanation is that the parties must have made some contract in relation to land such as the contract alleged. I read the speeches in *Maddison v Alderson* (1883) 8 App Cas 467 as having proceeded on that basis. Thus, in that part of his speech in which he said that it was settled that part payment of purchase price was not enough to amount to part performance, Lord Selborne said, at p. 479, that the best explanation of that was that the payment of money is an equivocal act, not (in itself) until the connection is established by parol testimony, "indicative of a contract concerning land." It is because of this that the taking of possession of land will often be considered to be an act having strong claims to be regarded as an act of part performance indicative of a contract concerning the land.

I turn then to the question whether the payment of £100 by the husband can be regarded as an act of part performance. In my view, it cannot possibly be. The money was paid by the husband to the petty sessional court in Bromley. It was paid after that court had made the order of 2 March 1972, in the terms which I have set out. The payment into court by a husband of a sum of money to be sent by the court to his wife does not, in my view, prove that there had been some contract between them: even more emphatically it does not prove that there had been any contract concerning land. The only inference that would be drawn from the payment of £100 into court by a husband in matrimonial proceedings would be that he was in arrears in regard to some payments that he had been ordered to make. Without a connection established by parol testimony the payment of the money would not begin to suggest or to establish either the existence of a contract or of a contract in relation to land.

The other suggested acts relied upon on behalf of the husband do not, in my view, possess any greater merit. Nor, in my view, if they fail to qualify as acts of part performance do they have an accrual of merit by being linked with other suggested acts which also fail to qualify. It was submitted that the fact of mentioning the agreed terms to the magistrates and inviting them to make orders can be regarded as an act of part performance. But in agreement with Edmund Davies LJ I consider that an act of part performance, in order to be such, must be an act in relation to that term of a contract (in a case where there are other terms) which alone is required to be in writing if it is to be enforceable as satisfying section 40. In the present litigation what is being considered is whether an oral and prima facie unenforceable contract in relation to land has been made enforceable by reason of there being some act of part performance which shows that there must have been a contract in relation to land. An oral statement (or concurrence in an oral statement) that there was such an oral contract cannot, in my view, suffice.

Nor do I consider that any abandonment on the part of the husband of any attempt to ask the magistrates to remit the whole amount of the arrears of maintenance he owed to his wife can qualify as an act of part performance in relation to land. The fact that he incurred legal costs and then caused a draft conveyance to be sent to his wife's solicitors (which she ignored after receiving it — indicating to her solicitors that she was very reluctant to agree the terms) could certainly indicate a belief on his part that there had been an oral contract or it could indicate a hope or expectation that agreement would in the future be reached. Without more I do not think that an act of part performance was established.

This is most unfortunate litigation. Having regard to the findings of fact which must be accepted, I much regret that I am reaching a different conclusion from that of your Lordships. The case is a very special one, but even so I consider that the decision of the majority in the Court of Appeal involves extending the law relating to part performance in a way which I do not consider to be warranted.

I would allow the appeal.

QUESTIONS
1. In negotiations for the purchase of land, X and Y orally agree terms and further agree to exchange contracts the next day. X then orally promises Y that he will enter into a formal contract if Y attends at X's office before 10 a.m. the next day and tenders his part of the contract duly signed together with a banker's draft for the deposit. When Y complies with the conditions, X refuses to exchange contracts.
   (a) Is there a valid oral contract between X and Y?
   (b) If so, does L.P.A. 1925, s. 40 apply to that contract?
   (c) If it does, is there a sufficient act of part performance by Y?
      Daulia Ltd v Four Millbank Nominees Ltd [1978] Ch 231, [1978] 2 All ER 557. [1978] Conv 375 (F.R. Crane); (1979) 38 CLJ 31 (C. Harpum and D.L. Jones).
2. Are the following sufficient acts of part performance?
   (a) As a result of an oral agreement with X that he will leave his house and contents to Y in his will, Y gives up her council flat and looks after X and his house for no wages. X dies without making provision for Y. *Kingswood Estate Co Ltd v Anderson* [1963] 2 QB 169, [1962] 3 All ER 593; *Wakeham v Mackenzie* [1968] 1 WLR 1175, [1968] 2 All ER 783.

(*b*) In a similar situation,

   (i) Y, instead of moving house, continues to keep house for X. *Maddison v Alderson* (1883) 8 App Cas 467.

   (ii) Y leaves X's house, and then, as a result of X's oral agreement, Y returns to X's house and to the kind of position and standing which Y had before. *Re Gonin* [1979] Ch 16, [1977] 2 All ER 720, (1977) 41 Conv (NS) 350 (F.R. Crane), (1978) 128 NLJ 449 (J.G. Miller).

(*c*) X orally agrees to take a lease of a flat from Y, who agrees to make, and does make, alterations to it in accordance with the wishes of X.

Rawlinson v Ames [1925] Ch 96.

(*d*) X orally agrees to transfer the matrimonial home to his wife, Y, in consideration of her covenanting with his mortgagees to pay to them the mortgage arrears and instalments. Y pays them, instructs her solicitors to prepare the transfer, and pays X's costs and disbursements.

Re Windle [1975] 1 WLR 1628, [1975] 3 All ER 987.

ii.   CONVEYANCE

a.   *Formalities*[10]

LAW OF PROPERTY ACT 1925

51. Lands lie in grant only. — (1) All lands and all interests therein lie in grant and are incapable of being conveyed by livery or livery and seisin, or by feoffment, or by bargain and sale[11]; and a conveyance of an interest in land may operate to pass the possession or right to possession thereof, without actual entry, but subject to all prior rights thereto.

52. Conveyances to be by deed. — (1) All conveyances of land or of any interest therein are void for the purpose of conveying or creating a legal estate unless made by deed.

(2) This section does not apply to —

(*a*) assents by a personal representative[12];

(*b*) disclaimers made in accordance with section fifty-four of the Bankruptcy Act, 1914, or not required to be evidenced in writing;

(*c*) surrenders by operation of law, including surrenders which may, by law, be effected without writing;

(*d*) leases or tenancies or other assurances not required by law to be made in writing;

(*e*) receipts not required by law to be under seal;

(*f*) vesting orders of the court or other competent authority;

(*g*) conveyances taking effect by operation of law[13].

---

[10] Cheshire, pp. 390–391, 752–756; M & W, p. 167; MM, pp. 313–314; s. 54 (1) follows Statute of Frauds, s. 1; and s. 52 (1) follows Real Property Act 1845, s. 3.

[11] For these old methods of conveyancing, see M & W, pp. 163–167, and Holdsworth, vol. 3, pp. 217–246, vol. 7, pp. 356–362.

[12] But assents to the vesting of a legal estate in land must be in writing, signed by the personal representative: A.E.A, 1925, s. 36 (4); *Re King's Will Trusts* [1964] Ch 542, [1964] 1 All ER 833.

[13] E.g. probates and letters of administration.

54. Creation of interests in land by parol. — (1) All interests in land created by parol and not put in writing and signed by the persons so creating the same, or by their agents thereunto lawfully authorised in writing, have, notwithstanding any consideration having been given for the same, the force and effect of interests at will only.

b. *Title*[14]

LAW OF PROPERTY ACT 1925

44. Statutory commencements of title. — (1) After the commencement of this Act thirty years shall be substituted for forty years as the period of commencement of title which a purchaser of land may require; nevertheless earlier title than thirty years may be required in cases similar to those in which earlier title than forty years might immediately before the commencement of this Act be required.

LAW OF PROPERTY ACT 1969

23. Reduction of statutory period of title. — Section 44 (1) of the Law of Property Act 1925 . . . shall have effect, in its application to contracts made after the commencement of this Act[15], as if it specified fifteen years instead of thirty years as the period of commencement of title which may be so required.

c. *Conveyance to Self*

LAW OF PROPERTY ACT 1925

72. Conveyances by a person to himself &c. — (3) After the commencement of this Act a person may convey land to or vest land in himself.

(4)[16] Two or more persons (whether or not being trustees or personal representatives) may convey, and shall be deemed always to have been capable of conveying, any property vested in them to any one or more of themselves in like manner as they could have conveyed such property to a third party . . .

d. *Savings*

LAW OF PROPERTY ACT 1925

55. Savings in regard to last two sections. — Nothing in the last two foregoing sections shall —
    (a) invalidate dispositions by will; or
    (b) affect any interest validly created before the commencement of this Act; or

---

[14] Cheshire, pp. 731–733; M & W, pp. 123–124; MM, pp. 59–60. See also Law Commission Interim Report on Root of Title to Freehold Land (1967), Law Com. No. 9.
[15] 1 January 1970; L.P.A. 1969, s. 31 (2).
[16] *Rye v Rye* [1962] AC 496, [1962] 1 All ER 146; p. 385, post.

   (c) affect the right to acquire an interest in land by virtue of taking possession; or

   (d) affect the operation of the law relating to part performance.

e.   *Precedent*

PRECEDENT OF A CONVEYANCE ON SALE OF A FREEHOLD[17]

THIS CONVEYANCE made the.......day of.......[*date*] BETWEEN *AB* of....... [*address and description*] (hereinafter called "the Vendor") of the one part and *CD* of.......[*address and description*] (hereinafter called "the Purchaser") of the other part.

WHEREAS the Vendor is seised for his own sole benefit of the property hereby conveyed for a legal estate in fee simple in possession free from incumbrances and has agreed with the Purchaser for the sale thereof to him for the sum of £.......[*price*].

NOW THIS DEED WITNESSETH as follows:

   1.   In pursuance of the said agreement and in consideration of the sum of £.......paid by the Purchaser to the Vendor (the receipt whereof the Vendor hereby acknowledges) the Vendor as beneficial owner HEREBY CONVEYS unto the Purchaser ALL.......[*parcels*] TO HOLD unto the Purchaser in fee simple.

   2.   The Vendor HEREBY ACKNOWLEDGES the right of the Purchaser to the production of the documents mentioned in the Schedule hereto (the possession of which is retained by the Vendor) and to delivery of copies thereof AND HEREBY UNDERTAKES with the Purchaser for the safe custody of the same documents.

   3.   It is hereby certified that the transaction hereby effected does not form part of a larger transaction or of a series of transactions in respect of which the amount or value or the aggregate amount or value of the consideration exceeds [£20,000] [£25,000] [£30,000] [£35,000].

IN WITNESS whereof the said parties hereto have hereunto set their respective hands and seals the day and year first above [*or* "before"] written.

THE SCHEDULE

[*Here list the documents acknowledged*]
[*To be executed by the Vendor* (*and, if desired, the Purchaser*) *and attested*]

iii.   LEASES

a.   *Formalities*

LAW OF PROPERTY ACT 1925

54.   Creation of interests in land by parol. — (2) Nothing in the foregoing provisions of this Part of this Act shall affect the creation by parol of leases taking effect in possession for a term not exceeding

---

[17] Reproduced from Hallett's *Conveyancing Precedents* (1965), p. 192.

three years (whether or not the lessee is given power to extend the term) at the best rent which can be reasonably obtained without taking a fine[18].

52. Conveyances to be by deed. — (2) (*d*), p. 72, ante.

b. Title
This is dealt with later[19].

c. Savings

LAW OF PROPERTY ACT 1925

55. Savings in regard to last two sections. — p. 73, ante.

B. Equitable Interests[20]

i. REQUIREMENT OF WRITING

LAW OF PROPERTY ACT 1925

53. Instruments required to be in writing.[1] — (1) Subject to the provisions hereinafter contained with respect to the creation of interests in land by parol —

(*a*) no interest in land can be created or disposed of except by writing signed by the person creating or conveying the same, or by his agent thereunto lawfully authorised in writing, or by will, or by operation of law;

(*b*) a declaration of trust respecting any land or any interest therein must be manifested and proved by some writing signed by some person who is able to declare such trust or by his will;

(*c*) a disposition of an equitable interest or trust subsisting at the time of the disposition, must be in writing[2] signed by the person disposing of the same, or by his agent thereunto lawfully authorised in writing or by will[3].

(2) This section does not affect the creation or operation of resulting, implied or constructive trusts[4].

---

[18] I.e. a premium paid on the granting of the lease and operating in reduction of the rent. M & W, p. 622 n. 58.

[19] See p. 412, post.

[20] Cheshire, pp. 754–756; M & W, pp. 449–452; MM, p. 222–224.

[1] See generally H & M pp. 156–164; M & B (T) pp. 32–41.

[2] This may be satisfied by joinder of documents: *Re Danish Bacon Co Ltd Staff Pension Fund Trusts* [1971] 1 WLR 248, [1971] 1 All ER 486; c.f. L.P.A. 1925 s. 40 (1), p. 58, ante; *Timmins v Moreland St Property Co Ltd* [1958] Ch 110, [1957] 3 All ER 265.

[3] *Grey v I. R. C* [1960] AC 1, [1959] 3 All ER 603, (1960) 76 LQR 197 (R.E. Megarry); *Oughtred v I R C* [1960] AC 206, [1959] 3 All ER 623; *Re Tyler* [1967] 1 WLR 1269, [1967] 3 All ER 389; *Vandervell v I R C* [1967] 2 AC 291 at pp. 310–312, [1967] 1 All ER 1, [1966] CLJ 19 (G. H. Jones), [1979] Conv 17 (G. Battersby).

[4] *Bannister v Bannister* [1948] 2 All ER 133; *Hodgson v Marks* [1971] Ch 892, [1971] 2 All ER 684; (1971) 35 Conv NS 251 at 260–266 (I. Leeming); *Binions v Evans* [1972] Ch 359, [1972] 2 All ER 70; *Ottaway v Norman* [1972] Ch 698, [1971] 3 All ER 1325; *Re Vandervell's Trusts (No. 2)* [1974] Ch 269, [1974] 3 All ER 205.

ii. SAVINGS

LAW OF PROPERTY ACT 1925

55. Savings in regard to last two sections. — p. 73, ante.

C. Creation and Transfer in Equity. Estate Contracts

i. AN ESTATE CONTRACT IS A GRANT IN EQUITY[5]

An enforceable contract to convey or create a legal estate in land is one of the categories of contract which equity will specifically enforce[6]. If that remedy is available in respect of a particular contract, equity looks on that as done which ought to be done, and treats the situation as if the land were already conveyed. Such a contract is thus effective as a conveyance in equity[7]. This differs in various ways from a conveyance at law; just as interests in equity differ from estates and interests at law. The doctrine is applicable to contracts for the sale of land, contracts to grant a lease, a mortgage, an easement or profit, indeed a contract to convey or create a legal estate in any hereditament, corporeal or incorporeal[8]. Such a contract is termed an estate contract, and is defined in, and made registrable by, the Land Charges Act 1972, s. 2 (4), Class C (iv)[9].

Sir George JESSEL MR, in *Lysaght v Edwards* (1876) 2 ChD 499 said at p. 506: ". . . the effect of a contract for sale has been settled for more than two centuries; certainly it was completely settled before the time of Lord Hardwicke, who speaks of the settled doctrine of the court as to it. What is that doctrine? It is that the moment you have a valid contract for sale the vendor becomes in equity a trustee for the purchaser of the estate sold, and the beneficial ownership passes to the purchaser, the vendor having a right to the purchase-money, a charge or lien on the estate for the security of that purchase-money, and a right to retain possession of the estate until the purchase-money is paid, in the absence of express contract as to the time of delivering possession."

---

[5] H & M Chap. 26.

[6] On specific performance, see H & M chap. 2; Snell, pp. 573–600; Spry, *Equitable Remedies* (1971).

[7] Cheshire, pp. 69, 125–128, 742; M & W, pp. 132, 574–578; *Lysaght v Edwards* (1876) 2 ChD 499, supra. See also *Earl of Egmont v Smith* (1877) 6 ChD 469; *Abdulla v Shah*, [1959] AC 124; (vendor must not remove parts of the realty after the date of the contract) *Clarke v Ramuz* [1891] 2 QB 456; (removal of soil by trespasser), *Phillips v Lamdin* [1949] 2 KB 33, [1949] 1 All ER 770 (removal of door); the risk passes to the purchaser who should therefore insure. *Paine v Meller* (1801) 6 Ves 349; *Rayner v Preston* (1881) 18 ChD 1; L.P.A. 1925 s. 47 (reversing the decision in *Rayner v Preston*); *Berkley v Poulett* (1976) 241 Estates Gazette 911, 242 Estates Gazette 39 (discussing the rights of a sub-purchaser); *Ware v Verderber* (1978) 247 Estates Gazette 1081 (duty of vendor to take reasonable care of property).

[8] As to the distinction between grants of interests in real property and sales of chattels see M & W 547–549. The distinction also arises under L.P.A. 1925, s. 40 with regard to the necessity for evidence in writing. See also chap. 9, post: *Wood v Manley* (1839) 11 A & E 34; *James Jones & Son Ltd v Earl of Tankerville* [1909] 2 Ch 440.

[9] See p. 31 ante.

WALSH *v* LONSDALE[10]
(1882) 21 ChD 9 (CA, Sir George JESSEL MR, COTTON and
LINDLEY LJJ)

On 29 May 1879, the defendant agreed to grant to the plaintiff a lease
of a mill for seven years at a rent which varied with the number of
looms operated by the plaintiff, and at a rate per loom which depended
on whether the lessor or lessee provided the steam power. The
minimum rent payable was calculated on the smallest number of looms
which the plaintiff was contractually bound to operate, and at the
lowest rate was £810. The rent was payable in advance if demanded.
The plaintiff entered and paid rent quarterly, not in advance. He was
in arrears with rent due in January, 1882, and in March the defendant
demanded a year's rent in advance. It was not paid, and the defendant
distrained. The plaintiff brought this action for damages for illegal
distress and also for specific performance of the agreement and for an
interim injunction to restrain the distress.

Held. The landlord (defendant) had a right to distrain. An injunction
to restrain the distress would be granted only on payment by the
plaintiff of £810, the lowest sum that could be due for rent under the
lease.

SIR GEORGE JESSEL MR: The question is one of some nicety. There is
an agreement for a lease under which possession has been given. Now
since the *Judicature Act*[11] the possession is held under the agreement.
There are not two estates as there were formerly, one estate at
common law by reason of the payment of the rent from year to year,
and an estate in equity under the agreement. There is only one court,
and the equity rules prevail in it. The tenant holds under an agreement
for a lease. He holds, therefore, under the same terms in equity as if a
lease had been granted, it being a case in which both parties admit that
relief is capable of being given by specific performance. That being so,
he cannot complain of the exercise by the landlord of the same rights
as the landlord would have had if a lease had been granted. On the
other hand, he is protected in the same way as if a lease had been
granted; he cannot be turned out by six months' notice as a tenant
from year to year. He has a right to say, "I have a lease in equity, and
you can only re-enter if I have committed such a breach of covenant
as would if a lease had been granted have entitled you to re-enter

---

[10] *Tottenham Hotspur Football & Athletic Co Ltd v Princegrove Publishers Ltd* [1974]
1 WLR 113, [1974] 1 All ER 17, (1974) 90 LQR 149 (M. Albery); *Warmington v Miller*
[1973] QB 877, [1973] 2 All ER 372; *Industrial Properties (Barton Hill) Ltd v
Associated Electrical Industries Ltd* [1977] QB 580, [1977] 2 All ER 293.
[11] Supreme Court of Judicature Act 1873 provided for the creation of the Supreme
Court of Judicature and for the application in all branches thereof of the rules both of
law and of equity. In s. 25 (1)–(10) rules applicable to particular points are laid down,
and sub-s. (11) (now Supreme Court of Judicature (Consolidation) Act 1925, s. 44)
provides:
"Generally in all matters not herein-before particularly mentioned in which there is
any conflict or variance between the Rules of Equity and the Rules of the Common
Law with reference to the same matter, the Rules of Equity shall prevail."

according to the terms of a proper proviso for re-entry." That being so, it appears to me that being a lessee in equity he cannot complain of the exercise of the right of distress merely because the actual parchment has not been signed and sealed.

In *Industrial Properties (Barton Hill) Ltd v Associated Electrical Industries Ltd* [1977] QB 580, [1977] 2 All ER 293, the Parker trustees agreed in 1959 to sell part of an industrial estate to the plaintiff company. The purchase money was paid and the contract registered as a land charge, but, in order to save stamp duty, the legal estate was never conveyed to the company. In 1966 the company, which was a mere equitable owner, entered into negotiations with the defendants for the grant of a lease, and their solicitors inadvertently stated that the plaintiffs were the freeholders. The lease contained a covenant to keep the premises in good and tenantable repair and condition and so to yield them up at the determination of the term. When the lease expired, the defendants gave up possession, leaving the premises badly out of repair. The plaintiff company brought an action for damages for breach of the covenant. The defendants argued that the plaintiff company had no legal title to the premises. The Court of Appeal (Lord DENNING MR, ROSKILL and LAWTON LJJ) held that the defendants were liable. There was a tenancy by estoppel under which the defendants were estopped from denying the plaintiff company's title[12]. The Court of Appeal also held that the defendants were liable under the doctrine of *Walsh v Lonsdale*. Lord DENNING said at p. 598:

"Thus far I have considered the position at common law. But in equity there is a much shorter way to a decision. It is quite plain that, if the lease to A.E.I. was defective in point of law, nevertheless it was good in equity, and for this simple reason. There were two agreements of which specific performance would be granted. One was the agreement by the Parker trustees to convey to the plaintiff company. The other was the agreement by the plaintiff company to grant a lease to A.E.I. In respect of each of these agreements, equity looks upon that as done which ought to be done. It follows that, by combining the two agreements, the tenants, A.E.I., hold upon the same terms as if a lease had actually been granted by the Parker trustees to A.E.I. This is, of course, an extension of the doctrine of *Walsh v Lonsdale* (1882) 21 ChD 9 where there was only one agreement. But I see no reason why the doctrine should not be extended to a case like the present, where there were two agreements, each of which was such that specific performance would be granted."

In *McManus v Cooke* (1887) 35 ChD 681, the plaintiff and defendant were owners of adjoining houses. Between them was a party wall to which were fixed the lower ends of skylights which provided light to the basements of both houses, the upper end of the skylights being fixed to the respective buildings.

---

[12] P. 381, post.

The parties planned to rebuild their respective premises, and orally agreed that the wall should be rebuilt, and improved, and that each party should be entitled to make a lean-to skylight with its lower end resting on the wall.

The plaintiff built the skylight as agreed, but the defendant erected his in such a way that it obstructed the access of light to the plaintiff's skylight. The plaintiff claimed an injunction to restrain the defendant from permitting his skylight to remain in its present position.

KAY J held that the oral agreement was enforceable under the doctrine of part performance, and that the plaintiff was entitled to an easement on the terms of the agreement. He made an exhaustive analysis of the authorities and said at p. 697: "These authorities seem to me to establish the following propositions: (1) The doctrine of part-performance of a parol agreement, which enables proof of it to be given notwithstanding the *Statute of Frauds*, though principally applied in the case of contracts for the sale or purchase of land, or for the acquisition of an interest in land, has not been confined to those cases. (2) Probably it would be more accurate to say it applies to all cases in which a Court of Equity would entertain a suit for specific performance if the alleged contract had been in writing. (3) The most obvious case of part-performance is where the defendant is in possession of land of the plaintiff under the parol agreement. (4) The reason for the rule is that where the defendant has stood by and allowed the plaintiff to fulfil his part of the contract, it would be fraudulent to set up the statute. (5) But this reason applies wherever the defendant has obtained and is in possession of some substantial advantage under a parol agreement which, if in writing, would be such as the court would direct to be specifically performed. (6) The doctrine applies to a parol agreement for an easement, though no interest in land is intended to be acquired.

I have no doubt that the present case comes within the principle of these decisions."

In *Mason v Clarke* [1955] AC 778, [1955] 1 All ER 914, a landlord (the appellant company) granted a lease of land to a farmer (the respondent). The landlord orally agreed to grant to Mason (the appellant) the right to catch rabbits on the land for the period of one year in consideration of the payment of £100. The farmer interfered with Mason's activities and took up his rabbit snares. On the assumption that there was no evidence of a grant to Mason which would satisfy the Law of Property Act 1925, section 40, Mason could only rely upon an oral grant followed by entry upon the land, and the setting of traps. One question was whether this could be the basis of a grant.

LORD MORTON OF HENRYTON said at p. 798: "A profit à prendre is an interest in land, and no legal estate therein can be created or conveyed except by deed (Law of Property Act 1925, s. 52). At the time when the respondent did the acts of which complaint is made, there had been no grant by deed of the profit à prendre to Mr. Mason, but prima facie he had the benefit of an oral agreement for the grant thereof, and he had entered into possession thereof in the only possible way, viz., by exercising his rights thereunder . . .

. . . I am inclined to agree that there was no sufficient memorandum until 30 December 1950, but it is unnecessary to examine the relevant documents in detail because I am quite satisfied that the acts of Mr. Mason, already described, were a part performance of the oral agreement of 11 October 1950. Mr. Mason set snares, took rabbits and paid helpers, and, in my view, the work done and expense incurred were exclusively referable to the oral agreement. Accordingly, at the relevant time Mr. Mason had a contract, specifically enforceable against the appellant company, for the grant of a profit a prendre, and had entered into possession thereof. In these circumstances he was clearly entitled to bring an action for trespass against the respondent: see *Holford v Pritchard* ((1849) 3 Exch 793) and *Fitzgerald v Firbank*, ([1897] 2 Ch 96)."

In *Ex parte Wright* (1812) 19 Ves 255 at 258 Lord ELDON LC said: "In that case [a deposit of deeds with a mortgage] the deposit is evidence of an agreement for a mortgage: and an equitable title to a mortgage is here as good as a legal title."

ii.   SPECIFIC PERFORMANCE IS DISCRETIONARY

COATSWORTH *v* JOHNSON[13]
(1886) 54 LT 520 (CA, Lord ESHER MR, LINDLEY and LOPES LJJ)

The plaintiff entered into possession of the defendant's farm under an agreement to execute a lease in accordance with a draft lease which had already been signed but not sealed. This draft contained, among other covenants, a covenant by the tenant to use the land in a good and husbandlike manner, and there was a power of re-entry on breach of any of the covenants.

The plaintiff failed to cultivate the farm properly, and the defendant, before any rent was due or paid, gave notice to quit and, acting under the power of re-entry, turned the plaintiff out of possession. The plaintiff brought this action for damages for trespass, claiming protection under section 14 Conveyancing Act 1881[14].

Held. The plaintiff was not entitled to the protection of the statute.

LOPES LJ: In this case the tenant, the plaintiff, who brings this action for trespass, is in possession of the land in question under an agreement for a lease. No rent has been paid, and that agreement contains a covenant to cultivate the land according to the approved course of husbandry — the usual covenant — and it has been found by the jury that that covenant has been broken. But, as I have said, no

---

[13] *Williams v Greatrix* [1957] 1 WLR 31, [1956] 3 All ER 705; *Cornish v Brook Green Laundry Ltd* [1959] 1 QB 394, [1959] 1 All ER 373, (1959) 75 LQR 168 (R. E. M.); *Kingswood Estate Co Ltd v Anderson* [1963] 2 QB 169, [1962] 3 All ER 593, (1963) 79 LQR 19 (R. E. M.); *Warmington v Miller* [1973] QB 877 at 887, [1973] 2 All ER 372; *Bell Street Investments v Wood* (1970) 216 Estates Gazette 585.

[14] L.P.A. 1925, s. 146, p. 397, post, giving relief to a tenant against forfeiture.

rent has been paid. If rent had been paid the position of things would have been very different. Then the plaintiff would have been a tenant from year to year on the terms of that agreement, so far as those terms are not inconsistent with a yearly tenancy. But no rent having been paid, I am clearly of opinion that the plaintiff is a tenant at will only.

But it is said in this case that he is more than a tenant at will, because the court of equity would have decreed specific performance of this agreement for a lease, and that he must be regarded as lessee for the term of years mentioned in that agreement on the ground that we must regard that as done which a court of equity would have done. No doubt that is perfectly correct. But then the point arises, would the court of equity have decreed specific performance under the particular circumstances of this case? The plaintiff, the tenant, when he went to the court of equity and asked for specific performance, would have had to admit that which has been proved here, namely, that he himself had failed to perform a material portion of the contract — in point of fact, that he had broken a portion of the agreement. I take it that, under those circumstances, it is perfectly clear that the court of equity would have refused specific performance. If that is so, he is only a tenant at will. The notice had been given; the tenancy was determined; and the landlord, the defendant, makes out the justification which he sets up in this action. It might have been that a very different and important question might have arisen under section 14 of the Conveyancing Act 1881. I do not think, however, that that arises under the circumstances of this case. It is not necessary for us to consider what the position of the tenant under the lease would have been, and I therefore do not give any opinion with regard to that section.

iii. REGISTRATION

Estate contracts, being interests in equity only, are liable to destruction by a bona fide purchaser of the legal estate for value without notice.

> Maitland, *Equity* (2nd edn.) p. 158:
>
> "An agreement for a lease is not equal to a lease. An equitable right is not equivalent to a legal right; between the contracting parties an agreement for a lease may be as good as a lease; just so between the contracting parties an agreement for the sale of land may serve as well as a completed sale and conveyance. But introduce the third party and then you will see the difference. I take a lease; my lessor then sells the land to X; notice or no notice my lease is good against X. I take a mere agreement for a lease, and the person who has agreed to grant the lease then sells and conveys to Y, who has no notice of my merely equitable right. Y is not bound to grant me a lease."

Estate contracts are registrable as land charges Class C (iv) under the Land Charges Act 1972[15].

---

[15] L.C.A. 1972, s. 2 (4), p. 31, ante.

QUESTIONS

1. It has often been said that the effect of the Judicature Act is to effect a fusion of procedure but not of substantive law. "But the two streams of jurisdiction, though they run in the same channel run side by side, and do not mingle their waters." Ashburner, *Principles of Equity*, (2nd edn. 1933) p. 18. What light is thrown on this question by the cases considered in this section? See also (1870) 14 Sol Jo 548; (1954) 70 LQR 326 (Lord Evershed); (1961) 24 MLR 126 (V.T.H. Delany); (1977) 93 LQR 529 (P.V. Baker); (1977) 6 AALR 119 (T.G. Watkin); H & M, pp. 17–20; Pettit, *Equity and the Law of Trusts* (4th edn. 1979), pp. 6–10; *United Scientific Holdings Ltd v Burnley Borough Council* [1978] AC 904, [1977] 2 All ER 62.

2. Work out, step by step, the way in which the *Walsh v Lonsdale* litigation would have proceeded before 1875. H & M p. 15.

3. Is a contract for a lease as good as a lease? p. 387, post. What is the effect of the Land Charges Act 1972 upon this?

IV.　Fixtures[16]

A.　What is Land?

Since land and chattels are treated differently by the law and since a chattel may, by being affixed to land, become part of the land, it is necessary to have a test to determine whether or not such a change has taken place. For example, a brick in a builder's yard is a chattel; once used to build a wall, it becomes part of the land; and if the wall is knocked down the bricks become chattels again. When land is sold, the conveyance includes the land but not the chattels[17]; but includes those things which were once chattels but which have become land.

The question whether a chattel remains a chattel or has become part of the land can arise in many contexts, namely; whether it passes to a purchaser[18], or sub-purchaser[19], on a sale of the land; whether it is included as part of the security on a mortgage of the land[20]; whether it is

---

[16] Cheshire, pp. 136–144 M & W, pp. 711–719; MM, pp. 347–350. L.P.A. 1925 s. 205 (1) (ix); S.L.A. 1925, s. 117 (1) (ix); T.A. 1925, s. 68 (6); L.R.A. 1925, s. 3 (viii); L.C.A. 1972, s. 17 (1); Interpretation Act 1978, s. 5, Sch. 1.

[17] By statute a conveyance includes a number of additional rights. L.P.A. 1925, s. 62, p. 530, post.

[18] *Colgrave v Dias Santos* (1823) 2 B & C 76 (fixtures, including those which a tenant could have removed, passed on sale of freehold); *Phillips v Lamdin* [1949] 2 KB 33, [1949] 1 All ER 770 (purchaser entitled to reinstatement of Adam door removed by vendor).

[19] *Berkley v Poulett* (1976) 241 Estates Gazette 911, 242 Estates Gazette 39.

[20] *Holland v Hodgson* (1872) LR 7 CP 328; *Hobson v Gorringe* [1897] 1 Ch 182, (machinery affixed. The judgment of SMITH LJ contains a resume of the cases up to that time); *Lyon & Co v London City and Midland Bank* [1903] 2 KB 135 (tip-up seats screwed to bolts fastened to floor and hired to mortgagors: held to be chattels); *Vaudeville Electric Cinema Ltd v Muriset* [1923] 2 Ch 74 (similar seats owned by mortgagor held to be land); *Reynolds v Ashby & Sons* [1904] AC 466 (machines bolted to the floor held to be land); *Hulme v Brigham* [1943] KB 152, [1943] 1 All ER 204 (heavy printing machinery resting by its own weight held by BIRKETT J to be chattels).

owned by the estate of a tenant for life or passes to the remainderman[1]; whether it is owned by a tenant for years or by the freeholder[2]; whether it passes on a death as realty or personalty[3]; and whether a drainpipe, placed underground in the exercise of an easement of drainage, remains the property of the party entitled to the easement[4].

A related but separate question follows[5]. There are some occasions in which the owner of a one-time chattel may remove it even though it has now become part of the land. A tenant for years has long been able to remove trade, ornamental and domestic fixtures, and may now, by statute, remove agricultural fixtures also[6]. A tenant for life was in the same position at common law, but has not been given the statutory right to agricultural fixtures.

BERKLEY *v* POULETT

(1976) 241 Estates Gazette 911, 242 Estates Gazette 39, CA (STAMP, SCARMAN and GOFF LJJ).

The eighth Earl Poulett agreed to sell the Hinton St. George Estate to Effold Ltd, and Effold Ltd agreed, as Earl Poulett knew, to sell Lot 1, which included the mansion house, to the plaintiff. The properties were duly conveyed.

Prior to the conveyance to Effold, the Earl removed a number of treasures from the house, and sold them. Effold Ltd was unconcerned; but the plaintiff claimed that, by virtue of the sub-contract between himself and Effold Ltd, he became the owner of the treasures.

The treasures in question were —

(i) a number of pictures which, while still in their frames, had been affixed by screws into the recesses in the panelling of the dining room:

(ii) a white marble statue of a Greek athlete, weighing half a ton, and a sundial; each resting by its own weight on a plinth or pedestal outside the house.

---

[1] *D'Eyncourt v Gregory* (1866) LR 3 Eq 382 (ornamental statues in park, resting by their weight on plinth, held to be part of realty); *Leigh v Taylor* [1902] AC 157 (tapestries stretched over canvas and tacked thereto held to remain chattels); *Re Lord Chesterfield's Settled Estates* [1911] 1 Ch 237 (proceeds of sale of ornamental wood carvings by Grinling Gibbons treated as capital money under S.L.A. 1882).

[2] *Culling v Tufnal* (1694) Bull NP 34; *Elwes v Maw* (1802) 3 East 38 (Dutch barn resting by own weight in hollow of brick foundations remained a chattel); *Webb v Frank Bevis Ltd* [1940] 1 All ER 247 (similarly a corrugated iron building held to floor by iron strips).

[3] *Bain v Brand* (1876) 1 App Cas 762 (machinery on colliery passed to heir and not to executor); *Re Whaley* [1908] 1 Ch 615 (pictures and tapestries in dining-room designed as a "complete specimen of Elizabethan dwelling-house" passed under devise of house and not under bequest of chattels).

[4] *Simmons v Midford* [1969] 2 Ch 415, [1969] 2 All ER 1269 (plaintiff's drainpipe under roadway held to be chattel with which neighbour claiming an easement of drainage could not interfere); cf. *Montague v Long* (1972) 24 P & CR 240 (bridge over river).

[5] The two questions are not always kept separate. *Leigh v Taylor* [1902] AC 157: compare Lords HALSBURY and MACNAGHTEN with Lord SHAND. In the Court of Appeal, *sub nom. Re De Falbe* [1901] 1 Ch 523, STIRLING LJ said: "It appears to me, therefore, both on principle and on authority that the exception from the rule extends to ornamental fixtures as well as to trade fixtures. Now, what are the objects as to which the dispute arises here? Tapestries. Photographs of some of them have been produced, and they shew that the tapestries are of an ornamental character, and, therefore, it appears to me that the exception from the rule applies."

[6] Agricultural Holdings Act 1948, s. 13.

The plaintiff claimed that these treasures were fixtures, The further question whether, assuming they were fixtures, the plaintiff was entitled to them by virtue of this sub-contract, is omitted here.

Held. The treasures were not fixtures.

SCARMAN LJ: As so often, the difficulty is not the formulation but the application of the law. I think there is now no need to enter into research into the case law prior to *Leigh v Taylor* [1902] AC 157. The answer today to the question whether objects which were originally chattels have become fixtures, that is to say part of the freehold, depends upon the application of two tests: (1) the method and degree of annexation; (2) the object and purpose of the annexation. The early law attached great importance to the first test. It proved harsh and unjust both to limited owners who had affixed valuable chattels of their own to settled land and to tenants for years. The second test was evolved to take care primarily of the limited owner, for example a tenant for life. In *Leigh v Taylor* the House of Lords invoked it to protect the interest of the tenant for life who had affixed large and valuable tapestries to the walls of the house for the purpose of adornment and enjoyment of them as tapestries. As I read that decision, it was held that she had not made them fixtures. "They remained chattels from first to last," said Lord Lindley at p. 164 of the report. In the law of landlord and tenant the law's protection went further: even if the chattel affixed by the tenant must be held to have become a fixture, that is to say part of the realty, a rule was evolved that it was to be treated as the property of the tenant and could be removed by him if it fell into a class recognised by law as "tenant's fixtures," that is to say if it be a trade, agricultural, or an ornamental fixture. We are not concerned, on the view I take of the case, with "tenant's fixtures." The governing relationship with which this case is concerned is that of a beneficial owner of the legal estate selling the freehold to a purchaser. Such a seller can sell as much or as little of his property as he chooses. Lord Poulett excluded certain named objects from the sale, but the contract was silent as to the objects claimed by the plaintiff. I think it was conceded by the defendants — certainly I so read the contract of sale — that, if the pictures, statue, and sundial were fixtures at the time of the contract, they were included in it as part of the freehold (subject of course to a valuation if they should prove to be tenant's fixtures). The preliminary, and basic, question is therefore whether these objects were at that time fixtures.

Since *Leigh v Taylor* the question is really one of fact. The two tests were explained in that case by the Lord Chancellor (see the report at pp. 158 and 159), who commented that not the law but our mode of life has changed over the years; that what has changed is "the degree in which certain things have seemed susceptible of being put up as mere ornaments whereas at our earlier period the mere construction rendered it impossible sometimes to sever the thing which was put up from the realty." In other words, a degree of annexation which in earlier times the law would have treated as conclusive may now prove nothing. If the purpose of the annexation be for the better enjoyment of the object itself, it may remain a chattel, notwithstanding a high degree of physical annexation. Clearly, however, it remains significant to discover the extent of physical disturbance of the building or the land involved in the removal of the object. If an object cannot be removed without serious damage to, or destruction of, some part of the realty, the case for its having become a fixture is a strong one. The relationship of the two tests to each other requires consideration. If there is no physical annexation there is no fixture. *Quicquid plantatur solo solo cedit.* Nevertheless an object, resting on the ground by its own weight alone, can be a fixture, if it be so heavy that there is no need to tie it into a foundation, and if it were put in place to improve the realty. *Prima facie,* however, an object resting on the ground by its own weight alone is not a fixture: see *Megarry and Wade,* p. 716. Conversely, an object affixed to realty but capable of being removed without much difficulty may yet be a fixture, if, for example, the purpose of its affixing be that "of creating a beautiful room as a whole" (Neville J in *In Re Whaley* [1908] 1 Ch 615 at 619). And in the famous instance of *Lord Chesterfield's Settled Estates* [1911] 1 Ch 237 Grinling Gibbons carvings, which had been affixed to a suite of rooms 200 years earlier, were held to be fixtures. Today so great are the technical skills of affixing and removing objects to land or buildings that the second test is more likely than the first to be decisive. Perhaps the enduring significance of the first test is a reminder that there must be some degree of physical annexation before a chattel can be treated as part of the realty.......

The 7th Earl decided in the early part of the 20th century to install in the two rooms the panelling and so designed it that there were recesses for pictures. It is this feature which lends plausibility to the suggestion that the pictures, fitted into the recesses left for them, were not to be enjoyed as objects in themselves but as part of the grand architectural design of the two rooms. The Vice-Chancellor rejected this view. So do I. When the panelling was installed in the two rooms the design was either panelled walls with recesses for pictures to be enjoyed as pictures, or rooms having walls which were a composite of panelling and pictures: in other words, the pictures were to be part of a composite mural. I think the former was the truth. The panelling was Victorian, the pictures a heterogeneous collection. According to Sothebys' expert they were of different dates in the 17th and 18th centuries, of different styles, by different hands, the sort of set anyone could put together at any time — very different, I would comment, from that unity of design, the "Elizabethan Room" in the case of *In re Whaley.* There was a particular Poulett family interest in "The Return" and in the two coronation portraits, but this interest focused attention not on the design of the room but on the pictures themselves. Notwithstanding the painstaking and attractive arguments of Mr. Millett for the plaintiff, I find, applying the second test, that the pictures were not fixtures. They were put in place on the wall to be enjoyed as pictures. The panelling presented a technical problem in putting them up. The way the carpenter, or whoever it was, solved the problem is not decisive in determining their legal character. But the purpose in putting them there is.

The statue and the sundial give rise in my judgment to no difficulty. Neither was at the time of the sale physically attached to the realty. The sundial was a small object and, once the Earl had detached it (as he did many years earlier) from its pedestal, it ceased to be part of the realty. The statue was heavy. It weighed 10 cwt and stood 5 ft 7 in high on its plinth. There is an issue as to whether it was cemented into the plinth or rested on its own weight. The question is not decisive, for, even if it was attached by a cement bond, it was (as events proved) easily removable. However, upon the balance of probability, I agree with the Vice-Chancellor in thinking it was not attached. The best argument for the statue being a fixture was its careful siting in the West Lawn so as to form an integral part of the architectural design of the west elevation of the house. The design point is a good one so far as it goes: it explains the siting of the plinth, which undoubtedly was a fixture. But what was put upon the plinth was very much a matter for the taste of the occupier of the house for the time being. We know that at one time the object on the plinth had been a sundial. At the time of the sale it was this statue of a Greek athlete. The plinth's position was architecturally important: it ensured that whatever stood on it would be correctly positioned. But the object it carried could be whatever appealed to the occupier for the time being. Sundial or statue — it did not matter to the design, so long as it was in the right place — a result ensured by the plinth which was firmly fixed into the ground. Being, as I think, unattached, the statue was, *prima facie*, not a fixture, but, even if it were attached, the application of the second test would lead to the same conclusion.

B.   What Fixtures may be Removed?

Even if a chattel is affixed to the land so as to become part of the land, the person who affixed it or his successors in title may have a right to remove it. At common law, a tenant for years and a tenant for life were entitled to remove trade[7], ornamental or domestic fixtures[8]. By Agricultural Holdings Act 1948, section 13, replacing earlier legislation, a tenant for years may also remove agricultural fixtures. As between devisee and personal representative, vendor and purchaser and mortgagor and mortgagee there is no right of removal, and the question of entitlement is dependent upon the question of annexation to the land[9].

---

[7] *Poole's Case* (1703) 1 Salk 368; *Climie v Wood* (1869) LR 4 Exch 328; *Penton v Robart* (1801) 2 East 88; *Wardell v Usher* (1841) 3 Scott NR 508; *Elliott v Bishop* (1854) 10 Exch 496; *Smith v City Petroleum Co Ltd* [1940] 1 All ER 260.

[8] *Grymes v Boweren* (1830) 6 Bing 437; *Buckland v Butterfield* (1820) 2 Brod & Bing 54; *Beck v Rebow* (1706) 1 P Wms 94; *Leach v Thomas* (1835) 7 C & P 327; *Spyer v Phillipson* [1931] 2 Ch 183; *Colegrave v Dias Santos* (1823) 2 B & C 76, 77; *Darby v Harris* (1841) 1 QB 895; *Lyde v Russell* (1830) 1 B & Ad 394.

[9] See p. 83, ante.

2. Registered Land[1]

I. Registered Conveyancing

We have seen that the basic doctrines of land law developed at common law under a system in which title to land was proved by the production of deeds recording the history of transactions affecting the land; and that the system is steadily being overtaken by a system which is based upon the registration of title to land. In areas in which the latter system is in operation, all transfers of legal title are required to be by registration of the transferee's name in the register; and gradually title to land in the area is entered on the register. The old cumbrous method of conveyancing by title deeds is dispensed with; and a registered title is thenceforth guaranteed by the State.

A system of registration of title was introduced into England as far back as 1862, but only on an optional basis. The revised system of registration of title contained in the Land Registration Acts 1925–1971[2] and Rules of 1925[3] — which must be kept wholly distinct from systems of registration of deeds[4] and charges (such as that under the Land Charges Act 1972) — is, however, in the process of being made, area by area, compulsory over the whole of England and Wales; com-

---

[1] Cheshire, pp. 103–112, 766–788; M & W, pp. 1054–1084; MM, pp. 513–528. The authoritative account is Ruoff and Roper (prior and present Chief Land Registrars respectively), *Law and Practice of Registered Conveyancing* (4th edn. 1979). Ruoff, *Concise Land Registration Practice* (2nd edn. 1967); Ruoff, *Land Registration Forms* (2nd edn. 1973); Encyclopaedia of Forms and Precedents (4th edn. 1970), vol. xvii. pp. 112–270 (R. B. Roper); Wolstenholme and Cherry, *Conveyancing Statutes* (13th edn. 1972); vol. 6. Barnsley, *Conveyancing Law and Practice* (1973), Chaps. 2, 3, 4, 12, 16; Hayton, *Registered Land* (2nd edn. 1977); Wontner's *Guide to Land Registry Practice* (13th edn. 1979). The Land Registry issues Practice Notes in conjunction with the Law Society (1972), and the Chief Land Registrar an Annual Report on H.M. Land Registry. The Law Commission is revising registered conveyancing. It has so far published four Working papers; No. 32 (leaseholds), No. 37 (overriding interests), No. 45 (identity and boundaries: and rectification and indemnity), and No. 67 (methods of protection of interests in land, including mortgages and charges). The Law Commission hopes to present it's report towards the end of 1980. Law Com. No. 97, Fourteenth Annual Report 1978–1979, para. 2.33.

[2] L.R.A. 1925, 1936, 1966 and Land Registration and Land Charges Act 1971, Parts I and III.

[3] There are further Rules in 1956, 1964, 1967, 1969, 1971, 1972, 1976, 1977 and 1978.

[4] The Yorkshire Deeds Registries are now closed: L.P.A. 1969, Part II.

pulsory in the sense that dealings in land after the given date must be carried out under the new and not the old system of conveyancing. Responsibility for making an area, from a given date, one of compulsory registration in this sense, now rests with the central, and not the local authorities[5].

The 1925 registration system provides for the *registration* of legal titles to land, and the *protection* of other interests in and over land. It is important to grasp the nature of this dichotomy. Only interests capable of subsisting at law under the Law of Property Act 1925, s. 1, are *registrable*. Other interests, called "minor interests", are protected, not by registration as separate titles, but by entry on the register by means of a notice, restriction, caution or inhibition. Each legal title has a separate card in the Registry[6] and that card will contain such entries as are appropriate. In 1977 a new computerised system was introduced for indexing the names of proprietors of registered land and registered charges[7], and it is anticipated that this index will be fully computerised by 1983[8]. In addition, however, there are overriding interests that are binding on purchasers irrespective of entry on the register. Overriding interests are those which are not capable of being fitted into a system of registration. Their existence prevents the register from being the sole source of title to rights affecting land. The landowner receives from the Registry a land certificate which reproduces the relevant entries on the register, but it is the register, not the land certificate, which establishes, and is, the source of title. There is no room in the registered land system for the doctrine of the bona fide purchaser of the legal estate for value without notice; but, in cases where the Act fails to provide an answer, the court, as has been seen[9], will fall back on general equitable principles.

We have already seen that the number of legal estates which can exist after 1925 is reduced to two by s. 1 of the Law of Property Act 1925. We will see in Part II that, under the 1925 legislation, equitable beneficial interests in land are not required to be disclosed in the title deeds. A purchaser knows that they exist, but does not need to know details of them, as he will "overreach" them — that is, he will buy the land free from them, and they will attach instead to the

[5] L.R.A. 1966, s. 1 (1). For compulsory registration areas, see Registration of Title Order 1977 (S.I. 1977 No. 828), p. 89, post and for present progress, see the Annual Report for 1978–1979, paras. 1–3. Voluntary registration in non-compulsory areas is now only possible in special cases. L.R.A. 1966, s. 1 (2); (1967) 31 Conv (NS) 7; Practice Leaflet No. 12 (1977) 41 Conv (NS) 147. The registered system now handles about half of all conveyancing in England and Wales. On 31 March 1979 there were 6,347,002 separate titles on the register, and during the year ended 31 March, 417,080 applications for first registration were completed. Annual Report 1978–1979 paras. 3, 15.

[6] The Headquarters is at Lincoln's Inn Fields, London. Registers of Titles are kept at twelve District Registries. L.R. (District Registries) Order 1979 (S.I. 1979 No. 1019). For a map showing their areas of responsibility, see (1979) 123 Sol Jo 766.

[7] Annual Report for 1977–78, paras. 20–22.

[8] Annual Report for 1978–79, para. 35.

[9] P. 26, ante; *Abigail v Lapin* [1934] AC at 500–502; *Strand Securities Ltd v Caswell* [1965] Ch 958 at 991, [1965] 1 All ER 820.

purchase money. Similarly with registered land, the purchaser will know that there are equitable interests affecting the land[10], but will not know, nor need to know, what they are. For, although equitable beneficial interests in land may be protected by entry on the register, they are "overreached" on a sale as they would be with unregistered land.

AREAS OF COMPULSORY REGISTRATION
as at 1 February 1978[11]

County (including Greater London)	Areas of compulsory registration
Avon	The districts of Bath, Bristol and Kingswood.
Bedfordshire	The districts of Luton, North Bedfordshire and South Bedfordshire.
Berkshire	The whole county.
Buckinghamshire	The district of Beaconsfield.
Cambridgeshire	The districts of Cambridge and Peterborough.
Cheshire	The whole county.
Cleveland	The whole county.
Cumbria	The district of Barrow-in-Furness.
Derbyshire	The districts of Bolsover, Chesterfield, Derby, Erewash and South Derbyshire.
Devon	The districts of East Devon, Exeter, Plymouth, South Hams, Teignbridge and Torbay.
Dorset	The districts of Bournemouth, Christchurch, Poole, Weymouth and Portland, and Wimborne.
Durham	The districts of Chester-le-Street, Darlington, Durham, Easington and Sedgefield.
Dyfed	The district of Llanelli.
East Sussex	The whole county.
Essex	The districts of Basildon, Brentwood, Epping Forest, Harlow, Southend-on-Sea and Thurrock.
Gloucestershire	The district of Gloucester.

[10] See L.R.A. 1925, s. 88 (1).
[11] Registration of Title Order 1977 (S.I. 1977, No. 828).

County (including Greater London)	Areas of compulsory registration
Greater London	The whole administrative area.
Greater Manchester	The whole county.
Gwent	The districts of Islwyn and Newport.
Hampshire	The districts of Eastleigh, Fareham, Gosport, Havant, Portsmouth, New Forest and Southampton.
Hereford and Worcester	The districts of Bromsgrove, Hereford and Worcester.
Hertfordshire	The districts of Broxbourne, East Hertfordshire, Hertsmere, St. Albans, Stevenage, Three Rivers, Watford and Welwyn Hatfield.
Humberside	The districts of Cleethorpes, Grimsby, Kingston upon Hull, North Wolds and Scunthorpe.
Kent	The whole county.
Lancashire	The districts of Blackburn, Blackpool, Burnley, Fylde, Preston and Rossendale.
Leicestershire	The districts of Blaby, Charnwood, Hinckley and Bosworth, Leicester, North West Leicestershire, and Oadby and Wigston.
Lincolnshire	The district of Lincoln.
Merseyside	The whole county.
Mid Glamorgan	The districts of Ogwr, Rhondda and Taff-Ely.
Norfolk	The district of Norwich.
Northamptonshire	The districts of Kettering and Northampton.
Northumberland	The districts of Blyth Valley and Wansbeck.
North Yorkshire	The district of York.
Nottinghamshire	The districts of Ashfield, Broxtowe, Gedling, Mansfield, Nottingham and Rusheliffe.
Oxfordshire	The districts of Oxford, South Oxfordshire and Vale of White Horse.
South Glamorgan	The whole county.
South Yorkshire	The whole county.

County (including Greater London)	Areas of compulsory registration
Staffordshire	The districts of Cannock Chase, Lichfield, Newcastle-under-Lyme, Stoke-on-Trent and Tamworth.
Suffolk	The district of Ipswich.
Surrey	The whole county.
Tyne and Wear	The whole county.
Warwickshire	The districts of North Warwickshire, Nuneaton, Rugby and Warwick.
West Glamorgan	The whole county.
West Midlands	The whole county.
West Sussex	The districts of Adur, Arun, Crawley, Mid Sussex and Worthing.
West Yorkshire	The whole county.

LAND REGISTRATION ACT 1925

123. Effect of Act in areas where registration is compulsory. — (1) In any area in which an Order in Council declaring that registration of title to land within that area is to be compulsory on sale is for the time being in force[12], every conveyance on sale of freehold land and every grant of a term of years absolute not being less than forty years from the date of the delivery of the grant, and every assignment on sale of leasehold land held for a term of years absolute having not less than forty years to run from the date of delivery of the assignment, shall (save as hereinafter provided), on the expiration of two months from the date thereof or any authorised extension of that period, become void so far as regards the grant or conveyance of the legal estate[13] in the freehold or leasehold land comprised in the conveyance, grant, or assignment, or so much of such land as is situated within the area affected, unless the grantee (that is to say, the person who is entitled to be registered as proprietor of the freehold or leasehold land) or his successor in title or assign has in the meantime applied to be registered as proprietor of such land: . . .[14].

LAND REGISTRATION RULES 1925

8. Index Map and Parcels Index. — (1) Index Maps shall be kept in the Registry which shall show the position and extent of every

---

[12] Compulsory registration does not apply to any area of land declared by the Registrar to be subject to a souvenir land scheme: L.R. & L.C.A. 1971, s. 4; L.R. (Souvenir Land) Rules 1972 (S.I. 1972 No. 985); W & C, Vol. 6, p. 130.

[13] But they are valid in equity, *E. S. Schwab & Co Ltd v McCarthy* (1975) 31 P & C R 196 at 212.

[14] For the effect of failure to register, see Ruoff and Roper, pp. 176–179; W & C vol. 6, pp. 104, 105.

registered estate, provided that, where practicable, the General Map shall be used for this purpose.

LAND REGISTRATION ACT 1925

3. **Interpretation.** —

(viii) "Land" includes land of any tenure (including land, subject or not to manorial incidents, enfranchised under Part V. of the Law of Property Act, 1922), and mines and minerals, whether or not held with the surface, buildings or parts of buildings (whether this division is horizontal, vertical or made in any other way) and other corporeal hereditaments; also a manor, an advowson, and a rent and other incorporeal hereditaments[15], and an easement, right, privilege, or benefit in, over, or derived from land[16], but not an undivided share in land; . . . .

(xi) "Legal estates" means the estates interests and charges in or over land subsisting or created at law which are by the Law of Property Act, 1925, authorised to subsist or to be created at law[17]; and "Equitable interests" mean all the other interests and charges in or over land or in the proceeds of sale thereof; an equitable interest "capable of subsisting at law" means such as could validly subsist at law if clothed with the legal estate;

(xxiv) "Registered land" means land or any estate or interest in land the title to which is registered under this Act or any enactment replaced by this Act, and includes any easement[18], right, privilege, or benefit which is appurtenant or appendant thereto, and any mines and minerals within or under the same and held therewith;

2. **What estates may be registered.** — (1) After the commencement of this Act, estates capable of subsisting as legal estates shall be the only interests in land in respect of which a proprietor can be registered and all other interests in registered land (except overriding interests[19] and interests entered on the register at or before such commencement) shall take effect in equity as minor interests[20] . . .

69. **Effect of registration on the legal estate.** — (1) The proprietor of land (whether he was registered before or after the commencement of this Act) shall be deemed to have vested in him without any conveyance, where the registered land is freehold, the legal estate in fee simple in possession, and where the registered land is leasehold the legal term created by the registered lease, . . .

---

[15] L.R.R. 1925, r. 50. In practice, rent means rentcharge only. See Cheshire, pp. 634–635.

[16] P. 591, post. Legal easements may only be registered as appurtenant to the registered title of the dominant tenement. L.R.R. 1925, r. 257.

[17] L.P.A. 1925, s. 1 (1)–(4), p. 6, ante.

[18] P. 591, post.

[19] P. 109, post.

[20] P. 125, post.

(4) The estate for the time being vested in the proprietor shall only be capable of being disposed of or dealt with by him in manner authorised by this Act.

19. Registration of disposition of freeholds. — (1) The transfer of the registered estate in the land or part thereof shall be completed by the registrar entering on the register[1] the transferee as the proprietor of the estate transferred, but until such entry is made the transferor shall be deemed to remain proprietor of the registered estate; . . .

(3) The general words implied in conveyances under the Law of Property Act, 1925[2], shall apply, so far as applicable thereto, to dispositions of a registered estate.

74. Notice of trust not to affect registered dealing. — Subject to the provisions of this Act as to settled land, neither the registrar nor any person dealing with a registered estate or charge shall be affected with notice of a trust express implied or constructive, and references to trusts shall, so far as possible, be excluded from the register.

101. Dispositions off register creating "minor interests". — (1) Any person, whether being the proprietor or not, having a sufficient interest or power in or over registered land, may dispose of or deal with the same, and create any interests or rights therein which are permissible in like manner and by the like modes of assurance in all respects as if the land were not registered, but subject as provided by this section.

(2) All interests and rights disposed of or created under subsection (1) of this section (whether by the proprietor or any other person) shall, subject to the provisions of this section, take effect as minor interests, and be capable of being overridden by registered dispositions for valuable consideration.

(3) Minor interests shall, subject to the express exceptions contained in this section, take effect only in equity, but may be protected by entry on the register of such notices, cautions, inhibitions and restrictions as are provided for by this Act or rules[3].

107. Power for proprietors to bind successors and to enforce contracts. — (1) Subject to any entry to the contrary on the register, the proprietor of any registered land or charge may enter into any contract in reference thereto in like manner as if the land or charge had not been registered, and, subject to any disposition for valuable consideration which may be registered or protected on the register before the contract is completed or protected on the register, the contract may be enforced as a minor interest against any succeeding proprietor in like manner and to the same extent as if the land or charge had not been registered[4].

---

[1] Registration is completed as of the day on which the application is delivered to the Registrar. L.R.R. 1925, r. 83 (2); as substituted by L.R.R. 1978, r. 8; see letter from the Registrar, cited in (1976) 40 Conv (NS) 307; p. 107, post.
[2] L.P.A. 1925, s. 62, p. 530, post.
[3] P. 125, post.
[4] See (1977) 93 L.Q.R. 541, at 550–552 (R. J. Smith).

PRECEDENT FOR TRANSFER OF FREEHOLD LAND[5]

H.M. LAND REGISTRY

Land Registration Acts 1925–1971

TRANSFER OF WHOLE

County and district: ....
(or name of Greater London   ....
borough where applicable)   ....
Title No.:   ....
Property: ....
Date: ....

In consideration of .... pounds (£.......) the receipt whereof is hereby acknowledged I, *AB*, of .... [*address and description*] [formerly of .... [*registered address*]] as Beneficial Owner HEREBY TRANSFER to *CD* of .... [*address and description*] the land comprised in the title above referred to

[It is hereby certified that the transaction hereby effected does not form part of a larger transaction or series of transactions in respect of which the amount or value or aggregate amount or value of the consideration exceeds [£15,000] [£20,000] [£25,000] [£30,000]]

Signed sealed and delivered by
the said *AB*   *[Signature and seal of AB]*
in the presence of
    Name ....
    Address ....
    ....
    Description ....

LAND REGISTRATION ACT 1925

63. Issue of land and charge certificates. — (1) On the first registration of a freehold or leasehold interest in land, and on the registration of a charge, a land certificate, or charge certificate, as the case may be, shall be prepared in the prescribed form: it shall state whether the title is absolute, good leasehold, qualified or possessory, and it shall be either delivered to the proprietor or deposited in the registry as the proprietor may prefer.

(2) If so deposited in the registry it shall be officially endorsed from time to time, as in this Act provided, with notes of all subsequent entries in the register affecting the registered land or charge to which it relates.

64. Certificates to be produced and noted on dealings. — (1) So long as a land certificate or charge certificate is outstanding, it shall be produced to the registrar —

    (*a*) on every entry in the register of a disposition by the proprietor
        of the registered land or charge to which it relates; and

---

[5] Reprinted from Hallett's *Conveyancing Precedents* (1965), p. 1247.

(*b*) on every registered transmission; and

(*c*) in every case (except as hereinafter mentioned) where under this Act or otherwise notice of any estate right or claim or a restriction is entered or placed on the register, adversely affecting the title of the proprietor of the registered land or charge, but not in the case of the lodgment of a caution or of an inhibition or of a creditors' notice, or of the entry of a notice of a lease at a rent without taking a fine, or a notice of a charge for capital transfer tax[6].

(2) A note of every such entry or transmission shall be officially entered on the certificate. . . .

SPECIMEN LAND CERTIFICATE[7]

---

[6] As amended by F.A. 1975 s. 52, Sched. 12 para. 5 (5).
[7] Reproduced by permission of the Chief Land Registrar.

H.M. LAND REGISTRY   SPECIMEN

Edition 1   opened 10.7.1977   TITLE NUMBER BLK00001   *This register consists of*   2   *pages*

A. PROPERTY REGISTER
containing the description of the registered land and the estate comprised in the Title

COUNTY	DISTRICT
BLANKSHIRE	NORTH CRUMPTON

The Freehold land shown and edged with red on the plan of the above Title filed at the Registry registered on 10 July 1977 known as 1 to 9 (odd numbers) Lincoln Way and 2 Park Road.

The land edged and numbered in green on the filed plan has been removed from this title and registered under the title number or numbers shown in green on the said plan. (15:5:1978)

NOTE:-A transfer of the land edged and numbered BLK00457 in green on the filed plan dated 6 May 1978 from Michael Moxhay (Transferor) to Percival Patman contains the following exception and reservation:-

"Except and reserving to the Transferor and the owner or owners for the time being of 7 Lincoln Way the free passage and running of water and soil therefrom through the drain at the rear of the garden under the land hereby transferred." (15:5:1978)

B. PROPRIETORSHIP REGISTER
stating nature of the Title, name, address and description of the proprietor of the land and any entries affecting the right of disposing thereof

TITLE ABSOLUTE

Entry number	Proprietor, etc.
1.	~~MICHAEL MOXHAY of 217 Lonsdale Street, Swelford, Blankshire, Builder, registered on 10 July 1977.~~
2.	ERNEST ELLISTON, Solicitor, and ENIS ELLISTON, his wife, both of Tithe Barn, Lincoln Way, North Crumpton, Blankshire, registered on 18 September 1979.
3.	RESTRICTION registered on 18 September 1979:-No disposition by one proprietor of the land (being the survivor of joint proprietors and not being a trust corporation) under which capital money arises is to be registered except under an order of the Registrar or of the Court.

Demand No. 8037440 11/79 W & W Ltd 1314

Register Model III

Any entries struck through are no longer subsisting

SPECIMEN

TITLE NUMBER BLK00001

	C. CHARGES REGISTER	
	containing charges, incumbrances etc., adversely affecting the land and registered dealings therewith	
Entry number	The date at the beginning of each entry is the date on which the entry was made on this edition of the register	Remarks
1.	10 July 1977—Nos 1 Lincoln Way and 2 Park Road (numbered 1 and 2 on the filed plan) are with other land subject to a perpetual yearly rent-charge of £27.10s. 3d. created by a Conveyance dated 3 December 1884 and made between (1) Andrew Austerberry (2) Benjamin Ballard. NOTE:—The Conveyance dated 6 July 1931 referred to in entry No. 3 below contains a covenant by the Vendor to pay the said rentcharge of £27.10s. 3d. in exoneration of 1 Lincoln Way and 2 Park Road and provides that in case of her default the Purchaser shall have rights of retainer, distress and entry for perception.	Rentcharge registered under BLK00002 Abstract issued with Certificate: abstract filed.
2.	10 July 1977—Lease dated 21 November 1916 of 9 Lincoln Way (numbered 3 on the filed plan) to Frederick Formby for 99 years from 29 September 1916 at the rent of £35.	Lessee's title registered under BLK00003.
3.	10 July 1977—A Conveyance dated 6 July 1931 of the land in this title and made between (1) Dorothy Duce (Vendor) (2) Michael Moxhay (Purchaser) contains the following covenants:— "The Purchaser hereby covenants with the Vendor for the benefit of her adjoining land known as 2, 4, 6 and 8 Lincoln Way to observe the stipulations specified in the Second Schedule hereto. <u>The Second Schedule</u> 1. NO house is to be erected of less value than £1000 the value of a house being the amount of its first net cost in material and labour of construction only estimated at the lowest current prices. 2. The land is not to be used for the purpose of carrying on the trade or business of an innkeeper or licensed victualler nor for a beer or spirit shop or for the retail of any liquors. 3. Nothing is to be done or permitted on the land which may be a nuisance or annoyance to the adjoining houses or to the neighbourhood.	
4.	~~10 July 1977—CHARGE dated 30 June 1977 registered on 10 July 1977 to secure the moneys including the further advances therein mentioned.~~	
5.	~~PROPRIETOR—THE WEYFORD BUILDING SOCIETY of Society House, The Avenue, Weyford, Blankshire, 1WY 2AB, registered on 10 July 1977.~~	
6.	18 September 1979—NOTICE of deposit of land certificate with Eastminster Bank Limited of 989 Old Street, London EC3A 4PH, registered on 18 September 1979.	

Any entries struck through are no longer subsisting

[There is also a map]

II.   Registration of Title[8]

Registration of title is concerned basically with legal title to corporeal land. It follows that the only registrable freehold estate is the fee simple absolute in possession. An incorporeal interest at law; such as a legal easement[9], is registrable only as appurtenant to registered land. A term of years absolute can be registered, provided it is a term of more than 21 years. In this case there will be two registrations of title affecting one piece of land, that of the fee simple, and that of the term of 21 or more years[10]. The register takes the form of a card index system, based on one card for each title, but divided into three parts, the property register, the proprietorship register and the charges register.

There are four classes of title, absolute, good leasehold, possessory and qualified[10a]. Provision is made for conversion from one class of title to another.

A.   What Title may be Registered

i.   FIRST REGISTRATION

a.   Freehold

LAND REGISTRATION ACT 1925

4.   Application for registration of freehold land. — Where the title to be registered is a title to a freehold estate in land —

   (*a*) any estate owner holding an estate in fee simple (including a tenant for life, statutory owner, personal representative, or trustee for sale) whether subject or not to incumbrances; or

   (*b*) any other person (not being a mortgagee where there is a subsisting right of redemption or a person who has merely contracted to buy land) who is entitled to require a legal estate in fee simple whether subject or not to incumbrances, to be vested in him;

may apply to the registrar to be registered in respect of such estate, or, in the case of a person not in a fiduciary position, to have registered in his stead any nominee, as proprietor with an absolute title or with a possessory title:

Provided that —

   (i) Where an absolute title is required the applicant or his nominee shall not be registered as proprietor until and unless the title is approved by the registrar;

   (ii) Where a possessory title is required the applicant or his nominee may be registered as proprietor on giving such evidence of title and serving such notices, if any, as may for the time being be prescribed; . . .

---

[8]   Cheshire, pp. 103–109, 768–769; M & W pp. 1057–1064; MM, pp. 515–520.
[9]   See p. 591, post.   [10] Pp. 427–433, post.
[10a]   On first registration of freehold land, over 99 per cent of applications are registered with absolute title. The majority of the remainder relate to titles founded purely on adverse possession. See [1980] Conv 7–9.

5. Effect of first registration with absolute title. — Where the registered land is a freehold estate, the registration of any person as first proprietor thereof with an absolute title shall vest in the person so registered an estate in fee simple in possession in the land, together with all rights, privileges, and appurtenances belonging or appurtenant thereto, subject to the following rights and interests, that is to say, —

(a) Subject to the incumbrances, and other entries, if any, appearing on the register[11]; and

(b) Unless the contrary is expressed on the register, subject to such overriding interests, if any, as affect the registered land; and

(c) Where the first proprietor is not entitled for his own benefit to the registered land subject, as between himself and the persons entitled to minor interests, to any minor interests of such persons of which he has notice,

but free from all other estates and interests whatsoever, including estates and interests of His Majesty.

6. Effect of first registration with possessory title. — Where the registered land is a freehold estate, the registration of any person as first proprietor thereof with a possessory title only shall not affect or prejudice the enforcement of any estate, right or interest adverse to or in derogation of the title of the first proprietor, and subsisting or capable of arising at the time of registration of that proprietor; but, save as aforesaid, shall have the same effect as registration of a person with an absolute title.

7. Qualified title. — (1) Where an absolute title is required, and on the examination of the title it appears to the registrar that the title can be established only for a limited period, or only subject to certain reservations, the registrar may, on the application of the party applying to be registered, by an entry made in the register, except from the effect of registration any estate, right, or interest —

(a) arising before a specified date, or

(b) arising under a specified instrument or otherwise particularly described in the register,

and a title registered subject to such excepted estate, right, or interest shall be called a qualified title.

(2) Where the registered land is a freehold estate, the registration of a person as first proprietor thereof with a qualified title shall have the same effect as the registration of such person with an absolute title, save that registration with a qualified title shall not affect or prejudice the enforcement of any estate, right or interest appearing by the register to be excepted.

---

[11] If an option to renew a lease is void for non-registration under L.C.A 1972 s. 4 (6), it cannot be revived by subsequent first registration of title under L.R.A. 1925 s. 9, and the entry of the lease containing the option on the charges register; *Kitney v M.E.P.C. Ltd* [1977] 1 WLR 981, [1978] 1 All ER 595; (1977) 41 Conv (NS) 356; [1978] CLJ 13 (D. J. Hayton).

b.   Leasehold

8.   Application for registration of leasehold land. — (1) Where the title to be registered is a title to a leasehold interest in land —

>   (*a*)   any estate owner (including a tenant for life, statutory owner, personal representative, or trustee for sale, but not including a mortgagee where there is a subsisting right of redemption), holding under a lease for a term of years absolute of which more than twenty-one are unexpired, whether subject or not to incumbrances, or

>   (*b*)   any other person (not being a mortgagee as aforesaid and not being a person who has merely contracted to buy the lease-hold interest) who is entitled to require a legal leasehold estate held under such a lease as aforesaid (whether subject or not to incumbrances) to be vested in him,

may apply to the registrar to be registered in respect of such estate, or in the case of a person not being in a fiduciary position to have registered in his stead any nominee, as proprietor with an absolute title, with a good leasehold title or with a possessory title:

Provided that —

>   (i)   Where an absolute title is required, the applicant or his nominee shall not be registered as proprietor until and unless the title both to the leasehold and to the freehold, and to any inter-mediate leasehold that may exist, is approved by the registrar;

>   (ii)   Where a good leasehold title is required, the applicant or his nominee shall not be registered as proprietor until and unless the title to the leasehold interest is approved by the registrar;

>   (iii)   Where a possessory title is required, the applicant or his nominee may be registered as proprietor on giving such evidence of title and serving such notices, if any, as may for the time being be prescribed;

>   (iv)   If on an application for registration with a possessory title the registrar is satisfied as to the title to the leasehold interest, he may register it as good leasehold, whether the applicant consents to such registration or not, but in that case no higher fee shall be charged than would have been charged for registration with possessory title.

(2)   Leasehold land held under a lease containing an absolute prohibition against all dealings therewith inter vivos shall not be registered in pursuance of this Act; and leasehold land held under a lease containing a restriction on any such dealings, shall not be registered under this Act unless and until provision is made in the prescribed manner for preventing any dealing therewith in contravention of the restriction by an entry on the register to that effect, or otherwise.

(3)   Where on an application to register a mortgage term, wherein no right of redemption is subsisting, it appears that the applicant is entitled in equity to the superior term, if any, out of which it was created, the registrar shall register him as proprietor of the superior term without any entry to the effect that the legal interest in that term

is outstanding, and on such registration the superior term shall vest in the proprietor and the mortgage term shall merge therein:

Provided that this subsection shall not apply where the mortgage term does not comprise the whole of the land included in the superior term, unless in that case the rent, if any, payable in respect of the superior term has been apportioned, or the rent is of no money value or no rent is reserved, and unless the covenants, if any, entered into for the benefit of the reversion have been apportioned (either expressly or by implication) as respects the land comprised in the mortgage term.

9. Effect of first registration with absolute title. — Where the registered land is a leasehold interest, the registration under this Act of any person as first proprietor thereof with an absolute title shall be deemed to vest in such person the possession of the leasehold interest described, with all implied or expressed rights, privileges, and appurtenances attached to such interest, subject to the following obligations, rights, and interests, that is to say, —

(a) Subject to all implied and express covenants, obligations, and liabilities incident to the registered land; and

(b) Subject to the incumbrances and other entries (if any) appearing on the register; and

(c) Unless the contrary is expressed on the register, subject to such overriding interests, if any, as affect the registered land; and

(d) Where such first proprietor is not entitled for his own benefit to the registered land subject as between himself and the persons entitled to minor interests, to any minor interests of such persons of which he has notice;

but free from all other estates and interests whatsoever, including estates and interests of His Majesty.

10. Effect of first registration with good leasehold title. — Where the registered land is a leasehold interest, the registration of a person as first proprietor thereof with a good leasehold title shall not affect or prejudice the enforcement of any estate, right or interest affecting or in derogation of the title of the lessor to grant the lease, but, save as aforesaid, shall have the same effect as registration with an absolute title[12].

13. Regulations as to examination of title by registrar. —

(c) If the registrar, upon the examination of any title, is of opinion that the title is open to objection, but is nevertheless a title the holding under which will not be disturbed, he may approve of such title, or may require the applicant to apply to the court, upon a statement signed by the registrar, for its sanction to the registration[13].

---

[12] L.R.A. 1925, ss. 11, 12 contain analogous provisions with regard to possessory and qualified title.

[13] (1976) 40 Conv (NS) 122 (C. T. Emery); *MEPC. Ltd v Christian-Edwards* [1978] Ch 281, [1978] 3 All ER 795, affd. [1979] 3 WLR 713, [1979] 3 All ER 752; [1978] Conv 382 (F. R. Crane).

LAND REGISTRATION RULES 1925

72. Dealings by persons having right to apply for first registration. —
(1) Where a person having the right to apply for registration as first
proprietor desires to deal with the land in any way permitted by the
Act before he is himself registered as proprietor he may do so in the
manner, and subject to the conditions, which would be applicable if
he were in fact the registered proprietor. In the case of a transfer, the
transferee shall be deemed to be the applicant for first registration and
shall be entered on the register accordingly.

ii.   REGISTERED DEALINGS WITH REGISTERED LAND

LAND REGISTRATION ACT 1925

20.   Effect of registration of dispositions of freeholds.[14] — (1) In the
case of a freehold estate registered with an absolute title, a disposition
of the registered land or of a legal estate therein, including a lease
thereof, for valuable consideration shall, when registered, confer on the
transferee or grantee an estate in fee simple or the term of years
absolute or other legal estate expressed to be created in the land dealt
with, together with all rights, privileges, and appurtenances belonging
or appurtenant thereto, including (subject to any entry to the contrary
in the register) the appropriate rights and interests which would,
under the Law of Property Act, 1925, have been transferred if the
land had not been registered, subject —

(*a*) to the incumbrances and other entries, if any, appearing on
the register and any charge for capital transfer tax subject
to which the disposition takes effect under section 73 of this
Act[15];

(*b*) unless the contrary is expressed on the register, to the overriding interests, if any, affecting the estate transferred or
created,

but free from all other estates and interests whatsoever, including
estates and interests of His Majesty, and the disposition shall operate
in like manner as if the registered transferor or grantor were (subject
to any entry to the contrary in the register) entitled to the registered
land in fee simple in possession for his own benefit.

(4) Where any such disposition is made without valuable consideration, it shall, so far as the transferee or grantee is concerned, be
subject to any minor interests subject to which the transferor or grantor held the same, but, save as aforesaid, shall, when registered, in all
respects, and in particular as respects any registered dealings on the
part of the transferee or grantee, have the same effect as if the disposition had been made for valuable consideration.

In *Peffer v Rigg* [1977] 1 WLR 285, [1978] 3 All ER 745[15a], Peffer
and Rigg (the first defendant) purchased, in 1962, 103 Leighton Road,
Kentish Town, London, as a home for their mother-in-law. Rigg was

---

[14] L.R.A. 1925, s. 20 (2), (3) contains analogous provisions with regard to qualified and
possessory title. Cf. s. 23 with regard to leaseholds, p. 429, post.
[15] As amended by F.A. 1975 s. 52, Sch. 2 para. 5 (2).

registered as sole proprietor, but it was agreed that Rigg should hold the house on trust for Peffer and himself as tenants in common in equal shares. In 1967 this was confirmed in a formal trust deed. Peffer's interest was not protected in the register (by way of restriction, notice or caution), nor had he an overriding interest. In 1971, as part of the financial arrangements between Mr. and Mrs. Rigg on their divorce, Rigg transferred the house to Mrs. Rigg (the second defendant) for £1. Mrs Rigg, who was "perfectly well aware" of the trust in favour of Peffer, was registered as proprietor.

GRAHAM J, in granting Peffer a declaration of his half-interest and an order for sale, said at p. 292:

"The purported transfer, however, of the whole of the beneficial interest in the property by the first defendant to the second defendant on the occasion of the divorce agreement in the light of their knowledge of the true facts as I have found them seems to me to be in a very different position. It was argued by Mr. Banks, for the second defendant, that the property was transferred to her for valuable consideration as part of the divorce agreement and that, therefore, the combined effect of sections 20 and 59 of the Land Registration Act 1925 protected the second defendant against any claim or interest of the plaintiff because there is no entry on the register in his favour prior to the transfer to the second defendant. This argument would be convincing if it were not for my finding that the second defendant at the time knew perfectly well that the first defendant could not transfer to her more than a half share of the property. It is this knowledge which seems to me to cause great difficulty to her and prevents her argument succeeding for a number of different reasons put forward by Mr. Poulton for the plaintiff at the second hearing. He argues first that the purported transfer from the first to the second defendant of the beneficial interest in the whole of the property, 103, Leighton Road, was expressed to be for the consideration of £1. This is nominal consideration and not valuable consideration and it follows that the second defendant is not protected by section 20 of the Land Registration Act 1925. In accordance with the provisions of section 20(4) she can only take subject to any minor interests subject to which the first defendant held the same. He was party to the trust deed of 30 May 1968, and clearly had notice of the plaintiff's half interest in the property. The second defendant can therefore only take subject to the minor interest of the plaintiff in the property subject to which the first defendant held it.

The argument to the contrary is that the transfer was only part of the whole agreement entered into by the first and second defendants on the occasion of the divorce and it is not therefore

[15a] (1977) 41 Conv (NS) 207 (F. R. Crane); 93 LQR 341 (R. J. Smith); [1977] CLJ 227 (D. Hayton). On constructive trusts and registered land see [1978] Conv 52 (J. Martin); Oakley, *Constructive Trusts* (1978), p. 16. See also *Orakpo v Manson Investments Ltd* [1977] 1 WLR 347, at 360, 370, [1977] 1 All ER 666; (1978) 94 LQR 239 (D. C. Jackson).

right to limit the consideration for the transfer to the £1 expressed to be therefor. The consideration there was a great deal more and included all the obligations undertaken by the second defendant. Such consideration was therefore not nominal but valuable within section 20 and the second defendant received the protection of the section. I do not see why, when the parties have chosen to express a transfer as being for a nominal consideration, the court should seek to hold that the consideration was in fact otherwise than as agreed and stated. If however, the proper view is that there was valuable consideration for the transfer, then it is argued as follows. There is a contrast between sections 20 and 59 of the Act. Section 20(1) protects any 'transferee' for valuable consideration. By section 18(5) 'transfer' and 'transferee' in relation to freehold land have very wide meanings but are not specifically defined in section 3. It is to be noted, however, that section 20, though it mentions valuable consideration, does not mention 'good faith' as being necessary on the part of the transferee, nor does it mention notice. It can be argued therefore that section 20 seems to be saying that a transferee whether he has good faith or not, and whether he has notice or not, takes free of all interests (other than overriding interests) provided he has given valuable consideration.

This at first sight seems a remarkable proposition and though undoubtedly the property legislation of 1925 was intended to simplify such matters of title as far as possible, I find it difficult to think that section 20 of this Act can have been intended to be as broad in scope as this. Similar doubt is expressed in *Brickdale & Stewart-Wallace's Land Registration Act 1925*, 4th edn. (1939), p. 107, note (1). The provisions for rectification in section 82 as against a proprietor in possession who has been a party to a fraud, mistake or an omission in consequence of which rectification of the register is sought also seems to me to show that section 20 must be read with some limitations; see also *Ruoff & Roper, Registered Conveyancing*, 3rd edn. (1972), p. 417. Section 59(6)[15b] on the other hand speaks of a 'purchaser' not being affected by matters which are not protected by a caution or other entry on the register. By definition, however (see section 3(xxi)). ' "Purchaser" means a purchaser in good faith for valuable consideration . . .' It seems clear therefore that as a matter of construction a purchaser who is not in fact one 'in good faith' *will* be concerned with matters not protected by a caution or other entry on the register, at any rate, as I hold, if he has notice thereof. If these sections 20 and 59 are read together in the context of the Act they can be reconciled by holding that if the "transferee" spoken of in section 20 is in fact a 'purchaser' he will only be protected if he has given valuable consideration and is in good faith. He cannot in my judgment be in good faith if he has in fact notice of something which affects his

---

[15b] P. 129, post.

title as in the present case. Of course if he and, a fortiori, if a purchaser from him has given valuable consideration and in fact has no notice he is under no obligation to go behind the register, and will in such a case be fully protected. This view of the matter seems to me to enable the two sections to be construed consistently together without producing the unreasonable result of permitting a transferee purchaser to take advantage of the Act, and divest himself of knowledge of defects in his own title, and secure to himself a flawless title which he ought not in justice to be allowed to obtain. This view of the Act produces a result which is also produced by applying the principles applicable in the case of a constructive trust which I will now consider.

On the evidence in this case I have found that the second defendant knew quite well that the first defendant held the property on trust for himself and the plaintiff in equal shares. The second defendant knew this was so and that the property was trust property when the transfer was made to her, and therefore she took the property on a constructive trust in accordance with general equitable principles: see *Snell's Principles of Equity* 27th edn. (1973), pp. 98–99. This is a new trust imposed by equity and is distinct from the trust which bound the first defendant. Even if, therefore, I am wrong as to the proper construction of sections 20 and 59, when read together, and even if section 20 strikes off the shackles of the express trust which bound the first defendant, this cannot invalidate the new trust imposed on the second defendant.

On this assumption it seems to me that the ground is properly laid for granting rectification of the register under section 82. The second defendant, even though in possession, comes within the exceptions of subsection (3) and this would in my judgment be a case where rectification could properly be ordered against her. Mr. Reid, for the first defendant, supported the propositions of Mr. Poulton and adopted his argument. In addition he referred to *Jones v Lipman* [1962] 1 WLR 832, [1962] 1 All ER 442, which, he submitted, could only have been decided on the basis that the company in that case could not escape from, or divest itself of, its knowledge by reason of sections 20 and 59. It seems that this must be so, and Russell J mentions and rejects the argument at p. 837. . . . .

It follows that in my judgment the second defendant holds the property in question in trust for herself and the plaintiff and that the latter is entitled to appropriate relief."

B. Conversion to Another Title

77. Conversion of possessory into absolute or good leasehold title. — (2) Where the registrar is satisfied as to the title he may, on a transfer for valuable consideration of land registered with a qualified, good leasehold or possessory title, enter the title of a transferee or grantee as absolute or good leasehold, as the case may require or admit, . . .

(3) The following provisions shall apply with respect to land registered with a qualified or possessory title:—

    (*b*) Where the land has been registered, if freehold land, for fifteen years, or if leasehold land, for ten years, with a possessory title, the registrar shall, if satisfied that the proprietor is in possession, and after giving such notices, if any, as may be prescribed, enter the title of the proprietor of the freehold land as absolute, and the title of the proprietor of the leasehold land as good leasehold. . . .

(4) Where the land has been registered with a good leasehold title for at least ten years, the registrar may, subject to the payment of any additional insurance fee and to any advertisements or inquiries which may be prescribed, and if he is satisfied that the proprietor or successive proprietors has or have been in possession during the said period, at the request of the proprietor enter his title as absolute.

(6) Any person, other than the proprietor, who suffers loss by reason of any entry on the register made by virtue of this section shall be entitled to be indemnified under this Act as if a mistake had been made in the register.

C.   The Registers[16]

i.   TRIPARTITE

LAND REGISTRATION RULES 1925

2.   Parts of register and title number. — The register shall consist of three parts, called the Property Register, the Proprietorship Register, and the Charges Register. The title to each registered property shall bear a distinguishing number.

3.   Property Register. — The Property Register shall contain —

(1) The description of the land and estate comprised in the title. . . .

(2) Such notes as have to be entered relating —

    (*b*) to exemption from any of the overriding interests mentioned in Section 70 of the Act[17];

    (*c*) to easements[18], rights, privileges, conditions and covenants for the benefit of the land[19], and other like matters.

5.   Leasehold land, rentcharges and land subject thereto. — (1) In the case of leasehold land there shall be entered in the Property Register a reference to the registered lease, and such particulars of the lease, and of the exceptions or reservations therefrom (if any) as the applicant may desire, and the Registrar approve; and a reference to the lessor's title, if registered.

---

[16] See Ruoff; Appx. "A" for Model Registers and Plans.
[17] See pp. 102–112, post.
[18] See p. 111, post.
[19] See p. 591, post.

(2) In the case of rentcharges created by an instrument, that instrument shall be referred to in the Property Register.

(3) Where land is acquired in consideration of the reservation of a rentcharge and the grant of the land contains any exceptions or reservations, that grant shall be referred to in the Property Register.

6. Proprietorship Register. — The Proprietorship Register shall state the nature of the title, and shall contain the name, address, and description of the proprietor of the land, and cautions, inhibitions, and restrictions affecting his right of disposing thereof.

7. Charges Register. — The Charges Register shall contain —
  (a) incumbrances subsisting at the date of first registration;
  (b) subsequent charges, and other incumbrances (including notices of leases and other notices of adverse interests or claims permitted by the Act);
  (c) such notes as have to be entered relating to covenants, conditions, and other rights adversely affecting the land;
  (d) all such dealings with registered charges and incumbrances as are capable of registration.

10.[20] List of pending applications for first registration. — Until the estate in land comprised in a pending application for first registration is shown on the Index Map, the title number and a short description of the land shall be entered in a list known as the list of pending applications for first registration.

ii. DELIVERY AND DATE OF APPLICATIONS

LAND REGISTRATION RULES 1925

83.[1] Delivery of applications. — (1) Every application shall be delivered at the proper office and when so delivered, shall be allocated an official reference number and shall be dated as of the day on which it is deemed under rule 85 of these rules to have been delivered.

(2) The application shall be completed by registration as of the day on which and subject to the effect of any provision of the Act or of any rules made thereunder, of the priority in which it is deemed to have been delivered.

85.[1] Date of delivery of applications. — Every application delivered at the proper office after 11.00 hours on one day and before or at 11.00 hours on the next day shall be deemed to have been delivered at the same time, namely, immediately after 11.00 hours on the second day.

---

[20] As substituted by L.R.R. 1978 r. 4.
[1] As substituted by L.R.R. 1978, rr. 8, 10. For priority of applications where two or more applications are deemed to have been delivered at the same time, see r. 84, as substituted by L.R.R. 1978, r. 9. See (1978) L.S. Gaz. 1173-1174 (R. B. Roper).

iii.   PRIVACY[2]

LAND REGISTRATION ACT 1925

112.   Inspection of register and other documents at land registry. —
Subject to section 112 A below and[3] to the provisions of this Act as to
furnishing information to Government departments and local
authorities[4] and to such regulations and exceptions and to the
payment of such sums as may be made or fixed by general rules, any
person registered as proprietor of any land or charge, and any person
authorised by any such proprietor, or by an order of the court, or by
general rule, but no other person, may inspect and make copies of and
extracts from any register or document in the custody of the registrar
relating to such land or charge.

LAND REGISTRATION RULES 1925

287.   Authority to inspect the register. — Subject to the provisions of
sections 59, 61[5] and 112 of the Act, any entry in the register, and any
document in the custody of the Registrar and referred to in the
register, may be inspected by or under the authority of the proprietor
of the land or of any charge or incumbrance thereon[6].

**288.   Inspection of Property Register only and of other entries after
notice to proprietor.** — (1) The Property Register and the filed plan of
any title may be inspected by any person interested in the land or in
any adjoining land or in a charge or incumbrance thereon.

(2) Other entries in the register and documents referred to therein,
and the statutory declaration in support of a caution, may be inspected
by any person interested, on giving three days' notice to the proprietor
or on satisfying the Registrar that, by reason of the death of a sole
proprietor, or for any other sufficient reason, he cannot obtain the
requisite authority for or consent to such inspection, and that such
inspection is reasonable and proper.

iv.   SEARCHES

LAND REGISTRATION (OFFICIAL SEARCHES) RULES 1978[7]

5.   Official Search by Purchaser. — When a purchaser[8] has applied in
accordance with these rules for an official search, any entry which is

---

[2] Cf. the position in unregistered land, where there is no general duty on an estate
owner to produce his title deeds, but where anyone can search for possible land
charges merely by paying the appropriate fee. See Law Commission Working Paper
No. 32, paras. 70–94.

[3] As amended by A.J.A. 1977 s. 25 (2). S. 112A refers to inspection in connection with
criminal proceedings.

[4] L.R.A. 1925, s. 129 (including the Commissioners of Inland Revenue). L.R.R. 1925,
rr. 287–297. The Index Maps, the General Map and the Parcels Index are open to
inspection, L.R.R. 1925, r. 12 (1), as amended by L.R.R. 1978 r. 5.

[5] The sections entitle a judgment creditor, official trustee or trustee in bankruptcy to
inspect the register.

[6] See also L.R.R. 1967, r. 3 (3).

[7] See (1978) L.S. Gaz. 1173–1174 (R. B. Roper).

[8] "Any person (including a lessee or chargee) who in good faith and for valuable
consideration acquires or intends to acquire a legal estate in land" (r. 2).
On the meaning of good faith, see *Smith v Morrison* [1974] 1 WLR 659, [1974]
1 All ER 957.

made in the register during the priority period[9] relating to that search shall be postponed to a subsequent application to register the instrument effecting the purchase and, if the purchase is dependent on a prior dealing, to a subsequent application to register the instrument effecting that dealing provided each such subsequent application:

   (i) is deemed to have been delivered at the proper office within the priority period;

   (ii) affects the same land or charge as the postponed entry; and

   (iii) is in due course completed by registration.

6. — (1) Where a purchaser has obtained an official certificate of search but will be unable to deliver an application for the registration of the instrument effecting the purchase within the priority period, he may apply on the prescribed form for an extension[10] of the priority conferred by the official search[11].

11. Official Search without priority. — (1) A person (not being a purchaser requiring an official search under rule 3 of these rules) who has authority to inspect a register may apply on form 94C for an official search of that register.

(2) Form 94C shall be delivered in duplicate to the proper office and on completion of the search an official certificate of search shall be issued in form 94D but this certificate shall not confer upon the applicant priority for the registration of any dealing.

III. Overriding Interests[12]

Interests in land which cannot be registered as separate titles fall into the category of either overriding interests or minor interests. Overriding interests are enforceable without being protected on the register, and bind a registered proprietor and his transferee even though he does not know of their existence. They thus detract from the principle that the register should be a mirror of the title. They are listed in section 70 (1) of the Land Registration Act 1925 and have been added to by later enactments[13]. They consist of third party rights which on policy grounds should bind a purchaser, but which for some reason or other do not fit into the pattern of the register. If, however, an overriding interest does appear on the register[14], then its protection

---

[9] Of 20 working days (r. 2).

[10] When a purchaser obtains an extension under r. 6, postponement rules for the extended priority period (15 working days) similar to those in r. 5 apply (r. 7).

[11] A search may be made by telephone or teleprinter, but not by telegraph (rr. 9, 10). Such a search is not an official search for the purpose of indemnity under L.R.A. 1925, s. 83 (3), p. 139, post.

[12] Cheshire, pp. 109-110, 772-777; M & W, pp. 1064-1067; MM, pp. 520-521; Ruoff and Roper, chap. 6; W & C. Vol. 6 pp. 63-67; Barnsley, pp. 41-55; Farrand (2nd edn.), pp. 184-209; Hayton, pp. 79-119.

[13] L.R.R. 1925, r. 258, p. 112, post; Tithe Act 1936, s. 13 (11), p. 111, n. 2, post; Coal Act 1938, s. 41: Coal Industry Nationalisation Act 1946, ss. 5, 8, Sch. 1.

[14] And it often does. Ruoff and Roper, pp. 112–114, (1969) 32 M.L.R., at 129 (T. B. F. Ruoff). See *Re Dances Way, West Town, Hayling Island*, [1962] Ch 490, at 507; [1962] 2 All ER 42, per UPJOHN LJ.

under this category is superfluous; it ceases to bind as an overriding interest and its protection is then the protection of a minor interest entered on the register.

There has been criticism of the category of overriding interests[15], especially of the wide-ranging safety-net of paragraph (*g*), which accords protection to "the rights of every person in actual occupation of the land or in receipt of the rents and profits thereof, save where enquiry is made of such person and the rights are not disclosed". This paragraph protects an occupier who has failed either to register a title or to protect an interest by an entry on the register. This is diametrically opposed to the Draconian provisions of the Land Charges Act 1972 in the case of unregistered land under which a purchaser takes free of an unregistered land charge even if the person entitled thereto is in possession[16].

Section 70 (1) (*g*) is, in effect, an application of the rule in *Hunt v Luck*[17] to registered land; extended so as to include the rights of every person in receipt of the rents and profits of the land; and extended, it seems, in some of the decisions on the question of "actual occupation"[18]. On principle, this type of rule is sounder than the Land Charges Act rule. In most cases, of course, vacant possession will be given to the purchaser on completion, and the problem does not arise. Where the purchaser completes when some other person is in occupation, he will almost always, if he is careful, discover the occupation. In that situation, three solutions are possible; the purchaser takes subject to that interest; the purchaser takes free even though he has actual notice; or if he has constructive notice. The last solution would revive all the problems which registration is intended to avoid. The second solution (that of the Land Charges Act 1972) can cause great and obvious injustice. The first will nearly always produce the right result. It should not, it is submitted, be abandoned in favour of the logical symmetry of a complete system of registration.

LAND REGISTRATION ACT 1925

3. Interpretation. — (xvi) "Overriding interests" mean all the incumbrances, interests, rights, and powers not entered on the register but subject to which registered dispositions are by this Act to take effect, and in regard to land registered at the commencement of this Act include the matters which are by any enactment repealed by this Act declared not to be incumbrances; . . .

---

70. Liability of registered land to overriding interests. — (1) All registered land shall, unless under the provisions of this Act the contrary is expressed on the register, be deemed to be subject to such of the following overriding interests as may be for the time being

---

[15] Law Commission Published Working Paper No. 37 (1971).
[16] L.C.A. 1972, s. 4, p. 37, ante.
[17] [1901] 1 Ch 45; *affd.* [1902] 1 Ch 428; p. 41, ante.
[18] P. 118 et seq. post.

subsisting in reference thereto, and such interests shall not be treated as incumbrances within the meaning of this Act (that is to say):—

(a) Rights of common[19], drainage rights, customary rights (until extinguished), public rights, profits à prendre, rights of sheep-walk, rights of way, watercourses, rights of water, and other easements not being equitable easements required to be protected by notice on the register[20];

(b) Liability to repair highways by reason of tenure, quit-rents, crown rents, heriots, and other rents and charges (until extinguished) having their origin in tenure;

(c) Liability to repair the chancel of any church[1];

(d) Liability in respect of embankments, and sea and river walls;

(e) . . . . ,[2] payments in lieu of tithe, and charges or annuities payable for the redemption of tithe rentcharges;

(f) Subject to the provisions of this Act, rights acquired or in course of being acquired under the Limitation Acts[3];

(g) The rights of every person in actual occupation of the land or in receipt of the rents and profits thereof, save where enquiry is made of such person and the rights are not disclosed[4];

---

[19] Commons Registration Act 1965, s. 1 (1), (2), p. 53, ante.

[20] As to whether equitable easements are overriding interests, see Ruoff and Roper 97; W & C, vol. 6, p. 64; Barnsley, pp. 43–44; Farrand (2nd edn.), pp. 180–190; Hayton, pp. 86–88, *Poster v Slough Estates Ltd* [1969] 1 Ch 495, at 507, [1968] 3 All ER 257, per CROSS J; *Payne v Adnams* [1971] CLY 6486.

[1] The Law Commission is enquiring into the incidence of liability to repair chancels. Sixth Annual Report 1970–1971 (Law Com No. 47), para. 27. For the liability in unregistered land, see *Hauxton Parochial Church Council v Stevens* [1929] P. 240; *Chivers & Sons Ltd v Air Ministry and Queen's College, Cambridge* [1955] Ch 585, [1955] 2 All ER 607.

[2] As amended by Tithe Act 1936, s. 48, Sch. IX, and Finance Act 1963, ss. 68, 73 (8) *(b)*, Sch. 14, Pt. VI. As from 2 October 1977, tithe redemption annuities are extinguished; F.A. 1977 s. 56.

[3] L.R.A. 1925, s. 75, p. 180, post. *Re Chowood's Registered Land* [1933] Ch 574, at 581; *Bridges v Mees* [1957] Ch 475, [1957] 2 All ER 577.

[4] *National Provincial Bank Ltd v Ainsworth* [1965] AC 1175, [1965] 2 All ER 472, p. 113, post (deserted wife's equity not overriding interest); *Strand Securities Ltd v Caswell* [1965] Ch 958, [1965] 1 All ER 820, p. 117, post (step-daughter's occupation on her own account of flat by gratuitous licence from step-father lessee not actual occupation); *Webb v Pollmount Ltd* [1966] Ch 584, [1966] 1 All ER 481, p. 113, post (option to purchase freehold reversion contained in lease held to be overriding interest); *London and Cheshire Insurance Co Ltd v Laplagrene Property Co Ltd* [1971] Ch 499, [1971] 1 All ER 766, p. 124, post (unpaid vendor's lien under lease-back from purchaser held to be overriding interest); *Hodgson v Marks* [1971] Ch 892, [1971] 2 All ER 684, p. 118, post (equitable fee simple under bare trust held to be overriding interest); *Lee-Parker v Izzett (No. 2)*, [1972] 1 WLR 775, [1972] 2 All ER 800 (overriding interest conceded where purchaser-occupier expended money at request of vendor in belief induced by vendor that purchaser was beneficial owner under contract of sale, later held void for uncertainty); *Epps v Esso Petroleum Co Ltd* [1973] 1 WLR 1071, [1973] 2 All ER 465 (intermittent parking of car on undefined space not actual occupation); *E.S. Schwab & Co Ltd v McCarthy* (1976) 31 P & C R 196 ("receipt" means "actual receipt" of rent from a tenant); *Williams and Glyn's Bank Ltd v Boland* [1979] Ch 312, [1979] 2 All ER 697 (wife held to be in actual occupation of matrimonial home registered in sole name of husband); p. 122, post.

See also *Bridges v Mees*, supra (overlap between para. *(f)* and para. *(g)*. For statutory exclusions from para. *(g)*, see Matrimonial Homes Act 1967, s. 2 (7) (spouse's right of occupation); Leasehold Reform Act 1967, s. 5 (5) (tenant's right to acquire freehold or apply for extended lease).

(*h*) In the case of a possessory, qualified, or good leasehold title[5], all estates, rights, interests, and powers excepted from the effect of registration;

(*i*) Rights under local land charges unless and until registered or protected on the register in the prescribed manner[6];

(*j*) Rights of fishing and sporting, seignorial and manorial rights of all descriptions (until extinguished), and franchises;

(*k*) Leases for any term or interest not exceeding twenty-one years, granted at a rent without taking a fine[7,8]; . . .

Provided that, where it is proved to the satisfaction of the registrar that any land registered or about to be registered is exempt from land tax, or tithe rentcharge or payments in lieu of tithe, or from charges or annuities payable for the redemption of tithe rentcharge, the registrar may notify the fact on the register in the prescribed manner.

(2) Where at the time of first registration any easement, right, privilege, or benefit created by an instrument and appearing on the title adversely affects the land, the registrar shall enter a note thereof on the register[9].

(3) Where the existence of any overriding interest mentioned in this section is proved to the satisfaction of the registrar or admitted, he may (subject to any prescribed exceptions) enter notice of the same or of a claim thereto on the register, but no claim to an easement, right, or privilege not created by an instrument shall be noted against the title to the servient land if the proprietor of such land (after the prescribed notice is given to him) shows sufficient cause to the contrary.

LAND REGISTRATION RULES 1925

197.   Notice of freedom from or the existence of overriding interests. —
(1) Where any person desires to have an entry made in the register of the freedom from or the existence of an overriding interest mentioned in Section 70 of the Act, the application shall be made in writing and shall state the particulars of the entry required to be made[10].

(6) Any entry showing that the registered land is free from any one or more of the liabilities, rights, or interest, mentioned in Section 70 of the Act, shall be made in the Property Register.

258.   Adverse easements treated as overriding interests. — Rights, privileges, and appurtenances appertaining or reputed to appertain to land or demised, occupied, or enjoyed therewith or reputed or known as part or parcel of or appurtenant thereto, which adversely affect

---

[5] L.R.A. 1925, ss. 6, 7, 10, 11, 12, pp. 99, 101, ante.

[6] L.R.A. s. 49 (1) *(c)*, p. 127, post; s. 59 (2), p. 128, post; p. 46, ante.

[7] This does not include an agreement for a lease: *City Permanent Building Society v Miller* [1952] Ch 840, [1952] 2 All ER 621. But a person in possession under an agreement for a lease may be protected under para. *(g)*. No application can be made for the entry of a notice of a lease for 21 years or less; L.R.A. 1925, s. 48 (1).

[8] Para. *(l)* specifies certain rights to mines and minerals existing before 1926.

[9] See p. 591, post.

[10] See *Re Dances Way, West Town, Hayling Island* [1962] Ch 490 at 510, per DIPLOCK LJ; and cf. Ruoff and Roper, p. 115.

registered land, are overriding interests within section 70 of the Act, and shall not be deemed incumbrances for the purposes of the Act.

In *National Provincial Bank Ltd v Ainsworth* [1965] AC 1175, [1965] 2 All ER 472, Lord WILBERFORCE said, at p. 1261: "[The Land Registration] Act is a registration Act concerned (in this instance) to provide that certain rights are to be binding without registration and without the necessity for actual notice. To ascertain what 'rights' come within this provision, one must look outside the Land Registration Act and see what rights affect purchasers under the general law. To suppose that the subsection makes any right, of howsoever a personal character, which a person in occupation may have, an overriding interest by which a purchaser is bound, would involve two consequences: first that this Act is, in this respect, bringing about a substantive change in real property law by making personal rights bind purchasers; second, that there is a difference *as to the nature of the rights by which a purchaser may be bound* between registered and unregistered land; for purely personal rights including the wife's right to stay in the house (if my analysis of this is correct) cannot affect purchasers of unregistered land even with notice. One may have to accept that there is a difference between unregistered land and registered land as regards what kind of notice binds a purchaser, or what kind of inquiries a purchaser has to make. But there is no warrant in the terms of this paragraph or elsewhere in the Act for supposing that the nature of the rights which are to bind a purchaser is to be different, excluding personal rights in one case, including them in another. The whole frame of section 70, with the list that it gives of interests, or rights, which are overriding, shows that it is made against a background of interests or rights whose nature and whose transmissible character is known, or ascertainable, aliunde, i.e., under other statutes or under the common law. So, if the right of a deserted wife is a purely personal claim against her husband, not specifically related to the house in question, but merely, at its highest, to be provided with a home, there is no difficulty in seeing that this type of right cannot, any more than any purely contractual right, be an overriding interest[11]."

WEBB *v* POLLMOUNT LTD
[1966] Ch 584, [1966] 1 All ER 481 (ChD, UNGOED-THOMAS J)

The plaintiff held under a lease granted by the defendant's predecessor in title. The lease gave to the plaintiff the option to purchase the freehold but, as the register contained no mention of the option, the defendant claimed that it could not be exercised as against him. The issue was whether the option constituted an overriding interest within section 70 (1) (g).

---

[11] See also *Murray v Two Strokes Ltd* [1973] 1 WLR 823 at 827, per GOULDING J, [1973] 3 All ER 357 (right of first refusal held not an interest in land, and therefore not capable of protection as a minor interest by a caution); *Pritchard v Briggs* [1979] 3 WLR 868, [1980] 1 All ER 294.

Held. The option was an overriding interest[12].

UNGOED-THOMAS J: The defendant submits that overriding interests or rights in section 70 (1) (*g*) are limited to rights of a person in an estate in the land, and he makes this submission with a view to establishing that the plaintiff's overriding interest is here limited to his leasehold estate exclusive of the option to purchase. It was first sought to establish this by limiting "land" in sub-paragraph (*g*) to an estate in the land. . . .

As a matter of first impression, "land" in section 70 (1) (*g*) does not appear to me to refer to an estate in land, but to the physical land. The references which are contained in the sub-paragraph to "actual occupation" and "receipt of the rents and profits thereof" indicate this conclusion: and (*g*) is not limited to the rights of every tenant or estate owner, but extends to the rights of every person in actual occupation. "Registered land" and "land" are by definition not limited to estates in land, but include physical land. . . .

As the definition of "overriding interests" expressly excludes matters entered on the register, it indicates that matters registrable, but not registered, are not excluded. Overriding interests may include registrable matters, provided they have not been entered on the register . . . .

The opening words of section 70 (1) provide a further limit on overriding interests within the section, namely, that they be "for the time being subsisting in reference" to the registered land. The result is that, so far as material to this case, rights within section 70 (1) (*g*) must fall within such rights as (1) are "not entered on the register", (2) are "affecting the estate transferred" to the defendant, (3) "may be for the time being subsisting in reference" to the registered land. The option was not entered on the register, and there is no difficulty about the first of these limitations. So, the question in this case is whether the option to purchase contained in the lease affects the reversion transferred to the defendant and subsists in reference to the registered land. The statute itself does not answer this question: it raises it. The answer is only to be found by reference to the general law in whose context the statute was enacted.

In *National Provincial Bank Ltd v Ainsworth* ([1965] AC 1175, [1965] 2 All ER 472), the House of Lords, in considering the rights of a deserted wife in respect of the matrimonial home, dealt with section 70. Russell LJ's observations in the Court of Appeal in that case were quoted with approval in the House of Lords. He said:

"It seems to me that section 70 in all its parts is dealing with rights in reference to land which have the quality of being capable of enduring through different ownerships of the land, according to normal conceptions of title to real property."

---

[12] For the desirability of protecting such an option by notice, see *Registered Land Practice Notes* (1972), pp. 30–31.

Lord Upjohn said:

> ". . . notice itself does not create the right. To create a right over the land of another that right must (apart from statute) create a burden on the land, i.e., an equitable estate or interest in the land."

Thus, for a right to be within section 70 (1) (*g*), it must be an "interest in the land" "capable of enduring through different ownerships of the land according to normal conceptions of title to real property."

An option to purchase is an interest in the land in respect of which it is exercisable, whether contained in a lease or not. If contained in a lease, it differs from such an option not so contained only in that the parties are landlord and tenant and it is part of the terms on which the lease is granted. Though contained in a lease, it is collateral and does not "touch" or "concern" or "affect" the land "regarded as the subject-matter of the lease", but is "wholly outside the relation of landlord and tenant", e.g. so that it does not bind the assignees of the reversion under the Grantees of Reversions Act, 1540, and thus escapes any application of the rule against perpetuities. Though it is subject to the rule against perpetuities, this is a feature it has in common with other equitable interests, and the rule against perpetuities is not relevant for the present purposes, except in so far as consideration of what may "touch", "concern" or "affect" the land may be material: see *London and South Western Rly Co v Gomm* ((1882) 20 ChD 562); *Woodall v Clifton* ([1905] 2 Ch 257); *Griffith v Pelton* ([1958] Ch 205, [1957] 3 All ER 75)[13].

As an option to purchase is an interest in land, it was capable before 1926 of being exercised and enforced against the land in the hands of any person who acquired it other than a purchaser for value without notice. It could be enforced against a purchaser with notice (see *Wright v Dean* ([1948] Ch 686, [1948] 2 All ER 415), *Griffith v Pelton*). This general law, as so far stated, I understand to be accepted by the parties without, at any rate, any significant differences; but the last proposition of law introduces the element of notice and brings me to the part which notice has in this law.

It is vital at this stage to bear in mind that what we are seeking to ascertain at present is whether options to purchase are overriding interests or rights within section 70 (1) (*g*), and not what may constitute notice of those rights. Notice may be constituted in different ways, at different times, under different statutes. Russell LJ, in the passage (in *National Provincial Bank Ltd v Ainsworth*) from which I have already quoted, said:

> "Nor should the mind be in any way distracted by the fact that the owner of the rights under section 70 (1) (*g*) is identified as a person in actual occupation. It is the rights of such a person which constitute the overriding interest and must be examined, not his occupation."

---

[13] P. 335, post.

Lord Wilberforce, in his speech in the same case in the House of Lords, said:

> "One may have to accept that there is a difference between unregistered land and registered land as regards what kind of notice binds a purchaser, or what kind of inquiries a purchaser has to make. But there is no warrant in the terms of this paragraph or elsewhere in the Act for supposing that the nature of the rights which are to bind the purchaser is to be different, excluding personal rights in one case, including them in another."

In section 70 (1) (*g*) itself, notice is covered by the concluding words "save where inquiry is made of such person and the rights are not disclosed". Thus, in this very subsection, "the rights" are contrasted with and therefore are not defined or ascertained by reference to what constitutes notice of these rights. Notice, before the Act, is replaced by the express provision relating to notice in sub-paragraph (*g*) itself. So, it seems to me, that the question whether an option to purchase is a right within section 70 (1) (*g*) has to be decided independently of what constitutes notice of those rights. But, were it necessary, for the purposes of this case, to decide what has not hitherto been decided, whether before 1926 occupation by the lessee gave constructive notice of an option to purchase contained in his lease, I would decide that it did so (in accordance with the statement in Williams on Vendor and Purchaser, 4th edn., (1936) vol. 1, p. 636, and the judgments in *Hunt v Luck* ([1902] 1 Ch 428) and *Barnhart v Greenshields* ((1853) 9 Moo PCC 18).

It was suggested for the defendant that "the right of every person in actual occupation of the land" should be construed as the right by virtue of which a person is in actual occupation of the land. The short answer to this, it seems to me, is that it does not say so; and the wording is in marked contrast with the wording in section 14 of the Law of Property Act 1925, where reference is made to the interest of a person in possession or occupation of land "to which he may be entitled in right of such possession or occupation". It is neither, in my view, consistent with the wording of section 70 (1) (*g*) of the Land Registration Act 1925, nor with the authorities from which I have quoted.

Although an option to purchase does not, like an option to renew, "touch", "concern" or "affect" "the land demised and regarded as the subject-matter of the lease" (so as, e.g., to bind the reversion under the Grantees of Reversions Act 1540), what we are concerned with here is not whether it so "affects" "the land demised" and is within the relationship of landlord and tenant as considered in the judgment of the Court of Appeal in *Woodall v Clifton*, but whether within section 20 (1) (*b*)[14] it is an interest "affecting the estate transferred" to the defendant. That it is capable of affecting the estate transferred to the defendant is not disputed; e.g., if the defendant had notice of it before

---

[14] See p. 102, ante.

transfer to him. So, it seems to me to fall within Russell LJ's test in *National Provincial Bank Ltd v Ainsworth* of "being capable of enduring through different ownerships of the land according to normal conceptions of title to real property". And if it, thus, in the circumstances of this case, is a right "affecting the estate transferred", within the requirement of section 20 (1) (*b*), it seems to me that it is "for the time being subsisting in reference to" registered land within the requirement of section 70 (1). My conclusion, therefore, is that subject to deciding the question as to the effect of section 59[15], the option to purchase appears to be an overriding interest.

STRAND SECURITIES LTD *v* CASWELL
[1965] Ch 958, [1965] 1 All ER 820 (CA, Lord DENNING MR and HARMAN and RUSSELL LJJ)

The first defendant was the sub-lessee of a flat, the 42-year head lease of which had been registered with good leasehold title. The sub-lease of 39¼ years, less three days, was not, at the material date, entered in any way on the register. The question arose whether the first defendant had an overriding interest within section 70 (1) (*g*) which prevailed against a purchaser from the freeholders[16]. He lived in the country but used the flat as a London base. He allowed his stepdaughter, the second defendant (who had been deserted by her husband) to live in the flat rent free.

Held. The first defendant had no overriding interest.

LORD DENNING MR: Section 70 (1) (*g*) is an important provision. Fundamentally its object is to protect a person in actual occupation of land from having his rights lost in the welter of registration. He can stay there and do nothing. Yet he will be protected. No one can buy the land over his head and thereby take away or diminish his rights. It is up to every purchaser before he buys to make inquiry on the premises. If he fails to do so, it is at his own risk. He must take subject to whatever rights the occupier may have. Such is the doctrine of *Hunt v Luck* ([1901] 1 Ch 45) for unregistered land. Section 70 (1) (*g*) carries the same doctrine forward into registered land but with this difference. Not only is the actual occupier protected, but also the person from whom he holds. It is up to the purchaser to inquire of the occupier, not only about the occupier's own rights, but also about the rights of his immediate superior. The purchaser must ask the occupier: "To whom do you pay your rent?" And the purchaser must inquire what the rights of that person are. If he fails to do so, it is at his own risk for he takes subject to "the rights of every person in actual occupation of the land or in receipt of the rents and profits thereof".

In this case it is clear that the second defendant was in actual occupation of the flat. The plaintiffs, therefore, took subject to her

---

[15] See p. 128, post.
[16] L.R.A. 1925, s. 70 (1) *(k)* did not apply; the first defendant's sub-lease exceeded 21 years; the second defendant was a gratuitous licensee.

rights, whatever they were; see *National Provincial Bank Ltd v Hastings Car Mart Ltd* ([1964] Ch 665, [1964] 3 All ER 93, n). She was not a tenant but only a licensee; see *Foster v Robinson* ([1951] 1 KB 149, [1950] 2 All ER 342); *Cobb v Lane* ([1952] 1 All ER 1199). She had no contractual right to stay there. Her licence could be determined at any time and she would have to go in a reasonable time thereafter; see *Minister of Health v Bellotti* ([1944] KB 298, [1944] 1 All ER 238). So the plaintiffs could get her out, provided always that they could get rid of the first defendant's sublease.

But although the second defendant was in actual occupation, it is said that the first defendant was also in actual occupation. We have had several cases lately in which we have held that "possession in law is, of course, single and exclusive but occupation may be shared with others or had on behalf of others"; see *Hills (Patents) Ltd v University College Hospital Board of Governors* ([1956] 1 QB 90, 99, [1955] 3 All ER 365) and *Willis v Association of Universities of the British Commonwealth* ([1965] 1 QB 140). In this case it is said that the first defendant did share the actual occupation of the flat with the second defendant.

I would like to hold that the first defendant was sharing the occupation of the flat with the second defendant. But I cannot bring myself to this conclusion. The truth is that he allowed her to be in actual occupation, and that is all there is to it. She was a licensee rent free and I fear that it does not give him protection. It seems to be a very rare case — a case which the legislature did not think of. For it is quite clear that if the second defendant had paid a token sum as rent, or for use and occupation, to the first defendant, he would be "in receipt of the rents and profits" and his rights would be protected under section 70 (1) (*g*). Again if the first defendant put his servant or caretaker into the flat, rent free[17], he would be protected because his agent would have actual occupation on his behalf. It is odd that the first defendant is not protected simply because he let his stepdaughter in rent free. Odd as it is, however, I fear the words of the statute do not cover this case and the first defendant does not succeed on this point. But he does on the other[18]. And on that ground I would allow this appeal.

HODGSON *v* MARKS[19]
[1971] Ch 892, [1971] 2 All ER 684 (CA, RUSSELL, BUCKLEY and CAIRNS LJJ)
Mrs. Hodgson, an elderly widow, voluntarily transferred the title of her house to Evans, her lodger. They orally arranged that the house,

---

[17] See also *E. S. Schwab & Co Ltd v McCarthy* (1976) 31 P & C R 196, at 213, 214–215; (1977) 41 Conv (NS) 3.
[18] When the first defendant had made application for first registration of his sub-lease, he was unable to produce the head-lessor's land certificate. CA held that there was no need to produce it (p. 430, post), and that the register should be rectified. This gave the sub-lease priority over the transfer of the head-lease to the purchaser, which had not been registered until after the date of the first defendant's application.
[19] (1971) 35 Conv (NS) 255 (I. Leeming); (1973) 36 MLR 25 (R. H. Maudsley).

though it was registered in Evans's name, should remain hers, and she and Evans continued to reside there as before. Evans then sold it to Marks who became the registered proprietor and executed a mortgage in favour of a building society; neither Marks nor the mortgagee had any knowledge of the arrangement between Mrs. Hodgson and Evans. Mrs. Hodgson claimed that Evans held the house as a bare trustee for her, that she was entitled to the beneficial interest in it, and that Marks and his mortgagee took subject to her rights as "a person in actual occupation" within L.R.A. 1925, section 70 (1) (*g*), when Marks became the registered proprietor.

Held (reversing UNGOED-THOMAS J). Mrs. Hodgson had an overriding interest, and the register should be rectified in her favour.

RUSSELL LJ: I turn first to the question whether at the relevant time the plaintiff was in "actual occupation" of the house. For years it had been her property and her home. Mr. Evans was taken in by her as a lodger. I now quote from the findings of the judge ante, p. 912c:

"So I will now come to the facts which bear on whether Mrs. Hodgson was, independently of the context of section 70 (1) (*g*) of the Land Registration Act 1925, in actual occupation in this case. Before Mrs. Hodgson's transfer of the house to Mr. Evans and its registration in his name, it is undisputed and indisputable that Mrs. Hodgson was in actual occupation of it. After the registration, she continued to live there to all appearances and as a physical fact in exactly the same way as before; and so did Mr. Evans. They lived and ate and slept in the house exactly as before. The financial arrangements of payment by Mr. Evans to Mrs. Hodgson for board and lodging and by Mrs. Hodgson to Mr. Evans for investment for her and for the payment of bills continued unchanged. Mrs. Hodgson continued too as the rateable occupier. There was no change in the physical appearance of occupation nor was there any other change at all, except that Mrs. Hodgson transferred the house to Mr. Evans upon oral trust for herself and that Mr. Evans was registered as proprietor. Except that Mr. Evans held the legal estate on trust for Mrs. Hodgson, the transfer and registration made no difference as between Mrs. Hodgson and Mr. Evans. She was absolutely beneficially entitled and could at any time call for a transfer of the legal estate and then be registered as proprietor. Mr. Evans as bare trustee of the legal estate for Mrs. Hodgson was not entitled to occupy the house, but she as absolute beneficial owner was so entitled. After, as before Mr. Evans' registration, Mr. Evans' presence in the house was exclusively as lodger and Mrs. Hodgson's presence was in virtue of being absolute owner, legally and beneficially before the registration, and beneficially afterwards. She could terminate Mr. Evans' presence in the house after the registration just as she could before. As between Mrs. Hodgson and Mr. Evans, her occupation and her dominion over the house was the same after the registration as before.

So at all material times, Mrs. Hodgson was in fact in physical occupation of the premises and, more, had the right to occupy them. It seems to me that in general (if this matter can be considered at all independently of context) such physical occupation, even apart from such right to occupy, would constitute what would be meant by actual occupation generally."

With those findings I entirely agree.

But the judge then proceeded to attach a different and special meaning to the words "in actual occupation" in section 70 (1) (*g*). He took as a starting point to justify departure from the ordinary meaning of the words first the fact that every person in actual occupation could not include the vendor himself; but that only puts a gloss on the words "every person" and, indeed, assumes the ordinary meaning of "actual occupation"; moreover, it is not in the context a special construction of "every person" to exclude the vendor who ex hypothesi has transferred his rights to the purchaser. Secondly, the judge relied upon the correct conclusion that "the land" included part of the land. I cannot see that this can properly be used as a justification for departure from the ordinary meaning of the words "in actual occupation". Having by this means freed himself from the fetters of the golden rule, he then, after considering the circumstances in which in the case of unregistered land a purchaser would be fixed with constructive notice of the rights of persons in occupation of the land sold, concluded that "actual" should be construed in the sense of "actual and apparent". I do not see that this adds to or detracts from the words in the section. In connection with the word "apparent" I remark on the phrase of the judge that, after the registration of the transfer to Mr. Evans, "to all appearances" the plaintiff continued in actual occupation. I am prepared, for the purposes of this case, to assume (without necessarily accepting) that section 70 (1) (*g*) of the Land Registration Act 1925 is designed only to apply to a case in which the occupation is such, in point of fact, as would in the case of unregistered land affect a purchaser with constructive notice of the rights of the occupier; and it is [to] be observed that the words "actual occupation" are used in section 14 of the Law of Property Act 1925 and were used in *Barnhart v Greenshields* (1853) 9 Moo PCC 18 at 34. But, nevertheless, how can it be said that the plaintiff was not in actual occupation of the house? The judge said that in all fairness a purchaser of this house (if unregistered) should not be fixed with notice of the plaintiff's rights. But why not? It is a principle of law (and of the Land Registration Act 1925) that a person in occupation is protected in his rights by that occupation, unless, of course, the rights are such that they require registration if they are to be protected. A purchaser must pay heed to anyone in occupation if he is to be sure of getting a good title. It was argued, on the basis of a quotation from the judgment of Vaughan Williams LJ in *Hunt v Luck* [1902] 1 Ch 428 at 432 that this does not apply when the vendor is in occupation, and that (as is the fact) there is no reported case of unregistered land where a purchaser was fixed with constructive notice of the rights of any other occupier when the vendor was in occupation, and that any other view would lead to an impossible burden of inquiry on a purchaser and more particularly on a lender of money on mortgage such as the building society. (As to the defendant building society it is plain that it made no inquiries on the spot save as to repairs; it relied on Mr. Marks, who lied to it; and I waste no tears on it.) I do not think this is a real problem. Conveyancing is conducted generally upon a basis of good faith, with something of a long stop in the shape of covenants for title. Moreover, I do not consider that it is correct in law to say that any rights of a person who is in occupation will be overridden whenever the vendor is, or appears to be, also in occupation.

I do not think it desirable to attempt to lay down a code or catalogue of situations in which a person other than the vendor should be held to be in occupation of unregistered land for the purpose of constructive notice of his rights, or in actual occupation of registered land for the purposes of section 70 (1) (*g*). It must depend on the circumstances, and a wise purchaser or lender will take no risks. Indeed, however wise he may be he may have no ready opportunity of finding out; but, nevertheless, the law will protect the occupier. Reliance upon the untrue ipse dixit of the vendor will not suffice. Take the present case — though the test of occupation must be objective. Mr. Evans was only a lodger, and whether in law he was in occupation at all is at least doubtful. But the plaintiff was there for Mr. Marks to see and he saw her on two occasions. He did not introduce himself to her as an intending purchaser. He made no inquiry of her. He assumed her to be Mr. Evans' wife who knew all about the proposed purchase. This assumption may well have stemmed from a lie told by Mr. Evans, though neither Mr. Marks nor Mrs. Marks actually said so. Nonetheless, there was the plaintiff de facto living in the house as her house, and, if the judge's gloss were to be accepted, I should say just as much in apparent actual occupation of it as before the transfer to Mr. Evans; and, indeed, if Mr. Evans had stopped lodging there before the registration in Mr. Marks' name she would unquestionably have been in actual occupation. In short, unless it can be established in law that a person is not to be regarded as in actual occupation for the purposes of section 70 (1) (*g*) merely because the vendor appears also to be occupying the property, it seems to me that the judge's decision on this point cannot be supported. (I observe that it was necessary for the defendants' argument on actual occupation to contend that if the plaintiff had said in conversation to Mr. Marks that it was her house and Mr. Evans her lodger, and Mr. Marks had believed Mr. Evans when he said, "The old lady has a bee in her bonnet and is talking rubbish," her interest would not have been enforceable against Mr. Marks because she was not in actual occupation and, accordingly, without an overriding interest.) I do not accept that proposition of law. Accordingly, I would hold that the plaintiff was at all material times a person in actual occupation of the property. . . .

I would only add that I do not consider it necessary to this decision to pronounce on the decision in *Caunce v Caunce* [1969] 1 WLR 286, [1969] 1 All ER 722. In that case the occupation of the wife may have been rightly taken to be not her occupation but that of her husband. In so far, however, as some phrases in the judgment might appear to lay down a general proposition that inquiry need not be made of any person on the premises if the proposed vendor himself appears to be in occupation, I would not accept them.

Accordingly, I would allow the appeal with such order as may be consequential on the establishment by the plaintiff of her overriding beneficial entitlement to the premises.

WILLIAMS AND GLYN'S BANK LTD *v* BOLAND
WILLIAMS AND GLYN'S BANK LTD *v* BROWN[20]
[1979] Ch 312, [1979] 2 All ER 697 (CA, Lord DENNING MR,
ORMROD and BROWNE LJJ)

In each of two cases the husband was registered as sole proprietor of the matrimonial home where he and his wife lived. The wife had made a substantial contribution to the purchase, which entitled her to a share in the house. She had not protected her interest by entering a notice, caution or restriction on the register. The husband, without the wife's consent, charged the house to the plaintiff bank to secure his business indebtedness. The bank made no enquiry as to whether the wife had any interest in the house. It now claimed repayment of the loan and possession of the house. In both cases the wife claimed an overriding interest under Land Registration Act 1925, section 70 (1) (*g*).

Held. The wife had an overriding interest.

LORD DENNING MR:

Land Registration Act 1925
Once it is held that the wife has an equitable interest in the land[1] — and not merely in the proceeds of sale — it is easy to apply the provisions of the Land Registration Act 1925. Her interest is then a "minor interest" because it is capable of being overridden by a sale by the trustees for sale: see section (xv). But it may also be an "overriding interest" if it comes within section 70 (1) (*g*). Being an equitable interest in the land, it is clearly an interest "subsisting in reference" to the land[2]. It also affects "the estate transferred" within section 20 (1) (*b*). The crucial question therefore is whether it can be shown to be an "overriding interest" within section 70 (1) (*g*) which protects:

> "The rights of every person in actual occupation of the land or in receipt of the rents and profits thereof, save where inquiry is made of such person and the rights are not disclosed; . . ."

---

[20] (1979) 95 LQR 501 (R. J. Smith); 42 MLR 567 (W. T. Murphy);123 Sol Jo 411 (C. J. Allen); 129 NLJ 700 (H. W. Wilkinson).
[1] P. 243, post.
[2] See ORMORD LJ at pp. 563–565; p. 231, post.

"Actual occupation"

The wife clearly has rights. The only question is whether she is nerself a person "in actual occupation of the land." In construing those words, "actual occupation", it is no use looking at the meaning of occupation in other branches of the law, such as "rateable occupation" or occupation for the purposes of occupier's liability. I would only say that occupation need not be in one single person. Two persons can be in actual occupation, by themselves jointly or each of them severally.

In *Caunce v Caunce* [1969] 1 WLR 286[3] Stamp J seems to have held that, when a wife was living in the matrimonial home with her husband, it was the husband alone who was in actual occupation of it. The wife was not. Stamp J said at p. 293 that she:

"... was not in apparent occupation or possession. She was there, ostensibly, because she was the wife, and her presence there was wholly consistent with the title offered by the husband to the bank."

This was followed by Templeman J in *Bird v Syme-Thomson* [1979] 1 WLR 440 when he said, at p. 444A:

"In my judgment, when a mortgagor is in actual occupation of the matrimonial home, it cannot be said that his wife also is in actual occupation."

He followed it also in the present case when he said:

"actual occupation for the purposes of section 70 (1) (g) does not include the position of the wife of the legal owner who is in occupation."

Any other view, he said, would lead to chaos.

I profoundly disagree. Such statements would have been true a hundred years ago when the law regarded husband and wife as one: and the husband as that one. But they are not true today.

I do not think those statements can stand with the decision of this court in *Hodgson v Marks* [1971] Ch 892, [1971] 2 All ER 684: nor with the standing of women in our society today. Most wives now are joint owners of the matrimonial home — in law or in equity — with their husbands. They go out to work just as their husbands do. Their earnings go to build up the home just as much as their husband's earnings. Visit the home and you will find that she is in personal occupation of it just as much as he is. She eats there and sleeps there just as he does. She is in control of all that goes on there — just as much as he. In no respect whatever does the nature of her occupation differ from his. If he is a sailor away for months at a time, she is in actual occupation. If he deserts her, she is in actual occupation. These instances all show that "actual occupation" is matter of fact, not matter of law. It need not be single. Two partners in a business can be in actual occupation. It does not depend on title. A squatter is often in actual occupation. Taking it simply as matter of fact, I would conclude that in the cases before us the wife is in actual occupation just as the old lady Mrs. Hodgson was in *Hodgson v Marks*.

---

[3] P. 230, post.

Once it is found that a wife is in actual occupation, then it is clear that in the case of registered land, a purchaser or lender would be well advised to make inquiry of the wife. If she then discloses her rights, he takes subject to them. If she does not disclose them, he takes free of them. I see no reason why this should cause any difficulty to conveyancers. Nor should it impair the proper conduct of businesses. Anyone who lends money on the security of a matrimonial home nowadays ought to realise that the wife may have a share in it. He ought to make sure that the wife agrees to it, or to go to the house and make inquiries of her. It seems to me utterly wrong that a lender should turn a blind eye to the wife's interest or the possibility of it — and afterwards seek to turn her and the family out — on the plea that he did not know she was in actual occupation. If a bank is to do its duty, in the society in which we live, it should recognise the integrity of the matrimonial home. It should not destroy it by disregarding the wife's interest in it — simply to ensure that it is paid the husband's debt in full — with the high interest rate now prevailing. We should not give monied might priority over social justice. We should protect the position of a wife who has a share — just as years ago we protected the deserted wife. In the hope that the House of Lords will not reverse us now as it did then[4].

Mr. Boland's appeal

It seems to me that Mr. Boland has a case to be considered under section 36 of the Administration of Justice Act 1970[5]. No order for possession should be made against him at this stage.

Conclusion

In my opinion each of the wives, Mrs. Brown and Mrs. Boland, is entitled to be protected in her occupation of the matrimonial home. The bank is not entitled to throw these families out into the street — simply to get the last penny of the husband's debt. I would allow the appeals accordingly.

In *London and Cheshire Insurance Co Ltd v Laplagrene Property Co Ltd* [1971] Ch 499, [1971] 1 All ER 766[6], the unpaid vendors of registered land who remained in occupation under a leaseback by the purchasers, had an overriding interest under section 70 (1) (*g*). This entitled the vendors to enforce their lien against chargees of the purchaser, even though they had gone out of occupation subsequent to the purchase[7]. BRIGHTMAN J said at p. 505: "I can see nothing in

---

[4] *National Provincial Bank Ltd v Ainsworth* [1965] AC 1175, [1965] 2 All ER 472; p. 500, post.
[5] P. 640, post.
[6] (1971) 35 Conv (NS) 188 (F. R. Crane).
[7] The relevant date for occupation is that of the registration of the title of the transferee. *Re Boyle's Claim* [1961] 1 WLR 339, [1961] 1 All ER 620.

section 20[8], read with section 70, which causes a paragraph (g) over-riding interest, subject to which a disposition was made, to be extinguished merely because the owner of the right ceases occupation after that disposition but before there has been any other material dealing with the land. The extinction of the overriding interest in such a case, for the fortuitous benefit of the proprietor of the land, seems to me both unsupported by the wording of the Act and an unreasonable result. A right exists as an overriding interest for the very good reason that the owner of the right is in occupation of the land, ought to have been asked to define his rights by the intending transferee or grantee, but is ignored and has no inquiry made of him. In such circumstances, it is reasonable to provide that the transferee or grantee takes subject to the right as an overriding interest. The transferee or grantee has no one but himself to blame for that result. If the overriding interest were extinguished when the owner of the right went out of occupation, that would be a windfall for the transferee or grantee. He would be freed from a burden for no good reason that I can discern."

QUESTION

X, the registered owner of a house in London, orally agreed to sell it to Y. On the evening before the contract was signed, he wrote out and signed a declaration of trust under which he declared that he held the house in trust for his wife, his two year old son and his aunt Matilda (all of whom lived in the house) in equal shares. The contract for sale, subsequently signed, provided that completion should take place on 1 January following, and vacant possession on 1 June, the purchase price being discounted accordingly.

On 1 June, Y claimed possession, but Mrs. X, the baby, and aunt Matilda resisted on the ground of their prior interests. What result?

Hodgson v Marks [1971] Ch 892, [1971] 2 All ER 684; (1973) 36 MLR 25; *Williams and Glyn's Bank Ltd v Boland* [1979] Ch 312, [1979] 2 All ER 697.

IV. Minor Interests[9]

As we have seen, overriding interests do not stand in need of protection on the register, but minor interests do need entry on the register of the land affected if they are to bind purchasers for value. As in unregistered land, actual notice of the interest which should be

---

[8] P. 102, ante.

[9] Cheshire, pp. 105-106, 109-110, 777-783; M & W, pp. 1067-1073; MM, pp. 522-523; Ruoff and Roper, chaps. 7, 34-39. For detailed discussion of priorities of minor interests, see [1976] CLP 26, at 37 et seq. (D. J. Hayton), (1977) 93 LQR 541 (R. J. Smith); p. 687, post.

protected, but is not so protected, is irrelevant[10]. An entry on the register may be made by way of notice, restriction, caution or inhibition[11].

A notice is entered on the charges register of the land affected, and gives protection to and information about such interests as leases, agreements for leases, restrictive covenants and estate contracts[12]. Before a notice can be entered, the land certificate must be lodged at the Registry[13], and for this the registered proprietor's co-operation is required. But production is not necessary where the land is subject to a registered charge; in this case the land certificate will already be deposited at the Registry[14]. Nor is it necessary where a lease has been granted at a rent without taking a fine[15]. If a notice has been entered, any disposition of the land affected takes effect subject to the estate or interest protected by the notice, but only if and so far as such estate or interest may be valid[16].

A restriction is an entry on the proprietorship register, which prevents dealings in registered land until certain conditions and requirements have been complied with[17]. A common example of a restriction is when it is used to ensure that a purchaser of the land complies with the rules relating to the overreaching provisions of the Settled Land Act 1925[18] and the Law of Property Act 1925[19], thereby protecting the interests of the beneficiaries. Normally only the registered proprietor may enter a restriction, but other persons may do so, if they can persuade him to produce the land certificate[20].

A caution against dealings is entered on the proprietorship register. The land certificate need not be produced[1] and therefore the co-operation of the registered proprietor is unnecessary. Its effect is merely to achieve "no dealing with the land", without notice being first served on the cautioner, so as to give him an opportunity to object[2].

An inhibition rarely occurs, except where a bankruptcy inhibition is automatically entered by the Registrar[3].

---

[10] P. 41, ante, L.R.A. 1925, s. 59 (6); *Hodges v Jones* [1935] Ch 657 at 671, per LUXMOORE J; *De Lusignan v Johnson* (1973) 117 Sol Jo 854; but doubts have been cast upon this proposition by *Peffer v Rigg* [1977] 1 WLR 285, [1978] 3 All ER 745 p. 103, ante.

[11] L.R.A. 1925, s. 101 (3), p. 93, ante; (1953) 17 Conv (NS) 105 (T. B. F. Ruoff); (1958) 22 Conv (NS) 14 (F. R. Crane). For a chart showing the registration machinery which replaces that of L.C.A. 1972, see Ruoff and Roper, pp. 702–703; pp. 131–133, post.

[12] L.R.A. 1925, ss. 48–51, 59 (2), 59 (5), pp. 127–129, post.

[13] L.R.A. 1925, s. 64, p. 94, ante.

[14] L.R.A. 1925, s. 65, p. 684, post.

[15] L.R.A. 1925, s. 64 (1) (c) p. 95, ante.

[16] L.R.A. 1925, s. 52 (1), p. 128, post.

[17] L.R.A. 1925, s. 58 (1), p. 129, post.

[18] P. 258, post.

[19] P. 189, post.

[20] L.R.A. 1925, s. 58 (5); L.R.R. 1925, r. 236, p. 129, post.

[1] L.R.A. 1925, s. 64 (1) (c).

[2] L.R.A. 1925, ss. 54, 56, p. 130, post.

[3] L.R.A. 1925, s. 57, p. 130, post.

LAND REGISTRATION ACT 1925

3. Interpretation. —

(xv) "Minor interests" mean the interests not capable of being disposed of or created by registered dispositions and capable of being overridden (whether or not a purchaser has notice thereof) by the proprietors unless protected as provided by this Act, and all rights and interests which are not registered or protected on the register and are not overriding interests, and include —

(*a*) in the case of land held on trust for sale, all interests and powers which are under the Law of Property Act, 1925, capable of being overridden by the trustees for sale, whether or not such interests and powers are so protected; and

(*b*) in the case of settled land, all interests and powers which are under the Settled Land Act, 1925, and the Law of Property Act, 1925, or either of them, capable of being overridden by the tenant for life or statutory owner, whether or not such interests and powers are so protected as aforesaid; . . .

A. Notices

LAND REGISTRATION ACT 1925

48(1). Registration of notice of lease. — P. 430, post.

49. Rules to provide for notices of other rights, interests and claims. — (1) The provisions of the last foregoing section shall be extended by the rules[4] so as to apply to the registration of notices of or of claims in respect of —

(*a*) The grant or reservation of any annuity or rentcharge in possession, either perpetual or for a term of years absolute:

(*b*) The severance of any mines or minerals from the surface, except where the mines and minerals severed are expressly included in the registration:

(*c*) Land charges[5] until the land charge is registered as a registered charge:

(*d*) The right of any person interested in the proceeds of sale of land held on trust for sale or in land subject to a settlement to require that (unless a trust corporation is acting as trustee) there shall be at least two trustees of the disposition on trust for sale or of the settlement:

(*e*) The rights of any widow in respect of dower or under the Intestates' Estates Act, 1890, and any right to free bench or other like right saved by any statute coming into force concurrently with this Act (which rights shall take effect in equity as minor interests):

---

[4] L.R.R. 1925, r. 190.
[5] "Land charge" means a land charge of any class described in s. 2 of L.C.A. 1972 or a local land charge; L.R.A. 1925 s. 3 (ix), as substituted by L.L.C.A. 1975 s. 17, Sch. 1.

(f) Creditors' notices and any other right, interest, or claim which it may be deemed expedient to protect by notice instead of by caution, inhibition, or restriction:

(g) Charging orders (within the meaning of the Charging Orders Act 1979) which in the case of unregistered land may be protected by registration under the Land Charges Act 1972 and which, notwithstanding section 59 of this Act, it may be deemed expedient to protect by notice instead of by caution[6].

(2) A notice shall not be registered in respect of any estate, right, or interest which (independently of this Act) is capable of being over-ridden by the proprietor under a trust for sale or the powers of the Settled Land Act, 1925, or any other statute, or of a settlement, and of being protected by a restriction in the prescribed manner:

Provided that notice of such an estate right or interest may be lodged pending the appointment of trustees of a disposition on trust for sale or a settlement, and if so lodged, shall be cancelled if and when the appointment is made and the proper restriction (if any) is entered.

50.   Notices of restrictive covenants. — P. 777, post.

52.   Effect of notices. — (1) A disposition by the proprietor shall take effect subject to all estates, rights, and claims which are protected by way of notice on the register at the date of the registration or entry of notice of the disposition, but only if and so far as such estates, rights, and claims may be valid[7] and are not (independently of this Act) overridden by the disposition.

(2) Where notice of a claim is entered on the register, such entry shall operate by way of notice only, and shall not operate to render the claim valid whether made adversely to or for the benefit of the registered land or charge.

59.   Writs, orders, deeds of arrangement, pending actions, &c. — (1) A writ, order, deed of arrangement, pending action[8], or other interest which in the case of unregistered land may be protected by registration under the Land Charges Act, 1925, shall, where the land affected or the charge securing the debt affected is registered, be protected only by lodging a creditor's notice, a bankruptcy inhibition or a caution against dealings with the land or the charge.

(2) Registration of a land charge (other than a local land charge) shall, where the land affected is registered, be effected only by register-ing under this Act a notice caution or other prescribed entry: . . .

(5) The foregoing provisions of this section shall apply only to writs and orders, deeds of arrangement, pending actions and land charges which if the land were unregistered would for purposes of protection be required to be registered or re-registered after the commencement of

---

[6] As added by Charging Orders Act 1979, s. 3 (3). See also s. 7 (4). pp. 246–247, post.
[7] *Cator v Newton and Bates* [1940] 1 KB 415, [1939] 4 All ER 457 (entry that freehold land is subject to positive convenant does not make convenant enforceable).
[8] *Greenhi Builders Ltd v Allen* [1979] 1 WLR 156, [1978] 3 All ER 1163.

this Act under the Land Charges Act, 1925[9], and for the purposes of this section a land charge does not include a puisne mortgage or an Inland Revenue charge.

(6) Subject to the provisions of this Act relating to fraud and to the title of a trustee in bankruptcy, a purchaser acquiring title under a registered disposition, shall not be concerned with any pending action, writ, order, deed of arrangement, or other document, matter, or claim (not being an overriding interest) or a charge for capital transfer tax subject to which its disposition takes effect under section 73 of this Act[9a] which is not protected by a caution or other entry on the register, whether he has or has not notice thereof, express, implied, or constructive[10].

LAND REGISTRATION RULES 1925

199. Entry as to trivial rights not required. — The Registrar shall not be required to enter notice of any liability, right, or interest which shall appear to him to be of a trivial or obvious character, or the entry of which on the register is likely to cause confusion or inconvenience.

B. Restrictions

LAND REGISTRATION ACT 1925

58. Power to place restrictions on register. — (1) Where the proprietor of any registered land or charge desires to place restrictions on transferring or charging the land or on disposing of or dealing with the land or charge in any manner in which he is by this Act authorised to dispose of or deal with it, or on the deposit by way of security of any certificate, the proprietor may apply to the registrar to make an entry in the register that no transaction to which the application relates shall be effected, unless the following things, or such of them as the proprietor may determine, are done —

    (a) unless notice of any application for the transaction is transmitted by post to such address as he may specify to the registrar;

    (b) unless the consent of some person or persons, to be named by the proprietor, is given to the transaction;

    (c) unless some such other matter or thing is done as may be required by the applicant and approved by the registrar: . . .

(2) The registrar shall thereupon, if satisfied of the right of the applicant to give the directions, enter the requisite restriction on the register, and no transaction to which the restriction relates shall be effected except in conformity therewith; . . .

(5) Rules may be made to enable applications to be made for the entry of restrictions by persons other than the proprietor[11].

---

[9] Now L.C.A 1972.
[9a] As amended by F.A. 1975 s. 52, Sch. 12 para. 5 (4).
[10] See *Peffer v Rigg* [1977] 1 WLR 285, at 294, per GRAHAM J.
[11] L.R.R. 1925, r. 236.

C. Inhibitions

57. Power for court or registrar to inhibit registered dealings. —
(1) ... The registrar ... may ... issue an order or make an entry
inhibiting for a time, or until the occurrence of an event to be named
in such order or entry, or generally until further order or entry, the
registration or entry of any dealing with any registered land or
registered charge.

(2) The court or registrar may make or refuse to make any such
order or entry, and annex thereto any terms or conditions the court or
registrar may think fit, and discharge such order or cancel such entry
when granted, with or without costs, and generally act in the premises
in such manner as the justice of the case requires.

(4) The court or the registrar may, in lieu of an inhibition, order a
notice or restriction to be placed on the register.

D. Cautions

53. Cautions against first registration. — (1) Any person having or
claiming such an interest in land not already registered as entitles
him to object to any disposition thereof being made without his
consent, may lodge a caution with the registrar to the effect that the
cautioner is entitled to notice in the prescribed form, and to be served
in the prescribed manner, of any application that may be made for the
registration of an interest in the land affecting the right of the
cautioner.

(3) After a caution has been lodged in respect of any estate, which
has not already been registered, registration shall not be made of such
estate until notice has been served on the cautioner to appear and
oppose, if he thinks fit, such registration, and the prescribed time has
elapsed since the date of the service of such notice, or the cautioner has
entered an appearance, whichever may first happen.

54. Cautions against dealings. — (1) Any person interested under
any unregistered instrument, or interested as a judgment creditor, or
otherwise howsoever, in any land or charge registered in the name of
any other person, may lodge a caution with the registrar to the effect
that no dealing with such land or charge on the part of the proprietor
is to be registered until notice has been served upon the cautioner[12]:

Provided that a person whose estate, right, interest, or claim has
been registered or protected by a notice or restriction shall not be
entitled (except with the consent of the registrar) to lodge a caution
in respect of such estate, right, interest, or claim, but this provision

---

[12] *Re White Rose Cottage* [1965] Ch 940, [1965] 1 All ER 11, (equitable charge), p. 133,
post; *Parkash v Irani Finance Ltd* [1970] Ch 101, [1969] 1 All ER 930 (charging order),
p. 134, post, *Elias v Mitchell* [1972] Ch 652, [1972] 2 All ER 153 (equitable tenant in
common under trust for sale), p. 241, post; cf. *Murray v Two Strokes Ltd* [1973]
1 WLR 823, [1973] 3 All ER 357, p. 113, n. 11, ante, *Myton Ltd v Schwab-Morris*
[1974] 1 WLR 331, [1974] 1 All ER 326.

shall not operate to prevent an incumbrancer or assignee of a life interest, remainder, reversion or executory interest, from lodging a priority caution in a specially prescribed form.

55. Effect of cautions against dealings. — (1) After any such caution against dealings has been lodged[13] in respect of any registered land or charge, the registrar shall not, without the consent of the cautioner, register any dealing or make any entry on the register for protecting the rights acquired under a deposit of a land or charge certificate or other dealing by the proprietor with such land or charge until he has served notice on the cautioner, warning him that his caution will cease to have any effect after the expiration of the prescribed number of days next following the date at which such notice is served; and after the expiration of such time as aforesaid the caution shall cease unless an order to the contrary is made by the registrar, and upon the caution so ceasing the registered land or charge may be dealt with in the same manner as if no caution had been lodged.

Ruoff and Roper: *Law and Practice of Registered Conveyancing* (4th edn., 1979), pp. 702–703:

REGISTRATION MACHINERY REPLACING THAT OF THE LAND CHARGES ACT

Instrument or matter as defined in the Land Charges Act 1972	Normal method of protection against registered land	Some other possible alternative methods	Reference to the Land Registration Act 1925
Pending land, action.	Caution.	Inhibition if the court so orders.	ss. 59 (1), 54, 57.
Petition in bankruptcy.	Creditor's notice entered automatically by Chief Land Registrar.	None other necessary.	ss. 59 (1), 61 (1).
Writ or order for enforcing judgment against land.	Caution.	Notice, if the land certificate can be produced.	ss. 49, 59 (1) (3), 54.
Receiving order in bankruptcy.	Bankruptcy inhibition entered automatically by Chief Land Registrar.	None other necessary.	ss. 59 (1), 61 (3).
Deed of arrangement affecting land.	Substantive registration of the trustee as proprietor pursuant to a transfer.	Caution.	ss. 59 (1), 54.
Land charge, class A (created by applicant).	Substantive registration of the charge.	Notice or caution.	ss. 26, 49 (1) (c), 59 (2), 54.
Land charge, class B (arising automatically).	Substantive registration of the charge.	Notice or caution.	ss. 26, 49 (1) (c), 59 (2), 54.

---

[13] *Smith v Morrison* [1974] 1 WLR 659 at 682, [1974] 1 All ER 957 at 978.

Instrument or matter as defined in the Land Charges Act 1972	Normal method of protection against registered land	Some other possible alternative methods	Reference to the Land Registration Act 1925
Land charge, class C (i) (puisne mortgage).	Substantive registration of the charge.	Notice or caution.	ss. 26, 49 (1) (c), 54, 59 (5), and 106
Land charge, class C (ii) (limited owner's charge).	Caution or restriction.	Presumably a notice cannot be used as the charge can be overridden.	ss. 49 (1) (c), 49 (2), 54, 58 (1).
Land charge, class C (iii) (general equitable charge).	Notice.	Caution or notice of [intended] deposit.	ss. 49 (1) (c), 59 (2), 54, 66 and 106 (as amended)
Land charge, class C (iv) (estate contract).	Notice; but it is usually considered that no protection is necessary if possesion is taken immediately or if completion is to be soon.	Caution or restriction.	ss. 49 (1) (c), 59 (2), 54, 58 (1).
Land charge, class D (i) (Inland Revenue charge for capital transfer tax).	Notice.	None.	ss. 73, 59 (5)[14].
Land charge, class D (ii) (restrictive covenant).	Notice (entered automatically by Chief Land Registrar if the covenant is disclosed on first registration, and if created by a transfer of registered land, entered on registration of the transfer).	Caution.	ss. 5, 19 (2), 20 (1), 50 and 54.
Release or modification of restrictive covenant.	Notice.	None; unless the effectiveness of the release, etc., is strictly proved, when the original entry may be cancelled.	ss. 40, 50.
Land charge, class D (iii) (equitable easement)	Notice.	Caution.	ss. 49 (1) (c), 70 (1) (a), 59 (2), 54.

---

[14] L.R.A. 1925, ss. 59 (5) and 73 have been amended by FA 1975, ss. 52, 59; Schs. 12 and 13. L.R.A. 1925, s. 106 has been amended by A.J.A. 1977, s. 26 (which substituted a new section), p. 682 post.

Instrument or matter as defined in the Land Charges Act 1972	Normal method of protection against registered land	Some other possible alternative methods	Reference to the Land Registration Act 1925
Land charge, class E (old annuities).	Notice, provided the annuity cannot be overridden.	Caution.	ss. 49 (1) (c), 49 (2), 59 (2), 54.
Land charge, class F (rights of occupation of matrimonial home)[15].	Applicant applies for notice or caution. Chief Land Registrar will enter notice when the property is subject to a registered charge or, if it is not, when the land certificate is produced. Otherwise, caution.	None.	ss. 49 (1) (c), 54.
Renewal of class F charge[16].	Notice or caution, according to method already in use.	None.	ss. 49 (1) (c), 54.

RE WHITE ROSE COTTAGE
[1965] Ch 940, [1965] 1 All ER 11 (CA, Lord DENNING MR, HARMAN and SALMON LJJ)

The proprietor of land registered with an absolute title executed a memorandum of deposit of the land certificate with a bank to secure advances, and undertook to execute a legal charge on request. Notice of the deposit was entered on the charges register. The bank later wished to enter on the register notice of the equitable charge created by the memorandum, but Chippendale Workshops Ltd (the contractors), who were creditors of the proprietor of the land, and had meanwhile lodged cautions, objected.

Held. The contractors were not entitled to object to the registration.

LORD DENNING MR: Once the bank got the equitable charge, together with the land certificate, on 3 May 1962, the position about registration was as follows:

(1) The bank could not register the charge as a *substantive charge* on the property[17]. In order to make a substantive registration, so as to get special priority, one must have a *legal* charge. An equitable charge will not do: see sections 25 to 36 of the Land Registration Act, 1925. . . .

(2) The bank could apply to the registrar to register *notice* of the charge as a *land charge*, provided they produced the land certificate to him as well: see sections 48 (1)[18], 49 (1) (c)[19] and 64 (1)[20] of the Act of

---

[15] Matrimonial Homes Act 1967, ss. 1 (1), 2 (1) (7).
[16] Matrimonial Homes Act 1967, s. 5 (3); Land Registration (Matrimonial Homes) Rules 1967, r. 4.
[17] For an account of the types of mortgage and charge allowed in registered and unregistered land, see p. 601–605, 681–682, post.
[18] P. 430, post.
[19] P. 127, ante.
[20] P. 94, ante.

1925. Where the charge is protected by a *notice* of this kind, it means that every subsequent purchaser or incumbrancer is deemed to be affected with notice of the charge: see section 52[1].

(3) The bank could lodge a *caution* with the registrar: see section 54 of the Act[2]. A caution gives the cautioner this right: he is entitled to have notice, and to be heard, before any subsequent dealing is registered. After a hearing "the registrar shall make such order in the matter as he shall think just" (see rule 220 (3)); bearing in mind that a caution gives a protection to the cautioner in that it gives notice of his interest: see section 59[3].

(4) The bank could give a *notice* that the land certificate had been *deposited* with them. It is true that they had an equitable charge by deed. But they had also the land certificate. It had been deposited with them as security. And I see no reason why they should not give notice of the deposit. Indeed rule 239 (1) is quite clear and contemplates it. Such a notice operates as a caution: see rule 239 (4).

In this case, on 7 May 1962, the bank chose course (4). They gave notice of deposit of the land certificate. I think it was open to them to do so. It operated as a caution at the land registry warning all persons who looked at the register that the land certificate had been deposited with them as security for money. I think it took effect in priority to the subsequent charges by the contractors. The contractors are not entitled to object to the registration by the bank of notice of their charge.

HARMAN LJ: It is, I think, quite right to say that the deposit of the land certificate did not create the charge: that was done by the memorandum and the correct course would have been to seek to enter notice of the memorandum under section 49 of the Act of 1925. Nevertheless the entry on the register was in my opinion a sufficient notice to all the world that the land certificate was in the hands of someone as security for money and this is enough to put the subsequent encumbrancer on enquiry which can only lead to ascertaining the true facts[4].

PARKASH *v* IRANI FINANCE LTD
[1970] Ch 101, [1969] 1 All ER 930 (ChD PLOWMAN J)

In January 1967 one Kalra, who was registered as proprietor of No. 205 Wexham Road, Slough, with an absolute title, agreed to sell it to the plaintiff, subject to contract. No formal contract was ever signed. On 2 July the plaintiff went into possession. On 7 July the defendants obtained a charging order on the property under the County Courts Act 1959, to secure a judgment debt, and on 10 July lodged a caution with the Land Registry. On 27 July the Land Registry issued to the plaintiff's solicitors an official search without mentioning the caution.

---

[1] P. 128, ante.
[2] P. 130, ante.
[3] P. 128, ante.
[4] It would seem that the deposit of the land certificate alone would have been sufficient to give notice to a subsequent purchaser: *Barclays Bank Ltd v Taylor* [1974] Ch 137, [1974] 1 All ER 752; p. 687, post.

On 10 August Kalra transferred the property to the plaintiff and on 14 August the transfer was lodged for registration. The defendant then received notice of this application and objected.

The Chief Land Registrar referred to the Court the question whether the caution should continue to have effect or be cancelled.

Held. The defendant's caution continued to have effect.

PLOWMAN J: The plaintiff's case, in a nutshell, is this: while conceding that he could not establish any prior equity as against Irani (since he never had a specifically enforceable contract for the purchase of the property), he submits that he is entitled to pray in aid the doctrine of purchaser of a legal estate for value without notice and therefore to take free of the equitable charge created by the charging order. At first sight this submission is a little surprising, since one of the essential features of registration of title is to substitute a system of registration of rights for the doctrine of notice. In the circumstances it is necessary to examine the statutory provisions affecting the present case in order to see whether cautions are anomalous.

[His Lordship then referred to ss. 54 (1), 55, 56 (2) and 59 (1) Land Registration Act 1925 and continued:]

The effect of the registration of a caution, therefore, is that the cautioner's order (in this case a charging order) is "protected" (to quote section 59 (1))[5] by the fact that no dealing can be registered without notice to him so that he can, if he wishes, assert his right and challenge the proposed registration. Conversely, a purchaser of the property, who has a statutory right to an authority from his vendor to inspect the register (see section 110 (1) of the Land Registration Act 1925), will find that no transfer can be registered in his favour without notice to the cautioner. He will not know the precise nature of the cautioner's rights, nor will he probably inquire; his course, in the ordinary way, will be to call upon his vendor to procure either the withdrawal of the caution or the consent of the cautioner to the registration of the intended transfer. No doubt that is what would have happened here, if the plaintiff had made a personal instead of an official search. If the vendor had failed to comply, the plaintiff would presumably have declined to go on with his purchase.

There is one further provision in the Land Registration Act 1925, to which I must refer and that is section 59 (6)[6].

It is true, as was stressed in the argument before me, that what the subsection says is that a purchaser is *not* affected by notice, express, implied or constructive, of matters capable of protection by a caution and not so protected and that (unlike the case of a notice of lease under section 48 (1) of the Act)[7] it does not say in terms that a purchaser *is* affected by a notice of matters capable of protection by caution, which *are* so protected, but that, in my judgment, is implicit in the scheme of the Act and in the subsection.

---

[5] See p. 128, ante.
[6] P. 129, ante.
[7] P. 430, post.

The effect of the statutory provisions to which I have referred is, in my judgment, this: first, that the appropriate form of protection for a charging order is a caution; secondly, that once the caution is registered, the cautioner can only lose his protection either by virtue of section 55 (1)[8] or by withdrawing his caution, or consenting to its cancellation or by order of the Chief Land Registrar or this court; and, thirdly, that therefore he does not lose it merely because a purchaser of the property does not know of its existence, even if the purchaser's ignorance is the result of a mistake of the Land Registry, short of a failure to act on an application to register the caution in the first place.

There are certain dicta in the Court of Appeal which, even if they be obiter, seem to me to support the view which I have expressed. The case in question is *Re White Rose Cottage* ([1965] Ch 940, [1965] 1 All ER 11).

I, therefore, reach the conclusion that . . . Irani has not lost the protection given to it by its caution.

In *Webb v Pollmount Ltd* [1966] Ch 584, [1966] 1 All ER 481[9], UNGOED-THOMAS J said at p. 599: "So, I come to section 59[10]. The defendant's submission is that it provides that an option to purchase can only be protected by registration. But it will be convenient, by way of introduction to it, to refer briefly to certain provisions relating to the registration of options under the Land Charges Act 1925[11], and the Land Registration Act 1925. An option to purchase relating to unregistered land is an estate contract within section 10 (1), Class C (iv), of the Land Charges Act 1925[11], and may thus under section 10 (1) be registered as a land charge and under section 13 (2)[12] it is void against a purchaser of the land unless registered before completion of the purchase. Section 23[13] excludes (inter alia) land charges, not including local land charges, from the Act so far as they can be protected under the Land Registration Act 1925, 'by lodging or registering a creditor's notice, restriction, caution, inhibition or other notice'. All land charges can be so protected under the Land Registration Act 1925, by notice, under section 49 (1)[14] until registered as a registered charge, or by caution under section 54[15]. Therefore, the Land Charges Act 1925[16], does not apply to this option to purchase. . . .

---

[8] P. 113, ante.
[9] P. 128, ante. The question was whether an option to purchase held by a tenant in actual occupation was valid as an overriding interest.
[10] P. 128, ante.
[11] Now L.C.A. 1972, s. 2 (4).
[12] Now L.C.A. 1972, s. 4 (6).
[13] Now L.C.A. 1972, s. 14.
[14] P. 127, ante.
[15] P. 130, ante.
[16] Now L.C.A. 1972.

The crucial word in section 59 (1), for the purposes of the defendant's argument, is the word 'only' which is relied on to establish that an option to purchase cannot be protected otherwise than by a caution, the creditor's notice or bankruptcy inhibition which it mentions being inapplicable.

Subsection (1) is curiously worded in view of subsection (5). . . .

. . . no explanation seems clearly convincing. But it does seem reasonably clear that if section 59 were read as an exhaustive statement of the only exclusive methods of protecting land charges, it would be inconsistent with other substantial specific sections, and I am convinced that it should not be so read. . . .

I, therefore, respectfully agree with the conclusion of Harman J, in *Bridges v Mees* ([1957] Ch 475, 487, [1957] 2 All ER 577), that section 59 (1) does not establish that it is only by registration in accordance with the subsection that any of the interests, therein mentioned, even though they would otherwise be overriding interests, can be protected."

QUESTION

Legal and equitable estates in land existed for centuries. Since 1925, we speak of legal estates and equitable interests. To what extent is this nomenclature meaningful in the context of:

(a) Interests and charges registered under the Land Charges Act 1972;

(b) Registered Land?

See Maitland, *Equity,* pp. 210–215.

V. Rectification of the Register and Indemnity[17]

LAND REGISTRATION ACT 1925

82. **Rectification of the register.** — (1) The register may be rectified pursuant to an order of the court or by the registrar, subject to an appeal to the court, in any of the following cases, but subject to the provisions of this section:—

(a) Subject to any express provisions of this Act to the contrary, where a court of competent jurisdiction has decided that any person is entitled to any estate right or interest in or to any registered land or charge, and as a consequence of such decision such court is of opinion that a rectification of the register is required, and makes an order to that effect[18],

---

[17] Cheshire, pp. 109, 770–772; M & W, pp. 1079–1084; MM, p. 528; Farrand (2nd edn.), pp. 209–220; Ruoff and Roper, Chap. 40; (1968) 84 LQR 528 (S. M. Cretney and G. Dworkin); (1969) 32 MLR 138–141 (T. B. F. Ruoff); (1971), 35 Conv (NS) 390 (T. B. F. Ruoff and P. Meehan). Law Commission Working Paper No. 45, pp. 36–74.

[18] *Chowood Ltd v Lyall (No. 2)* [1930] 2 Ch 156 (rectification ordered to give effect to overriding interest acquired by adverse possession to part of land registered in name of proprietor); *Calgary and Edmonton Land Co Ltd v Discount Bank (Overseas) Ltd* [1971] 1 WLR 81, [1971] 1 All ER 551 (caution removed).

(*b*) Subject to any express provision of this Act to the contrary, where the court, on the application in the prescribed manner of any person who is aggrieved by any entry made in, or by the omission of any entry from, the register, or by any default being made, or unnecessary delay taking place, in the making of any entry in the register, makes an order for the rectification of the register[19];

(*c*) In any case and at any time with the consent of all persons interested;

(*d*) Where the court or the registrar is satisfied that any entry in the register has been obtained by fraud[20];

(*e*) Where two or more persons are, by mistake, registered as proprietors of the same registered estate or of the same charge;

(*f*) Where a mortgagee has been registered as proprietor of the land instead of as proprietor of a charge and a right of redemption is subsisting[1];

(*g*) Where a legal estate has been registered in the name of a person who if the land had not been registered would not have been the estate owner[2]; and

(*h*) In any other case where, by reason of any error or omission in the register, or by reason of any entry made under a mistake, it may be deemed just to rectify the register[3].

(2) The register may be rectified under this section, notwithstanding that the rectification may affect any estates, rights, charges, or interests acquired or protected by registration, or by any entry on the register, or otherwise.

(3)[4] The register shall not be rectified, except for the purpose of giving effect to an overriding interest[5] or an order of the court so as to affect the title of the proprietor who is in possession —

(*a*) unless the proprietor has caused or substantially contributed to the error or omission by fraud or lack of proper care; or

(*c*) unless for any other reason, in any particular case, it is considered that it would be unjust not to rectify the register against him[6].

---

[19] *Chowood Ltd v Lyall (No. 2)* supra at pp. 168–169, per LAWRENCE LJ; *Calgary and Edmonton Land Co Ltd v Discount Bank (Overseas) Ltd* supra; *Lester v Burgess* (1973) 26 P & C R 536 (caution removed).

[20] *Re Leighton's Conveyance* [1936] 1 All ER 667 (fraudulent misrepresentation and undue influence). L.R.A 1925, s. 114.

[1] Cf. for unregistered land L.P.A. 1925, ss. 85 (2), (3), 86 (2), (3), p. 601, post.

[2] *Chowood v Lyall (No. 2)* supra.

[3] *Re Dances Way, West Town, Hayling Island* [1962] Ch 490, [1962] 2 All ER 42; p. 593, post (notice of adverse easement cancelled).

[4] As amended by A.J.A. 1977 s. 24, which came into force on 29 August 1977; see Law Com Working Paper No. 45 (1972) pp. 36–74.

[5] *Re Chowood's Registered Land*, [1933] Ch 574, p. 145, post; *Epps v Esso Petroleum Ltd* [1973] 1 WLR 1071, [1973] 2 All ER 465, p. 139, post.

[6] *Epps v Esso Petroleum Co Ltd* supra.

83. Right to indemnity in certain cases[7]. — (1) Subject to the provisions of this Act to the contrary, any person suffering loss by reason of any rectification of the register under this Act shall be entitled to be indemnified[8].

(2) Where an error or omission has occurred in the register, but the register is not rectified, any person suffering loss by reason of such error or omission, shall, subject to the provisions of this Act, be entitled to be indemnified.

(3) Where any person suffers loss by reason of the loss or destruction of any document lodged at the registry for inspection or safe custody or by reason of an error in any official search, he shall be entitled to be indemnified under this Act.

(4) Subject as hereinafter provided, a proprietor of any registered land or charge claiming in good faith under a forged disposition shall, where the register is rectified, be deemed to have suffered loss by reason of such rectification and shall be entitled to be indemnified under this Act.

(5) No indemnity shall be payable under this Act in any of the following cases:—

   (a) Where the applicant or a person from whom he derives title (otherwise than under a disposition for valuable consideration which is registered or protected on the register) has caused or substantially contributed to the loss by fraud or lack of proper care[9];

(11) ... when a claim to indemnity arises in consequence of the registration of an estate in land with an absolute or good leasehold title, the claim shall be enforceable only if made within six years from the date of such registration, ...[10].

EPPS *v* ESSO PETROLEUM LTD
[1973] 1 WLR 1071, [1973] 2 All ER 465[11] (ChD, TEMPLEMAN J)

In 1935 Alfred Clifford owned 4 Darland Avenue, Gillingham, Kent, and, on the North side of it, the adjoining Darland Garage. In that year he leased both to Mr. Jones. In 1955 his personal representatives conveyed the house to Mrs. Jones in fee simple, together with an extra 11 foot strip of frontage on the north side of the wall dividing the home

---

[7] The indemnity is payable by the Chief Land Registrar out of moneys provided by Parliament. L.R. & L.C.A. 1971, s. 1. See (1971) 35 Conv (NS) 390 (T. B. F. Ruoff and P. Meehan); Barnsley, pp. 69–71. During 1978–1979, £54,669 was paid in respect of 109 claims; these included £9,500 for three claims for erroneous inclusion of land on first registration (double conveyance), and £20,416 for four claims arising out of registration of forged transfers. Annual Report for 1978–1979, paras. 23–24. Viewed against a fee revenue of about £36 million for the year 1978–1979, the sums paid by way of indemnity "fade almost into insignificance".
[8] *Re Chowood's Registered Land* [1933] Ch 574.
[9] As substituted by L.R. & L.C.A. 1971, s. 3 (1). (1971) 35 Conv (NS) 390.
[10] Then follow special provisions for the date at which the six years start in cases of minors, settlements, covenants, and mortgages.
[11] (1973) 37 Conv (NS) 284 (F. R. Crane).

from the garage. The object was to provide space for a garage at the home. Mrs. Jones covenanted to erect a new wall on the new boundary, but never did. In 1956 Clifford's personal representatives granted a new lease of Darland Garage to Mr. Jones, and in error the plan included the 11 foot strip. In 1959 they conveyed the garage, subject to the lease, to Julian Ball, and included the strip. The Land Registration Act 1925 had become applicable, and Ball became first registered proprietor of the garage and strip, with the consequence that L.R.A. 1925, section 5 deprived Mrs. Jones of the strip and vested it in Ball, subject to any overriding interests affecting the strip. In 1964 Ball conveyed the garage and strip to the defendants who became the second registered proprietors with absolute title. In 1968 the personal representatives of Mrs. Jones conveyed 4 Darland Avenue and the strip to Mr. and Mrs. Epps, who obtained first registration of the house without the strip.

On a summons by Mr. and Mrs. Epps for rectification of the register, so as to exclude the strip from the defendant's title on the register, the plaintiffs argued that Mrs. Jones was in possession of the strip at the time of the conveyance to the defendant in 1964; and, therefore, Mrs. Jones and her estate had an overriding interest under L.R.A. 1925, section 70 (1) (*g*) by virtue of that possession.

Held. Rectification refused.

TEMPLEMAN J: Section 82 (1) of the Land Registration Act provides that the register may be rectified where, inter alia, as in the present case, a legal estate has been registered in the name of a person who, if the land had not been registered, would not have been the estate owner. That describes the defendants. Section 82 (3), limits the exercise of the power of rectification conferred by section 82 (1). The limitation is in these terms:

"The register shall not be rectified, except for the purpose of giving effect to an overriding interest, so as to affect the title of the proprietor who is in possession — unless . . ."

and then it specifies three conditions[12], one of which must be satisfied, if rectification is to be granted. . . . . . .

Condition (*c*) provides for rectification — and I quote:

"unless for any other reason, in any particular case, it is considered that it would be unjust not to rectify the register against . . ." [the registered proprietor.]

Mr. Cullen, for the plaintiffs, submitted that when Mrs. Jones was deprived of her legal estate in fee simple by the mistaken registration of Mr. Ball as proprietor, Mrs. Jones retained or acquired, and her successors in title, down to and including the plaintiffs, acquired an equitable interest in fee simple. The registered proprietor, first Mr. Ball and now the defendants, acquired the legal estate, subject to the equitable interest of Mrs. Jones and her successors. Effect should be given to that equitable interest by rectification. The limitation on the

---

[12] Now only two. A. J. A. 1977, s. 24; p. 138, ante.

exercise of the power of rectification, which is to be found in section 82 (3), does not apply where rectification is required to give effect to an overriding interest. The equitable interest of Mrs. Jones and her successors in title is an overriding interest.

By section 70 (1) (*g*) overriding interests include the rights of every person in actual occupation of the land or in receipt of the rents and profits thereof, save where inquiry is made of such person and the rights are not disclosed. Mrs. Jones and her successors in title were in actual occupation, because Mr. Jones, and later the plaintiffs, parked a car on the disputed strip. Mr. Ball and the defendants acquired the disputed strip subject to the overriding interests of Mrs. Jones and her successors constituted by an equitable interest protected by actual occupation. The defendants never were in possession or, at any rate, ceased to be in possession when the plaintiffs erected their fence in 1968. Thus far Mr. Cullen. . . . . . .

The claim put forward by Mr. Cullen on behalf of the plaintiffs to an overriding interest depends on whether Mr. Jones was in actual occupation of the disputed strip when the defendants became the registered proprietor of the disputed strip in 1964. The contention put forward by Mr. Cullen that the defendants were not in possession depends on whether they went into possession of the disputed strip when they became the registered proprietor and remained in possession until after the plaintiffs completed their purchase in 1968. Mr. Brodie for the defendants took up a position at the opposite pole. He submitted that even if Mr. Jones was in actual occupation he occupied in his capacity as tenant of Mr. Ball. Alternatively, the occupation of Mr. Jones could not protect any equitable interest vested in the probate judge at the date when the defendants became the registered proprietors of the disputed strip in 1964.

I reject these submissions of Mr. Brodie. If Mr. Jones was in actual occupation when the defendants completed their purchase of the disputed strip then his occupation in the present circumstances sufficed to assert and protect any equitable interest of Mrs. Jones and her estate so as to constitute an overriding interest, and sufficed also to defeat the claim by the defendants to be in possession. . . . . . .

In my judgment, the fact that the defendants were not the original proprietors, but subsequent transferees, is only one element to be considered in the exercise of the discretion conferred by section 82 (1) and section 82 (3) (*c*) of the Land Registration Act 1925. In the confrontation envisaged by section 82 (1) and in particular by section 82 (1) (*g*), between, on the one hand, the registered proprietor, who is a victim of double conveyancing, and the first purchaser or his successors, deprived of the legal estate by registration, the court must first determine whether the registered proprietor is in possession. If the registered proprietor is not in possession then section 82 (3) does not apply, and the court will normally grant rectification: see *Chowood Ltd v Lyall (No. 2)* [1930] 2 Ch 156. A fortiori if the registered proprietor is not in possession but the applicant has an overriding interest constituted by an equitable interest protected by actual occupation, the court will grant rectification: see *Bridges v Mees* [1957] 1 Ch 475 at 486. However, the power of rectification given by section 82 (1) never ceases to be discretionary, so that where section 82 (3) does not apply there may still be circumstances which defeat the claim for rectification.

If the registered proprietor is in possession, the applicant for rectification will not normally be in actual occupation, and one of the conditions specified in section 82 (3) must be satisfied if rectification is to be granted. . . . . . .

It follows that the crucial questions in the present case are, first, whether Mr. Jones was in actual occupation of the disputed strip when the defendants completed purchase in 1964; secondly, whether the defendants were in possession at the date when the plaintiffs completed their purchase of 4 Darland Avenue in 1968; and if those questions are decided in favour of the defendants, thirdly, whether it would be unjust not to rectify against them.

In *Hodgson v Marks* [1971] Ch 892 at 931, Russell LJ said, on actual occupation as an ingredient of an overriding interest, that he was prepared for the purpose of that case to assume, without necessarily accepting, that section 70 (1) (*g*) of the Land Registration Act 1925 is designed only to apply to a case in which the occupation is such in point of fact as would in the case of unregistered land affect a purchaser with constructive notice of the rights of the occupier. Then Russell LJ said, at p. 932:

"I do not think it desirable to attempt to lay down a code or catalogue of situations in which a person other than the vendor should be held to be in occupation of unregistered land for the purpose of constructive notice of his rights, or in actual occupation of registered land for the purposes of section 70 (1) (*g*). It must depend on the circumstances, and a wise purchaser or vendor will take no risks. Indeed, however wise he may be he may have no ready opportunity of finding out; but, nevertheless, the law will protect the occupier."

In my judgment Mr. Jones was not in actual occupation of the disputed strip when the defendants completed their purchase of Darland Garage and was not thereafter in actual occupation.

Mr. Jones gave evidence that every night he parked his car on the disputed strip, and sometimes the car was there during the day. Mr. Jones's recollection, not unnaturally, was not very reliable, and I find that he sometimes parked his car on the disputed strip, but how often and when no one can now determine with any certainty. But even if Mr. Jones regularly parked his car on the disputed strip I do not consider that this constituted actual occupation of the disputed strip in the circumstances of the present case. I reach this conclusion for the following reasons: first, the parking of a car on a strip 11 feet wide by 80 feet long does not actually occupy the whole, or a substantial, or any defined part of that disputed strip for the whole or any defined time. Secondly, the parking of a car on an unidentified piece of land, apparently comprised in garage premises, is not an assertion of actual occupation of anything.

In addition to these two reasons there are circumstances which show that, not only was Mr. Jones not in actual occupation, but on the contrary that the defendants were.

[His Lordship reviewed the evidence and continued:]

In my judgment, therefore, section 82 (3) does apply because the Jones's and the plaintiffs had no overriding interest protected by actual occupation and because the defendants were in possession. There remains the question, under condition (c) of section 82 (3) whether it would be unjust not to rectify against the defendants.

In my judgment, justice in the present case lies wholly with the defendants and not with the plaintiffs. . . .

In my judgment, whereas the defendants bought the disputed strip, the plaintiffs bought a law suit, thanks to the default of their vendor in not taking steps to assert ownership and possession of the disputed strip, and thanks to the failure of the plaintiffs to make before completion the inquiries which they made immediately after completion.

Mr. Cullen put forward one additional circumstance which he argued, with some force, tilted the balance of justice in favour of rectification. That circumstance, he submitted, was that if the register is rectified the defendants can recover compensation based on the 1973 value of the disputed strip, but if the register is not rectified the plaintiffs cannot recover compensation. This argument is founded on section 83 of the Land Registration Act 1925 which deals with compensation. Section 83 (1) provides that, subject to the provisions of the Act to the contrary, any person suffering loss by reason of any rectification of the register under the Act shall be entitled to be indemnified. That will be the position of the defendants if I rectify. Section 83 (2) provides that where an error or omission has occurred in the register but the register is not rectified, any person suffering loss by reason of such error or omission shall, subject to the provisions of the Act, be entitled to be indemnified. That is the position of the plaintiffs, if I do not rectify.

By section 83 (6) where indemnity is paid in respect of the loss of an estate or interest in or charge on land the amount so paid shall not exceed (a), where the register is not rectified the value of the estate interest or charge at the time when the error or omission which caused the loss was made. In other words, if I do not rectify then the plaintiffs' indemnity is reduced to the value of the disputed strip as at 1959 when the error was made. Subsection (6) (b), on the other hand, says that where the register is rectified the indemnity is not to exceed the value if there had been no rectification of the estate, interest or charge immediately before the time of rectification. This would apply to the defendants. So that the legislature provides 1959 values for the plaintiffs and 1973 values for the defendants. The matter does not end there, however, because by subsection (11) there is a further limitation on indemnity. Subsection (11) provides that a liability to pay indemnity under the Act shall be deemed a simple contract debt and for the purposes of the Limitation Act the cause of action shall be deemed to arise at the time when the claimant knows or, but for his own default, might have known of the existence of his claim. Whether or not that applies to the plaintiffs, it clearly does not affect the defendants; first, because they are not claimants; and, secondly, because they must have been in complete innocence of anything wrong until the plaintiffs came on the scene and raised the question of where the true boundary lay. Then there is a proviso:

"Provided that, when a claim to indemnity arises in consequence of the registration of an estate in land with an absolute or good leasehold title, the claim shall be enforceable only if made within six years from the date of such registration, except in the following cases . . ."

and then it sets out cases involving infants or settled land, which plainly do not apply. Clearly, that proviso operates to deprive the plaintiffs of compensation, because their claim to indemnity is made more than six years from the date of the 1959 registration. Mr. Cullen submits that it does not apply to the defendants. First, he says that the proviso only applies to section 83 (2); and, secondly, he says that the claim to indemnity will only arise so far as the defendants are concerned in consequence of the registration which will follow upon any order for rectification.

Mr. Brodie, on the other hand, submits that the proviso applies to the defendants and that if it does not, the matter is obscure, and any decision I make on it will not be binding, and the defendants should not be left in the uncertainty of knowing whether that decision is right.

I can only peer through my own spectacles and, in my judgment, the proviso does not apply to the defendants. It is intended only to apply to a claimant who has the means and opportunity of finding out and asserting his claim, and therefore there is no reason why the six-year period should not operate. In the case of the defendants, however, who are in possession and who have got the title, I do not consider that the proviso applies; they will not suffer and their claim to indemnity will not arise unless and until an order for rectification is made. Accordingly, the foundation for Mr. Cullen's submission is established. This is a case, in my judgment, in which if an order for rectification is made the defendants will be entitled to indemnity on 1973 values, and if the claim for rectification is refused then they will keep the land, but the plaintiffs will not get compensation.

The question I have to determine is whether that is sufficient to upset the justice of the defendants' claim that there should not be rectification in the present instance. Is it sufficient — and this is the test — to make it unjust not to rectify the register against the defendants? Mr. Cullen pointed out that as far as the defendants are concerned the disputed strip formed, he calculated, 4 per cent. of the garage premises. He said it could not make a lot of difference to the defendants' garage; on the other hand, it was of importance to 4 Darland Avenue because it provided a private garage, an asset which is important in commuter territory.

In my judgment, however, this cannot be solved merely on the question of money. The defendants bought the land; they bought it to exploit for their commercial purposes; they did not buy it in order to sell a strip for a 1973 value, which in real terms will not, in my judgment, adequately indemnify them. Although the strip is at the back of the garage, in the same way as it could be used as a private garage for 4 Darland Avenue, so it could be used by the defendants for commercial purposes, and in fact they say now they intend to use it in connection with a car wash; if they are deprived of it they will be in considerable difficulty, and will not have all the facilities which a modern garage requires. I think that may be putting it a bit high, but the fact of the matter is that this strip is worth more to the defendants than the pounds, shillings and pence which they will receive by indemnity, even on a 1973 basis.

Accordingly, in my judgment, that argument is not sufficient to overturn all the other arguments in favour of the defendants, and I decline to order rectification of the register.

RE CHOWOOD'S REGISTERED LAND[13]
[1933] Ch 574 (ChD, CLAUSON J)

Lyall had, before the registration of Chowood Ltd (the purchaser of certain freeholds from Ralli) as proprietor of those freeholds with an absolute title, acquired a right under the Limitation Acts to a part thereof. The register was rectified and Chowood Ltd claimed an indemnity under section 83.

Held. Chowood Ltd was not entitled to be indemnified.

CLAUSON J: Chowood's title was all along subject to the rights which Lyall has succeeded in establishing; and the loss, if it may properly be so called, which Chowood has suffered is that they have not got, and since the Act of 1925 came into force (whatever may have been the position before) have never had title to the strip, except subject to an overriding right in Lyall. That loss was occasioned by Chowood failing to ascertain that, when they bought, Lyall was in possession, and in possession under such circumstances that Ralli could not make a title to the strip. The loss was occasioned by paying Ralli for a strip to which Ralli could not make title. The rectification of the register merely recognized the existing position, and put Chowood in no worse a position than they were in before.

In these circumstances I must hold that Chowood have suffered no loss by reason of the rectification of the register.

-----

[13] Followed in *Re Boyle's Claim* [1961] 1 WLR 339, [1961] 1 All ER 620.

In *Freer v Unwins Ltd* [1976] Ch 288, [1976] 1 All ER 634[14], the owners of unregistered land, which was laid out as a parade of shops, sold and conveyed shop No. 2 in 1913 to Freer with the benefit of a covenant imposed on the remaining shops in the Parade, restraining them from selling tobacco and sweets. The burden of the restrictive covenant was registered as a land charge under the Land Charges Act 1925. Later the titles to the servient land were registered, but no notice of the covenant was entered on the title to No. 11 nor was any other entry made to protect it.

In 1969 the then registered proprietor of No. 11 leased it for 21 years to Shaws Laundries Ltd. In 1974 Shaws assigned their lease to the defendants, who were vintners selling also tobacco and sweets. The defendants investigated not only the leasehold but also the freehold registered title, and found no restrictions which would affect their business. In 1975 Freer sought an injunction against the defendants, but were met with the complete defence that the covenant was not protected on the register and was therefore not binding (L.R.A. 1925, sections 20 (1) and 59 (6)). Freer then obtained rectification of the register of No. 11 from the Land Registrar, and a new edition of the register was opened on 28 April 1975. The question was whether this entry on the register was effective to make the covenant binding on the defendants, even though they had taken an assignment of the lease in 1974. WALTON J held that it was not. He said at p. 297:

"It seems to me that the scheme of the Act requires one to look in every case at the date of the notice of the restrictive covenant on the register. Section 50 (2) provides:

'When such a notice is entered' — and that, I think, must mean when the notice is entered and not from any earlier date — 'the proprietor of the land and the persons deriving title under him . . .' — and then there is the exception which I will come back to in a moment — 'shall be deemed to be affected with notice of the covenant or agreement as being an incumbrance on the land.'

But there is excepted in clear language:

'. . . (except incumbrancers or other persons who at the time when the notice is entered may not be bound by the covenant or agreement) . . .'

What [counsel for the plaintiff] has submitted to me is that those words are inconsistent with the general scheme of the Land Registration Act 1925 and should therefore be given a very narrow ambit. I am not myself persuaded in any way that those words are inconsistent with the general scheme of the Act. It appears to me that the general scheme of the Act is that one obtains priority according to the date of registration, and one is subject, or not subject, to matters appearing on the register according to whether they were there before or after one took one's interest, whatever that interest might be. That seems to me to be the only sensible way in which the provisions of the Act can all be

---

[14] (1976) 40 Conv (NS) 304 (F. R. Crane), (1977) 41 Conv (NS) 1, (1976) 35 CLJ 211 (D. Hayton), (1976) 92 LQR 338 (R. J. Smith), (1976) 126 NLJ 523 (S. M. Cretney).

made to mesh together. For example, supposing that now, for the first time, the defendants' landlords, the registered proprietors, were to impose a restrictive covenant on the land, which they are fully entitled to do, that restrictive covenant would then have to be protected by notice on the register, and it would have the effect stated in section 50 (2):

> 'When such a notice is entered the proprietor of the land and the persons deriving title under him (except incumbrancers or other persons who at the time when the notice is entered may not be bound by the covenant or agreement) . . .'

and that exception surely must include a lessee who was not a party to the covenant or agreement and who has taken his lease prior to the date when the notice was entered.

So it seems to me that so far from it being an exception to the scheme of the Act, those words are fully consistent with it and especially in view of the extremely simple example that I have given, which all must concede, I think, could not possibly result in the lessee being bound by the subsequent restrictive covenant. . . . . . .

So, in my view at the end of the day, the matter comes down to the fact that, for better or for worse, the date which is given in the charges register for the entry of this notice of the restrictive covenant is April 28, 1975. . . .

The entry of the notice being subsequent to the date of the lease of December 8, 1969, in my judgment Shaws Laundries Ltd. took free from that notice, therefore free from the restrictive covenant to which it related, and their assignees, the defendants, are in an exactly similar position. Therefore, it appears to me that the plaintiff, for whom I have the greatest possible sympathy, in fact is not entitled to enforce this covenant quoad the defendants. I realise that this is a very curious result, in that it appears that the plaintiff would have no claim to any indemnity against anybody because of the fact that he cannot enforce this restrictive covenant against the defendants, but it seems to me that if that is the position, that is a defect in the Act, and that the Act is clear in its general outlines and specific provisions, under which it is only matters that are actually registered at the time that the disposition is made which affect the person who derives title under the registered proprietor. Of course, I should like to make it clear that in other cases that may not be the end of the story. In the present case one is dealing with a lease which is not registrable, and therefore has not been registered, and therefore there is no proprietorship register in relation to it because it is not separately registered as leasehold land with a title of its own. But if there were to be a lease of that nature, then it might very well be that rectification would be available against that title, as well as the title of the freehold; but, of course, equally in that case the provisions of section 82 (3) (c) would apply, and I cannot, as at present advised, think that a lessee who has taken every precaution to see that he is entitled to use the land for the purpose for which he wishes to use it, so far as he can see, would have the title rectified against him, because so far from it being unjust not to rectify the register against him — at any rate, in the usual case which is likely to happen — it seems to me that it would be most unjust to rectify the register against him. Vigilantibus non dormientibus servit aequitas; 'Equity aids the vigilant and not the indolent,' and here the defendants have been very vigilant — although I am not ascribing to the plaintiff any sleeping on his rights. But the defendants having been vigilant, even if they had had a separate registered title, I do not think there would have been any prospect of rectification as against them."

VI.　Powers of Registrar[15]

The Chief Land Registrar has wide administrative and judicial powers under the Act. They are contained in a number of sections scattered throughout the Act[16]. Those of a general nature are set out below.

LAND REGISTRATION ACT 1925

127.　Conduct of business by registrar. — Subject to the provisions of this Act, the Chief Land Registrar shall conduct the whole business of registration under this Act, and shall frame and cause to be printed and circulated or otherwise promulgated such forms and directions as he may deem requisite or expedient for facilitating proceedings under this Act.

140.　Power of registrar to state case for the court[17]. — (1) Whenever, upon the examination of the title to any interest in land, the registrar entertains a doubt as to any matter of law or fact arising upon such title, he may (whether or not the matter has been referred to a conveyancing counsel in the prescribed manner), upon the application of any party interested in such land —

(a) refer a case for the opinion of the High Court and the court may direct an issue to be tried before a jury for the purpose of determining any fact;

(b) name the parties to such case;

(c) give directions as to the manner in which proceedings in relation thereto are to be brought before the court.

(2) The opinion of any court to whom any case is referred by the registrar shall be conclusive on all the parties to the case, unless the court permits an appeal.

LAND REGISTRATION RULES 1925

298.　Hearing before the Registrar. — (1) If any question, doubt, dispute, difficulty or complaint arises before the Registrar upon any application or during any investigation of title —

---

[15] Curtis and Ruoff, chap. 41.
[16] E.g. L.R.A 1925, ss. 13, 17, 82, 128.
[17] For the registrar's power to summon witnesses and compel production of documents, see L.R.A 1925, s. 128.

(*a*) as to the registration of a title, incumbrance, or charge,

(*b*) as to any dealing with any registered title, incumbrance, or charge, or any matter entered or noted in or omitted from the register, or

(*c*) as to the amendment or withdrawal from the register or production to the Registrar of any certificate or other document, or

(*d*) in any registration or other proceedings in the Registry, or

(*e*) as to any claim for indemnity[18],

(whether such questions relate to the construction, validity, or effect of any instrument, or the persons interested, or the nature or extent of their respective interests or powers, or as to order of priority, or the mode in which any entry should be made or dealt with in the register or otherwise), the Registrar shall hear and determine the matter and, subject to appeal to the Court, make such order in the matter as he shall think just.

(2) But the Registrar may, if he thinks fit, instead of deciding the question himself, refer the matter at any stage, or any question thereon, for the decision of the Court[19].

299. Appeal to the Court. — Any person aggrieved by an order or decision of the Registrar may appeal to the Court.

322. Power to relax regulations, etc. — (1) The Registrar, if he so thinks fit, may, in any particular case, extend the time limited, or relax the regulations made by general rules, for any purpose; and may at any time adjourn any proceeding, and make any new appointment[20].

(2) If at any time he is of opinion that the production of any further documents, or evidence, or the giving of any further notices is necessary or desirable, he may refuse to complete or proceed with a registration, or to do any act, or make any entry until such further documents, or evidence, or notices have been supplied or given.

QUESTIONS

1. Compare the position of a purchaser under the registered and the unregistered systems. Should there be any differences? If not, how should be existing differences be resolved? Cheshire, *Modern Real Property*, 12th edn. (1976), pp. 110–112, 776–777; (1977) 41 Conv (NS) 405 (J.G. Riddall), [1978] Conv 248 (P.R. Gelling): (1976) CLP 26 (D.J. Hayton).

---

[18] See now L.R. & L.C.A. 1971, s. 2 (4).
[19] L.R.R. 1925, r. 220 (4). See *Re White Rose Cottage* [1965] Ch 940, [1965] 1 All ER 11; p. 133, ante; *Barclays Bank Ltd v Taylor*, [1974] Ch 137, [1973] 1 All ER 752, (1956), 20 Conv (NS) 194 (G. H. Curtis).
[20] *Morelle Ltd v Wakeling* [1955] 2 QB 379, [1955] 1 All ER 708; *Smith v Morrison*, [1974] 1 WLR 659, [1974] 1 All ER 957.

2. How far is a purchaser bound, and how far should he be bound, by an unregistered registrable interest of which he actually knows?

   (a) Unregistered Land. L.P.A. 1925, section 199; L.C.A. 1972, section 4; *Hollington Brothers Ltd v Rhodes* [1951] 2 TLR 691; p. 41 ante; *Industrial Properties (Barton Hill Ltd) v Associated Electrical Industries Ltd* [1977] 1 QB 580 at 608–609, per ROSKILL LJ *Midland Bank Trust Co Ltd v Green* [1979] 3 WLR 167; [1979] 3 All ER 28; p. 45 ante.

   (b) Registered Land. *Hodges v Jones* [1935] Ch 657 at 671, per LUXMOORE J; *De Lusignan v Johnson* (1973) 117 Sol Jo 854; p. 126 ante; *Peffer v Rigg* [1977] 1 WLR 285; p. 103 ante, and articles in n. 9 p. 125 ante.

3. Compare the meaning in registered land of transferee (L.R.A. 1925, section 20 (1)) and purchaser (section 59 (6)) with that of purchaser in unregistered land (L.C.A. 1925, section 4, 17 (1). *Peffer v Rigg* [1977] 1 WLR 285; p. 103 ante; *Midland Bank Trust Col Ltd v Green,* supra.

3. Limitation of Actions

I. Introduction[1]

The Limitation Acts 1939–1980 amend and consolidate the law of limitation of civil actions[2]. The general principle is that no action may be brought for the recovery of land after the expiration of a prescribed period from the time when the right of action first accrues. This period is now in general twelve years[3], and sections 5–9 of the 1939 Act deal specifically with the accrual of the right of action in the case of present interests, future interests, settled land and land held under trust for sale, forfeiture or breach of condition, and tenancies. For an action to accrue, and consequently for time to start running, there must be an "adverse possessor" against whom an action can be brought[4].

The policy of limitation was stated by Streatfeild J, in *R. B. Policies at Lloyd's v Butler*[5]: "It is a policy of the Limitation Acts that those who go to sleep upon their claims should not be assisted by the courts recovering their property, but another, and, I think, equal policy behind these Acts, is that there shall be an end of litigation ..." What is the effect of such a policy? What is the effect of the expiration

---

[1] Cheshire, pp. 883–909; M & W, pp. 1003–1033; MM, pp. 488–499; Preston and Newsom, *Limitation of Actions* (3rd edn., 1953); Franks, *Limitation of Actions* (1959). For the history of the old law: Holdsworth, Vol. iv, pp. 484–486, Vol. vii, p. 29, et seq.; Simpson, *Introduction to History of Land Law* (1961), pp. 141–145; Hayes, *Introduction to Conveyancing* (5th edn.), p. 222 et seq.

[2] The 1939 Act came into force on 1 July 1940, and has been amended by Law Reform (Limitation of Actions & c.) Act 1954 and Limitation Act 1975 (which do not alter the land law), and Limitation Amendment Act 1980. Main previous statutes were: Limitation Act 1623; Civil Procedure Act 1833; Real Property Limitation Acts 1833, 1874; Public Authorities Protection Act 1893. See Law Reform Committee 21st Report (Final Report on Limitations of Actions) 1977 Cmnd 6923, for a valuable discussion of all aspects of limitation. It forms the basis of the Limitation Amendment Act 1980. See also (1977) 244 Estates Gazette 291, 375, 881, 955 (D. Brahams).

[3] Limitation Act 1939, s. 4 (3); the general period of 20 years, fixed by the Real Property Limitation Act 1833, was reduced to 12 years by the Real Property Limitation Act 1874.

[4] Limitation Act 1939, s. 10, *Leigh v Jack* (1879) 5 Ex D 264, p. 156, post; *Treloar v Nute* [1976] 1 WLR 1295, [1977] 1 All ER 230, p. 157, post.

[5] [1950] 1 KB at p. 81, [1949] 2 All ER, at p. 229; *A'Court v Cross* (1825) 3 Bing at p. 332, per BEST CJ "It is ... an Act of peace. Long dormant claims have often more of cruelty than of justice in them."

of the limitation period on D (the person who has been dispossessed or has discontinued his possession) and on A (the adverse possessor)[6]?

a.   On D

The effect of the Limitation Act is purely negative. Not only is D's right of action to recover the land from A extinguished, but also his title to the land[7]. D cannot revive his title by a later acknowledgment or payment made to him[8], or by a judgment obtained by default[9]. He cannot restore his position by re-entry on the land (in this case, he can only regain it by lapse of time as an adverse possessor), and if he brings an action for recovery of the land, A need not plead the Limitation Act[10].

b.   On A

Here the Act is silent. It is now clear that D's title is not transferred to A: there is no "Parliamentary Conveyance"[11]. But by a combination of the negative effect of the Act on D's title, and the positive effect of his adverse possession, A has a new estate of his own, a fee simple subject to the unextinguished rights of other persons[12]. If D is a fee simple owner, then, as Megarry and Wade say[13], "A's possession at once gives all the rights and powers of ownership[14]. A has, in fact, a legal estate, a fee simple absolute in possession. But so also has D, until such time as his title is extinguished by limitation. . . . There is thus no absurdity in speaking of two or more[15] adverse estates in the land, for their validity is relative. If D allows his title to become barred by lapse of time, A's title becomes the better, and A then becomes 'absolute owner'. But if D brings his action within the time allowed, he can successfully assert his better title based on his prior possession; as against D, A's legal estate is nothing."

If D is a lessee of L, and A has been in adverse possession for twelve years, A's possession extinguishes D's title. This has no effect on L's

---

[6] Cheshire, pp. 900–904; M & W, pp. 1004–1010, 1027–1032; MM, pp. 488, 496–498; Pollock and Wright, *Possession* (1888), pp. 93–100; Preston and Newsom, pp. 77–84; Franks, pp. 131–133, 141–143; (1925) 41 LQR 139 (S. A. Wiren); (1940) 56 LQR 376 (A. D. Hargreaves), 479 (W. S. Holdsworth); (1962) 78 LQR 541 (H. W. R. Wade); (1964) 80 LQR 63 (B. Rudden); (1973) 32 Conv (NS) 85 (J. A. Omotola); Section VI, post.

[7] Limitation Act 1939, s. 16.

[8] *Sanders v Sanders* [1881] 19 ChD 373; p. 172, post; *Nicholson v England* [1926] 2 KB 93.

[9] *Irish Land Commission v Ryan* [1900] 2 IR 565.

[10] *Dawkins v Lord Penrhyn* (1878) 4 App Cas 51; *Dismore v Milton* [1938] 3 All ER 762; Franks, pp. 131, 265.

[11] *Tichborne v Weir* (1892) 67 LT 735, p. 178, post.

[12] Co Litt 271a (also 2a, 297a) "For a disseisor, abator, intruder, usurper, etc., have a fee simple, but it is not a lawful fee". *Leach v Jay* (1878) 9 ChD at pp. 44, 45; *Rankin v M'Murtry* (1889) 24 LR Ir 290, (1962) 78 LQR at pp. 543–5.

[13] At p. 1007. The symbols have been changed.

[14] If A dies, the land passes under his will or intestacy. *Asher v Whitlock* (1865) LR 1 QB 1, p. 173, post; *Allen v Roughley* (1955) 94 CLR 98, [1956] CLJ 177. (H. W. R. Wade).

[15] In the case of successive adverse possessors, the last in possession may be evicted by an earlier adverse possessor, until that possessor's title has itself been extinguished by lapse of time.

title, because L's right of action does not accrue until the end of the lease[16]. "A has a legal estate (probably a fee simple . . .) subject to L's right of entry at the end of the original term[17]." But A may be evicted before then (*a*) by L, if he has taken a surrender of the lease from D[18], or if he has forfeited the lease[19], (*b*) by D, if he has taken a conveyance of the fee simple from L[20]. If, however, A acknowledges L as the freeholder, he may become a tenant for a term of years, or a yearly tenant or a tenant at will[1].

Whatever interest A gets, it is subject to the legal and equitable rights of third parties which run with the land and have not themselves been independently extinguished e.g. easements and restrictive covenants[2]. If the land is leasehold and A has extinguished the title of the lessee but not that of the lessor, he is not an assignee of the lease, and so is not bound by any covenants in the lease, unless they are enforceable as restrictive covenants. If A pays rent to the lessor and becomes a yearly tenant, he is not, by the mere payment of rent, estopped from denying that he is bound by the terms of the original lease[3].

The Limitation Act 1939, then, operates negatively; not positively as does the Prescription Act 1832. It does not create a title in A, it merely prevents D from enforcing his. The effect of this as between vendor and purchaser is that a title based on adverse possession alone for the limitation period or longer is not necessarily a good title. The claims of a reversioner or a remainderman may have yet to be extinguished[4]: the reversion may be on a 99 year lease, the remainderman's interest may not vest in possession for over 100 years[5]. But if a vendor can establish that the flaw in an otherwise good title is one that can be cured by the running of time in his favour under the Act, he can force a purchaser to take the title[6]. Proof that rival claims have been extinguished by the lapse of time may be very difficult, and in practice a purchaser often agrees to accept an imperfect title.

---

[16] Limitation Act 1939, s. 6, p. 160, post.

[17] M & W, p. 1030.

[18] *Fairweather v St. Marylebone Property Co Ltd* [1963] AC 510, [1962] 2 All ER 288; see p. 174, post.

[19] *Tickner v Buzzacott* [1965] Ch 426, [1964] 1 All ER 131 (adverse possessor not entitled to apply to court for relief against forfeiture of lease for non-payment of rent).

[20] *Taylor v Twinberrow* [1930] 2 KB 16.

[1] For an analysis of the situation where A is a tenant for life, see M & W, pp. 1028–1029.

[2] *Re Nisbet and Potts' Contract* [1906] 1 Ch 386, p. 179, post; *Scott v Scott* (1854), 4 HL Cas. 1065.

[3] *Tichborne v Weir* (1892) 67 LT 735; p. 178, post and p. 179, n. 13, post.

[4] Limitation Act 1939, s. 6. Time runs against the landlord even if the lease is immediately renewed; p. 167, post.

[5] *Cadell v Palmer* (1833) 1 Cl & Fin 372: vesting postponed for over 100 years (note to *Re Villar* [1928] Ch 471, 478).

[6] *Re Atkinson's and Horsell's Contract* [1912] 2 Ch 1; *Re Spencer and Hauser's Contract* [1928] Ch 598; distinguished in *George Wimpey & Co Ltd v Sohn* [1967] Ch 487, [1966] 1 All ER 232; Farrand, pp. 104–106.

LIMITATION ACT 1939

10. Right of action not to accrue or continue unless there is adverse possession. — (1) No right of action to recover land shall be deemed to accrue unless the land is in the possession of some person in whose favour the period of limitation can run (hereafter in this section referred to as "adverse possession") and where under the foregoing provisions of this Act any such right of action is deemed to accrue on a certain date and no person is in adverse possession on that date, the right of action shall not be deemed to accrue unless and until adverse possession is taken of the land.

(2) Where a right of action to recover land has accrued and thereafter, before the right is barred, the land ceases to be in adverse possession, the right of action shall no longer be deemed to have accrued and no fresh right of action shall be deemed to accrue unless and until the land is again taken into adverse possession[7].

(3) For the purposes of this section —

(a) possession of any land subject to a rentcharge by a person (other than the person entitled to the rentcharge) who does not pay the rent shall be deemed to be adverse possession of the rentcharge; and

(b) receipt of rent under a lease by a person wrongfully claiming, in accordance with subsection (3) of the last foregoing section[8], the land in reversion shall be deemed to be adverse possession of the land[9].

(4)[10] For the purpose of determining whether a person occupying any land is in adverse possession of the land it shall not be assumed by implication of law that his occupation is by permission of the person entitled to the land merely by virtue of the fact that his occupation is not inconsistent with the latter's present or future enjoyment of the land.

This provision shall not be taken as prejudicing a finding to the effect that a person's occupation of any land is by implied permission of the person entitled to the land in any case where such a finding is justified on the actual facts of the case.

---

[7] Enacting the rule in *Trustees Executors and Agency Co Ltd v Short* (1888) 13 App Cas 793.

[8] See p. 163, post.

[9] *Bligh v Martin*, [1968] 1 WLR 804, [1968] 1 All ER 1157.

[10] As added by Limitation Amendment Act 1980, s. 4. This reverses the doctrine of implied licence suggested by Lord DENNING MR in "*Wallis's Cayton Bay Holiday Camp Ltd v Shell Mex and BP Ltd* [1975] 1 QB 94, [1974] 3 All ER 575; *Gray v Wykeham-Martin and Goode* [1977] Bar Library Transcript No. 10A (CA, affirming the decision of Goulding J, who had followed *Wallis* by implying a licence without any factual basis); *Powell v McFarlane* (1979) 38 P & CR 452—Slade J held he was bound by these cases if necessary to find an implied or hypothetical licence, but actually found that possession had not been taken. The contrary approach, along traditional lines, was demonstrated in *Treloar v Nute* [1976] 1 WLR 1295 [1977], 1 All ER 230." Law Reform Committee 21st Report (1977) paras. 3.47–3.52, n. 24. For a full discussion of these cases see (1977) 244 Estates Gazette 291, 375 (D. Brahams).

31. Interpretation. — (1) ...

"Land" includes corporeal hereditaments, tithes and rentcharges, and any legal or equitable estate or interest therein, including an interest in the proceeds of the sale of land held upon trust for sale, but save as aforesaid does not include any incorporeal hereditament[10a];

(4) A person shall be deemed to claim through another person, if he became entitled by, through, under, or by the act of that other person to the right claimed, and any person whose estate or interest might have been barred by a person entitled to an entailed interest in possession shall be deemed to claim through the person so entitled:

Provided that a person becoming entitled to any estate or interest by virtue of a special power of appointment shall not be deemed to claim through the appointor.

II. Accrual of Right of Action[11]

A. Present Interests

LIMITATION ACT 1939

5. Accrual of right of action in case of present interests in land. — (1) Where the person bringing an action to recover land, or some person through whom he claims, has been in possession thereof, and has while entitled thereto been dispossessed or discontinued his possession, the right of action shall be deemed to have accrued on the date of the dispossession or discontinuance.

(2) Where any person brings an action to recover any land of a deceased person, whether under a will or on intestacy, and the deceased person was on the date of his death in possession of the land or, in the case of a rentcharge created by will or taking effect upon his death, in possession of the land charged, and was the last person entitled to the land to be in possession thereof, the right of action shall be deemed to have accrued on the date of his death.

(3) Where any person brings an action to recover land, being an estate or interest in possession assured otherwise than by will to him, or to some person through whom he claims, by a person who, at the date when the assurance took effect, was in possession of the land or, in the case of a rentcharge created by the assurance, in possession of the land charged, and no person has been in possession of the land by virtue of the assurance, the right of action shall be deemed to have accrued on the date when the assurance took effect.

[10a] As amended by Limitation Amendment Act 1980 s. 13 (1) Sch. 1 para. 12(a).
[11] Cheshire, pp. 886–900; M & W, pp. 1012–1023; MM, pp. 489–493. For the accrual of the right of action where there are defects in the construction of a building, see *Sparham-Souter v Town and Country Developments (Essex) Ltd* [1976] QB 858, [1976] 2 All ER 65; *Anns v Merton London Borough Council* [1978] AC 728, [1977] 2 All ER 492, (1978) 94 LQR 60 (I.N. Duncan Wallace); *Lewisham London Borough v Leslie & Co Ltd* (1979) 250 Estates Gazette 1289; Law Reform Committee 21st Report (1977), paras. 2.1–2.38. See also Defective Premises Act 1972, s. 1 (5).

LEIGH v JACK
(1879) 5 Ex D 264 (CA, COCKBURN CJ, BRAMWELL and COTTON LJJ)

In 1854 J. S. Leigh conveyed to the defendant a plot of land on the South side of an intended street, on which the defendant built an iron foundry. In 1857 Leigh conveyed to the Mersey Dock Trustees the plot of land on the North side of the intended street, which in 1872 was conveyed by them to the defendant. The intended street was never dedicated to the public as a highway. From 1854 the defendant placed on it materials used at the foundry so as to close it to all except pedestrians: in 1865 he enclosed an oblong portion of it, and in 1872 fenced in the ends. In 1876 the plaintiff, who was tenant for life of all Leigh's lands, brought an action to recover the site of the intended street.

Held. The plaintiff's title was not barred by the Real Property Limitation Act 1883: there had been no dispossession or discontinuance of possession.

BRAMWELL LJ: The second point relates to the true construction of the Statute of Limitations, section 3[12]. Two things appear to be contemplated by that enactment, dispossession and discontinuance of possession. It is difficult to suppose a case where it can be doubtful whether there has been a discontinuance of possession as to a house; if any chair or table, or other small article of furniture be left, there is strong evidence of an intention that there shall be no discontinuance of possession; but it is possible to conceive a case of discontinuance of possession as to a piece of land where the former owner does nothing to it for the space of twenty years. In the present case, if the plaintiff and her predecessors had done nothing for twenty years to Grundy Street and Napier Place, it might have been possible to argue that there had been a discontinuance of possession. But, after all, it is a question of fact, and the smallest act would be sufficient to shew that there was no discontinuance. . . . The circumstance that J. S. Leigh within twenty years before suit repaired the fence separating Grundy Street from Regent Road is strong to shew that there was no discontinuance. I do not think that there was any dispossession of the plaintiff by the acts of the defendant; . . . in order to defeat a title by dispossessing the former owner, acts must be done which are inconsistent with his enjoyment of the soil for the purposes for which he intended to use it: that is not the case here, where the intention of the plaintiff and her predecessors in title was not either to build upon or to cultivate the land, but to devote it at some future time to public purposes. The plaintiff has not been dispossessed, nor has she discontinued possession, her title has not been taken away, and she is entitled to our judgment.

------

[12] Now Limitation Act 1939, s. 5 (1), p. 155, ante.

TRELOAR *v* NUTE [1976] 1 WLR 1295, [1977] 1 All ER 230[13]
(CA, STAMP, ORMROD LJJ and Sir John PENNYCUICK)

In 1961 the plaintiff owned a derelict plot of land at Halwin, Cornwall, comprising about one-seventh of an acre. In the same year the defendant's father bought adjacent land, believing that the derelict plot formed part of the purchase. The plot was included in the conveyance of September 1962. Between 1961 and September 1962 (when the limitation period began), the defendant's father had used the plot for grazing a couple of cows and a yearling, storing timber and stone, and filling in a gully, and his children rode motor cycles on it. In 1963 he erected a fence, and when the plaintiff removed it, re-erected it. In 1965 the defendant conveyed it to his son as a gift, and in 1974 the son started to build a bungalow on it. The plaintiff had made no use of the land since the father took possession in 1961, and there was no evidence of her having any special purpose in mind for the future use of the plot. She sought an injunction, damages for trespass and a declaration of her title. The defendant pleaded the Limitation Act.

Held, (reversing the County Court judge) The plaintiff's title was barred by Limitation Act 1939, section 10.

SIR JOHN PENNYCUICK: The particular acts found by the judge are we think rather on the borderline of what can properly be regarded as constituting possession, always apart from the consideration of adverse possession. Whether or not a person has taken possession of land is a question of fact depending on all the particular circumstances. The test is well put by Lord O'Hagan in *Lord Advocate v Lord Lovat* (1880) 5 App Cas 273 (a case not otherwise in point) in the following words, at p. 288:

"As to possession, it must be considered in every case with reference to the peculiar circumstances. The acts, implying possession in one case, may be wholly inadequate to prove it in another. The character and value of the property, the suitable and natural mode of using it, the course of conduct which the proprietor might reasonably be expected to follow with a due regard to his own interests—all these things, greatly varying as they must, under various conditions, are to be taken into account in determining the sufficiency of a possession."

In the present case the disputed land is extremely small, about one-seventh of an acre and admitted of very limited agricultural use, but would be a convenient site for a small house or bungalow. The

---

[13] *Littledale v Liverpool College* [1900] 1 Ch 19; *Moses v Lovegrove* [1952] 2 QB 533, [1952] 1 All ER 1279; *Jessamine Investment Co v Schwartz* [1978] QB 264; *Williams Brothers Direct Supply Co Ltd v Raftery* [1958] 1 QB 159; *George Wimpey and Co Ltd v Sohn* [1967] Ch 487, [1966] 1 All ER 232; *Bligh v Martin* [1968] 1 WLR 804, [1968] 1 All ER 1157; *Tecbild Ltd v Chamberlain* (1969) 20 P & C R 633; *Wallis's Cayton Bay Holiday Camp Ltd v Shell-Mex and B P Ltd* [1975] QB 94, [1974] 3 All ER 575, (1975) 39 Conv (NS) 57 (F. R. Crane); *Basildon District Council v Manning* (1975) 237 Estates Gazette 878 (erecting fence and dumping poultry manure held to be acts too trivial for adverse possession); *Red House Farms (Thorndon) Ltd v Catchpole;* (1977) 244 Estates Gazette 295 (where the plaintiff had allowed land to become derelict by letting a bridge fall into disrepair); *Powell v Mcfarlane* (1979) 38 P & CR 452.

defendant's father did put it to some small agricultural use by grazing two cows and a yearling. Much more important, in our view, is the change in the surface of the land by placing soil in the gully, thereby setting in train the levelling of the land upon which a bungalow could be built. It seems to us that these acts were sufficient to support a finding of possession and indeed on the material before us we would be disposed to reach the same conclusion. The other acts relied upon are of very little weight.

We turn then to the law. We will quote from three sections of the Limitation Act 1939:

[His Lordship quoted from sections 4 (3), 5 (1) and 10 (1) and continued:]

It is not in doubt that under the Act of 1939 as under the previous law, the person claiming by possession must show either (1) discontinuance by the paper owner followed by possession or (2) dispossession (or as it is sometimes called "ouster") of the paper owner. Clearly, possession concurrent with the paper owner is insufficient. On the other hand, where the person claiming by possession establishes possession in the full sense of exclusive possession, that by itself connotes absence of possession on the part of the paper owner and I doubt if there is any real difference in the concept of taking possession and the concept of dispossession except in the special type of case where the owner, although not technically in possession, has some purpose to which he intends to put the land in the future. We will refer to this special type of case in a moment.

The law, as we understand it, always apart from that special type of case, is that if a squatter takes possession of land belonging to another and remains in possession for 12 years to the exclusion of the owner that represents adverse possession and accordingly at the end of the 12 years the owner's title is extinguished. That is the plain meaning of the statutory provisions which I have quoted and no authority to the contrary has been quoted to us. The simple question is, "Did the squatter acquire and remain in exclusive possession?"

The literal application of the statutory provisions has been adapted by this court to meet one special type of case. It sometimes happens that the owner of a piece of land retains it with a view to its utilisation for some specific purpose in the future and that meanwhile some other person has physical possession of it. When that state of affairs exists, the owner is not treated as dispossessed: see *Leigh v Jack* (1879) 5 ExD 264, where factory materials were placed upon a strip of land intended by the owner to be dedicated as a road; in particular *per* Cockburn CJ, at p. 271 and *per* Bramwell LJ, where the latter said, at p. 273:

"... in order to defeat a title by dispossessing the former owner, acts must be done which are inconsistent with his enjoyment of the soil for the purposes for which he intended to use it: that is not the case here, where the intention of the plaintiff and her predecessors in title was not either to build upon or to cultivate the land, but to devote it at some future time to public purpose."

See also *Williams Brothers Direct Supply Ltd v Raftery* [1958] 1
QB 159, [1957] 3 All ER 593 where a strip of land intended by the
owner for development was used during and after the war for growing
vegetables and keeping greyhounds.

The principle was restated and applied by the majority of the Court
of Appeal in the recent case, *Wallis's Cayton Bay Holiday Camp Ltd v
Shell-Mex and BP Ltd* [1975] QB 94. In that case a strip of land was
intended by the owner to be the site of a garage which would front
upon a projected road, which in fact never materialised, and meanwhile
was occupied successively as part of a farm and part of a holiday camp.
The Court of Appeal held that the owner had not been dispossessed.
Lord Denning MR stated the principle in the following terms, at
p. 103:

> "There is a fundamental error in that argument. Possession by
> itself is not enough to give a title. It must be *adverse* possession.
> The true owner must have discontinued possession or have
> been dispossessed and another must have taken it adversely to
> him. There must be something in the nature of an ouster of the
> true owner by the wrongful possessor. That is shown by a series of
> cases in this court which, on their very facts, show this proposition
> to be true. When the true owner of land intends to use it for a
> particular purpose in the future, but meanwhile has no immediate
> use for it, and so leaves it unoccupied, he does not lose his title
> to it simply because some other person enters on it and uses it for
> some temporary purpose, like stacking materials; or for some
> seasonal purpose, like growing vegetables. Not even if this
> temporary or seasonal purpose continues year after year for 12
> years, or more: see *Leigh v Jack* (1879) 5 ExD 264; *Williams
> Brothers Direct Supply Ltd v Raftery* [1958] 1 QB 159; and
> *Tecbild Ltd v Chamberlain* [1969] 20 P & CR 633. The reason is
> not because the user does not amount to actual possession. The
> line between acts of user and acts of possession is too fine for
> words."

The subsequent passage has clearly no application to the facts of the
present case. Stamp L.J. dissented, holding that upon the facts the
case could not be brought within the principle of *Leigh v Jack*. Ormrod
LJ in company with Lord Denning MR held that applying the
principle of *Leigh v Jack* there was upon the facts no dispossession of
the owner. He makes a rather broad statement at p. 114. But the
theme of purpose, i.e. the purpose to which the owner intends to put
the land in the future, runs throughout his judgment and we do not
read him as saying that in the absence of such purpose there can be no
dispossession merely by reason that the owner has no present use for
the land. We have referred at length to this case because it was much
relied upon by counsel for the plaintiff and although the judge does not
specifically mention it we think it is clear that he had it in mind in the
critical passage where he refers to the defendant's possession as not
being adverse.

It is worth observing that all these cases were concerned with a
narrow strip of land of such a character that the acquisition of a

possessory title to it would not fall within the ordinary purview of the statute and the court was clearly anxious not to put too literal a construction upon the words of the statute. The same observation applies to *Littledale v Liverpool College* [1900] 1 Ch 19, a case distinguishable on other grounds.

A full statement of the law as it stood before *Wallis's Cayton Bay Holiday Camp Ltd v Shell-Mex and BP Ltd* will be found in *Preston and Newsom's Limitation of Actions* 3rd edn. (1953), pp. 88 et seq., and in *Halsbury's Laws of England* 3rd edn. vol. 24 (1958), pp. 251 et seq.

We return then to the present case. The judge found, as we read his judgment, that the defendant's father took possession of the disputed land outside the limitation period but that this possession was not adverse by reason that it caused no inconvenience to the plaintiff. In our judgment the second part of this finding is contrary to the plain terms of section 10 of the Act of 1939 which in effect defines adverse possession as possession of some person in whose favour the period of limitation can run. It is not permissible to import into this definition a requirement that the owner must be inconvenienced or otherwise affected by that possession. Apart from the case relating to special purpose no authority has been cited to us which would support the requirement of inconvenience to the owner and we are not ourselves aware of any such authority. On the contrary, so far as our own experience goes, the typical instance in which a possessory title is treated as having been acquired is that in which a squatter establishes himself upon a piece of land for which the owner has no use. Indeed, if inconvenience to the owner had to be established it would be difficult indeed ever to acquire a possessory title since the owner if inconvenienced would be likely to take proceedings.

We conclude that, once it is accepted that the judge found, and could properly find, that the defendant's father took possession of the disputed land before the commencement of the limitation period, and in the absence of any evidence of special purpose on the part of the plaintiff, time began to run from such taking of possession, irrespective of whether the plaintiff suffered inconvenience from the possession, and that the defendant must be treated as having acquired a possessory title before the commencement of this action. . . .

We would allow the appeal.

B. Future Interests

LIMITATION ACT 1939

6. Accrual of right of action in case of future interests. — (1) Subject as hereafter in the section provided, the right of action to recover any land shall, in a case where the estate or interest claimed was an estate or interest in reversion or remainder or any other future estate or interest and no person has taken possession of the land by virtue of the estate or interest claimed, be deemed to have accrued on the date on which the estate or interest fell into possession by the determination of the preceding estate or interest.

(2) If the person entitled to the preceding estate or interest, not being a term of years absolute, was not in possession of the land on the date of the determination thereof, no action shall be brought by the person entitled to the succeeding estate or interest after the expiration of twelve years from the date on which the right of action accrued to the person entitled to the preceding estate or interest, or six years from the date on which the right of action accrued to the person entitled to the succeeding estate or interest, whichever period last expires:

Provided that, where the Crown or a spiritual or eleemosynary corporation sole is entitled to the succeeding estate or interest, the foregoing provisions of this subsection shall have effect with the substitution for the reference to twelve years of a reference to thirty years, and for the reference to six years of a reference to twelve years.

(3) The foregoing provisions of this section shall not apply to any estate or interest which falls into possession on the determination of an entailed interest and which might have been barred by the person entitled to the entailed interest[14].

C. Settlements and Trusts for Sale

LIMITATION ACT 1939

7. Provisions in case of settled land and land held on trust[15]. — (1) Subject to the provisions of subsections (1) and (1A) of section nineteen of this Act, the provisions of this Act shall apply to equitable interests in land, including interests in the proceeds of the sale of land held upon trust for sale, in like manner as they apply to legal estates, and accordingly a right of action to recover the land shall, for the purposes of this Act but not otherwise, be deemed to accrue to a person entitled in possession to such an equitable interest in the like manner and circumstances and on the same date as it would accrue if his interest were a legal estate in the land[16].

(2) Where the period prescribed by this Act has expired for the bringing of an action to recover land by a tenant for life or a statutory owner of settled land, his legal estate shall not be extinguished, if and so long as the right of action to recover the land of any person entitled to a beneficial interest in the land either has not accrued or has not been barred by this Act, and the legal estate shall accordingly remain vested in the tenant for life or statutory owner and shall devolve in accordance with the Settled Land Act 1925; but if and when every such right of action as aforesaid has been barred by this Act, the said legal estate shall be extinguished.

---

[14] See too ss. 4 (3), 31 (4). M & W, p. 1016. The combined effect of these three sections is that a "reversioner or remainderman expectant upon an entail in possession is not entitled to the alternative six-year period, if his interest could have been barred by the tenant in tail".

[15] *Gray v Wykeham-Martin and Goode* [1977] Bar Library Transcript No. 10A.

[16] As amended by Limitation Amendment Act 1980 s. 5 (2).

(3) Where any land is held upon trust including a trust for sale, and the period prescribed by this Act has expired for the bringing of an action to recover the land by the trustees, the estate of the trustees shall not be extinguished if and so long as the right of action to recover the land of any person entitled to a beneficial interest in the land or in the proceeds of sale either has not accrued or has not been barred by this Act, but if and when every such right of action has been so barred, the estate of the trustees shall be extinguished.

(4) Where any settled land is vested in a statutory owner or any land is held upon trust, including a trust for sale, an action to recover the land may be brought by the statutory owner or trustees on behalf of any person entitled to a beneficial interest in possession in the land or in the proceeds of sale whose right of action has not been barred by this Act, notwithstanding that the right of action of the statutory owner or trustees would apart from this provision have been barred by this Act.

(5) Where any settled land or any land held on trust for sale is in the possession of a person entitled to a beneficial interest in the land or in the proceeds of sale, not being a person solely and absolutely entitled thereto, no right of action to recover the land shall be deemed for the purposes of this Act to accrue during such possession to any person in whom the land is vested as tenant for life, statutory owner or trustee, or to any other person entitled to a beneficial interest in the land or the proceeds of sale[17].

19.   Limitation of actions in respect of trust property. — (1) No period of limitation prescribed by this Act shall apply to an action by a beneficiary under a trust, being an action—

> (*a*) in respect of any fraud or fraudulent breach of trust to which the trustee was a party or privy; or
>
> (*b*) to recover from the trustee trust property or the proceeds thereof in the possession of the trustee, or previously received by the trustee and converted to his use.

[18](1A) Where a trustee who is also a beneficiary under the trust receives or retains trust property or its proceeds as his share on a distribution of trust property under the trust, his liability in any action brought by virtue of paragraph (*b*) of the foregoing subsection to recover that property or its proceeds after the expiration of the period of limitation prescribed by this Act for bringing an action to recover trust property shall be limited to the excess over his proper share.

This subsection only applies if the trustee acted honestly and reasonably in making the distribution.

(2) Subject as aforesaid, an action by a beneficiary to recover trust property or in respect of any breach of trust, not being an action for which a period of limitation is prescribed by any other provision of this

---

[17] *Bridges v Mees* [1957] Ch 475, [1957] 2 All ER 577; *Re Cussons Ltd* (1904) 73 LJ Ch 296; M & W, p. 1021.

[18] As added by Limitation Amendment Act 1980 s. 5. See Law Reform Committee 21st Report (1977) paras. 3.81–3.84.

Act, shall not be brought after the expiration of six years from the date on which the right of action accrued:

Provided that the right of action shall not be deemed to have accrued to any beneficiary entitled to a future interest in the trust property, until the interest fell into possession.

D. Forfeiture

LIMITATION ACT 1939

8. Accrual of right of action in case of forfeiture or breach of condition. — A right of action to recover land by virtue of a forfeiture or breach of condition shall be deemed to have accrued on the date on which the forfeiture was incurred or the condition broken:

Provided that, if such a right has accrued to a person entitled to an estate or interest in reversion or remainder and the land was not recovered by virtue thereof, the right of action to recover the land shall not be deemed to have accrued to that person until his estate or interest fell into possession, as if no such forfeiture or breach of condition had occurred.

E. Tenancies

i. PERIODIC TENANCIES

LIMITATION ACT 1939

6. Accrual of right of action in case of future interests.
(1) and (2) p. 160, ante.

9. Accrual of right of action in case of certain tenancies[19]. (2) A tenancy from year to year or other period, without a lease in writing, shall, for the purposes of this Act, be deemed to be determined at the expiration of the first year or other period, and accordingly the right of action of the person entitled to the land subject to the tenancy shall be deemed to have accrued at the date of such determination[20]:

Provided that, where any rent has subsequently been received in respect of the tenancy, the right of action shall be deemed to have accrued on the date of the last receipt of rent.

(3) Where any person is in possession of land by virtue of a lease in writing by which a rent of not less than ten pounds a year[21] is reserved, and the rent is received by some person wrongfully claiming to be entitled to the land in reversion immediately expectant on the determination of the lease, and no rent is subsequently received by the person rightfully so entitled, the right of action of the last-named person to recover the land shall be deemed to have accrued at the date

---

[19] Section 9 (1), which provided a special rule for accrual in respect of the reversion on a tenancy at will, was repealed by Limitation Amendment Act 1980 ss. 3 (1), 13 (2), Sch. 2. See Law Reform Committee 21st Report (1977), paras. 3.53–3.58.

[20] *Moses v Lovegrove* [1952] 2 QB 533, [1952] 1 All ER 1279, *Jessamine Investment Co v Schwartz* [1978] QB 264, [1976] 3 All ER 521.

[21] As substituted by Limitation Amendment Act 1980 s. 3 (2) (3) (4).

when the rent was first received by the person wrongfully claiming as aforesaid and not at the date of the determination of the lease.

(4) Subsection (3) of this section shall not apply to any lease granted by the Crown[1].

10.   Right of action not to accrue or continue unless there is adverse possession.

(3) (*b*) p. 154, ante.

In *Hayward v Chaloner,* [1968] 1 QB 107, the Saville Estate leased in 1938 to the rector of the parish of Bilsthorpe part of Redcote Farm for use as a garden on an oral tenancy at a rent of 10s. a year. The rent was paid by successive rectors until 1942, but not subsequently. In 1955 the plaintiffs purchased Redcote Farm including the part let to the rector.

In 1966 the incumbent rector, the defendant, claimed title under the Limitation Act 1939. The plaintiff's application for possession failed before the Court of Appeal (Lord DENNING dissenting). RUSSELL LJ said at p. 122:

"In the present case there was a periodic tenancy, not in writing: the last payment of rent was in May, 1942, by the then rector, Mr. McCormick, so that the right of action must by section 9 (2) for the purposes of the Limitation Act be deemed to have then accrued, and the plaintiffs' action in 1966 to recover possession was clearly forbidden by section 4 (3)[2].

It was argued for the plaintiffs, and the argument found favour with the county court judge, that section 10 (1) operated to prevent the right of action being deemed to accrue at any time because no person was in adverse possession at any time, adverse possession being the label applied by section 10 to 'the possession of some person in whose favour the period of limitation can run.' I do not think it necessary to discuss here the history of the conception of 'adverse possession' beyond a reference to Preston and Newsom's Limitation of Actions, 3rd edn. (1953), p. 86. I have no doubt that for this purpose the possession of a tenant is to be considered adverse once the period covered by the last payment of rent has expired so that section 10 (1) does not bear further upon section 9 (2). Nor do I doubt the applicability of section 9 (2) to the present case just because the freeholders were content that the rector should not pay his rent and did not bother to ask for it for all those years. In *Moses v Lovegrove* ([1952] 2 QB 533), in this court it was assumed on all hands that when section 9 apparently operates, adverse possession starts: see especially Lord Evershed, and Romer LJ, (ibid., 538–540, 543). The principle clearly accepted was that once the period covered by the last payment of rent expired, the tenant ceased to be regarded by the Limitation Acts as the tenant. This case was not cited to the county court judge. A similar assumption was made in *Nicholson v England,* ([1926] 2 KB 93), under the then existing

---

[1] As amended by Limitation Amendment Act 1980 s. 3 (2) (3) (4).
[2] See p. 168, post.

principles which section 10 (1) was designed to embody. Textbooks to the same effect include Cheshire's Modern Law of Real Property, 9th edn. (1962), pp. 797, 798; Megarry and Wade's Textbook of the Law of Real Property, 3rd edn. (1966), p. 1010; and Preston and Newsom on Limitation of Actions, 3rd edn. (1953), p. 89. I am not aware that the contrary view has been anywhere expressed, and in my judgment the cases relied upon by the county court judge of *Leigh v Jack* ((1879) 5 ExD 264), and *Williams Bros Direct Supply Ltd v Raftery* ([1958] 1 QB 159, [1957] 3 All ER 593), have no bearing on a question arising under section 9 (2) of the Act. In my judgment, therefore, a possessory title has been acquired to this property. . . .

The generous indulgence of the plaintiffs and their predecessors in title, loyal churchmen all, having resulted in a free accretion at their expense to the lands of their church, their reward may be in the next world. But in this jurisdiction we can only qualify them for that reward by allowing the appeal and dismissing their action."

ii. OCCUPATION FOR BENEFIT OF LANDLORD

SMIRK *v* LYNDALE DEVELOPMENTS LTD [1975] Ch 317, [1975] 1 All ER 690 (ChD, PENNYCUICK V-C, and CA, CAIRNS and LAWTON LJJ and WALTON J)

A tenant of a house, first of British Railways, and, from 1967, of the defendants, occupied other land belonging to British Railways which adjoined the house (the blue land) and enclosed it. The defendants in 1973 began to develop the blue land, and the plaintiff brought this action claiming (i) that he had a good possessory title to the land, or alternatively (ii) that he held it as an extension of the tenanted land.

Held. (i) (expressly agreeing with PENNYCUICK V-C) the plaintiff held the land as an addition to the demised land; and (ii) (reversing PENNYCUICK V-C) the purchase of the blue land by the defendants in 1967 did not, on the facts, operate as a surrender and regrant of the lease.

PENNYCUICK V-C[3]: I turn now to the law applicable where a tenant takes possession of adjoining land — a tenant, during the currency of his tenancy, who takes possession of adjoining land belonging to his landlord. The law on this point, if I may respectfully say so, has got into something of a tangle. [His Lordship referred to *Kingsmill v Millard* (1855) 11 Exch 313 and, quoted from the judgments of Alderson and Parke BB and continued:]

It will be observed that in his judgment Parke B in terms states that the presumption that the tenant has inclosed for the benefit of the landlord applies, irrespective of whether the inclosed land is part of the waste or belongs to the landlord; and indeed he uses the word "encroachment" as appropriate in either case. He then goes on to state in terms, following and agreeing what Alderson B said in the course of

---

[3] The present extract covers the judgment of PENNYCUICK V-C on the first point.

the argument, that in order to displace the presumption there must be communication to the landlord. That decision of high authority seems to me to be in accordance with justice and common sense, and unless I were compelled to do otherwise by subsequent authority, I would certainly adopt it. I should add, as is perhaps obvious, as appears in some of the later cases, that the presumption may be rebutted by any form of express or implied agreement or, in some cases, as Parke B says, by estoppel.

The next case is *Whitmore v Humphries* (1871) LR 7 CP 1, where Willes J says, at pp. 4–5:

"This case raises a question upon a branch of the law which involves considerations of some nicety. By the rule of law applicable to this subject the landlord is entitled at the determination of the tenancy to recover from the tenant, not only the land originally demised, but also any land which the tenant may have added to it by encroachment from the waste, such encroachment being deemed to be made by him as tenant as an addition to his holding, and consequently for the benefit of his landlord, unless it is made under circumstances which show an intention to hold it for his own benefit alone, and not as part of his holding under the landlord. This rule undoubtedly applies when the encroachment is made over land belonging to the landlord, and no inquiry appears ever to have been made in such cases, whether it was made with the consent of the landlord or not. In such cases the reasonableness of the rule is very obvious; it only gives back to the landlord that which is rightly his, and prevents the tenant, who has taken advantage of his tenancy to encroach, from keeping that which it would be a breach of the duty arising from the relation of landlord and tenant not to give up. The rule, however, goes further than this. It is not confined to cases where the encroachment is upon land to which the landlord is entitled, it applies to cases where the land encroached upon does not belong to the landlord"

and he then goes on to deal with the position where the encroachment is upon land to which the landlord is not entitled. Willes J. continues, at p. 5:

"The rule is based upon the obligation of the tenant to protect his landlord's rights, and to deliver up the subject of his tenancy in the same condition, fair wear and tear excepted, as that in which he enjoyed it. There is often great temptation and opportunity afforded to the tenant to take in adjoining land which may or may not be his landlord's and it is considered more convenient and more in accordance with the rights of property that the tenant who has availed himself of the opportunity afforded him by his tenancy to make encroachments, should be presumed to have intended to make them for the benefit of the reversioner, except under circumstances pointing to an intention to take the land for his own benefit exclusively. The result is to avoid questions which would otherwise frequently arise as to the property in land, and to exclude persons who have come in as tenants, and who are likely to encroach, from raising such questions. The reason of the rule appears on the one hand to be entirely independent of any notion of encroachment being a wrong done, and so also on the other hand it appears to be quite independent of the question, whether the encroachment was made with the assent of the landlord."

[This principle was applied also in *Tabor v Godfrey* (1895) 64 LJQB 245. But statements in other cases *(Lord Hastings v Saddler* (1898) 79 LT 355 and *J.F. Perrott & Co Ltd v Cohen* [1951] 1 KB 705, [1950] 2 All ER 939) apply the presumption only to cases where the land occupied by the tenant is waste and adjacent to the demised land.

Having been through the authorities I propose, as I have said earlier, to adopt and apply the principle laid down in *Kingsmill v Millard* (1855) 11 Exch 313.

To return to the present case, there is nothing on the facts which could in any way rebut the presumption, which it seems to me is applicable here, namely, that the tenant, the plaintiff, was occupying the plots by way of an addition to land comprised with his tenancy, and not otherwise adversely to the landlord. I need only add on this point that if, contrary to my view, the unilateral intention of the plaintiff was relevant, the plaintiff's very candid evidence of intention would be fatal to his own case.

iii.   TIME RUNS EVEN IF THE LEASE IS IMMEDIATELY RENEWED

In *Gray v Wykeham-Martin and Goode* [1977] Bar Library Transcript No. 10A GEOFFREY LANE LJ said: "A person coming to this type of situation freshly may well wonder by what possible rule of law a life tenant[4] could be affected [where there have been continual renewals]. It would seem to the uninitiated that the land has been in the possession of tenants throughout and that even if the freeholder had wanted to remove the chicken houses or the rabbit hutches from the land and to ensure thereby that the plaintiff had no claim to the land, he could not have done so. Such it seems is not the case; because it is not disputed by the defendants that the decision of the House of Lords in *Ecclesiastical Comrs of England and Wales v Rowe* (1880) 5 App Cas 736 governs the situation and that, where a tenancy comes to an end, even if it is followed immediately by a fresh tenancy, there is a moment of time, however short, in which the freeholder notionally regains possession of the land and a moment when time can start to run against the freeholder or life tenant; . . . . Consequently if during that moment of time, or one of those moments of time, the squatter is in the necessary adverse possession of the disputed land, time under the Limitation Act starts to run against the life tenant."

---

[4] The landlord.

III.   Limitation Period[5]

LIMITATION ACT 1939

2.   Limitation of actions of contract and tort, and certain other actions. — (1) The following actions shall not be brought after the expiration of six years from the date on which the cause of action accrued, that is to say:

(a) actions founded on simple contract or on tort; . . .

(3) An action upon a specialty shall not be brought after the expiration of twelve years from the date on which the cause of action accrued:

Provided that this subsection shall not affect any action for which a shorter period of limitation is prescribed by any other provision of this Act.

(7) This section shall not apply to any claim for specific performance of a contract or for an injunction or for other equitable relief, except in so far as any provision thereof may be applied by the Court by analogy in like manner as the corresponding enactment repealed by this Act has heretofore been applied[6].

4.   Limitation of actions to recover land. — (1) No action shall be brought by the Crown to recover any land after the expiration of thirty years from the date on which the right of action accrued to the Crown or, if it first accrued to some person through whom the Crown claims, to that person[7]:

Provided that an action to recover foreshore may be brought by the Crown at any time before the expiration of sixty years from the said date. . . .

(3) No action shall be brought by any other person to recover any land after the expiration of twelve years from the date on which the right of action accrued to him or, if it first accrued to some person through whom he claims, to that person:

Provided that, if the right of action first accrued to the Crown . . . the action may be brought at any time before the expiration of the period during which the action could have been brought by the Crown . . . or of twelve years from the date on which the right of action accrued to some person other than the Crown . . ., whichever period first expires.

12.   Limitation of redemption actions. — When a mortgagee of land has been in possession of any of the mortgaged land for a period of twelve years, no action to redeem the land of which the mortgagee has been so in possession shall thereafter be brought by the mortgagor or any person claiming through him[8].

---

[5] Cheshire, pp. 885–886; M & W, pp. 1011–1012; MM, p. 489.
[6] This preserves the equitable doctrine of laches. Snell, pp. 33–36. See too Limitation Act 1939, s. 29.
[7] The same period applies in the case of a spiritual or eleemosynary corporation sole.
[8] *Young v Clarey* [1948] Ch 191, [1948] 1 All ER 197.

17. Limitation of actions to recover rent[9]. — No action shall be brought, or distress made, to recover arrears of rent, or damages in respect thereof, after the expiration of six years from the date on which the arrears became due.

18. Limitation of actions to recover money secured by a mortgage or charge or to recover proceeds of the sale of land. — (1) No action shall be brought to recover any principal sum of money secured by a mortgage or other charge on property, whether real or personal, or to recover proceeds of the sale of land, after the expiration of twelve years from the date when the right to receive the money accrued.

(3) The right to receive any principal sum of money secured by a mortgage or other charge and the right to foreclose on the property subject to the mortgage or charge shall not be deemed to accrue so long as that property comprises any future interest or any life insurance policy which has not matured or been determined.

(4) Nothing in this section shall apply to a foreclosure action in respect of mortgaged land, but the provisions of this Act relating to actions to recover land shall apply to such an action.

(5) No action to recover arrears of interest payable in respect of any sum of money secured by a mortgage or other charge payable in respect of proceeds of the sale of land, or to recover damages in respect of such arrears shall be brought after the expiration of six years from the date on which the interest became due:

Provided that—

    (*a*) where a prior mortgagee or other incumbrancer has been in possession of the property charged, and an action is brought within one year of the discontinuance of such possession by the subsequent incumbrancer, he may recover by that action all the arrears of interest which fell due during the period of possession by the prior incumbrancer or damages in respect thereof, notwithstanding that the period exceeded six years;

    (*b*) where the property subject to the mortgage or charge comprises any future interest or life insurance policy and it is a term of the mortgage or charge that arrears of interest shall be treated as part of the principal sum of money secured by the mortgage or charge, interest shall not be deemed to become due before the right to receive the principal sum of money has accrued or is deemed to have accrued.

IV. Effect of Disability, Fraud, Concealment and Mistake[10]

LIMITATION ACT 1939

22. Extension of limitation period in case of disability. — If on the date when any right of action accrued for which a period of limitation

---

[9] As amended by Limitation Amendment Act 1980 s. 13(1), Sch. 1, para. 7.
[10] Cheshire, pp. 904–906; M & W, pp. 1023–105; MM, pp. 494–495.

is prescribed by this Act, the person to whom it accrued was under a disability, the action may be brought at any time before the expiration of six years, ... from the date when the person ceased to be under a disability or died, whichever event first occurred, notwithstanding that the period of limitation has expired:
   Provided that—
   (a) this section shall not affect any case where the right of action first accrued to some person (not under a disability) through whom the person under a disability claims;
   (b) when a right of action which has accrued to a person under a disability accrues, on the death of that person while still under a disability, to another person under a disability, no further extension of time shall be allowed by reason of the disability of the second person;
   (c) no action to recover land or money charged on land shall be brought by virtue of this section by any person after the expiration of thirty years from the date on which the right of action accrued to that person or some person through whom he claims; ...

31. Interpretation. — (2) For the purposes of this Act a person shall be deemed to be under a disability while he is an infant, or of unsound mind. ...[11]

26. Postponement of limitation period in case of fraud, concealment or mistake[12]. — (1) Subject to subsection (3) of this section, where in the case of any action for which a period of limitation is prescribed by this Act, either—
   (a) the action is based upon the fraud of the defendant; or
   (b) any fact relevant to the plaintiff's right of action has been deliberately concealed from him by the defendant[13] or
   (c) the action is for relief from the consequences of a mistake[14];
the period of limitation shall not begin to run until the plaintiff has discovered the fraud, concealment or mistake (as the case may be) or could with reasonable diligence have discovered it.

---

[11] As amended by Statute Law Repeals Act 1969, s. 1, Sch., Part VII. For a definition of unsound mind, see s. 31(3), as amended by Limitation Amendment Act 1980 s. 13(1), Sch. 1, para. 13. If a cause of action against an infant arose before 1 January 1970, the change from 21 to 18 years for the age of majority does not affect the time for bringing actions. Family Law Reform Act 1969, s. 1(4), Sch. 3, para. 8.
[12] As substituted by Limitation Amendment Act 1980 s. 7. See Law Reform Committee 21st Report (1977) paras. 2.5–2.48, 3.17–3.18.
[13] *Rains v Buxton* (1880) 14 ChD 537; *Vane v Vane* (1872) 8 Ch App 383; *Clark v Woor* [1965] 1 WLR 650, [1965] 2 All ER 353; *Eddis v Chichester-Constable* [1969] 2 Ch 345, [1969] 2 All ER 912; *Applegate v Moss* [1971] 1 QB 406, [1971] 1 All ER 747; *King v Victor Parsons and Co* [1973] 1 WLR 29, [1973] 1 All ER 206.
[14] *Phillips-Higgins v Harper* [1954] 1 QB 411, [1954] 2 All ER 51.

(2) For the purposes of the last foregoing subsection, deliberate commission of a breach of duty in circumstances in which it is unlikely to be discovered for some time amounts to deliberate concealment of the facts involved in that breach of duty.

(3) Nothing in this section shall enable any action—
- (*a*) to recover, or recover the value of, any property; or
- (*b*) to enforce any charge against, or set aside any transaction affecting, any property;

to be brought against the purchaser of the property or any person claiming through him in any case where the property has been purchased for valuable consideration by an innocent third party since the fraud or concealment or (as the case may be) the transaction in which the mistake was made took place.

(4) A purchaser is an innocent third party for the purposes of this section—
- (*a*) in the case of fraud or concealment of any fact relevant to the plaintiff's right of action, if he was not a party to the fraud or (as the case may be) to the concealment of that fact and did not at the time of the purchase know or have reason to believe that the fraud or concealment had taken place; and
- (*b*) in the case of mistake, if he did not at the time of the purchase know or have reason to believe that the mistake had been made.

(5) References in this section to the defendant include references to the defendant's agent and to any person through whom the defendant claims and his agent.

V. Effect of Acknowledgment and Part Payment[15]

LIMITATION ACT 1939

23. Fresh accrual of action on acknowledgment or part payment. — (1) Where there has accrued any right of action (including a foreclosure action) to recover land or an advowson[16] . . . and—
- (*a*) the person in possession of the land, . . . acknowledges the title of the person to whom the right of action has accrued; or
- (*b*) in the case of a foreclosure or other action by a mortgagee, the person in possession as aforesaid or the person liable for the mortgage debt makes any payment in respect thereof, whether of principal or interest;

---

[15] Cheshire, pp. 907–908; M & W, pp. 1026–1027; MM, pp. 495–496.
[16] Limitation Act 1939, s. 14.

the right shall be deemed to have accrued on and not before the date of the acknowledgment or payment.

(3) Where a mortgagee is by virtue of the mortgage in possession of any mortgaged land and either receives any sum in respect of the principal or interest of the mortgage debt or acknowledges the title of the mortgagor, or his equity of redemption, an action to redeem the land in his possession may be brought at any time before the expiration of twelve years from the date of the payment or acknowledgment.

(4) Where any right of action has accrued to recover any debt or other liquidated pecuniary claim[17], or any claim to the personal estate of a deceased person or to any share of interest therein, and the person liable or accountable therefor acknowledges the claim[18] or makes any payment in respect thereof, the right shall be deemed to have accrued on and not before the date of the acknowledgment or payment[19]:

Provided that a payment of a part of the rent or interest due at any time shall not extend the period for claiming the remainder then due, but any payment of interest shall be treated as a payment in respect of the principal debt.

(5)[20] Subject to the proviso to the last foregoing subsection, a current period of limitation may be repeatedly extended under this section by further acknowledgments or payments, but a right of action, once barred by this Act, shall not be revived (under this section or otherwise) by any subsequent acknowledgment or payment.

24. Formal provisions as to acknowledgments and part payments. — (1) Every such acknowledgment as aforesaid shall be in writing and signed by the person making the acknowledgment.

(2) Any such acknowledgment or payment as aforesaid may be made by the agent of the person by whom it is required to be made under the last foregoing section, and shall be made to the person, or to an agent of the person, whose title or claim is being acknowledged or, as the case may be, in respect of whose claim the payment is being made[1].

25. Effect of acknowledgment or part payment on persons other than the maker or recipient. — (1) An acknowledgment of the title to any land . . . by any person in possession thereof shall bind all other persons in possession during the ensuing period of limitation.

---

[17] As, for example, rent due under a lease.
[18] *Good v Parry* [1963] 2 QB 418, [1963] 2 All ER 59; *Dungate v Dungate* [1965] 1 WLR 1477 [1965] 3 All ER 818; *Surrendra Overseas Ltd v Government of Sri Lanka* [1977] 1 WLR 565, [1977] 2 All ER 481; *Kamouh v Associated Electrical Industries International Ltd* [1979] 2 WLR 795.
[19] As amended by Limitation Amendment Act 1980, s. 6(2).
[20] As amended by Limitation Amendment Act 1980, s. 6(1). See Law Reform Committee 21st Report (1977), paras. 2.62–2.71; *Sanders v Sanders* [1881] 19 ChD 373; *Nicholson v England* [1926] 2 KB 93.
[1] *Edginton v Clark* [1964] 1 QB 367, [1963] 3 All ER 468 (letter to owner's agent offering to purchase land held to be an acknowledgment).

(2) A payment in respect of a mortgage debt by the mortgagor or any other person liable for the debt or by any person in possession of the mortgaged property shall, so far as any right of the mortgagee to foreclose or otherwise to recover the property is concerned, bind all other persons in possession of the mortgaged property during the ensuing period of limitation[2].

VI. Effect of Expiration of Limitation Period[3]

LIMITATION ACT 1939

16. Extinction of title after expiration of period. — Subject to the provisions of section seven[4] of this Act and of section seventy-five of the Land Registration Act, 1925[5], at the expiration of the period prescribed by this Act for any person to bring an action to recover land (including a redemption action)[6] or an action to enforce an advowson[7], the title of that person to the land or advowson shall be extinguished.

ASHER *v* WHITLOCK
(1865) LR 1 QB 1 (Ct Exch Ch, COCKBURN CJ and MELLOR and LUSH JJ)

In 1842 Williamson enclosed some manorial land, which he occupied until his death in 1860. At that time (the period of limitation being 20 years) the title of the Lord of the Manor was not yet extinguished. He devised the land by will to his widow so long as she remained unmarried, with remainder to his daughter in fee simple. After his death the widow remained in possession, and in 1861 married the defendant, who came to live with the widow and daughter. The daughter died in February and the widow in May 1863. The defendant remained in possession of the property, and in 1865 the daughter's heir-at-law brought ejectment against him.

Held. The heir-in-law was entitled to recover the property.

COCKBURN CJ: Assuming the defendant's possession to have been adverse, we have then to consider how far it operated to destroy the right of the devisee and her heir-at-law. . . . I take it as clearly established, that possession is good against all the world except the person who can shew a good title: and it would be mischievous to change this established doctrine. In *Doe d. Hughes v Dyeball* ((1829) Mood & M 346) one year's possession by the plaintiff was held good against a person who came and turned him out; and there are other authorities to the same effect. Suppose the person who originally inclosed the land had been expelled by the defendant, or the defendant had obtained possession without force, by simply walking in at the

---

[2] As amended by Limitation Amendment Act 1980 s. 13(1), Sch. 1, para. 9(a).
[3] See p. 152, n. 6, ante.
[4] See p. 161, ante.
[5] See p. 180, post.
[6] Limitation Act 1939, s. 12; p. 168, ante.
[7] Limitation Act 1939, s. 14.

open door in the absence of the then possessor, and were to say to him, "You have no more title than I have, my possession is as good as yours", surely ejectment could have been maintained by the original possessor against the defendant. All the old law on the doctrine of disseisin was founded on the principle that the disseisor's title was good against all but the disseisee. It is too clear to admit of doubt, that if the devisor had been turned out of possession he could have maintained ejectment. What is the position of the devisee? There can be no doubt that a man has a right to devise that estate, which the law gives him against all the world but the true owner, Here the widow was a prior devisee, but *durante viduitate* only, and as soon as the testator died, the estate became vested in the widow; and immediately on the widow's marriage the daughter had a right to possession; the defendant however anticipates her, and with the widow takes possession. But just as he had no right to interfere with the testator, so he had no right against the daughter, and had she lived she could have brought ejectment; although she died without asserting her right, the same right belongs to her heir. Therefore I think the action can be maintained, inasmuch as the defendant had not acquired any title by length of possession. The devisor might have brought ejectment, his right of possession being passed by will to his daughter, she could have maintained ejectment, and so therefore can her heir, the female plaintiff. We know to what extent encroachments on waste lands have taken place; and if the lord has acquiesced and does not interfere, can it be at the mere will of any stranger to disturb the person in possession? I do not know what equity may say to the rights of different claimants who have come in at different times without title; but at law, I think the right of the original possessor is clear. On the simple ground that possession is good title against all but the true owner, I think the plaintiffs entitled to succeed[8]. . . .

FAIRWEATHER v ST. MARYLEBONE PROPERTY CO LTD
[1963] AC 510, [1962] 2 All ER 288 (HL, Lords RADCLIFFE, DENNING, MORRIS OF BORTH-Y-GEST[9] and GUEST)

LORD DENNING: My Lords, at the back of a leasehold house in Hampstead there is a shed. In the year 1920 the next-door neighbour, Mr. Millwood, saw it was unused and out of repair. He went in and repaired it and has treated it as his own ever since. Mr. Millwood has actually sub-let it as part of his own house. Now a property company has bought the freehold of the property on which the shed stands and wants to recover possession of the shed. Can it do so? or is it barred by the Statutes of Limitation? There are three important persons to consider:

---

[8] *Perry v Clissold* [1907] AC 73.
[9] Lord MORRIS dissented. For criticism of the majority view; see (1962) 78 LQR 541 (H. W. R. Wade).

(1) The *freeholder* who, in 1893, let the premises on which the shed stands on a lease for 99 years at a ground rent with a repairing covenant and a proviso for re-entry. The 99 years will not expire till 1992.

(2) The *leaseholder* who has taken no steps for more than 12 years to recover possession of the shed which stands on part of his leasehold premises. His right of action first accrued in 1920. So the 12 years for him to sue expired in 1932.

(3) The *squatter,* who has been in possession of the shed since 1920, by himself or his sub-tenants.

And there is one important event to consider: The *surrender* in 1959 by the *leaseholder* to the *freeholder* of the rest of the term of 99 years. Whereupon the freeholder claims that he is entitled to possession of the shed. But the *squatter* says he is entitled to stay in it until 1992.

It is quite clear from the Statutes of Limitation that in the year 1932 the "title" of the leaseholder to the land was "extinguished". What does this mean? There are four suggestion to consider.

The first suggestion is that the title of the leaseholder to the shed is extinguished completely, not only against the squatter, but also against the freeholder. So that the leasehold interest disappears altogether, and the freeholder becomes entitled to the land. I reject this suggestion completely. It would mean in this case that the freeholder would have become entitled to possession of the shed in the year 1932 and time would have begun to run against him from 1932. So that 12 years later the title of the freeholder to the shed would have been extinguished, that is, in 1944. That cannot be right, and it was not seriously suggested. In 99 cases out of 100, the freeholder has no knowledge that the squatter is on the premises at all. It would be utterly wrong if the title of the freeholder could be eroded away during the lease without his knowledge. The correct view is that the freehold is an estate in reversion within section 6 (1) of the Act of 1939, and time does not run against the freeholder until the determination of the lease: see *Doe d. Davy v Oxenham* ((1840) 7 M & W 131).

The second suggestion is that the title of the leaseholder to the shed is extinguished so far as the leaseholder is concerned—so that he is no longer entitled to the shed—but that the leasehold interest itself persists and is vested in the squatter. In other words, the squatter acquired a title which is "commensurate" with the leasehold interest which has been extinguished. This suggestion was made in 1867 in the first edition of Darby and Bosanquet's book [Statutes of Limitation] at p. 390, and it was accepted in 1889 as correct by the court in Ireland in *Rankin v M'Murtry* ((1889) 24 LR Ir 290). But it has since been disapproved. If it were correct, it would mean that the squatter would be in the position of a statutory assignee of the shed, and he would by reason of privity of estate, be liable on the covenants and subject to the conditions of the lease. I reject this suggestion also: for the simple reason that the operation of the Statutes of Limitation is merely negative. It destroys the leaseholder's title to the land but does not vest it in the squatter. The squatter is not liable on the repairing covenants: see *Tichborne v Weir* ((1892) 67 LT 735). Nor, when the leasehold is a tenancy from year to year, does he step into the shoes of the tenant so as to be himself entitled to six months' notice to quit: see *Taylor v Twinberrow* ([1930] 2 KB 16).

The third suggestion is that the *title* of the leaseholder is extinguished but that his *estate* in the land is not. This is too fine a distinction for me. And so it was for Parliament. For Parliament itself uses the two words as if they meant the same: see section 16 of the Limitation Act 1939, and section 75 of the Land Registration Act 1925.

The fourth suggestion is that the title of the leaseholder to the shed is extinguished as *against the squatter,* but remains good as *against the freeholder.* This seems to me the only acceptable suggestion . If it is adopted, it means that time does not run against the freeholder until the lease is determined—which is only just. It also means that until that time the freeholder has his remedy against the leaseholder on the covenants, as he should have; and can also re-enter for forfeiture, as he should be able to do: see *Humphry v Damion* ((1612) 3 Cro Jac 300), and can give notice to determine on a "break" clause or notice to quit, as the case may be. Further, it means that if the leaseholder should be able to induce the squatter to leave the shed— or if the squatter quits and the leaseholder resumes possession—the leaseholder is at once in the same position as he was originally, being entitled to the benefits and subject to the burdens of the lease in regard to the shed. All this seems to me eminently reasonable but it can only be achieved if, despite the presence of the squatter, the title of the leaseholder remains good as against the freeholder.

On this footing it is quite apparent that at the date of the surrender, the leaseholder had something to surrender. He still had his title to the shed as against the freeholder and was in a position to surrender it to him. The maxim nemo dat quod non habet has no application to the case at all.

But there still remains the question: What was the effect of the surrender? There are here two alternatives open:

(1) On the one hand, it may be said that the surrender operated to *determine* the term, just as a forfeiture does. If this is correct, it would mean that the freeholder would be entitled to possession at once as soon as the leaseholder surrendered the house. He could evict the squatter by virtue of his freehold estate against which the squatter could say nothing. And time would begin to run against the freeholder as soon as the surrender took place. This view is based on *Ecclesiastical Commissioners of England and Wales v Rowe* ((1880) 5 App Cas 736), and section 6 (1) of the Limitation Act 1939.

(2) On the other hand, it may be said that the surrender operated as an *assignment* by the leaseholder to the freeholder of the rest of the 99 years. If this is correct, it would mean that the freeholder could not evict the squatter because the freeholder would be "claiming through" the leaseholder and would be barred for the rest of the 99 years, just as

the leaseholder would be: see section 4 (3) of the Limitation Act. Time would not begin to run against the freeholder until the 99 years expired. This view is based on *Walter v Yalden* ([1902] 2 KB 304).

My Lords, I have come to the clear conclusion that a surrender operates as a determination of the term. It is not an assignment of it. I am aware that no less an authority than Lindley LJ, once said that "the surrender of the term only operated as an assignment of the surrenderor's interest in it": see *David v Sabin* ([1893] 1 Ch 523, 533). But if that be true, it is not by any rule of the common law, only by force of statute: and then only in the case of underleases, not in the case of trespasser or squatter.

At common law, if a leaseholder made an underlease and afterwards surrendered his term to the freeholder, then the freeholder could not evict the underlessee during the term of the underlease: see *Pleasant (Lessee of Hayton) v Benson* ((1811) 14 East 234). But this was not because there was any assignment from surrenderor to surrenderee. It is clear that, upon the surrender, the head term was determined altogether. It was extinguished completely, so much so that the freeholder could not sue the underlessee on the covenants or enforce the proviso for re-entry: see *Webb v Russell* ((1789) 3 Term Rep 393). The underlessee could enjoy the property without payment of rent and without performance of the covenants and conditions until the end of the term of the underlease: see *Ecclesiastical Commissioners for England v Treemer* ([1893] 1 Ch 166). This was remedied by the statutes of 1740 and 1845, which have been re-enacted in sections 139 and 150 of the Law of Property Act 1925. Under those statutes, on a surrender of the head lease, an underlessee becomes a direct tenant of the freeholder on the terms of his underlease. So that the surrender does operate as if it were an assignment of the surrenderor's interest. But those statutes have no application to trespassers or squatters.

The question may be asked: why did the common law on a surrender protect the underlessee from eviction? The answer is to be found in Coke upon Littleton II, p. 338b, where it is said that "having regard to the parties to the surrender, the estate is absolutely drowned . . . But having regard to strangers, who were not parties or privies thereunto, lest by a voluntary surrender they may receive prejudice touching any right or interest they had before the surrender, the estate surrendered hath in consideration of law a continuance." This passage applies in favour of an underlessee so as to protect him from eviction during the term of his underlease: but it does not apply in favour of a trespasser. The reason for the difference is because the underlessee comes in under a grant from the lessee; and the lessee cannot, by a surrender, derogate from his own grant: see *Davenport's* case ((1608) 8 Co Rep 144b) and *Mellor v Watkins* ((1874) LR 9 QB 400, 405), by Blackburn J. But a trespasser comes in by wrong and not by grant of the lessee. If the lessee surrenders his term, the freeholder is at once entitled to evict the trespasser for the simple reason that, on the surrender, the lease is determined, and there is no bar whatever to the freeholder recovering possession: see *Ecclesiastical Commissioners of England and Wales v Rowe* ((1880) 5 App Cas 736). And I see no reason why the same reasoning should not apply even though, at the date of the surrender, the trespasser is a squatter who has been there more than 12 years. For, as against the freeholder, he is still a trespasser. The freeholder's right to possession does not arise until the lease is determined by the surrender. It then comes into being and time begins to run against him under section 6 (1) of the Limitation Act, 1939.

The only reason, it seems to me, which can be urged against this conclusion is that it means that a squatter's title can be destroyed by the leaseholder and freeholder putting their heads together. It is said that they can by a surrender—or by a surrender and regrant—destroy the squatter's title completely and get rid of him. So be it. There is no way of preventing it. But I would point out that, if we were to deny the two of them this right, they could achieve the same result in another way. They could easily do it by the leaseholder submitting to a forfeiture. If the leaseholder chooses not to pay the rent, the freeholder can determine the lease under the proviso for re-entry. The squatter cannot stop him. He cannot pay the rent without the authority of the leaseholder. He cannot apply for relief against forfeiture. The squatter's title can thus be defeated by a forfeiture—or by a forfeiture and regrant—just as it can by a surrender—or by a surrender and regrant. So there is nothing in the point.

My Lords, so far as these questions under the Limitation Acts are concerned, I must say that I see no difference between a surrender or merger or a forfeiture. On each of those events the lease is determined and the freeholder is entitled to evict the squatter, even though the squatter has been on the land during the lease for more than 12 years: and on the determination of the lease, time then begins to run against the freeholder. It follows that, in my opinion, *Walter v Yalden* ([1902] 2 KB 304) was wrongly decided and *Taylor v Twinberrow* ([1930] 2 KB 16) was rightly decided. . . . I would dismiss this appeal[10].

In *Tichborne v Weir*, (1892) 67 LT 735[11] KAY LJ, said, at p. 737: "On the occasion of the conveyance [between Giraud and Weir] Giraud made a statement that he had no assignment of the lease, but only a title by a possession of forty years. The question is, what is the effect of that title. There is no doubt that covenants running with the land would bind anyone coming into possession of the estate which Baxter had, and if the lease is anyhow vested in the defendant, he would be bound by such covenants. Therefore the question is, whether Baxter's estate is vested in the defendant. It was argued that the effect of the

---

[10] *Jessamine Investment Co v Schwartz* [1978] QB 264, [1976] 3 All ER 521 (sub-tenant, protected as statutory tenant under Rent Acts, acquired possessory title against his immediate landlord, whose title continued to exist as against the freeholder until head lease expired. Sub-tenant held still protected under Rent Acts thereafter against freeholder. (1977) 41 Conv (NS) 213 (F. R. Crane).

[11] See p. 709, post, where the facts are given.

statute was to transfer the term from Baxter to Giraud, and so it would be vested in the defendant. Under section 34 of 3 & 4 Will 4, c 27[12], 'the right and title' of Baxter to 'the land' (which by the interpretation clause includes chattel interest) was 'extinguished'. That is the operation of the section, and we are now asked to construe the Act of Parliament so as to make it say that Baxter's right and title was transferred to Giraud. . . . The defendant got an estate in the land which he has admitted, by paying rent, is not the fee simple, and by operation of the statute Baxter's right to claim the term was extinguished. It follows that Giraud during the rest of the term was free from liability to Baxter or anyone claiming under him, but it does not follow that he acquired Baxter's estate. There is another point as to whether the defendant is estopped from denying that he was in possession of Baxter's lease. He admits he is in possession of the land, he and Giraud have paid rent agreed on in the lease of 1802, and they have claimed possession for the rest of the term. The landlord's title to the land has been completely admitted, but there is no other evidence of the defendant's being bound by all the terms of the lease, or of his holding all Baxter's estate. There being no such admission, either express or implied, we must hold that there is no evidence of such an extensive estoppel as that which has been contended for[13]. I think that the defendant, for the reasons I have stated, is not liable on the covenants of the lease, and that this appeal should be dismissed."

In *Re Nisbet and Potts' Contract*, [1906] 1 Ch 386[14] COZENS-HARDY LJ said, at p. 409:

"The suggestion which is at the root of the appellant's argument is this, that a squatter can wholly disregard restrictive covenants affecting a building estate. That is so startling a proposition, and so wide-reaching, that it must be wrong. The value of estates in the neighbourhood of London and all large towns, and the amenity of those estates, depend almost entirely upon the continuance of the mutual restrictive covenants affecting the user and the enjoyment of the property; and when we are told that the squatter, notwithstanding that he is a mere trespasser, is to be in a better position than that occupied by a person deriving a title strictly through the original covenantor, one feels that there must be an answer to the argument; and I think the authorities, when carefully examined, make the answer quite plain. The benefit of a restrictive covenant of this kind is a paramount right in the nature of a negative easement not in any way capable of being affected by the provisions of the Statute of Limitations on which the squatter relies. The only rights extinguished for the benefit of the squatter under section 34[15] are those of persons who

---

[12] Reproduced with amendments as Limitation Act 1939, s. 16.
[13] *Tickner v Buzzacott* [1965] Ch 426, [1964] 1 All ER 131 (payment of rent due under lease not estoppel): *Ashe v Hogan* [1920] 1 IR 159; *O'Connor v Foley* [1906] 1 IR 20.
[14] P. 710, post, where the facts are given.
[15] Reproduced with amendments as Limitation Act 1939, s. 16.

might, during the statutory period, have brought, but did not in fact bring, an action to recover possession of the land. But the person entitled to the benefit of a restrictive covenant like this never had any cause of action which he could have brought, because unless and until there is a breach, or a threatened breach, of such a covenant, it is impossible for the person entitled to the benefit of it to bring any action. It appears, therefore, so far as the squatter is himself concerned, that both during the currency of the twelve years and after the expiration of the twelve years, there could be no possible answer to the claim of anyone seeking to enforce the covenant. In fact, there would, so far as he is concerned, be no difference between this covenant, which is in the nature of an equitable easement, and a legal easement strictly and properly so called. But although the squatter took the property subject to this equitable burden, it may be that the present vendor, who purchased from or through the squatter, is able to say that the burden does not affect the property in his hands. But what must he prove in order to claim this exemption? He must prove that he is a purchaser for value of the legal estate without notice. . . . Now can the present vendor allege and prove that he was a purchaser for value without notice? I think not."

VII.   Registered Land[16]

LAND REGISTRATION ACT 1925

70.   Liability of registered land to overriding interests. — (1) . . . (*f*) Subject to the provisions of this Act, rights acquired or in course of being acquired under the Limitation Acts[17].

75.   Acquisition of title by possession. — (1) The Limitation Acts shall apply to registered land in the same manner and to the same extent as those Acts apply to land not registered, except that where, if the land were not registered, the estate of the person registered as proprietor would be extinguished, such estate shall not be extinguished but shall be deemed to be held by the proprietor for the time being in trust for the person who, by virtue of the said Acts, has acquired title against any proprietor, but without prejudice to the estates and interests of any other person interested in the land whose estate or interest is not extinguished by those Acts.

(2) Any person claiming to have acquired a title under the Limitation Acts to a registered estate in the land may apply to be registered as proprietor thereof.

(3) The registrar shall, on being satisfied as to the applicant's title, enter the applicant as proprietor either with absolute, good leasehold,

---

[16] Cheshire, pp. 908–909; M & W, pp. 1078–1079; MM, pp. 521, 527; Ruoff and Roper, pp. 648–656.
[17] P. 111, ante. For overlap with para. (*g*), see *Bridges v Mees,* [1957] Ch 475, [1957] 2 All ER 577.

qualified, or possessory title, as the case may require, but without prejudice to any estate or interest protected by any entry on the register which may not have been extinguished under the Limitation Acts, and such registration shall, subject as aforesaid, have the same effect as the registration of a first proprietor; but the proprietor or the applicant or any other person interested may apply to the court for the determination of any question arising under this section.

In *Fairweather v St Marylebone Property Co Ltd* [1963] AC 510, [1962] 2 All ER 288, Lord DENNING said, p. 548: "One word about section 75 (1) of the Land Registration Act 1925. That point was not raised in the county court and its availability depends on facts which were not proved. I do not think it is open to the appellant here. But in any case I doubt if that puts registered land on a very different footing from unregistered land. It is machinery so as to apply the Limitation Acts to registered land but it does not alter the substantive position very materially. The registered leaseholder clearly remains liable on the covenants and subject to the conditions of the lease, including the proviso for re-entry: and I do not see why, on a surrender, the freeholder should not recover possession from a squatter, just as he can on a forfeiture. The freeholder has no notice of the trust in favour of the squatter and his interests are not to be prejudiced by the fact that the leasehold is registered. I say no more because the point is not available here."

In *Jessamine Investment Co v Schwartz* [1978] QB 264, [1976] 3 All ER 521, Sir John PENNYCUICK said at p. 275: "I should be very reluctant to introduce a substantive distinction in the application of a provision of the Limitation Act to registered and unregistered land respectively, based upon what is plainly a conveyancing device designed to adopt that provisions to the former class of land."

QUESTIONS

1. What weight do you think should be given, in determining whether adverse possession has been taken, to the fact that
   (a) the owner did not currently need the land but had plans for future development
   (b) the trespasser did or did not intend to acquire the land as his own
   (c) the owner knew or did not know or should have known of the trespass?
2. Consider the very difficult questions which arise in determining whether the owner (plaintiff) impliedly permitted the defendant to occupy; and whether an earlier express permission is still operative. A similar question arises in connection with the acquisition of easements by prescription. *Healy v Hawkins* [1968] 1 WLR 1967; [1968] 3 All ER 836; p. 554, post. Limitation Act 1939, s. 10(4); Law Reform Committee 21st Report (1977), 3.47–3.52.

Part Two. Family Interests

4. Trusts for Sale

I. Successive and Concurrent Interests[1]

A system of private ownership of property must provide for something more sophisticated than absolute ownership of the property by one person. A property owner needs to be able to do more than own it during his lifetime and pass it on to someone else on his death. He may wish to give it to his children, subject to an annuity for his widow, or to give a life interest to the widow and a remainder to the children; or to provide, on his son's marriage, a life interest for his son, and after his death for the daughter-in-law and after her death for their children. He may wish to set up a form of family dynasty, such as was popular among the aristocracy in the 17th, 18th and 19th centuries. The law should make possible the satisfaction of an owner's reasonable wishes on these lines. Limits are imposed on the extent to which property can be tied up in this way. We will see that dispositions are void unless they vest within the period of a life in being plus twenty-one years, or, if a fixed period of years is chosen, a period not exceeding eighty years.

But a system which allows successive interests in property necessarily raises a number of problems. Who is to manage the property during the period of the working out of the various interests? Above all, who is the person to take the decision to sell the property and to transfer title? And what is to happen, when the land is sold, to the interests of the beneficiaries?

The problem is simplest with a fund of money. The common law never developed a system of limited estates in personalty. But in equity a fund could be vested in trustees, who would receive the income and pay it to the income beneficiary and hand over the capital to the person who was absolutely entitled at the conclusion of the

---

[1] Cheshire, pp. 99–103, 165–166, 789–799; M & W, pp. 285–288, 293–295, 358–371, 377–383; MM, pp. 137–138, 142–144, 173–179. H & M Chap. 13, Harvey, *Settlements of Land* (1973).

limited interests. Similarly there was no problem in equity with investments. The trustees could buy and sell them, the purchaser taking a good title from the trustees, and the purchase money being added as capital to the trust fund. Chattels can be held in trust; but there has always been doubt as to the forms of limited ownership which could exist in personalty; and heirlooms used to be settled on trusts conforming as far as possible to the devolution of the land with which they were connected[2]. In a trust, it is important to state what powers are to be given to the trustees; powers of management and investment, and the power to sell and to give a good receipt to the purchaser free from the trusts of the settlement. Much of this is now covered by statute.

Successive interests in land of course provided a special case. The common law system of estates provided for life estates, fees tail, remainders and reversions. When uses and trusts of land developed, equity, generally speaking, followed the law, and allowed similar interests in equity behind a use or a trust. But, when the legal fee simple of land was split up between successive limited owners, there was no provision for the proper management of the land and, above all, no provision for selling. If land were limited to A for life, with remainder to B for life, with remainder to C in fee simple, who would sell the land? The same problem arose if similar limitations were created behind a trust; for, unless special powers were given to the trustees, they could not give a clear title to anyone other than a purchaser of the legal estate for value without notice, because any other purchaser would take the legal estate with notice of the trusts and would be bound by them[3]. Of course, all the legal estate owners in the case of a limitation of legal estates, or all the beneficiaries in the case of a trust, could combine to sell. That might not be difficult where there was a simple limitation, such as one to A for life with remainder to B. But it becomes highly impracticable if there is a long series of limitations, and impossible if the limitations include an entail in an minor or if they create interests which are designed to vest on the happening of some contingencies which have not yet been worked out[4].

What is needed therefore is a system which meets both these difficulties; which allows a property owner to create future successive and contingent interests in the property (always within the perpetuity rule[5]) and, at the same time, provides for proper management of the fund and the power to sell and to pass a good title to the purchaser free from the trusts affecting the property. The problem is most acute where the capital consists of one single unique piece of property, like a

---

[2] *Shelley v Shelley* (1868) LR 6 Eq 540; *Re Morrison's Settlement* [1974] Ch 326, [1973] 3 All ER 1094.
[3] P. 24, ante.
[4] [1972] Duke Law Journal 517 (W. M. Fratcher); (1977) 42 Missouri LR 355 (R. H. Maudsley).
[5] Chap. 7, p. 290, post.

piece of land. How to reconcile the interests of the beneficiaries and those of a purchaser?

The solution is found by the application of the principle of "overreaching", and this is applied in each of two forms of procedure used for the purpose, the strict settlement and the trust for sale. "Overreaching" is a principle by which, on a sale of property which is subject to successive interests, the interests of the beneficiaries leave the property and attach to the purchase money. The interests of the beneficiaries are said to be overreached. The beneficiaries do not lose economically out of the sale. A ton of feathers weighs the same as a ton of lead. A life interest in remainder in £50,000 worth of land is worth exactly the same as the same interest in £50,000; indeed, more valuable if the money is invested more profitably; less valuable, though, if the land proved to be the better investment. The question is one of choice of investment of the family capital.

The two procedures or methods by which this result can be achieved are the strict settlement and the trust for sale. In the context of family holdings of land, the strict settlement is historically the more significant; because it was in this way that the great families held their ancestral lands. Legislation providing for the application of the overreaching principle to successive interests in land first came in 1882[6]. Now, under the Settled Land Act 1925, where there are successive interests in land, the legal estate is to be vested in the tenant for life (the income beneficiary) and he has the powers of management and of sale of the fee simple; and on such a sale the beneficial interests in the land are overreached and thus transferred from the land to the proceeds of sale.

Our emphasis will however be upon the other method, the trust for sale. Land held on trust for sale is vested in trustees upon trust to sell and to hold the income until sale and the proceeds of the sale on trust for the beneficiaries according to their interests under the terms of the limitation. Under the doctrine of conversion, by which land subject to a trust for sale is treated in equity as being personalty, the interests of the beneficiaries are already interests in personalty. Overreaching is therefore automatic, but the Law of Property Act 1925, section 2 makes express provision for it[7]. The existence of the trust for sale does not mean that the trustees must sell forthwith, for they are given by statute a discretionary power to postpone sale; and they can retain the land under this power as long as they wish. They are also given the same powers of management and sale as the tenant for life in the case of a settlement. The trust for sale is thus an alternative method of dealing with successive interests in land. It is more convenient than a strict settlement for various reasons, the most important of which are: land and personalty can be held together, and most family trusts

---

[6] S.L.A. 1882.

[7] It makes provision also for overreaching interests prior to the trust for sale where the trustees are either two or more individuals approved or appointed by the court or a trust corporation. L.P.A. 1925, s. 2 (2), p. 190, post.

contain each; decisions are taken by a group of persons in a fiduciary position and not by one interested beneficiary; it is equally convenient where there are concurrent as opposed to successive interests; and it proved more flexible and able to accommodate special forms of trusts developed to reduce tax and estate duty liability[8]. Most inter vivos trusts have this objective in mind in modern times. The law in the tax field has recently been subject to basic changes, and it is impossible at the time of writing to know how it will develop[9].

Concurrent interests used to create a similar problem for a purchaser. To get a good title, he had to buy from all the co-owners. This problem is overcome in 1925 by providing that all concurrent interests, other than landholding by trustees, exist only behind a trust for sale[10]. There cannot be more than four trustees of land[11]. So, even if land is beneficially owned by 130 tenants in common, the purchaser buys from not more than four trustees for sale, who pass the title, as with successive interests, free from the beneficial interests of the co-owners. Their interests attach to the purchase money. A statutory trust for sale is imposed also in the case of intestacy[12].

All cases of successive or concurrent ownership are thus subject to either a trust for sale or a strict settlement. Conveyancers use the trust for sale almost exclusively at the present day, and, for this reason, it will be given prominence here. But many titles, especially those deriving from large family landholdings, are still dependent upon the Settled Land Act conveyancing, and each of the methods needs to be understood.

The interests of the beneficiaries under the strict settlement are by statute treated as interests in land after the sale[13]; while, under a trust for sale they are, by the operation of the doctrine of conversion, interests in personalty even before the land is sold. But the logic of the theory is not always followed with land subject to a trust for sale. This is a complex matter which will best be considered after concurrent interests and statutory trusts for sale have been examined.

II.   Express and Statutory Trusts for Sale[14]

Trusts for sale may be created expressly or by statute. In the former case, it is important to distinguish between a trust for sale, and a mere power of sale. The overreaching provisions apply only in the case of a

---

[8] Cheshire, pp. 204–209; M & W, p. 384; MM, pp. 186–188; H & M, p. 305; (1928) 166 LT 45; (1938) 85 LJ News 353 (J.M.L.); (1938) 54 LQR 576 (M. M. Lewis); (1944) 8 Conv (NS) 147 (H. Potter); (1957) CLP 152 (E. H. Scamell); (1961) 24 MLR 123 (G. A. Grove); (1962) CLP 104 (E. C. Ryder).
[9] Finance Act 1975; (1974) Cmnd 5705; Wealth Tax (1974) Cmnd 5704.
[10] P. 218, post.
[11] T.A. 1925, s. 34.
[12] A.E.A. 1925, s. 33.
[13] S.L.A. 1925, s. 75 (5).
[14] Cheshire, pp. 196–209; M & W, pp. 362–364; MM, pp. 216–217; H & M chap. 13.

trust for sale. The distinction is simple in most cases, but difficult questions can arise[15].

Statutory trusts for sale can arise in various situations. The most important are[16] —

Co-ownership: Law of Property Act 1925, sections 34–36 (p. 218, post).

Intestacy: Administration of Estates Act 1925, sections 33, 47.

LAW OF PROPERTY ACT 1925

35. Meaning of the statutory trusts. — For the purposes of this Act land held upon the "statutory trusts" shall be held upon the trusts and subject to the provisions following, namely, upon trust to sell the same and to stand possessed of the net proceeds of sale, after payment of costs, and of the net rents and profits until sale after payment of rates, taxes, costs of insurance, repairs, and other outgoings, upon such trusts, and subject to such powers and provisions, as may be requisite for giving effect to the rights of the persons (including an incumbrancer of a former undivided share or whose incumbrance is not secured by a legal mortgage) interested in the land [and the right of a person who, if the land had not been made subject to a trust for sale by virtue of this Act, would have been entitled to an entailed interest in an undivided share in the land, shall be deemed to be a right to a corresponding entailed interest in the net proceeds of sale attributable to that share[17].]

[Where —
- (a) an undivided share was subject to a settlement, and
- (b) the settlement remains subsisting in respect of other property, and
- (c) the trustees thereof are not the same persons as the trustees for sale,

then the statutory trusts include a trust for the trustees for sale to pay the proper proportion of the net proceeds of sale or other capital money attributable to the share to the trustees of the settlement to be held by them as capital money arising under the Settled Land Act, 1925[18].]

III. Effect of Sale. Overreaching[19]

LAW OF PROPERTY ACT 1925

2. Conveyances overreaching certain equitable interests and powers. — (1) A conveyance to a purchaser of a legal estate in land shall over-

---

[15] Cheshire, pp. 197–198; M & W, pp. 294–295, 359; MM, pp. 143, 173; H & M, p. 277; *Re Newbould* (1913) 110 LT 6; *Re Smith and Lonsdale's Contract* (1934) 78 Sol Jo 173; *Re White's Settlement* [1930] 1 Ch 179; L.P.A. 1925, s. 25 (4); S.L.A. 1925, s. 30 (1) (i).

[16] See also L.P.A. 1925, s. 19 (2) infant entitled to legal estate with person of full age); s. 28 (4) (infant entitled under partition); s. 31 (right of redemption barred); s. 32 (personalty settlement).

[17] The words in square brackets were added by L.P. (Entailed Interests) A. 1932, s. 1.

[18] The words in square brackets were added by L.P. (A.) A. 1926, Sch.

[19] Cheshire, pp. 81–82, 796–797; M & W, pp. 377–379; MM, pp. 182–183.

reach any equitable interest or power affecting that estate, whether or not he has notice thereof, if —

(ii) the conveyance is made by trustees for sale and the equitable interest or power is at the date of the conveyance capable of being overreached by such trustees under the provisions of subsection (2) of this section or independently of that subsection[20], and the statutory requirements respecting the payment of capital money arising under a disposition upon trust for sale are complied with;

(iii) the conveyance is made by a mortgagee or personal representative in the exercise of his paramount powers, and the equitable interest or power is capable of being overreached by such conveyance, and any capital money arising from the transaction is paid to the mortgagee or personal representative;

(iv) the conveyance is made under an order of the court and the equitable interest or power is bound by such order, and any capital money arising from the transaction is paid into, or in accordance with the order of, the court.

(2)[1] Where the legal estate affected is subject to a trust for sale, then if at the date of a conveyance made after the commencement of this Act under the trust for sale or the powers conferred on the trustees for sale, the trustees (whether original or substituted) are either —

(a) two or more individuals approved or appointed by the court or the successors in office of the individuals so approved or appointed; or

(b) a trust corporation[2],

---

[20] *Re Ryder and Steadman's Contract* [1927] 2 Ch 62.

[1] This subsection was amended by L.P. (A.) A. 1926, Sch. The trust for sale then becomes "ad hoc" with additional overreaching powers. See S.L.A. 1925, s. 21, p. 260, post for "ad hoc" settlements.

[2] Defined in L.P.A. 1925, s. 205 (1) (xxviii) as follows: "Trust corporation" means the Public Trustee or a corporation either appointed by the court in any particular case to be a trustee or entitled by rules made under subsection (3) of section four of the Public Trustee Act, 1906, to act as custodian trustee.

Corporations which are entitled under the Public Trustee Rules 1912 r. 30, as substituted by the Public Trustee (Custodian Trustee) Rules 1975 (S.I. 1975 No. 1189), include companies "constituted under the law of the United Kingdom and empowered by its constitution to undertake trust business and having one or more places of business there", and being a registered company "having a capital (in stock or shares) for the time being issued of not less than £250,000, of which not less than £100,000, has been paid up in cash".

The definition was extended by L.P. (A.) A. 1926, s. 3 to include the "Treasury Solicitor, the Official Solicitor, and any person holding any other official position prescribed by the Lord Chancellor, and, in relation to the property of a bankrupt and property subject to a deed of arrangement, includes the trustee in bankruptcy and the trustee under the deed respectively, and, in relation to charitable, ecclesiastical and public trusts, also includes any local or public authority so prescribed, and any other corporation constituted under the laws of the United Kingdom or any part thereof which satisfies the Lord Chancellor that it undertakes the administration of any such trusts without remuneration, or that by its constitution it is required to apply the whole of its net income after payment of outgoings for charitable, ecclesiastical or public purposes, and is prohibited from distributing, directly or indirectly, any part thereof by way of profits amongst any of its members, and is authorised by him to act in relation to such trusts as a trust corporation." See also S.L.A. 1925, s. 117 (1) (xxx); T.A. 1925, s. 68 (18); A.E.A. 1925, s. 55 (1) (xxvi).

any equitable interest or power having priority to the trust for sale, shall, notwithstanding any stipulation to the contrary, be overreached by the conveyance, and shall, according to its priority, take effect as if created or arising by means of a primary trust affecting the proceeds of sale and the income of the land until sale.

(3) The following equitable interests and powers are excepted from the operation of subsection (2) of this section, namely —

(i) Any equitable interest protected by a deposit of documents relating to the legal estate affected;

(ii) The benefit of any covenant or agreement restrictive of the user of land;

(iii) Any easement, liberty, or privilege over or affecting land and being merely an equitable interest (in this Act referred to as an "equitable easement");

(iv) The benefit of any contract (in this Act referred to as an "estate contract") to convey or create a legal estate, including a contract conferring either expressly or by statutory implication a valid option to purchase, a right of pre-emption, or any other like right;

(v) Any equitable interest protected by registration under the Land Charges Act, 1925[3], other than —

(a) an annuity within the meaning of Part II. of that Act;

(b) a limited owner's charge or a general equitable charge within the meaning of that Act.

(4) Subject to the protection afforded by this section to the purchaser of a legal estate, nothing contained in this section shall deprive a person entitled to an equitable charge of any of his rights or remedies for enforcing the same.

(5) So far as regards the following interests, created before the commencement of this Act (which accordingly are not within the provisions of the Land Charges Act, 1925)[3], namely —

(a) the benefit of any covenant or agreement restrictive of the user of the land;

(b) any equitable easement;

(c) the interest under a puisne mortgage within the meaning of the Land Charges Act, 1925[3], unless and until acquired under a transfer made after the commencement of this Act;

(d) the benefit of an estate contract, unless and until the same is acquired under a conveyance made after the commencement of this Act;

a purchaser of a legal estate shall only take subject thereto if he has notice thereof, and the same are not overreached under the provisions contained or in the manner referred to in this section.

---

[3] Now L.C.A. 1972. The annuity referred to in (a) is one created before 1926 and registered in the Register of Annuities which then existed. L.C.A. 1972, Sch. 1.

IV.   Definition[4]

LAW OF PROPERTY ACT 1925

205.   General definitions. — (1) . . .

    (xxix) "Trust for sale", in relation to land, means an immediate binding trust for sale, whether or not exercisable at the request or with the consent of any person, and with or without a power at discretion to postpone the sale; "trustees for sale" mean the persons (including a personal representative) holding land on trust for sale; and "power to postpone a sale" means power to postpone in the exercise of a discretion.

The definition of a trust for sale has created a number of problems. It is vital to distinguish a trust for sale from a settlement; for the trustees in the former and the tenant for life in the latter are the persons to make title, and to exercise the powers of management until sale. It will be seen that wherever there are successive interests in land, or where a fee simple is subject to a family rentcharge, there is a settlement unless the land is held upon trust for sale[5]. The definition of trust for sale in terms of itself is not helpful, and problems have arisen on the construction of the words "immediate" and "binding".

A.   Immediate[6]

RE HERKLOTS' WILL TRUSTS
[1964] 1 WLR 583, [1964] 2 All ER 66 (ChD, UNGOED-THOMAS J)

By clauses 4 and 5 of her will, the testatrix left the residue of her estate on trust for sale, and by clause 7 directed the income to be paid to Miss Gordon for life with permission to "reside in my said house during her life for so long as she wishes". A codicil directed that the plaintiff could, if he wished, claim the house instead of a share of the residue given to him by the will. Miss Gordon proposed to sell the house, and the plaintiff brought this action to restrain her.

Held. Injunction granted. The house was held under a trust for sale subject to the consent of both Miss Gordon and the plaintiff.

UNGOED-THOMAS J: It is submitted on behalf of the plaintiff that with regard to the house, 8 Cannon Place, first, there was a trust for sale with a prohibition against sale in the lifetime of Miss Gordon without the plaintiff's consent and, secondly, that, even if that were not so, nonetheless the will and codicil declared a purpose, namely, that the plaintiff should on Miss Gordon's death have the house if he wished to have it, and that purpose must prevail over the trust for sale with the result that the property cannot be sold in the plaintiff's lifetime without his consent.

---

[4] Cheshire, p. 197–199; M & W, pp. 358–362; MM, pp. 173–174; H & M, p. 283.
[5] S.L.A. 1925, s. 1 (7), p. 250, post.
[6] See also *Re Hanson* [1928] Ch 96; *Bacon v Bacon* [1947] P. 151, [1947] 2 All ER 327.

On the other hand, it is submitted on behalf of the defendants that, on the proper construction of this will, and having regard to the law which is applicable to it, the house is settled land and not subject to a trust for sale at all. The result of it being settled land would be that Miss Gordon, as tenant for life, could sell the property under her Settled Land Act powers, and that the proceeds of sale would constitute capital and, it is submitted for the trustees, consequently become subject to the option which the plaintiff was given by the . . . codicil of the testatrix's will in exactly the same way as if the house had not been sold. . . .

I was referred to *Re Hanson* ([1928] 1 Ch 96) which dealt with the question whether or not a provision for residence requires that the property should be treated as settled land rather than as being subject to a trust for sale. In that case the testator directed the trustees of his will to purchase a dwelling-house for his wife as a residence for herself until his son David should attain 25 "if she should so long continue the testator's widow". On David attaining 25, or on the second marriage of his widow (whichever happened first) the house was to fall into and form part of the testator's residuary estate, and it was devised to trustees upon trust for sale. There was no provision in the terms of the will for a trust for sale followed by a direction that the donee should have the power to reside in the house for a specified period. There was simply a direction that a house should be bought followed by a provision that at the end of the specified period there should be a trust for sale. That case turned largely on the application in those circumstances of section 32 of the Law of Property Act 1925, which provides by subsection (1): "Where a settlement of personal property or of land held upon trust for sale contains a power to invest money in the purchase of land, such land shall, unless the settlement otherwise provides, be held by the trustees on trust for sale." In *Re Hanson* there was a settlement of personal property; there was a power to invest money in the purchase of land, namely, the house for the widow, and, therefore, it would follow that the land would, under the provisions of section 32 (1), be held by the trustees upon trust for sale "unless the settlement otherwise provides". Astbury, J., in the course of his judgment, said (at p. 99): "The only question therefore is whether the will settlement 'otherwise provides'. . . . I imagine that the testator's direction to the trustees to purchase a dwelling-house for the widow's residence until David attained 25 or she remarried is inconsistent with there being an immediate trust for sale. Such a trust for sale would no doubt oust the Settled Land Act, 1925. But in my view the testator has otherwise provided within section 32 of the Law of Property Act 1925. He could not have intended that a dwelling-house, expressly directed to be purchased for the widow's residence, should be liable to be sold over her head." What he was considering there was whether or not, on the construction of that will, the will otherwise provided. He held, that on the construction of that will, there was a contrary intention, in that the testator had himself provided that no trust for sale should operate before the time indicated in the will.

Here, on the other hand, the testatrix provided, by clauses 4 and 5, for there to be a trust for sale. The question here, therefore, is different, namely, whether, on the construction of this will, the testatrix takes out of the trust for sale, which she has declared, the house which was the subject of the gift in this case. Looking again at clause 7 of the will, it does not appear to me that the provision that Miss Gordon should be permitted to reside in this house so long as she wished is inconsistent with the trust for sale for which the testatrix had expressly provided. I have to construe the will and, so far as possible, to reconcile the provisions of the will in accordance with what, so far as I can gather from the terms of the will and codicil, are the testatrix's intentions. Reading this provision for residence in clause 7 of the will, coming as it does in the clause which deals with the income of the investments of the trust, it does not appear to me that the testatrix there contemplated that the provision for residence should take this property out of the trust for sale. It is certainly reconcilable with the trust for sale because the effect would simply be that if Miss Gordon wished to reside in this house, it was not to be sold. I find nothing in the fact that her consent to the sale was required in that way inconsistent with the definition of trust for sale contained in section 205 (1) (xxix) of the Law of Property Act 1925.

[His Lordship then held that the intention of the testatrix was that the house should not be sold without the plaintiff's consent.]

B. Binding

The basic problem has been to know whether or not the word "binding" means merely that the trust is valid as a binding trust to sell, as opposed to a power of sale, or whether it has greater significance.

The difficulty usually arises where the fee simple in land, subject to family charges, is left by will to trustees on trust for sale. Is there a binding trust for sale subject to the family charges? Or is it a settlement within the Settled Land Act 1925, section 1 (1) (v)? *Re Leigh's Settled Estates* ([1926] Ch 852)[7] was a case of this type.

Mrs. Tenison was tenant in tail of land which was subject to an equitable jointure rentcharge. In 1923, Mrs. Tenison disentailed and conveyed the fee simple, subject to the charge, to trustees on trust for sale. The question was whether or not, on 1 January 1926, the land was settled land or was subject to "an immediate binding trust for sale". Tomlin J, held that it was settled land because the trust for sale was not "binding" on every interest in the land. He said at p. 859: "The question is what is meant by 'an immediate binding trust for sale'. Of course an immediate trust for sale is an intelligible conception where

---

[7] The case was tried a second time after the trustees for sale had been approved by the court. The trustees for sale were then given powers to overreach the rentcharge (L.P.A. 1925, s. 2 as amended by L.P. (A.) A. 1926, Sch. and Tomlin J, then held that it was a binding trust for sale. *Re Leigh's Settled Estates (No. 2)* [1927] 2 Ch 13.

immediate is used as distinct from future; a binding trust for sale in its simplest form would be something the opposite of one that was not binding, but it is difficult to suppose that this is the contrast which was intended to be indicated by the use of this phrase. There must be, it seems to me, some significance in the word 'binding' here. It is incredible that the word should have no meaning. It has presumably been inserted for some definite purpose, and it is the duty of the Court to attribute to it some intelligible meaning. The expression 'unless the land is subject to an immediate binding trust for sale' must I think mean unless the land that is the total subject matter of the settlement is subject to a trust for sale which operates in relation to the whole subject matter of the settlement and is immediately exercisable, although possibly with the limitation, that it is treated as immediately exercisable 'whether or not exercisable at the request or with the consent of any person and with or without a power at discretion to postpone the sale'. If that be the meaning of the phrase it may well be that, where the subject matter of the settlement is the whole unencumbered fee simple, there is no immediate binding trust for sale so long as there is not a trust for sale which is capable of over-riding all charges having under the settlement priority to the trust for sale. In the present case there is no trust for sale capable of overriding all prior charges.''

In *Re Parker's Settled Estates* [1928] Ch 247[8], the question was whether land held by trustees on trust for sale, subject to prior *legal* charges to secure portions, was settled land, or land subject to an immediate binding trust for sale. ROMER J disapproved TOMLIN J's construction of the definition of "trust for sale", but held that, because there were prior legal charges, the land was settled land. He said at p. 257: "Now 'trust for sale' is defined as meaning, in relation to land, an immediate binding trust for sale whether or not exercisable at the request or with the consent of any person, and it was contended before me that the land is not held upon an immediate binding trust for sale within the meaning which it was said had been given to those words by Tomlin J, in *Re Leigh's Settled Estates* ([1926] Ch 852). In that case the learned judge came to the conclusion that where the subject-matter of a settlement is the whole unincumbered fee simple, 'the land' is not 'subject to an immediate binding trust for sale', so long as there is not a trust for sale which is capable of overriding all charges having, under the settlement, priority to the trust for sale. At the time that this decision was given the Law of Property (Amendment) Act 1926, had not been passed, so that the learned judge was not dealing with subsection 7 of section 1 of the Settled Land Act[9]. He was merely dealing with section 20, subsection 1 (viii), of the Act. But I feel some little doubt as to whether the learned judge held that 'the land' in the case

---

[8] (1928) 65 LJ News 248, 272, 293 (J.M.L.).
[9] P. 250, post.

before him was not subject to any trust for sale, inasmuch as the
subject-matter of the trust was merely the fee simple subject to the
incumbrance, or whether he held that no land can ever be subject to a
binding trust for sale, unless the trustees have power to overreach
prior equitable interests. If the latter be the real reason of his decision,
I find myself, with the greatest respect unable to follow it. For it
means that there cannot be, within the meaning of the Settled Land
Act, any trust for sale of land that is subject to equitable interests,
unless the trustees have a legal estate and are either two or more
individuals approved or appointed by the court, or the successors in
office of such individuals or a trust corporation. . . .

The conclusion, however, that I come to as a result of a consideration
of all the Acts is that the words 'trust for sale', when used in reference
to land that is subject to a prior equitable interest, are not confined to
cases where that equitable interest can be overreached by the trustees.
It may be said that in that case no effect is given to the word 'binding'.
But the word may quite conceivably have been inserted to meet a case
of a revocable trust for sale such as existed in *Re Goodall's Settlement*
([1909] 1 Ch 440), and even if this be not so I should prefer to treat the
word as mere surplusage, inserted ex majore cautela, rather than to
give it a meaning that would exclude from being trusts for sale
innumerable trusts which are indubitably trusts for sale, as that
phrase has always been understood by lawyers hitherto, and which
would either exclude them without any apparent reason from a very
large number of the general provisions of the Acts relating to 'trusts
for sale' or would necessitate the court holding that the context
required some other meaning to be attributed to that expression.

There is therefore, in my opinion, a trust for sale in the present case
affecting the legal estate in fee simple vested in the trustees of the
1924 deed. But is there a trust for sale that brings the present case
within the exception to section 1 of the Settled Land Act introduced
by the new subsection 7? In my opinion there is not. It is, I think,
reasonably clear that that subsection only applies where 'the land'
that would otherwise be the subject of a settlement under subsection 1
is held upon trust for sale.

[Here however, because there was an outstanding legal term of 1,000
years to secure portions] the whole legal estate which is the subject-
matter of the settlement is not therefore subjected to a trust for sale,
and in my opinion subsection 7 has no application to the case."

RE NORTON[10]
[1929] 1 Ch 84 (ChD, ROMER J)

On 31 December 1925, lands stood limited to Lord Norton for life
and, after his death, subject to certain equitable charges, to trustees
on trust for sale. A vesting deed was executed in favour of Lord

---

[10] (1929) 67 LJ News 24, 44 (J.M.L.).

Norton. He died in December 1926, and probate, limited to settled land, was granted to the trustees of the compound settlement[10a] as his special representatives. One question was whether the land remained settled or was held upon trust for sale.

Held. The legal estate was vested in Lord Norton as tenant for life under the Settled Land Act[11].

ROMER J: The first question that arises upon this summons is whether the compound settlement came to an end on the death of the second Lord Norton. The solution of that question depends upon the answer to be given to the further question whether, on the death of Lord Norton, the land, which previously had been the subject-matter of the settlement, was held upon trust for sale within the meaning of section 3 of the Settled Land Act 1925[12]. [His Lordship read section 3 and continued:] It is quite clear from that, that this land remains settled land after the death of the second Lord Norton, unless upon the happening of that event the land became held upon trust for sale. I had occasion recently in the case of *Re Parker's Settled Estates* ([1928] Ch 247) to consider the meaning of the phrase "trust for sale" as used in subsection 7 of section 1 of the Settled Land Act, and for reasons that I then gave I came to the conclusion that land was not settled land where the whole legal estate, which would be otherwise subject to a settlement, was held upon trust for sale. But I also came to the conclusion that the land in question there was settled land, because there was outstanding in certain trustees a legal etate in a term of years for securing portions. The whole legal estate subject to the settlement was not therefore held upon trust for sale.

That being so, what I have to consider here is whether, on the death of Lord Norton, the legal estate in the whole subject-matter of the settlement, which undoubtedly had existed up to that date, was thereafter held upon trust for sale. Up to his death he had had the legal estate in fee simple, and that was the legal estate which was the subject of the settlement. On his death it vested in his personal representatives, his special representatives to whom probate had been granted, and was not vested in the trustees for sale. I must accordingly turn to section 7 of the Act which is the section that provides what is to be done with the legal estate which becomes vested in his personal representatives on the death of a tenant for life, and for the purposes of the present case I need only refer to subsection 5, which is in these terms: "If any person of full age becomes absolutely entitled to the settled land (whether beneficially, or as personal representative, or as trustee for sale, or otherwise) free from all limitations, powers, and charges taking effect under the settlement, he shall be entitled to require the trustees of the settlement, personal representatives, or other persons in whom the settled land is vested, to convey the land to him" But the trustees for sale in this case have not

---

[10a] P. 250, post.
[11] P. 261, post.
[12] See p. 286, post.

become absolutely entitled to the settled land free from all charges taking effect under the settlement. There are certain equitable rent-charges which take effect in priority to the trust for sale. That being so, it appears to me that not only was the whole legal estate the subject-matter of the settlement not held upon trust for sale upon the death of the second Lord Norton, but that the trustees for sale as such had not, and have not now, a right to call for the legal estate. So far, I must, as it seems to me, come to the conclusion that on the death of the second Lord Norton, the land did not cease to be settled land, but continued to be settled land and is still settled land[13].

V. Powers of Trustees for Sale[14]

A. Postponement of Sale

LAW OF PROPERTY ACT 1925

25. Power to postpone sale. — (1) A power to postpone sale shall, in the case of every trust for sale of land, be implied unless a contrary intention appears.

(2) Where there is a power to postpone the sale, then (subject to any express direction to the contrary in the instrument, if any, creating the trust for sale) the trustees for sale shall not be liable in any way for postponing the sale, in the exercise of their discretion, for any indefinite period; nor shall a purchaser of a legal estate be concerned in any case with any directions respecting the postponement of a sale.

(3) The foregoing provisions of this section apply whether the trust for sale is created before or after the commencement or by virtue of this Act.

(4) Where a disposition or settlement coming into operation after the commencement of this Act contains a trust either to retain or sell land the same shall be construed as a trust to sell the land with power to postpone the sale.

In *Re Rooke* [1953] Ch 716, [1953] 2 All ER 110, the testator directed his trustees to sell his farm "as soon as possible after my death", the proceeds of sale to fall into residue. In spite of the fact that the will contained an express power to retain "investments" not authorised by law, HARMAN J, held that the earlier direction constituted a "contrary intention" under section 25 (1) as regards the farm[15].

In *Re Mayo* [1943] Ch 302, [1943] 2 All ER 440, an application was made by the testator's son, one of three trustees holding land on

---

[13] See also *Re Ryder and Steadman's Contract* [1927] 2 Ch 62; *Re Beaumont's Settled Estates* [1937] 2 All ER 353; *Re Sharpe's Deed of Release* [1939] Ch 51, [1938] 3 All ER 449; (1928) 65 LJ News 294; (1929) 67 LJ News 24, 44.

[14] Cheshire, pp. 200–202, 227; M & W, pp. 365–371; MM, pp. 176–179; H & M pp. 288–291.

[15] Referring to *Scriven v Sandom* (1862) 2 John & H 743; *Re Doherty-Waterhouse* [1918] 2 Ch 269; *Re Smith* [1896] 1 Ch 171; *Re Ball* (1930) 74 Sol Jo 298. See also *Re Atkins' Will Trusts* [1974] 1 WLR 761, [1974] 2 All ER 1, p. 312, post.

statutory trusts for sale, asking the court to exercise its discretion under the Law of Property Act 1925, section 30[16] to order a sale. The other two trustees were not willing to agree to sell.

SIMONDS J, made the order, saying: "The result of the residuary devise, having regard to the provisions of section 36 of the Settled Land Act 1925, was that the property was held on trust for sale, but, superadded to that trust, there is a statutory power of postponement. It appears to me that the judicial discretion conferred by section 30 of the Law of Property Act 1925, must be exercised in the same way as the discretion which is exercisable by the court in the case of an instrument containing an express trust for sale. The trust for sale will prevail, unless all three trustees agree in exercising the power to postpone. The principle is established by *Re Roth* ((1896) 74 LT 50), and *Re Hilton* ([1909] 2 Ch 548). Here there is no suggestion of mala fides on the part of the testator's son, who claims that the sale should not be postponed. If that were established, the position would be different, but in the present case I think that the son is reasonable in asking for the property to be sold. It has been urged that the same considerations should influence the court as those by which it would have been influenced before 1925 on applications under the Partition Acts. I do not think that the analogy is in any way of assistance. Here there is an express trust for sale imposed by the statute with a power to postpone the sale. I cannot exercise the discretion in any other way than I should have exercised it if there had been an express trust for sale, with a power of postponement, in the will. I must direct the trustees to concur with the testator's son in taking all necessary steps for the sale of the property."

B. Management and Sale

i. SETTLED LAND ACT POWERS GIVEN TO TRUSTEES FOR SALE

LAW OF PROPERTY ACT 1925

28. Powers of management, &c. conferred on trustees for sale. — (1) Trustees for sale shall, in relation to land ... and to the proceeds of sale, have all the powers of a tenant for life and the trustees of a settlement under the Settled Land Act, 1925[17], including in relation to the land the powers of management conferred by that Act during a

---

[16] See p. 207, post.

[17] S.L.A. 1925, pp. 264, et seq., post; the question arises whether the powers of the trustees for sale are indefeasible like those of a tenant for life under S.L.A. 1925, s. 106, p. 265, post. Apart from the possibility of the powers being restricted by the imposition of a requirement of consents to a sale under L.P.A. 1925, s. 26, p. 205, post, it would appear that they are. See *Re Davies' Will Trusts*, [1932] 1 Ch 530, holding that a life interest to a nephew, "so long as he shall reside upon and assist in the management of the ... farm", would not be forfeited by the exercise of powers inconsistent with such condition. The decision related to statutory trusts under L.P.A. 1925, s. 35 but there appears to be no reason why the powers given to the trustees should not be irreducible powers like those of the tenant for life under a settlement; [1978] Conv 229 (P. Smith).

minority[18]: [and where by statute settled land is or becomes vested in the trustees of the settlement upon the statutory trusts, such trustees and their successors in office shall also have all the additional or larger powers (if any) conferred by the settlement on the tenant for life, statutory owner, or trustees of the settlement[19]], and (subject to any express trust to the contrary) all capital money arising under the said powers shall, unless paid or applied for any purpose authorised by the Settled Land Act, 1925[20], be applicable in the same manner as if the money represented proceeds of sale arising under the trust for sale.

All land acquired under this subsection shall be conveyed to the trustees on trust for sale.

The powers conferred by this subsection shall be exercised with such consents (if any) as would have been required on a sale under the trust for sale[1], and when exercised shall operate to overreach any equitable interests or powers which are by virtue of this Act or otherwise made to attach to the net proceeds of sale as if created by a trust affecting those proceeds[2].

(2) Subject to any direction to the contrary in the disposition on trust for sale in the settlement of the proceeds of sale, the net rents and profits of the land until sale, after keeping down costs of repairs and insurance and other outgoings shall be paid or applied, except so far as any part thereof may be liable to be set aside as capital money under the Settled Land Act, 1925, in like manner as the income of investments representing the purchase money would be payable or applicable if a sale had been made and the proceeds had been duly invested.

ii. POWERS OF THE TENANT FOR LIFE UNDER THE SETTLED LAND ACT 1925[3]

SETTLED LAND ACT 1925

38. Power of sale and exchange. — A tenant for life —
   (i) May sell the settled land, or any part thereof, or any easement, right or privilege of any kind over or in relation to the land; and
   (iii) May make an exchange of the settled land, or any part thereof, or of any easement, right, or privilege of any kind, whether or not newly created, over or in relation to the settled land, or any part thereof, for other land, or for any easement, right or privilege of any kind, whether or not newly created, over or in relation to other land, including an exchange in consideration of money paid for equality of exchange[4].

---

[18] S.L.A. 1925, s. 26, p. 263, post; s. 102.
[19] The words in square brackets were added by L.P. (A.) A. 1926, Sch.
[20] E.g., for certain improvements, p. 278, post.
[1] L.P.A. 1925, s. 26, p. 205, post.
[2] L.P.A. 1925, s. 2 (1) (ii), p. 190, ante.
[3] See the whole of S.L.A. 1925, Part II.
[4] For further details concerning the powers of sale and exchange, see ss. 39, 40.

41. Power to lease for ordinary or building or mining or forestry purposes. — A tenant for life may lease the settled land, or any part thereof, or any easement, right, or privilege of any kind over or in relation to the land, for any purpose whatever, whether involving waste or not, for any term not exceeding —

(i) In case of a building lease, nine hundred and ninety-nine years;

(ii) In case of a mining lease, one hundred years;

(iii) In case of a forestry lease, nine hundred and ninety-nine years;

(iv) In case of any other lease, fifty years[5].

51. Power to grant options. — (1) A tenant for life may at any time, either with or without consideration, grant by writing an option to purchase or take a lease of the settled land, or any part thereof, or any easement, right, or privilege over or in relation to the same at a price or rent fixed at the time of the granting of the option[6].

(2) Every such option shall be made exercisable within an agreed number of years not exceeding ten.

71. Power to raise money by mortgage. — (1) Where money is required for any of the following purposes namely:—

(i) Discharging an incumbrance on the settled land or part thereof;

(ii) Paying for any improvement authorised by this Act or by the settlement;

(iii) Equality of exchange;

(vi) Redeeming a compensation rentcharge in respect of the extinguishment of manorial incidents and affecting the settled land;

(vii) Commuting any additional rent made payable on the conversion of a perpetually renewable leasehold interest into a long term;

(viii) Satisfying any claims for compensation on the conversion of a perpetually renewable leasehold interest into a long term by any officer, solicitor, or other agent of the lessor in respect of fees or remuneration which would have been payable by the lessee or under-lessee on any renewal;

(ix) Payment of the costs of any transaction authorised by this section or either of the two last preceding sections;

the tenant for life may raise the money so required, on the security of the settled land, or of any part thereof, by a legal mortgage, and the money so raised shall be capital money for that purpose, and may be paid or applied accordingly.

---

[5] For further details concerning the power of leasing, see ss. 42–48 [1979] Conv 258 (M. Dockray.).

[6] *Re Morgan's Lease* [1972] Ch 1, [1971] 2 All ER 235.

iii.   DELEGATION

LAW OF PROPERTY ACT 1925

29.   Delegation of powers of management by trustees for sale. — (1) The powers of and incidental to leasing, accepting surrenders of leases and management, conferred on trustees for sale whether by this Act or otherwise, may, until sale of the land, be revocably delegated from time to time, by writing, signed by them, to any person of full age (not being merely an annuitant) for the time being beneficially entitled in possession to the net rents and profits of the land during his life or for any less period: and in favour of a lessee such writing shall, unless the contrary appears, be sufficient evidence that the person named therein is a person to whom the powers may be delegated, and the production of such writing shall, unless the contrary appears, be sufficient evidence that the delegation has not been revoked.

(2) Any power so delegated shall be exercised only in the names and on behalf of the trustees delegating the power.

(3) The persons delegating any power under this section shall not, in relation to the exercise or purported exercise of the power, be liable for the acts or defaults of the person to whom the power is delegated, but that person shall, in relation to the exercise of the power by him, be deemed to be in the position and to have the duties and liabilities of a trustee.

(4) Where, at the commencement of this Act, an order made under section seven of the Settled Land Act, 1884, is in force, the person on whom any power is thereby conferred shall, while the order remains in force, exercise such power in the names and on behalf of the trustees for sale in like manner as if the power had been delegated to him under this section[7].

C.   General Powers for the Benefit of the Settled Land

SETTLED LAND ACT 1925

64.   General power for the tenant for life to effect any transaction under an order of the court. — (1) Any transaction affecting or concerning the settled land, or any part thereof, or any other land (not being a transaction otherwise authorised by this Act, or by the settlement) which in the opinion of the court could be for the benefit of the settled land, or any part thereof, or the persons interested under the settlement, may, under an order of the court, be effected by a tenant for life, if it is one which could have been validly effected by an absolute owner.

(2) In this section "transaction" includes any sale, . . . grant, lease . . . or other disposition, and any purchase or other acquisition, and

---

[7] Cheshire, p. 201, n. 2; M & W, pp. 294, 369; MM, p. 178.

any covenant, contract, or option, and any application of capital money . . ., and any compromise or other dealing, or arrangement[8] . . .;

This section is applicable both to settlements and trusts for sale[9].

The wide definition of "transaction" has enabled the power given by the section to be exercised in the following situations:

In *Re White-Popham Settled Estates* [1936] Ch 725, [1936] 2 All ER 1486, approval was given to a scheme for paying off debts incurred in keeping up the estate. The Court of Appeal (reversing EVE J) held that the section was wide enough to cover schemes which were for the benefit of persons interested under the settlement as well as those for the benefit of the settled land.

In *Re Scarisbrick Re-Settlement Estates* [1944] Ch 229, [1944] 1 All ER 404, approval was given to a scheme to raise £10,000 out of capital to enable the tenant for life to continue to live in the mansion house.

In *Re Earl of Mount Edgcumbe* [1950] Ch 615, [1950] 2 All ER 242, approval was given to the expenditure of £10,000, being compensation for chattels and heirlooms destroyed by war, upon such furniture and chattels for a rebuilt mansion house as the trustees (other than the tenant for life) thought suitable.

In *Re Rycroft's Settlement* [1962] Ch 263, [1961] 3 All ER 581, intended leases were held to be outside the statutory powers of the tenant for life, and WILBERFORCE J, said: at p. 273 "Therefore it must either be discarded altogether or it must be brought forward by means of some individual scheme justified on its merits and sanctioned by the court, either under the general provisions of section 64 of this Act, or . . . the rather more special provisions which apply to building leases contained in section 46."

This section also enables the court to approve on behalf of those who, because minor, incompetent or unborn, cannot consent to schemes which adjust beneficial interests under a settlement[10], where the object of the adjustment is to reduce liability to taxation. Its jurisdiction is wider than that of the Trustee Act 1925, section 57[11]. However, the Variation of Trusts Act 1958, section 1 gives the court power to approve an "arrangement" varying the trusts or the powers of the trustees on behalf of persons covered by the section: this section is now most commonly used for the ordinary case of adjustment or re-distribution of capital for the purpose of reducing liability to taxation[12]. If the 1958 Act does not apply to a particular case, and if the settlement includes land, Settled Land Act 1925, section 64 may be used.

---

[8] Sub-s. 2 has been amended by Settled Land and Trustee Acts (Court's General Powers) Act 1943, s. 2. See also s. 1.

[9] *Re Simmons* [1956] Ch 125, [1955] 3 All ER 818.

[10] *Re Downshire Settled Estates* [1953] Ch 218, [1953] 1 All ER 103.

[11] *Chapman v Chapman* [1954] AC 429, [1954] 1 All ER 798.

[12] H & M chap. 23; Snell, pp. 231–235; M & B (T) chap. 16; Harris, *Variation of Trusts* (1975).

VI.　Capital Money

A.　Rights and Duties of Purchasers

LAW OF PROPERTY ACT 1925

27.　Purchaser not to be concerned with the trusts of the proceeds of sale which are to be paid to two or more trustees or to a trust corporation. — (1) A purchaser of a legal estate from trustees for sale shall not be concerned with the trusts affecting the proceeds of sale of land subject to a trust for sale (whether made to attach to such proceeds by virtue of this Act or otherwise), or affecting the rents and profits of the land until sale, whether or not those trusts are declared by the same instrument by which the trust for sale is created.

(2) Notwithstanding anything to the contrary in the instrument (if any) creating a trust for sale of land or in the settlement of the net proceeds, the proceeds of sale or other capital money shall not be paid to or applied by the direction of fewer than two persons as trustees for sale, except where the trustee is a trust corporation, but this subsection does not affect the right of a sole personal representative as such to give valid receipts for, or direct the application of, proceeds of sale or other capital money, nor, except where capital money arises on the transaction, render it necessary to have more than one trustee[13].

B.　Investment

LAW OF PROPERTY ACT 1925

28.　Powers of management, &c., conferred on trustees for sale. — (1), (2), pp. 199–200, ante.

The Settled Land Act 1925, section 73 gives a list of investments or other authorised applications of capital money under the Act[14]. There are 21 such headings, of which the most important are:

(i) In investment in Government securities, or in other securities in which the trustees of the settlement are by the settlement or by law authorised to invest trust money of the settlement;

(ii) In discharge, purchase, or redemption of incumbrances affecting the whole estate the subject of the settlement . . .

(iii) In payment for any improvement authorised by this Act;

(xi–xii) In purchase of land in fee simple, or of leasehold land held for sixty years or more unexpired at the time of purchase, or with or without mines and minerials; or mines and minerals separately, convenient to be held or worked with the settled land;

(xxi) In any other mode authorised by the settlement with respect to money produced by the sale of the settled land.

---

[13] Sub-s. 2 was substituted by L.P. (A.) A. 1926, s. 7 and Sch. See also T.A. 1925, s. 14.
[14] See also Coal Mining (Subsidence) Act 1957, s. 11 (7); Housing (Financial Provisions) Act 1958, s. 35 (3); Leasehold Reform Act 1967, s. 6 (5), Sch. 2., para. 9.

The Trustee Investments Act 1961 gives wider powers of investment to trustees. In short, it allows trustees to divide the fund into two parts "equal in value at the time of the division" and to invest one part in "narrower-range" investments (those falling within Parts I and II of the First Schedule, and consisting of a modernised form of the old trustee investments); and the other part in "wider-range" investments (those falling within Part III and permitting investment in ordinary shares of companies quoted on a recognised stock exchange[15], having a paid up share capital of at least one million pounds, and which have in each of the immediately preceding five years paid a dividend). The Act should be consulted for further details[16].

In *Re Wakeman* [1945] Ch 177, [1945] 1 All ER 421, UTHWATT J, held that trustees for sale who sold *all* the land which was subject to the trust for sale did not have power to apply the proceeds of sale in the purchase of land. Such a purchase would not be an authorised investment for ordinary trustees; and the trustees in *Re Wakeman*, having sold all the land, could not rely upon Law of Property Act 1925, section 28 because they were no longer "persons holding land on trust for sale", and therefore not trustees for sale[17]. In *Re Wellsted's Will Trusts* [1949] Ch 296, the Court of Appeal held that trustees for sale who do retain some land may, under section 28, apply the proceeds of sale of land, and investments traceable to such proceeds, in the purchase of land; and COHEN LJ, desired "to reserve the question of what the position would be if at the time when the question of investment arose no land was held upon the trusts of the settlement"[18].

VII. Consents to Sale

LAW OF PROPERTY ACT 1925

26. Consents to the execution of a trust for sale. — (1) If the consent of more than two persons is by the disposition made requisite to the execution of a trust for sale of land, then, in favour of a purchaser, the consent of any two of such persons to the execution of the trust or to the exercise of any statutory or other powers vested in the trustees for sale shall be deemed sufficient.

(2) Where the person whose consent to the execution of any such trust or power is expressed to be required in a disposition is not sui juris or becomes subject to disability, his consent shall not, in favour of a purchaser, be deemed to be requisite to the execution of the trust or the exercise of the power; but the trustees shall, in any such case, obtain the separate consent of the parent or testamentary or other

---

[15] As defined by Prevention of Frauds (Investments) Act 1958.
[16] H & M pp. 456–466; Snell, pp. 206–217; M & B (T) pp. 477–489.
[17] L.P.A. 1925, s. 205 (1) (xxix) p. 192, ante.
[18] At p. 319, Lord GREENE MR, analysed L.P.A. 1925, s. 28 in detail and considered some of the difficulties to which it gives rise. See also *Re Gray* [1927] 1 Ch 242; *Re Smith* [1930] 1 Ch 88.

guardian of an infant or of the receiver (if any) of a person suffering from mental disorder[19].

(3) infra.

28. Powers of management, &c., conferred on trustees for sale. — (1) p. 199, ante.

30. Powers of court where trustees for sale refuse to exercise powers. — p. 207, post.

In *Re Inns* [1947] Ch 576, [1947] 2 All ER 308 there was an application by a widow under the Inheritance (Family Provision) Act 1938, section 1 for an increased provision from her deceased husband's very substantial estate. The widow argued that it was the testator's intention that she should reside during widowhood in a luxurious mansion "Springfield" which was expensive to run and would consume more than the financial provision made for her. The house was held on trust for sale, but could only be sold with the consent both of the widow and of the Stevenage Urban District Council, to whom the house was to be offered, on the widow's remarriage or death, for use as a hospital, with £10,000 in addition for maintenance and equipment if they accepted the gift.

WYNN-PARRY J refused to hold, on the facts, that the financial provision for the widow was unreasonable, but at no stage was doubt cast upon the validity of the requirement of the consent of the widow and of the Council. WYNN-PARRY J said, at p. 582:

"After an exhaustive consideration of all the circumstances I come to the conclusion that while, if I had been sitting in the testator's armchair, I might well have avoided tying up 'Springfield' so that only the plaintiff's consent to its sale in her lifetime would have been required, and I might well have provided a somewhat larger fund than the 85,000*l* in view of the size of the estate; yet, bearing in mind the principles upon which I am directed to proceed by the authorities which I regard as binding on me, and with which I am respectfully in agreement, I cannot bring myself to the conclusion that what has been provided is so little as to be unreasonable. From the plaintiff's point of view the provisions regarding 'Springfield' are unfortunate in that neither she nor the trustees can bring about a sale during her lifetime. . . ."

VIII.   The Beneficiaries under a Trust for Sale

A.   Consultation

LAW OF PROPERTY ACT 1925

26. Consents to the execution of a trust for sale. — (3)[20] Trustees for sale shall so far as practicable consult the persons of full age for the

---

[19] As amended by Mental Health Act 1959, s. 149, Sch. 7, Part I.
[20] Substituted for the original subsection by L.P. (A.) A. 1926, Sch.; *Waller v Waller* [1967] 1 WLR 451, [1967] 1 All ER 305; *Caunce v Caunce* [1969] 1 WLR 286, [1969] 1 All ER 722.

time being beneficially interested in possession in the rents and profits of the land until sale, and shall, so far as consistent with the general interest of the trust, give effect to the wishes of such persons, or, in the case of dispute, of the majority (according to the value of their combined interests) of such persons, but a purchaser shall not be concerned to see that the provisions of this subsection have been complied with.

In the case of a trust for sale, not being a trust for sale created by or in pursuance of the powers conferred by this or any other Act, this subsection shall not apply unless the contrary intention appears in the disposition creating the trust[1].

B. Application to Court for Exercise of Powers

LAW OF PROPERTY ACT 1925

30. Powers of court where trustees for sale refuse to exercise powers. — If the trustees for sale refuse to sell or to exercise any of the powers conferred by either of the last two sections[2], or any requisite consent cannot be obtained, any person interested[3] may apply to the court for a vesting or other order for giving effect to the proposed transaction or for an order directing the trustees for sale to give effect thereto, and the court may make such order as it thinks fit[4].

The leading case for many years on the exercise of the court's jurisdiction was *Jones v Challenger* [1961] 1 QB 176, [1960] 1 All

---

[1] I.e. the rule relating to consultation of the beneficiaries applies to statutory trusts for sale. In an express trust for sale, the trustees are bound by the testator's wishes. If there are no special provisions, apart from the trust to sell, the trustees may, if they wish, postpone the sale, (L.P.A. 1925, s. 25), but unless they all agree to do so, they must sell, *Re Mayo* [1943] Ch 302, p. 198, ante; see also *Bull v Bull* [1955] 1 QB 234, 238–239, [1955] 1 All ER 253 at 256. See (1973) 117 Sol Jo 518 (A. M. Prichard).

[2] L.P.A. 1925, s. 28, p. 199, ante s. 29, p. 202, ante.

[3] *Stevens v Hutchinson* [1953] Ch 299 at 305, [1953] 1 All ER 699 at 701 ("a person interested in some proprietary right under the trust for sale" per UPJOHN J.); *Re Solomon* [1967] Ch 573, [1966] 3 All ER 255.

[4] *Rawlings v Rawlings* [1964] P 398, [1964] 2 All ER 804; *Rivett v Rivett* (1966) 200 Estates Gazette 858; *Cullingford v Cullingford* (1967) 204 Estates Gazette 471; *Barclay v Barclay* [1970] 2 QB 677, [1970] 2 All ER 676; *Re John's Assignment Trusts* [1970] 1 WLR 955, [1970] 2 All ER 210; *Re Hardy's Trust* (1970) 114 Sol Jo 864; *Jackson v Jackson* [1971] 1 WLR 1539, [1971] 3 All ER 774, (1971) 87 LQR 153 (P.V.B.); *Burke v Burke,* [1974] 1 WLR 1063, [1974] 2 All ER 944, *Mayes v Mayes* [1969] EGD 501; *Browne v Pritchard* [1975] 1 WLR 1366, [1975] 3 All ER 721; *Hayward v Hayward* (1974) 237 Estates Gazette 577; *Williams v Williams* [1976] Ch 278, [1977] 1 All ER 28; *Jones v Jones* [1977] 1 WLR 438, [1977] 2 All ER 231, (1972) 36 Conv (NS) 99, [1978] Conv 301 (J. G. Miller), p. 209, post; (1977) 93 LQR 176 (M. W. Bryan). Cf. *Re 90 Thornhill Rd., Tolworth, Surrey,* [1970] Ch 261, [1969] 3 All ER 685 (sale not ordered under S.L.A. 1925, s. 93, where joint tenants for life disagreed as to the exercise of the power of sale). For another remedy available in the husband and wife situation, see Domestic Violence and Matrimonial Proceedings Act 1976 ss. 3, 4 (4), p. 234, post. For cases where the trustee in bankruptcy asks for an order under s. 30, see *Re Solomon* [1967] Ch 573, [1966] 3 All ER 255; *Re Turner* [1974] 1 WLR 1556, [1975] 1 All ER 5; *Re McCarthy* [1975] 1 WLR 807, [1975] 2 All ER 857; *Re Densham* [1975] 1 WLR 1519, [1975] 3 All ER 726; *Re A Debtor* (No. 24 of 1971) [1976] 1 WLR 952, [1976] 2 All ER 1010; *Re Bailey* [1977] 1 WLR 278, [1977] 2 All ER 26; p. 213, post.

ER 785. A husband and wife had contributed equally to the purchase of a joint tenancy in the matrimonial home. The wife deserted the husband who remained in occupation. An order for sale was made on the wife's application. DEVLIN LJ said at p. 183:

"In the case we have to consider, the house was acquired as the matrimonial home. That was the purpose of the joint tenancy and, for so long as that purpose was still alive, I think that the right test to be applied would be that in *Re Buchanan-Wollaston's Conveyance* [1939] Ch 738. But with the end of the marriage, that purpose was dissolved and the primacy of the duty to sell was restored. No doubt there is still a discretion. If the husband wanted time to obtain alternative accommodation, the sale could be postponed for that purpose, but he has not asked for that. If he was prepared to buy out the wife's interest, it might be proper to allow it, but he has not accepted a suggestion that terms of that sort should be made. In these circumstances, there is no way in which the discretion can properly be exercised except by an order to sell, because, since they cannot now both enjoy occupation of the property, that is the only way whereby the beneficiaries can derive equal benefit from their investment, which is the primary object of the trust."

Wolstenholme and Cherry, *Conveyancing Statutes* (13th edn. 1972), vol. 1, pp. 89–90:

"The power of the court to make an order under this section is exercisable in accordance with general equitable principles, e.g., in the same way as it exercises its discretion where there is an express trust for sale (see *Re Roth* (1896) 74 LT 50; *Re Hilton* [1909] 2 Ch 548), i.e., it will generally order a sale. (*Re Mayo* [1943] Ch 302; *Jones v Challenger* [1961] 1 QB 176; also *Re Steed's Will Trusts* [1960] Ch 407 and *Barclay v Barclay* [1970] 2 QB 677 CA). But regard will be had to all the circumstances of the case and an order will be made only when it is right and proper that it should be made in the particular circumstances (*Re Buchanan-Wollaston's Conveyance* [1939] Ch 738). Thus the court will not aid one of the parties to break his contractual obligations (same case; also *Re Hyde's Conveyance* (1952) 102 LJ 58).

In practice, the primary purpose of purchases of land by co-owners (who necessarily become trustees for sale), will mostly not be sale at all but, for example, the provision of a home, often but not always matrimonial. Even though no contractual obligations are undertaken, so long as that purpose subsists, a sale will *not* be ordered, particularly if an innocent party would be deprived of a home (see *Bull v Bull* [1955] 1 QB 234 and *Bedson v Bedson* [1965] 2 QB 666). But when that purpose is no longer supportable, e.g., because the marriage between the co-owners has ended in divorce or breakdown, the court will be prepared to order a sale (see *Jones v Challenger* [1961] 1 QB 176; *Rawlings v Rawlings* [1964] P 398; and *Re Solomon* [1967] Ch 573). However, even in such a case, where the property concerned is the matrimonial home, it is not clear that the court will order a sale on the application of a husband in desertion. In *Jackson v Jackson* [1970] 3 All ER 854, Plowman J did order a sale, taking the view that the inability of a husband in desertion to turn the wife out of the matrimonial home was commensurate with his duty to maintain her and that, in the case, the cost to the husband of allowing his wife to remain in the matrimonial home was far in excess of anything he could be ordered to pay by way of maintenance in matrimonial proceedings. Nevertheless, in *Re Hardy's Trust* (1970) 114 Sol Jo 864 (decided one week later than *Jackson v Jackson*, (supra, which was not apparently cited), Stamp J refused to order a sale unless and until the husband provided some alternative accommodation for the wife who had a right to have a roof over her head provided by the husband.

In *Re John's Assignment Trusts* [1970] 1 WLR 955, another case where the matrimonial home was jointly owned but the parties had divorced, Goff J held that this section did not enable the court to order the grant of a tenancy to one of the parties, although there was jurisdiction to authorise such a grant, on such terms as might be agreed between the parties, notwithstanding their fiduciary capacities."

The exercise of the court's jurisdiction has become dominated in recent years by questions arising out of the matrimonial situation; and particularly by the availability of a much wider discretionary power in the court to deal with matrimonial property, in the context of divorce, nullity or judicial separation under the Matrimonial Causes Act 1973[5].

[1978] Conv 301 at pp. 302–306 (J. G. Miller)

"The presence of children
In *Rawlings v Rawlings* Salmon LJ expressed the view, obiter, that the presence of children for whom the property might continue to provide a home, might justify the postponement of a sale. He said[6]:

'If there were young children the position would be different. One of the purposes of the trust would no doubt have been to provide a home for them, and whilst that purpose still existed a sale would not generally be ordered. But when these children are grown up and the marriage is dead, the purposes of the trust have failed.'

This factor was taken into account by Goff J in *Mayes v Mayes*[7] when he refused a wife's application for an order for sale, but in *Burke v Burke*[8] the Court of Appeal appeared, at first sight at least, to take a narrower view of the purpose of a matrimonial home. In that case Buckley LJ acknowledged that in considering whether or not to postpone sale the court must have regard to the situation of both beneficial owners and personal problems affecting those beneficiaries relevant to that question. However, the interests of the children

---

[5] See *Fielding v Fielding* [1977] 1 WLR 1146 n., [1978] 1 All ER 267.
[6] [1964] P 398, 419.
[7] [1969] *EGD* 50.
[8] [1974] 1 WLR 1063.

in that case were only incidentally to be taken into consideration, namely, only in so far as they affected the equities of the matter between the two spouses as beneficial owners. He emphasised that '. . . it is not . . . right to treat this case as though the husband was obliged to make provision for his children by agreeing to retain the property unsold. To do this is . . . to confuse with a problem relating to property considerations which are relevant to maintenance[9].'

The possibility of future variation

However, the disposition of the matrimonial home on the breakdown of a marriage will frequently be the dominating factor in the financial arrangements to be made. A point which seemed to remain open after *Jackson v Jackson*[10] was the extent to which it was permissible for the court to take into account the possibility of a variation of property rights on a subsequent divorce in deciding whether or not to order a sale. Even prior to the introduction of the present wide powers of property adjustment by the M.P.P.A. 1970, the court had power to vary an *ante-* or *post*-nuptial settlement on the granting of a decree of divorce or nullity[11]. In *Rawlings v Rawlings*[12] Harman LJ took the view that this possibility was not a matter which should be allowed to affect the exercise of the court's discretion, but in *Bedson v Bedson*[13] both Lord Denning and Russell LJ thought that it was. In *Jackson v Jackson*, where there was in any event little likelihood of divorce proceedings, no mention was made of this factor, but the desirability of maintaining the status quo until the whole financial position of the parties can be considered, at least when proceedings are pending, was recognised by the Law Commission in Working Paper No. 42 on Family Property[14].

The point became of greater significance when the courts acquired much wider powers of property adjustment on divorce, nullity and judicial separation. In *Brown v Brown*[15] Lord Denning emphasised that it was now undesirable that an application for sale should be dealt with under section 17 alone. Such an application ought to be heard together with applications under section 4 of the Matrimonial Proceedings and Property Act 1970[16] whereby the court dealt with the whole matter and could make any order for transfer of property, payment of money or for securing any payment, which might be just in all the circumstances. In *Williams v Williams*[17] the Court of Appeal took the same view in relation to applications under section 30. Lord Denning said[18]:

---

[9] [1974] 1 WLR 1063, 1067.
[10] [1971] 1 WLR 1539.
[11] Matrimonial Causes Act 1965, s. 17 (1).
[12] [1964] P 348, 415.
[13] [1965] 2 QB 666, 679 and 697 respectively.
[14] P. 112.
[15] (1974) 5 Fam Law 51.
[16] Now s. 24 of the Matrimonial Causes Act 1973.
[17] [1976] Ch 278.
[18] Ibid, at p. 286.

'An application about a matrimonial home should not be restricted to section 30 of the Law of Property Act 1925. In view of the wide powers of transfer and adjustment which are available under the new matrimonial property legislation it seems to me that the applications should be made to the Family Division under the relevant provisions. If taken out in another division, they should be transferred to a judge of the Family Division.'

In *Williams v Williams* it was some time after the marriage of the parties had been terminated by a decree absolute of divorce that the former husband applied in the Chancery Division under section 30 for an order that the wife should concur in the sale of the former matrimonial home which was vested in their joint names and was occupied by the former wife and four sons of the marriage. Foster J rejected the wife's argument that sale should be postponed so that, in particular, the youngest son could remain in the same area until he had finished his schooling. He ordered a sale so that the husband should have his money even though it meant that the wife would have to leave.

In the Court of Appeal Lord Denning described the approach exemplified by *Jones v Challenger* and *Burke v Burke* as outdated and said[19]:

'When judges are dealing with the matrimonial home, they nowadays have great regard to the fact that the house is bought as a home in which the family is to be brought up. It is not treated as property to be sold nor as an investment to be realised for cash. That was emphasised by this court in the recent case of *Browne* (formerly *Pritchard*) *v Pritchard* [1975] 1 WLR 1366. The court, in executing the trust should regard the primary object as being to provide a home and not a sale. Steps should be taken to preserve it as a home for the remaining partner and children, but giving the outgoing partner such compensation, by way of a charge or being bought out, as is reasonable in the circumstances.'

He considered that it would not be proper at this stage to order the sale of the house unless it were shown that alternative accommodation could be provided at a cheaper rate and some capital released. That had not been done. The order for sale was set aside and the matter remitted for further consideration by a judge of the Family Division when an application had been taken out under the matrimonial property legislation. [sic].

On the other hand, in the later case of *Bigg v Bigg*[20] Court of Appeal unheld an order for sale under section 30 and considered it unnecessary to await divorce proceedings when the court could exercise its powers of property adjustment. In that case the parties had married in 1967 when the husband, then a bachelor, was over 60 and the wife, who had been previously married, was in her fifties. They purchased a house in Hampshire in joint names though the wife provided the larger portion

---

[19] Ibid, at p. 285.
[20] (1976) 6 Fam Law 56.

of the purchase price. Some three or four years later the wife purchased a house in Minorca for the benefit of her health and with a view to them both retiring there in due course. However, the marriage subsequently broke down and the wife went to live there herself. She lived on the interest from her capital and sought an order for the sale of the Hampshire house. The parties had lived apart for two years, but divorce proceedings had not been started. Lord Denning rejected the argument that the right approach was to look forward to the time when there was a divorce when the court, under the Matrimonial Causes Act 1973, might let the husband stay in the house. It was not necessary for the husband to stay in the house in order to keep a roof over his head. He would have sufficient capital (some £5,000–£6,000) and income to be able to find a niche somewhere and would be able to move his driving school which he had carried on from the house. There was no reason why the wife should not have her small amount of capital released. Lawton L.J. said that if a divorce was likely it was wise and convenient to adjourn section 30 proceedings, but the judge had this factor in mind and said so.

Some conclusions may now be drawn from these decisions. First, if divorce proceedings have already been commenced the position is covered by the statements in *Williams v Williams* and the disposition of the matrimonial home should not be considered in proceedings under section 17 or section 30 alone but in conjunction with applications under the Matrimonial Causes Act 1973. However, it must be remembered that if a party has remarried after divorce without making an application under section 24 of the Matrimonial Causes Act then no application by that party under that section will then be possible[1]. If no application is possible under the Matrimonial Causes Act for this or any other reason, then obviously the disposition of the former matrimonial home will have to be dealt with under section 17 or section 30 alone.

Secondly, if no basis for proceedings for divorce or judicial separation yet exists, or if the immediate possibility of divorce is uncertain, the court should, in proceedings under section 17 or section 30 bear in mind the possibility of the court exercising its powers under the Matrimonial Causes Act in favour of a party or the children in due course. If an adjustment of property rights which would safeguard occupation of the former home is likely, then disturbance of the status quo would not seem justified simply to give effect to existing strict property rights. Two factors may be relevant in this context. First, in cases like *Bigg v Bigg*, where the parties are not young, it is in any event by no means certain that divorce proceedings will be started at all or at any rate in the immediate future. This is obviously something that has to be taken into account for if there is no real prospect of the

---

[1] S. 28. It is sufficient for an application to be commenced before remarriage and it is not also necessary for it to be adjudicated upon before remarriage: *Jackson v Jackson* [1973] Fam 99, [1973] 2 All ER 395. The Court now has power to order sale of property under Matrimonial Causes Act 1973, s. 24, and without specific application under M.W.P.A. 1882, s. 17 or L.P.A. 1925, s. 30. Practice Note [1980] 1 WLR 4 Fam.

court being able to consider the disposition of the matrimonial home under the Matrimonial Causes Act then it will have to deal with the matter under section 17 or section 30. A second factor, however, is the extent to which protection seems called for in any event. An important perhaps crucial factor in *Bigg v Bigg* seems to have been that even under the Matrimonial Causes Act it was unlikely that the trust for sale would have been postponed so as to allow the husband to remain in occupation. Unless one party and/or the children seem to merit protection which might be more effectively provided in proceedings under the Matrimonial Causes Act, there is no reason why the court should not deal with the matter under section 17 or section 30.''

Different considerations may apply where a trustee in bankruptcy of one spouse seeks an order for the sale of the matrimonial home against the other spouse. In *Re Bailey (A Bankrupt)* (No. 25 of 1975) [1977] 1 WLR 278, [1977] 2 All ER 26, a husband and wife, now divorced, were joint tenants of the former matrimonial home. The husband became bankrupt. His main asset was his half share in the house, the equity of which, after deduction of the mortgage, was worth about £12,000. The wife lived in the house with their 16 year old son, of whom she had custody; he was about to re-sit his O level examinations and had at the same time started on his A level course. The trustee in bankruptcy obtained an order for the sale of the house under section 30 of the Law of Property Act 1925. The wife appealed, claiming that the sale should be postponed until the son's school education was completed. MEGARRY V-C and WALTON J dismissed the appeal. MEGARRY V-C said at p. 279:

"We have had put before us a considerable wealth of authorities, some on bankruptcy, some on the general matrimonial law. The main bankruptcy authorities put before us were *Re Solomon (A Bankrupt)* [1967] Ch 573, [1966] 3 All ER 255; *Re Turner (A Bankrupt)* [1974] 1 WLR 1556, [1975] 1 All ER 5, and *Re Densham (A Bankrupt)* [1975] 1 WLR 1519, [1975] 3 All ER 726. It is a plain from these cases that there is considerable authority in support of the proposition that there is no automatic rule, but that it is the duty of the court to exercise a proper discretion in deciding whether to order a sale or not, and that in exercising that discretion the court is under a duty to consider all the circumstances of the case. . . .

Apart from *Re Densham,* the cases have concerned husband and wife, and the claims of children have not been before the court. In *Burke v Burke* [1974] 1 WLR 1063, [1974] 2 All ER 944, which was a matrimonial case in the Court of Appeal not involving bankruptcy, Buckley LJ at p. 1067 expressed the view that the interests of the children in a husband and wife case were interests which were only incidentally to be taken into consideration, as affecting the equities as between husband and wife: and *Re Densham* applied that view in bankruptcy. Under a trust for sale in which the husband and wife are entitled equally the children, of course, are not beneficiaries. However, it has been forcefully argued before us by Mr. Worsley that that approach has now to be reconsidered in the light of the decision of a different division of the Court of Appeal in *Williams v Williams* [1976] Ch 278, [1977] 1 All ER 28. That, again, was not a bankruptcy case, but a husband and wife case. There, Lord Denning MR emphasised that where a house had been bought as a home for the family to be brought up in, then in disputes between husband and wife as to whether the home should be sold great weight had to be given to the interests of the family as a whole. The decision of the trial judge in that case was said to have gone back to the older view related to property rights, without giving effect to the modern view which requires regard to be paid to the needs of the family as a whole before a sale of the house is ordered. In that case the wife and the four sons were living in the house, the youngest son being only 13.

Let me accept for the purposes of this appeal that the view of one division of the Court of Appeal, based as it was on the approach that the Matrimonial Proceedings and Property Act 1970 and the Matrimonial Causes Act 1973 had transformed the law, has rightly displaced the views of another division of the Court of Appeal in *Burke v Burke* also decided after those statutes had been passed. Assume that, and yet one must bear in mind that these were decisions within the sphere of matrimonial property, concerning the property disposition of the property rights of husband and wife under statutory provisions giving a very wide discretion to the court to adjust those property rights as was thought proper. They were not cases in which matters of commercial obligation arose, as in the case of bankruptcy. In bankruptcy one must, of course, consider the claims of the creditors as asserted through the trustee in bankruptcy. The fact that bankruptcy has a somewhat special position in relation to property rights in a matrimonial home is brought out by two statutes to which Mr. Crystal made reference, namely, the Matrimonial Homes Act 1967, section 2 (5) and the Matrimonial Causes Act 1973, section 39. I do not propose to read these sections; but they make it plain that bankruptcy has, in relation to the matrimonial home, its own claim to protection.

I return in a sense to the point where I started. There is a discretion in this court which has to be exercised on proper grounds. One has to weigh, on the one hand, the claims of the trustee in bankruptcy and the creditors; against those, one must put into the scales all that can properly be put there on behalf of the other spouse of the marriage and any children. In this case the creditors and the trustee clearly have a strong claim to the realisation of the husband's share in this house, which is the only real asset in the bankruptcy. If the sale is postponed, then it is true that the creditors will, if the assets suffice (as apparently they will), receive the statutory interest; but under section 33 (8) of the Bankruptcy Act 1914 that is unhappily still a mere 4 per cent. So far as the wife is concerned, the sale of this property would give her a substantial capital sum. Her half-share in equity, after discharging the mortgage on the property, would be of the order of some £6,000 or more. As against that, £6,000 is not a very large sum with which to seek some other home, and she would plainly have the difficulties of finding somewhere else to live with her son. So far as the son is concerned, he is not, as I have mentioned, a beneficiary under the trust for sale at all. The evidence about the interference with his educational prospects is very slight. It seems improbable that he would have to move from his school. Other accommodation would be more likely to be obtained within the catchment areas of his school than elsewhere. It is, after all, some 18 months or so before the actual examinations at A-level will have to be taken, and there is nothing to suggest that there are any special circumstances, apart from the inevitable disruption of having to move one's home, that will affect his prospects in education.

Putting these competing interests into the balance on one side and the other, and looking at the facts of the case as a whole, the only conclusion I can reach is that the claims of the wife and the son do not suffice to outweigh the claims of the trustee in bankruptcy to an immediate sale of this house. When I say "immediate sale" I am not suggesting that it should be sold tomorrow. The precise terms of any order will have to be settled after any further submissions by counsel have been heard; but I cannot think that this is a case that in any way justifies postponing the sale until the summer of 1978. Accordingly, I would dismiss the appeal."

IX. Termination of Trusts for Sale

LAW OF PROPERTY ACT 1925

23. Duration of trusts for sale. — Where land has, either before or after the commencement of this Act, become subject to an express or implied trust for sale, such trust shall, so far as regards the safety and protection of any purchaser thereunder, be deemed to be subsisting until the land has been conveyed to or under the direction of the persons interested in the proceeds of sale.

This section applies to sale whether made before or after the commencement of this Act, but operates without prejudice to an order of any court restraining a sale.

X. Registered Land[2]

Title to land subject to a trust for sale must be registered in the name of the trustees for sale (not exceeding four in number), and the purchaser is informed of the necessity to pay capital moneys to at least two trustees for sale or to a trust corporation by entry of a restriction in Form 62[3] (as amended from the statutory form by the Chief Land Registrar[4]).

---

[2] Cheshire, p. 203; M & W, pp. 1072–1073; MM, p. 523; Ruoff and Roper, Chap. 20.
[3] P. 216, post.
[4] Ruoff and Roper, p. 380.

LAND REGISTRATION ACT 1925

74. Notice of trust not to affect registered dealing. — Subject to the provisions of this Act as to settled land, neither the registrar nor any person dealing with a registered estate or charge shall be affected with notice of a trust express, implied or constructive, and references to trusts shall, so far as possible, be excluded from the register.

94. Land held on trust for sale. — (1) Where registered land is subject to a trust for sale, express or implied, whether or not there is power to postpone the sale, the land shall be registered in the names of the trustees for sale.

95. Restriction on number of trustees. — The statutory restrictions affecting the number of persons entitled to hold land on trust for sale and the number of trustees of a settlement apply to registered land[5].

49. Rules to provide for notices of other rights, interests and claims. — (2) p. 128, ante.

58. Power to place restrictions on register. — (3) In the case of joint proprietors the restriction may be to the effect that when the number of proprietors is reduced below a certain specified number no disposition shall be registered except under an order of the court, or of the registrar after inquiry into title, subject to appeal to the court, and, subject to general rules, such an entry under this subsection as may be prescribed, shall be obligatory unless it is shown to the registrar's satisfaction that the joint proprietors are entitled for their own benefit, or can give valid receipts for capital money, or that one of them is a trust corporation.

(5) Rules may be made to enable applications to be made for the entry of restrictions by persons other than the proprietor[6].

LAND REGISTRATION RULES 1925
Statutory Form 62
Entry restraining a disposition by a sole surviving proprietor

No disposition by one proprietor of the land (being the survivor of joint proprietors and not being a trust corporation) under which capital money arises is to be registered except under an order of the registrar or of the court.

QUESTION

Having read so far, would you suppose that an interest under a trust for sale:

(i) passed under a testamentary gift of realty? or of personalty? *Re Newman* [1930] 2 Ch 409; p. 221, post.

---

[5] Trustee Act 1925, s. 34; L.P.A., 1925, s. 27 (2), p. 204, ante; S.L.A. 1925, ss. 18 (1), 94 (1), pp. 256, 279, post.
[6] See L.R.R. 1925, rr. 235, 236.

(ii) came within L.P.A. 1925, s. 40, requiring evidence in writing of contracts concerning an interest in land? *Cooper v Critchley* [1955] Ch 431, [1955] 1 All ER 520; p. 240, post.

(iii) was a minor interest if the legal title is registered? *Elias v Mitchell* [1972] Ch 652, [1972] 2 All ER 153; p. 241, post.

(iv) if in possession, was binding on a purchaser of a legal estate for value with constructive notice? L.P.A. 1925, s. 27 (2); T.A. 1925, s. 14 (1); *Caunce v Caunce* [1969] 1 WLR 286, [1969] 1 All ER 722; p. 230, post.

5. Concurrent Interests After 1925[1]

I. The Scheme of the 1925 Legislation

The sections of the 1925 legislation applicable to concurrent interests are a further manifestation of the basic principles of that legislation. They attempt to simplify conveyancing by presenting to the purchaser a single title, however numerous and complicated the beneficial interests are, and by applying the overreaching principle to beneficial interests. In short, this is achieved by providing that the only form of co-ownership that can exist *at law* is a form of un-severable joint tenancy such as trustees hold. This is held on trust for sale, and every form of *beneficial* co-ownership can only exist behind the trust for sale.

LAW OF PROPERTY ACT 1925

1. Legal estates and equitable interests. — (6) p. 7, ante.

26. Consents to the execution of a trust for sale. — (3) p. 206, ante.

34. Effect of future dispositions to tenants in common. — (1) An undivided share in land shall not be capable of being created except as provided by the Settled Land Act, 1925[2], or as hereinafter mentioned.

(2) Where, after the commencement of this Act, land is expressed to be conveyed to any persons in undivided shares and those persons are of full age, the conveyance shall (notwithstanding anything to the contrary in this Act) operate as if the land had been expressed to be conveyed to the grantees, or, if there are more than four grantees, to the four first named in the conveyance, as joint tenants upon the

---

[1] Cheshire, pp. 210–236; M & W, pp. 391–437; MM, pp. 192–214. For the nature and characteristics of different types of co-ownership, and for the pre-1926 law, see Cheshire 210–220; M & W, pp. 391–407, 421–423, 429–434; MM, pp. 192–199, 202–203, 207–213. The present chapter assumes an understanding of this material.

[2] S.L.A. 1925, s. 36 (1), (2), p. 220, post.

statutory trusts hereinafter mentioned and so as to give effect to the rights of the persons who would have been entitled to the shares had the conveyance operated to create those shares:

Provided that, where the conveyance is made by way of mortgage the land shall vest in the grantees or such four of them as aforesaid for a term of years absolute (as provided by this Act) as joint tenants subject to cesser on redemption in like manner as if the mortgage money had belonged to them on a joint account, but without prejudice to the beneficial interests in the mortgage money and interest.

(3) A devise bequest or testamentary appointment, coming into operation after the commencement of this Act, of land to two or more persons in undivided shares shall operate as a devise bequest or appointment of the land to the trustees (if any) of the will for the purposes of the Settled Land Act, 1925, or, if there are no such trustees, then to the personal representatives of the testator, and in each case (but without prejudice to the rights and powers of the personal representatives for purposes of administration) upon the statutory trusts hereinafter mentioned.

35. Meaning of the Statutory trusts. — p. 189, ante.

36. Joint tenancies. — (1) Where a legal estate (not being settled land)[3] is beneficially limited to or held in trust for any persons as joint tenants, the same shall be held on trust for sale, in like manner as if the persons beneficially entitled were tenants in common, but not so as to sever their joint tenancy in equity.

(2) No severance of a joint tenancy of a legal estate, so as to create a tenancy in common in land, shall be permissible, whether by operation of law or otherwise, but this subsection does not affect the right of a joint tenant to release his interest to the other joint tenants, or the right to sever a joint tenancy in an equitable interest whether or not the legal estate is vested in the joint tenants:

Provided that, where a legal estate (not being settled land) is vested in joint tenants beneficially, and any tenant desires to sever the joint tenancy in equity[4], he shall give to the other joint tenants a notice in writing[5] of such desire or do such other acts or things as would, in the case of personal estate, have been effectual to sever the tenancy in equity, and thereupon under the trust for sale affecting the land the net proceeds of sale, and the net rents and profits until sale, shall be held upon the trusts which would have been requisite for giving effect to the beneficial interests if there had been an actual severance.

---

[3] The definition of settled land is the same as that in S.L.A. 1925, s. 1, p. 248, post. *Re Gaul and Houlston's Contract* [1928] Ch 689.

[4] See *Bedson v Bedson* [1965] 2 QB 666 at 678; *Re Draper's Conveyance* [1969] 1 Ch 486, [1967] 3 All ER 853, p. 222, post; *Burgess v Rawnsley* [1975] Ch 429, [1975] 3 All ER 142, p. 225, post.

[5] *Re 88 Berkeley Road, NW 9* [1971] Ch 648, [1971] 1 All ER 254, (notice properly served by recorded delivery, even if not received by addressee). L.P.A. 1925, s. 196 (4), (1971) 87 L.Q.R. 155.

[Nothing in this Act affects the right of a survivor of joint tenants, who is solely and beneficially interested, to deal with his legal estate as if it were not held on trust for sale.][6]

37.   Rights of husband and wife. — A husband and wife shall, for all purposes of acquisition of any interest in property, under a disposition made or coming into operation after the commencement of this Act, be treated as two persons.

SETTLED LAND ACT 1925

36.   Undivided shares to take effect behind a trust for sale of the land. — (1) If and when, after the commencement of this Act, settled land is held in trust for persons entitled in possession under a trust instrument[7] in undivided shares, the trustees of the settlement (if the settled land is not already vested in them) may require the estate owner in whom the settled land is vested (but in the case of a personal representative subject to his rights and powers for purposes of administration), at the cost of the trust estate, to convey the land to them, or assent to the land vesting in them as joint tenants, and in the meantime the land shall be held on the same trusts as would have been applicable thereto if it had been so conveyed to or vested in the trustees.

(2) If and when the settled land so held in trust in undivided shares is or becomes vested in the trustees of the settlement, the land shall be held by them (subject to any incumbrances affecting the settled land which are secured by a legal mortgage, but freed from any incumbrances affecting the undivided shares or not secured as aforesaid, and from any interests, powers and charges subsisting under the trust instrument which have priority to the trust for the persons entitled to the undivided shares) upon the statutory trusts.

(4) An undivided share in land shall not be capable of being created except under a trust instrument or under the Law of Property Act, 1925, and shall then only take effect behind a trust for sale.

(6) For the purposes of this section land held upon the statutory trusts shall be held upon the trusts and subject to the provisions following, namely, upon trust to sell the same, with power to postpone the sale of the whole or any part thereof, and to stand possessed of the net proceeds of sale, after payment of costs, and of the net rents and profits until sale, after payment of rates, taxes, costs of insurance, repairs, and other outgoings, upon such trusts and subject to such powers and provisions as may be requisite for giving effect to the rights of the persons interested in the settled land, [and the right of a person who, if the land had not been made subject to a trust of sale by virtue of this Act, would have been entitled to an entailed interest in an undivided share in the land, shall be deemed to be a right to a

---

[6] The words in square brackets were added by L.P. (A.) A. 1926, s. 7 and Sch.
[7] P. 252, post.

corresponding entailed interest in the net proceeds of sale attributable to that share[8]].

The scheme of the Act is to subject to a trust for sale all forms of concurrent ownership except for joint owners taking as tenants for life, in which case the land remains settled land[9]. The question arises, however, of the position of a form of concurrent ownership which does not come within the terms of the Law of Property Act 1925, sections 34 and 36[10]. For example, land conveyed in undivided shares to an adult and an infant; or where a tenancy in common exists although the land is not "expressed to be conveyed in undivided shares".

In *Bull v Bull* [1955] 1 QB 234, [1955] 1 All ER 253, land was conveyed to X, the purchase money being paid partly by him and partly by his mother. The Court of Appeal (DENNING, HODSON and PARKER LJJ) treated this as a case of beneficial tenancy in common; the Settled Land Act 1925, section 36 (4) permitted tenancy in common only behind a trust for sale[11].

In *Re Buchanan-Wollaston's Conveyance* [1939] Ch 217 (FARWELL J), *affd*, [1939] Ch 738, a conveyance to purchasers as joint tenants (who provided the purchase money in unequal shares) was treated as coming within the Law of Property Act 1925, section 36 (1), although this does violence to the requirement for the application of that section that the legal estate should be "beneficially limited to . . . persons as joint tenants."

In *Re Kempthorne* [1930] 1 Ch 268[12], the testator, by a will dated 1911, left "all my freehold and copyhold property" to A, and " . . . all my personal estate and effects . . . " to B. He died in 1928, entitled to undivided shares in freehold land and freehold minerals. The Court of Appeal (Lord HANWORTH MR, LAWRENCE and RUSSELL LJJ) held that the undivided shares, being subjected to the statutory trusts by the Law of Property Act 1925, section 36 on 1 January 1926, passed as personalty to B.

A different construction might have been possible if the words of the will had shown an intention to give to A his interests in the freeholds, whatever they might be[13]; and such a construction would be easier to apply if the will were executed after 1925, or, if executed before 1926, was republished by a codicil dated after 1925[14].

---

[8] The words in square brackets were added by L.P. (Entailed Interests) Act 1932, s. 1 (1)

[9] S.L.A. 1925, s. 19 (2), p. 261, post.

[10] (1945) 9 Conv (NS) 37; (1963) 27 Conv (NS) 51 (B. A. Rudden).

[11] A similar situation arises where a matrimonial home, to whose purchase both spouses contribute, is conveyed to one, p. 228, post.

[12] *Re Newman* [1930] 2 Ch 409.

[13] *Re Mellish* [1929] 2 KB 82 n; "All his share and interest in an estate known as the Rushall Estate . . ." *Re Wheeler* [1929] 2 KB 81n: "My interest in an undivided moiety of the real estate in the county of York".

[14] *Re Warren* [1932] 1 Ch 42 (codicil expressly confirming); *Re Harvey* [1947] Ch 285, [1947] 1 All ER 349 (codicil impliedly confirming).

II. Severance

LAW OF PROPERTY ACT 1925

36.   Joint Tenancies. — (1), (2) p. 219, ante.

The provision in Law of Property Act 1925, section 36 (2) for the severance of equitable joint tenancies by the giving of notice to the other joint tenants was new in 1925; and is additional to other methods of severance.

RE DRAPER'S CONVEYANCE[15]
[1969] 1 Ch 486, [1967] 3 All ER 853 (ChD, PLOWMAN J)

A house was conveyed to a husband and wife as joint tenants. The wife obtained a divorce, and issued a summons under section 17 of the Married Women's Property Act 1882, asking for an order that the house be sold and the proceeds distributed according to the interests of the spouses. The order was made but the husband remained in occupation. The husband died and the question was whether the wife was entitled to the house absolutely by survivorship or whether she and her husband's estate were entitled in equal shares.

Held. The wife held the legal estate on trust for herself and her husband's estate in equal shares.

PLOWMAN J: It is common ground that the answer to the question asked by originating summons in this case depends upon whether a beneficial joint tenancy which subsisted between two persons who were formerly husband and wife in a certain house was severed in the lifetime of the husband .... Mr. Cooke, on behalf of the defendants, submits that the joint tenancy was severed, and he puts the matter in two ways, either that it was severed by notice in writing, or it was severed by conduct, and in order to explain those submissions I should, I think, refer to section 36 (2) of the Law of Property Act 1925. ...

Mr. Cooke, as I say, puts it in two ways: first, he submits that the wife's conduct was such as to effect a severance of the joint tenancy, and in relation to that matter he relies on the summons of 11 February 1966, in the Probate, Divorce and Admiralty Division, coupled with the orders which were made by that court, coupled with the plaintiff's solicitor's letter of 7 June 1966. And he says, either as a result of those three matters or as a result of any of them, the joint tenancy became severed by conduct, and he referred me to the decision of Havers J in *Hawkesley v May* ([1956] 1 QB 304, [1955] 3 All ER 353). The part of that case which is relevant for present purposes depends upon these facts, which I read from the headnote: "A settled fund was held by trustees upon trusts under which on attaining the age of 21 the

---

[15] (1968) 84 LQR 462 (P.V.B.); *Cedar Holdings Ltd v Green* [1979] 3 WLR 31; (dictum at p. 35 that a mortgage of a joint tenant's beneficial interest would effect a severance).

plaintiff and his younger sister became absolutely entitled as joint tenants." The question was whether that joint tenancy had become severed, and Havers J, said:

"The joint tenancy was capable of being severed by the plaintiff on attaining the age of 21. There are a number of ways by which a joint tenancy may be severed. In *Williams v Hensman* ((1861) 1 John & H 546) Page Wood V-C, in the course of his judgment, said: 'A joint-tenancy may be severed in three ways: in the first place, an act of any one of the persons interested operating upon his own share may create a severance as to that share[16]. The right of each joint-tenant is a right by survivorship only in the event of no severance having taken place of the share which is claimed under the jus accrescendi. Each one is at liberty to dispose of his own interest in such manner as to sever it from the joint fund — losing, of course, at the same time, his own right of survivorship. Secondly, a joint-tenancy may be severed by mutual agreement. And, in the third place, there may be a severance by any course of dealing sufficient to intimate that the interests of all were mutually treated as constituting a tenancy in common. When the severance depends on an inference of this kind without any express act of severance, it will not suffice to rely on an intention, with respect to the particular share, declared only behind the backs of the other persons interested'."

Havers J continued:

"The first method indicated, namely, an act of any one of the persons interested operating upon his own share, obviously includes a declaration of intention to sever by one party."

Then, after referring to *Walmsley v Foxhall* ((1870) 40 LJ Ch 28) he said:

"This being the state of the authorities, I hold that on the plaintiff attaining the age of 21 he was entitled to the income of his share of the fund. As regards the severance, I hold that when the sister wrote the letter dated 18 March 1942, in which she said: 'Thank you for your letter of 17th instant with the particulars of the investments. I should like the dividends to be paid into my account at Martins Bank, 208 Kensington High Street' (which was a letter in reply to the first defendant), that was a sufficient act on her part to constitute a severance of the joint tenancy. If I am wrong about that, there clearly was a severance when her share of the trust funds were transferred to her in September 1942."

So from that case I derive this; a declaration by one of a number of joint tenants of his intention to sever operates as a severance. Mr. Cooke also, as I have said, relied upon the notice in writing which under section 36 (2) of the Law of Property Act 1925, is allowed in the case of a joint tenancy in land, although not in personalty, and he submits that the summons to which I have already referred, although not signed, amounted to a notice in writing on the part of the wife that

---

[16] *Re Rushton* [1972] Ch 197, [1971] 2 All ER 937.

she desired to sever the joint tenancy in equity. I say "although not signed by the wife or by anybody on her behalf" because there is no requirement in the subsection of a signature.

Dealing with the matter there, and ignoring for a moment certain matters which were submitted by Mr. McCulloch, it seems to me that Mr. Cooke's submissions are right whether they are based on the new provision in section 36 (2) of the Law of Property Act, 1925, or whether they are based on the old law which applied to severing a joint tenancy in the case of a personal estate. It seems to me that that summons, coupled with the affidavit in support of it, clearly evinced an intention on the part of the wife that she wished the property to be sold and the proceeds distributed, a half to her and a half to the husband. And if that is right then it seems to me that that is wholly inconsistent with the notion that a beneficial joint tenancy in that property is to continue, and therefore, apart from these objections to which I will refer in a moment, I feel little doubt that in one way or the other this joint tenancy was severed in equity before the end of February 1966, as a result of the summons which was served on the husband and as a result of what the wife stated in her affidavit in support of the summons.

But then certain matters were submitted to me by Mr. McCulloch on behalf of the wife, which I think fall under two heads. In the first place I was referred to certain observations which were made by Lord Denning MR, in *Bedson v Bedson* [1965] 2 QB 666, [1965] 3 All ER 307. That was a case in which a wife, in September 1964, applied to the County court under section 17 of the Married Women's Property Act 1882, for an order that the property together with the fixtures, fittings, car, stock and goodwill be sold, and the proceeds divided between herself and her husband in equal shares. And then the headnote goes on to state that no matrimonial proceedings had at any relevant date been begun.

But Lord Denning in the course of his judgment had certain things to say about the severance of the joint tenancy in the matrimonial home. He said:

"(3) So long as the house is in the possession of the husband and wife as joint tenants or one of them, there can be no severance of their equitable interests: see section 36 (1) (3)." That is a reference to the Law of Property Act 1925. "Neither of them can sell his or her equitable interest separately. If he or she could do so, it would mean that the purchaser could insist on going into possession himself — with the other spouse there — which is absurd. It would mean also that one of them could, of his own head, destroy the right of survivorship which was the essence of the joint tenancy. That cannot be correct."

If I may say so, it is not easy to understand what it is in section 36 (1) and (3) of the Law of Property Act 1925, on which Lord Denning was relying as authority for the proposition that so long as the house is in the possession of the husband and wife as joint tenants or one of them there can be no severance of their equitable interests.

Then Lord Denning, MR, added:

"One further point: I am of opinion that, while the husband is in possession of the house, there can be no severance of the joint tenancy. The wife cannot sell her interest separately. In case I am wrong about this, I think we should make an order restraining the wife from doing so. It would be quite intolerable that she should, for instance, be able to sell her interest to her mother and get her to turn him out. The jurisdiction in this behalf is amply covered by *Lee v Lee*, [1952] 2 QB 489n, [1952] 1 All ER 1299, which has been approved by the House of Lords."

Mr. McCulloch points out that in the present case the husband continued in possession until January of 1967 which was some time after the orders of the Divorce court had been made. However, Russell LJ in the same case took a different view about the severance of beneficial joint tenancies. He said:

"I am unable to accept the legal proposition of Lord Denning MR, that when husband and wife are joint tenants of the legal estate in the matrimonial home and also beneficial joint tenants in respect of it, neither can, so long as one is in possession, sell his or her beneficial interest therein or otherwise sever the beneficial joint tenancy. The proposition is, I think, without the slightest foundation in law or in equity. If anything, it appears to be an attempt to revive to some extent the long defunct tenancy by entireties which, as I have already remarked, was doomed by the Married Women's Property Act 1882, itself. It may indeed be that either the wife's claim in this case, or the notation in the business accounts of the husband of her interest has long since operated as a severance."

If I have to choose between those two statements I respectfully express my preference for that of Russell LJ[17]. It is interesting to note that he referred to the possibility that the wife's claim in that case might have operated by itself as a severance, and, as I have already stated, I take the view that in this case the summons issued by the wife in the Divorce Division coupled with the affidavit which she swore in support of that summons did operate to sever her beneficial joint tenancy.

In *Burgess v Rawnsley* [1975] Ch 429, [1975] 3 All ER 142[18], a house had been transferred to the defendant, Mrs. Rawnsley, and Mr. Honick as joint tenants. Mr. Honick had intended the house to be the matrimonial home, but the plaintiff never intended to marry him. When this became clear, he attempted to buy her share from her, but the price could not be agreed. Mr. Honick died, and the question was whether his estate was entitled to a half share in the house.

---

[17] See also (1966) 82 LQR 29 (R.E.M.); (1976) 40 Conv (NS) 77 (J. F. Garner).
[18] (1975) 39 Conv (NS) 433 (F. R. Crane); (1976) CLJ 20 (D. J. Hayton); (1977) 41 Conv (NS) 243 (S. M. Bandali).

The Court of Appeal, affirming Judge Granville-Smith, found that the joint tenancy had been severed. Lord DENNING MR, said at p. 438:

"Was there a severance of the beneficial joint tenancy? The judge said:

'I hold that there has been a severance of the joint tenancy brought about by the conduct of the defendant in asking £750 for her share which was agreed to.'

In making that statement the judge made a little slip. She did not ask £750. But it was a slip of no importance. The important finding is that there was an agreement that she would sell her share to him for £750. Almost immediately afterwards she went back upon it. Is that conduct sufficient to effect a severance?

Mr. Levy submitted that it was not. He relied on the recent decision of Walton J in *Nielson-Jones v Fedden* [1975] Ch 222, [1974] 3 All ER 38, given subsequently to the judgment of the judge here. Walton J held that no conduct is sufficient to sever a joint tenancy unless it is irrevocable. Mr. Levy said that in the present case the agreement was not in writing. It could not be enforced by specific performance. It was revocable and was in fact revoked by Mrs. Rawnsley when she went back on it. So there was, he submitted, no severance.

Walton J founded himself on the decision of Stirling J in *Re Wilks* [1891] 3 Ch 59. He criticised *Hawkesley v May* [1956] 1 QB 304, [1955] 3 All ER 353 and *Re Draper's Conveyance* [1969] 1 Ch 486, [1967] 3 All ER 853, and said that they were clearly contrary to the existing well-established law. He went back to *Coke upon Littleton*, 189a, 299b and to *Blackstone's Commentaries*. Those old writers were dealing with legal joint tenancies. *Blackstone* said, 8th edn. (1778), vol. II, pp. 180, 185:

'The properties of a joint estate are derived from its unity, which is fourfold; the unity of interest, the unity of title, the unity of time, and the unity of possession: . . . an estate in joint tenancy may be severed and destroyed . . . by destroying any of its constituent unities.'

and he gives instances of how this may be done. Now that is all very well when you are considering how a legal joint tenancy can be severed. But it is of no application today when there can be no severance of a legal joint tenancy; and you are only considering how a beneficial joint tenancy can be severed. The thing to remember today is that equity leans against joint tenants and favours tenancies in common.

Nowadays everyone starts with the judgment of Sir William Page Wood V-C in *Williams v Hensman* (1861) 1 John & H 546, 557, where he said:

'A joint tenancy may be severed in three ways: in the first place, an act of any one of the persons interested operating upon his own share may create a severance as to that share. . . . Secondly, a joint tenancy may be severed by mutual agreement. And, in the third place, there may be a severance by any course of dealing sufficient to intimate that the interests of all were mutually treated as constituting a tenancy in common. When the severance depends on an inference of this kind without any express act of severance, it will not suffice to rely on an intention, with respect to the particular share, declared only behind the backs of the other persons interested. You must find in this class of cases a course of dealing by which the shares of all the parties to the contest have been effected, as happened in the cases of *Wilson v Bell* (1843) 5 Ir Eq R 501 and *Jackson v Jackson* (1804) 9 Ves 591.'

In that passage Page Wood V-C distinguished between severance 'by mutual agreement' and severance by a 'course of dealing.' That shows that a 'course of dealing' need not amount to an agreement, expressed or implied, for severance. It is sufficient if there is a course of dealing in which one party makes clear to the other that he desires that their shares should no longer be held jointly but be held in common. I emphasise that it must be made clear to the other party. That is implicit in the sentence in which Page Wood V-C says:

'it will not suffice to rely on an intention, with respect to the particular share, declared only behind the backs of the other persons interested.'

Similarly it is sufficient if both parties enter on a course of dealing which evinces an intention by both of them that their shares shall henceforth be held in common and not jointly. As appears from the two cases to which Page Wood V-C referred of *Wilson v Bell* (1843) 5 Ir Eq R 501 and *Jackson v Jackson* (1804) 9 Ves 591.

I come now to the question of notice. Suppose that one party gives a notice in writing to the other saying that he desires to sever the joint tenancy. Is that sufficient to effect a severance? I think it is.

[His Lordship read L.P.A. 1925, section 36 (2)[19] and continued:]

The word 'other' is most illuminating. It shows quite plainly that, in the case of personal estate one of the things which is effective in equity to sever a joint tenancy is 'a notice in writing' of a desire to sever. So also in regard to real estate.

Taking this view, I find myself in agreement with Havers J in *Hawkesley v May* [1956] 1 QB 304, 313–314, and of Plowman J in *Re Draper's Conveyance* [1969] 1 Ch 486. I cannot agree with Walton J [1975] Ch 222, 234–235, that those cases were wrongly decided. It would be absurd that there should be a difference between real estate and personal estate in this respect. Suppose real estate is held on a joint tenancy on a trust for sale and is sold and converted into personal property. Before sale, it is severable by notice in writing. It would be ridiculous if it could not be severed afterwards in like manner. I look upon section 36 (2) as declaratory of the law as to severance by notice and not as a new provision confined to real estate. A joint tenancy in personal estate can be severed by notice just as a joint tenancy in real estate.

[His Lordship referred to *Nielson-Jones v Fedden* [1975] Ch 222 and *Re Wilks* [1891] 3 Ch 59, and continued:]

It remains to apply these principles to the present case. I think there was evidence that Mr. Honick and Mrs. Rawnsley did come to an agreement that he would buy her share for £750. That agreement was

---

[19] P. 219, ante.

not in writing and it was not specifically enforceable. Yet it was sufficient to effect a severance. Even if there was not any firm agreement but only a course of dealing, it clearly evinced an intention by both parties that the property should henceforth be held in common and not jointly.

On these grounds I would dismiss the appeal."[20]

III.   Legal Estate in One Person with Beneficial Interest in Two or More

Complicated situations arise where the legal estate in land is held by one person, but the beneficial interest is held by two or more. Such a case occurs usually, but not exclusively, in the context of the matrimonial home. A number of problems can arise, and it will sometimes be relevant to determine the true nature of the beneficiary's interest. Thus, a husband takes a conveyance, in his own name, of a house which is paid for partly by him and partly by his wife, or where there has been an agreement to hold to joint names[21]. Or, as in *Bull v Bull*[22], where a house was conveyed to the plaintiff who provided the bulk of the purchase money, but his mother, the defendant, also contributed. The plaintiff married, and he attempted to evict his mother. Or, as in *Barclay v Barclay*[1], a trust for sale in a will provided for the sale of a bungalow and division of the proceeds. The sole trustee was a daughter-in-law of the testator. She wished to sell with vacant possession, but one of the beneficiaries, the testator's son, remained in possession throughout.

A.   Co-ownership in Equity

In these situations, the first question is whether there is co-ownership in equity of the house. In *Bull v Bull*[2], there was, because the mother had provided part of the purchase money, and was entitled in equity to a share of the beneficial ownership, which related to her share of the purchase money. Similarly, in the matrimonial situation. A spouse may obtain a beneficial interest by making a contribution directly or indirectly, in money or money's worth, to the purchase price, whether towards the initial deposit[3] or to the mortgage instalments[4]; or by substantially contributing in money or money's worth to the improvement of the property[5]. If some person, other than the legal estate owner, is entitled to a beneficial proprietary interest in the house, there is co-ownership in equity.

---

[20] Cf. *Greenfield v Greenfield* (1979) 38 P & CR 570 (where the plaintiff failed to establish severance by a course of dealing).
[21] *Caunce v Caunce* [1969] WLR 286, [1969] 1 All ER 722.
[22] [1955] 1 QB 234, [1955] 1 All ER 253.
[1] [1970] 2 QB 677, [1970] 2 All ER 676.
[2] Supra.   [3] *Caunce v Caunce,* supra.
[4] *Gissing v Gissing* [1971] AC 886, [1970] 2 All ER 780.
[5] Matrimonial Proceedings and Property Act 1970, s. 37.

B. Statutory Trust for Sale

The next question is whether or not such co-ownership in equity creates a statutory trust for sale. We have seen that the courts are willing to hold that it does; even though the provisions of Law of Property Act 1925, section 34, or section 36 may have to be strained in order to reach this result[6]. Beneficial joint tenancy or tenancy in common can only exist in equity; and we have seen that a tenancy in common can only take effect behind a trust for sale[7].

C. Right to Possession Against Trustee

Assuming that there is a trust for sale, express, as in *Barclay v Barclay*[8], or statutory, a further question is whether the equitable co-owners can remain in possession as against the trustee. In *Bull v Bull*[9], and in *Barclay v Barclay*, the sole trustee sued for possession. The action failed in the former case because Mrs. Bull, it was said, had an interest in the land; but succeeded in the latter because, it was said, the brother-in-law had an interest only in the proceeds of sale[10]. Thus, a conceptual analysis can reach either result. The question is whether a beneficiary under a trust for sale is entitled to possession as against the trustee. Before 1926, this depended very much on the discretion of the trustees.

(1955) 19 Conv (NS) 146, at p. 147 (F. R. Crane)

"Before 1926 beneficiaries with equitable interests in land under trusts were not entitled to possession as of right[11] but only in the discretion of the trustees, duly controlled by the court, which was fairly ready to give possession (see *Re Earl of Stamford and Warrington* [1925] Ch 162, reviewing the earlier authorities). The same rules applied to beneficiaries under trusts for sale (*Re Bagot's Settlement* [1894] 1 Ch 177). . . .

It is therefore respectfully submitted that the law laid down in *Re Bagot* now applies to both express and statutory trusts for sale; beneficiaries are not entitled to possession as of right, though the trustee should give it in proper cases, especially where section 26 (3) of the Law of Property Act applies."

D. Overreaching on Sale

Where a trustee for sale is suing a beneficiary for possession, he usually does so in order to be able to sell with vacant possession. He

---

[6] P. 221, ante.
[7] S.L.A. 1925, s. 36 (4); p. 220, ante.
[8] [1970] 2 QB 677, [1970] 2 All ER 676.
[9] [1955] 1 QB 234, [1955] 1 All ER 253.
[10] [1970] 2 QB at p. 684, per Lord DENNING MR. See *Irani Finance Ltd v Singh*, [1971] Ch 59 at pp. 79–80, (1970) 34 Conv (NS) 344 (F. R. Crane).
[11] Nor can one tenant in common claim rent from another who is in possession, unless there is an "ouster"; rent received from a stranger will be shared: *Jones v Jones* [1977] 1 WLR 438, [1977] 2 All ER 231, (1978) 41 MLR 208 (J. Alder).

does not need possession in order to be able to sell. For a sale by trustees for sale overreaches the interests of the beneficiaries, including the interest of a beneficiary in possession; even if that interest is valid against the trustee's claim for possession, it would have no effect against the purchaser. But, to effect a sale as trustees for sale, there must be at least two trustees[12]. A second trustee therefore needs to be appointed. A sale could then be made; though it would leave the purchaser with the unattractive problem of evicting the remaining beneficiary, and that would reduce the price which could be obtained.

E.   Order of Court under Law of Property Act 1925, section 30

The 1925 legislation on co-ownership assumes that the beneficial co-owners (or the first four mentioned) are the trustees[13]. This assumption fails in this type of case because the trust for sale is imposed without, as has been seen, direct statutory language to require it. If the house had been conveyed to the Bulls or the Barclays as joint tenants, or had been expressed to be conveyed in undivided shares, then they would have been the trustees.

They would have to agree upon a sale. If they disagreed, there could be an application to the court under the Law of Property Act 1925, section 30, and on the principles which have emerged in its operation[14].

If there is one trustee for sale only and more than one beneficial owner, as where the legal title is in a husband and he and his wife are beneficial owners, a second trustee for sale should be appointed in order to effect a sale. The wife would be appropriate. But if there is disagreement, she cannot insist on being appointed. She may, however, as a "person interested", apply to the court under Law of Property Act 1925, section 30 for an order for sale.

F.   Sale by Single Owner

i.   UNREGISTERED LAND

A further problem arises if the sale is made by one trustee only. The overreaching provisions do not apply[14a]. This was illustrated in *Caunce v Caunce* [1969] 1 WLR 286, [1969] 1 All ER 722, where a husband and wife agreed that the wife would make a capital payment towards the purchase of a house, that the husband would pay the instalments to the building society, and that the conveyance would be in their joint names. The house was, however, conveyed to the husband alone, and, without the wife's knowledge, he further charged it in favour of Lloyds Bank. On the husband's bankruptcy, one question was whether the bank took subject to, or free from, the wife's equitable interest. STAMP J held that the bank took free, as a bona fide purchaser of a legal estate

---

[12]   L.P.A. 1925, s. 27; p. 204, ante.
[13]   L.P.A. 1925, s. 34 (2); p. 218, ante.
[14]   P. 207 et seq., ante.
[14a]   See *Williams and Glyn's Bank v Boland* [1979] 2 WLR 550 at 588, per LORD DENNING MR.

for value without notice. Thus, in that situation, whether or not a purchaser is bound by the interest of the beneficial co-owner depends upon the application of the old doctrine of the bona fide purchaser without notice. Presumably, if the bank had had notice, actual or constructive, of the wife's interest, the mortgage would have been subject to it; though that assumes that the wife's interest as tenant in common in equity behind a trust for sale is an interest in the land. If it were treated as an interest in the proceeds of sale only, the bank would take free of that interest, even if it had notice.

ii. REGISTERED LAND

This type of situation arises in a different form in the case of registered land. Notice there is irrelevant; or should be. The question is whether the wife has an overriding interest under Land Registration Act 1925, section 70 (1) (*g*)[15]. Such an interest must be in the nature of a proprietary interest "subsisting in reference to" the land, and not merely in the notional purchase money; and the spouse claiming it must be in actual occupation. On the first point, ORMROD LJ in *Williams and Glyn's Bank Ltd v Boland*[16] [1979] 2 WLR 550, [1979] 2 All ER 697, said at p. 564:

"In my judgment, the rights of an equitable tenant in common are not accurately described as an interest in a sum of money, simpliciter. So long as the land remains unsold he has the same rights against his co-tenant in respect of the land as a legal tenant in common before the legislation of 1925 came into effect: *Bull v Bull* [1955] 1 QB 234. Such rights include the right not to be dispossessed by his co-tenant and the right, if his share is 50 per cent. or more, to prevent the land from being sold, subject to the overriding power of the court to order a sale, which power may not and will not be exercised if to do so would defeat the object of the trust: see again Farwell J in *Re Buchanan-Wollaston's Conveyance* [1939] 1 Ch 217. In the instant cases the object of the trust was to provide a joint home and the last thing the parties contemplated was that the house would be sold and the cash divided between them.

In converting such a relationship into a trust for sale the legislation of 1925 created, in effect, a legal fiction, at least in so far as the implied trusts are concerned. This may have been an inescapable consequence of the method adopted to achieve its primary objective, that is, the simplification of conveyancing. But to press this legal fiction to its logical conclusion and beyond the point which is necessary to achieve the primary objective is not justifiable, particularly when it involves the sacrifice of the interests of a class or classes of person. The consequence is that the interests of persons in the position of the wives ought not to be dismissed as a mere interest in the proceeds of sale except where it is essential to the working of the scheme to do so.

---

[15] P. 109, ante. Interests under a strict settlement can never be overriding interests L.R.A. 1925, s. 86 (2), (1958) 22 Conv (NS) 14, at pp. 23–24 (F. R. Crane); p. 288, post.
[16] P. 122, ante.

It follows that in construing this, and other legislation closely connected with it, it is permissible, and indeed necessary, to construe the relevant phraseology so as to do the least possible violence to the rights of holders of equitable interests in the property.

[His Lordship referred to *Irani Finance Ltd v Singh* [1971] Ch 59, [1970] 3 All ER 199; p. 244 post, and *Elias v Mitchell* [1972] Ch 652, [1972] 2 All ER 153; p. 241 post, and continued:]

In the present case the relevant words (combining paragraph (*g*) and the opening words of section 70 (1)) are 'Rights subsisting in reference to registered land.' In my judgment, these words are apt to include the interests of a co-owner or equitable tenant in common whose rights are not fully described, for reasons already stated, as an interest in the proceeds of sale."

G.   Right of Occupation

A wife however has a further means of protection. She may rely, not upon her ownership, but upon the statutory right of occupation given to spouse under the Matrimonial Homes Act 1967, section 1[17]. She may protect this against purchasers by registration of a land charge Class F in the case of unregistered land. With registered land, the right must be protected by entry of a notice or a caution[18]. In these situations, that is to say, in respect of the statutory protection given to the wife under the Matrimonial Homes Act 1967, all depends on following the correct procedure for protection. Failure to register or to protect by notice or caution involves the loss of the right against a purchaser. But the loss of that right still leaves open any claim which the wife may have in respect of her beneficial ownership.

MATRIMONIAL HOMES ACT 1967[19]

1.   Protection against eviction, etc., from matrimonial home of spouse not entitled by virtue of estate, etc., to occupy it. — (1) Where one spouse is entitled to occupy a dwelling house by virtue of any estate or interest or contract or by virtue of any enactment[20] giving him or her the right to remain in occupation, and the other spouse is not so entitled, then, subject to the provisions of this Act, the spouse not so entitled shall have the following rights (in this Act referred to as "rights of occupation"):—

(*a*) if in occupation, a right not to be evicted or excluded from the dwelling house or any part thereof by the other spouse except with the leave of the court given by an order under this section;

---

[17] As amended by Matrimonial Proceedings and Property Act 1970, s. 38; and by Domestic Violence and Matrimonial Proceedings Act 1976 s. 3.

[18] It cannot be an overriding interest under, L.R.A. 1925, s. 70 (1) (*g*). Matrimonial Homes Act 1967, s. 2 (7).

[19] Bromley, *Family Law* (5th edn. 1976), pp. 477–487; Cretney, *Principles of Family Law* (3rd edn. 1979), pp. 205–215; (1968) 32 Conv (NS) 85 (F. R. Crane); *Wroth v Tyler* [1974] Ch 30, [1973] 1 All ER 897. See Law Commission Third Report on Family Property (Law Com No. 86, 1978) pp. 241–334.

[20] E.g. Rent Act 1968; *Penn v Dunn* [1970] 2 QB 686, [1970] 2 All ER 858.

(*b*) if not in occupation[21], a right with the leave of the court so given to enter into and occupy the dwelling house[1].

(2) So long as one spouse has rights of occupation, either of the spouses may apply to the court for an order declaring, enforcing, restricting or terminating those rights or prohibiting, suspending or restricting the exercise by either spouse of the right to occupy the dwelling house, or requiring either spouse to permit the exercise by the other of that right[2].

(3) On an application for an order under this section the court may make such order as it thinks just and reasonable having regard to the conduct of the spouses in relation to each other and otherwise, to their respective needs and financial resources, to the needs of any children and to all the circumstances of the case, . . .

(8) This Act shall not apply to a dwelling house which has at no time been a matrimonial home of the spouses in question; and a spouse's rights of occupation shall continue only so long as the marriage subsists and the other spouse is entitled as mentioned in subsection (1) above to occupy the dwelling house, except where provision is made by section 2 of this Act for those rights to be a charge on an estate or interest in the dwelling house.

(9)[3] It is hereby declared that a spouse who has an equitable interest in a dwelling house or in the proceeds of sale thereof, not being a spouse in whom is vested (whether solely or as a joint tenant) a legal estate in fee simple or a legal term of years absolute in the dwelling house, is to be treated for the purpose only of determining whether he or she has rights of occupation under this section as not being entitled to occupy the dwelling house by virtue of that interest.

2. Effect of statutory rights of occupation as charge on dwelling house. — (1) Where, at any time during the subsistence of a marriage, one spouse is entitled to occupy a dwelling house by virtue of an estate or interest, then the other spouse's rights of occupation shall be a charge on that estate or interest, having the like priority as if it were an equitable interest created at whichever is the latest of the following dates, that is to say,—

(*a*) the date when the spouse so entitled acquires the estate or interest;

(*b*) the date of the marriage; and

(*c*) the commencement of this Act.

---

[21] *Hoggelt v Hoggelt* (1980) 39 P & CR 121 at 127.

[1] *Watts v Waller* [1973] QB 153, [1972] 3 All ER 257; cf. *Rutherford v Rutherford* [1970] 1 WLR 1479, [1970] 3 All ER 422.

[2] As amended by Domestic Violence and Matrimonial Proceedings Act 1976, s. 3. [1979] Conv 330 at 335–337 (J. G. Miller).

[3] Added by Matrimonial Proceedings and Property Act 1970, s. 38.

(2) Notwithstanding that a spouse's rights of occupation are a charge on an estate or interest in the dwelling house, those rights shall be brought to an end by —

(a) the death of the other spouse, or

(b) the termination (otherwise than by death) of the marriage,

unless in the event of a matrimonial dispute or estrangement the court sees fit to direct otherwise by an order made under section 1 above during the subsistence of the marriage.

(5) Where a spouse's rights of occupation are a charge on the estate or interest of the other spouse, and the other spouse —

(a) is adjudged bankrupt or makes a conveyance or assignment of his or her property (including that estate or interest) to trustees for the benefit of his or her creditors generally; or

(b) dies and his or her estate is insolvent;

then, nothwithstanding that it is registered under section 2 of the Land Charges Act 1972[4] or subsection (7) below[4a], the charge shall be void against the trustee in bankruptcy, the trustees under the conveyance or assignment, or the personal representatives of the deceased spouse, as the case may be.

(7) Where the title to the legal estate by virtue of which a spouse is entitled to occupy a dwelling house is registered under the Land Registration Act 1925 or any enactment replaced by that Act, registration of a land charge affecting the dwelling house by virtue of this Act shall be effected by registering a notice or caution under that Act[5], and a spouse's rights of occupation shall not be an overriding interest within the meaning of that Act affecting the dwelling house notwithstanding that the spouse is in actual occupation of the dwelling house.

6. Release of rights of occupation and postponement of priority of charge. — (1) A spouse entitled to rights of occupation may by a release in writing release those rights or release them as respects part only of the dwelling house affected by them.

(3) A spouse entitled by virtue of section 2 above to a charge on an estate or interest of the other spouse may agree in writing that any other charge on, or interest in, that estate or interest shall rank in priority to the charge to which that spouse is so entitled.

DOMESTIC VIOLENCE AND MATRIMONIAL PROCEEDINGS ACT 1976

4. Order restricting occupation of matrimonial home. — (1) Where each of two spouses is entitled, by virtue of a legal estate vested in them jointly, to occupy a dwelling-house in which they have or at any

---

[4]   As a Class F land charge; p. 33, ante.

[4a]   As amended by L.C.A. 1972, Sch. 3, para. 8.

[5]   *Miles v Bull (No. 2)* [1969] 3 All ER 1585 (held that, where wife failed to register right of occupation, purchaser with notice took free under L.R.A. 1925, s. 20 (1)). See pp. 125 et seq., post. In 1977–1978 these averaged 122 a week; Class F land charges in respect of unregistered land averaged 206; Report on H.M. Land Registry 1977–78 para. 11.

time have had a matrimonial home, either of them may apply to the court, with respect to the exercise during the subsistence of the marriage of the right to occupy the dwelling-house, for an order prohibiting, suspending or restricting its exercise by the other or requiring the other to permit its exercise by the applicant.

(2) In relation to orders under this section, section 1 (3), (4) and (6) of the Matrimonial Homes Act 1967 (which relate to the considerations relevant to and the contents of, and to the jurisdiction to make, orders under that section) shall apply as they apply in relation to orders under that section; and in this section "dwelling-house" has the same meaning as in that Act.

(3) Where each of two spouses is entitled to occupy a dwelling-house by virtue of a contract, or by virtue of any enactment giving them the right to remain in occupation, this section shall apply as it applies where they are entitled by virtue of a legal estate vested in them jointly.

In *Wroth v Tyler* [1974] Ch 30, [1973] 1 All ER 897, MEGARRY J said at p. 46: "At this stage I may summarise my conclusions as to the essentials of the right given by the Act to an occupying spouse as follows. The right is in essence a personal and non-assignable statutory right not to be evicted from the matrimonial home in question during marriage or until the court otherwise orders; and this right constitutes a charge on the estate or interest of the owning spouse which requires protection against third parties by registration. For various reasons, the right may be said to be one which readily fits into no category known to conveyancers before 1967; the phrase sui generis seems apt, but of little help."

IV. Conveyance to Joint Tenants, One of Whom Dies

From the purchaser's position, this situation is the converse of that in the previous section. If land were conveyed to A and B as joint tenants a purchaser would see that a trust for sale was created by virtue of Law of Property Act 1925, section 36. He would therefore expect to deal with two trustees and to hand the purchase money over to them[6]. Suppose A dies. The absence of two trustees was met, as has been seen[7] by the addition to section 36 of the words: "Nothing in this Act affects the right of a survivor of joint tenants, who is solely and beneficially interested, to deal with his legal estate as if it were not held on trust for sale." The successor, B, will only be "solely and beneficially interested" if he remains a joint tenant until A's death; and he can only satisfy the purchaser of this by establishing the negative proposition that there has been no severance of the joint tenancy in equity. This problem is dealt with, as will be seen, by the Law of Property (Joint Tenants) Act 1964.

---

[6] L.P.A. 1925, s. 27, p. 204, ante.
[7] See p. 220, ante.

RE COOK

[1948] Ch 212, [1948] 1 All ER 231 (ChD, HARMAN J)

Before 1926 a freehold house was conveyed to H and W as joint tenants. H died in January 1944 and W, by her will made in March 1944, left "all my personal estate" to her nephews and nieces, and died in September 1944 still possessed of the house.

The question was whether the house passed under the gift of personalty in the will.

Held. Although the freehold was subjected to a trust for sale on 1 January 1926 under the Law of Property Act 1925, section 36, it was reconverted to its natural state on the death of H and did not pass as personalty under the will of W.

HARMAN J: The question to be decided is this: Did the trust for sale imposed by section 36 come to an end on the husband's death? After that date there is no doubt that the entire interest in the property, both legal and equitable, became vested in the testatrix. It is said by Mr. Danckwerts for the Custodian of Enemy Property that, according to the ordinary and well-known rule in *Re Selous* ([1901] 1 Ch 921) per Farwell J, the legal estate swallows up the equitable, that there is a merger between the two, and that from January, 1944, onwards the testatrix was merely the owner of this property and no trust for sale could exist, because A cannot be trustee for A. I think Mr. Alcock, who argued on behalf of the beneficiaries under the will of the testatrix, would admit that to be so if this were anything but what is known as a statutory trust, but he submits that, this trust being the creature of statute, statute must put an end to it and without any statutory ending it goes on, and he points out that under section 23 of the Law of Property Act 1925, a trust for sale may, at any rate so far as protection of a purchaser is concerned, be deemed to go on indefinitely. Even so, I think he would be in great difficulty but for the addition to section 36 of the Law of Property Act 1925 made by the Law of Property (Amendment) Act 1926 in these terms: "Nothing in this Act affects the right of a survivor of joint tenants, who is solely and beneficially interested" — that is the position of the testatrix in this case — "to deal with his legal estate as if it were not held on trust for sale".

Mr. Alcock argues, and I think with force, that the inference from that is inevitable, namely, that the legal estate is held on trust for sale, although the owner of it is given leave by the Act to deal with it as if it were not. If that were the true meaning of it, he says it follows that a trust for sale still does affect the property until it is dealt with in some way inconsistent with that position. I feel the force of that, but I do not think it is enough to alter the view which I should have taken if it were not there. This sentence is an after-thought introduced into the Act ex cautela because of some danger, real or imaginary, that was thought to exist after the Act of 1925 had come into force, and in my judgment it is not enough to alter the prima facie rule that you cannot have a trust existing when nobody is interested under it except the trustee, because nobody can enforce it and there is, in fact, no trust in existence.

I get some assistance also from section 36, subsection 1 itself, because there are found the words "shall be held on trust for sale, in like manner as if the persons beneficially entitled were tenants in common". As soon as only one person is beneficially entitled there are no persons who would be tenants in common, because there is only one person interested. The phrase "persons beneficially entitled" must, as Mr. Freeman submitted to me, mean what it says, namely, "persons", in the plural, and therefore the subsection does not apply as soon as there is but one person interested in the entirety of the property. Consequently, I hold that upon the death of the husband the testatrix became the absolute owner of this property and there was no trust for sale subsisting beyond that date. . . .

If I am right so far, this property was at the time of her will and at the time of her death real estate to which she was entitled in fee simple. . . . It may well be that she thought "personal estate" meant "all my worldly goods"; I do not know. In the absence of something to show that the phrase ought not to be so construed, I must suppose that she used the term "personal estate" in its ordinary meaning as a term of art. Consequently, I hold that the testatrix only succeeded in disposing of what the lawyers would call her "personal estate" and she did not dispose of this house, . . . which therefore devolves as on an intestacy.

LAW OF PROPERTY (JOINT TENANTS) ACT 1964[8]

1. Assumptions on sale of land by survivor of joint tenants. — (1) For the purposes of section 36 (2) of the Law of Property Act 1925, as amended by section 7 and the Schedule to the Law of Property (Amendment) Act 1926, the survivor of two or more joint tenants shall, in favour of a purchaser of the legal estate, be deemed to be solely and beneficially interested if he conveys as beneficial owner or the conveyance includes a statement that he is so interested.

Provided that the foregoing provisions of this subsection shall not apply if, at any time before the date of the conveyance by the survivor —

(a) a memorandum of severance (that is to say a note or memorandum signed by the joint tenants or one of them and recording that the joint tenancy was severed in equity on a date therein specified) had been endorsed on or annexed to the conveyance by virtue of which the legal estate was vested in the joint tenants; or

(b) a receiving order in bankruptcy made against any of the joint tenants, or a petition for such an order, had been registered under the Land Charges Act 1925[9], being an order or petition of which the purchaser has notice, by virtue of the registration, on the date of the conveyance by the survivor.

---

[8] W & C, Vol. 2, pp. 149–151; (1964) 28 Conv (NS) 329, (1966) 30 Conv (NS) 27 (P. Jackson).
[9] Now L.C.A. 1972.

(2) The foregoing provisions of this section shall apply with the necessary modifications in relation to a conveyance by the personal representatives of the survivor of joint tenants as they apply in relation to a conveyance by such a survivor.

2. Retrospective and transitional provisions. — Section 1 of this Act shall be deemed to have come into force on 1st January 1926, and for the purposes of that section in its application to a conveyance executed before the passing of this Act a statement signed by the vendor or by his personal representatives that he was solely and beneficially interested shall be treated as if it had been included in the conveyance.

3. Exclusion of registered land. — This Act shall not apply to any land the title of which has been registered under the provisions of the Land Registration Acts 1925 and 1936.

V.   Nature of Interests of Beneficiaries under a Trust for Sale

As we have seen[10], the doctrine of conversion applies as soon as a trust for sale comes into operation; the interests of the beneficiaries are thus automatically interests in the proceeds of sale of land and not in the land itself. CROSS LJ said in *Irani Finance Ltd v Singh* [1971] Ch 59 at 80, [1970] 3 All ER 199 at 204: "The whole purpose of the trust for sale is to make sure, by shifting the equitable interests away from the land and into the proceeds of sale, that a purchaser of the land takes free from the equitable interests. To hold these to be equitable interests in the land itself would be to frustrate this purpose. Even to hold that they have equitable interests in the land for a limited period, namely, until the land is sold, would, we think, be inconsistent with the trust for sale being an 'immediate' trust for sale working an immediate conversion, which is what the Law of Property Act 1925, envisages (see section 205 (1) (xxix))[11]."

But this view has given rise to difficulties and in certain situations it has been found undersirable to apply the full logic of the doctrine of conversion.

A.   General[12]

(1971) 34 MLR 441 (S. M. Cretney)

"A beneficiary under a trust for sale of land can be said to have an interest in the land itself at least in the following ways. (1) He may, with the concurrence of the other beneficiaries, compel the transfer of the land to himself[13]. (2) If the trust is imposed by law, he has a right

---

[10] P. 187, 189, ante.
[11] P. 192, ante.
[12] See also (1971) CLJ 44 (M.J. Prichard), [1978] Conv 194 (H. Forrest).
[13] *Saunders v Vautier* (1841) 4 Beav 115; cf. the trustees' power to partition land held on trust for tenants in common: s. 28 (3) of the Law of Property Act 1925.

to be consulted by the trustees as to the exercise of their powers over
the land; they are obliged to give effect to the beneficiaries' wishes[14].
(3) Even if some of the trustees wish to execute the trust (rather than
use their power to postpone sale) the court may refuse to permit this
(contrary to the general principle that even a minority may compel the
execution of an imperative obligation[15]) if some particular purpose for
which the land was acquired still subsists, or it would be inequitable to
do so[16]. (4) For purposes of construction, although a devise of 'all my
freehold and copyhold land' is inapt to carry an interest under a trust
for sale[17] yet a gift of a 'share and interest' in land has been held to
suffice[18].

It is thus chimerical to suppose that a single 'correct' answer can be
given to the problem whether the beneficiary's interest is or is not an
'interest in land': in some ways it is, in others it is not. It is submitted
that the right approach is therefore to ask for what purposes the land
has been subjected to the trust, and what is the policy of the legislation under which the question arises.

The realistic process of considering the purpose of the settlement is
well illustrated by the three cases[19] in which the Court of Appeal has
held that a person jointly interested in a dwelling-house had a right to
possession (or at least a right not to be ousted from possession). It is
quite clear that an equitable beneficiary had no such right prior to
1926[20], when it was a matter of choice[1] whether to interpose a trust
between the legal estate and the beneficiaries. It is incredible to
suppose that the legislature could, in pursuance of its aim of simp-

---

[14] L.P.A. 1925, s. 26 (3), which applies only to trusts imposed by statute: L.P. (A) A.
1926, Sch. It could be argued that this shows legislative recognition of the need
to distinguish between cases where the trust for sale should be regarded as
machinery, on the one hand, and those where it has been expressly chosen, when its
logical consequences may be implemented.

[15] *Re Mayo* [1943] Ch 302, [1943] 2 All ER 440; cf. *Re 90 Thornhill Road., Tolworth
Surrey* [1970] Ch 261.

[16] *Re Buchanan-Wollaston's Conveyance* [1939] Ch 738, [1939] 2 All ER 302; *Re Hyde's
Conveyance* (1950) noted in 102 LJ 58; *Bedson v Bedson* [1965] 2 QB 666, [1965] 3 All
ER 307; *Rawlings v Rawlings* [1964] P 398, [1964] 2 All ER 804.

[17] *Re Kempthorne* [1930] 1 Ch 268.

[18] *Re Newman* [1930] 2 Ch 409, see particularly per FARWELL J at p. 414; and see also
Re Warren [1932] 1 Ch 42.

[19] *Bull v Bull* [1955] 1 QB 234, [1955] 1 All ER 253; *Cook v Cook* [1962] P 235; *Gurasz v
Gurasz* [1970] P 11, [1969] 3 All ER 822; *Bull v Bull* was a controversial decision:
see (1955) 19 Conv (NS) 146 (Crane), (1970) 34 Conv (NS) 344 (Crane), (1955) 18 MLR
303 (Latham); ibid 408 (Gray), (1956) 19 MLR 312 (Forrest), [1955] CLJ 156. The
view that an equitable beneficiary might be held "entitled to occupy a dwelling-house
by virtue of any estate or interest . . ." (Matrimonial Homes Act 1967, s. 1) led the
Law Commission, *ex abundante cautela*, to recommend an amendment of the Act;
Matrimonial Proceedings and Property Act 1970, s. 38; Law Com No. 25, para. 59,
and explanatory note to draft cl. 28.

[20] *Re Wythes* [1893] 2 Ch 369 at 374; *Re Newen* [1894] 2 Ch 297; *Re Bagot* [1894] 1
Ch 177; *Re Earl of Stamford and Warrington* [1925] Ch 162.

[1] There is evidence in the old cases that the intention of the settlor was of paramount
importance in determining whether the beneficiary be allowed into possession or not:
thus in *Tidd v Lister* (1820) 5 Madd 429 Sir J. LEACH V-C, pointed out that the
nature of the property (e.g., a family residence) might indicate that the beneficiary
should not be excluded.

lifying conveyancing, have intended to deprive all existing owners of undivided shares in land of their right to possession, leaving this to the discretion of a trustee (perhaps even the Public Trustee)[2]. If the clear intention is that a dwelling-house should be occupied by the joint purchasers it is absurd to deny them, because of conveyancing machinery, any sufficient interest in the house; *Bull v Bull*[3]; if, on the other hand, there is an express trust for sale (not created on the purchase of the property), and it is clear that the intention was that the property be sold and the proceeds divided, it is equally absurd to claim that any single beneficiary is entitled to frustrate this object by retaining possession as against the trustee: *Barclay v Barclay*[4].

This is a more attractive approach than simply to ask the abstract question whether the beneficiaries have an interest in the land itself. Unfortunately it did not attract the division of the Court of Appeal which decided *Irani Finance Ltd v Singh. . .*"[5]

B.　Statutory Definitions of Land

The question whether a reference in a statute to "land" includes an interest under a trust for sale is primarily one of statutory interpretation. Sometimes a statute deals expressly with the point. Under the Limitation Act 1939, for example, land includes "an interest in the proceeds of the sale of land held upon trust for sale[6]."

Questions of interpretation have arisen in connection with the following statutes.

i.　LAW OF PROPERTY ACT 1925, SECTION 40[7]

In *Cooper v Critchley* [1955] Ch 431, [1955] 1 All ER 520[8], the question arose whether a contract by one of two tenants in common in equity to sell his interest to the other was a contract for the sale of "land or any interest in land", and, to be enforceable, needed a memorandum in writing. VAISEY J and the Court of Appeal (EVERSHED MR, JENKINS and HODSON LJJ) held that there was no contract, and then considered what the position would have been if there had been one. JENKINS LJ said at p. 439: "The definition of land in section 205 (1) (ix) of this Act does, in so many words, exclude an undivided share in land; but that does not, to my mind, conclude the matter. The interest here in question is not an undivided share in land: it is a right to a share of the proceeds to arise from a sale of land, and paragraph (ix) does not say that such a right is not an interest in land, while paragraph (x) classes together as 'equitable interests' interests in land or the proceeds of

[2] L.P.A. 1925, Sch. 1, Part IV, paras. 1 (3), 1 (4).
[3] See p. 239, n. 19.
[4] [1970] 2 QB 677, noted (1970) 34 Conv (NS) 344.
[5] [1971] Ch 59, [1970] 3 All ER 1455, p. 244, post.
[6] Ss. 18 (1), 31 (1). See also A.E.A. 1925, s. 3 (1) (ii).
[7] P. 58, ante.
[8] (1955) 71 LQR 177 (R.E.M.); Farrand, pp. 33–35; *Steadman v Steadman* [1974] QB 161, [1973] 3 All ER 977; affd, [1976] AC 536, [1974] 2 All ER 977.

sale thereof. Moreover, the definitions in section 205 of the Act of 1925 are assigned subject to the qualification 'unless the context otherwise requires.' Section 40 of the Act of 1925, as is well known, replaced section 4 of the Statute of Frauds, and there is to my mind little doubt that, before the Law of Property Act, 1925, an interest in the proceeds to arise from a sale of land would, notwithstanding the equitable doctrine of conversion, have ranked as an interest in land for the purposes of section 4 of the old statute. I am reluctant to construe section 40 of the Act of 1925 as altering the law in this respect.

Accordingly, I would be disposed to hold that a share in the proceeds to arise from a sale of land is an interest in land within the meaning of section 40. But if I am wrong in my inclination to accept the pro- position in these general terms, I think that in a case such as this, where the transaction to which the contract relates is a sale by one to the other of two legal joint tenants of land, each of whom is beneficially entitled to one-half of the proceeds to arise from its sale, and who, moreover, as joint lessors under a lease to which the property is subject, and by virtue of the transaction the purchaser will acquire. subject to and with the benefit of the lease, the whole estate, legal and beneficial, in the entirety of the land, the contract cannot well be regarded as anything else than a contract for the sale of an interest in land and, were it necessary for us to do so, I would so hold[9]."

ii. LAND REGISTRATION ACT 1925, SECTION 54 (1)

In *Elias v Mitchell* [1972] Ch 652, [1972] 2 All ER 153[10], PENNYCUICK V-C was asked to decide in interlocutory proceedings whether a person interested in the proceeds of sale of registered land had a minor interest which could be protected by the entry of a caution. Under a partnership deed of 1967 Elias and Mitchell were business partners of freehold property in Ealing. Mitchell was registered as sole proprietor. The deed provided that the partners would stand possessed of the property for themselves in equal shares. In August 1970, Mitchell determined the partnership, and in October executed a transfer of the property to Mohammed Yousaf Dar, who, having no notice of the partnership, paid the purchase price to Mitchell as registered proprietor. Mohammed unfortunately did not present the transfer for registration until March 1971. Meanwhile in December 1970 Elias lodged a caution in respect of the property. Mohammed thereupon sought to remove the caution on the ground that Elias had no locus standi to lodge it. PENNYCUICK V-C, in holding that Elias was a person interested in land within section 54 (1) and so was entitled to lodge a caution, said at p. 659:

---

[9] Cf. *Re Rayleigh Weir Stadium* [1954] 1 WLR 786, [1954] 2 All ER 283 (such a contract held not registrable under L.C.A. 1925). See also *Georgiades v Edward Wolfe & Co Ltd* [1965] Ch 487, [1964] 3 All ER 433 (charge on deposit of proceeds of sale of land not registrable as Class C (iii) land charge); *Taylor v Taylor* [1968] 1 WLR 378, [1968] 1 All ER 843; *Thomas v Rose* [1968] 1 WLR 1797, [1968] 3 All ER 765.
[10] (1972) 36 Conv (NS) 206 (D. J. Hayton).

"I will first consider this matter apart from authority. When one reads the definition of 'minor interests' in section 3 (xv)[11] it seems to me perfectly clear that although what is defined is simply 'minor interests,' that is intended as a definition of minor interests in land. The opening words 'interests not capable of being disposed of or created by registered dispositions and capable of being overridden . . . by the proprietors unless protected as provided by this Act . . .' relate straight back to section 2 (1): '. . . all other interests in registered land . . . shall take effect in equity as minor interests. . . .' Reading those two subsections together it seems to me clear that the entire subject matter of the definition of 'minor interests' consists of interests in land. Then one finds in section 3 (xv) (*a*) that interests under a trust for sale are expressly included among minor interests; and it follows that those particular interests under a trust for sale are treated, for the purpose of this Act, as being minor interests in land.

Then one comes to section 54 (1): 'Any person interested . . . howsoever, in any land . . . may lodge a caution. . . .' If it is right to say that an interest in the proceeds of sale being by definition a minor interest is, within the intendment of this Act, an interest in land, then there is no doubt that a person interested in the proceeds of sale is a person interested in land for the purpose of section 54 (1) and can accordingly lodge a caution. If there were any doubt on this point, it would, I think, be set at rest by section 101 (3) which provides that minor interests may be protected by entry on the register of cautions. So that subsection in terms provides that minor interests, which by definition include interests under a trust for sale, may be protected by entry on the register, and that means that such interests are interests in land within the scope of section 54. . . .

Apart from authority then, I conclude that the plaintiff, having an interest in the proceeds of sale under this trust for sale, is a person interested in the land within the meaning of section 54 and as such is in a position to lodge a caution. That seems to me an entirely sensible provision in accordance with the general scheme of the Act. Indeed, it would be strange if a person having an interest in the proceeds of sale of land were not in a position to obtain a protection against some threatened misapplication of the land by the registered proprietor.

I turn now to the authorities which I propose to go through fairly briefly. They deal with comparable provisions contained in other parts of the legislation of 1925.

[His Lordship referred to *Stevens v Hutchinson* [1953] Ch 299, [1953] 1 All ER 699; *Cooper v Critchley* [1955] Ch 431, [1955] 1 All ER 520; *Georgiades v Edward Wolfe & Co Ltd* [1965] Ch 487, [1964] 3 All ER 433; *Taylor v Taylor* [1968] 1 WLR 378, [1968] 1 All ER 843; *Thomas v Rose* [1968] 1 WLR 1797, [1968] 3 All ER 765; *Irani Finance Ltd v Singh* [1971] Ch 59, [1970] 3 All ER 1455 and continued:]

---

[11] P. 127, *ante.*

It seems to me that the general principle to be applied in this connection is, if I may say so, correctly set out in the obiter statement made by Jenkins LJ in *Cooper v Critchley* [1955] Ch 431, at 439, [1955] 1 All ER 520, 524[12]. One must look at the particular Act and see whether in the context of that particular Act an expression such as 'interest in land' is or is not apt to cover an interest in the proceeds of sale of land. I do not find anything in the other authorities which I have cited which leads me to a different conclusion from that which I have expressed on the construction of the relevant sections of the Land Registration Act viewed in the context of that Act."

iii.   LAND REGISTRATION ACT 1925, SECTION 70 (1)

In *Williams and Glyn's Bank Ltd v Boland* [1979] 2 WLR 550, [1979] 2 All ER 697 the Court of Appeal held that an interest under a trust for sale was an "interest subsisting in reference to" registered land for the purposes of an overriding interest under section 70 (1) (*g*). See the judgment of ORMROD LJ at p. 558 (p. 231, ante).

iv.   LAW OF PROPERTY ACT 1925, SECTION 63

In *Cedar Holdings Ltd v Green* [1979] 3 WLR 31, [1979] 3 All ER 117[13] the Greens (the first and second defendants) were joint beneficial owners of the matrimonial home. They were divorced in 1971. Mrs. Green continued to live in the home with their four children.

Mr. Green wished to raise money by a mortgage of the property. The plaintiffs required the documents to be executed by both defendants. Mr. Green did not tell his wife, but attended the plaintiffs' offices with another woman, who executed the documents in the name of Mrs. Green. The question was whether the transaction was effective to charge Mrs. Green's share of the beneficial interest in the house. In holding that the charge was ineffective, BUCKLEY LJ said at p. 35:

"Under the Law of Property Act 1925, section 36, the legal estate in 12, Preston Road was vested in the first and second defendants as joint tenants upon the statutory trusts set out in section 35. The plaintiffs' contention in the present case is that either by the legal charge itself, or by a pre-existing contract to create the legal charge arising out of the written application for a loan and the plaintiffs' acceptance of it, the first defendant effectively severed the joint tenancy in the proceeds of sale subsisting under the statutory trusts so as to become entitled to an undivided half-share of the proceeds of sale. If the effect of either the legal charge itself or of a contract to create the legal charge was, in the one case, to occasion a disposal by the first defendant of his beneficial interest under the statutory trust or, in the other, to oblige the first defendant to dispose of that interest, there can, I think, be no doubt that the legal charge or the contract would have effected a severance of the joint beneficial ownership. The legal charge or the contract would constitute an act by one of the joint owners operating upon his own share. This would fall within the first

---

[12] P. 240, ante.
[13] [1979] Conv 372 (F. R. Crane); 38 CLJ 251 (M. J. Prichard) 43 MLR 225 (B. Berkovits).

of the three methods of severance mentioned by Page Wood V-C in
Williams v Hensman (1861) 1 John & H 546 at 557 (p. 223 ante). The
effect of such an act is to destroy the unity of interest theretofore
existing between the joint owners and so to put an end to the joint
ownership.

Mr. Millett, for the plaintiffs, relies in this respect, first, upon the
Law of Property Act 1925, section 63, and, secondly, upon the
principle that where a vendor contracts to grant a particular interest
in property which is in fact greater than the interest which he is
competent to grant, the purchaser can elect to affirm the contract and
compel the vendor to grant such less interest in the property as he is
competent to grant.

Section 63 of the Act of 1925 provides:

'(1) Every conveyance is effectual to pass all the estate, right,
title, interest, claim and demand which the conveying parties
respectively have, in, to, or on the property conveyed, or expressed
or intended so to be, or which they respectively have power to
convey in, to, or on the same' . . .

Was the first defendant's beneficial interest under the statutory trusts
an interest in that property?

In *Irani Finance Ltd v Singh* [1971] Ch 59, [1970] 3 All ER 199 this
court had to consider whether the beneficial interests of joint tenants
under the statutory trust for sale could be the subject matter of a
charging order under the Administration of Justice Act 1956, section
35[14], which enables a court, for the purpose of enforcing a judgment or
order for the payment of money, to impose by order 'on any such land
or interest in land' of the debtor as may be specified in the order a
charge for securing payment of the moneys due. Cross LJ, delivering
the judgment of the court, said, at pp. 79–80:

'No doubt such tenants in common are interested in the land in a
general sense, as was remarked by Russell LJ in *Re Kempthorne*
[1930] 1 Ch 268, 292. But that is not the same thing as their
being owners of equitable interests in the realty. The whole
purpose of the trust for sale is to make sure, by shifting the
equitable interests away from the land and into the proceeds of
sale, that a purchaser of land takes free from the equitable
interests. To hold these to be equitable interests in the land itself
would be to frustrate this purpose. Even to hold that they have
equitable interests in the land for a limited period, namely, until
the land is sold, would, we think, be inconsistent with the trust for
sale being an "immediate" trust for sale working an immediate
conversion, which is what the Law of Property Act 1925, envisages
(see section 205 (1) (xxix)), though of course, it is not in fact only
such a limited interest that the plaintiffs are seeking to charge.'

The Court of Appeal held in that case that the interests of the joint
beneficial owners under the statutory trusts were not interests in land
for the relevant purpose. It is true that in that case the legislative
history of the statutory provision in question played a considerable

---

[14] See now Charging Orders Act 1979, p. 246, post.

part in the reasoning of the judgment, as also did references to the Land Charges Act 1925 and the Land Registration Act 1925 contained in the section under consideration. Consequently, in my opinion, that case and the authorities referred to in it are not by any means directly in point in the present case. . . .

[His Lordship referred to *Cooper v Critchley* [1955] Ch 431; [1955] 1 All ER 520; p. 240 ante, and *Stevens v Hutchinson* [1953] Ch 299, [1953] 1 All ER 699 and continued:]

In my judgment, upon the true construction of section 63 a beneficial interest in the proceeds of sale of land held upon the statutory trusts is not an interest in that land within the meaning of the section and a conveyance of that land is not effectual to pass a beneficial interest in the proceeds of sale. It follows that, in my judgment, in the present case the legal charge executed by the first defendant was not effectual to charge his beneficial interest in the proceeds of sale of 12, Preston Road.

I turn therefore to the other way in which Mr. Millett presents his argument. Where a vendor is unable to make a good title to the whole of what he has contracted to sell, the purchaser may, as a rule, elect to enforce the contract in respect of so much as he can get with an appropriate abatement of the purchase price . . .

The doctrine . . . is, in my opinion, directed to ensuring that the grantee shall obtain, if he so elects, as much of the subject matter contracted to be granted as the grantor can convey, whether the deficiency be in respect of the physical extent of the subject matter or of the estate or interest of the grantor in the subject matter. It does not enable the grantee to demand a grant of some different subject matter in lieu of that contracted for.

In the present case the plaintiffs contracted for a mortgage of the freehold estate in 12, Preston Road. Neither the plaintiffs nor the first defendant contemplated a mortgage of the first defendant's share of the proceeds of sale of the property. Both the application for a loan and the legal charge itself explicitly refer to the freehold estate in the whole of the property. If the plaintiffs had realised that the first defendant was competent to charge no more than a half-share in the proceeds of sale, the transaction would never have taken place. Nevertheless, had the first defendant been competent to charge some estate or interest in 12, Preston Road less than the freehold, such as a leasehold interest, the plaintiff would, I think, have been entitled to elect to claim specific enforcement of the creation of a charge upon that lesser interest. The first defendant, however, has no interest in 12, Preston Road; his interest is confined to a half-share of the proceeds of sale of the house and of any rents and profits until sale. That interest is, in my opinion, an entirely different subject matter from that which the first defendant contracted to mortgage. Accordingly, in my judgment, the principle in accordance with which such cases as *Basma v Weekes* [1950] AC 441 and *Thellusson v Liddard* [1900] 2 Ch 635 were decided has no application to the present case."

v.   ADMINISTRATION OF JUSTICE ACT 1956, SECTION 35

Section 35 (1) gave power to the High Court or County Court to make a charging order on, inter alia, "any such land or interest in land of the debtor as may be specified in the order". The question arose whether the Court's power applied in relation to an interest under a trust for sale. A distinction was drawn between the case where the charging order was made against the separate interest of one beneficiary[15], and that where the order was made against both joint tenants together[16]. Section 35 has been repealed[17], and the jurisdiction is now widened to cover both cases.

CHARGING ORDERS ACT 1979

2.   Property which may be charged.— (1) Subject to subsection (3) below, a charge may be imposed by a charging order only on —

(a)   any interest held by the debtor beneficially —

   (i)   in any asset of a kind mentioned in subsection (2) below, or

   (ii)   under any trust; or

(b)   any interest held by a person as trustee of a trust ("the trust"), if the interest is in such an asset or is an interest under another trust and —

   (i)   the judgment or order in respect of which a charge is to be imposed was made against that person as trustee of the trust, or

   (ii)   the whole beneficial interest under the trust is held by the debtor unencumbered and for his own benefit, or

   (iii)   in a case where there are two or more debtors all of whom are liable to the creditor for the same debt, they together hold the whole beneficial interest under the trust unencumbered and for their own benefit.

(2)   The assets referred to in subsection (1) above are —

(a)   land,

(b)   securities of any of the following kinds —

   (i)   government stock,

   (ii)   stock of any body (other than a building society) incorporated within England and Wales,

   (iii)   stock of any body incorporated outside England and Wales or of any state or territory outside the United Kingdom, being stock registered in a register kept at any place within England and Wales,

   (iv)   units of any unit trust in respect of which a register of the unit holders is kept at any place within England and Wales, or

---

[15] Where there was no jurisdiction. *Irani Finance Ltd v Singh* [1971] Ch 59, [1970] 3 All ER 1455.
[16] Where there was jurisdiction. *National Westminster Bank Ltd v Allen* [1971] 2 QB 718, [1971] 3 All ER 201.
[17] Charging Orders Act 1979, s. 7 (2). See generally (1980) 124 Sol Jo 91, 110, 136 (A. J. Shipwright).

(*c*) funds in court.

(3) In any case where a charge is imposed by a charging order on any interest in an asset of a kind mentioned in paragraph (*b*) or (*c*) of subsection (2) above, the court making the order may provide for the charge to extend to any interest or dividend payable in respect of the asset.

3. Provisions supplementing sections 1 and 2. — (2) The Land Charges Act 1972[18] and the Land Registration Act 1925[19] shall apply in relation to charging orders as they apply in relation to other orders or writs issued or made for the purpose of enforcing judgments.

vi. DEVELOPMENT LAND TAX ACT 1976

(1976) 40 Conv (NS) 394

"CONVERSION INVERSION

"Now, we conveyancers all know that in the eyes of equity where there is a trust for sale of land, personalty will be owned, so that in cases of concurrent ownership a beneficiary's interest will normally be in the proceeds of sale not in the land[20]. Equally we recall that where there is a strict settlement the beneficiaries' interests are always in land[21]. But for DLT purposes, forget it — all is *vice versa*: beneficial joint tenants or tenants in common will always have interests in the land[22], whilst even the tenant for life under a strict settlement will never enjoy an 'interest in land[23].' There is nothing quite like operating within the areas of feudal property law!"

QUESTIONS

1. What effect would the abolition of the doctrine of conversion have on the nature of beneficial interests under a trust for sale? (1970) 34 Conv (NS) 50, 421 (F. R. Crane), (1955) 71 LQR 179 (R.E.M.) (1971) 34 MLR 441 (S. M. Cretney). Survey of the Land Law of Northern Ireland (1971), para. 359.
2. Compare the protection accorded to beneficiaries under a trust for sale of unregistered and registered land. (1958) 22 Conv (NS) 14, 22–26; Wolstenholme and Cherry, vol. 6, pp. 65–66; Barnsley, *Conveyancing Law and Practice* (1973), pp. 49–50, 316; (1973) 117 Sol Jo 115, 136 (G. Miller); L.R.A., 1925 sections 74 (p. 216, ante), 86 (2), p. 288, n. 1, post; *Elias v Mitchell* [1972] Ch 652, [1972] 2 All ER 153; p. 241, ante.

---

[18] P. 30, ante.
[19] P. 128, ante.
[20] See *Irani Finance Ltd v Singh* [1971] Ch 59; [1970] 3 All ER 1455.
[21] See S.L.A. 1925, s. 75 (5).
[22] See Development Land Tax Act 1976, ss. 28 (4) (*a*), 46 (4).
[23] See ibid. s. 46 (2) (*c*).

6. Strict Settlements[1]

A settlement exists whenever successive interests exist in land (not being land held upon trust for sale). Successive interests are interests less than a fee simple, and cannot exist as legal estates. They are therefore equitable interests, existing behind a trust. These elementary propositions are the key to understanding the definition of a settlement for the purposes of the Settled Land Act 1925. With a single exception, it will be seen that the definition in section 1 includes an element of successive ownership. The exception is the case where land is held by a minor; the Settled Land Act machinery is then imposed in order to make possible dealings with the legal estate.

It should also be noted that by virtue of subsection 7 of section 1, settlements and trusts for sale are alternatives.

I.   Definition of a Settlement under the Settled Land Act 1925[2]

SETTLED LAND ACT 1925

1. What constitutes a settlement. — (1) Any deed, will, agreement for a settlement or other agreement[3], Act of Parliament, or other

---

[1] Cheshire, pp. 165–196, 789–795, 797–799; M & W, pp. 282–285, 288–293, 295–358, 371–377, 379–390; MM pp. 135–137, 138–142, 144–173, 179–182, 186–190; Harvey, *Settlements of Land* (1973).

[2] Cheshire, pp. 165–170; M & W pp. 314–320; MM, pp. 139, 151–154.

[3] *Bacon v Bacon* [1947] P 151, [1947] 2 All ER 327 (a separation agreement giving the wife the right to remain in the house for her life).

instrument[4], or any number of instruments, whether made or passed before or after, or partly before and partly after, the commencement of this Act, under or by virtue of which instrument or instruments any land, after the commencement of this Act, stands for the time being —

(i) limited in trust for any persons by way of succession; or

(ii) limited in trust for any person in possession —

    (*a*) for an entailed interest whether or not capable of being barred or defeated;

    (*b*) for an estate in fee simple or for a term of years absolute subject to an executory limitation, gift, or disposition over on failure of his issue or in any other event;

    (*c*) for a base or determinable fee or any corresponding interest in leasehold land;

    (*d*) being an infant, for an estate in fee simple or for a term of years absolute; or

(iii) limited in trust for any person for an estate in fee simple or for a term of years absolute contingently on the happening of any event; or . . .

(v) charged, whether voluntarily or in consideration of marriage or by way of family arrangement, and whether immediately or after an interval, with the payment of any rentcharge for the life of any person, or any less period[5], or of any capital, annual, or periodical sums for the portions, advancement, maintenance, or otherwise for the benefit of any persons, with or without any term of years for securing or raising the same;

creates or is for the purposes of this Act a settlement and is in this Act referred to as a settlement, or as the settlement, as the case requires:

Provided that, where land is the subject of a compound settlement, references in this Act to the settlement shall be construed as meaning such compound settlement, unless the context otherwise requires.

(2) Where an infant is beneficially entitled to land for an estate in fee simple or for a term of years absolute and by reason of an intestacy or otherwise there is no instrument under which the interest of the infant arises or is acquired, a settlement shall be deemed to have been made by the intestate, or by the person whose interest the infant has acquired.

(4) An estate or interest not disposed of by a settlement and remaining in or reverting to the settlor, or any person deriving title under him, is for the purposes of this Act an estate or interest comprised in the subject of the settlement and coming to the settlor or such person under or by virtue of the settlement.

(5) Where —

    (*a*) a settlement creates an entailed interest which is incapable of being barred or defeated, or a base or determinable fee,

---

[4] *Martin v Martin* [1978] Fam 12, [1977] 3 All ER 762, [1978] Conv 229 (P. Smith); *Griffiths v Williams* (1977) 248 Estates Gazette 947; p. 494, post.

[5] See *Re Austen* [1929] 2 Ch 155.

whether or not the reversion or right of reverter is in the Crown, or any corresponding interest in leasehold land; or

(b) the subject of a settlement is an entailed interest, or a base or determinable fee, whether or not the reversion or right of reverter is in the Crown, or any corresponding interest in leasehold land;

the reversion or right of reverter upon the cesser of the interest so created or settled shall be deemed to be an interest comprised in the subject of the settlement, and limited by the settlement.

(6) Subsections (4) and (5) of this section bind the Crown.

(7) This section does not apply to land held upon trust for sale[5a].

2. What is settled land. — Land which is or is deemed to be the subject of a settlement is for the purposes of this Act settled land, and is in relation to the settlement referred to in this Act as the settled land.

The Law of Property (Amendment) Act 1926, Schedule, amending Law of Property Act 1925, section 7 (1), provides that "a fee simple subject to a legal or equitable right of entry or re-entry is for the purposes of this Act a fee simple absolute[6]".

Other types of settlement also arise:

i.   Compound settlements[7]: Where new trusts are declared of land which is already subject to a settlement, as, for example, where a settlement is followed by a resettlement, the land is subject to a compound settlement. Normally the same person would be tenant for life under both settlements; but, even if he was tenant for life under the resettlement only, he could act as tenant for life under the compound settlement. The Settled Land Act 1925, section 31 (1)[8] provides that the trustees of the original settlement or, if there are none[9], the trustees of the resettlement shall be trustees of the compound settlement.

ii.   Referential settlements: i.e. a settlement which incorporates by reference an earlier settlement[10].

iii.   Derivative settlements: i.e. a settlement which is created out of the beneficial interest of one of the beneficiaries of another settlement.

[5a]   Sub-s. 7 was added by L.P. (A) A. 1926, Sch.
[6]   See p. 7, n. 17, ante, where this amendment is commented upon.
[7]   Cheshire, pp. 169, 190; M & W , pp. 327–330; MM, pp. 157–159.
[8]   See p. 276, post. The section is retrospective. *Re Symons* [1927] 1 Ch 344.
[9]   This provision was added by L.P. (A.) A. 1926, Sch.
[10]   S.L.A. 1925, s. 32, also retrospective.

In *Re Ogle's Settled Estates* [1927] 1 Ch 229, ROMER J, held that where the owner of an estate subject to family charges sold plots subject to the charges, the land retained and the plots sold were subject to separate settlements. ROMER J, said at p. 232: "In some parts of the Act no doubt 'settlement' means merely the document or documents creating the settlement: see, for example, sections 1 subsection 4, 47 and 64. But in general a settlement, for the purposes of the Act, is a state of affairs in relation to certain land, brought about, or deemed to have been brought about by one or more documents, the particular state of affairs being one or more of those specified in subsections (i) to (v) of section 1 subsection 1. A document may, therefore, create more than one settlement. If by means of one and the same document, Blackacre and Whiteacre stand limited in trust for A. and his children in strict succession, and for B. and his children in strict succession respectively, there are two settlements."

II. Machinery. The Curtain Principle[11]

The Settled Land Act 1925 introduced the "curtain principle", shutting off the purchaser's view of matters which do not concern him, such as the beneficial interests, and providing him with all the information he needs for the purpose of being certain to obtain the legal estate.

Dealings with the legal estate and equitable interests are contained in separate documents.

SETTLED LAND ACT 1925

4. Authorised method of settling land inter vivos. — (1) Every settlement of a legal estate in land inter vivos, shall, save as in this Act otherwise provided, be effected by two deeds, namely, a vesting deed and a trust instrument and if effected in any other way shall not operate to transfer or create a legal estate.

(2) By the vesting deed the land shall be conveyed to the tenant for life or statutory owner (and if more than one as joint tenants) for the legal estate the subject of the intended settlement:

Provided that, where such legal estate is already vested in the tenant for life or statutory owner, it shall be sufficient, without any other conveyance, if the vesting deed declares that the land is vested in him for that estate.

(3) The trust instrument shall —

- (a) declare the trusts affecting the settled land;
- (b) appoint or constitute trustees of the settlement;
- (c) contain the power, if any, to appoint new trustees of the settlement;

---

[11] Cheshire, pp. 170–175, 789–795; M & W, pp. 298–306; MM, pp. 146–151.

(*d*) set out, either expressly or by reference, any powers intended to be conferred by the settlement in extension of those conferred by this Act;

(*e*) bear any ad valorem stamp duty which may be payable (whether by virtue of the vesting deed or otherwise) in respect of the settlement.

TRUST INSTRUMENT ON THE SETTLEMENT OF LAND[12]

This Trust Instrument is made [&c.] between *John H.* of [&c.] (hereinafter called the Settlor) of the first part, *Jane W.* of [&c.] of the second part, and *X* of [&c.], *Y* of [&c.], and *Z* of [&c.] (hereinafter called the trustees) of the third part.

Whereas by a deed (hereinafter called the Vesting Deed) bearing even date with but executed contemporaneously with these presents, and made between the same parties and in the same order as these presents, certain hereditaments situated at . . . . in the county of . . . . were vested in the Settlor Upon the trusts declared concerning the same by a trust instrument of even date therein referred to (meaning these presents).

Now in consideration of the intended marriage between the Settlor and *Jane W.*, this Deed witnesseth as follows:—

1.   The Settlor hereby agrees that he will hold the hereditaments and property comprised in the Vesting Deed In trust for himself until the solemnisation of the said marriage and thereafter Upon the trusts following, that is to say:—

2.   Upon trust for the Settlor during his life without impeachment of waste with remainder Upon trust if *Jane W.* survives him that she shall receive out of the premises during the residue of her life a yearly jointure rentcharge of [&c.] and subject thereto Upon trust for the trustees for a term of 800 years from the date of the death of the Settlor without impeachment of waste Upon the trusts hereinafter declared concerning the same. And subject to the said term and the trusts thereof Upon trust for the first and other sons of the said intended marriage successively according to seniority in tail male with remainder [&c.] *with an ultimate remainder in trust for the Settlor in fee simple.*

[*Here add the requisite trusts of the portions term, and any other proper provisions including the appointment of the trustees to be trustees of the settlement for the purposes of the Settled Land Act, 1925, extension of Settled Land Act powers, and a power for the tenant for life for the time being of full age to appoint new trustees of the settlement.*]

---

[12] S.L.A. 1925, 1st Sch. Form No. 3.

In witness [&c.].

[NOTE.—The Vesting Deed and the Trust Instrument can be executed as escrows till the marriage.]

---

5. **Contents of vesting deeds.** — (1) Every vesting deed for giving effect to a settlement or for conveying settled land to a tenant for life or statutory owner during the subsistence of the settlement (in this Act referred to as a "principal vesting deed") shall contain the following statements and particulars, namely:—

(a) A description, either specific or general, of the settled land;

(b) A statement that the settled land is vested in the person or persons to whom it is conveyed or in whom it is declared to be vested upon the trusts from time to time affecting the settled land;

(c) The names of the persons who are the trustees of the settlement;

(d) Any additional or larger powers conferred by the trust instrument relating to the settled land which by virtue of this Act operate and are exercisable as if conferred by this Act on a tenant for life;

(e) The name of any person for the time being entitled under the trust instrument to appoint new trustees of the settlement.

(2) The statements or particulars required by this section may be incorporated by reference to an existing vesting instrument, and, where there is a settlement subsisting at the commencement of this Act, by reference to that settlement and to any instrument whereby land has been conveyed to the uses or upon the trusts of that settlement, but not (save as last aforesaid) by reference to a trust instrument nor by reference to a disentailing deed.

(3) A principal vesting deed shall not be invalidated by reason only of any error in any of the statements or particulars by this Act required to be contained therein[13].

VESTING DEED ON THE SETTLEMENT OF LAND[14]

This Vesting Deed made [&c.] between *John H.* of [&c.] of the first part, *Jane W.* of [&c.] of the second part, and *X* of [&c.], *Y* of [&c.], and *Z* of [&c.] (hereinafter called the trustees) of the third part.

Witnesseth and it is hereby declared as follows:—

1.   In consideration of the intended marriage between *John H.* and *Jane W* the said *John H.* as Settlor hereby declares that

All that (*setting out the parcels by reference to a schedule or otherwise*) are vested in *John H.* in fee simple (*or in the case of leaseholds refer to the terms*).

---

[13] S.L.A. 1925, s. 110 (2); see p. 281, post.
[14] S.L.A. 1925, 1st Sch. Form No. 2.

Upon the trusts declared concerning the same by a Trust Instrument bearing even date with but intended to be executed contemporaneously with these presents and made between the same parties and in the same order as these presents or upon such other trusts as the same ought to be held from time to time.

2.   The trustees are the trustees of the settlement for the purposes of the Settled Land Act, 1925.

3.   The following additional or larger powers are conferred by the said trust instrument in relation to the settled land and by virtue of the Settled Land Act, 1925, operate and are exercisable as if conferred by that Act on a tenant for life. [*Here insert the additional powers.*]

4.   The power of appointing a new trustee or new trustees of the settlement is vested in the said [*John H.*] during his life.

In witness [&c.].

---

6.   Procedure in the case of settlements by will. — Where a settlement is created by the will of an estate owner who dies after the commencement of this Act —

    (*a*) the will is for the purposes of this Act a trust instrument; and

    (*b*) the personal representatives of the testator shall hold the settled land on trust, if and when required so to do, to convey it to the person who, under the will, or by virtue of this Act, is the tenant for life[15] or statutory owner[16], and, if more than one, as joint tenants[17].

8.   Mode and costs of conveyance, and saving of rights of personal representatives and equitable chargees. — (1) A conveyance by personal representatives under either of the last two preceding sections[18] may be made by an assent in writing signed by them which shall operate as a conveyance[19].

9.   Procedure in the case of settlements and of instruments deemed to be trust instruments. — (1) Each of the following settlements or instruments shall for the purposes of this Act be deemed to be a trust instrument, and any reference to a trust instrument contained in this Act shall apply thereto, namely:—

    (i) An instrument executed, or, in case of a will, coming into operation, after the commencement of this Act which by virtue of this Act is deemed to be a settlement;

    (ii) A settlement which by virtue of this Act is deemed to have been made by any person after the commencement of this Act[20];

---

[15] S.L.A. 1925, ss. 19, 20; see pp. 261–264, post.

[16] S.L.A. 1925, s. 20.

[17] S.L.A. 1925, s. 19 (2).

[18] For s. 7, see p. 279, post.

[19] The vesting assent performs the same function as a vesting deed; but it need not be sealed, and 50p stamp duty is thereby saved. A.E.A. 1925, s. 36.

[20] For instruments deemed to be settlements or settlements deemed to have been made after the commencement of the Act, see S.L.A. 1925, ss. 1 (2), (3), 20 (3), 29 (1).

(iii) An instrument inter vivos intended to create a settlement of a legal estate in land which is executed after the commencement of this Act, and does not comply with the requirements of this Act with respect to the method of effecting such a settlement; and

(iv) A settlement made after the commencement of this Act (including a settlement by the will of a person who dies after such commencement) of any of the following interests —

   (a) an equitable interest in land which is capable, when in possession, of subsisting at law; or

   (b) an entailed interest; or

   (c) a base or determinable fee or any corresponding interest in leasehold land,

   but only if and when the interest settled takes effect free from all equitable interests and powers under every prior settlement (if any).

(2) As soon as practicable after a settlement, or an instrument which for the purposes of this Act is deemed to be a trust instrument, takes effect as such, the trustees of the settlement may, and on the request of the tenant for life or statutory owner shall, execute a principal vesting deed, containing the proper statements and particulars, declaring that the legal estate in the settled land shall vest or is vested in the person therein named, being the tenant for life or statutory owner, and including themselves if they are the statutory owners, and such deed shall, unless the legal estate is already so vested, operate to convey or vest the legal estate in the settled land to or in the person or persons aforesaid and, if more than one, as joint tenants.

(3) If there are no trustees of the settlement, then (in default of a person able and willing to appoint such trustees) an application under this Act shall be made to the court for the appointment of such trustees.

III. Dispositions of Settled Land

A. No Vesting Instrument. Paralysis

SETTLED LAND ACT 1925

13. Dispositions not to take effect until vesting instrument is made. — Where a tenant for life or statutory owner has become entitled to have a principal vesting deed or a vesting assent executed in his favour, then until a vesting instrument is executed or made pursuant to this Act in respect of the settled land, any purported disposition thereof inter vivos by any person, other than a personal representative (not being a disposition which he has power to make in right of his equitable interests or powers under a trust instrument), shall not take effect except in favour of a purchaser of a legal estate [without notice of such tenant for life or statutory owner having become so entitled as aforesaid][1], but, save as aforesaid, shall operate only as a contract for valuable consideration to carry out the transaction after the requisite vesting instrument has been executed or made, and a purchaser of a legal estate shall not be concerned with such disposition unless the contract is registered as a land charge[2].

By virtue of Law of Property (Amendment) Act 1926, section 1, a person beneficially entitled in possession to land for an estate in fee simple or term of years absolute subject to charges[3] which would normally make the land settled land[4] may sell the land subject to such charges without complying with the Settled Land Act procedure and section 13. Alternatively he can overreach the charges by complying with the statutory procedure.

B.   Subject to Vesting Instrument

SETTLED LAND ACT 1925

18.   Restrictions on dispositions of settled land where trustees have not been discharged. — (1) Where land is the subject of a vesting instrument and the trustees of the settlement have not been discharged under this Act, then —

(a) any disposition by the tenant for life or statutory owner of the land, other than a disposition authorised by this Act or any other statute, or made in pursuance of any additional or larger powers mentioned in the vesting instrument, shall be void, except for the purpose of conveying or creating such equitable interests as he has power, in right of his equitable interests and powers under the trust instrument, to convey or create; and

(b) if any capital money is payable in respect of a transaction, a conveyance to a purchaser of the land shall only take effect under this Act if the capital money is paid to or by the direction of the trustees of the settlement or into court; and

(c) notwithstanding anything to the contrary in the vesting instrument, or the trust instrument, capital money shall not, except where the trustee is a trust corporation, be paid to or by the direction of fewer persons than two as trustees of the settlement[5].

(2) The restrictions imposed by this section do not affect —

(a) the right of a personal representative in whom the settled land may be vested to convey or deal with the land for the purposes of administration;

---

[1] As amended by L.P. (A.) A. 1926, Sch.
[2] See W & C, vol. 3, pp. 54-57.
[3] S.L.A. 1925, s. 20 (1) (ix).
[4] S.L.A. 1925, s. 1 (1) (v).
[5] See also S.L.A. 1925, s. 94; and as to receipts, s. 95, p. 277, post.
   For the definition of a Trust Corporation see p. 190. n. 2, ante.

(*b*) the right of a person of full age who has become absolutely
entitled (whether beneficially or as trustee for sale or personal
representative or otherwise) to the settled land, free from all
limitations, powers, and charges taking effect under the trust
instrument, to require the land to be conveyed to him.

The question arises of the position of the purchaser if he fails to
comply with these requirements in circumstances in which he did
not know and could not have known that the land was subject to a
settlement. Is the conveyance "void" under section 18? Or, should a
purchaser be protected under section 110 (1)[6]?

In *Weston v Henshaw* [1950] Ch 510, three generations of Westons,
W 1, W 2, and W 3, were successively interested in Blackacre. In 1921
W 1 sold Blackacre to W 2, who in 1927 sold it back to W 1. By his will
W 1 settled it on Mrs W 1 for life and then on W 2 for life and to a
grandson (W 3) contingently on attaining the age of 25. W 1 died in
1931, and Mrs W 1 in 1940, and on her death the fee simple was vested
by vesting assent in W 2.

W 2 charged Blackacre to the defendants by way of legal mortgage
to secure a number of personal advances, making title on each occasion
by showing the deeds up to the sale to him in 1921, and suppressing all
subsequent documents. Thus, W 2 appeared to be the absolute owner
of the fee simple. In reality, he was only a tenant for life. There was no
way in which the defendant, by enquiries, could have found out.

W 3 brought this action, after the death of W 2, as his administrator,
for a declaration that the charges were void against him.

DANCKWERTS J held that they were, because the land was settled
land, and the mortgagee had not complied with the provisions of
section 18. The mortgagee was by any standards a bona fide purchaser
of the legal estate for value without notice; and, if the decision is
correct, his position, under an Act which was intended to help him, is
worse than it was before 1926.

The decision was doubted in *Re Morgan's Lease*[7], [1972] Ch 1, [1971]
2 All ER 235, where UNGOED-THOMAS J said, at p. 7. "I come now to
the third issue on the first question, whether section 110 of the Settled
Land Act 1925 only applies if the purchaser knows that the other
party to the transaction is a tenant for life. The landlords' submission
was founded on *Weston v Henshaw* [1950] Ch 510.

[His Lordship referred to *Mogridge v Clapp* [1892] 3 Ch 382 which
"unfortunately was not brought to DANCKWERTS J's notice" and
continued:]

Here Kay, LJ, sitting in the Court of Appeal with Lindley LJ and
Bowen LJ, seems to me to treat it as self-evident that a person dealing
with a life tenant without knowing that he was a life tenant would be

---

[6] P. 281, post.
[7] (1971) 87 LQR 338 (D. W. Elliott). (1973) 36 Mod LR at p. 28 (R. H. Maudsley).

entitled to rely on section 110 of the Settled Land Act 1925; and, with the greatest respect for the decision in *Weston v Henshaw* [1950] Ch 510, that is the conclusion to which I would come independently of authority. There is, in the section, no express provision limiting its benefit to a purchaser who knows that the person with whom he is dealing is a tenant for life. On its face it reads as free of limitation and as applicable to a person without such knowledge as to a person who has it. There is a limitation, namely, that the purchaser must act in good faith; but that limitation reads as applicable to a purchaser with such knowledge as without. So, despite the insertion of the limitation of good faith on the part of the purchaser, there is no insertion of the limitation for which the landlords contend. Thus my conclusion is that section 110 applies whether or not the purchaser knows that the other party to the transaction is tenant for life."

IV.   Overreaching[8]

A.   Under an Ordinary Conveyance

If the correct machinery is used, a sale by a tenant for life "over-reaches" the beneficial interests under the settlement and passes the title to a purchaser free from them. The beneficial interests are transferred from the land to the purchase money[9].

LAW OF PROPERTY ACT 1925

2.   Conveyances overreaching certain equitable interests and powers. — (1) A conveyance to a purchaser of a legal estate in land shall over-reach any equitable interest or power affecting that estate, whether or not he has notice thereof, if —

  (i) the conveyance is made under the powers conferred by the Settled Land Act, 1925[10], or any additional powers conferred by a settlement, and the equitable interest or power is capable of being overreached thereby, and the statutory requirements respecting the payment of capital money arising under the settlement are complied with[11];

SETTLED LAND ACT 1925

72.   Completion of transactions by conveyance. — (1) On a sale, exchange, lease, mortgage, charge, or other disposition, the tenant for life may, as regards land sold, given in exchange, leased, mortgaged, charged, or otherwise disposed of, or intended so to be, or as regards

---

[8] Cheshire, pp. 80, 792–793, 796–797; M & W, pp. 148–150, 371–377, 379–383; MM, pp. 77–79, 179–186.
[9] S.L.A. 1925, s. 75 (5), p. 278, post.
[10] S.L.A. 1925, s. 72.
[11] S.L.A. 1925, s. 18 (1) (*b*), p. 256, ante.

easements or other rights or privileges sold, given in exchange, leased, mortgaged, or otherwise disposed of, or intended so to be, effect the transaction by deed to the extent of the estate or interest vested or declared to be vested in him by the last or only vesting instrument affecting the settled land or any less estate or interest, in the manner requisite for giving effect to the sale, exchange, lease, mortgage, charge, or other disposition, but so that a mortgage shall be effected by the creation of a term of years absolute in the settled land or by charge by way of legal mortgage, and not otherwise.

(2) Such a deed, to the extent and in the manner to and in which it is expressed or intended to operate and can operate under this Act, is effectual to pass the land conveyed, or the easements, rights, privileges or other interests created, discharged from all the limitations, powers, and provisions of the settlement, and from all estates, interests and charges subsisting or to arise thereunder, but subject to and with the exception of —

(i) all legal estates and charges by way of legal mortgage having priority to the settlement; and

(ii) all legal estates and charges by way of legal mortgage which have been conveyed or created for securing money actually raised at the date of the deed; and

(iii) all leases and grants at fee-farm rents or otherwise, and all grants of easements, rights of common, or other rights or privileges which —

(a) were before the date of the deed granted or made for value in money or money's worth, or agreed so to be, by the tenant for life or statutory owner, or by any of his predecessors in title, or any trustees for them, under the settlement, or under any statutory power, or are at that date otherwise binding on the successors in title of the tenant for life or statutory owner; and

(b) are at the date of the deed protected by registration under the Land Charges Act, 1925[12], if capable of registration thereunder.

(3) Notwithstanding registration under the Land Charges Act, 1925[12], of —

(a) an annuity within the meaning of Part II. of that Act;

(b) a limited owner's charge or a general equitable charge within the meaning of that Act;

a disposition under this Act operates to overreach such annuity or charge which shall, according to its priority, take effect as if limited by the settlement.

(4) Where a lease is by this Act authorised to be made by writing under hand only, such writing shall have the same operation under this section as if it had been a deed.

---

[12] Now L.C.A. 1972.

B.   Ad Hoc Settlements

SETTLED LAND ACT 1925

21.   Absolute owners subject to certain interests to have the powers of tenant for life. — (1) Where a person of full age is beneficially entitled in possession to a legal estate subject to any equitable interests or powers, then, for the purpose of overreaching such interests or powers, he may, notwithstanding any stipulation to the contrary, by deed (which shall have effect as a principal vesting deed within the meaning of this Act) declare that the legal estate is vested in him on trust to give effect to all equitable interests and powers affecting the legal estate, and that deed shall be executed by two or more individuals approved or appointed by the court or a trust corporation[13], who shall be stated to be the trustees of the settlement for the purposes of this Act.

Thereupon so long as any of the equitable interests and powers are subsisting the following provisions shall have effect:—

(*a*) The person so entitled as aforesaid and each of his successors in title being an estate owner shall have the powers of a tenant for life and the land shall be deemed to be settled land;

(*b*) The instrument (if any) under which his estate arises or is acquired, and the instrument (if any) under which the equitable interests or powers are subsisting or capable of taking effect shall be deemed to be the trust instrument:

   Provided that where there is no such instrument as last aforesaid then a deed (which shall take effect as a trust instrument) shall be executed contemporaneously with the vesting deed, and shall declare the trusts affecting the land;

(*c*) The persons stated in the principal vesting deed to be the trustees of the settlement for the purposes of this Act shall also be the trustees of the trust instrument for those purposes; and

(*d*) Capital money arising on any disposition of the land shall be paid to or by the direction of the trustees of the settlement or into court, and shall be applicable towards discharging or providing for payment in due order of any principal money payable in respect of such interests or charges as are overreached by such disposition, and until so applied shall be invested or applied as capital money under the trust instrument, and the income thereof shall be applied as the income of such capital money, and be liable for keeping down in due order any annual or periodical sum which may be overreached by the disposition.

(2) The following equitable interests and powers are excepted from the operation of subsection (1) of this section, namely —

(i) an equitable interest protected by a deposit of documents relating to the legal estate affected;

---

[13] See p. 190, n. 2, ante.

(ii) the benefit of a covenant or agreement restrictive of the user of land;

(iii) an easement, liberty or privilege over or affecting land and being merely an equitable interest;

(iv) the benefit of a contract to convey or create a legal estate, including a contract conferring either expressly or by statutory implication a valid option of purchase, a right of pre-emption, or any other like right;

(v) any equitable interest protected by registration under the Land Charges Act, 1925[14], other than —

(a) an annuity with the meaning of Part II. of that Act;

(b) a limited owner's charge or a general equitable charge within the meaning of that Act.

(3) Subject to the powers conferred by this Act on a tenant for life, nothing contained in this section shall deprive an equitable chargee of any of his rights or of his remedies for enforcing those rights.

V. The Tenant for Life[15]

A. Who is Tenant for Life and Who has Powers of Tenant for Life

i. TENANT FOR LIFE AND OTHER LIMITED OWNERS

SETTLED LAND ACT 1925

19. Who is tenant for life. — (1) The person of full age who is for the time being beneficially entitled under a settlement to possession of settled land for his life is for the purposes of this Act the tenant for life of that land and the tenant for life under that settlement.

(2) If in any case there are two or more persons of full age so entitled as joint tenants, they together constitute the tenant for life for the purposes of this Act.

(3) If in any case there are two or more persons so entitled as joint tenants and they are not all of full age, such one or more of them as is or are for the time being of full age is or (if more than one) together constitute the tenant for life for the purposes of this Act, but this subsection does not affect the beneficial interests of such of them as are not for the time being of full age.

(4) A person being tenant for life within the foregoing definitions shall be deemed to be such notwithstanding that, under the settlement or otherwise, the settled land, or his estate or interest therein, is incumbered or charged in any manner or to any extent, and notwithstanding any assignment by operation of law or otherwise of his estate or interest under the settlement, whether before or after it came into possession, other than an assurance which extinguishes that estate or interest.

---

[14] Now L.C.A. 1972.
[15] Cheshire, pp. 174–189; M & W, pp. 320–324, 330–357; MM, pp. 140–141, 144–146, 154–155, 159–171.

20. Other limited owners having powers of tenant for life. — (1) Each of the following persons being of full age shall, when his estate or interest is in possession, have the powers of a tenant for life under this Act, (namely):—

(i) A tenant in tail, including a tenant in tail after possibility of issue extinct, and a tenant in tail who is by Act of Parliament restrained from barring or defeating his estate tail, and although the reversion is in the Crown, but not including such a tenant in tail where the land in respect whereof he is so restrained was purchased with money provided by Parliament in consideration of public services;

(ii) A person entitled to land for an estate in fee simple or for a term of years absolute with or subject to, in any of such cases, an executory limitation, gift, or disposition over on failure of his issue or in any other event;

(iii) A person entitled to a base or determinable fee, although the reversion or right of reverter is in the Crown, or to any corresponding interest in leasehold land;

(iv) A tenant for years determinable on life, not holding merely under a lease at a rent;

(v) A tenant for the life of another, not holding merely under a lease at a rent;

(vi) A tenant for his own or any other life, or for years determinable on life, whose estate is liable to cease in any event during that life, whether by expiration of the estate, or by conditional limitation, or otherwise, or to be defeated by an executory limitation, gift, or disposition over, or is subject to a trust for accumulation of income for any purpose;

(vii) A tenant by the curtesy;

(viii) A person entitled to the income of land under a trust or direction for payment thereof to him during his own or any other life, whether or not subject to expenses of management or to a trust for accumulation of income for any purpose, or until sale of the land, or until forfeiture, cesser or determination by any means of his interest therein, unless the land is subject to an immediate binding trust for sale;

(ix) A person beneficially entitled to land for an estate in fee simple or for a term of years absolute subject to any estates, interests, charges, or powers of charging, subsisting or capable of being exercised under a settlement[16];

117. Definitions. — (1) . . .

(xxviii) "Tenant for life" includes a person (not being a statutory owner) who has the powers of a tenant for life under this Act, and also (where the context requires) one of two or more

---

[16] Such persons may, however, convey the land subject to a prior interest as if the land had not been settled land. L.P. (A.) A. 1926, s. 1.

persons who together constitute the tenant for life, or have the powers of a tenant for life[17]; . . .

ii. STATUTORY OWNERS

SETTLED LAND ACT 1925

23. Powers of trustees, &c. when there is no tenant for life. — (1) Where under a settlement there is no tenant for life, nor, independently of this section, a person having by virtue of this Act the powers of a tenant for life then —

    (a) any person of full age on whom such powers are by the settlement expressed to be conferred[18]; and

    (b) in any other case the trustees of the settlement;

shall have the powers of a tenant for life under this Act[19].

26. Infants, how to be affected.[20] — (1) Where an infant is beneficially entitled in possession to land for an estate in fee simple or for a term of years absolute or would if of full age be a tenant for life of

---

[17] *Re Jefferys* [1939] Ch 205, [1938] 4 All ER 120 (an annuitant is not tenant for life); *Re Carne's Settled Estates* [1899] 1 Ch 324 ("to occupy the land rent free so long as she might wish to do so," held to be a tenant for life); *Ayer v Benton* (1967) 204 Estates Gazette 359; *Re Catling*, [1931] 2 Ch 359 (wife as tenant at a nominal annual sum, the tenancy not to be determined so long as she made the property her principal place of residence: held, not to be a tenant for life; and indeed there was no settlement); *Re Waleran Settled Estates* [1927] 1 Ch 522 (a term to a woman "for 99 years if she should so long live", held to be a tenant for life); *Re Ogle's Settled Estates* [1927] 1 Ch 229, p. 251, ante; *Re Cayley and Evans' Contract* [1930] 2 Ch 143; *Re Gallenga Will Trusts*, [1938] 1 All ER 106. Questions also arise in connection with settlements on divorce: *Morss v Morss* [1972] Fam 264, [1972] 1 All ER 1121 (agreement incorporated in court order allowing a wife the use of house "rent free for her life or until . . . debarred by court from access to the children"; held a licence); *Martin v Martin* [1978] Fam 12, [1977] 3 All ER 762 (court order giving house on trust to wife for life or until remarriage or such earlier date as she should cease to live there, and thereafter on trust for the parties in equal shares. This would presumably make the wife a tenant for life; the incoveniences of such a decision are pointed out in [1978] Conv 229 (P. Smith). See also *Allen v Allen* [1974] 1 WLR 1171, [1974] 3 All ER 385, where a similar result was achieved through the machinery of a trust for sale. A similar problem arises where the court gives protection to a licensee for the period of his life; p. 498, post; (1977) 93 LQR 561 (J.A. Hornby).

[18] *Re Craven Settled Estates* [1926] Ch 985; *Re Norton* [1929] 1 Ch 84, p. 196, ante; *Re Beaumont's Settled Estates* [1937] 2 All ER 353.

[19] S.L.A. 1925, s. 104 (1) provides that the powers of a tenant for life are not capable of assignment or release. A person who becomes a "statutory owner" under s. 23 (1) may release his powers, and the trustees then become statutory owners. *Re Craven Settled Estates* [1926] Ch 985, p. 268, post.

[20] S.L.A. 1925, ss. 1 (1) (ii) (d), 1 (2), 102. The Family Law Reform Act 1969, s. 1 provides that as from January 1, 1970, "a person shall attain full age on attaining the age of eighteen instead of on attaining the age of twenty-one; and a person shall attain full age on that date if he has then already attained the age of eighteen but not the age of twenty-one". On minors generally see Cheshire, pp. 915–922; M & W, pp. 988–993. MM, pp. 480–483. A minor cannot hold a legal estate in land, although he may hold an equitable interest: L.P.A. 1925, s. 1 (6). L.R.A. 1925, s. 3 (iv). For the effect of a conveyance of a legal estate to a minor, L.P.A. 1925, s. 19; S.L.A. 1925, s. 27. L.R.A. 1925, s. 111. He cannot be appointed a trustee: L.P.A. 1925, s. 20, nor an executor: Judicature Act 1925, s. 165, nor an administrator: *In Re Manuel* (1849) 13 Jur 664. He cannot make a will: Wills Act 1837, s. 7, except as provided by Wills (Soldiers and Sailors) Act 1918. Any disposition by a minor of any interest in land is voidable at his option, on his attaining his majority, or within a reasonable time thereafter.

or have the powers of a tenant for life over settled land, then, during the minority of the infant —

    (*a*) if the settled land is vested in a personal representative, the personal representative, until a principal vesting instrument has been executed pursuant to the provisions of this Act; and

    (*b*) in every other case, the trustees of the settlement;

shall have, in reference to the settled land and capital money, all the powers conferred by this Act and the settlement on a tenant for life, and on the trustees of the settlement.

117. Definitions. — (1) . . .

(xxvi) "Statutory owner" means the trustees of the settlement or other persons who, during a minority, or at any other time when there is no tenant for life, have the powers of a tenant for life under this Act, but does not include the trustees of the settlement, where by virtue of an order of the court or otherwise the trustees have power to convey the settled land in the name of the tenant for life;

B. Powers of the Tenant for Life

i. TENANT FOR LIFE AND TRUSTEES FOR SALE

The tenant for life's powers are given in detail in Settled Land Act 1925, Part II. The same powers are given to trustees for sale by Law of Property Act 1925, section 28, and the most important sections are set out at pp. 200–201, ante.

ii. NOTICE TO TRUSTEES

When a tenant for life exercises his powers of sale, exchange, leasing, mortgaging, charging or granting an option, he is usually required to give notice to the trustees[1]. In the case of the sale of a mansion house, their consent is required.

iii. SPECIAL CONSENTS[2]

SETTLED LAND ACT 1925

65. Power to dispose of mansion. — (1) The powers of disposing of settled land conferred by this Act on a tenant for life may be exercised as respects the principal mansion house, if any, on any settled land, and the pleasure grounds and park and lands, if any, usually occupied therewith:

  Provided that those powers shall not be exercised without the consent of the trustees of the settlement or an order of the court —

    (*a*) if the settlement is a settlement made or coming into operation before the commencement of this Act and the settlement does not expressly provide to the contrary; or

---

[1] S.L.A. 1925, s. 101.

[2] See also s. 66 (1) (cutting and sale of timber by tenant for life impeachable for waste); s. 58 (compromising claims): s. 67 (3) (order of the court needed for the sale of settled chattels); s. 64 (general power to effect any transaction under a court order: p. 202, ante).

(*b*) if the settlement is a settlement made or coming into operation after the commencement of this Act and the settlement expressly provides that these powers or any of them shall not be exercised without such consent or order.

(2) Where a house is usually occupied as a farmhouse, or where the site of any house and the pleasure grounds and park and lands, if any, usually occupied therewith do not together exceed twenty-five acres in extent, the house is not to be deemed a principal mansion house within the meaning of this section, and may accordingly be disposed of in like manner as any other part of the settled land.

C. Reductions from and Additions to the Powers of the Tenant for Life

SETTLED LAND ACT 1925

106[3]. Prohibition or limitation against exercise of powers void, and provision against forfeiture. — (1) If in a settlement, will, assurance, or other instrument executed or made before or after, or partly before and partly after, the commencement of this Act a provision is inserted —

(*a*) purporting or attempting, by way of direction, declaration, or otherwise, to forbid a tenant for life or statutory owner to exercise any power under this Act, or his right to require the settled land to be vested in him; or

(*b*) attempting, or tending, or intended, by a limitation, gift, or disposition over of settled land, or by a limitation, gift, or disposition of other real or any personal property, or by the imposition of any condition, or by forfeiture, or in any other manner whatever, to prohibit or prevent him from exercising, or to induce him to abstain from exercising, or to put him into a position inconsistent with his exercising any power under this Act, or his right to require the settled land to be vested in him;

that provision, as far as it purports, or attempts, or tends, or is intended to have, or would or might have, the operation aforesaid, shall be deemed to be void.

(2) For the purposes of this section an estate or interest limited to continue so long as a person abstains from exercising any such power or right as aforesaid shall be and take effect as an estate or interest to continue for the period for which it would continue if that person were to abstain from exercising the power or right, discharged from liability to determination or cesser by or on his exercising the same.

(3) Notwithstanding anything in a settlement, the exercise by the tenant for life or statutory owner of any power under this Act shall not occasion a forfeiture.

---

[3] [1978] Conv 229 (P. Smith).

108.   Saving for and exercise of other powers. — (1) Nothing in this Act shall take away, abridge, or prejudicially affect any power for the time being subsisting under a settlement, or by statute or otherwise, exercisable by a tenant for life, or (save as hereinafter provided) by trustees with his consent, or on his request, or by his direction, or otherwise, and the powers given by this Act are cumulative.

(2) In case of conflict between the provisions of a settlement and the provisions of this Act, relative to any matter in respect whereof the tenant for life or statutory owner exercises or contracts or intends to exercise any power under this Act, the provisions of this Act shall prevail; and, notwithstanding anything in the settlement, any power (not being merely a power of revocation or appointment) relating to the settled land thereby conferred on the trustees of the settlement or other persons exercisable for any purpose, whether or not provided for in this Act, shall, after the commencement of this Act, be exercisable by the tenant for life or statutory owner as if it were an additional power conferred on the tenant for life within the next following section of this Act and not otherwise.

109.   Saving for additional or larger powers under settlement. — (1) Nothing in this Act precludes a settlor from conferring on the tenant for life, or (save as provided by the last preceding section) on the trustees of the settlement, any powers additional to or larger than those conferred by this Act.

(2) Any additional or larger powers so conferred shall, as far as may be, notwithstanding anything in this Act, operate and be exercisable in the like manner, and with all the like incidents, effects, and consequences, as if they were conferred by this Act, and, if relating to the settled land, as if they were conferred by this Act on a tenant for life.

In *Re Jefferys* [1939] Ch 205, [1938] 4 All ER 120; FARWELL J, held that a power given to an annuitant to restrain a sale by trustees of the settlement as statutory owners was not a "power exercisable by trustees with" the consent of the tenant for life[4] and was not therefore saved by section 108 (1); the annuitant's power to restrain a sale was thus in conflict with the powers given to the statutory owners by the Act[5]. The statutory power of sale thus prevailed under section 108 (2); and, even if the annuitant consented, sales by the statutory owners were sales under their statutory power, and the provisions of the Settled Land Act 1925 as to capital money must be complied with[6].

In *Re Ames* [1893] 2 Ch 479, personalty was bequeathed for the upkeep of settled land, the surplus income being applicable to the

---

[4] See p. 263, n. 17, ante.
[5] See p. 265, ante.
[6] S.L.A. 1925, s. 18 (1), p. 256, ante; s. 73, p. 204, ante; s. 75, p. 277, post; (1939) 55 LQR 22 (H.P.).

tenant for life, but, if the tenant for life should become disentitled to the possession or income of the settled land, the settled personalty should fall into residue.

NORTH J, held the proviso void under the Settled Land Act 1882, section 51 (the predecessor of section 106) and the tenant for life continued to be entitled to the income of the personalty after the sale of the settled land.

In *Re Acklom* [1929] 1 Ch 195, the testator gave his leasehold house and its contents on trust for Mrs. Hawkins for life; with a direction to the trustees that if "and when she shall not wish to reside or continue to reside there", the house should be sold, and the proceeds divided between certain charities.

The testator died in 1918 and Mrs. Hawkins went into possession. In 1925, she went abroad for health reasons, and her return was delayed by a serious illness in the spring of 1926. In 1927 she sold the premises in exercise of her Settled Land Act powers and the trustees sold the contents.

In holding that she had not forfeited her interest in the property, and could receive the income from the proceeds of sale, MAUGHAM J. said at p. 198: "There is no doubt at all that under section 106 of the Settled Land Act, 1925, which applies to the provisions of wills made before and after the Act, a provision which limits or prevents the tenant for life from exercising his power of sale is void. Accordingly it is reasonably clear to my mind in this case that if Mrs. Hawkins was in a position to exercise the powers of a tenant for life on 29 June 1927, a provision whereby the proceeds of sale should under the terms of the will pass to the charities is void. If authority were needed for that it would be found in *Re Paget's Settled Estates* ((1885) 30 ChD 161), *Re Trenchard* ([1902] 1 Ch 378) and *Re Gibbons* ([1920] 1 Ch 372). B parity of reasoning it cannot be denied that so long as Mrs. Hawkins was a person having the powers of a tenant for life she was entitled to let Wiseton Court without incurring any forfeiture even if she ceased thereupon to reside or to continue to reside within the meaning of the words contained in the clause I have read. The argument for the charities does not dispute this proposition. They maintain that on the evidence and in the events which happened Mrs. Hawkins must be taken to have ceased to reside or to continue to reside at a date considerably anterior to the sale, and accordingly that she had forfeited her interest in the property prior to the sale, and therefore that they are entitled to the proceeds of sale. Now the evidence as to this is unsatisfactory; ... I have no evidence that at any particular date it can be established that prior to the sale she had finally and irrevocably decided not only not to continue to reside, but not to let the house under her powers as tenant for life. The question of intention is affected by section 106; and if a tenant for life or person entitled to possession, so long as he enjoys it, is careful to exercise the powers as under the Act so that section 106 applies, the intention is wholly immaterial. I hold that Mrs. Hawkins was entitled temporarily to give up possession if it was for the purpose of exercising her powers under the Settled Land Act or of procuring a tenant or effecting a sale, and that on the evidence before me Mrs. Hawkins has so acted that the trustees had not the power of sale of the property. Of course it is material in that connection to bear in mind that they never purported to exercise any such power. They are to be presumed to have allowed her to sell without interference by any one. Accordingly I answer the first question by saying that she has not forfeited her interest in the proceeds of sale of the leasehold property[7].''

D. Non-Assignability

SETTLED LAND ACT 1925

104. Powers not assignable, and contract not to exercise powers void. — (1) The powers under this Act of a tenant for life are not capable of assignment or release, and do not pass to a person as being, by operation of law or otherwise, an assignee of a tenant for life, and remain exercisable by the tenant for life after and notwithstanding any assignment, by operation of law or otherwise, of his estate or interest under the settlement.

This subsection applies notwithstanding that the estate or interest of the tenant for life under the settlement was not in possession when the assignment was made or took effect by operation of law.

(2) A contract by a tenant for life not to exercise his powers under this Act or any of them shall be void.

(4) Where such an assignment for value[8] is made or comes into operation after the commencement of this Act, the consent of the assignee shall not be requisite for the exercise by the tenant for life of any of the powers conferred by this Act:

Provided that —

(a) the assignee shall be entitled to the same or the like estate or interest in or charge on the land, money, or securities for the time being representing the land, money, or securities comprised in the assignment, as he had by virtue of the assignment in the last-mentioned land, money, or securities; and

(b) if the assignment so provides, or if it takes effect by operation of the law of bankruptcy, and after notice thereof to the trustees of the settlement, no investment or application of capital money for the time being affected by the assignment shall be made without the consent of the assignee, except an

---

[7] See also *Re Orlebar* [1936] Ch 147; and *Re Aberconway's Settlement Trusts* [1953] Ch 647, [1953] 2 All ER 350.

[8] I.e., an assignment for value of the beneficial interest of the tenant for life (sub-s. 3).

investment in securities authorised by statute for the investment of trust money[9], and

(c) notice of the intended transaction shall, unless the assignment otherwise provides, be given to the assignee, but a purchaser shall not be concerned to see or inquire whether such notice has been given.

(10) An assignment by operation of the law of bankruptcy, where the assignment comes into operation after the commencement of this Act, shall be deemed to be an assignment for value for the purposes of this section.

105. Effect of surrender of life estate to the next remainderman. — (1) Where the estate or interest of a tenant for life under the settlement has been or is absolutely assured with intent to extinguish the same, either before or after the commencement of this Act, to the person next entitled in remainder or reversion under the settlement[10], then, the statutory powers of the tenant for life under this Act shall, in reference to the property affected by the assurance, and notwithstanding the provisions of the last preceding section, cease to be exercisable by him, and the statutory powers shall thenceforth become exercisable as if he were dead, but without prejudice to any incumbrance affecting the estate or interest assured, and to the rights to which any incumbrancer would have been entitled if those powers had remained exercisable by the tenant for life. . . .

In *Re Shawdon Estates Settlement* [1930] 2 Ch 1, it was held by the Court of Appeal (Lord HANWORTH MR, LAWRENCE and ROMER LJJ, affirming EVE J) that section 105 (1) applied also to the case where the "assurance" was made by the trustee in bankruptcy of the tenant for life. The tenant for life refused to execute a vesting deed in favour of the tenant in tail in remainder, the "person next entitled", who was held to be entitled to call for a vesting order in his favour under the Settled Land Act 1925, section 12 (1) (a).

SETTLED LAND ACT 1925

24. As to a tenant for life who has parted with his interest. — (1) If it is shown to the satisfaction of the court that a tenant for life, who has by reason of bankruptcy, assignment, incumbrance, or otherwise ceased in the opinion of the court to have a substantial interest in his estate or interest in the settled land or any part thereof, has unreasonably refused to exercise any of the powers conferred on him by this Act, or consents to an order under this section, the court may,

---

[9] S.L.A. 1925, ss. 73, 74; Trustee Investments Act 1961, p. 205, ante; L.P.A. 1925, s. 28 (2), p. 200, ante.
[10] A remainderman or reversioner does not qualify if there is an intervening limitation which may take effect. *Re Maryon-Wilson's Instruments* [1971] Ch 789, [1969] 3 All ER 558.

on the application of any person interested in the settled land or the part thereof affected, make an order authorising the trustees of the settlement, to exercise in the name and on behalf of the tenant for life, any of the powers of a tenant for life under this Act, in relation to the settled land or the part thereof affected, either generally and in such manner and for such period as the court may think fit, or in a particular instance, and the court may by the order direct that any documents of title in the possession of the tenant for life relating to the settled land be delivered to the trustees of the settlement.

(2) While any such order is in force, the tenant for life shall not, in relation to the settled land or the part thereof affected, exercise any of the powers thereby authorised to be exercised in his name and on his behalf, but no person dealing with the tenant for life shall be affected by any such order, unless the order is for the time being registered as an order affecting land[11].

(3) An order may be made under this section at any time after the estate or interest of the tenant for life under the settlement has taken effect in possession, and notwithstanding that he disposed thereof when it was an estate or interest in remainder or reversion.

RE THORNHILL'S SETTLEMENT

[1941] Ch 24, [1940] 4 All ER 83, 249 (ChD, BENNETT J, affirmed in five lines by CA Sir Wilfrid GREENE MR, CLAUSON and GODDARD LJJ).

Michael Christopher Wright McCreagh, the tenant for life, was bankrupt. He neglected the management of the property, and the mansion house and three farms were derelict.

The summons asked that the Public Trustee, as trustee of the settlement, should be authorised by order under the Settled Land Act 1925, section 24 (1) to exercise the tenant for life's powers of leasing and sale.

Held. The tenant for life had unreasonably refused to exercise his powers, and the order should be made.

BENNETT J: The real question which I have to determine is whether the applicant has satisfied me that the tenant for life, the bankrupt, has unreasonably refused to exercise the powers which the Settled Land Act 1925 gives to him as a tenant for life. . . .

There is evidence which satisfies me that for some years past the land comprised in the settlement has been neglected. . . .

The fact that the land has been allowed to fall into this deplorable condition is not a ground for exercising the jurisdiction which section 24 of the Settled Land Act 1925 confers on this court. I have to be satisfied by evidence that the tenant for life has unreasonably refused to exercise the powers which that Act gives him — namely the powers of sale and the powers of leasing and other powers concerned with the disposal of the land comprised in the settlement.

---

[11] L.C.A. 1972, s. 6 p. 38, ante.

There are three respects in which, in my judgment, the applicant has proved that the bankrupt has unreasonably refused to exercise his powers . . .

[His Lordship referred to occasions on which the bankrupt unreasonably refused to let farms, to sell to the War Office land which they had requisitioned, and to let some allotments. The tenant for life was acting in this way because he felt aggrieved that the settlor, his mother, had given him only a life interest under the settlement.]

On the evidence I think that it is plain that in the interests of everybody interested in the settled land an order should be made authorizing the trustees of the settlement to exercise on behalf of the tenant for life some of the tenant for life's powers. I do not propose, as at present advised and on the evidence before me, to make an order which will authorize the trustees of the settlement to exercise powers of sale over the whole of the settled land, because, as I understand it, the settled land has been in the possession of the ancestors of the present tenant for life since the days of King John. It may well be that the bankrupt might have objections founded on reason against the whole of the estate being disposed of. The order which I propose to make under the section is one which will enable the Public Trustee, as trustee of the settlement, to exercise in the name and on behalf of the tenant for life the powers of sale in relation to any of the land comprised in the settlement and requisitioned by or on behalf of the War Office, and the powers of the tenant for life to lease any part of the settled land and to exercise all powers conferred on a tenant for life by the Act ancillary to the powers of leasing. I will also make an order on the tenant for life to deliver to the trustee documents of title in his possession relating to the settled land. I will authorize the trustee to exercise the powers of the tenant for life to make a contract to sell the land requisitioned by the War Office and to sell it, and I will vest in the trustee the power to direct investment.

E. Fiduciary Nature of the Powers of the Tenant for Life

SETTLED LAND ACT 1925

107. Tenant for life trustee for all parties interested. — (1) A tenant for life or statutory owner shall, in exercising any power under this Act, have regard to the interests of all parties entitled under the settlement, and shall, in relation to the exercise thereof by him, be deemed to be in the position and to have the duties and liabilities of a trustee for those parties.

In *Wheelwright v Walker* (1883) 23 ChD 752, the defendant was tenant for life of land which was settled within the Settled Land Act 1882, and his daughter was entitled in remainder[12]. The daughter sold

---

[12] Subject to partial divestment if, as was most unlikely, her father had further children.

her interest in remainder to the plaintiff. The defendant intended to sell under his Settled Land Act powers, the result of such sale being to deprive the plaintiff of his right to occupy the land when the defendant died[13]. No Settled Land Act trustees had been appointed.

PEARSON J, granted an injunction on the ground that, since no Settled Land Act trustees had been appointed, the provisions of the Act would not be complied with. On the question of the tenant for life's power to sell, he said at p. 758:

"So far as I can see, there is no restriction whatever in the Act on the power of a tenant for life to sell. There is nothing that I can see in the Act to enable the Court to restrain him from selling, whether he desires to sell because he is in debt, and wishes to increase his income; or whether, without being in debt, he thinks he can increase his income; or whether he desires to sell from mere unwillingness to take the trouble involved in the management of landed property; or whether he acts from worse motives, as from mere caprice or whim, or because he is desirous of doing that which he knows would be very disagreeable to those who expect to succeed him at his death. There is not, so far as I can see, any power either in the Court or in trustees to interfere with his power of sale. . . . Now if *Elizabeth France,* instead of selling the property to the Plaintiff *J. W. Wheelwright,* had simply settled it, on her marriage, on herself as tenant for life, with remainder to her children, I am of opinion that this Act would have applied, and her father, as tenant for life under the will, could have exercised the power of sale as tenant for life under the Act. I think it makes no difference that *Elizabeth France* simply sold to the Plaintiff *J. W. Wheelwright* instead of settling her interest. I find nothing whatever in the Act which gives any person entitled in remainder any power of any sort or description to interfere with the right of the tenant for life to sell. So far as I can see, the object of the Act is to enable the tenant for life of real estate comprised in a settlement to take it out of the settlement, and to substitute for it, *ex mero motu,* the value of it in pounds, shillings, and pence. I come now to the next question which has been raised. It was said that the tenant for life may have a power to sell, but that there are no trustees here; that trustees are required to be in existence under the Act, and that the tenant for life cannot sell unless there be trustees under the Act, because he is required to give them notice. . . . Although I do not see exactly what power or control they have over the tenant for life in regard to selling the property, it is quite plain from the whole scope of the Act that the trustees are considered as having an important duty to perform; at all events, I think it clear that even as regards a sale they have this important duty to perform, that if a tenant for life attempted to commit what may be called a fraud, and proposed to sell the property for something infinitely below its real value, it would be the duty of the trustees to come to the Court and ask for an injunction to restrain a sale. I do not think it would be

---

[13] The plaintiff's interest would be overreached on sale and transferred to the purchase money. S.L.A. 1882, s. 22 (5); 1925, s. 75 (5), p. 278, *post.*

right for them to leave the remainderman to take the objection at some remote period when the evidence might be very conflicting as to the circumstances under which the sale was made, and as to the value of the property; but I think it would be the trustees' duty to bring the matter before the Court, and the Court would have power in that case of controlling the sale, and the more so because the 53rd section of the Act[14] states that 'a tenant for life shall in exercising any power under this Act . . . be deemed to be in the position and to have the duties and liabilities of a trustee for' all parties. I assent to Mr. *William Pearson's* argument that a tenant for life in selling under the Act must sell as fairly as trustees must sell for the tenant for life and for those in remainder. . . . Now, there are certainly no trustees here who come within the meaning of the Act. But by the 38th section[15] power is given to 'the tenant for life', or any other person having an interest in the settled land, to come to the Court, and then the Court 'may, if it thinks fit, . . . appoint fit persons to be trustees under the settlement for the purposes of this Act'. I think, therefore, that *John Walker,* the tenant for life, has himself power to sell the fee simple and inheritance of this property if he should comply with the provisions of the Act, but I also think that he has been proceeding, up to the present moment, precipitately, because there are no trustees to whom he can give notice, and therefore I shall grant an injunction to restrain him from selling or offering for sale the property until such time as there shall have been appointed proper trustees of the will for the purposes of the Act, to whom notice can be given and until due notice shall have been given to them of the intention to sell.''

In *Middlemas v Stevens* [1901] 1 Ch 574, the defendant was entitled under her deceased husband's will to the enjoyment of a house during widowhood and so long as she resided therein. Intending to marry again, she proposed to grant, under her Settled Land Act powers, a 21 year lease to her intended husband. The remainderman objected, and JOYCE J, held that her proposed action was not a bona fide exercise of her powers.

JOYCE J said: "I have no doubt in this case. A tenant for life in exercising any of the powers conferred by the Settled Land Acts must have regard to the interests of all parties entitled under the settlement. Here is a lady who is tenant for life during widowhood. Apart from any question as to her relationship to the gentleman who is the intended lessee, if I found a person, whose interest in the settled property would come to an end to-morrow, persisting in granting a lease which was objected to by all those entitled in remainder, I should regard the case with considerable suspicion. But this case goes beyond suspicion. It is clear from the correspondence that the real object of the lady in granting the lease is that she may herself continue in occupation of the

---

[14] Replaced by S.L.A. 1925, s. 107 (1); p. 271, ante.
[15] Replaced by S.L.A. 1925, s. 34; p. 276, post.

premises. That, in my opinion, is not a bona fide exercise of her powers as tenant for life. But it does not rest there, because it is admitted by the correspondence that she has no intention of granting the lease in the event of her not marrying the gentleman in question. I think the plaintiffs are entitled to an injunction restraining the defendant from granting the lease without their consent or the sanction of the Court[16].''

Subject to restrictions, the tenant for life may however deal with the settled land for his own purposes.

SETTLED LAND ACT 1925

68. Provision enabling dealings with tenant for life. — (1) In the manner mentioned and subject to the provisions contained in this section —

(a) a sale, grant, lease, mortgage, charge or other disposition of settled land, or of any easement, right, or privilege over the same may be made to the tenant for life; or

(b) capital money may be advanced on mortgage to him; or

(c) a purchase may be made from him of land to be made subject to the limitations of the settlement; or

(d) an exchange may be made with him of settled land for other land; and

(e) any such disposition, advance, purchase, or exchange as aforesaid may be made to, from, or with any persons of whom the tenant for life is one.

(2) In every such case the trustees of the settlement shall, in addition to their powers as trustees, have all the powers of a tenant for life in reference to negotiating and completing the transaction, and shall have power to enforce any covenants by the tenant for life, or, where the tenant for life is himself one of the trustees, then the other or others of them shall have such power, and the said powers of a tenant for life may be exercised by the trustees of the settlement in the name and on behalf of the tenant for life[17].

(3) This section applies, notwithstanding that the tenant for life is one of the trustees of the settlement, or that an order has been made authorising the trustees to act on his behalf, or that he is [suffering from mental disorder][18], but does not apply to dealings with any body of persons which includes a trustee of the settlement, not being the tenant for life, unless the transaction is either previously or subsequently approved by the court.

---

[16] See also later proceedings in *Wheelwright v Walker* (1883) 31 WR 912, where a malicious attempt to sell at a deflated price was restrained; *Re Handman and Wilcox's Contract* [1902] 1 Ch 599 (best rent not obtained as required by S.L.A., 1882, s. 7, now S.L.A. 1925, s. 42); *Re Earl Somers* (1895) 11, T.L.R. 567. (lease of public house by teetotal tenant for life containing a term that intoxicating liquid should not be sold).

[17] See *Re Pennant's Will Trusts* [1970] Ch 75, [1969] 2 All ER 862.

[18] Amended by the Mental Health Act 1959, s. 149 (1) and Sch. 7, Part I.

VI. Trustees of the Settlement[19]

SETTLED LAND ACT 1925

30. Who are trustees for purposes of Act. — (1) Subject to the provisions of this Act, the following persons are trustees of a settlement for the purposes of this Act, and are in this Act referred to as the "trustees of the settlement" or "trustees of a settlement", namely —

  (i) the persons, if any, who are for the time being under the settlement, trustees with power of sale of the settled land (subject or not to the consent of any person), or with power of consent to or approval of the exercise of such a power of sale, or if there are no such persons; then

 (ii) the persons, if any, for the time being, who are by the settlement declared to be trustees thereof for the purposes of the Settled Land Acts 1882 to 1890, or any of them, or this Act, or if there are no such persons; then

(iii) the persons, if any, who are for the time being under the Settled Land Acts, 1882 to 1890, or any of them, or this Act, other land comprised in the settlement and subject to the same limitations as the land to be sold or otherwise dealt with, or with power of consent to or approval of the exercise of such a power of sale, or, if there are no such persons; then

 (iv) the persons, if any, who are for the time being under the settlement trustees with future power of sale, or under a future trust for sale of the settled land, or with power of consent to or approval of the exercise of such a future power of sale, and whether the power or trust takes effect in all events or not, or, if there are no such persons; then

  (v) the persons, if any, appointed by deed to be trustees of the settlement by all the persons who at the date of the deed were together able, by virtue of their beneficial interests or by the exercise of an equitable power, to dispose of the settled land in equity for the whole estate the subject of the settlement.

  (2) Paragraphs (i) (iii) and (iv) of the last preceding subsection take effect in like manner as if the powers therein referred to had not by this Act been made exercisable by the tenant for life or statutory owner.

  (3) Where a settlement is created by will, or a settlement has arisen by the effect of an intestacy, and apart from this subsection there would be no trustees for the purposes of this Act of such settlement, then the personal representatives of the deceased shall, until other trustees are appointed, be by virtue of this Act the trustees of the settlement, but where there is a sole personal representative, not being a trust corporation, it shall be obligatory on him to appoint an additional trustee to act with him for the purposes of this Act, and the provisions of the Trustee Act, 1925[20], relating to the appointment of new trustees and the vesting of trust property shall apply accordingly.

---

[19] Cheshire, pp. 189–192; M & W, pp. 324–330, 357–358, 452–457; MM, pp. 155–159, 172–173.
[20] T.A. 1925, ss. 36–44.

31. As to trustees of compound settlements. — (1) Persons who are for the time being trustees for the purposes of this Act of an instrument which is a settlement, or is deemed to be a subsisting settlement for the purposes of this Act, shall be the trustees for the purposes of this Act of any settlement constituted by that instrument and any instruments subsequent in date or operation.

[Where there are trustees for the purposes of this Act of the instrument under which there is a tenant for life or statutory owner but there are no trustees for those purposes of a prior instrument, being one of the instruments by which a compound settlement is constituted, those trustees shall, unless and until trustees are appointed of the prior instrument or of the compound settlement, be the trustees for the purposes of this Act of the compound settlement[1].]

34. Appointment of trustees by court. — (1) If at any time there are no trustees of a settlement, or where in any other case it is expedient, for the purposes of this Act, that new trustees of a settlement be appointed, the court may, if it thinks fit, on the application of the tenant for life, statutory owner, or of any other person having, under the settlement, an estate or interest in the settled land, in possession, remainder or otherwise, or, in the case of an infant, of his testamentary or other guardian or next friend, appoint fit persons to be trustees of the settlement.

(2) The persons so appointed, and the survivors and survivor of them, while continuing to be trustees or trustee, and, until the appointment of new trustees, the personal representatives or representative for the time being of the last surviving or continuing trustee, shall become and be the trustees or trustee of the settlement.

35. Procedure on appointment of new trustees. — (1) Whenever a new trustee for the purposes of this Act is appointed of a trust instrument or a trustee thereof for the purposes aforesaid is discharged from the trust without a new trustee being appointed, a deed shall be executed supplemental to the last or only principal vesting instrument containing a declaration that the persons therein named, being the persons who after such appointment or discharge, as the case may be, are the trustees of the trust instrument for the purposes aforesaid, are the trustees of the settlement for those purposes; and a memorandum shall be endorsed on or annexed to the last or only principal vesting instrument in accordance with the Trustee Act, 1925.

(2) Every such deed as aforesaid shall, if the trustee was appointed or discharged by the court, be executed by such person as the court may direct, and, in any other case, shall be executed by —

   (i) the person, if any, named in the principal vesting instrument as the person for the time being entitled to appoint new trustees of the settlement, or if no person is so named, or the person is dead or unable or unwilling to act, the persons who if the principal vesting instrument had been the only instru-

---

[1] The words in square brackets were added by L.P. (A.) A., 1926, Sch.

ment constituting the settlement would have had power to appoint new trustees thereof;

(ii) the persons named in the deed of declaration as the trustees of the settlement; and

(iii) any trustee who is discharged as aforesaid or retires.

(3) A statement contained in any such deed of declaration as is mentioned in this section to the effect that the person named in the principal vesting instrument as the person for the time being entitled to appoint new trustees of the settlement is unable or unwilling to act, or that a trustee has remained outside the United Kingdom for more than twelve months, or refuses or is unfit to act, or is incapable of acting, shall in favour of a purchaser of a legal estate be conclusive evidence of the matter stated.

95. Trustees' receipts. The receipt or direction in writing of or by the trustees of the settlement, or where a sole trustee is a trust corporation, of or by that trustee, or of or by the personal representatives of the last surviving or continuing trustee, for or relating to any money or securities, paid or transferred to or by the direction of the trustees, trustee, or representatives, as the case may be, effectually discharges the payer or transferor therefrom, and from being bound to see to the application or being answerable for any loss or misapplication thereof, and, in case of a mortgagee or other person advancing money, from being concerned to see that any money advanced by him is wanted for any purpose of this Act, or that no more than is wanted is raised.

Provisions relating to the protection of trustees are contained in Settled Land Act 1925, sections 96-98.

VII. Capital Money[2]

A. Application

SETTLED LAND ACT 1925

75. Regulations respecting investment, devolution, and income of securities, &c.[3] — (1) Capital money arising under this Act[4] shall, in order to its being invested or applied as aforesaid, be paid either to the trustees of the settlement or into court at the option of the tenant for life, and shall be invested or applied by the trustees, or under the direction of the court, as the case may be, accordingly.

(2) The investment or other application by the trustees shall be made according to the direction of the tenant for life, and in default thereof according to the discretion of the trustees, but in the last-mentioned case subject to any consent required or direction given by

---

[2] Cheshire, pp. 193-196; M & W, pp. 345-350, 375-377; MM, pp. 165-167, 181-182.
[3] As to investment of capital money see S.L.A. 1925, ss. 73, 74 and Trustee Investments Act 1961, p. 205, ante.
[4] For the meaning of capital money, see W & C, vol. 2, pp. 156-157.

the settlement with respect to the investment or other application by the trustees of trust money of the settlement, and any investment shall be in the names or under the control of the trustees.

(3) The investment or other application under the direction of the court shall be made on the application of the tenant for life, or of the trustees.

(4) Any investment or other application shall not during the subsistence of the beneficial interest of the tenant for life be altered without his consent.

(5) Capital money arising under this Act while remaining uninvested or unapplied, and securities on which an investment of any such capital money is made shall for all purposes of disposition, transmission and devolution be treated as land, and shall be held for and go to the same persons successively, in the same manner and for and on the same estates, interests, and trusts, as the land wherefrom the money arises would, if not disposed of, have been held and have gone under the settlement.

(6) The income of those securities shall be paid or applied as the income of that land, if not disposed of, would have been payable or applicable under the settlement.

(7) Those securities may be converted into money, which shall be capital money arising under this Act.

(8) All or any part of any capital money paid into court may, if the court thinks fit, be at any time paid out to the trustees of the settlement.

B.   Improvements

SETTLED LAND ACT 1925

83. Description of improvements authorised by Act. — Improvements authorised by this Act are the making or execution on, or in connexion with, and for the benefit of settled land, of any of the works mentioned in the Third Schedule to this Act, or of any works for any of the purposes mentioned in that Schedule, and any operation incident to or necessary or proper in the execution of any of those works, or necessary or proper for carrying into effect any of those purposes, or for securing the full benefit of any of those works or purposes.

84. Mode of application of capital money. — (1) Capital money arising under this Act may be applied in or towards payment for any improvement authorised by this Act or by the settlement, without any scheme for the execution of the improvement being first submitted for approval to, or approved by, the trustees of the settlement or the court.

The Third Schedule is divided into three Parts:
I   Improvements, the costs of which are not liable to be replaced by instalments.

II Improvements, the costs of which the trustees of the settlement or the court may require to be replaced by instalments.

III Improvements, the costs of which the trustees of the settlement or the court must require to be replaced by instalments.

C. Receipts

SETTLED LAND ACT 1925

94. Number of trustees to act. — (1) Notwithstanding anything in this Act, capital money arising under this Act shall not be paid to fewer than two persons as trustees of the settlement, unless the trustee is a trust corporation[5].

D. Investments (Pp. 204–205, ante)

VIII. Change of Ownership

SETTLED LAND ACT 1925

7. Procedure on change of ownership. — (1) If, on the death of a tenant for life or statutory owner, or of the survivor of two or more tenants for life or statutory owners, in whom the settled land was vested, the land remains settled land, his personal representatives shall hold the settled land on trust, if and when required to do so, to convey it to the person who under the trust instrument or by virtue of this Act becomes the tenant for life or statutory owner and, if more than one, as joint tenants.

(2) If a person by reason of attaining full age becomes a tenant for life for the purposes of this Act of settled land, he shall be entitled to require the trustees of the settlement, personal representatives, or other persons in whom the settled land is vested, to convey the land to him.

(3) If a person who, when of full age, will together with another person or other persons constitute the tenant for life for the purposes of this Act of settled land attains that age, he shall be entitled to require the tenant for life, trustees of the settlement, personal representatives or other persons in whom the settled land is vested to convey the land to him and the other person or persons who together with him constitute the tenant for life as joint tenants.

(4) If by reason of forfeiture, surrender, or otherwise the estate owner of any settled land ceases to have the statutory powers of a tenant for life and the land remains settled land, he shall be bound forthwith to convey the settled land to the person who under the trust instrument, or by virtue of this Act, becomes the tenant for life or statutory owner and, if more than one, as joint tenants.

---

[5] See S.L.A. 1925, s. 95, p. 277, ante.

(5) If any person of full age becomes absolutely entitled to the settled land (whether beneficially, or as personal representative, or as trustee for sale, or otherwise) free from all limitations, powers, and charges taking effect under the settlement, he shall be entitled to require the trustees of the settlement, personal representatives, or other persons in whom the settled land is vested, to convey the land to him, and if more persons than one being of full age become so entitled to the settled land they shall be entitled to require such persons as aforesaid to convey the land to them as joint tenants.

8.   Mode and costs of conveyance, and saving of rights of personal representatives and equitable chargees. — (1) A conveyance by personal representatives under either of the last two preceding sections[6] may be made by an assent in writing signed by them which shall operate as a conveyance.

(4) Where the land is or remains settled land a conveyance under either of the last two preceding sections[6] shall —

    (*a*) if by deed, be a principal vesting deed; and

    (*b*) if by an assent, be a vesting assent, which shall contain the like statements and particulars as are required by this Act in the case of a principal vesting deed.

ADMINISTRATION OF ESTATES ACT 1925

22.   Special executors as respects settled land. — (1) A testator may appoint, and in default of such express appointment shall be deemed to have appointed, as his special executors in regard to settled land, the persons, if any, who are at his death the trustees of the settlement thereof, and probate may be granted to such trustees specially limited to the settled land.

In this subsection "settled land" means land vested in the testator which was settled previously to his death and not by his will[7].

(2) A testator may appoint other persons either with or without such trustees as aforesaid or any of them to be his general executors in regard to his other property and assets.

24.   Power for special personal representatives to dispose of settled land. — (1) The special personal representatives may dispose of the settled land without the concurrence of the general personal representatives, who may likewise dispose of the other property and assets of the deceased without the concurrence of the special personal representatives.

(2) In this section the expression "special personal representatives" means the representatives appointed to act for the purposes of settled land and includes any original personal representative who is to act with an additional personal representative for those purposes.

---

[6] For s. 6, see p. 254, ante.

[7] *Re Bridgett and Hayes' Contract* [1928] Ch 163; p. 283, post. For similar result in the case of intestacy see Judicature Act 1925, s. 162, as amended by Administration of Justice Act 1928, s. 9. See too W & C, vol. 5, pp. 36–38.

IX. Protection of Purchasers[8]

SETTLED LAND ACT 1925

110. Protection of purchasers, &c. — (1) On a sale, exchange, lease, mortgage, charge, or other disposition, a purchaser dealing in good faith with a tenant for life or statutory owner shall, as against all parties entitled under the settlement, be conclusively taken to have given the best price, consideration, or rent, as the case may require, that could reasonably be obtained by the tenant for life or statutory owner, and to have complied with all the requisitions of this Act[9].

(2) A purchaser of a legal estate in settled land shall not, except as hereby expressly provided, be bound or entitled to call for the production of the trust instrument or any information concerning that instrument or any ad valorem stamp duty thereon, and whether or not he has notice of its contents he shall, save as hereinafter provided, be bound and entitled if the last or only principal vesting instrument contains the statements and particulars required by this Act to assume that —

(a) the person in whom the land is by the said document vested or declared to be vested is the tenant for life or statutory owner and has all the powers of a tenant for life under this Act, including such additional or larger powers, if any, as are therein mentioned;

(b) the persons by the said instrument stated to be the trustees of the settlement, or their successors appearing to be duly appointed, are the properly constituted trustees of the settlement;

(c) the statements and particulars required by this Act and contained (expressly or by reference) in the said instrument were correct at the date thereof;

(d) the statements contained in any deed executed in accordance with this Act declaring who are the trustees of the settlement for the purposes of this Act are correct;

(e) the statements contained in any deed of discharge, executed in accordance with this Act, are correct;

Provided that, as regards the first vesting instrument executed for the purpose of giving effect to —

(a) a settlement subsisting at the commencement of this Act; or

(b) an instrument which by virtue of this Act is deemed to be a settlement[10]; or

---

[8] Cheshire, pp. 791–795; M & W, pp. 306–311; MM, pp. 161, 172.

[9] See *Weston v Henshaw* [1950] Ch 510, p. 257, ante; *Re Morgan's Lease* [1972] Ch 1, [1971] 2 All ER 235, p. 257, ante; see also *Gilmore v O'Conor* [1947] IR 462; *Davies v Hall* [1954] 1 WLR 855, [1954] 2 All ER 330; raising the question whether the purchaser can claim to be acting in good faith when the tenant for life's failure to observe the statutory requirements was discoverable. *Re Handman and Wilcox's Contract* [1902] 1 Ch 599 (transferee from lessee).

[10] See p. 254, n. 20, ante.

(*c*) a settlement which by virtue of this Act is deemed to have been made by any person after the commencement of this Act; or

(*d*) an instrument inter vivos intended to create a settlement of a legal estate in land which is executed after the commencement of this Act and does not comply with the requirements of this Act with respect to the method of effecting such a settlement;

a purchaser shall be concerned to see —

(i) that the land disposed of to him is comprised in such settlement or instrument;

(ii) that the person in whom the settled land is by such vesting instrument vested, or declared to be vested, is the person in whom it ought to be vested as tenant for life or statutory owner;

(iii) that the persons thereby stated to be the trustees of the settlement are the properly constituted trustees of the settlement.

(3) A purchaser of a legal estate in settled land from a personal representative shall be entitled to act on the following assumptions:—

(i) If the capital money, if any, payable in respect of the transaction is paid to the personal representative, that such representative is acting under his statutory or other powers and requires the money for purposes of administration;

(ii) If such capital money is, by the direction of the personal representative, paid to persons who are stated to be the trustees of a settlement, that such persons are the duly constituted trustees of the settlement for the purposes of this Act, and that the personal representative is acting under his statutory powers during a minority;

(iii) In any other case, that the personal representative is acting under his statutory or other powers.

(4) Where no capital money arises under a transaction, a disposition by a tenant for life or statutory owner shall, in favour of a purchaser of a legal estate, have effect under this Act notwithstanding that at the date of the transaction there are no trustees of the settlement.

(5) If a conveyance of or an assent relating to land formerly subject to a vesting instrument does not state who are the trustees of the settlement for the purposes of this Act, a purchaser of a legal estate shall be bound and entitled to act on the assumption that the person in whom the land was thereby vested was entitled to the land free from all limitations, powers, and charges taking effect under that settlement, absolutely and beneficially, or, if so expressed in the conveyance or assent, as personal representative, or trustee for sale or otherwise, and that every statement of fact in such conveyance or assent is correct.

The scheme of the Settled Land Act 1925 with the exceptions as shown in the proviso to section 110 (2), is based on the assumption that the purchaser of settled land is unaffected by the beneficial interests of the settlement. The scheme assumes that the appropriate machinery is correctly used; and the Act does not provide answers to the problems that will arise if mistakes are made[11]. Problems are most likely to arise in connection with a vesting instrument. Fraudulent suppression of deeds is another hazard, not however confined to settled land[12].

(1946) 62 LQR 168–169, (A. H. Withers):

"Conveyancers also assume that, in connexion with settled land, abstracted documents purporting to be vesting deeds, vesting assents by personal representatives of deceased tenants for life, deeds of declaration and deeds of discharge operate according to their tenor, except (1) in the case of the first vesting instrument made to give effect to a pre-1926 settlement, and (2) where facts or events are disclosed which suggest that some mistake has been made. In practice conveyancers must make these assumptions, though . . . unless section 110 of the Settled Land Act 1925 is benevolently construed by the court, such assumptions are not justified."

RE BRIDGETT AND HAYES' CONTRACT

[1928] Ch 163 (ChD, ROMER J)

At the date of her death on 17 January 1926, Mrs. Thornley was tenant for life of settled land, and Jackson was sole surviving trustee of the settlement, which came to an end on Mrs. Thornley's death.

Mrs. Thornley appointed Bridgett as her sole executor, and he entered into an agreement to sell the land to Hayes. Hayes objected on the ground that title should have been made by Mrs. Thornley's special representative under the Administration of Estates Act 1925, section 22 (1).

Held. Bridgett was able to give a good title to the land.

ROMER J: It is common ground that up to the date of her death Mrs. Emily Margaret Thornley, who was the tenant for life of the property now in question, had vested in her the legal estate in the property. It is common ground that, that being so, on her death this legal estate passed to her personal representative by virtue of sub-sections 1 and 3 of section 1 of the Administration of Estates Act 1925. But then it is said that by virtue of section 22, subsection 1, of that Act, in such a case as this the lady must be deemed to have appointed as her special executor in regard to this land the person who up to the date of her death was sole surviving trustee for the purposes

---

[11] Similar problems have arisen in connection with A.E.A. 1925, s. 36 (1): *Re Duce and Boots Cash Chemists (Southern) Ltd's Contract* [1937] Ch 642, [1937] 3 All ER 788; *Re Alefounder's Will Trusts* [1927] 1 Ch 360.

[12] *Pilcher v Rawlins* (1872) 7 Ch App 259, p. 27, ante; *Weston v Henshaw* [1950] Ch 510, p. 257, ante.

of the Settled Land Act. Let me assume that that was so. On 17 January 1926, she died, and on 7 April 1926, a general grant of probate of her will was made to Thomas William Bridgett, a person whom she had thereby appointed as executor. As from that date, at any rate, wherever the legal estate in this property may have been as between the date of her death and this act of probate, the legal estate in this land vested in Thomas William Bridgett, and, while that act of probate remains unrevoked, he can in my opinion properly convey the legal estate to the purchaser. Section 204 of the Law of Property Act 1925, subsection 1, says this: "An order of the Court under any statutory or other jurisdiction shall not, as against a purchaser, be invalidated on the ground of want of jurisdication, or of want of any concurrence, consent, notice, or service, whether the purchaser has notice of any such want or not". Section 22, subsection 1 (if the purchaser is right as to its application at all to this case), provided that probate might have been granted to this sole surviving trustee. In point of fact the Court of Probate did not grant probate to him, but granted probate to Thomas William Bridgett. That being so, it appears to me that section 204 of the Law of Property Act applies to the case with regard to the taking of a conveyance from the legal personal representative. Further, the purchaser would be protected in the event of any subsequent revocation of that grant of probate by section 37, subsection 1, of the Administration of Estates Act 1925. It can hardly be doubted that in this case, if the purchaser does take a conveyance from the person to whom the grant of probate was granted, he would be acting in good faith, within the meaning of section 55, subsection 1 (xviii), of the Act. . . .

The point still remains as to whether section 22, subsection 1, applies to the present case, it being conceded on both sides that on the death of this lady the settlement came to an end.

[His Lordship read section 22 (1) and continued:]

Section 22 is the first of three sections which are introduced under the general heading "Special Provisions as to Settled Land". In sections 23 and 24 it is I think reasonably clear that "settled land" means land which after the death of the testator continues to be settled land, and the words in section 22, subsection 1, "'settled land' means land vested in the testator which was settled previously to his death and not by his will" refer in terms only to that particular subsection. I cannot help thinking that these words were merely designed for the purpose of making it clear that section 22, subsection 1, did not apply to a case where the land was settled by the will of a testator. However, I have to deal with the words as I find them, and that being so I must read the earlier part of the sub-section as follows: "A testator may appoint and in default of such express appointment shall be deemed to have appointed as his special executors in regard to land vested in the testator which was settled previously to his death the persons if any who are at his death the trustees of the settlement thereof." So far down to the words "previously to his death" the section applies to the present case, because here land was vested in the testatrix and it had been settled previously to her death. Then the sub-section says she shall be deemed to have appointed as her special executors the persons, if any, who are at her death the trustees of the settlement. Now before any one can go to the Court of Probate and get probate specially limited to the settled land granted to him, he must be in a position to say to the Court that he is to be deemed to have been appointed special executor of this land, because at the death of the testator he was trustee of the settlement thereof. But in my opinion he is not in a position to make that statement if the settlement comes to an end the moment the testator dies. It is to be observed that the sub-section does not refer to the persons who immediately before the death of the testator were the trustees of the settlement, but to the persons who at his death are the trustees of the settlement.

The words "persons who are at his death the trustees of the settlement" connote to my mind persons who are trustees notwithstanding his death, especially when it is realized that the section is dealing with the testator's will, which comes into operation only when he is dead.

For these reasons I think this sub-section does not apply in a case like the present, where, upon the death of the testatrix in question, the settlement existing up to that date comes to an end.

It has been seen that difficulties can arise where a vesting instrument is executed by those who appear to the purchaser to be the wrong persons. Similarly there may be doubt as to whether or not the land is settled land and whether, if it is settled, it has been vested in the right person as tenant for life. There seems little doubt that a purchaser who follows the correct Settled Land Act machinery is intended to be protected; but, as he is a purchaser with notice of the existence of trusts affecting the land, statutory authority is needed to protect him. And if he discovers the flaw on the title by extraneous enquiries or by chance and objects to the title, it will be odd if he is compelled to take a bad title[13].

Megarry and Wade, *Law of Real Property* (4th edn.), p. 307:

"Suppose, for example, that a testator leaves his land by his will to his widow, W, for life or until remarriage, with remainder to X in fee simple; and that the widow remarries, and then nevertheless purports (as tenant for life) to sell the land to P, P duly paying the purchase-money to the trustees. If P had been allowed to inspect the trust instrument he would have discovered that W was no longer tenant for life and consequently had no power to sell to him. But he cannot discover it from the vesting deed or assent, which is all he is allowed to

---

[13] See (1939) 83 Sol Jo 45, (A. H. Withers); (1946) 10 Conv (NS) 135 (H. Potter); (1947) 11 Conv (NS) 91 (H. Potter), 159 (B. B. Benas); (1958) 22 Conv (NS) 78 (F. R. Crane).

see. He must assume what is untrue, that W is still tenant for life. He probably obtains the legal estate, for that was vested in W and should pass by her conveyance. But it seems unlikely that P can rely upon section 110 (2), mentioned above, for on W's remarriage the settlement came to an end, and P is not 'a purchaser of a legal estate in settled land.' P is a purchaser with constructive notice of the trust in favour of X, which W (not being tenant for life) has no power to overreach[14]. P therefore takes a bad title. This disaster would be avoided only if 'settled land' could be held to mean 'land which appears to be settled land but is not'[15]. If that were possible, P could plead purchase of a legal estate without notice that W was not still tenant for life and so empowered to sell."

X.   Termination of Settlements[16]

A.   Duration

SETTLED LAND ACT 1925

3.   Duration of settlements. — Land [not held upon trust for sale][17] which has been subject to a settlement shall be deemed for the purposes of this Act to remain and be settled land, and the settlement shall be deemed to be a subsisting settlement for the purposes of this Act so long as —

(a) any limitation, charge, or power of charging under the settlement subsists, or is capable of being exercised; or

(b) the person who, if of full age, would be entitled as beneficial owner to have that land vested in him for a legal estate is an infant.

7.   Procedure on change of ownership. — (5), p. 280, ante.

B.   Deed of Discharge

SETTLED LAND ACT 1925

17.   Deed of discharge on termination of settlement. — (1) Where the estate owner of any settled land holds the land free from all equitable interests and powers under a trust instrument, the persons who in the last or only principal vesting instrument or the last or only endorsement on or annex thereto are declared to be the trustees of the settlement or the survivors of them shall, save as hereinafter mentioned, be bound to execute, at the cost of the trust estate, a deed

---

[14] S.L.A. 1925, s. 72 (p. 258, ante): cf. ss. 7 (4), 19.

[15] "For a somewhat similar interpretation of another section of the Act (s. 36), see p. 425": (M & W, p. 308, n. 20).

[16] Cheshire, pp. 790–791; M & W, pp. 311–313; MM, pp. 171–172.

[17] The words in square brackets were inserted by L.P. (A.) A. 1926, s. 7 and Sch.

declaring that they are discharged from the trust so far as regards that land: . . .

Where the land is affected by a derivative settlement or trust for sale, the deed of discharge shall contain a statement that the land is settled land by virtue of such vesting instrument as aforesaid and the trust instrument therein referred to, or is held on trust for sale by virtue of such conveyance as aforesaid, as the case may require.

(3) Where a deed or order of discharge contains no statement to the contrary, a purchaser of a legal estate in the land to which the deed or order relates shall be entitled to assume that the land has ceased to be settled land, and is not subject to any trust for sale.

110. Protection of purchasers, &c. — (5) p. 282, ante.

QUESTIONS

(a) T died in 1916, having appointed the Public Trustee sole trustee of her will, and devising land to her husband for life, and after his death to her sister A, and on A's death to the Public Trustee on trust to sell and divide the proceeds between six nieces of her husband. Her husband died in 1929. A vesting assent duly vested the legal estate in A as tenant for life. A, after giving notice to the Public Trustee, sold the land to various purchasers at a time of rapidly rising prices and in circumstances which showed that the sales were commercially most imprudent. The nieces did not know of the sales until A's death. Advise the nieces whether they have a basis of complaint against A's estate, the Public Trustee, or the purchasers.

If the nieces had known of the intention to sell, could they have prevented the sale?

See *England v Public Trustee* (1967) 205 Estates Gazette 651, where SELLERS LJ suggested that it would be desirable to provide that notice of an intended sale should be given to the beneficiaries under a settlement. See also Settled Land Act 1925, sections 30 (3) 97, 101.

(b) What arguments would you put forward on behalf of the purchaser in the hypothetical case on p. 285, ante?

(c) Would a purchaser from personal representatives obtain a good title on facts which were identical with those of *Re Bridgett and Hayes' Contract* except for the fact that, as the purchaser later discovered, the settlement had not come to an end?

(d) A purported to convey land to B for life and after B's death to C in fee. Later A executed a vesting deed vesting the land in B as tenant for life under the settlement and executed also a trust instrument. B, relying on the vesting deed, sold the land to X. Is X entitled to the protection of the Settled Land Act 1925, section 110 (2)? See Settled Land Act, sections 4, 5, 9, 110 (2); (1946) 10 Conv (NS) 139–40.

XI. Registered Land[18]

Settled land is registered in the name of the estate owner. The beneficial interests under the settlement are included in the definition of minor interests (L.R.A. 1925, section 3 (xv), p. 127, ante), but they will be overridden (i.e. overreached) on a sale by the estate owner in the same way as they would be with unregistered land. A purchaser will discover that the land is settled land by means of a restriction[19] which, in whatever form is appropriate (Statutory Forms 9, 10, 11, Land Registration Rules 1925. See Form 9, p. 289, post), is required to be entered on the register.

LAND REGISTRATION ACT 1925

74.   Notice of trust not to affect registered dealing. — P. 93, ante.

86.   Registration of settled land. — (1) Settled land shall be registered in the name of the tenant for life or statutory owner.

(2) The successive or other interests created by or arising under a settlement shall (save as regards any legal estate which cannot be overridden under the powers of the Settled Land Act, 1925[20], or any other statute) take effect as minor interests and not otherwise . . .[1]

(3) There shall also be entered on the register such restrictions[2] as may be prescribed, or may be expedient, for the protection of the rights of the persons beneficially interested in the land, and such restrictions shall (subject to the provisions of this Act relating to releases by the trustees of a settlement and to transfers by a tenant for life whose estate has ceased in his lifetime)[3] be binding on the proprietor during his life, but shall not restrain or otherwise affect a disposition by his personal representative.

(5) References in this Act to the "tenant for life" shall, where the context admits, be read as referring to the tenant for life, statutory owner, or personal representative who is entitled to be registered.

49.   Rules to provide for notices of other rights, interest and claims. — (2) A notice shall not be registered in respect of any estate, right, or interest which (independently of this Act) is capable of being overridden by the proprietor under a trust for sale[4] or the powers of the Settled Land Act, 1925[5], or any other statute, or of a settlement, and of being protected by a restriction in the prescribed manner: . . .

---

[18] Cheshire, p. 203; M & W, pp. 1072–1073, 1076; MM, pp. 522–523; Ruoff and Roper, Chap. 19.

[19] P. 129, ante.

[20] S.L.A. 1925, s. 72 (2), p. 259, ante.

[1] See (1958) 22 Conv (NS) 14, at pp. 23–24 (F. R. Crane), where it is suggested that, if no restriction is entered, a beneficiary in possession of settled land cannot claim an overriding interest under L.R.A. 1925, s. 70 (1) (g).

[2] P. 129, ante.'

[3] L.R.A. 1925, s. 87 (4), (6).

[4] L.P.A. 1925, s. 2, p. 189, ante; s. 27, p. 204, ante.

[5] S.L.A. 1925, s. 72, p. 258, ante; s. 110, p. 281, ante.

LAND REGISTRATION RULES 1925

104. Duty to apply for restrictions when land is settled. — (1) On the creation of a settlement it shall be the duty of the proprietor, or (if there is no proprietor) the personal representative of a deceased proprietor, to apply to the Registrar for the entry of such restrictions or inhibitions or notices as may be appropriate to the case.

The application shall state that they are required for the protection of the minor interests under the settlement.

Statutory Form 9

Restriction where Tenant for Life is registered as proprietor

No disposition under which capital money arises is to be registered unless the money is paid to . . . (the trustees of the settlement . . .), or into Court.

Except under an order of the Registrar, no disposition is to be registered, unless authorised by the Settled Land Act, 1925.

QUESTION

Should the strict settlement be abolished? If so, should land held for successive interests be subjected to a trust for sale? [1952] CLP 152 (E. H. Scamell). Or vested in trustees with statutory overreaching powers? (1961) 24 MLR at p. 127 (G. A. Grove); Survey of the Land Law of Northern Ireland (1971), paras. 88–100; H & M p. 305; Cheshire, pp. 204–209.

7. Perpetuities and Accumulations

I. General[1]

The policy of the law has always been to prevent property from being tied up in perpetuity. The problem has been met in various forms. Conditions preventing alienation are void[2], as are non-charitable trusts

---

[1] Cheshire, pp. 312–361; M & W, pp. 199–281; MM, pp. 95–134; Gray, *Rule Against Perpetuities* (4th edn., 1942); Maudsley, *Modern Law of Perpetuities* (1979); Morris and Leach, *Rule Against Perpetuities* (2nd edn., 1962 and 1st supplement, 1964); *Theobald on Wills* (13th edn., 1971) chap. 42; Holdsworth, HEL, Vol. vii, pp. 81–144, 193–238; Simpson, *Introduction to the History of the Land Law,* pp. 195–224.

[2] Litt s. 360; Co Litt 206b, 223a; and cases quoted in Cheshire, pp. 371–372; M & W, pp. 78–79; MM, pp. 31–32.

of perpetual duration[3]; estates tail have been barrable since *Taltarum's Case* in 1472[4], in which a condition against barring was held void[5]; and the subsequent device of the creation of successive life estates was prevented by a rule which is one aspect of the rule against double possibilities, but which is better known under its 19th century title of the rule in *Whitby v Mitchell*[6]. The emergency of the modern rule against perpetuities was inevitable once it was established that executory limitations were valid at law, and were indestructible by a tortious feoffment by the tenant in possession[7]; the power to project estates into the future was unlimited.

The rule was therefore concerned with the extent to which estates could be made to vest in the future, and the period finally established was that of a life or lives in being plus 21 years plus a period of gestation in respect of a life in being or of a beneficiary if a posthumous child were born[8].

A. Relationship between Vesting and Living Persons

Gray's famous and authoritative statement of the Rule is: "No interest is good unless it must vest, if at all, not later than twenty-one years after some life in being at the creation of the interest". This is one author's formulation and not a statute. There are special situations, dealt with below[9], where exceptions have to be made. It does not mean, of course, that an interest will be invalid, unless it is certain to vest within the period of a life in being plus 21 years. The Rule is concerned with contingent interests, and, by definition, such an interest may never vest at all. The point is that, to comply with the Rule, the interest must be such that, if it does vest in the future, it must necessarily do so within the period. Put another way, and in a way which is sometimes thought to be easier to comprehend, an interest is void if it might by any possibility vest outside the period.

It is amazing that the Rule, so simple on its face, has caused such difficulty in its operation. What has to be appreciated is that the Rule requires the *recognition of a relationship* between the vesting and the lives of living people. The question is: is it certain that the interest

---

[3] *Carne v Long* (1860) 2 De GF & J 75; *Gilmour v Coats* [1949] AC 426, [1949] 1 All ER 848; *Leahy v A-G for New South Wales* [1959] AC 457, [1959] 2 All ER 300; *Macaulay v O'Donnell* [1943] Ch 435 n; M & B (T) chap. 9; H & M, chap. 16; Maudsley, pp. 166–178; Morris and Leach, pp. 307–327.

[4] (1472), YB 12 Edw 4 Ed 19.

[5] *Corbet's Case* (1600) 1 Co Rep 83b; *Mildmay's Case* (1605) 6 Co Rep 40a; *Portington's Case* (1613) 10 Co Rep 35b.

[6] (1889) 42 ChD 494; *affd.* (1890) 44 ChD 85. The rule was abolished in 1925. L.P.A. 1925, s. 161.

[7] *Pells v Brown* (1620) Cro Jac 590; Gray, s. 159; Morris and Leach, Chap. 1.

[8] *Duke of Norfolk's Case* (1681) 3 Cas in Ch 1; *Lloyd v Carew* (1697) Show Parl Cas 137, 1 Moo PC 133n; *Stephens v Stephens* (1736) Cas temp Talb 228; *Thellusson v Woodford* (1805) 11 Ves 112; *Cadell v Palmer* (1883) 1 Cl & Fin 372; *Re Wilmer's Trusts* [1903] 2 Ch 411; *Re Stern* [1962] Ch 732, [1961] 3 All ER 1129.

[9] P. 339, post.

must vest, if it vest at all, within 21 years of the death of some person now living? That is a simple legal formulation. The difficulty is in the recognition of the *relationship* between the vesting and the lives, that is, in being able to say for certain whether a particular contingent interest is certain to vest within 21 years of someone's death; or, to put it the other way, whether the contingent interest might vest outside the period.

As will be seen in the discussion which follows, there is no need to attempt to define who the "lives in being" may be. Anyone will do; so long as the interest must vest, if at all, within 21 years of the dropping of that life. The life (or lives) in being is (are), therefore, that person (those persons) within 21 years of whose death (deaths) the interest must vest, if it vest at all. They are the lives who validate the gift. There are no "lives in being" in the case of void gifts. The only problems in relation to "lives in being" are those in which the settlor has himself expressly selected the persons whose lives are to be used for the purpose.

Thus a gift

   (i) to the first child of A (who is alive) to marry was void at common law, because the first child of A to marry might be a future born child, and that future born child was not certain to marry, if at all, within 21 years of the death of a person living at the date of the gift.

  (ii) to the first child of A to attain the age of 21. This is valid whether A is alive or dead. If A is alive, it is valid because A's first child must attain the age of 21 within 21 years of A's death (a period of gestation is added in the case of posthumous children). A is the "life in being". If A is dead, the first child to attain the age of 21 must be a child of A living at the date of the gift. The child is the "life in being".

 (iii) to the first great-grandchild of A to go for a walk with X. This is valid, because it must happen, if at all (and however unlikely in fact), during X's lifetime. X is the "life in being".

 (iv) to the first child of A (who is alive) to marry a person now living. This is valid, because the marriage must take place, if at all, within the lifetime of a living person (though not yet identified).

  (v) to the first grandchild of A (who is alive) to attain the age of 21. This is void, because the first grandchild of A to attain the the age of 21 might be a child of a future born child of A, and may attain the age of 21 more than 21 years after the death of any person alive at the date of the gift.

 (vi) to the first grandchild of A (who is deceased) to attain the age of 21. This is valid, because any grandchild of A, whether born at the date of the gift or not, must attain the age of 21 within 21 years of the death of a child of A. A's children are the "lives in being". If a child (or all the children) of A be dead, his (their) children must be alive and they would be the "lives in being".

B. Vesting in Interest. Vesting in Possession

The requirement of vesting is that the gift must vest in interest but not necessarily in possession. This means that the beneficiary or beneficiaries must be ascertained and that all prior conditions have been satisfied[10]. In the case of class gifts, the size and the share of each beneficiary must be known before the class gift is considered to vest for the purposes of the perpetuity rule[11]; a class gift does not therefore vest for this purpose until there can be no possibility of the membership of the class increasing or decreasing. Thus, a gift "to the children of A" does not "vest", as a class gift in this context, until A dies; for A may have further children after the date of the gift. And a gift "to the children of A who survive both their parents" does not vest, as a class gift in this context, until the death of both parents; for, although there can be no more children of those parents after the death of either of them, the number of members of the class may be reduced at any time before the death of the survivor, and this possibility prevents vesting until that time.

C. Remorseless Application

The rule has been applied remorselessly[12], defeating the intention of the testator, and has invalidated many gifts because of the recognition of the most extreme and unlikely possibilities, which would allow an interest to vest outside the period. This converted the rule into an object of ridicule; and one of the worst aspects of arbitrary application is, as Professor Leach has pointed out, that the vice of a void limitation is one that could have been prevented by competent drafting. The fault is the lawyer's, but the intended beneficiary is the sufferer[13]. However, apart from these anomalous cases which have become well-known draftsman's 'traps', the rule has by and large performed a useful function in holding a balance between the claims of the property owner to control the disposition of his property, and the policy in favour of free alienation[14].

D. Subject Matter

A remarkable feature of its history is that it was established in the context of the control and disposition of family land, and has survived the change from land to stocks and shares as the basic form of capitalistic wealth. In this new context, the question of the tying up of property appears in a new light; in the old context of the tying up of land, the particular piece of land was inalienable during the period of

---

[10] Maudsley, p. 10; Morris and Leach, p. 1.
[11] See p. 319, post; *Pearks v Moseley* (1880) 5 App Cas 714; *Re Dawson* (1888) 39 ChD 155; *Ward v Van der Loeff* [1924] AC 653.
[12] See pp. 304. et seq., post; Maudsley, p. 36.
[13] (1952) 68 L.Q.R. 35 (W. B. Leach).
[14] Simes, *Public Policy and the Dead Hand*; (1953) 52 Mich LR 179, (1955) 103 U of Penn LR 707.

the family settlement. In a settlement of stocks and shares, no property is tied up or made inalienable; for, even if successive interests under the settlement continued in perpetuity, the stocks and shares which formed the trust would remain alienable by the trustees, and would be bought and sold as the trustees decided to vary the investments.

E. Reform

In spite of much criticism, the rule proved itself obstructive to reform, and various attempts over the years to amend it in the United States have met with difficulties, and many states abandoned the attempt and re-established the common law rule[15]. In recent years, largely through Leach's influence, various jurisdictions in the Common-wealth and the United States have, in various ways, passed legislation reforming the Rule[16]. The methods selected are basically of three types, though some jurisdictions combine the methods —

    (i) Patching Up: that is to say, to provide specific solutions to the specific situations which have caused problems in the working of the Rule. The most common situation is that in which the vesting is postponed to an age greater than 21 and the interest thereby invalidated. England dealt with this case in 1925[17].

    (ii) Cy-Près: that is, to give to a court the power, on the analogy of the cy-près power in connection with charitable trusts, to alter the terms of a void gift so as to make it conform to the Rule. After all, the testator did not intend to make a void gift. Altering the terms would meet his intention. This solution was considered by the Law Reform Committee in 1956, and rejected.

    (iii) Wait and See. This, on its face, is the most attractive solution. Much of the criticism directed at the common law rule related to cases where the interest was held void on the ground that it might conceivably vest outside the period, but did in fact vest next year. Thus, to return to example (i) above, assume that A is a lady of 56 and has three children, all engaged to be married. They all marry within the year. But the gift would be void at common law because of the possibility that A's present children may die, A may have another child, and the first child of A to marry may do so outside the period. The policy behind the Rule is to prevent remote vesting; not to hold void gifts which vest within the period merely because they might have vested outside. Why not, therefore, wait and see whether or not the gift vests within the period; and hold it valid if it does, but void if it does not? This is the

---

[15] Morris and Leach, pp. 13, 33.
[16] Maudsley, Appendix D.
[17] L.P.A. 1925 s. 163; p. 317, post.

principle recommended by the Law Reform Committee and
adopted by the Perpetuities and Accumulations Act 1964;
along with some "patching up" provisions also.

F. Perpetuities and Accumulations Act 1964

The Perpetuities and Accumulations Act 1964 came into force on
16 July 1964, and applies only to instruments coming into effect on
or after that date[18]. The common law rule still applies to other
limitations. Litigation on pre-1964 dispositions will become less likely
as the years go by; but will remain possible for many years because
questions for decision do not arise until the time for payment arrives,
and this may await the termination of a life interest or the attainment
of a specified age by beneficiaries.

Further, Wait and See applies, according to the terms of the Act, to
void gifts; that is, to dispositions which are void under the common
law rule on the ground that they might vest outside the period. To
follow this method, it is necessary to apply the common law rule first,
in order to discover whether the disposition is valid or void under the
common law rule. Thus, there are two rules to apply; and the common
law rule still survives in spite of the introduction of Wait and See.

The question is whether the retention of the common law rule was
necessary or sensible; whether, in other words, there is any advantage
in knowing that a disposition complies with the common law rule.
It is submitted here that compliance with the common law rule is
irrelevant once Wait and See is enacted; and it should be noted that all
jurisdictions which have enacted Wait and See, except those which
have effectively copied the English Act, have abolished the common
law rule and relied solely on Wait and See. In these circumstances, the
common law rule would phase peacefully out, and validity would
depend on Wait and See alone.

The issue turns on the question whether or not, in a Wait and See
jurisdiction, there is any advantage in knowing whether a disposition
complies with the common law rule. The legislators assumed that
there was. The contrary view, argued in detail elsewhere[19], can only be
presented shortly here. The point is that a contingent interest which is
valid under the common law rule remains contingent; the beneficiary
does not take until the contingency occurs. Thus, before paying out,
even with "valid" gifts, you have to wait and see whether they do in
fact vest. If the gift is to the first child of A to attain the age of 21, and
A has a child of 16, then, you wait and see if the child attains 21. If he
does, you pay out; if he does not, the gift fails. The current value of the
gift depends on the statistical likelihood of vesting. Similarly with all
gifts under a Wait and See system. Treat the gift as valid until it is

---

[18] Section 15 (5). An arrangement under the Variation of Trusts Act 1958 will, with
the court order approving it, constitute an "instrument" for the purposes of
the subsection. *Re Holt's Settlement* [1969] 1 Ch 100, [1968] 1 All ER 470.
[19] Maudsley, chap. 4.

known that it will not vest within the period, and in the meantime wait
and see whether it vests within the period. The value of the interest
depends on the statistical likelihood of vesting within the period.
Presumably, "valid" gifts are more likely to vest within the period
than "void" gifts; but the added value which they acquire is due to
their increased likelihood of vesting, and not to their happening to
comply with the Rule. Compare two gifts:—

(i) To such of the children and grandchildren of A as shall return
from the Moon within 21 years of the death of X. A has 2
children and 4 grandchildren (none of them astronauts).

(ii) To the first grandchild of A (who is alive) to attain the age of
21. A has 2 children and also 4 grandchildren, all healthy and
aged 20.

The first gift is valid under the common law rule, because it must
vest, if at all, during X's lifetime; but it would be valueless to the
children and grandchildren, because the trustees would be unlikely to
make an advancement, and the grandchildren would be unable to offer
it as security for a loan. The second gift is void (see above), but would
have value, especially in the case of the eldest grandchild. In the era of
Wait and See, compliance with the common law rule is irrelevant.
Likelihood of vesting is crucial.

The common law rule is logically irrelevant, because Wait and See
necessarily takes it over. The common law rule asks and answers the
question: Is the limitation one which must vest, if at all, within the
period? Wait and See asks whether it does in fact vest within the
period. If an interest *must* vest, if at all, within the period, then it *will*
vest, if at all, within the period. Wait and See takes over the common
law rule. Unless, that is, you can detect situations in which the periods
are different: as where a life in being might validate the gift at common
law, but is not a person whom the statute allows to be used as a
measuring life under Wait and See. There are, tragically, a few such
situations under the English Act. That should be dealt with either by
adding such lives to the statutory list of measuring lives applicable to
Wait and See; or by letting the disposition stand or fall by the use of
the statutory lives alone. It makes no sense to perpetuate for ever the
learning of the common law rules just to deal with such situations. We
should look, one way or another, to a system in which we have to deal
with Wait and See alone.

G.　Impact of Taxation

However you look at it, the great days of the perpetuity rule are over.
There is a further reason for simplification. It is indeed paradoxical
that, after waiting so long for reform of the law of perpetuities, the Act
eventually comes when wealthy families no longer attempt to provide
a series of successive limited interests projecting into the future. It
was noted above that the problem of perpetuity became less acute
when family settlements became settlements of variable securities
rather than a specific piece of land; and, in the last few decades, the

severity of the rates of estate duty, coupled with the rule that duty was payable at a life tenant's death upon the full value of the capital sum, greatly decreased the attractiveness of settlements containing successive limited interests. Discretionary settlements in various forms, which had substantial fiscal attractions prior to the Finance Act 1969, involve the use of the perpetuity rule only in respect of the measurement of the duration of the discretionary trust; and the provision of an alternative period of 80 years in section 1 of the Perpetuities and Accumulations Act 1964 is most welcome in this respect as an escape from a period based upon royal lives. The capital transfer tax system, introduced in the Finance Act 1975, makes the tying-up of property in family settlements even less attractive.

H. Common Law Rule To-day

But, for the present, it remains necessary to understand the working of the common law rule. Questions may still arise relating to dispositions taking effect before 16 July 1964, to which the Act does not apply[20]. And, as has been seen, the form of the Act does not follow the line of reasoning in this text. The Act was based on the contrary assumption; namely that it is still important to test every disposition by the common law rule; and to introduce Wait and See only if the disposition is void under the common law rule. The textbooks on Land Law all so assume. An outline of the working of the common law rule is therefore included here, along with the provisions of the Act.

II. The Perpetuity Period

A. At Common Law[1]

In *Cadell v Palmer* ((1833) 1 Cl & Fin 372), BAYLEY B, in tendering advice to the House of Lords, discussed a number of cases[2] and continued at p. 416: "We would not wish the House to suppose, that there were not expressions in other cases about the same period, from which it might clearly be collected, that minority was originally the foundation of the limit[3], and to raise some presumption that the limit of 21 years after a life in being was confined to cases in which there was such a minority; but the manner in which the rule was expressed in the

---

[20] P.A.A. 1964, s. 15 (5).

[1] Cheshire, pp. 315–317; M & W, pp. 207–208; MM, pp. 104–107; Maudsley, pp. 42–45; Morris and Leach, pp. 56–70. *Duke of Norfolk's Case* (1681) 3 Cas in Ch 1; *Lloyd v Carew* (1697) Show Parl Cas 137; *Stephens v Stephens* (1736) Cas temp Talb 228; *Thellusson v Woodford* (1805) 11 Ves 112.

[2] *Lloyd v Carew*, supra; *Marks v Marks* (1719) 10 Mod Rep 419; *Taylor v Biddal* (1677) 2 Mod Rep 289; *Stephens v Stephens*, supra; *Goodtitle d Gurnall v Wood* (1740) Willes 211; *Thellusson v Woodford*, supra; *Goodman v Goodright* (1759) 2 Burr 873; *Buckworth v Thirkell* (1785) 3 Bos & P 654n; *Jee v Audley* (1787) 1 Cox Eq Cas 324; *Long v Blackall* (1797) 7 Term Rep 100; *Wilkinson v South* (1798) 7 Term Rep 555.

[3] To 21 years.

instances to which I have referred, as well as in text writers, appears to us to justify the conclusion, that it was at length extended to the enlarged limit of a life or lives in being, and 21 years afterwards. It is difficult to suppose, that men of such discriminating minds, and so much in the habit of discrimination, should have laid down the rule, as they did, without expressing minority as a qualification of the limit, particularly when, in many of the instances, they had minority before their eyes, had it not been their clear understanding, that the rule of 21 years was general, without the qualification of minority.

[His Lordship then referred to *Beard v Westcott* ((1813) 5 Taunt 393), in which the Court of Common Pleas upheld an executory limitation which was not to take effect until 21 years after a life in being; but Lord ELDON sent the case to the King's Bench ((1822) 5 B & Ald 801) where it was held void, on the ground however that it followed a prior void limitation. He continued:]

Upon the direct authority, therefore, of the decision of the Court of Common Pleas, in *Beard v Westcott*, and the *dicta* by L. C. Justice Willes, Lord Mansfield and Lord Kenyon, and the rules laid down in Blackstone and Fearne, we consider ourselves warranted in saying that the limit is a life or lives in being, and 21 years afterwards, without reference to the infancy of any person whatever. This will certainly render the estate unalienable for 21 years after lives in being, but it will preserve in safety any limitations which may have been made upon authority of the *dicta* or text writers I have mentioned; and it will not tie up the alienation an unreasonable length of time.

Upon the second and third questions proposed by your Lordships, whether a limitation by way of executory devise is void, as too remote, or otherwise, if it is not to take effect until after the determination of a life or lives in being, and upon the expiration of a term of 21 years afterwards, together with the number of months equal to the ordinary or longest period of gestation, but the whole of such years and months to be taken as a term in gross, and without reference to the infancy of any person whatever, born or *en ventre sa mere*, the unanimous opinion of the Judges is, that such a limitation would be void, as too remote. They consider 21 years as the limit, and the period of gestation to be allowed in those cases only in which the gestation exists."

Their Lordships affirmed the decision of the court below[4].

B.   Perpetuities and Accumulations Act 1964

PERPETUITIES AND ACCUMULATIONS ACT 1964

1.   Power to specify perpetuity period[5]. — (1) Subject to section 9 (2) of this Act and subsection (2) below, where the instrument by which

---

[4] *Sub nom Bengough v Edridge* (1827) 1 Sim 173. See note to ASTBURY J's judgment in *Re Villar* [1928] Ch 471; p. 302, n. 12, post.
[5] This section does not apply to options: s. 9 (2); Morris and Leach, Supplement, pp. 2–3; Cheshire, p. 348; M & W, pp. 220–221; MM, p. 109–110; Maudsley, pp. 111–115.

any disposition is made so provides, the perpetuity period applicable to the disposition under the rule against perpetuities, instead of being of any other duration, shall be of a duration equal to such number of years not exceeding eighty as is specified in that behalf in the instrument.

(2) Subsection (1) above shall not have effect where the disposition is made in exercise of a special power of appointment, but where a period is specified under that subsection in the instrument creating such a power the period shall apply in relation to any disposition under the power as it applies in relation to the power itself.

15. **Short title, interpretation and extent.** — (2) In this Act —
"disposition" includes the conferring of a power of appointment and any other disposition of an interest in or right over property, and references to the interest disposed of shall be construed accordingly[6];

(6) This Act shall apply in relation to a disposition made otherwise than by an instrument as if the disposition had been contained in an instrument taking effect when the disposition was made.

III. Lives in Being at Common Law[7]

A. Validating Lives

(1955) University of Florida LR at p. 470 (B.M. Sparks)[8]:

"There are possibly those who will say . . . that they can never figure out this business about lives in being. They will ask how they are to determine who are the measuring lives. The best answer to that is that you may determine the measuring lives any way you desire. Do the lives have to be named in the instrument? No. Do the lives have to be lives of persons taking an interest under the will or deed? No. Is there a limit to the number of lives? No, not so long as they are reasonably ascertainable. Instead of searching for measuring lives it will probably be more profitable to concentrate on an examination of the property interest you are creating. The proper question to ask is: Can I point to some person or persons now living and say that this interest will by the very terms of its creation be vested in an identified individual within twenty-one years after that person dies?"

American Bar Association Legislation Handbook (3rd edn. 1967) p.4:

". . . at common law, if vesting were certain to occur within 21 years after *any* life in being, it was valid. But if *no* person could be identified,

---

[6] *Re Thomas Meadows & Co Ltd and Subsidiary Companies (1960) Staff Pension Scheme Rules* [1971] Ch 278, [1971] 1 All ER 239 (entry of employees' names in register for pension purposes held to be a disposition).

[7] Cheshire, pp. 319–320; M & W, pp. 218–220; MM, pp. 104–107; Maudsley, pp. 88–92; Morris and Leach, pp. 60–63, 67–68.

[8] Used by permission; Copyright 1955, by the University of Florida Law Review.

within 21 years of whose death an interest was certain to vest, the interest was void."

RE GAITE'S WILL TRUSTS

[1949] 1 All ER 459 (ChD, ROXBURGH J)

A testatrix left gifts by will in favour of such of the grandchildren of Mrs. Gaite "as shall be living at my death or born within five years therefrom who shall attain the age of 21 years or being female marry under that age in equal shares". At the date of the death, there were two children and one grandchild of Mrs. Gaite alive.

Held. The gifts were valid as no grandchildren could take outside the perpetuity period unless that grandchild was born, within 5 years of the testatrix's death, of a child of Mrs. Gaite born after the textatrix's death; this was legally impossible as it is not lawful to marry under the age of 16 years.

ROXBURGH J: I must assume that Mrs. Hagar Gaite, who was alive at the date of the death of the testatrix, might have had a child within five years after the death of the testatrix. What is impossible is that the child of Mrs. Hagar Gaite, *ex hypothesi* born after the death of the testatrix, could itself have had a child within that period of five years, and that is essential to qualify for membership of the class. I do not base my judgment on physical impossibility. I leave all questions of that sort open for consideration when they arise because the matter is, in my judgment, concluded — and counsel for the second defendant admitted it was concluded — by the Age of Marriage Act 1929, section 1 (1)[9], which provides:

"A marriage between persons either of whom is under the age of sixteen shall be void."

Ex hypothesi, the child of Mrs. Hagar Gaite born after the death of the testatrix must be under the age of 16 years at the expiration of five years from the death of the testatrix, and, therefore, that child could not lawfully be married and have lawful children. In construing the rule, I must have regard to the statute law of England, and, therefore, I hold that the rule is not infringed[10].

Who were the lives in being? Who were the persons within 21 years of whose death (children of future-born children being eliminated) the interest must vest if at all?

---

[9] Now Marriage Act 1949, s. 2.

[10] For criticisms of the reasoning of ROXBURGH J, see (1949) 13 Conv (NS) 289 (J. H. C. Morris); Morris and Leach, pp. 85–86; *Theobald on Wills* (13th edn., 1971), para. 1485; (1952) 68 LQR 35, 46 (W. B. Leach). In respect of dispositions made on or after 1 January 1970, Family Law Reform Act 1969, s. 15, provides that, in the absence of a contrary intention, references to children and other relatives include references to illegitimate persons and persons descended through illegitimate persons.

Mrs. Gaite's living children were the lives in being, though nowhere mentioned in the instrument (nor in the judgment). Further grandchildren of Mrs. Gaite might attain the age of 21 more than 21 years after the death of the testatrix and Mrs. Gaite; but it was certain that they would do so, if at all, within 21 years of the death of the living children of Mrs. Gaite.

B. Expressly Selected Lives

The same principle applies where the settlor or testator selects the persons within 21 years of whose death the interest must vest, if at all. It will be seen that this was done in the following cases in this section. A gift would be void if it were made, for example, to "such of the great-grandchildren of A (who is alive) as shall attain the age of 25. The measuring lives for the purposes of this limitation shall be X, Y and Z." The vesting is not, in that situation, *related* to the lives. Where it is so related, there is the further question of the number and complexity of the lives who may be selected.

RE VILLAR

[1928] Ch 471 (ASTBURY J); affd., [1929] 1 Ch 243 (CA, Lord HANWORTH, LAWRENCE and RUSSELL LJJ)

By a will dated 1921 and confirmed by a codicil of 1926 the testator, who died in 1926, left his property upon certain trusts and provided that interests in the capital should not vest until the termination of the period of restriction which was defined as "the period ending at the expiration of 20 years from the day of the death of the last survivor of all the lineal descendants of Her late Majesty Queen Victoria who shall be living at the time of my death".

It was established that, in view of the fact that there were about 120 known descendants of Queen Victoria, some of whom had been dispersed and might be living in obscurity, and some whose fate was unknown[11], the ascertainment of the date of the dropping of these lives would be extremely difficult and expensive. The question was whether the testator could properly select such lives in 1926.

Held. The ascertainment of the lives was not impracticable and the trust was valid.

ASTBURY J: The real question is whether the period of restriction is one that can be given effect to in the circumstances. I feel the gravest doubt as to the validity of this will, having regard to the period of restriction and the circumstances now surrounding the lineal descendants of the late Queen Victoria. This form of restriction has appeared in many books of forms for many years, and the testator in 1921 adopted this form, which having regard to the war and the events during the war and subsequent thereto, is extremely difficult to carry out . . .

---

[11] For example, the Grand Duchess Anastasia.

The whole matter turns upon the true meaning of the law as explained in *Thellusson v Woodford*. In that case the judges were called in to advise the House of Lords, and their unanimous opinion was pronounced by Macdonald CB. It is upon the true meaning of that opinion and that of Lord Eldon LC, that the question must be decided . . .

The joint effect [of the tests applied by Lord Eldon LC and Macdonald CB in *Thellusson v Woodford* ((1799) 4 Ves 227; *affd.* (1805) 11 Ves 112)] is that, if, in the circumstances of the particular gift and the lives selected, it is substantially impracticable to ascertain the date of the extinction of the lives described, the gift is bad; but if, although the lives are numerous and the ascertainment of the date of the survivor's death is or may be difficult and expensive, the gift will not be rendered invalid if ordinary legal testimony can be applied, and will be available to determine that date.

Now in this case the testator has in 1921 used an old form or precedent, restraining the distribution of his estate to a period expiring twenty years from the death of the last survivor of all the lineal descendants of the late Queen Victoria living on 6 September 1926. That must postpone the vesting for a very long period, but having regard to the character of this class, I have come to the conclusion that I cannot say it will be impracticable, having regard to the legal testimony probably available, to ascertain the period when the capital becomes distributable twenty years after the survivor's death. The expense involved will probably be very great. The trust operates very hardly upon the testator's five children. If I could have seen my way to hold this tying up invalid I would gladly have done so, but in my opinion I am not at liberty to do so.

It must be borne in mind that there are probably many other gifts and trusts now in existence with similar limitations. Years ago this was a very common form of limitation. Its application has presented increasing difficulties as time has gone on, and now, having regard to the war, the difficulties are still more serious. But I feel myself unable to hold that the determination of the period of vesting is beyond the scope of legal testimony in the ordinary sense, and for these reasons this capital gift is good. There will be liberty to apply for an inquiry to ascertain the existing descendants, but that inquiry will be unncessary if, as I hope, my judgment is reversed on appeal[12].

---

[12] It was not. A footnote to the case at [1928] Ch 478 adds: "For a somewhat similar impracticability argument see *Cadell v Palmer* (1833) 1 Cl & F 372, 397; *Tudor's Real Property Cases* 3rd edn., pp. 424, 443. In that case the testator died in April 1818, and on 16 May 1918, his estate was finally wound up by Astbury J, in *Bengough v Edridge*, a few months after the period of 28 lives and 20 years had expired." For other cases on royal lives, see *Re Leverhulme* (No. 2) [1943] 2 All ER 274 (testator died in 1925 and life tenant in 1943. MORTON J held the gift valid, but warned testators not to use the descendants of Queen Victora in the future); *Re Warren's Will Trusts* (1961) 105 Sol Jo 511 (gift upheld in spite of MORTON J's warning. Testator died in 1944). Modern precedents use the descendants of King George V (or, preferably a period not exceeding 80 years; p. 298, ante).

In *Re Moore* [1901] 1 Ch 936, an attempt was made to stretch the period of perpetuity to the utmost: "for the longest period allowed by law, that is to say, until the period of twenty-one years from the death of the last survivor of all persons who shall be living at my death." JOYCE J, held the gift void for uncertainty[13]. The gift was for the maintenance of a tomb.

In *Re Kelly* [1932] IR 255, the question concerned the validity of a bequest to expend "£4 sterling on the support of each of my dogs per year ... and on the death of the last of my dogs" any balance to charitable purposes. MEREDITH J, held that the gift was void for remoteness, and said, at p. 260:

"It will be more convenient to deal first with the gift of any possible surplus remaining over on the death of the last of the dogs. Here the question, so far as there can be any question, is strictly one of remoteness. If the lives of the dogs or other animals could be taken into account in reckoning the maximum period of 'lives in being and twenty-one years afterwards' any contingent or executory interest might be properly limited, so as only to vest within the lives of specified carp, or tortoises, or other animals that might live for over a hundred years, and for twenty-one years afterwards, which, of course, is absurd. 'Lives' means human lives. It was suggested that the last of the dogs could in fact not outlive the testator by more than twenty-one years. I know nothing of that. The court does not enter into the question of a dog's expectation of life. In point of fact neighbour's dogs and cats are unpleasantly long-lived; but I have no knowledge of their precise expectation of life. Anyway the maximum period is exceeded by the lives of specified butterflies and twenty-one years afterwards. And even, according to my decision — and, I confess, it displays this weakness on being pressed to a logical conclusion — the expiration of the life of a single butterfly, even without the twenty-one years, would be too remote, despite all the world of poetry that may be thereby destroyed. In *Robinson v Hardcastle* ((1786) 2 Bro CC at 30) Lord Thurlow defined a perpetuity in these words: 'What is a perpetuity, but the extending the estate beyond a life in being, and twenty-one years after?' Of course by a 'life' he means lives; and there can be no doubt that 'lives' means lives of human beings, not of animals or trees in California.

[His Lordship then considered the gift for the support of the dogs and said:] I adhere to the view that in the present case there is a valid severable trust for twenty-one years succeeding the death of the testator, provided any of the dogs live so long."

---

[13] And not even valid for 21 years, e.g., *Muir v IRC* [1966] 1 WLR 1269, at p. 1282, [1966] 3 All ER 38 at p. 44.

If there are no lives in being, the period of 21 years may be allowed. In *Re Hooper* [1932] 1 Ch 38, a gift for the upkeep of certain monuments "so far as they [the trustees] legally can do so . . ." was upheld by MAUGHAM J, for a period (in respect of non-charitable objects) of 21 years.

A child en ventre sa mere may be a life in being, and a period of gestation, if it exists[14], may also be added to the perpetuity period of a life in being plus 21 years. BUCKLEY J, in *Re Wilmer's Trusts* [1903] 1 Ch 874; *(affd)*. [1903] 2 Ch 411 said, at 886: "*Thellusson v Woodford* is to be found again reported in 11 Ves 112, and at 143 Macdonald CB says: 'The case of *Long v Blackall* ((1797) 7 Term Rep 100) seems to have decided that an infant in ventre matris is a life in being. The established length of time, during which the vesting may be suspended, is during a life or lives in being, the period of gestation, and the infancy of such posthumous child'."

IV.　Possible Not Actual Events: The Requirement of Certainty[15]

The rule requires that the interest must be certain to vest, if it vest at all, within the period. This requirement has been applied remorselessly; and limitations have been struck down where the only chance of vesting outside the period is fantastic, and even physically impossible. A number of such limitations are now well known.

A.　The Fertile Octogenarian[16]; or the Conclusive Presumption of Fertility[17]

i.　THE COMMON LAW RULE

In *Jee v Audley* ((1787) 1 Cox Eq Cas 324) the testator gave £1,000 "unto my niece Mary Hall and the issue of her body lawfully begotten, and to be begotten, and in default of such issue, I give the same £1,000 to be equally divided between the daughters then living of my kinsman John Jee and his wife Elizabeth Jee".

---

[14] *Cadell v Palmer* (1833) 1 Cl & Fin 372, p. 297, ante; *Re Stern* [1962] Ch 732, [1961] 3 All ER 1129 (conception equivalent to birth).

[15] Cheshire, pp. 320–325 M & W, pp. 208–214; MM, pp. 100–103; Maudsley, pp. 35, 45–56; Morris and Leach, pp. 70–95.

[16] Prof. Barton Leach labelled these categories. (1938) 51 HLR 1329, (1952) 65 HLR 721, (1952) 68 LQR 44; *Re Dawson* (1888) 39 ChD 155, p. 320, post.

[17] On the law's different approach to this matter in a non-perpetuity context, see *Re Widdow's Trusts* (1871) LR 11 Eq 408; *Re White* [1901] 1 Ch 570; *Re Eve* [1909] 1 Ch 796; *Re Fletcher* [1949] Ch 473, [1949] 1 All ER 732; *Re Wohlgemuth* [1949] Ch 12, [1948] 2 All ER 882; *Re Herwin* [1953] Ch 701, [1953] 2 All ER 782; *Re Gilpin* [1954] Ch 1, [1953] 2 All ER 1218; *Re Westminster Bank's Declaration of Trust* [1963] 1 WLR 820, [1963] 2 All ER 400n; *Re Pettifor's Will Trusts* [1966] Ch 257, [1966] 1 All ER 913.

Mary Hall was about 40 and the Jees were 70, and had four living daughters. But, because the provision related to a general failure of issue (i.e. failure at any time in the future) it was theoretically possible that Mary Hall's issue might die at a time in the future, and because the daughters of the Jees *then* living might include a future born daughter of that old couple, the gift was held void[18].

WARD *v* VAN DER LOEFF

[1924] AC 653 (HL, Viscounts HALDANE LC and CAVE, Lords DUNEDIN, PHILLIMORE and BLANESBURGH)

By his will the testator devised and bequeathed his residuary real and personal estate on trust for his widow for life and then for their children, and, if none (as happened), on trust for the children of his brothers and sisters.

By a codicil he declared that his widow's life interest should be terminable on her remarriage unless such remarriage should be with a natural born British subject; and that on her death the trustees should hold the residuary estate on trust for the children of his brothers and sisters who should be living at the death of his wife or born at any time afterwards before any one of them .... attained a vested interest and who being a son attained 21 or being a daughter attained that age or married. The widow married a Dutchman.

At the date of the testator's death (without issue) his parents were both aged 66. All his brothers and sisters were over 30 years old and all had infant children, one of whom was born after the remarriage of the widow.

Held. (i) The gift in the codicil was void for perpetuity, (ii) The codicil did not revoke the gift in the will which was valid.

VISCOUNT HALDANE LC: On the construction of the will and codicil, two questions arise. The first is, whether the limitation in favour of children, contained in the concluding words of the codicil, is valid, having regard to the rule against perpetuities. The second is whether, if invalid, this new limitation and the wording of the codicil have been at all events efficacious as expressing a revocation of his bequest to children contained in the will. If the limitation to children in the codicil be invalid, and that in the will has not been revoked, then a further question arises, whether the gift in the will operated in favour of any children of the brothers and sisters who were not born until after the testator's death. Philip Ponsonby Burnyeat, who is one of the parties to these appeals, was a son of the testator's brother, Myles Fleming Burnyeat, but was not born until after the testator's death and the remarriage of his widow. It is argued against his claim that the life interest of the widow was effectively determined by the provision in the codicil and that the class of children to take was finally ascertained at that date as the time of distribution. If this be so, Philip Ponsonby Burnyeat is excluded.

---

[18] *Re Sayer's Trusts* (1868) LR 6 Eq 319; *Re Deloitte* [1926] Ch 56.

P. O. Lawrence J was the judge before whom this summons came in the first instance. He decided that the gift in the codicil in favour of the children of the testator's brothers and sisters was so framed as to be void for perpetuity. He held further, that the codicil operated to revoke the residuary gift in the will only so far as the substituted provision in the codicil was valid, and that the gift in the will in favour of these children, therefore, took effect, but merely in favour of such of the children as were born before the remarriage of the testator's widow. Philip Ponsonby Burnyeat was thus excluded. A majority of the Court of Appeal, Lord Sterndale MR and Warrington LJ, agreed with him in holding that the gift in the codicil in favour of the children of brothers and sisters was void for perpetuity, but held that the codicil revoked the gift in their favour contained in the will, and that there was an intestacy as regarded the residuary estate of the testator as from the remarriage of his widow. Atkin LJ dissented, holding that the testator must be taken, as matter or construction, to have been referring in his codicil only to the brothers and sisters of the whole blood in existence when he died, just as if he had designated them individually. The provision in the codicil was therefore valid, that in the will having been revoked.

My Lords, the principle to be applied in construing instruments for the purpose of ascertaining whether the direction they contain infringes the rule against perpetuity is a well settled one. It was repeated with emphasis in this House in *Pearks v Moseley* ((1880) 5 App Cas 714), where it was laid down that in construing the words the effect of the rule must in the first instance be left out of sight, and then, having in this way defined the intention expressed, the court had to test its validity by applying the rule to the meaning thus ascertained. It is only therefore if, as matter of construction, the words in the codicil, taken in the natural sense in which the testator used them, do not violate the rule that they can be regarded as giving a valid direction. Looking at the language of the testator here, I am wholly unable to read it as not postponing the ascertainment of possible members of the class beyond the period of a life in being and twenty-one years afterwards. No doubt if we were warranted in interpreting the testator as having referred only to the children of those of his brothers and sisters who were alive at his death we might read his language in a way which would satisfy the law. But for so restricting the natural meaning of his words there is no justification in the language used in the context. He speaks of his brothers and sisters generally, and there is no expression which excludes the children of other possible brothers and sisters of the whole or half blood who might in contemplation of law be born. He has nowhere indicated an intention that his words are not to be construed in this, their natural meaning. I think, therefore, that the class to be benefited was not one all the members of which were, as a necessary result of the words used, to be ascertained within the period which the law prescribes, and that the gift in the codicil in favour of children of brothers and sisters is wholly void.

The next question is whether the codicil, although inoperative to this extent, was yet operative to revoke the gift to children of brothers and sisters contained in the will. After consideration, I have come to the conclusion that it was not so operative. There is indeed a revocation expressed in the codicil, but it is confined to the power of appointment given to the wife. It does not extend to what follows. That is, in terms, an attempt at a substantive and independent gift, and, as it is wholly void, I think, differing on this point from the Court of Appeal, that the provision in the will stands undisturbed. There is nothing else in the codicil which purports to affect it. It can make no difference that the class of children is a new and different class if the constitution of the new class is wholly inoperative in law. If it fails, then unless an independent and valid intention to revoke has been independently of it expressed, no revocation can take place. There is no such independent expression of intention here.

The only other point is at what period the class of children of brothers and sisters who took under the will is to be ascertained. I think that according to a well-known rule, the period is that of distribution; in other words, taking the valid alteration in the codicil into account, the remarriage of the widow with a foreign subject. Philip Ponsonby Burnyeat is thus excluded.

The result is that the judgment of P. O. Lawrence J should be restored. As the difficulty has been entirely caused by the testator himself, I think that the costs here and below should be taxed as between solicitor and client and paid out of the residuary estate.

LORD BLANESBURGH. My Lords, I too have arrived at the same conclusions as the rest of your Lordships. I am of opinion that the ultimate gift of residue contained in this testator's codicil is void as transgressing the rule against perpetuities, and I think it is also inoperative to revoke those residuary dispositions of his will which rank subsequent to the interest thereby given to his widow.

We have in this case, my Lords, an extreme but by no means uncommon illustration of the stringency — I might even describe it as the penal character — of this rule. At no time was there here any practical possibility that a perpetuity could eventuate as a result of the complete fulfilment of the terms of the gift in question; while, by the time any contest as to the validity of the gift arose, it had become, by reason of the death of the testator's father, inconceivable that any infraction of the rule could be involved in it. If we consider matters as they stood at the testator's death, which is, of course, the really relevant date, it was necessary before anything obnoxious to the rule could take place in connection with this residuary gift, that the following remarkable conjunction of events should supervene. The testator's father and mother were then each upwards of sixty-six years of age; to them, after a family of five, no child had been born for more than thirty years. It was, nevertheless, necessary that they should have another child. Alternatively it was necessary that their marriage should be dissolved otherwise than by the death of the father, and that he should marry again, and have a child by the second marriage. That child, in turn, had to have a child born after the death of the testator's widow — one born in her lifetime would not have been excluded by the rule. And even a child so born would have brought about an infraction of the rule, only if it had also eventuated that no one of the already substantial and apparently increasing families of the testator's four living brothers and sisters had survived his widow having married or attained twenty-one.

So much, as matters stood at the testator's death, had to happen before any nephew or niece excluded by the rule could appear. By the date of the summons on which the orders under appeal were made, this new event had to take place before the rule could be infringed. The testator's mother had survived her husband; she, then a widow lady of upwards of seventy-two years of age, had to marry again and have issue.

It is, I think, only fair to the draftsman of this codicil, manifestly prepared under severe pressure of time, to give this indication of the apparent remoteness of any provision contained in it from the danger of a perpetuity. It is quite certain, I make bold to say, that no idea of such a possibility entered anybody's mind. In its application to the present case, the rule has been really a snare, useless so far as its legitimate purpose is concerned, but operative in the view of the Court of Appeal and operative also in the view of this House (but for a fortunate accident for which the rule is entitled to no credit), to produce an intestacy under which certainly one person would greatly benefit, whose interests it was the permissible and express purpose of the testator by his codicil to circumscribe and reduce.

In my own experience nearly all modern manifestations of the rule are of this character, and have this result. The rule has so schooled testators into compliance with, perhaps even into approval of, its requirements, that deliberate attempts to push their privileges beyond its strict limits are now rarely made. So far as the Courts are concerned, the existence of the rule in these days is usually made manifest only in cases where nothing of the kind having been desired or suspected, and where by nothing short of a miracle could a perpetuity at any time have supervened, even that possibility has, by the time of the contest, ceased to be existent. All the same in these cases the rule is fatal even to gifts so innocuous, and I cannot doubt that such a result is both mischievous and unfortunate, in many directions — in this notably, that it brings a sound principle into entirely gratuitous discredit. Nevertheless I most fully agree that the rule is not to be whittled away by the Courts even for such a reason as that. It is too well authenticated in all its recognised incidents to be any longer under the control of any Court. It is the Legislature alone, which, maintaining the salutary purpose of the rule in its proper application, can, if it pleases, remove from it those incidents or excrescences which, without assisting to achieve its legitimate object, have done much mischief in other directions.

In the present case, and notwithstanding the actual conditions to which I have referred, I am, like the rest of your Lordships, satisfied that on the construction of the words here used by the testator, it is impossible to say that this gift is not within the prohibition of the rule as we have inherited it. It is agreed that the only conceivable means of escape is, either by construction or otherwise, to confine the apparently general expression "my brothers and sisters" to the brothers and sisters of the testator in being at the date of his codicil. On construction it is not, I think, open to your Lordships so to limit these words. Nor is it, in my judgment, permissible, by reference to surrounding circumstances, to confine them, as Atkin LJ thought he could, to those same brothers and sisters as being the only brothers and sisters the testator knew, and as being in consequence and in the circumstances those with reference to whom alone he must be taken to have spoken[19].

The problem of the "precocious toddler", dealing with the minimum age of reproduction, is dealt with in *Re Gaite's Will Trusts* ([1949] 1 All ER 459, p. 300, ante).

ii. PERPETUITIES AND ACCUMULATIONS ACT 1964[20]

PERPETUITIES AND ACCUMULATIONS ACT 1964

2. Presumptions and evidence as to future parenthood. — (1) Where in any proceedings there arises on the rule against perpetuities a question which turns on the ability of a person to have a child at some future time, then —

(a) subject to paragraph (b) below, it shall be presumed that a male can have a child at the age of fourteen years or over, but not under that age, and that a female can have a child at the age of twelve years or over, but not under that age or over the age of fifty-five years; but

(b) in the case of a living person evidence may be given to show that he or she will or will not be able to have a child at the time in question.

(2) Where any such question is decided by treating a person as unable to have a child at a particular time, and he or she does so, the High Court may make such order as it thinks fit for placing the persons interested in the property comprised in the disposition, so far as may be just, in the position they would have held if the question had not been so decided.

(3) Subject to subsection (2) above, where any such question is decided in relation to a disposition by treating a person as able or unable to have a child at a particular time, then he or she shall be so treated for the purpose of any question which may arise on the rule against perpetuities in relation to the same disposition in any subsequent proceedings.

---

[19] *Cooper v Laroche* (1881) 17 ChD 368; *Re Dawson* (1888) 39 ChD 155, p. 320, post.
[20] (1964) 80 LQR 489-491; Cheshire, pp. 343-344; M & W, p. 217-218; MM, p. 102; Maudsley, pp. 116-118; Morris and Leach Supp., pp. 3-4.

(4) In the foregoing provisions of this section references to having a child are references to begetting or giving birth to a child, but those provisions (except subsection (1) (*b*)) shall apply in relation to the possibility that a person will at any time have a child by adoption[1], legitimation[2] or other means[3] as they apply to his or her ability at that time to beget or give birth to a child.

QUESTIONS

1. As a lawyer who is trained to construe a will in accordance with the intention of the testator, how would you have construed the will in *Ward v Van der Loeff*?

    See Morris and Leach 79; Restatement of Property, vol. 4, section 377, comment (*c*); *Re Powell* [1898] 1 Ch 227; *Re Cockle's Will Trusts* [1967] Ch 690, [1967] 1 All ER 391.

2. Redraft the codicil in *Ward v Van der Loeff* so as to comply with the testator's true intention.

3. (For thought now; answer later). If the codicil was void in *Ward v Van der Loeff*, why was the will not void too?

4. What would be the decision on the facts of *Re Gaite's Will Trusts* if the testatrix had died in 1970 — i.e. after the coming into force of Family Law Reform Act 1969, section 15?

B.   The Unborn Widow under the Common Law Rule

RE FROST

(1889) 43 ChD 246 (ChD, KAY J)

The testator devised a freehold estate to his spinster daughter Emma for life, and after her decease, to the use of any husband she may hereafter marry for his life and, subject to a power of appointment, to the use of such of Emma's children as should be living at the death of the survivor of Emma and such husband . . . with further gifts over. The question was whether, on the death of Emma and her husband, without issue, the subsequent limitations were valid.

Held. All the limitations subsequent to the life interests to the spouses were void.

KAY J: [Emma] might have married after the death of the testator a person who was not born in his lifetime, and it might therefore have been a limitation to *Emma Frost* for life, remainder to an unborn person for his life, with a contingent remainder over to the children of *Emma Frost* living at the death of that unborn person, or such of them as should be then dead leaving issue then living, and an alternative limitation to other persons, still to be living at the death of that unborn person, or leaving issue then living. That clearly would be a limitation which would offend against the rule of perpetuity, because

---

[1] Children Act 1975, s. 8, Sch. 1, paras. 3–5. See Adoption Act 1976, s. 39 (the Act is not yet in force).

[2] Legitimacy Act 1976, ss. 5, 11, Schs., 1, 2.

[3] See, for illegitimate children, Family Law Reform Act 1969, ss. 14, 15; Law Commission Working Paper No. 47 (1979).

it would tie up the estate, not merely during the life of *Emma Frost*, who was in existence at the death of the testator, but during the life of *Emma Frost's* husband, who might possibly not be living at the death of the testator. So that it would not merely be tied up for a life in being and twenty-one years after, but for a life in being, with remainder for a life not in being, with a contingent gift over[4].

In *Re Garnham* [1916] 2 Ch 413, the limitation was to A (a bachelor) for life, then to any woman he might marry for life, and then to the children of A at 21 or on marriage, and in default of children (as happened) then to certain other persons. The gift was upheld. It differed from *Re Frost*, in that, as NEVILLE J, at p. 416, said: "It seems to me that upon the determination of the tenancy for life given to an existing person the class is ascertained, although the enjoyment may be postponed during a life tenancy of a person who may have been unborn at the date of the gift." In other words, in this case, the limitation vested in interest on the death of A, and not, as in *Re Frost*, on the death of the survivor. The vesting in possession would be the same in either case, but this is not relevant in the application of the perpetuity rule.

This distinction was further illustrated in *Re Garnham*. The land was to be held on trust for sale on the death of the survivor of A and such wife. NEVILLE J, decided that the trust for sale was void and that the property was received by those entitled to it in its unconverted form.

The Perpetuities and Accumulations Act 1964 makes provision for dealing with the unborn widow problem in section 5[5]. The section however applies only where the gift has not been saved under the "wait and see" principle introduced in section 3. The sections will be considered in the order in which they are to be applied.

C. Administrative Contingencies under the Common Law Rule

In *Re Wood* [1894] 2 Ch 310; *affd.* [1894] 3 Ch 381[6], the testator, a gravel contractor, directed his trustees to "carry on my said business of a gravel contractor until my gravel-pits are worked out," and then to sell them and to hold the proceeds of sale among his children "then living" and the living issue of (deceased) children who being sons attain 21, or, being daughters, attain 21 or marry.

---

[4] The limitation was void also under the rule in *Whitby v Mitchell* (1890) 44 ChD 85. If Emma was married at the date of the gift, it would be a question of construction whether the gift to the husband was limited to her present husband, who would be a life in being, or would include other future husbands who might not be.

[5] (1964) 80 LQR 512–515; Cheshire, pp. 350–351; M & W, pp. 227–228; MM, p. 109; p. 324, post; Maudsley, pp. 146–148; Morris and Leach Supp., pp. 12–13.

[6] *Thomas v Thomas* (1902) 87 LT 58. This is so, even if the gift is charitable; *Re Lord Stratheden and Campbell* [1894] 3 Ch 265, (annuity of £100 to be provided to the Central London Rangers on the appointment of the next lieutenant-colonel.)

At the date of the will it was clear that the testator knew that the gravel pits would soon be worked out and they were in fact worked out within six years. KEKEWICH J, and the Court of Appeal held the gift void for perpetuity because the gravel pits might not have been worked out within the perpetuity period.

In *Re Atkins' Will Trusts* [1974] 1 WLR 761, [1974] 2 All ER 1, a testator, who died in 1957, devised his farm on trust to allow his stepson, Ernest Alexander Double, to have the full use and enjoyment thereof and on his death or his ceasing to work the farm the trustees were directed to sell it "and to divide the net proceeds of sale equally and per capita amongst such of the following as shall be living at the date of the completion of the said sale", namely, the grandchildren of a deceased brother of the testator, a niece of the testator and the four children of another niece. After the death of the stepson on 30 March 1972, the bulk of the farm was sold on 7 September 1972. In holding that the remainder was valid. PENNYCUICK V-C said, at p. 767:

"Having reached the conclusion which I have expressed on the first two points — namely, that the proceeds of sale of the farm became divisible amongst the beneficiaries living at the date of completion of the sale and that the duty of the bank was to sell within one year, at latest, from the death of Ernest Alexander Double — then one comes to the question: was such a disposition void on the ground of perpetuity, namely, that the interests of the beneficiaries might not vest within 21 years from the death of Ernest Alexander Double, who was a life in being at the death of the testator?

Counsel for the last two defendants stressed, as is undoubtedly true, that in applying the rule against perpetuities as it stood before the Perpetuities and Accumulations Act 1964, one must look at possible and not actual events (see, for instance, *Theobald, Wills*, 13th edn. (1971), para. 1483), and there is no doubt that the court over the years has sometimes taken into account some very remote possibilities. Counsel relied in particular on *Re Wood* [1894] 3 Ch 381, in the Court of Appeal, a decision which has come in for a good deal of textbook criticism since, but which I suppose in comparable circumstances I should be bound to follow. It seems to me, however, that there is a critical distinction to be made between the possibility of delay owing to physical causes such as were considered in *Re Wood* and the possibility of delay owing to a breach of trust on the part of the trustee concerned. In the former case one must, I suppose, take into account anything physically capable of happening. I should myself wish to reserve consideration on that matter in relation to certain highly improbable events. On the other hand, where there is a possibility that delay can arise only should there be a breach of trust, that is a possibility which it seems to me the court must clearly disregard. The court will act on the basis that equity regards that as done which ought to be done, and it will treat the trustees as having done whatever they were bound to do. It will not allow the rights of beneficiaries to be defeated because the trustees failed to carry out their fiduciary duties.

So, in the present case, the duty of the trustee was to sell this farm immediately, and that means at the latest, as I have held, within one year of the death of Ernest Alexander Double, and the court should not and cannot properly take into account the possibility that the bank, in breach of trust, might fail to realise within the time in which it was bound to realise. The result is that one must treat the sale as something which must be completed within, at the most, 12 months from the death of Ernest Alexander Double, and accordingly the vesting of the interests of the beneficiaries would take effect within one year of the death of Ernest Alexander Double, and there can be no question of a perpetuity."

V. Wait and See

A. General

It will be observed that all of the limitations in the examples given which failed did so because they *might* have vested outside the perpetuity period; not because they did so. This was necessitated by the common law rule's requirement of certainty; an interest is valid under the common law rule only if it is possible to postulate, at the date when the gift takes effect, that *if* the gift ever vests, it *must* do so within the perpetuity period. Of course, it may never vest at all. This is the risk of all contingent interests. The common law rule is concerned with the time within which it *must* vest if it ever does.

We have seen that, by making a judicious selection of measuring lives, a competent draftsman can extend the rule to its fullest extent. It will be observed that all the illustrations so far given could have been validated if the draftsman had made use of the opportunities available to him. He could have made use of selected lives; or, he could have included a simple catch-all provision, such as "provided that no beneficiary shall be entitled to take unless his interest shall vest within 21 years of the death of . . ."[7]. Such a provision would not restrict the donor's freedom of disposition, because in nearly all the cases the interests given will in fact vest within the period. It should be appreciated that, however many lives are selected, the period is the same: a life in being plus 21 years. For, as Twisden used to say, "the candles are all lighted at once"[8].

What, then, is the sense in holding void a gift which vests within the period, merely because it might have vested outside; but did not? We saw that a gift to the first child of A to marry is void, if A is alive and has no married child; because A's first child to marry *might* do so more

---

[7] (1961) 74 HLR 1141 (W. B. Leach and J. K. Logan).
[8] *Scattergood v Edge* (1699) 1 Salk 229.

than 21 years after the death of any persons now living. But if the gift is made on the eve of A's eldest daughter's wedding day, and she does marry on that day, why should the gift be held void for perpetuity?

In other words, why insist on certainty of vesting, if at all, within the period? Why not wait and see whether the disposition does in fact vest within the period? The adoption of a wait and see rule was enacted by the Perpetuities and Accumulations Act 1964, section 3.

PERPETUITIES AND ACCUMULATIONS ACT 1964

3.[9] **Uncertainty as to remoteness.** — (1) Where, apart from the provisions of this section and sections 4 and 5 of this Act, a disposition would be void on the ground that the interest disposed of might not become vested until too remote a time, the disposition shall be treated, until such time (if any) as it becomes established that the vesting must occur, if at all, after the end of the perpetuity period, as if the disposition were not subject to the rule against perpetuities; and its becoming so established shall not affect the validity of anything previously done in relation to the interest disposed of by way of advancement, application of intermediate income or otherwise.

(2) Where, apart from the said provisions, a disposition consisting of the conferring of a general power of appointment would be void on the ground that the power might not become exercisable until too remote a time, the disposition shall be treated, until such time (if any) as it becomes established that the power will not be exercisable within the perpetuity period, as if the disposition were not subject to the rule against perpetuities.

(3) Where, apart from the said provisions, a disposition consisting of the conferring of any power, option or other right would be void on the ground that the right might be exercised at too remote a time, the disposition shall be treated as regards any exercise of the right within the perpetuity period as if it were not subject to the rule against perpetuities and, subject to the said provisions, shall be treated as void for remoteness only if, and so far as, the right is not fully exercised within that period.

B. Measuring Lives[10]

The introduction of the Wait and See principle requires a total reconsideration of the question of measuring lives. The common law lives obviously will not do; because the only persons recognised as common law lives are those who have already validated the gifts. If we only used them, we "would never wait and see at all"[11]. If the statute

---

[9] (1964) 80 LQR 492–495, Cheshire, pp. 344–347; M & W, pp. 214–216; MM, pp. 102–103, Maudsley, pp. 120–122; Morris and Leach Supp., pp 5–8. For the first judicial application see *Re Thomas Meadows & Co Ltd and Subsidiary Companies (1960) Staff Pension Scheme Rules* [1971] Ch 278, [1971] 1 All ER 239.

[10] Maudsley, pp. 87–109, 123–139.

[11] (1965) 81 LQR 106, 108 (D. E. Allan).

does not make some selection, it could be argued that any living person would do[12]; but this "would send potential beneficiaries ransacking the registers of births and deaths throughout the world[11]" in order to find a centenarian capable of validating a gift which vested after 121 years.

It is obvious that the lives to be used should be known, and known precisely. If gifts are to be held valid or void, dependent on whether or not they do in fact vest within a period of lives in being plus 21 years, the system can only operate if you know how long the period is, and you only know that, if you know whose lives are to be used. The statute enacting Wait and See must lay down who the measuring lives are. They need have no relation to common law lives; it is best to discard all thoughts based on the common law situation; and to consider what, in the new situation, is required of the measuring lives. The new situation is trying to allow a limitation to be effective if it vests within a life in being plus 21 years (or 80 years). Any life? No, because of the inconvenience of following up every life; but the policy is to include every life that is reasonably connected with the limitation and identifiable at the date of the gift. In a gift "to the grandchildren of A" (a living person) why not include a present living grandchild if such inclusion enables the limitation to be valid, or allows the testator's intention to be more accurately followed; or, indeed, the donee of a power? On the other hand, an "unborn widow" is not included even if she turns out to have been alive at the date of the gift, because of the clearly sound principle that lives in being must be ascertainable at the beginning of the period. The Act of 1964 was the first in the world to recognize the problem and to produce a workable list[13].

C. Perpetuities and Accumulations Act 1964[14]

PERPETUITIES AND ACCUMULATIONS ACT 1964

3. Uncertainty as to remoteness. —

(4) Where this section applies to a disposition and the duration of the perpetuity period is not determined by virtue of section 1 or 9 (2) of this Act, it shall be determined as follows:—

(*a*) where any persons falling within subsection (5) below are individuals in being and ascertainable at the commencement of the perpetuity period the duration of the period shall be determined by reference to their lives and no others, but so that the lives of any description of persons falling within paragraph (*b*) or (*c*) of that subsection shall be disregarded if

---

[12] (1953) 52 Mich LR 179 (L. M. Simes); (1963) 6 U of WALR 21 (L. M. Simes); 27 (D. E. Allan); (1965) 81 LQR 106. (D. E. Allan) (1970) 80 LQR 357 (R. H. Maudsley).

[13] And followed, with or without minor changes, in Northern Ireland, Alberta, British Columbia and New Zealand; Maudsley, Appendix D.

[14] Cheshire, pp. 348–350; M & W, pp. 220–226; MM, pp. 107–110; Maudsley, pp.123–139; Morris and Leach Supp., pp. 8–10; Morris and Wade, (1964) 80 L.Q.R. 495–508.

the number of persons of that description is such as to render it impracticable to ascertain the date of death of the survivor;

(b) where there are no lives under paragraph (a) above the period shall be twenty-one years.

(5) The said persons are as follows:—

(a) the person by whom the disposition was made;

(b) a person to whom or in whose favour the disposition was made, that is to say —

(i) in the case of a disposition to a class of persons, any member or potential member of the class;

(ii) in the case of an individual disposition to a person taking only on certain conditions being satisfied, any person as to whom some of the conditions are satisfied and the remainder may in time be satisfied;

(iii) in the case of a special power of appointment exercisable in favour of members of a class, any member or potential member of the class;

(iv) in the case of a special power of appointment exercisable in favour of one person only, that person or, where the object of the power is ascertainable only on certain conditions being satisfied, any person as to whom some of the conditions are satisfied and the remainder may in time be satisfied;

(v) in the case of any power, option or other right, the person on whom the right is conferred;

(c) a person having a child or grandchild within sub-paragraphs (i) to (iv) of paragraph (b) above, or any of whose children or grandchildren, if subsequently born, would by virtue of his or her descent, fall within those sub-paragraphs;

(d) any person on the failure or determination of whose prior interest the disposition is limited to take effect.

15.   Short title, interpretation and extent. —

(3) For the purposes of this Act a person shall be treated as a member of a class if in his case all the conditions identifying a member of the class are satisfied, and shall be treated as a potential member if in his case some only of those conditions are satisfied but there is a possibility that the remainder will in time be satisfied.

With this compare:

(i) Victoria Perpetuities and Accumulations Act 1968, section 6 (4):

"Nothing in this section[15] makes any person a life in being for the purposes of ascertaining the perpetuity period unless the life of that person is one expressed or implied as relevant for this purpose by the terms of the disposition and would have been reckoned a life in being for such purpose if this section had not been enacted:

---

[15] Introducing a "wait and see" rule.

Provided however that in the case of a disposition to a class of persons or to one or more members of a class, any person living at the date of the disposition whose life is so expressed or implied as relevant for any member of the class may be reckoned a life in being in ascertaining the perpetuity period."

(ii) Kentucky Rev. Stats. § 381.216.[16]

318.216 Wait-and-See doctrine; reformation. In determining whether an interest would violate the rule against perpetuities the period of perpetuities shall be measured by actual rather than possible events; provided, however, the period shall not be measured by any lives whose continuance does not have a causal relationship to the vesting or failure of the interest. Any interest which would violate said rule as thus modified shall be reformed, within the limits of that rule, to approximate most closely the intention of the creator of the interest.

VI. Reduction of Age Contingencies

A. Before 1964[17]

A common cause of violation of the rule was the postponement of vesting until an age greater than 21.

LAW OF PROPERTY ACT 1925

163. Validation of certain gifts void for remoteness. — (1) Where in a will, settlement or other instrument the absolute vesting either of capital or income of property, or the ascertainment of a beneficiary or class of beneficiaries, is made to depend on the attainment by the beneficiary or members of the class of an age exceeding twenty-one years, and thereby the gift to that beneficiary or class or any member thereof, or any gift over, remainder, executory limitation, or trust arising on the total or partial failure of the original gift, is, or but for this section would be, rendered void for remoteness, the will, settlement, or other instrument shall take effect for the purposes of such gift over, remainder, executory limitation, or trust as if the absolute vesting or ascertainment aforesaid had been made to depend on the beneficiary or member of the class attaining the age of twenty-one years, and that age shall be substituted for the age stated in the will, settlement, or other instrument.

(2) This section applies to any instrument executed after the commencement of this Act and to any testamentary appointment (whether made in exercise of a general or special power), devise, or bequest contained in the will of a person dying after such commencement, whether the will is made before or after such commencement.

---

[16] (1960) 49 Kentucky LR 62 (J. Dukeminier): Dukeminier, *Perpetuities in Action*; Maudsley, p. 107 n. 13, 14.

[17] Cheshire, pp. 325–326; M & W, pp. 234–236; MM, pp. 106–107; Morris and Leach, pp. 52–56.

(3) This section applies without prejudice to any provision whereby the absolute vesting or ascertainment is also made to depend on the marriage of any person, or any other event which may occur before the age stated in the will, settlement, or other instrument is attained.

B.   Perpetuities and Accumulations Act 1964[18]

A different solution was needed after the introduction of a principle of "wait and see" into the perpetuity rule by the 1964 Act.

PERPETUITIES AND ACCUMULATIONS ACT 1964

4.   Reduction of age and exclusion of class members to avoid remoteness. — (1) Where a disposition is limited by reference to the attainment by any person or persons of a specified age exceeding twenty-one years, and it is apparent at the time the disposition is made or becomes apparent at a subsequent time —

(a) that the disposition would, apart from this section, be void for remoteness, but

(b) that it would not be so void if the specified age had been twenty-one years,

the disposition shall be treated for all purposes as if, instead of being limited by reference to the age in fact specified, it had been limited by reference to the age nearest to that age which would, if specified instead, have prevented the disposition from being so void.

(2) Where in the case of any disposition different ages exceeding twenty-one years are specified in relation to different persons —

(a) the reference in paragraph (b) of subsection (1) above to the specified age shall be construed as a reference to all the specified ages, and

(b) that subsection shall operate to reduce each such age so far as is necessary to save the disposition from being void for remoteness.

(6) Section 163 of the Law of Property Act 1925 (which saves a disposition from remoteness arising out of a condition requiring the attainment of an age exceeding twenty-one years) is hereby repealed.

(7)[19] For the avoidance of doubt it is hereby declared that a question arising under section 3 of this Act or subsection (1) (a) above of whether a disposition would be void apart from this section is to be determined as if subsection (6) above had been a separate section of this Act.

---

[18] (1964) 80 LQR 508–510. Cheshire, pp. 351–353; M & W, pp. 236–238; MM, pp. 108–109; Maudsley, pp. 139–143; Morris and Leach Supp., pp. 10–12.

[19] As added by Children Act 1975, s. 108, Sch. 3, para. 43. (1965) 81 LQR 346 (J. D. Davies); (1976) 120 Sol Jo 498 (F.A.R. Bennion).

VII. Class Gifts[20]

A. The Common Law Rule

Many of the gifts which have been held void, in the illustrations so far discussed, have been class gifts; and they have been held void because there was a theoretical possibility that the interest of a member of the class might vest outside the period. The fact that the interests of most (and probably all) the members of the class vested well within the period did not help the gift, nor did it help the prospects of those whose interests did in fact vest. When the rule says that "an interest ... must vest", it refers in the case of a class gift to the vesting of the class and not to the interests of individual members[1]. It means that the composition of the class and the share of each member must be known within the period. The gift is void if, outside the period, the number of members of the class might increase and the size of each share thus be reduced; or if the number of members of the class might be reduced, and the size of each share be increased[2].

It is important to appreciate that the question of "vesting", when asked in a perpetuity context, is different from that asked in the more usual context unaffected by the perpetuity rule; when, for example, the question is whether or not one member is yet qualified to claim an admittedly valid gift, and whether it is therefore safe for an executor or trustee to pay a share to him. For example: "To the children of A at 21." When A's eldest son is 21, he will have a "vested" interest and can be paid his share. If the question were whether or not the gift had "vested" in a perpetuity context, however, the answer would have to be "no; the gift will not vest until 21 years from the death of A". For until A's death, there may be more children so as to increase the class; and, after A's death, there may be fewer, if some die under 21, and this would reduce the membership.

To return to the trustee paying out under the gift to the children of A at 21. What share can he properly pay to the eldest son? There may be more children. Either the eldest must wait until A's death, at which time the maximum number of claimants would be known; and for this purpose it does not matter that the number may be later reduced[3]; or the eldest must be allowed to claim his share now, based upon the existing number of children, and to the exclusion of later born

---

[20] Cheshire, pp. 326–329; M & W, pp. 228–234; MM, pp. 113–114; Maudsley, pp. 15–25, 36–39; Morris and Leach, pp. 101–133; (1938) 51 HLR 1329 (W. B. Leach).
[1] Lord SELBORNE LC, in *Pearks v Moseley* (1880) 5 App Cas at p. 723 said: "A gift is said to be to a 'class' of persons, when it is to all those who shall come within a certain category or description defined by a general or collective formula, and who, if they take at all, are to take one divisible subject in proportionate shares; and the rule is, that the vice of remoteness affects the class as a whole, if it may affect an unascertained number of its members." See also Restatement of Property, Ch 22.
[2] *Jee v Audley* (1787) 1 Cox Eq Cas 324; *Leake v Robinson* (1817) 2 Mer 363; *Pearks v Moseley* (1880) 5 App Cas 714; *Ward v Van der Loeff* [1924] AC 653 and cases cited in this section.
[3] For the share of each would then be increased.

children. The problem would be presented more dramatically if the limitation were "to all the grandchildren of X at 21." X has died, leaving a grandchild Y who is 21, and a son Z who is 10. Must Y wait until the death of all his uncles and aunts, including Z, and perhaps a further 21 years before claiming? For only then will it be known how many grandchildren of X will attain 21.

The law solves the problem by closing the class of potential takers to those possible claimants who are alive at the period of distribution — i.e. when the trustees wish to start paying out. This provides a maximum number of takers and the smallest possible share; and this is what the trustees need to know. Those who are alive at that time will be paid when they vest; future born are excluded. The rule is only a rule of construction, and gives way to an expression of contrary intention and it seems that the courts are becoming more ready to find such contrary intention[4]. It is known as the rule of convenience; it is highly convenient for the trustees and for those who are alive at the period of distribution; highly inconvenient for future born. The class-closing rules have been much criticized[5]. It is important to appreciate that they are arbitrary; and inevitable.

Finally, let it be noted that the rule against perpetuities and the class-closing rules sometimes inter-act. Sometimes, as it were by a fluke, a class artificially closed must vest, if at all, within the period, although if left to close naturally, members might join outside. Some of these cases will be examined at pp. 325 et seq., post.

RE DAWSON

(1888) 39 ChD 155 (ChD, CHITTY J)

A testator, by his will, provided an annuity for the plaintiff, his daughter, and after her death the residue was to be held on trust for her children at 21, or (being daughters) at that age or marriage, and also for such child or children of any son of the plaintiff who should die under 21 as shall live to attain the age of 21, or being daughters live to attain that age or marry, such children to take their parent's share.

---

[4] *Re Bleckly* [1951] Ch 740, [1951] 1 All ER 1064; *Re Cockle's Will Trusts* [1967] Ch 690, [1967] 1 All ER 391; *Re Kebty-Fletcher's Will Trusts* [1969] 1 Ch 339, [1967] 3 All ER 1076; *Re Harker's Will Trusts* [1969] 1 WLR 1124, [1969] 3 All ER 1; *Re Henderson's Trusts* [1969] 1 WLR 651, [1969] 3 All ER 769. *Re Edmondson's Will Trusts* [1972] 1 WLR 183, [1972] 1 All ER 444; *Re Deeley's Settlement* [1974] Ch 454, [1973] 3 All ER 1127, (1970) 34 Conv (NS) 393 (J. G. Riddall); *Re Chapman's Settlement Trusts* [1977] 1 WLR 1163, [1978] Conv 73 (F. R. Crane).

[5] For a statement of the class-closing rules, see Cheshire, pp. 327–329, 855–856; M & W, pp. 231–233, 500–503; MM, pp. 259–261; Maudsley, pp. 17–25; Morris and Leach, pp. 109–125; (1954) 70 LQR 61, (J. H. C. Morris); [1958] C.L.J. 39, (S. J. Bailey); *Theobald on Wills* (13th edn. 1971) Chap. 30., and note that where the members of a class are to take vested interests at birth and no member of the class exists at the time when the property is available for distribution, the class remains open indefinitely. *Shepherd v Ingram* (1764) Amb 448, (1954) 70 LQR 66, 67. Otherwise the first born would automatically take the whole at birth. On balance that would be less satisfactory than the inconvenience of allowing the class to remain open; *Re Bleckly*, supra.

The plaintiff was 60 years of age on the testator's death, and her children were all over 21.

She brought this action claiming that the trusts of the will subsequent to her death were void for remoteness.

Held. Since the plaintiff could in law give birth to further children, membership of the class would not be determined until a time beyond the period and the whole class gift was void.

CHITTY J: The question in this case is whether the trust in favour of the children and grandchildren of the testator's daughter, the Plaintiff *Mary Elizabeth Johnston*, is or is not void for remoteness.

Putting aside for a moment the question that has been argued as to the admissibility of evidence to shew that the daughter was at the time of the testator's death past child-bearing, it appears to me to be clear this trust is void. The gift is in favour of one class, but made up of two generations. The first generation is the daughter's own children. As to that no objection can be raised. The children are to take at twenty-one as to sons and as to daughters on attaining twenty-one or marriage. But the limitation in favour of the next generation, that is the daughter's grandchildren, is plainly void. The gift, to read it shortly, is for such children of any son of the daughter who should die under the age of twenty-one as shall live to attain the age of twenty-one years, or being a daughter or daughters live to attain that age or marry. Admitting the possibility of the testator's daughter having a son born after the testator's death, then I should get to a life not in being at his death; and as that child might die under twenty-one more than twenty-one years after the death of the testator that limitation to his children at twenty-one is obviously too remote[6]. . . .

Then it is argued that the Court in applying the rule against perpetuities looks at the state of things as they existed at the testator's death, and it appears that the testator's daughter at his death was sixty years and three months old, or thereabouts; and thereupon it is said that she was past child-bearing, and consequently that there could be no son of hers born after the testator's death. . . .

[His Lordship, relying especially on *Jee v Audley* ((1787) 1 Cox Eq Cas 324 (at p. 304, ante)) and *Re Sayer's Trusts* ((1868) LR 6 Eq 319), held that evidence as to capacity for child-bearing was inadmissible, and then continued:]

Another argument was adduced with reference to what appears to be the practice of the Court of Chancery in former times and of the Chancery Division of the High Court in the present day with reference to payment out where there is a married woman whose children are to take and the lady has attained a certain age. Those are cases I think, when examined from the beginning down to the present time, in which the Court does not assume the impossibility of issue, but as a mere matter of convenience of administration regards the high degree of

---

[6] The question so far was the same as that decided by the House of Lords in *Pearks v Moseley* (1880) 5 App Cas 714, where however there was not the complication of the physical impossibility of the appearance of new members.

improbability, and it has come now to be fixed somewhere about the age of fifty-four, although the circumstances may still be inquired into[7]. But with regard to the rule against perpetuities a high degree of probability or improbability will not do. The rule with regard to perpetuities is that the limitation must be such that every member of the class, where it is a question of a class gift, must of necessity take within the time allowed.

In *Re Hooper's Settlement Trusts* [1948] Ch 586, [1948] 2 All ER 261[8] the same fate befell a gift where the limitation was for the sons and daughters of the settlor . . . "provided always that if any son of the settlor shall die . . . leaving surviving him a child or children who shall attain the age of twenty-one years . . ." JENKINS J, held that the fact that the grandchildren were introduced by way of proviso was not sufficient to distinguish the case from *Pearks v Moseley* ((1880) 5 App Cas 714).

However, a different construction may save parts of the gift.

In *Cattlin v Brown* (1853) 11 Hare 372, WOOD VC, said at p. 373: "The question arises on a short devise to *Thomas Bannister Cattlin* for life, and after his decease to all and every his children or child, for their lives, in equal shares, and after the decease of any or either of them, the part or share of the child so dying unto his, her, or their children or child, and his, her or their heirs for ever . . .

The fifth and last rule to which I need to advert is this, — that where there is a gift or devise of a given sum of money or property to each member of a class, and the gift to each is wholly independent of the same or similar gift to every other member of the class, and cannot be augmented or diminished whatever be the number of the other members, then the gift may be good as to those within the limits allowed by law. This was settled in the case of *Storrs v Benbow*[9]. . . .

The testator devises the estate to *Thomas Bannister Cattlin* for life, with remainder to all his children as tenants in common for life, with remainder as to every share of every child to the children of that child in fee. Now, to follow the respective shares of the property, suppose *Thomas Bannister Cattlin* to have four sons, A. B. C. and D. and A. and B. to be living at the testator's death and the others to be born afterwards. A. and B. on the testator's death take an immediate vested interest in remainder for life, expectant on their father's death, with remainder to their respective children in fee, subject to their respective moieties being diminished on the birth of C. and D., but their exact shares are ascertained within the legal limits at the death of their father, and neither their life interests nor the remainder in fee are capable of being wholly divested in favour of any party beyond the legal limits, neither could any one intended by the testator to take an

---

[7] See p. 304, n. 17, ante.
[8] *Re Lord's Settlement* [1947] 2 All ER 685; *Haworth v IRC* [1974] STC 378.
[9] (1853) 3 De GM & G 390; *Wilkinson v Duncan* (1861) 30 Beav 111.

interest, but at a period beyond the legal limits, possibly take in lieu of A. or B.; their shares are not therefore within the third rule, or governed by the judgment in the case of *Lord Dungannon v Smith* ((1846) 12 Cl & Fin 546) as might have been the case if the devise had been to the sons of *Thomas Bannister Cattlin* living at his decease, with remainder to their sons in fee, for then there might possibly, at the death of *Thomas Bannister Cattlin*, have been no son who was in existence at the testator's death. Neither, again, can any possible event happening after the death of *Thomas Bannister Cattlin*, augment or diminish the share of A. or B. Here then A. and B. are respectively persons in esse at the death of the testator, who are to take a share that must be ascertained in a manner incapable of augmentation or diminution at the expiration of another life in esse. What is there to prevent the limitation of that share to him for life, with remainder to his children in fee? for this share must of necessity vest, if at all, within the legal limits, and complies, therefore, with the rule. It is in reality the case of *Storrs v Benbow*, substituting a given share for a given sum of money. . . .

The limitation as to the shares of C. and D. in the case I have supposed would be clearly void, as their children might be born at a period exceeding the limits which the law allows, they themselves not being in esse at the death of the testator. . . .

The declaration will be that the estate was by the will of the testator well limited in fee to the children of those children of *Thomas Bannister Cattlin* who were living at the death of the testator."

In *Re Russell* [1895] 2 Ch 698[10] there was a gift to all the daughters of Mary Dorrell who shall attain 21 . . . provided that . . . the share of any daughter shall be held on trust for her for life and after her death on trust for her children.

Mary Dorrell's only daughter, the plaintiff, who was born in the testator's lifetime and had attained 21, claimed that the proviso was void and that she was entitled absolutely.

The Court of Appeal (Lord HALSBURY LC, LINDLEY and RIGBY LJJ,) construed the proviso as being a condition of defeasance of the original gift to the daughters; and held it to apply independently to the separate share of each daughter; so that, while it would have been void in the case of a daughter born after the testator's death, it was valid in the plaintiff's case.

B. Perpetuities and Accumulations Act 1964[11]

PERPETUITIES AND ACCUMULATIONS ACT 1964

4. Reduction of age and exclusion of class members to avoid remoteness. —

(2) p. 318, ante.

---

[10] *Re Morrison's Will Trusts* [1940] Ch 102, [1939] 4 All ER 332.
[11] Cheshire, pp. 353–354; M & W, pp. 233–234, 238; MM, p. 114; Maudsley, pp. 140–143; (1964) 80 LQR 510–512; Morris and Leach Supp., pp. 10–12.

(3) Where the inclusion of any persons, being potential members of a class or unborn persons who at birth would become members or potential members of the class, prevents the foregoing provisions of this section[12] from operating to save a disposition from being void for remoteness, those persons shall thenceforth be deemed for all the purposes of the disposition to be excluded from the class, and the said provisions shall thereupon have effect accordingly.

(4) Where, in the case of a disposition to which subsection (3) above does not apply, it is apparent at the time the disposition is made or becomes apparent at a subsequent time that, apart from this subsection, the inclusion of any persons, being potential members of a class or unborn persons who at birth would become members or potential members of the class, would cause the disposition to be treated as void for remoteness, those persons shall, unless their exclusion would exhaust the class, thenceforth be deemed for all the purposes of the disposition to be excluded from the class.

(5) Where this section has effect in relation to a disposition to which section 3 above applies[13], the operation of this section shall not affect the validity of anything previously done in relation to the interest disposed of by way of advancement, application of intermediate income or otherwise.

---

5. Condition relating to death of surviving spouse. — Where a disposition is limited by reference to the time of death of the survivor of a person in being at the commencement of the perpetuity period and any spouse of that person, and that time has not arrived at the end of the perpetuity period, the disposition shall be treated for all purposes, where to do so would save it from being void for remoteness, as if it had instead been limited by reference to the time immediately before the end of that period.

QUESTIONS

1. Do you prefer the English, or the Victorian or the Kentucky treatment of the problem of the selection of measuring lives for the purposes of the perpetuity rule in a "wait and see" context?
2. Which limitations, if any, are valid at common law, but may be void under "wait and see"? Should the statutory list be made to include everyone who would be implied as a life in being at common law? If this were done, would there be any need to apply to instruments coming into operation after 15 July 1964, any parts of the common law rule, other than those relating to the selection of "express" lives in being. See Maudsley pp. 156–160: (1975) 60 Cornell LR 355. M & W, pp. 223–225.
3. Which measuring lives do you think should be used for Wait and See?

---

[12] Section 4 (1) (2), p. 318, ante, relating to reduction of age contingencies.
[13] P. 314, ante.

VIII.   Class Closing Rules[14]

It may sometimes happen that a class gift is saved at common law by the fortuitous operation of the class closing rules discussed above[15]. It cannot be emphasised too strongly that the purpose of the class closing rules is to do something quite different. But it sometimes has this effect.

PICKEN *v* MATTHEWS

(1878) 10 ChD 264 (ChD, MALINS VC)

The testator gave real and personal property on trust for the children of his daughters Helen and Charlotte who should attain 25. At the date of the testator's death Helen had three children, one of whom had attained 25 and Charlotte had two infant children.

Held. A valid gift to such of the daughters' children living at the testator's death who should attain 25.

MALINS VC: If the two daughters of the testator had had no children living at his death, the gift would have been void for remoteness; because it would not be certain that the property would vest within a life or lives in being and twenty-one years after. But this is a gift to living grandchildren. . . . Now, the rules . . . applicable to this case are, first, that a gift to a class not preceded by any life estate is a gift to such of the class as are living at the death of the testator. . . .

The second rule is, that where you have a gift for such of the children of *A.* as shall attain a specified age, only those who are in esse when the first of the class attains the specified age can take. All afterborn children are excluded. This also is a rule of convenience . . .

Here there is a gift to such of a class as shall attain twenty-five. The class was ascertained at the death of the testator because one of them had then attained twenty-five. The two infant children of *Charlotte* . . . who were alive at the death of the testator are entitled to take provided they attain the age of twenty-five years . . .

Here I hold that there is a valid gift because one of the children of *Helen* . . . had attained twenty-five at the death of the testator; the maximum number to take was, therefore, then ascertained, and the gift in question is not void for remoteness."

A class may be closed by the existence of the estate of a deceased member of the class who held a vested interest before his death.

In *Re Chartres* [1927] 1 Ch 466, the testator gave two-fifths of the residue, after the expiration of 21 years, in trust for the children or remoter issue of his son Richard as Richard should by will appoint, and

---

[14] Cheshire, pp. 327–329, 855–856; M & W, pp. 231–233, 500–503; MM, pp. 259–261; Maudsley, pp. 17–25, 36–39, 145–146; Morris and Leach, pp. 109–125; (1954) 70 LQR 61 (J. H. C. Morris); [1958] CLJ 39 (S. J. Bailey); *Theobald on Wills* (13th edn. 1971) chap. 30; see p. 320, n. 5, ante.

[15] See pp. 319–320, ante.

in default of appointment in trust for all Richard's children who being sons attain 21 or being daughters attain 21 or marry.

On 11 March 1905 the testator died, so that the 21 year period expired on 11 March 1926.

On 18 March 1916, Richard's only child, Archibald, attained 21.

On 12 March 1924, Richard released his testamentary power.

On 26 February 1925, Archibald died having bequeathed his property to Richard.

Richard was still alive and the question was whether, having released his testamentary power, he could claim the two-fifths of the estate given to his children. ASTBURY J held that the class closed at the period of distribution, which would be at the expiry of the 21 year period, or the attainment of 21 by one of Richard's children, whichever was the later. Archibald's interest had "vested"; the period of distribution was therefore the expiry of the 21 year period on 11 March 1926, and the trustees were to pay the money over to Archibald's estate, to the exclusion of possible future born children of Richard[16]. The two-fifths share thus passed under Archibald's will to Richard.

The Perpetuities and Accumulations Act 1964 makes no reference to the class closing rules. They will apply in exactly the same way as they did before the Act. Where they would previously have saved a gift from invalidity, their effect now is to avoid the necessity of applying the Act.

Where a limitation is void at common law and consequently the wait and see rule applies under section 3 (1), there is new scope for the operation of the class closing rules. A class gift which comes within section 3 (1) may remain open for lives in being plus 21 years, and after that time potential members who have not yet joined the class will be excluded: section 4 (4). Many class gifts will not however wait so long; for, at the period of distribution, the class will close to include only those potential members who are in being at the time.

Thus, suppose a gift: "To such of the grandchildren of A. (a living person), as shall attain the age of 21." A. has two sons, B. and C., and a grandson X., all of whom will be measuring lives under section 3 (5). Without rules for artificial closing of the class, any grandchildren could join it who attained 21 within 21 years of the dropping of the last of those lives. However on X.'s 21st birthday, he will be able to demand payment of his share; and the class will close to include only those grandchildren who are alive at the time[17].

---

[16] See the criticism of the application of the class-closing rules to a case where a life interest is released; *Re Kebty-Fletcher's Will Trusts* [1969] 1 Ch 339, [1967] 3 All ER 1076; *Re Harker's Will Trusts* [1969] 1 WLR 1124, [1969] 3 All ER 1; (1970) 34 Conv (NS) 393, 398, 407 (J. G. Riddall).

[17] If there is no grandchild alive at the testator's death, there is some doubt whether or not the class closes when the first grandchild attains 21. The better view is that it does. *Pearse v Catton* (1839) 1 Beav 352; Morris and Leach, p. 114; (1954) 70 LQR 61, 68–69, (J. H. C. Morris); *Re Bleckly* [1951] Ch 740 at p. 749, [1951] 1 All ER 1064.

QUESTIONS

1. On what principle was the gift in the will in *Ward v Van der Loeff* held valid?
2. What alteration in the facts would have enabled the gift in the codicil to be upheld on the same ground as that on which the gift in the will was upheld? (1954) 70 LQR 61, 84 (J. H. C. Morris); *Re Cockle's Will Trusts* [1967] Ch 690, [1967] 1 All ER 391; Maudsley pp. 53–56.
3. A testator bequeathed his residuary estate upon trust to be divided equally between such of his nephews and nieces as were living at the date of his death for their lives and after the death of any such nephew or niece upon trust for the child or children of such nephews or nieces who shall attain the age of 21 years.

   One nephew, Geoffrey, having no need of the income, released to the trustees all his interest to the intent that the trustees should hold the income on the same trusts as would be applicable if he were dead. The elder of Geoffrey's two daughters attained the age of 21. Is she entitled to claim half of the fund? See *Re Kebty-Fletcher's Will Trusts* [1969] 1 Ch 339, [1967] 3 All ER 1076; *Re Harker's Will Trusts* [1969] 1 WLR 1124, [1969] 3 All ER 1.
4. What would be the solution to *Ward v Van der Loeff* ([1924] AC 653) if the testator had died after 1964?

IX.   Powers of Appointment

A.   Before 1964[18]

i.   GENERAL POWERS

a.   *Validity of Power*

A general power is one by which the donee of the power may appoint to any person, including himself. Thus, the giving of a general power to a donee is, in a sense, equivalent to giving the property to him. Hence, a general power is valid if it must become exercisable by the donee, if at all, within the perpetuity period. It is not relevant that he may exercise it outside the period.

b.   *Validity of Exercise of Power*

In the case of a general power, the perpetuity period runs from the time of the exercise of the power.

ii.   SPECIAL POWERS

a.   *Validity of Power*

A special power is one in which the class of appointees is restricted. The donor of the power is exercising an element of control over the appointment. A stricter rule applies.

---

[18] Cheshire, pp. 329–333; M & W, pp. 250–258; MM, pp. 117–122; Maudsley, pp. 59–64; Morris and Leach, pp. 134–163.

In *Re De Sommery* [1912] 2 Ch 622, PARKER J said, at p. 630: "A special power which, according to the true construction of the instrument creating it, is capable of being exercised beyond lives in being and twenty-one years afterwards is, by reason of the rule against perpetuities, absolutely void; but if it can only be exercised within the period allowed by the rule, it is a good power, even although some particular exercise of it might be void because of the rule.

If a power be given to a person alive at the date of the instrument creating it, it must, of course, if exercised at all, be executed during his life, and is therefore valid. Again, if a power can be exercised only in favour of a person living at the date of the instrument creating it, it must, if exercised at all, be exercised during the life of such person, and is therefore unobjectionable. Further, the instrument itself may expressly limit a period, not exceeding the legal limits, for the exercise of the power. Lastly, where the settlor has used language from which the Court may fairly infer that he contemplated the creation, not of a single power, but of two distinct powers, one of which only is open to objection because of the rule against perpetuities, the Court will avoid the latter only and will give effect to the power which is not open to this objection. Thus, although a power vested in the trustees for the time being of a settlement has, so far as I can discover, been uniformly looked on as a single and indivisible power, it may be otherwise if the power be limited to A. and B. or other the trustees of the settlement for the time being. In this case the Court may treat the settlor as having created one power vested in A. and B. while trustees, and a distinct power vested in their successors, in which case the power vested in A. and B. would be open to no objection on the ground of remoteness: *Attenborough v Attenborough* ((1855) 1 K & J 296).

In the present case the testatrix devised all her real and residuary personal estate to two named persons, thereinafter called her 'trustees', upon trust for sale, and, after payment of her debts and funeral and testamentary expenses and a certain charitable legacy, to divide the proceeds into thirteen parts, and, as to two such parts, to hold the same, upon trust to pay the capital and income thereof, or neither, to her nephew Eugene de Sommery, or to apply the capital or income thereof for his benefit, or for the benefit of his wife or any child or children of his, as her trustees should consider advisable, and, subject thereto, to pay any capital or income which might remain in their hands under that trust to such of her nephews and nieces, and in such shares, as her trustees should think proper. In my opinion, the power or powers thus created in favour of Eugene de Sommery, his wife and children, are conferred on the trustees of the will for the time being, and not on the original trustees only (see *Re Smith* [1904] 1 Ch 139); and this being so, there is, I think, no possibility of applying the principle of *Attenborough v Attenborough*. Further, if there be one power only vested in these trustees, it is fairly obvious that it may, according to the true construction of the will, be exercised during the life of any child of Eugene de Sommery, whether alive at the testatrix's death or born afterwards, and would therefore be avoided by the rule against perpetuities. I have come to the conclusion, however, that there are in fact two powers vested in the trustees for the time being of the will — first, a power of paying either capital or income to Eugene de Sommery, which is only capable of being exercised during his life, and, secondly, a power of applying either capital or income for the benefit of Eugene de Sommery, his wife or children, which is capable of being exercised beyond the period allowed by law. I see no reason on principle which precludes me from upholding the former and rejecting the latter power."

b. Validity of Exercise of Power

The appointment must be read back into the instrument containing the power; that is the perpetuity period must run from the date of the creation of the power.

RE BROWN AND SIBLY'S CONTRACT

(1876) 3 ChD 156 (ChD, MALINS VC)

By a marriage settlement of 1821, land was conveyed to trustees to the use of W.M. for life and after his death as he shall appoint among his issue with a gift over in default.

W.M. appointed by will in 1867 to his son W.E.M. in fee; but in case W.E.M. should have no child who should attain 21, then in fee to W.M.B. (a grandson through a daughter, and unborn at the date of the settlement).

W.E.M. sold part of the land to Brown, who then entered into a contract with Sibly to sell part of the land to him. The question was whether W.E.M. could give a good title to the fee simple without the concurrence of W.M.B.

Held. He could; because the executory gift over to W.M.B. was void for remoteness.

MALINS VC: The point I have to decide under this settlement is free from doubt. The law is settled, that where a person takes property by virtue of the execution of a special or limited power of appointment, he takes directly under the instrument creating the power. Consequently, when *W. Metford* made his will, it was the same as if the words he there used had formed part of the settlement, and as if the property had been conveyed by that settlement to trustees to the use of himself for life, with remainder to the use of his (unborn) son in fee, with a direction that in case his son should have no child who should attain twenty-one, then that the estate should, after the son's death, go over to the settlor's grandson in fee. That is an attempt to make the property inalienable for a period which might extend to twenty-one years after the determination of the life of a person not in being at the date of the settlement. The law does not allow a man to tie up property for longer than a life or lives in being and twenty-one years; and this is clearly an attempt to do what is contrary to the law.

I need not do more than refer to my decision in *Stuart v Cockerell*, ((1869) LR 7 Eq 363), afterwards affirmed on appeal ((1870) 5 Ch App 713), which shews that the law is as I have stated it. My opinion, therefore, is that the appointment by the testator to his son in fee is good, and the attempt to give the estate over is void. It is precisely the same as if a man were to give property to his son for life, and after his decease to his son's children, as tenants in common in fee, with a proviso that if any of the children should die under twenty-five the property should go over. In that case the proviso carrying over the shares would be void. The gift to the son in fee is therefore good, and the executory devise over is void[19].

But the court will take into consideration certain facts existing at the date on which the appointment is made.

In *Re Paul* [1921] 2 Ch 1, a testator who died in 1895 left a share of his residuary estate to his daughter Mrs. A. for life and after her death as she should appoint by will among her children.

Mrs. A., by will, appointed the share to her son A.J.A. on attaining 25 years. She died in 1919 when A.J.A. was 18 or 19.

SARGANT J upheld the appointment and said, at p. 5: "There is ample and quite conclusive authority in favour of the appointment being good. *Wilkinson v Duncan* ((1861) 30 Beav 111) and *Von Brockdorff v Malcolm* ((1885) 30 ChD 172) are direct decisions in favour . . . Having regard to the fact that the son in this case was 18 or 19 years old at the time of his mother's death, so that his interest must vest in him in six or seven years after her death, I decide that the gift to him is good, contingently, of course, on his attaining the age of 25 years. . . ."

In *Wilkinson v Duncan* (1861) 30 Beav 111[20], there was a bequest to such of the children of George Wilkinson as he should appoint. He appointed the fund upon trust to pay £2,000 to each of his daughters as and when they attained 24, and to divide the residue among his sons equally as and when they attained 24. George Wilkinson left ten children, two of whom were under the age of three years at his death. Sir John ROMILLY MR, held that the gift to the sons was void; but the gift to the daughters was valid in respect of such of the daughters as were three years old at his death.

---

[19] The same principle was applied to a statutory power of advancement (T.A. 1925, s. 32) in *Pilkington v IRC* [1964] AC 612, 642, [1962] 3 All ER 622: "I think that the important point for the purpose of the rule against perpetuities is that the new settlement is only effected by the operation of a fiduciary power which itself 'belongs' to the old settlement." *Re Hastings-Bass* [1975] Ch 25, [1974] 2 All ER 193.

[20] *Permanent Trustee Co of New South Wales Ltd v Richardson* (1948) 48 SR (NSW) 313.

B. Perpetuities and Accumulations Act 1964[1]

PERPETUITIES AND ACCUMULATIONS ACT 1964

1. Power to specify perpetuity period. — (2) p. 299, ante.

3. Uncertainty as to remoteness. — (2) p. 314, ante.

(3) p. 314, ante.

7. Powers of appointment. — For the purposes of the rule against perpetuities, a power of appointment shall be treated as a special power unless —

(a) in the instrument creating the power it is expressed to be exercisable by one person only, and

(b) it could, at all times during its currency when that person is of full age and capacity, be exercised by him so as immediately to transfer to himself the whole of the interest governed by the power without the consent of any other person or compliance with any other condition, not being a formal condition relating only to the mode of exercise of the power:

Provided that for the purpose of determining whether a disposition made under a power of appointment exercisable by will only is void for remoteness, the power shall be treated as a general power where it would have fallen to be so treated if exercisable by deed[2].

15. Short title, interpretation and extent. — (2) In this Act ... "power of appointment" includes any discretionary power to transfer a beneficial interest in property without the furnishing of valuable consideration; ...

(5) The foregoing sections of this Act ... in the case of an instrument made in the exercise of a special power of appointment shall apply only where the instrument creating the power takes effect after [the commencement of the Act].

Provided that section 7 above shall apply in all cases for construing the foregoing reference to a special power of appointment.

X. Administrative Powers of Trustees[3]

PERPETUITIES AND ACCUMULATIONS ACT 1964

8. Administrative powers of trustees. — (1) The rule against perpetuities shall not operate to invalidate a power conferred on trustees or other persons to sell, lease, exchange or otherwise dispose of any property for full consideration, or to do any other act in the administration (as opposed to the distribution) of any property, and

---

[1] Cheshire, pp. 345–347, 354–355; M & W, pp. 250–258; MM, pp. 117–122; Maudsley, pp. 162–166; (1964) 80 LQR 518–521; Morris and Leach Supp., pp. 7, 14–15.

[2] Thus avoiding the difficulties in cases such as *Re Churston Settled Estate* [1954] Ch 334, [1954] 1 All ER 725; *Re Earl of Coventry's Indentures* [1974] Ch 71, [1973] 3 All ER 1, (joint power and consent power held special power for purposes of the rule).

[3] Cheshire, pp. 341–342; M & W, pp. 251–252; MM, pp. 117–118; Maudsley, pp. 58–59, 183–185; Morris and Leach, pp. 232–242.

shall not prevent the payment to trustees or other persons of reasonable remuneration for their services.

(2) Subsection (1) above shall apply for the purpose of enabling a power to be exercised at any time after the commencement of this Act notwithstanding that the power is conferred by an instrument which took effect before that commencement.

XI.   Expectant and Dependent Limitations

A.   Before 1964[4]

In *Re Hubbard's Will Trusts* [1963] Ch 275, [1962] 2 All ER 917, the testator gave a share of the "sisters' fund" to each of his sisters and their issue (clause 9 (iv)) by trusts which included discretionary trusts in favour of the sisters' grandchildren, which were void for remoteness (clause 9 (v)). The will, by clause 9 (vi), directed that, on the failure or determination of any of the sisters' shares, there should be an accruer to the other shares, and, subject thereto, the property was given to charity.

The question was whether the gifts over on the failure of the discretionary trusts were valid. BUCKLEY J held that the accruer provision, being dependent upon the same provision as that which terminated the trusts, was void. But the gift to charity was a vested gift, not dependent, and was valid. He said, at p. 283: "It is said that it is settled law that any limitation dependent or expectant on a prior limitation which is void for remoteness is itself invalid (*Re Abbott* ([1893] 1 Ch 54), and *Re Canning's Will Trusts* ([1936] Ch 309), but it is not very easy to discover from the authorities what is meant by the expression 'dependent or expectant on' in this context. In *Re Thatcher's Trusts* Sir John Romilly MR used the following language ((1859) 26 Beav 365 at 370): 'On the other hand if the limitations are ulterior to or expectant upon limitations which are too remote, they are void also, although made to a person in existence at the date of the will.'

It is clear from the comparatively modern decision of *Re Coleman*, ([1936] Ch 528, [1936] 2 All ER 225), that the mere fact that a trust is ulterior to another which is invalid for remoteness, in the sense that the benefit under the former trust can only fall into possession when any possible benefit under the latter, had it been valid, would have ceased, is not sufficient to render the ulterior trust invalid. Accordingly, I think that it is necessary to look at the cases to see to what kind of case the rule applies. . . .

I think that the cases in which the problem with which I am concerned has been considered, where the trusts were such that

---

[4] Cheshire, pp. 333–336; M & W, pp. 238–242; MM, pp. 110–111; Maudsley, pp. 64–67; Morris and Leach, pp. 173–181; (1950) 10 CLJ 392 (J. H. C. Morris); (1950) 14 Conv (NS) 148 (A. K. Kiralfy).

successive interests existed or could have come into existence, can be divided into three categories.

If a testator or other settlor settles property in such a way as to create a series of successive interests, each intended to take effect upon and only upon the exhaustion or termination of all antecedent interests in the chain, and one of those interests is void for remoteness, all the ulterior interests will fail, and this will be so even in the case of such an interest as a life interest given to a living person which, if it were ever to take effect at all, would necessarily do so within the limits of perpetuity. In such a case the invalidity of one of the successive interests for perpetuity breaks the chain and all interests below the point of fracture fall away. This rule seems to be based on the intention of the settlor demonstrated by the nature of the trusts. It was explained by Stirling J in *Re Abbott* ([1893] 1 Ch 54 at 57), as follows: 'The reason appears to be that the persons entitled under the subsequent limitation are not intended to take unless and until the prior limitation is exhausted; and as the prior limitation which is void for remoteness can never come into operation, much less be exhausted, it is impossible to give effect to the intentions of the settlor in favour of the beneficiaries under the subsequent limitation.'

In such a case, if an ulterior interest were accelerated to fill the void created by the failure of the preceding interest on the ground of perpetuity, the result would be that some one would be in possession whom the settlor did not mean to be in possession in the existing circumstances. Alternatively, the gap might be left void. Each alternative would be contrary to the intention of the settlor.

The leading case on this subject is *Beard v Westcott* ((1822) 5 B & Ald 801), explained in *Monypenny v Dering* ((1852) 2 De GM & G 145). Sir John Romilly MR, in *Re Thatcher's Trusts* treated himself as following *Beard v Westcott*, and Astbury J in *Re Hewett's Settlement* [1915] 1 Ch 810 purported to follow both *Beard v Westcott* and *Re Thatcher's Trusts*. *Re Backhouse* ([1921] 2 Ch 51), was presumably decided on similar grounds; and see *Re Mortimer*, ([1905] 2 Ch 502), where a vested legal remainder subsequent to a remote estate tail was held to fail. So far as these authorities result in an interest which, if it ever falls into possession, must do so within the perpetuity period being rendered invalid by the remoteness of some earlier interest in the chain, they have been subjected to criticism in Gray on Perpetuities, 4th edn., pp. 276–281, paras. 252–257, which seems to me to be cogent, but there is no doubt that they are binding on me. In such cases the ulterior interest may truly be said to fail by reason of contagion with or of dependency on the remote interest if, as in *Beard v Westcott*, the ulterior interest is one which is expressed to take effect on some contingency which is not itself remote. This is, I believe, the only kind of case to be found in the books in which this rule has been applied. They are to be distinguished from the kinds of cases which I now proceed to notice.

Where the testator or settlor so frames his trusts as to create an interest which will not take effect in possession until a future date but must vest in interest within the perpetuity limit, either on a stated date or on some event which must occur within that limit, and the enjoyment of that interest in possession is not dependent on the prior exhaustion of the antecedent interests, such future interest will be unaffected by remoteness in any of the antecedent interests. Thus in *Re Coleman* ([1936] Ch 528, [1936] 2 All ER 225), where a testator settled a share of his residue on discretionary trusts for his son W. during his life, and after his death on similar discretionary trust for any widow W. might leave and for all or any of the children of W. and after the death of such widow on trust for the children of W. at 21 or marriage, in equal shares, it was held that though the discretionary trust in favour of W.'s widow was void for remoteness, as W. might marry a woman who was not born at the death of the testator, the ultimate trust in favour of W.'s children being vested, and not contingent or dependent on the void trust, was valid. . . .

Another case falling within this class is *Re Allan* ([1958] 1 WLR 220, [1958] 1 All ER 401), where although the interest there in question was expressed to take effect "on the determination of the trusts hereinbefore declared," Danckwerts J construed those words as equivalent to 'on the death of such widow'.

A third class of cases is exemplified by *Re Abbott* ([1893] 1 Ch 54), and *Re Canning's Will Trusts* ([1936] Ch 309). Where a testator or settlor gives property to A. either immediately or at some future date which is not too remote, but so frames his trusts that the interest of A. may be displaced by the exercise of some power or discretion, the interest of A. will be unaffected by any invalidity of that power or discretion on the ground of remoteness.

[His Lordship referred to *Re Abbott* and to *Re Canning's Will Trusts* and continued:]

I now return to considering the testator's will. As I have pointed out, the accruer provision in clause 9 (vi) must take effect, if at all, while the trusts declared by clause 9 (iv) and (v) remain in operation in respect of the appropriated share of one of the testator's sisters. That is to say, it must take effect, if at all, while a sister of the testator or a child of a sister of the testator is alive. It must and could only take effect in respect of a particular share upon there ceasing to be a sister of the testator or any child of hers entitled in respect of that share under clause 9 (iv) and, ignoring perpetuity for the present purpose, any grandchild of that sister entitled in respect of that share under clause 9 (v). In other words, it could only take effect upon the exhaustion of the objects of the preceding trusts. The accruer provision is, in my judgment, dependent on the preceding trusts and expectant on their failure, as indeed the opening words of clause 9 (vi) suggest.

The disposition of capital in the second half of clause 9 (vi)[5], however, appears to me to stand on a different footing. The earlier trusts

---

[5] I.e., the gift over to charity.

are trusts for a limited period which must end on or before an ascertainable date, namely, the death of the last survivor of the testator's sisters and their children. This event is not dependent on the exhaustion of objects of the antecedent trusts. The fact that theoretically this date might be more than 21 years after the end of a life in being at the testator's death is, I think, irrelevant: *Re Coleman*. The gift of the capital of the sisters' fund contained at the end of clause 9 (vi) is the only disposition of the capital of this fund, it vested in interest immediately on the death of the testator, and the enjoyment by the charities of that interest in possession is merely postponed because and to the extent that the testator has for a limited time given the income elsewhere. I see no ground upon which this gift could be said itself to fail for perpetuity, nor do I think that the facts of the case bring it within the principle of what I may call dependent invalidity.

The only case which may perhaps be said to be awkward to reconcile with this view is *Re Backhouse* ([1921] 2 Ch 51). . . .

If *Re Backhouse* and *Re Coleman* conflict, I prefer the decision of Clauston J in *Re Coleman*. At any rate, *Re Backhouse* is clearly distinguishable on its facts from the present case, and as Eve J gave no reasons for the relevant part of his decision in that case I am not embarrassed by it[6]."

B. Perpetuities and Accumulations Act 1964

PERPETUITIES AND ACCUMULATIONS ACT 1964[7]

6. Saving and acceleration of expectant interests. — A disposition shall not be treated as void for remoteness by reason only that the interest disposed of is ulterior to and dependent upon an interest under a disposition which is so void, and the vesting of an interest shall not be prevented from being accelerated on the failure of a prior interest by reason only that the failure arises because of remoteness.

XII. Contracts and Options

A. Before 1964[8]

In *Woodall v Clifton* [1905] 2 Ch 257, the question was whether the rule applied to a covenant in a 99 year lease to purchase the fee simple, in such a way as to prevent the assignee of the lease from being able to enforce the covenant against an assignee of the freehold.

---

[6] On the question whether "failure" of the trusts includes failure because of the application of the perpetuity rule, see *Re Robinson's Will Trusts* [1963] 1 WLR 628, [1963] 1 All ER 777 (held to include); *Re Buckton's Settlement Trusts* [1964] Ch 497, [1964] 2 All ER 487 (held not to include); (1964) 80 LQR 323 (R. E. Megarry).
[7] Cheshire, pp. 355–356; M & W, p. 242; MM, p. 111; Maudsley, p. 185; (1964) 80 LQR, pp. 517–518. Morris and Leach Supp., pp. 13–14.
[8] Cheshire, pp. 338–339; M & W, pp. 258–263; MM, pp. 122–123; Maudsley, p. 72–75; Morris and Leach, pp. 219–228; (1954) 18 Conv (NS) 576 (J. H. C. Morris and W. B. Leach).

WARRINGTON J, held that it did. In the Court of Appeal the result was affirmed on the ground that the covenant did not run with the reversion under 32 Hen 8, c 34[9]; the perpetuity question was not referred to in the judgments on appeal.

LONDON AND SOUTH WESTERN RAILWAY CO *v* GOMM

(1882) 20 ChD 562 (CA, JESSEL MR, Sir James HANNEN, LINDLEY LJ)

In 1865 the London and South Western Rail Co conveyed to Powell for £100 the fee simple of certain land which was no longer required for the purposes of the railway. Powell covenanted with the company that he, his heirs and assigns would at any time thereafter whenever the land might be required for the railway and upon receiving £100, reconvey the land to the company. In 1879 Gomm purchased the land from Powell's heir with notice of the covenant, and in 1880 the company brought an action for specific performance of the covenant.

Held (inter alia). The covenant was void, as it created an interest in land and might be exercised outside the perpetuity period.

JESSEL MR: If then the rule as to remoteness applies to a covenant of this nature, this covenant clearly is bad as extending beyond the period allowed by the rule. Whether the rule applies or not depends upon this as it appears to me, does or does not the covenant give an interest in the land? If it is a bare or mere personal contract it is of course not obnoxious to the rule, but in that case it is impossible to see how the present Appellant can be bound. He did not enter into the contract, but is only a purchaser from *Powell* who did. If it is a mere personal contract it cannot be enforced against the assignee. Therefore the company must admit that it somehow binds the land. But if it binds the land it creates an equitable interest in the land. The right to call for a conveyance of the land is an equitable interest or equitable estate. In the ordinary case of a contract for purchase there is no doubt about this, and an option for repurchase is not different in its nature[10]. A person exercising the option has to do two things, he has to give notice of his intention to purchase, and to pay the purchase-money; but so far as the man who is liable to convey is concerned, his estate or interest is taken away from him without his consent, and the right to take it away being vested in another, the covenant giving the option must give that other an interest in the land.

It appears to me therefore that this covenant plainly gives the company an interest in the land, and as regards remoteness there is no distinction that I know of (unless the case falls within one of the recognised exceptions, such as charities) between one kind of equitable

---

[9] See p. 416, post.

[10] *Mountford v Scott* [1975] Ch 258, [1973] 3 WLR 884, [1974] 1 All ER 248; *affd.* [1975] 2 WLR 114, [1975] 1 All ER 198, (option to purchase); *George Wimpey & Co Ltd v IRC* [1974] 1 WLR 975, [1974] 2 All ER 602; cf. *Murray v Two Strokes Ltd* [1973] 1 WLR 823, [1973] 3 All ER 357 (right of pre-emption); (1973) 89 LQR 462 (M. Albery); *Pritchard v Briggs* [1979] 3 WLR 868, [1980] 1 All ER 294; Barnsley, *Land Options* (1978), chap. 7.

interest and another kind of equitable interest. In all cases they must take effect as against the owners of the land within a prescribed period.

Specific performance was held to be obtainable between the original contracting parties (*Hutton v Watling*[11] ([1948] Ch 26, [1947] 2 All ER 641); affd. on other grounds ([1948] Ch 398, [1948] 1 All ER 803)); and even if the defendant is no longer in possession of the land, damages for breach of contract could be obtained (*Worthing Corpn v Heather* ([1906] 2 Ch 532))[12].

B. Perpetuities and Accumulations Act 1964[13]

PERPETUITIES AND ACCUMULATIONS ACT 1964

9. Options relating to land. — (1) The rule against perpetuities shall not apply to a disposition consisting of the conferring of an option to acquire for valuable consideration an interest reversionary (whether directly or indirectly) on the term of a lease if —

(*a*) the option is exercisable only by the lessee or his successors in title, and

(*b*) it ceases to be exercisable at or before the expiration of one year following the determination of the lease.

This subsection shall apply in relation to an agreement for a lease as it applies in relation to a lease, and "lessee" shall be construed accordingly.

(2) In the case of a disposition consisting of the conferring of an option to acquire for valuable consideration any interest in land, the perpetuity period under the rule against perpetuities shall be twenty-one years, and section 1 of this Act shall not apply:

Provided that this subsection shall not apply to a right of pre-emption conferred on a public or local authority in respect of land used or to be used for religious purposes where the right becomes exercisable only if the land ceases to be used for such purposes.

10. Avoidance of contractual and other rights in cases of remoteness. — Where a disposition inter vivos would fall to be treated as void for remoteness if the rights and duties thereunder were capable of transmission to persons other than the original parties and had been so transmitted, it shall be treated as void as between the person by whom it was made and the person to whom or in whose favour it was made or any successor of his, and no remedy shall lie in contract or otherwise for giving effect to it or making restitution for its lack of effect.

---

[11] (1948) 12 Conv (NS) 258 (E. O. Walford).

[12] See also *South Eastern Rly Co v Associated Portland Cement Manufacturers (1900) Ltd* [1910] 1 Ch 12; *Dunn v Blackdown Properties Ltd* [1961] Ch 433, [1961] 1 All ER 62.

[13] Cheshire, pp. 347–348, 356–357; M & W, pp. 261–263; MM, p. 123; Maudsley, pp. 186–189; (1964) 80 LQR, pp. 522–525; Morris and Leach Supp., pp. 16–17.

XIII.   Possibilities of Reverter and Conditions Subsequent[14]

A.   Before 1964[15]

LAW OF PROPERTY ACT 1925

4.   Creation and disposition of equitable interests. — (3) All rights of entry affecting a legal estate which are exercisable on condition broken or for any other reason may after the commencement of this Act, be made exercisable by any person and the persons deriving title under him, but, in regard to an estate in fee simple (not being a rentcharge held for a legal estate) only within the period authorised by the rule relating to perpetuities[16].

The rule was usually held not to apply to a possibility of reverter[17]. An executory gift over, outside the period, will of course be void; the interest reverts to the grantor who can dispose of it by a grant *inter vivos* or by his will (*Brown v Independent Baptist Church of Woburn*[18]). The view was strongly held before 1964 that the rule ought to be applied to possibilities of reverter; and in *Hopper v Liverpool Corpn* (1944) 88 Sol Jo 213, the Vice-Chancellor of the Lancaster County Palatine Court held that it did.

B.   Perpetuities and Accumulations Act 1964[19]

PERPETUITIES AND ACCUMULATIONS ACT 1964[19]

12.   Possibilities of reverter, conditions subsequent, exceptions and reservations. — (1) In the case of —
   (a) a possibility of reverter on the determination of a determinable fee simple, or
   (b) a possibility of a resulting trust on the determination of any other determinable interest in property,
the rule against perpetuities shall apply in relation to the provision causing the interest to be determinable as it would apply if that

---

[14] For the distinction between a determinable and a conditional fee see Cheshire, pp. 362–370; M & W, pp. 74–82; MM, pp. 29–33; see also p. 23, ante.

[15] Cheshire, pp. 341, 363–364, 369; M & W, pp. 244–248; MM, pp. 114–116; Maudsley, pp. 69–71; Morris and Leach, pp. 209–219.

[16] *Re Trustees of Hollis' Hospital and Hague's Contract* [1899] 2 Ch 540; *Re Da Costa* [1912] 1 Ch 337; *Re Bowen* [1893] 2 Ch 491; *Re Peel's Release* [1921] 2 Ch 218.

[17] *Re Randell* (1888) 38 ChD 213; *Re Blunt's Trusts* [1904] 2 Ch 767; *Re Chardon* [1928] Ch 464; *Re Wightwick's Will Trusts* [1950] Ch 260, [1950] 1 All ER 689; *Re Chambers' Will Trusts* [1950] Ch 267; *Re Cooper's Conveyance Trusts* [1956] 1 WLR 1096, [1956] 3 All ER 28.

[18] 325 Mass 645, 91 NE (2d) 922 (1950); (1952) 65 HLR 721, 741 (W. B. Leach) (a residuary gift held in Massachusetts to include such an interest).

[19] Cheshire, pp. 363–364, 369–370; M & W, pp. 246–248; MM, p. 116; Maudsley, pp. 190–191; (1964) 80 LQR 525–527; Morris and Leach Supp., p. 18.

provision were expressed in the form of a condition subsequent giving rise, on breach thereof, to a right of re-entry or an equivalent right in the case of property other than land, and where the provision falls to be treated as void for remoteness the determinable interest shall become an absolute interest.

(2) Where a disposition is subject to any such provision, or to any such condition subsequent, or to any exception or reservation, the disposition shall be treated for the purposes of this Act as including a separate disposition of any rights arising by virtue of the provision, condition subsequent, exception and reservation.

XIV. Exceptions to the Rule[20]

Morris and Leach, *The Rule Against Perpetuities* (2nd edn. 1962), pp. 242–243

"It may be useful to enumerate here some of the more important exceptions to the Rule. Most of these have already been considered[1].
  (1) Gifts over from one charity to another[86].
  (2) Limitations which must vest at or before the termination of an entailed interest[87].
  (3) Contracts, unless they create contingent interests in land or other property[88].
  (4) Covenants for renewal in leases[89].
  (5) Mortgages[90].
  (6) Certain easements[91].
  (7) Certain rights of entry for non-payment of rentcharges[92].
  (8) Trusts for the payment of debts[93].
  (9) Accumulations for reducing the National Debt[94].
  (10) Trusts of 'registered funds' the main purpose of which is to provide superannuation allowances or widows' pensions or children's allowances for employees or the assurance of capital sums on the death of employees[95]."

---

[20] Cheshire, pp. 338–343; M & W, pp. 263–266; MM, pp. 123–125.
  [1] The footnotes refer to pages in Morris and Leach.
  [86] Ante, pp. 189–194.
  [87] Ante, pp. 195–196.
  [88] Ante, pp. 219, 227, 228.
  [89] Ante, p. 223.
  [90] Ante, p. 227.
  [91] Ante, pp. 229–230.
  [92] L.P.A. 1925, ss. 121 (6), 162; ante, p. 218.
  [93] Ante, pp. 240–241.
  [94] Superannuation and Other Trust Funds (Validation) Act, 1927, s. 9 (now replaced by Social Security Act 1973; Maudsley, p. 191).
  [95] Social Security Act 1973, s. 69. Similar legislation is in force in many other parts of the British Commonwealth.

XV.   Accumulations[2]

A.   Introduction

The rule against accumulations was introduced by the Accumulations Act 1800, as a result of *Thellusson v Woodford* ((1799) 4 Ves 227; affd. (1805) 11 Ves 112; see p. 341, post), and these statutory provisions were re-enacted and amended by sections 164–166, Law of Property Act 1925. The general effect is to limit those accumulations, to which the Act applies[3], to any one of four periods: first, the life of the grantor or settlor; second, twenty-one years from the death of the grantor, settlor or testator, and third and fourth, two alternative periods of certain specified minorities. The main differences between the third and fourth periods[4] are that the third is limited to persons alive at the death of the testator or settlor, while the fourth period includes accumulations (a) during the minorities of persons born after the death of the grantor, settlor or testator, provided that accumulation is not directed to begin until such person is born and (b) during successive minorities; but it is confined to the minorities of those who would, if of full age, have been entitled to the income which is being accumulated[5].

Two further periods of accumulation were added by the Perpetuities and Accumulations Act 1964, section 13 (1)[6] for the benefit of a living settlor, namely twenty-one years from the date of the disposition, and the minority or respective minorities of any person or persons in being at that date. This provision offered considerable advantages to a settlor who wished to establish an inter vivos discretionary trust for his family. Previously the only periods applicable to inter vivos trusts were accumulations during minorities (third and fourth periods); or during the life of the settlor (first period) which attracted estate duty on the settlor's death[7]. Under the new tax system, capital transfer tax is payable when a capital distribution is made from a trust. In the case of discretionary trusts, there is deemed to be a distribution of the whole of the capital of the trust on each tenth anniversary of the transfer of the property to the trust; but tax is chargeable at only 30% of the rate which would be chargeable upon actual distribution[8].

The effect of a direction which breaks the rule against accumulations depends on whether it also breaks the rule against perpetuities. If

---

[2] Cheshire, pp. 357–361; M & W, pp. 277–281; MM, pp. 127–133; Gray, ss. 671–679. 1, Appendix B. ss. 686–714: Maudsley, chap. 7; Morris and Leach, pp. 266–306. *Theobald on Wills* (13th edn., 1971), paras. 1544–1556, (1953) 17 Conv (NS) 199 (G. B. Graham); [1958] CLJ 39 (S. J. Bailey); Law Reform Committee Fourth Report Section C.

[3] For exceptions see L.P.A. 1925, s. 164 (2) p. 347, post.

[4] *Re Cattell* [1914] 1 Ch 177; see p. 344, post. For the relationship between L.P.A. 1925, s. 165, as interpreted in *Re Maber* [1928] Ch 88 and the fourth period under s. 164, see Morris and Leach, pp. 276–278.

[5] *Re Cattell* [1914] 1 Ch 177, at p. 189; see p. 344, post.

[6] Following the recommendation of the Law Reform Committee Fourth Report, paras. 56, 57; (1964) 80 LQR 529–530. Morris and Leach Supp., 19.

[7] F.A. 1894, s. (1) (*b*) (*iv*).

[8] F.A. 1975, Sch. 5, para. 12. See also para. 15, excluding accumulation and maintenance trusts from this provision.

it breaks both rules, then the direction is totally void i.e. there is no accumulation at all[9]. If, however, it satisfies the rule against perpetuities but only breaks the rule against accumulations, then it is good pro tanto and only void as to the excess beyond the appropriate statutory period. There is, then, a gap from the end of the statutory period until the end of the period chosen during which the income is in effect undisposed of; during this gap the income so released either reverts to the settlor or his representatives or falls into residue or goes to the next of kin. There is no acceleration of the interests of those entitled after the accumulation is over[10].

B. Before 1964

THELLUSSON *v* WOODFORD[11]

(1805) 11 Ves 112 (HL, Lord ELDON LC)

Peter Thellusson, who died in 1797, devised real estates of the annual value of about £1,000, and other estates, directed to be purchased with the residue of the personal estate, amounting to above £600,000 to trustees upon trust to accumulate the rents and profits at compound interest during the lives of his sons, grandsons and great-grandsons living at his death or born in due time[12] afterwards, and on the death of the survivor to divide the said estates into three lots, each of which was to be strictly settled on the eldest male lineal descendant then living of each of his three sons. He directed that the trustees should stand seised, upon the failure of male lineal descendants, upon trust to sell and pay the produce to His Majesty, his heirs, and successors, to the use of the Sinking Fund: and that all the persons becoming entitled should use the surname of Thellusson only. At the time of the testator's death, there were alive his widow, three sons and four grandsons: two more grandsons, who were en ventre at the time of his death, were born later.

Held, (affirming the decision of Lord LOUGHBOROUGH ((1799) 4 Ves 227). The limitations and the direction to accumulate were valid, being confined to lives in being.

Counsel for the appellants: "Mr. *Thellusson*'s will is morally vicious; as it was a contrivance of a parent to exclude every one of his issue from the enjoyment even of the produce of his property during almost a century; and it is politically injurious; as during the whole of that period it makes an immense property unproductive both to individuals and the community at large; and by the time, when the accumulation shall end, it will have created a fund, the revenue of which will be greater than the civil list; and will therefore give its possessor the means of disturbing the whole economy of the country. The probable

---

[9] Is the "wait and see" rule applicable? Consider P. & A.A. 1964, s. 3 (1), (3); Maudsley, pp. 206–208; M & W, pp. 275–276.

[10] *Green v Gascoyne* (1864) 4 De GJ & Sm 565; see p. 348, post.

[11] For a general history of the Thellusson family litigation, see (1970) 21 NILQ 131 (G. W. Keeton).

[12] I.e., the period of gestation.

amount of the accumulated fund, in the events, which have happened, is stated in the Appellant's bill, and admitted in the answer, to be 19,000,000*l*; and in case any of the persons, answering the description of heir male, when the period of suspense ends, should be a minor, and his minority should continue 10 years, it would increase the amount of that third to the sum of 10,802,373*l*; so that, if the whole property should centre in one person, and that person should have a minority of 10 years, after the end of the period of suspense (a circumstance by no means improbable, particularly as Mr. *George Woodford Thellusson* has been long married and has no son), the whole accumulated fund will amount to 32,407,120*l*[13]."

LORD ELDON LC: Another question arises out of this will; which is a pure question of equity: Whether a testator can direct the rents and profits to be accumulated for that period, during which he may direct, that the title shall not vest, and the property shall remain unalienable; and, that he can do so, is most clear law. A familiar case may be put. If this testator had given the residue of his personal estate to such person as should be the eldest male descendant of *Peter Isaac Thellusson* at the death of the survivor of all the lives, mentioned in this will, without more, that simple bequest would in effect have directed accumulation, until it should be seen, what individual would answer the description of that male descendant; and the effect of the ordinary rule of law, as applied in equity, would have supplied everything, that is contained in this will, as to accumulation; for the first question would be, Is the executory devise of the personal estate to the future individual, so described, good? If it is, wherever a residue of personal estate is given, the interest goes with the bulk; and there is no more objection to giving that person, that, which is only forming another capital, than to giving the capital itself. But the constant course of a Court of Equity is to accumulate interest from time to time without a direction, and to hand over the accumulation to that person, who is to take the capital. Take another instance of accumulation: Suppose, the nine persons, named in this will, had been lunatics: without any direction there would have been an accumulation of the interest and profits of all these estates. In truth there is no objection to accumulation upon the policy of the law, applying to perpetuities: for the rents and profits are not to be locked up, and made no use of, for the individuals, or the public. The effect is only to invest them from time to time in land: so that the fund is, not only in a constant course of accumulation, but also in a constant course of circulation. To that application what possible objection can there be in law? . . . Therefore, as to giving the property at the expiration of nine lives and the accumulation, I never could doubt upon these points.

---

[13] "On the death of the last surviving grandson in 1856, the estate was divided (not without more litigation) between the two male representatives of the two of Peter Thellusson's sons who had left issue. But owing to mismanagement and costs of litigation, the estate realised a comparatively small amount." Holdsworth, vii, p. 230; (1970) 21 NILQ at pp. 169–174.

LAW OF PROPERTY ACT 1925

164. General restrictions on accumulation of income. — (1) No person[14] may by any instrument or otherwise settle or dispose of any property in such manner that the income thereof shall, save as hereinafter mentioned, be wholly or partially accumulated for any longer period than one of the following, namely:—

(a) the life of the grantor or settlor; or

(b) a term of twenty-one years from the death of the grantor, settlor or testator; or

(c) the duration of the minority[15] or respective minorities of any person or persons living or en ventre sa mere at the death of the grantor, settlor or testator; or

(d) the duration of the minority[15] or respective minorities only of any person or persons who under the limitations of the instrument directing the accumulations would, for the time being, if of full age, be entitled to the income directed to be accumulated[16].

In every case where any accumulation is directed[17] otherwise than as aforesaid, the direction shall (save as hereinafter mentioned) be void; and the income of the property directed to be accumulated shall, so long as the same is directed to be accumulated contrary to this section, go to and be received by the person or persons who would have been entitled thereto if such accumulation had not been directed.

(3) The restrictions imposed by this section apply to instruments made on or after the twenty-eighth day of July, eighteen hundred, but in the case of wills only where the testator was living and of testamentary capacity after the end of one year from that date.

165. Qualification of restrictions on accumulation. — Where accumulations of surplus income are made during a minority under any statutory power or under the general law, the period for which such accumulations are made is not (whether the trust was created or the accumulations were made before or after the commencement of this Act) to be taken into account in determining the periods for which accumulations are permitted to be made by the last preceding section, and accordingly an express trust for accumulation for any other permitted period shall not be deemed to have been invalidated or

---

[14] A corporate settlor is not a "person" within the section; *Re Dodwell & Co Ltd's Trust Deed* [1979] Ch 301, [1978] 3 All ER 738.

[15] In the case of dispositions taking effect after 1969, minority ends at the age of 18; Family Law Reform Act 1969, s. 1. There are transitional provisions so that the change from 21 to 18 shall not invalidate any direction for accumulation in a settlement or other disposition made by a deed, will or other instrument, which was made before 1970. Ibid., ss. 1, 4, Sch. 3, para. 7.

[16] See *Re Cattell* [1914] 1 Ch 177; p. 344; post.

[17] This includes a power to accumulate. P.A.A. 1964, s. 13 (2), p. 346, post; affirming *Re Robb* [1953] Ch 459, [1953] 1 All ER 920. The same point was recently so decided in Scotland under Trusts (Scotland) Act 1961, s. 5 (2); *Baird v Lord Advocate* [1979] AC 666, [1979] 2 All ER 28.

become invalid, by reason of accumulations also having been made as aforesaid during such minority[18].

166.   Restriction on accumulation for the purchase of land. — (1) No person may settle or dispose of any property in such manner that the income thereof shall be wholly or partially accumulated for the purchase of land only, for any longer period than the duration of the minority or respective minorities of any person or persons who, under the limitations of the instrument directing the accumulation, would for the time being, if of full age, be entitled to the income so directed to be accumulated.

(2) This section does not, nor do the enactments which it replaces, apply to accumulations to be held as capital money for the purposes of the Settled Land Act, 1925, or the enactments replaced by that Act, whether or not the accumulations are primarily liable to be laid out in the purchase of land.

(3) This section applies to settlements and dispositions made after the twenty-seventh day of June eighteen hundred and ninety-two.

In *Re Cattell* [1914] 1 Ch 177, the question was whether an accumulation was limited to the minority of persons born in the life time of the testator. The Court of Appeal (LORD PARKER OF WADDINGTON, LORD SUMNER and WARRINGTON J) held that the fourth period extended to the minorities of persons born after the testator's death and to successive minorities. Lord PARKER OF WADDINGTON said at p. 186: "In construing the Thellusson Act, it must be remembered that it is not an enabling but a disabling Act. Prior to the passing of the Act a testator had the right to direct an accumulation for any period he chose, provided he did not exceed the time which was allowed by the perpetuity rule — that is to say, lives in being, and twenty-one years afterwards. The Act was passed in order to disable testators from taking full advantage of the liberty which they had hitherto enjoyed in that respect. The terms of the Act are 'That no person or persons shall after the passing of this Act, by any deed or deeds, surrender or surrenders, will, codicil or otherwise howsoever, settle or dispose of any real or personal property so and in such manner that the rents, issues, profits or produce thereof shall be wholly or partially accumulated for any longer term than' — then there are four alternative periods given, and it has been held, and I think rightly held, that of those four periods one only can be selected by the testator. The difficulty arises in this case in regard to the fourth period. The first contemplates the case of a man who settles property otherwise than by will, in which case he may direct that the rents and

---

[18] See p. 343, n. 15, ante.

profits be accumulated during his life. The settlor cannot direct an accumulation during his life and some further period. The second period contemplates an accumulation which is to commence from the death of the settlor, and includes the case of a settlor by will. No such accumulation is to go on for more than twenty-one years. Then the third alternative is a period — almost the same period of twenty-one years from the death of the settlor — during the minority or respective minorities of any person or persons 'who shall be living or in (*sic*) ventre sa mère' at the time of the death of the settlor. That of course must be limited to twenty-one years, and some further period representing gestation in the case of a child yet unborn. Then there is the fourth alternative, which gives rise to the difficulty in the present case . . . [His Lordship read the fourth period[19] and continued:] It is to be observed that this last alternative clause closely follows and seems to be contrasted with the alternative with regard to the minority or respective minorities of any person or persons who should be living or en ventre sa mere at the time of the death of the settlor. One would not therefore expect it to be limited (as contended by the appellant) to children living or en ventre sa mère at the settlor's death. Indeed if so limited it would in effect add nothing to the preceding alternative. The reason urged in support of the appellant's contention rests mainly on certain decisions which it is said we ought to follow and to which I will now refer.

[His Lordship referred to *Haley v Bannister* ((1819) 4 Madd 275), *Ellis v Maxwell* ((1841) 3 Beav 587) and *Bryan v Collins* ((1852) 16 Beav 14) and continued:] In my opinion the fourth alternative period covers not only children who are born or en ventre sa mère at the death of the settlor, but children who are subsequently born, and I think the fact that the fourth alternative comes immediately after, and in contrast with, the third alternative, which refers only to born children, and children en ventre sa mère, at the time of the death of the settlor, points strongly to this conclusion. . . .

It is said — and I think said with some truth — that in this case if we adopt the construction which allows a child who is not born at the death of the settlor to be one of the children during whose minority or respective minorities the accumulations are directed to be made, then we allow successive accumulations to be made of what practically, if not theoretically, is the same fund, which accumulations taken together may last for a considerable time. I think that may be true, but at the same time it is worth bearing in mind that though these periods may when added together amount to a considerable time, yet the periods in question are not really within the vice against which the Act is directed . . . and there being nothing in the express words of the Act to prevent us giving effect to the old powers which were possessed by testators before the Act, there is no reason to construe the fourth alternative in any other way than I have

---

[19] Which is in substance the same as L.P.A., s. 164 (1) (*d*), p. 343, *ante*.

suggested. It is well known that settlements are and have been drawn up on this footing. A testator may often direct a settlement of property upon A. for life, and after his death upon his children on attaining twenty-one, and if he goes on to provide that during the minority or respective minorities of his children the income of the property shall be accumulated, it is only a clause in common form. I have never known any doubt to be thrown on the validity of such a clause, but if the appellant's contention prevailed its validity would be open to question. It seems to me, therefore, that Neville J was right in his decision, and that this appeal ought to be dismissed.

See also Trustee Act 1925, section 31, which gives power to trustees to apply income for the maintenance of beneficiaries, vested or contingent, during their minority, and requires the unapplied part of the income to be accumulated[20].

C. Perpetuities and Accumulations Act 1964[1]

PERPETUITIES AND ACCUMULATIONS ACT 1964

13. Amendment of s. 164 of Law of Property Act 1925. — (1) The periods for which accumulations of income under a settlement or other disposition are permitted by section 164 of the Law of Property Act 1925 shall include —

  (a) a term of twenty-one years from the date of the making of the disposition, and

  (b) the duration of the minority or respective minorities[2] of any person or persons in being at that date.

(2) It is hereby declared that the restrictions imposed by the said section 164 apply in relation to a power to accumulate income whether or not there is a duty to exercise that power, and that they apply whether or not the power to accumulate extends to income produced by the investment of income previously accumulated.

14. Right to stop accumulations. — Section 2 above shall apply to any question as to the right of beneficiaries to put an end to accumulations of income under any disposition as it applies to questions arising on the rule against perpetuities[3].

-----

[20] H & M, pp. 499–504; Snell, pp. 262–271; M & B (T), pp. 541–548.
[1] Cheshire, p. 358; M & W, p. 273; MM, pp. 127–129; Maudsley, pp. 204–211; (1964) 80 LQR, pp. 529–530; Morris and Leach Supp., p. 19.
[2] See p. 345, n. 15, ante.
[3] Beneficiaries of full age holding an absolute beneficial interest in a trust fund may terminate the accumulation and the trust and require the trustees to pay the capital of the fund to them. (*Saunders v Vautier* (1841) Cr & Ph 240). *Re Deloitte* [1926] Ch 56 had held that evidence of infertility was inadmissible to help beneficiaries to terminate a trust under this rule.

Compare, with these provisions:

VICTORIA PERPETUITIES AND ACCUMULATIONS ACT 1968

19(1). Accumulation of income:—

Where property is settled or disposed of in such manner that the income thereof may be or is directed to be accumulated wholly or in part the power or direction to accumulate that income shall be valid if the disposition of the accumulated income is or may be valid but not otherwise.

D. Exemptions from Restrictions on Accumulation

i. BY STATUTE

LAW OF PROPERTY ACT 1925

164. General restrictions on accumulation of income:—

(2) This section does not extend to any provision —

- (i) for payment of the debts of any grantor, settlor, testator or other person;
- (ii) for raising portions for —
  - (a) any child, children or remoter issue of any grantor, settlor or testator; or
  - (b) any child, children or remoter issue of a person taking any interest under any settlement or other disposition directing the accumulations or to whom any interest is thereby limited;
- (iii) respecting the accumulation of the produce of timber or wood; and accordingly such provisions may be made as if no statutory restrictions on accumulation of income had been imposed.

ii. OTHER EXEMPTIONS

Maudsley, Modern Law of Perpetuities, pp. 210–211

"COMMERCIAL ARRANGEMENTS; CONTRACTS OF INSURANCE; UNIT TRUSTS

Various commercial arrangements have been held to be outside the Act, even though they involve in some sense an accumulation. Thus, in the leading case of *Bassil v Lister*[4] a testator directed his trustees to pay the premiums on a policy of insurance on his son's life out of the income of the residuary estate. Turner VC held that this was not an accumulation of the type to which the Thellusson Act was directed; and that it was valid for the son's life, and not merely for a period of 21 years. In *Re AEG Unit Trust (Managers) Ltd's Trust Deed*[5], the question concerned a provision in a trust deed to the effect that surplus income in any accounting period, over and above that available

---

[4] (1851) 9 Hare 177; similarly with a partnership agreement: (1851) 9 Hare at 184; [1957] Ch 415 at 421.
[5] [1957] Ch 415, [1957] 2 All ER 506.

for distribution to unit holders, should be added to capital and should thereupon cease to be available for distribution. Again, this, in a sense, involved an accumulation of such income. Wynn-Parry J held that the Law of Property Act 1925, section 164, did not apply. An investor, purchasing units in a unit trust, did not "settle or dispose" of property, nor was such a transaction within the scope of the section. Nor could the section be applicable where the unit holders were able at any time to amend or terminate the trust[6]. Nor does the section apply where a corporation is the settlor[7].

MAINTENANCE OF PROPERTY[8]
A provision for the application of income for the upkeep of property is also outside the scope of the Act. This is not really an exception; for it covers only the maintenance of the value of depreciating property, whether by way of provision for repairs[9], or by way of provision for the replacement of leaseholds as they expire[10]. It does not include a fund for the accumulation of income for the improvement of land, or by the construction of buildings on it[11]. Where the exception applies, the provision must of course comply with the perpetuity period[12]."

E. Excessive Accumulations

GREEN v GASCOYNE
(1864) 4 De GJ & Sm 565 (Lord WESTBURY LC)

LORD WESTBURY LC: The case is that of a testator directing an accumulation during the lives of his wife and sister and the life of the survivor of them of the rents and profits of certain freehold estates.

The first question is, what is the operation of the statute upon that trust for accumulation? The second, what will be its effect upon the construction and interpretation of the will?

The first effect of the statute I apprehend to be that the trust for accumulation is reduced to a term of twenty-one years, and that I must take the trust as if it had been expressed "for a period of twenty-one years, provided my wife and my sister *Sarah* or the survivor of them shall so long live". Secondly, I take it that the words of the statute which direct that the rents released by its effect from the operation of the trust for accumulation shall "go to and be received by such person or persons as would have been entitled thereto if such accumulation had not been directed", must be construed to mean "if such excessive accumulation had not been directed". The meaning of the words therefore is brought to be the same as it would have been had the accumulations been directed for twenty-one years only.

---

[6] [1957] Ch 415 at 421; *Wharton v Masterman* [1895] AC 186.
[7] *Re Dodwell & Co Ltd's Trust Deed* [1979] Ch 301, [1978] 3 All ER 738.
[8] See generally M & W, p. 281; Morris and Leach, p. 280.
[9] *Vine v Raleigh* [1891] 2 Ch 13; *Re Mason* [1891] 3 Ch 467.
[10] *Re Gardiner* [1901] 1 Ch 697; *Re Hurlbatt* [1910] 2 Ch 553.
[11] *Vine v Raleigh* [1891] 2 Ch 13 at 26; *Re Gardiner* [1901] 1 Ch 697 at 700.
[12] *Curtis v Lukin* (1842) 5 Beav 147.

I am not at liberty to apply or use the statute so as in any manner to accelerate the enjoyment of any gift or disposition contained in the will, nor can I use the statute for the purpose of giving to any term or description contained in the will a meaning which it would not have had had the trust for accumulation been good instead of bad. Although the trust for accumulation is cut down and reduced to a limited period, the whole of the rest of the will remains in point of disposition, in point of the meaning, effect and true interpretation of its language, precisely as if there had been no such operation performed by the statute. . . .

The result is that there is a hiatus between the period when the accumulation ceases by law and the period when the accumulation is directed to cease by the will; there is nothing in the will to catch the rents which arise during that hiatus; and those rents accordingly belong to the heir at law.

———————

Sometimes the problem is to know which of the permitted periods should be applied.

In *Re Ransome* [1957] Ch 348, [1957] 1 All ER 690, there was a testamentary direction in a will coming into operation in 1935 that "the income . . . shall be accumulated until the youngest child of my [living grandson R] shall attain the age of 21 years." R had by his first marriage a son D, who attained 21 in 1951. By R's second marriage in 1953, there were no children at the date of the proceedings. UPJOHN J held that the gift did not vest absolutely in D on his attaining 21. This meant that the direction to accumulate was excessive, and one question was the proper period of accumulation.

UPJOHN J said at p. 361: "The next question is as to the impact of the rule against accumulations on the direction to accumulate until the youngest child attains 21. Plainly, that direction infringes the rule and it is necessary to determine for what period the term is valid. The test is stated to be that you have first to determine which of the four periods set out in section 164 the testatrix has seemingly selected, determining that question according to the language employed and the facts of the case; see *Re Watt's Will Trusts* ([1936] 2 All ER at 1562). That seems to me an artificial and difficult test. The trouble in this case and in most cases dealing with the rule against accumulations is that the testatrix has given directions clearly not having the rule in mind at all. The competing periods in this case are section 164 (1) (*b*), a term of 21 years from the death of the testatrix, which brings the period of valid accumulation to an end on 6 July 1956, on the one hand, and, on the other, sub-paragraph (*c*) of the section, the duration of the minority or respective minorities of anyone living at the death of the testatrix. If that period is selected, it is submitted that it came to an end when the eldest child, David, attained 21 on 24 June 1951.

Neither sub-paragraph fits in, in the least degree with, the directions of the testatrix. However, in directing accumulations until Robert's youngest child should attain 21, the testatrix can hardly have contemplated that the period of accumulations would in fact come to an end by the attainment by Robert's eldest child of the age of 21 years, and I propose to hold that sub-paragraph (*b*) is the relevant paragraph; the difference is not of great importance."

QUESTIONS

1. What periods would you expect to be applied in the following testamentary dispositions:
   (*a*) ". . . during the minority of the children of Gerald.": *Re Watt's Will Trusts* [1936] 2 All ER 1555.
   (*b*) ". . . so much of the dividends as shall accrue due to Elizabeth Mary Griffiths (a beneficiary) during the life of John Griffiths, her husband, . . . shall be accumulated.": *Griffiths v Vere* (1803) 9 Ves 127.
   (*c*) "to be accumulated . . . until the decease of the last survivor of the said several annuitants, or during such portion of such surviving annuitant's life as the rules of law will permit . . .": *Talbot v Jevers* (1875) LR 20 Eq 255.
   (*d*) Upon trust "to invest the same in the Funds, so as the same might accumulate, by way of Compound Interest until (the testator's) Great Nephew, Philip Crawley, [aged 3] shall attain 25.": *Longdon v Simson* (1806) 12 Ves 295; *Crawley v Crawley* (1835) 7 Sim 427.
   (*e*) "To my wife during widowhood, but if she should marry again, then from and after such marriage, I direct that all bequests in her favour shall cease, and that in lieu thereof the trustees shall pay to my wife an annuity of £500 and shall accumulate the surplus income during the remainder of the life of my wife": *Weatherall v Thornburgh* (1878) 8 ChD 261.
   (*f*) ". . . as and when each of them the said Ann Webb and William Adams shall respectively die, the annuity and annuities so given by me to or for her or him respectively as aforesaid, shall be laid out from time to time, until the death of the last survivor of them the said two last-named annuitants, as an addition to the said capital of the said rest, residue, and remainder of my said stock of three per cent. consolidated Bank annuities . . . shall be and shall be taken as an increase and accumulation to the said capital stock, until the death of the last survivor of them, the said two last-mentioned annuitants.": *Webb v Webb* (1840) 2 Beav 493.
   (*g*) And a gift inter vivos:
   ". . . to receive and accumulate the dividends . . . during the joint lives of James Campbell and Jane, his wife, and, after the death of James Campbell, if his wife should survive him . . . for her life, and, after her decease, whether the same should happen in the lifetime or after the decease of her husband, to

stand possessed of the capital and accumulations in trust for their daughter, Charlotte Campbell . . .": *Re Lady Rosslyn's Trust* (1848) 16 Sim 391.

(*h*) By a settlement dated 6 December 1951 "to accumulate the income during the life of the settlor or until the beneficiary [born 1950] attains the age of 22.": *Re Erskine's Settlement Trusts* [1971] 1 WLR 162, [1971] 1 All ER 572. Would the answer be different if all the facts had taken place after 1964?

2. Do you think that restrictive rules, such as those currently applicable, are required? The present trend in countries abroad is to return to the common law rule. Maudsley p. 202, Appendix D.

3. Does Wait and See apply to the question of the validity, under the Perpetuity rule, of a provision for the accumulation of income? Can you see any reason why, if Wait and See is introduced in respect of disposition generally, it should not also apply to accumulations? M & W, pp. 275–276, Maudsley, pp. 206–208. See Victoria Perpetuities and Accumulations Act 1968 section 19 (1), p. 347, ante; and others included in Maudsley, Appendix D.

Part Three. Commercial Interests

8. Terms of Years[1]

I. General Background

Other than the estate in fee simple absolute in possession, the only
legal estate which can subsist after 1925 is the term of years absolute[2].
These two legal estates are different in nature, in that the former is a
freehold, the latter a leasehold estate; the former, in other words, is
held, theoretically, of a feudal superior by freehold tenure, the latter is
held of the freeholder by leasehold tenure. The two estates can
therefore exist contemporaneously in one piece of land[3], the fee simple

---

[1] Cheshire, pp. 38–40, 381–512, M & W, pp. 43–47, 613–742, 1108–1156; MM, pp. 19–
20, 310–350, 355–364; Foa, *Law of Landlord and Tenant* (8th edn., 1957); Hill and
Redman, *Law of Landlord and Tenant* (15th edn., 1970); Woodfall, *Landlord and
Tenant* (28th edn., 1978); Evans, *Law of Landlord and Tenant* (1974); Partington,
Landlord and Tenant (1975). The Law Commission hopes to produce a Landlord and
Tenant Code. This will be preceded by three interim reports. The Report on Obligations of Landlords and Tenants was published in 1975 (Law Com No. 67). The
remaining two will be on Covenants against Dispositions, Alterations and Change of
User, and on the Termination of Tenancies. Law Commission 13th Annual Report
1977– 1978 (Law Com No. 92, Paras. 2.34–36).
[2] L.P.A. 1925, s. 1 (1) p. 358, post.
[3] L.P.A. 1925, s. 1 (5).

being held by the freeholder (commonly called the owner), the leasehold estate by the leaseholder (commonly called the tenant).

It was essential for the feudal system of landholding that one person or a group of feoffees to uses should be responsible for each piece of land; as freeholders they were protected, in the days before the action of trespass, by the Real Actions, the Writs of Right, Writs of Entry and the Possessory Assizes, all of which were available to, and only to, persons seised[4]. The leaseholder's position was not important to the feudal system, and he never received the protection of the Real Actions; his interest never became 'Real' property, and is, to the present day, personalty; he was never seised; he was originally left to his action on the covenant against his landlord, the freeholder, if he were evicted[5].

Better remedies became available to the leaseholder as soon as remedies dependent on *possession*, as opposed to *seisin*, were developed in the King's Court. Trespass was such an action, and a leaseholder, being *possessed* of the land, could bring the writ of trespass, without being *seised*[6]. By the thirteenth century[7], the action of trespass *quare clausum fregit* was available to persons in possession of land and lay for damages against anyone who was guilty of unlawful physical interference with land. This was an improvement, but the leaseholder needed something more than damages; he needed an action by which he could recover his lease. This came with Ejectment at the end of the fifteenth century[8]. From that time a leaseholder has had a "real" remedy; but leasehold property was already established as "personalty" and it was too late then for it to become "realty" for the purposes of the general law.

The tables were now turned on the freeholder. He had a "real" remedy, but it was cumbrous and old-fashioned. The leaseholder now had a modern action for specific recovery, the action of Ejectment. Freeholders began to use this action by alleging a fictitious lease. This practice began in the sixteenth century, and continued until the abolition of the old Real Actions in the first half of the nineteenth century. Ejectment now lies in respect of any wrongful deprivation of possession of land[9].

This chapter deals with some of the principles of the law relating to leases. Superimposed upon the general law is a large body of statutory

---

[4] Maitland, *Forms of Action at Common Law*, pp. 20 et seq; Simpson, *Introduction to the History of the Land Law*, pp. 24–43; M & W pp. 1167–1169.
[5] Pollock and Maitland, *History of English Law*, (2nd edn., Reissued 1968) vol. ii, pp. 106–117; Plucknett, *A Concise History of the Common Law* (5th edn., 1956), pp. 570–574; Jouon des Longrais, *La conception Anglaise de la Saisine*, pp. 141–148; Simpson, pp. 68–73.
[6] In the ordinary case of land being owned by A, the freeholder, and leased to B, the leaseholder, A is seised and B possessed of the land.
[7] Maitland, *Forms of Action*, p. 48. Cheshire, pp. 29–31; M & W, pp. 1167–1169.
[8] *Trespass de ejectione firmae*; Pollock and Maitland, op. cit., p. 109: Simpson, pp. 135–136.
[9] Maitland, *Forms of Action*, pp. 57–60; Cheshire, p. 89; M & W, pp. 1170–1172; Simpson, pp. 136–141.

material dealing with specialised topics. The general policy of these statutes is to limit the rent which a landlord can obtain, and restrict his right to recover possession of the premises at the end of the lease. The Leasehold Reform Act 1967 goes further, and grants to certain long leaseholders of residential premises at low rents the right to acquire their freehold or an extended lease[10]. These statutes and books dealing with them must be consulted before a working knowledge of the law of leaseholds can be obtained; but lack of space forbids their treatment here[11].

Department of the Environment: Review of the Rent Acts — A Consultation Paper (January 1977), paragraph 7[12].

"The decline of private renting

7. In 1914, nine families out of every ten lived in houses which they rented from private landlords. Since then, the number of privately rented houses has fallen by more than half and only about one sixth of all households now live in housing of this type. Most of the reduction in the stock has occurred since 1939 and is accounted for by such factors as slum clearance, bombing during the Second World War, demolition for development, and (particularly in recent years) sale for owner-occupation. During the same period, the total number of houses has roughly doubled, mainly as a result of new building of owner-occupied and council houses, which have generally been of markedly higher quality than the rented houses which they have supplemented or replaced. Relatively few new houses have been built for private renting since 1945, although a fair number of private houses and flats

---

[10] See p. 700, post.

[11] Cheshire, pp. 468–509; M & W, pp. 1108–1156; MM, pp. 544–569.

The main statues are:

(a) Agricultural holdings. Agricultural Holdings Act 1948; Agriculture Act 1958; Agriculture (Miscellaneous Provisions) Act 1976; Rent (Agriculture) Act 1976; Agricultural Holdings (Notices to Quit) Act 1977; Rent (Agriculture) Amendment Act 1977. Muir Watt: *Agricultural Holdings* (12th edn., 1967); Woodfall, Chap. 21: Hill and Redman, Part V.

(b) Business tenancies. Landlord and Tenant Act 1954, Part II. L.P.A. 1969, Part I. Woodfall, Chap. 22: Hill and Redman, Part II.

(c) Residential lettings. Rent Act 1977. Megarry, *Rent Acts* (10th edn., 1967); Woodfall, Chap. 23: Hill and Redman, Part III; Farrand, *Rent Act 1977* (1978); Pettit, *Landlord and Tenant Under the Rent Act 1977* (1978). Report of the Committee on the Rent Acts (Francis Report) 1971 (Cmnd. 4609).

The Department of the Environment is conducting a Review of the Rent Acts. A consultation paper was issued in January 1977.

(d) Long tenancies. Landlord and Tenant Act 1954, Part I. Leasehold Reform Act 1967, Part I: Leasehold Reform Act 1979. Barnes, *The Leasehold Reform Act 1967;* Hague, *Leasehold Enfranchisement;* Megarry, *Rent Acts,* pp. 130–132, 235–243; Woodfall, Chap. 24; Hill and Redman, Part IV.

(e) Mobile Homes. Caravan Sites and Control of Development Act 1960; Caravan Sites Act 1968; Mobile Homes Act 1975. Gordon, *Caravans and the Law* (1978).

[12] See also Paley, *Attitudes to Letting in 1976* (a survey undertaken for the Department of the Environment). In 1978 the Department began issuing consultation papers on public sector tenancies. For a summary, see (1979) 129 NLJ 210, 388 (H.E. Markson).

were built and let in the 1930s. The following table shows how private renting has fallen as a proportion of all tenures over the last 60 years.

	1914* (GB)	1947* (GB)	1961+ (England & Wales)	1966+ (E&W)	1971+ (E&W)
Number in all tenures	9m	13m	14.5m	15.5m	16.5m
	%	%	%	%	%
Owner-occupied	10	26	42	46	50
Local authority rented	NIL	13	24	26	28
Private rented (including other tenures)	90	61	34	28	22

(* estimate.   + census estimate. Censuses before 1961 did not record tenure)."

II.   General Characteristics

A.   A Lease may be a Legal Estate

LAW OF PROPERTY ACT 1925

1.   Legal estates and equitable interests. — (1) The only estates in land which are capable of subsisting or of being conveyed or created at law are —

(*a*) An estate in fee simple absolute in possession[13];

(*b*) A term of years absolute.

205.   General definitions. — (1) . . . (xxvii) "Term of years absolute" means a term of years (taking effect either in possession or in reversion whether or not at a rent) with or without impeachment for waste[14], subject or not to another legal estate, and either certain or liable to determination by notice, re-entry[15], operation of law, or by a provision for cesser on redemption[16], or in any other event (other than the dropping of a life, or the determination of a determinable life interest); but does not include any term of years determinable with life or lives or with the cesser of a determinable life interest[17], nor, if created after the commencement of this Act, a term of years which is not expressed to take effect in possession within twenty-one years after the creation thereof where required by this Act to take effect within that period[18]; and in this definition the expression "term of years" includes a term for less than a year[19], or for a year or years and a fraction of a year or from year to year.

---

[13] See p. 4, ante.
[14] See p. 18, ante.
[15] See p. 390, post.
[16] See p. 601–602, post.
[17] L.P.A. 1925, s. 149 (6) p. 363, post.
[18] L.P.A. 1925, s. 149 (3) p. 361, post.
[19] See *Re Land and Premises at Liss, Hants* [1971] Ch 986 at 991, per GOULDING J.

B. "Time Certain"[20]

A lease must commence at[1], and exist for, a "time certain", or at or for a time which can be rendered certain.

LACE *v* CHANTLER
[1944] KB 368 (CA, Lord GREENE MR, MACKINNON and LUXMOORE LJJ)

In a sublease of furnished premises for 16s. 5d. a week, the rent-book stated certain conditions, one of which was that the premises were taken "furnished for duration", meaning the duration of the war. A notice to quit was served and was valid to determine a weekly tenancy, but not to determine a lease for the duration of the war. The question was whether such a lease could be, and had been, created.

Held. It was not possible to create a lease for the duration of the war.

LORD GREENE MR: Normally there could be no question that this was an ordinary weekly tenancy, duly determinable by a week's notice, but the parties in the rent-book agreed to a term which appears there expressed by the words "furnished for duration", which must mean the duration of the war. The question immediately arises whether a tenancy for the duration of the war creates a good leasehold interest. In my opinion, it does not. A term created by a leasehold tenancy agreement must be expressed either with certainty and specifically or by reference to something which can, at the time when the lease takes effect, be looked to as a certain ascertainment of what the term is meant to be. In the present case, when this tenancy agreement took effect, the term was completely uncertain. It was impossible to say how long the tenancy would last. Mr. Sturge in his argument has maintained that such a lease would be valid, and that, even if the term is uncertain at its beginning when the lease takes effect, the fact that at some future time it will be rendered certain is sufficient to make it a good lease. In my opinion, that argument is not to be sustained.

I do not propose to go into the authorities on the matter, but in Foa's Landlord and Tenant (6th edn.), p. 115, the law is stated in this way, and, in my view, correctly: "The habendum in a lease must point out the period during which the enjoyment of the premises is to be had; so that the duration, as well as the commencement of the term, must be stated. The certainty of a lease as to its continuance must be ascertainable either by the express limitation of the parties at the time the lease is made, or by reference to some collateral act which may, with equal certainty, measure the continuance of it, otherwise it is void. If the term be fixed by reference to some collateral matter, such matter must either be itself certain (e.g., a demise to hold for 'as many

---

[20] Cheshire, pp. 382–388; M&W, pp. 630–633, 642–645; MM, pp. 317–318, 322–325.
[1] *Harvey v Pratt* [1965] 1 WLR 1025, [1965] 2 All ER 786 (a contract for a lease failed to specify the date of its commencement); *James v Lock* (1977) 246 Estates Gazette 395.

years as A. has in the manor of B.') or capable before the lease takes effect of being rendered so (e.g., for 'as many years as C. shall name').'' The important words to observe in that last phrase are the words "before the lease takes effect". Then it goes on : "Consequently, a lease to endure for 'as many years as A. shall live', or 'as the coverture between B. and C. shall continue', would not be good as a lease for years, although the same results may be achieved in another way by making the demise for a fixed number (ninety-nine for instance) of years determinable upon A.'s death, or the dissolution of the coverture between B. and C." In the present case, in my opinion, this agreement cannot take effect as a good tenancy for the duration of the war. . . .[2]

In *Re Midland Rly Co's Agreement*[3] [1971] Ch 725, [1971] 1 All ER 1007, the Midland Railway Company in 1920 granted a half-yearly tenancy at £1 a year of 100 square yards of land in Luton, Bedfordshire. Clause 2 provided that the lease could be determined by either party on giving to the other three months' written notice. A proviso to clause 2 stated that "this agreement shall not be so terminated by the company until they shall require the said premises for the purposes of their undertaking". In 1969 the British Railways Board, the successors to the landlords, gave notice to the tenant to terminate the tenancy under Landlord and Tenant Act 1954, section 25. They did not require the premises for the purpose of their undertaking, but claimed that clause 2 was void, on the ground of uncertainty of duration and repugnancy. The Court of Appeal held that the clause was valid, and the notice of termination void.

RUSSELL LJ said at p. 732:

"Now it appears to us that [*Lace v Chantler*] is confined to a case in which that which was purported to be done was simply to create a leasehold interest for a single and uncertain period. The applicability of this matter of certainty to a periodic tenancy was not under consideration. If *Lace v Chantler* had been a case in which there was simply a periodic tenancy with a proviso that the landlord would not give notice during the continuance of the war, this court might not have concluded that such an agreement, which would of course have left the tenant free to determine on notice at any time, was inoperative to create a leasehold. There is nothing in the reasoning of the judgments to lead to the necessary conclusion that such must have been so.

If you have an ordinary case of a periodic tenancy (for example, a yearly tenancy), it is plain that in one sense at least it is uncertain at the outset what will be the maximum duration of the term created,

---

[2] Leases and agreements for a lease for the duration of the Second World War were converted by Validation of War-time Leases Act 1944, s. 1. into leases, or agreements for a lease, for ten years, subject (usually) to determination by one month's notice given after the end of the war.

[3] (1971) CLJ 198 (D. Macintyre).

which term grows year by year as a single term springing from the original grant. It cannot be predicated that in no circumstances will it exceed, for example, 50 years; there is no previously ascertained maximum duration for the term; its duration will depend upon the time that will elapse before either party gives notice of determination. The simple statement of the law that the maximum duration of a term must be certainly known in advance of its taking effect cannot therefore have direct reference to periodic tenancies."

i. INTERESSE TERMINI

LAW OF PROPERTY ACT 1925

149. Abolition of interesse termini, and as to reversionary leases and leases for lives. — (1) The doctrine of interesse termini is hereby abolished.

(2) As from the commencement of this Act all terms of years absolute shall, whether the interest is created before or after such commencement, be capable of taking effect at law or in equity, according to the estate interest or powers of the grantor, from the date fixed for commencement of the term, without actual entry.

ii. REVERSIONARY LEASES[4]

LAW OF PROPERTY ACT 1925

149. Abolition of interesse termini, and as to reversionary leases and leases for lives. — (3) A term, at a rent or granted in consideration of a fine[5], limited after the commencement of this Act to take effect more than twenty-one years from the date of the instrument purporting to create it, shall be void, and any contract made after such commencement to create such a term shall likewise be void; but this subsection does not apply to any term taking effect in equity under a settlement, or created out of an equitable interest under a settlement, or under an equitable power for mortgage, indemnity or other like purposes.

RE STRAND AND SAVOY PROPERTIES LTD[6]
[1960] Ch 582, [1960] 2 All ER 327 (ChD, BUCKLEY J)

A 35 year lease contained a provision that the lessors would "at the written request of the lessee made 12 months before the expiration of the term hereby created" grant a further term of 35 years at the same rent.

The tenants took out a summons to determine whether the Law of Property Act 1925, section 149 (3) invalidated their option to renew the lease on the ground that it was a contract to take effect more than 21 years from the date of the lease granting the option.

---

[4] I.e., a lease which is to take effect at a future time. This must not be confused with a lease of the reversion (or a concurrent lease); p. 384, post.

[5] P. 75, n. 18, ante.

[6] (1960) 76 LQR 352 (R. E. M.).

Held. The option for renewal was valid.

BUCKLEY J: Sir Milner Holland, who appears for the tenants, . . . says that subsection (3) makes it impossible for any man to create a reversionary term — that is to say, a term to take effect more than 21 years from the date of the instrument creating the term — and that it also invalidates any contract by which a man undertakes to create a reversionary term, that is to say, a term which will not commence until 21 years after the date of the instrument creating such a term. He says that the subsection does not invalidate a contract to create a lease, at however remote a date in the future, which, when it is granted, will create a term which will take effect within 21 years of the date of that lease. . . .

Mr. Albery, on the other hand, points out that the contention advanced by Sir Milner really gives no operative effect to that part of subsection (3) which deals with contracts at all, because if a lease granting a term to commence at a date later than 21 years from the date of the lease is void, a contract to grant such a lease must also necessarily be void without any express provision to that effect in the statute. . . .

On [its true] terms the subsection is confined, so far as contracts are concerned, to contracts to create terms which, when created, will only take effect more than 21 years from the dates of the instruments creating them; that is to say, it invalidates contracts for the granting of leases which will, when granted, be reversionary leases, the postponement of the commencement of the term being for more than 21 years from the date of the lease.

WEG MOTORS LTD *v* HALES
[1962] Ch 49, [1961] 3 All ER 181 (CA, Lord EVERSHED MR, HARMAN and DONOVAN LJJ)

In July 1938 the plaintiffs were granted a lease of premises for a term of 21 years from December 1938, with an option of "taking a further lease" of the premises for a period of 21 years from the date of the exercise of the option; and the option was expressed to be exercisable at any time before 25 December 1959. The defendants claimed that the option agreement was void under section 149 (3).

Held. The option agreement was valid.

LORD EVERSHED MR: The question is, in our judgment, an extremely short one — namely, does the option agreement of July, 1938, fall within the scope of the language in subsection (3) of section 149 of the Act of 1925 as being a contract "to create such a term" as therein mentioned? The view of the learned author of the note to the section in volume 1 of Wolstenholme and Cherry's *Conveyancing Statutes*, 12th edn. (1932), p. 497, appears clearly to have been that a contract to create a term of years, which might begin to take effect more than 21 years from the date of the contract, fell within the vice of the subsection. It was this view that Buckley J rejected in the case already cited[7]; and he did so upon the basis that the phrase "such a term" could in its context refer, and refer only, to a term commencing more than 21 years from the instrument purporting to create the term, that is to say, the lease executed in pursuance of the contract and not the contract itself. We must not be taken to be expressing any doubt of the correctness of Buckley J's decision. But in the present case we are concerned not with a contract, that is a binding agreement, to grant and take a lease but with an option which might never be exercised and cannot, until exercised, be in any event said, in our judgment, to create a term of years at all. It follows, therefore, in our view, that the option agreement with which we are concerned cannot be said to be such a contract as is comprehended in section 149 (3) of the Act of 1925. The challenge to the plaintiffs based upon that section must, therefore, fail.

iii.   LEASES FOR LIVES

LAW OF PROPERTY ACT 1925

149. Abolition of interesse termini, and as to reversionary leases and leases for lives. — (6) Any lease or underlease, at a rent, or in consideration of a fine[8], for life or lives or for any term of years determinable with life or lives, or on the marriage of the lessee, or any contract therefor, made before or after the commencement of this Act, or created by virtue of Part V. of the Law of Property Act, 1922, shall take effect as a lease, underlease or contract therefor, for a term of ninety years determinable after the death or marriage (as the case may be) of the original lessee, or of the survivor of the original lessees, by at least one month's notice in writing given to determine the same on one of the quarter days applicable to the tenancy, either by the lessor or the persons deriving title under him, to the person entitled to the leasehold interest, or if no such person is in existence by affixing the same to the premises, or by the lessee or other persons in whom the leasehold interest is vested to the lessor or the persons deriving title under him:

Provided that —

(a) this subsection shall not apply to any term taking effect in equity under a settlement or created out of an equitable interest under a settlement for mortgage, indemnity, or other like purposes; . . .

(d) if there are no quarter days specially applicable to the tenancy, notice may be given to determine the tenancy on one of the usual quarter days.

iv.   PERPETUALLY RENEWABLE LEASES

Perpetually renewable leases are converted into terms of 2,000 years; those existing on 1 January 1926 date from the commencement of the

---

[7] *Re Strand and Savoy Properties Ltd* p. 361, ante.
[8] Thus excluding beneficial life tenancies under a settlement. These are equitable interests and subject to S.L.A. 1925; p. 248, ante.

existing tenancy, and those created after 1925 from the date fixed for the commencement of the tenancy. Perpetually renewable subleases are converted into terms of 2,000 years less one day[9].

In *Caerphilly Concrete Products Ltd v Owen* [1972] 1 WLR 372, [1972] 1 All ER 248[10] a grant in 1963 of a five year term of 4,800 square feet in an industrial area of Caerphilly at £10 a year contained a provision that "the landlord will on the written request of the tenant . . . grant to him a lease of the said demised land for the further term of five years from the expiration of the said term hereby granted at the same rent and containing the like covenants and provisos as are herein contained (including an option to renew such lease for the further term of five years at the expiration thereof)". The Court of Appeal (RUSSELL, SACHS and STAMP LJJ) held that the grant took effect as a lease for 2,000 years. SACHS LJ said, at p. 375:

"I, too, have underlined the words in brackets. It is trite to say that when construing a document such as a lease it is the prime purpose of the courts to seek to adopt a meaning that conforms to the intentions of the parties. Not even the most impeccable conveyancing logic, however neatly expressed, can convince me that in the instant case it was the mutual intention of the parties that the lease should be perpetually renewable. So far as the landlord is concerned it seems to me highly unlikely that he really intended that this particular lease could or should be "for ever". My doubts on that question of intention extend also to the tenant — for I would acquit him of any intent to lay a trap through the operation of the words enclosed in the brackets, which we know to have been added to the draft at the very last moment by his solicitors. It is difficult indeed, at any rate so far as I am concerned, to think that two business men would be talking in terms of five years if both — or indeed either — of them truly meant that a lease should be granted which went on ad infinitum.

Were I in a position to give effect to the views just expressed that would result in the landlord succeeding in this appeal: but it is necessary to consider whether the authorities which were so fully and so helpfully cited to us permit such a result. An examination of the relevant decisions discloses an area of law in which the courts have manoeuvred themselves into an unhappy position . . . [They] appear to have bound themselves to hold that the use of a certain set of words (to which I will refer as "the formula") causes the lease to be perpetually renewable, even when no layman — at least if he has some elementary knowledge of business — would dream of granting such a lease and, if aware of the technical meaning of the particular phraseology would almost certainty be aghast at its devastating effect and refuse to sign. One reason for the courts so binding themselves is said to be that the formula is one the effect of which is well known to trained conveyancers, and that this is advantageous, however much of a trap it may constitute for others.

---

[9] L.P.A. 1922, s. 145 and Sch. 15.
[10] (1972) 88 LQR 173.

As already mentioned, the prime purpose of the courts when construing a lease is to interpret it according to the true intentions of the parties. Already 20 years ago judicial unease at having to determine those intentions in cases of the instant type by a blinkered approach is reflected in the judgments in *Parkus v Greenwood*, both at first instance [1950] Ch 33, [1949] 2 All ER 743 and on appeal [1950] Ch 644, [1950] 1 All ER 436.

[His Lordship referred to *Green v Palmer* [1944] Ch 328, [1944] 1 All ER 670 and continued:]

The judicial unease of 1950 is, so far as I am concerned, by now increased by two factors. First, more and more leases over the two succeeding decades have tended to come from pens not fully trained in the art of conveyancing. Secondly, over the same period the value of the pound sterling has been decreasing rapidly, thus making it even more unlikely that a man of business in the course of a normal transaction would knowingly part 'for ever' with his rights over land in return for a static rent. Moreover, when residential property is concerned a landlord could indeed now find himself in the position of having to relinquish a freehold when the document which he signed appeared on the face of it to be a lease for relatively short periods of years.

In those circumstances I, too, have great sympathy with the line of approach adopted by Uthwatt J[11] and Harman J[12]. I could wish that the courts had followed the apparent preference of Lord FitzGerald in *Swinburne v Milburn* (1884) 9 App Cas 844 at 855 for confining interpretations of perpetual renewability to leases where words such as 'for ever' or 'from time to time for ever hereafter' or some equivalent were used in the relevant document. This approach would have avoided that sort of path by which good logic can on occasion make bad law, and would have been in accord with the aphorism that at times 'logic is only the art of going wrong with confidence'.

Having, however, examined the authorities, I feel bound in this court to say that the matter is concluded by them in that the words in brackets, as inserted at the last moment, have in law the same effect as those considered in *Parkus v Greenwood* [1950] Ch 644, [1950] 1 All ER 436.''

C. Certainty of Rent

The rent must be certain. That does not mean that it must be certain at the date of the lease. Rent is sufficiently certain if it can be calculated with certainty at the time when payment comes to be made[13]. This

---

[11] In *Green v Palmer* [1944] Ch 328, [1944] 1 All ER 670.
[12] In *Parkus v Greenwood* [1950] Ch 644, [1950] 1 All ER 436.
[13] *Greater London Council v Connolly* [1970] 2 QB 100, [1970] 1 All ER 870 ("rent liable to be increased or decreased on notice being given" held to be valid); *C. H. Bailey Ltd v Memorial Enterprises Ltd* [1974] 1 WLR 728, [1974] 1 All ER 1003 (increased rent ascertained retrospectively).

problem has recently been considered in connexion with options to
renew a lease and rent revision at the time of renewal[14].

BROWN *v* GOULD[15]
[1972] Ch 53, [1971] 2 All ER 1505 (ChD, MEGARRY J)

In 1949 Margaret Gould leased part of Albion Granaries, 250 High
Road, Loughton, Essex to Frank Brown[16] for 21 years from 29
September 1949, at a rent of £500 a year. Clause 3 (c) of the lease
granted to the tenant an option to renew the tenancy for a further term
of 21 years at a rent "to be fixed having regard to the market value of
the premises at the time of exercising the option taking into account to
the advantage of the tenant any increased value of such premises
attributable to structural improvements made by the tenant during
the currency of this present lease." Frank Brown spent nearly £30,000
rebuilding the premises, and in 1969 served notice in accordance with
the terms of the lease purporting to exercise the option. The trustees of
Margaret Gould, in whom the reversion had vested on her death,
contended that the option was void for uncertainty.

Held. The option was valid.

MEGARRY J: The landlords . . . contend that the option for renewal
contained in the lease is void for uncertainty. That is the sole question
that I have to determine. Stated briefly, the proper approach, I think,
is that the court is reluctant to hold void for uncertainty any provision
that was intended to have legal effect. In this case it is very properly
accepted that the option was intended to have business efficacy.

In an unreported case, *Re Lloyd's Trust Instruments* (1970) 24th
June, to which I referred counsel, I endeavoured to state the basic
principles applicable in cases of uncertainty. What I said there was:

"I think the starting point on any question of uncertainty must
be that of the court's reluctance to hold an instrument void for
uncertainty. Lord Hardwicke LC once said 'A court never construes a
devise void, unless it is so absolutely dark, that they cannot find out
the testator's meaning': *Minshull v Minshull* (1737) 1 Atk 411 at 412.
Lord Brougham said: 'The difficulty must be so great that it amounts
to an impossibility, the doubt so grave that there is not even an
inclination of the scales one way': *Doe d Winter v Perratt* (1843) 9 Cl &
F 606 at 689. In a well-known statement, Sir George Jessel MR said
that the court would not hold a will void for uncertainty 'unless it is
utterly impossible to put a meaning upon it. The duty of the court is to
put a fair meaning on the terms used, and not, as was said in one case,

---

[14] As to time being of the essence in rent review clauses, see *United Scientific Holdings
Ltd v Burnley Borough Council* [1978] AC 904, [1977] 2 All ER 62; Conv Prec 5–57;
Dean and Chapter of Chichester Cathedral v Lennards Ltd (1977) 35 P & CR 309.
Drebbond Ltd v Horsham District Council (1979) 37 P & CR 237. See generally
Barnsley, *Land Options* (1978), Chap. 10.

[15] (1972) 36 Conv (NS) 317 (P. Robertshaw).

[16] "He had the good fortune to live at Arabin House, High Beech, Essex", at p. 55. See
Megarry, *Arabinesque-at-law* (1969), p. xi.

to repose on the easy pillow of saying that the whole is void for uncertainty': *Re Roberts* (1881) 19 ChD 520 at 529. That this is not a doctrine confined to wills but is one which applies to other instruments, such as planning permissions, is shown by cases such as *Fawcett Properties Ltd v Buckingham County Council* [1961] AC 636, [1960] 3 All ER 503, where, by a majority, the delphic language of a condition in a planning permission escaped from being held void for uncertainty largely because of its resemblance to a section to be found in a modern Act of Parliament. The second question is that of the types of uncertainty. The basic type (and on one view the only true type) is uncertainty of concept, as contrasted with mere difficulty of application: see, for example, *Re Gape* [1952] Ch 418, affirmed at 743, where the question was one of a condition subsequent, in which special considerations apply. In *Fawcett's* case [1961] AC 636 at 670, [1960] 3 All ER 503 at 513, Lord Keith of Avonholm said: 'The point is one of uncertainty of concept. If it is impossible, on construction of the condition, to reach a conclusion as to what was in the draftsman's mind, the condition is meaningless and must be read as pro non scripto.' Putting it another way, the question is one of linguistic or semantic uncertainty, and not of difficulty of ascertainment: see *Re Baden's Deed Trusts* [1971] AC 424 at 457, [1970] 2 All ER 228, per Lord Wilberforce. If there is a trust for 'my old friends,' all concerned are faced with uncertainty as to the concept or idea enshrined in these words. It may not be difficult to resolve that 'old' means not 'aged' but 'of long standing'; but then there is the question how long is 'long'. Friendship, too, is a concept with almost infinite shades of meaning. Where the concept is uncertain, the gift is void. Where the concept is certain, then mere difficulty in tracing and discovering those who are entitled normally does not invalidate the gift.''

To the authorities mentioned in that passage must now be added *Greater London Council v Connolly* [1970] 2 QB 100, [1970] 1 All ER 870, a landlord and tenant case concerning a condition on the rent card of a council tenant. This condition provided that the rent and other sums shown on the rent card "are liable to be increased or decreased on notice being given"; and the Court of Appeal unanimously held that the condition was not void for uncertainty. Lord Denning MR said, at p. 108: "The courts are always loath to hold a condition bad for uncertainty. They will give it a reasonable interpretation whenever possible. It is possible here." . . . No doubt there may be cases in which the draftsman's ineptitude will succeed in defeating the court's efforts to find a meaning for the provision in question; but only if the court is driven to it will it be held that a provision is void for uncertainty.

With that in mind, I approach the attack made on the present clause. Mr. Scamell [counsel for the defendants] concentrated on three phrases in the clause, the words "a rent to be fixed", the words "having regard to" the market value of the premises at the time of exercising the option, and the words "taking into account" to the advantage of the tenant any increased value of the premises attributable to his structural improvements. In addition, he pointed to the absence of any machinery for working out this formula, by contrast with the other provisions in the lease that I have mentioned. Taken together, he said, these considerations showed that the clause provided neither a clear basis for determining the rent nor any means of quantifying that basis, and accordingly the option was void for uncertainty.

At least three types of option may be distinguished. First, the option may be for renewal simply "at a rent to be agreed". In that case, no formula for quantifying the rent is laid down, and prima facie the option will, as in *King's Motors (Oxford) Ltd v Lax* [1970] 1 WLR 426, [1969] 3 All ER 665, be void as being a mere contract to make a contract, or, perhaps more properly, as being an agreement to make a contract, or a contract dependent upon the making of an agreement[17]. In *Smith v Morgan*, ... [1971] 1 WLR 803, [1971] 2 All ER 1500, my brother Brightman held that a right of pre-emption in a conveyance "at a figure to be agreed upon" was not void for uncertainty, but imposed upon the person granting it an obligation to offer the land to the grantee at the price at which she was willing to sell it. On this, I would make two comments. First, it illustrates the attitude of the court in striving to avoid holding a provision void for uncertainty. Second, it illustrates one of the differences between an option and a right of pre-emption. Under an option, only one step is normally needed to constitute a contract, namely, the exercise of the option. Under a right of pre-emption, two steps will usually be necessary, the making of the offer in accordance with the right of pre-emption, and the acceptance of that offer. The failure to provide either a price or a formula for ascertaining the price is accordingly far more serious in the case of an option than under a pre-emption: he who exercises such an option may well be virtually signing a blank cheque, whereas he who is entitled to a right of pre-emption can at least refrain from accepting the grantor's offer if the price be too high.

The second type of option is one that is expressed to be exercisable at a price to be determined according to some stated formula, without any effective machinery being in terms provided for the working out of that formula. That is the present case. Thirdly, the option may be one which provides both a formula and the machinery, as, for example, arbitration. In this last case, it may be that the machinery can do something to cure defects in the formula: I do not have to decide that. What is before me is a formula that is assailed for its uncertainty, and the absence of any specified machinery that can do anything to cure that uncertainty. I shall consider the question of machinery first.

[His Lordship rejected the landlords' argument that there was no adequate machinery for determining the rent, and continued:]

I readily accept that the words of clause 3 (c) might have been more precise. But that is not the point: the point is whether it is void for uncertainty. If one approaches the formula stated in the clause with

---

[17] See also *Courtney and Fairbairn Ltd v Tolaini Bros (Hotels) Ltd* [1975] 1 WLR 297, [1975] 1 All ER 716 (agreement "to negotiate fair and reasonable contract sums" held invalid).

reasonable goodwill, as I think I am entitled and, indeed, required to do, does it appear to embody such uncertainty of concept as to make it void? Without saying that there is no room for argument on the details, I would answer No to that question, or, indeed, to any other reasonable way of formulating the question that I can conceive. The question is not, I think, whether the clause is proof against wilful misinterpretation, but whether someone genuinely seeking to discover its meaning is able to do so. To that question I would answer Yes[18]."

D. Lease and Licence[19]

i. THE DISTINCTION

It used to be said that the critical issue was whether the party in question had exclusive possession of the land[20]; that a person in exclusive possession (other than a freeholder or copyholder) was a lessee[1]. The point has been under discussion in litigation over the last 30 years on a variety of matters including the revocability of a party's right to remain on land[2], the application of the Rent Acts[3] and the Landlord and Tenant Acts[4] and, until 1980, the operation of the

---

[18] See also *Talbot v Talbot* [1968] Ch 1, [1967] 2 All ER 920 (option to purchase "at a reasonable valuation" held valid by CA).

[19] Cheshire, pp. 384–386; 470; M & W, pp. 618–620, 776–777; MM, pp. 312–313.

[20] The giving of a right of exclusive possession should be distinguished from the giving of an exclusive or sole right to use the premises for a particular purpose which has never been held to create a tenancy. *Hill v Tupper* (1863) 2 H & C 121; *Wilson v Tavener* [1901] 1 Ch 578; *Clore v Theatrical Properties Ltd and Westby & Co Ltd* [1936] 3 All ER 483.

[1] In *Lynes v Snaith* [1899] 1 QB 486, LAWRENCE J said: "As to the first question, I think it is clear [the defendant] was a tenant at will and not a licensee; for the admissions state that she was in exclusive possession, a fact which is wholly inconsistent with her having been a mere licensee."

[2] *Errington v Errington and Woods* [1952] 1 KB 290, [1952] 1 All ER 149; p. 452, post. *Tanner v Tanner* [1975] 1 WLR 1346, [1975] 3 All ER 776 (joint licence from mother to son and daughter in law); *Hardwick v Johnson* [1978] 1 WLR 683, [1978] 2 All ER 935, p. 448, post; *Chandler v Kerley* [1978] 1 WLR 693, [1978] 2 All ER 942, p. 443, post; *Rossvale Ltd v Green* (1978) 250 Estates Gazette 1183.

[3] *Foster v Robinson* [1951] 1 KB 149, [1950] 2 All ER 342; *Murray, Bull & Co Ltd v Murray* [1953] 1 QB 211, [1952] 2 All ER 1079; *Marcroft Wagons Ltd v Smith* [1951] 2 KB 496, [1951] 2 All ER 271; *Crane v Morris* [1965] 1 WLR 1104, [1965] 3 All ER 77; *Abbeyfield (Harpenden) Society Ltd v Woods* [1968] 1 WLR 374, [1968] 1 All ER 352; *Luganda v Services Hotel Ltd* [1969] 2 Ch 209, [1969] 2 All ER 692; *Barnes v Barratt* [1970] 2 QB 657, [1970] 2 All ER 483; *R v South Middlesex Rent Tribunal, Ex parte Beswick* (1976) 32 P & CR 67; *Marchant v Charters* [1977] 1 WLR 1181, [1977] 3 All ER 918 p. 370, post; *Somma v Hazelhurst* [1978] 1 WLR 1014, [1978] 2 All ER 1011; p. 373, post; *Aldrington Garages v Fielder* (1978) 37 P & CR 461; *Walsh v Griffiths-Jones* [1978] 2 All ER 1002; *O'Malley v Seymour* (1978) 250 Estates Gazette 1083; *Demuren v Seal Estates Ltd* (1978) 249 Estates Gazette 440. Megarry, *Rent Acts* (10th edn.), pp. 53–64; Pettit, *Landlord and Tenant under the Rent Act 1977*, pp. 8–15.

[4] *Facchini v Bryson* [1952] 1 TLR 1386; *Addiscombe Garden Estates Ltd v Crabbe* [1958] 1 QB 513, [1957] 2 All ER 563; *Bracey v Read* [1963] Ch 88, [1962] 3 All ER 472; *Shell-Mex and BP Ltd v Manchester Garages Ltd* [1971] 1 WLR 612, [1971] 1 All ER 841; *Parcar Utilities Ltd v Fordamsted Ltd and W.J. Brown Ltd* (1967) 204 Estates Gazette 1027; *Wang v Wei* (1975) 237 Estates Gazette 657, 119 Sol Jo 668 at 688, (1977) 121 Sol Jo 804 (H.E. Markson).

Limitation Act 1939[5]. The question now depends on the intention of the parties to be inferred from all the circumstances[6]. An arrangement will never be construed as a lease unless exclusive possession is given[7]; but, contrary to the views expressed in many of the older cases[8] exclusive possession does not necessarily mean that the person in enjoyment must be a tenant and not a licensee.

In *Barnes v Barratt* [1970] 2 QB 657, [1970] 2 All ER 483, SACHS LJ summarised at p. 669 the present attitude of the Court of Appeal to the distinction between a lease and a licence: "Whether any given arrangement does, in law, produce a tenancy or, on the other hand, a licence is rarely easy to determine though perhaps not so difficult as it was some 20 years ago. In this case, as always, it is necessary to give weight to the fact that exclusive possession has been given to the occupiers. That, however, is a factor which is no longer conclusive and, indeed, appears nowadays to have diminishing weight. Weight has also to be given to the words of potential technical import used by the parties. Again, however, these are not conclusive either when written or spoken. In the end it is the substance of the transaction to which the court must have regard and when deciding its intended effect it applies to that substance the law and not the label of either of the parties[9]. In this way, the law has adapted itself so as to deal with the complexities of the Rent Acts without causing patently unintended injustice to landlords, whilst guarding against improper avoidance by the latter of the provisions of those Acts."

MARCHANT *v* CHARTERS
[1977] 1 WLR 1181, [1977] 3 All ER 918 (CA, Lord DENNING MR, ORR and WALLER LJJ)

LORD DENNING MR: No. 131 Clapton Common is an ordinary sort of house. It is owned by Mrs. Marchant. It was at one time a private

---

[5] *Cobb v Lane* [1952] 1 All ER 1199, *Hughes v Griffin* [1969] 1 WLR 23, [1969] 1 All ER 460, *Heslop v Burns* [1974] 1 WLR 1241, [1974] 3 All ER 406; Limitation Amendment Act 1980 s. 3 (1), p. 163 ante.

[6] *Booker v Palmer* [1942] 2 All ER 674 at 677; *Errington v Errington and Woods* (supra); *Gorham (Contractors) Ltd v Field* [1952] CPL 266; *Cobb v Lane* (supra); *Murray, Bull & Co Ltd v Murray* (supra); *Isaac v Hotel de Paris Ltd* [1960] 1 WLR 239, [1960] 1 All ER 348; *Appah v Parncliffe Investments Ltd* [1964] 1 WLR 1064, [1964] 1 All ER 838; *Strand Securities Ltd v Caswell* [1965] Ch 958 at 980; *Barnes v Barratt* (supra); *Binions v Evans* [1972] Ch 359, [1972] 2 All ER 70; *Heslop v Burns* (supra); *Shell-Mex and BP Ltd v Manchester Garages Ltd* (supra); *R v Tao* [1977] QB 141, [1976] 3 All ER 65; and cases in section ii p. 373, post. See also (1976) Conv (NS) 5.

[7] *Smith v St. Michael's, Cambridgeshire Overseers* (1860) 3 E & E 383; *Hill v Tupper* (supra); *Watkins v Milton-next-Gravesend Overseers* (1868) LR 3 QB 350 (a barge in a river), *London and North Western Rly Co v Buckmaster* (1874) LR 10 QB 70 at 76 (licence to use stables); *Rendell v Roman* (1893) 9 TLR 192 (a stall at an exhibition); *Wells v Kingston-upon-Hull Corpn* (1875) LR 10 CP 402; *Clore v Theatrical Properties Ltd and Westby & Co Ltd* [1936] 3 All ER 483 (front of the house rights in a theatre).

[8] (1953) 69 LQR 466 (A. D. Hargreaves).

[9] See also *Facchini v Bryson* [1952] 1 TLR 1386; *Addiscombe Gardens Estates Ltd v Crabbe* [1958] 1 QB 513, [1957] 3 All ER 563.

dwelling house, but for the last 23 years she has let it off in single rooms to men only. She has regularly put the same advertisement in the local newspaper: "Attractive Bachelor Service Apartments, Superior House, Resident Housekeeper, Every convenience. . . ."

There are seven bed-sitting rooms. Each room is simply but nicely furnished with a bed, table, a couple of chairs and so forth. Each room has, of course, its gas ring and grill, so that the residents can do a little cooking on their own as meals are not included. The bathroom and lavatory are shared. The housekeeper cleans the rooms every day and provides clean linen every week. It is a very usual sort of arrangement. Many young people live in bed-sitting rooms like this.

The question is whether the occupation of such a bed-sitting room has security of tenure. . . .

On that evidence the final question is, was Mr. Charters a tenant or only a licensee? The law on this subject has been developed greatly in the last 25 years. I might almost say revolutionised. In 1952 I collected several of the cases in *Errington v Errington and Woods* [1952] 1 KB 290 and since that time there have been many more. The difference is very important under the Rent Acts (including the Act of 1974) because a "tenant" is given complete security of tenure, but a licensee is not. There are four or five cases, somewhat like the present, to which we have been referred. The first is *Appah v Parncliffe Investments Ltd* [1964] 1 WLR 1064. A house had been split up into 17 different rooms, each with its own Yale lock and key. The rooms were furnished. No meals were provided, but the rooms were cleaned daily, and beds made. Fresh linen was provided. A lady took one of the rooms, but owing to the negligence of the owners, someone was able to break into her room and steal her belongings. It was held that she was not a tenant but a licensee for reward: and so able to sue the owner for negligence.

The next case is *Abbeyfield (Harpenden) Society Ltd v Woods* [1968] 1 WLR 374. A charitable society had converted a big house into an old people's home with 12 rooms. They let one of the rooms unfurnished to an old man of 85. He furnished it himself. The society provided food in a common dining room and so forth. There was a resident housekeeper. It was held that the old man was only a licensee and not a tenant. So he was not protected by the Rent Acts and had to go.

The nearest case to the present case is *Luganda v Service Hotels Ltd* [1969] 2 Ch 209. A student was reading for the Bar. He took a furnished room in a building called the Queensborough Court Hotel. There were 88 rooms. They were said to be "let" out to tenants. Every student had a Yale key for his room. It was a bed-sitting room with a double gas ring. He got his own meals and provided his own towels and soap. The chambermaids came in every day and made the bed and cleaned the room. Every week they changed the linen. It was held that he was a contractual licensee and not a tenant: see p. 219C. But as he had applied to the rent tribunal, he was protected for a limited period from being evicted: see p. 219H.

The next case arose under the Planning Acts: *Mayflower Cambridge Ltd v Secretary of State for the Environment* (1975) 30 P & CR 28. A building in Cambridge had been erected for students to stay; but it was not needed for them. So it was used for visitors who wanted to come to Cambridge. The question was whether the change of use was to an "hotel." Lord Widgery CJ said, at p. 32: "The essence of a hotel is that it takes transient passengers." That may well be a test under the Planning Acts but it is not a test for seeing whether there is a tenancy or a licence.

The last case is *R v South Middlesex Rent Tribunal*, ex parte *Beswick* (1976) 32 P & CR 67. A young lady lived in a single room at a Y.W.C.A. hostel. It was a furnished room. It was her sole home. She was permanent, not temporary. In common with other residents, she had the use of a kitchen, dining room, living room, laundry room, bathroom and toilet. It was held that she was not a tenant but a licensee. So the fair rent was to be fixed, not by the rent officer, but by the rent tribunal.

Gathering the cases together, what does it come to? What is the test to see whether the occupier of one room in a house is a tenant or a licensee? It does not depend on whether he or she has exclusive possession or not. It does not depend on whether the room is furnished or not. It does not depend on whether the occupation is permanent or temporary. It does not depend on the label which the parties put upon it. All these are factors which may influence the decision but none of them is conclusive. All the circumstances have to be worked out. Eventually the answer depends on the nature and quality of the occupancy. Was it intended that the occupier should have a stake in the room or did he have only permission for himself personally to occupy the room, whether under a contract or not? In which case he is a licensee.

Looking at the position in this case, in my opinion Mr. Charters was not a tenant of this one room. He was only a licensee. A contractual licensee, no doubt, but still only a licensee. So he does not have security of tenure under the Rent Acts. He is not protected against eviction. On this point I differ from the judge. It is sufficient for the deciding of this case. Mr. Charters has no right to stay.

On the other hand, in *Bracey v Read* [1963] Ch 88, [1962] 3 All ER 472, the plaintiff, in 1957, agreed to lease to the defendants land on which to train and exercise racehorses. The lease was to be for a term of three years, after which it was to continue on a yearly tenancy. The plaintiff gave notice ending the right on 31 December 1961. The notice was adequate if the agreement of 1957 created a licence, but inadequate under the Landlord and Tenant Act 1954, Part II, if a lease[10].

---

[10] A lease of an incorporeal hereditament is not within Part II; *Land Reclamation Co Ltd v Basildon District Council* [1979] 1 WLR 106, at 111, [1978] 2 All ER 1162, at 1166.

CROSS J holding that the agreement of 1957 created a lease referred to "the question whether the defendant is entitled to protection under legislation which applies to tenancies, but does not apply to licences", and said ([1962] 3 All ER at 475): "In the case of a business transaction like this I think that the question whether a man ought to be considered as a licensee or a tenant depends principally, if not entirely, on whether he has exclusive possession of the property in question. Under arrangements which are not of an ordinary business character, one very often has a man in exclusive possession of the property in question, who is yet not a tenant but only a licensee; but no case was cited to me, and I do not know of any case, where a man who is in exclusive possession under an ordinary business agreement has been held not to be a tenant but only a licensee. . . . I think, on the whole, that the proper conclusion from the facts is that the defendant was in possession of the gallops as tenant."

ii. GENUINE OR SHAM
In an attempt to avoid the application of the Rent Acts, some landlords have drafted occupational agreements in terms which are designed to ensure that the premises are occupied under a licence and not under a lease. The court examines these agreements to determine whether they are genuine or sham.

SOMMA *v* HAZELHURST
[1978] 1 WLR 1014, [1978] 2 All ER 1011 (CA, STEPHENSON. GEOFFREY LANE and CUMMING-BRUCE LJJ)[11]

In 1976 Mr. Hazelhurst, "an educated man employed as a computer programmer", and Miss Savelli, an Italian "who also had a job", were looking for accommodation in which to live together in London. They entered into separate but identical written agreements with Miss Somma, the owner of 4 Cornwall Mansions, W.14. Each agreement was for the use of a double bed sitting room for a period of 12 weeks for £116.40, payable in three four-weekly instalments. It began:
"Whereas the licensor is not willing to grant the licensee exclusive possession of any part of the rooms hereinafter referred to.
And whereas the licensee is anxious to secure the use of the rooms notwithstanding that such use be in common with the licensor and such other licensees or invitees as the licensor may permit from time to time to use the said rooms.
And whereas this licence is entered into by the licensor and the licensee solely upon the above basis.

---

[11] Leave to appeal was refused by H L (1978) 128 NLJ 624. The case was followed in *Aldrington Garages Ltd v Fielder* (1979) 37 P & CR 461. Similar agreements were held to be sham in *Walsh v Griffiths-Jones* [1978] 2 All ER 1002; *Demuren v Seal Estates Ltd* (1978) 249 Estates Gazette 440 ("There is something so badly wrong with this agreement that one is bound to look at it with the gravest suspicion", at p. 443 per MEGAW LJ); *O'Malley v Seymour* (1978) 250 Estates Gazette 1083; p. 376, post. See [1978] Conv 397, (1979) 42 MLR 331 (M. Partington), 38 CLJ 38 (K.J. Gray); [1980] Conv 27 (P. Robson and P. Watchman).

By this licence the licensor licenses the licensee to use (but not exclusively) all those rooms. . . .''

The couple entered into occupation after each had signed the agreement and each had paid separately the instalments. They then applied to the rent officer to get the instalments reduced, claiming a tenancy within the Rent Acts.

Held (reversing the County Court judge) The agreement was a licence, and the Rent Acts did not apply.

CUMMING-BRUCE LJ (who delivered the judgment of the Court): We are confronted with one more attempt by an owner of housing accommodation to provide it at a profit for those in great need of it without the restrictions imposed by Parliament on his or her contractual right to charge for it and regain possession of it. The attempt which has led to this appeal is made by a document drawn up by one, or a combination, of those who seem to have studied all the efforts, recorded in a welter of cases decided in every court from the county court to the House of Lords, to avoid letting a dwelling house or part of it by arranging to licence or to share the occupation of it. On the particular facts of this case has this attempt failed as the judge held?

Each document which we have to consider is on its face a licence to each respondent to share occupation — of one double-bed-sitting room for 12 weeks. But the obligation which the document imposes on each respondent is an obligation to share with (1) the owner (described as the licensor), (2) the other respondent (described as a person permitted by the licensor but identified, by reading the respondents' documents with each other, as the other respondent). And the document so repeatedly proclaims itself a licence, and the relationship it creates between the appellant and each respondent as being that of licensor and licensee, that it raises the question why it should be necessary to protest so much and whether so many labels so clearly written all over it give a true or a false description of its real contents.

Our first task is to examine closely the course of the proceedings in the county court. The next to observe and analyse findings made by the judge. . . .

It seems to us that the reasoning behind the judge's ultimate conclusion is that (1) although there are on the face of it two documents here which if taken separately would give neither grantee exclusive possession, this is not fatal to the claim of the occupants that this was a tenancy, because the two documents must be construed together and if that is done they are apt to confer on the couple a joint interest of some sort in the room. (2) The other clauses which appear to make the occupation non-exclusive are illegal possibly on the grounds of public policy and therefore are not binding upon the grantees. (3) Consequently, one is left with a joint and exclusive occupation. (4) The nature of the occupation is a tenancy because there are "heaps of indications" which show that the parties if they applied their minds to it conferred on these people a joint tenancy or the equivalent rights. He does not say what these indications may be.

We find ourselves unable to come to the same conclusion as the judge. Lord Gifford, basing himself on the judgment of Denning LJ in *Facchini v Bryson* [1952] 1 TLR 1386 at 1389 and the reasoning in *Marchant v Charters* [1977] 1 WLR 1181 at 1185, submits that in a "Rent Act" situation, any permission to occupy residential premises exclusively must be a tenancy and not a licence, unless it comes into the category of hotels, hostels, family arrangements or service occupancy or a similar undefined special category. We can see no reason why an ordinary landlord not in any of these special categories should not be able to grant a licence to occupy an ordinary house. If that is what both he and the licensee intend and if they can frame any written agreement in such a way as to demonstrate that it is not really an agreement for a lease masquerading as a licence, we can see no reason in law or justice why they should be prevented from achieving that object. Nor can we see why their common intentions should be categorised as bogus or unreal or as sham merely on the ground that the court disapproves of the bargain. [His Lordship referred to Buckley LJ in *Shell-mex and BP Ltd v Manchester Garages Ltd* [1971] 1 WLR 612 at 619 and continued:]

There seem to us to be two questions which we have to answer: (1) did the parties intend to be bound by the written agreement? and (2) can it be said from the words which they used in those agreements that they intended to create a tenancy rather than a licence? As to the first question there is a clear finding of the judge that Mr. Hazelhurst and Miss Savelli "knew what they were letting themselves in for"; also that they were both educated and that they both signed the document. It is plain from these findings that the judge was of the opinion that they knew what they were signing and nevertheless voluntarily signed it. The second question is really the nub of the whole case, namely, do the terms of the two documents show an agreement for a licence rather than an agreement for a tenancy. Immediately one faces the problem of the two separate agreements, one with Mr. Hazelhurst and the other with Miss Savelli. If they are truly separate then it must follow that neither Mr. Hazelhurst nor Miss Savelli has the necessary exclusive occupation of the room on which to found a tenancy. . . . It is impossible to reconstruct the separate obligations into one joint obligation without doing violence to the obvious intentions of the parties, particularly of the two grantees, Mr. Hazelhurst and Miss Savelli. For example, if one takes clause 1 which deals with the consideration which the grantees are bound to pay, it would be necessary as we see it, either to have a joint interest coupled with a several liability for half the weekly amounts, which is something of a logical inconsistency[12], or else to redraw the terms of the agreements to make each grantee jointly and severally liable for the full four-weekly instalment of

---

[12] See *Demuren v Seal Estates Ltd* (1978) 249 Estates Gazette 440 at 444, (held not "logically inconsistent", where the landlord had secured for himself the whole amount due from both occupants by means of post-dated cheques).

£77.60, as against the contractual liability resting on each under the agreement of £38.80. This is not construing the agreement between the parties it is rewriting it in the absence of any claim for rectification or any allegation of fraud. . . . We find it impossible to say that on the contents of these two documents, even adding the fact that the two grantees made their bid for the room together, a joint interest was created in their favour. That is really the end of the matter, because if the rights of the parties are several as opposed to joint, it is impossible to say that either has the necessary exclusive possession to found a tenancy. . . .

In *O'Malley v Seymour* (1978) 250 Estates Gazette 1083, the defendant "a sophisticated and literate person", in 1976, signed an agreement purporting to be a licence of a flat for six months. Clause (1) stated: "In consideration of the sum of £520 payable by the licensee to the owner as hereinafter mentioned, the owner grants to the licensee the right to use in common with others who have been granted or will be granted the like right to the premises known as . . . 13 Ribblesdale Road, Crouch End, London N.8." In evidence the plaintiff "was honest enough to admit that he never contemplated for a moment foisting other persons on the defendant. He knew that Mr. Seymour wanted exclusive possession for his own purposes. There was no suggestion ever made in the six months that Mr. Seymour should accept any other person". The plaintiff claimed possession of the flat. The Court of Appeal held (upholding the County Court judge) that the agreement for a licence was a sham, and the Rent Acts applied to protect the defendant.

GEOFFREY LANE LJ said at p. 1088: This appeal demonstrates how much each case of this sort must depend upon its own particular facts. The owner of the premises here was trying to put forward the same sort of arguments as did the owners in *Somma's* case, decided in March of this year and the *Aldrington Garages'* case, decided on 7 July. Here however, the basic, if not the only, problem which had to be decided was whether the written document which was proffered by the plaintiff and signed by the defendant purporting to record the agreement already reached between the parties was a genuine attempt to record the agreed terms or whether it was a sham. In other words, was it an attempt to disguise what was truly a tenancy in the trappings of a licence? The document itself, which was signed by the defendant, bore many similarities to the equivalent documents in the two cases which I have mentioned, but here there was, to say the very least of it, ample evidence that the document was indeed a sham. The plaintiff's own answers in cross-examination to which my Lords have already referred really concluded the matter against him, because he effectively conceded that the prior oral agreement was firmly concluded and, secondly, that it was in the terms of tenancy and not in the terms of a licence. The opposite contention was, on the evidence, scarcely arguable. There was plainly a tenancy here and not a licence. I would dismiss the appeal accordingly.

III. Creation[13]

A. Statutory Requirements

LAW OF PROPERTY ACT 1925

54. Creation of interest in land by parol. — (1) p. 73, ante.

(2) p. 74, ante.

52. Conveyances to be by deed. — (1) p. 72, ante.

(2) (*d*) p. 72, ante[14].

Special provisions relate to the creation and disposition of leaseholds in registered land and these are set out below[15].

B. Tenancies at Common Law

i. TENANCIES AT WILL AND AT SUFFERANCE

Entry into possession as a tenant, or holding over with the landlord's consent after the expiration of the tenancy, creates a tenancy at will[16].

A tenant who holds over without the landlord's consent becomes a tenant at sufferance. Both such tenancies would expand to become weekly, monthly or yearly tenancies where rent was paid and accepted, the length of the tenancy being related to the period in respect of which the rent was paid[17].

In *Wheeler v Mercer* [1957] AC 416, [1956] 3 All ER 631 Viscount SIMONDS said at p. 426: "It may, I think, be truly said that, since a tenant at will is regarded at law as being in possession by his own will and at the will, express or implied, of his landlord, he is a tenant by their mutual agreement. . . . He is distinguished from a tenant at sufferance in that such a tenant is said to be in possession without either the agreement or disagreement of the landlord. . . . A tenancy at will . . . has been properly described as a personal relation between the landlord and his tenant: it is determined by the death of either of them or by any one of a variety of acts, even by an involuntary alienation, which would not affect the subsistence of any other tenancy[18]."

---

[13] Cheshire, pp. 388–405; M & W, pp. 620–650; MM, pp. 313–325.

[14] This includes a lease for a period exceeding three years even though it may be determinable within the period. *Kushner v Law Society* [1952] 1 KB 264, [1952] 1 All ER 404.

[15] See pp. 100–102, ante, pp. 427–433, post.

[16] It is occasionally created by express agreement; *Morgan v William Harrison Ltd* [1907] 2 Ch 137; *Manfield & Sons Ltd v Botchin* [1970] 2 QB 612, [1970] 3 All ER 143; *Hagee (London) Ltd v A. B. Erikson and Larson* [1976] QB 209, [1975] 3 All ER 234 (a tenancy at will avoids the provisions of L. & T. A. 1954 Part II). On its "apt legal mechanism to protect an occupier during a period of transition", see *Heslop v Burns* [1974] 1 WLR 1241 at 1253, per SCARMAN LJ.

[17] *Clayton v Blakey* (1798) 8 Term Rep 3; *Dougal v McCarthy* [1893] 1 QB 736.

[18] Cheshire, pp. 398–404; M & W, pp. 638–642; MM, pp. 321–322.

ii.   YEARLY BASIS

ADLER *v* BLACKMAN
[1952] 2 All ER 41 (QBD, ORMEROD J)[19]

Blackman had held shop premises under a weekly tenancy until December 1947, from which date the tenancy was changed to a yearly tenancy on the following terms: "To hold for the term of one year . . . at the exclusive weekly rent of £3 payable weekly . . .". After the expiration of the year, Blackman held over and Adler served on him a notice to quit, which was valid if he held a weekly, void if he held a yearly, tenancy. The notice to quit was first accepted by Blackman, whose first reaction was to claim compensation or a new lease under the Landlord and Tenant Act 1927. He subsequently claimed that the notice was invalid.

Held. Notice valid, as Blackman was a weekly tenant.

ORMEROD J: The questions to be decided are: Was the tenant holding these premises as a tenant from year to year, in which case, of course, this notice was invalid, or was he holding them on a weekly tenancy, in which case admittedly the notice is good? Secondly, even if the notice was invalid, as the tenant elected to treat it as valid by taking proceedings under the Landlord and Tenant Act, 1927, can he now say that the notice was invalid and that he is entitled to remain in possession of the premises? So far as the first point is concerned, it is clearly established that, if a tenant holds over with the consent of the landlord at the expiration of a period reserved by a lease or tenancy agreement, an implied tenancy is set up, and the presumption is that that tenancy is a yearly tenancy on the terms of the instrument creating the original tenancy so far as they are consistent with a yearly tenancy, but that presumption may be rebutted by various circumstances including, of course, the terms of the agreement itself. I am asked by the landlord to say that the fact that the original tenancy was admittedly a weekly tenancy is a circumstance which should be taken into account in rebutting this presumption. The agreement for a tenancy for twelve months, in which the rent was expressed to be payable by the week and was calculated by the week and not by the year, says the landlord, is also a very strong circumstance to take into account. Further, he says that the conduct of the parties after the expiration of the period of tenancy, and, particularly, when the notice to quit was served by the landlord on the tenant, establishes beyond doubt the inference that the tenancy was not a tenancy from year to year. . . .

In *Covered Markets Ltd v Green* ([1947] 2 All ER 140) a tenant held over at the expiration of a tenancy for seven years at a rent of £3, payable weekly. Macnaghten J, decided that the presumption was that

---

[19] Affirmed by CA (SOMERVELL, JENKINS and HODSON LJJ) [1953] 1 QB 146, [1952] 2 All ER 945, where the decision of MACNAGHTEN J, in *Covered Markets Ltd v Green* [1947] 2 All ER 140 was overruled.

the tenancy was a yearly one, and he saw no reason to rebut that presumption. He distinguished that case from Maugham J's decision on the ground that the premises were a fishmonger's shop, whereas the premises in the *Ladies' Hosiery* case ([1930] 1 Ch 304) were merely a piece of ground. I find it difficult to appreciate the distinction, but Macnaghten J very clearly held that the proper inference from the circumstances was that there was a yearly tenancy on the termination of the seven years.

I have to consider whether in the present case there is a yearly tenancy or whether the circumstances are such that the presumption of a yearly tenancy has been rebutted and the tenant holds the premises on a weekly tenancy only. I have come to the conclusion that I ought to hold that the presumption has been rebutted and that the tenancy is a weekly one. I am not influenced by the situation before the agreement for a yearly tenancy was entered into. I do not think I ought to regard that as relevant to the consideration of the circumstances because it may well be that the parties decided that they would have the tenancy on an entirely new basis. There is no evidence about that one way or the other. The terms of the tenancy under the agreement were very different from the terms of the tenancy before it, including the rent, the terms relating to repairs, and so on, but I do take into consideration strongly the fact that the rent was expressed to be the rent of £3 per week and was never calculated by reference to a yearly sum. It was always paid weekly, and, after the term of the agreement had expired, it continued to be paid weekly right up to the time when the notice to quit was given. . . . The notice to quit was served on the basis that the tenancy was a weekly one, and was accepted without question by the tenant. Clearly the tenant's view was that he was holding on a weekly tenancy and not on a yearly tenancy, and I see no reason why that should not be taken into account in deciding whether the presumption of a yearly tenancy has been rebutted. Even if that were not the case, however, I think that, where as here, the original tenancy is not for a period of years, but is for only one year, and where the rent payable is expressed as a weekly sum and not by reference to a yearly rent, the presumption is rebutted that there is a yearly tenancy and the tenant must be taken to be holding over on the basis of a weekly tenancy on the terms of the agreement so far as they are consistent therewith. It follows that the notice was valid and the landlord is entitled to succeed in this action.

[ORMEROD J found it unnecessary to decide the second question. If it had been necessary to decide it, he would have held that the tenant, by claiming a new lease under the Landlord and Tenant Act 1927, had elected to accept the notice and could not now say that it was invalid.]

iii. THE TERMS OF A YEARLY TENANCY

Where a tenant obtains a yearly (or other periodic) tenancy by entry followed by payment of rent in pursuance of an agreement to grant a lease or of a purported grant which is void for lack of a seal, the terms of the tenancy include such of those of the void grant as are consistent with a tenancy for the period in question[20].

iv.   CERTAINTY OF TIME.   REPUGNANCY

CENTAPLOY LTD *v* MATLODGE LTD
[1974] Ch 1, [1973] 2 All ER 720 (ChD, WHITFORD J)

In 1968 the defendant landlords' predecessors in title agreed to let to the plaintiffs a lock-up garage and workshop premises in Ashburn Mews, London on the written terms: "Ground floor garage. Received from Centaploy Ltd the sum of £12 being one week's rent on 25 Ashburn Mews, S.W.7, the tenancy to continue thus on the same terms until determined by the lessee."

In 1971 the defendants purported to determine the tenancy by giving the plaintiffs a week's notice to quit. The question was whether, in view of the terms of the agreement, they were entitled to do so.

Held. The agreement was void for repugnancy, and the notice to quit was valid.

WHITFORD J: The Court of Appeal has held in *Re Midland Railway Co's Agreement* [1971] Ch 725, [1971] 1 All ER 1007[1], that the simple statement of the law that if a term is to be validly created the maximum duration of that term must be ascertained before the term takes effect, cannot have direct application to periodic tenancies. It is, apparently, enough if you know when it could be brought to an end even if you do not know exactly when it will be brought to an end.

The law is evolutionary. In the evolution of life it is common enough to find that forms which were at one time successful have died out completely or changed radically. The defendants accept that a fetter can be placed on the right to determine a periodic tenancy for a certain period. They also accept, in this court, though they expressly reserve the point for a higher court, that, on the authority of *Re Midland Railway Co's Agreement*, it must be accepted here such a fetter can be placed upon the right to determine for an uncertain period. The defendants base themselves further on a decision given by the Court of King's Bench in *Doe d Warner v Browne* (1807) 8 East 165, where it was decided that it was repugnant to the nature of a tenancy from year to year that the right to determine should rest solely with the tenant, a decision approved by the Court of Appeal in *Cheshire Lines Committee v Lewis & Co* (1880) 50 LJQB 121.

Uncertainty and repugnancy were the defendants' main ground of attack assuming agreements in other respects unimpeachable. The submission of the plaintiffs on repugnancy was basically that this must be considered to be a ghost of the past and I was urged to pass on unafraid. In fact both the plaintiffs and the defendants relied upon the judgment of the Court of Appeal in *Re Midland Railway Co's Agreement*, ...

---

[20] *Doe d Rigg v Bell* (1793) 5 Term Rep 471; *Doe d Thomson v Amey* (1840) 12 Ad & El 476; Cheshire, pp. 403–404; M & W, pp. 623, 634–635; MM, pp. 314, 319.
[1] P. 360, ante.

In the present case the position on uncertainty is somewhat different. Here we have a period growing week by week and there is never going to be any possibility of knowing, on the landlord's side, its maximum length, for there is never going to be a right in the landlords to determine.

In *Re Midland Railway Co's Agreement*, counsel for the defendants submitted that a periodic tenancy is only an exception to the uncertainty rule, because if both sides are going to be able to determine there is no relevant uncertainty: see [1971] Ch 725, 730. In the present case a stronger case can be made out on the defendants' side than was made out in *Re Midland Railway Co's Agreement*. It can be urged that as the landlord cannot ever be certain when the agreement is going to be brought to an end there must be a relevant uncertainty. As I understand the judgment in the Court of Appeal, what has been held in relation to the issue of uncertainty is that it is better to enforce a clearly expressed bargain than to attempt to introduce yet further refinements into a field where the lines have perhaps already been rather over-finely drawn. On this basis I have reached the conclusion, having regard to what was said in the Court of Appeal in *Re Midland Railway Co's Agreement*, that I must reject the defendants' argument on the basis of uncertainty which, but for *Re Midland Railway Co's Agreement*, I would have been prepared to accept. . . .

In *Re Midland Railway Co's Agreement* the point which I have to consider — the ghost of the past — was expressly left unlaid. Here we have a case where the tenant is saying that on the bargain struck the landlord cannot ever determine the tenancy.

Now counsel for the plaintiffs was able to say, and to say quite rightly, that great inroads have been made on the application of this idea of repugnancy since 1807, as the passage I have just read shows, and there is no need for me to go into the cases between *Doe d Warner v Browne* and *Re Midland Railway Co's Agreement*, for it is now plain that a fetter for a period, even a period of uncertain duration, cannot necessarily be considered as repugnant to the grant of a periodic tenancy. It nevertheless appears to me that it must be basic to a tenancy that at some stage the person granting the tenancy shall have the right to determine and a tenancy in which the landlord is never going to have the right to determine at all is, as I see it, a complete contradiction in terms. Unless, therefore, some greater estate than a weekly tenancy was created by the agreements, the determination provisions must, in my view, be regarded as repugnant and on this aspect the defendants are entitled to succeed.

v. TENANCY BY ESTOPPEL[2]

In *Webb v Austin* (1844) 7 Man & G 701, TINDAL CJ said at p. 724: "The doctrine on this subject, as it has been generally understood by

---

[2] Spencer Bower and Turner, *The Law Relating to Estoppel by Representation* (3rd edn., 1977) pp. 191-211; Cheshire, pp. 404-405; M & W, pp. 645-648; MM, pp. 324-325; (1964) 80 LQR 370 (A. M. Prichard); *Industrial Properties (Barton Hill) Ltd v Associated Electrical Industries Ltd* [1977] QB 580, [1977] 2 All ER 293, p. 78 ante; (1977) 40 MLR 718 (P. Jackson), [1978] Conv 137 (J. Martin).

the profession, may be collected from Mr. *Preston's Treatise on Abstracts*, vol. ii, p. 210, and the authorities there cited. That general understanding appears to be, that 'An indenture of lease, or a fine *sur concessit*, for years, will be an estoppel only during the term. It first operates by way of estoppel, and finally, when the grantor obtains an ownership, it attaches on the seisin and creates an interest, or produces the relation of landlord and tenant; and there is a term *commencing* by estoppel, but *for all purposes* it becomes an estate or interest. It binds the estate of the lessor, &c., and therefore continues in force against the lessor, his heirs, &c. It also binds the assigns of the lessor and of the lessee'."

CHURCH OF ENGLAND BUILDING SOCIETY *v* PISKOR
[1954] Ch 553, [1954] 2 All ER 85 (CA, EVERSHED MR, BIRKETT and ROMER LJJ)

In September 1946, the defendants contracted to purchase leasehold premises at No. 32, Harold Road, Croydon, and were allowed to go into possession before completion. Early in November they purported to grant a weekly tenancy of part of No. 32 to a Captain Hamilton. On 25 November the purchase was completed by an assignment of the lease to the defendants. On the same day they executed a legal charge in favour of the plaintiffs, which stated that No. 32 "is now vested in the mortgagors free from incumbrances for the unexpired residue of the term", and also that the mortgagor's power of leasing under Law of Property Act 1925, section 99 (1) was excluded. Captain Hamilton then sub-let to Miss Hunnex, who was protected by the Rent Acts. The plaintiffs (the mortgagees) claimed possession on the ground that they had a legal title paramount to her tenancy.

Held (affirming VAISEY J). The plaintiffs were not entitled to possession.

ROMER LJ: I agree. The theory that a purchase, which is completed by payment of money which has been provided in part by a third party, and a mortgage by the purchaser of the property sold to secure the repayment of that money to the lender, constitutes only one transaction, if the instruments are executed at more or less the same time, is a conception which has a prima facie appeal, but it does not, on analysis, in my opinion, truly reflect the legal effect of what takes place. The mortgage of the purchased property cannot have any operation in law (whatever rights it may give rise to in equity or by estoppel) unless and until the purchaser is in a position to vest a legal term in the property, as security, in the mortgagee, and he is not and cannot be in a position to do this until he himself has acquired from the vendor the legal estate out of which the mortgage term is capable of being created. From this it follows that the execution and delivery of the conveyance (if the property is freehold) or of the assignment (in the case of a leasehold) by the vendor to the purchaser must of necessity constitute an essential preliminary to the vesting in the mortgagee of a subsidiary interest in the property. Mr. Lightman pressed upon us the necessity of looking at the substance rather than the form of the transaction which took place in the present case and referred us to such cases as *Meux v Smith* ((1843) 11 Sim 410) in support of that proposition. I am very willing to do so, but the substance of the transaction was that the purchasers were to purchase property with money lent in part by the building society and give the society a mortgage on the property for the loan. All this has in fact been done and the society has got its security but, look at it how one will, the fact remains that the purchasers could not have given the society the legal charge which the society required unless, at the time when the charge was executed, the purchasers were the owners of the legal interest in the property charged. That this was recognised by the society itself is sufficiently shown by the fact that there appears in the schedule to the charge the statement that the premises were then (that is to say, at the moment of the delivery of the charge) vested in the mortgagors — a circumstance of evidence upon which Danckwerts J relied in *Woolwich Equitable Building Society v Marshall*, ([1952] Ch 1). I agree with Danckwerts J that the plaintiffs, having inserted that statement in the charge, cannot very well complain if the statement is regarded as true. Even without this element, however, I should still regard the legal interest in the purchased premises as having become vested in the purchasers prior to the execution of the charge for, as I say, unless this sequence of interests is observed, the charge would have been wholly ineffective in law to achieve its immediate purpose. I agree with Mr. Alcock's submission that a composite transaction cannot be regarded as being one transaction, unless it is not only one but one and indivisible; and that two transactions, each possessing a legal individuality of its own, do not coalesce into one merely because they are dependent on each other.

The whole object of the plaintiffs in trying to displace the view which is both logical and in conformity with conveyancing practice, namely, that the completion of the purchase preceded by however short a time the execution and delivery of the mortgage, is to defeat the claim of the sitting tenants. But for the Rent Restriction Acts the point would have had no importance and would, I suppose, never have been taken at all, for the society could have determined the tenancies by the service of notices to quit; and I find myself unable to treat as one what were, in law, two palpably distinct transactions merely for the purpose of enabling the society to evict persons, who were already in occupation, but whose existence or rights the society had never troubled to inquire about at all. . . .

For the above reasons, and those given by the Master of the Rolls, I agree that the appeal should be dismissed[3].

---

[3] See *Security Trust Co v Royal Bank of Canada* [1976] AC 503, [1976] 1 All ER 381.

vi.   CONCURRENT LEASES[4]

LAW OF PROPERTY ACT 1925

149.   Abolition of interesse termini, and as to reversionary leases and leases for lives. —

(2) See p. 361, ante.

(5) Nothing in this Act affects the rule of law that a legal term, whether or not being a mortgage term, may be created to take effect in reversion expectant on a longer term, which rule is hereby confirmed.

When a landlord grants a lease, and then later grants another lease of the same land (for more or less than the period of the first lease), there are concurrent leases, and he is said to have granted a lease of the reversion[5]. This creates the relationship of landlord and tenant between the first and second lessees; the second lessee does not need to go into possession[6], but, by virtue of his legal estate, he can as reversioner claim rent, distrain, and enforce covenants. This is so, even if the second lease is for a term shorter than the first one[7]. If his lease continues after the end of the first lease, he is entitled to possession when the first lease terminates.

In *Re Moore and Hulm's Contract* [1912] 2 Ch 105, leaseholds were mortgaged by sub-demise for the residue of the original term less one day. Afterwards by another mortgage they were sub-demised to a second mortgagee (Worrell) for the same period, subject to the first mortgage. The second mortgage was paid off during the continuance of the first mortgage and the deed effecting the second mortgage was handed back to the mortgagor. A purchaser of the freeholds from the mortgagor declined to complete without a formal surrender being obtained of the term created by the second mortgage. JOYCE J held that a surrender was necessary: "[Counsel for the vendor] says, first, that there was no necessity or reason for Worrell, the second mortgagee, to surrender the term granted to him by the second mortgage because no legal term or interest passed to him. Bearing in mind, however, the cases cited to me by [counsel for the purchaser], I think that a legal estate or interest did pass to the second mortgagee. I think that Worrell acquired a legal reversion upon the term created by the first mortgage. I think that he got a legal term under his mortgage. If the money secured by the earlier mortgage had been paid to the first mortgagee on the date fixed for payment I think that the second mortgagee would have had a right to the actual possession of the leasehold premises[8], and if the lease granted by the first mortgage had been terminated in any manner during the continuance of the

---

[4] M & W, pp. 648–650.
[5] Distinguish a reversionary lease, p. 361, ante.
[6] L.P.A. 1925, s. 149 (2), p. 361, ante.
[7] *Neale v Mackenzie* (1836) 1M & W 747; *Re Moore and Hulm's Contract* [1912] 2 Ch 105.
[8] For a mortgagee's right to possession, see p. 638, post.

second mortgage, the second mortgagee would have been entitled to possession for the rest of the term created by his mortgage. Therefore I think that the argument for the vendor on the first point fails. . . .

There must be a declaration that the vendor is bound to obtain a surrender of the term created by the second mortgage."

C. Lease to Self

LAW OF PROPERTY ACT 1925

72. Conveyances by a person to himself, &c. —
(3) See p. 73, ante.
(4) See p. 73, ante.

RYE *v* RYE[9]
[1962] AC 496, [1962] 1 All ER 146 (HL, Viscount SIMONDS, Lords MACDERMOTT, REID, RADCLIFFE and DENNING)

In 1942 Arthur Rye, the appellant, and his brother Frank, who were in partnership as solicitors, became owners of freehold premises in London as tenants in common in equal shares. They decided to transfer the practice there and orally agreed that the firm should be granted a yearly tenancy of the premises at a rent of £500 a year to be paid out of the partnership assets. In 1948 Frank died, and the freehold was vested in Arthur and the two trustees of Frank's will, one of whom was Frank's son, Ralph, the respondent. In 1950 Arthur took Ralph into a partnership, which was dissolved in 1957. Ralph refused to leave the premises, where he continued to occupy a room. Arthur claimed possession of the room, on the ground that the firm was the tenant under the oral yearly tenancy of 1942, and that he was the surviving partner.

Held (affirming CA). No tenancy was created in 1942, and, therefore, the claim for possession failed.

VISCOUNT SIMONDS: The first [question] is whether it is competent for two persons orally to grant to themselves an annual tenancy of premises of which they are the owners. . . .

It is common ground, my Lords, that before the Law of Property Act 1925, came into force it could not [be granted]. But the appellant claims that the law has been altered by the combined effect of sections 72 and 205 of that Act. In the courts below the meaning and effect of section 205 (1) (ii)[10] has been the main topic of discussion, and it appears to have been readily assumed that, if "conveyance" includes the oral grant (or agreement to make a grant) of an annual tenancy, then either subsection (3) or subsection (4) of section 72 validates the transaction. I do not differ from those of your Lordships who think that section 205 (1) (ii) has not this effect, nor do I think that any assistance is given by section 52 or section 54. But I would briefly

---

[9] (1962) 78 LQR 175 (P. V. B.), 177 (R. E. M.).
[10] See p. 8, ante.

examine the position if the contrary view prevails and an oral grant of a tenancy is a "conveyance" within the meaning of the Act and "convey" has a corresponding meaning.

I turn, then, to section 72 ... Let me take subsection (4) first. In this subsection I do not find it provided that two persons may convey property to themselves or three persons to themselves. On the contrary, I read the subsection literally as meaning that where property is vested in two persons they may convey it to one of themselves and where it is vested in three persons they may convey it to one or two of themselves. I see no reason for giving a more extended meaning to this subsection, and I would point out that, if it did have the meaning claimed for it, it would add nothing to subsection (3) except to provide a plain inconsistency in respect of the date of commencement. I come back to subsection (3). I accept that in this subsection the singular "person" must include the plural so that two persons may now convey land to, or vest land in, themselves. What, then, is the scope of this subsection? It is said on behalf of the appellant that it enables A., the owner of property, to grant a lease of it to himself and similarly enables A. and B., the joint owners of property, to grant a lease of it to themselves. It was not, I think, suggested that A. and B. could do what A. could not do. The question, then, can conveniently be examined by asking whether the subsection enables A. to grant a lease to himself of land of which he is the owner, or, in other words, to carve out of his larger estate a lesser estate which creates (I know not how to put it otherwise) the relationship of landlord and tenant between himself and himself. I find this a strange conception. In *Grey v Ellison* ((1859) 1 Giff 436, 444), Stuart, V-C describes as fanciful and a whimsical transaction the proposal that a man should grant a lease to himself. He had, no doubt, in mind that a lease is in one aspect contractual. Of things necessary to a lease, says Sheppard's Touchstone of Assurances (see 7th edn., vol II, p. 268), one is that: "There must be an acceptance, [actual or presumed], of the thing demised." Yet it is meaningless to say that a man accepts from himself something which is already his own. I recognise that a lease not only has a contractual basis between lessor and lessee, but operates also to vest an estate in the lessee. But what sort of estate is in these circumstances vested in the lessee? I will assume that it will not at once merge in the higher estate from which it springs, though I see no reason why it should not. Yet it must be an estate hitherto unknown to the law. Even a bare demise implies certain covenants at law: but to such an estate as this no covenants can be effectively attached. Nor can the common law remedy of distress operate to enable the lessor to distrain on his own goods. Again, at law in the absence of some special provision the lessee is entitled to exclusive possession of the demised premises. What meaning is to be attributed to this where the lessee is also the lessor? My Lords, my mind recoils against an interpretation of the Act which leads to so fanciful and whimsical a result, and it appears to me to be quite unnecessary.

If, then, it is asked what meaning can be given to the subsection, I think that the answer is that it is intended partly to supersede the old conveyancing device of a conveyance to uses or of a grant and regrant and partly to provide an essential step in the new machinery set up by the series of Acts passed in 1925. To the latter the word "vest" itself supplies a clue. It appears to refer to the statutory provisions for vesting the legal estate in a tenant for life or statutory owner, which are to be found, for example, in Schedule II, paragraph 1, to the Settled Land Act 1925.

Thirty-five years have now passed since the Law of Property Act came into operation. I have not found in any of the textbooks that I have been able to consult dealing with real property or the relation of landlord and tenant any suggestion that section 72 of the Act has given birth to such a monstrous child . . . I am not prepared in this case to give it currency, and for this reason I would dismiss this appeal.

D. The Position in Equity

Where there is an enforceable agreement to grant a lease, of which equity is prepared, in the circumstances, to grant specific performance, equity (following the maxim that equity looks on that as done which ought to be done) will treat the intended tenant as having already, inequity, a lease. This is so where there is

(i) an agreement evidenced in writing as required by the Law of Property Act 1925, section 40, p. 58, ante; or

(ii) a "void" lease, i.e. a lease in writing for more than three years which is void at law owing to the lack of a seal, but is construed in equity as an agreement for a lease[11], or

(iii) an agreement proved by oral evidence and supported by acts of part performance[12].

E. The Doctrine of Walsh v Lonsdale[13]

This doctrine is one aspect of the general doctrine of estate contracts which is discussed in detail above[14]. A question which is commonly discussed is the extent to which an agreement for a lease is as good as a lease.

F. The Differences between a Lease and an Agreement for a Lease[15]

i. THE BONA FIDE PURCHASER

An agreement for a lease is an equitable interest, and, as such, liable to destruction by a bona fide purchaser of a legal estate for value without notice[16]. The doctrine of the bona fide purchaser is modified, in the case

---

[11] *Parker v Taswell* (1858) 2 De G & J 559; *Bond v Rosling* (1861) 1 B & S 371; *Tidey v Mollett* (1864) 16 CBNS 298.

[12] See p. 62, ante.

[13] (1882) 21 ChD 9. See p. 76, ante.

[14] See pp. 57 et seq., ante.

[15] Cheshire, pp. 394–398; M & W, pp. 626–629; MM, pp. 316–317.

[16] *Pilcher v Rawlins* (1872) 7 Ch App 259, p. 27, ante. Maitland, p. 158; p. 81, ante.

of unregistered land, by the introduction of a system of registration of land charges by the Land Charges Acts 1925-1972[17]; and has no part to play in the context of registered land[18].

ii.   LAW OF PROPERTY ACT 1925, SECTION 62

An agreement for a lease is not a "conveyance" within the meaning of the Law of Property Act 1925, section 62[19].

BORMAN *v* GRIFFITH
[1930] 1 Ch 493 (ChD, MAUGHAM J)

In 1923 James agreed to grant a lease to Borman of a house which was situated in a large park containing a mansion. The house was approached only by the drive leading to the mansion and not by a public road. The agreement contained no express grant of a right of way over the drive. In 1926 James leased the mansion to Griffith for 14 years.

Subsequent to the agreement of 1923, James constructed an unmetalled road to the rear of Borman's house. The road was not adequate for heavy traffic, and was unsuitable for Borman's trade as a poultry dealer, and Borman continued to use the drive. In 1928 Griffith obstructed Borman's use of the drive, and Borman sued to establish his right of way.

Held. (i) Section 62 of the Law of Property Act 1925 did not apply to an agreement for a lease, and the plaintiff could not claim an easement on that ground.

(ii) The plaintiff was entitled to claim the right of way under the rule in *Wheeldon v Burrows* ((1879) 12 ChD 31 (p. 525, post)).

MAUGHAM J: . . . The date of the contract is a date before the coming into force of the Law of Property Act 1925, and is a date at which the Conveyancing Act 1881, was still in force. The plaintiff relies on section 62, subsections 1 and 2 of the Law of Property Act 1925, under which certain general words are deemed to be included in a conveyance, and, in particular, the words "ways . . . reputed to appertain to the land, houses, etc." and "reputed or known as part or parcel of or appurtenant to, the land, houses, etc.": and he asserts that the way along the drive in the front of his house, and the branch drive leading directly to the back of his house, were ways enjoyed with the premises demised by the contract; and he points out that under subsection 6, the section applies to conveyances executed after 31 December 1881, and that "conveyance" is defined in section 205, subsection 1 (ii), to

---

[17] P. 29, ante.

[18] P. 26, ante.

[19] "Conveyance" is defined in L.P.A. 1925, s. 205 (1) (ii), p. 8, ante; s. 62 is set out at p. 530, post. On the operation of this section, see also *Wright v Macadam* [1949] 2 KB 744, [1949] 2 All ER 565; *Goldberg v Edwards* [1950] Ch 247; *Phipps v Pears* [1965] 1 QB 76, [1964] 2 All ER 35; *Ward v Kirkland* [1967] Ch 194, [1966] 1 All ER 609; *Green v Aschco Horticulturist Ltd* [1966] 1 WLR 889, [1966] 2 All ER 232; *White v Taylor* (No. 2) [1969] 1 Ch 160, [1968] 1 All ER 1015 (profit à prendre); *Crow v Wood* [1971] 1 QB 77, [1970] 3 All ER 425; *Penn v Wilkins* (1974) 236 Estates Gazette 203; *Sovmots Investments Ltd v Secretary of State for the Environment* [1979] AC 144, [1977] 2 All ER 385 p. 540, post.

include "a lease ... and every other assurance of property or of an interest therein by any instrument, except a will". . . .

On the whole, I think that it is not a "conveyance", because it is not an "assurance of property or of an interest therein". It is true that, under the decision in *Walsh v Lonsdale* ((1882) 21 ChD 9 at 14) it has been held that, where there is an agreement for a lease under which possession has been given, the tenant holds, for many purposes, as if a lease had actually been granted. [His Lordship then quoted from the judgment of Jessel MR (p. 77, ante and continued:] That is the well known judgment of Sir George Jessel MR, with which Cotton and Lindley LJJ agreed. But no court has yet declared that an agreement for a lease for a term of more than three years is an "assurance". It has to be borne in mind that a lease for any term of more than three years must be by deed, and it is well known that, under section 3 of the Real Property Act 1845, ". . . a lease, required by law to be in writing, of any tenements or hereditaments . . . shall . . . be void at law unless made by deed." (See now section 52 of the Law of Property Act 1925, and the repeal section.)

In my opinion, a contract for a lease exceeding a term of three years does not come within the meaning of the phrase "assurance of property or of an interest therein" as that phrase is used in section 205, subsection 1 (ii), of the Law of Property Act 1925: and accordingly I am unable to construe the agreement of 10 October 1923, as if the general words of section 62 of that Act were included in it . . .

In my view, the principles laid down in such cases as *Wheeldon v Burrows* ((1879) 12 ChD 31); *Brown v Alabaster* ((1887) 37 ChD 490); and *Nicholls v Nicholls* ((1899) 81 LT 811) are applicable. Without going through all those cases in detail, I may state the principle as follows — namely, that where, as in the present case, two properties belonging to a single owner and about to be granted are separated by a common road, or where a plainly visible road exists over the one for the apparent use of the other, and that road is necessary for the reasonable enjoyment of the property, a right to use the road will pass with the quasi-dominant tenement, unless by the terms of the contract that right is excluded: and in my opinion, if the present position were that the plaintiff was claming against the lessor specific performance of the agreement of 10 October 1923, he would be entitled to be given a right of way for all reasonable purposes along the drive, including the part that passes the farm on the way to the orchard.

iii.   AVAILABILITY OF SPECIFIC PERFORMANCE[20]

The doctrine of *Walsh v Lonsdale* is dependent upon the availability of specific performance, which is discretionary.

---

[20] *Coatsworth v Johnson* (1886) 55 LJQB 220, p. 80, ante; *Foster v Reeves* [1892] 2 QB 255; *Cornish v Brook Green Laundry Ltd* [1959] 1 QB 394, [1959] 1 All ER 373, (1959) 75 LQR 168 (R. E. M.); *Kingswood Estate Co Ltd v Anderson* [1963] 2 QB 169, [1962] 3 All ER 593, (1963) 79 LQR 19 (R. E. M.); *Rushton v Smith* [1976] QB 480, [1975] 2 All ER 905; *Industrial Properties (Barton Hill) Ltd v Associated Electrical Industries Ltd* [1977] QB 580, [1977] 2 All ER 293, p. 78, ante. *Warmington v Miller* [1973] QB 877 at 887, [1973] 2 All ER 372; *Bell Street Investments v Wood* (1970) 216 Estates Gazette 585.

iv.   THE EFFECT OF AN ASSIGNMENT. See p. 420, post.

See p. 420, post.

IV.   Remedies of the Landlord

It is not possible, in the available space, to deal with all the landlord's remedies. This section will be confined to a consideration of some of the restrictions upon the landlord's right to recover possession of the demised premises.

A.   Statutory Restrictions on Recovery of Possession[1]

When a lease comes to an end, whether by the expiry of the term or by notice to quit, the landlord's common law right to recover possession is subject to certain statutory restrictions.

> (*a*) The landlord may be liable criminally, under Criminal Law Act 1977, section 6[2], and under Protection from Eviction Act 1977, section 1[3], for unlawful eviction and harassment.
>
> (*b*) The tenant may be protected under the Agricultural Holdings Act 1948, the Landlord and Tenant Act 1954, the Leasehold Reform Act 1967 and the Rent Act 1977.
>
> (*c*) Or, more generally, under the following provisions.

PROTECTION FROM EVICTION ACT 1977[4]

2.   Restriction on re-entry without due process of law. — Where any premises are let as a dwelling on a lease which is subject to a right of re-entry or forfeiture it shall not be lawful to enforce that right other. wise than by proceedings in the court while any person is lawfully residing in the premises or part of them.

3.   Prohibition of eviction without due process of law. — (1) Where any premises have been let as a dwelling under a tenancy which is not a statutorily protected tenancy and —

> (*a*) the tenancy (in this section referred to as the former tenancy) has come to an end, but
>
> (*b*) the occupier continues to reside in the premises or part of them,

it shall not be lawful for the owner to enforce against the occupier, otherwise than by proceedings in the court, his right to recover possession of the premises[5].

---

[1] Cheshire, pp. 463, 468–469, 483; Report of the Committee on the Rent Acts (1971) (Cmnd 4609), pp. 105–106.

[2] The Forcible Entry Acts 1381–1623 were abolished by s. 13. See Law Com. Report, Conspiracy and Criminal Law Reform, Part II (Law Com. No. 76, 1976).

[3] The section does not give rise to a statutory cause of action in tort for damages. *McCall v Abelesz* [1976] QB 585, [1976] 1 All ER 727. Existing remedies in tort are available; s. 1 (5); *Drane v Evangelou* [1978] 1 WLR 455, [1978] 2 All ER 437 (exemplary damages for landlord's "monstrous behaviour").

[4] Farrard, *Protection from Eviction Act 1977* (1978).

[5] *Warder v Cooper* [1970] Ch 495, [1970] 1 All ER 1112.

(2) In this section "the occupier", in relation to any premises, means any person lawfully residing in the premises or part of them at the termination of the former tenancy.

(3) This section shall, with the necessary modifications, apply where the owner's right to recover possession arises on the death of the tenant under a statutory tenancy within the meaning of the Rent Act 1977 or the Rent (Agriculture) Act 1976[6].

5. Validity of notices to quit. — (1) No notice by a landlord or a tenant to quit any premises let (whether before or after the commencement of this Act) as a dwelling shall be valid unless —

(a) it is in writing and contains such information as may be prescribed, and

(b) it is given not less than 4 weeks before the date on which it is to take effect.

(2) In this section "prescribed" means prescribed by regulations made by the Secretary of State by statutory instrument, and a statutory instrument containing any such regulations shall be subject to annulment in pursuance of a resolution of either House of Parliament[7].

(3) Regulations under this section may make different provision in relation to different descriptions of lettings and different circumstances.

8. Interpretation. — (1) In this Act "statutorily protected tenancy" means —

(a) a protected tenancy within the meaning of the Rent Act 1977 or a tenancy to which Part I of the Landlord and Tenant Act 1954 applies;

(b) a protected occupancy or statutory tenancy as defined in the Rent (Agriculture) Act 1976;

(c) a tenancy to which Part II of the Landlord and Tenant Act 1954 applies;

(d) a tenancy of an agricultural holding within the meaning of the Agricultural Holdings Act 1948.

(2) For the purposes of Part I of this Act a person who, under the terms of his employment, had exclusive possession of any premises other than as a tenant shall be deemed to have been a tenant and the expressions "let" and "tenancy" shall be construed accordingly.

(3) In Part I of this Act "the owner", in relation to any premises, means the person who, as against the occupier, is entitled to possession thereof.

9. The court for purposes of Part I. — (3) Nothing in this Act shall affect the jurisdiction of the High Court in proceedings to enforce a lessor's right of re-entry of forfeiture[8] or to enforce a mortgagee's right

---

[6] S. 4 contains special provisions for agricultural employees.

[7] See Notice to Quit (Prescribed Information) (Protected Tenancies and Part VI Contracts) Regulations 1975 (S.I. 1975 No. 2196).

[8] *Borźak v Ahmed* [1965] 2 QB 320, [1965] 1 All ER 808.

of possession in a case where the former tenancy was not binding on the mortgagee[9].

B.   Forfeiture and Relief against Forfeiture[10]

A lease usually includes a forfeiture clause which provides for the landlord's right to forfeit the remainder of the lease if there is a breach by the tenant of any covenants in the lease.

Unlimited application of such a clause could inflict hardship on the tenant out of all proportion to the damage suffered by the landlord. For example, a tenant, who is in arrears with his rent, may subsequently pay everything that is due with interest; a breach of a covenant to insure may cause no loss to the landlord, but it used to be treated as sufficient to produce forfeiture under a forfeiture clause.

It has long been settled that equity will relieve a tenant against forfeiture in respect of non-payment of rent, but as a general rule not in other cases. The position is now regulated by statute.

i.   NON-PAYMENT OF RENT

COMMON LAW PROCEDURE ACT 1852

210. Proceedings in ejectment by landlord for non-payment of rent. — In all cases between landlord and tenant, as often as it shall happen that one half year's rent shall be in arrear, and the landlord or lessor, to whom the same is due, hath right by law to re-enter for the non-payment thereof, such landlord or lessor shall and may without any formal demand or re-entry, serve a writ in ejectment for the recovery of the demised premises, which service shall stand in the place and stead of a demand and re-entry[11]; and in case of judgment against the defendant for non-appearance, if it shall be made appear to the court where the said action is depending, by affidavit, or be proved upon the trial in case the defendant appears, that half a year's rent was due before the said writ was served, and that no sufficient distress was to be found on the demised premises, countervailing the arrears then due, and that the lessor had power to re-enter, then and in every such case the lessor shall recover judgment and execution, in the same manner as if the rent in arrear had been legally demanded, and a re-entry made; and in case the lessee or his assignee, or other person claiming or deriving under the said lease, shall permit and suffer judgment to be had and recovered on such trial in ejectment, and execution to be executed thereon, without paying the rent and arrears, together with full costs, and without proceeding for relief in equity within six months after such execution executed, then and in such case the said lessee, his assignee, and all other persons claiming and deriving under the said lease, shall be barred and foreclosed from all

---

[9] See p. 636, post.
[10] Cheshire, pp. 435–449; M & W, pp. 654–667; MM, pp. 326–333.
[11] See *Canas Property Co Ltd v KL Television Services Ltd* [1970] 2 QB 433, [1970] 2 All ER 795; *Richards v De Freitas* (1975) 29 P & CR 1.

relief or remedy in law or equity, other than by bringing error for reversal of such judgment, in case the same shall be erroneous, and the said landlord or lessor shall from thenceforth hold the said demised premises discharged from such lease . . .

211. Lessee proceeding in equity not to have injunction or relief without payment of rent and costs. — In case the said lessee, his assignee, or other person claiming any right, title, or interest, in law or equity, of, in, or to the said lease, shall, within the time aforesaid, proceed for relief in any court of equity, such person shall not have or continue any injunction against the proceedings at law on such eject-ment, unless he does or shall, within forty days next after a full and perfect answer shall be made by the claimant in such ejectment, bring into court, and lodge with the proper officer such sum and sums of money as the lessor or landlord shall in his answer swear to be due and in arrear over and above all just allowances, and also the costs taxed in the said suit, there to remain till the hearing of the cause, or to be paid out to the lessor or landlord on good security, subject to the decree of the court; and in case such proceedings for relief in equity shall be taken within the time aforesaid, and after execution is executed, the lessor or landlord shall be accountable only for so much and no more as he shall really and bona fide, without fraud, deceit, or wilful neglect, make of the demised premises from the time of his entering into the actual possession thereof; and if what shall be so made by the lessor or landlord happen to be less than the rent reserved on the said lease, then the said lessee or his assignee, before he shall be restored to his possession, shall pay such lessor or landlord what the money so by him made fell short of the reserved rent for the time such lessor or landlord held the said lands[12].

212. Tenant paying all rent, with costs, proceedings to cease. — If the tenant or his assignee do or shall, at any time before the trial in such ejectment, pay or tender to the lessor or landlord, his executors or administrators, or his or their attorney in that cause, or pay into the court where the same cause is depending, all the rent and arrears[13], together with the costs, then and in such case all further proceedings on the said ejectment shall cease and be discontinued; and if such lessee, his executors, administrators, or assigns, shall, upon such proceedings as aforesaid, be relieved in equity, he and they shall have, hold, and enjoy the demised lands, according to the lease thereof made, without any new lease.

LAW OF PROPERTY ACT 1925

146. Restrictions on and relief against forfeiture of leases and underleases. — (4) p. 397, post.

---

[12] The granting of relief is discretionary. *Stanhope v Haworth* (1886) 3 TLR 34.
[13] *Standard Pattern Co Ltd v Ivey* [1962] Ch 432, [1962] 1 All ER 452 (limiting the tenant's right to cases where at least half a year's rent is in arrear); (1962) 78 LQR 168 (R. E. Megarry).

SUPREME COURT OF JUDICATURE (CONSOLIDATION) ACT 1925

46.   Relief against forfeiture for non-payment of rent. — In the case of any action for a forfeiture brought for non-payment of rent, the High Court or a judge thereof shall have power to give relief in a summary manner, and subject to the same terms and conditions in all respects as to payment of rent, costs, and otherwise as could formerly have been imposed in the Court of Chancery, and if the lessee, his executors, administrators or assigns are so relieved they shall hold the demised premises according to the terms of the lease and without the necessity of any new lease.

In *Belgravia Insurance Co Ltd v Meah* [1964] 1 QB 436, [1963] 3 All ER 828, Lord DENNING MR reviewed the law relating to the right to relief for non-payment of rent and said at p. 443:

"The first thing to notice is that the ground of forfeiture was *for non-payment of rent*. Relief from such a forfeiture is treated differently from relief for other breaches, such as disrepair and so forth. In case of non-payment of rent, relief is still based fundamentally on the jurisdiction of Courts of Equity to grant relief, subject to the limitations imposed by sections 210 and 212 of the Common Law Procedure Act 1852. In case of other breaches, relief is based on section 146 of the Law of Property Act 1925.

In the case of a *lessee* himself seeking relief from forfeiture for non-payment for rent, the relevant principles have been stated recently by this court in *Gill v Lewis* ([1956] 2 QB 1, [1956] 1 All ER 844). But here we are concerned with the position of an *under-lessee* to whom somewhat different considerations apply. I say an *under-lessee* because, although the applicant is a *mortgagee* holding a charge by way of legal mortgage, he is to be treated as if he held a mortgage by sub-demise (see section 87 of the Law of Property Act 1925, and *Grand Junction Co Ltd v Bates* ([1954] 2 QB 160, [1954] 2 All ER 385)), that is, as if he was an under-lessee[14].

When an under-lessee or a mortgagee by sub-demise (as all mortgagees are now) claims relief from *forfeiture for non-payment of rent*, he can *either* claim under the equitable jurisdiction (which is preserved by section 46 of the Judicature Act of 1925) *or* under section 146 (4) of the Law of Property Act 1925. The applicant claimed under both. It was suggested before us that there was some difference between the principles applicable. I do not think there is. I will deal with them separately.

First, the application under section 46 of the Judicature Act of 1925.

The jurisdiction to give relief under section 46 of the Judicature Act of 1925 is founded on the jurisdiction of the old Court of Chancery. The Court of Chancery from its earliest days held that, wherever

---

[14] P. 603, post.

the court could fully compensate the party entitled for breach of a condition, i.e., wherever it could ensure that the party would get all that was due to him, it would grant relief against a forfeiture. It was so held in 1682 by Lord Nottingham LC, in *Popham v Bampfeild* ((1682) 1 Vern 79, 83), and in 1707 by Lord Cowper LC, in *Grimston v Lord Bruce* ((1707) 1 Salk 156). In accordance with this principle it granted relief not only to lessees, but also to under-lessees and to mortgagees by assignment or by sub-demise, provided always that all the covenants were performed. A good instance was in 1689 when the then Lord Salisbury granted a lease at a certain rent and the lessee convenanted to repair. The lessee granted a hundred under-leases to a hundred sub-tenants. The lessee did not pay the rent nor perform the covenant to repair. So Lord Salisbury re-entered. Six out of the one hundred sub-tenants applied for relief, joining the lessee and Lord Salisbury as parties. The court granted relief on the terms that the six sub-tenants *paid the whole rent in arrear and repaired the premises*: see *Webber v Smith* ((1689) 2 Vern 103)[15]. It would seem that the principle of that case was applied to mortgagees, whether by assignment or by sub-demise. For it was expressly recognised by the legislature in the Landlord and Tenant Act 1730. . . . In 1852 the statute was re-enacted in virtually the same terms in section 210 of the Common Law Procedure Act 1852. In 1860, by section 1 of the Common Law Procedure Act 1860, the courts of common law were given the same powers as the Court of Chancery. And in 1895, when the common law courts came to apply these powers, they applied them in precisely the same way as the Courts of Chancery had done. In *Newbolt v Bingham* ((1895) 72 LT 852) the lessee was in arrear with his rent and had let the premises fall into disrepair. The landlord forfeited the lease for non-payment of rent. A mortgagee by sub-demise applied for relief and he was granted it *on condition that he paid all rent in arrear and did all the repairs and paid all the costs.* . . .

The principle was thus clearly established that, in case of forfeiture for non-payment of rent, a Court of Chancery would, in the ordinary way, grant relief to an under-lessee or a mortgagee by sub-demise, if he paid all the rent in arrear and performed all the covenants and paid all the costs. The court, however, as a rule only granted relief if the original lessee was made a party (see *Hare v Elms* ([1893] 1 QB 604)) though this rule could be relaxed for good cause: see *Humphreys v Morten* ([1905] 1 Ch 739).

Secondly, the application under section 146 (4) of the Law of Property Act 1925.

During the nineteenth century it was held (following Lord Eldon, L.C.'s views in *Hill v Barclay* ((1810) 16 Ves 402, 405; see p. 407, post)). that the Court of Chancery had no jurisdiction to grant a lessee relief

---

[15] Compare *Chatham Empire Theatre* (1955) *Ltd v Ultrans Ltd* [1961] 1 WLR 817, [1961] 2 All ER 381, where SALMON J, without referring to *Webber v Smith*, granted relief on payment of a proportionate share by the applicant sub-lessees.

from forfeiture for any breaches except non-payment of rent. This was remedied in 1881 by section 14 of the Conveyancing Act 1881 (which did not apply to non-payment of rent). But that section did not apply to under-lessees. So Parliament enacted section 4 of the Conveyancing Act 1892, so as to include them. But this section was held to apply, not only to other breaches, but also to non-payment of rent: see *Gray v Bonsall* ([1904] 1 KB 601). In 1925 the whole law, as so evolved, was consolidated in section 146 of the Law of Property Act 1925. Section 146 (4) enabled the court to grant relief to an under-lessee, not only in case of other breaches but also non-payment of rent, on such conditions 'as the court in the circumstances of each case may think fit'. It seems to me that, in exercising this discretion, the court will, in the ordinary way, grant relief to an under-lessee on the terms of paying the rent in arrear, performing the covenants, and paying all the costs: see *Gray v Bonsall* (ibid., at p. 608), *per* Romer LJ. In short, on the same terms as the old Court of Chancery would have done. The only difference is that it is not necessary to make the lessee a party.

Thirdly, power to refuse relief.

In any case, whether under the old Chancery jurisdiction or under section 146 (4) of the Law of Property Act 1925, it is clear that the court may always refuse relief, if the conduct of the applicant is such as to make it inequitable that relief should be given to him: see *Bowser v Colby* ((1841), 1 Hare 109, 134) *per* Wigram V-C, and *Gill v Lewis*, ([1956] 2 QB 1, 17) *per* Hodson LJ[16].''

ii.   BREACH OF COVENANTS OTHER THAN NON-PAYMENT OF RENT

Before a landlord can enforce a right of forfeiture for breach of covenant other than one for the payment of rent, he must serve a notice on the tenant under section 146 (1) of the Law of Property Act 1925. Whether a breach is capable of remedy under para. (*b*) has given rise to difficulty. If the covenant is positive, e.g. to repair, the breach is clearly capable of remedy. In the case of a negative covenant, the Court of Appeal held in *Scala House and District Property Co Ltd v Forbes* [1974] QB 575, [1973] 3 All ER 308, that the breach of a covenant not to assign underlet or part with possession was incapable of remedy. "It is a complete breach once for all[17].'' The Court also considered that the breach of a user covenant, e.g. not to use the premises for illegal or immoral purposes, where the user has ceased before the service of a section 146 notice, is also incapable of remedy. Hitherto the test applicable to such breaches had been whether or not the stigma attaching to the premises could be removed by mere cesser of

---

[16] See *Lovelock v Margo* [1963] 2 QB 786, [1963] 2 All ER 13, holding that, under the ancient jurisdiction of the Court of Chancery, the court has power, independent of statute, to grant relief from forfeiture where there has been a peaceable entry. *Public Trustee v Westbrook* [1965] 1 WLR 1160, [1965] 3 All ER 398; *Thatcher v C. H. Pearce & Sons (Contractors) Ltd* [1968] 1 WLR 748 (tenant granted relief, in spite of bringing action six months and four days after landlord regained possession).

[17] At p. 588, per RUSSELL LJ, p. 404, post.

the immoral or illegal user[18]. It might be preferable to revert to the "attractive and easy[19]" ratio of Mackinnon J in *Rugby School (Governors) v Tannahill*[20] and to hold that all negative covenants are incapable of remedy, and that recovery of possession by the landlord depends solely on whether the tenant can persuade the court to grant relief from forfeiture under section 146 (2).

LAW OF PROPERTY ACT 1925

146. Restrictions on and relief against forfeiture of leases and under-leases. — (1) A right of re-entry or forfeiture under any proviso or stipulation in a lease for a breach of any covenant or condition in the lease shall not be enforceable, by action or otherwise, unless and until the lessor serves on the lessee a notice —

(a) specifying the particular breach complained of; and

(b) if the breach is capable of remedy, requiring the lessee to remedy the breach; and

(c) in any case, requiring the lessee to make compensation in money for the breach;

and the lessee fails, within a reasonable time thereafter, to remedy the breach, if it is capable of remedy, and to make reasonable compensation in money, to the satisfaction of the lessor, for the breach.

(2) Where a lessor is proceeding[1], by action or otherwise[2], to enforce such a right of re-entry or forfeiture, the lessee[3] may, in the lessor's action, if any, or in any action brought by himself, apply to the court for relief; and the court may grant or refuse relief, as the court, having regard to the proceedings and conduct of the parties under the foregoing provisions of this section, and to all the other circumstances, thinks fit; and in case of relief may grant it on such terms, if any, as to costs, expenses, damages, compensation, penalty, or otherwise, including the granting of an injuction to restrain any like breach in the future, as the court, in the circumstances of each case, thinks fit.

(4) Where a lessor is proceeding by action or otherwise to enforce a right of re-entry or forfeiture under any convenant, proviso, or stipulation in a lease, or for non-payment of rent, the court may, on

---

[18] *Rugby School (Governors) v Tannahill* [1935] 1 KB 87, p. 401, post. *Egerton v Esplanade Hotels, London Ltd* [1947] 2 All ER 88; *Hoffmann v Fineberg* [1949] Ch 245, [1948] 1 All ER 592; *Borthwick-Norton v Romney Warwick Estates Ltd* [1950] 1 All ER 798; *Glass v Kencakes Ltd* [1966] 1 QB 611, [1964] 3 All ER 807, p. 402, post.

[19] *Hoffmann v Fineberg* [1949] Ch 245, [1948] 1 All ER 592, per HARMAN J.

[20] [1934] 1 KB 695, 700–701.

[1] The right to relief, unlike that in respect of breach of a covenant to pay rent, terminates upon re-entry by the lessor. *Rogers v Rice* [1892] 2 Ch 170. The lessor may not, of course, re-enter without serving the notice required by sub-s. (1).

[2] I.e., by the service of a notice under s. 146. *Pakwood Transport Ltd v 15 Beauchamp Place Ltd* (1978) 36 P & CR 112.

[3] Where there are joint lessees, relief cannot be granted on the application of only one of them *T. M. Fairclough & Sons Ltd v Berliner* [1931] 1 Ch 60.

application by any person claiming as under-lessee any estate or interest in the property comprised in the lease or any part thereof, either in the lessor's action (if any) or in any action brought by such person for that purpose, make an order vesting, for the whole term of the lease or any less term, the property comprised in the lease or any part thereof in any person entitled as under-lessee to any estate or interest in such property upon such conditions as to execution of any deed or other document, payment of rent, costs, expenses, damages, compensation, giving security, or otherwise, as the court in the circumstances of each case may think fit, but in no case shall any such under-lessee be entitled to require a lease to be granted to him for any longer term than he had under his original sub-lease.

(5) For the purposes of this section —

(a) "Lease" includes an original or derivative under-lease; also an agreement for a lease where the lessee has become entitled to have his lease granted; also a grant at a fee farm rent, or securing a rent by condition;

(b) "Lessee" includes an original or derivative under-lessee, and the persons deriving title under a lessee; also a grantee under any such grant as aforesaid and the persons deriving title under him;

(c) "Lessor" includes an original or derivative under-lessor, and the persons deriving title under a lessor; also a person making such grant as aforesaid and the persons deriving title under him;

(d) "Under-lease" includes an agreement for an under-lease where the under-lessee has become entitled to have his under-lease granted;

(e) "Under-lessee" includes any person deriving title under an under-lessee.

(8) This section does not extend —

(i) To a convenant or condition against assigning, underletting, parting with the possession, or disposing of the land leased where the breach occurred before the commencement of this Act; or

(ii) In the case of a mining lease, to a covenant or condition for allowing the lessor to have access to or inspect books, accounts, records, weighing machines or other things, or to enter or inspect the mine or the workings thereof.

(9) This section does not apply to a condition for forfeiture on the bankruptcy of the lessee[4] or on taking in execution of the lessee's interest if contained in a lease of —

(a) Agricultural or pastoral land;

(b) Mines or minerals;

---

[4] But it does apply on the bankruptcy of a lessee's surety; *Halliard Property Co Ltd v Jack Segal Ltd* [1978] 1 WLR 377, [1978] 1 All ER 1219.

   (*c*) A house used or intended to be used as a public-house or beershop;

   (*d*) A house let as a dwelling-house, with the use of any furniture, books, works of art, or other chattels not being in the nature of fixtures;

   (*e*) Any property with respect to which the personal qualifications of the tenant are of importance for the preservation of the value or character of the property[5], or on the ground of neighbourhood to the lessor, or to any person holding under him.

(10) Where a condition of forfeiture on the bankruptcy of the lessee or on taking in execution of the lessee's interest is contained in any lease, other than a lease of any of the classes mentioned in the last subsection, then —

   (*a*) if the lessee's interest is sold within one year from the bankruptcy or taking in execution, this section applies to the forfeiture condition aforesaid;

   (*b*) if the lessee's interest is not sold before the expiration of that year, this section only applies to the forfeiture condition aforesaid during the first year from the date of the bankruptcy or taking in execution.

(11) This section does not, save as otherwise mentioned, affect the law relating to re-entry or forfeiture or relief in case of non-payment of rent.

(12) This section has effect notwithstanding any stipulation to the contrary.

LANDLORD AND TENANT ACT 1927

18. Provisions as to covenants to repair. — (2) A right of re-entry or forfeiture for a breach of any such covenant or agreement as aforesaid shall not be enforceable, by action or otherwise, unless the lessor proves that the fact that such a notice as is required by section one hundred and forty-six of the Law of Property Act, 1925, had been served on the lessee was known either —

   (*a*) to the lessee; or

   (*b*) to an under-lessee holding under an under-lease which reserved a nominal reversion only to the lessee; or

   (*c*) to the person who last paid the rent due under the lease either on his own behalf or as agent for the lessee or under-lessee;

and that a time reasonably sufficient to enable the repairs to be executed had elapsed since the time when the fact of the service of the notice came to the knowledge of any such person.

   Where a notice has been sent by registered post[6] addressed to a person at his last known place of abode in the United Kingdom, then,

---

[5] *Earl of Bathurst v Fine* [1974] 1 WLR 905, [1974] 2 All ER 1160, (1974) 90 LQR 441.

[6] The recorded delivery service may be used as an alternative to registered post; Recorded Delivery Service Act 1962, s. 1 (1).

for the purposes of this subsection, that person shall be deemed, unless the contrary is proved, to have had knowledge of the fact that the notice had been served as from the time at which the letter would have been delivered in the ordinary course of post.

This subsection shall be construed as one with section one hundred and forty-six of the Law of Property Act, 1925.

LAW OF PROPERTY (AMENDMENT) ACT 1929

1. Relief of under-lessees against breach of covenant. — Nothing in subsection (8), subsection (9) or subsection (10) of section one hundred and forty-six of the Law of Property Act, 1925 ... shall affect the provisions of subsection (4) of the said section.

In the case of a covenant "to keep or put the premises in repair," there are further provisions, under the Leasehold Property (Repairs) Act 1938[7]. "This Act applies to premises, other than an agricultural holding, which have been let for a period of not less than seven years, of which at least three years remain unexpired. The landlord must serve on the tenant a notice under section 146 of the Law of Property Act 1925 not less than one month before the commencement of the action, and inform him in that notice of his right to serve a counter-notice[8]. The tenant may within 28 days of receiving the notice serve a counter-notice on the landlord claiming the benefit of the Act.

The effect of a counter-notice is that no proceedings whatsoever may be taken by the landlord for the enforcement of any right of re-entry or forfeiture, or for the recovery of damages, in respect of a breach of the repairing covenant, unless he first obtains the leave of the County Court"[9].

SCALA HOUSE AND DISTRICT PROPERTY CO LTD v FORBES[10]
[1974] QB 575, [1973] 3 All ER 308 (CA, RUSSELL and JAMES LJJ and PLOWMAN J)

By a lease dated February 1968, the lessees convenanted not to assign underlet or part with the possession of a shop in Dean Street, London, without the permission of the landlords. The lease contained a proviso for re-entry on breach of covenant. In March the lease was assigned to the first defendant with the landlords' consent. He used

---

[7] As amended by Landlord and Tenant Act 1954, s. 51 (1).
[8] *Middlegate Properties Ltd v Messimeris* [1973] 1 WLR 168, [1973] 1 All ER 645; *BL Holdings Ltd v Marcott Investments Ltd* (1979) 249 Estates Gazette 849.
[9] Cheshire, p. 445. For the special provisions relating to internal decorative repair see L.P.A. 1925, s. 147.
[10] (1973) 89 LQR 460 (P.V.B.), (1973) 37 Conv (NS) 445 (D. Macintyre); *David Blackstone Ltd v Burnetts (West End) Ltd* [1973] 1 WLR 1487, [1973] 3 All ER 782.

the premises as a restaurant, and then in November entered into an agreement with Pierto and Elisa Delpoio, the second and third defendants, to manage the restaurant for him. This agreement, which was intended to be a management agreement, in fact created a sublease in breach of the covenant. The plaintiff, who had acquired the reversion of the lease, served on the defendants[11] a notice under Law of Property Act 1925, section 146 (1), requiring them to remedy the breach, and 14 days later then issued a writ for possession. NIELD J held that the breach was capable of remedy, and since 14 days was insufficient time for the defendants to remedy the breach, dismissed the action. On appeal by the plaintiff.

Held. (i) The breach was not capable of remedy, and therefore 14 days was a sufficient time.

(ii) Relief from forfeiture was granted to the first defendant.

RUSSELL LJ: It is a remarkable fact that this case raises questions under section 146 of the Law of Property Act 1925, which, except in a case at first instance reported only in the Estates Gazette Digest[12], have never been considered for decision . . .

So the first question is whether a breach of covenant such as is involved in the present case is capable of remedy. If it is capable of remedy, and is remedied in reasonable time, the lessor is unable to prove that a condition precedent to his ability to seek to forfeit by action or otherwise has been fulfilled. Here at once is a problem. An unlawful subletting is a breach once and for all. The subterm has been created.

I turn to the authorities. In *Jackson v Simons* [1923] 1 Ch 373 there was a breach of a covenant against sharing the premises let: such a breach was not excluded from section 14 of the Act of 1881: no notice at all was served before the writ for possession issued and this was fatal to the action. The sharing apparently ended shortly after the writ: but there was no discussion whether a subsequent notice based on a "past" breach, followed by a writ, would have resulted in either forfeiture or relief. *Rugby School (Governors) v Tannahill* [1935] 1 KB 87 was a case of user by the lessee for immoral purposes contrary to covenant in the lease sought to be forfeited. Apparently before the section 146 notice the prostitutes had left and the premises had ceased to be used for immoral purposes. The notice did not call upon the lessee to remedy the breach. At first instance the judge decided in favour of the lessor on the short ground that breach of a negative covenant could never be remedied. This court did not call upon counsel for the lessor, who thus had no opportunity to support the judge's short ground: this court expressed the view that breach of negative covenants might be capable of remedy, but not this one, on the ground that the stigma attaching to the premises would not be removed by mere cesser of the immoral user. I observe that it does not appear to have been con-

---

[11] It is not sufficient to serve the notice on the assignor only; *Old Grovebury Manor Farm Ltd v W. Seymour Plant Sales and Hire Ltd* (No. 2) [1979] 1 WLR 1397; [1979] 3 All ER 504.

[12] *Capital and Counties Property Co Ltd v Mills*, [1966] EGD 96.

sidered whether the breach in that case was incapable of remedy on another ground, viz.: that the wrongful user had ceased before the section 146 notice. It might perhaps be argued that reliance by this court on the "stigma" point suggests that it was considered that a wrongful user in breach wholly in the past, without continuing adverse effect, would not entitle the lessor to seek to forfeit at all. But the question does not seem to have been canvassed.

[His Lordship referred to *Borthwick-Norton v Romney Warwick Estates Ltd* [1950] 1 All ER 798; and continued:]

In *Hoffmann v Fineberg* [1949] Ch 245, [1948] 1 All ER 592 (Harman J), the lessee, in breach of user covenants, allowed the premises to be used for illegal gambling, for which there were convictions. The section 146 notice did not call for the breach to be remedied. It is not clear whether the illegal user continued at the date of the notice. Again the decision was based on the "stigma" aspect as making the breach incapable of remedy within a reasonable time. Harman J said, at p. 257: ". . . on the facts of this case this is a breach where mere cesser is no remedy." The judgment referred to another immoral user case of *Egerton v Esplanade Hotels London Ltd* [1947] 2 All ER 88 (Morris J), in which the notice did not call for the breach to be remedied: it was decided on the stigma point, on the facts of that case, that the breach was not capable of remedy within a reasonable time. Morris J said, at p. 91: "Merely desisting from the wrongful user or not continuing to commit further breaches is not, . . . on the facts of this case, a way of remedying the breach." Neither case was considered on the possible shorter ground that a user covenant breach when the user had ceased before the section 146 notice was incapable of remedy for that very reason.

Glass v Kencakes Ltd [1966] 1 QB 611, [1964] 3 All ER 807, a decision of Paull J, was of this nature. The lease forbade the use of the upper part of the premises otherwise than for residential purposes. The lessee sublet that part to D, who caused and permitted their use for the business of prostitution unknown to the lessee. The sublease contained a similar covenant. The section 146 notice was simply based upon the fact of business use. It asserted that the breach was incapable of remedy. The judge held that the breach of the sublease by D was incapable of remedy by him: apparently he considered that the person who caused or permitted such a use could not, by the cesser of such use, remedy the breach, because the stigma on the premises could not be blotted out within a reasonable time so long as the man responsible remained subtenant. He therefore could not remedy his breach. Paull J pointed out that in the *Rugby School* case, [1934] 1 KB 695, in *Egerton v Esplanade Hotels London Ltd* [1947] 2 All ER 88 (both cases of immoral user) and in *Hoffmann v Fineberg* [1949] Ch 245, [1948] 1 All ER 592 (the illegal gambling case) it was in each case the tenant under the lease sought to be forfeited who was directly responsible for the breach: and that in the *Borthwick-Norton* case, [1950] 1 All ER 798 the lessee had in breach suffered and permitted the immoral user by a subtenant. Paull J decided, however, that where the breach alleged was merely of a user by a subtenant for which the lessee whose lease was sought to be forfeited could not be said to have permitted or suffered or to be in any way responsible for, the breach was not incapable of remedy by that lessee, the remedy required being not only the cesser of the user in breach but also the ending of the subterm with all expedition by forfeiture. Paull J was much impressed by the argument that where there was a lease for a large block of flats, one of which, without any fault of the lessee, was used for a short time in breach of the user covenant in the lease by a subtenant, he should not be put in the situation that he was not capable of remedying the breach and must therefore be put to the expense of seeking relief from forfeiture. He held in that case that the notice was bad since it asserted that the breach was not capable of remedy.

Two points are to be noticed in that case. First: Paull J did not address his mind, particularly in the case of the large block of flats mentioned, to the possible situation of the lessee if the subletting in question, and therefore the unlawful user, had come to an end before discovery by the head lessor, when no remedial step would have been available to the lessee, and whether in such case the lessee could only have sought relief. Second: the decision in terms says nothing of a case (other than "stigma" cases) where the lessee is directly responsible for the breach by a business user contrary to covenant. . . .

In summary upon the cases we have therefore a number of cases of user of premises in breach of covenant in which the decision that the breach is not capable of remedy has gone upon the "stigma" point, without considering whether a short answer might be — if the user had ceased before the section 146 notice — that it was ex hypothesi incapable of remedy, leaving the lessee only with the ability to seek relief from forfeiture and the writ unchallengeable as such. If a user in breach has ceased before the section 146 notice (quite apart from the stigma cases) then either it is incapable of remedy and after notice there is nothing in the way of a writ: or the cesser of use has somehow deprived the lessor of his ability to seek to forfeit though he has done nothing to waive the breach, a situation in law which I find extremely difficult to spell out of section 146. But whatever may be the position in user breach cases, which are of a continuing nature, there is no authority, other than that of *Capital and Counties Property Co Ltd v Mills* [1966] EGD 96 to suggest that the creation of a subterm in breach of covenant is capable of remedy. I would make two particular comments on that decision, as reported. First: I find it difficult to see how a breach is said to be capable of remedy because the lessor can waive the breach, which would be involved in the suggestion that he could post hoc consent to the subletting. Second: I do not see how a breach by unlawful subletting can be said to be remedied by the lessee when he does nothing except wait for the subterm to come to an end by effluxion of time.

After this review of the cases I come to the conclusion that breach by an unlawful subletting is not capable of remedy at all. In my judgment the introduction of such breaches into the relevant section for the first time by section 146 of the Act of 1925 operates only to confer a statutory ability to relieve the lessee from forfeiture on that ground. The subterm has been effectively created subject only to risks of forfeiture: it is a complete breach once for all: it is not in any sense a continuing breach. If the law were otherwise a lessee, when a subtenancy is current at the time of the section 146 notice, would have a chance of remedying the situation without having to apply for relief. But if the unlawful subletting had determined before the notice, the lessee could only seek relief from forfeiture. The only escape from that wholly unsatisfactory difference would be to hold that in the second example by some analogy the lessor was disabled from issuing a writ for possession. But I can find nothing in the section to justify that limitation on the common law right of re-entry, bearing especially in mind that a lessor might discover a whole series of past expired unlawful sublettings which might well justify a refusal to grant relief in forfeiture proceedings.

I stress again that where there has been an unlawful subletting which has determined (and which has not been waived) there has been a breach which at common law entitles the lessor to re-enter: nothing can be done to remedy that breach: the expiry of the subterm has not annulled or remedied the breach: in such case the lessor plainly need not, in his section 146 notice, call upon the lessee to remedy the breach which is not capable of remedy, and is free to issue his writ for possession, the possibility of relief remaining. Can it possibly be that, while that is the situation in such case, it is otherwise if the lessee has failed to get rid of the subterm until after a notice served? Is the lessee then in a stronger position and the lessor in a weaker position? In my judgment not so. These problems and questions arise only if such a breach is capable of remedy, which in my judgment it is not. I consider that *Capital and Counties Property Co Ltd v Mills* [1966] EGD 96, if correctly reported, was wrongly decided. I should add that I find some support for my opinion in the comments of Fraser J in *Abrahams v Mac Fisheries Ltd* [1925] 2 KB 18, 35, who expressed the view that the exceptions in section 14 (6) of the Act of 1881 (as to, inter alia, subletting) were made to cover cases where the breach cannot be remedied specifically.

In those circumstances in judging whether the 14 days that here elapsed between the section 146 notice and the writ, the time which it might reasonably take the lessee to come to terms with the subtenants, the second and third defendants, so as to end the subterm, which in fact was done in June 1972, is irrelevant. In those circumstances it is in my view plain that the writ was not prematurely issued, even assuming, as with all familial piety I must having regard to *Civil Service Co-operative Society Ltd v McGrigor's Trustee*, [1923] 2 Ch 347, citing *Horsey Estate Ltd v Steiger* [1899] 2 QB 79, that reasonable time in the case of an irremediable breach is related to something other than making compensation in money, notwithstanding the language of the section.

In *Plymouth Corporation v Harvey* [1971] 1 WLR 549, [1971] 1 All ER 623, the tenant executed an undated deed of surrender in escrow. When he was in breach, the landlord dated the deed and demanded possession. The deed was held void as being a device to circumvent section 146. The statutory notices were required. "A forfeiture in the guise of a surrender . . . remains a forfeiture for the purposes of section 146," said PLOWMAN J.

iii. WAIVER

In *Matthews v Smallwood* [1910] 1 Ch 777, PARKER J said at p. 786: "I think that the law on the subject of waiver is reasonably clear. The right to re-enter is a legal right which, apart from release or abandonment or waiver, will exist and can be exercised, at any time within the period fixed by the Statutes of Limitation; and if a defendant in an action of ejectment based upon that right of re-entry alleges a release or abandonment or waiver, logically speaking the onus ought to lie on him to shew the release or the abandonment or the waiver. Waiver of a right of re-entry can only occur where the lessor, with knowledge of the facts upon which his right to re-enter arises, does some unequivocal act recognizing the continued existence of the lease. It is not enough that he should do the act which recognizes, or appears to recognize, the continued existence of the lease, unless, at the time when the act is done, he has knowledge of the facts under which, or from which, his right of entry arose. Therefore we get the principle that, though an act of waiver operates with regard to all known breaches, it does not operate with regard to breaches which were unknown to the lessor at the time when the act took place. It is also, I think, reasonably clear upon the cases that whether the act, coupled with the knowledge, constitutes a waiver is a question which the law decides, and therefore it is not open to a lessor who has knowledge of the breach to say 'I will treat the tenancy as existing, and I will receive the rent, or I will take advantage of my power as landlord to distrain; but I tell you that all I shall do will be without prejudice to my right to re-enter, which I intend to reserve.' That is a position which he is not entitled to take up. If, knowing of the breach, he does distrain, or does receive the rent, then by law he waives the breach, and nothing which he can say by way of protest against the law will avail him anything. Logically, therefore, a person who relies upon waiver ought to shew, first, an act unequivocally recognizing the subsistence of the lease, and, secondly, knowledge of the circumstances from which the right of re-entry arises at the time when the act is performed[13].

---

[13] *Goodright d Charter v Cordwent* (1795) 6 Term Rep 219; *Dendy v Nicholl* (1858) 4 CBNS 376; *Ward v Day* (1864) 5 B & S 359; *Grimwood v Moss* (1872) LR 7 CP 360; *Segal Securities Ltd v Thoseby* [1963] 1 QB 887, [1963] 1 All ER 500 (demand for rent made without prejudice held to be waiver). *Central Estates (Belgravia) Ltd v Woolgar (No. 2)* [1972] 1 WLR 1048, [1972] 3 All ER 610; *David Blackstone Ltd v Burnetts (West End) Ltd* [1973] 1 WLR 1487, [1973] 3 All ER 782; *Welch v Birrane* (1975) 29 P & CR 102; *Brikom Investments Ltd v Carr* [1979] QB 467, [1979] 2 All ER 753. See (1976) 40 Conv (NS) 327, (1977) 41 Conv (NS) 220 (E. L. G. Tyler).

LAW OF PROPERTY ACT 1925

148. Waiver of a covenant in a lease. — (1) Where any actual waiver
by a lessor or the persons deriving title under him of the benefit of any
covenant or condition in any lease is proved to have taken place in any
particular instance, such waiver shall not be deemed to extend to any
instance, or to any breach of covenant or condition save that to which
such waiver specially relates, nor operate as a general waiver of the
benefit of any such covenant or condition.

(2) This section applies unless a contrary intention appears and
extends to waivers effected after the twenty-third day of July,
eighteen hundred and sixty.

iv. RELIEF AGAINST FORFEITURE

In *Shiloh Spinners Ltd v Harding* [1973] AC 691, [1973] 1 All ER 90[14],
Lord WILBERFORCE said, at p. 722; "There cannot be any doubt that
from the earliest times courts of equity have asserted the right to
relieve against the forfeiture of property. The jurisdiction has not been
confined to any particular type of case. The commonest instances concerned mortgages, giving rise to the equity of redemption, and leases,
which commonly contained re-entry clauses; but other instances are
found in relation to copyholds, or where the forfeiture was in the
nature of a penalty. Although the principle is well established, there
has undoubtedly been some fluctuation of authority as to the self-
limitation to be imposed or accepted on this power. There has not been
much difficulty as regards two heads of jurisdiction. First, where it is
possible to state that the object of the transaction and of the insertion
of the right to forfeit is essentially to secure the payment of money,
equity has been willing to relieve on terms that the payment is made
with interest, if appropriate, and also costs (*Peachy v Duke of
Somerset* (1721) 1 Stra 447 and cases there cited). Yet even this head
of relief has not been uncontested: Lord Eldon LC in his well-
known judgment in *Hill v Barclay* (1811) 18 Ves 56 expressed his
suspicion of it as a valid principle, pointing out, in an argument which
surely has much force, that there may be cases where to oblige
acceptance of a stipulated sum of money even with interest, at a date
when receipt had lost its usefulness, might represent an unjust
variation of what had been contracted for: see also *Reynolds v
Pitt* (1812) 19 Ves 140. Secondly there were the heads of fraud,
accident, mistake or surprise, always a ground for equity's intervention, the inclusion of which entailed the exclusion of mere
inadvertence and a fortiori of wilful defaults.

Outside of these there remained a debatable area in which were
included obligations in leases such as to repair and analogous
obligations concerning the condition of property, and covenants to

---

[14] P. 34, ante. See also *Scala House and District Property Ltd v Forbes* [1974] QB 575
at 584, [1973] 3 All ER 308. For a case where relief was granted in favour of a tenant
who was in breach of a covenant against immoral user, see *Central Estates (Belgravia)
Ltd v Woolgar (No. 2)* [1972] 1 WLR 1048, [1972] 3 All ER 610.

insure or not to assign. As to covenants to repair and cases of waste, cases can be quoted before the 19th century in which relief was granted: see *Webber v Smith* (1689) 2 Vern 103 and *Nash v Earl of Derby* (1705) 2 Vern 537. There were hostile pronouncements. In *Wadman v Calcroft* (1804) 10 Ves Jun 67 both Sir William Grant MR and Lord Eldon LC are found stating it to be clear that relief cannot be given against the breach of other covenants — i.e. than covenants to pay rent.

It was soon after that the critical divide or supposed divide occurred, between the liberal view of Lord Erskine LC in *Sanders v Pope* (1806) 12 Ves Jun 282 and the strict view of Lord Eldon LC in *Hill v Barclay*. The latter case came to be followed as the true canon; the former was poorly regarded in Lincoln's Inn, but it is important to observe where the difference lay. This was not, as I understand it, in any disagreement as to the field in which relief might be granted, for both cases seem to have accepted that, in principle, relief from forfeiture might be granted when the covenant was to lay out a sum of money on property: but rather on whether equity would relieve against a wilful breach. The breach in *Sanders v Pope* was of this kind but Lord Erskine LC said, at p. 293: 'If the covenant is broken with the consciousness, that it is broken, that is, if it is wilful, not by surprise, accident, or ignorance, still if it is a case, where full compensation can be made, these authorities say, not that it is imperative upon the court to give the relief, but that there is a discretion.' To this Lord Eldon LC answers, 18 Ves Jun 56, 63: '. . . with regard to other cases,' (sc. waste or omitting repairs) 'the doctrine I have repeatedly stated is all wrong, if it is to be taken, that relief is to be given in case of a wilful breach of covenant.' The emphasis here, and the root of disagreement, clearly relates to wilful breaches, and on this it is still Lord Eldon LC's view which holds the field.

The suggestion that relief could not be granted against forfeiture for breach of other covenants was not one that followed from either case: relief was so granted in *Bargent v Thomson* (1864) 4 Giff 473. Equally in *Barrow v Isaacs & Son* [1891] 1 QB 417, a case of a covenant against underletting without consent, a high water mark of the strict doctrine, the emphasis is not so much on the nature of the breach which may or may not be relieved against, but on the argument that it is enough to show that compensation can be given: '. . . it was soon recognised that there would be great difficulty in estimating the proper amount of compensation; and, since the decision of Lord Eldon LC in *Hill v Barclay* it has always been held that equity would not relieve, merely on the ground that it could give compensation, upon breach of any covenant in a lease except the covenant for payment of rent' (*per* Kay LJ, at p. 425).

We are not bound by these decisions, certainly not by every shade of opinion they may reflect, but I am entirely willing to follow them in their main lines.

As regards the present appeal it is possible to disengage the following considerations. In the first place there should be put on one side cases where the court has been asked to relieve against conditions contained in wills or gifts inter vivos. These raise considerations of a different kind from those relevant to contractual stipulations. Secondly, no decision in the present case involves the establishment or recognition directly or by implication of any general power — that is to say, apart from the special heads of fraud, accident, mistake or surprise — in courts exercising equitable jurisdiction to relieve against men's bargains. Lord Eldon LC's firm denial of any such power in *Hill v Barclay* does not call for any revision or review in this case. Equally there is no need to qualify Kay LJ's proposition in *Barrow v Isaacs & Son* (cited above). I would fully endorse this: it remains true today that equity expects men to carry out their bargains and will not let them buy their way out by unconvenanted payment. But it is consistent with these principles that we should reaffirm the right of courts of equity in appropriate and limited cases to relieve against forfeiture for breach of covenant or condition where the primary object of the bargain is to secure a stated result which can effectively be attained when the matter comes before the court, and where the forfeiture provision is added by way of security for the production of that result. The word 'appropriate' involves consideration of the conduct of the applicant for relief, in particular whether his default was wilful, of the gravity of the breaches, and of the disparity between the value of the property of which forfeiture is claimed as compared with the damage caused by the breach.

Both as a matter of history and by the nature of things, different considerations apply to different covenants. As regards covenants to pay rent, in spite of Lord Eldon LC's reservations, the matter has, subject to qualifications which need not be discussed, been taken over by statute, first by 4 Geo 2 c 28 then by later Acts leading up to the Law of Property Act 1925. The same is true of covenants to insure and other covenants in leases. I shall consider shortly the implications of the legislation as regards other covenants than those expressly mentioned. As regards covenants to repair and analogous covenants concerning the condition of property, other than those now dealt with by Act of Parliament, it is not necessary to overrule *Hill v Barclay* any more than it was necessary for Lord Eldon LC to do more than to distinguish *Sanders v Pope*. Lord Eldon LC's decision was in fact based partly upon the circumstance that he was concerned with a wilful default and partly upon the impossibility of speculating whether the later doing of the repairs would compensate the landlord: such considerations remain relevant. Where it is necessary, and, in my opinion, right, to move away from some 19th century authorities, is to reject as a reason against granting relief, the impossibility for the courts to supervise the doing of work. The fact is a reality, no doubt, and explains why specific performance cannot be granted of agreements to this effect but in the present context it can now be seen (as it was seen by Lord Erksine LC in *Sanders v Pope*) to be an irrelevance: for what the court has to do is to satisfy itself, ex post facto, that the convenanted work has been done, and it has ample machinery, through certificates, or by enquiry, to do precisely this. This removes much of the support from one of the more formidable authorities, viz.: the majority judgment in *Bracebridge v Buckley* (1816) 2 Price 200.

There remain two other arguments which cannot be passed over. First it is said that the strict view (that there should be no relief except under the two classical headings) has been endorsed in this House in *Hughes v Metropolitan Rly Co* (1877) 2 App Cas 439. There is no substance in this. The basis of decision in this House was that the landlord's notice was suspended in operation by acquiescence, so that there was no effective breach. The opinion invoked is that of Lord Cairns LC, in which there appears this portion of a sentence, at p. 448: 'it could not be argued, that there was any right of a court of equity, . . . to give relief in cases of this kind, by way of mercy, or by way merely of saving property from forfeiture, . . .' words which have only to be re-read to show that they are no sort of denial of the jurisdiction now invoked.

Secondly, a point of more difficulty arises from the intervention of Parliament in providing specific machinery for the granting of relief against forfeiture of leases: see Law of Property (Amendment) Act 1859 (22 & 23 Vict c 35), Common Law Procedure Act 1852, Law of Property Act 1925, Leasehold Property (Repairs) Act 1938 and other statutes. This, it is said, negatives an intention that any corresponding jurisdiction should exist outside the case of leases. I do not accept this argument. In my opinion where the courts have established a general principle of law or equity, and the legislature steps in with particular legislation in a particular area, it must, unless showing a contrary intention, be taken to have left cases outside that area where they were under the influence of the general law. To suppose otherwise involves the conclusion that an existing jurisdiction has been cut down by implication, by an enactment moreover which is positive in character (for it amplifies the jurisdiction in cases of leases) rather than negative. That legislation did not have this effect was the view of Kay LJ in *Barrow v Isaacs & Son* [1891] 1 QB 417, 430, when he held that covenants against assigning — excluded from the Conveyancing Act 1881 — were left to be dealt with according to the ordinary law. The Occupiers' Liability Act 1957 gave rise to a similar problem since it legislated as to one part of a larger total field; I may perhaps refer to what I said in *Herrington v British Railways Board* [1972] AC 877, [1972] 1 All ER 749.

The present case, in my opinion, falls within the class of case in which it would be possible for a court of equity to intervene. When the appellants assigned a portion of their leased property, retaining the rest, which adjoined and was supported by the portion assigned, they had an essential interest in securing adequate protection for their buildings, in having the entire site fenced, in preventing unauthorised access through the assigned property. The covenants were drafted accordingly. The power of re-entry was inserted by way of reinforcement of the contractual obligation which it must have been perceived might cease to be enforceable as such. Failures to observe the covenants having occurred, it would be right to consider whether the assignor should be allowed to exercise his legal rights if the essentials of the bargain could be secured and if it was fair and just to prevent him from doing so. It would be necessary, as stated above, to consider the conduct of the assignee, the nature and gravity of the breach, and its relation to the value of the property which might be forfeited. Established and, in my opinion, sound principle requires that wilful breaches should not, or at least should only in exceptional cases, be relieved against, if only for the reason that the assignor should not be compelled to remain in a relation of neighbourhood with a person in deliberate breach of his obligations.

In this light should relief have been granted? The respondent's difficulty is that the Vice-Chancellor, who heard the witnesses and went into all the facts, clearly took the view that the case was not one for relief. I should be reluctant, in any event, except on clear conviction to substitute a different view of my own. But I have examined in detail the evidence given, the correspondence over a period of four years, the photographs and plans of the site. All this material establishes a case of clear and wilful breaches of more than one covenant which, if individually not serious, were certainly substantial: a case of continuous disregard by the respondent of the appellants' rights over a period of time, coupled with a total lack of evidence as to the respondent's ability speedily and adequately to make good the consequences of his default, and finally a failure to show any such disproportion between the expenditure required and the value of the interest involved as to amount to a case of hardship. In my opinion the case is not, on established principles, one for relief.

For all these reasons I would allow the appeal."

In *Richard Clarke & Co Ltd v Widnall* [1976] 1 WLR 845, [1976] 3 All ER 301, the plaintiffs leased the Stag's Head, Great Warford, Cheshire to the defendants. The lease contained a clause with a marginal side-note "Forfeiture" which provided that, if the tenant committed a breach of certain covenants including the covenant to pay rent, the landlords could terminate the lease either by re-entering (clause 13 (4) (i)) or by serving a three months notice specifying the breach (14 (4) (ii)). When the defendant's rent was in arrear for three quarters, the plaintiffs served a notice under (ii), whereupon the defendant paid up all arrears and the then current quarter. The plaintiffs then claimed possession on expiry of the notice. The Court of Appeal (MEGAW and ORR LJJ and MILMO J) held that the clause was a forfeiture clause and that the defendants were entitled to relief. MEGAW LJ said at p. 849:

". . . The landlords did not choose to act under the provisions of sub-paragraph (i) of clause 13 (4). They chose to proceed under sub-paragraph (ii). The consequence, the landlords say and the judge in the court below accepted, is that no question of relief against forfeiture arises because sub-paragraph (ii) does not involve forfeiture. It involves an ordinary contractual right to terminate on the expiry of a contractually provided period of notice, which notice was duly given. There is no forfeiture; there is no right of relief against forfeiture; and also the tenant cannot rely on waiver consisting of the demand for, and acceptance of, rent.

The question raised is simply stated. Does a notice to terminate given under clause 13 (4) (ii) by reason of a breach of the covenant to pay rent constitute, or have the same effect in law as, a forfeiture? If the answer is 'Yes', the tenant succeeds in this appeal; he is entitled to relief. If the answer is 'No', then the landlords are entitled, as the judge has held, to possession on the expiry of three months' notice. . . .

The doctrine of relief against forfeiture for breach of covenant to pay rent is a long-established doctrine in the law. The reasons for its existence are not in doubt. In *Chandless-Chandless v Nicholson* [1942] 2 KB 321. Lord Greene MR said, at p. 323:

> 'The court, in exercising its jurisdiction to grant relief in cases of non-payment of rent is, of course, proceeding on the old principles of the court of equity which always regarded the condition of re-entry as being merely security for payment of the rent and gave relief if the landlord could get his rent.'

So the 'condition of re-entry' in clause 13 (4) (i) is 'regarded . . . as being merely security for payment of the rent'; and therefore the tenant would have his right of relief. Is there any reason, first, in logic why the 'condition of re-entry' in clause 13 (4) (ii) should be regarded as something essentially different in character and legal consequence, merely because there is a contractual provision for a period of notice before the landlord's right to re-enter is to be effected? In my judgment, there is no such logical reason.

Is there, then, secondly, any practical reason why different legal consequences should be attributed to clause 13 (4) (ii), as contrasted with clause 13 (4) (i), affecting the tenant's right to claim relief? Again, I can see no practical reason. On the contrary, I think there are strong practical reasons why no distinction should be drawn in respect of the right to relief as between sub-paragraph (i) and sub-paragraph (ii). If the landlords were right, it would mean that both (in a case such as the present) the long-established doctrine of equity as to relief against forfeiture and also (in cases falling within section 146 of the Law of Property Act 1925) the statutory requirement as to relief from forfeiture, could be evaded by the mere insertion in the tenancy agreement of a provision for short notice — perhaps one day's notice — in the event of a breach of covenant. That cannot be right. The answer suggested by Mr. Simpson for the landlords is that the court could, perhaps, disregard the provision for a short period of notice if in the view of the court it was, as it was put, 'illusory' or 'merely a sham.' It would then become a question of degree, to be decided on the basis of some undefined and, I suspect, undefinable criterion; unless, indeed, the criterion were to be whether the motive for the insertion of the clause was to enable the landlord to avoid the possibility that the tenant might be entitled to relief in respect of a breach of covenant. If that were the criterion, could the present provision of clause 13 (4) (ii) escape the category of 'illusory'? I think not.

I would hold that, whether or not technically clause 13 (4) (ii) is to be described as a 'forfeiture clause,' its effect in law, as regards the tenant's right of relief for breach of covenant to pay rent, is no different from the effect of a clause which provides for forfeiture operating immediately upon the landlord indicating his intention to act on it. The inclusion of a period of notice before the lease terminates, being a period unilateral to the landlord and less than the general period of notice available to either party, does not deprive the tenant of his right to claim relief where, as here, the event on which the landlord relies as giving rise to his right to terminate is a breach by the tenant of his covenant to pay rent.

Accordingly, I would allow the appeal as regards the order for possession.''

V.   The Title to the Freehold[15]

LAW OF PROPERTY ACT 1925

44.   Statutory commencements of title. — (2) Under a contract to grant or assign a term of years, whether derived or to be derived out of freehold or leasehold land, the intended lessee or assign shall not be entitled to call for the title to the freehold.

(3) Under a contract to sell and assign a term of years derived out of a leasehold interest in land, the intended assign shall not have the right to call for the title to the leasehold reversion.

(4) On a contract to grant a lease for a term of years to be derived out of a leasehold interest, with a leasehold reversion, the intended lessee shall not have the right to call for the title to that reversion.

(5) Where by reason of any of the three last preceding subsections, an intending lessee or assign is not entitled to call for the title to the freehold or to a leasehold reversion, as the case may be, he shall not, where the contract is made after the commencement of this Act, be deemed to be affected with notice of any matter or thing of which, if he had contracted that such title should be furnished, he might have had notice.

SHEARS *v* WELLS
[1936] 1 All ER 832 (ChD, Luxmoore J)

The first defendant was the owner, and the second defendant, Cooper, the tenant of premises under a tenancy commencing in 1929[16]. The

---

[15] Cheshire, pp. 734–736; M & W, pp. 705–708; MM pp. 508–509.
[16] In the statement of facts this date is given as 1931 but this is at variance with the date given in the judgment which is used here.

plaintiff brought this action for an injunction to restrain the breach of a restrictive covenant contained in the conveyance to the first defendant. The second defendant pleaded that he had no notice of the restrictive covenant. On the question of his liability,

Held. By virtue of the Law of Property Act 1925, section 44 (5), the second defendant was only bound by matters of which the plaintiff could prove he had notice at the commencement of his tenancy.

LUXMOORE J: I think that Cooper is not liable under the covenant at all. He took the tenancy of the garage in 1929 after the passing of the Law of Property Act 1925. Section 44 enacts as follows:— [His Lordship read section 44 (2), (4), (5);] It follows that the onus of proving that the defendant Cooper had notice when he took the tenancy is on the plaintiff. There is no evidence here that he had notice and the onus is not discharged. The defendant Cooper is therefore not subject to the covenants in the deed.

———————

This case illustrates the reversal of the rule in *Patman v Harland* (1881) 17 ChD 353, where Sir George JESSEL MR held that a tenant had constructive notice of a restrictive covenant affecting the freehold, which covenant was disclosed in the deeds. The tenant was not protected even if the lessor told her that there was no such covenant, nor by the Vendor and Purchaser Act 1874, section 2 which provides "subject to any stipulation to the contrary" that "under a contract to grant or assign a term of years, whether derived or to be derived out of a freehold or leasehold estate, the intended lessee or assign shall not be entitled to call for the title to the freehold."

Shears v Wells does not, however, solve all the problems. The person entitled to the benefit of the covenant needs to ensure that the lessee has notice of the covenant. Presumably he could do this by registration and rely on the provisions of the Law of Property Act 1925, section 198 (1) that registration is deemed to constitute "actual notice . . . to all persons . . . connected with the land affected[17]." The result is not satisfactory; for the procedure for registration under the Land Charges Act 1925 provides for registration under personal names and not under the land concerned. Unless therefore the incumbrance is registered against the present lessor, the tenant (a fortiori, a sub-tenant), not seeing the earlier deeds, will not know under whose name to search. And neither pre-1926 covenants nor covenants originally entered into between landlord and tenant are registrable[18].

———————

[17] In *White v Bijou Mansions* [1937] Ch 610 at 619, SIMONDS J suggested "that s. 198 . . . appears, notwithstanding the unqualified language of s. 44, sub-s. 5, to affect a lessee with notice of all those charges which are registered under the Land Charges Act 1925". For registered land, see p. 777, n. 18, post.

[18] (1940) 56 LQR 361 (D. W. Logan), [1956] CLJ 230–234 (H. W. R. Wade).

VI.   The Effect of Assignment on Covenants[19]

A.   Covenants which "Touch and Concern" the Land

The only covenants which can be enforced by or against assignees of
the leasehold estate or the reversion, are those which touch and
concern the land[20]; or (which means the same thing) have "reference to
the subject-matter of the lease[1]." In Lord Ellenborough's words, the
test is satisfied if the covenant "affected the nature, quality or value of
the thing demised, independently of collateral circumstances; or
if it affected the mode of enjoying it[2]." The simplest test is that
put forward by Cheshire[3], that is to consider whether the covenant
affects "the landlord *qua* landlord or the tenant *qua* tenant". No
single definition seems adequate to explain all the cases. Textbooks
commonly list examples of covenants falling on either side of the line,
and it is not proposed to enter into details here[4].

B.   Covenants Running with the Leasehold Estate

The common law rule was that covenants which touched and concerned the land were enforceable by and against the assignee of the
tenant. There was however an exception to the effect that a covenant
relating to something not in esse at the date of the covenant only ran
with the leasehold estate if assigns were expressly mentioned; this
exception was abolished in 1925[5].

SPENCER'S CASE
(1583) 5 Co Rep 16a (KB)

Spencer and his wife leased land to S for 21 years. S covenanted
for him, his executors and administrators that he, his executors,
administrators, or assigns would build a brick wall thereon. He
assigned his lease to J, who assigned it to the defendant Clark. The
question is as to the liability of Clark on the covenant to build.

Held. Since the covenant was in respect of something to be done on
the land demised, and was not made expressly on behalf of the assigns
the defendant was not liable.

The report records that after many arguments at the Bar, the case
was excellently argued and debated by the Justices at the Bench.
Three of the resolutions were:

---

[19] Cheshire, pp. 449–461; M & W, pp. 628–629, 650–652, 723–742; MM, pp. 315, 325,
356–364.
[20] *Spencer's Case* (1583) 5 Co Rep 16a; 1 Smith's Leading Cases (13th edn., 1929), Vol. 1,
p. 51.
[1] L.P.A. 1925, ss. 141, 142; *Davis v Town Properties Investment Corporation Ltd*
[1903] 1 Ch 797.
[2] *Congleton Corpn v Pattison* (1808) 10 East 130, 135.
[3] Cheshire, p. 451, and approved in *Breams Property Investment Co Ltd v Stroulger*
[1948] 2 KB 1 at 7, [1948] 1 All ER 758.
[4] Woodfall (28th edn., 19), paras. 1.1130–1131; Cheshire, pp. 451–453; M & W, pp.
724–727; MM, pp. 356–357.
[5] L.P.A. 1925, s. 79, p. 416, post.

"1. When the covenant extends to a thing *in esse*, parcel of the demise, the thing to be done by force of the covenant is *quodammodo* annexed and appurtenant to the thing demised, and shall go with the land, and shall bind the assignee although he be not bound by express words: but when the covenant extends to a thing which is not in being at the time of the demise made, it cannot be appurtenant or annexed to the thing which hath no being: as if the lessee covenants to repair the houses demised to him during the term, that is parcel of the contract, and extends to the support of the thing demised, and therefore is *quodammodo* annexed appurtenant to houses, and shall bind the assignee although he be not bound expressly by the covenant: but in the case at bar, the covenant concerns a thing which was not *in esse* at the time of the demise made, but to be newly built after, and therefore shall bind the covenantor, his executors, or administrators, and not the assignee, for the law will not annex the covenant to a thing which hath no being.

2. It was resolved that in this case, if the lessee had covenanted for him and his assigns, that they would make a new wall upon some part of the thing demised, that for as much as it is to be done upon the land demised, that it should bind the assignee; for although the covenant doth extend to a thing to be newly made, yet it is to be made upon the thing demised, and the assignee is to take the benefit of it, and therefore shall bind the assignee by express words. So on the other side, if a warranty be made to one, his heirs and assigns, by express words, the assignee shall take benefit of it, and shall have a *Warrantia chartae*. . . . But although the covenant be for him and his assigns, yet if the thing to be done be merely collateral to the land, and doth not touch or concern the thing demised in any sort, there the assignee shall not be charged. As if the lessee covenants for him and his assigns to build a house upon the land of the lessor which is no parcel of the demise, or to pay any collateral sum to the lessor, or to a stranger, it shall not bind the assignee, because it is merely collateral, and in no manner touches or concerns the thing that was demised, or that is assigned over; and therefore in such case the assignee of the thing demised cannot be charged with it, no more than any other stranger.

4. It was resolved, that if a man makes a feoffment by this word *dedi*, which implies a warranty, the assignee of the feoffee shall not vouch; but if a man makes a lease for years by this word *concessi* or *demisi*, which implies a covenant, if the assignee of the lessee be evicted, he shall have a writ of covenant; for the lessee and his assignee hath the yearly profits of the land which shall grow by his labour and industry for an annual rent, and therefore it is reasonable when he hath applied his labour, and employed his cost upon the land, and be evicted (whereby he loses all), that he shall take such benefit of the demise and grant, as the first lessee might, and the lessor hath no other prejudice than what his special contract with the first lessee hath bound him to."

LAW OF PROPERTY ACT 1925[6]

78. Benefit of covenants relating to land. — (1) A covenant relating to any land of the covenantee shall be deemed to be made with the covenantee and his successors in title and the persons deriving title under him or them, and shall have effect as if such successors and other persons were expressed.

For the purposes of this subsection in connexion with covenants restrictive of the user of land "successors in title" shall be deemed to include the owners and occupiers for the time being of the land of the covenantee intended to be benefited.

(2) This section applies to covenants made after the commencement of this Act, but the repeal of section fifty-eight of the Conveyancing Act, 1881, does not affect the operation of covenants to which that section applied.

79. Burden of covenants relating to land. — (1) A covenant relating to any land of a covenantor or capable of being bound by him, shall, unless a contrary intention is expressed, be deemed to be made by the covenantor on behalf of himself his successors in title and the persons deriving title under him or them, and, subject as aforesaid, shall have effect as if such successors and other persons were expressed.

This subsection extends to a covenant to do some act relating to the land, notwithstanding that the subject-matter may not be in existence when the covenant is made.

(2) For the purposes of this section in connection with covenants restrictive of the user of land "successors in title" shall be deemed to include the owners and occupiers for the time being of such land.

(3) This section applies only to covenants made after the commencement of this Act.

C. Covenants Running with the Reversion

At common law the benefit and burden of covenants other than "usual" or "implied" covenants did not run with the landlord's reversion. Statutory provision was made in 32 Hen 8 c 34 and in the Conveyancing Act 1881. These provisions were superseded by the Law of Property Act 1925.

LAW OF PROPERTY ACT 1925

141. Rent and benefit of lessee's covenants to run with the reversion. — (1) Rent reserved by a lease, and the benefit of every covenant or provision therein contained, having reference to the subject-matter

---

[6] See also pp. 711–712, 713–717, 723–726, 729, post.

thereof, and on the lessee's part to be observed or performed, and every condition of re-entry and other condition therein contained, shall be annexed and incident to and shall go with the reversionary estate in the land, or in any part thereof, immediately expectant on the term granted by the lease, notwithstanding severance of that reversionary estate, and without prejudice to any liability affecting a covenantor or his estate.

(2) Any such rent, covenant or provision shall be capable of being recovered, received, enforced, and taken advantage of, by the person from time to time entitled, subject to the term, to the income of the whole or any part, as the case may require, of the land leased.

(3) Where that person becomes entitled by conveyance or otherwise, such rent, covenant or provision may be recovered, received, enforced or taken advantage of by him notwithstanding that he becomes so entitled after the condition of re-entry or forfeiture has become enforceable, but this subsection does not render enforceable any condition of re-entry or other condition waived or released before such person becomes entitled as aforesaid.

(4) This section applies to leases made before or after the commencement of this Act, but does not affect the operation of —
  (a) any severance of the reversionary estate; or
  (b) any acquisition by conveyance or otherwise of the right to receive or enforce any rent covenant or provision;
effected before the commencement of this Act.

142. Obligation of lessor's covenants to run with reversion. — (1) The obligation under a condition or of a covenant entered into by a lessor with reference to the subject-matter of the lease shall, if and as far as the lessor has power to bind the reversionary estate immediately expectant on the term granted by the lease, be annexed and incident to and shall go with that reversionary estate, or the several parts thereof, notwithstanding severance of that reversionary estate, and may be taken advantage of and enforced by the person in whom the term is from time to time vested by conveyance, devolution in law, or otherwise; and, if and as far as the lessor has power to bind the person from time to time entitled to that reversionary estate, the obligation aforesaid may be taken advantage of and enforced against any person so entitled.

(2) This section applies to leases made before or after the commencement of this Act, whether the severance of the reversionary estate was affected before or after such commencement:

Provided that, where the lease was made before the first day of January eighteen hundred and eighty-two, nothing in this section shall affect the operation of any severance of the reversionary estate effected before such commencement.

This section takes effect without prejudice to any liability affecting a covenantor or his estate.

RE KING[7]
[1963] Ch 459, [1963] 1 All ER 781 (CA, DENNING MR, UPJOHN and
DIPLOCK LJJ)

In 1895 Edward Graves-Tagg granted a lease of land and a factory in
Bethnal Green to Mrs. Elven, who covenanted for herself, her
executors, administrators and assigns (a) to keep the premises in
repair, (b) to insure the premises and keep them insured against loss or
damage by fire and (c) to lay out all moneys received under any such
policy in rebuilding or repairing the premises destroyed or damaged by
fire and, if necessary, to reinstate the premises. In 1907 the lease was
assinged to King. In 1944 the factory was severely damaged by fire,
but could not be repaired or rebuilt owing to wartime restrictions. The
insurance moneys were duly paid. In 1946 Edward Graves-Tagg
assigned his reversion to Edward Ernest Graves-Tagg ("Tagg") and in
1949 King died. The factory had never been repaired or rebuilt. In 1960
Tagg assigned his reversion to the London County Council as a result
of a compulsory purchase order. In 1961, during negotiations between
the London County Council and King's executors for the transfer of
the lease to the London County Council, King's executors issued a
summons to determine, inter alia, whether Tagg could still sue them
for the breach of the covenant to repair and to reinstate, which had
occurred before the assignment of 1960. If he could, then King's
executors argued that an indemnity by the London County Council
should be included in the transfer of the lease.

   Held. King's executors were not liable to Tagg.

   UPJOHN LJ: The first question may be briefly stated in this way:
Can a landlord, who has assigned his reversion to a lease, after the date
of such assignment, sue the lessee in respect of breaches of covenant
which occurred before the assignment? . . .

   This case is concerned with express covenants in a lease, and in
such case it cannot possibly be doubted that section 141 of the
Law of Property Act 1925 governs the situation. [His Lordship read
sections (1) and (2) and continued:]

   I turn, then, to a consideration of the meaning of section 141 and
construe the language used in its ordinary and natural meaning, which
seems to me quite plain and clear. To illustrate this, consider the case
of a lease containing a covenant to build a house according to certain
detailed specifications before a certain day. Let me suppose that after
that certain day the then lessor assigns the benefit of the reversion to
an assignee, and at the time of the assignment the lessee has failed to
perform the covenant to build. Who can sue the lessee for breach of
covenant? It seems to me clear that the assignee alone can sue. Upon
the assignment the benefit of every covenant on the lessee's part to be
observed and performed is annexed and incident to and goes with the
reversionary estate. The benefit of that covenant to build, therefore,

---

[7] (1966) 30 Conv (NS) 429 (D. Macintyre).

passed; as it had been broken, the right to sue also passed as part of the benefit of the covenant and, incidentally, also the right to re-enter, if that has not been waived. I protest against the argument that because a right to sue is itself a chose in action it, therefore, has become severed from, and independent of, the parent covenant; on the contrary it remains part of it. The right to sue on breach is merely one of the bundle of rights that are contained in the concept "benefit of every covenant". . . . To return to my example. Suppose the right to sue for breach of that covenant did not pass, and that right remained in the assignor, then the assignee would take the lease without the benefit of that covenant and he could never enforce it. So he has not got the benefit of every covenant contained in the lease and the words of the section are not satisfied. That cannot be right. . . .

Then suppose the lease contains a covenant to keep in repair which is broken at the date of the assignment, and that at all material times the premises were out of repair; that is, a continuing breach. It is an a fortiori case to the example I have just dealt with. Indeed, with all respect to the argument to the contrary, you cannot give any sensible meaning to the words of the section unless the entire benefit of a repairing covenant has passed, leaving the assignor without remedy against the lessee. Look at the absurd results if that were not so. The assignor of the reversion remains at liberty to sue the lessee for breaches down to the moment of the assignment. After assignment he sues and obtains judgment for certain damages. But then the premises are still out of repair and the breach continues. The assignee claims to re-enter or to sue because the premises are out of repair. What is the situation of the lessee? Either he has to pay damages twice or pay damages to the assignor and then reinstate the premises because otherwise the assignee will re-enter. This is impossible. Alternatively, the assignee's right to re-enter or to sue in respect of post-assignment breaches is in some way adversely affected by reason of the fact that the assignor has recovered a judgment for damages for pre-assignment breaches; therefore, the benefit of the covenant to keep in repair did not pass wholly to him even in respect of post-assignment breaches. That directly contradicts the words of the section. . . .

In my judgment Tagg's claims fail and I would allow this part of the appeal . . .

In *London and County (A and D) Ltd v Wilfred Sportsman Ltd* [1971] Ch 764, [1970] 2 All ER 600 the Court of Appeal held that section 141 should be similarly interpreted in the case of a covenant to pay rent. RUSSELL LJ said, at p. 784: "The language of section 141 (substantially re-enacting the earlier legislation from 1881 onwards) is such as, in my judgment, to indicate plainly that an assignee of the reversion may sue and re-enter for rent in arrear at the date of the assignment when the right of re-entry has arisen before the assignment[8]. The decision in *Rickett v Green* [1910] 1 KB 253 was, therefore, correct[9]."

D.   Privity of Estate

i.   ASSIGNEES AND SUB-TENANTS

Subject to the situation discussed in *ii* below, liability under, and the right to sue upon, covenants running with the land or the reversion exists only between persons between whom there is privity of estate. The original contracting parties are liable to each other contractually and remain so liable[10] assignees are liable and able to sue only if, and so long as, they hold the estate with which the covenant runs; and such persons must be assignees and not sub-lessees[11] or squatters[12].

In *South of England Dairies v Baker* [1906] 2 Ch 631, the freeholder of certain property demised it for 21 years and covenanted to pay all rates and taxes (except one third of the water rate). In the following year, the lessee sub-demised the premises to the plaintiff (a company formed by the lessee) for the remainder of his term less three days. Seven years later the freeholder sold the fee simple subject to the lease to the defendant, who in the following year accepted the surrender of the lease from the original lessee. The plaintiff, the sub-tenant, was compelled by the Local Authority to pay the rates, and sought to recover damages from the defendant under the landlord's covenant to pay all rates and taxes. JOYCE J held that the defendant was not liable since the plaintiff was not an assignee of the original lessee and was unable therefore to enforce the covenant originally given to the lessee.

In *Milmo v Carreras* [1946] KB 306, [1946] 1 All ER 288, the plaintiff was tenant of a flat under a 7 year lease, expiring on 28 November 1944. In October 1943, he agreed to sublet the flat to the defendant for one year from 1 November 1943, "and thereafter quarterly until such time as" one of the parties should give three months notice to terminate. The plaintiff gave such notice on returning from active service in 1945.

The Court of Appeal (Lord GREENE MR, MORTON and BUCKNILL LJJ) held that the notice was bad because the plaintiff retained no reversion. Lord GREENE said at p. 310:

"For the purposes of this case, I think it is sufficient to say that, in accordance with a very ancient and established rule, where a lessee, by a document in the form of a sub-lease, divests himself of everything that he has got (which he must necessarily do if he is transferring to his so-called sub-lessee an estate as great as, or purporting to be

---

[8] *Arlesford Trading Co Ltd v Servansingh* [1971] 1 WLR 1080, [1971] 3 All ER 113 (assignee of reversion recovered rent against lessee who had assigned his lease before the reversion was assigned).

[9] See p. 424, post.

[10] On the continuing liability of an original lessee to the lessor for rent which falls due after assignment of the lease, see *Warnford Investments Ltd v Duckworth* [1979] Ch 127, [1978] 2 All ER 517.

[11] *South of England Dairies Ltd v Baker* [1906] 2 Ch 631.

[12] *Tichborne v Weir* (1892) 67 LT 735; p. 709, post.

greater than, his own) he from that moment is a stranger to the land, in the sense that the relationship of landlord and tenant, in respect of tenure, cannot any longer exist between him and the so-called sub-lessee. That relationship must depend on privity of estate. I myself find it impossible to conceive of a relationship of landlord and tenant which has not got that essential element of tenure in it, and that implies that the tenant holds of his landlord, and he can only do that if the landlord has a reversion. You cannot have a purely contractual tenure. Tenure exists by reason of privity of estate. That seems to me to be the effect of all the decisions, and that position is recognised by all the decisions.''

ii.   AGREEMENTS FOR LEASES

The question of the enforcement of covenants after assignment raises different issues where there has been no grant of a lease, but merely an agreement for a lease[13]. First, it used to be said that covenants could run with land at common law only if created under seal[14], but this rule has since been changed[15]. Secondly, there is no privity of estate between persons who have entered into a contract for a lease or between their assigns[16]; nor between the lessor and one who has contracted to take an assignment from a lessee[17].

Since the benefit of a covenant can be assigned at law, there is no difficulty in holding that the benefit of a covenant runs with the freehold reversion[18]; and it appears that the benefit will run also by virtue of Law of Property Act 1925, section 141[19], and, if this is so, the burden will run also with the reversion under section 142. It is usually held that the benefit but not the burden of covenants will run on the assignment of an agreement for a lease[20]; an assignee may be liable under an implied agreement if he enters into possession and pays rent[1]; or on grounds of estoppel[2]. His freedom from liability under the covenant may cause great hardship to the lessor, and the question is whether this is a necessary limitation.

The rule seems to have developed from the independence of law and equity before the Judicature Act. There could be no liability at law after the assignment because there was no privity of estate; in equity, the question was whether or not specific performance of the agreement

---

[13] See pp. 76, 387, ante.
[14] *Manchester Brewery Co v Coombs* [1901] 2 Ch 608; p. 422, post.
[15] L.P.A. 1925, s. 154. *Boyer v Warbey* [1953] 1 QB 234, [1952] 2 All ER 976; p. 426, post.
[16] *Purchase v Lichfield Brewery Co* [1915] 1 KB 184; p. 425, post.
[17] *Cox v Bishop* (1857) 8 De GM & G 815; *Friary, Holroyd, and Healey's Breweries Ltd v Singleton* [1899] 1 Ch 86.
[18] *Manchester Brewery Co v Coombs*, supra.
[19] *Rickett v Green*, [1910] 1 KB 253; *Rye v Purcell* [1926] 1 KB 446; *London and County (A and D) Ltd v Wilfred Sportsman Ltd* [1971] Ch 764, [1970] 2 All ER 600.
[20] *Marquis of Camden v Batterbury* (1860) 7 CBNS 864; *Purchase v Lichfield Brewery Co* supra.
[1] *Buckworth v Simpson* (1835) 1 Cr M & R 834; *Cornish v Stubbs* (1870) LR 5 CP 334 at 338–339.
[2] *Ashe v Hogan* [1920] 1 IR 159; *Rodenhurst Estates Ltd v W. H. Barnes Ltd* [1936] 2 All ER 3.

would be given, and the question of monetary liability under the covenants pending the grant of specific performance did not arise. There appears to be no reason why, since the Judicature Act, the doctrine of *Walsh v Lonsdale* should not be applied and the monetary liability of the defendant determined *as if* the decree of specific performance had been granted. The dicta in *Boyer v Warbey* ([1953] 1 QB 234, [1952] 2 All ER 976; p. 426, post) indicate that "nowadays" the rules relating to the running of covenants should be the same, whether the lease which has been assigned is legal or equitable. Further, as has been seen, the Court of Appeal in *Industrial Properties (Barton Hill) Ltd v Associated Electrical Industries Ltd* ([1977] QB 580, [1977] 2 All ER 293; p. 78, ante) held, as an alternative ground for supporting the judgment, that the doctrine of *Walsh v Lonsdale* applied where an equitable owner had purported to grant a lease; the effect was to treat the equitable lease as a legal lease, and thus enable the owner to sue for damages for breach of covenant in the lease.

The older cases are to the contrary. The only case in which the issue appears to have arisen since the Judicature Act is *Purchase v Lichfield Brewery* ([1915] 1 KB 184), which was, however, one of assignment by way of mortgage. It is submitted that the trend of the modern cases should be supported, and that the court should hold that the liability, both of the assignee of an equitable lease and that of the equitable assignee of a legal lease, is the same as it would be if specific performance had been granted[3].

a. Benefit

MANCHESTER BREWERY CO *v* COOMBS
[1901] 2 Ch 608 (ChD, FARWELL J)

By an agreement under seal dated 10 December 1892 between the defendant and Broadbents Ltd, who were brewers, the defendant, who alone executed the deed, undertook to take a yearly tenancy of a hotel, and covenanted with "Broadbents Ltd and their successors in business" to buy all his liquor from them. The covenant did not mention "assigns".

In June 1899, Broadbents sold their business to the plaintiffs, who gave notice of this purchase to the defendant. The defendant continued to take his supplies from the plaintiffs until December, when he ceased to buy from them. They brought this action for an injunction to restrain a breach of the covenant contained in the deed of 1892.

Held. The plaintiffs were entitled to the benefit of the covenant.

FARWELL J (after holding that the covenant was not, on its construction, a mere personal covenant confined to beer brewed at the original brewery which no longer operated): The last point taken by Mr. Younger rests on the fact that the agreement of 10 December 1892, was not executed by the landlords. Having regard to the construction that I have put on the covenant, it could not be contended

---

[3] [1978] Camb LJ 98 (R. J. Smith).

that it is not of such a nature as to run with the land. But it is said that, in order to arrive at the conclusion that it does run with the land, the Court must first find that an estate has been duly created at law in the land with which the covenant can run, or, in other words, that there must be privity of estate between lessor and lessee, and that such estate can only be created by deed duly executed by the lessor, and that this is borne out by 32 Hen 8, c 34, which applies only to leases by deed. This is undoubtedly sound — e.g., it has been held that a lease by mortgagor and mortgagee, in which the covenants to repair were with the mortgagor and his assigns, did not enable an assign of the mortgagee to maintain an action on the covenant: [His Lordship referred to *Webb v Russell* ((1789) 3 Term Rep 393) per Lord Kenyon at 402, and to *Standen v Chrismas* ((1847) 10 QB 135), and continued:] . . . But it by no means follows that the plaintiffs would have failed in every form of action, even before the Judicature Acts; still less that they must fail now. Before the Judicature Acts the plaintiffs might have succeeded if they had sued on the new contract implied from the conduct of the tenant and the assignee of the landlord, instead of suing on the original contract between the tenant and the landlord.

[His Lordship then found that the defendant agreed that the plaintiffs should occupy the position of landlords to him in the same way as Broadbents Ltd had done, and continued:]

There is, moreover, another point which is fatal to the defendant. The defendant holds under an agreement for a lease from Broadbents Limited, under which he has been in possession and paid rent for several years. The whole contract has been performed up to the present time, except that the legal estate has not been actually demised. The defendant would have no defence to an action for specific performance, the sole object of which would be to compel him to accept the legal estate. If Broadbents Limited, had not parted with the legal estate, I see no reason why they should not now execute the deed in order to complete the transaction. The present plaintiffs are the assigns of the benefit of the agreement both by implication from the conveyance of the land subject to the lease, and by the express words of clause 26 of the agreement of 29 March 1899. The plaintiffs could, therefore, obtain specific performance in this court of the contract so far as it is incomplete . . . Holding, therefore, as I do, that the plaintiffs could obtain specific performance against the defendant, I find it laid down by the Court of Appeal that since the Judicature Acts there are not in such a case as this two estates as there were formerly, one at common law by reason of the payment of the rent, and another in equity under the agreement, but the tenant holds under the same terms, and has the same rights and liabilities as if a lease had been granted: *Walsh v Lonsdale* ((1882) 21 ChD 9), approved by Cotton LJ in *Lowther v Heaver* ((1889) 41 ChD 248, 264), and explained by Lord Esher in *Swain v Ayres* ((1888) 21 QBD 289, at 292) and *Foster v Reeves* ([1892] 2 QB 255). Although it has been suggested that the decision in *Walsh v Lonsdale* takes away all differences between the legal and equitable estate, it, of course, does nothing of the sort, and the limits of its applicability are really somewhat narrow. It applies only to cases where there is a contract to transfer a legal title, and an act has to be justified or an action maintained by force of the legal title to which such contract relates. It involves two questions: (1) Is there a contract of which specific performance can be obtained? (2) If Yes, will the title acquired by such specific performance justify at law the act complained of, or support at law the action in question? It is to be treated as though before the Judicature Acts there had been, first, a suit in equity for specific performance, and then an action at law between the same parties; and the doctrine is applicable only in those cases where specific performance can be obtained between the same parties in the same court, and at the same time as the subsequent legal question falls to be determined. Thus, in *Walsh v Lonsdale*, the landlord under an agreement for a lease for a term of seven years distrained. Distress is a legal remedy and depends on the existence at law of the relation of landlord and tenant; but the agreement between the same parties, if specifically enforced, created that relation. It was clear that such an agreement would be enforced in the same court and between the same parties: the act of distress was therefore held to be lawful. So in the present case I have already stated that specific performance can be granted between the parties to this action. I must treat it therefore as granted, and I then find that the result justifies this action. It is not necessary to call in aid this doctrine in matters that are purely equitable; its existence is due entirely to the divergence of legal and equitable rights between the same parties, nor does it affect the rights of third parties. Thus, a contract by a landowner to sell the fee simple of land in possession to A. would not enable A. to maintain an action of ejectment or trespass against a third person, because such actions are purely legal actions requiring the legal estate and possession respectively to support them, and the contract relied on is not made with the defendant. . . .

I hold, therefore, on this point, that the plaintiffs, being clearly entitled in this court against the defendant to specific performance of the agreement under which the defendant has been for years and still is in possession of the land, can sue him on the covenants in the same manner as they could have done if Broadbents had actually executed the original agreement. . . .

The result is that I grant the injunction as asked, and order the defendant to pay the costs of the action.

In *Rickett v Green* [1910] 1 KB 253, one of the questions was whether or not the plaintiff, as assignee of the freehold, was entitled to demand rent from the defendant who held the premises under an agreement for a lease. DARLING and PHILLIMORE JJ held that he was entitled to sue by virtue of the Conveyancing Act 1881, section 10 (now Law of Property Act 1925, section 141). DARLING J said at p. 259: ". . . the question occurred to [the county court judge] whether this tenancy agreement was a 'lease' within the meaning of section 10 of the Act of 1881, inasmuch as the agreement was dated 19 December 1907, and the three years were to run from 25 December 1907, so that the lease was one exceeding three years from the making thereof and, not being under seal, was void at law under section 3 of the Real Property Act 1845. Though at law it may be void as a lease, still in equity it is looked upon as a lease, and in my judgment it must be treated, as between the parties, as if it were a lease under seal. A Court of Equity would look upon the matter as if a lease under seal had been granted. Upon the case to which we have been referred the county court judge came to a right conclusion upon this point, and the agreement must be treated as a 'lease' for the purposes of section 10 of the Act of 1881, and for other purposes also.''

b. Burden

In *Cox v Bishop* (1857) 8 De G M & G 815, the freeholder brought an action for rent due and for breaches of covenant in a lease. The lessees had contracted to assign the lease to persons who assigned to the defendants. KNIGHT BRUCE and TURNER LJJ, held that the defendants were not liable on the covenants, TURNER LJ, saying at p. 823: "If, on the other hand, these Defendants are not at law liable to the Plaintiffs, what are the grounds alleged by this bill upon which they are in equity to be made liable? Simply that they have contracted to purchase interests in the lease and have been in possession. The contracts to purchase, however, are not contracts with the Plaintiffs, and there is nothing in the bill to shew that the Plaintiffs are in any manner entitled to the benefit of those contracts, and if the Defendants are liable by virtue of their possession, the liability, as I apprehend, is to be enforced at law and not in equity. Courts of equity do not, as I think, in ordinary cases, decree the payment of rent or the performance of covenants upon a mere agreement for a lease. In such cases the Court does not treat the relation of landlord and tenant as completed by the agreement, and decree the rent to be paid and the covenants to be performed accordingly, but it decrees the execution of the lease, and leaves the parties to their remedies at law consequent upon the relation created by the execution of it. To take, however, a case more near to the present, suppose, in the case of an agreement for a lease, the intended lessee has assigned the benefit of the contract, can this Court, at the instance of the intended lessor, enforce the payment of the rent or the performance of the covenants by the assignee of the contract. I take it most clearly not; for there is no privity of contract between the lessor and the assignee; but if this cannot be done where there is a mere contract for a lease, upon what principle is it to be done where there is an actual lease and the lessee has agreed to assign."

PURCHASE v LICHFIELD BREWERY CO.
[1915] 1 KB 184 (KBD, HORRIDGE and LUSH JJ)

The plaintiff, in writing but not under seal, purported to grant to Lunnis a 15-year lease of a house, the agreement containing a proviso that Lunnis would not assign the term without the plaintiff's consent, such consent not to be unreasonably refused.

On the following day Lunnis assigned by way of mortgage his interest to the defendant, who never went into possession. The rent being unpaid, the plaintiff claimed from the defendant (mortgagee) the rent due under the agreement.

Held. In the absence of privity of contract or estate the defendant was not liable.

LUSH J (agreeing with HORRIDGE J): I am of the same opinion. The only point which the county court judge decided was that the present case was governed by *Williams v Bosanquet* ((1819) 1 Brod & Bing 238). In my view that case does not apply. The lease in question there was under seal. It was assigned by deed to mortgagees. That was a valid assignment. The only question was whether the mortgagees, not having taken possession, were bound by the covenants in the lease. It was held that they were bound. In this case there was no lease under seal. No term was created as between lessor and lessee. Therefore the question decided in *Williams v Bosanquet* does not arise in this case. Consequently the judgment of the county court judge cannot stand on the grounds on which he has based it.

Then can the judgment be supported on other grounds? I do not think it is necessary to say how the case might have stood if the defendants had ever taken possession. They are liable, if at all, on the principle of *Walsh v Lonsdale* ((1882) 21 ChD 9). In that case the tenant was in possession under the agreement. In the present case the defendants never did take possession. The agreement contained a provision against assigning. The defendants were only mortgagees. It does not follow from *Walsh v Lonsdale* that a court of equity would decree specific performance against mere mortgagees who only took an assignment by way of security. In my opinion it would leave the parties to their position at law. Accordingly the matter stands thus: A tenant under an agreement, whose only title to call himself a lessee depends on his right to specific performance of the agreement, assigns his right to assignees. The assignees never had a term vested in them because no term was ever created; therefore there was never privity of estate. They never went into possession or were recognised by the landlord; therefore there was never privity of contract. It is impossible that specific performance of a contract can be decreed against a person with whom there is neither privity of contract nor privity of estate. Therefore these assignees are not liable to perform the terms of the agreement and this appeal must be allowed.

In *Boyer v Warbey* [1953] 1 QB 234, [1952] 2 All ER 976 (CA, EVERSHED MR, DENNING and ROMER LJJ), one question was whether a covenant by a tenant in a written lease of a flat within the Rent Restriction Acts to pay £40 towards the cost of redecoration "immediately after the expiration or determination of the tenancy" was binding on an assignee of the tenant.

The lease was for 3 years; within nine days of the expiration of the term, the lessee assigned the lease to the defendant who, on the expiry of the nine days, became a statutory tenant, subject to all the terms of the original tenancy "so far as the same are consistent with the provisions of this Act[4]." It was held, *inter alia*, that the covenant to pay the £40 became a term of the statutory tenancy.

DENNING LJ said, at p. 245: "Seeing that the agreement touched and concerned the thing demised, it ran with the land so as to bind the assignee, the tenant, as soon as he entered into possession. I know that before the Judicature Act 1873, it was said that the doctrine of covenants running with the land only applied to covenants under seal and not to agreements under hand. See *Elliot v Johnson* ((1868) LR 2 QB 120). But since the fusion of law and equity, the position is different. The distinction between agreements under hand and covenants under seal has been largely obliterated. There is no valid reason nowadays why the doctrine of covenants running with the land — or with the reversion — should not apply equally to agreements under hand as to covenants under seal; and I think we should so hold, not only in the case of agreements for more than three years which need the intervention of equity to perfect them, but also in the case of agreements for three years or less which do not."

QUESTION

A. agreed to grant a lease for 99 years to B. of valuable land at a rent of £25,000 a year. B. assigned his interest to C., and disappeared. C. has not yet taken possession. Is he liable for the rent? See Cheshire, p. 396; M & W, pp. 628–629, 727–728; MM, pp. 316, 358; *Purchase v Lichfield Brewery Co* [1915] 1 KB 184; (1978) 37 CLJ 90 (R. J. Smith).

VII. Registered Land[5]

We have already seen that a term of years absolute can be registered as a separate title, provided that it is a term of more than 21 years[6]. In addition, a notice of the lease itself must be entered on the register of the lessor's title[7]. Where the lease is registered as a separate title, the notice is entered automatically by the Registrar at the time of registration[8]. But where a lease is incapable of registration, because it is a lease of 21 years or less, a distinction is drawn between leases

---

[4] Increase of Rent and Mortgage Interest (Restrictions) Act 1920, s. 15 (1); now Rent Act 1977, s. 3 (1).
[5] Cheshire, pp. 105, 509–512; M & W, pp. 1059–1063, 1065–1066; MM, pp. 516–519; Ruoff, and Roper, Chap. 23; Law Commission Working Paper, No. 32 (1971).
[6] P. 100, ante.
[7] L.R.A. 1925, s. 19 (2), p. 428, post; s. 22 (2).
[8] L.R.R. 1925, r. 46.

granted at a rent without taking a fine, and other leases, such as are granted with a premium (or fine). With the latter, the lessee must apply for the entry of a notice on the register[9]. The former are overriding interests under section 70 (1) (*k*) of the Land Registration Act 1925[10], and no other protection is necessary. "To prevent the register from being cluttered by notices of leases which are overriding interests the Chief Land Registrar can refuse to enter such notices[11]. In practice it is very rarely that application is made to register notice of leases that are overriding interests[12]." Where the lease has not been noted on the register, a lessee who is in actual occupation will also be protected by virtue of an overriding interest under section 70 (1) (*g*) of the Land Registration Act 1925[13].

LAND REGISTRATION ACT 1925

3.   Interpretation. — (x) "Lease" includes an under-lease and any tenancy or agreement for a lease, under-lease or tenancy[14].

   8.   Application for registration of leasehold land. — p. 100, ante.

   9.   Effect of first registration with absolute title. — p. 101, ante.

   10.   Effect of first registration with good leasehold title. — p. 101, ante.

   123.   Effect of Act in areas where registration is compulsory. — (1) p. 91, ante.

   19.   Registration of disposition of freeholds[15]. — (2) All interests transferred or created by dispositions by the proprietor, other than a transfer of the registered estate in the land, or part thereof, shall, subject to the provisions relating to mortgages, be completed by registration in the same manner and with the same effect as provided by this Act with respect to transfers of registered estates and notice thereof shall also be noted on the register:
   Provided that nothing in this subsection —
   (*a*) shall authorise the registration of a lease granted for a term not exceeding twenty-one years, or require the entry of a notice of such a lease if it is granted at a rent without taking a fine[16]; or

---

[9] L.R.A. 1925, s. 48, p. 430, post.
[10] P. 112, ante.
[11] L.R.A. 1925, ss. 19 (2) (*a*), 22 (2) (*a*); L.R.R. 1925, r. 199: cf. L.R.A. 1925, s. 70 (3), p. 112, ante.
[12] Ruoff and Roper, p. 452.
[13] P. 111, ante.
[14] Accordingly, notice of a sub-lease is properly entered on the intermediate lessor's title. See *Strand Securities Ltd v Caswell* [1965] Ch 958, [1965] 1 All ER 820. The subsection is misleading, however, in including an agreement for a lease; *City Permanent Building Society v Miller* [1952] Ch 840, [1952] 2 All ER 621, p. 112, n. 7, ante.
[15] For almost identical provisions relating to dispositions by registered proprietors of leaseholds, see L.R.A. 1925, s. 22 (2).
[16] This is protected as an overriding interest under L.R.A. 1925, s. 70 (1) (*k*), p. 112, ante.

(*b*) shall authorise the registration of a mortgage term where there is a subsisting right of redemption; . . .

Every such disposition shall, when registered, take effect as a registered disposition, and a lease made by the registered proprietor under the last foregoing section which is not required to be registered or noted on the register shall nevertheless take effect as if it were a registered disposition immediately on being granted.

22. Registration of dispositions of leaseholds. — (1) A transfer of the registered estate in the land or part thereof shall be completed by the registrar entering on the register the transferee as proprietor of the estate transferred, but until such entry is made the transferor shall be deemed to remain the proprietor of the registered estate; and where part only of the land is transferred, notice thereof shall also be noted on the register.

(3) The general words implied in conveyances under the Law of Property Act, 1925[17], shall apply, so far as applicable thereto, to transfers of a registered leasehold estate.

23. Effect of registration of dispositions of leaseholds[18]. — (1) In the case of a leasehold estate registered with an absolute title, a disposition (including a subdemise thereof) for valuable consideration shall, when registered, be deemed to vest in the transferee or underlessee the estate transferred or created to the extent of the registered estate, or for the term created by the subdemise, as the case may require, with all implied or expressed rights, privileges, and appurtenances attached to the estate transferred or created, including (subject to any entry to the contrary on the register) the appropriate rights and interests which would under the Law of Property Act, 1925, have been transferred if the land had not been registered, but subject as follows:—

(*a*) To all implied and express covenants, obligations, and liabilities incident to the estate transferred or created; and

(*b*) To the incumbrances and other entries (if any) appearing on the register and any charge for capital transfer tax subject to which the disposition takes effect under section 7 (3) of this Act[19];

(*c*) Unless the contrary is expressed on the register, to the overriding interests, if any, affecting the estate transferred or created,

but free from all other estates and interests whatsoever, including estates and interests of His Majesty; and the transfer or subdemise shall operate in like manner as if the registered transferor or sublessor were (subject to any entry to the contrary on the register) absolutely entitled to the registered lease for his own benefit.

---

[17] L.P.A. 1925, s. 62, p. 530, post.

[18] Sub-ss. (2), (3) and (4) contain analogous provisions with regard to good leasehold, qualified, and possessory titles. Cf. s. 20 with regard to freeholds; p. 102, ante.

[19] As amended by F.A. 1975, s. 52, Sch. 12 para. 5 (3).

(5) Where any such disposition is made without valuable consideration it shall, so far as the transferee or underlessee is concerned, be subject to any minor interests subject to which the transferor or sublessor held the same; but, save as aforesaid, shall, when registered, in all respects, and in particular as respects any registered dealings on the part of the transferee or underlessee, have the same effect as if the disposition had been made for valuable consideration.

48.   Registration of notice of lease. — (1) Any lessee or other person entitled to or interested in a lease of registered land, where the term granted is not an overriding interest[20], may apply to the registrar to register notice of such lease in the prescribed manner, and when so registered, every proprietor and the persons deriving title under him shall be deemed to be affected with notice of such lease, as being an incumbrance on the registered land in respect of which the notice is entered. . . .

STRAND SECURITIES LTD *v* CASWELL[1]
[1965] Ch 958, [1965] 1 All ER 820, (CA, DENNING MR, HARMAN and RUSSELL LJJ)

LORD DENNING MR: The case raises the question: What is the proper course for the Land Registrar to take when he is asked to register a leasehold interest (for more than 21 years) which has never been registered before? The present case concerns a sublease derived out of a superior lease, but the question is the same in the case of a lease derived out of the freehold. Sections 4, 19 and 20 of the Land Registration Act 1925 (which relate to freeholds) are in all material respects the same as sections 8, 22 and 23 (which relate to leaseholds). It is, however, much more simple to state the position when a freeholder grants a lease: and I will, therefore, take that case. These are the steps which, in my opinion, should be taken on first registration of a lease:

(1) The lessee must apply to be registered as the first proprietor of his leasehold interest. His application must be accompanied by his own lease, but it need not be accompanied by the freeholder's land certificate. We are told that the registrar insists that the lessee shall produce the freeholder's land certificate showing the freeholder's title to his freehold. If it is not produced, the registrar treats the application by the lessee as insufficient and incomplete. In my opinion that practice is wrong. In the absence of express agreement, a lessee has no right to call for his lessor's title. Likewise he has no right to call for his lessor's land certificate. The registrar should not insist on the lessee producing a document to which he has no right. The application is complete without it. . . .

---

[20] I.e. under L.R.A., s. 70 (1) (*k*), p. 112, ante.
[1] P. 117, ante. (1965) Law Soc Gaz 507 (T. B. F. Ruoff).

The judge was much influenced by the practice of the Land Registry. He thought he ought to give weight to it, just as to the practice of conveyancers. I do not agree with this. We cannot allow the registrar by his practice to make bad law and it is bad law to insist on the lessee producing his landlord's land certificate — to which he has no right.

(2) As soon as the application to register the leasehold interest is received, the registrar must enter it in the list of pending applications, which is open to the public, see rules 10 and 12 of the Land Registration Rules 1925[2]. Thereafter anyone who makes a search of the freeholder's register is told that there is a pending application affecting it and the nature of the application, namely, to register a lease. . . .

(3) It is desirable, however, that before the lease is registered, some enquiry should be made of the freeholder, so as to see that the lease is genuine. If it is genuine, it is desirable that an entry should be made in the freeholder's register. Else a purchaser might buy the freehold without knowledge of the lease. The Act and rules make provision for this. As soon as the registrar receives the application from the lessee to register the lease, he must give notice to the freeholder. This appears from rule 46 where "is registered" clearly means "is being registered". The freeholder has seven days in which to object. In the ordinary way he will not object because it will be he who has granted the lease. In that case, there being no objection, the registrar should proceed to enter the lease as a first registration. He should give it a new title number, and enter the lessee as the proprietor of this new leasehold interest. But he should also, at the same time, enter a notice in the charges section of the freeholder's register (see rule 7 (b)) to the effect that the lease has been granted out of the freehold. The lease then is an incumbrance on the freehold and the freeholder, and all persons deriving title under him, are affected by notice of it, see rule 46 (2) and section 48.

(4) The important thing to notice is that, when the registration is eventually effected of the lease, it takes effect as of the date on which the application was delivered at the Land Registry, see rule 83, and the note on the freeholder's register also takes effect as a notice effected on that day. The reason is because section 19 (2) for freeholds (the corresponding section for leaseholds is section 22 (2)) treats the registration and the noting as contemporaneous and rule 46 (2) equates the noting under that rule with a notice under section 48 which takes effect as of the date of application, see rule 83[3].

(5) Thus far we have got the note about the lease on the freeholder's register which is kept in the Land Registry. But it is desirable that this note about the lease should also be entered on the freeholder's land certificate. The freeholder holds this himself and the registrar has no

---

[2] See L.R.R. 1925 rr. 7A (entry in the day list) and 10 (list of pending applications for first registration), p. 107, ante. R. 7A was added and r. 10 substituted by L.R.R. 1978.
[3] See new rule 83, as substituted by L.R.R. 1978 r. 8.

right to call for this. Section 64 (1) (c) makes it clear that it need not be produced. There is no reason, however, why the registrar should not ask the freeholder to produce it voluntarily and, if it is forthcoming as it usually will be, he can enter the notice on it. If it is not forthcoming, all that the registrar can do is to wait until the freeholder's land certificate comes into the Land Registry on some other matter and then enter the notice on it.

(6) Here I will go back a little to paragraph 3 above. If the freeholder within the seven days, objects to the lease being entered on the freeholder's register, then the registrar should hear and determine the objection, subject to an appeal to the court, see rule 298. If the objection is disallowed, the registration and noting will proceed and will take effect as of the date of application. If the objection is upheld, then the lease should not be registered and no note be made on the freeholder's register.

(7) It is obvious that some time may elapse between the date of the application to register the lease and the eventual registration and the noting on the freeholder's register. Suppose in the interval the freeholder agrees to transfer his freehold or to grant a lease to someone else. The transferee or lessee, before completing, will of course search at the registry. Upon this search, he will be told of any pending application which affects the land. In particular he will be told that there is an application to register a lease as a first registration and he will know that, if this application is granted, it will date back to the date of the original application. So it will take priority over the transfer or lease which is then in contemplation. So it does appear that under the steps I have stated there is good protection against fraud.

Registered Land Practice Notes (1972) pp. 14–15

Protection of lessee where lease not an overriding interest — registration of leases and assignments of leases

(a) *Where the freeholder or superior leasehold is registered (whether in the compulsory areas or not)*

A grant of a term of more than twenty-one years by the registered proprietor must be completed by registration if the grantee is to obtain a legal estate (sections 20 and 23). It is emphasised that this refers to substantive registration of the lessee's term under section 19 (2) or 22 (2).

Notice of the grant should be entered against the freehold or superior leasehold title (section 48) and it is desirable that the land certificate of the title of the freeholder or superior leaseholder should be produced. The land certificate must be produced if the lessor takes a premium (section 64 (1) (c)).

(b) *Where the freehold or superior leasehold is not registered (compulsory areas only)*

(i) A grant of a term of forty years or more or an assignment on sale of leasehold land where the lease has not less than forty years to run at the date of the delivery of the assignment *must* be completed by registration within two months from the date of the grant or the assignment, if the lessee or assignee is to obtain the legal estate (section 123).

(ii) A grant of a term of more than twenty-one years but less than forty years, or an assignment of a term having less than forty years but more than twenty-one years unexpired, *may* be registered.

(c) *Position where lessee fails to register*

(i) As stated above, the lessee will not obtain the legal estate in the lease.

(ii) A lessee who has not protected himself in accordance with the foregoing provisions, may nevertheless have an overriding interest under section 70 (1) (g) whilst in actual occupation of the land or in receipt of the rents and profits thereof, but, if these circumstances change, the overriding interest may well cease (see *Strand Securities Ltd v Caswell* [1965] Ch 958).

(iii) If a lessee or assignee has failed to register in accordance with paragraph (b) (i) above, and application is made for the registration of the freehold or superior leasehold, the existence of the lease ought to be disclosed in the application, and if it is, notice of it will be entered on the register automatically. If the grantee or assignee subsequently applies for registration, he will have no difficulty in obtaining an order under section 123, provided more than twenty-one years of his lease are unexpired (section 8 (1) (a)).

(iv) If a head lessee fails to register in any case where registration is compulsory, he cannot confer a legal estate on a sub-lessee (*British Maritime Trust v Upsons Ltd* [1931] WN 7).

(d) *The following interests are incapable of registration:—*

(i) A lease with only twenty-one years (or less) to run at the time of application (section 8 (1) (a)).

(ii) A lease originally granted for twenty-one years (or less) (section 19 (2), proviso (a)).

(iii) A mortgage term where there is a subsisting right of redemption (section 8 (1) and section 19 (2), proviso (b)).

(iv) A lease containing an absolute prohibition against alienation *inter vivos* (section 8 (2)).

(v) An agreement for a lease (section 8 (1) (b)).

The interests referred to in items (i), (iv) and (v) should be protected on the register by notice, but such protection is not required in the case of the lease mentioned in (ii), if it was granted at a rent without taking a fine (section 19 (2), proviso (a), and section 70 (1) (k)).

9. Licences[1]

I. Introduction[2]

In its simplest form, a licence is a permission to enter upon land. It makes lawful what would otherwise be a trespass[3]; and, in the absence of special circumstances, is revocable at the will of the licensor. It is not a proprietary interest, and is not the subject matter of a grant.

But there are many ways in which a licence has progressed from this simplistic form. Since the Judicature Act 1873, equitable remedies became available to protect a licensee in suitable cases. The years since World War II have seen a rapid development of their use, and this development is not fully worked out. The earlier cases focussed on the question whether the licensee was to be protected against the licensor, by an injunction restraining the licensor from revoking the licence. Protection of the licensee against the licensor inevitably gave rise to the next question; whether the licensee was also to be protected against third parties, who would usually be the successors in title of the licensor. Protection against third parties further gave rise to the question whether such a licence had acquired proprietary characteristics. It may be that a licence which protects the licensee against third parties should be regarded as "proprietary" in nature, or it may be that an interest should only be regarded as proprietary if it is capable of being assigned, bought and sold, and of passing through the estate of a deceased person. There have not yet been cases in which a

---

[1] Cheshire, pp. 577-589; M & W, pp. 776-786, MM, pp. 351-354; H & M, pp. 650-669; Dawson and Pearce; *Licences Relating to the Occupation or Use of Land* (1979).
[2] (1954) 70 LQR 326 (Lord EVERSHED).
[3] VAUGHAN CJ, in *Thomas v Sorrell* (1673), Vaughan 330 at 351.

protected licensee has purported to "sell" his licence. But there are cases in which licensees have been held to be entitled to an order transferring to them an easement, or a life interest, or a fee simple in the land[4]; or have been held, even in the absence of such order, to be entitled to compensation, in their capacity as licensees, under statutory provisions authorising the payment of compensation to persons having interests in the land[5]. The question of the proper nature of a licence in modern law will not be answered in this book; but it is one which should be borne in mind in reading the cases.

The facts of the cases will show in what a wide variety of circumstances questions of protection of licensees can arise. And it will not be a matter of surprise to recognise that a large percentage of current cases are dealing with arrangements for the occupation of family homes, using "family" in a sense wide enough to include mistresses. This question is related to that discussed in the context of Trusts for Sale[6]. Where a proprietary interest is found by the application of trust doctrines (usually resulting or constructive trust), in the party who is not the legal owner, a beneficial co-ownership is created; and various questions then arise as to the determination of the rights of the parties, as by sale of the premises, or by their retention as a home for (usually) the woman and children. Where a non-owner has no such proprietary interest, protection may be given, by restraining the legal owner from evicting the licensee.

The litigation on the protection of licensees has generally concerned licences of four main types: contractual licences; licences by estoppel; licences arising under a constructive trust; and, for the short period of their recognition, the deserted wife's licence[7]. Each of these will be looked at in turn; but it will be useful, first of all, to lay down some of the basic propositions of the common law. The modern development has been by way of the application of equitable principles and remedies to that situation.

II. The Common Law Rules[8]

A. A Bare and Gratuitous Licence is Revocable at the Will of the Licensor

The licensee here avoids being a trespasser only because of the licensor's permission to enter. Such is the position of a guest at dinner,

---

[4] P. 478, post.

[5] P. 475, post.

[6] P. 228, ante.

[7] Dawson and Pearce use nine categories of licences: Bare Licences; Contractual Licences; Licences by Estoppel; Licences arising under the doctrine of benefit and burden; Licences arising under the doctrine against derogation from grant; Licences and section 62 L.P.A. 1925; Licences arising by operation of law; Licences coupled with an interest; Licences as interests under a constructive trust.

[8] Cheshire, pp. 578–579; M & W, pp. 776–782; MM, pp. 351–352; Dawson and Pearce, pp. 22–24, 68–73.

or of a picnic party in a friend's garden. The licensor is free to
withdraw his permission, as is a bailor in the case of gratuitous
bailment. The licensee then becomes a trespasser, but is allowed a
reasonable time in which to collect his goods, if any, and to leave the
land[9].

B.   Entry upon a Licence does not make it Irrevocable

There is also a doctrine[10] of long standing, little relied on, to the effect
that, if a licence has been acted upon, it is not revocable. Such an
argument would prove too much, for it disregards the many cases in
which licensees are permitted to be evicted after entry[11], and also
disregards the reasoning in other cases in which the licensee has been
protected on other grounds. *Tayler v Waters*[12], one of the leading cases
in support of this theory, was disapproved in *Wood v Leadbitter*
and described as being "to the last degree unsatisfactory"[13]. If the
principle of *Tayler v Waters* had developed, it "would go close to
reversing the general rule of the revocability of licences"[14]. The cases
have been explained as illustrations of the principle of estoppel,
discussed below[15]. But there is no indication that the judges in the
cases so thought, and no express reference to that principle. A related
but distinct concept appears in modern law in the rule formulated by
Lord EVERSHED in *Armstrong v Sheppard and Short Ltd* ([1959] 2 QB
384 at 399, [1959] 2 All ER 651): "If A gives authority to B for the
doing of an act on A's land, and the act is done and completed, then,
whatever be the strict description of the authority . . . it is, generally
speaking at any rate, too late for A . . . to complain of it.[16]"

C.   A Licence is not the Subject Matter of a Grant

This and the following proposition are closely related, and are both
based upon the elementary rule that a grant of property is not

---

[9] *Minister of Health v Bellotti* [1944] KB 298, [1944] 1 All ER 238; *Canadian Pacific
   Rly Co v R* [1931] AC 414; *Australian Blue Metal Ltd v Hughes* [1963] AC 74, [1962]
   3 All ER 335.
[10] *Webb v Paternoster* (1619) Palm 71; *Wood v Lake* (1751) Say 3; *Winter v Brockwell*
   (1807) 8 East 308; *Tayler v Waters* (1817) 7 Taunt 374; *Wallis v Harrison* (1838) 4 M &
   W 538 at 544; *Feltham v Cartwright* (1839) 5 Bing NC 569; *Wood v Manley* (1839)
   11 Ad & El 34 where, however, the licence was coupled with an interest, for the
   licensee was the owner of the hay; *Bendall v McWhirter* [1952] 2 QB 466 at 479, per
   DENNING LJ, [1952] 1 All ER 1307; *Armstrong v Sheppard and Short Ltd* [1959] 2 QB
   384, [1959] 2 All ER 651; *Hounslow London Borough Council v Twickenham Garden
   Developments Ltd* [1971] Ch 233 at 255, [1970] 3 All ER 326; (1965) 29 Conv (NS) 19
   (M. C. Cullity).
[11] E.g. *Winter Garden Theatre (London) Ltd v Millennium Productions Ltd* [1948] AC
   173, [1947] 2 All ER 331; see p. 441, post.
[12] (1817) 7 Taunt 374.
[13] (1845) 13 M & W 838 at 852.
[14] (1965) 29 Conv (NS) 19, 31.
[15] P. 463, post. See Dawson and Pearce, p. 31.
[16] See *Hounslow London Borough Council v Twickenham Gardens Development Ltd*
   [1971] Ch 233 at 255, [1970] 3 All ER 326 at 343.

revocable. A conveyance transfers to the grantee the subject matter of the grant, and it is beyond the grantor's power to recall.

But, of course, to be effective, the conveyance must have concerned something which the law recognises as being the subject matter of a grant and capable of being conveyed. A licensee, as stated above, is merely "not a trespasser". A licence is not a piece of property. But a licence may be coupled with a grant of an interest in property, real or personal, and, as shown in D below[17], it will then be irrevocable.

In *Wood v Leadbitter* (1845) 13 M & W 838, the plaintiff bought a ticket entitling him to enter the grandstand at Doncaster racecourse. On account of alleged malpractices on a previous occasion, he was ordered by the defendant, who was the servant of Lord Eglintoun, the steward of the course, to leave the racecourse. On his refusal, he was physically removed, no more force being used than was reasonably necessary. His action for assault and false imprisonment failed. He was a licensee only; and not a grantee of an interest in land. ALDERSON B, delivering the judgment of the Court of Exchequer, said, at p. 845: "It may further be observed, that a license under seal (provided it be a mere license) is as revocable as a license by parol; and, on the other hand, a license by parol, coupled with a grant, is as irrevocable as a license by deed, provided only that the grant is of a nature capable of being made by parol. But where there is a license by parol, coupled with a parol grant, or pretended grant, of something which is incapable of being granted otherwise than by deed, there the licence is a mere licence; it is not an incident to a *valid* grant, and it is therefore revocable."

LATHAM CJ in *Cowell v Rosehill Racecourse Co Ltd* (1937) 56 CLR 605, said at 616: "Fifty thousand people who pay to see a football match do not obtain fifty thousand interests in the football ground."

This may be logical; but hardly satisfactory. Where a licensee has paid to enter premises for a period of time, and he observes the terms and conditions of the license, is it right that the licensor should be allowed to break the contract and turn the licensee into a trespasser?

In *Hurst v Picture Theatres Ltd* [1915] 1 KB 1, the plaintiff bought a ticket for 6d. to watch a cinema show at a theatre of the defendants. During the performance, the plaintiff was requested to leave on the ground, as the defendant incorrectly believed, that he had not paid for his ticket. He refused, and was ejected forcibly, but without the use of unnecessary violence. His action for assault and false imprisonment succeeded by a majority of 2 to 1. The majority (BUCKLEY and KENNEDY LJJ) found that he had an interest in the land. Since the Judicature Act, an interest in land could be granted without a deed. A

---

[17] P. 438, post.

contract for valuable consideration of which equity would decree specific performance would suffice.

The fallacy of this reasoning was shown by PHILLIMORE LJ, dissenting. The doctrine of *Walsh v Lonsdale*[18], he said, is that a man "has the estate which equity thinks he ought to have. That has no bearing on the question if there is no estate, and no interest in land given by the document relied on".

In short, contractual licences are not grants. They are contracts, and should be treated as such.

D.   A Licence Coupled with a Grant (or an Interest) is Irrevocable

It is an anciently established rule that a licence coupled with a proprietary interest (in land or in a chattel) is irrevocable[19]. The interest must, of course, have been correctly granted[20]. In the grant of incorporeal hereditaments in realty at common law, a seal was needed; but, since the Judicature Act, an agreement for valuable consideration suffices[1]. It is, indeed, somewhat artificial to speak of a licence coupled with an interest in realty; for if the interest is properly granted and is one which involves entry upon another's land, the grantee enters by force of the grant and does not need to rely on a licence.

In the case of licences coupled with a chattel interest, that interest must again be properly granted, usually by gift or sale. Thus, where the occupier gives or sells a stack of coal on the land to a purchaser, the donee or purchaser is entitled to enter the land to take away the coal, and the donor or seller cannot deny him the right[2]. And a contract to cut and carry away timber on the Earl of Tankerville's Estate[3] created a chattel interest in the cut timber and a realty interest in the growing trees.

III.   Licences for Consideration: Contractual Licences[4]

A.   Damages for Breach of Contract

It has been seen that much confusion has been caused by the inability of the common law to give protection to a contractual licensee unless he has a proprietary interest in the land or chattels upon it. This

---

[18] P. 76, ante.

[19] *Webb v Paternoster* (1619) Palm 71; *Wood v Manley* (1839) 11 Ad & El 34, *James Jones & Sons Ltd v Earl of Tankerville* [1909] 2 Ch 440.

[20] On the question whether certain interests need to be regarded as realty or personalty for the purpose of a grant or of compliance with L.P.A. 1925, s. 40, see M & W, pp. 547–549; MM, p. 293; see also p. 58, ante.

[1] *Walsh v Lonsdale* (1882) 21 ChD 9; see p. 77, ante.

[2] *Wood v Manley* (1839) 11 Ad & El 34.

[3] *James Jones & Sons Ltd v Earl of Tankerville* [1909] 2 Ch 440.

[4] Cheshire, pp. 578–581; M & W pp. 780–783; MM, pp. 352–354; Dawson and Pearce, pp. 24–38, 73–97, 133–144, 153–161, 167. See MEGARRY J's summary in *Hounslow London Borough Council v Twickenham Garden Developments Ltd* [1971] Ch 233 at 254, [1970] 3 All ER 326 at 343; *Chandler v Kerley* [1978] 1 WLR 693, [1978] 2 All ER 942.

position, based upon *Wood v Leadbitter*, meant that the licensor could, without giving any reason, turn out at will any watchers of a cinema show, horse race or football match[5]. The only difference between a contractual and a gratuitous licence was that, in the former, the licensor must pay damages. These were commonly assumed to be the price which the licensee had paid to enter. But there seems to be no reason why the damages should not reflect the loss of the licensee's expectation under the contract[6].

In *Tanner v Tanner* [1975] 1 WLR 1346, [1975] 3 All ER 776[7] the plaintiff and defendant had baby daughters. They were not married. The plaintiff purchased a house for the defendant, and she accordingly left her rent-controlled flat. The time came when the plaintiff, having changed his affections, decided to turn out the defendant and the children. She stayed, claiming that she should be allowed to remain in the house with the children until they had finished school. In the County court, an order for possession was made, and the defendant was rehoused by the local authority.

The Court of Appeal held that she was a licensee entitled to protection. She should have been entitled to stay in the house with the children until they left school, if the house continued to be needed for that purpose. But, as they had left, damages were awarded, compensating her for her loss. Lord DENNING MR said p. 1350: "It seems to me that enables an inference to be drawn, namely that in all the circumstances it is to be implied that she had a licence — a contractual licence — to have accommodation in the house for herself and the children so long as they were of school age and the accommodation was reasonably required for her and the children. There was, it is true, no express contract to that effect, but the circumstances are such that the court should imply a contract by the plaintiff — or, if need be impose the equivalent of a contract by him — whereby they were entitled to have the use of the house as their home until the girls had finished school. . . . . .

If therefore the defendant had sought an injunction restraining the plaintiff from determining the licence, it should have been granted. The order for possession ought not to have been made." . . . . .

But the order for possession had been made and the defendant had moved out. His Lordship continued at p. 1351: "What is to be done? The judge ordered possession in six weeks. Thereupon the local housing authority (as they usually do when an order for possession is made) provided accommodation for the defendant and the children. She moved out in pursuance of the order and does not ask to be put back now. Seeing that the order ought not to have been made and we reverse it, what is to be done? It seems to me that this court has ample

---

[5] Per PHILLIMORE LJ, in *Hurst v Picture Theatres Ltd* [1915] 1 KB 1, p. 437, ante; *Cowell v Rosehill Racecourse Co Ltd* (1937) 56 CLR 605.

[6] *Kerrison v Smith* [1897] 2 QB 445.

[7] (1976) 92 LQR 168 (J.L. Barton).

power, when it reverses an order of the court below, to do what is just and equitable to restore the position as fairly as it can in the circumstances. The plaintiff has obtained an unjust benefit and should make restitution. In the circumstances the court can and should assess compensation to be payable by him. . . . . It seems to me a reasonable sum for loss of this licence (which the defendant ought not to have lost) would be £2,000."[8]

B. Injunction To Restrain Breach of Contract

The more realistic question, however, is whether a licensee may obtain a remedy to prevent the revocation of the licence; as the defendant in *Tanner v Tanner* would have done if she had not previously been rehoused. The plain fact is that the common law had no appropriate remedy; and this may explain the development of the tenuous and unsatisfactory common law doctrine that a licence, once entered upon, was irrevocable[9].

After the Judicature Act, equitable remedies became available. We saw that, in *Hurst's* case[10], the Court of Appeal found that the licensee should be protected; but only by reasoning the weakness of which is shown in the dissenting judgment of PHILLIMORE LJ. The availability of equitable rights and remedies is vital in this situation. But the relevant remedy is not a decree of specific performance, but an injunction to restrain the licensor from breaking the contract. Such a remedy has the effect of course of requiring the licence to continue; this is a form of "negative specific performance"[11]; and the terminology of specific performance is sometimes used in contractual licence cases[12]. But if such references mean that a decree of specific performance will issue, then the question is raised again of determining what proprietary interest was being transferred, and would signal a return to the heresy of Hurst's case.

The crucial question in considering the revocability of contractual licences is whether the licence is revocable according to the proper construction of the contract[13]. Express provision will often be made. In its absence, the right to revoke will depend upon the intention of the parties as gathered from all the surrounding circumstances. There is

---

[8] No contract was implied in similar circumstances in *Horrocks v Forray* [1976] I WLR 230, [1976] 1 All ER 737 (described in (1976) 40 Conv (NS) 362 (M. Richards) as "*Tanner v Tanner* in a middle class setting").

[9] P. 436, ante.

[10] [1915] 1 KB I, p. 437, ante. The plaintiff received £150 as damages for assault and false imprisonment.

[11] *Lumley v Wagner* (1852) 1 DeG M & G 604; Ames: *Lectures on Legal History*, p. 370; H & M pp. 101–102.

[12] E.g. MEGARRY J in *Hounslow London Borough Council v Twickenham Garden Developments Ltd* [1971] Ch 233 at p. 254, [1970] 3 All ER 326 at 343; Lord DENNING MR in *Binions v Evans* [1972] Ch 359 at p. 367, [1972] 2 All ER 70 at 75.

[13] *Winter Garden Theatre (London) Ltd v Millennium Productions Ltd* [1948] AC 173, [1947] 2 All ER 331.

no presumption one way or the other[14]; but it will presumably be more difficult to establish the non-revocability of a licence unlimited in time than it would be in the case of a licence for a specific period. The court may find that the licensor has a right to revoke upon giving reasonable notice, and will determine what that period is. If the licensor has no right to revoke, the question is whether the case is one in which it is appropriate to protect the licensee by an injunction restraining the licensor from breaking the contract, or whether the licensee should be left to his remedy in damages.

A licensee who is himself in breach of the terms of the contractual licence will not be protected[15]; nor presumably if the effect of the injunction would be to compel people to live together in intolerable circumstances[16]. And it was recently held that a licensee, whose occupation of premises was dependent upon his employment, was not protected where he was dismissed in breach of contract[17].

In *Winter Garden Theatre (London) Ltd v Millennium Productions Ltd* [1948] AC 173, [1947] 2 All ER 331, the appellant granted to the respondent a licence to use and present plays in the Winter Garden Theatre in Drury Lane for a period of six months, from 6 July 1942 with an option to renew for a further six months at an increased payment. The licence provided that on the expiration of these periods the respondents should have the option to continue the licence for an unstated period, terminable by them at a month's notice. No provision was made for termination by the appellants. The options were duly exercised. The appellants retained possession of the bars and cloakrooms. After three years the appellants wished to terminate the licence, and on 11 September 1945 served a notice requiring the respondents to vacate the theatre on 13 October 1945. The respondents refused to leave and brought an action for a declaration that the licence was not revocable; or, alternatively, if it was, that a reasonable period after the service of the notice had not expired.

The House of Lords held that, on the proper construction of the contract, the licence was terminable on giving reasonable notice, and that the notice given was reasonable. The question of wrongful revocation did not arise. But, on that subject, Lord UTHWATT said, at p. 202:

"My view as to the construction of the agreement renders it unnecessary to consider whether *Hurst v Picture Theatres Ltd* ([1915]

---

[14] Ibid at p. 203, per Lord MACDERMOTT; *Re Spenborough UDC's Agreement* [1968] Ch 139 , [1967] 1 All ER 959; *Beverley Corpn v Richard Hodgson and Sons Ltd* (1972) 225 Estates Gazette 799. Lord PORTER said at p. 195 that a licence was prima facie revocable.

[15] *Thompson v Park* [1944] KB 408, [1947] 2 All ER 477, where the defendant had "been guilty at least of riot, affray, wilful damage, forcible entry, and, perhaps, conspiracy", per GODDARD LJ at p. 409. The defendant was a preparatary school master who had moved, with his pupils, to the plaintiff's school when the defendant's premises were unavailable because of the war.

[16] Ibid, per GODDARD LJ at p. 409.

[17] *Ivory v Palmer* [1975] ICR 340. For a consideration of the question of the circumstances in which misbehaviour by a licensee by estoppel will allow his licence to be terminated, see *Williams v Staite* [1979] Ch 291, [1978] 2 All ER 928; p. 500, post.

1 KB 1)[18] was rightly decided, or to express any concluded opinion on the question of the remedies now open in every court to a bare licensee who claims that the licensor has in breach of his bargain affected to revoke it. I merely confess my present inability to see any answer to the propositions of law stated by the Master of the Rolls in his judgment in the case under appeal[19]. The settled practice of the courts of equity is to do what they can by an injunction to preserve the sanctity of a bargain. To my mind, as at present advised, a licensee who has refused to accept the wrongful repudiation of the bargain which is involved in an unauthorized revocation of the licence is as much entitled to the protection of an injunction as a licensee who has not received any notice of revocation; and, if the remedy of injunction is properly available in the latter case against unauthorised interference by the licensor, it is also available in the former case. In a court of equity, wrongful acts are no passport to favour.

I would allow the appeal.''

The Court of Appeal in this case had been faced with the question of the proper solution to the problem of the protection of a contractual licensee under a contract which was construed as irrevocable; it had taken a different view from the House of Lords of the construction of the contract. The statement of the law by Lord GREENE MR, referred to by Lord Uthwatt is as follows ([1946] 1 All ER 678, at p. 684):

"The next question which I must mention is this. The respondents[20] have purported to determine the licence. If I have correctly construed the contract their doing so was a breach of contract. It may well be that, in the old days, that would only have given rise to a right to sue for damages. The licence would have stood revoked, but after the expiration of what was the appropriate period of grace the licensees would have been trespassers and could have been expelled, and their right would have been to sue for damages for breach of contract, as was said in *Kerrison v Smith* ([1897] 2 QB 445). But the matter requires to be considered further, because the power of equity to grant an injunction to restrain a breach of contract is, of course, a power exercisable in any court. The general rule is that, before equity will grant such an injunction, there must be, on the construction of the contract, a negative clause express or implied. In the present case it seems to me that the grant of an option which, if I am right, is an irrevocable option, must imply a negative undertaking by the licensor not to revoke it. That being so, in my opinion, such a contract could be enforced in equity by an injunction. Then the question would arise, at what time can equity interfere? If the licensor were threatening to revoke, equity, I apprehend, would grant an injunction to restrain him

---

[18] See p. 437, ante.
[19] Infra.
[20] I.e., *Winter Garden Theatre (London) Ltd* who became the appellants in the House of Lords.

from carrying out that threat. But supposing he has in fact purported to revoke, is equity then to say: 'We are now powerless. We cannot stop you from doing anything to carry into effect your wrongful revocation?' I apprehend not. I apprehend equity would say: 'You have revoked and the licensee had no opportunity of stopping you doing so by an injunction; but what the court of equity can do is to prevent you from carrying that revocation into effect and restrain you from doing anything under it.' In the present case, nothing has been done. The appellants are still there. I can see no reason at all why, on general principles, equity should not interfere to restrain the licensors from acting upon the purported revocation, that revocation being, as I consider, a breach of contract.

Looking at it in that rather simple way, one is not concerned with the difficulties which are suggested to arise from the decision of this court in *Hurst v Picture Theatres Ltd* ([1915] 1 KB 1)[1]. Counsel for the respondents agreed that in this court he could not ask us to take a different view to the view there taken. It is a decision which has not satisfied everybody, but, quite apart from that decision, the simple propositions which I have just enunciated, which I cannot help thinking are right, would appear to me to get round any difficulties which might be felt as to the reasoning in *Hurst v Picture Theatres Ltd*. We are not concerned here with a licence coupled with a grant. Nothing of that kind is suggested. It is not suggested that that type of licence is in question here. It is a pure licence and nothing else, and the breach of the licence contract by the licensor could be restrained by a court of equity, and a court of equity would interfere to prevent the licensor taking steps pursuant to his wrongful revocation. That seems to me to put the matter right so far as this case is concerned[2]."

CHANDLER *v* KERLEY
[1978] 1 WLR 693, [1978] 2 All ER 942 (CA, Lord SCARMAN, MEGAW and ROSKILL LJJ)[3]

LORD SCARMAN read the following judgment. This appeal is concerned with the right to occupy a dwelling-house, 300 Salisbury Road, Testwood, Totton, in Hampshire. The plaintiff owns it: the defendant, with her two children, occupies it. She will not leave, because she says the plaintiff has agreed that she may stay there as long as she pleases.

---

[1] See p. 437, ante.
[2] See also *Hounslow London Borough Council v Twickenham Garden Developments Ltd* [1971] Ch 233, at p. 254, [1970] 3 All ER 326 where MEGARRY J summarizes the law relating to contractual licenses. (1971) 87 LQR 309; *Mayfield Holdings Ltd v Moana Reef Ltd* [1973] 1 NZLR 309.
[3] *Roach v Johannes* [1976] CLY 1549 (licence of "paying guest" terminable on giving reasonable notice, which in the circumstances was not less than 21 days); *Piquet v Tyler* (1978) unreported [1978] CLY 119 CA (irrevocable licence for life of defendants, who had, by arrangement with plaintiff, surrendered protected tenancy to look after plaintiff's aged mother).

The plaintiff went to the Southampton County Court with a claim for possession, alleging that the defendant was a trespasser, her licence having been terminated. The defendant not only resisted the claim, but also counterclaimed for a declaration that she is a tenant for life, alternatively that "she is the beneficiary under a trust ... upon terms that she is entitled to remain therein with her children for as long as she wishes." In this court the defendant was allowed, the plaintiff not opposing, to amend her counterclaim by adding in the further alternative that she is a licensee for life, or for so long as her children remain in her custody and the younger is of school age and so long as she does not remarry, or for a period terminable only by reasonable notice.

On 26 May 1977, Judge McCreery dismissed the plaintiffs' claim and gave judgment for the defendant on the counterclaim, declaring that the defendant is a beneficiary under a trust upon terms that she is entitled to occupy the house for her life or for so long as she pleases. The plaintiff now appeals.

The facts are unusual. The plaintiff, Mr. Chandler, acquired the house from the defendant, Mrs. Kerley, and her husband in the following circumstances. In 1972 Mr. and Mrs. Kerley jointly bought the house for £11,000, intending it to be their family home. The purchase was partly financed by a building society mortgage for £5,800. Mr. Kerley paid the mortgage instalments. They have two children, both of whom are now living with their mother. In 1974 the marriage broke down. In May of that year Mr. Kerley left home, not to return. However, he continued to pay the building society instalments. The defendant and the children continued to live in the house.

At about the time Mr. Kerley left home, the defendant met the plaintiff. They became friends: sexual intercourse followed, and the defendant became the plaintiff's mistress. This relationship continued until January 1976, when it ended.

Early in 1975 Mr. Kerley stopped paying the building society: he said he could not afford it. He and his wife put the house on the market for £14,950, but failed to find a buyer — even when in the autumn they reduced the asking price to £14,300. Meanwhile the building society was threatening to foreclose. The defendant naturally told the plaintiff of her anxieties. He wanted to help, and said he could afford £10,000, but no more. Finally it was agreed that the Kerleys should sell the house to the plaintiff for that figure, and the house was sold to him in December 1975. The net proceeds of sale, after they had paid off the debt to the building society, were divided — £1,000 to the defendant and £1,800 to Mr. Kerley. The defendant accepted less than her half-share because she understood that the plaintiff was going to let her live in the house.

The arrangement between the plaintiff and the defendant which made all this possible was, according to the judge's findings, the following. The plaintiff agreed to buy the house for £10,000 (a figure substantially less than the asking price) upon the understanding that the defendant would continue to live in it indefinitely till he moved in.

For at this time, 1975, they contemplated living together in the house as man and wife once they were free to do so, that is to say, after a divorce between Mr. and Mrs. Kerley. The defendant, very sensibly, did ask the plaintiff what would happen if they parted: he replied that he could not put her out.

Within six weeks of the purchase of the house, the plaintiff had brought their relationship to an end. It was not suggested, however, that he did so in order to get the defendant out of the house. Nevertheless he did purport in 1976 to serve a notice terminating her licence. It was given by solicitors' letter dated April 29 requiring the lady to quit on May 28.

The judge found that the plaintiff had granted the defendant an express licence and that the notice was not effectual to terminate it. There is now no challenge to these findings. The defendant is, therefore, a licensee whose right to occupy has not yet been terminated. In so far, therefore, as the appeal is against the dismissal of the plaintiff's claim for possession, it must fail. The true dispute, however, between the parties arises on the counterclaim. There are two substantial issues: (1) the terms of the licence; and (2) whether the defendant has an equitable interest arising under a constructive trust; and, if so, what is the extent of the interest.

The judge's findings as to the terms of the licence are obscure. He rejected the submission made on behalf of the defendant that she had an implied licence to remain in the house all her life: yet he also held (and I quote from the notes of judgment) "that there was an express agreement between the two and, as a result, there was a constructive trust with Mr. Chandler as trustee and Mrs. Kerley being the beneficiary." It is possible, though certainly not clear to me, that the judge is here finding an express agreement that she may remain for life: for he certainly granted her a declaration that she had an equity to that effect. But, whatever the finding as to the terms of the agreement, the reasoning of the judge in this passage is, in my judgment, unsound. If the defendant can establish a licence for life, there is neither room nor need for an equitable interest. Since the fusion of law and equity, such a legal right can be protected by injunction: see *Hurst v Picture Theatres Ltd* [1915] 1 KB 1, *Winter Garden Theatre (London) Ltd v Millennium Productions Ltd* [1948] AC 173, [1947] 2 All ER 331 and *Foster v Robinson* [1951] 1 KB 149, [1950] 2 All ER 342, *per* Lord Evershed MR, at p. 156. If she cannot establish such a licence (express or implied), she cannot establish an equity: for no question of estoppel arises in this case. It is simply a case of what the parties envisaged by their arrangement: see *Dodsworth v Dodsworth* (1973) 228 Estates Gazette 1115, where the Court of Appeal considered it not right to confer upon the defendants a greater interest than was envisaged by the parties. In the present case the parties certainly intended that the arrangement between them should have legal consequences. If, therefore, they agreed upon a right of occupation for life, there is a binding contract to that effect: if they did not so agree, there is nothing to give rise to an equity to that effect.

In a case such as the present, the role of equity is supportive and supplementary. Where the parties have contracted for a licence, equity will today provide an equitable remedy to protect the legal right, for example by injunction, which may be by interlocutory order, if the court considers it just and convenient: see section 45, Supreme Court of Judicature (Consolidation) Act 1925. If, however, the legal relationship between the parties is such that the true arrangement envisaged by the parties will be frustrated if the parties are left to their rights and duties at law, an equity will arise which the courts can satisfy by appropriate equitable relief. An old illustration of equity at work in this way was given by Parker J in *Jones v Earl of Tankerville* [1909] 2 Ch 440 at 443 (quoted in *Hurst's* case [1915] 1 KB 1 at 9). Likewise in another old case, *Frogley v Earl of Lovelace* (1859) John 333, Page Wood V-C granted an injunction to restrain the defendant from interfering with the plaintiff shooting over his land "until the defendant shall have executed a proper legal grant of the right claimed by the plaintiff."

The judge in the present case believed he was constrained by the decision in *Bannister v Bannister* [1948] 2 All ER 133 to declare the existence of a right of occupation for life, even though he had rejected an implied contractual right to that effect. But, when analysed, *Bannister v Bannister* is no more than an illustration of the supportive and supplementary role of equity. It was a case in which the plaintiff gave an oral undertaking that the defendant would be allowed to live in the cottage rent-free for as long as she desired. The defendant could not show a legal right: but she did establish the existence of an understanding or arrangement with the plaintiff which, though giving rise to no legal right, brought into existence an equity which the court thought it just to satisfy by declaring the defendant had an equitable life interest in the cottage with the plaintiff as her trustee. The court treated this life interest as the equivalent to a tenancy for life under the Settled Land Act 1925.

Errington v Errington and Woods [1952] 1 KB 290, [1952] 1 All ER 149 is a decision which follows the same pattern. The arrangement in that case was oral. The father bought a house, put his son and daughter-in-law into occupation and promised them that if they paid the instalments on the mortgage the house would be theirs when the last instalment was paid. The Court of Appeal held that the arrangement conferred upon the daughter-in-law (father having died, son having left his wife and she continuing to pay the instalments) a contractual right of occupation which carried with it an equity which on payment of the last instalment would give her a good equitable title to the house. The case may be said to be a classic illustration of equity supplementing a contractual right so as to give effect to the intention of the parties to the arrangement. *Binions v Evans* [1972] Ch 359, [1972] 2 All ER 70 is to the same effect.

The defendant in this appeal, however, relied strongly on *Bannister v Bannister* [1948] 2 All ER 133 to support a submission that she has a tenancy for life. Like Megaw L.J. in *Binions v Evans* at 370, I find great difficulty in understanding how the court in *Bannister's* case came to conclude that there was in that case a tenancy for life under the Act. It was, however, a matter which depended upon the particular facts of the case.

As Russell LJ commented in *Dodsworth v Dodsworth* (1973) 228 Estates Gazette 1115, there is a risk that such an inference may fall foul of the Settled Land Act 1925, which confers a power of sale and of leasing upon the tenant — powers which cannot, for instance, have been in the minds of the parties in the present case. The present is *not*, in my judgment, a case of life tenancy: and in this respect *Bannister v Bannister* is a decision to be treated as turning on the particular facts of that case.

The most recent case to which we were referred is the decision of the Court of Appeal in *Tanner v Tanner* [1975] 1 WLR 1346, [1975] 3 All ER 776. It is close on its facts to the present case, in that the defendant was found to have no proprietary interest in the house but did have a contractual right to live in it until her two children, of whom the plaintiff was the father, were no longer of school age. The defendant had been the mistress of the plaintiff, who had bought the house (when she had been a tenant protected by the Rent Act) to provide accommodation for her and their two children. The court held it to be a case of contractual licence, Lord Denning MR saying at p. 1350:

> "It was a contractual licence of the kind which is specifically enforceable on her behalf: and which he can be restrained from breaking: and he could not sell the house over her head so as to get her out in that way."

It is yet another case of a contractual licence supported by equity so far, and only so far, as is necessary to give effect to the expectations of the parties when making their arrangement.

Accordingly, the task in this case is to determine what were the terms of the arrangement, express and implied, between the parties. I agree with the judge that it is not possible to imply a licence to the defendant to occupy the house for her life. The plaintiff had invested £10,000 in the house and, in the absence of express stipulation, cannot be supposed in the circumstances to have frozen his capital for as long as the defendant pleased or for the duration of her life. On the other hand, the plaintiff was well aware that the defendant wanted the house as a home for her children as well as for herself. It would be wrong, however, to infer, in the absence of an express promise, that the plaintiff was assuming the burden of housing another man's wife and children indefinitely, and long after his relationship with them had ended. The balance of these factors leads me to the conclusion that the defendant's contractual licence was terminable upon reasonable notice, and that the notice must be such as to give the defendant ample opportunity to re-house herself and her children without disruption. In my judgment 12 calendar months' notice is reasonable in the circumstances.

For these reasons I do not think this is a case in which it is necessary to invoke the support of any equitable doctrine. The defendant is entitled to 12 months' notice. It follows that the appeal against the dismissal of the claim to possession fails in my judgment, the licence not yet having been determined. The order upon the counterclaim should, in my judgment, be varied so as to substitute for the declaration granted by the judge a declaration that the defendant's licence is terminable upon reasonable notice and that reasonable notice is one of 12 calendar months from its service.

In *Hardwick v Johnson* [1978] 1 WLR 683, [1978] 2 All ER 935, a mother purchased a house for occupation by her son and daughter-in-law as their home. Rent of £7 per week was payable, but it ceased to be paid after a month or two, and the mother did not demand it. Within a year, marriage was collapsing, and the son was about to leave his wife. The mother sued for possession and arrears of rent. The daughter-in-law gave birth to a child, and claimed to be entitled to remain in possession on paying £7 a week. The Court of Appeal held that the licence was irrevocable. The daughter-in-law was not in breach in respect of the arrears because the mother had indicated no desire to claim the rent. ROSKILL LJ said at p. 690:

"When one looks at the correspondence before action brought and indeed at the pleadings, one sees an ever increasing number of legal arguments being founded upon a perfectly simple family arrangement; but in my judgment this case can be decided upon one very short ground. It is plain, as the deputy judge said, that there was here never any tenancy. It is equally plain, in my judgment, that there was here a licence; and for my part, with respect to Lord Denning MR, I prefer to call it a contractual licence rather than an equitable licence.

The only question we have to decide is what was the nature of that contractual licence. Was it a licence to both the son and his future wife as joint licensees or was it a licence to the son alone? Nobody contemplated the possibility that this marriage would break down as soon as it did. Nobody comtemplated that the son would within a couple of years or so go off and have an affair with another woman, abandoning his wife with the child of the marriage who remained in the house. What the parties would have agreed upon if they had thought of that possibility in March 1973 no one can tell; but the court, as Lord Denning MR has said and as has been said many times before (and Lord Diplock also said it in *Pettitt v Pettitt* [1970] AC 777 at 821–823, [1969] 2 All ER 385), has in those circumstances to impute to the parties a common intention to make some arrangement in the events which have occurred, albeit unexpectedly. I cannot, for my part, think that anybody would impute to these parties an intention that if the marriage broke down as soon as it did and the husband went off with another woman the wife would be liable to be ejected from the home together with the child of the marriage. It seems to me that the arrangement was perfectly straightforward: it was a joint contractual licence to the husband and wife to live there. It was not conditional upon the marriage succeeding. It was not conditional upon a number of other possibilities.

I am disinclined to express any opinion on what if any events that licence is now determinable. Suffice it to say that in my judgment it is not determinable in the event which has occurred, namely, that the husband has left the wife — no divorce proceedings are pending, as Lord Denning MR has said — since that licence was not given only to the husband. It seems to me that no event has yet taken place which justifies the bringing to an end of this contractual licence; and therefore, for that reason, I think the deputy circuit judge reached the right conclusion in a careful and closely reasoned judgment."

Lord DENNING said that the licence was a licence by estoppel. BROWNE LJ, agreed with ROSKILL LJ.

QUESTION

Could you decide, with any confidence, whether a licence will, in these types of circumstances, be held to be a contractual licence, or a licence by estoppel? Does it make any difference? Might it be that the court categorizes the licence according to the result which it hopes to reach?

C. Enforcement of Contractual Licences Against Third Parties[4].

The next question is whether a contractual licence, which is irrevocable by the licensor, is binding on a third party. On the one hand, it is well settled that, subject to exceptions, contractual rights are binding on, and enforceable by the parties to the contract only[5]. On the other hand, the protection given to the licensee may be of little use if a transfer of the land to a third party leaves that third party free to claim possession, and leaves the licensee to his remedy in damages against the original licensor. Further, a licensee's right to protection by injunction against the licensor gives him some sort of equity, and it is arguable that such an equity should give him protection against all but bona fide purchasers for value without notice.

Whether or not contractual licences should be held to be binding on third parties is ultimately a policy question. So it has been in other areas of the law. Contractual restrictions on the use of chattels have been held not to be binding on third parties even though they have express notice of the restriction[6]. The great case of *Tulk v Moxhay*[7] decided that a covenant restricting the user of land was binding on

---

[4] Dawson and Pearce, pp. 153–161.

[5] *Dunlop Pneumatic Tyre Co Ltd v Selfridge & Co Ltd* [1915] AC 847; *Beswick v Beswick* [1968] AC 58, [1967] 2 All ER 1197.

[6] *De Mattos v Gibson* (1859) 4 De G & J 276; *Lord Strathcona SS Co Ltd v Dominion Coal Co. Ltd* [1926] AC 108; *Port Line Ltd v Ben Line Steamers Ltd* [1958] 2 QB 146, [1958] 1 All ER 787.

[7] (1848) 2 Ph 774; p. 704 post.

successors in title of the convenantor taking with notice. It was soon found that so wide a doctrine would create burdens on land for which there was no justification, and the basis of the doctrine was later changed so as to limit the running of the burden to cases in which the continuation of the covenant was necessary to protect land capable of benefiting; more like a negative equitable easement[8]. The point is that the whole question whether an equity enforceable against one contracting party is enforceable against third parties is determined, not by a rule of thumb, but by an examination of the policy questions applicable to the particular situation.

On this basis, it would seem clear that contractual licences should not, in the ordinary case, be binding on third parties. Otherwise, thousands of minor personal arrangements, like hotel bookings, contracts for lodgings, car parking contracts, and a host of other minor non-proprietary arrangements would in effect come on to the title; with no effective way of determining the question whether or not the third party had notice. After all, the contractual licensee has his remedy in damages.

Authority is to the same effect[9]. But there are a few special situations in which contractual licences have been held binding on third parties. *Errington v Errington and Woods* ([1952] 1 KB 290, [1952] 1 All ER 149)[10] is generally accepted as being a case of a contractual licence. But there is clearly an estoppel situation also, and it will be discussed under that heading. Further, in *Binions v Evans* ([1972] Ch 359, [1972] 2 All ER 70)[11], the conveyance was made expressly subject to the contractual right of the licensee; and this was held to create a constructive trust.

Similarly in *DHN Food Distributors Ltd v Tower Hamlets London Borough Council* [1976] 1 WLR 852, [1976] 3 All ER 462[12], an irrevocable contractual licence was said, as one of three rationes in the case, to give rise to a constructive trust, and to "give to D.H.N. a sufficient interest in the land to qualify them for compensation for disturbance" upon compulsory purchase by the local authority.

i.   THIRD PARTIES TAKING WITH NOTICE

KING *v* DAVID ALLEN AND SONS, BILLPOSTING LTD
[1916] 2 AC 54 (HL, Lord BUCKMASTER LC Earl LOREBURN and Lord ATKINSON)

By an agreement of 1 July 1913, the appellant gave the respondents an exclusive permission to affix advertisements for a stated period to the walls of a cinema which was to be built.

---

[8] P. 709, post.
[9] *Clore v Theatrical Properties Ltd and Westby & Co Ltd* [1936] 3 All ER 483; *King v David Allen & Sons, Billposting Ltd* [1916] 2 AC 54.
[10] P. 452, post.
[11] P. 455, post.
[12] (1977) 93 LQR 170 (D. Sugarman and F. Webb); (1977) 41 Conv (NS) 73. See also *Re Sharpe* [1980] 1 WLR 219, [1980] 1 All ER 198 (plaintiff entitled under constructive trust as against trustee in bankruptcy to remain in house until repaid sums advanced to brankrupt).

In September 1913 the appellant executed a lease of the property to the cinema company, but the lease, disregarding arrangements previously made, contained no reference to the agreement of 1 July. The company refused to allow the advertisement to be posted and the respondents brought an action against the appellant King, for breach of the agreement of 1 July.

Held. The appellant (the licensor) was liable in damages.

EARL LOREBURN: My Lords, I agree in the opinion expressed by the Lord Chancellor, and with him I greatly regret the position in which Mr. King has been placed, which seems to me to be hard upon him. He has behaved perfectly honestly in the whole business, and one cannot help regretting the expense to which he has been put.

I have very little to add to what has been said, but I look at the case in this way. The plaintiffs say that Mr. King promised them for four years the use of a certain wall for advertising purposes by the agreement of 1 July 1913, and they say that after that Mr. King demised that land, and that Mr. King's lessees refused to make good the promise in regard to advertisement. Well, if the agreement of 1 July, which purports to be on the face of it a licence, was equivalent to creating an incorporeal hereditament or a sufficient interest in land, Mr. King did not break his contract in making the lease, and would not be responsible for any trespasses that were committed by his licensees. But we must look at the document itself, and it seems to me that it does not create any interest in land at all; it merely amounts to a promise on the part of Mr. King that he would allow the other party to the contract to use the wall for advertising purposes, and there was an implied undertaking that he would not disable himself from carrying out his contract. Now Mr. King has altered his legal position in respect of his control of this land. Those to whom he granted the lease have disregarded his wishes and refused to allow his bargain to be carried out, and they have been practically enabled to do so by reason of the demise that he executed. In these circumstances it seems to me that there has been a breach in law of the contract of 1 July, and Mr. King has disabled himself from giving effect to it as intended by parting with his right to present possession. That is enough to establish a case for damages against Mr. King. There may be a remedy over against the lessees. I say nothing of that, because they are not here, and I do not wish either to encourage or to discourage any further proceedings; but this I think is clear: that the existence of such a remedy, if remedy there be, does not release Mr. King from his liability to answer for breaking the contract which he made.

In *Clore v Theatrical Properties Ltd and Westby & Co Ltd* [1936] 3 All ER 483, an indenture provided that "the lessor doth hereby demise and grant unto the lessee the free and exclusive use of all the refreshment rooms ... of the theatre ... for the purpose only of the supply to and the accommodation of the visitors to the theatre and for

no other purpose whatsoever". The definition clause stated that
the terms "lessor" and "lessee" should include their executors,
administrators and assigns. Both parties assigned and the assignees
of the lessor sought to prevent the assignees of the lessee from
exercising any of the rights conferred upon the lessee by the indenture.
The action was brought by the plaintiff (Clore) for a declaration that
the defendants could not exercise rights given to the licensees by the
indenture.

The Court of Appeal (Lord WRIGHT MR, ROMER and GREENE
LJJ) held that the indenture was not a lease, but a licence, and
that it could only be enforced between the parties to it. They upheld
CLAUSON J, in making the declaration.

Lord WRIGHT MR, said at p. 485: "I think that this court is bound
by the decisions in previous cases[13] to hold that this document does
not convey any interest in land but is merely a personal contract
embodying a licence. On that ground the learned judge decided this
matter and I agree with him and in particular with his final conclusion
in that the rights mentioned in the document are purely contractual.
It follows from this that there is no circumstance which enables the
present appellants to assert any rights against the present respondent
because there is no contractual nexus between them".

ii.   SPECIAL CASES. ESTOPPEL; CONSTRUCTIVE TRUST

ERRINGTON *v* ERRINGTON AND WOODS
[1952] 1 KB 290, [1952] 1 All ER 149 (CA, SOMERVELL, DENNING and
HODSON LJJ)

In 1936 a father bought a house through a building society, paying a
lump sum of £250 and leaving the balance of £500 on mortgage. He
told his daughter-in-law shortly after her marriage to his son, that the
property would be theirs when they had paid the last instalment on the
mortgage, gave the daughter-in-law the building society's book, and
allowed them to go into occupation.The father, however, took the
conveyance in his own name and paid the rates. The young couple paid
the instalments as they became due, but the payments were not all
completed when the father died in 1945 leaving all his property,
including the house in question, to his widow. The son then left his wife
and went to live with his mother; his mother now claimed possession
of the house from her daughter-in-law, who had remained in the
house with her sister, the second defendant, and continued to pay the
instalments.

Held. The daughter-in-law was a licensee who was entitled to
protection against the plaintiff.

DENNING LJ: It is to be noted that the couple never bound themselves to pay the instalments to the building society; and I see no
reason why any such obligation should be implied. It is clear law that
the court is not to imply a term unless it is necessary; and I do not

---

[13] *Edwardes v Barrington* (1901) 85 LT 650, HL affirming SC *sub nom Daly v Edwardes*
(1900) 83 LT 548; *Frank Warr & Co Ltd v LCC,* [1904] 1 KB 713.

see that it is necessary here. Ample content is given to the whole arrangement by holding that the father promised that the house should belong to the couple as soon as they paid off the mortgage. The parties did not discuss what was to happen if the couple failed to pay the instalments to the building society, but I should have thought it clear that, if they did fail to pay the instalments, the father would not be bound to transfer the house to them. The father's promise was a unilateral contract — a promise of the house in return for their act of paying the instalments. It could not be revoked by him once the couple entered on performance of the act, but it would cease to bind him if they left it incomplete and unperformed, which they have not done. If that was the position during the father's lifetime, so it must be after his death. If the daughter-in-law continues to pay all the building society instalments, the couple will be entitled to have the property transferred to them as soon as the mortgage is paid off; but if she does not do so, then the building society will claim the instalments from the father's estate and the estate will have to pay them. I cannot think that in those circumstances the estate would be bound to transfer the house to them, any more than the father himself would have been.

What is the result in law of those facts? The relationship of the parties is open to three possible legal constructions: (i) That the couple were tenants at will paying no rent. That is what the judge thought they were. He said that, in this case, just as in *Lynes v Snaith* ([1899] 1 QB 486), the defendant "was in exclusive possession and was therefore not a mere licensee but in the position of a tenant at will". But in my opinion it is of the essence of a tenancy at will that it should be determinable by either party on demand, and it is quite clear that the relationship of these parties was not so determinable. The father could not eject the couple as long as they paid the instalments regularly to the building society. It was therefore not a tenancy at will. I confess that I am glad to reach this result; because it would appear that, if the couple were held to be tenants at will, the father's title would be defeated after the lapse of 13 years[13a], long before the couple paid off the instalments, which would be quite contrary to the justice of the case. (ii) That the couple were tenants at a rent of 15s. 0d. a week, that rent being for convenience paid direct to the building society instead of to the father, and the tenancy being either a weekly tenancy or a tenancy for the duration of the mortgage repayments. But I do not think that the 15s. 0d. can possibly be regarded as rent, for the simple reason that the couple were not bound to pay it. If they did not pay it, the father could not sue for it or distrain for it. He could only refuse to transfer the house to them. If the 15s. 0d. was not rent, then it affords no ground for inferring a tenancy. (iii) That the couple were licensees, having a permissive occupation short of a tenancy, but with a contractual right, or at any rate, an equitable right to remain so long as they paid the instalments, which would grow into a good equitable title to the house itself as soon as the mortgage was paid. This

---

[13a] See now Limitation Amendment Act 1980, ss. 3 (1), 13 (2), p. 163, ante.

is, I think, the right view of the relationship of the parties. I will explain how I arrive at it.

The classic definition of a licence was propounded by Vaughan CJ in the seventeenth century in *Thomas v Sorrell* ((1673) Vaugh 330, at 351): "A dispensation or licence properly passeth no interest nor alters or transfers property in any thing, but only makes an action lawful, which without it had been unlawful." The difference between a tenancy and a licence is, therefore, that, in a tenancy, an interest passes in the land, whereas, in a licence, it does not. . . .

The result of all these cases is that, although a person who is let into exclusive possession is prima facie to be considered to be a tenant, nevertheless he will not be held to be so if the circumstances negative any intention to create a tenancy. Words alone may not suffice. Parties cannot turn a tenancy into a licence merely by calling it one. But if the circumstances and the conduct of the parties show that all that was intended was that the occupier should be granted a personal privilege, with no interest in the land, he will be held to be a licensee only. In view of these recent cases I doubt whether *Lynes v Snaith* ([1899] 1 QB 486), and the case of the gamekeeper referred to therein (unreported case; Kennedy J), would be decided the same way today.

Applying the foregoing principles to the present case, it seems to me that, although the couple had exclusive possession of the house, there was clearly no relationship of landlord and tenant. They were not tenants at will but licensees. They had a mere personal privilege to remain there, with no right to assign or sub-let. They were, however, not bare licensees. They were licensees with a contractual right to remain. As such they have no right at law to remain, but only in equity, and equitable rights now prevail. I confess, however, that it has taken the courts some time to reach this position. At common law a licence was always revocable at will, notwithstanding a contract to the contrary: *Wood v Leadbitter* ((1845) 13 M & W 838)[14]. The remedy for a breach of the contract was only in damages. That was the view generally held until a few years ago: see, for instance, what was said in *Booker v Palmer* ([1942] 2 All ER 674, 677), and *Thompson v Park* ([1944] KB 408, 410, [1944] 2 All ER 477). The rule has, however, been altered owing to the interposition of equity.

Law and equity have been fused for nearly 80 years, and since 1948 it has been clear that, as a result of the fusion, a licensor will not be permitted to eject a licensee in breach of a contract to allow him to remain: see, *London Millennium Productions Ltd v Winter Garden Theatre per* Lord Greene ([1946] 1 All ER 678, 680)[15], and in the House of Lords *per* Lord Simon ([1948] AC 173, 191, [1947] 2 All ER 342); nor in breach of a promise on which the licensee has acted, even though he gave no value for it: see *Foster v Robinson* ([1951] 1 KB 149, 156, [1950] 2 All ER 342), where Sir Raymond Evershed MR said that as a

---

[14] See p. 437, ante.
[15] See p. 442, ante.

result of the oral arrangement to let the man stay, he was entitled as licensee to occupy the premises without any payment of rent for the rest of his days. This infusion of equity means that contractual licences now have a force and validity of their own and cannot be revoked in breach of the contract. Neither the licensor nor anyone who claims through him can disregard the contract except a purchaser for value without notice. . . .

In the present case it is clear that the father expressly promised the couple that the property should belong to them as soon as the mortgage was paid, and impliedly promised that so long as they paid the instalments to the building society they should be allowed to remain in possession. They were not purchasers because they never bound themselves to pay the instalments, but nevertheless they were in a position analogous to purchasers. They have acted on the promise, and neither the father nor his widow, his successor in title, can eject them in disregard of it. The result is that in my opinion the appeal should be dismissed and no order for possession should be made.

BINIONS *v* EVANS[16]
[1972] Ch 359, [1972] 2 All ER 70 (CA, Lord DENNING MR, MEGAW and STEPHENSON LJJ)

The trustees of the Tredegar Estate in Monmouthshire and South Wales entered into an agreement with Mrs. Evans, the 79 year old widow of an employee of the Estate. The trustees agreed to permit her to reside in and occupy a cottage on the estate for the remainder of her life as tenant at will rent free. She agreed to keep it in a proper manner and "personally occupy and live in it as a private residence only and not assign, sub-let or part with the possession" of it. Two years later the trustees sold the cottage to the plaintiffs expressly subject to Mrs. Evans's tenancy agreement, a copy of which was handed to the purchasers. Six months later the plaintiffs gave Mrs. Evans notice to quit as a mere tenant at will and claimed possession of the cottage.

Held. Order for possession refused. Per MEGAW and STEPHENSON LJJ: Mrs. Evans was tenant for life under the Settled Land Act 1925.

LORD DENNING MR (having held that Mrs. Evans was not a tenant at will, nor a lessee nor a tenant for life under the Settled Land Act):

An equitable interest
Seeing that the defendant has no legal estate or interest in the land, the question is what right has she? At any rate, she has a contractual right to reside in the house for the remainder of her life or as long as she pleases to stay. I know that in the agreement it is described as a tenancy: but that does not matter. The question is: What is it in

---

[16] (1972) 88 LQR 336 (P.V.B.); (1972) 36 Conv (NS) 266 (J. Martin); 277 (D.J. Hayton); (1973) CLJ 123 (R.J. Smith); (1973) 117 Sol Jo 23 (B. W. Harvey); (1977) 93 LQR 561 (J.A. Hornby).

reality? To my mind it is a licence, and no tenancy. It is a privilege which is personal to her. On all the modern cases, which are legion, it ranks as a contractual licence, and not a tenancy: see *Shell-Mex and BP Ltd v Manchester Garages Ltd* [1971] 1 WLR 612, [1971] 1 All ER 841.

What is the status of such a licence as this? There are a number of cases in the books in which a similar right has been given. They show that a right to occupy for life, arising by contract, gives to the occupier an equitable interest in the land: just as it does when it arises under a settlement: see *Re Carne's Settled Estates* [1899] 1 Ch 324 and *Re Boyer's Settled Estates* [1916] 2 Ch 404. The courts of equity will not allow the landlord to turn the occupier out in breach of the contract: see *Foster v Robinson* [1951] 1 KB 149, 156, [1950] 2 All ER 342; nor will they allow a purchaser to turn her out if he bought with knowledge of her right — *Errington v Errington and Woods* [1952] 1 KB 290, 299; [1952] 1 All ER 149.

It is instructive to go back to the cases before the Supreme Court Judicature Act 1873. They show that, if a landlord, by a memorandum in writing, let a house to someone, let us say to a widow, at a rent, for her life or as long as she pleased to stay, the courts of equity would not allow the landlord to turn her out in breach of his contract. If the landlord were to go to the courts of law and obtain an order in ejectment against her, as in *Doe d Warner v Browne* (1807) 8 East 165, the courts of equity would grant an injunction to restrain the landlord from enforcing his rights at law, as in *Browne v Warner* (1808) 14 Ves 409. The courts of equity would give the agreement a construction, which Lord Eldon LC called an "equitable construction," and construe it as if it were an agreement to execute a deed granting her a lease of the house for her life — *Browne v Warner* (1907) 14 Ves 156, 158. They would order the landlord specifically to perform the contract, so construed, by executing such a deed. This court did so in *Zimbler v Abraham* [1903] 1 KB 577. This means that she had an equitable interest in the land. So much so that if a purchaser wished to buy her interest from her, he had to pay her its full value as such. Malins V-C so held in *Re King's Leasehold Estate* (1873) LR 16 Eq 521, 527, where he described it as an "equitable interest." It follows that, if the owner sold his reversion to another, who took with notice of the widow's interest, his successor could not turn her out any more than he could. She would have, I should have thought, at least as strong a case as the occupier in *Webb v Paternoster* (1619) Poph 151, which received the blessing of Lord Upjohn in *National Provincial Bank Ltd v Hastings Car Mart Ltd* [1965] AC 1175, 1239, [1965] 2 All ER 472.

Suppose, however, that the defendant did not have an equitable interest at the outset, nevertheless it is quite plain that she obtained one afterwards when the Tredegar Estate sold the cottage. They stipulated with the plaintiffs that they were to take the house "subject to" the defendant's rights under the agreement. They supplied the plaintiffs with a copy of the contract: and the plaintiffs paid less because of her right to stay there. In these circumstances, this court will impose on the plaintiffs a constructive trust for her benefit: for the simple reason that it would be utterly inequitable for the plaintiffs to turn the defendant out contrary to the stipulation subject to which they took the premises. That seems to me clear from the important decision of *Bannister v Bannister* [1948] 2 All ER 133, which was applied by the judge, and which I gladly follow.

The imposing of a constructive trust is entirely in accord with the precepts of equity. As Cardozo J once put it: "A constructive trust is the formula through which the conscience of equity finds expression," see *Beatty v Guggenheim Exploration Co* (1919) 225 NY 380, 386: or, as Lord Diplock put it quite recently in *Gissing v Gissing* [1971] AC 886, 905, [1970] 2 All ER 780, a constructive trust is created "whenever the trustee has so conducted himself that it would be inequitable to allow him to deny to the cestui que trust a beneficial interest in the land acquired."

I know that there are some who have doubted whether a contractual licensee has any protection against a purchaser, even one who takes with full notice. We were referred in this connection to Professor Wade's article Licences and Third Parties in (1952) 68 LQR 337, and to the judgment of Goff J in *Re Solomon, A Bankrupt, ex parte Trustee of the Property of the Bankrupt v Solomon* [1967] Ch 573, [1966] 3 All ER 255. None of these doubts can prevail, however, when the situation gives rise to a constructive trust. Whenever the owner sells the land to a purchaser, and at the same time stipulates that he shall take it "subject to" a contractual licence, I think it plain that a court of equity will impose on the purchaser a constructive trust in favour of the beneficiary. It is true that the stipulation (that the purchaser shall take it subject to the rights of the licensee) is a stipulation for the benefit of one who is not a party to the contract of sale; but, as Lord Upjohn said in *Beswick v Beswick* [1968] AC 58, 98, [1967] 2 All ER 1197, that is just the very case in which equity will "come to the aid of the common law." It does so by imposing a constructive trust on the purchaser. It would be utterly inequitable that the purchaser should be able to turn out the beneficiary. It is to be noticed that in the two cases which are said to give rise to difficulty *King v David Allen & Sons, Billposting Ltd* [1916] 2 AC 54 and *Clore v Theatrical Properties Ltd and Westby & Co Ltd* [1936] 3 All ER 483, there was no trace of a stipulation, express or implied, that the purchaser should take the property subject to the right of the contractual licensee. In the first case, if Mr. King had protected himself by stipulating that the company should take the lease "subject to the rights of David Allen," I cannot think that he would have been held liable to damages. In the second case the documents were exceedingly complicated, but if Mr. Clore had acquired the theatre "subject to the rights of the licensees," I cannot suppose that this court would have allowed him to disregard those rights.

In many of these cases the purchaser takes *expressly* "subject to" the rights of the licensee. Obviously the purchaser then holds the land on an imputed trust for the licensee. But, even if he does not take expressly "subject to" the rights of the licensee, he may do so *impliedly.* At any rate when the licensee is in actual occupation of the land, so that the purchaser must know he is there, and of the rights which he has: see *Hodgson v Marks* [1971] Ch 892, [1971] 2 All ER 684. Whenever the purchaser takes the land impliedly subject to the rights of the contractual licensee, a court of equity will impose a constructive trust for the beneficiary. So I still adhere to the proposition I stated in *Errington v Errington and Woods* [1952] 1 KB 290, 299, [1952] 1 All ER 149, and elaborated in *National Provincial Bank Ltd v Hastings Car Mart Ltd* [1964] Ch 665, 686–689, [1964] 1 All ER 688, namely, that, when the licensee is in actual occupation, neither the licensor nor anyone who claims through him can disregard the contract except a purchaser for value without notice.

Conclusion
In my opinion the defendant, by virtue of the agreement, had an equitable interest in the cottage which the court would protect by granting an injunction against the landlords restraining them from turning her out. When the landlords sold the cottage to a purchaser "subject to" her rights under the agreement, the purchaser took the cottage on a constructive trust to permit the defendant to reside there during her life, or as long as she might desire. The courts will not allow the purchaser to go back on that trust. I entirely agree with the judgment of Judge Bulger. I would dismiss this appeal.

STEPHENSON LJ: Apart from authority, I would not have thought that such an interest could be understood to amount to a tenancy for life within the meaning of the Settled Land Act 1925, and I would have thought that the other terms of her tenancy (as I think it ought properly to be called) are inconsistent with a power to ask for the legal estate to be settled on her or to sell the cottage. But *Bannister v Bannister* [1948] 2 All ER 133 is a clear decision of this court that such words as have been used in this agreement (excepting, I must concede, the words "as tenant at will of them") create a life interest determinable (apart from the special considerations introduced by the Settled Land Act 1925) on the beneficiary ceasing to occupy the premises and the landlords hold the cottage on trust to permit her to occupy it "during her life or as long as she lives," as Judge Bulger held, and subject thereto in trust for them.

I therefore find it unnecessary to consider or decide the vexed questions (1) whether this agreement is or creates an irrevocable contractual licence to occupy, and (2) whether such a licence has been elevated to a status equivalent to an estate or interest in land by decisions of this court such as *Errington v Errington and Woods* [1952] 1 KB 290, [1952] 1 All ER 149 or *Foster v Robinson* [1951] 1

KB 149, [1950] 2 All ER 342 or still awaits legislation before it can so achieve transmissibility to subsequent purchasers with notice: see the rival views set out by Goff J in *Re Solomon, A Bankrupt, ex parte Trustee of the Property of the Bankrupt v Solomon* [1967] Ch 573, 582–586 [1966] 3 All ER 255.

QUESTION

Have contractual licences become interests in land? (1953) 16 MLR 1 (G.C.Cheshire); (1952) 16 Conv (NS) 323 (F.R.Crane); (1953) 17 Conv (NS) 440 (L.A.Sheridan); Dawson and Pearce Chap. 11.

IV. Constructive Trusts

Before dealing with the major topic of Licences by Estoppel, it will be useful to refer to the doctrine, which has already been met in *Binions v Evans*[17] and *DHN Food Distributors Ltd v Tower Hamlets London Borough Council*[18], (both of which cases could be included in this section) and which will appear again in many of the estoppel cases: that of the constructive trust in favour of the licensee. Equity finds a constructive trust, in various circumstances, on the principle of unjust enrichment. In the present context, the finding of a constructive trust in favour of the licensee creates an equitable interest in his favour. This solution has sometimes been too readily applied; without appreciating the conveyancing problems which follow; as has been explained. This development stems back to *Bannister v Bannister* in 1948[19], where the facts provided a compelling situation for the protection of an old lady who had no proprietary interest in the premises. This was before the High Trees doctrine of promissory estoppel had been widely recognised, and before licensees were protected on the ground of estoppel. The advantage of an estoppel theory is that, as will be seen, the court has available to it a much wider choice of remedy. *Bannister v Bannister* would probably be so treated at the present day[20].

BANNISTER *v* BANNISTER
[1948] 2 All ER 133 (CA, SCOTT and ASQUITH LJJ and JENKINS J)

The defendant was the owner of two cottages, Nos. 30 and 31. In 1943, she sold them to the plaintiff, her brother-in-law, for £250 (£150 below

---

[17] [1972] Ch 359, [1972] 2 All ER 70; p. 455, ante.
[18] [1976] 1 WLR 852, [1976] 3 All ER 462; p. 450, ante.
[19] [1948] 2 All ER 133.
[20] (1977) 93 LQR 561 (J.A. Hornby): see also *Binions v Evans* [1972] Ch 359, [1972] 2 All ER 70 p. 455, ante; *DHN Food Distributors Ltd v Tower Hamlets London Borough Council* [1976] 1 WLR 852, [1976] 3 All ER 462, p. 450, ante; *Re Sharpe* [1980] 1 WLR 219, [1980] 1 All ER 198, p. 450 n. 12, ante.

the market price) under an oral arrangement by which the brother-in-law would "let you stay [in No. 30] as long as you like, rent free". No mention of this arrangement was made in the conveyance. The defendant lived in the cottage until 1945 when she gave up possession of all except one downstairs room. In 1947, the plaintiff claimed possession of that, on the ground that she was a tenant at will only.

Held. The plaintiff was entitled to a life interest determinable upon her ceasing to reside in the cottage under a constructive trust created by the oral agreement.

SCOTT LJ: It is, we think, clearly a mistake to suppose that the equitable principle on which a constructive trust is raised against a person who insists on the absolute character of a conveyance to himself for the purpose of defeating a beneficial interest, which, according to the true bargain, was to belong to another, is confined to cases in which the conveyance itself was fraudulently obtained. The fraud which brings the principle into play arises as soon as the absolute character of the conveyance is set up for the purpose of defeating the beneficial interest, and that is the fraud to cover which the Statute of Frauds or the corresponding provisions of the Law of Property Act 1925, cannot be called in aid in cases in which no written evidence of the real bargain is available. Nor is it, in our opinion, necessary that the bargain on which the absolute conveyance is made should include any express stipulation that the grantee is in so many words to hold as trustee. It is enough that the bargain should have included a stipulation under which some sufficiently defined beneficial interest in the property was to be taken by another. The above propositions are, we think, clearly borne out by the cases to which we were referred of *Booth v Turle* (1873) LR 16 Eq 182, *Chattock v Muller* (1878) 8 ChD 177, *Re Duke of Marlborough* [1894] 2 Ch 133, and *Rochefoucauld v Boustead* [1897] 1 Ch 196.

We see no distinction in principle between a case in which property is conveyed to a purchaser on terms that the entire beneficial interest in some part of it is to be retained by the vendor (as in *Booth v Turle*) and a case, like the present, in which property is conveyed to a purchaser on terms that a limited beneficial interest in some part of it is to be retained by the vendor. We are, accordingly, of opinion that the third ground of objection to the learned county court judge's conclusion also fails. His finding that there was no fraud in the case cannot be taken as meaning that it was not fraudulent in the plaintiff to insist on the absolute character of the conveyance for the purpose of defeating the beneficial interest which he had agreed the defendant should retain. The conclusion that the plaintiff was fraudulent, in this sense, necessarily follows from the facts found, and, as indicated above, the fact that he may have been innocent of any fraudulent intent in taking the conveyance in absolute form is for this purpose immaterial. . . . The plaintiff holds No. 30 in trust during the life of the defendant to permit the defendant to occupy the same for so long as she may desire to do so, and subject thereto in trust for the plaintiff.

A trust in this form has the effect of making the beneficiary a tenant for life within the meaning of the Settled Land Act 1925.

In *Hussey v Palmer* [1972] 1 WLR 1286, [1972] 3 All ER 744[1], Mrs. Hussey, an elderly widow, was invited to live with her daughter and son-in-law. To accommodate her, an additional bedroom was built on to the house, and Mrs. Hussey paid £607, the cost of the construction.

Differences arose, and Mrs. Hussey left. She claimed recovery of the money. Lord DENNING MR, in upholding the claim, said, at p. 1289: "If there was no loan, was there a resulting trust? and, if so, what were the terms of the trust?

Although the plaintiff alleged that there was a resulting trust, I should have thought that the trust in this case, if there was one, was more in the nature of a constructive trust: but this is more a matter of words than anything else. The two run together. By whatever name it is described, it is a trust imposed by law whenever justice and good conscience require it. It is a liberal process, founded upon large principles of equity, to be applied in cases where the legal owner cannot conscientiously keep the property for himself alone, but ought to allow another to have the property or the benefit of it or a share in it. The trust may arise at the outset when the property is acquired, or later on, as the circumstances may require. It is an equitable remedy by which the court can enable an aggrieved party to obtain restitution. It is comparable to the legal remedy of money had and received which, as Lord Mansfield said, is 'very beneficial and therefore, much encouraged' [*Moses v MacFerlan* (1760) 2 Burr 1005 at 1012]. Thus we have repeatedly held that, when one person contributes towards the purchase price of a house, the owner holds it on a constructive trust for him, proportionate to his contribution, even though there is no agreement between them, and no declaration of trust to be found, and no evidence of any intention to create a trust. Instances are numerous where a wife has contributed money to the initial purchase of a house or property; or later on the payment of mortgage instalments; or has helped in a business: see *Falconer v Falconer* [1970] 1 WLR 1333, [1970] 3 All ER 449; *Heseltine v Heseltine* [1971] 1 WLR 342, [1971] 1 All ER 952 and *Re Cummins* [1972] Ch 62, [1971] 3 All ER 782. Similarly, when a mistress has contributed money, or money's worth, to the building of a house: *Cooke v Head* [1972] 1 WLR 518, [1972] 2 All ER 38. Very recently we held that a purchaser, who bought a cottage subject to the rights of an occupier, held it on trust for her benefit: *Binions v Evans* [1972] Ch 359, [1972] 2 All ER 70. In all those cases it would have been quite inequitable for the legal owner to take the property for himself and exclude the other from it. So the law imputed or imposed a trust for his or her benefit.

---

[1] (1973) 89 LQR 2.

The present case is well within the principles of those cases. Just as a person, who pays part of the purchase price, acquires an equitable interest in the house, so also he does when he pays for an extension to be added to it. Mr. Owen has done a lot of research and has found a case in 1858 to that very effect. It is *Unity Joint Stock Mutual Banking Association v King* (1858) 25 Beav 72. A father had land on which he built a granary. His two sons built two other granaries on it at a cost of £1,200. Sir John Romilly MR held that the two sons had a lien or charge on the property as against the father, and any person claiming through him. The father had never promised to pay the sons £1,200. He was not indebted to them in that sum. He had never engaged or promised to make over the land to them or to give them a charge on it. Yet they had a lien or charge on the land. That case was approved by the Privy Council in *Chalmers v Pardoe* [1963] 1 WLR 677, 681–682, [1963] 3 All ER 552, where it was said to be based on the 'general equitable principle that ... it would be against conscience' for the owner to take the land without repaying the sums expended on the buildings. To this I would add *Inwards v Baker* [1965] 2 QB 29, [1965] 1 All ER 446, when a son built a bungalow on his father's land in the expectation that he would be allowed to stay there as his home, though there was no promise to that effect. After the father's death, his trustees sought to turn the son out. It was held that he had an equitable interest which was good against the trustees. In those cases it was emphasised that the court must look at the circumstances of each case to decide in what way the equity can be satisfied. In some by an equitable lien. In others by a constructive trust. But in either case it is because justice and good conscience so require.

In the present case Mrs. Hussey paid £607 to a builder for the erection of this extension. It may well be, as the defendant says, that there was no contract to repay it at all. It was not a loan to the son-in-law. She could not sue him for repayment. He could not have turned her out. If she had stayed there until she died, the extension would undoubtedly have belonged beneficially to the son-in-law. If, during her lifetime, he had sold the house, together with the extension, she would be entitled to be repaid the £607 out of the proceeds. He admits this himself. But he has not sold the house. She has left, and the son-in-law has the extension for his own benefit and could sell the whole if he so desired. It seems to me to be entirely against conscience that he should retain the whole house and not allow Mrs. Hussey any interest in it, or any charge upon it. The court should, and will, impose or impute a trust by which Mr. Palmer is to hold the property on terms under which, in the circumstances that have happened, she has an interest in the property proportionate to the £607 which she put into it. She is quite content if he repays her the £607. If he does not repay the £607, she can apply for an order for sale, so that the sum can be paid to her. But the simplest way for him would be to raise the £607 on mortgage and pay it to her. But, on the legal point raised, I have no doubt there was a resulting trust, or, more accurately, a constructive trust, for her, and I would so declare. I would allow the appeal, accordingly."

V. Licences by Estoppel[2]

The doctrine of estoppel, which is of general application at law and in equity, has played a significant part in the modern development of the law of licences. The basic principle of the doctrine is that a person who makes, by word or conduct, a representation to another, intending that other to act on it, and the other does so to his detriment[3], will not be allowed subsequently to take a position inconsistently with the representation. At common law, the representation had to be one of existing fact[4]. The estoppel acted like a rule of evidence. The representor could not subsequently allege, in dealings with the representee, that the facts were different from those represented. The estoppel did not however give rise to any independent cause of action.

The doctrine widened in equity so as to cover a representation, not only of fact, but of intention, or a promise. This is promissory estoppel; which became well known through *Central London Property Trust Ltd v High Trees House Ltd* (1946)[5] in 1947, and was firmly established in later years. Promissory estoppel also gives negative protection only, and is not a cause of action[6].

The past few years have seen a remarkable growth, in the context of licences, of a different, but related doctrine: called proprietary estoppel. The doctrine deals with the equities arising out of a situation in which one party (O) knowingly encourages another to act (A), or acquiesces in his acting to his detriment and in infringement of O's rights, O but not A being aware both of the infringement, and of A's ignorance of it. O will be unable to complain later of the infringement; and may indeed be required to make good A's expectations in respect of the rights exercised. Thus, unlike other estoppels, this doctrine may create a claim, and an entitlement to property rights in or over land[7]. Authoritative statements laying down the requirements for the operation of the doctrine appear below.

These estoppel doctrines have been applied to many cases involving licences. The licence may be gratuitous or contractual. The categories of licences may therefore overlap[8]. If the licence is contractual, the

---

[2] Cheshire, pp. 581-583, 585-586; M & W, pp. 778-779; MM, pp. 352-353; Spencer Bower and Turner, *Estoppel by Representation* (3rd edn., 1977) passim, and especially Chap. 12; Dawson and Pearce, pp. 29-36, 97-99, 144-145, 161-163.
[3] As by expenditure of money, or giving up present accommodation.
[4] *Jorden v Money* (1854) 5 H L Cas 185.
[5] [1947] KB 130, [1956] 1 All ER 256.
[6] *Combe v Combe* [1951] 2 KB 215, [1951] 1 All ER 767.
[7] *Western Fish Products Ltd v Penwith District Council* (1979) 38 P & CR 7.
[8] In *Hardwick v Johnson* [1978] 1 WLR 683, [1978] 2 All ER 935, p. 448, ante, the Court of Appeal divided 2-1 on the question of the type of licence. But that made no difference to the result.

licensee may be protected under the doctrines relating to contractual licences, discussed above; and it may be unnecessary to invoke the doctrine of estoppel[9]. Where, however, the licensee is seeking protection against a third party, a licence by estoppel is more effective. It will be seen that the courts appear to have these factors in mind in categorizing licences.

Decisions to protect licensees of all kinds raise a number of difficulties. Some of these have been seen in the context of contractual licences. With licences by estoppel, the courts recognise their power and duty in these cases as being to "look at the circumstances in each case to decide in what way the equity can be satisfied"[10]. The court may decide to protect the licensee by means of an injunction restraining the licensor from interfering; and in cases of estoppel by representation, this may be the only choice[11]. Such a solution produces conveyancing difficulties; for it leaves the licensee in possession with no title. His equity is good, not only against the licensor, but also against third parties other than a bona fide purchaser for value without notice[12]. In such a situation, it seems that, in the case of unregistered land, the licence not being registrable, we are thrown back on the hazards of notice[13]. With registered land, a licensee in occupation will presumably have an overriding interest, and may be able to acquire protection by entering a caution or a notice[14].

The negative protection under the classical estoppel principle has advantages in situations where the time is not yet ripe for a final settlement; as where a licensee is protected in occupation which may only be temporary and something less than a permanent solution is required; as where a son builds a bungalow on his father's land in the expectation of being allowed to stay there for the rest of his life[15]; or parents give up a home and move in to look after an aged grandparent[16]; or a mistress requires a home until the children are of school age[17]; or a garage is built which overlaps a neighbour's boundary[18].

---

[9] *Tanner v Tanner* [1975] 1 WLR 1346, [1975] 3 All ER 776; p. 439, ante.
[10] *Plimmer v Wellington Corpn* (1884) 9 App Cas 699 at 714; *Chalmers v Pardoe* [1963] 1 WLR 677 at 682, [1963] 3 All ER 552; *Inwards v Baker* [1965] 2 QB 29 at 37, [1965] 1 All ER 446; *E.R. Ives Investment Ltd v High* [1967] 2 QB 379 at 395, [1967] 1 All ER 504; *Crabb v Arun District Council* [1976] Ch 179 at 188, [1975] 3 All ER 865.
[11] Unless a constructive trust is found; *Bannister v Bannister* [1948] 2 All ER 133; *Hussey v Palmer* [1972] 1 WLR 286, [1972] 3 All ER 744; p. 461, ante.
[12] *Hopgood v Brown* [1955] 1 WLR 213, [1955] 1 All ER 550.
[13] Which may not be a serious problem if the licensee is in occupation; but could be if the licensee's rights were only exercisable periodically; (1956) 20 Conv (NS) 281 (R.H. Maudsley); Dawson and Pearce, p. 162.
[14] Cheshire, pp. 588–589; Dawson and Pearce, pp. 194–200.
[15] *Inwards v Baker* [1965] 2 QB 29, [1965] 1 All ER 446; p. 469, post.
[16] *Piquet v Tyler* (1978) unreported [1978] CLY 119; CA. *Dodsworth v Dodsworth* (1973) 228 Estates Gazette 1115, *Williams v Staite* [1979] Ch 291, [1978] 2 All ER 928; *Griffiths v Williams* (1978) 248 Estates Gazette 947.
[17] *Tanner v Tanner* [1975] 1 WLR 1346, [1975] 3 All ER 776 a contractual licence also; damages were awarded because the licensee had already been rehoused; p. 439, ante.
[18] *Hopgood v Brown*, supra.

In several of the recent cases, the court, applying the doctrine of proprietary estoppel, has found it best to declare that some interest is to be vested in the licensee. If the proper documentation follows, the conveyancing difficulties are avoided; but until that time, they exist as before; perhaps more acutely; for it is one thing for a purchaser to buy land which is subject to a licensee's temporary rights of protection; and another to find that he has taken title from a non-owner, or has bought settled land from someone other than the tenant for life. Some of these difficulties were not foreseen in the earlier cases; but the courts, as will be seen from the cases, are now aware of the problems, especially that of the application of the Settled Land Act 1925[19] and attempt to avoid them.

The court exercises wide discretionary powers in seeking the just solution. Negative protection may be hazardous and inadequate. A positive solution, ordering a transfer of the land to the licensee, may do injustice to the legal owner; as where a prior owner promised a gift, failed to make it, and a conveyance is ordered, without payment, by the successor owner[20]. The court has power to order a transfer, subject to payment by the licensee of the value of the site; or to order compensation to the licensee for his expenditure; and it may in some circumstances be best to give to the licensee the choice. This situation indeed "displays equity at its most flexible[1]." The court has to bear in mind the equities between the parties involved in all the circumstances; and also the effect of its order upon the conveyancing system. The extent to which these principles have been observed should be considered in the cases which follow.

In *Ramsden v Dyson* (1866) LR 1 HL 129, Lord KINGSDOWN in a dissenting speech, where however the difference of opinion was on the application of the principle to the facts, and not on the statement of the principle, said at p. 170:

"If a man, under a verbal agreement with a landlord for a certain interest in land, or, what amounts to the same thing, under an expectation, created or encouraged by the landlord, that he shall have a certain interest, takes possession of such land, with the consent of the landlord, and upon the faith of such promise or expectation, with the knowledge of the landlord, and without objection by him, lays out money upon the land, a Court of equity will compel the landlord to give effect to such promise or expectation."

Spencer Bower and Turner: *The Law Relating to Estoppel by Representation* (3rd edn. 1977).

"*Encouragement or acquiescence*

289. 'Encouragement' or 'acquiescence' may provide a foundation for estoppels in an interesting variety of circumstances. In the first

---

[19] See (1977) 93 LQR 561 (J.A. Hornby), [1978] Conv 250.
[20] *Dillwyn v Llewelyn* (1862) 4 De G F & J 517.
[1] Snell, p. 568.

edition of this work acquiescence was treated simply as an example of the general doctrine of estoppel by representation, no distinction being made between this manifestation of the principle of estoppel and any other. It is difficult or impossible, however, to maintain this attitude in its entirety; as will presently be seen, it will be submitted in this chapter that in at least two important respects estoppels arising from encouragement or acquiescence may be regarded as different from normal estoppels. The first is the degree of actual knowledge which must be possessed by the party to be bound[2]; the second is the use which may be made of the doctrine of acquiescence to found a cause of action[3]. . . . .

The principle stated

290. The general principle may thus be stated: Where A has a right or title which B is in fact infringing under a mistaken belief that his acts are not acts of infringement at all, and A is aware of his own title or right, and also aware of B's invasion of that title or right, and of his erroneous belief that he is not encroaching thereon, but is lawfully exercising rights of his own, and yet, with that knowledge, A so conducts himself, or so abstains from objection, protest, warning, or action, as to foster and maintain the delusion under which he knows that B is labouring, and induce B to act to his prejudice on the faith of the acknowledgement to be implied from such conduct or inaction, A is not permitted afterwards to assert his own rights against B, or contest B's rights against himself. . . .

Willmott v Barber[4]

292. Finally, in a passage which is always referred to in this connection, and which, like the first of those already cited, is not limited to encroachments on land, but is framed with the utmost generality, SIR EDWARD FRY deduced from the previous authorities in his judgment in *Willmott v Barber*[5] the following condensed statement of the requisites of a good case of acquiescence or encouragement. 1. In the first place, the plaintiff — in the case before him, the person said to have been 'encouraged' happened to be the plaintiff[6] — must have made a mistake as to his legal rights. 2. Secondly, the plaintiff must have expended some money, or must have done some act . . . on the faith of his mistaken belief. 3. Thirdly, the defendant, the possessor of the legal right, must know of the existence of his own right which is inconsistent with the right claimed by the plaintiff. If he does not know of it, he is in the same position as the plaintiff . . . 4. Fourthly, the defendant, the possessor of the legal right, must know of the plaintiff's mistaken belief of his rights[6a]. If he does not, there is nothing

---

[2] See para. 293.
[3] See para. 307.
[4] (1880) 15 ChD 96.
[5] (1880) 15 ChD 96 at 105–106.
[6] This requirement may be thought especially significant when contrasted with the proposition in Chapter 1 that estoppel "emphatically is not a cause of action in itself, nor does it create one"; see para. 307.
[6a] This was said not to be essential in *Taylor Fashions Ltd v Liverpool Victoria Friendly Society* (1979) 251 Estates Gazette 159 at 161.

to call upon him to assert his own rights. 5. Lastly, the defendant, the possessor of the legal right, must have encouraged the plaintiff in his expenditure of money or in the other acts which he has done, either directly or by abstaining from asserting his legal rights[7].

Proprietary estoppel

308. It has recently become fashionable to use the term 'proprietary estoppel' to signify the doctrine which we have been discussing above under the name of estoppel by encouragement or acquiescence[8]; and, so long as it is understood that this terminology does not produce a new estoppel, but is effective only to assign a new name to an old and well-established one, there can be no objection to the new term. It may easily enough come about, however, that a relaxation in the terminology of a subject may induce a corresponding relaxation in the systematic thought of its philosophers; and it is already possible, in the estoppel cases, to find traces of a distinct tendency loosely to 'lump together' the doctrines of acquiescence, or 'proprietary estoppel', and of promissory estoppel, as if they were one, or took their origin from the same source, or were regulated by the same principles[9]. It is for this reason that the term has not been adopted in this treatise; by keeping to the old terms this book has been able, it is hoped, to adhere more clearly to the presentation of these two doctrines as two, and not one.

The doctrines of acquiescence on the one hand, and of promissory estoppel on the other, must be separately stated, and separately applied, whether they are examined historically or analytically. If the approach be historical, estoppel by acquiescence dates back at least

---

[7] In *Willmott v Barber* at pp. 105-106. The propositions there laid down by FRY J were adhered to and confirmed by him three years later in *Russell v Watts* (1883) 25 ChD 559 at pp. 585-586 CA. After nearly a century SCARMAN LJ is to be found relisting them in *Crabb v Arun District Council* [1976] Ch 179 at 194-195, [1975] 3 All ER 865. *Cf.* the speech of Lord DIPLOCK in *Kammins Ballrooms Co Ltd v Zenith Investments (Torquay) Ltd* [1971] A.C. 850 at 884, [1970] 2 All ER 871, in which the five probanda are noted as positively indispensable. *Cf.*, in Australia, *Wilson v Stewart* (1889) 15 VLR 781. In New Zealand, see *Wellington City Corporation v Rod* [1919] NZLR 595.

[8] E.g., per Lord DENNING MR in *Crabb v Arun District Council,* [1976] Ch 179 at 187, [1975] 3 All ER 865, per SCARMAN LJ in the same case, at p. 193. In *Moorgate Mercantile Co Ltd v Twitchings* [1976] QB 225, at 243, [1975] 3 All ER 314, (later reversed by the House of Lords) Lord DENNING again uses the term. *Cf. Snell's Principles of Equity,* 27th edn., p. 564.

[9] SCARMAN LJ permitted himself to consider the two estoppels in one breath in *Crabb v Arun District Council,* at p. 193. "I do not find helpful the distinction", he says, "between promissory and proprietary estoppel. This distinction may indeed be valuable for those who have to teach or expound the law, but I do not think that in solving the particular problem raised by a particular case, putting the law into categories is of the slightest assistance." To some readers such a reluctance to adhere to a systematic approach to legal doctrine may seem to come perilously close to the abandonment of strict principle. *Cf. per* Lord DENNING MR at p. 187 — a passage which, although it begins by speaking of promissory estoppel and proprietary estoppel as separate conceptions, goes on to deal with the cases supporting these separate doctrines in a paragraph in which it becomes impossible to distinguish one doctrine from the other. It is to be noted, however, that notwithstanding the note *cur. adv. vult.* at p. 868 of [1975] 3 All ER 865, the judgments were in fact apparently delivered extempore — see the corrigenda page of the same volume of the Reports.

as far as 1880, the year of FRY LJ's celebrated judgment in *Willmott v Barber*[10], the five classic probanda in which are still listed as a matter of course in any acquiescence case presenting difficulties in principle. The new promissory estoppel, on the other hand, had never been heard of until 1946, when DENNING J's judgment in *Central London Property Trust Ltd v High Trees House Ltd* was delivered: and even if one goes back to *Hughes v Metropolitan Rly Co*[11] and *Birmingham and District Land Co v London and North Western Rly Co*[12], the two earlier cases from which DENNING J's new doctrine professedly took its origin, it is at once obvious that the doctrine which Lord CAIRNS LC was expounding in the first of these, and which BOWEN LJ expanded in the second, had nothing whatever to do with *Willmott v Barber*. History, then, shows the two doctrines to have originated separately from entirely different kinds of situations, and gives no justification for any attempt at fusion nearly a century afterwards[13].

Authority furnishes the same answer. Till the loose use of the term 'proprietary estoppel' began to encourage such a step, no judge or textbook writer of eminence had thought of confusing these two doctrines. Such a confusion seems logically unjustifiable as soon as the essentials of each doctrine are examined and compared; and if only one point be used as a touchstone, it is obvious that in the case of acquiescence it has always been permissible to use the same facts as give rise to the estoppel as a *cause of action in equity*[14]. Promissory estoppel, on the other hand, does not permit this[15]. This one difference alone should make it impossible for a careful thinker to speak of the two doctrines in one breath; and there are other differences which lead to the same conclusion, the enunciation and consideration of which must be omitted here for reasons of space. The crucial distinction between the doctrines, however, is not a matter upon which the textbook writers are in any disagreement[16].''

Snell's Principles of Equity (27 edn. 1973), p. 567
"*Conferment of title.* The doctrine has, however, been carried beyond any mere use of an estoppel by way of defence[17]. Thus, if O has made an imperfect gift of the land to A, as by merely signing an informal memorandum[18] or uttering words of abandonment[19], the court will compel O to perfect the gift by conveying the land to A[20]. In such cases

---

[10] (1880) 15 ChD 96.
[11] (1877) 2 App Cas 439 HL.
[12] (1888), 40 ChD 268 CA.
[13] The contrast is noticed in the judgment of Lord DIPLOCK in *Kammins Ballrooms Co Ltd v Zenith Investments (Torquay) Ltd* [1971] AC 850, at 883, [1970] 2 All ER 871.
[14] See p. 305.
[15] See Chapter XIV, para. 350.
[16] See, for instance, *Snell's Principles of Equity*, 27th edn., pp. 564 et seq.
[17] *Quaere* why in *Cullen v Cullen* [1962] IR 268 the equity was held to give more than a defence.
[18] *Dillwyn v Llewelyn* (1862) 4 De GF & J 517.
[19] *Thomas v Thomas* [1956] NZLR 785 (husband and wife).
[20] Contrast ante, p. 122 (dealing with imperfect gifts).

the court may act by analogy with the specific performance of contracts: A's expenditure with O's knowledge plays the part both of valuable consideration and of part performance[1]. If the circumstances do not suggest a gift, O may be compelled to convey the land on being paid its unimproved value[2]. Or the circumstances may indicate that A is to have a lease[3], a perpetual easement[4], a perpetual licence[5] or a licence as long as he desires to use the premises as his home[6]; and a lessor may be compelled to grant a licence to assign[7]. Alternatively, A may be given an equitable lien on the property for his expenditure[8], or for the value of his improvements[9]; and in such a case he will be treated as a mortgagee in possession[10]. Or it may appear that A has already had "sufficient satisfaction" for his expenditure, and so is entitled to no relief[11]. The doctrine thus displays equity at its most flexible[12]".

A. Negative Protection[13]

INWARDS v BAKER[14]

[1965] 2 QB 29, [1965] 1 All ER 446 (CA, DENNING MR, DANCKWERTS and SALMON LJJ)

In 1931, the younger Mr. Baker wished to build a bungalow for himself on land which he hoped to purchase, but the project was beyond his means. His father said "Why not put the bungalow on my land and make the bungalow a little bigger?" The son did so, building the bungalow largely through his own labour and expense. He lived there continuously until his father's death in 1951, and also from his father's death until the proceedings began.

---

[1] See *Dillwyn v Llewelyn*, at pp. 521, 522; and see Lord RUSSELL OF KILLOWEN'S restrictive interpretation of *Ramsden v Dyson*, in *Ariff v Jadunath Majumdar* (1931) LR 58 Ind App 91 at 102, 103.

[2] *Duke of Beaufort v Patrick* (1853) 17 Beav 60.

[3] *Stiles v Cowper* (1748) 3 Atk 692; and see *Gregory v Mighell* (1811) 18 Ves 328; *Ramsden v Dyson* (1866) LR 1 H.L. 129.

[4] *Ward v Kirkland* [1967] Ch 194, [1966] 1 All ER 609; *E. R. Ives Investment Ltd v High* [1967] 2 QB 379, [1967] 1 All ER 504.

[5] *Plimmer v Wellington Corpn* (1884) 9 App Cas 699.

[6] *Inwards v Baker* [1965] 2 QB 29, [1965] 1 All ER 446 (son builds bungalow on father's land).

[7] *Willmott v Barber* (1880) 15 ChD 96 (where the claim failed).

[8] *Unity Joint Stock Mutual Banking Association v King* (1858) 25 Beav 72 (land); *Re Foster, Hudson v Foster (No. 2)* [1938] 3 All ER 610 (life insurance policy): and see *Veitch v Caldicott* (1945) 173 LT 30; *Taylor v Taylor* [1956] NZLR 99; *Hussey v Palmer* [1972] 1 WLR 1286, [1972] 3 All ER 744 (trust interest proportionate to expenditure); *sed quaere;* see (1973) 89 LQR 2.

[9] *Raffaele v Raffaele* [1962] WAR 29, discussed by D. E. Allan (1963) 79 LQR 238.

[10] *Neesom v Clarkson* (1845) 4 Hare 97.

[11] *A-G v Balliol College, Oxford* (1744) 9 Mod Rep 407 at 412, per Lord HARDWICKE LC (expenditure by lessee).

[12] See *E. R. Ives Investment Ltd v High* [1967] 2 QB 379 at 399, citing this section.

[13] (1976) 40 Conv (NS) 416 (A.M. Everton). See also *Jones v Jones* [1977] 1 WLR 438, [1977] 2 All ER 231, p. 473, post. It is not clear whether the case fits best into this category or the later one.

[14] (1965) 81 LQR 183 (R. H. Maudsley); *Ward v Kirkland* [1967] Ch 194 at 235–243, [1966] 1 All ER 609; *E. R. Ives Investment Ltd v High* [1967] 2 QB 379, [1967] 1 All ER 504; *Siew Soon Wah v Yong Tong Hong* [1973] AC 836.

The land was left elsewhere in a will dated 1922, and in 1963 the trustees for sale of the land brought proceedings for possession.

Held. The son could not be disturbed.

LORD DENNING MR: The trustees say that at the most Jack Baker had a licence to be in the bungalow but that it had been revoked and he had no right to stay. The judge has held in their favour. He was referred to *Errington v Errington and Woods* ([1952] 1 KB 290)[15] but the judge held that that decision only protected a contractual licensee. He thought that, in order to be protected, the licensee must have a contract or promise by which he is entitled to be there. The judge said: "I can find no promise made by the father to the son that he should remain in the property at all — no contractual arrangement between them. True the father said that the son could live in the property, expressly or impliedly, but there is no evidence that this was arrived at as the result of a contract or promise — merely an arrangement made casually because of the relationship which existed and knowledge that the son wished to erect a bungalow for residence." Thereupon, the judge, with much reluctance, thought the case was not within *Errington's* case, and said the son must go.

The son appeals to this court. We have had the advantage of cases which were not cited to the county court judge, — cases in the last century, notably *Dillwyn v Llewelyn* ((1862) 4 De GF & J 517)[16], and *Plimmer v Wellington Corpn* ((1884) 9 App Cas 699)[17]. This latter was a decision of the Privy Council which expressly affirmed and approved the statement of the law made by Lord Kingsdown in *Ramsden v Dyson* ((1866) LR 1 HL 129, 170). It is quite plain from those authorities that if the owner of land requests another, or indeed allows another, to expend money on the land under an expectation created or encouraged by the landlord that he will be able to remain there, that raises an equity in the licensee such as to entitled him to stay. He has a licence coupled with an equity. Mr. Goodhart urged before us that the licensee could not stay indefinitely. The principle only applied, he said, when there was an expectation of some precise legal term. But it seems to me, from *Plimmer's* case in particular, that the equity arising from the expenditure on land need not fail "merely on the ground that the interest to be secured has not been expressly indicated . . . the court must look at the circumstances in each case to decide in what way the equity can be satisified."

So in this case, even though there is no binding contract to grant any particular interest to the licensee, nevertheless the court can look at the circumstances and see whether there is an equity arising out of the expenditure of money. All that is necessary is that the licensee should, at the request or with the encouragement of the landlord, have spent the money in the expectation of being allowed to stay there. If so, the court will not allow that expectation to be defeated where it

---

[15] See p. 452, ante.
[16] See p. 490, post.
[17] See p. 475, post.

would be inequitable so to do. In this case it is quite plain that the father allowed an expectation to be created in the son's mind that this bungalow was to be his home. It was to be his home for his life or, at all events, his home as long as he wished it to remain his home. It seems to me, in the light of that equity, that the father could not in 1932 have turned to his son and said: "You are to go. It is my land and my house." Nor could he at any time thereafter so long as the son wanted it as his home.

Mr. Goodhart put the case of a purchaser. He suggested that the father could sell the land to a purchaser who could get the son out. But I think that any purchaser who took with notice would clearly be bound by the equity. So here, too, the present plaintiffs, the successors in title of the father, are clearly themselves bound by this equity. It is an equity well recognised in law. It arises from the expenditure of money by a person in actual occupation of land when he is led to believe that, as the result of that expenditure, he will be allowed to remain there. It is for the court to say in what way the equity can be satisfied. I am quite clear in this case it can be satisfied by holding that the defendant can remain there as long as he desires to as his home.

I would allow the appeal accordingly and enter judgment for the defendant.

DANCKWERTS LJ: I agree and I will add only a few words. It seems to me the claim of the defendant in respect of this property is amply covered by *Errington v Errington and Woods*, *Dillwyn v Llewelyn*, and *Plimmer v Wellington Corpn*. Further, it seems to me to be supported by the observations of Lord Kingsdown in *Ramsden v Dyson*. It is true that in that case Lord Kingsdown reached a result on the facts of the case which differed from that reached by the other members of the House of Lords, but Lord Kingsdown's observations which are relevant in the present case have received support since that case was decided; and, in particular, I would like to refer to the observations in the judgment of the Privy Council in *Plimmer v Wellington Corpn*. It is said there ((1884) 9 App Cas 699 at 713): "Their Lordships consider that this case falls within the principle stated by Lord Kingsdown as to expectations created or encouraged by the landlord, with the addition that in this case the landlord did more than encourage the expenditure, for he took the initiative in requesting it."

There are similar circumstances in the present case. The defendant was induced to give up his project of building a bungalow on land belonging to somebody else other than his father, in which case he would have become the owner or tenant of the land in question and thus have his own home. His father induced him to build on his, the father's, land and expenditure was made by the defendant for the purpose of the erection of the bungalow.

In my view the case comes plainly within the proposition stated in the cases. It is not necessary, I think, to imply a promise. It seems to me that this is one of the cases of an equity created by estoppel, or equitable estoppel, as it is sometimes called, by which the person who has made the expenditure is induced by the expectation of obtaining protection, and equity protects him so that an injustice may not be perpetrated.

I am clearly of opinion that the appeal should be allowed and judgment should be entered for the defendant.

In *Hopgood v Brown*[18] [1955] 1 WLR 213, [1955] 1 All ER 550, adjoining plots of land (here called plots A and B) were conveyed to a purchaser in 1932 by separate conveyances. The common boundary was not precisely indicated, reference being made in each conveyance to a plan "for the purpose of facilitating identification only". Both plots were later sold, B to the defendant, and A, to the North of it, to a company of which the defendant was a director. The defendant engaged the company to build a bungalow and a garage on his plot, which, in accordance with plans agreed with the company, encroached on plot A beyond the line which would form the boundary between these plots if the boundary between them were a line drawn parallel to their other lateral boundaries. When the garage had been built, it gave the appearance of forming the boundary, but, if the boundary were such a parallel line, it covered also a wedge shaped area belonging to plot A. Plot A was sold to one Lester in April 1952 and by him to the plaintiff, in November 1952, and these conveyances described the plot in the same terms as the conveyance of 1932 had done. The plaintiff began to build a bungalow on plot A, and, after the building had reached an advanced stage, he discovered that it was not possible for a car to pass between his bungalow and the southern boundary of his plot because of the encroachment made by the defendant's garage.

The plaintiff sought to eject the defendant from the encroachment, and to require him to remove the garage, and damages.

The Court of Appeal (Lord EVERSHED MR, JENKINS and MORRIS LJJ) affirming Judge Howard, at Ilford County Court, held that the defendant was entitled to remain. Lord EVERSHED MR said at p. 224:

"In my judgment, there was, beyond a peradventure, a representation by the company to the defendant which has all the qualities which Mr. Spencer Bower[19] enumerated, and which had, therefore, all its consequences. In effect, and by way of paraphrase only, the defendant was saying to his northern neighbour, the company: 'Our boundary shown on the small plan has never been marked out on the land. I want to build a bungalow and garage. I have made plans, and I believe that the boundary goes as it is shown on my plans. I want to build accordingly. It may be that I shall take a little bit of your land or that you will take a little bit of mine, or both, but do you assent to the boundary being so assumed and fixed?' and the company said: 'Yes.

---

[18] *Penfold and Penfold v Cooke* (1978) NLJ 736 not following *Hopgood v Brown* because there was no sufficient reason, on the facts, to raise the equity.
[19] Spencer Bower on Estoppel (1923), pp. 9–10; (3rd edn., 1977), pp. 4–6.

What is more, we will assist you to carry out your purpose and build for you at your cost your house and garage'. . . . Is it really suggested (for this must, I think, follow from an argument to the contrary) that the company, having assented to what had been proposed, having participated in what followed, and having taken the sum of £2,200 from the defendant for building the garage and his house in the places which he had identified, could tell the defendant next day that they had now measured the plot more accurately, and that he must take down that part of the garage which encroached upon the company's land, and which they had just built at his entire expense? It seems to me that such a suggestion would, indeed, shock common sense and be contrary to the realities of the case.

If that is right, the only other question is whether the disability on the company's part from averring the boundary to be in any place other than that where they, with the defendant, had put it, is equally binding on the plaintiff. In my judgment, that can also be answered in favour of the defendant; and I accept the passage which Mr. Holdsworth [counsel for the defendant] read from the judgment of Mansfield CJ, in *Taylor v Needham* ((1810) 2 Taunt 278). That was a case of estoppel between lessor and lessee, but the principle is the same. Mansfield CJ (at p. 282) said: 'Then the question comes, whether the assignee of the lease may be allowed to controvert the title of the lessor, when the lessee, under whom he derives, could not controvert the title of the lessor; so that the assignee should have a better right than he from whom he derives it. Exclusive of all the dicta, it would be a very odd thing in the law of any country, if A could take, by any form of conveyance, a greater or better right than he had who conveys it to him; it would be contrary to all principle. But it does not rest merely on the general principle; for if you look into all the books upon estoppel, you find it laid down that parties and privies are estopped, and he who takes an estate under a deed, is privy in estate, and therefore never can be in a better situation than he from whom he takes it.' My conclusion, therefore, is that Mr. Lester has failed to satisfy me that there are any good grounds for differing from the judge's decision."

Jones v Jones [1977] 1 WLR 438, [1977] 2 All ER 231[20] is difficult to classify. The Court of Appeal avoided a decision on the question whether the defendant should be given a life interest. He already owned ¼ share as tenant in common. In that case, Mr. Jones encouraged his son Frederick to move from Kingston-upon-Thames to Blundeston in Suffolk in order to have the family closer. He purchased a house there for £4,000. Frederick gave up his job at Kingston, moved to the house at Blundeston, and paid £1,000 to his father. He paid the rates, but no rent.

---

[20] (1977) 41 Conv (NS) 279 (F.R. Crane); (1978) 41 MLR 208 (J. Alder).

The father's will, made before these circumstances took place, left his residuary estate to his second wife, Alice, stepmother to Frederick. She unsuccessfully attempted to evict Frederick, and that litigation established that Frederick owned a 25% interest in the house by reason of the money paid, and that Alice owned 75%. Alice now sued for rent, to be calculated on the basis of 75% of the market rental. This claim failed, on the ground that one tenant in common is not entitled to claim rent from another. The Court of Appeal held that Frederick was entitled, as against his co-tenant in common, to remain in possession of the house rent free for the rest of his life. Lord DENNING MR said, at p. 442:

"Second, the order for sale. Here comes into play the doctrine of proprietary estoppel. It has been considered by this court in *Inwards v Baker* [1965] 2 QB 29, [1965] 1 All ER 446 and *Crabb v Arun District Council* [1976] Ch 179, [1975] 3 All ER 865. It is quite plain that the principles of those cases apply here.

Old Mr. Jones' conduct was such as to lead his son Frederick reasonably to believe that he could stay there and regard Philmona as his home for the rest of his life. On the basis of that reasonable expectation, the son gave up his work at Kingston-upon-Thames and moved to Blundeston. He paid the £1,000 too in the same expectation. He did work on the house as well. It was all because he had been led to believe that his father would never turn him out of the house: it would be his family's home for the rest of his life. He and the rest of the family thought that the father would alter his will or make over the house to the son. The father did not do it, but nevertheless he led the son to believe that he could stay there for the rest of his life. On those two cases it is clear that old Mr. Jones would be estopped from turning the son out. After his death the plaintiff is equally estopped from turning the defendant out.

Similarly, the plaintiff is not entitled to an order for the property to be sold. Nor for any payment to be made by Frederick to her pending sale. Even though there is an implied trust for sale, nevertheless, the courts will not allow it to be used so as to defeat the purposes contemplated by the parties. That appears from *Bedson v Bedson* [1965] 2 QB 666, [1965] 3 All ER 307: see what I said at 679, and *per* Russell LJ, at pp. 697 and 698. No order for the sale of this property should be made because that would defeat the very purpose of the acquisition, namely that the son Frederick would be able to be there for his life and remain in it as his home.

The two doctrines go hand in hand to show that no order should be made so as to disturb the son in his possession of the house: nor should he be made to pay anything for staying there.

The ultimate result of the case is that the son has a proprietary interest of a one-quarter share in the house. He is able to stay there for life by virtue of his interest in it, and the plaintiff is estopped from turning him out. Nor can it be sold without his consent. The appeal should be allowed and an order made accordingly."

ROSKILL LJ said at p. 443:

"I would mention one other thing. It was suggested by Mr. Sunnucks that if we took the view which we do we ought to order a life interest to be created in favour of the defendant. In my judgment, at this stage it would be wrong so to do. This does not seem to have been the subject of argument below, and it seems to me that the defendant's real case was that he should not pay the rent, and not to seek the creation of a life interest."

B. Acquisition of Proprietary Interests

i.   ACQUISITION OF INTEREST FOR PURPOSES OF STATUTE

PLIMMER *v* WELLINGTON CORPORATION[1]
(1884), 9 App Cas 699, (JC, Lord WATSON, Sir Barnes PEACOCK, Sir Robert P COLLIER, Sir Richard COUGH and Sir Arthur HOBHOUSE)

Plimmer moored an old hulk on the foreshore of Wellington Bay and used it as a wharf and store by permission of the Crown. An earthquake raised the level of the land and necessitated the building of a jetty, which Plimmer built. Between 1856 and 1861, at the instance of the Provincial Government, Plimmer extended the jetty. Subsequently the Government took possession of the jetty under statutory powers, and Plimmer and another claimed compensation under the Public Works Loans Act 1882 under which any person who "had any estate or interest in, to or out of the lands . . . vested in the Corporation . . . shall be entitled to . . . compensation".

Held. The equitable right so acquired is an "estate or interest in, to or out of land" within the meaning of the Act of 1882.

SIR ARTHUR HOBHOUSE: The law relating to cases of this kind may be taken as stated by Lord Kingsdown in the case of *Ramsden v Dyson* ((1866) LR 1 HL 129). The passage is at p. 170: "If a man, under a verbal agreement with a landlord for a certain interest in land, or, what amounts to the same thing, under an expectation created or encouraged by the landlord that he shall have a certain interest, takes possession of such land with the consent of the landlord, and upon the faith of such promise or expectation, with the knowledge of the landlord and without objection by him, lays out money upon land, a Court of Equity will compel the landlord to give effect to such promise or expectation. This was the principle of the decision in *Gregory v Mighell* ((1811) 18 Ves 328), and, as I conceive, is open to no doubt. If at the hearing of the cause there appears to be such uncertainty as to the particular terms of the contract as might prevent a Court of Equity from giving relief if the contract had been in writing but there had been no expenditure, a Court of Equity will nevertheless, in the case which is above stated, interfere in order to prevent fraud, though

---

[1] Cf *DHN Food Distributors Ltd v Tower Hamlets London Borough Council* [1976] 1 WLR 852, [1976] 3 All ER 462; p. 450, ante (a case of a contractual licence).

there has been a difference of opinion amongst great judges as to the nature of the relief to be granted. Lord Thurlow seems to have thought that the Court would ascertain the terms by reference to the Master, and if they could not be ascertained would itself fix reasonable terms. Lord Alvanley and Lord Redesdale, and perhaps Lord Eldon, thought this was going too far; but I do not understand any doubt to have been entertained by any of them that, either in the form of a specific interest in the land, or in the shape of compensation for the expenditure, a Court of Equity would give relief, and protect in the meantime the possession of the tenant. If, on the other hand, a tenant being in possession of land, and knowing the nature and extent of his interest, lays out money upon it in the hope or expectation of an extended term or an allowance for expenditure, then, if such hope or expectation has not been created or encouraged by the landlord, the tenant has no claim which any Court of Law or Equity can enforce. This was the principle of the decision in *Pilling v Armitage* ((1805) 12 Ves 78), and, like the decision in *Gregory v Mighell*, seems founded on plain rules of reason and justice. . . .''

In the present case, the equity is not claimed because the landowner has stood by in silence while his tenant has spent money on his land. This is a case in which the landowner has, for his own purposes, requested the tenant to make the improvements. The Government were engaged in the important work of introducing immigrants into the colony. For some reason, not now apparent, they were not prepared to make landing-places of their own, and in fact they did not do so until the year 1863. So they applied to John Plimmer to make his landing-place more commodious by a substantial extension of his jetty and the erection of a warehouse for baggage. Is it to be said that, when he had incurred the expense of doing the work asked for, the Government could turn round and revoke his licence at their will? Could they in July, 1856, have deprived him summarily of the use of the jetty? It would be in a high degree unjust that they should do so, and that the parties should have intended such a result is, in the absence of evidence, incredible. . . .

Their Lordships will not be the first to hold, and no authority has been cited to them to shew that after such a landowner has requested such a tenant to incur expense on his land for his benefit, he can without more and at his own will take away the property so improved. Their Lordships consider that this case falls within the principle stated by Lord Kingsdown as to expectations created or encouraged by the landlord, with the addition that in this case the landlord did more than encourage the expenditure, for he took the initiative in requesting it. . . .

The question still remains as to the extent of interest which Plimmer acquired by his expenditure in 1856. Referring again to the passage quoted from Lord Kingsdown's judgment, there is good authority for saying what appears to their Lordships to be quite sound in principle, that the equity arising from expenditure on land need not fail merely on the ground that the interest to be secured has not been expressly indicated.

In such a case as *Ramsden v Dyson*, the evidence (according to Lord Kingsdown's view) shewed that the tenant expected a particular kind of lease, which Vice-Chancellor Stuart decreed to him, though it does not appear what form of relief Lord Kingsdown himself would have given. In such a case as the *Duke of Beaufort v Patrick* ((1853) 17 Beav 60), nothing but perpetual retention of the land would satisfy the equity raised in favour of those who spent their money on it, and it was secured to them at a valuation. In such a case as *Dillwyn v Llewelyn* ((1862) 4 De G F & J 517), nothing but a grant of the fee simple would satisfy the equity which the Lord Chancellor held to have been raised by the son's expenditure on his father's land. In such a case as that of the *Unity Joint-Stock Mutual Banking Association v King* ((1858) 25 Beav 72), the Master of the Rolls, holding that the father did not intend to part with his land to his sons who built upon it, considered that their equity would be satisfied by recouping their expenditure to them. In fact, the Court must look at the circumstances in each case to decide in what way the equity can be satisfied.

In this case their Lordships feel no great difficulty. In their view, the licence given by the Government to John Plimmer, which was indefinite in point of duration but was revocable at will, became irrevocable by the transactions of 1856, because those transactions were sufficient to create in his mind a reasonable expectation that his occupation would not be disturbed; and because they and the subsequent dealings of the parties cannot be reasonably explained on any other supposition. Nothing was done to limit the use of the jetty in point of duration. The consequence is that Plimmer acquired an indefinite, that is practically a perpetual, right to the jetty for the purposes of the original licence, and if the ground was afterwards wanted for public purposes, it could only be taken from him by the legislature.

An analogy to this process may be found in such cases as *Winter v Brockwell* ((1807) 8 East 308) and *Liggins v Inge* ((1831) 7 Bing 682). These cases shew that where a landowner permits his neighbour to execute works in his (the neighbour's land), and the licence is executed, it cannot be revoked at will by the licensor. If indefinite in duration, it becomes perpetual. Their Lordships think that the same consequence must follow where the licence is to execute works on the land of the licensor, and owing to some supervening equity the licence has become irrevocable.

There are perhaps purposes for which such a licence would not be held to be an interest in land. But their Lordships are construing a statute which takes away private property for compensation, and in such statutes the expression "estate or interest in, to or out of land" should receive a wide meaning. Indeed the statute itself directs that, in ascertaining the title of anybody to compensation, the Court shall not be bound to regard strict legal rights only, but shall do what is reasonable and just. Their Lordships have no difficulty in deciding that the equitable right acquired by John Plimmer is an interest in land carrying compensation under the Acts of 1880 and 1882[2].

ii.   ACQUISITION OF INCORPOREAL INTEREST

(a) As Between the Parties

CRABB *v* ARUN DISTRICT COUNCIL
[1976] Ch 179, [1975] 3 All ER 865[3] (CA, Lord DENNING MR, LAWTON and SCARMAN LJJ)

The plaintiff owned two acres of land. The outlet to the road was through a point of access (point A) to a lane owned by the defendants, and by a right of way over that lane in a northerly direction to the road.

He decided to divide his land into two parts, and to sell them separately. This would require another point of access to the South, together with an additional right of way over the lane, to serve the Southern part. This was negotiated with the defendants at a meeting in July 1967, at which there was an oral agreement in principle that the plaintiff should have another access at point B; but no formal agreement was signed. The defendants, in accordance with the terms of the informal agreement, fenced the boundary between their land and the plaintiff's, leaving gaps at A and B, and erected gates at these points, the gateposts being set in concrete.

The plaintiff sold the Northern part, together with the right of way and access from point A. Differences arose between the plaintiff and defendants. The defendants uprooted the gatepost at point B, continued the fence to cover the gateway, and left the Southern part of the plaintiff's land landlocked. They offered access at point B and right of way for £3,000. The action was for a declaration and injunction, claiming that the defendants were estopped by their conduct from denying the plaintiff a right of access at point B and a right of way.

Held. Rights of access and way awarded to the plaintiff without payment.

SCARMAN LJ: I agree that the appeal should be allowed. The plaintiff and the defendants are adjoining landowners. The plaintiff asserts that he has a right of way over the defendants' land giving access from his land to the public highway. Without this access his land is in fact landlocked, but, for reasons which clearly appear from the narration of the facts already given by my Lords, the plaintiff cannot claim a right of way by necessity. The plaintiff has no grant. He has the benefit of no enforceable contract. He has no prescriptive right. His case has to be that the defendants are estopped by their

---

[2] Cf. *Canadian Pacific Rly Co v R* [1931] AC at 428–429; *Lee-Parker v Izzet (No. 2)* [1972] 1 WLR 775 at 780–781, [1972] 2 All ER 800.
[3] (1976) 40 Conv (NS) 156 (F.R. Crane); (1976) 92 LQR 174 (P.S. Atiyah); 342 (P.J. Millett).

conduct from denying him a right of access over their land to the public highway. If the plaintiff has any right, it is an equity arising out of the conduct and relationship of the parties. In such a case I think it is now well settled law that the court, having analysed and assessed the conduct and relationship of the parties, has to answer three questions. First, is there an equity established? Secondly, what is the extent of the equity, if one is established? And, thirdly, what is the relief appropriate to satisfy the equity? See *Duke of Beaufort v Patrick* (1853) 17 Beav 60; *Plimmer v Wellington Corpn* (1884) 9 App Cas 699 and *Inwards v Baker* [1965] 2 QB 29, [1965] 1 All ER 446, a decision of this court, and particularly the observations of Lord Denning MR at p. 37. Such therefore I believe to be the nature of the inquiry that the courts have to conduct in a case of this sort. In pursuit of that inquiry I do not find helpful the distinction between promissory and proprietary estoppel. This distinction may indeed be valuable to those who have to teach or expound the law; but I do not think that, in solving the particular problem raised by a particular case, putting the law into categories is of the slightest assistance.

Nor do I think it necessary in a case such as this to inquire minutely into the law of agency. These defendants could, of course, only act through agents; but, as I have already made clear, from the very nature of the case, there would be no question of grant, no question of legally enforceable contract. We are in the realm of equity; and within that realm we find that equity, to its eternal credit, has developed an immensely flexible, yet perfectly clear, doctrine: see *E. R. Ives Investment Ltd v High* [1967] 2 QB 379, [1967] 1 All ER 504, *per* Danckwerts LJ at 399. The approach of equity, when there is a question of agency in a field such as this, must I think be a very simple one. It will merely be that, within reasonable limits, those to whom a defendant entrusts the conduct of negotiations must be treated as having the authority, which, within the course of the negotiations, they purport to exercise. I put it in that way in the light of the comments of Lord Denning MR in *Moorgate Mercantile Co Ltd v Twitchings* [1976] QB 225, 243, [1975] 3 All ER 314 comments which were themselves made upon a judgment to the same effect in *Attorney-General to the Prince of Wales v Collom* [1916] 2 KB 193, 203. I would add only one reservation to this broad proposition. The defendant, if he thinks that an agent has exceeded his instructions, can always so inform the plaintiff before the plaintiff acts to his detriment in reliance upon what the agent has said or done. If a defendant has done so, the plaintiff cannot then establish the equity: for the defendant will have intervened to prevent him acting to his detriment. Nothing of that sort happened in this case. After the meeting in July 1967, to which both my Lords have referred, the plaintiff was left to form his own conclusions as to the intentions of the defendants.

I come now to consider the first of the three questions which I think in a case such as this the court have to consider. What is needed to establish an equity? In the course of an interesting addition to his submissions this morning, Mr. Lightman cited *Ramsden v Dyson* (1886) LR 1 HL 129, 142, to support his proposition that in order to establish an equity by estoppel there must be a belief by the plaintiff in the existence of a right created or encouraged by the words or actions of the defendant. With respect, I do not think that that is today a correct statement of the law. I think the law has developed so that today it is to be considered as correctly stated by Lord Kingsdown in his dissenting speech in *Ramsden v Dyson*. Like Lord Denning MR, I think that the point of dissent in *Ramsden v Dyson* was not on the law but on the facts. Lord Kingdsown's speech, in so far as it dealt with propositions of law, has been often considered, and recently followed by this court in *Inwards v Baker* [1965] 2 QB 29, [1965] 1 All ER 446. So what is the effect of looking to Lord Kingsdown's speech for a statement of the law? Lord Kingsdown said, LR 1 HL 129, 170:

> "The rule of law applicable to the case appears to me to be this: If a man, under a verbal agreement with a landlord for a certain interest in land, or, what amounts to the same thing, *under an expectation, created or encouraged by the landlord*," — my italics — "that he shall have a certain interest, takes possession of such land, with the consent of the landlord, and upon the faith of such promise or expectation, with the knowledge of the landlord, and without objection by him, lays out money upon the land, a court of equity will compel the landlord to give effect to such promise or expectation."

That statement of the law is put into the language of landlord and tenant because it was a landlord and tenant situation with which Lord Kingsdown was concerned; but it has been accepted as of general application. While *Ramsden v Dyson* may properly be considered as the modern starting-point of the law of equitable estoppel, it was analysed and spelt out in a judgment of Fry J in 1880 in *Willmott v Barber* (1880) 15 ChD 96, a decision to which Pennycuick V-C referred in his judgment. I agree with Pennycuick V-C in thinking that the passage from Fry J's judgment, from p. 105, is a valuable guide as to the matters of fact which have to be established in order that a plaintiff may establish this particular equity. Moreover, Mr. Lightman for the defendants sought to make a submission in reliance upon the judgment. Fry J said, at pp. 105–106:

> "It has been said that the acquiescence which will deprive a man of his legal rights must amount to fraud, and in my view that is an abbreviated statement of a very true proposition. A man is not to be deprived of his legal rights unless he has acted in such a way as would make it fraudulent for him to set up those rights. What, then, are the elements or requisites necessary to constitute fraud of that description? In the first place the plaintiff must have made a mistake as to his legal rights[3a]. Secondly, the plaintiff must have expended some money or must have done some act (not necessarily upon the defendant's land) on the faith of his mistaken belief. Thirdly, the defendant, the possessor of the legal right,

---

[3a] In *E and L Berg Homes Ltd v Grey* (1979) 253 Estates Gazette 473, this plaintiff failed because he was unable to satisfy this requirement.

must know of the existence of his own right which is inconsistent with the right claimed by the plaintiff. If he does not know of it he is in the same position as the plaintiff, and the doctrine of acquiescence is founded upon conduct with a knowledge of your legal right. Fourthly, the defendant, the possessor of the legal rights, must know of the plaintiff mistaken belief of his rights[3b]. If he does not, there is nothing which calls upon him to assert his own rights. Lastly," — if I may digress, this is the important element as far as this appeal is concerned — "the defendant, the possessor of the legal right, must have encouraged the plaintiff in his expenditure of money or in the other acts which he has done, either directly or by abstaining from asserting his legal right."

Mr. Lightman, in the course of an interesting and vigorous submission, drew the attention of the court to the necessity of finding something akin to fraud before the equity sought by the plaintiff could be established. "Fraud" was a word often in the mouths of those robust judges who adorned the bench in the 19th century. It is less often in the mouths of the more wary judicial spirits today who sit upon the bench. But it is clear that whether one uses the word "fraud" or not, the plaintiff has to establish as a fact that the defendant, by setting up his right, is taking advantage of him in a way which is unconscionable, inequitable or unjust. It is to be observed from the passage that I have quoted from the judgment of Fry J, that the fraud or injustice alleged does not take place during the course of negotiation, but only when the defendant decides to refuse to allow the plaintiff to set up his claim against the defendants' undoubted right. The fraud, if it be such, arises after the event, when the defendant seeks by relying on his right to defeat the expectation which he by his conduct encouraged the plaintiff to have. There need not be anything fraudulent or unjust in the conduct of the actual negotiations — the conduct of the transaction by the defendants.

The court therefore cannot find an equity established unless it is prepared to go as far as to say that it would be unconscionable and unjust to allow the defendants to set up their undoubted rights against the claim being made by the plaintiff. In order to reach a conclusion upon that matter the court does have to consider the history of the negotiations under the five headings to which Fry J referred. I need not at this stage weary anyone with an elaborate statement of the facts. I have no doubt upon the facts of this case that the first four elements referred to by Fry J exist. The question before the judge and now in this court is whether the fifth element is present: have the defendants, as possessor of the legal right, encouraged the plaintiff in the expenditure of money or in the other acts which he has done, either directly or by abstaining from asserting their legal rights? The first matter to be considered is the meeting on site of 26 July 1967. Pennycuick V-C made a finding of fact about the meeting; and for myself I am not prepared to dissent from his finding. But the

---

[3b] Though this was said not to be essential in *Taylor Fashions Ltd v Liverpool Victoria Friendly Society* (1979) 251 Estates Gazette 159, at 161, p. 466, ante.

substance of the finding of fact has to be regarded; not its phrasing
One must not be misled by words or phrases into mis-construing the
nature of the finding. Pennycuick V-C found there was no definite
assurance given by the defendants' representative to the plaintiff and
his architect.

[His Lordship summarized the evidence and continued:]

That was a finding that there was acceptance in principle that there
should be access and a right of way over the defendants' land at
point B; and I am content to go no further and to base my judgment on
what I believe to be that finding of Pennycuick V-C. Clearly the
plaintiff and Mr. Alford came away from that meeting in the confident
expectation that a right would in due course be accorded to the
plaintiff. Mr. Alford did foresee "further processes." Of course, there
would be further processes. The nature of the legal right to be granted
had to be determined. It might be given by way of licence. It might be
granted by way of easement. Conditions might be imposed. Payment
of a sum of money might be required. But those two men, the plaintiff
and his architect, came away from the meeting in the confident
expectation that such a right would be granted upon reasonable
conditions. What happened? By August — a month or less, after the
meeting — posts for a fence were already on the ground, though
not erected. There was already an indication, at about that time, I
think —if not then, certainly soon after — of the presence of a gap at
point B, that being the point of access agreed in principle. During the
later months of 1967 nothing relevant transpired in the conduct of
the negotiations between the plaintiff and the defendants. I accept
Mr. Lightman's submission that relationship as well as conduct is
relevant: but during this period their relationship did not develop at
all. They remained adjoining landowners, one of whom had agreed in
principle at a meeting upon the site that there should be a right of way
from point B over his land to the public road. Yet, things were
happening. In the later months of 1967 the defendants, who were the
local authority, were busy developing on neighbouring land, which the
plaintiff's predecessor in title had sold them, a council housing estate.
Lorries were being used for carting building materials, removing
debris and so forth; and these lorries were in fact going upon the land
of the plaintiff. Unfortunately materials on the land, the property of
the plaintiff, were being pilfered. And so there came a meeting in
January 1968, the point of which was to draw the attention of the
defendants' officers to the situation which was developing. By the
time the meeting took place the fence, which the defendants were
obliged under the conveyance of their estate to erect between their
land and the plaintiff's land, was substantially in position with gaps at
point A, the access to the northern land, and at point B, the access in
dispute. Nobody on behalf of the defendants gave the slightest
indication to the plaintiff and his representatives at that meeting that
there was going to be any difficulty or was likely to be any difficulty
about access at point B. The confident expectation with which the

plaintiff and Mr. Alford left the meeting in July remained remarkably undisturbed by the meeting of January 1968. Indeed it was reinforced because there on the ground, plain for all to see, was a fence with gaps which accorded exactly with the agreement in principle reached in the previous July. Ten days later the defendants ordered gates, and by March the gates were installed. I ask myself: as at March 1968 had these defendants encouraged the plaintiff to think that he had or was going to be given a right? To use the language of Fry J, had they done it directly or had they done it by abstaining from asserting a legal right? Their encouragement of the belief in the mind of the plaintiff and Mr. Alford was both direct and indirect. It was direct because of what they had done on the ground. It was indirect because ever since the July meeting they had abstained from giving the plaintiff or his architect any indication that they were standing on their rights, or had it in mind to go back, as, of course, they were entitled at that stage to go back, upon the agreement in principle reached at that meeting. And so matters proceeded until September 1968. By now, be it observed, over a year had passed since that first meeting when there was agreement in principle. Nothing had been done to disabuse the minds of the plaintiff and Mr. Alford of the expectation reasonably induced by what the defendants' engineer then said: and there had been the direct encouragement of the gates. In September 1968, without telling the defendants or giving them any notice, so far as I am aware, the plaintiff entered into a contract to sell the northern piece of land without reservation over that land of any right of way. This was the act which was detrimental to the interests of the plaintiff. He did it in the belief that he had or could enforce a right of way and access at point B in the southern land.

One of the points taken by Mr. Lightman is that the defendants had no notice of the sale, and therefore no opportunity to correct what on his case was a false belief in the mind of the plaintiff. Mr. Millett in the course of his submissions conceded that he had not found in the books any case in which the sort of estoppel which we are here considering had arisen when the fact known to the defendants was an intention and not the realisation of that intention. That is, of course, what differentiates this case from one such as *E. R. Ives Investment Ltd v High* [1967] 2 QB 379, [1967] 1 All ER 504. There the party who was found to be estopped did have notice of what the other party was doing at the time he was doing it. Therefore I think Mr. Lightman rightly invites us to face this question: Does the fact that the defendants had no notice of the sale of the northern land before it was completed destroy the equity? Mr. Lightman will concede, as I understand this part of his argument, no more than this: that the plaintiff might have been able to establish an equity if he had referred to the defendants before binding himself to the purchaser of the northern land: for that would have given the defendants an opportunity of disabusing the mind of the plaintiff before he acted to his detriment. The point is worthy of careful consideration. I reject it because, in my judgment, in this sort of proceedings, the court must be careful to avoid generalisation. I can conceive of cases in which it would be absolutely appropriate for a defendant to say: "But you should not have acted to your detriment until you had had a word with me and I could have put you right." But there are cases in which it is far too late for a defendant to get himself out of his pickle by putting upon the plaintiff that sort of duty; and this, in my judgment, is one of those cases. If immediately following the July meeting the clerk to the defendant authority had written saying: "I have had a report of the meeting with the assistant engineer and I must inform you that whether or not there is to be an easement or a licence is a matter which can only be decided by the council," the plaintiff would not now establish his equity: in selling the northern land without reservation of a right of way, he would have acted at his own risk. But one has to look at the whole conduct of the parties and the developing relationship between them. By September 1968, 13½ months after the initial meeting, the plaintiff must really and reasonably have been attaching importance to the abstention of the defendants from declaring to him in correspondence, or by telephone to his agent, their true position, namely, that there would be no acceptance in principle of a right until the matter had been considered by the authority itself. By that time there had been, as well, the laying out of the fence and the installing of the gates. It is for those reasons — the passage of time, the abstention and the gates — that I think the defendants cannot rely upon the fact that the plaintiff acted, without referring to the defendants, on his intention — an intention of which they had had notice ever since their agent was informed of it at the meeting in July 1967. I think therefore an equity is established.

I turn now to the other two questions — the extent of the equity and the relief needed to satisfy it. There being no grant, no enforceable contract, no licence, I would analyse the minimum equity to do justice to the plaintiff as a right either to an easement or to a licence upon terms to be agreed. I do not think it is necessary to go further than that. Of course, going that far would support the equitable remedy of injunction which is sought in this action. If there is no agreement as to terms, if agreement fails to be obtained, the court can, in my judgment, and must, determine in these proceedings upon what terms the plaintiff should be put to enable him to have the benefit of the equitable right which he is held to have. It is interesting that there has been some doubt amongst distinguished lawyers in the past as to whether the court can so proceed. Lord Kingsdown refers in fact to those doubts in a passage, which I need not quote, in *Ramsden v Dyson* (1866) LR 1 HL 129 at 171. Lord Thurlow clearly thought that the court did have this power. Other lawyers of that time did not. But there can be no doubt that since *Ramsden v Dyson* the courts have acted upon the basis that they have to determine not only the extent of the equity, but also the conditions necessary to satisfy it, and they have done so in a great number and variety of cases. I need refer only to the interesting collection of cases enumerated in *Snell's Principles of Equity*, 27th edn. (1973), at pp. 567–568, para. 2 (b).

In the present case the court does have to consider what is necessary now in order to satisfy the plaintiff's equity. Had matters taken a different turn, I would without hesitation have said that the plaintiff should be put upon terms to be agreed if possible with the defendants, and, if not agreed, settled by the court. But, as already mentioned by Lord Denning MR and Lawton LJ, there has been a history of delay, and indeed high-handedness, which it is impossible to disregard. In January 1969 the defendants, for reasons which no doubt they thought good at the time, without consulting the plaintiff, locked up his land. They removed not only the padlocks which he had put on the gates at point B, but the gates themselves. In their place they put a fence — rendering access impossible save by breaking down the fence. I am not disposed to consider whether or not the defendants are to be blamed in moral terms for what they did. I just do not know. But the effect of their action has been to sterilise the plaintiff's land; and for the reasons which I have endeavoured to give, such action was an infringement of an equitable right possessed by the plaintiff. It has involved him in loss, which has not been measured; but, since it amounted to sterilisation of an industrial estate for a very considerable period of time, it must surpass any sort of sum of money which the plaintiff ought reasonably, before it was done, to have paid the defendants in order to obtain an enforceable legal right. I think therefore that nothing should now be paid by the plaintiff and that he should receive at the hands of the court the belated protection of the equity that he has established. Reasonable terms, other than money payment, should be agreed: or, if not agreed, determined by the court.

For those reasons I also would allow the appeal.

(b) As Against a Purchaser. The Problem of Notice.

E. R. IVES INVESTMENT LTD *v* HIGH[4]
[1967] 2 QB 379, [1967] 1 All ER 504 (CA, DENNING MR, DANCKWERTS and WINN LJJ)

In 1949, the defendant, High, began to build a house on a plot of land. Soon after, Westgate, his neighbour, started to erect to block of flats in such a way that their foundations encroached by about one foot upon the defendant's land. The defendant and Westgate agreed that the foundations could remain, and that the defendant should have a right of way for his car across Westgate's yard. The agreement for the right of way was never registered.

Westgate sold the block to Flt.-Lt. and Mrs. Wright who knew of the agreement, and also knew that in 1959 the defendant erected a garage so sited that it could only be approached across the yard. In 1960, the defendant contributed to the surfacing of the yard.

---

[4] *Montague v Long* (1972) 24 P & CR 240.

In 1962 the Wrights sold the flats to the plaintiffs, expressly subject to the right of way. The plaintiffs sued the defendant for trespass to the yard, claiming that the defendant had no legal right of way, and that if he was entitled to an equitable easement, it was void against them because it was not registered.

Held. The defendant was entitled to use the way across the yard.

LORD DENNING MR: One thing is quite clear. Apart from this point about the Land Charges Act 1925, Mr. High would have in equity a good right of way across the yard. This right arises in two ways:

1. *Mutual benefit and burden.* The right arises out of the agreement of 2 November 1949, and the subsequent action taken on it: on the principle that "he who takes the benefit must accept the burden." When adjoining owners of land make an agreement to secure continuing rights and benefits for each of them in or over the land of the other, neither of them can take the benefit of the agreement and throw over the burden of it. This applies not only to be original parties, but also to their successors. The successor who takes the continuing benefit must take it subject to the continuing burden. This principle has been applied to neighbours who send their water into a common drainage system: see *Hopgood v Brown* ([1955] 1 WLR 213, [1955] 1 All ER 550), and to purchasers of houses on a building estate who had the benefit of using the roads and were subject to the burden of contributing to the upkeep: see *Halsall v Brizell* ([1957] Ch 169, [1957] 1 All ER 371)[5]. The principle clearly applies in the present case. The owners of the block of flats have the benefit of having their foundations in Mr. High's land. So long as they take that benefit, they must shoulder the burden. They must observe the condition on which the benefit was granted, namely, they must allow Mr. High and his successors to have access over their yard: cf. *May v Belleville* ([1905] 2 Ch 605). Conversely, so long as Mr. High takes the benefit of the access, he must permit the block of flats to keep their foundations in his land.

2. *Equity arising out of acquiescence.* The right arises out of the expense incurred by Mr. High in building his garage, as it is now, with access only over the yard: and the Wrights standing by and acquiescing in it, knowing that he believed he had a right of way over the yard. By so doing the Wrights created in Mr. High's mind a reasonable expectation that his access over the yard would not be disturbed. That gives rise to an "equity arising out of acquiescence." It is available not only against the Wrights but also their successors in title. The court will not allow that expectation to be defeated when it would be inequitable so to do. It is for the court in each case to decide in what way the equity can be satisfied: see *Inwards v Baker* ([1965] 2 QB 29, [1965] 1 All ER 446); *Ward v Kirkland* ([1967] Ch 194, [1966] 1 All ER 609) and the cases cited therein. In this case it could only be satisfied by allowing Mr. High and his successors to have

---

[5] P. 699, post.

access over the yard so long as the block of flats has its foundations in his land.

The next question is this: was that right a land charge such as to need registration under the Land Charges Act 1925? For if it was a land charge, it was never registered and would be void as against any purchaser: see section 13 of the Act[6]. It would, therefore, be void against the plaintiffs, even though they took with the most express knowledge and notice of the right.

It was suggested that the agreement of 2 November 1949, was "an estate contract" within Class C (iv). I do not think so. There was no contract by Mr. Westgate to convey a legal estate of any kind.

It was next suggested that the right was an "equitable easement" within Class D (iii). This class is defined as "any easement right or privilege over or affecting land created or arising after the commencement of this Act, and being merely an equitable interest." Those words are almost identical with section 2 (3) (iii) of the Law of Property Act 1925, and should be given the same meaning. They must be read in conjunction with sections 1 (2) (*a*), 1 (3) and 4 (1) of the Law of Property Act 1925. It then appears that an "equitable easement" is a proprietary interest in land such as would before 1926 have been recognised as capable of being conveyed or created *at law*, but which since 1926 only takes effect as an equitable interest. An instance of such a proprietary interest is a profit à prendre for life. It does not include a right to possession by a requisitioning authority: see *Lewisham Borough Council v Maloney* ([1948] 1 KB 50, [1947] 2 All ER 36). Nor does it include a right, liberty or privilege arising in equity by reason of "mutual benefit and burden," or arising out of "acquiescence," or by reason of a contractual licence: because none of those before 1926 were proprietary interests such as were capable of being conveyed or created *at law*. They only subsisted *in equity*. They do not need to be registered as land charges, so as to bind successors, but take effect in equity without registration: see an article by Mr. C. V. Davidge on "Equitable Easements" in (1937) 53 Law Quarterly Review, p. 259 and by Professor H. W. R. Wade in [1956] Cambridge Law Journal, pp. 225-226[7].

The right of Mr. High to cross this yard was not a right such as could ever have been created or conveyed at law. It subsisted only in equity. It therefore still subsists in equity without being registered. Any other view would enable the owners of the flats to perpetrate the grossest injustice. They could block up Mr. High's access to the garage, whilst keeping their foundations in his land. That cannot be right.

I am confirmed in this construction of the statute when I remember that there are many houses adjoining one another which have drainage systems in common, with mutual benefits and burdens. The statute cannot have required all these to be registered as land charges.

---

[6] Now L.C.A. 1972, s. 2 (6).
[7] P. 32, ante; p. 519, post.

I know that this greatly restricts the scope of Class D (iii) but this is not disturbing[8]. A special committee has already suggested that Class D (iii) should be abolished altogether: see the report of the Committee on Land Charges ((1956) Command Paper 9825, para. 16)[9].

iii.   ACQUISITION OF FEE SIMPLE ESTATE

PASCOE *v* TURNER[10]

[1979] 1 WLR 431, [1979] 2 All ER 945 (CA, ORR, LAWTON and CUMMING-BRUCE LJJ)

The plaintiff and defendant lived together in the plaintiff's home. Later, the plaintiff purchased another house and they moved in. He told the defendant that the house was hers, and everything in it. In reliance on this gratuitous promise, she expended, to the plaintiff's knowledge, her own money on repairs, improvements and redecoration; and also on furniture.

Later, when the relationship ended, the plaintiff gave to the defendant two month's notice to determine the licence.

Held. The defendant occupied the house as a licensee. There was a gift of the contents, but no valid gift or declaration of trust of the house. But an estoppel operated in her favour, and this could most properly be satisfied by a conveyance of the house to the defendant.

CUMMING-BRUCE LJ:

The issues

The appeal raises three issues about the house: (a) Did the defendant prove the trust found by the judge? (b) Did she prove such facts as prevented the plaintiff by estoppel from asserting his legal title? (c) If the answer to that question is yes, what is the equitable relief to which she is entitled? In respect of the contents of the house, did the defendant prove that they were given to her by the plaintiff's voluntary gift? . . . .

The judge found that the plaintiff had made a gift to her of the contents of the house. I have no doubt that he was right about that. She was already in possession of them as a bailee when he declared the gift. Counsel for the plaintiff submitted that there was no gift because it was uncertain what he was giving her. He pointed to a safe and to the defendant's evidence that she had sent round an orange bedroom suite to the plaintiff so that he should have a bed to sleep on. The answer is that he gave her everything in the house, but later, recognising his need, she gave back some bits and pieces to him. So much for the contents.

Her rights in the realty are not quite so simply disposed of because of section 53 and section 54 of the Law of Property Act 1925. There

---

[8] See *Shiloh Spinners Ltd v Harding* [1973] AC 691 at 719–720, [1973] 1 All ER 90, p. 34, ante.

[9] P. 520, n. 5, post.

[10] [1979] Conv 379 (F.R. Crane); (1979) 42 M.L.R. 574 (B. Sufrin). Cf. *Dillwyn v Llewelyn* (1862) 4 De G.F. & J. 517.

was nothing in writing. The judge considered the plaintiff's declarations, and decided that they were not enough to found an express trust. We agreed. But he went on to hold that the beneficial interest in the house had passed under a constructive trust inferred from words and conduct of the parties. He relied on the passage in *Snell's Principles of Equity*, 27th edn. (1973), p. 185, in which the editors suggest a possible definition of a constructive trust. But there are difficulties in the way. The long and short of events in 1973 is that the plaintiff made an imperfect gift of the house. There is nothing in the facts from which an inference of a constructive trust can be drawn. If it had not been for section 53 of the Law of Property Act 1925 the gift of the house would have been a perfect gift, just as the gift of the contents was a perfect gift. In the event it remained an imperfect gift and, as Turner LJ said in *Milroy v Lord* (1862) 4 De G F & J 264 274: "there is no equity in this court to perfect an imperfect gift." So matters stood in 1973, and if the facts had stopped there the defendant would have remained a licensee at will of the plaintiff.

But the facts did not stop there. On the judge's findings the defendant, having been told that the house was hers, set about improving it within and without. Outside she did not do much: a little work on the roof and an improvement which covered the way from the outside toilet to the rest of the house, putting in a new door there, and Snowcem to protect the toilet. Inside she did a good deal more. She installed gas in the kitchen with a cooker, improved the plumbing in the kitchen and put in a new sink. She got new gas fires, putting a gas fire in the lounge. She redecorated four rooms. The fitted carpets she put in the bedrooms, the stair carpeting, and the curtains and the furniture that she bought are not part of the realty, and it is not clear how much she spent on those items. But they are part of the whole circumstances. There she was, on her own after he left her in 1973. She had £1,000 left of her capital, and a pension of some kind, Having as she thought been given the house, she set about it as described. On the repairs and improvement to the realty and its fixtures she spent about £230. She had £300 of her capital left by the date of the trial, but she did not establish in evidence how much had been expended on refurbishing the house with carpets, curtains and furniture. We would describe the work done in and about the house as substantial in the sense that that adjective is used in the context of estoppel. All the while the plaintiff not only stood by and watched but encouraged and advised, without a word to suggest that she was putting her money and her personal labour into his house. What is the effect in equity?

The cases relied upon by the plaintiff are relevant for the purpose of showing that the judge fell into error in deciding that on the facts a constructive trust could be inferred. They are the cases which deal with the intention of the parties when a house is acquired. But of those cases only *Inwards v Baker* [1965] 2 QB 29, [1965] 1 All ER 446 is in point here. For this is a case of estoppel arising from the encouragement and acquiescence of the plaintiff between 1973 and 1976 when, in reliance upon his declaration that he was giving and, later, that he had given the house to her, she spent a substantial part of her small capital upon repairs and improvements to the house. The relevant principle is expounded in *Snell's Principles of Equity*, 27th edn., p. 565 in the passage under the heading "Proprietary Estoppel," and is elaborated in *Spencer Bower and Turner, Estoppel by Representation*, 3rd edn. (1977), chapter 12 entitled "Encouragement and Acquiescence."

The cases in point illustrating that principle in relation to real property are *Dillwyn v Llewelyn* (1862) 4 De G F & J 517; *Ramsden v Dyson* (1866) LR 1 HL 129 and *Plimmer v Wellington Corpn* (1884) 9 App Cas 699. One distinction between this class of case and the doctrine which has come to be known as "promissory estoppel" is that where estoppel by encouragement or acquiescence is found on the facts, those facts give rise to a cause of action. They may be relied upon as a sword, not merely as a shield. In *Ramsden v Dyson* the plaintiff failed on the facts, and the dissent of Lord Kingsdown was upon the inferences to be drawn from the facts. On the principle, however, the House was agreed, and it is stated by Lord Cranworth LC and by Lord Wensleydale as well as by Lord Kingsdown. Likewise in *Plimmer's* case the plaintiff was granted a declaration that he had a perpetual right of occupation.

The final question that arises is: to what relief is the defendant entitled upon her counterclaim? In *Dillwyn v Llewelyn* (1862) 4 De G F & J 517 there was an imperfect gift of land by a father who encouraged his son to build a house on it for £14,000. Lord Westbury LC said, at p. 521:

"About the rules of the court there can be no controversy. A voluntary agreement will not be completed or assisted by a court of equity, in cases of mere gift. If anything be wanting to complete the title of the donee, a court of equity will not assist him in obtaining it; for a mere donee can have no right to claim more then he has received. But the subsequent acts of the donor may give the donee that right or ground of claim which he did not acquire from the original gift. Thus, if A gives a house to B, but makes no formal conveyance, and the house is afterwards, on the marriage of B, included, with the knowledge of A, in the marriage settlement of B, A would be bound to complete the title of the parties claiming under that settlement. So if A puts B in possession of a piece of land, and tells him, 'I give it to you that you may build a house on it,' and B on the strength of that promise, with the knowledge of A, expends a large sum of money in building a house accordingly, I cannot doubt that the donee acquires a right from the subsequent transaction to call on the donor to perform that contract and complete the imperfect donation which was made."

In *Plimmer's* case (1884), 9 App Cas 699 the Privy Council pose the question, how should the equity be satisfied? (See pp. 713, 714). And the Board declare that on the facts a licence revocable at will became irrevocable as a consequence of the subsequent transactions. So in *Thomas v Thomas* [1956] NZLR 785 the Supreme Court of New Zealand ordered the defendant to execute a proper transfer of the property.

In *Crabb v Arun District Council* [1976] Ch 179, [1975] 3 All ER 865 this court had to consider the principles upon which the court should give effect to the equity: see Lord Denning MR at p. 189. Lawton and Scarman LJJ agreed with the remedy proposed by Lord Denning MR. On the facts of that case Scarman LJ expressed himself thus at pp. 198–199:

[His Lordship quoted the paragraph set out on p. 484, ante, beginning "I turn now to . . .'' and continued:]

So the principle to be applied is that the court should consider all the circumstances, and the counterclaimant having at law no perfected gift or licence other than a licence revocable at will, the court must decide what is the minimum equity to do justice to her having regard to the way in which she changed her position for the worse by reason of the acquiescence and encouragement of the legal owner. The defendant submits that the only appropriate way in which the equity can here be satisfied is by perfecting the imperfect gift as was done in *Dillwyn v Llewelyn*.

Counsel for the plaintiff on instructions has throughout submitted that the plaintiff is entitled to possession. The only concession that he made was that the period of notice given in the letter of 9 April 1976 was too short. He made no submission upon the way the equity, if there was an equity, should be satisfied save to submit that the court should not in any view grant a remedy more beneficial to the defendant than a licence to occupy the house for her lifetime.

We are satisfied that the problem of remedy on the facts resolves itself into a choice between two alternatives: should the equity be satisfied by a licence to the defendant to occupy the house for her lifetime, or should there be a transfer to her of the fee simple?

The main consideration pointing to a licence for her lifetime is that she did not by her case at the hearing seek to establish that she had spent more money or done more work on the house than she would have done had she believed that she had only a licence to live there for her lifetime. But the court must be cautious about drawing any inference from what she did not give in evidence as the hypothesis put is one that manifestly never occurred to her. Then it may reasonably be held that her expenditure and effort can hardly be regarded as comparable to the change of position of those who have constructed buildings on land over which they had no legal rights.

This court appreciates that the moneys laid out by the defendant were much less than in some of the cases in the books. But the court has to look at all the circumstances. When the plaintiff left her she was, we were told, a widow in her middle fifties. During the period that she lived with the plaintiff her capital was reduced from £4,500 to

£1,000. Save for her invalidity pension that was all that she had in the world. In reliance upon the plaintiff's declaration of gift, encouragement and acquiescence she arranged her affairs on the basis that the house and contents belonged to her. So relying, she devoted a quarter of her remaining capital and her personal effort upon the house and its fixtures. In addition she bought carpets, curtains and furniture for it, with the result that by the date of the trial she had only £300 left. Compared to her, on the evidence the plaintiff is a rich man. He might not regard an expenditure of a few hundred pounds as a very grave loss. But the court has to regard her change of position over the years 1973 to 1976.

We take the view that the equity cannot here be satisfied without granting a remedy which assures to the defendant security of tenure, quiet enjoyment, and freedom of action in respect of repairs and improvements without interference from the plaintiff. The history of the conduct of the plaintiff since 9 April 1976 in relation to these proceedings leads to an irresistible inference that he is determined to pursue his purpose of evicting her from the house by any legal means at his disposal with a ruthless disregard of the obligations binding upon conscience. The court must grant a remedy effective to protect her against the future manifestations of his ruthlessness. It was conceded that if she is granted a licence, such a licence cannot be registered as a land charge, so that she may find herself ousted by a purchaser for value without notice. If she has in the future to do further and more expensive repairs she may only be able to finance them by a loan, but as a licensee she cannot charge the house. The plaintiff as legal owner may well find excuses for entry in order to do what he may plausibly represent as necessary works and so contrive to derogate from her enjoyment of the licence in ways that make it difficult or impossible for the court to give her effective protection.

Weighing such considerations this court concludes that the equity to which the facts in this case give rise can only be satisfied by compelling the plaintiff to give effect to his promise and her expectations. He has so acted that he must now perfect the gift.

iv. SOLUTION ADJUSTED TO ALL THE CIRCUMSTANCES

In *Dodsworth v Dodsworth* (1973) 228 Estates Gazette 1115 [10a], giving the judgment of the court, RUSSELL LJ said: "In this case the plaintiff, aged over 70, owned in 1967 a bungalow near Boston, Lincolnshire, and lived there alone. Her younger brother and his wife — the two defendants — returned to England from Australia and were looking for a house to acquire as their home. The plaintiff persuaded them to join her in her bungalow. The judge held on the evidence that the defendants spent a sum of over £700 on improvements to the plaintiff's bungalow in the expectation, encouraged and induced by the plaintiff, that the defendants and the survivor of them would be able to remain in the bungalow as their home — sharing of course with the plaintiff while she lived — for as

---

[10a] *Re Sharpe* [1980] 1 WLR 219, [1980] 1 All ER 198, p. 450, n. 12, ante.

long as they wished to do so, in circumstances that raised an equity in favour of the defendants on the footing of principles exemplified in a passage from Lord Kingsdown's speech in *Ramsden v Dyson* (1866) LR 1 HL 129, and in other cases since then. The judge, however, held on the evidence that the parties did not intend to create a legal relationship. Not many months after the defendants moved into the bungalow, the plaintiff repented of her invitation for reasons, or alleged reasons, which need not be rehearsed. She started proceedings for possession: the defendants counterclaimed to assert an equity. The plaintiff did not appear at the hearing, and her claim for possession was non-suited. The question on the counterclaim was whether the proper way in which the equity should be satisfied would be to make some order which would assure the defendants in their occupation of the bungalow as their home for as long as they wished, or on the other hand to declare in effect that possession could only be obtained against them by the plaintiff if they were repaid their outlay on improvements to the bungalow.

The judge decided upon the latter as the appropriate course. His main ground was this. The plaintiff was anxious to sell the bungalow and buy a smaller and less expensive one for herself. She could not do this, having no other capital asset, if the defendants were entitled to stay rent free. She would therefore have to continue sharing her home for the rest of her life with the defendants, with whom she was, or thought she was, at loggerheads. Against this the defendants would, on leaving, recover and have available towards another home the expenditure which they laid out in the expectation, albeit encouraged by the plaintiff, of ability to stay there as their home. We think that the judge in balancing these considerations was entitled, and right, to come to that decision. We do not accept that the judge was wrong on the ground submitted to us that where the extent of the expectations was defined, though without intention to creat a legal relationship, between the parties, compensation for outlay could not be an appropriate satisfaction of the equity. On the appeal, the plaintiff having died intestate after notice of appeal, leave was given to the respondents, who are her administrators under a grant of letters of administration, to be joined as parties to the appeal. They do not contend that there was not an equity. They support the view, in the changed circumstances, of the judge that it was proper to satisfy the defendants' equity by protecting their occupation unless and until their expenditure was reimbursed.

Now it is clear that the ground upon which the judge mainly decided upon the appropriate remedy has, by the plaintiff's death, disappeared. But what is the situation now? Apart from the equity, the situation is this. The estate vested in the legal personal representatives consists only of the bungalow. This is subject to a standing mortgage of some £200 to £300. Its value free of any occupation rights in the defendants might be £5,000. Under the Administration of Estates Act 1925 the administrators hold the bungalow on trust for sale and to pay out of the proceeds of sale debts, duties, if any, and administration expenses (which must include their costs of this appeal), and then to divide among ten stirpes of beneficiaries, the first defendant in fact being one stirps. The immediate problem seems to be this. If immediate and direct effect is given to the expectations of the defendants, to take effect in priority to the respondents' entitlement and statutory duties, we cannot see but that it will lead, by virtue of the provisions of the Settled Land Act, to a greater and more extensive interest than was ever contemplated by the plaintiff and the defendants. The defendants would necessarily become joint tenants for life. As such they could sell the property, or quit and let it. In the one case, they would be entitled to the income of the invested proceeds of sale for life and the life of the survivor: in the other, they would be entitled to the net rents. None of these possibilities could conceivably have been embodied in the expectations giving rise to the equity in question, and we do not think that it can be right to satisfy such an equity by conferring upon the defendants a greater interest in the property than was envisaged by the parties. This, we should say, is a point which appears to have been overlooked in *Inwards v Baker* [1965] 2 QB 29, [1965] 1 All ER 446.

Is it possible in the present case to give effect to the expectation without falling foul of the impact of the Settled Land Act? . . ." Yes it was. "In short therefore we do not see how we can sensibly, and without awarding to the defendants a greater interest in law than was within the induced expectation, satisfy this equity save by securing their occupation until this expenditure has been reimbursed, which was the effect of the judge's order or declaration."

GRIFFITHS *v* WILLIAMS
(1977) 248 Estates Gazette 947 (CA, MEGAW, ORR and GOFF LJJ).

No I Gordon Villa, in Hereford, was owned by Mrs. Cole, who was the mother of Mrs. Williams, who was the mother of Mrs. Griffiths. Mrs. Williams was a school teacher, who had lived most of her life at the house.

Mrs. Cole had always indicated her intention of leaving Mrs. Williams a life interest in the house, and made a will to that effect in 1971. But in 1974, she changed her will, and left the house absolutely to Mrs. Griffiths.

Mrs. Williams looked after Mrs. Cole in her latter years, and expended her money on repairs and improvements to the house. she did so primarily for the care of her mother, but also in the belief that she would be entitled to live in the house for the rest of her life.

Held. Mrs. Williams was protected under the doctrine of estoppel. The award of a life interest was not appropriate, because that might create a settlement under the Settled Land Act 1925. Mrs. Williams should receive (with all the parties' agreement) a lease determinable upon death, with no power to assign, and at a nominal rent which did not exceed two thirds of the rateable value.

GOFF LJ: [The] equity is said to arise because the grandmother had repeatedly assured Mrs. Williams that she would be allowed to live in the house for the whole of her life, and because, on the faith of those assurances, Mrs. Williams had expended money upon the property which otherwise she would not have done. It emerged at the trial that she had spent in all, out of her own moneys, a sum of £2,000. Part of that was spent upon improvements to the property which consisted of putting in a bathroom and an indoors toilet, rewiring for electricity, concreting the yard, and repairs to one of the walls; but part of it had been spent in paying outgoings. In so far as the expenditure was of the latter character, I doubt whether it would raise an equity in Mrs. Williams' favour, because it could be regarded simply as current payment for the benefits which she was enjoying by being allowed to live in the house. But in so far as money was spent upon permanent improvements such as I have mentioned, it would be capable of creating what is known as a promissory estoppel. It seems that a grant in aid towards the improvements was obtained from the local authority; but, even so, as I read the evidence Mrs. Williams did incur expenditure out of her own money on improvements. But the evidence does not show how the £2,000 should be broken down between expenditure of that character and expenditure on current repairs.

In these circumstances, in my judgment, we have to determine three questions, which were propounded by Scarman LJ in his judgment in the case of *Crabb v Arun District Council* [1976] Ch 179, [1975] 3 All ER 865, the relevant passage being at page 193/A. I will read them from another case where they were cited, namely, *Jones v Jones* [1977] 1 WLR 438, [1977] 2 All ER 231, because there Roskill LJ answered those questions — of course, on the facts of the case before him, but the answers I think throw light on the nature of the questions and what the approach to answering them should be. I cite from the judgment of Roskill LJ at page 443/D, where his Lordship said:

"As for the rest, Lord Denning MR has referred to the decision of this court, consisting of himself and Lawton and Scarman LJJ, in *Crabb v Arun District Council* [1976] Ch 179. I would refer to the three questions, posed by Scarman LJ at the beginning of his judgment, which the court has to ask in relation to the now well-settled law of estoppel, at p. 193. 'First, is there an equity established?' The answer here is unquestionably Yes. 'Secondly, what is the extent of the equity, if one is established?' — and the answer, shortly, is that the equity is of a possessory nature entitling the defendant to remain in this house —"

and then (though not relevant for present purposes)

"but it would not, in my judgment, extend to the defendant's wife. 'And, thirdly, what is the relief appropriate to satisfy the equity?'"

Then he went on to answer that question, saying:

"All the members of the court in *Crabb v Arun District Council* thought that in some circumstances a court might impose the making of payment of some form or another as a condition of giving effect to the equity, but in the present case it seems to me that it would be wrong to impose as a condition of protecting the equity that the defendant should pay rent to the plaintiff for the following reasons. . . ." which he then set out.

That indicates to my mind that the third question is one upon which the court has to exercise a discretion. If it finds that there is an equity, then it must determine the nature of it, and then, guided by that nature and exercising discretion in all the circumstances, it has to determine what is the fair order to make between the parties for the protection of the claimant.

So I direct my mind to the first question: Was there here an equity? Mr. McCarthy says that there was not, because the defendant failed to prove, and the learned judge did not find, that the grandmother at the time the improvements were effected knew that Mrs. Williams was making a mistake as to her position. He relied on the passage in *Snell's Equity*, 27th edn. at p. 566/C, where it is said:

"Knowledge of the mistake makes it dishonest for him to remain wilfully passive in order afterwards to profit by the mistake he might have prevented. The knowledge must accordingly be proved by 'strong and cogent evidence.'"

He also points to the learned judge's judgment, where he said:

"It was clear that Mrs. Williams — and I think this would apply to most sensitive people in her position — was reluctant to admit, even to herself, that in spending her own money on housekeeping and house improvement, she was thinking predominantly of her own inheritance rather than the care and comfort of her mother. What she did say, however, was that had it occurred to her that her enjoyment and benefit of these improvements, or rather of the house as improved (a house that she had always regarded as her home) would be limited to her mother's life span, she would have had to think whether she was not obliged to look more closely to her own future. . . . It was equally clear, however, that none of this occurred to her at the time, or perhaps even not until it was put to her in this court."

In so far as it is necessary to prove that Mrs. Williams made a mistake, I think the mistake is to be found in her belief that she would be allowed to live in the house for the whole of her life. But I do not myself think that it really depends upon mistake. The equity is based upon the fact that where one has made a representation on the faith of which another party has expended his money, then the man who made the representation will not, to the prejudice of the other, be allowed to go back on it and assert his strict legal rights if to do so would be unconscionable. I cite this passage from the judgment of Lord Denning MR in *Inwards v Baker* [1965] 2 QB 29 at 37/C:

[His Lordship quoted the paragraph set out on p. 470, ante, beginning "So in this case . . .", and continued:].

The facts in that case were different, but the principle appears to me to apply precisely to the facts of the present case. Mrs. Williams' evidence, which the learned judge preferred to that of Mrs. Griffiths, was as follows: "Whenever the question arose in any discussion Mrs. Williams had always been assured that the house was her home for life. That was always what was said and she never expected more than a life interest." That does not read as if it was the lady giving evidence, but the notes of the evidence appear throughout in that form, and this was obviously a record which the learned judge was making of the evidence which had given before him. Then Mr. Hedley Williams, whose evidence the learned judge also accepted, said — or the effect of his evidence is recorded — as follows: "He had always understood that the house was his mother's for life, and this had been said to, or in front of, him over many years by both his grandmother and his mother"; and, again, "As to the improvements etc there was no objection by the grandmother and he had never heard any mention (prior to his grandmother's death) of his mother leaving, or being asked to leave." So when the learned judge speaks of what Mrs. Williams would have thought had it occurred to her, it is clear that it would have occurred to her but for the fact that Mrs. Cole, the testatrix, was throughout repeatedly assuring Mrs. Williams that she could live in the house for the rest of her life. It seems to me, on this evidence, clear that Mrs. Williams expended her money on the faith of those repeated assurances, and it is, I think, an irresistible inference that Mrs. Cole knew that Mrs. Williams was relying on the assurances which she herself was repeatedly making to her daughter. In my judgment, therefore, there is no doubt at all in this case but that an equity is made out.

I therefore pass to the second question, and that is: What is the equity? That must be an equity to have made good, so far as may fairly be done between the parties, the representation that Mrs. Williams should be entitled to live in the house rent-free for the rest of her life.

So I come to the third question, which is really the one which gives rise to such difficulties as there are in this case. In *Dodsworth v Dodsworth* (1973) (228 Estates Gazette 1115) this court unanimously decided that if an equity of this nature were implemented by giving the claimant the right to occupy the house (as it was in that case) for his life, the result would be to create a tenancy for life within the meaning of the Settled Land Act, and so the party setting up the equity would get more than it was ever represented that he should have, because he would get all the statutory powers of a tenant for life under the Act: he could sell the property and take the income of the proceeds for his life, or he could grant a long lease. In that case the court does not seem to have considered what may in such cases be a difficult problem, namely, what is the "settlement?" I think there are many authorities which establish that a right to occupy property for one's life is the equivalent of a tenancy for life under the Act. But the Act defines "settlement" in section 1 in these terms:

"Any deed, will, agreement for a settlement or other agreement, Act of Parliament, or other instrument, or any number of instruments, whether made or passed before or after, or partly before and partly

after, the commencement of this Act, under or by virtue of which instrument or instruments any land, after the commencement of this Act, stands for the time being. . . ."
and then follow the various limitations which make it settled land.

Where the interest arises under a contract or other agreement, of course, there is no difficulty, because that falls fairly and squarely within the words of subsection (1) of section 1. But where what is set up is an equity arising from acting upon a representation, it is not obvious how that can be brought within the terms of section 1 (1). There are two other cases in which this type of problem was considered by this court, namely, *Binions v Evans* [1972] Ch 359, [1972] 2 All ER 70 and *Bannister v Bannister* [1948] 2 All ER 133. In *Binions v Evans* the Master of the Rolls thought that such an equity would not in any event create a settlement; but, with all respect, I think his reasoning leads to difficulties, because at p. 367 he reached the conclusion that it created an equitable interest, and once that is established then the ground on which he said (at p. 366) there was no settlement appears to me to be undermined. The other two Lord Justices who heard that case, Megaw LJ and Stephenson LJ, felt that they were bound by the earlier decision in *Bannister v Bannister* to hold that there was a settlement; but they did not direct themselves to any question under section 1; nor, I think, need they have done so, because in *Binions v Evans* and the earlier case of *Bannister v Bannister* there was actually an agreement. So that the difficulty which in my view arises, on the case of *Dodsworth v Dodsworth* and upon the present case, of seeing whether there can be a settlement when you have an interest which appears to give you a tenancy for life but there does not obviously appear to be anything which is a "settlement" within the Act, did not arise in those two earlier cases. If it were necessary, we would have to decide what is, I think, a serious problem — whether *Dodsworth v Dodsworth* is binding upon us or whether it was decided strictly *per incuriam* because the learned Lord Justices who heard it did not advert to section 1 of the Settled Land Act, and, if it be not binding upon us, whether in truth it be right, and if so, what is the answer to the conundrum posed by subsection (1) of section 1. It may be that in such a case there is a settlement, and it is the order of the court declaring the equity, which is an "instrument" and, therefore, the "settlement" within the meaning of that subsection.

Happily, by the good sense of the parties in accepting a solution of the problem which I propounded for their consideration, it is unnecessary for this court to resolve those problems. In *Dodsworth v Dodsworth*, having decided that a right of occupation for the whole life of the claimant would be a wrong way of giving effect to the equity because it would create a settlement under the Settled Land Act and give the claimant too much, the court then adopted an alternative suggestion of compensation by recouping the claimant his expenditure (I think with interest) and giving him possession until payment. They recognised that that really went too far the other way; and certainly it would not be appropriate in this case — if for no other reason, because of the difficulty of quantification. But it seems to me that *Dodsworth v Dodsworth* proceeded upon the basis which I have spelt out of *Crabb's* case — that the third problem is one of discretion: the court ought to see, having regard to all the circumstances, what is the best and fairest way to secure protection for the person who has been misled by the representations made to him and subsequently repudiated.

In the present case, it seemed to me, and I suggested to the parties, that the fairest way of dealing with the matter would be to direct the plaintiffs to grant Mrs. Williams a long lease, determinable upon her death, at a nominal rent, since that would give her the right of occupation for her whole life and could not in any event give her the statutory powers under the Settled Land Act. The nominal rent would be an obligation not contemplated when the representations were made to her, but perfect equity is seldom possible.

There appeared to be only two objections to this course. One was that she might assign the lease; but that can be dealt with by including in the lease an absolute covenant not to assign, and by her giving an undertaking to this court, which I understand she is prepared to do, not to assign. The other difficulty was that, if she were to marry again, her husband might be able to claim a protected tenancy under the Rent Acts. I know that to Mrs. Williams that appears a flight of fantasy; but we have to take precautions to see that what we propose is something which will not go wrong in an event which is not impossible and could happen. Counsel have made inquiries and they assure us that the husband would not be entitled to protection under the Rent Acts if the rent did not exceed two-thirds of the rateable value at the relevant date; and they have ascertained that that rateable value is £46 per annum. Therefore, if we direct the lease to be at a rent of £30 per annum we will have served the two ends of keeping it below two-thirds of the rateable value and making it nominal; and that is what I would propose. I took the precaution of making it clear to counsel, and they have made it clear to the parties, that, while we might order that as a term after deciding whether or not a life interest would be a "settlement" within the meaning of the Act, if we were to decide that it was not a settlement within the Act Mrs. Williams would be entitled to claim a full life interest without reservation of any rent, and therefore we could only adopt this course of a long lease at this stage if the parties consented to it, otherwise we must first determine the problem which I have mentioned and then consider what it would be right to order in the light of that determination. Counsel, having withdrawn and consulted with their clients and taken instructions, say that they are content that we should adopt the solution proposed by me.

I would therefore allow the appeal, discharge the order of the learned deputy circuit judge, and direct the plaintiffs to grant to Mrs. Williams the lease which I have indicated.

QUESTIONS

1. Is a licence by estoppel an interest in land? Can it be sold? Would it pass with the land? Dawson and Pearce, pp. 144–145 and Chap. 11.

2. (a) Consider the solutions reached in the various cases in this section, and compare them with those reached in sections III and IV.

   (b) Do you think that the equities were satisfied in the best possible way? See also *Dillwyn v Llewelyn* (1862) 4 De GF & J 517; *Duke of Devonshire v Elgin* (1851) 14 Beav 530; *Unity Joint Stock Mutual Banking Association v King* (1858) 25 Beav 72; *Duke of Beaufort v Patrick* (1853) 17 Beav 60; *Raffaele v Raffaele* [1962] WAR 29; *Thomas v Thomas* [1956] NZLR 785.

3. To what extent is a licensee's right to protection affected by his conduct (a) before and (b) after his licence is established? Why are contractual licences and licences by estoppel treated differently? *Thompson v Park* [1944] KB 408; *Williams v Staite* [1979] Ch 291, [1978] 2 All ER 928; Dawson and Pearce, pp. 223–224.

VI. Deserted Wives. A Historical Note

Brief mention should be made here of a body of doctrine which grew up in the nineteen-fifties, with the object of protecting a deserted wife in the occupation of the family home. If a husband owns the matrimonial home and deserts his wife, does the wife become a trespasser, liable to eviction by the husband; or by a third party, if the husband has transferred the title? In a number of cases, the deserted wife was protected on the theory that she was a licensee under a licence which was irrevocable by the husband, or by a transferee other than a bona fide purchaser of a legal estate for value without notice[11]. There is no need now to enter into the complexities and controversies which this situation created; for the House of Lords held in *National Provincial Bank, Ltd. v Ainsworth*[12] that she had no interest capable of enforcement against a third party; and the short but active career of "the deserted wife's equity" came to an end. "The deserted wife therefore," said Lord Wilberforce, "cannot resist a claim from a 'purchaser' from her husband whether the 'purchase' takes place after or before the desertion. As regards transactions subsequent to the desertion this disability is somewhat mitigated by three factors. First, if it appears that the husband is threatening to dispose of the house in such a manner as to defeat her rights, she may be able to obtain an injunction

---

[11] *Bendall v McWhirter* [1952] 2 QB 466, [1952] 1 All ER 1307; *Ferris v Weaven* [1952] 2 All ER 233; *Street v Denham,* [1954] 1 WLR 624, [1954] 1 All ER 532; *Lee v Lee,* [1952] 2 QB 489n, [1952] 1 All ER 1299; *Jess B. Woodcock & Sons Ltd v Hobbs* [1955] 1 WLR 152, [1955] 1 All ER 445; *Westminster Bank Ltd v Lee* [1956] Ch 7, [1955] 2 All ER 883; *Miles v Bull* [1969] 1 QB 258, [1968] 3 All ER 632.

[12] [1965] AC 1175, [1965] 2 All ER 472.

to restrain him from doing so (*Lee v Lee* ([1952] 2 QB 489n, [1952] 1 All ER 1299)). An injunction is, of course, a discretionary remedy and it does not follow that the wife will be granted it in every case, but in suitable circumstances she has this protection. Secondly, the courts have ample powers to detect, and to refuse to give effect to, sham or fraudulent transactions — such as that which was attempted in *Ferris v Weaven* ([1952] 2 All ER 233). Thirdly. . . .''

A deserted wife (spouse) has, in recent years, earned protection under different theories. She is not merely a licensee of her husband in the family home. Her contributions to the establishment of the home have been more and more readily treated as an entitlement to a share in the ownership of the family home. Regardless of any property ownership, however, she has a right of occupation, and may protect this against third parties by registration, as has been seen, under the Matrimonial Homes Act 1967[13]. Further, her shared ownership, together with her occupation of the home, along with her husband, has been held to be sufficient to entitle her to an overriding interest[14]. It remains to be seen whether occupation based upon a licence by estoppel would be similarly treated. And, where the wife has protection, the mistress does not follow far behind.

---

[13] P. 232, ante.
[14] *Williams and Glyn's Bank Ltd v Boland* [1979] Ch 312, [1979] 2 All ER 697; p. 122, ante.

10. Easements and Profits A Prendre[1]

I. General

Easements and profits a prendre are interests entitling their owners to exercise certain rights over the land of another. They may be legal[2] or equitable. They are distinguishable in that a profit entitles its owner to take away something capable of ownership from the servient land, while an easement does not; and also in that a profit may exist "in gross", while an easement must always be appurtenant to land. Little will be said of profits, owing to lack of available space; or, indeed, of commons[3].

II. Nature of Easements[4]

A. General Characteristics

The detailed characteristics of an easement are discussed in the text-books and need not be repeated here. In short, an easement is

---

[1] Cheshire, pp. 513–591; M & W, pp. 805-884; MM, pp. 386–426, *Gale on Easements* (14th edn., 1972); Jackson, *Law of Easements and Profits* (1978); (1964) 28 Conv (NS) 450 (M. A. Peel).

[2] L.P.A. 1925, ss. 1 (2), 187.

[3] For registration of commons under Commons Registration Act 1965, see p. 53, ante.

[4] Cheshire, pp. 516–526; M & W, pp. 805–827; MM, pp. 386–398, Gale, pp. 3–60; Jackson, 1-27, 39–49.

a right, appurtenant to one piece of land and exercisable over another piece of land, and capable of forming the subject matter of a grant. Indeed, all easements, other than those created by statute, are either granted expressly or impliedly, or are presumed to have been granted. An easement must be distinguished from a licence in that it is a proprietary interest and must be appurtenant to land; from a lease in that it does not give the owner of the easement any possessory rights over the land of another; from local customary rights in that there cannot be a grant without a capable grantee; and from natural rights in that these need no grant; from the covenant in that it must be a right capable of being granted. Thus rights which are properly licences, leases, customary rights, natural rights or covenants may look very much like easements, but they may be very different. If X, the owner of Whiteacre, tells Y, the owner of Blackacre, that Y's son may enter Whiteacre to collect a lost ball, that is clearly a licence; but if X were to permit the owner of Blackacre to enter Whiteacre at any time for pleasure and recreation, it might create an easement[5]. Again, a letting of a garage on a weekly tenancy is clearly in no sense an easement; but a right to park vehicles on a neighbour's ground without interfering with his user of the land looks more like an easement[6], and the right to fix a signboard on a neighbour's house can be an easement[7]. Again, local inhabitants of a particular area may have the right to pass across another's land on the way to church[8], or to dry their nets on someone's land[9]; but these rights rely on custom and not on grant and cannot be easements. Again, every landowner has the right of support from his neighbour to his land in its natural state[10]. A right of support to buildings on land is, however, a right which must be claimed as the result of a grant[11]. A covenant not to use land as a fish shop is clearly no easement; but an arrangement permitting the owner of neighbouring land to walk across it in perpetuity to the road is capable of being an easement. In connection with this comparison between easements and covenants, the anomalous position of the easement of light may be noted[12]. For this easement is more like a negative right; the grantor does not grant the light; he is rather under an obligation not to obstruct it. One can only suppose that in the times of narrow streets, poor lighting and small windows, some way of protecting the access of light to houses in towns was necessary. Until

---

[5] *Horton v Tidd* (1965) 196 Estates Gazette 697: *Re Ellenborough Park* [1965] Ch 131, [1955] 3 All ER 667; see p. 507, post; *Miller v Jackson* [1977] QB 966, [1977] 3 All ER 338, (1977) 93 LQR 481.
[6] Compare *Copeland v Greenhalf* [1952] Ch 488, [1952] 1 All ER 809; see pp. 512–514, post.
[7] *Re Webb's Lease* [1951] Ch 808, [1951] 2 All ER 131; see p. 545, post.
[8] *Brocklebank v Thompson* [1903] 2 Ch 344.
[9] *Mercer v Denne* [1905] 2 Ch 538; *Alfred F. Beckett Ltd v Lyons* [1967] Ch 449. [1967] 1 All ER 833.
[10] *Hunt v Peake* (1860) John 705; *Backhouse v Bonomi* (1851) 9 HL Cas 503.
[11] *Dalton v Angus* (1881) 6 App Cas 740; *Ray v Fairway Motors (Barnstaple) Ltd* (1969) 20 P & CR 261.
[12] See p. 582, post.

1848[13], there was no way of providing that a negative covenant between freeholders should run with the land, and the only way in which a landowner could be protected was by regarding him as the owner of an easement. It seems, however, more natural to look upon that situation as one of covenant — one in which the neighbour is under an obligation not to build, rather than one in which he has granted the landowner a right "not to have his light obstructed". Nevertheless it is so treated historically. A similar situation arises in the case of an easement of support[14]. A further anomaly exists in the case of an easement to repair a fence. The general principle is that the servient owner is under no obligation to expend money on the maintenance of any property over which an easement is exercised. The dominant owner may enter to effect the necessary repair. Thus the easement of fencing is unusual in that the servient owner is under a duty to take positive steps to maintain the fence, including the expenditure of money[15]. There may also be cases where the parties have expressly or impliedly agreed that the servient owner shall bear the burden; as where a local authority, which owned a high-rise block of flats, let them to tenants. Easements of access over the common parts of the building retained by the local authority were implied in favour of the tenants (the dominant owners). And the authority was held liable, as on an implied contract, to maintain those parts[16].

While the essential characteristics of an easement are reasonably clear, and no right which fails to comply with them can exist as an easement, it is not possible to say that the law will recognise as an easement every right that does comply. An easement can be described rather than defined, and lists of those judicially recognised are collected in the books[17]. New ones may arise: "The category of servitudes and easements must alter and expand with the changes that take place in the circumstances of mankind[18]." Whether or not a new right, complying with the accepted requirements of an easement, will be judicially recognised or not is very difficult to forecast[19]. Inevitably the cases in this section are a random selection.

---

[13] *Tulk v Moxhay* (1848) 2 Ph 774; see p. 704, post.

[14] *Dalton v Angus* (1881), 6 App. Cas. 740.

[15] *Lawrence v Jenkins* (1873), L.R. 8 QB 274 (a 'spurious easement'); *Jones v Price*, [1965] 2 QB 618, [1965] 2 All ER 625; *Crow v Wood* [1971] 1 QB 77, [1970] 3 All ER 425; see p. 518, post; other rights cannot be easements if they involve expenditure by the servient owner, *Regis Property Co Ltd v Redman* [1956] 2 QB 612, [1956] 2 All ER 335 (supply of hot water cannot be an easement so as to pass under L.P.A. 1925, s. 62).

[16] *Liverpool City Council v Irwin* [1977] AC 239; cf. *Stokes v Mixconcrete* (Holdings) Ltd (1979) 38 P & CR 488.

[17] Cheshire, pp. 522–525; M & W, pp. 810–813, 880–881; MM, pp. 389–390, 424; Gale, pp. 35–37.

[18] *Dyce v Lady James Hay* (1852) 1 Macq 305, 312–313, per Lord St. Leonards.

[19] *A-G of Southern Nigeria v John Holt & Co (Liverpool) Ltd* [1915] AC 599; *Miller v Emcer Products* [1956] Ch 304, [1956] 1 All ER 237, (1956) 72 LQR 172 (R. E. M.); *Phipps v Pears* [1965] 1 QB 76, [1964] 2 All ER 35, (1964) 80 LQR 318 (R. E. M.), see p. 516, post; *Dowty Boulton Paul Ltd v Wolverhampton Corpn* (No. 2) [1976] Ch 13, [1973] 2 All ER 491.

i. CAPABILITY OF EXISTENCE AS EASEMENT

HILL *v* TUPPER
(1863) 2 H & C 121 (Exch, POLLOCK CB, MARTIN and BRAMWELL BB)

The Company of Proprietors of the Basingstoke Canal Navigation leased premises on the bank of the canal to the plaintiff, a boat proprietor. The lease to the plaintiff purported to give to him, inter alia, "the sole and exclusive right or liberty to put or use boats on the said canal, and let the same for hire for the purpose of pleasure only". It was alleged that the defendant, the landlord of an inn adjoining the canal, had interfered with the plaintiff's right by putting boats on the canal. The judge refused an application to nonsuit the plaintiff. A rule *nisi* was obtained to enter a nonsuit.

Held. Rule made absolute. The plaintiff was a licensee only and was not entitled to an easement.

POLLOCK CB: We are all of opinion that the rule must be absolute to enter the verdict for the defendant on the second plea. After the very full argument which has taken place, I do not think it necessary to assign any other reason for our decision, than that the case of *Ackroyd v Smith* ((1850) 10 CB 164) expressly decided that it is not competent to create rights unconnected with the use and enjoyment of land, and annex them to it so as to constitute a property in the grantee. This grant merely operates as a licence or covenant on the part of the grantors, and is binding on them as between themselves and the grantee, but gives him no right of action in his own name for any infringement of the supposed exclusive right. It is argued that, as the owner of an estate may grant a right to cut turves, or to fish or hunt, there is no reason why he may not grant such a right as that now claimed by the plaintiff. The answer is, that the law will not allow it. So the law will not permit the owner of an estate to grant it alternately to his heirs male and heirs female. A new species of incorporeal hereditament cannot be created at the will and pleasure of the owner of property; but he must be content to accept the estate and the right to dispose of it subject to the law as settled by decisions or controlled by Act of Parliament. A grantor may bind himself by covenant to allow any right he pleases over his property, but he cannot annex to it a new incident, so as to enable the grantee to sue in his own name for an infringement of such a limited right as that now claimed.

BRYANT *v* LEFEVER
(1879) 4 CPD 172 (CA, BRAMWELL, BRETT and COTTON LJJ)

The plaintiff and defendants were occupiers of adjoining houses which were of approximately equal height. The houses had remained in the same condition for much more than twenty years before 1876 when the defendants re-built their house in such a way that a new wall structure, adjoining the plaintiff's chimneys, made it possible for the defendants to stack timber on their roof. This structure caused the plaintiff's chimneys to smoke. The plaintiff brought this action, claiming that he had a right to the free access of air to his chimneys and for nuisance.

Held. The action failed. The right claimed was not capable of existing as an easement.

COTTON LJ: This is an appeal of the defendants from a judgment of Lord Coleridge in favour of the plaintiff in respect of the interruption of air to the plaintiff's chimney caused by the defendants.

The jury have found, first, that there had been for more than twenty years free access of air to the chimneys of the plaintiff's house; secondly, that the defendants interfered with it; thirdly, that the erection of the defendants' wall sensibly and materially interfered with the comfort of human existence in the plaintiff's premises; fourthly, that the plaintiff sustained damage 40*l* by the building of the defendants' wall.

The first question is, whether the plaintiff has, either as a natural right of property or as an easement, a right as against the defendants to have the access of air to his chimney without any interruption by the defendants. In my opinion he has no such right.

In my opinion it would be a contradiction in terms to say that a man has a natural right against his neighbour in respect of a house which is an artificial addition to, and not a user of, the land. That the owner of a house has, as against his neighbour, no natural rights in respect of his house, is shewn by the cases as to subjacent and lateral support. These shew that while every owner of property has, independently of user, a natural right to support for his land, if he adds buildings to his land and thereby requires an increased support, he, in the absence of express grant, can only acquire a right to such support by user, that is, by way of easement. The right (if any) of the plaintiff to the uninterrupted flow of air to his chimney must therefore be by way of easement. Cases to prevent, or to claim damages for, interference with ancient lights, are frequently spoken of as cases of light and air, and the right relied on as a right to the access of light and air. But this is inaccurate. The cases, as a rule, relate solely to the interference with the access of light, and in no case has any injunction been granted to restrain interference with the access of air. It is unnecessary to say whether, if the uninterrupted flow of air through a definite aperture or channel over a neighbour's property has been enjoyed as of right for a sufficient period, a right by way of easement could be acquired. No such point is made in this case, and I am of opinion that a right by way of easement to the access of air over the general unlimited surface of a neighbour cannot be acquired by mere enjoyment. For this *Webb v Bird* ((1862) 13 CBNS 841) is an authority, and as the last decision in that case was in the Exchequer Chamber, it would be sufficient to rely upon the authority of that case. But I think it better to say that I entirely agree with that decision and with the reasons given in this case by Bramwell LJ. In my opinion, therefore, the plaintiff has no right in respect of the flow of air to or from his chimney.

[His Lordship held that no action lay in nuisance because the defendants had not sent impure air on to the plaintiff's land: they had merely blocked the escape of the plaintiff's own impure air[20].]

In *Cable v Bryant* [1908] 1 Ch 259, it was held that an easement could exist which entitled the dominant owner to the access of air through a defined aperture (a ventilator), although there was no defined channel across the servient tenement through which the air flowed[1].

RE ELLENBOROUGH PARK
[1956] Ch 131, [1955] 3 All ER 667 (ChD, DANCKWERTS J and CA, EVERSHED MR, BIRKETT and ROMER LJJ)

In 1855 the White Cross Estate, which included Ellenborough Park, was being developed for building purposes. Purchasers of the several plots surrounding the Park were given in their conveyances certain rights of user over the Park; and for the purposes of the present action it was agreed to take as typical of all these conveyances, one dated 1864 conveying a plot to John Porter. The material part of this conveyance was as follows: "Together with . . . and also full enjoyment at all times hereafter in common with the other persons to whom such easements may be granted of the pleasure ground set out and made in front of the said plot of land . . . in the centre of the square called Ellenborough Park . . . but subject to the payment of a fair and just proportion of the costs charges and expenses of keeping in good order and condition the said pleasure ground." John Porter covenanted to pay a fair proportion of the expenses of the upkeep of the Park, and the vendors covenanted to keep the Park as an ornamental pleasure ground. The Park became vested in the plaintiffs on statutory trusts for sale.

During the Second World War, the Park was requisitioned, and subsequently the War Office paid sums of money in respect of compensation rental and on account of dilapidations. Various questions arose, concerning the rights of the original purchasers and their successors in title to use the Park, and concerning the allocation of compensation money from the War Office. The question was whether the surrounding owners had lost a legal right, for which they would be entitled to be compensated.

Held (affirming DANCKWERTS J). The right of enjoyment was an easement appurtenant to the plots bought by the original purchasers, and the plaintiffs were therefore entitled to compensation.

---

[20] See also *Harris v De Pinna* (1886) 33 ChD 238. The right may arise under the doctrine of non-derogation from grant (*Aldin v Latimer, Clark, Muirhead & Co* [1894] 2 Ch 437).

[1] *Wong v Beaumount Property Trust Ltd* [1965] 1 QB 173, [1964] 2 All ER 119, see p. 527, post.

EVERSHED MR: The substantial question in the case, which we have briefly indicated, is one of considerable interest and importance. It is clear from our brief recital of the facts that, if the house owners are now entitled to an enforceable right in respect of the use and enjoyment of Ellenborough Park, that right must have the character and quality of an easement as understood by, and known to, our law. It has, therefore, been necessary for us to consider carefully the qualities and characteristics of easements, and, for such purpose, to look back into the history of that category of incorporeal rights in the development of English real property law. It may be fairly assumed that, in the case of *Duncan v Louch* ((1845) 6 QB 904), the Court of Queen's Bench in the year 1845, and particularly Lord Denman CJ, who delivered the first judgment in the court, was of opinion that such a right as the respondent claims was capable of fulfilling the qualifying conditions of an easement. And Buckley J, in the case in 1904 of *Keith v Twentieth Century Club Ltd* ((1904) 73 LJ Ch 545), answered certain questions which Byrne J had ordered to be set down to be argued before the court, themselves depending upon the assumption that such a right could exist in law. On the other hand, Farwell J, a judge peculiarly experienced and learned in real property law, on two occasions, namely, in 1903 in the case of *International Tea Stores Co v Hobbs* ([1903] 2 Ch 165 at 172), and in 1905 in *A-G v Antrobus* ([1905] 2 Ch 188 at 198), used language appearing to treat as axiomatic the proposition, that a right, which should properly be described as a jus spatiandi, was a right excluded by English law, as by Roman law, from the company of servitudes.

The four cases which we have mentioned must be considered hereafter at greater length. But it can be said at once that, with the possible exception of the first, none of them constitutes or involves a direct decision upon the question now before us: and although the existence of gardens surrounded by houses, the owners or occupiers of which enjoy in practice the amenities of the gardens, is a well-known feature of town development throughout the country, no other case appears to have come before the courts in which the validity of the rights in fact enjoyed in the gardens has ever been tested. . . .[2]

For the purposes of the argument before us, Mr. Cross and Mr. Goff [counsel for each side] were content to adopt, as correct, the four characteristics formulated in Dr. Cheshire's *Modern Real Property* 7th edn., pp. 456[3] et seq. They are (1) there must be a dominant and a servient tenement: (2) an easement must "accommodate" the dominant tenement: (3) dominant and servient owners must be different persons[4], and (4) a right over land cannot amount to an

---

[2] Lord EVERSHED referred to Holdsworth, *Historical Introduction to Land Law* (1927), p. 265.

[3] 12th edn., pp. 517 et seq.

[4] This is not strictly true. A tenant may grant an easement, for a period not exceeding that of his lease, in favour of another tenant of the same landlord; and an easement of light may be so acquired by prescription: *Morgan v Fear* [1907] AC 425, (1949) 13 Conv (NS) 104 (A. K. R. Kiralfy), (1958) 74 LQR 82 (V. T. H. Delany); M & W, p. 809.

easement, unless it is capable of forming the subject-matter of a grant. . . .

We pass, accordingly, to a consideration of the first of Dr. Cheshire's conditions — that of the accommodation of the alleged dominant tenements by the rights as we have interpreted them. For it was one of the main submissions by Mr. Cross on behalf of the appellant that the right of full enjoyment of the park, granted to the purchaser by the conveyance of 23 December 1864, was insufficiently connected with the enjoyment of the property conveyed, in that it did not subserve some use which was to be made of that property; and that such a right accordingly could not exist in law as an easement. In this part of his argument Mr. Cross was invoking a principle which is, in our judgment, of unchallengeable authority, expounded, in somewhat varying language, in many judicial utterances, of which the judgments in *Ackroyd v Smith* ((1850) 10 CB 164) are, perhaps, most commonly cited. We think it unnecessary to review the authorities in which the principle has been applied; for the effect of the decisions is stated with accuracy in Dr. Cheshire's *Modern Real Property* 7th edn, p. 457[5]. After pointing out that "one of the fundamental principles concerning easements is that they must be not only apppurtenant to a dominant tenement, but also connected with the normal enjoyment of the dominant tenement" and referring to certain citations in support of that proposition the author proceeded: "We may expand the statement of the principle thus: a right enjoyed by one over the land of another does not possess the status of an easement unless it accommodates and serves the dominant tenement, and is reasonably necessary for the better enjoyment of that tenement, for if it has no necessary connexion therewith, although it confers an advantage upon the owner and renders his ownership of the land more valuable, it is not an easement at all, but a mere contractual right personal to and only enforceable between the two contracting parties."

[His Lordship rejected the argument, based on an observation of WILLES J, in *Bailey v Stephens* ((1862) 12 CB NS 91) to the effect that a right could only exist as an easement if it could benefit only the claimant to the easement and no other person, and continued:] Can it be said, then, of the right of full enjoyment of the park in question, which was granted by the conveyance of 23 December 1864, and which, for reasons already given, was, in our view, intended to be annexed to the property conveyed to Mr. Porter, that it accommodated and served that property? It is clear that the right did, in some degree, enhance the value of the property, and this consideration cannot be dismissed as wholly irrelevant. It is, of course, a point to be noted; but we agree with Mr. Cross's submission that it is in no way decisive of the problem; it is not sufficient to show that the right increased the value of the property conveyed, unless it is also shown that it was connected with the normal enjoyment of that property.

---

[5] 12th edn., p. 518.

It appears to us that the question whether or not this connexion exists is primarily one of fact, and depends largely on the nature of the alleged dominant tenement and the nature of the right granted. As to the former, it was in the contemplation of the parties to the conveyance of 1864 that the property conveyed should be used for residential and not commercial purposes. . . . As to the nature of the right granted, the conveyance of 1864 shows that the park was to be kept and maintained as a pleasure ground or ornamental garden. . . .

On these facts Mr. Cross submitted that the requisite connexion between the right to use the park and the normal enjoyment of the houses which were built around it or near it had not been established. He likened the position to a right granted to the purchaser of a house to use the Zoological Gardens free of charge or to attend Lord's Cricket Ground without payment. Such a right would undoubtedly, he said, increase the value of the property conveyed but could not run with it at law as an easement, because there was no sufficient nexus between the enjoyment of the right and the use of the house. It is probably true, we think, that in neither of Mr. Cross's illustrations would the supposed right constitute an easement, for it would be wholly extraneous to, and independent of, the use of a house as a house, namely, as a place in which the householder and his family live and make their home; and it is for this reason that the analogy which Mr. Cross sought to establish between his illustrations and the present case cannot, in our opinion, be supported. A much closer analogy, as it seems to us, is the case of a man selling the freehold of part of his house and granting to the purchaser, his heirs and assigns, the right, appurtenant to such part, to use the garden in common with the vendor and his assigns. In such a case, the test of connexion, or accommodation, would be amply satisfied; for just as the use of a garden undoubtedly enhances, and is connected with, the normal enjoyment of the house to which it belongs, so also would the right granted, in the case supposed, be closely connected with the use and enjoyment of the part of the premises sold. Such, we think, is in substance the position in the present case. The park became a communal garden for the benefit and enjoyment of those whose houses adjoined it or were in its close proximity. Its flower beds, lawns and walks were calculated to afford all the amenities which it is the purpose of the garden of a house to provide; and, apart from the fact that these amenities extended to a number of householders, instead of being confined to one (which on this aspect of the case is immaterial), we can see no difference in principle between Ellenborough Park and a garden in the ordinary signification of that word. It is the collective garden of the neighbouring houses, to whose use it was dedicated by the owners of the estate and as such amply satisfied, in our judgment, the requirement of connexion with the dominant tenements to which it is appurtenant. The result is not affected by the circumstances that the right to the park is in this case enjoyed by some few houses which are not immediately fronting on the park. The test for present purposes, no doubt, is that the park should constitute in a real and intelligible sense the garden (albeit the communal garden) of the houses to which its enjoyment is annexed. But we think that the test is satisfied as regards these few neighbouring, though not adjacent, houses. We think that the extension of the right of enjoyment to these few houses does not negative the presence of the necessary "nexus" between the subject-matter enjoyed and the premises to which the enjoyment is expressed to belong. . . .[6]

For the reasons which we have stated, we are unable to accept the contention that the right to the full enjoyment of Ellenborough Park fails in limine to qualify as a legal easement for want of the necessary connexion between its enjoyment and the use of the properties comprised in the conveyance of 1864, and in other relevant conveyances.

We turn next to Dr. Cheshire's fourth condition for an easement — that the right must be capable of forming the subject-matter of a grant. As we have earlier stated, satisfaction of the condition in the present case depends on a consideration of the questions whether the right conferred is too wide and vague, whether it is inconsistent with the proprietorship or possession of the alleged servient owners, and whether it is a mere right of recreation without utility or benefit.

To the first of these questions the interpretation which we have given to the typical deed provides, in our judgment, the answer; for we have construed the right conferred as being both well defined and commonly understood. In these essential respects the right may be said to be distinct from the indefinite and unregulated privilege which, we think, would ordinarily be understood by the Latin term "jus spatiandi", a privilege of wandering at will over all and every part of another's field or park, and which, though easily intelligible as the subject-matter of a personal licence, is something substantially different from the subject-matter of the grant in question, namely, the provision for a limited number of houses in a uniform crescent of one single large but private garden.

Our interpretation of the deed also provides, we think, the answer to the second question; for the right conferred no more amounts to a joint occupation of the park with its owners, no more excludes the proprietorship or possession of the latter, than a right of way granted through a passage, or than the use by the public of the gardens of Lincoln's Inn Fields (to take one of our former examples) amount to joint occupation of that garden with the London County Council, or involve an inconsistency with the possession or proprietorship of the council as lessees. . . .

[His Lordship referred to *Copeland v Greenhalf* ([1952] Ch 488, [1952] 1 All ER 809), discussed the nature of the right claimed in the present case and continued:]

---

[6] *Todrick v Western National Omnibus Co Ltd* [1934] Ch 561; *Birmingham, Dudley and District Banking Co v Ross* (1888) 38 ChD at 314; *Pugh v Savage* [1970] 2 QB 373, [1970] 2 All ER 353 (intervening land between dominant and servient tenements).

... The right to full enjoyment of Ellenborough Park, which was granted by the 1864 and other relevant conveyances, was, in substance, no more than a right to use the park as a garden in the way in which gardens are commonly used. In a sense, no doubt, such a right includes something of a jus spatiandi, inasmuch as it involves the principle of wandering at will round each part of the garden, except of course, such parts as comprise flower beds, or are laid out for some other purpose, which renders walking impossible or unsuitable. We doubt, nevertheless, whether the right to use and enjoy a garden in this manner can with accuracy be said to constitute a mere jus spatiandi. Wandering at large is of the essence of such a right and constitutes the main purpose for which it exists. A private garden, on the other hand, is an attribute of the ordinary enjoyment of the residence to which it is attached, and the right of wandering in it is but one method of enjoying it. On the assumption, however, that the right now in question does constitute a jus spatiandi, or that it is analogous thereto, it becomes necessary to consider whether the right, which is in question in these proceedings, is, for that reason, incapable of ranking in law as an easement.

[His Lordship referred to dicta of Farwell J in *International Tea Stores Co v Hobbs* ([1903] 2 Ch at 171), and in *A-G v Antrobus* ([1905] 2 Ch, at 198, 199, 205), which spoke of a jus spatiandi as being a right "not known to our law". These statements were obiter and "cannot be regarded as authoritative". His Lordship continued:]

Duncan v Louch ((1845) 6 QB 904), on the other hand, decided more than 100 years ago but not, as we have observed, quoted to Farwell J in either of the two cases which we have cited, is authoritative in favour of the recognition by our law as an easement of a right closely comparable to that now in question which, if it involves in some sense a jus spatiandi, is nevertheless properly annexed and appurtenant to a defined hereditament. ...

... We agree with Danckwerts J in regarding *Duncan v Louch* as being a direct authority in the defendant's favour. It has never, so far as we are aware, been since questioned, and we think it should, in the present case, be followed.

For the reasons which we have stated, Danckwerts J came, in our judgment, to a right conclusion in this case and, accordingly, the appeal must be dismissed.

ii.   EXCLUSIVE OR JOINT USER

COPELAND *v* GREENHALF[7]
[1952] Ch 488, [1952] 1 All ER 809 (ChD, UPJOHN J)

The plaintiff was the owner of an orchard and an adjoining house. Access to the orchard from the road was provided by a strip of land of varying width about 150 ft. long.

The defendant was a wheelwright whose premises were across the road from the plaintiff's land. The defendant proved that for 50 years

---

[7] Gale, pp. 30–34.

he and his father before him had to the plaintiff's knowledge used one side of the plaintiff's strip of land to store and repair vehicles in connection with his business as wheelwright; leaving always room for the plaintiff to have access to the orchard. He claimed a prescriptive right to do so. The plaintiff brought this action to restrain him.

Held. Such a right was not an easement, and the claim amounted to one for beneficial user of the land.

UPJOHN J: Mr. Horne, [for the plaintiff] ... says that there are two reasons why this cannot be a valid easement. First, he says that it is uncertain. He says that the court is not in a position to control the exercise of this easement. He relied on *Hill v Tupper* ((1863) 2 H & C 121; p. 505, ante), and he referred to the well-known passage in the judgment of Pollock CB, which says: "A new series of incorporeal hereditament cannot be created at the will and pleasure of the owner of property; but he must be content to accept the estate and the right to dispose of it subject to the law as settled by decisions or controlled by Act of Parliament. A grantor may bind himself by covenant to allow any right he pleases over his property, but he cannot annex to it a new incident, so as to enable the grantee to sue in his own name for an infringement of such a limited right as that now claimed."

He pressed me, of course, very strongly with the well-known case of *Dyce v Lady James Hay* ((1852) 1 Macq 305), in the House of Lords, in which the sidenote reads as follows: "There can be no prescriptive right in the nature of a servitude or easement so large as to preclude the ordinary uses of property by the owner of the lands affected. *Semble*, that where a claim in the nature of a servitude or easement is incapable of judicial control and restriction it cannot be sustained by prescription. It does not follow that rights sustainable by grant are necessarily sustainable by prescription. The law of Scotland agrees with the law of England in holding that the right to village greens and playgrounds stands upon a principle of original dedication to the use of the public. Where new inventions come into use they may have the benefit of servitudes and easements, the law accommodating its practical operation to the varying circumstances of mankind." ...

He contended that there is nothing novel in the business of a wheelwright, but that it is an entirely novel suggestion that a wheelwright or anyone else carrying on trade can have such a right as this. He pointed out the great width of the right claimed: vehicles can be left there for an indefinite time, for years, if necessary; they can be left in a vague and undefined part of the strip, leaving an ill-defined gangway, as it has been called, for the owner of the strip to use in getting to his land. He further pointed out that the defendant is really doing much more than an ordinary wheelwright's business; that he is doing repairs to every form of modern type of vehicle, such as motor lorries, and that that also makes the claim really too uncertain to be enforceable.

Mr. Horne's second point is this, that an easement must be for the benefit of the land, and not for a business carried on in connexion with the land. ...

I think that . . . the matter is concluded for me by the decision of
Fry J, in *Moody v Steggles* ((1879) 12 ChD 261) in which he said: "The
next point taken on behalf of the defendants is this: It is said that the
easement in question relates, not to the tenement, but to the business
of the occupant of the tenement, and that therefore I cannot tie the
easement to the house. It appears to me that that argument is of too
refined a nature to prevail, and for this reason, that the house can only
be used by an occupant, and that the occupant only uses the house for
the business which he pursues, and therefore in some manner (direct or
indirect) an easement is more or less connected with the mode in which
the occupant of the house uses it." Then he proceeds to illustrate that
by reference to certain cases. I also have in mind that the Judicial
Committee in the *Nigerian* case ([1915] AC 599) felt no difficulty in
principle in holding that there might be an easement in connexion with
a right to deposit trade goods.

So far, therefore, as that point is concerned, I decide that it does not
avail the plaintiff; but I must return to the point of uncertainty.

I think that the right claimed goes wholly outside any normal idea of
an easement, that is, the right of the owner or the occupier of a
dominant tenement over a servient tenement. This claim (to which no
closely related authority has been referred to me) really amounts to a
claim to a joint user of the land by the defendant. Practically, the
defendant is claiming the whole beneficial user of the strip of land on
the south-east side of the track there; he can leave as many or as few
lorries there as he likes for as long as he likes; he may enter on it
by himself, his servants and agents to do repair work thereon. In my
judgment, that is not a claim which can be established as an easement.
It is virtually a claim to possession of the servient tenement, if
necessary to the exclusion of the owner; or, at any rate, to a joint user,
and no authority has been cited to me which could justify the
conclusion that a right of this wide and undefined nature can be the
proper subject-matter of an easement. It seems to me that to succeed,
this claim must amount to a successful claim of possession by reason
of long adverse possession[8]. I say nothing, of course, as to the creation
of such rights by deeds or by covenant; I am dealing solely with the
question of a right arising by prescription.

In *Grigsby v Melville* [1972] 1 WLR 1355, [1973] 1 All ER 385[9], the
plaintiff and the defendants were neighbours. The defendants claimed
the right to store articles in a cellar beneath the plaintiff's drawing room
floor. BRIGHTMAN J, in rejecting the claim to an easement of storage,
said, at p. 1363: "There are, I think, two issues here: first, whether an
easement of unlimited storage within a confined or defined space is

---

[8] (1968) 32 Conv (NS) 270 (M. J. Goodman).
[9] Affirmed [1974] 1 WLR 81, [1973] 3 All ER 455, when CA held that there was no
  evidence to support the claim to an easement, and declined to "embark upon an
  analysis of the cases". (1973) 37 Conv (NS) 60 (D. J. Hayton).

capable of existing as a matter of law. Secondly, if so, whether such an easement was reserved in the present case.

[His Lordship referred to *Copeland v Greenhalf* [1952] Ch 488, [1952] 1 All ER 809 and continued:]

Mr. Ainger countered by observing that *Copeland v Greenhalf* was inconsistent with *Wright v Macadam* [1949] 2 KB 744, [1949] 2 All ER 565[10], an earlier decision of the Court of Appeal in which it was held that the right of a tenant to store domestic coal in a shed on the landlord's land could exist as an easement for the benefit of the demised premises. I am not convinced that there is any real inconsistency between the two cases. The point of the decision in *Copeland v Greenhalf* was that the right asserted amounted in effect to a claim to the whole beneficial user of the servient tenement and for that reason could not exist as a mere easement. The precise facts in *Wright v Macadam* in this respect are not wholly clear from the report and it is a little difficult to know whether the tenant had exclusive use of the coal shed or of any defined portion of it. To some extent a problem of this sort may be one of degree.

In the case before me, it is, I think, clear that the defendant's claim to an easement would give, to all practical intents and purposes, an exclusive right of user over the whole of the confined space representing the servient tenement. I think I would be at liberty, if necessary, to follow *Copeland v Greenhalf*. I doubt, however, whether I need express any concluded view on this aspect of the case."

[His Lordship then held that an easement was not reserved in the present case].

(1973) 37 Conv (NS) 62 (D. J. Hayton)

"On this footing it would appear, for example, that a right to park a car in a particular defined space amounts to a claim to whole beneficial user of the servient space and so cannot rank as an easement, whilst a right to park a car anywhere in a large area does not amount to a claim to whole beneficial user of any servient area and so can rank as an easement. Lawyers advising companies allocating car spaces in basements of flats for flat owners should thus use leases or licences or merely grant a general easement of parking in the basement but ensure that a practical *modus vivendi* is arrived at between the car-owning flat-occupiers. However, the law would adapt itself much better to 'the conditions of modern society and trade' to use Lord Shaw's words in the *Holt* case, [1915] AC 599, at p. 617 if it were to treat as valid easements of parking or of storage in particular defined places, as held by Judge Block in the case of parking in *Sweet and Maxwell Ltd v Michael-Michaels Advertising Ltd* [1965] CLY 2192."

---

[10] P. 530, post.

In *Miller v Emcer Products Ltd* [1956] Ch 304, [1956] 1 All ER 237[11], premises were demised to a tenant together with the right to use two lavatories on upper floors which were occupied by a third party. One question, inter alia, which arose was whether or not such a right could exist as an easement. As to this ROMER LJ, in a judgment with which Lord EVERSHED MR and BIRKETT LJ concurred, said: "In my judgment the right had all the requisite characteristics of an easement. There is no doubt as to what were intended to be the dominant and servient tenements respectively, and the right was appurtenant to the former and calculated to enhance its beneficial use and enjoyment. It is true that during the times when the dominant owner exercised the right, the owner of the servient tenement would be excluded, but this in greater or less degree is a common feature of many easements (for example, rights of way) and does not amount to such an ouster of the servient owner's rights as was held by Upjohn J to be incompatible with a legal easement in *Copeland v Greenhalf* ([1952] Ch 488, [1952] 1 All ER 809; p. 512, ante)[12]. No case precisely in point on this issue was brought to our attention, but the right to use a lavatory is not dissimilar, I think, to the right to use a neighbour's kitchen for washing, the validity of which as an easement was assumed without question in *Heywood v Mallalieu* ((1883) 25 ChD 357). No objection can fairly be made based upon uncertainty, and it follows, in my judgment, that the right may properly be regarded as an easement which the lessors were professing to grant for a term of years; and such an easement would rank as an interest in or over land capable of being created at law by virtue of section 1 (2) of the Law of Property Act 1925."

iii.   NEGATIVITY

In *Phipps v Pears*, [1965] 1 QB 76, [1964] 2 All ER 35[13], the question was whether a right to make use of a neighbour's house as protection from the weather could exist as an easement.

Two houses, Nos. 14 and 16 Market St., Warwick, were owned by a single owner. No. 16 was rebuilt, "with its flank wall flat up against the old wall of No. 14," the two walls not being bonded together. No. 16 was sold and then No. 14. No. 14 was demolished, and the flank wall of No. 16 was exposed to the weather, and damage resulted.

The owner of No. 16 argued that a right to protection passed to him on the purchase of No. 16 by virtue of Law of Property Act 1925, section 62[14].

On the question whether such a right could exist as an easement, Lord DENNING MR said at p. 82: "There are two kinds of easements

---

[11] (1956) 72 LQR 172 (R. E. M.).
[12] In *Ward v Kirkland* [1967] Ch 194, at 222, [1966] 1 All ER 609, a right to repair and maintain a wall was held to be an easement and not to amount to "the possession or joint possession of part of the servient property".
[13] (1964) 80 LQR 318 (R. E. M.).
[14] See p. 529, post.

known to the law: positive easements, such as a right of way, which give the owner of land *a right himself to do something* on or to his neighbour's land: and negative easements, such as a right of light, which gives him *a right to stop his neighbour doing something* on his (the neighbour's) own land. The right of support does not fall neatly into either category. It seems in some way to partake of the nature of a positive easement rather than a negative easement. The one building, by its weight, exerts a thrust, not only downwards, but also sideways on to the adjoining building or the adjoining land, and is thus doing something to the neighbour's land, exerting a thrust on it, see *Dalton v Angus* (1881) 6 App Cas 740, 793, *per* Lord Selborne LC. But a right to protection from the weather (if it exists) is entirely negative. It is a right to stop your neighbour pulling down his own house. Seeing that it is a negative easement, it must be looked at with caution. Because the law has been very chary of creating any new negative easements.

[His Lordship referred to the fact that the law recognised no easement to a view (*Bland v Moseley* (1587) cited in 9 Co Rep at 58a), nor to the passage of air through an undefined channel to the sails of a windmill[15] and continued:] The reason underlying these instances is that if such an easement were to be permitted, it would unduly restrict your neighbour in his enjoyment of his own land. It would hamper legitimate development, see *Dalton v Angus per* Lord Blackburn ((1881) 6 App Cas at 824). Likewise here, if we were to stop a man pulling down his house, we would put a brake on desirable improvement. Every man is entitled to pull down his house if he likes. If it exposes your house to the weather, that is your misfortune. It is no wrong on his part. Likewise every man is entitled to cut down his trees if he likes, even if it leaves you without shelter from the wind or shade from the sun, see the decision of the Master of the Rolls in Ireland in *Cochrane v Verner* ((1895) 29 ILT 571). There is no such easement known to the law as an easement to be protected from the weather. The only way for an owner to protect himself is by getting a covenant from his neighbour that he will not pull down his house or cut down his trees. Such a covenant would be binding on him in contract: and it would be enforceable on any successor who took with notice of it. But it would not be binding on one who took without notice[16]."

(1964) 80 LQR 321 (R. E Megarry)

"Finally, there seems to be at least one field in which the decision [*Phipps v Pears*] may cause difficulty, namely, that of freehold flats and maisonettes. If A sells the upper part of his house to B, the

---

[15] *Webb v Bird* (1861) 10 CB NS 268.
[16] Under Public Health Act 1961, s. 29 (5), a local authority may serve a notice on any-one demolishing a building, requiring him to weatherproof any surfaces of adjacent buildings exposed by the demolition.

conveyance may well provide for the grant of easements of support by A to B, and for the reservation of easements of shelter and protection by A against B: see, e.g. George, *The Sale of Flats* (2nd edn. 1959), pp. 27, 128. *Phipps v Pears* now seems to mean that the reservation by A creates no easement, and that B's successors in title will not be bound by it. Yet it would be most unsatisfactory to be compelled to hold that although A's successors in title may not remove the support from B's flat, B's successors in title may freely remove any or all of their flat and leave A's flat at the mercy of the elements. Even though a right 'to protection from the weather', *totidem verbis*, may well be too indefinite to be an easement, it is still questionable why such a right, if sufficiently and clearly defined in its ambit by the instrument granting it, should be refused recognition as an easement, and left to more complex and less potent means of enforcement such as covenants of indemnity and the doctrine of *Halsall v Brizell*, [1957] Ch 169, [1957] 1 All ER 371. In recent years many new rights have been accepted as easements, not least the right to use a lavatory: see *Miller v Emcer Products Ltd* [1956] Ch 304, [1956] 1 All ER 237. Is the law of easements not ample enough to match bodily relief with protection from the elements[17]?''

iv.   EXPENDITURE BY SERVIENT OWNER

In *Crow v Wood* [1971] 1 QB 77, [1970] 3 All ER 425[18], the parties farmed land adjoining a large sheep moor in the North Riding of Yorkshire. Each had the right to allow their sheep to stray on the moor. The defendant's sheep trespassed on the plaintiff's land by passing through the plaintiff's fence, which had not been repaired since 1966. There was no arrangement between the parties as to fencing, but the defendant claimed that he was entitled to an easement requiring the plaintiff to maintain the fence. Such an easement, if it existed, passed to the defendant under Law of Property Act 1925, section 62. LORD DENNING said, at p. 84: "The question is, therefore, whether a right to have a fence or wall kept in repair is a right which is capable of being granted by law. I think it is because it is in the nature of an easement. It is not an easement strictly so called because it involves the servient owner in the expenditure of money. It was described by Gale [*Easements*, 11th edn. (1932), p. 432] as a 'spurious kind of easement'. But it has been treated in practice by the courts as being an easement. Professor Glanville Williams on *Liability for Animals* (1939), says, at p. 209: 'If we put aside these questions of theory and turn to the practice of the courts, there seems to be little doubt that fencing is an easement.' In *Jones v Price*, [1965] 2 QB 618 at 633, Willmer LJ said: 'It is clear that a right to require the owner of adjoining land to keep the boundary fence in repair is a right which

---

[17] Many of the difficulties can be overcome by suitably drawn covenants. See p. 699, post.

[18] *Liverpool City Council v Irwin* [1977] AC 239, [1976] 2 All ER 39, p. 504, ante.

the law will recognise as a quasi-easement.' Diplock LJ, at p. 639, points out that it is a right of such a nature that it can be acquired by prescription which imports that it lies in grant, for prescription rests on a presumed grant.

It seems to me that it is now sufficiently established — or at any rate, if not established hitherto, we should now declare — that a right to have your neighbour keep up the fences is a right in the nature of an easement which is capable of being granted by law so as to run with the land and to be binding on successors. It is a right which lies in grant and is of such a nature that it can pass under section 62 of the Law of Property Act 1925[19].''

QUESTION

Having read the cases on the nature of easements, can you set out any guide-lines to help a court decide whether or not a right which complies with the accepted requirements of an easement is to be recognized judicially? Cheshire, pp. 524–525. *Dowty Boulton Paul Ltd v Wolverhampton Corpn (No. 2)* [1976] Ch 13 at 23 per RUSSELL LJ "A tendency in the past to freeze the categories of easements has been overtaken by the defrosting operation in *Re Ellenborough Park* [1956] Ch 131, [1955] 3 All ER 667".

B. Legal and Equitable Easements

LAW OF PROPERTY ACT 1925

1. **Legal estates and equitable interests.**
   (2) (*a*), p. 6, ante.
   (3)   p. 6, ante.

2. **Conveyances overreaching certain equitable interests and powers.**
   (3) (iii), p. 190, ante.

4. **Creation and disposition of equitable interests.**
   (1) p. 12, ante.

LAND CHARGES ACT 1972

2. **Register of land charges.**
   (4) Class C (iv), p. 32, ante.
   (5) Class D (iii), p. 32, ante.

An easement is a legal interest if it (a) complies with section 1 (2) (*a*), Law of Property Act 1925 and is held for "an interest equivalent to an estate in fee simple absolute in possession or a term of years absolute" and (b) is created either by statute, deed or prescription.

---

[19] An easement of fencing may also be acquired (i) as an easement by prescription: *Lawrence v Jenkins* (1873) LR 8 QB 274; *Jones v Price* [1965] 2 QB 618, [1965] 2 All ER 625, (ii) by custom: *Egerton v Harding* [1975] QB 62, [1974] 3 All ER 689.

An easement which fails to satisfy either (a) or (b) is not a legal, but an equitable, interest, e.g., if it is for the life of the grantee or created by an equitable owner (in which case it is registrable, if created after 1925, as a Land Charge Class D (iii)), or if it is granted informally or is the subject of a contract to grant (when it is registrable as an estate contract Class C (iv))[20].

In spite of some earlier views to the contrary[1], it is now settled that the definition of an equitable easement (which is defined in section 2 (3) (iii) of the Law of Property Act 1925 as "any easement, liberty[2], or privilege over or affecting land and being merely an equitable interest") is to be construed narrowly. This excludes such informal equitable rights as an equitable right of re-entry[3], or any rights arising in equity by reason of an estoppel licence or the doctrine of mutual benefit and burden[4]. These rights are therefore not registrable as land charges, and their enforcement against third parties depends solely on the doctrine of notice[5].

III. Acquisition[6]

Easements, like any other incorporeal hereditaments, lie in grant at common law. They could not, like corporeal hereditaments, pass by "livery of seisin", and, as an easement is real property, a deed of grant was required. Situations could arise, however, in which it was felt that the landowner should have an easement, but he could show no express grant. The common law, true to the basic rule that easements lie in grant, developed rules whereby the grant could be *implied* in a deed conveying land but making no mention of the easement, or could be *presumed* where there was no deed at all; this latter case deals with what is more commonly called prescription. As has been seen, an easement may be granted in equity. There are statutory provisions relating to various aspects of acquisition by grant[7]. And, on occasion,

---

[20] *McManus v Cooke* (1887) 35 ChD 681 (easement), p. 78, ante; *Mason v Clarke* [1955] AC 778, [1955] 1 All ER 914 (profit), p. 79, ante; *Lowe v J. W. Ashmore Ltd* [1971] Ch 545 at 557–558, [1971] 1 All ER 1057 (profit).

[1] (1935) 15 Bell Yard 18 (G. Cross); see also (1948) 12 Conv (NS) 202 (J. F. Garner).

[2] The definition in L.C.A. 1972, s. 2 (5) substitutes the word "right" for "liberty".

[3] *Shiloh Spinners Ltd v Harding* [1973] AC 691, [1973] 1 All ER 90, p. 34, ante.

[4] *E. R. Ives Investment Ltd v High* [1967] 2 QB 379, [1967] 1 All ER 504, p. 485, ante; followed in *Poster v Slough Estates Ltd* [1969] 1 Ch 495, [1968] 3 All ER 257 (right of entry to remove fixtures at end of lease); (1937) 53 LQR 259 (C. V. Davidge); (1969) 33 Conv (NS) 135 (P. Jackson). See also *Lewisham Borough Council v Maloney* [1948] 1 KB 50, [1947] 2 All ER 36 (requisitioning authority's right to possession).

[5] P. 24, ante. Report of the Committee on Land Charges (1956 Cmnd 9825), para. 16 suggested that Class D (iii) might be abolished. Law Commission Report on Land Charges affecting unregistered Land (1969 Law Com No. 18), para. 65, recommended its retention. Registrations in that class were than running at an annual rate of 2,500–3,500; there were 1,914 registrations during the year ending 31 March 1979; p. 33, ante.

[6] Cheshire, pp. 528–554; M & W, pp. 827–865; MM, pp. 398–417; Gale, pp. 75–192; Jackson, pp. 71–138, 189–194.

[7] L.P.A. 1925, s. 62; see p. 530, post.

statutes have been passed specifically creating easements between adjoining owners; the common example of this type of statute is an Inclosure Act which distributed among individual owners land which had been subject to rights of common and created certain easements among these owners.

A. Acquisition by Express Grant or Reservation[8]

i. AT LAW

Coke (Co Litt 9a): "And here is implyed a division of fee, or inheritance, *viz*, into corporeall, ... and incorporeall (which lie in grant, and cannot passe by livery, but by deede, as advowsons, commons &c., and of some is called haereditas incorporata, and, by the delivery of the deede, the freehold, and inheritance of such inheritance, as doth lie in grant, doth passe) comprehended in this word grant. And the deed of incorporeate inheritances doth equall the livery of corporeate."

LAW OF PROPERTY ACT 1925

52. Conveyances are to be by deed. — (1) p. 72, ante.

65. Reservation of legal estates. — (1) A reservation of a legal estate shall operate at law without any execution of the conveyance by the grantee of the legal estate out of which the reservation is made, or any regrant by him, so as to create the legal estate reserved, and so as to vest the same in possession in the person (whether being the grantor or not) for whose benefit the reservation is made.

(2) A conveyance of a legal estate expressed to be made subject to another legal estate not in existence immediately before the date of the conveyance, shall operate as a reservation, unless a contrary intention appears.

(3) This section applies only to reservations made after the commencement of this Act.

In *St. Edmundsbury and Ipswich Diocesan Board of Finance v Clark (No. 2)* [1975] 1 WLR 468, [1975] 1 All ER 772, the question arose whether on the reservation of an easement by a vendor the terms of the reservation were, in case of doubt, to be construed against the vendor or against the purchaser. The Court of Appeal laid down that it should be construed against the purchaser, as on a re-grant. Sir John PENNYCUICK said, at p. 477:

"Second, is the maxim 'omnia praesumuntur contra proferentem' applicable against the vendor or against the purchaser where there is a conveyance subject to the reservation of a new right of way? In view of the full discussion of this question by Megarry J, and of the fact that we do not agree with his conclusion, we think it right to

---

[8] Cheshire, pp. 528–532; M & W, pp. 828–830; MM, pp. 399–400; Gale, pp. 76–82; Jackson, pp. 108–109.

deal fairly fully with it. But it is necessary to make clear that this presumption can only come into play if the court finds itself unable on the material before it to reach a sure conclusion on the construction of a reservation. The presumption is not itself a factor to be taken into account in reaching the conclusion. In the present case we have indeed reached a sure conclusion, and on this footing the presumption never comes into play, so that the view which we are about to express upon it is not necessary to the decision of the present case.

The point turns upon the true construction of section 65 (1) of the Law of Property Act 1925 [His Lordship read the section (p. 521, ante) and continued:] . . . Formerly the law was that on a conveyance with words merely reserving an easement, the easement was held to be created, provided that the purchaser executed the conveyance, without the necessity for words of regrant. The law treated the language of the reservation as having the same effect as would the language of regrant though there was not in terms a regrant, and in those circumstances regarded the purchaser as the proferens for present purposes. This was a relaxation of the strict requirements for the creation of an easement. (An easement could be created without execution by the purchaser of a conveyance by reference to the Statute of Uses, once section 62 of the Conveyancing Act 1881 removed the technical objection that that statute could not operate to create an easement. This method disappeared with the repeal of the Statute of Uses in the 1925 property legislation. . .)

Section 65 must be read in the light, therefore, of two aspects of the preceding law. First: that previously the law was sufficiently relaxed from its prima facie stringency to permit the language of mere reservation to have the effect of a regrant though it was not in truth a regrant by its language. Second: that for this purpose the purchaser must execute the conveyance if an easement was to be created; that is to say, although a regrant in terms was not required. Against that background, are the words in section 65 "without . . . any regrant by" the purchaser to be regarded as altering the law so that the purchaser is no longer to be regarded as the relevant proferens? Or are they to be regarded as merely maintaining for the avoidance of doubt the situation that had been already reached by the development of the law, viz. that mere words of reservation could be regarded as having the same effect as would the language of regrant though without there being in terms any purported regrant by the purchaser? We would, apart from authority, construe the words in the latter sense, so that the only relevant change in the law is the absence of the requirement that the purchaser should execute the conveyance. We read the section as if it were in effect saying that whereas an easement could be created by mere words of reservation without any words of regrant by the purchaser, provided that the purchaser executes the conveyance, hereafter the easement can be created by mere words of reservation without any words of regrant by the purchaser even if he does not execute the conveyance: it is not to be said that in the latter event the previous relaxation of the strict law has disappeared, so that the language of the conveyance must be more than the mere language of reservation. It will be observed that that view keeps in line, on the relevant point, a post-1925 conveyance executed by the purchaser, which is apparently not touched by section 65, and one which is executed by him.

The above is our view apart from authority. What then of authority? We start with the fact that Sir Benjamin Cherry, architect of the 1925 property legislation, made no reference to this suggested change of principle in the law in the first edition of *Wolstenholme and Cherry's Conveyancing Statutes* after the 1925 property legislation. Further, in more than one case since 1925, judges of high authority took it for granted that the old principle still prevails: see *Bulstrode v Lambert* [1953] 1 WLR 1064 *per* Upjohn J at p. 1068; *Mason v Clarke* [1954] 1 QB 460, in the Court of Appeal, *per* Denning LJ at p. 467 and in the House of Lords *per* Lord Simonds [1955] AC 778, 786. In these cases the contrary was not argued and the judicial statements are not of binding authority. But in *Johnstone v Holdway* [1963] 1 QB 601, in the Court of Appeal, Upjohn LJ, giving the judgment of the court, not only in terms re-stated the old principle but made it part of the ratio decidendi of his judgment.

He said, at p. 612:

'that the exception and reservation of the mines and minerals was to the vendor, that is the legal owner, but the exception and reservation of the right of way was to the company, the equitable owner. If the reservation of a right of way operated strictly as a reservation, then, as the company only had an equitable title, it would seem that only an equitable easement could have been reserved. But it is clear that an exception and reservation of a right of way in fact operates by way of regrant by the purchaser to his vendor and the question, therefore, is whether as a matter of construction the purchaser granted to the company a legal easement or an equitable easement.'

The opposing view was expressed by Megarry J in *Cordell v Second Clanfield Properties Ltd* [1969] 2 Ch 9 (upon motion and without being referred to *Johnstone v Holdway* [1963] 1 QB 601) and in the present case (after a full review of the authorities, including *Johnstone v Holdway*). He distinguishes *Johnstone v Holdway* as a decision based on mistake and states his own conclusion in the following words [1973] 1 WLR 1572, 1591:

'The fair and natural meaning of section 65 (1) seems to me to be that if a vendor reserves an easement, the reservation is to be effective at law without any actual or notional regrant by the purchaser, and so without the consequences that flow from any regrant. At common law, the rule that a reservation of an easement was to be construed against the purchaser depended solely upon the notional regrant. Apart from that, the words of reservation, being the words of the vendor, would be construed against the vendor in accordance with the general principle stated in *Norton on Deeds*, 2nd edn. (1928), just as an exception or a reservation of a rent would; it was the fiction of a regrant which made reservations of easements stand out of line with exceptions and reservations in the strict sense. With the statutory abolition of the fictitious regrant, reservations of easements fall into line with the broad and sensible approach that it is for him who wishes to retain something for himself to see that there is an adequate statement of what it is that he seeks to retain; and if after considering all the circumstances of the case there remains any real doubt as to the ambit of the right reserved, then that doubt should be resolved against the vendor. Accordingly, in this case I hold that the words "subject also to a right of way over the land coloured red on the said plan to and from St. Botolphs Church" in the 1945 conveyance should, if their meaning is not otherwise resolved, be construed against the church authorities and so in favour of Mr. Clark.'

We see much force in this reasoning. But we find it impossible to accept Megarry J's analysis of the decision in *Johnstone v Holdway*. We are not prepared to infer from the report that experienced and responsible counsel misrepresented the terms of section 65 to the court and that the judge based his decision on the terms of the section as so misrepresented. It follows that the decision in *Johnstone v Holdway* is binding upon this court and that we ought to follow it."

ii.   IN EQUITY

An agreement for valuable consideration to grant an easement or a profit à prendre is a contract which equity will specifically enforce and is registrable as an estate contract. Equity looks on that as done which ought to be done and such an agreement operates as a grant in equity of an easement. Further, equity construes an informal (unsealed) grant as a contract to grant an easement. Such a contract, being an agreement for a disposition of an interest in land, is required to be evidenced in writing; but the doctrine of part performance applies, and, as in the case of an agreement for a lease, equity will construe a purported oral or written grant as an agreement to grant an easement.

McManus v Cooke (1887) 35 ChD 681, p. 78, ante[9].

B.   Acquisition by Implied Grant or Reservation[10]

When the owner of land grants part of it, or certain interests in part of it, to another person, there will be implied, in appropriate circumstances, (i) certain rights in favour of the grantee exercisable over the land retained (implied grant), and (ii) certain rights in favour of the grantor over the land granted (implied reservation). These rights are rights in the nature of easements, but which could not be easements

---

[9] See also *May v Belleville* [1905] 2 Ch 605; *Mason v Clarke* [1955] AC 778, [1955] 1 All ER 914 (profit à prendre) p. 79, ante.

[10] Cheshire, pp. 532–538 M & W, pp. 830–841; MM., pp. 401–404; Gale, pp. 82–132; Jackson pp. 70–109; Farrand (2nd edn.) pp. 377–392.

before the grant because all the land was under single ownership. These two cases — implied grant and implied reservation — are treated differently and must be dealt with separately.

i.   EASEMENTS IMPLIED IN FAVOUR OF THE GRANTEE

(a)   The Common Law Rule

Consistently with the principle that a grantor must not derogate from his grant[11], the law readily implies easements in favour of the grantee. The rule has been laid down in an obiter dictum in *Wheeldon v Burrows*, which has subsequently been accepted universally as a correct statement of the law, to the effect that in a grant of land there may be implied in favour of the grantee those rights in the nature of easements which (1) are "continuous and apparent" or "in other words all those easements which are necessary to the reasonable enjoyment of the property granted" and (2) have been and are, at the time of the grant, used by the grantor for the benefit of the part granted. Easements of necessity without which the property could not be enjoyed at all and easements which were clearly within the common intention of the parties[12] will also be implied in favour of the grantee; and sometimes in favour of the grantor also.

The doctrine of *Wheeldon v Burrows* has been shorn of much of its importance by section 62 of the Law of Property Act 1925. But it still remains available wherever, for one reason or another, a claimant cannot rely on section 62[13]. It always operates subject to the terms of the contract or conveyance[14], and to the circumstances existing at the date of the grant.

WHEELDON *v* BURROWS
(1879) 12 ChD 31 (CA, THESIGER, JAMES and BAGGALLAY LJJ)

Of land owned in 1875 by one Tetley, part was sold in January 1876 to the plaintiff's husband, William Wheeldon. Another part was sold in February 1876 to the defendant; on this part there was a shed containing, and lighted by, three windows which overlooked the plaintiff's land. In 1878 the plaintiff, then the widow and devisee of William Wheeldon, erected hoardings near the edge of her land facing the defendant's shed for the purpose of ascertaining her right to exclude the light from the shed. The defendant, claiming an easement of light, knocked down the hoardings, and this action was brought for trespass.

---

[11] (1964) 80 LQR 244 (D. W. Elliott); Gale 88–92; *Ward v Kirkland* [1967] Ch 194, at 226–227; [1966] 1 All ER 609; *Woodhouse & Co Ltd v Kirkland (Derby) Ltd* [1970] 1 WLR 1185, [1970] 2 All ER 587.
[12] *Pwllbach Colliery Co Ltd v Woodman* [1915] AC 634; *Keewatin Water Power Co Ltd v Lake of the Woods Milling Co Ltd* [1930] AC 640; *Wong v Beaumont Property Trust Ltd* [1965] 1 QB 173, [1964] 2 All ER 119; p. 527, post; *Nickerson v Barraclough* [1979] 3 WLR 562, [1979] 3 All ER 312.
[13] See p. 530, post.
[14] This may be expressed by a condition of sale; see *National Conditions of Sale* (19th edn., 1976) Condition 20; Law Society's *Contract and Conditions of Sale* 1973, Condition 4 (2) (c); Wilkinson, *Standard Conditions of Sale of Land* (2nd edn.), pp. 31–35; Hallett's *Conveyancing Precedents*, pp. 210, para. (4), 213, para. (3).

Held. The defendant had no right to knock down the hoardings because no right to the access of light to the windows of the shed had been reserved by Tetley on the sale of the land to the plaintiff's husband.

THESIGER LJ: We have had a considerable number of cases cited to us, and out of them I think that two propositions may be stated as what I may call the general rules governing cases of this kind. The first of these rules is, that on the grant by the owner of a tenement of part of that tenement as it is then used and enjoyed, there will pass to the grantee all those continuous[15] and apparent easements (by which, of course, I mean *quasi* easements), or, in other words, all those easements which are necessary to the reasonable enjoyment of the property granted, and which have been and are at the time of the grant used by the owners of the entirety for the benefit of the part granted. The second proposition is that, if the grantor intends to reserve any right over the tenement granted, it is his duty to reserve it expressly in the grant. Those are the general rules governing cases of this kind, but the second of those rules is subject to certain exceptions. One of those exceptions is the well-known exception which attaches to cases of what are called ways of necessity; and I do not dispute for a moment that there may be, and probably are, certain other exceptions, to which I shall refer before I close my observations upon this case.

Both of the general rules which I have mentioned are founded upon a maxim which is as well established by authority as it is consonant to reason and common sense, viz., that a grantor shall not derogate from his grant. It has been argued before us that there is no distinction between what has been called an implied grant and what is attempted to be established under the name of an implied reservation; and that such a distinction between the implied grant and the implied reservation is a mere modern invention and one which runs contrary, not only to the general practice upon which land has been bought and sold for a considerable time, but also to authorities which are said to be clear and distinct upon the matter. So far, however, from that distinction being one which was laid down for the first time by and which is to be attributed to Lord *Westbury* in *Suffield v Brown* ((1864) 4 De GJ & Sm 185), it appears to me that it has existed almost as far back as we can trace the law upon the subject; and I think it right, as the case is one of considerable importance, not merely as regards the parties, but as regards vendors and purchasers of land generally, that I should go with some little particularity into what I may term the leading cases upon the subject.

. . . These cases in no way support the proposition for which the appellant in this case contends; but, on the contrary, support the propositions that in the case of a grant you may imply a grant of such

---

[15] Cheshire, pp. 535–536; M & W, pp. 834–835; MM, p.402; Gale, pp. 92–99; Jackson pp. 77–79; Farrand (2nd edn.), pp. 383–384; *Polden v Bastard* (1865) LR 1 QB 156; *Hansford v Jago* [1921] 1 Ch 322; *cf.* MAUGHAM J, in *Borman v Griffith* [1930] 1 Ch 493, p. 388, ante; *Ward v Kirkland* [1967] Ch 194 at 224–225, [1966] 1 All ER 609.

continuous and apparent easements or such easements as are necessary to the reasonable enjoyment of the property conveyed, and have in fact been enjoyed during the unity of ownership, but that, with the exception which I have referred to of easements of necessity, you cannot imply a similar reservation in favour of the grantor of land[16].

In *Ward v Kirkland*, [1967] Ch 194, [1966] 1 All ER 609 UNGOED-THOMAS J referred to the discrepancy in the first and last paragraphs of THESIGER LJ's judgment. Of the first paragraph he said at p. 224: "There, it might appear that the words 'in other words' in that passage would indicate that the requirement, 'which are necessary to the reasonable enjoyment of the property granted', and the earlier words, 'continuous and apparent easements', refer to the same easements." Of the last paragraph he said: "Reading that passage on its own, on first impression, it would appear that the 'easements which are necessary to the reasonable enjoyment of the property conveyed' might be a separate class from 'continuous and apparent easements.' ... It has been suggested that perhaps the 'easements necessary to the reasonable enjoyment of the property conveyed' might refer to negative easements. ... I understand that there is no case in which positive easements which are not 'continuous and apparent' have been held to come within the doctrine of *Wheeldon v Burrows*[17]."

WONG *v* BEAUMONT PROPERTY TRUST LTD
[1965] 1 QB 173, [1964] 2 All ER 119 (CA, Lord DENNING MR PEARSON and SALMON LJJ)

In 1957, three cellars in Exeter were let to one Blackaby who covenanted to use the premises as a popular restaurant and to control all smells and odours according to health regulations and so as not to become a nuisance. To comply with these undertakings, it was necessary to construct a ventilation duct fixed to the outside wall of the landlords' premises. This was not realised by the parties at the time, and no duct was built.

In 1961 the plaintiff bought the remainder of the lease and developed the premises into a highly successful Chinese restaurant. The smells and odours caused the Midland Bank, who occupied the floor above, to complain and the public health inspector required the duct to be built. the defendants, assignees in 1962 of the original landlords, refused to allow the work to be done, and the plaintiff asked for a declaration of entitlement and damages.

Held (affirming Judge Pratt). Declaration that the plaintiff was entitled to an easement as an easement of necessity.

LORD DENNING MR: The question is: Has the plaintiff a right to put up this duct without the landlords' consent? If he is to have any right at

---

[16] *Aldridge v Wright* [1929] 2 KB 117; *Suffield v Brown* (1864) 4 De GJ & Sm 185; *Borman v Griffith* [1930] 1 Ch 493; see p. 388, ante.
[17] (1967) 83 LQR 240 (A. W. B. Simpson).

all, it must be by way of easement and not merely by way of implied contract. He is not the original lessee, nor are the defendants the original lessors. Each is a successor in title. As between them, a right of this kind, if it exists at all, must be by way of an easement. In particular, an easement of necessity. The law on the matter was stated by Lord Parker of Waddington in *Pwllbach Colliery Co Ltd v Woodman* ([1915] AC 634), where he said (at p. 646), omitting immaterial words, "The law will readily imply the grant or reservation of such easements as may be necessary to give effect to the common intention of the parties to a grant of real property, with reference to the manner or purposes in and for which the land granted . . . is to be used. But it is essential for this purpose that the parties should intend that the subject of the grant . . . should be used in some definite and particular manner. It is not enough that the subject of the grant . . . should be intended to be used in a manner which may or may not involve this definite and particular use." That is the principle which underlies all easements of necessity. If you go back to Rolle's Abridgment you will find it stated in this way: "If I have a field inclosed by my own land on all sides, and I alien this close to another, he shall have a way to this close over my land, as incident to the grant; for otherwise he cannot have any benefit by the grant."

I would apply those principles here. Here was the grant of a lease to the lessee for the very purpose of carrying on a restaurant business. It was to be a popular restaurant, and it was to be developed and extended. There was a covenant not to cause any nuisance; and to control and eliminate all smells; and to comply with the Food Hygiene Regulations. That was "a definite and particular manner" in which the business had to be conducted. It could not be carried on in that manner at all unless a ventilation system was installed by a duct of this kind. In these circumstances it seems to me that, if the business is to be carried on at all — if, in the words of Rolle's Abridgment, the lessee is to "have any benefit by the grant" at all — he must of necessity be able to put a ventilation duct up the wall. It may be that in Blackaby's time it would not have needed such a large duct as is now needed in the plaintiff's time. But nevertheless a duct of some kind would have had to be put up the wall. The plaintiff may need a bigger one. But that does not matter. A man who has a right to an easement can use it in any proper way, so long as he does not substantially increase the burden on the servient tenement. In this case a bigger duct will not substantially increase the burden.

There is one point in which this case goes further than the earlier cases which have been cited. It is this. It was not realised by the parties, at the time of the lease, that this duct would be necessary. But it was in fact necessary from the very beginning. That seems to me sufficient to bring the principle into play. In order to use this place as a restaurant, there must be implied an easement, by the necessity of the case, to carry a duct up this wall. The county court judge so held. He granted a declaration. I agree with him.

DANCKWERTS J in *Barry v Hasseldine* [1952] Ch 835 [1952] 2 All ER 317, said at p. 839, "In my opinion, however, if the grantee has no access to the property which is sold and conveyed to him except over the grantor's land or over the land of some other person or persons whom he cannot compel to give him any legal right of way, common sense demands that a way of necessity should be implied, so as to confer on the grantee a right of way, for the purposes for which the land is conveyed, over the land of the grantor; and it is no answer to say that a permissive method of approach was in fact enjoyed, at the time of the grant, over the land of some person other than the grantor because that permissive method of approach may be determined on the following day, thereby leaving the grantee with no lawful method of approaching the land which he has purchased."

QUESTION

Is there a difference between an easement of necessity, and an easement which is "necessary to give effect to the common intention of the parties?"

If there is a difference, is it relevant in either case that the parties did not realise that the necessity existed? See (1964) 80 LQR 322–323 (R. E. Megarry) and pp. 542–548, post. *Horn v Hiscock* (1972), 223 Estates Gazette 1437 at 1441; Nickerson v Barraclough [1979] 3 WLR 562, [1979] 3 All ER 312.

b. Law of Property Act 1925, section 62.

The Law of Property Act 1925, section 62 (replacing the Conveyancing Act 1881, section 6), has taken over much of the area formerly governed by the rule in Wheeldon v Burrows[18]. Its application is wider, in that the right need not be "continuous and apparent"[19] nor "necessary for the reasonable enjoyment of the property granted"[20]; it also applies to profits à prendre[1]. On the other hand, it does not apply where the dominant owner obtains his interest without a conveyance under seal (as by will or under contract)[2], or where there was previously no diversity of occupation of the two tenements[3].

---

[18] See p. 524, ante.
[19] *Ward v Kirkland* [1967] Ch 194, [1966] 1 All ER 609 (right to enter farmyard to maintain a wall held to be not continuous and apparent; but to be an easement created under s. 62). The right must of course be exercised at the date of the convevance: *Penn v Wilkins* (1974) 236 Estates Gazette 203 (passage of sewage, which ceased many years before conveyance, not covered by s. 62).
[20] *Goldberg v Edwards* [1950] Ch 247, p. 534, post.
[1] *Polden v Bastard* (1865) LR 1 QB 156; *White v Williams* [1922] 1 KB 727; *White v Taylor (No. 2)* [1969] 1 Ch 160, [1968] 1 All ER 1015; *Anderson v Bostock* [1976] Ch 312; [1976] 1 All ER 560; *Re Yateley Common, Hampshire* [1977] 1 WLR 840 at 850; *Re Broxhead Common, Whitehill, Hampshire* (1977) 33 P & CR 451.
[2] *Borman v Griffith* [1930] 1 Ch 493, p. 388, ante; *Schwann v Cotton* [1916] 2 Ch 459; *Horn v Hiscock* (1972) 223 Estates Gazette 1437.
[3] *Long v Gowlett* [1923] 2 Ch 177, p. 537, post; *Ward v Kirkland* [1967] Ch 194, [1966] 1 All ER 609; *Sovmots Investments Ltd v Secretary of State for the Environment* [1979] AC 144, [1977] 2 All ER 385, p. 540, post.

LAW OF PROPERTY ACT 1925

62. General words implied in conveyances.[4] — (1) A conveyance of land shall be deemed to include and shall by virtue of this Act operate to convey, with the land, all buildings, erections, fixtures, commons, hedges, ditches, fences, ways, waters, watercourses, liberties, privileges, easements, rights, and advantages whatsoever, appertaining or reputed to appertain to the land, or any part thereof, or, at the time of conveyance, demised, occupied, or enjoyed with[5] or reputed or known as part or parcel of or appurtenant to the land or any part thereof.

(2) A conveyance of land, having houses or other buildings thereon, shall be deemed to include and shall by virtue of this Act operate to convey, with the land, houses, or other buildings, all outhouses, erections, fixtures, cellars, areas, courts, courtyards, cisterns, sewers, gutters, drains, ways, passages, lights, watercourses, liberties, privileges, easements, rights, and advantages whatsoever, appertaining or reputed to appertain to the land, houses, or other buildings conveyed, or any of them, or any part thereof, or, at the time of conveyance, demised, occupied, or enjoyed with, or reputed or known as part or parcel of or appurtenant to, the land, houses, or other buildings conveyed, or any of them, or any part thereof.

(4) This section applies only if and as far as a contrary intention is not expressed in the conveyance, and has effect subject to the terms of the conveyance and to the provisions therein contained[6].

(6) This section applies to conveyances made after the thirty-first day of December, eighteen hundred and eighty-one.

WRIGHT *v* MACADAM[7]
[1949] 2 KB 744, [1949] 2 All ER 565 (CA, Tucker, Jenkins and Singleton LJJ)

In 1940, the defendant let a top floor flat at 13 Mount Ararat Road, Richmond, to Mrs. Wright for one week. After the expiration of that time Mrs. Wright continued in occupation by virtue of the Rent Acts.

In 1941, the defendant gave Mrs. Wright permission to use a shed in the garden for the storage of coal, and this permission was exercised.

In 1943, the defendant granted a new tenancy of the premises with an additional room to Mrs. Wright and her daughter by an unsealed document which made no reference to the use of the shed. The Wrights enjoyed the use of the shed until 1947 when the defendant suggested that 1s. 6d. a week should be paid for its use. They refused, and were denied the use of the shed. This action was brought for an injunction to restrain interference with their use of it and for £10 in damages.

---

[4] (1966) 30 Conv (NS) 340 (P. Jackson); Jackson, pp. 92–108.
[5] This is not synonymous with user; *Re Yateley Common,* supra.
[6] There are restrictions upon the exclusion of the section in a conveyance of a freehold to a tenant enfranchised under the Leasehold Reform Act 1967, s. 10 (1).
[7] (1950) 66 LQR 302 (R. E. M.). The section was applied to an easement of fencing in *Crow v Wood* [1971] 1 QB 77, [1970] 3 All ER 425, p. 518, ante.

Held. The right to use the coal-shed passed to the Wrights as an easement under section 62 of the Law of Property Act 1925 on the grant of the tenancy in 1943.

JENKINS LJ: The plaintiffs claimed an injunction to restrain the defendant from trespassing or otherwise interfering with their lawful use of the coal shed, a declaration that their tenancy of the flat included the right to use the coal shed, and damages limited to 10*l*. I may mention that, as matters stand at present, the last of those claims appears to be the only relevant one, inasmuch as we were informed in the course of the hearing that the defendant has in fact pulled down the coal shed. The question, therefore, is simply this: whether the plaintiffs, as tenants of the top floor flat at 13, Mount Ararat Road, were entitled to the use of the coal shed in question. It is argued for the plaintiffs that they were so entitled, by virtue of section 62 of the Law of Property Act, 1925, which is the section replacing the old section 6 of the Conveyancing Act 1881, and providing by statute the general words which it was formerly customary to insert in full in the parcels of conveyances and other dispositions of land. The plaintiffs claim that this section covers the case. The defendant, on the other hand, claims that, although the coal shed was admittedly used, it was used under no sufficiently definite arrangement; that it was used purely as a matter of personal licence and precariously; and that the arrangement under which it was used could not be said to confer a right in any way appurtenant to the flat, but was an arrangement of a kind to which section 62 of the Act had no application.

[His Lordship came to the conclusion that the tenancy agreement, being sufficient by virtue of the Law of Property Act 1925, sections 52, 54, to pass a legal estate, was a "conveyance" within the meaning given to that term in section 205 (1) (ii). There was therefore a "conveyance of land" within the meaning of section 62 (1). He continued:]

The question in the present case, therefore, is whether the right to use the coal shed was at the date of the letting of 28 August 1943 a liberty, privilege, easement, right or advantage appertaining or reputed to appertain, to the land, or any part thereof, or, at the time of the conveyance, demised, occupied or enjoyed with the land — that is the flat — or any part thereof. It is enough for the plaintiffs' purposes if they can bring the right claimed within the widest part of the subsection — that is to say, if they can show that the right was at the time of the material letting demised, occupied or enjoyed with the flat or any part thereof.

The predecessor of section 62 of the Act of 1925, in the shape of section 6 of the Act of 1881 has been the subject of a good deal of judicial discussion, and I think the effect of the cases can be thus summarized. First, the section is not confined to rights which, as a matter of law, were so annexed or appurtenant to the property conveyed at the time of the conveyance as to make them actual legally enforceable rights. Thus, on the severance of a piece of land in common ownership, the quasi easements de facto enjoyed in respect of it by one part of the land over another will pass although, of course, as a matter of law, no man can have a right appendant or appurtenant to one part of his property exercisable by him over the other part of his property[8]. Secondly, the right, in order to pass, need not be one to which the owner or occupier for the time being of the land has had what may be described as a permanent title. A right enjoyed merely by permission is enough. The leading authority for that proposition is the case of *International Tea Stores Co v Hobbs* ([1903] 2 Ch 165)[9]. That was a decision of Sir George Farwell as a judge of first instance. It was a case in which the defendant, who owned two houses, let one of them for business purposes and there had been a practice of giving permission to the successive managers of the property let to pass and re-pass with their servants and so forth across a yard which was part of the property and remained in the defendant's occupation. The part of the property which had been let was later sold to the tenants, nothing being said in the conveyance about the right of way. The purchasers claimed to exercise the right of way by virtue of section 6 of the Act of 1881. That claim was disputed, and the point was taken that it could not be a right which would pass under the implied general words inasmuch as it was only precariously enjoyed. The learned judge held that the fact that the way was permissive only was irrelevant for this purpose, and that by virtue of section 6 of the Act of 1881 the grant included a corresponding right of way in fee simple. Dealing with the question of licence or permission, the learned judge said this: "Unless I am prepared to say that in no case can a tenant obtain under the Conveyancing Act 1881, a right of way unless he has enjoyed it as of right, I must hold in this case that the fact of licence makes no difference. In all these cases the right of way must be either licensed or unlicensed. If it is unlicensed it would be at least as cogent an argument to say. 'True you went there, but it was precarious, because I could have sent a man to stop you or stopped you myself any day'. If it is by licence, it is precarious, of course, in the sense that the licence, being ex hypothesi revocable, might be revoked at any time; but if there be degrees of precariousness, the latter is less precarious than the former. But, in my opinion, precariousness has nothing to do with this sort of case, where a privilege which is by its nature known to the law — namely, a right of way — has been in fact enjoyed. Lord Coleridge's argument was founded upon a misconception of a judgment of mine in *Burrows v Lang* ([1901] 2 Ch 502), where I was using the argument of precariousness to show that the right which was desired to be enjoyed there was one which was unknown to the law — namely, to take water if and whenever the defendant chose to put water into a particular pond; such a right does not exist at law; but a right of way is well known to the law."

[His Lordship referred also to *Lewis v Meredith* ([1913] 1 Ch 571) and *White v Williams* ([1922] 1 KB 727) and continued:] There is, therefore,

---

[8] Compare *Long v Gowlett* [1923] 2 Ch 177; p. 537, post.
[9] See the remarks of Cross J in *Green v Ashco Horticulturist Ltd* [1966] 1 WLR 889 at 896–897, [1966] 2 All ER 232; *Ward v Kirkland* [1967] Ch 194, [1966] 1 All ER 609.

ample authority for the proposition that a right in fact enjoyed with property will pass on a conveyance of the property by virtue of the grant to be read into it under section 62, even although down to the date of the conveyance the right was exercised by permission only, and therefore was in that sense precarious.

The next proposition deducible from the cases is the one laid down in *Burrows v Lang,* which has been referred to in some of the passages I have already read. It is that the right in question must be a right known to the law.... For the purposes of section 62, it is only necessary that the right should be one capable of being granted at law, or, in other words, a right known to the law. If it is a right of that description it matters not, as the *International Tea Stores* case ([1903] 2 Ch 165) shows, that it has been in fact enjoyed by permission only. The reason for that is clear, for, on the assumption that the right is included or imported into the parcels of the conveyance by virtue of section 62, the grant under the conveyance supplies what one may call the defect in title, and substitutes a new title based on the grant.

[His Lordship also referred to *Birmingham, Dudley and District Banking Co v Ross* ((1888) 38 ChD 295) and continued:] I think those are all the cases to which I can usefully refer, and applying the principles deducible from them to the present case one finds, I think, this. First of all, on the evidence the coal shed was used by Mrs. Wright by the permission of Mr. Macadam, but *International Tea Stores Co v Hobbs* shows that that does not prevent section 62 from applying, because permissive as the right may have been it was in fact enjoyed.

Next, the right was, as I understand it, a right to use the coal shed in question for the purpose of storing such coal as might be required for the domestic purposes of the flat. In my judgment that is a right or easement which the law will clearly recognize[10], and it is a right or easement of a kind which could readily be included in a lease or conveyance by the insertion of appropriate words in the parcels. This, therefore, is not a case in which a title to a right unknown to the law is claimed by virtue of section 62. Nor is it a case in which it can be said to have been in the contemplation of the parties that the enjoyment of the right should be purely temporary. No limit was set as to the time during which the coal shed could continue to be used. Mr. Macadam simply gave his permission; that permission was acted on; and the use of the coal shed in fact went on down to 28 August 1943, and thereafter down to 1947. Therefore, applying to the facts of the present case the principles which seem to be deducible from the authorities, the conclusion to which I have come is that the right to use the coal shed was at the date of the letting of 28 August 1943 a right enjoyed with the top floor flat within the meaning of section 62 of the Law of Property Act 1925, with the result that (as no contrary intention was expressed in

---

[10] On easements of storage, cf. *Copeland v Greenhalf* [1952] Ch 488, [1952] 1 All ER 809, p. 512, *ante*; *Grigsby v Melville* [1972] 1 WLR 1355, [1973] 1 All ER 385, p. 514, *ante*.

the document) the right in question must be regarded as having passed
by virtue of that letting, just as it would have passed if it had been
mentioned in express terms in cl. 1, which sets out the subject-matter
of the lease. . . .

For these reasons I would allow the appeal and direct that, inasmuch
as the coal shed is now no longer in existence, judgment should be
entered for the plaintiffs for the sum of damages claimed.

GOLDBERG *v* EDWARDS
[1950] Ch 247 (CA, EVERSHED MR, COHEN and ASQUITH LJJ)

The first defendant was the owner of a house at Salford and of an
annexe consisting of two storeys at the rear. The annexe could be
reached by an uncovered passage to the East of the house, and this
approach had always been used by the tenants previous to the
plaintiffs. During the course of the negotiations with the plaintiffs,
Isadore Goldberg and Barnett Sewelson, for the letting of the annexe,
the first defendant agreed to give a personal privilege to the plaintiffs
to use another approach to the annexe which led through the front
door of the house, and to use the letter box in that door.

On 13 January 1947, an oral agreement for a lease of the annexe to
the plaintiffs was reached, and they went into possession on 18
January 1947. On 10 July 1947, the first defendant, pursuant to this
agreement, demised the annexe to the plaintiffs "with the appurtenances" for two years from 18 January 1947 with an option to renew
for a further two. From the time of taking possession the plaintiffs
took privileges beyond those given to them, but the first defendant
was held by the Vice-Chancellor of the County Palatine Court of
Lancaster to have consented to such acts for the period of time during
which she should be in possession of the house.

In January 1949, the first defendant agreed to let the house to the
second defendant who went into possession and obstructed the
plaintiffs in the enjoyment of these privileges. The action was to
restrain interference with the use of the passage through the front
door to the annexe by the plaintiffs their servants and agents.

Held, (reversing in part the Vice-Chancellor of the County Palatine).
The plaintiffs were entitled to the right of way because it was a right
appertaining to their premises on 10 July 1947, the date of the lease;
but not to the other privileges.

EVERSHED MR: The substance of the judge's finding is clearly this:
he found that there was a sharp and substantial distinction between
the privilege to the two plaintiffs themselves to go to and from the
annexe through the front door, on the one hand, and all the other
privileges on the other. [His Lordship quoted from the judge's judgment and continued:] The passage just read seems to me consistent
only with the view that in the Vice-Chancellor's opinion the privilege
given to the plaintiff tenants was intended to be one which otherwise
was capable of annexation to the demised property and therefore
capable of being caught by section 62 of the Law of Property Act 1925.

The claim of the plaintiffs . . . has been based on two grounds: first, implied grant, apart altogether from section 62 of the Law of Property Act 1925, and secondly section 62. In my judgment, the first ground cannot be sustained.

[His Lordship explained that the use of the front door and passage was not "necessary for the reasonable or convenient enjoyment" of the annexe, and a grant could not therefore be implied, and continued:] I therefore reject the argument based on implied grant, and turn to section 62.

The various rights here claimed are these: first, a right for the plaintiffs personally to pass through the front door and along the passage of the house. . . . Secondly, a right to maintain a signboard and an electric bell; thirdly, as a necessary corollary to that, a right for the plaintiffs' customers to use the front door and passage; and, fourthly, a right to use it for the passage of goods. . . . It is plain, in my view, that these rights, other than the plaintiffs' personal right of passage, were not within the language of section 62 so as to be covered by the demise to them.

That leaves only the personal right. . . . Having regard to his judgment, I think that I am bound to regard the view of the judge as having been that, in contra-distinction to the other rights, it was intended to be something which the plaintiffs should enjoy qua lessees during the term of the demise, though it should not be enjoyed by their servants, workmen or any other persons with their authority. Therefore, I think, to quote Jenkins LJ, in the recent case of *Wright v Macadam* ([1949] 2 KB 744 at 752, [1949] 2 All ER 565; p. 530, ante). "It is a right or easement of a kind which could be readily included in a lease or conveyance by the insertion of appropriate words in the parcels." What those would be I will state later, because, in the view which I take, it is necessary to see that the injunction or declaration to which the plaintiffs may be entitled is properly formulated.

Wright v Macadam was decided after the Vice-Chancellor gave judgment in this case. . . . The present privilege is in some ways indeed not dissimilar to that which in *Wright v Macadam* was held to be covered by section 62, namely, a privilege for the tenant to use a shed for storing her coal. I therefore think that, if the right which I have defined was one which was being enjoyed at the time of the conveyance, it is covered by section 62.

That therefore leaves the final point: what is the "time of conveyance" within the meaning of section 62, subsections 1 and 2? The arrangement about this use of the passage appears to have been made at various dates, the last of which was 13 January 1947. The plaintiffs went into occupation of the annexe on 18 January 1947. The fitting of the bell and signboard took place after that. Several months passed (why, I know not, and it is quite immaterial) before the lease was executed on 10 July 1947, though the term was expressed to run from 18 January. It is plain that before 10 July there was no written instrument whatever. Possession may no doubt have been attributable to an oral agreement of which, having regard to the position, specific performance might have been granted; but I fail to find any instrument in writing within the meaning of section 62 before the lease of 10 July. It seems to me, therefore, that the phrase "at the time of conveyance" must mean in this case 10 July. I am unable to accept the view that one should construe that as meaning at the time when the term granted by the lease is stated to have begun. On 10 July 1947, under the privilege granted, this right of ingress and egress was being enjoyed in fact. As I have held, though it is limited to the lessees themselves and does not extend to other persons, it would be capable of formulation and incorporation as a term of the lease, and it is, in my judgment, covered by section 62. To that extent, therefore, but to that limited extent only, the plaintiffs are entitled to succeed.

In *Phipps v Pears* [1965] 1 QB 76, [1964] 2 All ER 35[11], Lord DENNING MR, after holding that a right to protection from the weather could not exist as an easement, added at p. 84: "There is a further point. It was said that when the owner . . . conveyed No. 16 to Helena Field, the plaintiff's predecessor, there was implied in the conveyance all the general words of section 62 of the Law of Property Act 1925. The conveyance included all 'easements, rights and advantages whatsoever appertaining or reputed to appertain to the land'. On the conveyance of No. 16, Market Street, to the plaintiff's predecessor, there passed to him all these 'advantages' appertaining to No. 16. One of these advantages, it was said, was the benefit of having the old No. 14 there as a protection from the weather. I do not think this argument avails the plaintiff for the simple reason that, in order for section 62 to apply, the right or advantage must be one which is known to the law, in this sense, that it is capable of being granted at law so as to be binding on all successors in title, even those who take without notice, see *Wright v Macadam* ([1949] 2 KB 744, [1949] 2 All ER 565; p. 530, ante). A fine view, or an expanse open to the winds, may be an 'advantage' to a house but it would not pass under section 62. Whereas a right to use a coal shed or to go along a passage would pass under section 62. The reason being that these last are rights known to the law, whereas the others are not. A right to protection from the weather is not a right known to the law. It does not therefore pass under section 62."

Section 62 only applies, unlike the rule in *Wheeldon v Burrows*, if there has been a "diversity of occupation" before the sale or lease; that is to say that the section does not apply where a person who has been both owner and occupier of adjoining premises sells or leases one of them.

A number of problems would arise if the exercise of general rights of

---

[11] P. 516, ante.

ownership by the common owner and occupier over the part to be sold were treated as "rights and advantages" so as to give the purchaser an easement in respect of such of them as were capable of existing as easements.

In *Long v Gowlett* [1923] 2 Ch 177[12], Mrs. Nichols, the owner of land adjoining the River Granta at Linton, Cambridgeshire, sold the land in two lots by contemporaneous sales to two purchasers; Lot 1 to Gowlett and Lot 2 to Long's predecessor in title. The common owner had been accustomed to go from Lot 1, on which Hadstock Mill stood, to Lot 2 higher up the river, to repair the river bank and cut weeds therefrom, so as to ensure a free flow of water downstream to the Mill. Gowlett, the owner of Lot 1, claimed that an easement to enter Lot 2 to repair and cut had been created in his favour by the conveyance of 1909 under section 6 Conveyancing Act 1881 (now section 62 Law of Property Act 1925). Long sought an injunction and damages for trespass. In rejecting Gowlett's claim, SARGANT J said at p. 199:

"And on these facts it is contended for the defendant that this constituted a 'privilege easement right or advantage' over or in relation to Lot 2, which at the time of the conveyance was occupied or enjoyed with Lot 1; and accordingly, that this advantage passed to the defendant by virtue of the express words of the sub-section as included in the conveyance by virtue of the statute. The argument is not based in any way on the existence of any continuous and apparent easement existing over Lot 2 in favour of Lot 1; indeed, any such claim would be incompatible with the evidence, which clearly establishes that there was no defined way at all along the south bank. The claim is founded upon there having been a statutory introduction into the conveyance to the defendant of words equivalent to or identical with those either expressly contained or statutorily introduced in the corresponding conveyances in such cases as *James v Plant* (1836) 4 Ad & El 749; *Watts v Kelson* (1871) 6 Ch App 166; *Bayley v Great Western Rly Co* (1884) 26 ChD 434; and *White v Williams* [1922] 1 KB 727.

It is, therefore, necessary for the purpose of dealing with the matter on this footing to consider whether, during the common ownership and occupation of Lot 1 and Lot 2 by Mr. Nichols and his widow, and therefore at the date of the conveyance, there was a 'privilege, easement, right or advantage' of the kind now claimed, which can properly be said to have been 'demised, occupied or enjoyed' with Lot 1 over Lot 2. It is very difficult to see how this can have been the case. No doubt the common owner and occupier did in fact repair the bank of Lot 2, and cut the weeds there; and no doubt also this repair and cutting would enure not solely for the benefit of Lot 2 (which comprised, amongst other things, a lawn tennis court), so as to prevent its being flooded, but also and very likely to a greater extent for the benefit of Lot 1. But there is nothing to indicate that the acts done on

---

[12] See also *Ward v Kirkland*, [1967] Ch. 194, at pp. 228–231; [1966] 1 All ER 609; p. 529 n. 19, ante.

Lot 2 were done otherwise than in the course of the ownership and occupation of Lot 2, or that they were by way of using a 'privilege, easement or advantage' over Lot 2 in connection with Lot 1. The common owner and occupier of Whiteacre and Blackacre may in fact use Blackacre as an alternative and more convenient method of communication between Whiteacre and a neighbouring village. But it has never been held, and would I think be contrary to principle to hold, that (in default of there being a made road over Blackacre forming a continuous and apparent means of communication) a sale and conveyance of Whiteacre alone would carry a right to pass over Blackacre in the same way in which the common owner had been accustomed to pass. As it seems to me, in order that there may be a 'privilege, easement or advantage' enjoyed with Whiteacre over Blackacre so as to pass under the statute, there must be something done on Blackacre not due to or comprehended within the general rights of an occupying owner of Blackacre, but of such a nature that it is attributable to a privilege, easement, right or advantage, however precarious, which arises out of the ownership or occupation of Whiteacre, altogether apart from the ownership or occupation of Blackacre. And it is difficult to see how, when there is a common ownership of both Whiteacre and Blackacre, there can be any such relationship between the two closes as (apart from the case of continuous and apparent easements or that of a way of necessity) would be necessary to create a 'privilege, easement, right or advantage' within the words of section 6, subsection 2, of the statute. For this purpose it would seem that there must be some diversity of ownership or occupation of the two closes sufficient to refer the act or acts relied on not to mere occupying ownership, but to some advantage or privilege (however far short of a legal right) attaching to the owner or occupier of Whiteacre as such and de facto exercised over Blackacre. Let me illustrate my meaning from the latest case on the subject — namely, *White v Williams* [1922] 1 KB 727. . . .

Mr. Greene for the defendant was challenged to produce from the very many cases in which, on a conveyance of Whiteacre, an easement over Blackacre has been held to pass under the statutory words or their equivalent, a single case in which both the closes in question had been in common ownership and occupation, or in which there had not been an actual enjoyment over Blackacre on the part of an owner or occupier of Whiteacre who was not the owner and occupier of Blackacre. And neither from among the cases cited to me, nor from any other case in the books, was he able (with one solitary exception) to produce such a case as required. The exception, however, is one of high authority — namely, that of *Broomfield v Williams* [1897] 1 Ch 602 — and it is necessary to examine it with some attention.

In that case the common owner of a house and of adjoining land over which light had in fact been received through the windows of the house, sold and conveyed the house by a conveyance after the date of the Conveyancing Act 1881, but retained the adjoining land. It was held by the Court of Appeal that, although the retained land was

marked on the plan on the conveyance as 'building land', the vendor
was not at liberty subsequently to build on the retained land so as to
interfere substantially with the access of light to the windows of the
house. A. L. Smith L.J., it is true, based his judgment solely on the
principle that the grantor was not entitled to derogate from his grant;
and this was quite sufficient to support the actual decision. But the
other two members of the Court relied mainly, if not exclusively, on
the express words of section 6, subsection 2, of the Act; and the
decision is, therefore, undoubtedly binding on me with regard to the
access of light, and also with regard to any other 'privilege, easement,
right or advantage' that is on the same footing as 'light.'

But such an easement or advantage as is now claimed is, in my
judgment, very different from light, or a right to light. The access of
light to a window over adjoining land is a physical fact plainly visible
to any one buying a house. It is extremely similar to a continuous and
apparent easement. It is mentioned in the subsection in the midst of a
number of physical features ending with the word 'watercourses'; and
the special position of light to an existing window as compared with
other easements is fully recognized in the Prescription Act, which
makes the acquisition of an easement of light depend on the enjoyment
of the light simpliciter, and not, as in the case of other easements, on
enjoyment as of right. The fact, therefore, that the inclusion of light in
the subject matter of conveyance in section 6, subsection 2, has been
held to entitle the grantee to the light coming to an existing window,
does not necessarily involve the further inclusion of imperceptible
rights or advantages, corresponding with intermittent practice or user
as between two tenements of the common owner and occupier of both.
Such an intermittent and non-apparent user or practice stands, in my
judgment, on a completely different footing from the visible access of
light to an existing window.

The importance of such a distinction is specially obvious in a case
like the present, where there is a contemporaneous sale by a common
owner to two separate purchasers of adjoining lots completely divided
by a physical boundary. If the contention of the defendant is correct, it
would be necessary in any such case for the purchaser to inquire how
the common owner and occupier had been accustomed to make use of
each close in connection with the other. Would the plaintiff, for
instance, in this case be entitled, as against the defendant, to an
alternative way over Lot 1 to reach Lot 2, because while both lots
were in common ownership and occupation, it was the practice of Mr.
and Mrs. Nichols by way of Lot 1 to repair the south bank of Lot 2?
Any number of similar puzzles would arise, if the law were as the
defendant would have it. The fact that the common owner and occupier
sells two adjoining closes separately is, in my mind, a negation of the
intention to preserve access between them: compare such a case as
Midland Rly Co v Gribble [1895] 2 Ch 827.

The only two exceptions to this rule appear to be those of ways of
necessity and of continuous and apparent easements. Had the general
words of section 6, subsection 2, any such effect as is suggested

by the defendant — and it must be remembered that these words were not new, but represented conveyancing practice for many years previously — it is difficult, if not impossible, to understand how there have not been numerous cases in which, on a severance of two closes, a subsisting practice by the common owner and occupier of both has not been given effect to by way of legal easement as a result of general words of this kind."

In *Sovmots Investments Ltd v Secretary of State for the Environment* [1979] AC 144, [1977] 2 All ER 385[1] the House of Lords considered both the rule in *Wheeldon v Burrows* and section 62. The London Borough of Camden made a compulsory purchase order to acquire 36 residential maisonettes in Centre Point. The question was whether certain rights over and in respect of other parts of Centre Point, without which the maisonettes could not be used as housing accommodation, passed on the conveyance; and whether, if they did not pass, the Borough had power to make a compulsory purchase order to acquire the maisonettes which, without the additional rights, could not be used for housing purposes. In quashing the order, Lord WILBERFORCE said at p. 168[2]:

"The main argument before the inspector and in the courts below was that in this case and under the compulsory purchase order as made no specific power to require the creation of ancillary rights was necessary because these would pass to the acquiring authority under either, or both, of the first rule in *Wheeldon v Burrows* (1879) 12 ChD 31 ("the rule") or of section 62 of the Law of Property Act 1925. Under the rule (I apologise for the reminder but the expression of the rule is important)

'on the grant by the owner of a tenement of part of that tenement *as it is then used and enjoyed*, there will pass to the grantee all those continuous and apparent easements (by which, of course, I mean quasi-easements), or, in other words, all those easements which are necessary to the reasonable enjoyment of the property granted, and *which have been and are at the time of the grant used* by the owners of the entirety for the benefit of the part granted' (see *per* Thesiger LJ, at p. 49, my emphasis).

Under section 62 a conveyance of land operates to convey with the land all ways, watercourses, liberties, privileges, easements, rights and advantages whatsoever, appertaining or reputed to appertain to the land, or any part thereof, or, at the time of conveyance, demised, occupied or enjoyed with, or reputed or known as part or parcel or appurtenant to the land or any part thereof.

---

[1] (1977) 41 Conv (NS) 415; [1979] Conv 113 (C. Harpum); [1978] Conv 449 (P. Smith); 127 NLJ 695 (H. W. Wilkinson); Jackson, pp. 100–103.
[2] See also pp. 175–176, per Lord EDMUND-DAVIES.

My Lords, there are very comprehensive expressions here, but it does not take much analysis to see that they have no relevance to the situation under consideration.

The rule is a rule of intention, based on the proposition that a man may not derogate from his grant. He cannot grant or agree to grant land and at the same time deny to his grantee what is at the time of the grant obviously necessary for its reasonable enjoyment. To apply this to a case where a public authority is taking from an owner his land without his will is to stand the rule on its head: it means substituting for the intention of a reasonable voluntary grantor the unilateral, opposed, intention of the acquirer.

Moreover, and this point is relevant to a later argument, the words I have underlined[3] show that for the rule to apply there must be actual, and apparent, use and enjoyment at the time of the grant. But no such use or enjoyment had, at Centre Point, taken place at all.

Equally, section 62 does not fit this case. The reason is that when land is under one ownership one cannot speak in any intelligible sense of rights, or privileges, or easements being exercised over one part for the benefit of another. Whatever the owner does, he does as owner and until a separation occurs, of ownership or at least of occupation, the condition for the existence of rights, etc., does not exist: see *Bolton v Bolton* (1879) 11 ChD 968, 970 *per* Fry J and *Long v Gowlett* [1923] 2 Ch 177, 189, 198, in my opinion a correct decision.

A separation of ownership, in a case like the present, will arise on conveyance of one of the parts (e.g. the maisonettes), but this separation cannot be projected back to the stage of the compulsory purchase order so as, by anticipation to bring into existence rights not existing in fact."

[1978] Conv 499, at pp. 454–455 (P. Smith)

"In fact there is a considerable body of authority against [*Long v Gowlett*], both academic and precedent based, none of which was seriously considered by the House of Lords. There is no need to consider it in any detail as most readers will be aware of it[4]. The first limitation namely that section 62 has no ambit where there is no diversity of occupation, does not stand up to precedent for a start. In *Broomfield v Williams*[5] the Court of Appeal made no such limitation as suggested by Sargant J in *Long v Gowlett* and Lord Wilberforce and Lord Edmund-Davies in the *Sovmots* case. With respect to Lord Edmund-Davies and to Mr. Harpum[6], merely to state easements of

---

[3] As printed in italics.
[4] For starters Jackson (1966) 30 Conv (NS) 342–348 and thence Jackson, *The Law of Easements and Profits*, pp. 97–103; Megarry and Wade, *The Law of Real Property* (4th edn.), pp. 836, note 47 and 837–838; Farrand, *Contract and Conveyance* (2nd edn.), pp. 384–386; *Emmet*, p. 515; Barnsley, *Conveyancing Law and Practice*, pp. 484–485 (perhaps?); and *Gale on Easements* (14th edn.), pp. 125–126. The last book is particularly significant as the Thirteenth Edition of that book supported *Long v Gowlett* but was changed after Professor Jackson's article supra.
[5] [1897] 1 Ch. 602.
[6] (1977) 41 Conv (NS) 415.

light are different from other easements does not explain why section 62, apparently very widely drawn, applies to those easements and not to others when there is no diversity of occupation. There is absolutely nothing in the section to justify such a limitation. Furthermore the objection that the rights etc. do not exist at the relevant time, ignores the substantial body of case law where section 62 has turned a precarious right into a full legal easements[7]. . . .

The real problem now is what is left after *Sovmots*? It appears that one of the major opponents of the limitations imposed by the case is prepared to concede it now[8], but is such resignation necessary? Only two of the five law lords considered the point, no argument was addressed to them on the point and no cases cited.''

QUESTION

Is there good reason in principle or authority for requiring a diversity of occupation for the operation of section 62? What bearing does the *Sovmots* case have on the matter? And is there justification for applying a different rule to easements of light?

Jackson, pp. 92 et seq, [1978] Conv 499 (P. Smith); M & W, p. 836 n. 47; *Broomfield v Williams* [1897] 1 Ch 602.

Is there good reason for differentiating in this respect between the operation of the rule in *Wheeldon v Burrows* and the Law of Property Act 1925, section 62? See JENKINS LJ in *Wright v Macadam* ([1949] 2 KB 744, [1949] 2 All ER 565), p. 530, ante; Cheshire, pp. 531-532; M & W, p. 838; MM, p. 400; Gale pp. 125-126; Jackson pp. 100-103.

ii.   EASEMENTS IMPLIED IN FAVOUR OF THE GRANTOR

Generally, any rights which a grantor wishes to enjoy as easements in favour of the land he retains, and exercisable over the land sold, must be expressly reserved[9] or regranted. Otherwise he may not derogate from his grant[10]. In exceptional cases, however, easements will be implied in his favour. These are easements of necessity[11], and may be (a) "an easement without which the property retained cannot be used at all, and not one merely necessary to the reasonable enjoyment of that property[12], and (b) an easement which is required to carry out the common intention of the parties[13]. These are usually easements of

---

[7] See e.g. *Wright v Macadam* [1949] 2 KB 744, [1949] 2 All ER 565; *Goldberg v Edwards* [1950] Ch 247 and *International Tea Stores v Hobbs* [1903] 2 Ch 165. None of these cases featured in the *Sovmots case*.

[8] See Jackson, p. 100.

[9] L.P.A. 1925, s. 65; p. 521, ante.

[10] (1964) 80 LQR 244 (D. W. Elliott).

[11] (1973) 89 LQR 87 (E. H. Bodkin).

[12] *Union Lighterage Co v London Graving Dock Co* [1902] 2 Ch 557 at p. 573; *Pinnington v Galland* (1853) 9 Exch 1; *Deacon v South Eastern Rly Co* (1889) 61 LT 377; *Midland Rly Co v Miles* (1886) 33 ChD 632.

[13] *Richards v Rose* (1853) 9 Exch 218; *Shubrook v Tufnell* (1882) 46 LT 886; *Re Webb's Lease* [1951] Ch 808, [1951] 2 All ER 131; p. 545, post.

support, and such easements can only be claimed when the intention is clear. In each case the right which the grantor can claim is the minimum necessary to comply with the rule under which it is claimed[14].

CORPORATION OF LONDON *v* RIGGS
(1880) 13 ChD 798 (ChD, JESSEL MR)

In 1887, Heathcote, the owner of land in Essex, conveyed part of this land to London Corporation who declared that they would hold the land conveyed as an open space for ever. This land completely encircled a close of about two acres called Barn Hoppet which was owned also by Heathcote, and had been used up to that time for agricultural purposes only. No easements in favour of Barn Hoppet were reserved in the conveyance of the other land to London Corporation. In 1879 Riggs entered into possession of Barn Hoppet as tenant, and he made preparations for the erection of a house and of other buildings for the sale of refreshments to the public. The plaintiffs claimed a declaration that Riggs' right of way of necessity was limited to purposes sufficient to the use of Barn Hoppet for agricultural purposes only; and an injunction and damages. The action was tried on demurrer.

Held. The defendant's right of way was limited to the purposes for which it was used in 1877.

JESSEL MR: I am afraid that, whatever I may call my decision, it will, in effect, be making law, which I never have any desire to do; but I cannot find that the point is covered by any decided case, or even appears to have been discussed in any decided case. The only satisfaction I have in deciding the point is this, that it will in all probability be carried to a higher court, and it will be for that court to make the law, or, as we say, declare the law, and not for me.

The real question I have to decide is this — whether, on a grant of land wholly surrounding a close, the implied grant, or re-grant, of a right of way by the grantee to the grantor to enable him to get to the reserved, or excepted, or inclosed close, is a grant of a general right of way for all purposes, or only a grant of a right of way for the purpose of the enjoyment of the reserved or excepted close in its then state.

There is, as I have said, no distinct authority on the question. It seems to me to have been laid down in very early times — and I have looked into a great number of cases, and among others several black-letter cases — that the right to a way of necessity is an exception to the ordinary rule that a man shall not derogate from his own grant, and that the man who grants the surrounding land is in very much the same position as regards the right of way to the reserved close as if he

---

[14] Cheshire, pp. 534, 555; L & W, p. 874; MM, p. 421; *Corporation of London v Riggs* (1880) 13 ChD 798; *Nickerson v Barraclough* [1979] 3 WLR 562, [1979] 3 All ER 312, (1980) 130 NLJ 204 (H.W. Wilkinson).

had granted the close, retaining the surrounding land. In both cases there is what is called a way of necessity; and the way of necessity, according to the old rules of pleading, must have been pleaded as a grant, or, where the close is reserved, as it is here, as a re-grant. . . .

Well, now, if we try the case on principle — treating this right of way as an exception to the rule — ought it to be treated as a larger exception than the necessity of the case warrants? That of course brings us back to the question, What does the necessity of the case require? The object of implying the re-grant, as stated by the older Judges, was that if you did not give the owner of the reserved close some right of way or other, he could neither use nor occupy the reserved close, nor derive any benefit from it. But what is the extent of the benefit he is to have? Is he entitled to say, I have reserved to myself more than that which enables me to enjoy it as it is at the time of the grant? And if that is the true rule, that he is not to have more than necessity requires, as distinguished from what convenience may require, it appears to me that the right of way must be limited to that which is necessary at the time of the grant; that is, he is supposed to take a re-grant to himself of such a right of way as will enable him to enjoy the reserved thing as it is.

That appears to me to be the meaning of a right of way of necessity. If you imply more, you reserve to him not only that which enables him to enjoy the thing he has reserved as it is, but that which enables him to enjoy it in the same way and to the same extent as if he reserved a general right of way for all purposes: that is — as in the case I have before me — a man who reserves two acres of arable land in the middle of a large piece of land is to be entitled to cover the reserved land with houses, and call on his grantee to allow him to make a wide metalled road up to it. I do not think that is a fair meaning of a way of necessity: I think it must be limited by the necessity at the time of the grant; and that the man who does not take the pains to secure an actual grant of a right of way for all purposes is not entitled to be put in a better position than to be able to enjoy that which he had at the time the grant was made. I am not aware of any other principle on which this case can be decided.

I may be met by the objection that a way of necessity must mean something more than what I have stated, because, where the grant is of the inclosed piece, the grantee is entitled to use the land for all purposes, and should therefore be entitled to a right of way commensurate with his right of enjoyment. But there again the grantee has not taken from the grantor any express grant of a right of way: and all he can be entitled to ask is a right to enable him to enjoy the property granted to him as it was granted to him. It does not appear to me that the grant of the property gives any greater right. But even if it did, the principle applicable to the grantee is not quite the same as the principle applicable to the grantor: and it might be that the grantee obtains a larger way of necessity — though I do not think he does — than the grantor does under the implied re-grant.

I am afraid that I am laying down the law for the first time — that I am for the first time declaring the law; but it is a matter of necessity from which I cannot escape.

The demurrer must, therefore, be overruled, with costs.

RE WEBB'S LEASE
[1951] Ch 808, [1951] 2 All ER 131 (CA, EVERSHED MR, JENKINS and MORRIS LJJ)

The defendant (the landlord) was head lessee of a three storey building. He occupied the ground floor for his own business as a butcher, and leased the upper two storeys to the plaintiff (the tenant). The first letting was in 1939 for three years; the tenant remained in occupation until 1949 when he was granted a 21 year lease. Throughout all this time one side of the building contained an advertisement for the defendant's business, and another side (the west wall) one for Bryant and May's matches, both of which covered all or part of the external walls of the upper two storeys. None of the leases made any reservation of the right of the landlord to use the outer walls of the demised premises for this purpose. In 1950, the tenants began to make enquiries concerning the landlord's right so to use the walls and finally issued this summons to determine the question.

Held (reversing DANCKWERTS J). Without express reservation, the landlord had no right to claim the easement in question.

JENKINS LJ: The matter therefore stands thus: The landlord did not include in the provisions of the lease as executed any reservation of advertising rights over any part of the outer walls; but, at the date of the lease, the advertisements now in dispute were in their present positions on the walls and plainly to be seen. Moreover, they had existed in their present positions continuously since before the commencement of the tenant's original tenancy in 1939; and the tenant never objected to their presence at any time during his original tenancy, or at the time of the granting of the lease of 11 August 1949, or thereafter until January 1950. There is no evidence that either party ever even mentioned the subject of the advertisements to the other during the whole of this period of more than ten years.

This being in substance the whole of the available facts, the question is whether on those bare facts without more, the court can and ought as a matter of law to imply in favour of the landlord a reservation during the term of twenty-one years granted by the lease of 11 August 1949, of advertising rights over the outer walls demised, at all events to the extent required to enable him to maintain the existing advertisements and to retain for his own benefit any periodical payments receivable from the Borough Billposting Company in respect of the site of the "Brymay" poster.

As to the law applicable to the case, it is not disputed that as a general rule a grantor, whether by way of conveyance or lease, of part of a hereditament in his ownership, cannot claim any easement over the part granted for the benefit of the part retained, unless it is expressly reserved out of the grant. See (for instance) *Suffield v Brown* ((1864) 4 De GJ & Sm 185); *Crossley & Sons Ltd v Lightowler* ((1867) 2 Ch App 478); *Wheeldon v Burrows* (1879) 12 ChD 31; p. 525, ante).

There are, however, certain exceptions to the general rule. Two well-established exceptions relate to easements of necessity and mutual easements such as rights of support between adjacent buildings. But it is recognized in the authorities that these two specific exceptions do not exhaust the list, which is indeed incapable of exhaustive statement, as the circumstances of any particular case may be such as to raise a necessary inference that the common intention of the parties must have been to reserve some easement to the grantor, or such as to preclude the grantee from denying the right consistently with good faith, and there appears to be no doubt that where circumstances such as these are clearly established the court will imply the appropriate reservation.

[His Lordship quoted from the judgment of THESIGER LJ, in *Wheeldon v Burrows*, at p. 525, ante, referred to *Russell v Watts* ((1885) 10 App Cas 590); *Aldridge v Wright* ([1929] 2 KB 117); *Liddiard v Waldron* ([1934] 1 KB 435), and continued:] The most comprehensive statement of the area of potential exceptions is probably that contained in the speech of Lord Parker in *Pwllbach Colliery Co Ltd v Woodman* ([1915] AC 634), where his Lordship, after referring to the exception with respect to easements of necessity, said this: "The second class of cases in which easements may impliedly be created depends not upon the terms of the grant itself, but upon the circumstances under which the grant was made. The law will readily imply the grant or reservation of such easements as may be necessary to give effect to the common intention of the parties to a grant of real property, with reference to the manner or purposes in and for which the land granted or some land retained by the grantor is to be used. See *Jones v Pritchard* ([1908] 1 Ch 630), and *Lyttelton Times Co Ltd v Warners Ltd* ([1907] AC 476). But it is essential for this purpose that the parties should intend that the subject of the grant or the land retained by the grantor should be used in some definite and particular manner. It is not enough that the subject of the grant or the land retained should be intended to be used in a manner which may or may not involve this definite and particular use."

... The question is whether the circumstances of the case as proved in evidence are such as to raise a necessary inference that the common intention of the parties was to reserve to the landlord during the twenty-one years' term some, and if so what, rights in regard to the display of advertisements over the outer walls of the demised premises, or such as to preclude the tenant from denying the implied reservation to the landlord of some such rights consistently with good faith.

That question must be approached with the following principles in mind: (i) If the landlord intended to reserve any such rights over the demised premises it was his duty to reserve them expressly in the lease of 11 August 1949 (*Wheeldon v Burrows* (1879) 12 ChD 31); (ii) The landlord having failed in this duty, the onus was upon him to establish the facts to prove, and prove clearly, that his case was an exception to the rule (*Aldridge v Wright* [1929] 2 KB 117); (iii) The mere fact that the tenant knew at the date of the lease of 11 August 1949 that the landlord was using the outer walls of the demised premises for the display of the advertisements in question did not suffice to absolve the landlord from his duty of expressly reserving any rights in respect of them he intended to claim, or to take the case out of the general rule: see *Suffield v Brown* ((1864) 4 De GJ & Sm 185); *Crossley & Sons Ltd v Lightowler* ((1867) 2 Ch App 478).

Applying these principles to the present case, I ask myself whether the landlord has on the meagre facts proved discharged the onus which lies upon him of proving it an exception to the general rule. He can, so far as I can see, derive no assistance from the passage quoted above from Lord Parker's speech in the *Pwllbach Colliery* case ([1915] AC 634). It might, I suppose, be said to have been in the contemplation of the parties that the landlord would continue to use the ground floor of the premises for the purposes of his business as a butcher and provision merchant, but it cannot in my view be contended that the maintenance during the term of the lease of his advertisement over the door was a necessary incident of the user so contemplated. This applies a fortiori to the "Brymay" advertisement, the display of which on the outer wall of the demised premises by the Borough Billposting Company as licensees of the landlord was so far as I can see not related in any way to the use or occupation of the ground floor for the existing or any other purpose. The transaction with the Borough Billposting Company was simply a hiring out for reward of part of an outer wall of the demised premises for use as an advertising or billposting site or station.

The mere fact that the tenant knew of the presence of the advertisements at the date when the lease of 11 August 1949 was granted being, as stated above, beside the point, nothing is left beyond the bare circumstance that the advertisements were not only present at the date of the grant but had been continuously present without objection by the tenant since the commencement of his original tenancy in 1939. Does this circumstance suffice to raise a necessary inference of an intention common to both parties at the date of the lease that the landlord should have reserved to him the right to maintain these advertisements throughout the twenty-one years' term thereby granted? I cannot see that it does. The most that can be said is that the facts are consistent with such a common intention. But that will not do. The landlord must surely show at least that the facts are not reasonably consistent with any other explanation. Here he manifestly fails. . . .

In short, I can hold nothing more established by the facts proved than permissive user of the outer walls by the landlord for the display of the advertisements during the original tenancy and thereafter from the granting of the lease until the tenant's objection in January 1950; with nothing approaching grounds for inferring, as a matter of necessary inference, an intention common to both parties that such permissive user should be converted by the lease into a reservation to the landlord of equivalent rights throughout the twenty-one years' term thereby granted.

C. Acquisition by Presumed Grant, or Prescription[15]

i.   PRESCRIPTION AT COMMON LAW: TIME IMMEMORIAL

In *Bryant v Foot* (1867) LR 2 QB 161[16], the question was whether the rector of Horton, Buckinghamshire, could establish a claim based on long user, to a fee of 13s. for marriages performed in the parish church. User was proved since 1808, but there was no evidence prior to that time.

COCKBURN CJ, MELLOR and LUSH JJ, (BLACKBURN J, dissenting) held that the size of the fee made it impossible to believe that it existed in the time of Richard I. The presumption of immemorial legal existence which arose from user within living memory was rebutted. In discussing the methods of proof of immemorial user, COCKBURN CJ, said at p. 179: "The law of England ever has been and still is, in respect of prescriptive rights, in a most unsatisfactory state. The common law admitted of no prescription in the matter of real estate, or of any franchise which was matter of record, as not lying in grant. In respect of things incorporeal, lying in grant, it admitted of a species of prescription, not upon the ground that possession or enjoyment for a given period gave an indefeasible right, but on the assumption, when possession or enjoyment had been carried back as far as living memory would go, that a grant had once existed which had since been lost.

Practically speaking, by means of this presumption prescriptive rights were established in respect of matters which lay in grant. Protection, in respect of real estates, after continued and peaceable enjoyment, was effected, not by the law being that after possession for a given number of years the right of property should be absolutely acquired, but by the indirect contrivance of debarring the adverse claimant from the benefit of the procedure by which alone his right could be established. And here again our ancestors, instead of fixing a given number of years as the period within which legal proceedings to recover real property must be resorted to, had recourse to the singular expedient of making the period of limitation run from particular events or dates. From the time of Henry I. to that of Henry III., on a writ of right, the time within which a descent must be shewn was the time of King Henry I. (Co Litt 114b). In the 20th year of Henry III., by the Statute of Merton (c. 8) the date was altered to the time Henry II.

---

[18] Cheshire, pp. 538–554; M & W, pp. 841–865; MM, pp. 404–417; Gale, pp. 133–192; Jackson pp. 110–138; (1975) 38 MLR 641 (S. Anderson).

[19] *Duke of Norfolk v Arbuthnot* (1880) 5 CPD 390 (no prescription in respect of church built about 1380).

Writs of mort d'ancestor were limited to the time of the last return of King John into England; writs of novel disseisin to the time of the king's first crossing the sea into Gascony. In the previous reign, according to Glanville (Lib 13, c. 33), the disseisin must have been since the last voyage of King Henry II. into Normandy. So that the time necessary to bar a claim varied materially at different epochs. Thus matters remained till the 3 Edw. I. (Stat West 1 c. 39), when, as all lawyers are aware, the time within which a writ of right might be brought was limited to cases in which the seisin of the ancestor was since the time of King Richard I., which was construed to mean the beginning of that king's reign (2 Inst 238), a period of not less than eighty-six years. The legislature having thus adopted the reign of Richard I. as the date from which the limitation in a real action was to run, the courts of law adopted it as the period to which, in all matters of prescription or custom, legal memory, which till then had been confined to the time to which living memory could go back, should thenceforth be required to extend. Thus the law remained for two centuries and a half, by which time the limitation imposed in respect of actions to recover real property having long become inoperative to bar claims which had their origin posterior to the time of Richard I., and having therefore ceased practically to afford any protection against antiquated claims, the legislature, in 32nd of Henry VIII. (c. 2), again interfered, and on this occasion, instead of dating the period of limitation from some particular event or date, took the wiser course of prescribing a fixed number of years as the limit within which a suit should be entertained. The legislature having thus altered the period within which rights to real estate could be asserted by parties out of possession, the courts on this occasion omitted to follow the analogy of the recent statute as fixing the date from which legal memory was to commence, as they had done on the passing of the statute of the 3 Edw I., and adhered in all that related to prescription or custom to the previously established standard. It was of course impossible that as time went on the adoption of a fixed epoch, as the time from which legal memory was to run, should not be attended by grievous inconvenience and hardship. Possession, however long, enjoyment, however uninterrupted, afforded no protection against stale and obsolete claims, or the assertion of long abandoned rights. And as parliament failed to intervene to amend the law, the judges set their ingenuity to work, by fictions and presumptions, to atone for the supineness of the legislature, and to amend, so far as in them lay, the law, which I cannot but think they were bound to administer as they found it. They first laid down the somewhat startling rule that from the usage of a lifetime the presumption arose that a similar usage had existed from a remote antiquity. Next, as it could not but happen that, in the case of many private rights, especially in that of easements, which had a more recent origin, such a presumption was impossible, judicial astuteness to support possession and enjoyment, which the law ought to have invested with the character of rights, had recourse to the questionable theory of lost grants. Juries were first told that from user, during living memory, or even during twenty years, they might presume a lost grant or deed; next they were recommended to make such presumption; and lastly, as the final consummation of judicial legislation, it was held that a jury should be told, not only that they might, but also that they were bound to presume the existence of such a lost grant, although neither judge nor jury, nor any one else, had the shadow of a belief that any such instrument had ever really existed. In this manner the courts have endeavoured to supply the deficiency of the law in the matter of rights acquired by possession and enjoyment. When the doctrine of presumptions had proceeded far towards its development, the legislature at length interfered, and in respect of real property and of certain specified easements, fixed certain periods of possession or enjoyment as establishing presumptive rights. But with regard to all prescriptions or customs not provided for by statutory enactment the law remains as before."

In advising the House of Lords in *Dalton v Angus* ((1881) 6 App Cas at 773–4) where a claim to an easement of support for a building based upon 27 years user was upheld, FRY J, in a famous passage, based the doctrine of prescription upon acquiescence.

"But leaving such technical questions aside, I prefer to observe that, in my opinion, the whole law of prescription and the whole law which governs the presumption or inference of a grant or covenant rest upon acquiescence. The Courts and the Judges have had recourse to various expedients for quieting the possession of persons in the exercise of rights which have not been resisted by the persons against whom they are exercised, but in all cases it appears to me that acquiescence and nothing else is the principle upon which these expedients rest. It becomes then of the highest importance to consider of what ingredients acquiescence consists. In many cases, as, for instance, in the case of that acquiescence which creates a right of way, it will be found to involve, 1st, the doing of some act by one man upon the land of another; 2ndly, the absence of right to do that act in the person doing it; 3rdly, the knowledge of the person affected by it that the act is done; 4thly, the power of the person affected by the act to prevent such act either by act on his part or by action in the Courts; and lastly, the abstinence by him from any such interference for such a length of time as renders it reasonable for the Courts to say that he shall not afterwards interfere to stop the act being done. In some other cases, as, for example, in the case of lights, some of these ingredients are wanting; but I cannot imagine any case of acquiescence in which there is not shewn to be in the servient owner: 1, a knowledge of the acts done; 2, a power in him to stop the acts or to sue in respect of them; and 3, an abstinence on his part from the exercise of such power. That such is the nature of acquiescence and that such is the ground upon which presumptions or inferences of grant or covenant may be made appears to me to be plain both from reason, from maxim, and from the cases.

As regards the reason of the case, it is plain good sense to hold that a man who can stop an asserted right, or a continued user, and does not do so for a long time, may be told that he has lost his right by his delay and his negligence, and every presumption should therefore be made to quiet a possession thus acquired and enjoyed by the tacit consent of the sufferer. But there is no sense in binding a man by an enjoyment he cannot prevent, or quieting a possession which he could never disturb."

ii. USER AS OF RIGHT[17]

In *Diment v N. H. Foot Ltd* [1974] 1 WLR 1427, the plaintiff and defendant owned adjacent farms at Buckland Newton, in Dorset, known as Sanctions Farm and Bookham Farm respectively. On an outlying part, a gateway gave access from a "panhandle", or narrow tongue of land, on Bookham Farm through Field 415 on Sanctions Farm to the highway. From 1936 onwards Foot (the predecessor in title of the defendant) used this way across Mrs. Diment's land six to ten times a year. From 1936 to 1967 Mrs. Diment was absent from the farm, but visited it occasionally. During that time she let it on four separate agricultural tenancies, and employed a firm of chartered surveyors to act as her agent. She first heard of Foot's user on her final return in 1967, and in 1970 sought an injunction to restrain Foot's entry on her land. PENNYCUICK V-C held that Foot had not acquired an easement by prescription and said, at p. 1433:

"Coming to the facts of the present case, I have already held that the plaintiff had never heard that the defendant company or its predecessors had been using no. 415 for access to their own land, until Mr. Billen told her something in 1967. I have already made clear that I accept that evidence, so that she did not have actual knowledge at any time before 1967. Were the circumstances such that if she had followed up any clues she would have ascertained that the relevant act was being done? I have reached the clear conclusion that the plaintiff did not possess any such means of knowledge.

Mr. Bradburn contended that she must be treated as having such means of knowledge by reason of the existence of the gateway at point B, considered in connection with the lie of the land which made the extreme north-west tip of the panhandle virtually inaccessible to vehicles except through that gate. I am not at all certain that the plaintiff, doing all the acts which a diligent landowner could have done, would have even seen gate B when she made her inspections of Sanctions Farm during this period from 1936 to 1967. During this period the plaintiff came down to Buckland Newton perhaps once a

---

[17] M & W, p. 842, n. 86; "*Solomon v Vintners Co* (1859) 4 H & N 585 at 602 (common law prescription); *Sturges v Bridgman* (1879) 11 ChD 852, 863 (lost modern grant); *Tickle v Brown* (1836) 4 Ad & El. 369, 382 (prescription under the Prescription Act 1832; and see ss. 1, 2)."

year to look over Sanctions Farm. No. 415 was an outlying part of a large farm and there is no reason I can see why one should infer that the plaintiff, looking over the farm as a whole, should have walked up along the boundary to this outlying field. Even if she had done so, I am not persuaded that the mere site of a gate at point B leading to the panhandle would have put her on any further inquiry as to why that gate was there. There can be all sorts of reasons why a gate stands between two pieces of land which are not at present in common ownership and I should not have thought that the mere sight of the gate would have put her on inquiry as to whether the gate was in current use by the owner/occupier for the time being of Bookham Farm for the purposes of access over no. 415. I conclude that it is not possible to impute to the plaintiff personally any means of knowledge.

Mr. Bradburn put his contention of knowledge in one rather different way. I mention now the case to which I alluded earlier, namely, *Pugh v Savage* [1970] 2 QB 373, [1970] 2 All ER 353 in which Cross LJ said, at p. 384: 'When long user — here user for 36 years — of a way has been shown, I think, that the law should support it if it can, and that we ought to presume, in the absence of any evidence to the contrary, that the owners of 457 in the period 1932/1940 knew of the user and that Ralphs knew of it.' There Cross LJ — and both Harman and Salmon LJJ agreed — was stating that there is a presumption that the owner concerned knows of the relevant user of a way but, as he himself said, it is obvious that that presumption can be rebutted by evidence that the owner did not have such knowledge. The effect of that statement is to throw the burden of proof upon the owner concerned, that is to say instead of the other party having to establish affirmatively that he did have knowledge, he must establish that he did not have knowledge. That is I think an enlargement of the principle stated in the earlier case[1].

The plaintiff, herself, did not have such knowledge and so, as far as she is concerned, she has in the present case rebutted the presumption. But during these years the plaintiff employed a firm of chartered surveyors known as Henry Duke & Son of Dorchester to act for her in connection with Sanctions Farm including the making of agreements with the successive tenants in occupation of no. 415. Mr. Bradburn contended that any knowledge or imputed knowledge on the part of the plaintiff's agent must be treated for this purpose as her own knowledge as principal and that the presumption of knowledge applies as regards Messrs Henry Duke & Son, and could only be rebutted by showing that Henry Duke & Son did not in fact have knowledge of the user of the way, or means of such knowledge. I do not think the presumption can legitimately be carried so far where a landowner employs an agent in connection with the property. There cannot, I think, be a presumption, merely by reason of that relation and without reference to the particular circumstances, that the agent has know-

---

[1] *Dalton v Angus* (1881) 6 App Cas 740.

ledge or means of knowledge of any particular act upon the land. That would be carrying this presumption altogether beyond anything that was said in *Pugh v Savage* and would, I venture to think, lead to some very odd consequences. It seems to me that where one is concerned with an agent, the role of establishing knowledge or means of knowledge must rest on the other party concerned, who might discharge that burden by direct evidence or by inference — the inference depending upon all the particular circumstances. There was no evidence here as to the precise activities carried on by Henry Duke & Son apart from the fact that they were responsible for making the tenancies and dealing with matters of rents and so forth. There is no evidence as to what members of that firm or their representative did physically upon Sanctions Farm or no. 415 by way of inspection and I see no ground upon which I would be entitled to hold that Henry Duke & Son had knowledge or means of knowledge of the user of this way by Mr. Foot or the defendant company.

That is sufficient to decide this case because the defendant company has failed to establish that the plaintiff either had knowledge of the use of this way or the means of such knowledge and that is the third of Fry J's requirements."

Davies v Du Paver [1953] 1 QB 184, [1952] 2 All ER 991, p. 562, post.

GARDNER *v* HODGSON'S KINGSTON BREWERY CO LTD
[1903] AC 229 (HL, Lords HALSBURY, ASHBOURNE, MACNAGHTEN, DAVEY, ROBERTSON and LINDLEY)

For some 70 or 80 years, the owners of the plaintiff's house had been accustomed to use a way from their stable across the yard of the defendant's inn to reach a road. The user was open and uninterrupted, but, for a long period, and certainly since 1855, an annual payment of 15*s.* had been made.

The plaintiff claimed a declaration that she was entitled to a right of way.

Held. No claim could be made under the Prescription Act or under the doctrine of lost modern grant because the user, being by permission, was not "as of right".

LORD LINDLEY: The plaintiff's statement of claim is so drawn as to entitle her to succeed if she can bring herself within the Prescription Act, or failing that, if the facts warrant the presumption of a lost grant. Cozens-Hardy J considered that she was entitled to succeed under the Prescription Act; but that if not, a lost grant in her favour ought to be presumed. It is necessary to consider both of these methods of establishing her right; for the Prescription Act has not taken away any of the modes of claiming easements which existed before that Act was passed: see *Aynsley v Glover* ((1875) 10 Ch App 283).

I will take the Prescription Act first. Section 2 is the important section, and the last part of it is relied upon by the plaintiff. To bring herself within this enactment she must prove that she and her predecessors in title have enjoyed the way in question "claiming right thereto" without interruption for forty years. The difficulty is raised by the words "claiming right thereto", and by the payment of the 15s. a year. I understand the words "claiming right thereto" and the equivalent words "as of right", which occur in section 5, to have the same meaning as the older expression nec vi, nec clam, nec precario. A temporary permission, although often renewed, would prevent an enjoyment from being "as of right"; but a permanent, irrevocable permission attributable to a lost grant would not have the same effect. The common law doctrine is that all prescription presupposes a grant. But if the grant is proved and its terms are known, prescription has no place.

A title by prescription can be established by long peaceable open enjoyment only; but in order that it may be so established the enjoyment must be inconsistent with any other reasonable inference than that it has been as of right in the sense above explained. This, I think, is the proper inference to be drawn from the authorities discussed in the court below. If the enjoyment is equally consistent with two reasonable inferences, enjoyment as of right is not established; and this, I think, is the real truth in the present case.

The enjoyment is equally open to explanation in one of two ways, namely, by a lost grant of a right of way in consideration of a rent-charge on the plaintiff's land of 15s. a year, or by a succession of yearly licences not, perhaps, expressed every year, but implied and assumed and paid for[2].

––––––––––––

In *Healey v Hawkins* [1968] 1 WLR 1967, [1968] 3 All ER 836, the question arose of the effect of initial oral permission on user for the 20 year period under the Prescription Act 1832. GOFF J held that the user which was permissive in origin did not so continue and thus prevent the defendant from acquiring an easement of way. His Lordship said, at p. 1973:

"In principle it seems to me that once permission has been given, the user must remain permissive and not be capable of ripening into a right save where the permission is oral and the user has continued for 40 or 60 years, unless and until, having been given for a limited period only, it expires or, being general, it is revoked, or there is a change in circumstances from which revocation may fairly be implied. Moreover, *Gaved v Martyn* ((1865) 19 CBNS 732) appears to me to be a decision expressly in point and in accordance with the conclusion in Megarry and Wade (p. 850, para. 4 (iii)). In that case, oral permission had been given to use an artificial watercourse, and a

––––––––––––

[2] *Monmouth Canal Co v Harford* (1834) 1 Cr M & R 614.

successor who did not claim under the original licensee and who had no actual knowledge of permission having been given continued to exercise the privilege, but in circumstances which ought to, or might, have put him on inquiry, and the court held that there was evidence and, as Byles J at p. 747 thought, abundant evidence, on which the jury could find, as it had done, that the user even by the new occupier remained permissive.

Of course, when the user has continued for 40 or 60 years a prior parol consent affords no answer, because it is excluded by the express terms of section 2 of the Prescription Act, but, even so, permission given during the period will defeat the claimant because it negatives user as of right. That is, in my judgement, the explanation of the distinction drawn by the House of Lords in *Gardner v Hodgson's Kingston Brewery* ([1903] AC 229), between antecedent and current parol consents."

iii. USER IN FEE SIMPLE[3]

In *Kilgour v Gaddes* [1904] 1 KB 457, a dispute arose between two neighbouring tenants of Sir James Graham in connection with the use of a pump which was situated on the land occupied by the plaintiff. The defendant and his predecessors in title had used the pump for forty years before the action was brought.

The Court of Appeal held that there was no prescriptive right to use the pump, COLLINS MR, saying at p. 460: "The question in this case is whether, as between two persons who are termors of different tenements, a right of way to a pump has been acquired by prescription for the owner of one of the tenements over the other tenement under section 2 the Prescription Act 1832. I say a right for the owner, for it appears to me clear that under the section the right cannot be acquired merely by a tenant as against a tenant, but must be acquired by the owner of the fee in one of the tenements as against the owner of the fee in the other. Here the respective tenants of the so-called dominant and servient tenements hold under the same landlord; and, if the proposition be correct that a prescriptive right of way under section 2 of the Act must be acquired by the owner of the fee in one of the tenements as against the owner of the fee in the other, then in this case the defendant's contention would involve the result that the tenant of one of the tenements has acquired for his landlord a right of way over the landlord's own land; which is impossible and inconsistent with the essential notion of a right by prescription, namely, that the right is acquired by the owner of land over land belonging to another owner. I limit what I am saying to such an easement as a right of way, because questions with regard to the easement of light stand on a different footing, and depend on the provisions of section 3 of the

---

[3] M & W, p. 844, n. 4; "*Bright v Walker* (1834) Cr M & R 211, 221 (prescription at common law); *Wheaton v Maple & Co* [1893] 3 Ch 48 at 63 (lost modern grant); *Kilgour v Gaddes* [1904] 1 KB, 457 at 460 (Prescription Act 1832)." *Pugh v Savage* [1970] 2 QB 373, [1970] 2 All ER 353; *Davis v Whitby* [1973] 1 WLR 629, [1973] 3 All ER 403.

Act[4]. . . . 'If I am asked how it is consistent with the Prescription Act, I answer that such user and enjoyment is not as of right within the meaning of the 2nd section. It is a user by a termor, who, if he acquire the right, must acquire it as incident to the land of which he is termor, and thus for the benefit of his reversioner. Such user cannnot be as of right, unless a reversioner can in law by user acquire a right against himself[5].' That reasoning appears to me conclusive of the present case. There was a long discussion in the course of the argument as to the possibility of a termor under one landlord acquiring for his landlord an easement by user over land in the occupation of a termor under another landlord, and as to whether an easement in such a case could be acquired, unless and until the user had continued for the period of three years after the determination of the term in the servient tenement without interference by the reversioner[6]. That no doubt raises an interesting question, which appears to have been decided in Ireland in the case of *Beggan v M'Donald* ((1877) 2 LR Ir 560), contrary to the view expressed in this country in *Bright v Walker* ((1834) 1 Cr M & R 211) and also in *Wheaton v Maple & Co* ([1893] 3 Ch 48), in neither of which cases, however, was it necessary actually to decide the point. That question, however, is not the question raised in the present case. . . .

In the case of *Wheaton v Maple & Co* the view which I am expressing was very clearly stated by Lindley LJ in his judgment. He dealt first with the question of the possibility of acquiring an easement as against a tenant of land by a presumption of a lost grant as follows: 'I am not aware of any authority for presuming, as a matter of law, a lost grant by a lessee for years in the case of ordinary easements, or a lost covenant by such a person not to interrupt in the case of light, and I am certainly not prepared to introduce another fiction to support a claim to a novel prescriptive right. The whole theory of prescription at common law is against presuming any grant or covenant not to interrupt, by or with any one except an owner in fee. A right claimed by prescription must be claimed as appendant or appurtenant to land, and not as annexed to it for a term of years. Although, therefore, a grant by a lessee of the Crown, commensurate with his lease, might be inferred as a fact, if there was evidence to justify the inference, there is no legal presumption, as distinguished from an inference in fact, in favour of such a grant. This view of the common law is in entire accordance with *Bright v Walker* where this doctrine of presumption is carefully examined.' He was there dealing with the question of an implied grant.''

Claims to easements (other than easements of light, p. 582, post) under prescription at common law (*Bright v Walker* (1834) 1 Cr M & R,

---

4 P. 582, post.
5 Quoting Palles CB, in *Timmons v Hewitt* (1888) 22 LR Ir 627.
6 Prescription Act 1832, s. 8, p. 561, post.

at 221) or under the doctrine of implied grant must be based upon user against a fee simple owner. In *Wheaton v Maple & Co* ([1893] 3 Ch 48), the easement claimed was an easement of light, but the Crown was the freeholder of the servient tenement; Prescription Act 1832, section 3 (right to light) does not, as do sections 1 and 2, bind the Crown, and the plaintiff was thrown back on reliance on section 2 or upon the doctrine of lost modern grant.

Similarly, prescription (apart from easements of light) can operate only in favour of a fee simple estate, but the fee simple owner may take advantage of user enjoyed by a lessee or other limited owner in making a claim to an easement.

The rule is clear; but there appears to be no logical reason why the doctrine of the lost modern grant should not apply to cases of prescription by or against a lessee or other limited owner. The doctrine could apply so as to presume a grant to a lessee of the dominant tenement of an easement for the period of his tenancy; or to a grant either by the lessee of the servient tenement of an easement for years or by the fee simple owner of an easement in fee[7].

iv.   THE DOCTRINE OF LOST MODERN GRANT[8]

HULBERT *v* DALE
[1909] 2 Ch 570 (JOYCE J; CA, COZENS-HARDY MR, FLETCHER MOULTON and FARWELL LJJ)

By an Inclosure Award of 1804, a "private carriage road of the width of thirty feet" over Crown Farm (now owned by the plaintiff), was allotted to the predecessor in title of the defendant's lessor, owner of Fishmore Farm. The road was never made, and trees grew and buildings were built on the intended site. However the defendant and his predecessor in title or occupation had, since 1804, uninterruptedly used a private road running across the plaintiff's farm, parallel to the site of the awarded road and some 100 yards from it.

There had been unity of possession of the two farms from 1889 to 1905, while they were in the occupation of the same tenant.

The plaintiff brought this action for an injunction to restrain the defendant from using the road.

Held (affirming JOYCE J). A lost grant of a right of way should be presumed.

JOYCE J: There was a considerable conflict of evidence in the case, but, upon the whole, the result to my mind is that I come to the conclusion, and find as a fact, that for a period as far back as living memory extends the owners and occupiers for the time being of Fishmore Farm have openly and without interruption had an

---

[7] (1958) 74 LQR 82 (V. T. H. Delany).
[8] Holdsworth, Vol. vii, pp. 347–349; *Healey v Hawkins* [1968] 1 WLR 1967, [1968] 3 All ER 836 (grant of right of way presumed); *Oakley v Boston* [1976] QB 270, [1975] 3 All ER 405 (incumbent of glebe land is capable granter with consent of Ecclesiastical Commissioners).

unquestioned user until quite recently, when the dispute arose, of the now disputed road, and I should have held such user to have been as of right (or by persons claiming a right thereto) but for the circumstance that during the period between the years 1889 and 1905 there was unity of possession (not of ownership) of the two farms, Fishmore and Crown Farms, both being in the occupation of the same tenant or tenants.

This being so, the defendant could not make good any claim to a right of way along the disputed road by prescription under the 2nd section of the Prescription Act. Nor could he, I think, have succeeded upon a claim by prescription at common law, because I consider it to be tolerably plain, for various reasons, that the existence of the right of way claimed, if it does exist, originated and commenced at a date long subsequent to the reign of King Richard I — in fact very little more than one hundred years ago. The defendant, therefore, has to base his claim upon the existence of a grant not produced, and he contends that it is a case for presuming a grant, now lost, of the right to use the disputed road.

I must say that it seems to me that if ever there was a case in which some such presumption ought to be made, this is the case. For I am tolerably certain that the owners and occupiers of Fishmore Farm have had the use of the disputed road without interruption and with the full knowledge of the occupiers, and presumably of the owners, of Crown Farm, who have acquiesced in such use possibly because of the existence of the right of the awarded way, which right, if enforced, would have been much more disadvantageous to Crown Farm than the user of the disputed road by the owners and occupiers of Fishmore Farm.

In *Tehidy Minerals Ltd v Norman* [1971] 2 QB 528, [1971] 2 All ER 475, the defendants proved that they were accustomed to graze Tawna Down, Cardinham, Cornwall, from 19 January 1920 to 6 October 1941, a period of 21 years, eight and a half months. In holding that they had acquired a profit à prendre under the doctrine of lost modern grant, BUCKLEY LJ, in delivering the judgment of the Court of Appeal (SALMON, SACHS and BUCKLEY LJJ) said at p. 547: "The question is whether on the facts of this case enjoyment of this grazing for a period of upwards of 20 years preceding 6 October 1941 permits or requires us to presume that such enjoyment was had by virtue of grants made after 19 January 1920, but before 6 October 1921 (being 20 years before 6 October 1941), and subsequently lost, and whether we ought to act on such a presumption[9]. [His Lordship then analysed the judgments in *Angus v Dalton* ((1877) 3 QBD 85,

---

[9] The CA rejected an argument that, as the Prescription Act 1832 lays down longer periods for prescription in respect of profits than in respect of easements, so by analogy a longer period of enjoyment should be required in the case of a profit than in the case of an easement to support the prescription.

(1878) 4 QBD 162, (1881) 6 App Cas 740) "which in the course of its history enjoyed the attention of no less than 18 judges and members of the House of Lords, perhaps embodying a greater variety of judicial opinion than any other leading case", and continued:] In our judgment *Angus v Dalton* decides that, where there has been upwards of 20 years' uninterrupted enjoyment of an easement, such enjoyment having the necessary qualities to fulfil the requirements of prescription, then unless, for some reason such as incapacity on the part of the person or persons who might at some time before the commencement of the 20-year period have made a grant, the existence of such a grant is impossible, the law will adopt a legal fiction that such a grant was made, in spite of any direct evidence that no such grant was in fact made.

If this legal fiction is not to be displaced by direct evidence that no grant was made, it would be strange if it could be displaced by circumstantial evidence leading to the same conclusion, and in our judgment it must follow that circumstantial evidence tending to negative the existence of a grant (other than evidence establishing impossibility) should not be permitted to displace the fiction. Precisely the same reasoning must, we think, apply to a presumed lost grant of a profit à prendre as to an easement.

In the present case, if we are to presume lost grants, we must do so in respect of each of the four farms, Higher and Lower Hill, Cabilla and Pinsla Park. Each of the presumed grants must be supposed to have been made between 20 January 1920 and 5 October 1921, and to have been since lost in circumstances of which no one now has any recollection. This combination of circumstances seems to us to be exceedingly improbable, and we feel sympathy for the view expressed by Farwell J, in *A-G v Simpson* [1901] 2 Ch 671 at 698: 'It cannot be the duty of a judge to presume a grant of the non-existence of which he is convinced, nor can he be constrained to hold that such a grant is reasonably possible within the meaning of the authorities.' In view, however, of the decision in *Angus v Dalton* we consider that it is not open to us in the present case to follow this line."

v.   THE PRESCRIPTION ACT 1832[10]

PRESCRIPTION ACT 1832

Whereas the expression "time immemorial, or time whereof the memory of man runneth not to the contrary," is now by the Law of England in many cases considered to include and denote the whole period of time from the Reign of King Richard the First, whereby the title to matters that have been long enjoyed is sometimes defeated by shewing the commencement of such enjoyment, which is in many cases productive of inconvenience and injustice;

---

[10] For the history of prescription, see Holdsworth, Vol. vii, pp. 343 et seq; Simpson, *Introduction to the History of Land Law*, pp. 248–251.

[1.] Claims to right of common[11] and other profits à prendre, not to be defeated after thirty years enjoyment by merely showing the commencement of the right; after sixty years enjoyment the right to be absolute, unless had by consent or agreement. — No claim which may be lawfully made at the common law, by custom, prescription, or grant, to any right of common or other profit or benefit to be taken and enjoyed from or upon any land of our sovereign lord the King, or any land being parcel of the duchy of Lancaster or of the duchy of Cornwall, or of any ecclesiastical or lay person, or body corporate, except such matters and things as are herein specially provided for, and except tithes, rent, and services, shall, where such right, profit, or benefit shall have been actually taken and enjoyed by any person claiming right thereto without interruption for the full period of thirty years, be defeated or destroyed by showing only that such right, profit, or benefit was first taken or enjoyed at any time prior to such period of thirty years, but nevertheless such claim may be defeated in any other way by which the same is now liable to be defeated; and when such right, profit, or benefit shall have been so taken and enjoyed as aforesaid for the full period of sixty years, the right thereto shall be deemed absolute and indefeasible, unless it shall appear that the same was taken and enjoyed by some consent or agreement expressly made or given for that purpose by deed or writing.

2.   In claims of right of way or other easement the periods to be twenty years and forty years. — ... No claim which may be lawfully made at the common law, by custom, prescription, or grant, to any way or other easement, or to any watercourse, or the use of any water, to be enjoyed or derived upon, over, or from any land or water of our said lord the King, or being parcel of the duchy of Lancaster or of the duchy of Cornwall, or being the property of any ecclesiastical or lay person, or body corporate, when such way or other matter as herein last before mentioned shall have been actually enjoyed by any person claiming right thereto without interruption for the full period of twenty years, shall be defeated or destroyed by showing only that such way or other matter was first enjoyed at any time prior to such period of twenty years, but nevertheless such claim may be defeated in any other way by which the same is now liable to be defeated; and where such way or other matter as herein last before mentioned shall have been so enjoyed as aforesaid for the full period of forty years, the right thereto shall be deemed absolute and indefeasible, unless it shall appear that the same was enjoyed by some consent or agreement expressly given or made for that purpose by deed or writing.

4.[12]   Before mentioned periods to be deemed those next before suits. — Each of the respective periods of years herein-before

---

[11] P. 53, ante.

[12] Prescriptive claims to rights of common are not to be defeated by reason of interruptions due to requisition of the common land by a Government Department, or to inability to exercise a right to graze animals for reasons of animal health: Commons Registration Act 1965, s. 16. See Rights of Light Act 1959, s. 3 (6), p. 588, post.

mentioned shall be deemed and taken to be the period next before some suit or action wherein the claim or matter to which such period may relate shall have been or shall be brought into question; and that no act or other matter shall be deemed to be an interruption, within the meaning of this statute, unless the same shall have been or shall be submitted to or acquiesced in for one year after the party interrupted shall have had or shall have notice thereof, and of the person making or authorizing the same to be made.

7.[13]   **Proviso for infants &c.** — Provided also, that the time during which any person otherwise capable of resisting any claim to any of the matters before mentioned shall have been or shall be an infant, idiot, non compos mentis, feme covert, or tenant for life, or during which any action or suit shall have been pending, and which shall have been diligently prosecuted, until abated by the death of any party or parties thereto, shall be excluded in the computation of the periods here-before mentioned, except only in cases where the right or claim is hereby declared to be absolute and indefeasible.

8.[13]   **What time to be excluded in computing the term of forty years appointed by this Act.** — Provided always, that when any land or water upon, over, or from which any such way or other convenient[14] watercourse or use of water shall have been or shall be enjoyed or derived hath been or shall be held under or by virtue of any term of life, or any term of years[15] exceeding three years from the granting thereof, the time of the enjoyment of any such way or other matter as herein last before mentioned, during the continuance of such term, shall be excluded in the computation of the said period of forty years, in case the claim shall within three years next after the end or sooner determination of such term be resisted by any person entitled to any reversion expectant on the determination thereof.

Lord MACNAGHTEN in *Gardner v Hodgson's Kingston Brewery Co Ltd*[16] [1903] AC 229 said at p. 236: "I rather doubt whether the scope and effect of the Prescription Act have been always rightly apprehended. The Act was passed, as its preamble declares, for the purpose of getting rid of the inconvenience and injustice arising from the meaning which the law of England attached to the expressions 'time immemorial' and 'time whereof the memory of man runneth not to the contrary'. The law as it stood put an intolerable strain on

---

[13] See n. 12 supra.
[14] Probably a misprint for 'easement'. *Wright v Williams* (1836) Tyr & Gr 375 at 390; *Laird v Briggs* (1881) 19 ChD 22 at 33.
[15] *Palk v Shinner* (1852) 18 QB 568.
[16] See p. 553, ante.

the consciences of judges and jurymen. The Act was an Act 'for shortening the time of prescription in certain cases'. And really it did nothing more. A person who claims a right of way and invokes the protection of the Act must claim 'as of right'. But when the way in question has been used without interruption, as defined in the Act, for forty years 'as of right' — whether the claimant is really entitled of right or not — the claim cannot be defeated except by shewing that the right claimed was enjoyed 'by some consent or agreement expressly given or made for that purpose by deed or writing'. No parol consent will do. I fail to understand how that provision helps the appellant. The respondents do not set up a parol consent given before the period of forty years. They rely on the acknowledgment and recognition of their dominion over the property — their right to grant or withhold the grant of the way in question — involved in and evidenced by the annual payment accompanying the use of the way, and they point out that no other reasonable explanation of that payment is forthcoming."

(a) Interruption

In *Davies v Du Paver* [1953] 1 QB 184, [1952] 2 All ER 991, a dispute arose over the question whether the plaintiff had acquired a right (profit) by prescription based upon 60 years user to pasture sheep upon the defendant's land. Two main questions arose:

i.   The defendant in August 1950 completed a fence which excluded the sheep in spite of the plaintiff's vigorous protests. No further action was taken until the writ was issued in September 1951, and the defendant argued that the user was interrupted for more than a year.

ii.   During the first 55 of the 60 years during which user was proved, the defendant's land (servient tenement) had been in the possession of lessees.

The Court of Appeal (SINGLETON, BIRKETT and MORRIS LJJ) held that (SINGLETON LJ, dissenting):

i. there was no interruption within the Act, but ii. the plaintiff failed to show that the defendant had the knowledge or means of knowledge of the user and the power to object to it.

On the first point, MORRIS LJ, said at p. 206: "The first point raised by the defendant is that there was a fatal interruption of the enjoyment by the plaintiff of his alleged right of pasturage. In the notice of appeal this contention is formulated on the basis that there was no evidence that Mr. Davies 'had asserted his alleged rights or protested at the interruption of his alleged rights of pasturage' between 1 August 1950 and 28 September 1951, and 'that accordingly the judge was wrong in law in holding that the plaintiff Davies did not acquiesce in, or submit to, any interruption which had continued for more than one year'. This language raises the question as to the meaning of an 'assertion of rights or of a protest'. But the real question is not whether there was an assertion of rights or a protest during some period, but whether there was in this case a submission or an acquiescence. It is provided by the Prescription Act 1832, that no act or other matter is deemed to be an interruption within the meaning of the Act unless submitted to, or acquiesced in, for one year after the party interrupted has notice of the interruption and of the person making it or authorising it to be made.

There is no doubt that there was an actual interruption for more than a year before 27 September 1951. The question is whether there was acquiescence in such interruption or submission to it lasting for one year. This is, in my judgment, a question of fact. If a case were being tried with a jury it would be a question for the jury to determine: see *Bennison v Cartwright* ((1864) 5 B & S 1). . . .

The fence was completed on 9 August. Could it be said that the plaintiff had submitted to, or acquiesced in, the existence of the fence by that date? Having regard to the events that had happened, and to the correspondence, I would have thought, had it been for me to decide this question of fact, that the answer would be in the negative. The parties were breathing fury on each side of a newly erected fence. Could it be said that the challenging protests of the plaintiff must, as the August days passed, be deemed to have signified nothing, and that his former claims and assertions should be regarded as supplanted by submission and acquiescence? As time went by, it might well be that silence and inaction could be interpreted as submission or acquiescence. But the date when submission or acquiescence begins must be determined as a question of fact, having regard to all the circumstances. Had there been a beginning by 1 January 1951, or by 1 December 1950, or by 1 November 1950? These are all questions of fact. Unless it is held that there was submission or acquiescence by 27 September 1950, there would not be a period of one year. The judge referred to *Glover v Coleman* ((1874) LR 10 CP 108), and stated: 'On the evidence I hold that neither of the plaintiffs submitted to or acquiesced in the interruption.' This was a finding of fact which the judge was, in my view, entitled to make, and accordingly I consider that the first submission fails."

On the second point, the court appears to treat the question of the knowledge or means of knowledge of the user as being a matter related to user as of right. BIRKETT LJ, said at p. 206: " I see no evidence on which the judge could find that the common knowledge extended to the servient owner, or any evidence that the servient owner had the means of knowledge. It is on this ground that I would allow the appeal, for the claim 'as of right' cannot in these circumstances be established."

The user, as the judge found, was common knowledge; the defendant was unaware because he was the lessor, not in possession. The question should then be, it is submitted, not whether the user was as of right, but whether it was in fee simple. The answer to that question would be that, in the case of 40 years user for easements under the Prescription Act (60 years for profits), the fact that the servient tenement was in the occupation of a tenant for years was immaterial —

unless the period of user under the tenancy was excluded under the special defence provided by section 8[17].

(b) User as of Right is Necessary for Prescription under either period

Gardner v Hodgson's Kingston Brewery Co Ltd [1903] AC 229, p. 553, ante.

Healey v Hawkins [1968] 1 WLR 1967, [1968] 3 All ER 836, p. 554, ante.

Diment v N. H. Foot Ltd [1974] 1 WLR 1427, [1974] 2 All ER 785, p. 551, ante.

In *Union Lighterage Co v London Graving Dock Co* ([1902] 2 Ch 557), one question was whether the defendants could prescribe for an easement in respect of underwater support of a wharf, none of the metal supports except two nuts showing above the surface. The Court of Appeal (ROMER and STIRLING LJJ, VAUGHAN WILLIAMS LJ dissenting) held that there could be no prescription as the user was secret. ROMER LJ, said at p. 570: "Now, on principle, it appears to me that a prescriptive right to an easement over a man's land should only be acquired when the enjoyment has been open — that is to say, of such a character that an ordinary owner of the land, diligent in the protection of his interests, would have, or must be taken to have, a resonable opportunity of becoming aware of that enjoyment. And I think on the balance of authority that the principle has been recognised as the law, and ought to be followed by us."

(c) Next before Action Brought

HYMAN *v* VAN DEN BERGH

[1908] 1 Ch 167 (CA, COZENS-HARDY MR, FLETCHER MOULTON and FARWELL LJJ)

In 1877, one Cox, a former tenant of the plaintiff, built a cowshed with eight windows overlooking land subsequently purchased by the defendant. In 1896 and 1898, the defendant obstructed the windows by boards but these were quickly removed by the plaintiff. On 18 January 1899, Cox wrote a letter agreeing to pay 1s. per annum for the use of the light. In 1906, Cox left, and a dispute arose between the parties as to the right to the light.

Held. The plaintiff was not entitled to an easement although 22 years uninterrupted user had been enjoyed before the permission was given.

COZENS-HARDY MR: It is often asserted that an absolute right is obtained to access of light by reason merely of twenty years' undisturbed enjoyment, but I think this statement is too wide. Lord Macnaghten in *Colls v Home and Colonial Stores* ([1904] AC 179 at 189), after referring to certain "expressions not perhaps sufficiently

---

[17] *Wright v Williams* (1836) 1 M & W, 77 (not cited), (1956) 72 LQR 32 (R.E.M.). Compare *Kilgour v Gaddes* (p. 555, ante) where both tenements were owned by the same landlord.

guarded" which are to be found in the judgment in the House of Lords in *Tapling v Jones* ((1865) 11 HL Cas 290), said: "In that case Lord Westbury, Lord Cranworth, and Lord Chelmsford all assume that a period of twenty years' enjoyment of the access and use of light to a building creates an absolute and indefeasible right immediately on the expiration of the period of twenty years. No doubt section 3 says so in terms, but section 4 must be read in connection with section 3; and if the two sections are read together it will be seen than the period is not a period in gross, but a period next before some suit or action wherein the claim or matter to which such period may relate shall have been or shall be brought into question. Unless and until the claim or matter is thus brought into question, no absolute or indefeasible right can arise under the Act. There is what has been described as an inchoate right. The owner of the dominant tenement after twenty years' uninter-rupted enjoyment is in a position to avail himself of the Act if his claim is brought into question. But in the meantime, however long the enjoyment may have been, his right is just the same, as the origin of his right is just the same, as if the Act had never been passed. No title is as yet acquired under the Act. This point seems to have been much discussed shortly after the Act was passed. It was finally settled in a series of cases at common law, beginning, I think, with *Wright v Williams* ((1836) 1 M & W 77), and including *Richards v Fry* ((1837) 7 Ad & El 698) and *Cooper v Hubbuck* ((1862) 12 CB NS 456)." If this is to be regarded as a decision upon sections 3 and 4, it is of course binding upon us. If, however, it is to be regarded only as a dictum of Lord Macnaghten, I desire respectfully to say that I agree with it, and I accept it as an accurate statement of the law.

It only remains to apply the law to the facts of the present case. No action was brought by the plaintiff or any other person until the present action was commenced on 11 July 1906. The only material period to be considered is the period of twenty years prior to that date. No evidence as to what was the condition of the windows prior to that date can be regarded. Now during that period there was undoubtedly the actual enjoyment of light through the windows in question, but at the end of 1898 the windows were for a short time obstructed by the defendant. The then tenant in occupation having a doubt whether a right to light could be established, and being desirous of avoiding litigation, signed and addressed to the defendant the letter of 18 January 1899; thereupon the boards were removed, and the lights were thenceforth actually enjoyed. Under these circumstances I think it is clear that the light was enjoyed by "consent or agreement" expressly made or given for that purpose by writing. It is true that it was made or given, not to or with the freeholder, but to or with the tenant in occupation. The tenant in occupation was the proper person to make such agreement or to obtain such consent as the section requires. In my view it is a fallacy to say that the freeholder had an absolute right which his lessee ought not to be permitted to defeat. In truth he had only an inchoate right which never became an absolute

and indefeasible right. The judgment of Parker J so carefully deals
with the law applicable to the case under the Prescription Act that
I do not think I should be justified in saying anything more. In my
opinion this appeal must be dismissed with costs.

Hulbert v Dale [1909] 2 Ch 570, p. 557, ante.

In *Reilly v Orange* [1955] 2 QB 112, [1955] 2 All ER 369, neighbouring owners in 1934 came to an agreement whereby the defendant
could use a way over the plaintiff's land until the defendant should
construct a way of his own; this he did in 1953. In December 1953 the
plaintiff purported to terminate the defendant's right to use the way,
and began proceedings for this purpose; the defendant counterclaimed
for a declaration that, by reason of his user for over 19 years, he was
entitled to an easement.

The Court of Appeal (SINGLETON, JENKINS and MORRIS LJJ)
affirmed the county court judge in finding for the plaintiff, JENKINS
LJ, saying at p. 116: "Mr. Blease, for the defendant, very properly
admits that for the purpose of this appeal he must accept the deputy
judge's finding as to the nature and terms of the agreement, but he
says that notwithstanding this he is entitled to succeed. He says that
on two grounds: (1) that he has had 20 years' uninterrupted enjoyment
of the right claimed, as required by the Prescription Act 1832; (2) that
although the right he claims had its origin in the agreement of 1934,
and although that agreement, as found by the deputy judge, would
only give him a right to use the drive for domestic purposes, and only
until such time as he made a drive of his own, that permission did not
prevent the 20 years' user on which he relies from establishing his
right under the Prescription Act 1832. The second of those points can
only arise if Mr. Blease is entitled to succeed on the first. . . .

Mr. Blease's argument on this part of the case is of this nature: he
says that what must be shown is 20 years' uninterrupted user, and
that, according to section 4, no act or matter counts as an interruption
unless the same shall have been or shall be submitted to or acquiesced
in for one year. It follows, says Mr. Blease, that inasmuch as in this
case over 19 years' user down to the commencement of the action is
proved, the defendant's right is made good inasmuch as there could be
no interruption acquiesced in for one year between the date of the
commencement of the action and the completion of the full period of 20
years.

In support of that proposition he referred us to the well-known case
of *Flight v Thomas* ((1841) 8 Cl & Fin 231). In that case: 'A. had the
free access of light and air through a window of his house for nineteen
years and 330 days, and B. then raised a wall which obstructed the
light, and the obstruction was submitted to only for 35 days, when
A. brought an action to remove it.' It was held: 'that the right of action

was complete; that the twenty years' enjoyment was to be reckoned from the commencement of the enjoyment to the time of bringing the action; and that an interruption of the enjoyment, in whatever period of the twenty years it may happen, cannot be deemed an interruption within the meaning of the Act, unless it is acquiesced in for a whole year.'

Mr. Blease seeks to apply that to the present case in this way: he says that the commencement of the action constituted an interruption, and that, inasmuch as the action was not commenced until after the alleged easement had been enjoyed for more than 19 years, the interruption so constituted could not last for the required period of one year, so that his title was complete at the time of action brought. In my view that argument cannot prevail. What the Prescription Act requires, as appears from the combined effect of section 2 and section 4, is the full period of 20 years, being 'the period next before some suit or action wherein the claim or matter to which such period may relate shall have been or shall be brought into question'. The commencement of the suit or action in my view is clearly not an interruption within the meaning of section 4, but is the event marking the date down to which the requisite period of user must be shown. What must be shown is a full 20 years reckoned down to the date of action brought. That must be an uninterrupted period, but in considering whether it is an uninterrupted period or not, interruptions not acquiesced in for at least a year are not to be counted as interruptions."

In *Davis v Whitby* [1974] Ch 186, [1974] 1 All ER 806 (CA, LORD DENNING MR, STAMP and ORR LJJ), STAMP LJ said, at p. 192: "As the point is a somewhat novel one, I will express my views in my own words. The basis of prescription, as Lord Denning MR has pointed out, is that if long enjoyment of a right is shown, the court will strive to uphold the right by presuming that it had a lawful origin. Here, the owner of no. 51 (which, for the purpose of convenience, I will call 'the dominant tenement') has for upwards of 30 years enjoyed access from the rear of his house over no. 49 (which I will call 'the servient tenement'). During the first 15 years it was enjoyed over one path, and during the second period of over 15 years it was enjoyed partly over that path and partly over a substituted path. Viewed as the exercise of a right to pass and re-pass over the servient tenement, it has been enjoyed for upwards of 30 years, which is more than a sufficiently long period for it to be presumed that the right had a lawful origin. Viewed as a right so to pass and re-pass over a specified path, it has not. The question, as I see it, is which is the right way of looking at it. What happened was that in 1950 the new track or path over the back garden of the servient owner's house was established; but, using it, the dominant owner still used, as he had formerly done, the path at the side of the servient owner's house. Was the dominant owner then using the new way as of right and as of the same right as fomerly? I think he was. In substance, what was enjoyed as well before as after 1950 was access by the dominant owner to the back of his little house from the road in front of the terrace along the side of the servient owner's premises and across his back garden.

On the facts of this case, the use of the substituted route is, in my judgment, to be considered as substantially an exercise of the right claimed and enjoyed for the whole period of 30 years. It is not as though the servient owner had said: 'I will stop up the way you have been using over these last 15 years, but you may have a new defined way over a wholly different part of my land.' a situation about which I will say nothing.

I had at one time thought that the point taken that the agreement of 1950 by the servient owner amounted to a consent by him which interrupted the enjoyment as of right and so made the user 'precario' was a good point. But I accept Mr. Gidley Scott's submission that what was agreed in 1950 did not involve a simple consent to the user given by the owner of the dominant tenement, but is more consistent (as I think Burgess V-C thought) with the existence of a claim of right by the dominant owner settled by the servient owner affording a route less disadvantageous to him than a path crossing the middle of his garden; and I do not think that it was a case of consent, but rather of compromise.

I would, for these reasons, dismiss the appeal."

IV.   Content of Easements[18]

After establishing that an easement has been created, questions can still arise as to its content and extent. Such questions often relate to changes in the neighbourhood and, in connection with rights of way, to changes in methods of transportation. The principles applicable vary with the mode of creation of the easement.

A.   Easements Created by Express Grant

The extent of an easement is dependent upon the proper construction of the deed of grant. This is dependent upon the circumstances surrounding its execution, and they may be sufficient to restrict an apparently unlimited grant.

WILLES J, in *Williams v James* (1867) LR 2 CP 577, said at p. 581: "The distinction between a grant and prescription is obvious. In the case of proving a right by prescription the user of the right is the only evidence. In the case of a grant the language of the instrument can be referred to, and it is of course for the court to construe that language;

---

[18] Cheshire, pp. 554–555. As to easements of light, see p. 582, post. As to rights of way see M & W, pp. 873–875; MM, pp. 420–422; Gale, pp. 261–286; Jackson, pp. 139–155.

and in the absence of any clear indication of the intention of the parties, the maxim that a grant must be construed most strongly against the grantor must be applied."

In *White v Grand Hotel Eastbourne Ltd* [1913] 1 Ch 113[19], an unrestricted right of way to a public road granted to the owner of a private house was held not to be limited to the circumstances existing at the time of the grant. When the private house became the Grand Hotel, Eastbourne, the owners of the hotel were entitled to a right of way for the general purposes of the hotel.

In *Kain v Norfolk* [1949] Ch 163, [1949] 1 All ER 176, the rector of Bradwell had conveyed to a purchaser in 1919 land adjoining the rectory, together with a grant of the "right at all times hereafter with or without horses carts and agricultural machines and implements to go pass and repass" over a strip of land within the rectory grounds.

A sand and gravel pit was later opened, and substantial traffic of lorries carrying sand developed. The question was whether such user was within the terms of the grant of the easement; JENKINS J, relying on *White v Grand Hotel Eastbourne Ltd* held that it was.

In *Bulstrode v Lambert* [1953] 1 WLR 1064, [1953] 2 All ER 728[20], a reservation in the conveyance by the plaintiff's predecessor in title to the defendant's predecessor in title in 1944 had been made of a right of way as follows — "reserving unto the vendor his tenants and workmen and others authorized by him the right to pass and repass with or without vehicles over and along the land coloured brown on the . . . plan for the purpose of obtaining access to the building at the rear of the said premises and known as the auction mart."

At the date of the conveyance the route to the auction mart (coloured brown) was obstructed and could not be used by large vans. The obstructions were removed, and, on occasions when a better route was too crowded, the plaintiff made use of the route with furniture vans and pantechnicons for bringing goods to the mart. The defendant objected on the ground that the parked pantechnicons interfered with his business as a café and car hire proprietor, but UPJOHN J held that the plaintiff could use the way with pantechnicons which could park as long as was necessary for loading and unloading, this being an incident of a right of way.

---

[19] *United Land Co v Great Eastern Rly Co* (1875) 10 Ch App 586.
[20] *McIlraith v Grady* [1968] 1 QB 468, [1967] 3 All ER 625 (a right "to pass and repass through over and along "included a right for vehicles to stop for a reasonable time to load and unload).

KEEFE *v* AMOR
[1965] 1 QB 334, [1964] 2 All ER 517 (CA, SELLERS, RUSSELL and
DAVIES LJJ)

The plaintiff was the owner of one (No. 1) of two semi-detached houses
whose only outlet to the road was a strip of land to the rear. This land
and the other house (No. 2) were owned by the defendant.

The plaintiff's parents had bought No. 1 in 1930 from the previous
owner of both houses and the conveyance contained an express grant
of a right of way in the following terms: "Together also with a right
of way over the land shown and coloured brown on the plan hereto
annexed the purchasers paying a fair proportion in common with the
adjoining owners of the cost of keeping the said way in good repair and
condition subject to the liability of contributing (in common with the
adjoining owners) to the upkeep and repair of the wall on the west side
of the said right of way shown and marked with a T on the plan drawn
hereon."

At the date of the transfer there was at the frontage to the highway
a continuous wall, except for a gap four feet six inches wide between
two brick pillars. Inside, a gravelled strip eight feet wide led to a
doorway three feet wide to the plaintiff's property and to a gap some
seven feet wide leading to the remainder of the defendant's property.
In 1962 the defendant widened the entrance from the highway to
about seven feet six inches wide by rehanging the original gate and
hanging another, three feet wide, alongside, which she kept locked,
claiming the right so to do. The plaintiff sought a declaration that she
was entitled to a right of way for all purposes, including vehicular
traffic, over the whole of the strip of land coloured brown and an
injunction to restrain the defendant from interfering with her
reasonable enjoyment of this right.

The defendant contended that, in accordance with the circumstances
existing at the time of the grant, the right of way was a footway only,
or, at most, for such use as the four feet six inch gap permitted.

Held. On the proper construction of the grant, the right of way
included user by vehicular traffic.

RUSSELL LJ: What were the circumstances and the condition of the
property at the time of the grant? The inward end of the "brown strip"
abutted on the boundary wall of the plaintiff's property, No. 1 —
presumably a wall belonging to No. 1 — in which was a doorway about
three feet wide. Down one side of the "brown strip" was the wall
referred to in the transfer. Down the other side was a hedge, which, at
the inward end, left a gap of some seven feet or so, which afforded
access between the "brown strip" and No. 2. At the highway frontage
of the "brown strip" was a wall between the ends of the hedge and the
other wall, continuous except for the gap of about four feet six inches
between two 14-inch-square brick pillars suitable for a gateway; and
from this gateway to the inward end of the "brown strip" was a
gravelled strip appreciably wider than the gateway, with some kind of
edging of tiles, and on each side beyond that edging were garden beds

and bushes, though apparently not much kept up. In appearance it looked like a footpath rather than a roadway. During the tenancy of the plaintiff's parents (which had lasted since 1903), there did not appear to have been any vehicular use of the "brown strip" by them.

Bearing all those matters in mind, do they lead to the conclusion that the grant was of a footway only, or alternatively, if the grant was of a vehicular way, then that it was one limited as to the dimensions of the vehicle in the manner I have indicated? For myself, I think not. It is argued that that view, which I have just expressed, means that the plaintiff's parents could, had they been so minded, immediately after the transfer have insisted on the four feet six inch wide gap being widened, by pulling down a post and a part of the wall, if the vendor refused to do so, so as to enable a motor car, if they so wished, to come right up to their property, to enter and leave, and it is said that this surely would not have been a situation intended by the parties at the time of the grant. But there are several aspects of the transfer which I think lead to the conclusion that the greater right was intended.

First and foremost, the right of way was expressed to be over the strip whose whole 20-feet width was coloured brown. It would have been perfectly simple to define it more narrowly if that had been intended, or, of course, to define it as a footway, or as a right of way to and from the then existing gateway. Moreoever, the fact that the whole 20-feet width was regarded as available if necessary for the exercise of the right is stressed by the reference to the wall marked with a "T" as being "on the west side of the said right of way", showing that the whole of the 20-feet strip was being referred to as the right of way. Why (I ask myself) should the whole width be regarded as being available, if necessary, for the use as a right of way, if all that was intended was the restricted right suggested by the defendant?

I further observe that there was no obligation imposed to contribute to the upkeep of the frontage wall and, further, that an express grant of the footway alone would have been quite superfluous in the circumstances. I refer, of course, to the history of previous user; and, whether one speaks of it as a way of necessity or whether one speaks of it, as I think more correctly, as a grant which would have been implied having regard to the pre-existing user, in either event an express grant in 1930 was technically a superfluity.

Finally I would add that an obligation to pay a fair proportion of the cost of keeping the way in good repair and condition is at least unusual if all that was envisaged was the impact of human feet.

The county court judge decided against the defendant because he felt himself bound so to do by the decision of Upjohn J, in *Bulstrode v Lambert* ([1953] 1 WLR 1064, [1953] 2 All ER 728; p. 569, ante). In that case there was at the time of the grant a gateway and an overhead bar which would have limited the size of vehicles having access to the auction room premises and prevented the entry of furniture vans or pantechnicons. Nevertheless, in the judge's view that did not restrict the scope of the grant. I do not myself think that that case is conclusive of the present case, because the terms of the grant in that case were very particular, though I think that it is of use in approaching the alternative contention (which, if I may say so, was certainly not Mr. Poole's favourite of the two contentions), namely, the small-vehicle right.

Perhaps it would be desirable to stress what I have said by quoting from the judgment in that case where the judge says: "I am unable to accept that submission. Here is a perfectly plain, unambiguous reservation for 'the vendor, his tenants and workmen' — I think that is important — 'to pass and repass with or without vehicles' — there is no limitation whatever upon the vehicles — 'over and along the land coloured brown' on the plan. Pausing there, in my judgment the true effect of those words, that there is a right of way over and along the land coloured brown, cannot be affected by the circumstance that at the date of the grant there was this gate and bar across. The words of the grant are plain and unambiguous, and in my judgment the plaintiff plainly has a right over the whole of the yard coloured brown, and not merely a right to enter through the gates some six feet in width. Not only that: he has a right to enter it with vehicles. That must mean vehicles of any size appropriate to go down the yard, and as the yard is at no stage, until the garage is reached, less than eleven feet wide, there seems to be no reason why a pantechnicon should not use that yard."

The part that I have quoted there shows that there were particular considerations in the language of the grant in the *Bulstrode* case which are absent from the present case; and for my part I would not have thought that the judge was necessarily bound, simply as a result of that decision, to conclude that in the present case there was more than a footpath. However, as I say, I differ in the end from the conclusion at which, but for the *Bulstrode* decision the judge would have arrived. . . .

I would remark that it is sometimes thought that the grant of a right of way in respect of every part of a defined area involves the proposition that the grantee can object to anything on any part of the area which would obstruct passage over that part. This is a wrong understanding of the law. Assuming a right of way of a particular quality over an area of land, it will extend to every part of that area, as a matter, at least, of theory. But a right of way is not a right absolutely to restrict user of the area by the owner thereof. The grantee of the right could only object to such activities of the owner of the land, including retention of obstruction, as substantially interfered with the use of the land in such exercise of the defined right as for the time being is reasonably required. (I am, of course, talking now about private rights of way.)

This proposition is exemplified by the decision of this court in *Dyer v Mousley*[1], where the dominant owner asserted the right to clear and level the whole of the strip dedicated to the right of way, at a time

---

[1] (1962) unreported transcript No. 315.

when there was no need to do so for the current requirements of the dominant tenant.

For those reasons, in my judgment, this appeal fails.

In *Jelbert v Davis* [1968] 1 WLR 589, [1968] 1 All ER 1182, the plaintiff, in a conveyance of agricultural land to him in 1961, was granted "a right of way at all times and for all purposes over the driveway retained by the vendor leading to the main road in common with all other persons having the like right". In 1966 he obtained planning permission to use part of the land as a tourist and caravan site for up to 200 caravans or tents. The defendants, two neighbouring landowners, objected to the proposed use of the driveway for caravan traffic and put up notices warning off caravans and campers. The plaintiff sued for nuisance and slander of title, and the defendants counterclaimed for an injunction to restrain the plaintiff from using the driveway for access to the caravan site. The Court of Appeal held that the plaintiff was entitled to use the driveway for caravans, but not so as to cause substantial interference with its use by the defendants: the user by 200 caravans was excessive. DANCKWERTS LJ said at p. 597: "On the authorities, it is plain that the easement so granted is in such wide terms that the use by the plaintiff of it for caravans is permissible; but it is an easement which on its terms is a right which is to be used 'in common with all other persons having the like right'. That includes the defendants. A use of the right of way which is so excessive that it renders the rights of such other persons practically impossible, therefore, is not justified. The difficulty is to fix the limit in respect of such use. The test must be whether the interference is so substantial as to interfere with the rights of other persons in an unreasonable manner. It cannot be right that the others should be swamped by the traffic created by the plaintiff so as to amount to a legal nuisance. It is impossible to quantify this in figures, particularly as the problem relates to the future. These people are neighbours and share the right of way and there must be give and take and accommodation. Time will show what is practicable, and in the interests of both parties a practical solution must be found or a deadlock will result."

In *St. Edmundsbury and Ipswich Diocesan Board of Finance v Clark (No. 2)* [1975] 1 WLR 468, [1975] 1 All ER 772 land, including the former rectory of St. Botolph's Church, Iken, in Suffolk, was sold and conveyed in 1945 by the church authorities to the defendant. It then wholly surrounded the church and churchyard. Access from the village to the church porch was by Church Lane (a narrow public highway) which then became a path 100 yards long leading to the church porch. The first third of the path ("the disputed strip") crossed the rectory grounds, and the remainder ("the church path") was within the churchyard and church property. The first 7 yards of the disputed strip could be used by vehicles for access from the lane to a driveway leading to the rectory. The remainder ("the chestnut path") was not wider than 4 feet 6 inches and was a derelict gravel and sandy path covered with leaves. At the end of the chestnut path on the defendant's land was a gate between two gateposts, standing no more than 4 feet apart. There was no evidence that the path was used by vehicles before 1946.

On 31 December 1945 the land was conveyed to the defendant "subject to a right of way over the land coloured red on the said plan to and from St. Botolph's Church". The question was whether the right of way reserved by the church authorities was a right exercisable on foot only, or with vehicles also.

The Court of Appeal, construing the language of the conveyance in the light of all the surrounding circumstances, decided that it was a right of footway only. In explaining the correct approach in these matters, Sir John PENNYCUICK, said, at p. 476: "What is the proper approach upon the construction of a conveyance containing the reservation of a right of way? We feel no doubt that the proper approach is that upon which the court construes all documents; that is to say, one must construe the document according to the natural meaning of the words contained in the document as a whole, read in the light of surrounding circumstances."

A similar approach is adopted in the identification of the dominant tenement. In *Johnstone v Holdway* [1963] 1 QB 601, [1963] 1 All ER 432, George Horace Johnstone agreed in 1936 to sell land to the Trewithin Estates Company, but no conveyance was executed. In 1948 Trewithin Estates Company sold part of the land to Henry Bosustow, whereupon Johnstone as trustee and the company as beneficial owner conveyed it to Bosustow. The conveyance excepted and reserved to the company and its successors in title "a right of way at all times and for all purposes (including quarrying)" over the land conveyed from a point on its north-western boundary to a point on its south-eastern boundary. The conveyance failed to specify any dominant tenement for the right of way, but it was meant to be the quarry, retained as part of their land by the company. The plaintiffs, as successors in title of the company, claimed a right of way against the successors in title of Bosustow.

In holding that the plaintiffs were entitled to a legal easement, UPJOHN LJ said, at p. 609: "Mr. Seward, for the defendant ... submits that it is essential to the valid creation of every easement that the dominant tenement must be defined in the deed itself and that no extrinsic evidence is admissible to define it .... But the question we have to determine is whether that is essential to the validity of the easement or whether it is permissible to identify the dominant tenement by inferences from facts and circumstances which must have been known to the parties at the time of the conveyance ....

In our judgment, it is a question of the construction of the deed creating a right of way as to what is the dominant tenement for the benefit of which the right of way is granted and to which the right of way is appurtenant. In construing the deed the court is entitled to have evidence of all material facts at the time of the execution of the deed, so as to place the court in the situation of the parties .... It seems to us perfectly plain that in this case the dominant tenement was the land and quarry².''

B. Easements Created by Implied Grant

As explained above the rules for the creation of easements by implied grant vary with the question whether or not the easement is claimed by the grantor or grantee.

Easements implied in favour of the grantor are limited to cases of necessity or to cases where the intention of the parties is clear³. Easements of necessity are strictly limited to the circumstances of the necessity.

In the case of easements implied in favour of the grantee — where they are "continuous and apparent", "necessary for the reasonable enjoyment of the property granted", or where the common intention of the parties was clear — there seems to be little authority on the question of the extent of the easement. If tested at the time of the conveyance, no difficulty arises, for the same rules as govern implication will govern extent. But difficulties may arise if the matter is tested at a time when circumstances have changed. If, for example, a narrow track is sufficient to establish that a right of way is "continuous and apparent" in a conveyance of 1880, will this cover travellers on foot, horseback, by car or by lorry? The cases on easements by express grant would suggest that the extent of the easement will develop as circumstances change and that limitations will only be imposed where such a restriction is clearly justified⁴.

C. Easements Acquired by Prescription

Easements acquired by prescription are dependent upon user and their content is limited by the user proved. Small adjustments are allowed. Whether a variation is a new form of user or an extended example of that proved may be a difficult question.

---

² See p. 523, ante. (1963) 79 LQR 182 (R.E.M.); *The Shannon Ltd v Venner Ltd* [1965] Ch 682, [1965] 1 All ER 590; *Bracewell v Appleby* [1975] Ch 408, [1975] 1 All ER 993; (1975) 39 Conv (NS) 277 (F. R. Crane); *Land Reclamation Co Ltd v Basildon District Council* [1979] 1 WLR 106 at 110; Compare the judgment of UPJOHN J in *Newton Abbot Co-operative Society Ltd v Williamson and Treadgold Ltd* [1952] Ch 286, [1952] 1 All ER 279.

³ *Corporation of London v Riggs* (1880) 13 ChD 798; p. 543, ante; *Nickerson v Barraclough* [1979] 3 WLR 562, [1979] 3 All ER 312; *Re Webb's Lease* [1951] Ch 808, [1951] 2 All ER 131; p. 545, ante.

⁴ See however, *Milner's Safe Co Ltd v Great Northern and City Rly Co* [1907] 1 Ch 208.

BRITISH RAILWAYS BOARD *v* GLASS
[1965] Ch 538, [1964] 3 All ER 418 (CA, Lord DENNING MR, HARMAN
and DAVIES LJJ)

In 1847 the Wilts, Somerset and Weymouth Railway, predecessors in
title to the plaintiffs, constructed a railway line near a farm owned by
X, the defendant's predecessor in title, and through a field also owned
by him but occupied by a tenant Y. They purchased part of this field,
and the conveyance contained the following proviso (inter alia): "Save
and except that the . . . company and their successors shall and will at
all times hereafter allow unto . . . my heirs and assigns at all times . . .
a right of crossing the . . . railway to the extent of twelve feet in width
on the level thereof with all manner of cattle to and from one part of
the land . . . to the other part . . . severed by the . . . railway." To
provide for this right of way, the company constructed a level
crossing. For many years prior to 1942 one of the fields near the
crossing, formerly owned by X and occupied by Z (called the 'blue land')
was used for campers and caravanners and in 1942 there were six
caravans established on the site. Since then the numbers had grown,
and the traffic of vehicles and people over the crossing substantially
increased. The plaintiffs brought this action to limit 'the user of the
crossing.

It was conceded that (i) the right of way was not limited to linking
the separated parts of the field previously occupied by Y, but linked
the farm occupied by Z (which included the 'blue land') with the
severed part of that field and with a highway beyond, and (ii) the way
was not limited to foot passengers or cattle, but extended to vehicles.

Two main questions arose:
  (i) Whether the grant of the right of way covered the traffic of the
      caravanners;
 (ii) Whether, if not covered by the grant, there was a prescriptive
      right for all the caravanners, the defendant admitting a
      prescriptive right since 1942 for 6 caravanners.

Held, (affirming UNGOED-THOMAS J; Lord DENNING MR,
dissenting)
  (i) The right of way was general and not limited to agricultural
      purposes in the contemplation of the parties to the conveyance;
 (ii) A prescriptive right had been acquired for the use of the crossing
      by the caravanners, the increase in number of caravanners since
      1942 not being an excessive user.

The construction of the express grant of the right of way was
influenced by the fact that the conveyance of 1847 was stated to be in
compensation for, inter alia, the right to have certain "accommodation
works" carried out by the railway company in pursuance of their
duties under the Railways Clauses Consolidation Act 1845, section 68.
It was argued that the right of way should not be more extensive than
the company's duty in respect of the "accommodation works", for it
was an exception to them, and should therefore be limited to
agricultural or domestic purposes and those in the contemplation

of the parties in 1847. The Court of Appeal (LORD DENNING MR, dissenting), as stated above, rejected this argument. The present extracts from the judgments are limited to the issue of prescription.

LORD DENNING MR, (dissenting: ... *The Prescriptive Right*. The defendant says that alternatively he obtained a right by prescription. The judge found that for 20 years before the action, from 1942 to 1962, there had been six caravans on the site permanently, but that there had been 10 or 11 there at times from 1942 to 1945 and thereafter, and increased to 28 or 29 immediately before the issue of the writ. It is clear that by prescription there is a right of way for six caravans. But is there a right for 28 or 29 caravans?

It is quite clear that, when you acquire a right of way by prescription, you are not entitled to change the character of your land so as substantially to increase or alter the burden upon the servient tenement. If you have a right of way for your pasture land, you cannot turn it into a manufactory and claim a right of way for the purposes of the factory. If you have a right of way by prescription for one house, you cannot build two more houses on the land and claim a right of way for the purposes of those houses also. I think this rule is not confined to the character of the property. It extends also to the intensity of the user. If you use your land for years as a caravan site for six caravans and thereby gain a prescriptive right over a level crossing, you are not thereby entitled to put 30 caravans on the site and claim a right for those 30. As Baggallay JA said in *Wimbledon and Putney Commons Conservators v Dixon* ((1875) 1 ChD 362 at p. 374), "You must neither increase the burden on the servient tenement nor substantially change the nature of the user." This seems to me good sense. It would be very wrong that, because the plaintiffs have been so tolerant as to allow the occupants of six caravans to use the crossing, in consequence they are thereby to be saddled with the use of 30 caravans. Trains would be obstructed and delayed. Dangers would abound. After all, prescription is a presumed grant. No such grant for 30 caravans could ever be presumed from user for six.

On this part of the case, counsel for the defendant made a technical point. He said that the defendant had a prescriptive right to a "caravan site" and so phrased it in his defence: and that in the reply the plaintiffs had admitted that the field had been used "as a caravan site" since 1938. He says that, by this admission, the plaintiffs are debarred from saying that the defendant had a prescriptive right only for six caravans, and that the defendant has a right for as many caravans as the site will hold. I regard this as special pleading of the worst description. The facts and issues before the court are plain enough: and no one has been in the least misled by this verbal nicety. I would decide this case on the facts found, and I hold that the defendant had no prescriptive right to use the crossing for more than six caravans.

We were told that the local authority have taken steps to deal with this caravan site. They have exercised their statutory powers to see that it is gradually removed. All the caravans should be gone by 1966.

That is satisfactory, in a way. But I do not see why the local authority should be forced to do this: or to pay compensation to the defendant. I think the plaintiffs are entitled to come to the court and ask for protection on their own account. I think they are entitled to restrain the defendant from putting this greatly increased burden on the crossing.

I would allow the appeal and grant a declaration and injunction as asked in the notice of appeal.

HARMAN LJ: It appeared from the evidence that before the last war there were three caravans and a tent dwelling permanently situated upon the "blue land", and that this number increased after the war began, when the Admiralty moved some of its departments to Bath, to six permanent caravans and five more that came and went, and there was a further increase in the spring of 1942 after the first bombs fell on Bath, and that after the war there were further increases from time to time until shortly before the writ was issued the number of caravans had increased to 29 and it was of this burden that the plaintiffs not unnaturally complained. All the caravanners and those who visited them, and their suppliers, had no access to the blue land save over the level crossing.

This part of the case has become largely academic because the local planning authority has, by exercise of its statutory powers, ordered the gradual clearance of the site from caravans. At the date of the hearing in the court below the number had been reduced to 16 and will be reduced to none by the end of the year 1966 or thereabouts. Nevertheless the judge considered the state of things when the writ was issued, and rightly so, and he came to the conclusion that the plaintiffs could not complain of the state of things as it then existed. He reached this conclusion upon the admissions appearing upon the face of the pleadings. The plaintiffs admitted that the "blue land" was used "as a caravan site", that is to say, the whole of the "blue land" and not merely such portions of it as had in fact been the standings of caravans. I understand that in fact there were no such permanent standings, but that caravans coming and going occupied any part of the field they chose. The prescriptive claim was not made in the right of individual caravans, which would have been a claim by individual caravanners, but by the defendant as the owner of the whole of the "blue land" and on the footing that it constituted "the caravan site". It may be regrettable that this part of the case should turn on a point of pleading, as this to some extent was, but I do not think the judge could have come to his conclusion upon any other footing. The fact is that this expression "caravan site" has only recently come into prominence, and it was not perhaps fully appreciated until the recent decision of this court in *Biss v Smallburgh RDC* ([1965] Ch 335, [1964] 2 All ER 543), that it ought not to be used in a loose way. In that case a large area, which varied at various stages of the action from 70-odd acres to three or four, was claimed as being a "caravan site", but the court came to the conclusion that there was no caravan site at all within the meaning of that phrase in the Caravan Sites and Control of Development Act 1960[5], that the mere casual placing of caravans here and there on a large area did not constitute that area a "caravan site". So here, if the plaintiffs had not admitted that the "blue land" constituted a "caravan site", the defendant might have been in great difficulty in defining the area of the site. He was relieved of that difficulty by the pleadings and his case was that, admitting the whole "blue land" to be "a caravan site", the mere increase from, say, 10 to 29 caravans did not constitute such an increase in the burden of the prescriptive right as was a legitimate subject of complaint by the plaintiffs. The leading case on this subject is *Williams v James* ((1867) LR 2 CP 577). The headnote reads: "The defendant being entitled by immemorial user to a right of way over the plaintiff's land from field N, used the way for the purpose of carting from field N some hay stacked there, which had been grown partly there and partly on land adjoining. The jury found in effect that the defendant in so doing had used the way bona fide, and for the ordinary and reasonable use of field N as a field: *Held*, that the mere fact that some of the hay had not been grown on field N did not make the carrying of it over the plaintiff's land an excess in the user of the right of way." Bovill CJ says this (ibid. p. 580): "In all cases of this kind which depend upon user the right acquired must be measured by the extent of the enjoyment which is proved. When a right of way to a piece of land is proved, then that is, unless something appears to the contrary, a right of way for all purposes according to the ordinary and reasonable use to which that land might be applied at the time of the supposed grant. Such a right cannot be increased so as to affect the servient tenement by imposing upon it any additional burthen. It is also clear, according to the authorities, that where a person has a right of way over one piece of land to another piece of land, he can only use such right in order to reach the latter place. He cannot use it for the purpose of going elsewhere." Willes J says this (ibid. p. 582): "I agree with the argument of Mr. Jelf that in cases like this, where a way has to be proved by user, you cannot extend the purposes for which the way may be used, or for which it might be reasonably inferred that parties would have intended it to be used. The land in this case was a field in the country, and apparently only used for rustic purposes. To be a legitimate user of the right of way, it must be used for the enjoyment of the nine acre field, and not colourably for other closes. I quite agree also with the argument that the right of way can only be used for the field in its ordinary use as a field. The right could not be used for a manufactory built upon the field. The use must be the reasonable use for the purposes of the land in the condition in which it was while the user took place."

Applying that to the present case, you must do what the judge did, namely, base your conclusion on a consideration of what must have

---

[5] See p. 823, post.

been the supposed contents of the lost grant on which the prescription rests. If this be supposed to be a grant of the right to use the "blue land" as "a caravan site", then it is clear that a mere increase in the numbers of the caravans using the site is not an excessive user of the right. A right to use a way for this purpose or that has never been to my knowledge limited to a right to use the way so many times a day or for such and such a number of vehicles so long as the dominant tenement does not change its identity. If there be a radical change in the character of the dominant tenement, then the prescriptive right will not extend to it in that condition. The obvious example is a change of a small dwelling-house to a large hotel, but there has been no change of that character according to the facts found in this case. The caravan site never became a highly organised town of caravans with fixed standings and roads and all the paraphernalia attendant on such a place and in my opinion the judge was right in holding that there had been no such increase in the burden of the easement as to justify the plaintiffs in seeking as they did by injunction to restrict the user to three caravans or six or to prevent its use as what in the statement of claim is called "a caravan camp or site".

I, accordingly, hold that the judge was right in both branches of the case and that the appeal should be dismissed.

DAVIES LJ: If any prescriptive right has been acquired, it has been acquired not by any one or more caravans but by the "blue land" as dominant tenement. And it is not easy to contemplate an express grant of a right of way in respect of a specified or limited number of caravans. The "blue land" is still being used as a caravan site. Its use as such has been intensified. But there has been no alteration in the nature of its use ... So here, once it is admitted, as it has been admitted, that the "blue land" as "a caravan site" acquired by prescription a right of way, it does not seem to me that the plaintiffs can prevent a mere increase in the number of caravans upon the site and the consequent increase in the use of the right of way. An increase in the number of caravans on the site is quite a different thing from the erection of a number of new houses, though no doubt from the point of view of the servient tenement the effect is somewhat similar.

(1965) 81 LQR, at p. 18 (R. E. Megarry).

"Two cases that were not cited provide a little assistance on the point. First, in *Lock v Abercester Ltd* [1939] Ch 861, [1939] 3 All ER 562, the dominant owners had to rely on user for the prescriptive period mainly for horse-drawn vehicles delivering goods to the dominant tenement, a house previously used as a rectory. Within the last few years these owners had begun to keep cows, pigs and chickens on the land held with the house, and motor-vehicles brought the food stuffs for these animals as well as other goods. Despite this additional burden on the way, Bennett J held that the way established by prescription was wide enough to cover this user. The main point of the case was, of course, the question whether user by horse-drawn vehicles authorised enjoyment by horseless vehicles; but the element of the recent increase in agricultural user was mentioned in the judgment.

Secondly, there is *Cowling v Higginson* (1838) 4 M & W 245. This raised the question of the validity of a claim to a right of way for all purposes where the user proved was for a variety of purposes though not for every conceivable purpose. If the right were to be measured by the *de facto* user, then such a claim would fail; for the right would be 'confined to the identical carriages that have previously been used upon the road, and would not warrant even the slightest alteration in the carriage or the loading, or the purpose for which it was used': *Cowling v Higginson* (1838) 4 M & W at 254, per Parke B. On this footing, there might be 'a right to carry corn and manure, though not coals' (ibid., at p. 253). And so it was laid down that 'If a way has been used for several purposes, there may be a ground for inferring that there is a right of way for all purposes' (ibid., at p. 256, per Lord Abinger CB). As Parke B said during the argument, if the dominant owners 'shew that they have used [the way] time out of mind, for all the purposes that they wanted, it would seem to me to give them a general right' (p. 252). If user for a limited number of purposes can be generalised into a right to use for all purposes, it would be remarkable if on a claim to use the way for one purpose only there were to be imposed a strict quantitative restriction to the amount of use for that purpose during the prescriptive period. In the end, the point seems to come down to the difference between quantity and quality. It may well be that a change in quantity may be so vast as to amount to a change in quality; but short of such extremities, the distinction seems valid."

In *Woodhouse & Co Ltd v Kirkland (Derby) Ltd* [1970] 1 WLR 1185, [1970] 2 All ER 587, PLOWMAN J held that a considerable increase in the number of customers using a right of way was "a mere increase in user and not a user of a different kind or for a different purpose".

In *Giles v County Building Contractors (Hertford) Ltd* (1971) 22 P & CR 978, BRIGHTMAN J referred to HARMAN LJ in *British Railways Board v Glass* ([1965] Ch 538 at 562, [1964] 3 All ER 418, p. 578, ante) and said, at p. 987: "The important expressions, to my mind, are 'change of identity' and 'radical change in character'. In my view, the use of the convent site for the erection of seven modern dwelling units in place of the two existing houses, cannot properly be described as 'changing the identity' or 'radically changing the character' of the convent site. I think it is evolution rather than mutation."

QUESTION

A landlord granted to his tenant a right of way "at all times and for all purposes" over a roadway leading to the tenant's factory. The landlord then started to build over the roadway and planned to construct a long bridge or tunnel through which the tenant could have access to the factory. Although this would not affect the roadway itself, the freedom of manoeuvre, during loading and unloading from the tenant's vehicles, would be restricted, both vertically and laterally. Is the tenant entitled to an injunction to restrain the landlord from building in such a way as to restrict his freedom to load and unload as he had been accustomed to do? See *VT Engineering Ltd v Richard Barland & Co Ltd* (1968) 19 P & CR 890; *Hayns v Secretary of State for the Environment* (1977) 36 P & CR 317.

V.   Easement of Light[6]

PRESCRIPTION ACT 1832

3.   Claim to the use of light enjoyed for 20 years. — When the access and use of light to and for any dwelling house, workshop, or other building[7] shall have been actually enjoyed therewith for the full period of twenty years without interruption, the right thereto shall be deemed absolute and indefeasible, any local usage or custom to the contrary notwithstanding, unless it shall appear that the same was enjoyed by some consent or agreement expressly made or given for that purpose by deed or writing.

COLLS *v* HOME AND COLONIAL STORES LTD
[1904] AC 179 (HL, Earl of HALSBURY LC, Lords MACNAGHTEN, DAVEY, ROBERTSON and LINDLEY)

The Home and Colonial Stores were the lessees of a building in Shoreditch where they carried on their business. They brought an action for an injunction against Colls to restrain him from building on the opposite side of the road. JOYCE J found as a fact that, even after the erection of the building, the Home and Colonial Stores premises would be "well and sufficiently lighted for all ordinary purposes of occupancy as a place of business". JOYCE J refused an injunction and was reversed by the Court of Appeal.

Held, (reversing the Court of Appeal). Injunction refused.

LORD LINDLEY: The language of section 3 of the Prescription Act shews that in order to acquire a right to a light there must be — (1) Access and use of light, not access alone. Access here is understood to refer to free passage of light over the servient tenement (see per

---

[6] Cheshire, pp. 551–553; M & W, pp. 861–865, 875–878; MM, pp. 415–416, 422–423; Gale, pp. 147–152, 238–255; Jackson pp. 133–137, 156–166.
[7] *Allen v Greenwood* [1979] 2 WLR 187, [1979] 1 All ER 819, p. 585, post (green house).

Fry LJ, in *Scott v Pape* (1886) 31 ChD at 575, and per Kay J, in *Cooper v Straker* (1888) 40 ChD 26). (2) Such access and use must be to and for some dwelling-house, workshop, or other building (as to which see *Harris v De Pinna* ((1886) 33 ChD 238). (3) Such access and use must be actually enjoyed therewith. (4) Such enjoyment must be without interruption for twenty years. (5) If all these are proved, the right to the access and use of light so enjoyed becomes absolute and indefeasible, unless it can be explained by some deed or writing.

Pausing here for a moment, it will be observed that the statute does not in terms confer a right to light, but rather assumes its acquisition by use and enjoyment, and declares it to be "absolute and indefeasible".

Again, your Lordships will observe that nothing is said about enjoyment as of right; and notwithstanding section 5 of the Act, which refers to enjoyment as of right, it was early decided that as regards light claimed under section 3 enjoyment as of right need not be alleged or proved, and that the right, whatever it may be, is acquired by twenty years' use and enjoyment without interruption and without written consent: see *Truscott v Merchant Taylors' Co* ((1856) 11 Exch 855) and *Frewen v Phillips* ((1861) 11 CBNS 449); *Simper v Foley* ((1862) 2 John & H 555) and *Harbidge v Warwick* ((1849) 3 Exch 557). This was not so under the old law.

As regards use and enjoyment, there are some instructive decisions on unfinished and uninhabited houses, and on windows kept closed by shutters. These decisions shew·that a right to light may be acquired in respect of a house which has stood for twenty years without being occupied or even finished so as to be fit for occupation; and that the fact that shutters have been closed for some months at a time does not prevent the acquisition of a right to light through the windows: see *Courtauld v Legh* ((1869) LR 4 Exch 126); *Cooper v Straker* ((1888) 40 ChD 21); *Collis v Laugher* ([1894] 3 Ch 659); *Smith v Baxter* ([1900] 2 Ch 138).

These decisions did not, however, turn upon or settle with any precision the amount of light to which a right is acquired by twenty years' user. Nor is the statute clear upon this point. . . .

The doctrine laid down in *Back v Stacey* ((1826) 2 C & P 465), as I understand it, is the same as that laid down, although in somewhat different language, by the Court of Appeal in *Kelk v Pearson* ((1871) 6 Ch App 809) and *City of London Brewery Co v Tennant* ((1873) 9 Ch App 212), and must, I think, be taken as finally established and as good sound law, which your Lordships should adopt, notwithstanding the observations in the Irish case of *Mackey v Scottish Widows' Fund Assurance Society* ((1877) IR 11 Eq 541). That doctrine, as stated in *City of London Brewery Co v Tennant*, is that generally speaking an owner of ancient lights is entitled to sufficient light according to the ordinary notions of mankind for the comfortable use and enjoyment of his house as a dwelling-house, if it is a dwelling-house, or for the beneficial use and occupation of the house if it is a warehouse, a shop, or other place of business ((1873) 9 Ch App at 217). The expressions "the ordinary notions of mankind", "comfortable use and enjoyment", and "beneficial use and occupation" introduce elements of uncertainty; but similar uncertainty has always existed and exists still in all cases of nuisance, and in this country an obstruction of light has commonly been regarded as a nuisance, although the right to light has been regarded as a peculiar kind of easement. . . .

The expression "right to light" is sanctioned by the Prescription Act, and is convenient; but its use is apt to lead to error and to forgetfulness of the burden thrown on the servient tenement. This burden, however, ought never to be lost sight of in considering the extent of the right claimed in respect of the dominant tenement.

But the adoption of the more flexible standard of comfort and convenience has introduced difficulties of a serious nature, especially when dealing with places of business, and it is not surprising that different views on this subject should have been taken, and that the decisions upon it should be inconsistent with each other. . . .

There is no rule of law that if a person has 45 degrees of unobstructed light through a particular window left to him he cannot maintain an action for a nuisance caused by diminishing the light which formerly came through that window: *Theed v Debenham* ((1876) 2 ChD 165)[8]. But experience shews that it is, generally speaking, a fair working rule to consider that no substantial injury is done to him where an angle of 45 degrees is left to him, especially if there is good light from other directions as well. The late Lord Justice Cotton pointed this out in *Ecclesiastical Commissioners for England v Kino* ((1880) 14 ChD 213 at 228); see also *Parker v First Avenue Hotel Co* ((1883) 24 ChD 282).

As regards light from other quarters, such light cannot be disregarded; for, as pointed out by James V-C, in the *Dyer's Co v King* ((1870) LR 9 Eq 438), the light from other quarters, and the light the obstruction of which is complained of, may be so much in excess of what is protected by law as to render the interference complained of non-actionable. I apprehend, however, that light to which a right has not been acquired by grant or prescription, and of which the plaintiff may be deprived at any time, ought not to be taken into account. (See the case just cited.)

The purpose for which a person may desire to use a particular room or building in future does not either enlarge or diminish the easement which he has acquired. If he chooses in future to use a well-lighted room or building for a lumber-room for which little light is required, he does not lose his right to use the same room or building for some other purpose for which more light is required. *Aynsley v Glover* ((1875) 10 Ch App 283) is in accordance with this view. But if a room or building has been so built as to be badly lighted, the owner or occupier cannot by enlarging the windows or altering the purpose for which he uses it increase the burden on the servient tenement. *Martin v Goble* ((1808) 1

---

[8] Nor is there a rule of law that if half a room at table height is receiving one or more lumens the room as a whole is adequately lit: *Ough v King* [1967] 1 WLR 1547, [1967] 3 All ER 859.

Camp 320), where a malthouse was turned into a workhouse, may, I think, be upheld on this principle; and the observations of Wood V-C, on *Martin v Goble* in *Dent v Auction Mart Co* ((1866) LR 2 Eq 238) support this view. . . .

Joyce J, was asked for an injunction and he refused it, and, in my opinion, quite rightly. He came to the conclusion that although there would be a sensible diminution of light and some inconvenience to the plaintiffs, yet they had not established by twenty years' user a right to all the light which they had had, and that the obstruction complained of would not amount to an actionable nuisance, and so infringe the plaintiffs' right. The Court of Appeal, taking a different view of the amount of light to which the plaintiffs were entitled, reversed this decision, and ordered a partial demolition of the buildings erected by the defendants. For the reasons already given, I have come to the conclusion that this was wrong.

In *Allen v Greenwood* [1979] 2 WLR 187, [1979] 1 All ER 819[8a], the plaintiffs were the owners of 13 Woodtop Avenue, Rochdale, in which there was a greenhouse. After the greenhouse had been in use as an ordinary domestic greenhouse for more than 20 years, the defendants erected a fence on their adjoining property. This left sufficient light in the greenhouse for working in it, but insufficient for growing plants ("tomato, geraniums, stocks, antirrhinums, marigolds, zinnias, violets, pansies, the red ones that are rather tender"). The plaintiffs brought an action for injunctions to restrain the defendants from causing a nuisance by diminution of the access of light to the greenhouse.

In granting the injunctions, the Court of Appeal (BUCKLEY, ORR and GOFF LJJ) held that the light required for the normal use of a greenhouse is ordinary, and also that a right to a specially high degree of light may be acquired by prescription. The Court rejected "an overriding argument" that "in any event one can only prescribe a right to light, whether ordinary or special in degree, for purposes of illumination, not a right to the direct rays of the sun, or to heat, or to other beneficial properties from the sun's rays. GOFF LJ said at p. 196:

"In my judgment, therefore, the crux of this case at the end of the day is the overriding argument, which I must now consider.

The defendants argue on this as follows. (1) In *Colls'* case [1904] AC 179 the House of Lords was seeking to limit, or restrict, the extent of the right to light, so as to prevent undue restrictions on the development or improvement of surrounding land or buildings, and the court should be very chary of any extension of the right. (2) Although the standards prescribed by the speeches in *Colls'* case are expressed in terms susceptible of a wider interpretation, in their context they must be taken as referring to illumination only. (3) In all cases, at least since *Colls*, the right to light has been tested or measured in terms of illumination only. They refer, for example, to Mr. Waldram's

---

[8a] [1979] Conv 298 (F.R. Crane).

calculations and the theory of the 'grumble point:' see *Charles Semon & Co Ltd v Bradford Corpn* [1922] 2 Ch 737, 746–747, and to *Hortons' Estate Ltd v James Beattie Ltd* [1927] 1 Ch 75, where the question was whether the extent of the right to light should vary according to locality, and Russell J said, at p. 78: 'The human eye requires as much light for comfortable reading and sewing in Darlington Street, Wolverhampton, as in Mayfair.' Mr. Maddocks on the defendants' behalf, in his supporting argument, referred also to *Warren v Brown* [1900] 2 QB 722, 725, where the test was stated to be 'all ordinary purposes of inhabitancy or business,' and to the test applied by the Court of Appeal in *Ough v King* [1967] 1 WLR 1547, ordinary notions of contemporary mankind. These, however, I think, are at best neutral and possibly tell the other way, since a greenhouse is perfectly normal and ordinary in private gardens. . . . (6) In reality or in substance the injury here is not deprivation of light, but of heat or other energising properties of the sun and it is the plant life and not the human beings who are deprived.

I do not think this last point is in any case wholly accurate, as plants need light as well as heat, but it seems to me, with all respect to Blackett-Ord V-C and to counsel, to lead to an absurd conclusion. It cannot, I think, be right to say that there is no nuisance because one can see to go in and out of a greenhouse and to pot plants which will not flourish, and to pick fruit which cannot properly be developed and ripened, still less because one can see to read a book.

The plaintiffs answer all this simply by submitting that they are entitled, by virtue of their prescriptive right to light, to all the benefits of the light, including the rays of the sun. Warmth, they say, is an inseparable product of daylight, and they stress the absurd conclusion which I have already mentioned, to which the contrary argument inevitably leads. This reply commends itself to me, and I adopt it.

So the overriding argument, in my judgment, does not prevail, and for the reasons I have already given the plaintiffs are right, both on their primary and their alternative case, and I would allow this appeal. . . .

I desire, however, to add one important safeguarding proviso to this judgment. On other facts, particularly where one has solar heating (although that may not arise for some years) it may be possible and right to separate the heat, or some other property of the sun, from its light, and in such a case a different result might be reached. I leave that entirely open for decision when it arises. My judgment in this case is based upon the fact that this was a perfectly ordinary greenhouse, being used in a perfectly normal and ordinary manner, which user has, by the defendants' acts, been rendered substantially less beneficial than it was throughout the period of upwards of 20 years before action brought, and if necessary upon the fact that all this was known to the defendants and their predecessors for the whole of the relevant time."

In *Morgan v Fear* [1907] AC 425, it was held that a tenant could, by 20 years enjoyment of access to light from neighbouring land in the occupation of another tenant of the same landlord, prescribe for an easement of light under section 3. The House of Lords relied upon established authority. Lord LOREBURN LC, said at p. 428:

"The question . . . is whether a right can be acquired by a termor over land held by another termor under the same reversion, by virtue of section 3 of the Prescription Act. This has been decided in the affirmative as long ago as 1861, in *Frewen v Phillips* ((1861) 11 CB NS 449), and the same view was expressly indicated in *Mitchell v Cantrill* ((1887) 37 ChD 56). I think it is accurate to say that that rule of law has been acted upon for forty-six years. I cannot advise your Lordships to disturb so well settled a rule."

Prescription is in favour of the fee simple owner, and even in the case of an easement of light, there cannot be prescription in favour of a leaseholder[9].

QUESTION

Why can prescription not operate in favour of a leasehold estate? Compare:

Morgan v Fear [1907] AC 425;

Kilgour v Gaddes [1904] 1 KB 457, p. 555, ante;

Wheaton v Maple & Co [1893] 3 Ch 48, p. 556, ante.

RIGHTS OF LIGHT ACT 1959[10]

2. Registration of notice in lieu of obstruction of access of light. — (1) For the purpose of preventing the access and use of light from being taken to be enjoyed without interruption, any person who is an owner of land (in this and the next following section referred to as "the servient land") over which light passes to a dwelling-house, workshop or other building (in this and the next following section referred to as "the dominant building") may apply to the local authority in whose area the dominant building is situated for the registration of a notice under this section[11].

3. Effect of registered notice and proceedings relating thereto. — (1) Where, in pursuance of an application made in accordance with the last preceding section, a notice is registered thereunder, then, for the

---

[9] *Wheaton v Maple & Co* [1893] 3 Ch 48.

[10] This section is based on recommendations in the Report of the Committee on Rights of Light (1958; Cmnd 473); 1959 CLJ 182 (H. W. R. Wade). See *Hawker v Tomalin* (1969) 20 P & CR 550, at 551, per HARMAN LJ.

[11] Lands Tribunal Rules 1975 (S. I. 1975 No. 299); Local Land Charges Rules 1977 (S. I. 1977 No. 985). The application must be accompanied by a certificate from the Lands Tribunal. From 1959–1977, 842 definitive certificates were issued; see (1978) 122 Sol. Jo. 515, 534 (W. A. Greene).

purpose of determining whether any person is entitled (by virtue of the Prescription Act, 1832, or otherwise) to a right to the access of light to the dominant building across the servient land, the access of light to that building across that land shall be treated as obstructed to the same extent, and with the like consequences, as if an opaque structure, of the dimensions specified in the application, —

    (*a*) had, on the date of registration of the notice, been erected in the position on the servient land specified in the application, and had been so erected by the person who made the application, and

    (*b*) had remained in that position during the period for which the notice has effect and had been removed at the end of that period.

(2) For the purposes of this section a notice registered under the last preceding section shall be taken to have effect until either —

    (*a*) the registration is cancelled, or

    (*b*) the period of one year beginning with the date of registration of the notice expires, or

    (*c*) [the expiry of the period specified under a special procedure where the case is one of exceptional urgency,]

and shall cease to have effect on the occurrence of any one of those events.

(3) Subject to the following provisions of this section, any person who, if such a structure as is mentioned in subsection (1) of this section had been erected as therein mentioned, would have had a right of action in any court in respect of that structure, on the grounds that he was entitled to a right to the access of light to the dominant building across the servient land, and that the said right was infringed by that structure, shall have the like right of action in that court in respect of the registration of a notice under the last preceding section:

Provided that an action shall not be begun by virtue of this subsection after the notice in question has ceased to have effect.

(4) Where, at any time during the period for which a notice registered under the last preceding section has effect, the circumstances are such that, if the access of light to the dominant building had been enjoyed continuously from a date one year earlier than the date on which the enjoyment thereof in fact began, a person would have had a right of action in any court by virtue of the last preceding subsection in respect of the registration of the notice, that person shall have the like right of action in that court by virtue of this subsection in respect of the registration of the notice.

(6) For the purposes of section four of the Prescription Act, 1832 (under which a period of enjoyment of any of the rights to which that Act applies is not to be treated as interrupted except by a matter submitted to or acquiesced in for one year after notice thereof) —

    (*a*) as from the date of registration of a notice under the last preceding section, all persons interested in the dominant building or any part thereof shall be deemed to have notice of the registration thereof and of the person on whose application it was registered;

(b) until such time as an action is brought by virtue of subsection (3) or subsection (4) of this section in respect of the registration of a notice under the last preceding section, all persons interested in the dominant building or any part thereof shall be deemed to acquiesce in the obstruction which, in accordance with subsection (1) of this section, is to be treated as resulting from the registration of the notice;

(c) as from the date on which such an action is brought, no person shall be treated as submitting to or acquiescing in that obstruction:

Provided that if, in any such action, the court decides against the claim of the plaintiff, the court may direct that the preceding provisions of this subsection shall apply in relation to the notice as if that action had not been brought.

VI. Extinguishment[12]

Easements and profits may be extinguished by statute (e.g. under an Inclosure Act or as a result of failure to register under the Commons Registration Act 1965)[13], by release, express or implied, and by unity of both ownership and possession.

A. Implied Release

In *Tehidy Minerals Ltd v Norman* [1971] 2 QB 528, [1971] 2 All ER 475, BUCKLEY LJ said at p. 553: "Abandonment of an easement or of a profit à prendre can only, we think, be treated as having taken place where the person entitled to it has demonstrated a fixed intention never at any time thereafter to assert the right himself or to attempt to transmit it to anyone else."

MOORE *v* RAWSON[14]
(1824) 3 B & C 332 (Ct of KB, ABBOTT CJ, BAYLEY, HOLROYD and LITTLEDALE JJ)

The plaintiff's predecessor in title enjoyed easements of light and air in respect of certain windows in a wall of his house. He pulled down this wall and built another wall without any windows. Fourteen years later

---

[12] Cheshire, pp. 555–558, 568–571; M & W, pp. 867–872; MM, pp. 417–420; Gale, pp. 309–347; Jackson, pp. 195–200.

[13] S. 1 (2) p. 53 ante.

[14] *Crossley & Sons Ltd v Lightowler* (1867) 2 Ch App 478; *Cook v Bath Corporation* (1868) LR 6 Eq 177; *Ecclesiastical Commissioners for England v Kino* (1880) 14 ChD 213; *Swan v Sinclair* [1924] 1 Ch 254; affd [1925] AC 227; *Re Yateley Common, Hampshire* [1977] 1 WLR 840, [1977] 1 All ER 505.

the defendant erected a building opposite to the plaintiff's blank wall. After another three years the plaintiff opened a window in the blank wall in the place of one of the old windows, and then brought an action for obstruction.

Held. The plaintiff failed, because he had abandoned his rights.

HOLROYD J: I am of the same opinion. It appears that the former owner of the plaintiff's premises at one time was entitled to the house with the windows, so that the light coming to those windows over the adjoining land could not be obstructed by the owner of that land. I think, however, that the right acquired by the enjoyment of the light, continued no longer than the existence of the thing itself in respect of which the party had the right of enjoyment; I mean the house with the windows; when the house and the windows were destroyed by his own act, the right which he had in respect of them was also extinguished. If, indeed, at the time when he pulled the house down, he had intimated his intention of rebuilding it, the right would not then have been destroyed with the house. If he had done some act to shew that he intended to build another in its place, then the new house, when built, would in effect have been a continuation of the old house, and the rights attached to the old house would have continued. If a man has a right of common attached to his mill, or right of turbary attached to his house, if he pulls down the mill or the house, the right of common or of turbary will prima facie cease. If he shew an intention to build another mill or another house, his right continues. But if he pulls down the house or the mill without shewing any intention to make a similar use of the land, and after a long period of time has elapsed, builds a house or mill corresponding to that which he pulls down, that is not the renovation of the old house or mill, but the creation of a new thing, and the rights which he had in respect of the old house or mill, do not in my opinion attach to the new one. In this case, I think, the building of a blank wall is a stronger circumstance to shew that he had no intention to continue the enjoyment of his light than if he had merely pulled down the house. In that case he might have intended to substitute something in its place. Here, he does in fact substitute quite a different thing, a wall without windows. There is not only nothing to shew that he meant to renovate the house so as to make it a continuance of the old house, but he actually builds a new house different from the old one, thereby shewing that he did not mean to renovate the old house. It seems to me, therefore, that the right is not renewed as it would have been, if, when he pulled down the old house, he had shewn an intention to rebuild it within a reasonable time, although he did not do so eo instanti.

B. Unity of Ownership and Possession

Unity of both ownership and possession may cause extinguishment[15]. "An unity of possession merely suspends; there must be an unity of

---

[15] *Buckley v Coles* (1814) 5 Taunt 311 (easement); *Tyrringham's Case* (1584) 4 Co Rep 36b at 38a (profit).

ownership to destroy a prescriptive right"[16]. Similarly unity of ownership without unity of possession does not suffice; the easement continues until there is also unity of possession[17]. If an easement is extinguished, it may nevertheless be re-created under the doctrine of *Wheeldon v Burrows*[18] if the land is later severed into its original parts.

In *Richardson v Graham* [1908] 1 KB 39 BUCKLEY LJ said at p. 44[19]: "On 29 March 1906, the plaintiffs were entitled to a leasehold interest for a term of years in the dominant tenement. The reversion in the dominant tenement was in one Eadie. The dominant tenement enjoyed over the servient tenement which was vested in the defendant a prescriptive right to ancient light acquired by user for more than twenty years. On 29 March 1906, Eadie conveyed to the defendant the reversion in the dominant tenement. It is said that the effect of that conveyance was to destroy the easement of ancient light; that is to say, that by acts done by the plaintiff's lessor and by the owner of the servient tenement the rights enjoyed by the plaintiffs were destroyed.

In my opinion that is not the law. . . . So that it is perfectly plain on the authorities that if in this case the two tenements had belonged throughout, not to different owners, but to one owner, but the circumstances were such that a lessee of the dominant tenement had acquired a prescriptive right against the servient tenement, the right would have been good as against all the world. It is said, however, that this case is different because there was not a common owner of the dominant and servient tenement during the whole period, but common ownership of the two tenements arose after the right to light had been acquired. This seems to me an extravagant proposition."

VII. Registered Land[20]

Legal easements are among the list of overriding interests but they may nevertheless appear in the property register of the dominant land. A note should also appear on the register of the servient land.

"Equitable easements are not overriding interests. An example is an agreement to grant a right of way over a road until it is adopted by the local authority. They do not bind a purchaser for value of the legal estate in the servient tenement without notice of them. Equitable easements, therefore, require the protection of notice entered on the register at the instance of the dominant proprietor with the consent of

---

[16] *Canham v Fish* (1831) 2 Cn & J 126, per BAYLEY B.
[17] *Richardson v Graham* [1908] 1 KB 39.
[18] But not under LPA 1925 s. 62, since there would be no diversity of occupation; p. 536, ante.
[19] This was a case on the easement of light, but, in principle, the rule should apply generally. Cf. *Buckley v Coles*, supra, at 315, 316; M & W, p. 872, n. 35.
[20] Cheshire, pp. 586–589; M & W, pp. 1065, 1078–1079; MM, p. 521; Registered Land Practice Notes (1972) pp. 22–24.

the servient proprietor. If he will not concur, a caution against dealings should be registered[1]."

LAND REGISTRATION RULES 1925

257. Positive registration. — The benefit of an easement, right, or privilege shall not be entered on the register except as appurtenant to a registered estate, and then only if capable of subsisting as a legal estate.

252. Application for entry of appurtenant right on register. — (1) Where the proprietor wishes (whether on first registration or at any other time) to have a specific entry on the register of any appurtenant right, capable of subsisting as a legal estate, to which he may be entitled, he may apply to the Registrar in writing, signed by himself or his solicitor, for such an entry to be made.

254. Entry of appurtenant right and its effect. — (1) If the Registrar is satisfied that the right is capable of subsisting as a legal estate and appurtenant to the land, he may enter it as part of the description of the land in the Property Register, and the effect of such entry shall be to confer an absolute, good leasehold, qualified or possessory title to the right, according to the nature of the title to the land.

(2) If the Registrar is not satisfied that the right is appurtenant, he shall enter it with such qualification as he may deem advisable, or he may merely enter notice of the fact that the proprietor claims it.

251. Registration vests appurtenances. — The registration of a person as proprietor of land shall vest in him, together with the land, all rights, privileges, and appurtenances appertaining or reputed to appertain to the land or any part thereof, or, at the time of registration, demised, occupied, or enjoyed therewith, or reputed or known as part or parcel of, or appurtenant to the land or any part thereof, including the appropriate rights and interests which, had there been a conveyance of the land or manor, would under section 62 of the Law of Property Act, 1925[2], have passed therewith[3].

LAND REGISTRATION ACT 1925

70. Liability of registered land to overriding interests. — 1 (*a*) p. 111, ante.

(2) Where at the time of first registration any easement, right, privilege, or benefit created by an instrument and appearing on the

---

[1] Ruoff, p. 43; Ruoff and Roper, p. 97; W & C, vi, p. 64; Barnsley, *Conveyancing Law and Practice* (1973), pp. 43–44; Farrand (2nd edn.), pp. 188–190; Hayton, *Registered Land* (2nd edn., 1977), pp. 86–88; Jackson pp. 44–45; *Poster v Slough Estates Ltd* [1969] 1 Ch 495 at 507, [1968] 3 All ER 257, per CROSS LJ; *Payne v Adnams* [1971] CLY 6486.

[2] P. 530, ante.

[3] See L.R.A. 1925, s. 19 (3), p. 93, ante; s. 22 (3), p. 429, ante.

title adversely affects the land, the registrar shall enter a note thereof on the register.

LAND REGISTRATION RULES 1925

41. Adverse easements. — (1) Notice of an easement, right, or privilege created by an instrument and operating at law which appears to the Registrar to affect adversely the land shall, if the Registrar thinks fit, be entered in the register.

258. Adverse easements treated as overriding interests. — P. 112, ante.

LAND REGISTRATION ACT 1925

72. Appurtenances. — If before the registration of any freehold or leasehold interest in land with an absolute or good leasehold title any easement, right, or privilege has been acquired for the benefit thereof, then, on such registration, the easement, right, or privilege shall, subject to any entry to the contrary on the register, become appurtenant to the registered land in like manner as if it had been granted to the proprietor who is registered as aforesaid.

LAND REGISTRATION RULES 1925

250. Acquisition of adverse easements by prescription. — (1) . . . easements, rights and privileges adversely affecting registered land may be acquired in equity by prescription in the same manner and to the same extent as if the land were not registered.

(2) If any easement, right, or privilege so acquired is of such estate and nature as is capable of taking effect at law it shall take effect at law also, and in that case —

  (a) if it is an overriding interest, notice of it may be entered on the register if the Registrar thinks fit under subsection (3) of section 70 of the Act[4].

In *Re Dances Way, West Town, Hayling Island* [1962] Ch 490, [1962] 2 All ER 42; DIPLOCK LJ said at p. 508: "Section 70 (2) . . . is a mandatory requirement and is not in my view qualified by rule 41 which deals with easements, rights or privileges created by an instrument, without being restricted to those which appear on the title. These shall, but only if the registrar thinks fit, be entered in the register. It seems to me that the *discretionary* power to enter easements created by an instrument is limited to those which do not appear on the title; where they do appear on the title, it is a mandatory duty under section 70 (2) to enter them. That means that the registrar,

---

[4] P. 112, ante.

when the documents of title are submitted to him, must determine whether an instrument included among them and so appearing on the title does create an easement adversely affecting the land. That is a question of construction, and the material before him at the time that he makes the first entry will include only the documents of title and will not include evidence of surrounding circumstances which it is permissible to take into consideration in determining the question of construction. If the registrar, because of the absence of such evidence or for any other reason, misconstrues the document and so enters a note of an easement which was not created by an instrument and appearing on the title, it seems to me that there is then an error or a mistake in an entry, and section 82 (1) (*h*)[5] applies to that situation and entitles the registrar to rectify the error.''

VIII.   Law Reform Committee Report on Acquisition of Easements and Profits by Prescription (1966 Cmnd. 3100)[6]

There has been recent judicial criticism of the law relating to the acquisition of easements and profits by prescription. In *Tehidy Minerals Ltd v Norman* [1971] 2 QB 528, [1971] 2 All ER 475, BUCKLEY LJ said at p. 543: "The co-existence of three separate methods of prescribing is, in our view, anomalous and undesirable, for it results in much unnecessary complication and confusion. We hope that it may be possible for the Legislature to effect a long-overdue simplication in this branch of the law."

In 1966, the Law Reform Committee recommended the abolition of the prescriptive acquisition of easements (para. 32) and of profits à prendre (para. 98); in the former case by a majority of 8–6; in the latter unanimously.

The Committee, however, considered the ways in which prescriptive acquisition — if it should be retained for easements — should operate, and was unanimous on the new system which should be adopted.

The main recommendations, in brief outline, are:

(1) All existing methods of acquisition of easements and profits by prescription should be abolished. This recommendation includes the

---

[5] P. 138, ante.
[6] (1967) 30 MLR 189 (H. W. Wilkinson). The Law Commission will be publishing a series of reports over the next few years recommending changes in the law relating to easements, covenants (both negative and positive) and prescription. The first report will deal with covenants; (Law Com No. 78. Eleventh Annual Report 1975–1976, para. 17; Law Com No. 92. Thirteenth Annual Report 1977–1978, para. 2.30). A Working Paper (1971 No. 36) suggests that "easements and covenants should be assimilated along lines hitherto regarded as appropriate to easements" (para. 9); and, in relation to prescription, "as at present advised we are inclined to agree in principle with the majority, but only on the basis that some alternative to prescription can be found. In the meantime it will be assumed that prescription will continue" (para. 99). It should be reformed along the lines recommended by the Law Reform Committee. (Proposition 10.).

abolition of prescription at common law and under the doctrine of a lost modern grant, and the repeal of the Prescription Act 1832 (paras. 40, 98, 99 (1)–(3)).

(2) Under the new system (for easements only) (para. 99 (6)):

(*a*) The prescriptive period should be a period in gross of 12 years (*i.e.*, it need not be "next before action brought"), (paras. 41–43: Prescription Act 1832, section 4: *Hyman v Van den Bergh* [1908] 1 Ch 167, p. 564, ante).

(*b*) There should be no "disabilities" (para. 44: Prescription Act 1832, sections 7, 8: p. 561, ante).

(*c*) An easement should be capable of being acquired against the owner of a limited interest in the servient land so as to subsist as long as that servient owner's interest subsists (paras. 47–49: pp. 556, 587, ante). Prescription by the owner of a limited interest in the dominant land should continue, as at present, in favour of the freeholder (para. 50). A tenant should be able to prescribe against his landlord and vice-versa (para. 51).

(*d*) Enjoyment:

(i) by force should not count in favour of the dominant owner (para. 57);

(ii) must have been actually known to the servient owner or ought reasonably to have been known to him (para. 58);

(iii) must be of such a kind and frequency as would only be justified by the existence of an easement (para. 59);

(iv) by consent or agreement should not count. If so enjoyed for one year or more, the consent, like an interruption, would prevent earlier enjoyment being added to later enjoyment for the purpose of making up the required total of 12 years. A consent which is indefinite in duration should operate for one year (paras. 61–63).

(*e*) Notional interruption, on the lines of the Rights of Light Act 1959 (p. 587, ante), should be extended to easements generally: this should be by registration after notice given. Interruption, notional or actual, should endure for 12 months in order to be effective (as at present: Prescription Act 1832, section 4). (para. 75).

(*f*) An easement, acquired by prescription, should be lost by 12 years continuous non-user (para. 81).

(3) The Committee is unanimous about provisions to facilitate, subject to compensation where appropriate, the acquisition of easements of support for buildings by land or for buildings by buildings (paras. 89–95, 99 (8)–(11)).

(4) Shelter should be treated in the same way as support (paras. 96, 99 (12): *Phipps v Pears* [1965] 1 QB 76, [1964] 2 All ER 35, p. 516, ante).

(5) The Lands Tribunal should be empowered to discharge easements or substitute more convenient ones, subject to payment of compensation where appropriate (paras. 97, 99 (13)).

QUESTIONS

1. Consider the arguments for and against the abolition of the acquisition of easements and profits à prendre by prescription. How is the matter affected by the extension of the practice of Registration of Title to land? See the Report, paras. 30–38.
2. "We do not consider that it is necessary or appropriate for the same legal rules to apply to the acquisition of easements by prolonged enjoyment as apply to the acquisition of title to land by adverse possession". (Para. 36.)

    "In spite of the differences between adverse possession and prescription, the same fundamental considerations apply to them." (Para. 38 (*d*).)

    Law Reform Committee 14th Report (Acquisition of Easements and Profits by Prescription) (1966), Cmnd 3100.

With which of these two views do you agree?

3. How would the facts of *Copeland v Greenhalf* [1952] Ch 488, p. 512, post, have to be altered so as to establish a claim:
    (*a*) to an easement over the plaintiff's land;
    (*b*) to the plaintiff's land by adverse possession?
    (1968) 32 Conv (NS) 270 (M. J. Goodman).

11. Mortgages[1]

I. Introduction

The mortgage transaction has, throughout its history, been a collection of contradictions. Maitland described it as "one long suppressio veri and suggestio falsi"[2]. Before 1926, the usual form of mortgage of a fee simple was by conveyance of that fee simple subject to an undertaking by the mortgagee to reconvey on payment, at a stated time in the future, of all moneys due; mortgages of leaseholds were by assignment or by sub-demise. Since 1925, mortgages of freeholds may only be by way of demise and mortgages of leaseholds by sub-demise; or, in either case by charge by deed expressed to be by way of legal mortgage in accordance with section 87 (1) of the Law of Property Act 1925.

---

[1] Cheshire, pp. 636–719; M & W, pp. 885–987; MM, pp. 427–479. Coote, *Law of Mortgages* (9th edn., 1927); Fairest, *Mortgages* (1975); Fisher and Lightwood, *Law of Mortgage* (9th edn., 1977); Waldock, *Law of Mortgages* (2nd edn., 1950); (1978) 94 LQR 571 (P. Jackson).

[2] Maitland, p. 182; Simpson, *Introduction to the History of Land Law,* (1961), pp. 132–134, 225–229.

Statutory provision for the creation of charges by way of legal mortgage has at last made it possible for a mortgage transaction to appear to be what it really is — the charging of property as security for the repayment of a loan. The historical practice of conveying an estate in land to the mortgagee has hidden the true nature of the transaction, and has made it necessary for Courts of Chancery to make great exertions to prevent the mortgagee from using the property as something more than a security for the debt.

The legal mortgage before 1926 and the mortgage by demise or sub-demise were, and still are, drafted so as to appear to give the mortgagee something more than a security; they provide for reconveyance, or for cesser of the demise respectively, on repayment of all sums due at a time in the future. This is usually six months ahead, although in most cases there is no intention on the part of either party that the payment shall be made by that date. The mortgagor's legal right is then lost and the only protection that he receives is from equity; he is given an equitable right to redeem, and this right has been held by a series of cases to be absolute and inviolable[3].

In accordance with the proviso for redemption given by the mortgagee, the mortgagor has a legal, or contractual, right to redeem and to obtain a reconveyance of the property; and by virtue of his right to obtain specific performance of the mortgagee's covenant to reconvey, equity considered him to be the owner of the land subject to the mortgage. Equity's insistence upon the inviolability of the mortgagor's right to redeem, even after his contractual right had ended, led to the creation of an equitable right to redeem; and equity's willingness to enforce this right at any time on payment of all sums due meant that he continued to be the owner in equity subject to the mortgage. The equitable interest which he owns is called the Equity of Redemption; and just as, centuries earlier, equitable estates in land became proprietary by the protection given by equity to the cestui que use against everyone except the bona fide purchaser of the legal estate for value without notice[4], so also the equity of redemption was regarded as a proprietary interest which could be bought, sold, mortgaged, and, if it were personalty, pass to the Crown as bona vacantia[5].

Since the interest which the mortgagor retained after parting with the legal fee simple in a mortgage by conveyance before 1926 was merely equitable, all subsequent mortgages were of necessity equitable. In a mortgage by demise after 1925, the mortgagor retains an equitable interest in the term granted, the interest being the equity of redemption of the term; but he also retains the legal fee simple from which he can create subsequent legal mortgages taking effect subject to the prior mortgage and created either by legal charge or by demise for a period, usually a day longer than the first legal mortgage. The

---

[3] See pp. 665, et seq.
[4] See p. 24, ante.
[5] *Re Sir Thomas Spencer Wells* [1933] Ch 29. See p. 605, post.

change introduced in 1925 is one of form rather than substance. For, "the equity of redemption has in no way lost its importance. A fee simple giving the right to possession of land only when a lease for three thousand years has expired is of little value compared with the right to insist that the fee simple shall forthwith be freed from the term of three thousand years on payment of the money due[6]."

Courts of Equity have looked upon a mortgage transaction as one in which the terms were likely to be dictated by the mortgagee. In early days the mortgagor was at a disadvantage in that he was in need of money and must take it on the mortgagee's terms; it was a lender's market. And, while the law followed the maxim "caveat emptor" in the affairs of merchants and trade, equity not surprisingly took a different view in the case of mortgages. The fact that mortgagors were, in the early days, often members of great families and mortgagees were professional money lenders no doubt contributed to some extent to the development. A consideration of the changed position of borrowers and lenders in the capitalist society of the present day will suggest that the old cases should be accepted with some reserve. The cases on this subject show a continual struggle between the principle of binding precedent and the requirements of a changing society; they can only be understood with this in mind. Those which were decided about the turn of the present century do not create the principle they apply. That litigation was a challenge to the validity of the principle laid down in earlier centuries, but generally it succeeded only in re-affirming the old principles; it was not until 1914[7] that substantial progress was made.

The problem at the present day is the extent to which these old rules still hold good. A modern mortgage of land is usually a transaction between an individual house-buyer and a building society, or forms part of a development project embarked upon by property financiers. The small man is protected from unfair pressure by the high standards set by building societies[8] and also by statutory safeguards, and the financiers must look after themselves.

The mortgage industry is big business. The Chief Registrar of Friendly Societies reported that, at the end of 1978, the total assets of the 316 registered Building Societies were £39,538,400,000. Both the number and the amount of the advances were greater than in any previous year; 1,184,000 advances were made totalling £8,807,800,000[9]. In addition to Building Societies, there are three other substantial institutional lenders of money; Banks, Insurance Companies, and Local Authorities.

Furthermore a second mortgage market grew up, with householders taking advantage of the increased value of houses to borrow further

---

[6] M & W, p. 893.

[7] *Kreglinger v New Patagonia Meat and Cold Storage Co Ltd* [1914] AC 25, p. 622, post.

[8] P. 600, post.

[9] Report for the year 1978 pp. 2; 34–36, which contain a comparative summary of principal statistics for the years 1973–1978.

from "banks, finance houses and even moneylenders"[10]. The Consumer
Credit Act 1974[11] gives important protection to this type of borrower.

The rate of interest charged by Building Societies (and other
lenders) is related to interest rates applicable to the market generally.
The Minimum Lending Rate, currently 17%, moves according to
periodical political decisions by the Government; the present high
rates place a heavy burden on borrowers.

Difficult social questions arise if a building society has to take action
to enforce the security. The mortgagor has given as security, not an
investment, but his home. And a mortgagor who has defaulted with
one building society will have difficulty in borrowing money from
another[12].

Most of the litigation is in respect of applications for possession[13].
The mortgagee is, in law, entitled to possession "before the ink is dry
on the mortgage"[14]. A building society will not go into possession
without a court order; but it will go into possession before sale in order
to be able to give vacant possession to a purchaser. Applications for
possession are thus usually a preliminary to sale by the mortgagee. It
is in this context that questions arise at the present day concerning the
mortgagor's need for protection, and mortgagors of dwelling houses
now have statutory protection.

Cheshire: *Modern Law of Real Property* (12th edn. 1976) p. 717.

"BUILDING SOCIETY MORTGAGES[15]

Building societies are a special kind of mortgagee and have for many
years been the main source of finance for the purchase of houses in
owner-occupation. They are societies formed for raising, by the
subscription of the members, a fund for making advances to members
out of the funds of the society upon security by way of mortgage of
land[16]. The principal Act regulating such societies is the Building
Societies Act 1962. The general method of operation is to borrow
money from the general public at interest and then to lend that money
at interest by making advances to house purchasers on the security of
their houses. The mortgage is usually an instalment mortgage, that is

---

[10] Report for the year 1972–73 para. 18.
[11] See p. 632, post.
[12] Lord DIPLOCK in *Pettitt v Pettitt* [1970] AC 777 at 824, [1969] 2 All ER 385, referred
to "a real-property-mortgaged-to-a-building-society-owning democracy".
[13] See p. 638, post.
[14] *Per* HARMAN J, in *Four-maids Ltd v Dudley Marshall (Properties) Ltd* [1957] Ch 317
at 320.
[15] See Wurtzburg and Mills, *Building Society Law* (14th edn., 1976); Waldock, chap. 4;
Fisher and Lightwood, pp. 193–197; Part II of the Annual Reports of the Chief
Registrar of Friendly Societies. (1974) 118 Sol Jo 744, 768, 785, 803, 841; (1975) 125
NLJ 1149 (W. A. Greene).
[16] Building Societies Act 1962, s. 1 (1). The primary object is to assist the members in
obtaining a small freehold or leasehold property. See preamble to Building Societies
Act 1836.

to say, it is paid off by monthly payments at a rate which covers payment of interest and repayment of capital, so that the capital is paid off over an agreed period of time, for example, thirty years.

The general law of mortgage applies to these transactions. The main difference between a building society mortgage and any other is that the mortgagor is a member of a society, and, accordingly, the rules of the society will be incorporated in the mortgage. The rules usually require the mortgagor to obey the rules of the society and reserve the right to increase the rate of interest after giving notice to the mortgagor. Another important difference is that there are statutory limits on the lending powers of a building society. It may not advance money by way of second mortgage, unless the prior mortgage is in favour of the society[17]. And the right of a society to lend members more than £25,000 is restricted[18].

Finally, ... a building society, when selling as a mortgagee, must take reasonable care to ensure that the price is the best price which can reasonably be obtained[19]."

II. Methods of Creation

A. Legal Mortgages and Legal Charges[20]

LAW OF PROPERTY ACT 1925

85. Mode of mortgaging freeholds. — (1) A mortgage of an estate in fee simple shall only be capable of being effected at law either by a demise for a term of years absolute, subject to a provision for cesser on redemption, or by a charge by deed expressed to be by way of legal mortgage:

Provided that a first mortgagee shall have the same right to the possession of documents as if his security included the fee simple.

(2) Any purported conveyance of an estate in fee simple by way of mortgage made after the commencement of this Act shall (to the extent of the estate of the mortgagor) operate as a demise of the land to the mortgagee for a term of years absolute, without impeachment for waste, but subject to cesser on redemption, in manner following, namely:—

    (a) A first or only mortgagee shall take a term of three thousand years from the date of the mortgage:

    (b) A second or subsequent mortgagee shall take a term (commencing from the date of the mortgage) one day longer than

---

[17] Ibid., s. 32. See *Nash v Halifax Building Society* [1979] Ch 584, [1979] 2 All ER 19.

[18] Ibid., ss. 21, 22. Building Societies (Special Advances) Order 1979 (S.I. 1979 No. 1639).

[19] Ibid., s. 36; see p. 648, post.

[20] Cheshire, pp. 642–649; M & W, pp. 887–899, 902–904; MM, pp. 428–435; Waldock, pp. 19–43; Fisher and Lightwood, pp. 21–44.

the term vested in the first or other mortgagee whose security ranks immediately before that of such second or subsequent mortgagee: . . .

86.   Mode of mortgaging leaseholds. — (1) A mortgage of a term of years absolute shall only be capable of being effected at law either by a subdemise for a term of years absolute, less by one day at least than the term vested in the mortgagor, and subject to a provision for cesser on redemption, or by a charge by deed expressed to be by way of legal mortgage; and where a licence to subdemise by way of mortgage is required, such licence shall not be unreasonably refused:[1]

Provided that a first mortgagee shall have the same right to the possession of documents as if his security had been effected by assignment.

(2) Any purported assignment of a term of years absolute by way of mortgage made after the commencement of this Act shall (to the extent of the estate of the mortgagor) operate as a subdemise of the leasehold land to the mortgagee for a term of years absolute, but subject to cesser on redemption, in manner following, namely:—

(a) The term to be taken by a first or only mortgagee shall be ten days less than the term expressed to be assigned:

(b) The term to be taken by a second or subsequent mortgagee shall be one day longer than the term vested in the first or other mortgagee whose security ranks immediately before that of the second or subsequent mortgagee, if the length of the last mentioned term permits, and in any case for a term less by one day at least than the term expressed to be assigned: . . .

87.   Charges by way of legal mortgage. — (1) Where a legal mortgage of land is created by a charge by deed expressed[2] to be by way of legal mortgage, the mortgagee shall have the same protection, powers and remedies (including the right to take proceedings to obtain possession from the occupiers and the persons in receipt of rents and profits, or any of them) as if —

(a) where the mortgage is a mortgage of an estate in fee simple, a mortgage term of three thousand years without impeachment of waste had been thereby created in favour of the mortgagee; and

(b) where the mortgage is a mortgage of a term of years absolute, a sub-term less by one day than the term vested in the mortgagor had been thereby created in favour of the mortgagee.

---

[1] A charge probably dispenses with the need for a licence. *Gentle v Faulkner* [1900] 2 QB 267; *Matthews v Smallwood* [1910] 1 Ch 777; *Grand Junction Co Ltd v Bates* [1954] 2 QB 160, [1954] 2 All ER 385, p. 603, post. M & W, p. 898, n. 83.

[2] Such a statement is not required in the case of registered land: *Cityland and Property (Holdings) Ltd v Dabrah* [1968] Ch 166, [1967] 2 All ER 639.

LAW OF PROPERTY ACT 1925

FIFTH SCHEDULE
Forms of Instruments

Section 206   Form No. 1

CHARGE BY WAY OF LEGAL MORTGAGE

This Legal Charge is made [&c.] between *A.* of [&c.] of the one part and *B.* of [&c.] of the other part.

[*Recite the title of A. to the freeholds or leaseholds in the Schedule and agreement for the loan by B.*]

Now in consideration of the sum of............ pounds now paid by *B.* to *A.* (the receipt &c.) this Deed witnesseth as follows:—

1.   *A.* hereby covenants with *B.* to pay [*Add the requisite covenant to pay principal and interest*].

2.   *A.* as Beneficial Owner hereby charges by way of legal mortgage All and Singular the property mentioned in the Schedule hereto with the payment to *B.* of the principal money, interest, and other money hereby covenanted to be paid by *A.*

3.   [*Add covenant to insure buildings and any other provisions desired.*]

In witness [&c.] [*Add Schedule*].

Note. — *B.* will be in the same position as if a mortgage had been effected by a demise of freeholds or a subdemise of leaseholds.

In *Regent Oil Co Ltd v J. A. Gregory (Hatch End) Ltd* [1966] Ch 402, [1965] 3 All ER 673 the Court of Appeal held that an attornment clause in a charge by way of legal mortgage enabled covenants in the charge to be enforced against successors in title of the mortgagor. HARMAN LJ, said at p. 431:

"In my opinion, the new charge by way of legal mortgage created by section 87 was intended to be a substitute in all respects for a mortgage by demise, and anything which would be good in the one is good in the other. It would indeed be a trap if the rights of the mortgagee depended on whether his charge were created in one way or the other. Support for this view is to be found in *Grand Junction Co Ltd v Bates* ([1954] 2 QB 160, [1954] 2 All ER 385); I read from the judgment of Upjohn J (at p. 168): 'My approach to the problem is this: A charge by way of legal mortgage, as I have already said, was introduced as a conveyancing device by the Law of Property Act 1925, with a view to simplifying conveyancing, and it would be a pity to introduce subtle differences between one way of creating a charge and another way of creating a charge unless the words of the Act so required. It may be that there is the difference with regard to obtaining consent of the landlord to the charge, though that depends on the construction of the lease; but in any event that is no reason for making another difference between the two forms of creating a security, unless the Act so requires.' It was there held that the chargee by way of legal mortgage had a right to claim relief against forfeiture just as if he had been a mortgagee by sub-demise."

Whether or not section 87 vests a term in the chargee is a matter of doubt. In *Weg Motors Ltd v Hales* [1962] Ch 49, [1961] 3 All ER 181, DONOVAN LJ said, at p. 77:

"The section does not create even a notional term of years in the mortgagee but simply defines what protection, powers and remedies the mortgagee is to have."[3]

B.   Equitable Mortgages and Equitable Charges[4]

i.   MORTGAGE OF AN EQUITABLE INTEREST

This is created by assigning the equitable interest to the mortgagee with a proviso for reassignment on redemption. The assignment, if not made by will, must satisfy the requirements of section 53 (1) (*c*) of the Law of Property Act 1925[5].

ii.   AGREEMENT TO CREATE A LEGAL MORTGAGE

In accordance with the principle that Equity looks on that as done which ought to be done, an agreement to create a legal mortgage (or an imperfect legal mortgage) is treated as an actual mortgage[6], if it satisfies section 40 of the Law of Property Act 1925[7] or is supported by a sufficient act of part performance.

iii.   DEPOSIT OF TITLE DEEDS

Since *Russel v Russel*[8] in 1783 a deposit of title deeds, with the intention that the depositee shall hold them as a security, creates an equitable mortgage of the land. This is because such a deposit is construed as a contract to create a mortgage. No formalities are necessary, but it is usual for a memorandum of the agreement to accompany the deposit, and, if it is desired to enable the mortgagee to

---

[3] See also *Grand Junction Co Ltd v Bates* [1954] 2 QB 160 at 168, where it was said that a tenant who charges his lease is probably not in breach of a covenant against sub-letting without the landlord's consent. Nor does a chargee have a term so as to effect a transfer to him under L.P.A. 1925, s. 115 (*Cumberland Court (Brighton) Ltd v Taylor* [1964] Ch 29, [1963] 2 All ER 536); nor is it necessary to serve upon a chargee a notice under L.P.A. 1925, s. 146 (p. 397, ante nor under Leasehold Property (Repairs) Act 1938 (p. 400, ante; *Church Commissioners for England v Ve-Ri-Best Manufacturing Ltd* [1957] 1 QB 238, [1956] 3 All ER 777; *Ushers Brewery v P. S. King & Co (Finance) Ltd* (1969) 212 Estates Gazette 787; *Thompson v Salah* [1972] 1 All ER 530, W & C i., 177-178.

[4] Cheshire, pp. 649-652; M & W, pp. 899-902; MM, pp. 435-436; Waldock, pp. 43-59, 136-139; Fisher and Lightwood, pp. 44-51.

[5] See p. 75, ante.

[6] See p. 80, ante.

[7] See p. 58, ante.

[8] (1783) 1 Bro CC 269; *Dixon v Muckleston* (1872) 8 Ch App 155; *Re Wallis and Simmonds (Builders) Ltd* [1974] 1 WLR 391, [1974] 1 All ER 561.

pass a legal estate on sale, the mortgagor will execute a deed and insert in it a power of attorney or a declaration of trust, or both[9].

iv.   EQUITABLE CHARGE

This arises where property is charged in equity with the payment of a debt or some other obligation. In *Matthews v Goodday* (1861) 31 LJ Ch 282 KINDERSLEY V-C, said at p. 282:

"Suppose a man signed a written contract, by which he simply agreed that he thereby charged his real estate with 500*l* to A, what would be the effect of it? It would be no agreement to give a legal mortgage, but a security by which he equitably charged his land with the payment of a sum of money."

III.   The Equity of Redemption[10]

A.   The Equity of Redemption as a Proprietary Interest

In *Casborne v Scarfe* (1738) 1 Atk 603, Lord HARDWICKE LC, said at p. 605:

"An equity of redemption has always been considered as an estate in the land, for it may be devised, granted, or entailed with remainders, and such entail and remainders may be barred by a fine and recovery, and therefore cannot be considered as a mere right only, but such an estate whereof there may be a seisin; the person therefore entitled to the equity of redemption is considered as the owner of the land.... The interest of the land must be somewhere, and cannot be in abeyance, but it is not in the mortgagee, and therefore must remain in the mortgagor."

In *Re Sir Thomas Spencer Wells* [1933] Ch 29, the question was whether the Crown could claim, as bona vacantia, the equity of redemption of property owned by a company on its dissolution and not disposed of in its winding up. The property was leasehold land, and at the time of the dissolution, the rents received from it were insufficient to cover the interest on the mortgage money. The liquidator concluded that the equity of redemption was of no value. After a considerable time, the rents increased and were greater than the interest due on the mortgage to which the plaintiffs, as mortgagees, were entitled. All arrears of interest were paid off; the equity of redemption thus became of value. It was claimed by the plaintiffs on the ground that they were

---

[9] See p. 653, post. The right to create this kind of equitable mortgage is saved by L.P.A. 1925, s. 13. The mortgagee can retain the deeds until he is paid, but has no separate legal lien; *Re Molton Finance Ltd* [1968] Ch 325, [1967] 3 All ER 843; see also *Capital Finance Co Ltd v Stokes* [1969] 1 Ch 261 at 278.

[10] Cheshire, pp. 638–639, 653–662; M & W, pp. 890–892, 893, 937–948; MM, 429–430, 454–460; Waldock, pp. 170–223; Fisher and Lightwood, chap. 28.

the legal owners of the term of years and that, the mortgagor having ceased to exist, no-one was entitled to redeem. The Court of Appeal (Lord HANWORTH MR, LAWRENCE and ROMER LJJ) held (reversing FARWELL J) that the equity of redemption was a proprietary interest which had never passed to the mortgagees. The Crown was therefore entitled to claim the equity of redemption as bona vacantia.

B.   The Protection of the Mortgagor

Equity insists that unfair advantage shall not be taken of the mortgagor. It will be seen that mortgagors have been subjected to schemes which attempt to take away the right to redeem by providing that the mortgagee may purchase the mortgaged property, or that the mortgagor shall not be permitted to redeem it for a certain period of time, or that, even after redemption, certain advantages shall still be enjoyed by the mortgagee. The rules which equity has laid down have been developed during the centuries, and have been summarized in the words: "Once a mortgage, always a mortgage[11]".

i.   ONCE A MORTGAGE ALWAYS A MORTGAGE

Where a transaction is, on its proper construction, a mortgage, any provisions inserted for the advantage of the mortgagee which are inconsistent with the nature of a mortgage are void.

SAMUEL *v* JARRAH TIMBER AND WOOD PAVING CORPORATION LTD[12]
[1904] AC 323 (HL, Earl of HALSBURY LC, Lords MACNAGHTEN and LINDLEY)

First mortgage debenture stock of £30,000 was mortgaged to Samuel to secure an advance of £5,000 at 6%. The principal was to become payable with interest at thirty days' notice on either side; and the mortgagee, Samuel, was given "the option to purchase the whole or any part of such stock at 40% at any time within twelve months". Within that period Samuel claimed to exercise this option in respect of the whole stock. The Company claimed to redeem and to have a declaration that the option was illegal and void.

Held. The option was void, and the Company was entitled to redeem.

EARL OF HALSBURY LC: My Lords, I regret that the state of the authorities leaves me no alternative other than to affirm the judgment of Kekewich J and the Court of Appeal. A perfectly fair bargain made between two parties to it, each of whom was quite sensible of what they were doing, is not to be performed because at the same time a mortgage arrangement was made between them. If a day had inter-

---

[11] *Seton v Slade* (1802) 7 Ves 265, 273, per Lord ELDON LC.

[12] Followed in *Lewis v Frank Love Ltd* [1961] 1 WLR 261, [1961] 1 All ER 446, (1961) 77 LQR 163 (P. V. Baker). See also *Salt v Marquess of Northampton* [1892] AC 1, discussed by Lord DAVEY in *Noakes & Co Ltd v Rice* [1902] AC 24, see p. 618, post.

vened between the two parts of the arrangement, the part of the bargain which the appellant claims to be performed would have been perfectly good and capable of being enforced; but a line of authorities going back for more than a century has decided that such an arrangement as that which was here arrived at is contrary to a principle of equity, the sense or reason of which I am not able to appreciate, and very reluctantly I am compelled to acquiesce in the judgments appealed from.

LORD MACNAGHTEN: In *Vernon v Bethell* ((1762) 2 Eden 110, 113), however, Northington, L.C. (then Lord Henley) laid down the law broadly in the following terms: "This Court, as a Court of conscience, is very jealous of persons taking securities for a loan and converting such securities into purchases. And therefore I take it to be an established rule that a mortgagee can never provide at the time of making the loan for any event or condition on which the equity of redemption shall be discharged and the conveyance absolute. And there is great reason and justice in this rule, for necessitous men are not, truly speaking, free men, but to answer a present exigency will submit to any terms that the crafty may impose upon them."

This doctrine, described by Lord Henley as an established rule nearly 150 years ago, has never, so far as I can discover, been departed from since or questioned in any reported case. It is, I believe, universally accepted by text-writers of authority. Speaking for myself, I should not be sorry if your Lordships could see your way to modify it so as to prevent its being used as a means of evading a fair bargain come to between persons dealing at arms' length and negotiating on equal terms. The directors of a trading company in search of financial assistance are certainly in a very different position from that of an impecunious landowner in the toils of a crafty money-lender. At the same time I quite feel the difficulty of interfering with any rule that has prevailed so long, and I am not prepared to differ from the conclusion at which the Court of Appeal has arrived.

In *Reeve v Lisle* [1902] AC 461 property was mortgaged to secure a loan of money. At a later date it was agreed between the parties to the mortgage that, if within five years the mortgagees should elect to enter into partnership with the mortgagors, they should be entitled to do so on the terms, inter alia, that the mortgagors should be relieved of the liability to repay the loan and that a ship (which was part of the security) should be transferred free from the mortgage for the purposes of the partnership. The House of Lords (Earl of HALSBURY LC, and Lords MACNAGHTEN, BRAMPTION and LINDLEY) construed these two transactions as being separate and independent, and held that the agreement was binding on the mortgagor.

---

ii. CONTRACTUAL POSTPONEMENT OF THE RIGHT TO REDEEM

This section deals with cases in which the mortgagor covenants to postpone redemption for a substantial length of time. The situations cover a wide range between two extremes. On the one hand are cases in which the mortgagee, solely for his own benefit, insists on the postponement of redemption for so long a time that the security is virtually irredeemable. On the other hand are cases in which a fair business transaction includes, at the request of the mortgagor, a term postponing redemption for a certain period of time, and the mortgagor, finding that interest rates have gone down, makes use of these rules to escape from his bargain.

It used to be said that a postponement was valid if it were for a reasonable time. It is clear, however, since the *Knightsbridge* case[13], that this is not the proper test, whether "reasonableness" is judged in terms of mere length of time or in terms of all the circumstances of the case. Sir Wilfrid GREENE MR, laid down the test in that case as follows:[14] "Equity is concerned to see two things — one that the essential requirements of a mortgage transaction are observed, and the other that oppressive and unconscionable terms are not enforced." With the second requirement no-one could quarrel; it is possible, however, that the first one may some day be held to be too wide. In that case, the mortgagor covenanted not to redeem a mortgage of freehold land for 40 years, and the covenant was held valid. There was no suggestion of hardship or oppression. An interesting situation would have arisen if the property mortgaged had been a forty-one year lease[15]; assuming again that there was no hardship or oppression, the conflict between *Fairclough v Swan Brewery Co Ltd*[16] and *Santley v Wilde*[17] would then have to be resolved, and there is much to be said for the view that a business transaction of that nature ought to be upheld.

Cases falling within the present section should be distinguished from those dealt with in the next. The next section deals with cases where an advantage still remains to the mortgagee after redemption. Failure to appreciate this distinction has caused most of the misunderstanding of *Santley v Wilde*[17]. The criticism which that case received in the House of Lords[18], and particularly from Lord DAVEY, was directed against it on the assumption that it concerned a collateral advantage existing after redemption. It is clear, however, from the judgment of the case itself, that Lord LINDLEY treated it as a case of contractual postponement.

---

[13] *Knightsbridge Estates Trust Ltd v Byrne* [1939] Ch 441, [1938] 4 All ER 618; *affd.* [1940] AC 613, [1940] 2 All ER 401; p. 612, post.
[14] [1939] Ch at 457.
[15] See the question on p. 616, post.
[16] [1912] AC 565, p. 611, post.
[17] [1899] 2 Ch 474.
[18] Especially in *Noakes & Co Ltd v Rice* [1902] AC 24 at 33; p. 618, post.

SANTLEY *v* WILDE
[1899] 2 Ch 474 (CA, LINDLEY MR, Sir F. H. JEUNE, ROMER LJ
reversing BYRNE J [1899] 1 Ch 747)

The plaintiff, as sub-lessee of a theatre, had the option to take over the head lease on payment of £2,000. She arranged to borrow this money from the defendant Wilde, and mortgaged to him her sub-lease as security. The mortgage provided that the mortgagor should repay the capital by instalments under an arrangement which was not challenged, and that she should "during the residue of the term . . . notwithstanding that all principal moneys and interest may have been paid . . . pay . . . a sum equal to one-third part of the clear net profit rent or rents to be derived" from the lease. The proviso for cesser provided that the mortgage should determine on payment of the principal sum and interest, "and all other the moneys hereinbefore covenanted . . . to be paid . . ." etc. After certain payments had fallen into arrear, the plaintiff, on payment of all arrears, and on tender of the outstanding principal, interest and costs, claimed a declaration that she was entitled to redeem on payment of principal, interest and costs and that so far as the mortgage deed provided for payment of a share of the rents and profits or precluded her from redeeming on payment of principal and interest, it was invalid.

Held. The plaintiff could not redeem except by observing all the covenants for which her property was given as security, including the covenant to pay the profits.

LINDLEY MR: The question raised on this appeal is extremely important: I do not profess to be able to decide it on any principle which will be in harmony with all the cases; but it appears to me that the true principle running through them is not very difficult to discover, and I think that it can be applied so as to do justice in this case and in all other cases on the subject that may arise. The principle is this: a mortgage is a conveyance of land or an assignment of chattels as a security for the payment of a debt or the discharge of some other obligation for which it is given. This is the idea of a mortgage: and the security is redeemable on the payment or discharge of such debt or obligation, any provision to the contrary notwithstanding. That, in my opinion, is the law. Any provision inserted to prevent redemption on payment or performance of the debt or obligation for which the security was given is what is meant by a clog or fetter on the equity of redemption and is therefore void. . . . A clog or fetter is something which is inconsistent with the idea of security: a clog or fetter is in the nature of a repugnant condition. If I convey land in fee subject to a condition forbidding alienation, that is a repugnant condition. If I give a mortgage on a condition that I shall not redeem, that is a repugnant condition. The Courts of Equity have fought for years to maintain the doctrine that a security is redeemable. But when and under what circumstances? On the performance of the obligation for which it was given. If the obligation is the payment of a debt, the security is redeemable on the payment of that debt. That, in my opinion, is the true principle applicable to the cases, and that is what is meant when it is said there must not be any clog or fetter on the equity of redemption. If so, this mortgage has no clog or fetter at all. Of course, the debt or obligation may be impeachable for fraud, oppression, or over-reaching: there the obligation is tainted to that extent and is invalid. But, putting such cases out of the question, when you get a security for a debt or obligation, that security can be redeemed the moment the debt or obligation is paid or performed, but on no other terms.

Now, let us see what the contract here is. It is not suggested that there has been fraud or undue influence or over-reaching or hard bargaining. Here is a lady who has a lease, of which there are ten years to run, subject to a rent and covenants. She wants to carry on a theatre, and she wants to borrow a sum of 2,000*l.* for the purpose. What is the security she offers? The security of the lease is probably absolutely insufficient. A security of that sort, unless it is kept up for the ten years, is very shaky. The lender took that view. He says, "I will lend you the money, and you may have five years in which to pay it; and you shall pay me a sum equal to one-third part of the net profit rents to be derived from any underleases". What is the lender's position? It is obvious that his security depends not only on the solvency of the lady, but also on the success of the theatre. This is the kind of security proposed, and the lender says he will lend upon that. Accordingly the 2,000*l.* is lent, and the mortgagor by her security covenants to repay the money by instalments; the deed then further goes on as follows: [His Lordship read the second testatum and covenant by the mortgagor for payment to the mortgagee of one-third of the net profit rents to be derived from any underleases or undertenancies, and also the proviso for redemption: and continued:]

That means that this lease is granted or assigned by the mortgagor to the mortgagee as security not only for the payment of the 2,000*l.* and interest, but also for the payment of the one-third of the net profit rents to the end of the term. If I am right in the principle which I have laid down, that does not clog the right of redemption upon the performance of the obligation for which the security was given. That is the nature of the transaction, and the good sense of it.

But it is said that is not good law. Those, however, who say so lose sight of the true principle underlying the expression that there must be no clog or fetter on the equity of redemption. The plaintiff says, "I will pay off the balance of the 2,000*l.* and interest, and you will give me back the lease, and this is the end of my obligation". But the mortgagee says, "No; that is not the bargain: you cannot redeem on those terms. On the contrary, you may pay me the 2,000*l.* and interest, but if you do, you must also pay the one-third profit rents". On principle that is right: it follows from what I have said. That is the bargain, and there has been no oppression, and there is no reasonable legal ground for relieving this lady. . . .

FAIRCLOUGH *v* SWAN BREWERY CO LTD
[1912] AC 565 (PC, Lords MACNAGHTEN, ATKINSON, SHAW OF DUNFERMLINE, and MERSEY)

The appellant was lessee for 17½ years of a hotel owned by the respondent brewery. He executed a mortgage of his lease for £500 which contained a clause precluding him from redeeming the mortgage during the remainder of his term less six weeks, and from purchasing beer from any person other than the respondent brewery during the continuance of the mortgage. On the appellant's offering to redeem and claiming to be free to purchase beer elsewhere, the respondent brewery brought this action in Supreme Court of Western Australia for damages for breach of covenant and an injunction to restrain further breaches. The appellant argued that the covenant was void on the ground, inter alia, that it was a clog on his equity of redemption, and claimed that he was entitled to redeem.

Held. The covenant was void and the appellant was entitled to redeem.

LORD MACNAGHTEN: The arguments of counsel ranged over a very wide field[19]. But the real point is a narrow one. It depends upon a doctrine of equity, which is not open to question.

"There is", as Kindersley V-C said in *Gossip v Wright* ((1863) 32 LJ Ch. 648, at p. 653), "no doubt that the broad rule is this: that the Court will not allow the right of redemption in any way to be hampered or crippled in that which the parties intended to be a security either by any contemporaneous instrument with the deed in question, or by anything which this Court would regard as a simultaneous arrangement or part of the same transaction." The rule in comparatively recent times was unsettled by certain decisions in the Court of Chancery in England which seems to have misled the learned judges in the Full Court. But it is now firmly established by the House of Lords that the old rule still prevails and that equity will not permit any device or contrivance being part of the mortgage transaction or contemporaneous with it to prevent or impede redemption. The learned counsel on behalf of the respondents admitted, as he was bound to admit, that a mortgage cannot be made irredeemable. That is plainly forbidden. Is there any difference between forbidding redemption and permitting it, if the permission be a mere pretence? Here the provision for redemption is nugatory. . . . For all practical purposes this mortgage is irredeemable. It was obviously meant to be irredeemable. It was made irredeemable in and by the mortgage itself.

---

[19] Restraint of trade was also pleaded; at p. 566.

KNIGHTSBRIDGE ESTATES TRUST LTD *v* BYRNE
[1939] Ch 441, [1938] 4 All ER 618 (CA SIR WILFRID GREENE MR,
SCOTT and FARWELL LJJ)

The plaintiff company was the owner of certain freehold property in
London which had been mortgaged at 6½%. Wishing to pay off their
mortgage, they asked the defendant for a loan of £310,000 at 5¼%
repayable over forty years. The defendants agreed to make this loan,
repayment to be made by half-yearly instalments over forty years. The
deed so provided, and in it the defendant mortgagees undertook, if the
instalments were promptly paid, not to require repayment in any
other way.

The plaintiffs claimed, less than six years later, that they were
entitled to redeem on payment of all principal, interest and costs, on
the ground that, in so far as the term prevented them from redeeming
on making such payments, it was illegal and void as a clog on their
right to redeem and that it rendered the mortgage irredeemable for an
undue length of time.

Held (reversing LUXMOORE J, ([1938] Ch 741, [1938] 2 All ER 444)).
The plaintiffs were bound by the agreement and could only redeem in
accordance with its terms.

SIR WILFRID GREENE MR: We will deal first with the arguments
originally presented on behalf of the respondents. The first argument
was that the postponement of the contractual right to redeem for forty
years was void in itself, in other words, that the making of such an
agreement between mortgagor and mortgagee was prohibited by a rule
of equity. It was not contended that a provision in a mortgage deed
making the mortgage irredeemable for a period of years is necessarily
void. The argument was that such a period must be a "reasonable"
one, and it was said that the period in the present case was an
unreasonable one by reason merely of its length. This argument was
not the one accepted by the learned judge.

Now an argument such as this requires the closest scrutiny, for, if it
is correct, it means that an agreement made between two competent
parties, acting under expert advice and presumably knowing their own
business best, is one which the law forbids them to make upon the
ground that it is not "reasonable". If we were satisfied that the rule of
equity was what it is said to be, we should be bound to give effect to it.
But in the absence of compelling authority we are not prepared to say
that such an agreement cannot lawfully be made. A decision to that
effect would, in our view, involve an unjustified interference with the
freedom of business men to enter into agreements best suited to their
interests and would impose upon them a test of "reasonableness" laid
down by the Courts without reference to the business realities of the
case.

It is important to remember what those realities were. The respondents are a private company and do not enjoy the facilities for raising
money by a public issue possessed by public companies. They were the
owners of a large and valuable block of property, and so far as we know

they had no other assets. The property was subject to a mortgage at a high rate of interest and this mortgage was liable to be called in at any time. In these circumstances the respondents were, when the negotiations began, desirous of obtaining for themselves two advantages: (1) a reduction in the rate of interest, (2) the right to repay the mortgage moneys by instalments spread over a long period of years. The desirability of obtaining these terms from a business point of view is manifest, and it is not to be assumed that these respondents were actuated by anything but pure considerations of business in seeking to obtain them. The sum involved was a very large one, and the length of the period over which the instalments were spread is to be considered with reference to this fact. In the circumstances it was the most natural thing in the world that the respondents should address themselves to a body desirous of obtaining a long term investment for its money. The resulting agreement was a commercial agreement between two important corporations experienced in such matters, and has none of the features of an oppressive bargain where the borrower is at the mercy of an unscrupulous lender. In transactions of this kind it is notorious that there is competition among the large insurance companies and other bodies having large funds to invest, and we are not prepared to view the agreement made as anything but a proper business transaction.

But it is said not only that the period of postponement must be a reasonable one, but that in judging the "reasonableness" of the period the considerations which we have mentioned cannot be regarded; that the Court is bound to judge "reasonableness" by a consideration of the terms of the mortgage deed itself and without regard to extraneous matters. In the absence of clear authority we emphatically decline to consider a question of "reasonableness" from a standpoint so unreal. To hold that the law is to tell business men what is reasonable in such circumstances and to refuse to take into account the business considerations involved, would bring the law into disrepute. Fortunately we do not find ourselves forced to come to any such conclusion. . . .

Assuming therefore, without in any way deciding, that the period during which the contractual right of redemption is postponed must be a "reasonable" one (a question which we will now proceed to examine), we are of the opinion that the respondents have failed to establish (and the burden is on them) that there is anything unreasonable in the mere extension of the period of forty years in the circumstances of the present case.

But in our opinion the proposition that a postponement of the contractual right of redemption is only permissible for a "reasonable" time is not well-founded. Such a postponement is not properly described as a clog on the equity of redemption, since it is concerned with the contractual right to redeem. It is indisputable that any provision which hampers redemption after the contractual date for redemption has passed will not be permitted. Further, it is undoubtedly true to say that a right of redemption is a necessary element in a mortgage transaction, and consequently that, where the contractual right of redemption is illusory, equity will grant relief by allowing redemption. This was the point in the case of *Fairclough v Swan Brewery Co Ltd* ([1912] AC 565). . . .

Moreover, equity may give relief against contractual terms in a mortgage transaction if they are oppressive or unconscionable, and in deciding whether or not a particular transaction falls within this category the length of time for which the contractual right to redeem is postponed may well be an important consideration. In the present case no question of this kind was or could have been raised.

But equity does not reform mortgage transactions because they are unreasonable. It is concerned to see two things — one that the essential requirements of a mortgage transaction are observed, and the other that oppressive or unconscionable terms are not enforced. Subject to this, it does not, in our opinion, interfere. The question therefore arises whether, in a case where the right of redemption is real and not illusory and there is nothing oppressive or unconscionable in the transaction, there is something in a postponement of the con-tractual right to redeem, such as we have in the present case, that is inconsistent with the essential requirements of a mortgage transac-tion? Apart from authority the answer to this question would, in our opinion, be clearly in the negative. Any other answer would place an unfortunate restriction on the liberty of contract of competent parties who are at arm's length — in the present case it would have operated to prevent the respondents obtaining financial terms which for obvious reasons they themselves considered to be most desirable. It would, moreover, lead to highly inequitable results. The remedy sought by the respondents and the only remedy which is said to be open to them is the establishment of a right to redeem at any time on the ground that the postponement of the contractual right to redeem is void. They do not and could not suggest that the contract as a contract is affected, and the result would accordingly be that whereas the respondents would have had from the first the right to redeem at any time, the appellants would have had no right to require payment other-wise than by the specified instalments. Such an outcome to a bargain entered into by business people negotiating at arm's length would indeed be unfortunate, and we should require clear authority before coming to such a conclusion.

We will now turn to the relevant authorities cited in argument by counsel for the parties. The first in order of date is *Talbot v Braddill* ((1683) 1 Vern 183). [His Lordship referred also to *Cowdry v Day* (1859) 1 Giff 316; *Teevan v Smith* (1882) 20 ChD 724; *Biggs v Hoddinott* [1898] 2 Ch 307 at 311; *Bradley v Carritt* [1903] AC 253; *Williams v Morgan* [1906] 1 Ch 804; *Morgan v Jeffreys* [1910] 1 Ch 620; and to *Davis v Symons* [1934] Ch 442, and continued:]

The second ground upon which the respondents endeavoured to support the judgment of the Court below was that the postponement of the contractual right to redeem for a period of forty years offended the rule against perpetuities and was therefore invalid. The learned judge decided against the respondents on this question and in our judgment rightly. . . .

This decision was affirmed on appeal to the House of Lords [1940] AC 613, [1940] 2 All ER 401, on the ground that the mortgage was a debenture within the meaning of the Companies Act 1929, section 380[20] and, as such and by virtue of section 74 of that Act, not invalid by reason of postponement of the date for redemption. No views were expressed in the House of Lords on the reasoning of the Court of Appeal.

In *Kreglinger v New Patagonia Meat and Cold Storage Co Ltd* [1914] AC 25, Lord PARKER said, at p. 53:

"My Lords, I desire, in connection with what I have just said, to add a few words on the maxims in which attempts have been made to sum up the equitable principles applicable to mortgage transactions. I refer to the maxims, 'Once a mortgage, always a mortgage', or, 'A mortgage cannot be made irredeemable'. Such maxims, however convenient, afford little assistance where the Court has to deal with a new or doubtful case. They obviously beg the question, always of great importance, whether the particular transaction which the Court has to consider is, in fact, a mortgage or not, and if they be acted on without a careful consideration of the equitable considerations on which they are based, can only, like Bacon's idols of the market place, lead to misconception and error.

We will suppose that money is advanced to a company repayable at the expiration of fifteen years, not an unusual period, and that the company by way of security subdemises (as is often the case) to trustees for the lenders a number of leaseholds, some of which are held for terms less than fifteen years. It would, in my opinion, be a serious error to argue that this was an attempt to make an irredeemable mortgage. There would be the same error in objecting on the like ground to a mortgage of leaseholds to secure an annuity for a period exceeding the term of the lease. If the mortgage is irredeemable at all, this arises from the nature of the property mortgaged, and not from any penal or repugnant stipulation on the part of the mortgagee, and the maxim properly understood is in no way infringed."

---

[20] Now Companies Act 1948, s. 89.

QUESTION

X owned a 99-year lease in Blackacre. He wished to raise £100,000 in order to develop the land. His calculations showed that once the buildings were erected — estimated at 5 years — the income from the land would allow him to pay interest on the loan at 8% and repay £1,000 of the capital each year. As the capital outstanding and thus the interest payable each year was reduced, a sum, increasing annually, would be available for himself. His expectation was that interest rates would rise.

With this plan in mind, he suggested to Y that he borrow £100,000 at 8%, the capital repayable at the rate of £1,000 per annum starting five years hence, and £2,000 per annum in the last six years of the lease. Y agreed, saying that the repayment of capital was longer delayed than he wished, but that he was happy to help X.

Interest rates then declined to 6½%. X claimed to be entitled to pay off the capital forthwith, on the ground that the terms of the mortgage made it irredeemable and therefore void.

Will he succeed? What assistance could Y obtain from (a) *Knightsbridge Estates Trust Ltd v Byrne;* from (b) *Santley v Wilde?*

iii.   COLLATERAL ADVANTAGES EXISTING AFTER REDEMPTION

The cases in this section show how modifications have been made in recent times to the strict rule that an advantage or benefit collateral to the mortgage and in favour of the mortgagee is void in so far as it is to continue after redemption. A covenant is collateral where an obligation is placed on the mortgagor which is independent of that for the performance of which the land is charged. *Biggs v Hoddinott*[1] in 1898 held that such a collateral advantage was valid if it was to exist only until redemption; but covenants drafted so as to exist beyond redemption were struck down in *Noakes & Co Ltd v Rice*[2] and *Bradley v Carritt*[3], even though in the latter case the covenant was not of such a type that it could in any circumstances "run with" the property mortgaged. Inevitably the situation arose in which the strict application of this rule was not consistent with contemporary business requirements; and the speeches of Lords HALDANE and PARKER in *Kreglinger v New Patagonia Meat and Cold Storage Co Ltd*[4] show that the law has managed to conform both to the requirements of the day and to the precedents and rules of earlier times.

The most common method of reconciling the *Kreglinger* case with *Noakes & Co Ltd v Rice* and *Bradley v Carritt,* is to construe the covenant to sell the skins in the *Kreglinger* case as being a "contract, contained in the same document as constituted the security, but in

---

[1] [1898] 2 Ch 307.
[2] [1902] AC 24.
[3] [1903] AC 253.
[4] [1914] AC 25; followed in *Cityland and Property (Holdings) Ltd v Dabrah* [1968] Ch 166, [1967] 2 All ER 639.

substance independent of it[5]". Once it is so construed it must stand or fall on its own merits. It is difficult to see why a commercial contract, which is in itself valid, should become void because it is recorded in the same document as a mortgage. Where it can be construed as separate from the mortgage, the position is as if it were entered into on Monday and the mortgage on Tuesday[6]; the two are separate and incapable of infecting each other. It has already been seen that a covenant to do something other than repay principal, interest and costs may be part of the obligation for the performance of which the mortgage is given to secure; and a covenant of this type is not a 'collateral advantage' and cannot be affected by these rules[7]. Whether or not a contract is (i) part of the mortgage security, as in *Santley v Wilde,* (ii) entirely independent of the mortgage transaction, as in the *Kreglinger Case,* or (iii) part of the mortgage transaction without being part of the security, as in *Noakes & Co Ltd v Rice* and *Bradley v Carritt,* is a question of construction in each particular case. If the contract is of types (i) or (ii), it is not affected by the rules relating to collateral advantages. If it is of type (iii), which is in its nature between types (i) and (ii), then it is subjected to the authority of the cases declaring collateral advantages to be void. The selection of the correct category for any particular contract is a question for the court in each particular case, but the way is at least open now to the courts to permit the enforcement of bona fide business deals by construing them as falling outside the authority of *Noakes & Co Ltd v Rice*[8] and *Bradley v Carritt*[9].

BIGGS v HODDINOTT
[1898] 2 Ch 307 (CA, LINDLEY MR, CHITTY and COLLINS LJJ)

On 18 March 1896, the defendant Hoddinott, the owner of a public house, mortgaged it to Biggs, a brewer. The deed contained an undertaking by Hoddinott that during the continuance of the mortgage he would deal with the plaintiff only in his purchase of certain liquor; an undertaking by the plaintiff that during the continuance of the mortgage he would supply such liquor at the scheduled prices; and a provision that redemption should not take place, nor should the money be called in, for five years. About two years later, the defendant ceased to purchase liquor from the plaintiff who brought this action for an injunction, and the defendant claimed to be entitled to redeem the mortgage. ROMER J granted an injunction and refused to allow the defendant to redeem. On appeal on the question of the issue of the injunction.

Held. The covenant tying the public house during the continuance of the mortgage was valid.

---

[5] Per Lord HALDANE at p. 41; *Re Petrol Filling Station, Vauxhall Bridge Road, London* (1969) 20 P & CR 1, p. 631, post.
[6] See Lord HALSBURY in *Samuel v Jarrah Timber and Wood Paving Corpn Ltd* [1904] AC 323; p. 606, ante.
[7] Because it does not continue after redemption, *Santley v Wilde* [1899] 2 Ch 474.
[8] [1902] AC 24.
[9] [1903] AC 253.

LINDLEY MR: We have listened to a very ingenious and learned argument with the view of inducing us under pressure to lay down a proposition of law which would be very unfortunate for business men. The proposition contended for comes to this — that while two people are engaged in a mortgage transaction they cannot enter into any other transaction with each other which can possibly benefit the mortgagee, and that any such transaction must be before or after the mortgage and be independent of it, so that it cannot be said that the mortgagee got any additional benefit from the mortgage transaction. Mr. Farwell did not attempt to uphold this on any rational principle, but relied on authority. Of course, we must follow settled authorities whether we like them or not; but do they support this proposition? *Jennings v Ward* ((1705) 2 Vern 520) was the first case relied upon. That was a redemption suit, and the stipulation which was in question seriously interfered with the redemption of the mortgaged property, and the Master of the Rolls (Sir J. Trevor) decreed redemption without regard to that stipulation. He is reported to have said: "A man shall not have interest for his money, and a collateral advantage besides for the loan of it, or clog the redemption with any by-agreement." That has been understood as meaning exactly what was said, without regard to the circumstances of the case, and has found its way into the text-books as establishing that a mortgagee cannot have principal, interest, and cost, and also some collateral advantage. But that supposed rule has been departed from again and again. Take the case of West India mortgages: it has been repeatedly decided that the mortgagee, if not in possession, may stipulate that he shall be appointed consignee. The proposition stated in *Jennings v Ward* is too wide. If properly guarded it is good law and good sense. A mortgage is regarded as a security for money, and the mortgagor can always redeem on payment of principal, interest, and costs; and no bargain preventing such redemption is valid, nor will unconscionable bargains be enforce. There is no case where collateral advantages have been disallowed which does not come under one of these two heads. To say that to require such a covenant as that now in question is unconscionable is asking us to lay down a proposition which would shock any business man, and we are not driven to it by authority. . . .

The appeal will be dismissed.

NOAKES & CO LTD *v* RICE
[1902] AC 24, (HL, Earl of HALSBURY LC, Lords MACNAGHTEN, SHAND, DAVEY, BRAMPTON, ROBERTSON and LINDLEY)

Rice, the plaintiff, purchased, in 1897, the lease of a public house; the lease was to expire in 1923. Before this purchase, Noakes and Co, brewers, were mortgagees of the house and advanced money to Rice to enable him to purchase the leasehold premises which were mortgaged to them as security for the loan. Both this and the prior mortgage included a covenant, "so as to charge the premises into whose-soever possession the same may come ... and to the further intent that the obligation of this covenant may run with the land" that the mortgagor would not, during the continuance of the lease, "whether any principal moneys or interest shall or shall not be owing" under the mortgage, use any liquor that had not been purchased from Noakes and Co. Provision was made for payment of liquidated damages in case of breach.

Rice now wished to pay off the loan and claimed to redeem the property free from the covenant tying the house.

Held. On payment of all that was due, the plaintiff could recover the property free from the tie.

LORD DAVEY: My Lords, there are three doctrines of the Courts of Equity in this country which have been referred to in the course of the argument in this case. The first doctrine to which I refer is expressed in the maxim, "Once a mortgage always a mortgage". The second is that the mortgagee shall not reserve to himself any collateral advantage outside the mortgage contract; and the third is that a provision or stipulation which will have the effect of clogging or fettering the equity of redemption is void.

My Lords, the first maxim presents no difficulty: it is only another way of saying that a mortgage cannot be made irredeemable, and that a provision to that effect is void. In the case of *Salt v Marquess of Northampton* ([1892] AC 1) the question was whether a certain life policy, the premiums on which were charged against the mortgagor, was comprised in the mortgage security. That question having been decided in the affirmative, it was declared to be redeemable, notwithstanding an express provision to the contrary contained in the deed.

My Lords, the second doctrine to which I refer, namely that the mortgagee shall not reserve to himself any collateral advantage outside the mortgage contract, was established long ago when the usury laws were in force. The Court of Equity went beyond the usury laws, and set its face against every transaction which tended to usury. It therefore declared void every stipulation by a mortgagee for a collateral advantage which made his total remuneration for the loan indirectly exceed the legal interest. I think it will be found that every case under this head of equity was decided either on this ground, or on the ground that the bargain was oppressive and unconscionable. The abolition of the usury laws has made an alteration in the view the Court should take on this subject, and I agree that a collateral advantage may now be stipulated for by a mortgagee, provided that no unfair advantage be taken by the mortgagee which would render it void or voidable, according to the general principles of equity, and provided that it does not offend against the third doctrine. On these grounds I think the case of *Biggs v Hoddinott* ([1898] 2 Ch 307) in the Court of Appeal was rightly decided.

The third doctrine to which I have referred is really a corollary from the first, and it might be expressed in this form: Once a mortgage always a mortgage and nothing but a mortgage. The meaning of that is that the mortgagee shall not make any stipulation which will prevent a mortgagor, who has paid principal, interest, and costs, from getting back his mortgaged property in the condition in which he parted with it. I do not dissent from the opinion expressed by my noble and learned friend opposite (Lord Lindley), when Master of the Rolls, in the case of *Santley v Wilde* ([1899] 2 Ch 474). He says: "A clog or fetter is something which is inconsistent with the idea of security; a clog or fetter is in the nature of a repugnant condition," But I ask, "security" for what? I think it must be security for the principal, interest, and costs, and, I will add, for any advantages in the nature of increased interest or remuneration for the loan which the mortgagee has validly stipulated for during the continuance of the mortgage. There are two elements in the conception of a mortgage: first, security for the money advanced; and, secondly, remuneration for the use of the money. When the mortgage is paid off the security is at an end, and, as the mortgagee is no longer kept out of his money, the remuneration to him for the use of his money is also at an end. I confess I should have decided the case of *Santley v Wilde* differently from the way in which it was dealt with in the Court of Appeal. After the payment of principal and interest, and everything which had become payable up to the date of redemption, the property in that case remained charged with the payment to the mortgagee of one-third share of the profits, and the stipulation to that effect should, I think, have been held to be a clog or fetter on the right to redeem. The principle is this — that a mortgage must not be converted into something else; and when once you come to the conclusion that a stipulation for the benefit of the mortgagee is part of the mortgage transaction, it is but part of his security, and necessarily comes to an end on the payment off of the loan. In my opinion, every yearly or other recurring payment stipulated for by the mortgagee should be held to be in the nature of interest, and no more payable after the principal is paid off than interest would be. I apprehend a man could not stipulate for the continuance of payment of interest after the principal is paid, and I do not think he can stipulate for any other recurring payment such as a share of profits. Any stipulation to that effect, would, in my opinion be void as a clog or fetter on the equity of redemption.

LORD LINDLEY: The conclusion thus arrived at is not inconsistent with *Santley v Wilde* on which the appellants so strongly rely. Some of your Lordships think that case went too far. I do not think so myself: but I will not trouble your Lordships with its details, which were complicated. The principle on which the Court of Appeal decided the case was, I still think, sound. Whether it was properly applied in that case is now of no importance. I believe the true principle applicable to these cases to be that expounded by the Court of Appeal in *Biggs v Hoddinott* ([1898] 2 Ch 307) and *Santley v Wilde* ([1899] 2 Ch 474). That principle is perfectly consistent with a real pledge and with the maxim "Once a mortgage always a mortgage"; but it will not render valid the covenant which your Lordships have to consider in the present case.

In *Bradley v Carritt* [1903] AC 253, one Bradley, who was the owner of a controlling number of shares in the Sephinjuri Bheel Tea Company, mortgaged them to Carritt, a tea broker, who wished to become the sole broker for the sale of the company's teas. By a written agreement, Bradley undertook, in clause 4, to use his "best endeavours to secure that [Carritt, the plaintiff] shall always hereafter have the sale of all the company's teas as broker; and, in the event of any of the company's teas being sold otherwise than through" Carritt, to pay to him the commission which he would have earned if they had been sold through him. After the mortgage was paid off, the shares were again mortgaged to a different mortgagee, who took advantage of his voting-power to oust the plaintiff from his position as broker of the company. Carritt sued to recover, as damages for breach of contract, the amount of the commission.

By a bare majority, Lords MACNAGHTEN, DAVEY and ROBERTSON, with Lords SHAND and LINDLEY dissenting, the House of Lords reversed BIGHAM J and the Court of Appeal and held that the covenant was void as a clog on the equity of redemption, and that no action therefore lay.

The covenant was one that on its terms continued after redemption. The main question was whether or not it was a clog on the equity of redemption. It differed in this respect from the covenant in *Noakes v Rice*, for the covenant in that case was one that directly affected the property mortgaged; the mortgagor, having mortgaged a free house, would on redemption have received back a tied house. In this case, however, the covenant did not run with the tea shares; as Lord LINDLEY said at p. 276: "Clause 4 in no way fetters the right to redeem, nor obstructs the mortgagor in the practical exercise of that right, or of the use or enjoyment of his shares when he gets them back. He can then do what he likes with them, free from all control by the mortgagee." Lord DAVEY said at p. 268: ". . . Can it be said that the mortgagee does not retain a hold upon the shares which form the mortgaged property, or that the mortgagor has full redemption of it, when the latter is not free to exercise an important right in such manner as he may think most conducive to his own interests? . . . Again, the appellant could not part with or otherwise deal with his shares without losing the influence in the company's counsels which might enable him to secure the performance of the first part of the agreement, or running a serious risk of liability under the second part."

The speeches show again the different views of Lords LINDLEY and DAVEY upon the principles involved in the question of collateral advantages in particular and of the protection of the mortgagor in general.

KREGLINGER *v* NEW PATAGONIA MEAT AND COLD STORAGE CO LTD

[1914] AC 25 (HL, Viscount HALDANE LC, EARL of HALSBURY, Lords ATKINSON, MERSEY and PARKER OF WADDINGTON)

The appellants, a firm of woolbrokers agreed to lend £10,000 to the respondents, a firm of meat packers. Provided all interest was paid punctually and all the terms of the agreement observed, the appellants agreed not to call in the principal for five years, but the respondents were at liberty to pay off the loan whenever they wished. The loan was secured by a floating charge on the respondents' undertaking. Clause 8 of the agreement provided in sub-clause (A) that the respondents would not, for a period of five years, "sell any sheepskins to any person . . . other than the lenders so long as the lenders are willing to purchase the same at a price equal to the best price . . . offered . . . by any . . . other person . . ." Sub-clause (C) provided that the respondent company "will pay to the lenders a commission of 1% upon the sale price of all sheepskins sold by the company" to anyone other than the lenders.

After a few months over two years the respondents paid off the loan in accordance with the terms of the agreement, and disputed the right of the appellants to exercise their option to purchase the sheepskins. The appellants brought an action for an injunction to restrain the sale of sheepskins to other persons.

Held (reversing SWINFEN EADY J and the Court of Appeal[10] (COZENS-HARDY MR, BUCKLEY and KENNEDY LJJ)). Appellants entitled to an injunction.

VISCOUNT HALDANE LC: My Lords, the respondents have now, as they were entitled to do under the agreement, paid off the loan. They claim that such payment has put an end to the option of the appellants to buy the respondents' sheepskins. Under the terms of the agreement this option, as I have already stated, will, if it is valid, continue operative until 24 August 1915. What the respondents say is that the stipulation is one that restricts their freedom in conducting the undertaking or business which is the subject of the floating charge; that it was consequently of the nature of a clog on their right to redeem and invalid; and that, whether it clogged the right to redeem or was in the nature of a collateral advantage, it was not intended and could not be made to endure after redemption. The appellants, on the other hand, say that the stipulation in question was one of a kind usual in business, and that it was in the nature not of a clog but of a collateral bargain outside the actual loan, which they only agreed to make in order to obtain the option itself. They further say that even if the option could be regarded as within the doctrine of equity which forbids the clogging of the right to redeem, that doctrine does not in a case such as this extend to a floating charge.

---

[10] (1913) 29 TLR 393; 464.

... My Lords, before I refer to the decisions of this House which the Courts below have considered to cover the case, I will state what I conceive to be the broad principles which must govern it.

The reason for which a Court of Equity will set aside the legal title of a mortgagee and compel him to reconvey the land on being paid principal, interest, and costs is a very old one. . . .

The principle was . . . in the early days limited in its application to the accomplishment of the end which was held to justify interference of equity with freedom of contract. It did not go further. As established it was expressed in three ways. The most general of these was that if the transaction was once found to be a mortgage, it must be treated as always remaining a mortgage and nothing but a mortgage. That the substance of the transaction must be looked to in applying this doctrine and that it did not apply to cases which were only apparently or technically within it but were in reality something more than cases of mortgage, *Howard v Harris* ((1683) 1 Vern 190) and other authorities shew. It was only a different application of the paramount doctrine to lay it down in the form of a second rule that a mortgagee should not stipulate for a collateral advantage which would make his remuneration for the loan exceed a proper rate of interest. The Legislature during a long period placed restrictions on the rate of interest which could legally be exacted. But equity went beyond the limits of the statutes which limited the interest, and was ready to interfere with any usurious stipulation in a mortgage. In so doing it was influenced by the public policy of the time. That policy has now changed, and the Acts which limited the rate of interest have been repealed. The result is that a collateral advantage may now be stipulated for by the mortgagee provided that he has not acted unfairly or oppressively, and provided that the bargain does not conflict with the third form of the principle. This is that a mortgage . . . cannot be made irredeemable, and that any stipulation which restricts or clogs the equity of redemption is void. It is obvious that the reason for the doctrine in this form is the same as that which gave rise to the other forms. It is simply an assertion in a different way of the principle that once a mortgage always a mortgage and nothing else.

My Lords, the rules I have stated have now been applied by Courts of Equity for nearly three centuries, and the books are full of illustrations of their application. But what I have pointed out shews that it is inconsistent with the objects for which they were established that these rules should crystallize into technical language so rigid that the letter can defeat the underlying spirit and purpose. Their application must correspond with the practical necessities of the time. The rule as to collateral advantages, for example, has been much modified by the repeal of the usury laws and by the recognition of modern varieties of commercial bargaining. . . .

[His Lordship referred to *Biggs v Hoddinott* ([1898] 2 Ch 307) and to the dictum of TREVOR MR in *Jennings v Ward* ((1705) 2 Vern 520) and continued:]

Unless such a bargain is unconscionable it is now good. But none the less the other and wider principle remains unshaken, that it is the essence of a mortgage that in the eye of a Court of Equity it should be a mere security for money, and that no bargain can be validly made which will prevent the mortgagor from redeeming on payment of what is due including principal, interest, and costs. He may stipulate that he will not pay off his debt, and so redeem the mortgage, for a fixed period. But whenever a right to redeem arises out of the doctrine of equity, he is precluded from fettering it. This principle has become an integral part of our system of jurisprudence and must be faithfully adhered to.

My Lords, the question in the present case is whether the right to redeem has been interfered with. And this must, for the reasons to which I have adverted in considering the history of the doctrine of equity, depend on the answer to a question which is primarily one of fact. What was the true character of the transaction? Did the appellants make a bargain such that the right to redeem was cut down, or did they simply stipulate for a collateral undertaking, outside and clear of the mortgage, which would give them an exclusive option of purchase of the sheepskins of the respondents? The question is in my opinion not whether the two contracts were made at the same moment and evidenced by the same instrument, but whether they were in substance a single and undivided contract or two distinct contracts. Putting aside for the moment considerations turning on the character of the floating charge, such an option no doubt affects the freedom of the respondents in carrying on their business even after the mortgage has been paid off. But so might other arrangements which would be plainly collateral, an agreement, for example, to take permanently into the firm a new partner as a condition of obtaining fresh capital in the form of a loan. The question is one not of form but of substance, and it can be answered in each case by looking at all the circumstances, and not by mere reliance on some abstract principle, or upon the dicta which have fallen obiter from judges in other and different cases. . . .

My Lords, if in the case before the House your Lordships arrive at the conclusion that the agreement for an option to purchase the respondents' sheepskins was not in substance a fetter on the exercise of their right to redeem, but was in the nature of a collateral bargain the entering into which was a preliminary and separable condition of the loan, the decided cases cease to present any great difficulty. In questions of this kind the binding force of previous decisions, unless the facts are indistinguishable, depends on whether they establish a principle. To follow previous authorities, so far as they lay down principles, is essential if the law is to be preserved from becoming unsettled and vague. In this respect the previous decisions of a Court of co-ordinate jurisdiction are more binding in a system of jurisprudence such as ours than in systems where the paramount authority is that of a code. But when a previous case has not laid down any new principle but has merely decided that a particular set of facts illustrates an existing rule, there are few more fertile sources of fallacy than to search in it for what is simply resemblance in circumstances, and to erect a previous decision into a governing precedent merely on this account. To look for anything except the principle established or recognized by previous decisions is really to weaken and not to strengthen the importance of precedent. . . .

It is not, in my opinion, conclusive in favour of the appellants that the security assumed the form of a floating charge. A floating charge is not the less a pledge because of its floating character, and a contract which fetters the right to redeem on which equity insists as regards all contracts of loan and security ought on principle to be set aside as readily in the case of a floating security as in any other case. But it is material that such a floating charge, in the absence of bargain to the contrary effect, permits the assets to be dealt with freely by the mortgagor until the charge becomes enforceable[11]. . . . No doubt it is the fact that on redemption the respondents will not get back their business as free from obligation as it was before the date of the security. But that may well be because outside the security and consistently with its terms there was a contemporaneous but collateral contract, contained in the same document as constituted the security, but in substance independent of it. If it was the intention of the parties, as I think it was, to enter into this contract as a condition of the respondents getting their advance, I know no reason either in morals or in equity which ought to prevent this intention from being left to have its effect. What was to be capable of redemption was an undertaking which was deliberately left to be freely changed in its details by ordinary business transactions with which the mortgage was not to interfere. Had the charge not been a floating one, it might have been more difficult to give effect to this intention.

[His Lordship referred to *Noakes & Co Ltd v Rice* ([1902] AC 24), where "this difficulty is illustrated" and to *Bradley v Carritt* ([1903] AC 253), and continued:]

[The decision in *Bradley v Carritt*] certainly cannot, in my opinion, be taken as authoritatively laying down that the mere circumstances that after redemption the property redeemed may not, as the result of some bargain made at the time of the mortgage, be in the same condition as it was before that time, is conclusive against the validity of that bargain. To render it invalid the bargain must, when its substance is examined, turn out to have formed part of the terms of the mortgage and to have really cut down a true right of redemption. I think that the tendency of recent decisions has been to lay undue stress on the letter of the principle which limits the jurisdiction of equity in setting aside contracts. The origin and reason of the principle ought, as I have already said, to be kept steadily in view in applying it to fresh cases. There appears to me to have grown up a tendency to look to the letter rather than to the spirit of the doctrine. The true view

[11] See (1976) 40 Conv (NS) 397 (J. H. Farrar).

is, I think, that judges ought in this kind of jurisdiction to proceed cautiously, and to bear in mind the real reasons which have led Courts of Equity to insist on the free right to redeem and the limits within which the purpose of the rule ought to confine its scope. I cannot but think that the validity of the bargain in such cases as *Bradley v Carritt* and *Santley v Wilde* ([1899] 2 Ch 474) might have been made free from serious question if the parties had chosen to seek what would have been substantially the same result in a different form. . . .

LORD PARKER OF WADDINGTON: My Lords, the defendants in this case are appealing to the equitable jurisdiction of the Court for relief from a contract which they admit to be fair and reasonable and of which they have already enjoyed the full advantage. Their title to relief is based on some equity which they say is inherent in all transactions in the nature of a mortgage. They can state no intelligible principle underlying this alleged equity, but contend that your Lordships are bound by authority. That the Court should be asked in the exercise of its equitable jurisdiction to assist in so inequitable a proceeding as the repudiation of a fair and reasonable bargain is somewhat startling, and makes it necessary to examine the point of view from which Courts of Equity have always regarded mortgage transactions. . . .

My Lords, after the most careful consideration of the authorities I think it is open to this House to hold, and I invite your Lordships to hold, that there is now no rule in equity which precludes a mortgagee, whether the mortgage be made upon the occasion of a loan or otherwise, from stipulating for any collateral advantage, provided such collateral advantage is not either (1) unfair and unconscionable, or (2) in the nature of a penalty clogging the equity of redemption, or (3) inconsistent with or repugnant to the contractual and equitable right to redeem.

In the present case it is clear from the evidence, if not from the agreement of 24 August 1910 itself, that the nature of the transaction was as follows: The defendant company wanted to borrow 10,000*l*, and the plaintiffs desired to obtain an option of purchase over any sheepskins the defendants might have for sale during a period of five years. The plaintiffs agreed to lend the money in consideration of obtaining this option, and the defendant company agreed to give the option in consideration of obtaining the loan. The loan was to carry interest at 6 per cent. per annum, and was not to be called in by the plaintiffs for a specified period. The defendant company, however, might pay it off at any time. It was to be secured by a floating charge over the defendant company's undertaking. The option was to continue for five years, whether the loan was paid off or otherwise, and if the plaintiffs did not exercise their option as to any of the defendant company's skins, a commission on the sale of such skins was in certain events payable to the plaintiffs.

I doubt whether, even before the repeal of the usury laws, this perfectly fair and businesslike transaction would have been considered a mortgage within any equitable rule or maxim relating to mortgages.

The only possible way of deciding whether a transaction is a mortgage within any such rule or maxim is by reference to the intention of the parties. It never was intended by the parties that if the defendant company exercised their right to pay off the loan they should get rid of the option. The option was not in the nature of a penalty, nor was it nor could it ever become inconsistent with or repugnant to any other part of the real bargain within any such rule or maxim. The same is true of the commission payable on the sale of skins as to which the option was not exercised. Under these circumstances it seems to me that the bargain must stand and that the plaintiffs are entitled to the relief they claim[12].

In *Multiservice Bookbinding Ltd v Marden* [1979] Ch 84, [1978] 2 All ER 489[13], the plaintiffs in September 1966 charged their business premises to the defendant as security for a loan of £36,000, in order to purchase new premises in North London. The defendant was only willing to lend the money if he could be safeguarded against a decline in the purchasing power of sterling. The terms of the mortgage, which was created with solicitors' advice, were that (i) interest be payable at 2 per cent. above bank rate on the full capital sum for the duration of the mortgage (ii) arrears of interest be capitalized after 21 days (thus providing for interest on interest) (iii) the loan be neither called in nor redeemed for 10 years, and (iv) the value of the capital and interest be index-linked to the Swiss franc. ("the Swiss franc uplift" clause 6).

In September 1966 the Swiss franc was just over 12 to the pound but in October 1976, when a redemption statement was prepared, it had fallen to just over 4. The total capital repayment was £87,588, as against £36,000 lent, and the total interest due was £45,380 (£31,051 basic plus £14,329 uplift). The average rate of interest over the ten years would have been 16.01 per cent. On the other hand, the book value of the mortgaged property had more than doubled, and the plaintiff company's "growth had been considerable".

The plaintiffs took out a summons to determine how far the terms of the mortgage were enforceable. BROWNE-WILKINSON J held that all terms were valid. Having decided that an index-linked money obligation is not contrary to public policy, he continued at p. 109:

"I have dealt with these authorities [*Kreglinger v New Patagonia Meat and Cold Storage Co Ltd* [1914] AC 25; p. 622, ante; *Knightsbridge Estates Trust Ltd v Byrne* [1939] Ch 441, [1938] 4 All ER 618; p. 612, ante; *Biggs v Hoddinott* [1898] 2 Ch 307; p. 617, ante; *Davis v Symons* [1934] Ch 442] at some length because the sheet anchor of Mr. Nugee's argument, that mere unreasonableness is sufficient to invalidate a stipulation, is the use of the word unreasonable by Goff

---

[12] (1944) 60 LQR 191 (G. L. Williams).
[13] [1978] Conv 346 (H. W. Wilkinson); 432 (D. W. Williams).

J in *Cityland and Property (Holdings) Ltd v Dabrah* [1968] Ch 166. In that case the plaintiff company was the freehold owner of a house of which the defendant had been the tenant for 11 years. His lease expired and the plaintiff company sold the freehold to him for £3,500, of which the defendant paid £600 in cash and the balance of £2,900 was left by the plaintiff company on mortgage. The mortgage was in unusual terms in that it contained simply a covenant to pay, by instalments, the sum of £4,553, that is to say, a premium of 57 per cent. over the sum advanced. No explanation was given as to what this premium represented. The defendant defaulted in paying his instalments after only one year, and the plaintiff was seeking to enforce his security for the full sum of £4,553 less payments actually made. Not surprisingly Goff J refused to permit this on the grounds that the excess over £2,900 was an unlawful premium. Bearing in mind the relative strength of lender and borrower, the size of the premium and the lack of any explanation or justification for it, the premium in that case was unconscionable and oppressive. . . .

I therefore approach the second point on the basis that, in order to be freed from the necessity to comply with all the terms of the mortgage, the plaintiffs must show that the bargain, or some of its terms, was unfair and unconscionable: it is not enough to show that, in the eyes of the court, it was unreasonable. In my judgment a bargain cannot be unfair and unconscionable unless one of the parties to it has imposed the objectionable terms in a morally reprehensible manner, that is to say, in a way which affects his conscience.

The classic example of an unconscionable bargain is where advantage has been taken of a young, inexperienced or ignorant person to introduce a term which no sensible well-advised person or party would have accepted. But I do not think the categories of unconscionable bargains are limited: the court can and should intervene where a bargain has been procured by unfair means.

Mr. Nugee submitted that a borrower was, in the normal case, in an unequal bargaining position vis-à-vis the lender and that the care taken by the courts of equity to protect borrowers — to which Lord Parker referred in the passage I have quoted — was reflected in a general rule that, except in the case of two large equally powerful institutions, any unreasonable term would be 'unconscionable' within Lord Parker's test. I cannot accept this. In my judgment there is no such special rule applicable to contracts of loan which requires one to treat a bargain as having been unfairly made even where it is demonstrated that no unfair advantage has been taken of the borrower. No decision illustrating Mr. Nugee's principle was cited. However, if, as in the *Cityland* case [1968] Ch 166, there is an unusual or unreasonable stipulation the reason for which is not explained, it may well be that in the absence of any explanation, the court will assume that unfair advantage has been taken of the borrower. In considering all the facts, it will often be the case that the borrower's need for the money was far more pressing than the lenders need to lend: if this proves to be the case, then circumstances exist in which an unfair advantage could have been taken. It does not necessarily follow that what could have been done has been done: whether or not an unfair advantage has in fact been taken depends on the facts of each case.

Applying those principles to this case, first I do not think it is right to treat the 'Swiss franc uplift' element in the capital-repayments as being in any sense a premium or collateral advantage. In my judgment a lender of money is entitled to insure that he is repaid the real value of his loan and if he introduces a term which so provides, he is not stipulating for anything beyond the repayment of principal. I do not think equity would have struck down clause 6 as a collateral advantage even before the repeal of the usury laws. . . . .

Secondly, considering the mortgage bargain as a whole, in my judgment there was no great inequality of bargaining power as between the plaintiffs and the defendant. The plaintiff company was a small but prosperous company in need of cash to enable it to expand: if it did not like the terms offered it could have refused them without being made insolvent or, as in the *Cityland* case [1968] Ch 166, losing its home. The defendant had £40,000 to lend, but only, as he explained to the plaintiffs, if its real value was preserved. The defendant is not a professional moneylender and there is no evidence of any sharp practice of any kind by him. The borrowers were represented by independent solicitors of repute. Therefore the background does not give rise to any pre-supposition that the defendant took an unfair advantage of the plaintiffs.

Mr. Nugee's main case is based on the terms of the mortgage itself. He points to the facts that (1) the defendant's principal and interest is fully inflation proofed (2) that interest is payable at two per cent. above minimum lending rate and (3) that interest is payable on the whole £36,000 throughout the term of the loan. He says that although any one of these provisions by itself might not be objectionable, when all these are joined in one mortgage they are together 'unfair and unconscionable.' He adds further subsidiary points, amongst them that it is impossible to know the sum required for redemption when notice to redeem has to be given; that interest is payable in advance; that no days of grace were allowed for paying the instalments of capital and any expenses incurred by the lender are charged on the property and therefore under clause 6 subject to the Swiss franc uplift even though incurred long after 1966. He also contends that if there were capitalised arrears of interest, the Swiss franc uplift would be applied twice: once when the arrears are capitalised and again when the capitalised sum is paid: in my opinion this is not the true construction of the mortgage.

However, Mr. Nugee's other points amount to a formidable list and if it were relevant I would be of the view that the terms were unreasonable judged by the standards which the court would adopt if it had to settle the terms of a mortgage. In particular I consider that it was unreasonable both for the debt to be inflation proofed by reference to the Swiss franc and at the same time to provide for a rate of interest two per cent. above bank rate — a rate which reflects at least in part the unstable state of the pound sterling. On top of this interest on the whole sum advanced was to be paid throughout the term. The defendant made a hard bargain. But the test is not reasonableness. The parties made a bargain which the plaintiffs, who are businessmen, went into with their eyes open, with the benefit of independent advice, without any compelling necessity to accept a loan on these terms and without any sharp practice by the defendant. I cannot see that there was anything unfair or oppressive or morally reprehensible in such a bargain entered into in such circumstances. The need for the defendant to invest his money in a way which preserved its real purchasing power provides an adequate explanation of all the terms of the mortgage.''

The problem has also arisen in connection with the distribution of petroleum products through tied garages. In general terms, the garage proprietor undertakes to deal only in the products of a particular oil company. The oil company undertakes to supply the products and to allow a special rebate. Sometimes the oil company advances money to the garage proprietor, and in such a case the mortgage of the garage will include an undertaking to observe the terms of the agreement during the continuance of the mortgage.

A garage proprietor who wishes to pay off the mortgage before the due date and to be free of its provisions may attack its validity on two grounds. First, on the ground of the doctrine, previously discussed, which protects a mortgagor against oppression. Secondly, on the ground that the agreement is void as being in restraint of trade. This second ground is a matter for the law of contract and its details must be sought elsewhere[14]. We should, however, note here an argument that the doctrine of restraint of trade has no application to mortgages; that the mortgagor, being especially protected by equity, has equity's protection but no other. As would be expected, this argument has not been accepted[15].

Thus a mortgage is open to attack on both grounds. The two grounds must be kept distinct, for different evidence is relevant to each, and different rules are applicable; and, following the doctrine of the *Kreglinger Case*, the court may consider whether an operation is properly construed as a single transaction or as two separate transactions; one being a mortgage which is governed by the doctrine here discussed, and the other being a commercial agreement which is dealt with under the doctrine of restraint of trade.

---

[14] Cheshire and Fifoot (9th edn., 1976), pp. 368–378; Treitel, *Law of Contract* (5th edn., 197), pp. 337–358; (1969) 85 LQR 229 (J. D. Heydon); Heydon, *Restraint of Trade Doctrine* (1971), Chaps. 3, 9.

[15] *Esso Petroleum Co Ltd v Harper's Garage* [1968] AC 269; per Lord WILBERFORCE at p. 342.

RE PETROL FILLING STATION, VAUXHALL BRIDGE ROAD, LONDON
(1968) 20 P & CR 1 (ChD, UNGOED-THOMAS J)

The plaintiffs were owners of a petrol filling station, and entered into a twenty year contract on 9 April 1956 with the defendants, whereby the plaintiffs agreed to sell only the defendants' products, and were entitled to a rebate on the price in addition to the usual commission.

On 1 November 1956 the plaintiffs mortgaged their garage to the defendants in consideration of a loan which was required for the modernisation of the premises. The mortgage deed
(1) provided for the repayment of the loan over nineteen years;
(2) gave the defendants (the mortgagees) a right of pre-emption over the premises during the continuance of the mortgage;
(3) provided that the term of the contract of 9 April 1956 tying the petrol station should remain in force during the continuance of the mortgage.

The question was whether the plaintiffs were entitled to redeem, and to be free of the restrictions contained in the contract and the mortgage.

Held. The plaintiffs were bound by the terms of the mortgage.

UNGOED-THOMAS J: It is common ground that the ties in the November agreement are, in accordance with its express provisions, limited to the continuance of the security and that, therefore, on redemption they cease to operate and no question of clog can arise with regard to them. It is also common ground that the ties contained in the sales agreement are capable of constituting a clog on an equity of redemption if they are (and I purposely use vague words) sufficiently connected with it. Therefore, the only question for my decision becomes whether the ties imposed by the sales agreement of April are sufficiently connected with the equity of redemption of the legal charge of November as to constitute a clog upon it. . . .

If, in accordance with my view, the plaintiffs executed the sales agreement without there being any contract with regard to the loan, then it seems to me to follow that the sales agreement and the legal charge were what they appear on their face to be, namely, two separate contracts. Such a conclusion would be in line with the reliance, based on *De Beer's Consolidated Mines Ltd v British South Africa Co* [1912] AC 52, on the British South Africa Company's obligation to grant the licence being absolute and immediate and their granting of the mortgage being optional. This distinction in that case was relied on as itself establishing that there were two contracts, one with regard to the licence and one with regard to the mortgage, and not one contract comprehending them both.

Secondly, even if there were, contrary to my view, a binding contract with regard to the loan and with regard to the sales agreement before or at the time of the sales agreement, the question would still remain whether they constituted one or two contracts. Having regard to authorities and the evidence, which I have already considered, including the commercial nature of the ties in the sales agreement, it seems to me that at its highest the defendants' agreement to lend "in return for the plaintiffs' agreeing to enter into a petrol sales agreement" as stated by Mr. Pugh, was, in the words of Lord Haldane in the *Kreglinger Case* [1914] AC 25 "in consideration of being given" a petrol sales agreement, which was "a collateral bargain the entering into which was a preliminary and separable condition of the loan".

Thirdly, even if there were one contract, as the plaintiffs contend, I, for my part, if I were driven to it, would conclude that that contract comprehending the sales agreement and the agreement to lend on the legal charge was not in its "real nature and substance", as a whole, a mortgage transaction, nor, to use Lord Haldane's words, "a mere mortgage", and so falls outside the doctrine of once a mortgage always a mortgage, of which the clog on the equity of redemption is an emanation. I again quote Lord Haldane, where he said, at p. 37:

"That the substance of the transaction must be looked to in applying this doctrine and that it did not apply to cases which were only apparently or technically within it but were in reality something more than cases of mortgage."

If there were the one contract, as the plaintiffs say, then it was "something more than" a mortgage — it was a commercial transaction, of which the mortgage formed part, leaving at any rate the sales agreement part of the transaction with the sales agreement ties outside the ambit of the other part of the transaction, namely, the mortgage, altogether. As I have indicated, the effect on the ties specified in the document of legal charge if those ties were expressed to endure beyond redemption, does not arise.

My conclusion, therefore, is that the defendants succeed on the issue before me.

iv.   EXTORTIONATE CREDIT AGREEMENTS

Cheshire: *Modern Law of Real Property* (12th edn. 1976), pp. 718–719

"CONSUMER CREDIT AGREEMENTS

The Consumer Credit Act 1974[16] establishes a comprehensive code which regulates the supply of credit not exceeding £5,000 to an individual[17]. It includes provisions on advertising and canvassing; the licensing of credit and hire businesses; all aspects of the agreement; and judicial control over its enforcement.

To come within the Act, a mortgage must constitute a regulated consumer agreement, that is to say, a personal credit agreement by

---

[16] The Act is being implemented by stages. For progress see (1977) 121 Sol Jo 467, 484, 500 (F.A.R. Bennion), (1978) NLJ 604 (J. N. Adams). It will be supplemented by a mass of subordinate legislation. See Guest and Lloyd, *Consumer Credit Act 1974*, *Encyclopaedia of Consumer Credit Law* (1975), Goode, *Consumer Credit Act 1974*; (1975) 34 CLJ 79 (R. M. Goode); (1975) 39 Conv (NS) 94 (J. E. Adams); Fisher and Lightwood, chap. 9.

[17] This includes sole traders and partnerships, s. 189 (1).

which a creditor provides a debtor with a credit not exceeding £5,000[18]. There are, however, exempt agreements[19], of which the most important are loans made by a building society or local authority for house purchase. Banks are not exempt. We can only notice in very general terms the main areas where the ordinary law of mortgage is affected.

(A) Creation. If the formalities prescribed by the Act are not complied with[20], section 65 provides that an agreement which is "improperly-executed" can be enforced against the debtor on an order of the court[1] only.

(B) Rights of the Mortgagor. The most far-reaching provision for the protection of the mortgagor is the power given to the court to 're-open' a credit agreement if the credit bargain is extortionate[2]. This power extends to all credit bargains, whether regulated, exempt or above the £5,000 limit, other than those in which the debtor is a body corporate. A credit bargain is extortionate if the payments to be made under it are 'grossly exhorbitant' or if it 'otherwise grossly contravenes the ordinary principles of fair dealing.' The court is required to take into account interest rates prevailing when the bargain was made; factors in relation to the debtor, such as his age, experience and business capacity, and the degree to which he was under financial pressure when he made the bargain; and the degree of risk accepted by the creditor. The court has wide discretion 'to do justice between the parties'.

Under section 94, the debtor under a regulated agreement has the right, on giving notice to the creditor, to redeem prematurely at any time. Any provision in the agreement which limits his rights in this respect is void[3]. It would seem that if a provision to postpone the contractual right to redeem were included in a regulated agreement it would be void[4].

(C) Rights of the Mortgagee. Consonant with the object of the Act, these are curtailed. A security cannot be enforced by reason of any breach of a regulated agreement by the debtor, until the creditor has served a notice under section 87. This is similar to, but not identical with, the notice required by section 146 of the Law of Property Act 1925 in the case of the forfeiture of a lease[5]. Further, a land mortgage securing a regulated agreement is enforceable by an order of the court only[6]. This is a most important provision, since a mortgagee cannot exercise his rights of taking possession and of sale without such an

---

[18] S. 8.
[19] S. 16.
[20] Part V of the Act. See also s. 105.
[1] The County Court has exclusive jurisdiction, s. 141 (1). See also s. 127.
[2] Ss. 137–40, *cf. Cityland and Property (Holdings) Ltd v Dabrah* [1968] Ch 166, [1967] 2 All ER 639, p. 628, ante.
[3] S. 173 (1).
[4] *Knightsbridge Estates Trust Ltd v Byrne* [1939] Ch 441, [1938] 4 All ER 618; p. 612, ante.
[5] P. 397, ante.
[6] S. 126. For the orders which the court can make, see Part IX of the Act.

order. If, however, he sells without an order, it would seem that he can pass a good title to the purchaser[7].

Finally, under section 113, a creditor shall not derive from the enforcement of the security any greater benefit than he would obtain from enforcement of a regulated agreement, if the security were not provided. This would seem to deny the mortgagee the full benefit of foreclosure[8]."

CONSUMER CREDIT ACT 1974

Extortionate credit bargains[9]

137. — (1) If the court finds a credit bargain extortionate it may reopen the credit agreement so as to do justice between the parties.

(2) In this section and sections 138 to 140, —

    (a) "credit agreement" means any agreement between an individual (the "debtor") and any other person (the "creditor") by which the creditor provides the debtor with credit of any amount, and

    (b) "credit bargain" —

        (i) where no transaction other than the credit agreement is to be taken into account in computing the total charge for credit, means the credit agreement, or

        (ii) where one or more other transactions are to be so taken into account, means the credit agreement and those other transactions, taken together.

138. — (1) A credit bargain is extortionate if it —

    (a) requires the debtor or a relative of his to make payments (whether unconditionally, or on certain contingencies) which are grossly exorbitant, or

    (b) otherwise grossly contravenes ordinary principles of fair dealing.

(2) In determining whether a credit bargain is extortionate, regard shall be had to such evidence as is adduced concerning —

    (a) interest rates prevailing at the time it was made,

    (b) the factors mentioned in subsections (3) to (5), and

    (c) any other relevant considerations.

(3) Factors applicable under subsection (2) in relation to the debtor include —

    (a) his age, experience, business capacity and state of health; and

    (b) the degree to which, at the time of making the credit bargain, he was under financial pressure, and the nature of that pressure.

(4) Factors applicable under subsection (2) in relation to the creditor include —

---

[7] S. 177 (2).

[8] P. 655, ante. 39 Conv (NS) 94 at p. 108.

[9] These sections came into operation on 16 May 1977 and "apply to agreements and transactions whenever made". Consumer Credit Act 1974, s. 192 (1), Sch. 3, para. 42; Consumer Credit Act 1974 (Commencement No. 2) Order 1977 (S.I. 1977 No. 325) art. 2 (2). If the debtor or any surety alleges that the credit bargain is extortionate it is for the creditor to prove the contrary, s. 171 (7).

(a) the degree of risk accepted by him, having regard to the value of any security provided;

(b) his relationship to the debtor; and

(c) whether or not a colourable cash price was quoted for any goods or services included in the credit bargain.

IV. Statutory Provisions Affecting the Rights of the Mortgagor[8]

LAW OF PROPERTY ACT 1925

91. Sale of mortgaged property in action for redemption or foreclosure. — (1) Any person entitled to redeem mortgaged property may have a judgment or order for sale instead of for redemption in an action brought by him either for redemption alone, or for sale alone, or for sale or redemption in the alternative[9].

(2) In any action, whether for foreclosure, or for redemption, or for sale, or for the raising and payment in any manner of mortgage money, the court, on the request of the mortgagee, or of any person interested either in the mortgage money or in the right of redemption, and, notwithstanding that —

(a) any other person dissents; or

(b) the mortgagee or any person so interested does not appear in the action;

and without allowing any time for redemption or for payment of any mortgage money, may direct a sale of the mortgaged property, on such terms as it thinks fit, including the deposit in court of a reasonable sum fixed by the court to meet the expenses of sale and to secure performance of the terms[10].

95. Obligation to transfer instead of reconveying, and as to right to take possession. — (1) Where a mortgagor is entitled to redeem, then subject to compliance with the terms on compliance with which he would be entitled to require a reconveyance or surrender, he shall be entitled to require the mortgagee, instead of re-conveying or surrendering, to assign the mortgage debt and convey the mortgaged property to any third person, as the mortgagor directs; and the mortgagee shall be bound to assign and convey accordingly.

(2) The rights conferred by this section belong to and are capable of being enforced by each incumbrancer, or by the mortgagor, notwithstanding any intermediate incumbrance; but a requisition of an incumbrancer prevails over a requisition of the mortgagor, and, as between incumbrancers, a requisition of a prior incumbrancer prevails over a requisition of a subsequent incumbrancer.

(3) The foregoing provisions of this section do not apply in the case of a mortgagee being or having been in possession.

---

[8] Cheshire, pp. 662–665; M & W pp. 943–950; MM, pp. 456–460.

[9] He is apparently entitled to such an order as of right — *Clarke v Pannell* (1884) 29 Sol Jo 147.

[10] *Twentieth Century Banking Corpn Ltd v Wilkinson* [1977] Ch 99, [1976] 3 All ER 361.

(4) Nothing in this Act affects prejudicially the right of a mortgagee of land whether or not his charge is secured by a legal term of years absolute to take possession of the land, but the taking of possession by the mortgagee does not convert any legal estate of the mortgagor into an equitable interest.

(5) This section applies to mortgages made either before or after the commencement of this Act, and takes effect notwithstanding any stipulation to the contrary.

96. Regulations respecting inspection, production and delivery of documents, and priorities. — (1) A mortgagor, as long as his right to redeem subsists, shall be entitled from time to time, at reasonable times, on his request, and at his own cost, and on payment of the mortgagee's costs and expenses in this behalf, to inspect and make copies or abstracts of or extracts from the documents of title relating to the mortgaged property in the custody or power of the mortgagee.

This subsection applies to mortgages made after the thirty-first day of December, eighteen hundred and eighty-one, and takes effect notwithstanding any stipulation to the contrary.

98. Actions for possession by mortgagors. — (1) A mortgagor for the time being entitled to the possession or receipt of the rents and profits of any land, as to which the mortgagee has not given notice of his intention to take possession or to enter into the receipt of the rents and profits thereof, may sue for such possession, or for the recovery of such rents or profits, or to prevent or recover damages in respect of any trespass or other wrong relative thereto, in his own name only, unless the cause of action arises upon a lease or other contract made by him jointly with any other person.

(2) This section does not prejudice the power of a mortgagor independently of this section to take proceedings in his own name only, either in right of any legal estate vested in him or otherwise.

(3) This section applies whether the mortgage was made before or after the commencement of this Act.

V.   Rights Common to Mortgagor and Mortgagee[11]

LAW OF PROPERTY ACT 1925

91. Sale of mortgaged property in action for redemption or foreclosure. — p. 635, ante.

99. Leasing powers of mortgagor and mortgagee in possession. —
(1) A mortgagor of land while in possession shall, as against every incumbrancer, have power to make from time to time any such lease of the mortgaged land, or any part thereof, as is by this section authorised.

(2) A mortgagee of land while in possession shall, as against all prior incumbrancers, if any, and as against the mortgagor, have power to make from time to time any such lease as aforesaid.

---

[11] Cheshire, pp. 665–668, 679–680, 663; M & W, pp. 932–936; MM, pp. 451–454.

(3) The leases which this section authorises are —

   (i) agricultural or occupation leases for any term not exceeding twenty-one years, or, in the case of a mortgage made after the commencement of this Act, fifty years; and

   (ii) building leases for any term not exceeding ninety-nine years, or, in the case of a mortgage made after the commencement of this Act, nine hundred and ninety-nine years[12].

(5) Every such lease shall be made to take effect in possession not later than twelve months after its date.

(6) Every such lease shall reserve the best rent that can reasonably be obtained, regard being had to the circumstances of the case, but without any fine being taken.

(7) Every such lease shall contain a covenant by the lessee for payment of the rent, and a condition of re-entry on the rent not being paid within a time therein specified not exceeding thirty days.

(8) A counterpart of every such lease shall be executed by the lessee and delivered to the lessor, of which execution and delivery the execution of the lease by the lessor shall, in favour of the lessee and all persons deriving title under him, be sufficient evidence.

(11) In case of a lease by the mortgagor, he shall, within one month after making the lease, deliver to the mortgagee, or, where there are more than one, to the mortgagee first in priority, a counterpart of the lease duly executed by the lessee, but the lessee shall not be concerned to see that this provision is complied with.

(13) This section applies only if and as far as a contrary intention is not expressed by the mortgagor and mortgagee in the mortgage deed, or otherwise in writing, and has effect subject to the terms of the mortgage deed or of any such writing and to the provisions therein contained.

(14) The mortgagor and mortgagee may, by agreement in writing, whether or not contained in the mortgage deed, reserve to or confer on the mortgagor or the mortgagee, or both, any further or other powers of leasing or having reference to leasing; and any further or other powers so reserved or conferred shall be exercisable, as far as may be, as if they were conferred by this Act, and with all the like incidents, effects, and consequences. . . .

100. Powers of mortgagor and mortgagee in possession to accept surrenders of leases. — (1) For the purpose only of enabling a lease authorised under the last preceding section, or under any agreement made pursuant to that section, or by the mortgage deed (in this section referred to as an authorised lease) to be granted, a mortgagor of land while in possession shall, as against every incumbrancer, have, by virtue of this Act, power to accept from time to time a surrender of any lease of the mortgaged land or any part thereof comprised in the lease, with or without an exception of or in respect of all or any of the mines and minerals therein, and, on a surrender of the lease so far as it comprises part only of the land or mines and minerals leased, the rent may be apportioned.

---

[12] For further details, see sub-ss. 9, 10.

(2) For the same purpose, a mortgagee of land while in possession shall, as against all prior or other incumbrancers, if any, and as against the mortgagor, have, by virtue of this Act, power to accept from time to time any such surrender as aforesaid.

(5) No surrender shall, by virtue of this section, be rendered valid unless:—

    (a) An authorised lease is granted of the whole of the land or mines and minerals comprised in the surrender to take effect in possession immediately or within one month after the date of the surrender; and

    (b) The term certain or other interest granted by the new lease is not less in duration than the unexpired term or interest which would have been subsisting under the original lease if that lease had not been surrendered; and

    (c) Where the whole of the land mines and minerals originally leased has been surrendered, the rent reserved by the new lease is not less than the rent which would have been payable under the original lease if it had not been surrendered; or where part only of the land or mines and minerals has been surrendered, the aggregate rents respectively remaining payable or reserved under the original lease and new lease are not less than the rent which would have been payable under the original lease if no partial surrender had been accepted.

(7) This section applies only if and as far as a contrary intention is not expressed by the mortgagor and mortgagee in the mortgage deed, or otherwise in writing, and shall have effect subject to the terms of the mortgage deed or of any such writing and to the provisions therein contained.

VI.   Rights and Remedies of the Mortgagee[13]

A.   Possession of the Mortgaged Premises[14]

LAW OF PROPERTY ACT 1925

95.   Obligation to transfer instead of reconveying, and as to right to take possession.
    (4) p. 636, ante.

---

[13] Cheshire, pp. 668-679; M & W, pp. 904-932; MM, pp. 437-447; Waldock, pp. 224-295; Fisher and Lightwood, Chap. 18. The mortgagee's remedies are cumulative. *Rudge v Richens* (1873) LR 8 CP 358 (mortgagee, after exercising power of sale, may sue for balance on personal covenant): *Gordon Grant & Co Ltd v F. L. Boos* [1926] AC 781 (purchase of land (by leave) at auction and re-sale at a large profit still leaves personal action for balance not found at the auction sale) *Refuge Assurance Co Ltd v Pearlberg* [1938] Ch 687, [1938] 3 All ER 231 (a mortgagee in possession is not prevented from appointing a receiver). Foreclosure however puts an end to other remedies.

[14] Cheshire, pp. 676-678; M & W, pp. 914-919; MM, pp. 442-444; Fisher and Lightwood, Chap. 19. [1979] Conv (NS) 266 (R. J. Smith). Report of the Committee on the Enforcement of Judgment Debts 1969 (Cmnd. 3909), paras. 1363-1427. As to the right of an equitable mortgagee to possession, see M & W, pp. 923-924; (1955) 71 LQR 204 (H. W. R. Wade).

FOUR-MAIDS LTD *v* DUDLEY MARSHALL (PROPERTIES) LTD
[1957] Ch 317, [1957] 2 All ER 35 (ChD, HARMAN J)[15]

The legal charge provided that, if the interest payments were made punctually, the principal would not be called in for some 2 years 10 months. Six months after the loan was made interest was late and the lender called in the principal. Arrears of interest were then paid, but the lender claimed the whole sum due and took out an originating summons asking for possession.

Held. The mortgagee was entitled to possession.

HARMAN J: This is an originating summons for possession. . . . This subject is one which is constantly being agitated in this court. I have had my attention called to some observations I made on it recently in *Hughes v Waite* [1957] 1 WLR 713, [1957] 1 All ER 603, and even more recently in *Alliance Perpetual Building Society v Belrum Investments Ltd* [1957] 1 WLR 720, [1957] 1 All ER 635, which came before me on an application to commit the editor of the "Daily Mail" for comments on a mortgagee's action for possession of a sort exactly similar to the present. The comments and, indeed, the arguments of counsel for the newspaper showed an entire misapprehension of what an originating summons for possession is about. They all assumed that it involved some kind of default on the part of the mortgagor, but I said there, and I repeat now, that the right of the mortgagee to possession in the absence of some contract has nothing to do with default on the part of the mortgagor. The mortgagee may go into possession before the ink is dry on the mortgage unless there is something in the contract, express or by implication[16], whereby he has contracted himself out of that right. He has the right because he has a legal term of years in the property or its statutory equivalent. If there is an attornment clause, he must give notice. If there is a provision that, so long as certain payments are made, he will not go into possession, then he has contracted himself out of his rights. Apart from that, possession is a matter of course.

[An application for possession] has become a very fashionable form of relief because, owing to the conditions now prevailing, if it is desired to realize a security by sale, vacant possession is almost essential. Where, therefore, the mortgagor is in occupation, a summons for possession is taken out, and no other relief is sought, and where the mortgagee is in a position to exercise his power of sale, that is all the help he requires from the court. . . .

The mortgagor said here that his default was of a very small order. So it was. If this were a case where there was discretion in the matter, I should feel that it was a hard case. But the mortgagor has entered

---

[15] (1957) 73 LQR 300 (R. E. M.): *Birmingham Citizens' Permanent Building Society v Caunt* [1962] Ch 883, [1962] 1 All ER 163; see too *Alnwick RDC v Taylor* [1966] Ch 355, [1966] 1 All ER 899.

[16] See *Esso Petroleum Co Ltd v Alstonbridge Properties Ltd* [1975] 1 WLR 1474, [1975] 3 All ER 358; *Western Bank Ltd v Schindler* [1977] Ch 1, [1976] 2 All ER 393; p. 642, post.

into a contract with the mortgagee, and the mortgagee asks for his rights under the contract, and this court, in my judgment, has no power to refuse him those rights.

To this Draconian rule there is now a statutory exception in favour of the mortgagor of a dwelling-house. These additional powers can be exercised by the court whether or not the mortgagor is in default.

ADMINISTRATION OF JUSTICE ACT 1970

36.   Additional powers of court in action by mortgagee for possession of dwelling-house. — (1) Where the mortgagee under a mortgage of land which consists of or includes a dwelling-house[17] brings an action in which he claims possession of the mortgaged property, not being an action for foreclosure in which a claim for possession of the mortgaged property is also made, the court[18] may exercise any of the powers conferred on it by subsection (2) below if it appears to the court that in the event of its exercising the power the mortgagor is likely to be able within a reasonable period to pay[19] any sums due under the mortgage or to remedy a default consisting of a breach of any other obligation arising under or by virtue of the mortgage.

(2) The court —

    (a) may adjourn the proceedings, or

    (b) on giving judgment, or making an order, for delivery of possession of the mortgaged property, or at any time before the execution of such judgment or order, may —

        (i) stay or suspend execution of the judgment or order, or

        (ii) postpone the date for delivery of possession,

for such period or periods as the court thinks reasonable.

(3) Any such adjournment, stay, suspension or postponement as is referred to in subsection (2) above may be made subject to such conditions with regard to payment by the mortgagor of any sum secured by the mortgage or the remedying of any default as the court thinks fit.

(4) The court may from time to time vary or revoke any condition imposed by virtue of this section.

38A[20].   This part of this Act shall not apply to a mortgage securing an agreement which is a regulated agreement within the meaning of the Consumer Credit Act 1974.

---

[17] The fact that part is used as a shop or office or for business, trade or professional purposes does not prevent a house from being a dwelling-house: s. 39 (2).

[18] If the land is outside Greater London or the county palatine of Lancaster, and, if a County Court has jurisdiction, the action must be brought in the County Court: ss. 37–38. *Corbiere Properties Ltd v Taylor* (1971) 23 P & CR 289; *Trustees of Manchester Unity Life Insurance Collecting Society v Sadler* [1974] 1 WLR 770, [1974] 2 All ER 410; *Mornington Permanent Building Society v Ghai* (1975) 119 Sol Jo 592; *P. B. Frost Ltd v Green* [1978] 1 WLR 949, [1978] 2 All ER 206.

[19] *Royal Trust Co of Canada v Markham* [1975] 1 WLR 1416, [1975] 3 All ER 433.

[20] Added by Consumer Credit Act 1974 s. 192 Sch. 4, para. 30; p. 634, ante.

ADMINISTRATION OF JUSTICE ACT 1973

8. Extension of powers of court in action by mortgagee of dwelling house. — (1) Where by a mortgage of land which consists of or includes a dwelling-house, or by any agreement between the mortgagee under such a mortgage and the mortgagor, the mortgagor is entitled or is to be permitted to pay the principal sum secured by instalments or otherwise to defer payment of it in whole or in part, but provision is also made for earlier payment in the event of any default by the mortgagor or of a demand by the mortgagee or otherwise, then for purposes of section 36 of the Administration of Justice Act 1970 (under which a court has power to delay giving a mortgagee possession of the mortgaged property so as to allow the mortgagor a reasonable time to pay any sums due under the mortgage) a court may treat as due under the mortgage on account of the principal sum secured and of interest on it only such amounts as the mortgagor would have expected to be required to pay if there had been no such provision for earlier payment[1].

(2) A court shall not exercise by virtue of subsection (1) above the powers conferred by section 36 of the Administration of Justice Act 1970 unless it appears to the court not only that the mortgagor is likely to be able within a reasonable period to pay any amounts regarded (in accordance with subsection (1) above) as due on account of the principal sum secured, together with the interest on those amounts, but also that he is likely to be able by the end of that period to pay any further amounts that he would have expected to be required to pay by then on account of that sum and of interest on it if there had been no such provision as is referred to in subsection (1) above for earlier payment.

(3) Where subsection (1) above would apply to an action in which a mortgagee only claimed possession of the mortgaged property, and the mortgagee brings an action for foreclosure (with or without also claiming possession of the property), then section 36 of the Administration of Justice Act 1970 together with subsections (1) and (2) above shall apply as they would apply if it were an action in which the mortgagee only claimed possession of the mortgaged property, except that —

    (*a*) section 36 (2) (*b*) shall apply only in relation to any claim for possession. . . .

It is possible also to take possession for the purpose of receiving the income of the property. It is more usual, however, to appoint a receiver[2] if the object is to make up income in arrear, for a mortgagee

---

[1] Reversing the effect of *Halifax Building Society v Clark* [1973] 2 WLR 1, [1973] 2 All ER 33; but the grant of the statutory concession was unnecessary; *First Middlesbrough Trading and Mortgage Co Ltd v Cunningham* (1974) 28 P & CR 69; (1974) 38 Conv (NS) 309. See *Centrax Trustees Ltd v Ross* [1979] 2 All ER 952; [1979] Conv 371 (F. R. Crane).

[2] See p. 655, post.

in possession is made to account not only for what he received, but also for what he could, by prudent management, have received.

WESTERN BANK LTD *v* SCHINDLER
[1977] Ch 1, [1976] 2 All ER 393 (CA, BUCKLEY, SCARMAN and GOFF LJJ)

In 1973 the defendant mortgaged a dwelling-house to the plaintiffs to secure a loan of £32,000, and at the same time by a separate transaction took out an endowment policy in their favour as collateral security. The preliminary loan agreement provided for the payment of interest monthly in advance, and periodical payment of the premiums on the policy; also for repayment of the principal sum in 10 years time. The mortgage deed however failed to provide for monthly payments of interest, and provided instead that the principal and accrued interest be paid at the end of the 10 year period.

The defendant paid three monthly instalments of mortgage interest and three premiums under the policy, and then made no further payments. The policy lapsed, and the mortgagees sought possession of the dwelling-house. The mortgagor was not in breach of any term of the mortgage. GOULDING J, in the exercise of his discretion under Administration of Justice Act 1970, section 36 (1), made an order for possession to take effect one month after the order.

Held. (1) No term could be implied in the mortgage deed to exclude the mortgagees' common law right to possession.

(2) (GOFF LJ dubitante) section 36 (1) applied, even though the mortgagor was not in default.

SCARMAN LJ: I agree. This is an appeal by the mortgagor of a dwelling house against an order for possession within 28 days made by Goulding J in an action brought by the mortgagees. Owing to the strange but absolutely clear terms of the legal charge, the mortgagees were driven to base their claim for possession on the common law right which they enjoy by virtue of his legal estate: for they could allege no default, no arrears. Mr. Lightman, for the mortgagor, has put forward the case that, in the absence of a default by the mortgagor upon an obligation under the charge, or of arrears owed by him, the mortgagees have no right to possession; alternatively, that, if they have, the court has a discretion to postpone an order under section 36 of the Administration of Justice Act 1970, and should have exercised its discretion in favour of the mortgagor.

Mr. Lightman's argument for the mortgagor — presented, if I may respectfully say so, forcefully and cogently — falls into two parts. First, he submits that there should be implied into the terms of the legal charge a further term excluding the mortgagor's right to possession in the absence of arrears or default by the mortgagor. It is, he contends, a mortgage under which the mortgagee has expressly agreed to wait 10 years for repayment of his capital and for payment of interest (which, though it accrues from year to year, is not payable under this instrument until the date of repayment of capital): it is, therefore — he argues — consistent with the tenor of the parties' agreement to imply a term excluding the mortgagees' right to possession at least until that date, unless, of course, the mortgagor has defaulted upon any of his obligations. And there has been no such default. The second part of his argument raises an important question. He submits that, upon its true construction, section 36 (1) of the Administration of Justice Act 1970 (which applies only to mortgages of dwelling houses) excludes the common law right of the mortgagee to possession irrespective of default or arrears — a right which, in the absence of an agreement excluding it, a mortgagee enjoys by virtue of his estate: see *Fisher and Lightwood's Law of Mortgage*, 8th edn. (1969), p. 269.

If this construction of the subsection be not possible, he submits in the alternative that the subsection confers power upon the court by adjournment, or otherwise as specified in subsection (2), to delay the making or enforcement of an order for possession not only in cases of default or arrears, where the subsection expressly applies, but also in the case, not expressly mentioned in the subsection, where a mortgagee is relying on his common law right alone.

Mr. Lightman argues that, unless one or other of these constructions is placed upon the subsection, the section fails to provide the mortgagor of a dwelling house with the protection against eviction which Parliament plainly intended him to have.

I now deal with the argument based on contract. I do not think it possible to imply into this legal charge a term excluding the mortgagee's common law right to possession. . . .

I now turn to the argument based on statute. One may suppose that the section was passed to protect the mortgagors of dwelling houses from the full rigour of the decision in *Four-Maids Ltd v Dudley Marshall (Properties) Ltd* [1957] Ch 317 and *Birmingham Citizens Permanent Building Society v Caunt* [1962] Ch 883. If the section neither abrogates the common law right nor subjects it to the power of delay admittedly conferred upon the court in cases of default or arrears, the section fails in its purpose. The critical subsections are (1) and (2) [His Lordship read section 36 (1) (2) and continued:] Upon a first reading of these two subsections, I confess I thought it obvious that the powers conferred upon the court are exercisable only if it appears to the court that the mortgagor will be able within a reasonable time to pay off the arrears or remedy his default. In other words, there must be a default or arrears before the court can intervene. I thought so not only because of the wording of subsection (1) but because the powers of adjournment, suspension and postponement conferred by subsection (2) appear to be appropriate only to cases where there are arrears to be met or a default to be remedied. Subsection (2) does not, in terms, confer a power to adjourn generally or sine die, which is the sort of power needed to give effective protection against the unreasonable exercise of a mortgagee's common law right of possession, independent, as it is, of default or arrears. Mr. Lightman has, however, convinced me that it would be making a nonsense of the law so to read the two subsections. It would mean that a mortgagee could be prevented from taking possession when there was a default or arrears, but could not be so prevented if there were neither default nor arrears. Parliament cannot have intended so foolish a result.

Three courses are open to the court. The first is to treat the section as having a "casus-omissus," which only Parliament can fill. The second, and that for which Mr. Lightman principally contends (since it would give him victory outright), is to treat the section as excluding the common law right to possession from mortgages of dwelling houses. The third is to treat the section as giving the court a discretion to delay making an order in all cases where, upon whatever ground, a mortgagee is seeking possession of a mortgaged dwelling house.

Judicial legislation is not an option open to an English judge. Our courts are not required, as are, for instance, the Swiss courts (see the Swiss Civil Code, articles 1 and 2), to declare and insert into legislation rules which the judge would have put there, had he been the legislator. But our courts do have the duty of giving effect to the intention of Parliament, if it be possible, even though the process requires a strained construction of the language used or the insertion of some words in order to do so: see *Luke v Inland Revenue Commissioners* [1963] AC 557, *per* Lord Reid at p. 557. The line between judicial legislation, which our law does not permit, and judicial interpretation in a way best designed to give effect to the intention of Parliament is not an easy one to draw. Suffice it to say that before our courts can imply words into a statute the statutory intention must be plain and the insertion not too big, or too much at variance with the language in fact used by the legislature. The courts will strain against having to take the first of the three courses I mentioned; that is to say, leaving unfilled the "casus omissus." In the case of this section, is there an acceptable reading which would enable us to give effect to Parliament's intention within the principle which I think governs the problem?

It would be going too far, in my judgment, to adopt the second course. It would, indeed, be judicial legislation to read a section conferring discretionary powers upon the court as abrogating a common law right. I am not prepared to go that far in an attempt to make sense. If one had to go that far, then it would be for the legislature, not the courts, to take the step.

If the second course is not open, can we adopt the third course? Though it is straining the language, I find no great difficulty in construing subsection (1) so that it confers a power of delay upon the court in whatever circumstances the mortgagee of a dwelling house is seeking to obtain possession. It entails reading the conditional clause in the subsection as applicable only where there are arrears or default, and not as cutting down the width of the power conferred. The greater difficulty, I think, is in the wording of subsection (2) which requires that the limit of a reasonable period be set upon the delaying power of the court: see for illustration, *Royal Trust Co of Canada v Markham* [1975] 1 WLR 1416. It is appropriate to set such a limit when the problem is whether the mortgagor can find the necessary money or remedy the default. Nevertheless, though it is difficult, it is not impossible to envisage circumstances in which it would be appropriate to impose a time limit upon a mortgagee seeking possession by virtue only of his common law right. The danger to the security, which would be the reason for the mortgagee's application, might appear less imminent to the court than to the mortgagee; or the mortgagor might make proposals which the court would think ought to be given a chance. In either case it could be appropriate to adjourn proceedings for a period in order to see whether the mortgagee's fears were justified. For myself, I doubt whether the subsection empowers the court to adjourn a mortgagee's proceedings sine die or generally. But, upon the assumption that it does not, there is still sense, for the reasons given, in applying subsection (2) to cases where the mortgagee relies only on his estate and alleges no arrears or default.

Accordingly, I think that, within the general principle, it is open to the court to take the third course: and, in my opinion, the wording of the two subsections is not so difficult as to make it impossible to give effect to what was plainly the intention of Parliament, namely, to give the courts power, in their discretion, to protect the mortgagor of a dwelling house for a reasonable period against eviction by his mortgagee. I would therefore hold that the section applies as well where the mortgagee asserts his common law right as where he relies on arrears or default. Upon whatever ground the mortgagee of a dwelling house seeks possession, the court has, in my judgment, the discretion conferred by the section.

It follows, therefore, that the judge had the discretion which he believed he had. In ordering immediate or almost immediate possession, he cannot be shown to have exercised his discretion wrongly. I am not impressed with Mr. Lightman's ingenious argument that the risk to the security arises not from anything that has happened to the security but from the mortgagee's own acceptance of a date of repayment 10 years ahead.

For these reasons, I would dismiss the appeal.

WHITE *v* CITY OF LONDON BREWERY
(1889) 42 ChD 237 (CA, Lord ESHER MR, COTTON and FRY LJJ)

In 1868, the plaintiff, a publican, mortgaged his public house to the defendants in return for a loan. In 1869, when the plaintiff's financial affairs were in a serious condition, the defendants exercised their right to take possession, and leased the premises to a tenant who covenanted to purchase his ale, beer and porter from the defendants.

In 1879, the defendants sold the property, took what they claimed was due to them under the mortgage debt and paid the surplus to second mortgagees. The plaintiff, acting in the interests of the second mortgagees, brought this action for an account of what was due to the defendants. One question which arose was whether the defendants were chargeable, not merely with the rent which they received from their tenants, but with the rent which they would have obtained if the premises had been let free from the covenant to purchase ale, etc., from the defendants.

Held. The defendants were chargeable with the rent which they would have obtained if the tenant had not been so restricted.

COTTON LJ: There is then another point to be considered. A mortgagee in possession must account for the rents, which, but for his wilful default, he would have received. The plaintiff says that if he fails as to the brewers' profits yet he ought to have a larger sum in respect of the rents which the mortgagees would, but for their wilful default, have received. . . . The learned Judge has allowed an addition of £20 a year from 19 August 1874, down to the date of the sale, in addition to the rent obtained by the mortgagees. [His Lordship considered the evidence relating to the rent for which the public house could have been let, and continued:] The evidence on that question is of a some-what doubtful character, but I think the plaintiff has not established that more should be given him than what the learned Judge has allowed, *viz.* £20 a year, which comes altogether, as the Master of the Rolls has said, to £100."[3]

QUESTION

X, who owned a house, worth more than £30,000, mortgaged it to the Y Bank to secure a loan of £2,500. The mortgage deed prohibited the creation of a tenancy by X without Y's consent. In breach of that covenant, X let the house without Y's consent to Z, who became a statutory tenant protected by the Rent Acts. X, who wanted to sell the house with vacant possession, asked Y to bring an action for possession against Z, whose tenancy, though binding on X, was not binding on Y. Y refused. X's wife then paid off the money owing to Y and took a transfer from Y of the mortgage.

   1.   Can X's wife succeed in an action for possession at common law?

   2.   If so, is Z entitled to protection under A.J.A. 1970, section 36?

Quennell v Maltby [1979] 1 WLR 318, [1979] 1 All ER 568; (1979) 129 NLJ 457 (A. Waite); 38 CLJ 257 (R. A. Pearce).

B.   Powers to Grant and Accept Surrenders of Leases

LAW OF PROPERTY ACT 1925

99.   Leasing powers of mortgagor and mortgagee in possession. — p. 636, ante.

100.   Powers of mortgagor and mortgagee in possession to accept surrenders of leases. — p. 637, ante.

C.   Sale, Insurance, Appointment of Receiver, Cutting and Selling of Timber[4]

---

[3] See also *Hughes v Williams* (1806) 12 Ves 493; *Nelson v Booth* (1858) 3 De G & J 119: *Wrigley v Gill* [1905] 1 Ch 241; (1979) 129 NLJ 334 (H. E. Markson).

[4] The first mortgagee is entitled also to the custody of the title deeds; L.P.A. 1925, ss. 85 (1), 86 (1); p. 601, ante; on redemption by the mortgagor, the mortgagee must deliver the deeds to him, unless he has notice of a later mortgage, when he must deliver them to the mortgagee next in order of priority of whom he has notice. In this context, registration is not notice; L.P.A. 1925, s. 96 (2) as amended by L.P. (A) A. 1926, Sch.

LAW OF PROPERTY ACT 1925

101. Powers incident to estate or interest of mortgagee. — (1) A mortgagee, where the mortgage is made by deed, shall, by virtue of this Act, have the following powers, to the like extent as if they had been in terms conferred by the mortgage deed, but not further (namely):—

(i) A power, when the mortgage money has become due[5], to sell, or to concur with any other person in selling, the mortgaged property, or any part thereof, either subject to prior charges or not, and either together or in lots, by public auction or by private contract, subject to such conditions respecting title, or evidence of title, or other matter, as the mortgagee thinks fit, with power to vary any contract for sale, and to buy in at an auction, or to rescind any contract for sale, and to re-sell, without being answerable for any loss occasioned thereby; and

(ii) A power, at any time after the date of the mortgage deed, to insure[6] and keep insured against loss or damage by fire any building, or any effects or property of an insurable nature, whether affixed to the freehold or not, being or forming part of the property which or an estate or interest wherein is mortgaged, and the premiums paid for any such insurance shall be a charge on the mortgaged property or estate or interest, in addition to the mortgage money, and with the same priority, and with interest at the same rate, as the mortgage money; and

(iii) A power, when the mortgage money has become due, to appoint a receiver of the income of the mortgaged property, or any part thereof; or, if the mortgaged property consists of an interest in income, or of a rentcharge or an annual or other periodical sum, a receiver of that property or any part thereof; and

(iv) A power, while the mortgagee is in possession, to cut and sell timber and other trees ripe for cutting, and not planted or left standing for shelter or ornament, or to contract for any such cutting and sale, to be completed within any time not exceeding twelve months from the making of the contract.

(3) The provisions of this Act relating to the foregoing powers, comprised either in this section, or in any other section regulating the exercise of those powers, may be varied or extended by the mortgage deed, and, as so varied and extended, shall, as far as may be, operate in the like manner and with all the like incidents, effects, and consequences, as if such variations or extensions were contained in this Act.

---

[5] I.e., as soon as the contractual date for redemption has passed. If the mortgage money is payable by instalments the power of sale arises as soon as any instalment is in arrear. *Payne v Cardiff R.D.C.* [1932] 1 KB 241; c.p. *Twentieth Century Banking Corpn Ltd v Wilkinson* [1977] Ch 99, [1976] 3 All ER 361. See also A.J.A. 1973, s. 8, p. 641, ante.

[6] For amount and application of insurance money, see L.P.A. 1925, s. 108.

(4) This section applies only if and as far as a contrary intention is not expressed in the mortgage deed, and has effect subject to the terms of the mortgage deed and to the provisions therein contained.

i.   SALE[7]

a. *Legal Mortgagees*

LAW OF PROPERTY ACT 1925

101.   Powers incident to estate or interest of mortgagee.
> (i) p. 647, ante.

103.   Regulation of exercise of power of sale. — A mortgagee shall not exercise the power of sale conferred by this Act unless and until —
> (i) Notice requiring payment of the mortgage money has been served on the mortgagor or one of two or more mortgagors, and default has been made in payment of the mortgage money, or of part thereof, for three months after such service; or
> (ii) Some interest under the mortgage is in arrear and unpaid for two months after becoming due; or
> (iii) There has been a breach of some provision contained in the mortgage deed or in this Act, or in an enactment replaced by this Act, and on the part of the mortgagor, or of some person concurring in making the mortgage, to be observed or performed, other than and besides a covenant for payment of the mortgage money or interest thereon.

104.   Conveyance on sale. — (1) A mortgagee exercising the power of sale conferred by this Act shall have power, by deed, to convey the property sold, for such estate and interest therein as he is by this Act authorised to sell or convey or may be the subject of the mortgage, freed from all estates, interests, and rights to which the mortgage has priority, but subject to all estates, interests, and rights which have priority to the mortgage[8].

(2) Where a conveyance is made in exercise of the power of sale conferred by this Act, or any enactment replaced by this Act, the title of the purchaser shall not be impeachable on the ground —
> (a) that no case had arisen to authorise the sale; or
> (b) that due notice was not given; or
> (c) where the mortgage is made after the commencement of this Act, that leave of the court, when so required, was not obtained[9]; or
> (d) whether the mortgage was made before or after such commencement, that the power was otherwise improperly or irregularly exercised;

---

[7] Cheshire, pp. 669–673; M & W, pp. 908–914; MM, pp. 439–442; Fisher and Lightwood, Chap. 20. (1976) 73 L S Gaz 92, 654, (1977) 74 L S Gaz 493 (H. E. Markson).
[8] Compare L.P.A. 1925, s. 2 (1) (iii); p. 190, ante.
[9] See L.P.A. 1925, s. 110 (mortgagor a bankrupt and mortgage executed after 1925); (1944) 5 Conv YB, pp. 70–71.

and a purchaser is not, either before or on conveyance, concerned to see or inquire whether a case has arisen to authorise the sale, or due notice has been given, or the power is otherwise properly and regularly exercised; but any person damnified by an unauthorised, or improper, or irregular exercise of the power shall have his remedy in damages against the person exercising the power[10].

(3) A conveyance on sale by a mortgagee, made after the commencement of this Act, shall be deemed to have been made in exercise of the power of sale conferred by this Act unless a contrary intention appears.

105. Application of proceeds of sale. — The money which is received by the mortgagee, arising from the sale, after discharge of prior incumbrances to which the sale is not made subject, if any, or after payment into court under this Act of a sum to meet any prior incumbrance, shall be held by him in trust to be applied by him, first, in payment of all costs, charges, and expenses properly incurred by him as incident to the sale or any attempted sale, or otherwise; and secondly, in discharge of the mortgage money, interest, and costs, and other money, if any, due under the mortgage; and the residue of the money so received shall be paid to the person entitled to the mortgaged property[11], or authorised to give receipts for the proceeds of the sale thereof.

106. Provisions as to exercise of power of sale. — (1) The power of sale conferred by this Act may be exercised by any person for the time being entitled to receive and give a discharge for the mortgage money.

(2) The power of sale conferred by this Act does not affect the right of foreclosure.

88. Realisation of freehold mortgages. — (1) Where an estate in fee simple has been mortgaged by the creation of a term of years absolute limited thereout or by a charge by way of legal mortgage and the mortgagee sells under his statutory or express power of sale —

(*a*) the conveyance by him shall operate to vest in the purchaser the fee simple in the land conveyed subject to any legal mortgage having priority to the mortgage in right of which the sale is made and to any money thereby secured, and thereupon;

(*b*) the mortgage term or the charge by way of legal mortgage and any subsequent mortgage term or charges shall merge or be extinguished as respects the land conveyed;

---

[10] See *Price Bros (Somerford) Ltd v J. Kelly Homes (Stoke-on-Trent) Ltd* [1975] 1 WLR 1512, [1975] 3 All ER 369; *Northern Developments (Holdings) Ltd v UDT Securities Ltd* [1976] 1 WLR 1230; and generally Emmet, pp. 851–852.

[11] M & W point out (p. 913, n. 12) that these words literally refer to the purchaser; "but plainly the phrase must be read as 'to the person who *immediately before the sale* was entitled to the mortgaged property'," and this of course includes other mortgagees. But if the rights of the mortgagor and other encumbrancers have become extinguished by lapse of time (Limitation Act 1939, s. 12, p. 168, ante) the mortgagee may keep all the purchase money himself. *Young v Clarey* [1948] Ch 191, [1948] 1 All ER 197.

and such conveyance may, as respects the fee simple, be made in the name of the estate owner in whom it is vested.

89.   Realisation of leasehold mortgages. — (1) Where a term of years absolute has been mortgaged by the creation of another term of years absolute limited thereout or by a charge by way of legal mortgage and the mortgagee sells under his statutory or express power of sale, —

> (a) the conveyance by him shall operate to convey to the purchaser not only the mortgage term, if any, but also (unless expressly excepted with the leave of the court)[12] the leasehold reversion affected by the mortgage, subject to any legal mortgage having priority to the mortgage in right of which the sale is made and to any money thereby secured, and thereupon
>
> (b) the mortgage term, or the charge by way of legal mortgage and any subsequent mortgage term or charge, shall merge in such leasehold reversion or be extinguished unless excepted as aforesaid;

and such conveyance may, as respects the leasehold reversion, be made in the name of the estate owner in whom it is vested.

Where a licence to assign is required on a sale by a mortgagee, such licence shall not be unreasonably refused.

2.   Conveyances overreaching certain equitable interests and powers.

(1) (iii) p. 190, ante.

In *Lord Waring v London and Manchester Assurance Co Ltd* ([1935] Ch 310), the mortgagee had contracted to sell the property for £186,000. The mortgagor, who was negotiating elsewhere for a loan (on a mortgage of the property) of £200,000, sought an injunction to stop the sale.

CROSSMAN J refused, and said, at p. 317: "After a contract has been entered into, however, it is, in my judgment, perfectly clear (subject to what has been said to me to-day) that the mortgagee (in the present case, the company) can be restrained from completing only on the ground that he has not acted in good faith and that the sale is therefore liable to be set aside. Counsel for the plaintiff, who has argued the case most excellently, submitted that, notwithstanding that the company exercised its power of sale by entering into the contract, the plaintiff's equity of redemption has not been extinguished, as there has been no completion by conveyance, and that, pending completion, the plaintiff is still entitled to redeem, that is, to have the property reconveyed to him on payment of principal, interest, and costs. Counsel is relying, to some extent, on the provisions of the Law of Property Act 1925, which creates a statutory power of sale. In my judgment, section 101 of that Act, which gives to a mortgagee power to sell the mortgaged property, is perfectly clear, and means that the mortgagee has power to sell out

------

[12] This may be done to prevent the purchaser becoming liable upon the covenants in the lease.

and out, by private contract or by auction, and subsequently to complete by conveyance; and the power to sell is, I think, a power by selling to bind the mortgagor. If that were not so, the extraordinary result would follow that every purchaser from a mortgagee would, in effect, be getting a conditional contract liable at any time to be set aside by the mortgagor's coming in and paying the principal, interest and costs. Such a result would make it impossible for a mortgagee, in the ordinary course of events, to sell unless he was in a position to promise that completion should take place immediately or on the day after the contract, and there would have to be a rush for completion in order to defeat a possible claim by the mortgagor".[13]

CUCKMERE BRICK CO LTD *v* MUTUAL FINANCE LTD
[1971] Ch 949, [1971] 2 All ER 633 (CA, SALMON, CROSS and CAIRNS LJJ)

The plaintiffs owned some 2.6 acres of land on the outskirts of Maidstone, which they mortgaged to the defendants in 1961–62 for £50,000 and other money. They put it up for sale by public auction with planning permission for 33 houses, but without advertising the fact that there also existed planning permission for 100 flats; and they refused to postpone the sale when that was pointed out to them. However, they undertook to instruct the auctioneers to mention at the sale the existence of the permission for flats. The land was sold in June 1967 for £44,000, but was estimated by PLOWMAN J to be worth £65,000. The plaintiffs brought an action for negligence.

Held. The mortgagees owed a duty to take reasonable care to obtain a proper price (per SALMON LJ, the true market value); that (CROSS LJ dissenting) there had been a breach of that duty; and that (SALMON LJ dissenting) there should be an enquiry as to the damages sustained by the mortgagors.

SALMON LJ: It is well settled that a mortgagee is not a trustee of the power of sale for the mortgagor[14]. Once the power has accrued, the mortgagee is entitled to exercise it for his own purposes whenever he chooses to do so. It matters not that the moment may be unpropitious and that by waiting a higher price could be obtained. He has the right to realise his security by turning it into money when he likes. Nor, in my view, is there anything to prevent a mortgagee from accepting the best bid he can get at an auction, even though the auction is badly attended and the bidding exceptionally low. Providing none of those adverse factors is due to any fault of the mortgagee, he can do as he likes. If the mortgagee's interests, as he sees them, conflict with those

---

[13] Followed in *Property and Bloodstock Ltd v Emerton* [1968] Ch 94, [1967] 3 All ER 321. For the effect of a contract of sale by the mortgagor upon the mortgagee's powers, see *Duke v Robson* [1973] 1 WLR 267, [1973] 1 All ER 481, p. 653, post.
[14] But he cannot sell to himself: *Farrar v Farrars Ltd* (1888) 40 ChD 395 at 409; *Williams v Wellingborough Borough Council* [1975] 1 WLR 1327, [1975] 3 All ER 462 ("a see-through dress of a sale", at p. 1329, per RUSSELL LJ).

of the mortgagor, the mortgagee can give preference to his own interests, which of course he could not do were he a trustee of the power of sale for the mortgagor. . . .

It is impossible to pretend that the state of the authorities on this branch of the law is entirely satisfactory. There are some dicta which suggest that unless a mortgagee acts in bad faith he is safe. His only obligation to the mortgagor is not to cheat him. There are other dicta which suggest that in addition to the duty of acting in good faith, the mortgagee is under a duty to take reasonable care to obtain whatever is the true market value of the mortgaged property at the moment he chooses to sell it: compare, for example, *Kennedy v de Trafford* [1896] 1 Ch 762, [1897] AC 180 with *Tomlin v Luce* (1889) 43 ChD 191, 194.

The proposition that the mortgagee owes both duties, in my judgment, represents the true view of the law. Approaching the matter first of all on principle, it is to be observed that if the sale yields a surplus over the amount owed under the mortgage, the mortgagee holds this surplus in trust for the mortgagor. If the sale shows a deficiency, the mortgagor has to make it good out of his own pocket. The mortgagor is vitally affected by the result of the sale but its preparation and conduct is left entirely in the hands of the mortgagee. The proximity between them could scarcely be closer. Surely they are "neighbours". Given that the power of sale is for the benefit of the mortgagee and that he is entitled to choose the moment to sell which suits him, it would be strange indeed if he were under no legal obligation to take reasonable care to obtain what I call the true market value at the date of the sale. Some of the textbooks refer to the "proper price", others to the "best price". Vaisey J in *Reliance Permanent Building Society v Hardwood-Stamper* [1944] Ch 362, 364, 365, [1944] 2 All ER 75, seems to have attached great importance to the difference between these two descriptions of "price". My difficulty is that I cannot see any real difference between them. "Proper price" is perhaps a little nebulous, and "the best price" may suggest an exceptionally high price. That is why I prefer to call it "the true market value". . . .

I accordingly conclude, both on principle and authority, that a mortgagee in exercising his power of sale does owe a duty to take reasonable precautions to obtain the true market value of the mortgaged property at the date on which he decides to sell it. No doubt in deciding whether he has fallen short of that duty the facts must be looked at broadly, and he will not be adjudged to be in default unless he is plainly on the wrong side of the line[15].

---

[15] Cheshire, pp. 672–673; M & W, pp. 911–912; MM, p. 441; M & B (T), pp. 231–232: *Palmer v Barclays Bank Ltd* (1972), 23 P & CR 30; *Johnson v Ribbins* (1975) 235 Estates Gazette 757; c.p. *Barclays Bank Ltd v Thienel* (1978) 247 Estates Gazette 385 (no duty of care owed by mortgagee to surety of mortgagor to obtain true market value on sale); *Bank of Cyprus (London) Ltd v Gill* (1979) 2 Lloyd's Rep 508. A building society must take reasonable care to ensure that the price is the best price which can be reasonably obtained. Building Societies Act 1962, s. 36.

QUESTION

A mortgagor defaults and then contracts to sell the mortgaged property to X. The contract is registered as an estate contract under the Land Charges Act 1972, section 2 (4), Class C (iv). The mortgagee, under the statutory power of sale, contracts to sell the property to Y. Can X succeed in a claim for specific performance against the mortgagor and for an injunction against the mortgagee? *Duke v Robson* [1973] 1 WLR 267, [1973] 1 All ER 481; (1973) 37 Conv (NS) 210 (F.R. Crane).

b. *Equitable Mortgagees*

LAW OF PROPERTY ACT 1925

90. Realisation of equitable charges by the court. — (1) Where an order for sale is made by the court in reference to an equitable mortgage on land (not secured by a legal term of years absolute or by a charge by way of legal mortgage) the court may, in favour of a purchaser, make a vesting order conveying the land or may appoint a person to convey the land or create and vest in the mortgagee a legal term of years absolute to enable him to carry out the sale, as the case may require, in like manner as if the mortgage had been created by deed by way of legal mortgage pursuant to this Act, but without prejudice to any incumbrance having priority to the equitable mortgage unless the incumbrancer consents to the sale.

(2) This section applies to equitable mortgages made or arising before or after the commencement of this Act, but not to a mortgage which has been over-reached under the powers conferred by this Act or otherwise.

In the case of an equitable mortgage by deposit of title deeds, the mortgagee has no power of sale[16]. If he wishes to sell, he must apply to the court under Law of Property Act 1925, section 91 (2)[17]. The mortgagee's statutory power of sale becomes available if the mortgage is made by deed, and equitable mortgages are commonly accompanied by a memorandum under seal. Such a power, however, covers only "the mortgaged property"[18] — that is the equitable interest. In order to give the mortgagee power to sell the legal estate, the deed often includes a power of attorney, or a declaration of trust, or both.

In *Re White Rose Cottage* [1965] Ch 940, [1965] 1 All ER 11, one question was whether a sale by the mortgagor (the Kamerun company)

---

[16] Cheshire, pp. 685–686; M & W, pp. 922–923; MM, p. 446.
[17] See p. 635, ante.
[18] L.P.A. 1925, s. 101 (1) (i).

and the bank (an equitable mortgagee) gave a title free from or subject to an equitable charge in favour of a later equitable chargee. The Court of Appeal construed the sale as one by the mortgagor with the concurrence of the mortgagee, and the title which passed was therefore that held by the mortgagor and the purchaser took subject to the later chargee.

A different construction had been placed upon the sale by WILBERFORCE J, at first instance ([1964] Ch 483, [1964] 1 All ER 169); he treated it as being a sale by an equitable mortgagee.

The mortgagor had executed a memorandum under seal "in the usual form for effecting a charge to secure [an] advance. It was stated that the documents of title had been deposited as security for the money due. The liability under the charge was not to exceed £50,000. The Kamerun company gave an undertaking to execute a legal charge or mortgage on request and agreed to hold the property as trustee for executing such a charge, the bank having power to appoint a new trustee in the place of the . . . company at any time. An irrevocable power of attorney was given to the bank so that the bank, in the name and on behalf of the . . . company, could vest the legal estate in the property in any purchaser or other person in exercise of the statutory powers conferred on mortgagees free and discharged from all rights of redemption".

Both judgments of the Court of Appeal (Lord DENNING MR, and HARMAN LJ, with SALMON LJ, agreeing with both) expressed the view that, if they had construed the sale, as WILBERFORCE J did, as being a sale by an equitable mortgagee under a power of sale, the legal estate would have passed; and by virtue of Law of Property Act 1925, section 104 (1), would have passed to the purchaser free from the subsequent charge.

HARMAN LJ said at p. 955: "In other words, I think that an equitable mortgagee under a deed in the terms of the memorandum . . . can by virtue of the power of attorney contained in it convey to a purchaser the legal estate in the mortgaged property without first going through the form of calling for the execution by the mortgagor of a legal mortgage."

Lord DENNING MR said at p. 951: "Wilberforce J has held that that conveyance was an exercise by the bank of their statutory power of sale as mortgagees; and that selling as mortgagees they were entitled to sell the property freed from all charges subsequent to their own. If this be the correct construction of the conveyance, I would agree with him. [His Lordship referred to Law of Property Act 1925, section 104 (1) and continued:] The subject of the mortgage here was the property itself, both the legal and equitable estate in it: and I see no reason why an equitable mortgagee, exercising his power of sale, should not be able to convey the legal estate."[19]

---

[19] See W & C, Vol. 1, 212, where this view is doubted.

ii. APPOINTMENT OF RECEIVER[20]

LAW OF PROPERTY ACT 1925

101. (1) (iii). **Powers incident to estate or interest of mortgagee.** — P. 647, ante.

109. Appointment, powers, remuneration and duties of receiver. — (1) A mortgagee entitled to appoint a receiver under the power in that behalf conferred by this Act shall not appoint a receiver until he has become entitled to exercise the power of sale conferred by this Act, but may then, by writing under his hand, appoint such person as he thinks fit to be receiver.

(2) A receiver appointed under the powers conferred by this Act, or any enactment replaced by this Act, shall be deemed to be the agent of the mortgagor; and the mortgagor shall be solely responsible for the receiver's acts or defaults unless the mortgage deed otherwise provides.

(4) A person paying money to the receiver shall not be concerned to inquire whether any case has happened to authorise the receiver to act.

(8) Subject to the provisions of this Act as to the application of insurance money[1], the receiver shall apply all money received by him as follows, namely:

(i) In discharge of all rents, taxes, rates, and outgoings whatever affecting the mortgaged property; and

(ii) In keeping down all annual sums or other payments, and the interest on all principal sums, having priority to the mortgage in right whereof he is receiver; and

(iii) In payment of his commission, and of the premiums on fire, life or other insurances, if any, properly payable under the mortgage deed or under this Act, and the cost of executing necessary or proper repairs directed in writing by the mortgagee; and

(iv) In payment of the interest accruing due in respect of any principal money due under the mortgage; and

(v) In or towards discharge of the principal money if so directed in writing by the mortgagee;

and shall pay the residue, if any, of the money received by him to the person who, but for the possession of the receiver, would have been entitled to receive the income of which he is appointed receiver, or who is otherwise entitled to the mortgaged property.

D. Foreclosure[2]

LAW OF PROPERTY ACT 1925

88. Realisation of freehold mortgages. — (2) Where any such mortgagee obtains an order for foreclosure absolute, the order shall

---

[20] Cheshire, pp. 678–679; M & W, pp. 919–921; MM, pp. 444–445; Fisher and Lightwood, Chap. 18.

[1] L.P.A. 1925, s. 108.

[2] Cheshire, pp. 673–675; M & W, pp. 905–908; MM, pp. 437–439; Fisher and Lightwood, Chaps. 21, 22; (1978) L S Gaz 447; (1979) 129 NLJ 33 (H. E. Markson), 225 (C. M. Pepper).

operate to vest the fee simple in him (subject to any legal mortgage having priority to the mortgage in right of which the foreclosure is obtained and to any money thereby secured), and thereupon the mortgage term, if any, shall thereby be merged in the fee simple, and any subsequent mortgage term or charge by way of legal mortgage bound by the order shall thereupon be extinguished.

89.   Realisation of leasehold mortgages. — (2) Where any such mortgagee obtains an order for foreclosure absolute, the order shall, unless it otherwise provides, operate (without giving rise to a forfeiture for want of a licence to assign) to vest the leasehold reversion affected by the mortgage and any subsequent mortgage term in him, subject to any legal mortgage having priority to the mortgage in right of which the foreclosure is obtained and to any money thereby secured, and thereupon the mortgage term and any subsequent mortgage term or charge by way of legal mortgage bound by the order shall, subject to any express provision to the contrary contained in the order, merge in such leasehold reversion or be extinguished.

The mortgagee or any person interested may ask the court to order a sale instead of foreclosure; Law of Property Act 1925, section 91 (2), p. 635, ante[3].

In *Campbell v Holyland* (1877) 7 ChD 166, Blakely mortgaged a reversionary interest in a trust fund to Campbell and died insolvent. A foreclosure decree was made in 1876 ordering payment of the money by 4 January 1877. Blakely's administrator, Holyland, transferred the equity of redemption to X and Y who negotiated for the purchase of the interest of the mortgagee, Campbell; and failed to pay on 4 January 1877 because they thought, incorrectly, that they had purchased the interest. They discovered subsequently that Campbell had sold his interest on 3 January, to Ford, who was aware of the negotiations to sell to X and Y. The foreclosure decree was made absolute.

In March 1877, X and Y's executor moved to reopen the foreclosure decree, and JESSEL MR, allowed them to do so. He said at p. 171:

"I have no doubt that I ought to make the order asked for.

The question in dispute is really whether a mortgagor can be allowed to redeem after an order of foreclosure absolute, and I think, on looking at the authorities, that no Chancellor or Vice-Chancellor has ever laid down that any special circumstances are essential to enable a mortgagor to redeem in such a case.

Now what is the principle? The principle in a Court of Equity has always been that, though a mortgage is in form an absolute con-

---

[3] For the inter-relationship between the two remedies, see *Twentieth Century Banking Corpn Ltd v Wilkinson* [1977] Ch 99, [1976] 3 All ER 361.

veyance when the condition is broken, in equity it is always security; and it must be remembered that the doctrine arose at the time when mortgages were made in the form of conditional conveyance, the condition being that if the money was not paid at the day, the estate should become the estate of the mortgagee; that was the contract between the parties; yet Courts of Equity interfered with actual contract to this extent, by saying there was a paramount intention that the estate should be security, and that the mortgage money should be debt; and they gave relief in the shape of redemption on that principle. Of course that would lead, and did lead, to this inconvenience, that even when the mortgagor was not willing to redeem, the mortgagee could not sell or deal with the estate as his own, and to remedy that inconvenience the practice of bringing a foreclosure suit was adopted, by which a mortgagee was entitled to call on the mortgagor to redeem within a certain time, under penalty of losing the right of redemption. In that foreclosure suit the Court made various orders — interim orders fixing a time for payment of the money — and at last there came the final order which was called foreclosure absolute, that is, in form, that the mortgagor should not be allowed to redeem at all; but it was form only, just as the original deed was form only; for the Courts of Equity soon decided that, notwithstanding the form of that order, they would after that order allow the mortgagor to redeem. That is, although the order of foreclosure absolute appeared to be a final order of the Court, it was not so, but the mortgagee still remained liable to be treated as mortgagee and the mortgagor still retained a claim to be treated as mortgagor, subject to the discretion of the Court. Therefore everybody who took an order for foreclosure absolute knew that there was still a discretion in the Court to allow the mortgagor to redeem.

Under what circumstances that discretion should be exercised is quite another matter. The mortgagee had a right to deal with an estate acquired under foreclosure absolute the day after he acquired it; but he knew perfectly well that there might be circumstances to entitle the mortgagor to redeem, and everybody buying the estate from a mortgagee who merely acquired a title under such an order was considered to have the same knowledge, namely, that the estate might be taken away from him by the exercise, not of a capricious discretion, but of a judicial discretion by the Court of Equity which had made the order.

That being so, on what terms is that judicial discretion to be exercised? It has been said by the highest authority that it is impossible to say a *priori* what are the terms. They must depend upon the circumstances of each case. . . . In the first place the mortgagor must come, as it is said, promptly; that is, within a reasonable time. He is not to let the mortgagee deal with the estate as his own — if it is a landed estate, the mortgagee being in possession of it and using it — and then without any special reason come and say, 'Now I will redeem'. He cannot do that; he must come within a reasonable time.

What is a reasonable time? You must have regard to the nature of the property. As has been stated in more than one of the cases, where the estate is an estate in land in possession — where the mortgagee takes it in possession and deals with it and alters the property, and so on — the mortgagor must come more quickly than where it is an estate in reversion, as to which the mortgagee can do nothing except sell it. So that you must have regard to the nature of the estate in ascertaining what is to be considered reasonable time.

Then, again, was the mortgagee[4] entitled to redeem, but by some accident unable to redeem? Did he expect to get the money from a quarter from which he might reasonably hope to obtain it, and was he disappointed at the last moment? Was it a very large sum, and did he require a considerable time to raise it elsewhere? All those things must be considered in determining what is a reasonable time.

Then an element for consideration has always been the nature of the property as regards value[5]. For instance, if an estate were worth £50,000, and had been foreclosed for a mortgage debt of £5,000, the man who came to redeem that estate would have a longer time than where the estate was worth £5,100, and he was foreclosed for £5,000. But not only is there money value, but there may be other considerations. It may be an old family estate or a chattel, or picture, which possesses a special value for the mortgagor, but which possesses not the same value for other people; or it may be, as has happened in this instance, that the property, though a reversionary interest in the funds, is of special value to both the litigants: it may possess not merely a positive money value, but a peculiar value having regard to the nature of the title and other incidents, so that you cannot set an actual money value upon it. In fact, that is the real history of this contest, for the property does not appear to be of much more money value — though it is of some more — than the original amount of the mortgage. All this must be taken into consideration.

Then it is said you must not interfere against purchasers. As I have already explained, there are purchasers and purchasers. If the purchaser buys a freehold estate in possession after the lapse of a considerable time from the order of foreclosure absolute, with no notice of any extraneous circumstances which would induce the Court to interfere, I for one should decline to interfere with such a title as that; but if the purchaser bought the estate within twenty-four hours after the foreclosure absolute, and with notice of the fact that it was of much greater value than the amount of the mortgage debt, is it to be supposed that a Court of Equity would listen to the contention of such a purchaser that he ought not be interfered with? He must be taken to know the general law that an order for foreclosure may be opened

---

[4] Presumably "mortgagor" was intended here.
[5] *Lancashire and Yorkshire Reversionary Interest Co v Crowe* (1970) 114 Sol Jo 435. (Foreclosure decree made absolute in respect of mortgage of reversionary interest; and re-opened after the interest fell into possession on life tenant's death. The sum due was £3,000, and the fund £6,100.).

under proper circumstances and under a proper exercise of discretion by the Court; and if the mortgagor in that case came the week after, is it to be supposed a Court of Equity would so stultify itself as to say that a title so acquired would stand in the way? I am of opinion it would not.

Now I come to the circumstances of this case, and I must say they are very strong in favour of opening the foreclosure. . . .

The present purchaser, Mr. Ford, being very desirous to acquire the property for a collateral object[6] — I am not saying a wrong object, but a collateral object — had, before the time for foreclosure absolute had arrived, entered into a contract with the mortgagee to buy it. He was not a purchaser coming in even the day after foreclosure, but a purchaser coming in before foreclosure, and at that time of course he knew the property was redeemable. He bought a property certainly redeemable, for the day for redemption had not even arrived. That is the kind of purchase I am dealing with. He was aware on the day of redemption that it was not from unwillingness to redeem that the mortgagor failed to pay the money, but because the mortgagor was under the belief that he had acquired a right to take the property on paying less than the mortgage money, by reason of a contract of purchase with the mortgagee. . . .

I am of opinion, however, that such a sale as this ought to have no weight whatever, and that under the circusmtances the mortgagor is entitled to open the foreclosure on the usual terms, that is, on payment of principal, interest, and costs.''

E. Consolidation[7]

If the same mortgagor has mortgaged more than one property to the same mortgagee, and if one of the properties so mortgaged is worth less than the debt for the repayment of which it has been charged as security, it is in the mortgagor's interest to redeem the other properties but not that one. The mortgagor is, however, asking a favour of equity in being allowed to redeem any property after the contractual date for redemption has passed, and, in accordance with the maxim: "He who comes to Equity must do Equity", the mortgagor may be prevented from redeeming one mortgage without redeeming others. In other words, the mortgagee has a right in certain circumstances to consolidate the various mortgages against the mortgagor.

LAW OF PROPERTY ACT 1925

93. Restriction on consolidation of mortgages. — (1) A mortgagor seeking to redeem any one mortgage is entitled to do so without

---

[6] To obtain the property for Blakely's widow.

[7] Cheshire, pp. 680–684; M & W, pp. 926–932; MM, pp. 448–451; Waldock, pp. 284–295; Fisher and Lightwood, Chap. 27. As to whether the right amounts to a general equitable charge within L.C.A. 1972, s. 2 (4), Class C (iii); see (1948) 92 Sol Jo 736; W & C vol. 1, 189.

paying any money due under any separate mortgage made by him, or by any person through whom he claims, solely on property other than that comprised in the mortgage which he seeks to redeem.

This subsection applies only if and as far as a contrary intention is not expressed in the mortgage deeds or one of them.

(2) This section does not apply where all the mortgages were made before the first day of January, eighteen hundred and eighty-two.

(3) Save as aforesaid, nothing in this Act, in reference to mortgages, affects any right of consolidation or renders inoperative a stipulation in relation to any mortgage made before or after the commencement of this Act reserving a right to consolidate.

PLEDGE *v* WHITE
[1896] AC 187 (HL, LORD HALSBURY LC, WATSON and DAVEY)

There were mortgages on seven different properties; the properties will be referred to as Nos. 1–7. They were mortgaged by James Banks to various mortgagees between 1863 and 1866.

In 1866 James Banks the mortgagor made a second mortgage of Nos. 4–7 to Brockman: and in 1868 a third mortgage of these properties and a second mortgage of Nos. 1–3 to Brockman and Harrison. In 1885, Brockman and Harrison assigned their equities of redemption in all 7 properties to Pledge, the appellant.

Between 1871 and 1890, Brockman became the transferee of all the first mortgages except that on No. 3[8]. He died in 1877, and in 1890 his executors, the respondents, took an assignment of the first mortgage on No. 3.

In 1890 the appellants claimed to redeem No. 2 alone. The respondents refused to allow him to do so without redeeming the other six.

Held. The mortgagee was entitled to consolidate.

LORD HALSBURY LC: My Lords, I have had an opportunity of considering the judgment prepared by my noble and learned friend (Lord Davey) and I am not prepared to dissent from it. I use that form of expression because I confess I lament the conclusion to which it has been found necessary to come, although I believe the strict principle upon which it rests is founded in our law at present, and in dealing with a technical system it is better to adhere to a principle when once established, than to create greater confusion by dissenting from it. I think the principle laid down in *Vint v Padget* ((1858) 2 De G & J 611) has been so firmly established now by authority in our technical system, that I feel more mischief would be done by dissenting from it, than by acquiescing in it. . . .

LORD DAVEY: The question for your Lordships' decision is whether the respondents have the right of consolidation which they claim, notwithstanding that the mortgages which it is sought to consolidate

---

[8] The facts as given by Lord DAVEY do not explain how Brockman obtained the mortgages on Nos. 6 and 7.

were not united in title with the mortgage sought to be redeemed until after the assignment of the equity of redemption to the present appellant's predecessors in title. . . .

The equitable rule as to the consolidation of mortgages is not one of those doctrines of the Court of Chancery which has met with general approbation — at any rate as regards its later development. Originally it may have been a right of a mortgagee holding two separate mortgages on estates of the same mortgagor which have become absolute estates at law against the mortgagor and debtor personally to refuse to be redeemed as regards one estate without having his other debt also paid. But it has long been settled that the right of consolidation may be exercised by the transferee of the mortgages as well as by the original mortgagee, and may be exercised in respect of equitable mortgages as well as by a mortgagee holding the legal estate absolute at law; and on the other hand, that it may be asserted against the assignee of an equity of redemption from the mortgagor as well as against the mortgagor himself. . . .

The case of *Vint v Padget* came before Stuart V-C, in the first instance, whose judgment may be referred to as shewing how entirely that experienced judge considered the point to be settled. "In accepting", he says, "by way of security the equity of redemption of two separate estates, Mr. Lee deliberately incurred the risk of their uniting in one hand, and when that union has taken place there is only one single debt, and in order to redeem he must pay off both mortgages, each of which affects the entirety of both estates".

[His Lordship referred to: *Bovey v Skipwith* ((1671) 1 Cas in Ch 201); *Titley v Davies* ((1743) 2 Y & C Ch Cas 399); *Selby v Pomfret* ((1861) 3 De G F & J 595); *Beevor v Luck* ((1867) LR 4 Eq 537); *White v Hillacre* ((1839) 3 Y & C Ex 597); *Harter v Colman* ((1882) 19 ChD 630); *Jennings v Jordan* ((1881) 6 App Cas 698), and continued:]

It appears to me, my Lords, that an assignee of two or more equities of redemption from one mortgagor stands in a widely different position from the assignee of one equity only. He knows, or has the opportunity of knowing, what are the mortgages subject to which he has purchased the property, and he knows that they may become united by transfer in one hand. If the doctrine of consolidation be once admitted it appears to me not unreasonable to hold that a person in such a position occupies the place of the mortgagor or assignor to him towards the holders of the mortgages, subject to which he has purchased, although it may be unreasonable to hold that he can be affected by the transfer to such holders of mortgages to other persons by the same mortgagor on property which he has not purchased, and with the equity of redemption of which he has no concern. He does not investigate the title to such other property and cannot know in the latter case to what mortgages the property is subject. If your Lordships affirm the decree now under appeal, the doctrine of consolidation will be confined within at least intelligible limits. It will be applicable where at the date when redemption is sought all the mortgages are united in one hand and redeemable by the same person, or where after that state of things has once existed the equities of redemption have become separated[9]. If the purchaser of two or more equities of redemption desires to prevent consolidation, he has it in his power to redeem any one mortgage before consolidation takes place; but if for his own convenience he delays doing so, he runs the risk as his assignor ran of the mortgages becoming united by transfer in one hand.

I am of opinion that the application of the doctrine of consolidation to a case like the present has been too long considered part of the equitable jurisprudence of this country to be altered at the present time, and it is not so unreasonable as to demand a reversal of it by this House.

I move, therefore, that this appeal be dismissed with costs.

In *Cummins v Fletcher* (1880) 14 ChD 699, the trustees of a Building Society, who were mortgagees of two properties, refused to allow a bank, the second mortgagee of one of the properties, to redeem it, without also redeeming the other. All payments due under the first mortgage were up to date, but those on the second were in arrears.

The Court of Appeal (JAMES, COTTON and THESIGER LJJ, reversing HALL V-C) refused to allow the Building Society to consolidate, on the ground that consolidation arose only where the mortgagor was in default and was asking a favour of the Court of Equity. JAMES LJ said at p. 708: "The whole doctrine of consolidation, whatever may have been the particular circumstances under which it has been applied to different cases, arises from the power of the Court of Equity to put its own price upon its own interference as a matter of equitable consideration in favour of any suitor."

A further reason, mentioned by the court, was that the mortgagors were not the same in the two mortgages. In the first mortgage, the mortgagor was Vaugham and in the second Vaugham and Neesham, partners. This point was not necessary for the decision.

In *Hughes v Britannia Permanent Building Society* [1906] 2 Ch 607, A in 1894 mortgaged Blackacre to the defendants, the mortgage providing that A should not be entitled to redeem without paying all the moneys due by A to the defendants under any other mortgage.

A then mortgaged Whiteacre to the defendants, and gave a second mortgage to the plaintiffs, the defendants having notice of this mortgage; A subsequently mortgaged two separate properties to the defendants.

The plaintiffs claimed to redeem Whiteacre, and the question was whether the defendants could consolidate against the plaintiffs all

---

[9] It will not apply where the equities of redemption separated before the mortgages united in one hand. *Harter v Colman* (1882) 19 ChD 630.

their mortgages or only those made before the second mortgage of Whiteacre to the plaintiffs.

KEKEWICH J, held that the defendants could consolidate against the plaintiffs the mortgages on Blackacre and Whiteacre, but not those on the other properties. The mortgagor, by his express contract, would have been compelled to submit to consolidation of all the properties; and the plaintiffs would have been in the same position if the defendants, at the time of the later mortgages, had not had notice of the second mortgage on Whiteacre to the plaintiffs[10].

VII. Discharge of Mortgages

LAW OF PROPERTY ACT 1925

115. Reconveyances of mortgages by endorsed receipts. — (1) A receipt endorsed on, written at the foot of, or annexed to, a mortgage for all money thereby secured, which states the name of the person who pays the money and is executed by the chargee by way of legal mortgage or the person in whom the mortgaged property is vested and who is legally entitled to give a receipt for the mortgage money shall operate, without any reconveyance, surrender, or release —

(a) Where a mortgage takes effect by demise or subdemise, as a surrender of the term, so as to determine the term or merge the same in the reversion immediately expectant thereon;

(b) Where the mortgage does not take effect by demise or subdemise, as a reconveyance thereof to the extent of the interest which is the subject matter of the mortgage, to the person who immediately before the execution of the receipt was entitled to the equity of redemption;

and in either case, as a discharge of the mortgaged property from all principal money and interest secured by, and from all claims under the mortgage, but without prejudice to any term or other interest which is paramount to the estate or interest of the mortgagee or other person in whom the mortgaged property was vested.

(2) Provided that, where by the receipt the money appears to have been paid by a person who is not entitled to the immediate equity of redemption, the receipt shall operate as if the benefit of the mortgage had by deed been transferred to him; unless —

(a) it is otherwise expressly provided; or

(b) the mortgage is paid off out of capital money, or other money in the hands of a personal representative or trustee properly applicable for the discharge of the mortgage, and it is not expressly provided that the receipt is to operate as a transfer.

(3) Nothing in this section confers on a mortgagor a right to keep alive a mortgage paid off by him, so as to affect prejudicially any

---

[10] See too *Andrews v City Permanent Benefit Building Society* (1881) 44 LT 641.

subsequent incumbrancer; and where there is no right to keep the mortgage alive, the receipt does not operate as a transfer[11].

(4) This section does not affect the right of any person to require a reassignment, surrender, release, or transfer to be executed in lieu of a receipt.

(8) This section applies to the discharge of a charge by way of legal mortgage, and to the discharge of a mortgage, whether made by way of statutory mortgage or not, executed before or after the commencement of this Act, but only as respects discharges effected after such commencement.

(10) This section does not apply to the discharge of a charge or incumbrance registered under the Land Registration Act 1925[12].

116.   Cesser of mortgage terms. — Without prejudice to the right of a tenant for life or other person having only a limited interest in the equity of redemption to require a mortgage to be kept alive by transfer or otherwise, a mortgage term shall, when the money secured by the mortgage has been discharged, become a satisfied term and shall cease[13].

VIII.   Priority of Mortgages[14]

Very substantial alterations were made by the legislation of 1925 to the rules concerning the priority of mortgages. The rules which were in force before 1926 are still of importance as there are still circumstances in which they may apply. The two systems will be considered separately.

A   Before 1926

i.   MORTGAGES OF INTERESTS IN LAND

The basic rule was that priority depended on the time of creation. "*Qui prior est tempore, potior est jure.*" This rule could, however, be made inapplicable by the other principle that "Where the equities are equal, the law prevails". Where, for example, a legal mortgagee has no notice, actual or constructive, of a prior equitable mortgage, the equities are equal and the legal mortgagee will take priority. However, wrongful conduct (fraud, misrepresentation or gross negligence) may deprive the earlier mortgagee, even the holder of the legal estate, of his normal priority.

---

[11] *Otter v Lord Vaux* (1856) 6 De GM & G 638: *Parkash v Irani Finance Ltd* [1970] Ch 101, [1969] 1 All ER 930.

[12] Which can only be effected by a discharge entered on the register. L.R.A. 1925, s. 35, L.R.R. 1925, rr. 151, 267.

[13] *Edwards v Marshall-Lee* (1975) 235 Estates Gazette 901 (vacating receipt on a legal charge not complying with s. 115 held a valid discharge); (1976) 40 Conv (NS) 102.

[14] Cheshire, pp. 689–713; M & W, pp. 958–987; MM, pp. 465–479; Waldock, pp. 381–435; Fisher and Lightwood, Chap. 24, (1949) 7 CLJ 243 (R. E. Megarry).

These rules give rise to certain difficulties; inevitably, as they are conflicting. To decide which rule to apply is to determine the priority of the mortgages. And there is little guidance in the cases on the question of the tests to be applied in deciding whether the "equities are equal" or in defining how serious must be the conduct of the mortgagee before he will be postponed. A number of questions are not made clear.

First: it is not clear to what extent different rules for the displacement of the natural order of priority apply to the case of a prior equitable followed by a later legal mortgage from those applicable to a prior legal followed by a later equitable mortgage. Certainly the issues are different. The problem in the one case is to determine when the first rule is to be displaced by the second; in the other case both rules may be upset and the legal mortgagee who is first in time may be postponed[15].

In the latter type of case, the reason for the postponement of the legal mortgagee is usually fraud or estoppel; but gross negligence by the legal mortgagee in respect of the title deeds is usually said to be sufficient[16]. The addition of adjectives to negligence always causes difficulty, and there is no precise test to show what is signified by the adjective "gross".

Secondly: the requirement of negligence in the case of a later legal following a prior equitable mortgage is not clear. The position is sometimes said to be that the later legal mortgagee will take priority over a prior equitable unless he was grossly negligent. Sometimes it is said that he will do so if he enquires for the deeds (deposited with the equitable mortgagee) and receives a reasonable excuse for non-production[17]. The obvious way to treat the question, one would have thought, was to apply the ordinary rule relating to the bona fide purchaser for value and to postpone the later legal mortgagee unless he can pass that test[18]. But he has been more greatly favoured.

a. The Superiority of the Legal Estate[19]

HEWITT *v* LOOSEMORE
(1851) 9 Hare 449 (TURNER V-C)

Robert Loosemore, the mortgagor, was a solicitor; in 1834, he deposited his lease with the plaintiff as an equitable mortgage to secure the repayment of a sum of money. In 1838, he assigned the lease by way of legal mortgage to the defendant John Loosemore, who was a farmer, unacquainted with legal forms; John asked Robert whether the

---

[15] *Perry Herrick v Attwood* (1857) 2 De G & J 21; p. 669, post.
[16] *Colyer v Finch* (1856) 5 HL Cas 905; *Perry Herrick v Attwood,* supra; *Clarke v Palmer* (1882) 21 ChD 124; *Walker v Linom* [1907] 2 Ch 104, p. 671, post.
[17] *Hewitt v Loosemore* (1851) 9 Hare 449; *Agra Bank Ltd v Barry* (1874) LR 7 HL 135; *Oliver v Hinton* [1899] 2 Ch 264, p. 666, post.
[18] See p. 24, ante; *Pilcher v Rawlins* (1872) 7 Ch App 259.
[19] *Barnett v Weston* (1806) 12 Ves 130; *Agra Bank Ltd v Barry* supra; *Hewitt v Loosemore* supra; *Walker v Linom* supra; *Hudston v Viney* [1921] 1 Ch 98.

lease ought not to be delivered to him, and Robert said that it should, but that, as he was rather busy then, he would give it to John when he next came to market. The plaintiff brought this bill praying, inter alia, for a declaration that he was entitled to priority over the defendant.

Held. The defendant as legal mortgagee was entitled to priority.

TURNER V-C: [The question in this case is] whether an equitable mortgagee by deposit of title deeds is entitled to priority over a subsequent legal mortgagee of the property comprised in the deeds, who has not made all the inquiries after the deeds which could or might have been made. . . .

The law, . . . as I collect it from the authorities, stands thus:— That a legal mortgagee is not to be postponed to a prior equitable one upon the ground of his not having got in the title-deeds, unless there be fraud or gross and wilful negligence on his part. That the court will not impute fraud, or gross or wilful negligence to the mortgagee if he has bona fide inquired for the deeds, and a reasonable excuse has been given for the non-delivery of them; but that the court will impute fraud, or gross and wilful negligence to the mortgagee if he omits all inquiry as to the deeds. And I think there is much principle both in the rule and the distinctions upon it.

When this court is called upon to postpone a legal mortgagee its powers are invoked to take away a legal right; and I see no ground which can justify it in doing so except fraud, or gross and wilful negligence, which, in the eye of this court, amounts to fraud, and I think that in transactions of sale and mortgage of estates, if there be no inquiry as to the title-deeds, which constitute the sole evidence of the title to such property, the court is justified in assuming that the purchaser or mortgagee has abstained from making the inquiry, from a suspicion that his title would be affected if it was made, and is therefore bound to impute to him the knowledge which the inquiry, if made, would have imparted. But I think that where bona fide inquiry is made, and a reasonable excuse given, there is no ground for imputing the suspicion, or the notice which is consequent upon it.

Applying these principles to the present case, I am of opinion that the plaintiff has failed in making out a sufficient case for postponing the defendant, and that the only decree which I can make is the usual decree for redemption; but the plaintiff must pay the costs up to and including the decree. . . .

OLIVER *v* HINTON
[1899] 2 Ch 264 (ChD, ROMER J, and CA, LINDLEY MR, and
Sir F. H. JEUNE and RIGBY LJ)

The plaintiff, Mrs. Oliver, brought this action for a declaration that she was entitled to certain premises as equitable mortgagee as against the defendant Mrs. Hinton, who had purchased them. The circumstances were that in 1888, Hill, a solicitor, had deposited the deeds of the premises with the plaintiff under an equitable mortgage. In 1890, Hill conveyed the property to the defendant, who was represented by an agent who was not a solicitor. This agent asked Hill to see the deeds, but Hill replied that they could not be seen as they related also to other property.

Held. The plaintiff was entitled to priority over the defendant, the purchaser of the legal estate.

LINDLEY MR: In my opinion this case does not present any serious difficulty when once the facts are understood. The defendant has been cheated by Hill, but she has not been in any way cheated by the plaintiff. In 1888, Hill gave the plaintiff a mortgage of the three houses in question and two others. It was not a legal mortgage, but an equitable mortgage by deposit of title-deeds, accompanied by a memorandum of deposit, by which Hill agreed to execute a legal mortgage when requested by the plaintiff to do so. The plaintiff had a good equitable mortgage, and she cannot be charged with any neglect or breach of duty in not obtaining a legal mortgage. She ran, however, the risk of losing her priority in case the legal estate should be conveyed to a subsequent purchaser for value without notice of her charge. Who is it that now claims to override her charge? The only person who can do so, if he has acquired his title subsequently to hers, is a bona fide purchaser for value without notice of her charge. But this does not include a purchaser for value who is so grossly negligent as to take none of the ordinary precautions which ought to be taken in such a matter — who, in fact, takes no precautions whatever. He may be a bona fide purchaser for value without notice of a prior charge, but he is not entitled to the protection of the Court. I do not base my judgment upon constructive notice of the plaintiff's charge, nor do I mean to suggest that there was any fraud or complicity in fraud on the part of either the defendant or her agent, Price. Price gave his evidence with perfect candour. The defendant left the arrangement of the purchase entirely to him. He inquired about the title-deeds, and was told by Hill that they were in his possession, but that they would not be delivered up to the purchaser because they related also to other property. No abstract of title was asked for or delivered, and no further inquiry was made. Price in his evidence admitted that he made a mistake in not asking to see the deeds, but said that he relied upon Hill. Can a person whose agent acted in this way be regarded as a bona fide purchaser for value without notice who is entitled to the protection of the legal estate? To allow a purchaser who acts with such gross carelessness to deprive a prior innocent mortgagee of her priority would be the greatest injustice. . . .

In [*Hunt v Elmes* ((1860) 2 De GF & J 578)] and also in *Hewitt v Loosemore* ((1857) 9 Hare 449), it was said that to deprive a man of the protection of the legal estate he must have been guilty of either fraud or gross and wilful negligence. To deprive a purchaser for value without notice of a prior incumbrance of the protection of the legal estate it is not, in my opinion, essential that he should have been guilty of fraud; it is sufficient that he has been guilty of such gross negligence as would render it unjust to deprive the prior incumbrancer of his priority.

The appeal must be dismissed.

b.   The Effect of Fraud, Misrepresentation, Gross Negligence

(i) Fraud[20]

NORTHERN COUNTIES OF ENGLAND FIRE INSURANCE CO *v* WHIPP

(1884) 26 ChD 482 (CA, COTTON, BOWEN and FRY LJJ)

On two occasions in 1878, Crabtree, the manager of the plaintiff company, executed legal mortgages of freehold properties to the company and delivered to the company the title deeds which were locked in the safe. Crabtree was entrusted by the company with one of the two sets of keys to the safe, and, later in 1878, extracted the deeds, and, suppressing the mortgages, deposited them with the defendant, Mrs. Whipp, as security for a loan.

In an action by the company for foreclosure, Mrs. Whipp claimed that her security should take priority over that of the company.

Held (reversing the Vice-Chancellor of the Court of the County Palatine of Lancaster). The mortgage to the company took priority.

FRY LJ: The question which has thus to be investigated is — What conduct in relation to the title deeds on the part of a mortgagee who has the legal estate, is sufficient to postpone such mortgage in favour of a subsequent equitable mortgagee who has obtained the title deeds without knowledge of the legal mortgage? The question is not what circumstances may as between two equities give priority to the one over the other, but what circumstances justify the Court in depriving a legal mortgagee of the benefit of the legal estate. It has been contended on the part of the Plaintiffs that nothing short of fraud will justify the Court in postponing the legal estate. It has been contended by the Defendant that gross negligence is enough. . . .

The authorities which we have reviewed appear to us to justify the following conclusions:—

(1) That the Court will postpone the prior legal estate to a subsequent equitable estate: (*a*), where the owner of the legal estate has assisted in or connived at the fraud which has led to the creation of a subsequent equitable estate, without notice of the prior legal estate; of which assistance or connivance, the omission to use ordinary care in inquiry after or keeping title deeds may be, and in some cases has been, held to be sufficient evidence, where such conduct cannot otherwise be explained; (*b*), where the owner of the legal estate has constituted the mortgagor his agent with authority to raise money, and the estate thus created has by the fraud or misconduct of the agent been represented as being the first estate.

But (2) that the Court will not postpone the prior legal estate to the subsequent equitable estate on the ground of any mere carelessness or want of prudence on the part of the legal owner.

Now to apply the conclusions thus arrived at to the facts of the present case. That there was great carelessness in the manner in which

---

[20] *Thatched House Case* (1716) 1 Eq Cas Abr 321.

the Plaintiff company through its directors dealt with their securities seems to us to admit of no doubt. But is that carelessness evidence of any fraud? We think that it is not. Of what fraud is it evidence? The Plaintiffs never combined with *Crabtree* to induce the Defendant to lend her money. They never knew that she was lending it, and stood by. They can have had no motive to desire that their deeds should be abstracted and their own title clouded. Their carelessness may be called gross, but in our judgment it was carelessness likely to injure and not to benefit the Plaintiff company, and accordingly has no tendency to convict them of fraud. . . .

The rule, referred to in this case, which lays down that an earlier legal mortgagee may be postponed on the ground of fraud is undoubted. The rule however that an earlier legal mortgagee will never be postponed on the grounds of negligence (not amounting to fraud) is questioned by many writers and is inconsistent with some cases (p. 671, post). Much reconciliation can be effected by limiting the decision in *Whipp's* case to a situation where the negligence was in failure to *retain* the deeds. It is difficult however to justify in principle a distinction between a failure to obtain and a failure to retain the deeds.

(ii) Misrepresentation[1]

PERRY HERRICK *v* ATTWOOD
(1857) 2 De G & J 21 (Lord CRANWORTH LC)

In 1848 John Attwood was substantially indebted to the trustees of a family marriage settlement, and also to three of his sisters, the defendants. While he was being pressed for payment by the trustees, he executed a legal mortgage for the amount due to his sisters. The deeds, other than the mortgage, were, however, retained by the sisters' solicitor in order to enable John Attwood to execute a mortgage to secure his debts to the trustees. In April 1848, Attwood deposited the deeds with the solicitors for the trustees. Later, by employing those same solicitors, Attwood made several legal mortgages of the same property to various persons including the plaintiffs; the plaintiffs were also transferees of some of those mortgages.

The plaintiffs filed a bill to establish their mortgages as having priority over the mortgage to the Misses Attwood.

Held (affirming Sir John ROMILLY MR). The plaintiffs were entitled to priority.

LORD CRANWORTH LC: This case has occupied a long time in argument, and has given rise to the agitation of questions of great importance. It has been discussed how far a mortgagee, taking a

---

[1] *Briggs v Jones* (1870) LR 10 Eq 92; *Dixon v Muckleston* (1872) 8 Ch App at p. 160; *Brocklesby v Temperance Permanent Building Society* [1895] AC 173; *Rimmer v Webster* [1902] 2 Ch 163; *Abigail v Lapin* [1934] AC 491.

mortgage without taking the title deeds, does or does not postpone himself to persons who take a subsequent conveyance for value without notice of the mortgage, and obtain possession of the title deeds, and the cases on that subject have been referred to, the last being *Colyer v Finch* ((1856) 5 HL Cas 905), in the House of Lords.

I should think it very inexpedient now to treat it as a question open to discussion whether the law has or has not been correctly laid down on this subject, for I consider it to have been established beyond doubt that the law is, that the person having the legal estate without the title deeds is not to be postponed to a subsequent incumbrancer having the title deeds, unless he has been guilty of something which the law calls fraud or gross negligence. I agree that this rule may very often lead to great hardships on persons who have taken conveyances relying on the possession of the title deeds as evidence of unincumbered ownership in the conveying party. Such, however, is the law, and I must act upon it until it is otherwise settled. Still, if the present case had involved that principle, I should have taken time to consider my judgment, for it is difficult in each particular case to say what amounts to negligence, and still more is it difficult to say what constitutes negligence with the epithet of gross connected with it.

In my opinion no such question arises in the present case. I do not think there was here any fraud or any negligence, for I do not believe that any of the parties to the transaction of *January* 1848 intended that the mortgage then taken should interfere with any subsequent dealings for value which *Attwood* might have with his estate. If the parties did so intend, the transaction was a gross fraud on the part of *Attwood* and his solicitor, and of the ladies also, if they understood it.

The case is that: Mr. *Attwood* was a single man advanced in life, and living with two of his sisters, who were not young. He managed all their affairs. He was indebted to each of his three sisters, the two who lived with him and another who was married, in the sum of 10,000*l* each. At the end of 1847 and the beginning of 1848 he was pressed by creditors who were insisting on payment of large sums of money, amounting altogether to above 15,000*l*. He proposed to give them a mortgage, they refused it, and insisted on having payment of the money. That took place in the early part of *January* 1848. I do not go into the details of the evidence, but there were angry discussions going on and actions brought; and pending these proceedings, after issue of the writs and the delivery of pleas in the actions, Mr. *Attwood* executed the deed in question, for giving a security to his three sisters for the 30,000*l* that he owed to them, but intentionally did not give them the title deeds. . . . What does that prove the purport of the transaction to have been? That this security was given either with the intention (to put the worse construction on the conduct of the parties) that the ladies should have a pocket security of which they could avail themselves afterwards, when those who were to claim under subsequent conveyances by Mr. *Attwood* should assert their rights, or (to adopt a more favourable, and I hope and believe the true construction) that the deed was never intended to be set up against any subsequent dealing with the property by Mr. *Attwood* by way of mortgage, the title deeds being returned to him to be dealt with as he thought fit. I think it is clear.... that at this time it was contemplated by all parties that Mr. *Attwood* should raise money to pay off the creditors by whom he was then being sued. Taking that to be the intention, I agree with the view of the Master of the Rolls, in every part of whose judgment in this cause I entirely concur, that if a person taking a legal mortgage chooses to leave the deeds with the mortgagor, not through negligence or through fraud, but with the intention of enabling him to raise a sum of 15,000*l*, which is to take precedence of the legal mortgage, the mortgagee cannot, as against subsequent mortgagees, complain if, instead of 15,000*l* the mortgagor raises 50,000*l*, because he has himself put it into his power to raise any sum of money he pleases. That is the true nature of this transaction. It is not a case in which there was any negligence. It is not a case, as I am willing to believe, in which there was any fraud, but it is a case in which the mortgagees did deliberately and intentionally leave the deeds in the hands of the mortgagor, in order that he might raise money. To hold that a person who advances money on an estate, the title deeds of which are under such circumstances left in the hands of the mortgagor, is not to have preference, would be to shut our eyes to the plainest equity.

In *Clarke v Palmer* (1882) 21 ChD 124, the first mortgagee X failed to obtain possession of the deeds. Part of the property was then mortgaged to Y who believed that he was the first mortgagee, and the whole of the property to Z, who knew of Y, but not of X. HALL V-C, held that both Y and Z took priority over X; X's negligence had brought the principle of *Perry Herrick v Attwood* into play.

(iii) Gross Negligence
WALKER *v* LINOM
[1907] 2 Ch 104 (ChD, PARKER J)

In 1896 Walker conveyed land to trustees to be held on the trusts of his marriage settlement. The title deeds, with the exception of the conveyance to Walker, were handed over to the trustees, who were solicitors and who negligently failed to discover the omission.

Walker subsequently mortgaged the land to X, who sold it to Y. On the question (inter alia) of the competing claims of the trustees and the purchaser.

Held. The trustees by their negligence were postponed to the equitable interest of the purchaser.

PARKER J, reviewed in detail the judgment of FRY LJ, in *Northern Counties of England Fire Insurance Co v Whipp* ((1884) 26 ChD 482), and continued:

The conclusion he ultimately arrives at is that in order to postpone a prior legal to a subsequent equitable estate there must be fraud as apart from negligence, and this conclusion is stated in language wide enough to cover cases of postponement based upon the conduct of the holder of the legal estate in not getting possession of the title deeds as well as cases of postponement based upon the conduct of such holder in dealing with the title deeds after he has got them. It would seem at first sight that the Lord Justice uses the word "fraud" throughout this judgment as connoting a dishonest intent, notwithstanding that in the case of fraud to be gathered from conduct in relation to not getting in the title deeds he refers to such cases as *Le Neve v Le Neve* ((1747) Amb 436) and *Ratcliffe v Barnard* ((1871) 6 Ch App 652).

Now, as I have already said, I cannot under the circumstances of this case find that anyone concerned in the 1896 settlement, with the exception of George Church Walker, acted otherwise than honestly, and, if I treat Fry LJ's judgment as meaning that in no case can a prior legal estate be postponed to a subsequent equitable estate without the existence of fraud in its ordinary common law sense as necessarily connoting a dishonest intention, I must hold that the trustees are not postponed. There are, however, subsequent cases which suggest that at any rate in cases of postponement, based on no inquiry having been made for the deeds, fraud is not necessary. It is, for example, clear from the case of *Oliver v Hinton* ([1899] 2 Ch 264; p. 666, ante) that a purchaser obtaining the legal estate, but making no inquiry for the deeds, or making inquiry and failing to take reasonable means to verify the truth of the excuse made for not producing them or handing them over, is, although perfectly honest, guilty of such negligence as to make it inequitable for him to rely on his legal estate so as to deprive a prior incumbrancer of his priority. In this case Lindley MR, disapproves of the passage in the judgment of James LJ, in *Ratcliffe v Barnard*, quoted by Fry LJ in *Northern Counties of England Fire Insurance Co v Whipp*, and distinctly says that to deprive a purchaser for value without notice of a prior equitable incumbrance of the benefit of the legal estate it is not essential that he should have been guilty of fraud. And Sir F. H. Jeune, referring also to the judgment of James LJ in *Ratcliffe v Barnard*, comes to the conclusion that the word "fraud", as there used, did not mean such conduct as would justify a jury or judge in finding that there had been actual fraud, but such conduct as would justify the Court of Chancery in concluding that there had been fraud in some artificial sense. Similarly in *Berwick & Co v Price* ([1905] 1 Ch 632 at p. 640), Joyce J says: "The omission by a purchaser to investigate the title or to require delivery or production of the title-deeds is not to my mind either fraudulent or culpable, nor does it, since the judgment of Lindley MR in *Oliver v Hinton*, seem necessary to characterize it by any such epithet; but the consequence of such omission or wilful ignorance is that it is held to be unjust to prefer the purchaser to the previous mortgagee who has the deeds although such mortgage be equitable and the purchaser have the legal estate."

In both the cases last referred to the question was between a prior equitable and a subsequent legal estate, and I think the later case was actually decided on constructive or imputed notice. But the Master of the Rolls expressly refused to decide *Oliver v Hinton* on any such ground. The question, however, arises whether the principle laid down in *Oliver v Hinton* is equally applicable between the holder of the legal estate who has omitted to make inquiry for the title deeds and a subsequent equitable estate the creation of which has been rendered possible by such omission. In my opinion any conduct on the part of the holder of the legal estate in relation to the deeds which would make it inequitable for him to rely on his legal estate against a prior equitable estate of which he had no notice ought also to be sufficient to postpone him to a subsequent equitable estate the creation of which has only been rendered possible by the possession of deeds which but for such conduct would have passed into the possession of the owner of the legal estate. This must, I think, have been the opinion of Fry LJ in *Northern Counties of England Fire Insurance Co v Whipp* ((1884) 26 ChD 482); for he explains both *Worthington v Morgan* ((1849) 16 Sim 547) and *Clarke v Palmer* ((1882) 21 ChD 124), as based upon the same sort of fraud. I do not think, therefore, that there is anything in the authorities to preclude me from holding, and I accordingly hold, that the trustees, although they have the legal estate, are postponed to the defendant.

In *Grierson v National Provincial Bank* [1913] 2 Ch 18, George Franklin, a leaseholder, deposited his lease with Grant and Maddison's Bank as security for a loan. Later, he granted a legal mortgage to Grierson which was expressly stated to be subject to the prior equitable mortgage.

Franklin then redeemed the equitable mortgage, recovered the lease, and deposited it with the defendant Bank as security for a further loan. The defendant Bank knew nothing of the legal mortgage.

JOYCE J held that Grierson, the legal mortgagee, retained his priority.

ii.   MORTGAGES OF EQUITABLE INTERESTS IN PURE PERSONALTY
The priority of mortgages and assignments of interests in pure personalty (including interests under a trust for sale)[2] depended before 1926 upon the order in which notice was received by the legal owner of the personalty (i.e. usually by the trustees); however, a mortgagee who had actual or constructive notice of a prior mortgage when he lent his money could not gain priority by giving his notice first. The rule in *Dearle v Hall* was made applicable in 1925 to mortgages of all equitable interests, in land as well as pure personalty.

---

[2] *Lee v Howlett* (1856) 2 K & J 531.

DEARLE *v* HALL[3]
(1823) 3 Russ 1 (Sir Thomas PLUMER MR), *affd.* (1827) 3 Russ 48 (Lord
LYNDHURST LC)

Zachariah Brown was entitled under his father's will to a life interest
in a fund which produced £93 per annum. In 1808, he sold to William
Dearle an annuity of £37 to be paid out of this life interest, and
charged upon it. In 1809, he assigned in a similar manner an annuity of
£27 to Sherring. In 1812, he sold his life interest in the whole £93
to Hall. Hall's solicitors made all proper enquiries about Brown's
title, and obtained no information concerning the prior assignments.
Hall gave notice to the executors of the assignment to him. Later
the executors of Brown's father's will learned of the assignments
and refused to pay interest until the claimants' rights should be
ascertained.

Held. The assignment to Hall took priority.

SIR THOMAS PLUMER MR: It is observable, in the first place, that
the right which *Zachariah Brown* had under the will of his father was
simply a right to a chose in action. The legal interest in the residue was
vested in the executrix and executors. . . . Wherever it is intended to
complete the transfer of a chose in action, there is a mode of dealing
with it which a court of equity considers tantamount to possession,
namely, notice given to the legal depository of the fund. Where a contract, respecting property in the hands of other persons, who have a
legal right to the possession, is made behind the back of those in whom
the legal interest is thus vested, it is necessary, if the security is
intended to attach on the thing itself, to lay hold of that thing in the
manner in which its nature permits it to be laid hold of — that is, by
giving notice of the contract to those in whom the legal interest is. By
such notice, the legal holders are converted into trustees for the new
purchaser, and are charged with responsibility towards him; and the
cestui que trust is deprived of the power of carrying the same security
repeatedly into the market, and of inducing third persons to advance
money upon it, under the erroneous belief that it continues to belong to
him absolutely, free from incumbrance, and that the trustees are still
trustees for him, and for no one else. That precaution is always taken
by diligent purchasers and incumbrancers: if it is not taken, there is
neglect; and it is fit that it should be understood that the solicitor, who
conducts the business for the party advancing the money, is
responsible for that neglect. The consequence of such neglect is, that
the trustee of the fund remains ignorant of any alteration having taken
place in the equitable rights affecting it: he considers himself to be a
trustee for the same individual as before, and no other person is known
to him as his *cestui que trust*. The original *cestui que trust*, though he
has in fact parted with his interest, appears to the world to be the complete equitable owner, and remains in the order, management and

---

[3] For comment on the rule (mostly adverse), see *Ward v Duncombe* [1893] AC 369;
Lyle v Rosher [1959] 1 WLR 8, [1958] 3 All ER 597.

disposition of the property as absolutely as ever; so that he has it in his power to obtain, by means of it, a false and delusive credit. He may come into the market to dispose of that which he has previously sold; and how can those, who may chance to deal with him, protect themselves from his fraud? Whatever diligence may be used by a *puisne* incumbrancer or purchaser — whatever inquiries he may make in order to investigate the title, and to ascertain the exact state of the original right of the vendor, and his continuing right, — the trustees, who are the persons to whom application for information would naturally be made, will truly and unhesitatingly represent to all who put questions to them that the fund remains the sole absolute property of the proposed vendor. These inconveniences and mischiefs are the natural consequences of omitting to give notice to trustees; and they must be considered as foreseen by those who, in transactions of that kind, omit to give notice; for they are the consequences which in the experience of mankind usually follow such omissions. To give notice is a matter of no difficulty: and whenever persons, treating for a chose in action, do not give notice to the trustee or executor, who is the legal holder of the fund, they do not perfect their title; they do not do all that is necessary in order to make the thing belong to them in preference to all other persons; and they become responsible, in some respects, for the easily foreseen consequences of their negligence. . . .

The ground of this claim is priority of time. They rely upon the known maxim, borrowed from the civil law, which in many cases regulates equities — "*qui prior est in tempore, potior est in jure*". If, by the first contract, all the thing is given, there remains nothing to be the subject of the second contract, and priority must decide. But it cannot be contended that priority in time must decide, where the legal estate is outstanding. For the maxim, as an equitable rule, admits of exception and gives way, when the question does not lie between bare and equal equities. If there appears to be, in respect of any circumstances independent of priority of time, a better title in the *puisne* purchaser to call for the legal estate, than in the purchaser who precedes him in date, the case ceases to be a balance of equal equities, and the perference, which priority of date might otherwise have given, is done away with and counteracted. The question here is, — not which assignment is first in date, — but whether there is not, on the part of *Hall*, a better title to call for the legal estate than *Dearle* or *Sherring* can set up? Or rather, the question is, Shall these Plaintiffs now have equitable relief to the injury of *Hall*?

What title have they shown to call on a court of justice to interpose on their behalf, in order to obviate the consequence of their own misconduct? All that has happened is owing to their negligence (a negligence not accounted for) in forbearing to do what they ought to have done, what would have been attended with no difficulty, and what would have effectually prevented all the mischief which has followed. Is the Plaintiff to be heard in a court of equity, who asks its interposition in his behoof, to indemnify him against the effects of his

own negligence at the expense of another who has used all due
diligence, and who, if he is to suffer loss, will suffer it by reason of the
negligence of the very person who prays relief against him? The
question here is not, as in *Evans v Bicknell* ((1801) 6 Ves 174), whether
a court of equity is to deprive the Plaintiffs of any right — whether it
is to take from them, for instance, a legal estate, or to impose any
charge upon them. It is simply, whether they are entitled to relief
against their own negligence. They did not perfect their securities; a
third party has innocently advanced his money, and has perfected his
security as far as the nature of the subject permitted him: is this Court
to interfere to postpone him to them?

They say, that they were not bound to give notice to the trustees; for
that notice does not form part of the necessary conveyance of an
equitable interest. I admit, that, if you mean to rely on contract with
the individual, you do not need to give notice; from the moment of the
contract, he, with whom you are dealing, is personally bound. But if
you mean to go further, and to make your right attach upon the thing
which is the subject of the contract, it is necessary to give notice; and,
unless notice is given, you do not do that which is essential in all cases
of transfer of personal property. The law of *England* has always been,
that personal property passes by delivery of possession; and it is
possession which determines the apparent ownership. If, therefore, an
individual, who in the way of purchase or mortgage contracts with
another for the transfer of his interest, does not divest the vendor or
mortgagor of possession, but permits him to remain the ostensible
owner as before, he must take the consequences which may ensue
from such a mode of dealing. That doctrine was explained in *Ryall v
Rowles* ((1749) 1 Ves Sen 348) before Lord *Hardwicke* and three of the
Judges. If you, having the right of possession, do not exercise that
right, but leave another in actual possession, you enable that person to
gain a false and delusive credit, and put it in his power to obtain money
from innocent parties on the hypothesis of his being the owner of that
which in fact belongs to you. The principle has been long recognised,
even in courts of law. In *Twyne's* case ((1602) 3 Co Rep 80b), one of the
badges of fraud was, that the posssession had remained in the vendor.
Possession must follow right; and if you, who have the right, do not
take possession, you do not follow up the title, and are responsible for
the consequences.

In *Re Wyatt* [1892] 1 Ch 188, the question arose whether notice to
one of several trustees was a valid notice or not. The Court of Appeal
established the rule that notice to one of several trustees was valid
against incumbrancers who advanced money during the period of
office of such trustee. This was held in spite of the argument of E. S.
Ford, counsel for such an incumbrancer: "Now take this case: A first
mortgage is made, of which notice is given to A but not to B. Then a
second mortgage is made, of which notice is given to both. A then dies,
and a third mortgage is made, of which notice is given to B. The

respondents say, that 1 has priority over 2. But unquestionably 2 is prior to 3, for in each case complete notice was given, and priority of dates must settle the matter. Now, according to *Re Hall* ((1880) 7 LR Ir 180), 3 has priority over 1. If, therefore, the respondents are right, we get this circle: 1 prior to 2, 2 prior to 3, 3 prior to 1, which is a *reductio ad absurdum*; and this absurdity appears still more clearly where 1 is an absolute assignment, 2 is a mortgage, and 3 is an absolute assignment. If an assignee gives notice to all, he makes all his trustees. If he gives notice to one only, he makes only that one his trustee, and on his death the assignee has no longer a trustee and loses his priority."

As to this, LINDLEY LJ, delivering the judgment of the Court (drawn up by FRY LJ), said: "The solution of the difficulty is probably to be found in the view that the third incumbrancer is subrogated to the rights of the first to the extent of his charge, and to that extent, and that extent only, can take in priority of the second incumbrancer, by which the latter sustains no injury, but that as to any excess of the amount claimed by the third incumbrancer, he comes in after the second, so that the fund would be distributed as follows. First, to the third incumbrancer to the extent of the claim of the first. Secondly, to the second incumbrancer. Thirdly, to the third incumbrancer to the extent to which he might remain unpaid after the money he had received whilst standing in the shoes of the first incumbrancer: see *Benham v Keane* ((1861) 3 De GF & J 318) where a similar problem was similarly solved."

Re Wyatt was affirmed by the House of Lords (*sub nom Ward v Duncombe* [1893] AC 369) but there was no discussion of the solution of counsel's hypothetical case.

B. After 1925

i. MORTGAGES OF LEGAL ESTATES

The system of priority of mortgages which is in operation at the present day is the creation of the legislation of 1925. The paucity of litigation on the subject suggests that the system has, on the whole, worked reasonably well; though it may be due more to the considerable rise in land prices than to the merits of the system. It is however open to certain theoretical objections which are fully explained elsewhere. No more will be attempted here than to give the statutory enactments on which the system is based.

LAW OF PROPERTY ACT 1925

13. Effect of possession of documents. — This Act shall not prejudicially affect the right or interest of any person arising out of or consequent on the possession by him of any documents relating to a legal estate in land, nor affect any question arising out of or consequent upon any omission to obtain or any other absence of possession by any person of any documents relating to a legal estate in land.

97. Priorities as between puisne mortgages. — Every mortgage affecting a legal estate in land made after the commencement of this Act, whether legal or equitable (not being a mortgage protected by the deposit of documents relating to the legal estate affected) shall rank according to its date of registration as a land charge pursuant to the Land Charges Act, 1925.

This section does not apply to mortgages or charges to which the Land Charges Act 1972 does not apply by virtue of section 14 (3) of that Act (which excludes certain land charges created by instruments necessitating registration under the Land Registration Act 1925), or to mortgages or charges of registered land. . . .[4]

199. Restrictions on constructive notice.
(1) (i) p. 41, ante.

LAND CHARGES ACT 1972

2. The register of land charges.
(4) Class C, p. 31, ante[5].

4. Effect of land charges and protection of purchasers.
(5) p. 37, ante.

17. Interpretation.
(1) p. 37, ante.

ii.   MORTGAGES BY COMPANIES

LAND CHARGES ACT 1972

3. Registration of land charges. — (7) and (8) p. 51, ante.

COMPANIES ACT 1948

95. Registration of charges created by companies registered in England. — (1) (2) (7) (10) p. 51, ante.

iii.   MORTGAGES OF EQUITABLE INTERESTS

LAW OF PROPERTY ACT 1925

137. Dealings with life interests, reversions and other equitable interests. — (1) The law applicable to dealings with equitable things in action which regulates the priority of competing interests therein, shall, as respects dealings with equitable interests in land, capital money, and securities representing capital money effected after the commencement of this Act, apply to and regulate the priority of competing interests therein.

This subsection applies whether or not the money or securities are in court.

---

[4] As amended by L.C.A. 1972, s. 18 (1). Sch. 3, para. 1.
[5] As to whether a protected equitable mortgage is registrable as an estate contract (Class C (iv)), see Cheshire, p. 701; M & W, pp. 970–971; Waldock, pp. 425–428; (1962) 26 Conv (NS) 446–449 (R. G. Rowley).

(2) (i) In the case of a dealing with an equitable interest in settled land, capital money or securities representing capital money, the persons to be served with notice of the dealing shall be the trustees of the settlement; and where the equitable interest is created by a derivative or subsidiary settlement, the persons to be served with notice shall be the trustees of that settlement.

(ii) In the case of a dealing with an equitable interest in the proceeds of sale of land or in the rents and profits until sale the persons to be served with notice shall, as heretofore, be the trustees for sale.

(iii) In any other case the person to be served with notice of a dealing with an equitable interest in land shall be the estate owner of the land affected.

The persons on whom notice is served pursuant to this subsection shall be affected thereby in the same manner as if they had been trustees of personal property out of which the equitable interest was created or arose.

This subsection does not apply where the money or securities are in court.

(3) A notice, otherwise than in writing, given to, or received by, a trustee after the commencement of this Act as respects any dealing with an equitable interest in real or personal property, shall not affect the priority of competing claims of purchasers in that equitable interest.

(4) Where, as respects any dealing with an equitable interest in real or personal property —

(a) the trustees are not persons to whom a valid notice of the dealing can be given; or

(b) there are no trustees to whom a notice can be given; or

(c) for any other reason a valid notice cannot be served, or cannot be served without unreasonable cost or delay;

a purchaser may at his own cost require that —

(i) a memorandum of the dealing be endorsed, written on or permanently annexed to the instrument creating the trust;

(ii) the instrument be produced to him by the person having the possession or custody thereof to prove that a sufficient memorandum has been placed thereon or annexed thereto.

Such memorandum shall, as respects priorities, operate in like manner as if notice in writing of the dealing had been given to trustees duly qualified to receive the notice at the time when the memorandum is placed on or annexed to the instrument creating the trust.

(5) Where the property affected is settled land, the memorandum shall be placed on or annexed to the trust instrument and not the vesting instrument.

Where the property affected is land held on trust for sale, the memorandum shall be placed on or annexed to the instrument whereby the equitable interest is created.

(6) Where the trust is created by statute or by operation of law, or in any other case where there is no instrument whereby the trusts are

declared, the instrument under which the equitable interest is acquired or which is evidence of the devolution thereof shall, for the purposes of this section, be deemed the instrument creating the trust.

In particular, where the trust arises by reason of an intestacy, the letters of administration or probate in force when the dealing was effected shall be deemed such instrument.

(7) Nothing in this section affects any priority acquired before the commencement of this Act.

(8) Where a notice in writing of a dealing with an equitable interest in real or personal property has been served on a trustee under this section, the trustees from time to time of the property affected shall be entitled to the custody of the notice, and the notice shall be delivered to them by any person who for the time being may have the custody thereof; and subject to the payment of costs, any person interested in the equitable interest may require production of the notice.

(9) The liability of the estate owner of the legal estate affected to produce documents and furnish information to persons entitled to equitable interests therein shall correspond to the liability of a trustee for sale to produce documents and furnish information to persons entitled to equitable interests in the proceeds of sale of the land[6].

C.   Tacking after 1925[7]

LAW OF PROPERTY ACT 1925

94.   Tacking and further advances. — (1) After the commencement of this Act, a prior mortgagee shall have a right to make further advances to rank in priority to subsequent mortgages (whether legal or equitable) —

- (*a*) if an arrangement has been made to that effect with the subsequent mortgagees; or
- (*b*) if he had no notice of such subsequent mortgages at the time when the further advance was made by him; or
- (*c*) whether or not he had such notice as aforesaid, where the mortgage imposes an obligation on him to make such further advances.

The subsection applies whether or not the prior mortgage was made expressly for securing further advances.

(2) In relation to the making of further advances after the commencement of this Act a mortgagee shall not be deemed to have notice of a mortgage merely by reason that it was registered as a land charge . . . if it was not so registered at the [time when the original mortgage was created][8] or when the last search (if any) by or on behalf of the mortgagee was made, whichever last happened.

---

[6] This emasculates *Low v Bouverie* [1891] 3 Ch 82.
[7] Cheshire, pp. 693–695, 708–711; M & W, pp. 978–985; MM, pp. 475–479. The doctrine is of reduced importance after 1925. In relation to registered land, see L.R.A. 1925, s. 30; L.P. (A) A. 1926, s. 5, which adds sub-s. (3).
[8] The words in square brackets were substituted by L.P. (A) A. 1926, s. 7 and Sch.

This subsection only applies where the prior mortgage was made expressly for securing a current account or other further advances[9].

(3) Save in regard to the making of further advances as aforesaid, the right to tack is hereby abolished:

Provided that nothing in this Act shall affect any priority acquired before the commencement of this Act by tacking, or in respect of further advances made without notice of a subsequent incumbrance or by arrangement with the subsequent incumbrancer.

(4) This section applies to mortgages of land made before or after the commencement of this Act, but not to charges registered under the Land Registration Act, 1925, or any enactment replaced by that Act.

QUESTIONS

1. Is it possible to postulate a principle governing the system of priority of mortgages after 1925?
2. To what extent do the pre-1926 rules of priorities of mortgages still apply? In particular:
    (i) On what basis is priority calculated in the case of two mortgagees both claiming to be protected by deposit, and each having some of the deeds?
    (ii) Is any significance now attached, in the issue of priority, (whether in (i) above or otherwise) to the question whether a mortgage is legal or equitable?
    (iii) Is a first mortgagee, legal or equitable, whose mortgage is protected by deposit of the title deeds and is unregistered, liable to be defeated by a later mortgagee who is given a "reasonable" excuse for non-production of the title deeds?
3. Is it possible to find a satisfactory solution of the problem of the three mortgagees, each of whom has priority over the others? *Re Wyatt* [1892] 1 Ch 188, p. 676 ante; (1968) 32 Conv (NS) 325 (W.A.Lee): (1961) 71 Yale LJ 53 (G. Gilmore).

IX. Registered Land[10]

Mortgages of land may be effected in various ways:

i. Registered Charge. This is a legal mortgage which is effected by registration in the Charges Register of the lender as the proprietor of the charge. The land certificate is deposited at the registry, and a charge certificate is issued to the mortgagee.

ii. Mortgage of a Legal Estate by a method appropriate to unregistered land. This takes effect only in equity and needs to be

---

[9] (1958) 22 Conv (NS) 44 (R. G. Rowley).
[10] Cheshire, pp. 713–716; M & W, pp. 1076–1078; MM, pp. 525–527; Ruoff and Roper, Chaps. 25, 26; Fisher and Lightwood, Chap. 3.

protected as a minor interest. Such a mortgage can be converted into a registered charge by registration.

iii.   Mortgage by Deposit of the Land Certificate. This operates as an equitable mortgage; the mortgagee can be protected by a notice on the register which will operate as an ordinary caution.

iv.   Mortgage of an Equitable Interest. As with unregistered land, such mortgages are treated quite differently from mortgages of a legal estate. Mortgages of certain equitable interests may be entered upon a supplemental register of dealings in equitable interests. This is the Index of Minor Interests[11], and is completely separate from the Land Register. It is the registered land counterpart of the rule in *Dearle v Hall*[12].

v.   Equitable Charges which are, in unregistered land, capable of registration under the Land Charges Act 1972. These are minor interests, and may be protected as such[13].

LAND REGISTRATION ACT 1925

Creation and protection of mortgages of registered land.

106.[14] — (1) The proprietor of any registered land may, subject to any entry to the contrary on the register, mortgage, by deed or otherwise, the land or any part of it in any manner which would have been permissible if the land had not been registered and, subject to this section, with the like effect.

(2) Unless and until the mortgage becomes a registered charge, —

    (*a*) it shall take effect only in equity, and

    (*b*) it shall be capable of being overridden as a minor interest unless it is protected as provided by subsection (3) below.

(3) A mortgage which is not a registered charge may be protected on the register by —

    (*a*) a notice under section 49 of this Act,

    (*b*) any such other notice as may be prescribed, or

    (*c*) a caution under section 54 of this Act.

(4) A mortgage which is not a registered charge shall devolve and may be transferred, discharged, surrendered or otherwise dealt with by the same instruments and in the same manner as if the land had not been registered.

25.   Proprietor's power to create charges. — (1) The proprietor of any registered land may by deed —

---

[11] L.R.A. 1925, s. 102 (2), p. 684, post. Law Commission Working Paper No. 37, (1971), Part C recommends the abolition of the Index. Only 17 inspections were made between 1959 and 1970.

[12] See p. 673, ante.

[13] L.R.A. 1925, s. 59; p. 128, ante.

[14] As substituted by A.J.A. 1977, s. 26 (1). Under s. 26 (2), the Registrar may convert into a registered charge any mortgage protected by a mortgage caution entered before 29 August 1977; L.R.R. 1977 (S. I. 1977, No. 2089).

(*a*) charge the registered land with the payment at an appointed time of any principal sum of money either with or without interest; ...

(2) A charge may be in any form provided that —

(*a*) the registered land comprised in the charge is described by reference to the register or in any other manner sufficient to enable the registrar to identify the same without reference to any other document.

PRECEDENT: REGISTERED CHARGE[15]
H.M. LAND REGISTRY
Land Registration Acts 1925–1971

County and district: ....
(or name of Greater London borough where applicable)
Title No[s].: ....
Property: ....
Date: ....

In consideration of ..... pounds (£.....) the receipt whereof is hereby acknowledged I, *AB* of ..... [*address and description*] (hereinafter called "the Borrower" which expression shall where the context admits include all persons deriving title under the Borrower) as Beneficial Owner hereby charge by way of legal mortgage[16] the land comprised in the title[s] above referred to with the payment to *CD* of ..... [*address and description*] (hereinafter called "the Mortgagee" which expression shall where the context admits include all persons deriving title under the Mortgagee) on the ..... day of ..... of the principal sum of £..... with interest thereupon from the date hereof at ..... per cent. per annum payable half yearly on the ..... day of ..... and the ..... day of ..... in every year.

And it is hereby declared that:

[1. *Reduction of interest on punctual payment:*]

2. The Borrower HEREBY COVENANTS with the Mortgagee that at all times during the continuance of this security [*continue with Borrower's covenants*] ...

[3. *Warranty as to occupation:*] ...

[To be executed by both AB and CD and attested]

LAND REGISTRATION ACT 1925

26. Registration of charges. — (1) The charge shall be completed by the registrar entering on the register the person in whose favour the charge is made as the proprietor of such charge, and the particulars of the charge.

---

[15] The precedent is taken from Hallett, *Conveyancing Precedents*, p. 1207. The references in clauses 1, 2 and 3 are also to Hallett . See also L.R.R. 1925, r. 139 and Sch.

[16] Omit "by way of legal mortgage" if desired.

27. Terms of years implied in or granted by charges. — (1) A registered charge shall, unless made or taking effect by demise or subdemise, and subject to any provision to the contrary contained in the charge, take effect as a charge by way of legal mortgage.

(2) Subject to the provisions of the Law of Property Act, 1925, a registered charge may contain in the case of freehold land, an express demise, and in the case of leasehold land an express subdemise of the land to the creditor for a term of years absolute, subject to a proviso for cesser on redemption.

(3) Any such demise or subdemise or charge by way of legal mortgage shall take effect from the date of the delivery of the deed containing the same, but subject to the estate or interest of any person (other than the proprietor of the land) whose estate or interest (whenever created) is registered or noted on the register before the date of registration of the charge.

29. Priorities of registered charges. — Subject to any entry to the contrary on the register, registered charges on the same land shall as between themselves rank according to the order in which they are entered on the register, and not according to the order in which they are created.

102. Priorities as between minor interests. — (2) Priorities as regards dealings effected after the commencement of this Act between assignees and incumbrancers of life interests, remainders, reversions and executory interests shall be regulated by the order of the priority cautions or inhibitions lodged (in a specially prescribed form)[17] against the proprietor of the registered estate affected, but, save as aforesaid, priorities as between persons interested in minor interests shall not be affected by the lodgment of cautions or inhibitions[18].

34. Powers of proprietor of charge. — (1) Subject to any entry on the register to the contrary, the proprietor of a charge shall have and may exercise all the powers conferred by law on the owner of a legal mortgage.

65. Deposit at registry of certificate of mortgaged land. — Where a charge or mortgage (otherwise than by deposit) is registered, or is protected by a caution in a specially prescribed form, the land certificate shall be deposited at the registry until the charge or mortgage is cancelled.

LAND REGISTRATION RULES 1925

160. Registration of proprietor of incumbrances prior to first registration of land. — (1) Where it appears that any person is entitled to an incumbrance created prior to the first registration of land, the Registrar shall, on the application or with the consent of the person so

---

[17] In the Minor Interests Index.
[18] L.R.R. 1925, rr. 11, 229, 290 (2).

entitled and on due proof of his title and after notice to the proprietor of the land, register such person as the proprietor of such incumbrance.

(2) Where there are two or more such incumbrances, their relative priorities shall not be affected by the registration of some or one of them only, or by the order in which such of them as are registered are entered in the register.

LAND REGISTRATION ACT 1925

66. Creation of liens by deposit of certificates.[19] — The proprietor of any registered land or charge may, subject to the overriding interests, if any, to any entry to the contrary on the register, and to any estates, interests, charges, or rights registered or protected on the register at the date of the deposit, create a lien on the registered land or charge by deposit of the land certificate or charge certificate; and such lien shall, subject as aforesaid, be equivalent to a lien created in the case of unregistered land by the deposit of documents of title or of the mortgage deed by an owner entitled for his own benefit to the registered estate, or a mortgagee beneficially entitled to the mortgage, as the case may be.

LAND REGISTRATION RULES 1925

239. Notice of deposit of certificate. — (1) Any person with whom a land certificate or charge certificate is deposited as security for money may, by registered letter or otherwise, in writing give notice to the Registrar of such deposit, and of his name and address.

(3) On receipt of such notice the Registrar shall enter notice of the deposit in the Charges Register, and shall give a written acknowledgment of its receipt.

(4) Such notice shall operate as a caution under section 54 of the Act.

262. Form of charge certificate. — (1) A charge certificate shall certify the registration of the charge and shall contain —

   (*a*) an office copy of the charge,
   (*b*) a description (if no description is contained in the charge) of the land affected,
   (*c*) the name and address of the proprietor of the charge,
   (*d*) a list of the prior incumbrances (if any) appearing on the register.

(2) There shall also be added such further particulars, if any, as the Register shall think fit, and the Land Registry seal shall be affixed to it.

---

[19] See *Re White Rose Cottage* [1965] Ch 940, [1965] 1 All ER 11; p. 653, ante; (1966) 19 CLP 26 (E. C. Ryder). *Barclays Bank Ltd v Taylor* [1974] Ch 137, [1973] 1 All ER 752, (1973) 89 LQR 70 (P.V.B.); (1974) 124 NLJ 634 (S. Robinson).

(3) Notes of subsequent dealings affecting the charge shall from time to time be entered on the certificate, or a new certificate shall be issued in place thereof, as may be more convenient.

In *Grace Rymer Investments Ltd v Waite* [1958] Ch 831, [1958] 2 All ER 777, tenants under a lease for less than 21 years were in possession of the property at the date on which the lessor executed a legal charge in favour of a mortgagee. The charge was registered a few days later; an argument was addressed to the court as to the date from which the charge took effect.

Lord EVERSHED MR said at p. 849: "Apart from section 27 (3), it would appear therefore to be tolerably clear that the title of the purchaser or of the mortgagee, as the case may be, in the case of registered land is not perfected until registration, and that, when registration takes effect[20], it is subject to overriding interests which are anticipated by section 20[1], but more precisely defined by section 70. . . .[2]

The argument, as I follow it, appears to be: (1) that the time from which the mortgage shall take full effect must be treated as being the moment of the execution of the legal charge, which would put the legal estate in the chargee from that date; and (2) that the legal estate overrides all interests save those of persons whose estates or interests are registered or noted on the register. It seems to me that that cannot be right. If so, it would be inconsistent, so far as I can see, with the purpose and intention of the earlier sections to which I have already alluded, and which provide that until registration (in the case of a sale) the vendor remains the proprietor of the legal estate. I am unable to accept it that if the registered proprietor is to be treated as remaining the proprietor of the legal estate, a legal estate at the same time can also be created in favour of somebody else not on the register at all and not deriving title from someone on the register, although the earlier sections 19[3], 20[4] and 26[5] indicate that a charge is only completed by entry on the register. . . .

It would seem to me that it would be contrary to the whole tenor of the Act and indeed to general principle if, by reason of the reference in section 27[6] to estates or interests which are registered or noted on the register, you could produce the result that the plaintiffs could defeat the interests of a tenant of which they had notice when he took possession. According to general principles (and indeed it has not been contested) the plaintiffs had or must be treated as having had notice of

---

[20] See L.R.R. 1925 rr. 83–85, p. 107, ante.
[1] P. 101, ante.
[2] P. 110, ante.
[3] P. 93, ante.
[4] P. 101, ante.
[5] P. 683, ante.
[6] P. 684, ante.

the occupation of Mrs. Hitchen and her companions since there they were in occupation for all to see."

(1977) 93 LQR 541 at pp. 542–543, 558–560 (R. J. Smith)

"[*In Barclays Bank Ltd v Taylor* [1974] Ch 137, [1973] 1 All ER 752] the owner of land mortgaged it by deed; the mortgage was protected by a notice of deposit of the land certificate. At first instance[7], Goulding J held that a notice of deposit was not appropriate to protect the mortgage[8] which consequently was treated as unprotected. Subsequently, the mortgagor contracted to sell the land and this estate contract was protected by caution. When the mortgagee later sought to register its charge, the cautioner objected. Thus the question arose as to whether the protected estate contract had priority over the earlier, but unprotected, equitable mortgage. Goulding J held in favour of the estate contract. On appeal, Russell LJ, delivering the judgment of the court, asked[9] the not unreasonable question: 'what provision is there in the Act which reverses the ordinary rule that as between equities — for the [cautioners] have only an interest in equity under their contract of purchase — priority is governed by the time sequence?' It does not appear that the question, quite apart from an answer to it, had been raised before Goulding J. In the Court of Appeal, counsel for the cautioners was unable to offer any convincing answer and thus the appeal was allowed, giving priority to the mortgage.

It may be noted that the *ratio decidendi* supports two allied propositions. First, an unprotected minor interest does not automatically lose priority to a subsequent minor interest and, second, that an interest protected by caution does not have any automatic priority over earlier unprotected minor interests. . . . . .

There are, perhaps, two principal impressions one obtains from this examination of priority issues. The first is how confused and uncertain the law is and how difficult it is to abstract either general principles or comprehensible detailed provisions from the legislation. This is a serious charge to be made against legislation designed to simplify the law. The major problem is that the land registration system is designed for those with registered interests; for such persons it works well. However, the impact of its provisions on the holders of other interests has never been properly sorted out — unlike the unregistered system, one does not have familiar principles to illuminate one's way forward. Instead, there is a fog of obscure and conflicting detail. The

---

[7] [1973] Ch 63.
[8] Relying on L.R.A., s. 106 (2), by which a caution in a specially prescribed form was the only appropriate method of protection, short of registration of the charge under s. 26. This provision has now been repealed by the Administration of Justice Act 1977, s. 26.
[9] At p. 146.

second conclusion is more palatable; it is that many of the conclusions eventually reached make good sense and are quite workable.

Nevertheless, the uncertainty in the area borders upon the intolerable[10] and is clearly a suitable subject for reform. Particular points requiring attention are: the impact of protection by notice, the effect of section 107 and the special provisions relating to section 48 leases, restrictive covenants and liens by deposit of certificate (especially the priority accorded to the last two interests on creation).

The most important point of principle is whether a general priority rule based upon the order of protection on the register ought to be introduced. Where the second interest holder has searched the register, protected his interest and either paid over money to the proprietor or otherwise acted to his detriment, it seems a mockery of the system to subject him to an earlier unprotected minor interest[11]. Yet at present he could only succeed if, as urged above, he was protected by notice or could rely on the *Abigail v Lapin*[12] line of authority. It has already been argued that the latter possibility would lead to unfortunate uncertainty. It is submitted that there is a need for a statutory priority in favour of the second interest holder, for only legislation can provide the degree of precision required.

One obvious question is whether all minor interests should be affected by failure to protect them[13]. It is urged that it would be unfortunate to discriminate so that interests not commonly protected would not be so affected. The idea of a minor interest which one does not need to protect is odd and contrary to the ethos of the land registration system[14]. Nor is it right to accord priority only to those interests where money is usually handed over to the proprietor. There will always be cases where other interest holders have parted with money and so are equally deserving. It would be justifiable to limit the

---

[10] This is not, however, reflected in any mass of case law. On the contrary, the lack of reported cases makes one rely on pure statutory interpretation and analysis to a disconcerting extent. Perhaps the factual situations under discussion are relatively rare. More likely, the difficulties have not yet been fully appreciated. Certainly, the approach of the Court of Appeal in *Barclays Bank Ltd v Taylor* [1974] Ch 137 was radically different from that of Goulding J at first instance [1973] Ch 63 and that case involved the relatively simple problem of the effect of a caution.

[11] *Cf.* Robinson (1974) 124 NLJ 634, 635, who says of minor interests: "Until protected they are not and cannot be proprietary interests if the concept of a conclusive register is the plinth of the English system of title to land by registration."

[12] [1934] AC 491. (Privy Council, on appeal from the High Court of Australia). The case develops, in the registration context, the rule that as between two equitable interests the first in time only has priority if the equities are equal. The suggestion is that, if the first interest is not protected on the register, then the equities are not equal and so the second in time has priority. *Quaere* the need for detrimental reliance. In English law, the second interest, being registrable, could have had priority anyway if the register had been searched and the interest registered. The scope of *Abigail v Lapin* may well be limited by *J. and H. Just (Holdings) Pty Ltd v Bank of New South Wales* (1971) 45 ALJR 625.

[13] *Cf.* the Law Commision's Working Paper No. 67; Hayton, *Registered Land* (2nd edn.), pp. 147–157; (1976) 29 CLP 26.

[14] *Cf.* supra, p. 555. This is not an argument that where there is actual occupation then there should be no protection as an overriding interest under L.R.A., s. 70 (1) (*g*), for then there is a quite separate basis for binding the second interest holder.

priority to cases where the second interest holder has in fact paid over money or acted to his detriment, but it is submitted that to accord priority to all protected minor interests (subject to the holder not being a volunteer) would be simpler and preferable. This, then, is the reform urged: the priority of minor interests should be determined by the order of protection on the register.''

————————

QUESTION

What principles do you think are applicable to determine the priority of mortgages
   (*a*) pre–1926
   (*b*) post 1925 in unregistered land and
   (*c*) post 1926 in registered land?

Part Four. Control of Land

12. Covenants Between Freeholders[1]

I. Introduction

In considering to what extent covenants between freeholders may be enforced between persons who were not original parties to the covenant, two main distinctions must be made. First, different rules apply to the "running" of the benefit and the "running" of the burden. And, secondly, in connection both with the burden and the benefit, the rules of common law are different from those of equity. This is most marked in connection with the running of the burden, where the decision in equity of *Tulk v Moxhay* in 1848[2] provided the basis of the modern doctrine. The common law rules for the running of the benefit are still applicable, but they have been further developed in equity[3]. The burden and the benefit will be considered separately.

The common law rules for the running of the benefit are ancient. As with every case of a covenant running at common law, the covenant ran with the estate of the covenantee and not with the land[4], and it was necessary for the assignee of the covenantee to show that he had the

---

[1] Cheshire, pp. 592–623; M & W, pp. 720–723, 742–775; MM, pp. 364–379; Preston and Newsom, *Restrictive Covenants Affecting Freehold Land* (6th edn., 1976); Elphinstone, *Covenants Affecting Land* (1946); Farrand (2nd edn.), pp. 404–429; Maitland, pp. 162–178. For a historical account, see Simpson, *Introduction to the History of Land Law* (1961), pp. 109–111, 131–132, 238–243.

[2] (1848) 2 Ph 774. See p. 704, post.

[3] See p. 717, post.

[4] For covenants in leases, see p. 414, ante.

same legal estate as the original covenantee[5]. Equity, both with the benefit and the burden, developed a different concept of a covenant running with the land, and avoided the requirement that the assignee of the covenantee or covenantor should hold the same estate as his assignor[6].

These factors have to be considered when the question is whether or not an assignee of the covenantee can sue. He may be able to do so under the common law rules alone, as where there is no servient land[7]; he may be able to do so under either; or he may have to rely on the further developments in equity and under statute.[7a]

As indicated, the rules relating to the running of the burden of a covenant between freeholders are almost exclusively equitable. The origin of the rule is the equitable principle that a person cannot come to property with knowledge that a contract affecting the property is in existence and then ignore it. But there has been much development from the general principle in the case of restrictive covenants affecting land[8]. It is not in the general interest to allow burdens to be attached to land unless there is some corresponding benefit to be protected. And a covenant enforceable between adjoining freeholders is now looked upon as an interest which imposes a burden on one piece of land and confers a benefit on another; as something in the nature of an equitable negative easement[9].

This branch of equity grew with the great era of suburban development in the 19th century; control was in the hands of individual landowners. But, since the 1930s, this type of control has been largely superseded by public control in the hands of planning authorities exercised in the public interest[10]. It will be seen from the next Chapter that development or change of user may now only be carried out after planning permission has been obtained. Public planning control has thus overtaken the earlier method, both in influence and complexity. But the law relating to covenants between freeholders is still operative. The two methods of control are sometimes complementary,

---

[5] But see p. 713, post, *Smith and Snipes Hall Farm Ltd v River Douglas Catchment Board* [1949] 2 KB 500, [1949] 2 All ER 179; L.P.A. 1925, s. 78 (1).

[6] See p. 709, post, *Tichborne v Weir* (1892) 67 LT 735; *Re Nisbet and Potts' Contract* [1906] 1 Ch 386.

[7] *The Prior's Case* (1368) YB 42 Ed III, pl. 14, fol. 3A, discussed under *Spencer's Case* (1583) 5 Co Rep 16a; Smith's *Leading Cases* (13th edn., 1929), Vol. I, pp. 51, 65, 73; *Smith and Snipes Hall Farm Ltd v River Douglas Catchment Board*, supra, per Tucker LJ at p. 506.

[7a] L.P.A. 1925, s. 78 (1); *Federated Homes Ltd v Mill Lodge Properties Ltd* [1980] 1 WLR 594, [1980] 1 All ER 371; p. 722, post.

[8] For the operation of this principle in the case of chattels see Cheshire and Fifoot, *Law of Contract* (9th edn.) pp. 445–452, Treitel, *Law of Contract* (5th edn., pp. 477–481).

[9] *London and South Western Rly Co v Gomm* (1882) 20 ChD 562; *LCC v Allen* [1914] 3 KB 642; *Formby v Barker* [1903] 2 Ch 539; *Re Nisbet and Potts' Contract* [1906] 1 Ch 386.

[10] Town and Country Planning Act 1971; Land Compensation Acts 1961, 1973; Cheshire, pp. 935–981; M & W, pp. 1086–1108; MM, pp. 532–543. See Chapter 13, post.

sometimes contrary. They are cumulative, and a purchaser must satisfy himself in respect of both forms of restriction[11].

It has always been clear that no covenant will run with the land unless it "touches and concerns" the land. This requirement exists also in connection with covenants between landlord and tenant, and has been discussed in that connection[12]. An additional point of importance here is the view current before 1926 that section 5 Real Property Act 1845 (under which the benefit of a covenant in an indenture may be given to a person who was not a party to the indenture) applied only to cases of covenants which ran with the land[13]. This section is now repealed and replaced by Law of Property Act 1925, section 56, which has been said to be free from such restriction. The question whether a particular covenant "touches and concerns" the land is, therefore, not material in deciding whether the benefit of it can be given to a person not a party to it; it is material in deciding whether the benefit of the covenant so given will run with the land of the person to whom it was given.

This branch of the law is particularly concerned with covenants between freeholders. Covenants between landlord and tenant have already been discussed, and are governed by rules of their own. Where, however, a covenant between landlord and tenant is not enforceable under those special rules, it may, nevertheless, be enforceable under the rules discussed in this section where they are applicable[14].

Finally, it will be seen that the law relating to the passing of the benefit of restrictive covenants has become difficult and technical. But there is a tendency now to escape from many of the technicalities. This is shown by recent decisions in the context of annexation of the benefit of a covenant to the land of the covenantee[14a], and also in connection with schemes of development[14b]. "The tendency is ... to assimilate the law of covenants to the law of easements, where no formalities are required for establishing the right as appurtenant to the dominant tenement"[15]. This policy, as will be seen, is currently being pursued by the Law Commission[16].

---

[11] (1964) 28 Conv (NS) 190 (A. R. Mellows).
[12] See p. 414, ante. The position in connection with covenants between freeholders is not exactly the same, for in this situation there are two pieces of land involved. Preston and Newsom, pp. 23–25; *Rogers v Hosegood* [1900] 2 Ch 388; *Formby v Barker* [1903] 2 Ch 539, 554; *Dyson v Forster* [1909] AC 98; *Smith and Snipes Hall Farm Ltd v River Douglas Catchment Board* [1949] 2 KB 500, 506, [1949] 2 All ER 179; *Newton Abbot Co-operative Society Ltd v Williamson and Treadgold Ltd* [1952] Ch 286, [1952] 1 All ER 279; *Federated Homes Ltd v Mill Lodge Properties Ltd* [1980] 1 WLR 594, [1980] 1 All ER 371. The distinction is not kept clear by LINDLEY LJ in *Austerberry v Oldham Corporation* (1885) 29 ChD 750, 781.
[13] *Kelsey v Dodd* (1881) 52 LJ Ch 34, 39; *Forster v Elvet Colliery Co Ltd* [1908] 1 KB 629, affd. sub nom. *Dyson v Forster* [1909] AC 98; *Westhoughton UDC v Wigan Coal and Iron Co Ltd* [1919] 1 Ch 159; *Re Ecclesiastical Commissioners for England's Conveyance* [1936] Ch 430.
[14] *Hall v Ewin* (1887) 37 ChD 74, p. 702, n. 7, post; *Patman v Harland* (1881) 17 ChD 353; p. 413, ante.
[14a] *Federated Homes Ltd v Mill Lodge Properties Ltd*, supra.
[14b] *Re Dolphin's Conveyance* [1970] Ch 654, [1970] 2 All ER 664.
[15] (1972 B) 31 CLJ 157 at 163 (H. W. R.Wade). [16] P. 777, post.

II.   The Burden[17]

A.   Common Law

i.   THE GENERAL RULE

The general rule is that the burden of a covenant affecting land does not run with the land at common law. This is a basic principle, the existence of which has necessitated the development in equity of the doctrine of restrictive covenants. The rule is one of the many results of the wider principle of privity of contract, that a person may neither sue upon nor be made liable upon a contract unless he is a party to it. If, for instance, A sold Whiteacre, part of his land, to B who covenanted with A to lay out pleasure gardens on Whiteacre, A could sue B at law for damages if B refused to perform the covenant; but if B sold or gave the land to C, C could not be made liable on the covenant, because he was not a party to it. This is a matter of the greatest importance because, apart from cases in which specific performance will be decreed, equity only interferes, as will be seen, where the covenant is "restrictive". Positive covenants are therefore not enforceable by an action for damages against an assign of the covenantor.

It is questionable whether the policy behind such a rule is satisfactory, for it often has the effect of leaving a covenantee remediless. The matter was considered in 1965 by the Wilberforce Committee which recommended that, subject to certain conditions, the burden of positive covenants should run, but action upon the recommendation awaits a report by the Law Commission on the wider topic of Rights Appurtenant to Land[18]. The rule does not exist in such absolute form in most of the United States[19]. It is, however, possible in England to effect the observance of a positive covenant in other ways[20].

---

[17] Cheshire, pp. 594–605; M & W, pp. 752–760; MM, pp. 367–368, 374–377.

[18] Report of the Committee on Positive Covenants Affecting Land (1965) Cmnd 2719; Law Commission Report on Restrictive Covenants; No. 11 (1967); See also Law Commission Working Paper No. 36 (1971) which recommends that positive covenants to carry out or pay for work on land be enforceable as Land Obligations, (paras. 41–44: Propositions 5 and 6). The Law Commission will be publishing a series of reports over the next few years recommending changes in the law relating to easements, covenants (both negative and positive) and prescription. The first report will deal with positive and negative covenants. (Law Com No. 78, 11th Annual Report, 1975–76 para. 17; Law Com No. 92, 13th Annual Report 1977–78, para. 2.30; p. 776, post); (1972 B) 31 CLJ 157 (H. W. R. Wade).

[19] Clark, *Real Covenants* (2nd edn. 1947), pp. 231–232; (1943) 52 Yale LJ 699; (1945) 30 Cornell LQ 378; American Restatement (1944) Property: Vol. 5, Servitudes, Ch 45.

[20] *Brewster v Kitchell* (1697) 12 Mod 166, 169; *Morland v Cook* (1868) LR 6 Eq 252; *Aspden v Seddon* (1876) 1 Ex D 496; *Austerberry v Oldham Corporation* (1885) 29 ChD 750 per LINDLEY LJ at p. 781; *South Eastern Rly Co v Associated Portland Cement Manufacturers (1900) Ltd* [1910] 1 Ch 12; *Westhoughton UDC v Wigan Coal and Iron Co Ltd* [1919] 1 Ch 159; *Halsall v Brizell* [1957] Ch 169, [1957] 1 All ER 371, see p. 702, n. 7, post; (1954) 18 Conv (NS) 558–564 (E. H. Scamell). Preston and Newsom, pp. 65–66.

AUSTERBERRY *v* CORPORATION OF OLDHAM
(1885) 29 ChD 750 (CA, COTTON, FRY, LINDLEY LJJ)

In 1837 a company was formed for the purpose of acquiring land and building thereon a road, for the use of the public, on payment of a toll. The road was to pass over the land of John Elliott, who conveyed it to the trustees for the company who covenanted with him, his heirs and assigns to make up the road at their expense, and keep it at all times in repair. The trustees maintained the road until it was taken over by Oldham Corporation in 1880 under statutory powers. In 1868 the plaintiff purchased the land owned by John Elliott adjoining the road. The present dispute arose in connection with the payment of the expenses of 'making up' the street, liability for which is imposed upon the frontagers by the Public Health Act 1875. The plaintiffs argued, inter alia, that the Corporation had taken the land from the trustees with notice of the covenant to maintain, and were bound by that covenant to meet the expenses themselves.

Held. The covenant was not enforceable.

LINDLEY LJ (after dealing with a question arising under section 150 of the Public Health Act 1875[1]):

But then arises another and a totally different point. The Plaintiff says:— "You, the corporation, have bought or acquired this road under an Act of Parliament which places you in the position of, and in no better position than, those from whom you got it; you acquired it from certain trustees, and those trustees covenanted with my predecessors in title to keep this road open for the public, and to repair it: You are bound by that covenant to repair, and I am in a position to enforce against you that covenant." . . . That gives rise to one or two questions of law.

The first question which I will consider is whether that covenant runs with the land, as it is called — whether the benefit of it runs with the land held by the Plaintiff, and whether the burden of it runs with the land held by the Defendants; because, if the covenant does run at law, then the Plaintiff, so far as I can see, would be right as to this portion of his claim. Now, as regards the benefit running with the Plaintiff's land, the covenant is, so far as the road goes, a covenant to repair the road; what I mean by that is, there is nothing in the deed which points particularly to that portion of the road which abuts upon or fronts the Plaintiff's land — it is a covenant to repair the whole of the road, no distinction being made between the portion of that road which joins or abuts upon his land and the rest of the road; in other words, it is a covenant simply to make and maintain this road as a public highway; there is no covenant to do anything whatever on the Plaintiff's land, and there is nothing pointing to the Plaintiff's land in particular. Now it appears to me to be going a long way to say that the benefit of that covenant runs with the Plaintiff's land. I do not overlook the fact that the Plaintiff as a frontager has certain rights of

---

[1] See now Highways Act 1959, ss. 189, 190.

getting on to the road; and if this covenant had been so worded as to shew that there had been an intention to grant him some particular benefit in respect of that particular part of his land, possibly we might have said that the benefit of the covenant did run with this land; but when you look at the covenant it is a mere covenant with him, as with all adjoining owners, to make this road, a small portion of which only abuts on his land, and there is nothing specially relating to his land at all. I cannot see myself how any benefit of this covenant runs with his land.

But it strikes me, I confess, that there is a still more formidable objection as regards the burden. Does the burden of this covenant run with the land so as to bind the Defendants? The Defendants have acquired the road under the trustees, and they are bound by such covenant as runs with the land. Now we come to face the difficulty; does a covenant to repair all this road run with the land — that is, does the burden of it descend upon those to whom the road may be assigned in future? We are not dealing here with a case of landlord and tenant. The authorities which refer to that class of cases have little, if any, bearing upon the case which we have to consider, and I am not prepared to say that any covenant which imposes a burden upon land does run with the land, unless the covenant does, upon the true construction of the deed, containing the covenant, amount to either a grant of an easement, or a rent-charge, or some estate or interest in the land. A mere covenant, to repair or to do something of that kind, does not seem to me, I confess, to run with the land in such a way as to bind those who may acquire it.

It is remarkable that the authorities upon this point, when they are examined, are very few, and it is also remarkable that in no case that I know of, except one which I shall refer to presently, is there anything like authority to say that a burden of this kind will run with the land. That point has often been discussed, and I rather think the conclusion at which the editors of the last edition of *Smith's* Leading Cases have come to is right, that no case has been decided which does establish that such a burden can run with the land in the sense in which I am now using that expression. [His Lordship referred to *Holmes v Buckley* (1691) 1 Eq Cas Abr 27; *Morland v Cook* (1868) LR 6 Eq 252; *Cooke v Chilcott* (1876) 3 ChD 694; *Western v Macdermott* (1866) LR 1 Eq 499; affd. 2 Ch App 72, and continued:] I am not aware of any other case which either shews, or appears to shew, that a burden such as this can be annexed to land by a mere covenant, such as we have got here; and in the absence of authority it appears to me that we shall be perfectly warranted in saying that the burden of this covenant does not run with the land. After all it is a mere personal covenant. If the parties had intended to charge this land for ever, into whosesoever hands it came, with the burden of repairing the road, there are ways and means known to conveyancers by which it could be done with comparative ease; all that would have been necessary would have been to create a rent-charge and charge it on the tolls, and the thing would have been done. They have not done anything of the sort, and, therefore, it seems to me to shew that they did not intend to have a covenant which should run with the land. That disposes of the part of the case which is perhaps the most difficult.

The last point was this — that even if it did not run with the land at law, still, upon the authority of *Tulk v Moxhay* ((1848) 2 Ph 774), the Defendants, having bought the land with notice of this covenant, take the land subject to it. Mr. *Collins* very properly did not press that upon us, because after the two recent decisions in the Court of Appeal in *Haywood v Brunswick Permanent Benefit Building Society* ((1881) 8 QBD 403, see p. 703, post) and *London and South Western Rly Co v. Gomm* ((1882) 20 ChD 562), that argument is untenable. *Tulk v Moxhay* cannot be extended to covenants of this description. It appears to me, therefore, that upon all points the plaintiff has failed, and that the appeal ought to be dismissed with costs[2].

ii. METHODS OF CIRCUMVENTION

"A number of current techniques and devices by which lawyers attempt to surmount or circumvent the difficulties of enforcing positive covenants" are listed in the Report of the Committee on Positive Covenants Affecting Land[3]. They are:

(i) To lease land instead of selling it and to rely upon the enforceability of covenants between landlord and tenant[4].

(ii) Chains of Indemnity Covenants. A covenant could be taken by each successive purchaser and liability on the covenant will exist down the line of purchasers[5]. "But in practice this device sooner or later becomes ineffective, either in consequence of the death or disappearance of the original covenantor, or because a break occurs in the chain of indemnities."

(iii) Covenants against sale of registered land without the developer's consent[6].

(iv) The doctrine of *Halsall v Brizell*. "In some cases a positive covenant can be enforced in practice by the operation of the maxim *'qui sentit commodum sentire debet et onus'*. This obliges a person who wishes to take advantage of a service or facility (e.g. a road or drains) to comply with any corresponding obligation to contribute to the cost of providing or

---

[2] The burden of a positive covenant was held by MACNAGHTEN J (following the dicta in *Austerberry v Oldham Corporation*) not to run at law with the land of the covenantor in *E and G C Ltd v Bate* (1935) 79 LJo News 203.

[3] (1965) Cmd 2719. The quotations in (ii) and (iv) are from para. 8 of the Report. See Farrand (2nd edn.), pp. 422-427; George and George; *The Sale of Flats* (4th edn., 1978), pp. 14-16. 70-82; (1973) 37 Conv (NS) 194 (A. M. Prichard). *Precedents for the Conveyancer*, 5-22, 19-11; McCauslan, *Land, Law and Planning* (1975) pp. 292-302.

[4] See p. 414, ante.

[5] See Law Society's Conditions of Sale (1973 revision), Condition 11 (2); National Conditions of Sale (19th edn., 1976), Condition 19 (5) (6).

[6] L.R.A. 1925, s. 58; p. 129, ante.

maintaining it (*Halsall v Brizell* [1957] Ch 169, [1957] 1 All ER 371). The maxim cannot, however, be invoked where the burdened owner does not enjoy any service or facility to which his obligations attach or has no sufficient interest in the continuance of these benefits.'"[7]

(v) Easement of fencing[8].

(vi) On some occasions on which a long leasehold is converted into a freehold. Two statutes give such a right to a tenant:

(a) The Law of Property Act 1925, section 153, which provides for certain long leases[9] to be enlarged into free-holds, and for the freehold to be subject "to all the same covenants . . . as the term would have been subject to if it had not been so enlarged".

(b) The Leasehold Reform Act 1967 permits the tenant of a leasehold house[10] held on a long tenancy[11] at a low rent[12], which he has occupied as his residence for five years[13], to acquire the freehold[14] on fair terms and free from incumbrances[15], but "Burdens . . . in respect of the upkeep or regulation for the benefit of any locality of any land, building, structure, works, ways or watercourse[16] shall not be treated as incumbrances for purposes of this Part of this Act, but any conveyance executed to give effect to this section shall be made subject thereto . . ."[17].

(vii) Certain statutory powers which entitle Local Authorities to impose positive obligations on land and to enforce them upon successive owners[18].

---

[7] (1957) 73 LQR 154 (R. E. M.); [1957] CLJ 35 (H. W. R. Wade); (1957) 21 Conv (NS) 160 (F. R. Crane); *E. R. Ives Investment Ltd v High* [1967] 2 QB 379, [1967] 1 All ER 504, p. 485, ante; *Montague v Long* (1972) 24 P & CR 240. For a detailed discussion of the doctrine, see *Tito v Waddell* (No. 2) [1977] Ch 106 at 289–311, where MEGARRY V-C held at p. 303 that it covered not merely successors in title but also "anybody whose connection with the transaction creating the benefit and burden is sufficient to show that he has some claim to the benefit whether or not he has a valid title to it". See also (1977) 41 Conv (NS) 432–435 (F. R. Crane).

[8] *Crow v Wood* [1971] 1 QB 77, [1970] 3 All ER 425, p. 518, ante.

[9] Restricted to those: (i) which were originally created for at least 300 years of which not less than 200 years is unexpired; (ii) in which no rent or money value is payable; (iii) which are not liable to be determined by re-entry for condition broken. (1958) 22 Conv (NS) 101 (T. P. D. Taylor).

[10] Not a flat nor maisonette: s. 2.

[11] I.e., an original term of more than 21 years: s. 3.

[12] I.e., not more than two-thirds of the 1965 rateable value. The Act applies only to properties below certain rateable values. The provisions are complex. Put simply, the Act applies to "older" leases (i.e. granted on or before 18 February 1966) where rateable value does not exceed £1,500 in Greater London or £750 elsewhere. With "newer" leases the limits are £1,000 and £500 respectively. Housing Act 1974, s. 118.

[13] Or for 5 years within the last 10 years: s. 1.

[14] Or an extended lease for 50 years: ss. 1, 14.

[15] Section 8 (1). For restrictive covenants, see s. 10 (4) (a).

[16] This clearly includes provisions of the type found in *Halsall v Brizell* [1957] Ch 169, [1957] 1 All ER 371.

[17] Section 8 (3). There is an exception in the case of rent charges: s. 11.

[18] TCPA 1971, ss. 29, 30 and 52, pp. 794, 807, post; Highways Act 1971, s. 18. Housing Act 1974 s. 126; p. 702, n. 7, post and various Private Acts.

There are other possibilities.

(viii) Rentcharge. The creation of a rentcharge to secure the payment of money or contribution to the maintenance of property[19].

(ix) Right of re-entry. A right of re-entry may be reserved exercisable on events which amount to the breach of a positive covenant[20]. This right of re-entry runs with the land, but is subject to the rule against perpetuities[1].

B. Equity

It was held in the leading case of *Tulk v Moxhay* in 1848[2] that the purchaser of land with notice of a restrictive covenant affecting it would be restrained from using the land in a way inconsistent with that covenant. The vendor, who takes from a purchaser a covenant which restricts the way in which the land can be used, is entitled in appropriate circumstances to an injunction restraining improper use of the land, not only against the original covenantor, but also against other parties coming to the land. This right to an injunction is of course an equitable right, and is never enforceable against bona fide purchasers of the legal estate in the land for value without notice of the covenant[3], but it can be enforced against all other persons. The burden of such a covenant is then said to run with the land in equity.

The conditions on which the burden of a covenant will so run are established in the cases leading from *Tulk v Moxhay*, and these cases show that the basic principle on which such covenants are enforced has changed since 1848. *Tulk v Moxhay* was decided on the general equitable ground that it was contrary to conscience that a person should come to land with notice of a covenant affecting it, and act in a way inconsistent with the covenant. And this principle was applied in a number of subsequent cases[4]. It soon became clear, however, that such a policy would result in the imposition of burdens on land without there being any corresponding interest in the plaintiff which required protection. The end of the 19th century saw the change of emphasis[5]. There must be an intent that the burden of the covenant should run

---

[19] *Morland v Cook* (1868) LR 6 Eq 252. *Austerberry v Oldham Corporation* (1885) 29 ChD 750, 782. See p. 697, ante. Rentcharges Act 1977, s. 2 (3) (c), (4) (5). See George and George, pp. 76–82.

[20] *Shiloh Spinners Ltd v Harding* [1973] AC 691, [1973] 1 All ER 90, p. 34, ante. The possibility of relief against forfeiture reduces its effectiveness as a device.

[1] (1950) 14 Conv (NS) 350, 354–357 (S. M. Tolson).

[2] (1848) 2 Ph 774; following Lord COTTENHAM'S earlier decision in *Mann v Stephens* (1846) 15 Sim 377.

[3] *Pilcher v Rawlins* (1872) 7 Ch App 259. See p. 27, ante.

[4] *Luker v Dennis* (1877) 7 ChD 227; *Catt v Tourle* (1869) 4 Ch App 654; *Millbourn v Lyons* [1914] 2 Ch 231; *Clegg v Hands* (1890) 44 ChD 503; *De Mattos v Gibson* (1858) 4 De G & J 276; *Western v Macdermott* (1866) 2 Ch App 72; *Lord Strathcona SS Co Ltd v Dominion Coal Co Ltd* [1926] AC 108.

[5] *London and South Western Rly Co v Gomm* (1882) 20 ChD 562.

with the land⁶. There must also be land benefited by the covenant, and the plaintiff must show that he has an interest in that land⁷. On the question of benefit, the court does not apply its own standard, but takes a decision on expert evidence presented to it⁸. The onus is on the defendant to show that a covenant does not benefit the land⁹, either originally, or at the date of the action. "This means that if there were possible opinions either way, the defendant will still fail unless he can show that the opinions that the covenant benefits the land could not reasonably be held."¹⁰ The benefit of such a covenant then becomes associated with a piece of land in the way that an easement is appurtenant to the dominant tenement; and the phraseology of the law of easements is introduced into the law of restrictive covenants¹¹.

The doctrine of *Tulk v Moxhay* is applicable only to restrictive covenants; covenants, that is, which are negative in substance, even though positive in form: indeed, the covenant in *Tulk v Moxhay* itself was in positive form. But the boundary between those that are, and those that are not, negative in substance is not always easy to draw; for almost every positive covenant can, in some sense, be regarded negatively. Moreover, it is difficult to see any inherent distinction between negative and positive covenants so far as enforceability is concerned. Positive and negative undertakings may be contained in a single covenant, but "there cannot be any doctrine of contagious proximity whereby the presence of the positive inhibits the enforce-

---

⁶ This intent may be clear from the nature of the covenant or by virtue of L.P.A. 1925, s. 79 which will apply unless a contrary intention is shown. *Re Royal Victoria Pavilion (Ramsgate)* [1961] Ch 581, [1961] 3 All ER 83; *Tophams Ltd v Earl of Sefton* [1967] 1 AC 50, 73, 81, [1966] 1 All ER 1039; pp. 711–712, post.

⁷ *Formby v Barker* [1903] 2 Ch 539; *LCC v Allen* [1914] 3 KB 642; *Millbourn v Lyons* [1914] 2 Ch 231; *Kelly v Barrett* [1924] 2 Ch 379; *Re Ballard's Conveyance* [1937] Ch 473, [1937] 2 All ER 691; *Tophams Ltd v Earl of Sefton* [1967] 1 AC 50, 81, [1966] 1 All ER 1039 per Lord WILBERFORCE ("under what I am content for present purposes to take as accepted doctrine"). There are exceptions to this rule in Housing Act 1957, s. 151; National Trust Act 1937, s. 8; *Gee v The National Trust* [1966] 1 WLR 170, 174, [1966] 1 All ER 954; Town and Country Planning Act 1971, s. 52; Green Belt (London and Home Counties) Act 1938, s. 22; Water Act 1945, s. 15; Forestry Act 1967, s. 5 (2), National Park and Access to Countryside Act 1949, s. 16 (4); Endowments and Glebe Measure 1976 s. 22; and a number of local authorities have power under local Acts. See p. 808, post. There are further exceptions in the cases of (i) schemes of development, p. 742, post; (ii) the landlord's reversion on a tenancy; *Hall v Ewin* (1887) 37 ChD 74; *Teape v Douse* (1905) 92 LT 319; (iii) the mortgagee's interest in the land; *Regent Oil Co Ltd v J. A. Gregory (Hatch End) Ltd* [1966] Ch 402, [1965] 3 All ER 673; following *John Bros Abergarw Brewery Co v Holmes* [1900] 1 Ch 188. On the question whether a covenant to restrain the pursuance of a non-noxious trade so as to avoid competition with the plaintiff can benefit the plaintiff's land, see *Wilkes v Spooner* [1911] 2 KB 473, 485; *Newton Abbot Co-operative Society Ltd v Williamson and Treadgold Ltd* [1952] Ch 286, [1952] 1 All ER 279; *Re Royal Victoria Pavilion (Ramsgate)* [1961] Ch 581, [1961] 3 All ER 83.

⁸ *Marten v Flight Refuelling Ltd* [1962] Ch 115 at 137; *Earl of Leicester v Wells-next-the-Sea UDC* [1973] Ch 110, [1972] 3 All ER 77; *Wrotham Park Estate Co Ltd v Parkside Homes Ltd* [1974] 1 WLR 798, [1974] 2 All ER 321.

⁹ *Wrotham Park Estate Co Ltd v Parkside Homes Ltd* supra, at p. 808.

¹⁰ (1974) JPL at p. 133 (G. H. Newsom).

¹¹ Per Jessel MR in *London and South Western Rly Co v Gomm*, quoted at p. 709, post.

ment of the neighbouring negative."[12] The Report on Positive Covenants Affecting Land emphasises the inconvenience of the present law (under which the burden of positive covenants does not run) to adjoining owners of land and especially to owners of divided buildings and blocks of flats[13]. In some situations, such as a covenant to supply water to land in a waterless area, the economic and moral reasons for enforcing positive covenants are just as strong as in the case of negative covenants. The jurisdiction, however, is exclusively equitable, and is limited to the situations which are susceptible to equitable remedies.

The positive remedy of specific performance and the doctrine of estate contracts are not indeed aspects of the doctrine of *Tulk v Moxhay,* but they provide an interesting analogy. An option in a lease to purchase the freehold has been held to be one which does not touch and concern the land and therefore does not run with the estate upon assignment by the tenant[14]. But the option to purchase, if specifically enforceable, creates a proprietary interest in the grantee which is good against everyone coming to the land other than a bona fide purchaser of the legal estate for value without notice[15]: registration constituting notice since 1925. An assignee of the covenantor will therefore take subject to the option.[16]

However, the burden of a positive covenant does not run in equity any more than it ran at law. Such covenants may, as we have seen[17], be enforced on other grounds, and will, if the Report on Positive Covenants is adopted, be enforceable subject to certain conditions. In the early days of the *Tulk v Moxhay* doctrine, equity made gallant attempts to enforce some positive covenants by issuing an injunction restraining the defendant from omitting to perform the undertaking[18]. This development, not surprisingly, was brought to an abrupt halt five years later in *Haywood v Brunswick Permanent Benefit Building Society*[19]. It is, however, of interest in demonstrating the crucial

---

[12] *Shepherd Homes Ltd v Sandham (No. 2)* [1971] 1 WLR 1062 at 1067, [1971] 2 All ER 1267, per MEGARRY J; Preston and Newsom, pp. 67–70

[13] See p. 699, ante; Law Commission Report on Restrictive Covenants (No. 11, 1967).

[14] *Woodall v Clifton* [1905] 2 Ch 257, p. 335, ante; *Worthing Corpn v Heather* [1906] 2 Ch 532.

[15] See p. 24, ante.

[16] L.C.A. 1972, s. 2 (4) Class C (iv); *London and South Western Rly Co v Gomm* (1882) 20 ChD 562; *Hutton v Watling* [1948] Ch 26, [1947] 2 All ER 641. The option, unless it be an option for a lessee or his successors in title to acquire an interest reversionary on the term of a lease and which ceases to be exerciseable at or before the expiration of one year from the determination of the lease, must comply with the perpetuity rule, and the period, whether the issue is between the original contracting parties or not, is 21 years. Perpetuities and Accumulations Act 1964, ss. 9, 10. See p. 337, ante.

[17] See p. 699, ante.

[18] *Morland v Cook* (1868) LR 6 Eq 252; *Cooke v Chilcott* (1876) 3 ChD 694, which was expressly disapproved in *Haywood v Brunswick Permanent Benefit Building Society* (1881) 8 QBD 403; *Hall v Ewin* (1887) 37 ChD 74. In *Andrew v Aitken* (1882) 22 ChD 218, 220 FRY J, suggested that, in the case of a covenant to build, the covenantor and his assigns might be called upon to allow the covenantee to enter and carry out the work.

[19] (1881) 8 QBD 403.

importance of the scope of equitable remedies in the development of the doctrine of *Tulk v Moxhay*.

The burden of a covenant enforceable in equity under this doctrine is, unlike covenants between landlord and tenant, a burden on the land, and not on the estate held by the defendant[20]. Thus it is not necessary to show that the defendant holds the estate which the covenantor held; for the defendant is bound merely by coming to the land, whether as squatter, tenant at will, underlessee — as anyone indeed, other than bona fide purchaser of the legal estate for value without notice[1].

Provision is made in section 2 (5) of the Land Charges Act 1972 for the registration, as a land charge Class D (ii), of a restrictive covenant made after 1925 otherwise than between lessor and lessee[2]; and such registration, in accordance with the usual rules, is notice to all the world[3].

i. THE DOCTRINE OF *TULK V MOXHAY*

TULK *v* MOXHAY
(1848) 2 Ph 774 (Lord COTTENHAM LC)

In 1808, the plaintiff sold a vacant piece of land in Leicester Square to Elms, who covenanted for himself his heirs and assigns with the plaintiff his heirs and assigns that the purchaser would "at all times thereafter at his . . . own costs . . . keep and maintain the said piece of ground . . . in an open state, uncovered with any buildings, in neat and ornamental order . . ." The piece of land passed by divers conveyances to the hands of the defendant whose conveyance did not contain any such covenant, but who admitted that he had notice of the covenant in the deed of 1808. The defendant threatened to build on the land in contravention of the covenant. An injunction was granted by Lord Langdale, the Master of the Rolls. On a motion to discharge that order,

Held. The plaintiff was entitled to an injunction to restrain a breach of the covenant by the defendant.

LORD COTTENHAM: That this Court has jurisdiction to enforce a contract between the owner of land and his neighbour purchasing a part of it, that the latter shall either use or abstain from using the land purchased in a particular way, is what I never knew disputed. Here there is no question about the contract: the owner of certain houses in the Square sells the land adjoining, with a covenant from the

---

[20] *Tichborne v Weir* (1892) 67 LT 735; *Re Nisbet and Potts' Contract* [1905] 1 Ch 391; affd. [1906] 1 Ch 386; *Mander v Falcke* [1891] 2 Ch 554.

[1] *Pilcher v Rawlins* (1872) 7 Ch App 259; *Wilkes v Spooner* [1911] 2 KB 473.

[2] *Newman v Real Estate Debenture Corpn Ltd and Flower Decorations Ltd* [1940] 1 All ER 131, 149–150; *Dartstone Ltd v Cleveland Petroleum Co Ltd* [1969] 1 WLR 1807, [1969] 3 All ER 668, (1956) 20 Conv (NS) 370 (R. G. Rowley).

[3] L.P.A. 1925, s. 198 (1). See p. 29, ante; positive and negative covenants entered into with a local authority, a Minister of the Crown or Government Department (otherwise than as between landlord and tenant) are registrable as local land charges; L.L.C.A. 1975, ss. 1, 2, p. 46, ante.

purchaser not to use it for any other purpose than as a Square Garden. And it is now contended, not that the vendee could violate that contract, but that he might sell the piece of land, and that the purchaser from him may violate it without this Court having any power to interfere. If that were so, it would be impossible for an owner of land to sell part of it without incurring the risk of rendering what he retains worthless. It is said that, the covenant being one which does not run with the land, this Court cannot enforce it; but the question is, not whether the covenant runs with the land, but whether a party shall be permitted to use the land in a manner inconsistent with the contract entered into by his vendor, and with notice of which he purchased. Of course, the price would be affected by the covenant, and nothing could be more inequitable than that the original purchaser should be able to sell the property the next day for a greater price, in consideration of the assignee being allowed to escape from the liability which he had himself undertaken.

That the question does not depend upon whether the covenant runs with the land is evident from this, that if there was a mere agreement and no covenant, this Court would enforce it against a party purchasing with notice of it; for if an equity is attached to the property by the owner, no one purchasing with notice of that equity can stand in a different situation from the party from whom he purchased. . . .

I think the cases cited before the Vice-Chancellor and this decision of the Master of the Rolls perfectly right, and, therefore, that this injunction[4] must be refused with costs.

ii. THE NECESSITY FOR BENEFITED LAND

LONDON COUNTY COUNCIL *v* ALLEN
[1914] 3 KB 642 (CA, BUCKLEY and KENNEDY LJJ, SCRUTTON J)

In 1906, the defendant, M. J. Allen, a builder, applied to the L.C.C. for their permission to lay out certain land of which Allen was in possession under an option to purchase. He was treated in the Court of Appeal as if he were the owner. The L.C.C. gave permission subject to a condition that Allen would enter into a covenant not to build upon part of the land which was needed for the continuation of certain proposed streets. By a deed of 1907, Allen covenanted "for himself, his heirs and assigns, and other the persons claiming under him, and so far as practicable to bind the land and hereditaments herein mentioned into whosesoever hands the same may come" that he would not place any erection on the land, and that he would give notice of this covenant in every document dealing with the land.

The land was conveyed to Allen in 1908; and part mortgaged to Willcocks who, in 1911, conveyed it on redemption, with M. J. Allen's concurrence, to Emily Allen, M. J. Allen's wife. Emily Allen built three houses on the plot, and mortgaged it to Norris.

---

[4] Presumably 'motion' was intended here, and not 'injunction'. It is correct in (1848). 1 H & Tw 105 at 117.

The question was whether the covenant was binding on Emily Allen and Norris.

Held. Not binding, because the plaintiffs held no land for the benefit of which the covenant was taken.

SCRUTTON J: The question then is whether it is essential to the doctrine of *Tulk v Moxhay* that the covenantee should have at the time of the creation of the covenant, and afterwards, land for the benefit of which the covenant is created, in order that the burden of the covenant may bind assigns of the land to which it relates.

[His Lordship then reviewed the authorities, and referred to *Haywood v Brunswick Permanent Benefit Building Society* (1881) 8 QBD 403, *De Mattos v Gibson* (1858) 4 De G & J 276, *Luker v Dennis* (1877) 7 ChD 227, *London and South Western Rly Co v Gomm* (1882) 20 ChD 562, *Clegg v Hands* (1890) 44 ChD 503, *Catt v Tourle* (1869) 4 Ch App 654, and continued:]

I think the result of this long chain of authorities is that, whereas in my view, at the time of *Tulk v Moxhay* and for at least twenty years afterwards, the plaintiffs in this case would have succeeded against an assign on the ground that the assign had notice of the covenant, since *Formby v Barker* ([1903] 2 Ch 539), *Re Nisbet and Potts' Contract* ([1905] 1 Ch 391; *affd.* [1906] 1 Ch 386) and *Millbourn v Lyons* [1914] 1 Ch 34; *affd* [1914] 2 Ch 231) three decisions of the Court of Appeal, the plaintiffs must fail on the ground that they have never had any land for the benefit of which this "equitable interest analogous to a negative easement" could be created, and therefore cannot sue a person who bought the land with knowledge that there was a restrictive covenant as to its use, which he proceeds to disregard, because he is not privy to the contract. I think the learned editors of Dart on Vendors and Purchasers (7th edn.), Vol. ii., p. 769, are justified by the present state of the authorities in saying that "the question of notice to the purchaser has nothing whatever to do with the question whether the covenant binds him, except in so far as the absence of notice may enable him to raise the plea of purchaser for valuable consideration without notice". If the covenant does not run with the land in law, its benefit can only be asserted against an assign of the land burdened, if the covenant was made for the benefit of certain land, all or some of which remains in the possession of the covenantee or his assign, suing to enforce the covenant.... I regard it as very regrettable that a public body should be prevented from enforcing a restriction on the use of property imposed for the public benefit against persons who bought the property knowing of the restriction, by the apparently immaterial circumstance that the public body does not own any land in the immediate neighbourhood. But, after a careful consideration of the authorities, I am forced to the view that the later decisions of this court compel me so to hold[5].

---

[5] For exceptions to this rule see p. 702, n. 7, ante, especially the statutory exceptions in favour of local authorities.

In my opinion, therefore, the demurrer of Mr. Norris and of Mrs. Allen succeeds. This action against Mr. Norris must be dismissed with costs. I regret that I do not see my way to depriving Mrs. Allen of her costs, as, whatever may be her equitable rights, I am not at all favourably impressed with her conduct as a good citizen. . . .

FORMBY v BARKER

[1903] 2 Ch 539 (CA, VAUGHAN WILLIAMS, ROMER and
STIRLING LJJ)

In 1868, R. H. Formby sold all the land owned by him in Formby, Lancashire, to the Mutual Land Company Ltd, subject to various covenants restricting the user of the land. The defendant was an assignee of the company of part of the land, and took with notice of the covenants. R. H. Formby died in 1884, and letters of administration with the will annexed were granted to his widow, the plaintiff, to whom he had given all his property by his will. In 1902, the defendant began to erect certain shops which were alleged to be in breach of the covenant.

Held (affirming HALL V-C of the County Palatine of Lancaster).

(i) The building of the shops was not a breach of the covenant.

(ii) Even if it were, the plaintiff, having no land capable of benefiting, was unable to maintain the action.

VAUGHAN WILLIAMS LJ: The plaintiff sues in her individual capacity and also as administratix with the will annexed of R. H. Formby deceased.

[His Lordship held that, on its proper construction, the covenant had not been broken by the defendant, and continued:]

This view really puts an end to the plaintiff's case. But, as another defence was raised and was discussed by the learned Vice-Chancellor, I think it right to deal with that point also.

The learned Vice-Chancellor expressed an opinion that, even if the plaintiff's construction of the covenant was right, and there had been a breach of the covenant, nevertheless the plaintiff was not entitled to sue — that is, was not entitled to sue either as personal representative of R. H. Formby or as residuary devisee under his will. . . .

Before dealing with the question of the plaintiff's right to sue, I wish to point out that that which R. H. Formby conveyed was his whole estate, and that he had no contiguous estate which would be benefited by the covenant in question. Moreover, there is in the deed no re-entry clause under which the vendor could go in as of his old estate, or, indeed, as of any estate. . . .

It becomes necessary, therefore, to ascertain whether the principle of *Tulk v Moxhay* applies to a case in which the vendor sells his whole estate. I have not been able to find any case in which, after the sale of the whole of an estate in land, the benefit of a restrictive covenant has been enforced by injunction against an assignee of the purchaser at the instance of a plaintiff having no land retained by the vendor, although there are cases in which restrictive covenants seem to have been enforced at the instance of plaintiffs, other than the vendor, for the benefit of whose land it appears from the terms of the covenant, or can be inferred from surrounding circumstances, that the covenant was intended to operate. In all other cases the restrictive covenant would seem to be a mere personal covenant collateral to the conveyance. It is a covenant which cannot run with the land, either at law or in equity, and therefore the burden of the covenant cannot be enforced against an assignee of the purchaser.

In *Re Gadd's Land Transfer* [1966] Ch 56, [1965] 2 All ER 800, BUCKLEY J held that the retention only of a road to the land burdened by the covenant was sufficient to enable the covenantee to enforce a restrictive covenant.

BUCKLEY J said at p. 67: "The question must, I think, be what is the impact of the covenants on the owner of Bridle Lane in respect of its occupation or enjoyment of that property. . . .

If the use of the pink land is to be changed from agricultural use to use as a building estate of that kind, there will be a great increase in the traffic over the right-of-way. Now the increase in the traffic over the right-of-way must inevitably mean that the maintenance of the roadway will become a more burdensome expense than otherwise it would be. . . .

If the cost of maintaining Bridle Lane became very much heavier than at present because of a great increase in the traffic over the road, it seems to me that there would be a risk that cannot be regarded as non-existent that the frontagers may not all be able to honour their obligations to contribute towards the cost of maintenance. I cannot suppose that that risk is negligible. . . .

Moreover, I think there is substance in the suggestion that if the lane is not kept in a proper state of repair there will be a risk that the road will be taken over by the local authority and the defendant company would thereby be deprived of some element of its ownership in the road.

Now it may be that this road is not a readily saleable asset, but it is not, I think, inconceivable that the residents in the road under certain circumstances would want themselves to acquire the road from the defendant company with a view to preserving it as their private road. If the burden of maintaining the road were to be made substantially more onerous than it is at present owing to an increase of traffic, the likelihood of the defendant company being able to dispose of this asset in any such way as that would, I think, decrease. These may not be very substantial interests or benefits which result to the defendant company from possible enforcement of the restrictive covenants, but nevertheless I do not think they are wholly negligible; I do not think they are matters that the court ought to disregard and I think they are matters of sufficient significance to justify the view that the capacity to enforce the covenants is a matter which does affect the defendant company in its position as owner of Bridle Lane."

iii. THE NATURE OF A RESTRICTIVE COVENANT

In 1882, Sir George JESSEL MR described the doctrine of *Tulk v Moxhay* as follows: "The doctrine of that case, rightly considered, appears to me to be either an extension in equity of the doctrine of *Spencer's Case* to another line of cases, or else an extension in equity of the doctrine of negative easements; such, for instance, as a right to the access of light, which prevents the owner of the servient tenement from building so as to obstruct the light. The covenant in *Tulk v Moxhay* was affirmative in its terms, but was held by the Court to imply a negative. Where there is a negative covenant expressed or implied, as, for instance, not to build so as to obstruct a view, or not to use a piece of land otherwise than as a garden, the Court interferes on one or other of the above grounds. This is an equitable doctrine, establishing an exception to the rules of Common Law which did not treat such a covenant as running with the land, and it does not matter whether it proceeds on analogy to a covenant running with the land or on analogy to an easement."[6] In other words, the doctrine of *Spencer's Case* was to apply so as to impose liability between parties, between whom there was no privity of estate; or the concept of a negative easement was to be extended in equity to cover the burden imposed, not by grant but by covenant, upon one piece of land for the benefit of another piece of land.

The latter is the better analogy; for, under *Spencer's Case*, as with all covenants running with land at common law, the covenant ran with the estate and not with the land. A restrictive covenant under the doctrine of *Tulk v Moxhay*, like an easement, runs with the land, and not with the estate.

TICHBORNE *v* WEIR
(1892) 67 LT 735 (CA, Lord ESHER MR, BOWEN and KAY LJJ)

The plaintiff's predecessor in title was seised of a house in fee simple. In 1802 she leased it to Baxter for eighty-nine years. The lease contained a covenant to repair. Baxter made an equitable mortgage of the premises to Giraud, and Giraud entered on the premises in 1836. In 1836 Baxter disappeared, and Giraud remained in occupation of the premises till 1876. During that period he paid the rent reserved in Baxter's lease to the lessor. In 1876 Giraud purported to assign the lease to the defendant. The defendant entered and paid the rent till the term ended in 1891. He then delivered up possession to the plaintiff. The plaintiff sought to make him liable on the covenant to repair, but the Court of Appeal held that he was not liable.

The Real Property Limitation Act 1833 had barred the action and extinguished the right of Baxter; but it had not vested Baxter's lease in Giraud. The covenant to repair would run with the lease on an

---

[6] *London and South Western Rly Co v Gomm* (1882) 20 ChD at p. 583. (1971) 87 LQR 539 (D. J. Hayton).

assignment; but neither Giraud nor the defendant had taken Baxter's lease and the defendant was not bound by the covenant to repair[7].

To the argument that he was estopped by the payment of rent from denying that he had taken Baxter's estate, it was said that such payment estopped him from disputing the title of the plaintiff, but it did not estop him from denying that he was bound by the terms of the lease. It estopped him from denying that he was a lessee: it did not estop him from denying that he was the holder of Baxter's lease[8].

RE NISBET AND POTTS' CONTRACT
[1905] 1 Ch 391 (FARWELL J), [1906] 1 Ch 386 (CA, Sir RICHARD HENN COLLINS MR, ROMER and COZENS-HARDY LJJ)

A summons was taken out by Potts asking for a declaration that Nisbet, the vendor under a contract of sale, failed to produce a good title.

Nisbet had purchased in 1901 from X and Y who had themselves purchased in 1890 from Headde, whose title was based upon occupation since 1878. Nisbet agreed to accept a title commencing at that date. Restrictive covenants had been imposed on the land in 1867 and 1872; Nisbet knew nothing of these but would have discovered them if he had insisted on a forty years' title[9].

On Potts' complaint that Nisbet was unable to produce a good title because of the restrictive covenants, Nisbet replied:

    (i) that he had purchased without notice; and
    (ii) that, in any case, covenants would not be binding upon a title acquired by adverse possession.

FARWELL J, affirmed by the Court of Appeal, held that a party had constructive notice of all that he would have ascertained if he had made proper enquiries and searched back for forty years; and also that the restrictive covenants were an equitable burden on the land, and were not terminated by the adverse possession. He said at p. 396:

"But if the covenant be negative, so as to restrict the mode of use and enjoyment of the land, then there is called into existence an equity attached to the property of such a nature that it is annexed to and runs with it in equity ... This equity, although created by covenant or contract, cannot be sued on as such, but stands on the same footing with, and is completely analogous to, an equitable charge on real estate created by some predecessor in title of the present owner of the land charged."

QUESTION

K Ltd., a garage company, owning the site of a garage, mortgaged it to E, and entered into a "solus" agreement, under which they undertook

---

[7] See especially KAY LJ, at p. 737. See p. 178, ante.
[8] Much of this account of *Tichborne v Weir* is taken from Holdsworth, *Historical Introduction to the Land Law* (1927), pp. 286–287.
[9] The period of commencement of title which a purchaser could then require; see L.P.A. 1925, s. 44 (1), and L.P.A. 1969, s. 23, p. 73, ante.

to sell E's petrol only; and to extract similar undertakings from any person to whom they might sell the garage.

I H purchased all the shares in K Ltd., and took a conveyance of the site of the garage, with the intention of breaking the provision relating to the sale of the petrol. They did so. E owned no land capable of benefiting. E sues for an injunction, joining K Ltd. and I H as defendants. What result?

Esso Petroleum Co Ltd v Kingswood Motors (Addlestone) Ltd [1974] QB 142, [1973] 3 All ER 1057.

C. Law of Property Act 1925, section 79[10]

In *Tophams Ltd v Earl of Sefton* [1967] 1 AC 50, [1966] 1 All ER 1039, Lord UPJOHN said at p. 72: "If this matter was a live issue before your Lordships I conceive that it might indeed be difficult of solution, for I can see arguments both for and against the proposition that the covenant was intended to bind assigns of Tophams. . . . I will only add that upon this aspect of the matter I think too much significance was placed in the courts below upon the impact of section 79 (1) of the Law of Property Act 1925. During the course of the hearing before your Lordships it became common ground that, so far as relevant to any question that your Lordships have to decide, it does no more than render it unnecessary in the description of the parties to the conveyance to add after the respondent's name: 'his executors, administrators and assigns', and after Tophams' name: 'and their successors in title'. This can really have little or no weight in considering the liability of Tophams' assigns in relation to a restrictive covenant affecting land."

Unlike section 78,[11] section 79 applies only "unless a contrary intention is expressed". In *Re Royal Victoria Pavilion, Ramsgate* [1961] Ch 581, [1961] 3 All ER 83, PENNYCUICK J considered a covenant which began "The vendors hereby covenant with the purchasers that they the vendors will . . .". He said at p. 589:

"Here it is contended that no contrary intention is expressed in the conveyance, . . . and that, therefore, the covenant in clause 5 must be deemed to be made by Thanet Theatrical on behalf of itself and its successors in title. If the words 'unless the contrary intention is expressed' in section 79 mean: unless the instrument contains express provision to the contrary, this contention would, I think, be unanswerable. But it seems to me the words 'unless a contrary intention is expressed' mean rather: unless an indication to the contrary is to be found in the instrument, and that such an indication may be sufficiently contained in the wording and context of the instrument even though the instrument contains no provision expressly excluding

---

[10] Page 416, ante; M & W, pp. 723-724. See also *Federated Homes Ltd v Mill Lodge Properties Ltd* [1980] 1 WLR 594, 606; p. 726, post.
[11] See p. 416, ante; pp. 712-717, post.

successors in title from its operation. It can hardly be the intention of the section that a covenant which, on its natural construction, is manifestly intended to be personal only, must be construed as running with the land merely because the contrary is not expressly provided. . . .

So here, although the covenant contains no express provision to the effect that it is not made on behalf of successors in title, it does, as it seems to me, contain sufficient indication to this effect."

III.   The Benefit[12]

A.   Common Law

It has long been held that the benefit of a covenant will run with the land at law in certain circumstances[13]. The rule is thought to have its origin in the old warranties for title which were enforceable not only by the covenantee, but also by his heirs, and, later, by assigns; if the warranty were broken, the warrantor would be liable in some cases to provide lands of equal value, in other cases to pay damages[14]. The conditions which are necessary for the benefit of a covenant to run with the land at law are a matter of some doubt, owing to the paucity of modern authority; it is clear however that the covenant will run if the following conditions are complied with[15]:

(i)   The covenant must 'touch and concern' the land[16]. It may do this even though the covenantor is a stranger to the land, and there is no servient tenement to be bound by the covenant[17].

(ii)   The land to be benefited must be expressly identified by the deed containing the covenant. There appears to be no authority for this; if it is a requirement, it is weakened by the operation of the maxim '*id certum est quod certum reddi potest*'.[18]

(iii)   There must be an intention that the benefit should run with the land, owned by the covenantee at the date of the covenant[19].

---

[12] Cheshire, pp. 593–594, 605–616; M & W. pp. 744–748, 760–772; MM, pp. 365–367, 368–374.

[13] *The Prior's Case* (1368) YB 42 Ed III, pl. 14, fol. 3 A; Smith's *Leading Cases* (13th edn., 1929), Vol. i., pp. 51, 65, 73.

[14] Simpson, *Introduction to the History of the Land Law*, pp. 131–132.

[15] Much of this section is based on (1954) 18 Conv (NS) 546 (E. H. Scamell).

[16] See p. 695, n. 12, ante.

[17] *The Prior's Case*, see p. 694, n. 7, ante; *Smith and Snipes Hall Farm Ltd v River Douglas Catchment Board* [1949] 2 KB 500, [1949] 2 All ER 179; and for cases where there is a servient tenement which would not be bound by the covenant, see *Sharp v Waterhouse* (1857) 7 E & B 816; *Shayler v Woolf* [1946] Ch 320, [1946] 2 All ER 54.

[18] *Smith and Snipes Hall Farm Ltd v River Douglas Catchment Board* [1949] 2 KB at pp. 508, 517.

[19] *Rogers v Hosegood* [1900] 2 Ch 388 at p. 396; *Shayler v Woolf* [1946] Ch 320, [1946] 2 All ER 54; *Smith and Snipes Hall Farm Ltd v River Douglas Catchment Board* [1949] 2 KB at p. 506.

(iv) The covenant must have been entered into with the owner of the legal estate in the land to be benefited[20].

(v) Before 1926, it was necessary for a person seeking to enforce the covenant to have the same legal estate in the land as the original covenantee[1]. It has been held that section 78 (1) of the Law of Property Act 1925 excludes this last requirement[2]. It may be that the wide interpretation given to that section in *Federated Homes Ltd v Mill Lodge Properties Ltd*[3] will have the effect of excluding some of the others as well. This was a case dealing with the running of the benefit in equity, which is the context in which the question usually arises; because the burdened land will commonly have also been assigned.

The common law rules continue to apply in cases not covered by equity, as, for example, where there is no land upon which the burden of the covenant is imposed[4].

It should also be noted that, independently of the above rules, the benefit of a covenant can be assigned as a chose in action, under section 136 of the Law of Property Act 1925. To be effective at law, the assignment must be in writing, and express notice in writing given to the covenantor[5].

SMITH AND SNIPES HALL FARM LTD *v* RIVER DOUGLAS CATCHMENT BOARD
[1949] 2 KB 500, [1949] 2 All ER 179 (CA, TUCKER, SOMERVELL and DENNING LJJ)

The defendant Board was the Drainage Authority for a part of Lancashire. In 1938, the Board covenanted under seal with the freehold owners of land within that area that in consideration of the Board's widening, deepening and making good the banks of the Eller Brook, taking control thereof and maintaining for all time the work when it was completed, the landowners would contribute to the cost.

In 1940, Mrs. Ellen Smith, one of the owners, sold her land, expressly with the benefit of the covenant, to the first plaintiff, John Bruce Smith, who leased it to the second plaintiff under a yearly tenancy. Owing to the faulty work of the defendants, the brook broke its banks, and flooded the land of the plaintiffs. They brought this action in tort and for breach of contract.

---

[20] Litt Co 385a; *Webb v Russell* (1789) 3 Term Rep 393; compare *Rogers v Hosegood* [1900] 2 Ch 388.

[1] *Westhoughton UDC v Wigan Coal and Iron Co Ltd* [1919] 1 Ch 159; *Smith and Snipes Hall Farm Ltd v River Douglas Catchment Board* [1949] 2 KB 500, [1949] 2 All ER 179.

[2] *Smith and Snipes Hall Farm Ltd v River Douglas Catchment Board*, supra.

[3] [1980] 1 WLR 594, [1980] 1 All ER 371, where the plaintiff took an assignment of part only of the land from the original covenantee; see pp. 717, 722, post.

[4] See p. 694, n. 7, ante.

[5] Cheshire and Fifoot, *Law of Contract* (9th edn., 1976) pp. 492 et seq.

Held, (reversing MORRIS J ([1948] WN 414)). Both plaintiffs could succeed under the contract.

The action in tort did not therefore arise for decision and no decision was reached on that point. The plaintiffs would have found it necessary to distinguish the House of Lords case of *East Suffolk Catchment Board v Kent* [1941] AC 74, [1940] 4 All ER 527.

TUCKER LJ [having held that the defendants were in breach of the contract and that such breach caused the damage]: . . . It remains to consider whether, in these circumstances, the plaintiffs, or either of them, can sue in respect of this breach. It is said for the defendants that the benefit of the covenant does not run with the land so as to bind a stranger who has not and never had an interest in the land to be benefited and there being no servient tenement to bear the burden. Further, it is contended that such a covenant must by the terms of the deed in which it is contained relate to some specific parcel of land, the precise extent and situation of which can be identified by reference to the deed alone. It is first necessary to ascertain from the deed that the covenant is one which "touches or concerns" the land, that is, it must either affect the land as regards mode of occupation, or it must be such as per se, and not merely from collateral circumstances, affects the value of the land, and it must then be shewn that it was the intention of the parties that the benefit thereof should run with the land. In this case the deed shews that its object was to improve the drainage of land liable to flooding and prevent future flooding. The location of the land is described as situate between the Leeds and Liverpool Canal and the River Douglas and adjoining the Eller Brook. In return for lump sum payments the board covenants to do certain work to the banks of the Eller Brook, one of such banks being in fact situate upon and forming part of the plaintiff's lands, and to maintain for all time the work when completed. In my view the language of the deed satisfies both tests. It affects the value of the land per se and converts it from flooded meadows to land suitable for agriculture, and shows an intention that the benefit of the obligation to maintain shall attach thereto into whosesoever hands the lands shall come.

With regard to the covenantor being a stranger, the case of *The Prior* is referred to in *Spencer's* case, in these words: "In the case of a grandfather, father and two sons, the grandfather being seised of the manor of D, whereof a chapel was parcel: a prior, with the assent of his convent, by deed covenanted for him and his successors, with the grandfather and his heirs that he and his convent would sing all the week in his chapel, parcel of the said manor, for the lord of the said manor and his servants, etc.; the grandfather did enfeoff one of the manor in fee, who gave it to the younger son and his wife in tail; and it was adjudged that the tenants in tail, as terre-tenants (for the elder brother was heir), should have an action of covenant against the prior, for the covenant is to do a thing which is annexed to the chapel, which is within the manor, and so annexed to the manor, as it is there said." . . .

In Rogers v Hosegood ([1900] 2 Ch at 395), Farwell J, in a passage where he refers, amongst others, to *The Prior's* case — and I quote from Farwell J's judgment because, although this case went to the Court of Appeal, his judgment was approved, and the Court of Appeal had to deal with a rather different point — after stating what are the requirements in order that the covenant may run with the land, proceeds: "It is not contended that the covenants in question in this case have not the first characteristic, but it is said that they fail in the second. I am of opinion that they possess both. Adopting the definition of Bayley J, in *Congleton Corpn v Pattison* ((1808) 10 East at 135), the covenant must either affect the land as regards mode of occupation, or it must be such as per se, and not merely from collateral circumstances, affects the value of the land. It is to my mind obvious that the value of Sir J. Millais's land is directly increased by the covenants in question. If authority is needed, I would refer to *Mann v Stephens* ((1846 15 Sim 377), a case very similar to the present; *Vyvyan v Arthur* ((1823) 1 B & C 410), *The Prior's* case, *Fleetwood v Hull* ((1889) 23 QBD 35), *White v Southend Hotel Co* ([1897] 1 Ch 767). I see no difficulty in holding that the benefit of a covenant runs with the land of the covenantee, while the burden of the same covenant does not run with the land of the covenantor."

In this state of the authorities it seems clear, despite some dicta tending to the contrary view, that such a covenant if it runs with the land is binding on the covenantor though a mere stranger, and that this point will not avail the defendant board. As to the requirement that the deed containing the covenant must expressly identify the particular land to be benefited, no authority was cited to us and in the absence of such authority I can see no valid reason why the maxim "Id certum est quod certum reddi potest" should not apply, so as to make admissible extrinsic evidence to prove the extent and situation of the lands of the respective land owners adjoining the Eller Brook situate between the Leeds and Liverpool Canal and the River Douglas.

. . . I have accordingly arrived at the conclusion that the covenant by the board in the agreement of 25 April 1938 is one which runs with the land referred to therein, which land is capable of identification, and that it is binding on the defendant board; and, further, that by virtue of section 78 of the Law of Property Act 1925, it can be enforced at the suit of the covenantee and her successors in title and the persons deriving title under her or them, so that both the plaintiff Smith and the plaintiff company can sue in respect of the damage resulting to their respective interests therein by reason of the defendants' breach of covenant.

DENNING LJ: The law on this subject was fully expounded by Mr. Smith in his note to *Spencer's* case which has always been regarded as authoritative. Such covenants [relating to land] are clearly intended, and usually expressed, to be for the benefit of whomsoever should be the owner of the land for the time being; and at common law each successive owner has a sufficient interest to sue because he holds the same estate as the original owner. The reason which Lord Coke gave for this rule is the reason which underlies the whole of the principle now under consideration. He said in his work upon Littleton that it was "to give damages to the party grieved". If a successor in title were not allowed to sue it would mean that the covenantor could break his contract with impunity, for it is clear that the original owner, after he has parted with the land, could recover no more than nominal damages for any breach that occurred thereafter. It was always held, however, at common law that, in order that a successor in title should be entitled to sue, he must be of the same estate as the original owner. That alone was a sufficient interest to entitle him to enforce the contract. The covenant was supposed to be made for the benefit of the owner and his successors in title, and not for the benefit of anyone else. This limitation, however, was, as is pointed out in *Smith's* Leading Cases, capable of being "productive of very serious and disagreeable consequences", and it has been removed by section 78 of the Law of Property Act 1925, which provides that a covenant relating to any land of the covenantee shall be deemed to be made with the covenantee and his successors in title, "and the persons deriving title under him or them" and shall have effect as if such successors "and other persons" were expressed.

The covenant of the catchment board in this case clearly relates to the land of the covenantees. It was a covenant to do work on the land for the benefit of the land. By the statute, therefore, it is to be deemed to be made, not only with the original owner, but also with the purchasers of the land and their tenants as if they were expressed. Now if they were expressed, it would be clear that the covenant was made for their benefit; and they clearly have sufficient interest to entitle them to enforce it because they have suffered the damage. The result is that the plaintiffs come within the principle whereby a person interested can sue on a contract expressly made for his benefit.

In *Williams v Unit Construction Co Ltd*[6] the question again arose whether section 78 of the Law of Property Act 1925[7] allowed the benefit of a restrictive covenant to pass at law in favour of persons who did not hold the same legal estate as the original covenantee. Counsel argued that a decision to that effect could only be taken by a court which was prepared also to hold that section 79 would have the same effect upon the burden; in other words, to hold that, since 1925, "successors in title and persons deriving title under him or them" would be bound by the burden of the covenant. The Court of Appeal declined to express a view on the effect of section 79[8] upon the burden — the point not being before the court — and followed *Smith and Snipes Hall Farm Ltd v River Douglas Catchment Board.* Similarly, in *Federated Homes Ltd v Mill Lodge Properties Ltd* [1980]

---

[6] Unreported, but discussed in (1955) 19 Conv (NS) 262 (W. L. Blease); p. 726, post.
[7] See p. 416, ante.
[8] On the application of s. 79, see p. 711, ante.

1 WLR 594, [1980] 1 All ER 371, BRIGHTMAN LJ said at p. 606: "We were referred to observations in the speeches of Lord Upjohn and Lord Wilberforce in *Sefton v Tophams Ltd* [1967] 1 AC 50, 73 and 81, to the effect that section 79. . . achieved no more than the introduction of statutory shorthand into the drafting of covenants. Section 79, in my view, involves quite different considerations and I do not think that it provides a helpful analogy."

B. Equity

Where a person other than the original covenantee desires to enforce a covenant, he must show that he is the person entitled to the benefit of the covenant. He may do this by showing either that the benefit of the covenant has passed to him, or that he was made an original covenantee by section 56 of the Law of Property Act 1925. As has been seen, the benefit of a covenant would run at law in certain circumstances. But there are some situations outside the limits of the common law where the benefit would run in equity. Generally, equity follows the law, and this development is probably an elucidation of the rules of common law, rather than a separate contribution of equity[10].

The situations in which the equitable rules must be observed are these:

(i) where the plaintiff or the covenantee was an equitable owner[11];

(ii) (subject to section 78 of the Law of Property Act 1925) where the plaintiff does not have the same legal estate as the covenantee[12];

(iii) where the servient land has been assigned, and enforcement depends on the doctrine of *Tulk v Moxhay*[13];

(iv) where the plaintiff relies upon an express assignment of the benefit of the covenant without compliance with section 136 of the Law of Property Act 1925[14];

(v) where the plaintiff takes an assignment of part of the land only, for "at law, the benefit could not be assigned in pieces. It would have to be assigned as a whole or not at all"[15];

---

[9] The case held that s. 78 effected an annexation of the benefit of the covenant in equity; p. 723 post. See also M & W, p. 748; W & C i, 162-163; see also (1956) 20 Conv (NS) 43, 52 (D. W. Elliott); (1972 B) CLJ 157, at pp. 171-175, (H. W. R. Wade), p. 723, post; Emmet on Title pp. 603-604.

[10] (1938) 6 CLJ 339 (S. J. Bailey).

[11] *Fairclough v Marshall* (1878) 4 Ex D 37; *Rogers v Hosegood* [1900] 2 Ch 388 (a mortgagor before 1926) p. 719, post.

[12] *Taite v Gosling* (1879) 11 ChD 273; see also *Westhoughton UDC v Wigan Coal and Iron Co Ltd* [1919] 1 Ch 159; *Smith and Snipes Hall Farm Ltd v River Douglas Catchment Board* [1949] 2 KB 500, [1949] 2 All ER 179.

[13] *Renals v Cowlishaw* (1878) 9 ChD 125; *Re Union of London and Smith's Bank Ltd's Conveyance, Miles v Easter* [1933] Ch 611, per ROMER J, at 630; *Marten v Flight Refuelling Ltd* [1962] Ch 115, [1961] 2 All ER 696.

[14] See p. 730, post. *Re Union of London and Smith's Bank Ltd's Conveyance, Miles v Easter* [1933] Ch 611; *Newton Abbot Co-operative Society Ltd v Williamson and Treadgold Ltd* [1952] Ch 286, [1952] 1 All ER 279; *Stilwell v Blackman* [1968] Ch 508, [1967] 3 All ER 514, p. 729, post.

[15] *Re Union of London and Smith's Bank Ltd's Conveyance* (supra) at p. 630 per ROMER LJ; *Federated Homes Ltd v Mill Lodge Properties Ltd* [1980] 1 WLR 594, [1980] 1 All ER 371; p. 722, post.

(vi) where the plaintiff relies upon his land being part of a scheme of development[16].

A purchaser of land may show that the benefit of a restrictive covenant has passed to him in one of three ways.

In *Re Pinewood Estate* [1958] Ch 280[17], WYNN-PARRY J, said at p. 284: "I propose first to consider whether there is in existence what is known as a building scheme affecting this area of land which is clearly ascertained; because, if there is an existing building scheme, fulfilling the conditions laid down by Parker J, in *Elliston v Reacher* ([1908] 2 Ch 374; *affd*, [1908] 2 Ch 665; p. 743, post), then the respondent and the other persons interested will have the benefit of the covenants in the deed ... It is admitted by Mr. Newsom that she could claim the benefit of the restrictive covenants if it could be shown either that the benefit had been annexed by proper words of annexation, or that there was a complete chain of assignments of the benefit of the covenants; but it is conceded on behalf of the respondent that there are no words of annexation, and it is conceded that the chain is not complete. In those circumstances, what the respondent says is that she is entitled to the benefit of the restrictive provisions because it is a deed which shows clearly by its language an intention that the parties should be mutually bound by the restrictions, and that that element of mutuality is enough to carry the benefit of the restrictive stipulations. That means that they are endeavouring to set up a further method by which the benefit of restrictive stipulations can be transferred. ...

The real question is: Is there a fourth class at all? The first class is the *Elliston v Reacher* type of case; the second consists of cases where there are proper words of annexation; the third consists of cases where there is a continuous chain of express assignments. But is there a fourth class? ...

But I can find no authority, certainly none was cited to me, which establishes the fourth class suggested. In my opinion, therefore, it is not open either to the respondent or to anybody else upon this line of reasoning to rely on these restrictive covenants."

i.   BY EXPRESS ANNEXATION

Whether or not the benefit of a restrictive covenant has been annexed to the land of the covenantee depends upon the intention of the parties, as construed from the language of the conveyance. If such an intention were manifested, the benefit of the covenant is notionally annexed to the land to be benefited; and the benefit of the covenant then passed automatically on an assignment of the covenantee's land.

This situation was contrasted with a covenant whose terms failed to manifest such an intention. The benefit of such a covenant was available, by the contract, to the covenantee; but was only available to

---

[16] See p. 742, post.
[17] [1957] CLJ 146 (H. W. R. Wade). See p. 740, post.

successors in title of the covenantee if the benefit of the covenant was expressly assigned at the time of the conveyance; and, in the case of a series of assignments of the land, it was necessary to show that there was a similar "chain of assignments" of the benefit of the covenant.

The leading cases illustrating these rules were *Rogers v Hosegood* [1900] 2 Ch 388, where annexation was achieved; and *Renals v Cowlishaw* [1878] 9 ChD 125, where it failed. Describing the methods of annexation, GREENE L.J. said in *Drake v Gray* [1936] Ch 451, at p. 466:

"There are two familiar methods of indicating in a covenant of this kind the land in respect of which the benefit is to enure. One is to describe the character in which the covenantee receives the covenant. That is the form which is adopted here, a covenant with so and so, owners or owner for the time being of whatever the land may be. Another method is to state by means of an appropriate declaration that the covenant is taken 'for the benefit of' whatever the lands may be."

The language which succeeded in effecting an annexation in *Rogers v Hosegood* was in this form: "with intent that the covenants. . . might enure for the benefit of the [vendors] . . . their heirs and assigns and others claiming under them to all or any of their lands adjoining or near to the said premises." It has never been suggested that that form of words was necessary; what was needed was a manifestation of an intention to annex. Would annexation be effected if the covenant were made in the following form? "With the covenantee and his successors in title (including the owners and occupiers for the time being of the land of the covenantee intended to be benefited) and the persons deriving title under him or them." If such a covenant would be effective to annex the benefit of the covenant, annexation would appear to be effected in every case; for, by section 78 of the Law of Property Act 1925, every covenant "relating to the land of the covenantee" shall be deemed to be made in that form. And the problem of determining whether the language of the conveyance is sufficient to manifest an intention to annex would disappear. That is the decision in the recent case of *Federated Homes Ltd v Mill Lodge Properties Ltd* [1980] 1 WLR 594, [1980] 1 All ER 371, extracted below.

a. Construction of the Instrument

ROGERS *v* HOSEGOOD
[1900] 2 Ch 388 (FARWELL J; affd, CA Lord ALVERSTONE MR
RIGBY and COLLINS LJJ)

Four partners, carrying on business as builders, were the owners in fee simple, subject to a mortgage, of land at Palace Gate, Kensington. One plot was sold in 1869 to the Duke of Bedford who entered into a covenant "with intent that the covenants . . . might so far as possible bind the premises thereby conveyed and every part thereof and might enure to the benefit of [the vendors] . . . their heirs and assigns and others claiming under them to all or any of their lands adjoining or near to the said premises" . . . that "no more than one messuage or dwelling house . . . should at any one time be erected or be standing on the . . . plot . . .". In 1872, a nearby plot was sold, and in 1873 conveyed to Sir John Millais, who had no knowledge of the covenant given by the Duke. Successors in title of the Duke by purchase proposed, in breach of the restrictive covenant, to erect, on this and adjoining plots, a large building which was to be occupied as residential flats. Among various actions, the trustees of the will of Sir John Millais claimed an injunction to restrain the defendants from erecting the block of flats.

Held. The plaintiffs were entitled to enforce the covenant.

COLLINS LJ (reading the judgment of the court): This case raises questions of some difficulty, but we are of opinion that the decision of Farwell J is right, and ought to be affirmed. . . . The real and only difficulty arises on the question — whether the benefit of the covenants has passed to the assigns of Sir John Millais as owners of the plot purchased by him on 25 March 1873, there being no evidence that he knew of these covenants when he bought. Here, again, the difficulty is narrowed, because by express declaration on the face of the conveyances of 1869 the benefit of the two covenants in question was intended for all or any of the vendor's lands near to or adjoining the plot sold, and therefore for (among others) the plot of land acquired by Sir John Millais, and that they "touched and concerned" that land within the meaning of those words so as to run with the land at law we do not doubt. Therefore, but for a technical difficulty which was not raised before Farwell J, we should agree with him that the benefit of the covenants in question was annexed to and passed to Sir John Millais by the conveyance of the land which he bought in 1873. A difficulty, however, in giving effect to this view arises from the fact that the covenants in question in the deeds of May and July 1869, were made with the mortgagors only, and therefore in contemplation of law were made with strangers to the land: *Webb v Russell* ((1789) 3 Term Rep 393), to which, therefore, the benefit did not become annexed. That a court of equity, however, would not regard such an objection as defeating the intention of the parties to the covenant is clear; and, therefore, when the covenant was clearly made for the benefit of certain land with a person who, in the contemplation of such a court was the true owner of it, it would be regarded as annexed to and running with that land, just as it would have been at law but for the technical difficulty. . . .

These observations [referring to observations of Jessel MR, in *London and South Western Rly Co v Gomm* ((1882) 20 ChD at p. 583)] which are just as applicable to the benefit reserved as to the burden imposed, shew that in equity, just as at law, the first point to be determined is whether the covenant or contract in its inception binds the land. If it does, it is then capable of passing with the land to subsequent assignees . . . of the land. The benefit may be annexed to one plot and the burden to another, and when this has been once clearly done, the benefit and the burden pass to the respective assignees, subject, in the case of the burden, to proof that the legal estate, if acquired, has been acquired with notice of the covenant. . . .

[His Lordship then referred to *Renals v Cowlishaw* ((1878) 9 ChD 125, infra) and *Child v Douglas* ((1854) Kay 560).]

These authorities establish the proposition that, when the benefit has been once clearly annexed to one piece of land, it passes by assignment of that land, and may be said to run with it, in contemplation as well of equity as of law, without proof of special bargain or representation on the assignment. In such a case it runs, not because the conscience of either party is affected, but because the purchaser has bought something which inhered in or was annexed to the land bought. This is the reason why, in dealing with the burden, the purchaser's conscience is not affected by notice of covenants which were part of the original bargain or on the first sale, but were merely personal and collateral, while it is affected by notice of those which touch and concern the land. The covenant must be one that is capable of running with the land before the question of the purchaser's conscience and the equity affecting it can come into discussion. When, as in *Renals v Cowlishaw,* there is no indication in the original conveyance, or in the circumstances attending it, that the burden of the restrictive covenant is imposed for the benefit of the land reserved, or any particular part of it, then it becomes necessary to examine the circumstances under which any part of the land reserved is sold, in order to see whether a benefit, not originally annexed to it, has become annexed to it on the sale, so that the purchaser is deemed to have bought it with the land, and this can hardly be the case when the purchaser did not know of the existence of the restrictive covenant. But when, as here, it has been once annexed to the land reserved, then it is not necessary to spell an intention out of surrounding facts, such as the existence of a building scheme, statements at auctions, and such like circumstances, and the presumption must be that it passes on a sale of that land, unless there is something to rebut it, and the purchaser's ignorance of the existence of the covenant does not defeat the presumption. We can find nothing in the conveyance to Sir John Millais in any degree inconsistent with the intention to pass to him the benefit already annexed to the land sold to him. We are of opinion, therefore, that Sir John Millais's assigns are entitled to enforce the restrictive covenant against the defendant, and that his appeal must be dismissed.

Rogers v Hosegood is to be contrasted with *Renals v Cowlishaw* (1878) 9 ChD 125, the difference turning on the language of the covenant. In *Renals v Cowlishaw* trustees sold lands to a purchaser who covenanted "for himself, his heirs, executors and administrators" with the trustees "their heirs, executors, administrators and assigns" that he would not use the lands in certain ways. The lands purchased were later sold to other purchasers who took with notice of the covenant. And the trustees later sold their retained land to the plaintiffs, no mention being made of the covenant in this conveyance. The question was whether the benefit of the covenant had passed to the plaintiffs. HALL V-C, (affirmed by the Court of Appeal (1879) 11 ChD 866) held that it had not. There was no building scheme, no express assignment of the benefit of the covenant; and the language of the covenant was inadequate to annex the benefit of the covenant to the plaintiffs' land.

The modern practice is to draft the covenant so as to mainfest an intention to annex the benefit of the covenant to the land retained by the vendor; unless the vendor wishes to retain the power to choose which of his later purchasers shall be given the benefit (by expressly assigning it[1]). Correct drafting may no longer be important, because it has been held that section 78 of the Law of Property Act 1925 supplies the words necessary to effect annexation[2].

b.   Law of Property Act 1925, section 78

LAW OF PROPERTY ACT 1925

78.   Benefit of covenants relating to land — p. 416, ante.

FEDERATED HOMES LTD V MILL LODGE PROPERTIES LTD [1980] 1 WLR 594, [1980] 1 ALL ER 371 (CA, MEGAW, BROWNE and BRIGHTMAN LJJ)

Mackenzie Hill Ltd owned land which was to be the subject of a large development in Newport Pagnell in Buckinghamshire. Planning permission was obtained in 1970, and was valid for 3 years. The building programme was phased, and was subject to restrictions upon the overall density of the number of houses to be built on the area. The present litigation arises out of sales by Mackenzie Hill Ltd. of three parts of the land; the blue, the red and the green.

The blue land was sold to Mill Lodge Properties Ltd., the defendant company, subject to various conditions, the one relevant for present purposes being the following covenant:

"The Purchaser hereby covenants with the Vendor that. . . . (iv) in carrying out the development of the 'blue' land the Purchaser shall not build at a greater density than a total of 300 dwellings so as not to reduce the number of units which the Vendor might eventually erect on the retained land under the existing Planning Consent."

The red and green lands were also sold, and the plaintiff company eventually became the owner of each. It will be seen that the terms of the covenant were not such as, from the express language of the covenant, to annex the benefit of the covenant to the land of the covenantee under the rule in *Rogers v Hosegood.* There was, however, a complete chain of assignments of the benefit of the covenant, through the various purchasers to the plaintiff, in the case of the *green* land. But not in the case of the red.

The question was whether the plaintiffs could sue to restrain the breach of the defendants' covenant relating to building density.

---

[1] *Marquess of Zetland v Driver* [1937] Ch 651; [1939] Ch 1; *Federated Homes Ltd v Mill Lodge Properties Ltd* [1980] 1 WLR 594, [1980] 1 All ER 371 at p. 606 per BRIGHTMAN LJ.

[2] *Federated Homes Ltd v Mill Lodge Properties Ltd,* supra; (1980) JPL 371 (G.H. Newsom), 43 MLR 445 (D.J. Hayton), 130 NLJ 531 (T. Bailey).

Held. The plaintiff company was entitled to the benefit of the covenant in respect of the *green* land by reason of the completed chain of assignments; in respect of the *red* land, because section 78 (1) had the effect of annexing the benefit of the covenant to all or any part of the land of the covenantee.

BRIGHTMAN LJ: "In September 1978, after much prevarication on the part of Mill Lodge, the plaintiff issued a writ to restrain Mill Lodge from building on the blue land at a greater density than a total of 300 dwellings in breach, it was alleged, of clause 5 (iv) of the Mill Lodge conveyance. The defences raised by Mill Lodge so far as relied upon in this appeal were as follows: (1) the covenant in clause 5 (iv) was said to be personal to Mackenzie Hill so that the benefit thereof was incapable of assignment to the plaintiff; (2) alternatively, it was said that the covenant became spent when the 1970 planning permission became void at the end of the three-year period; and (3) it was said that, if the covenant was assignable and was not spent, then the benefit had not become vested in the plaintiff by assignment or otherwise.

That, in broad effect, was how the defence was pleaded so far as relevant for present purposes. In a reserved judgment Mr. Mills held that the covenant was not personal to Mackenzie Hill and was not spent when the original planning permission lapsed. As regards the transmission of the benefit of the covenant, he held that the benefit was not annexed to the red and the green land, so that it did not automatically pass upon conveyances of the red and the green land. However, he found, as was clearly the fact, that there was an unbroken chain of assignments between transferor and transferee of the green land, so that the benefit of the covenant was now vested, by reason of such assignments, in the plaintiff as the present owner of the green land. There was no such unbroken chain of assignments in the case of the red land; but the judge considered that section 62 of the Law of Property Act 1925, which implies general words into a conveyance of land, was apt to carry the benefit of the covenant from U.D.T. Properties Ltd., the previous assignee of such benefit, to the plaintiff when the registered transfer in its favour was made. The defence, therefore, failed. The judge rejected a submission that damages would be the proper remedy. He granted an injunction against building in excess of the permitted density and gave liberty to apply for a mandatory injunction.

I deal first with the question of construction, upon which two issues arise: whether the covenant was personal to Mackenzie Hill, and whether it is spent.

[His Lordship decided that the covenant was not personal to Mackenzie Hill; nor was the covenant "spent" by the lapse of the planning permission in 1973].

Having reached the conclusion that the restrictive covenant was capable of assignment and is not spent, I turn to the question whether the benefit has safely reached the hands of the plaintiff. The green land has no problem, owing to the unbroken chain of assignments. I am disposed to think that is sufficient to entitle the plaintiff to relief, and that the plaintiff's right to relief would be no greater at the present time if it were held that it also had the benefit of the covenant in its capacity as owner of the red land. However, the judge dealt with both areas of land and I propose to do the same.

An express assignment of the benefit of a covenant is not necessary if the benefit of the covenant is annexed to the land. In that event, the benefit will pass automatically on a conveyance of the land, without express mention, because it is annexed to the land and runs with it. So the issue of annexation is logically the next to be considered. . . .

In my judgment the benefit of this covenant was annexed to the retained land, and I think that this is a consequence of section 78 of the Act of 1925. . .

[His Lordship read this section and continued:]

Mr. Price submitted that there were three possible views about section 78. One view, which he described as "the orthodox view" hitherto held, is that it is merely a statutory shorthand for reducing the length of legal documents. A second view, which was the one that Mr. Price was inclined to place in the forefront of his argument, is that the section only applies, or at any rate only achieves annexation, when the land intended to be benefited is signified in the document by express words or necessary implication as the intended beneficiary of the covenant. A third view is that the section applies if the covenant in fact touches and concerns the land of the covenantee, whether that be gleaned from the document itself or from evidence outside the document.

For myself, I reject the narrowest interpretation of section 78, the supposed orthodox view, which seems to me to fly in the face of the wording of the section. Before I express my reasons I will say that I do not find it necessary to choose between the second and third views because, in my opinion, this covenant relates to land of the covenantee on either interpretation of section 78. Clause 5 (iv) shows clearly that the covenant is for the protection of the retained land and that land is described in clause 2 as "any adjoining or adjacent property retained by the vendor." This formulation is sufficient for annexation purposes: see *Rogers v Hosegood* [1900] 2 Ch 388 (p. 719, ante).

There is in my judgment no doubt that this covenant "related to the land of the covenantee," or, to use the old-fashioned expression, that it touched and concerned the land, even if Mr. Price is correct in his submission that the document must show an intention to benefit identified land. The result of such application is that one must read clause 5 (iv) as if it were written: "The purchaser hereby covenants with the vendor and its successors in title and the persons deriving title under it or them, including the owners and occupiers for the time being of the retained land, that in carrying out the development of the blue land the purchaser shall not build at a greater density than a total 300 dwellings so as not to reduce, etc." I leave out of consideration section 79 as unnecessary to be considered in this context, since Mill Lodge is the original covenantor.

The first point to notice about section 78 (1) is that the wording is significantly different from the wording of its predecessor section 58 (1) of the Conveyancing Act 1881. The distinction is underlined by section 78 (2), which applies section 78 (1) only to covenants made after the commencement of the Act. Section 58 (1) of the Act of 1881 did not include the covenantee's successors in title or persons deriving title under him or them, or the owner or occupiers for the time being of the land of the covenantee intended to be benefited. The section was confined, in relation to realty, to the covenantee, his heirs and assigns, words which suggest a more limited scope of operation than is found in section 78.

If, as the language of section 78 implies, a covenant relating to land which is restrictive of the user thereof is enforceable at the suit of (1) a successor in title of the covenantee, (2) a person deriving title under the covenantee or under his successors in title, and (3) the owner or occupier of the land intended to be benefited by the covenant, it must, in my view, follow that the covenant runs with the land, because ex hypothesi every successor in title to the land, every derivative proprietor of the land and every other owner and occupier has a right by statute to the covenant. In other words, if the condition precedent of section 78 is satisfied — that is to say, there exists a covenant which touches and concerns the land of the covenantee — that covenant runs with the land for the benefit of his successors in title, persons deriving title under him or them and other owners and occupiers.

This approach to section 78 has been advocated by distinguished textbook writers; see Dr. Radcliffe's article "Some Problems of the Law Relating to Restrictive Covenants" (1941) 57 LQR 203, Professor Wade's article, "Covenants — A Broad and Reasonable View" and the apt cross-heading "What is wrong with section 78?" [1972B] CLJ 151, 171, and *Megarry and Wade, The Law of Real Property,* 4th edn. (1975), p. 764. Counsel pointed out to us that the fourth edition of *Megarry and Wade* indicates a change of mind on this topic since the third edition.

Although the section does not seem to have been extensively used in the course of argument in this type of case, the construction of section 78 which appeals to me appears to be consistent with at least two cases decided in this court. The first is *Smith and Snipes Hall Farm Ltd v River Douglas Catchment Board* [1949] 2 KB 500, [1949] 2 All ER 179, (p. 713, ante.) In that case an agreement was made in April 1938 between certain landowners and the catchment board under which the catchment board undertook to make good the banks of a certain brook and to maintain the same, and the landowners undertook to contribute towards the cost. In 1940 the first plaintiff took a conveyance from one of the landowners of a part of the land together with an express assignment of the benefit of the agreement. In 1944 the second plaintiff took a tenancy of that land without any express assignment of the benefit of the agreement. In 1946 the brook burst its banks and the land owned by the first plaintiff and tenanted by the second plaintiff was inundated. The two important points are that the agreement was not expressed to be for the benefit of the landowner's successors in title; and there was no assignment of the benefit of the agreement in favour of the second plaintiff, the tenant. In reliance, as I understand the case, upon section 78 of the Act of 1925, it was held that the second plaintiff was entitled to sue the catchment board for damages for breach of the agreement. It seems to me that that conclusion can only have been reached on the basis that section 78 had the effect of causing the benefit of the agreement to run with the land so as to be capable of being sued upon by the tenant.

The other case, *Williams v Unit Construction Co Ltd* (unreported in the usual series of law reports but fully set out in 19 Conveyancer 262 (p. 716, ante)), was decided by this court in 1951. There a company had acquired a building estate and had underleased four plots to Cubbin for 999 years. The underlessors arranged for the defendant company to build houses on the four plots. The defendant covenanted with Cubbin to keep the adjacent road in repair until adopted. Cubbin granted a weekly tenancy of one house to the plaintiff without any express assignment of the benefit of the covenant. The plaintiff was injured owing to the disrepair of the road. She was held entitled to recover damages from the defendant for breach of the covenant.

We were referred to observations in the speeches of Lord Upjohn and Lord Wilberforce in *Setfon v Tophams Ltd* [1967] 1 AC 50, 73 and 81, to the effect that section 79 of the Act of 1925, relating to the burden of covenants, achieved no more than the introduction of statutory shorthand into the drafting of covenants. Section 79, in my view, involves quite different considerations and I do not think that it provides a helpful analogy.

It was suggested by Mr. Price that, if this covenant ought to be read as enuring for the benefit of the retained land, it should be read as enuring only for the benefit of the retained land as a whole and not for the benefit of every part of it; with the apparent result that there is no annexation of the benefit to a part of the retained land when any severance takes place. He referred us to a passage in *In re Union of London and Smith's Bank Ltd's Conveyance* [1933] Ch 611, 628, (p. 730) which I do not think it is necessary for me to read"....

I find the idea of the annexation of a covenant to the whole of the land but not to a part of it a difficult conception fully to grasp... [The discussion of this question is postponed to section (d) below].

In the end, I come to the conclusion that section 78 of the Law of Property Act 1925 caused the benefit of the restrictive covenant in question to run with the red land and therefore to be annexed to it, with the result that the plaintiff is able to enforce the covenant against Mill Lodge, not only in its capacity as owner of the green land, but also in its capacity as owner of the red land.

For these reasons I think that the judge reached the correct view on the right of the plaintiff to enforce the covenant, although in part he arrived there by a different route.

c. *Annexation to the Whole of the Covenantee's Land*

The covenantee may enforce the covenant against the covenantor or his assigns, so long as the covenantee has some land capable of benefiting. But, when the question concerns the annexation of the benefit of the covenant to the dominant land, so as to make the benefit run with the land on a conveyance, it has been held that this can only be done at law or in equity, if substantially the whole of the "dominant" land is capable of benefiting; it is not possible for the court to effect a severance and allow the covenant to be annexed to such land as is capable of benefiting[19].

The difficulty, however, disappears if the covenant is correctly drafted, so as to show an intention to annex the benefit to the whole or *any part or parts of* the estate, for the benefit will then be annexed to such parts as are in fact benefited[20]. It has been held that the court will hear evidence as to the capability of the land to be benefited by the covenant[21].

d. Annexation to Part of the Covenantee's Land

Even if the whole of the dominant land is capable of benefiting, and if the benefit of the covenant is annexed to the whole, it has usually been held that the benefit of the covenant will only run in favour of the purchaser of a *part* of the land, if he can show that the benefit was annexed to the part which he purchased, or to each portion of the whole.

"For instance, A, the owner of a large property, sells part of it to Y and takes a covenant that no public house shall be opened on it. This covenant is annexed to A's land. Later A sells part of the dominant land to B. If B seeks to enforce the covenant by virtue of its annexation to A's land, he must prove that its benefit was annexed to each and every part of those lands or to the very part bought by him."[22]

In *Drake v Gray* ([1936] Ch 451, [1936] 1 All ER 363)[23], the Court of Appeal (SLESSER, ROMER and GREENE, LJJ) held that a covenant taken with the other parties to the deed . . . "and other the owners or owner for the time being of the remaining hereditaments so agreed to be partitioned" operated to annex the covenant to each portion of the land, so as to allow the benefit of the covenant to run with each portion of the partitioned land.

SLESSER LJ said at p. 461: "I recognise, and I accept entirely, what was said by this Court in *Re Union of London and Smith's Bank Ltd's Conveyance, Miles v Easter* ([1933] Ch 611; p. 731, post) that it must be shown that the benefit was intended to enure to each portion of the land, and it is true that it has been held that the use of the words 'or any part thereof' may be apt for that purpose; but I cannot read that case as meaning that those words, and those words only, are the sole means by which a conveyance may show that the benefit was intended to enure to each portion. In this case, the intention, as gathered from the documents and the recital of the whole history of the case, is clear that the benefit of the covenant was to enure to the owner of any part

---

[19] *Re Ballard's Conveyance* [1937] Ch 473, [1937] 2 All ER 691; 57 LQR at p. 210 (G. R. Y. Radcliffe); Elphinstone, *Covenants Affecting Land,* (1946) p. 60; *Marten v Flight Refuelling Ltd* [1962] Ch 115 at 137, [1961] 2 All ER 696; p. 736, post.

[20] *Marquess of Zetland v Driver* [1937] Ch 651, [1939] Ch 1; (1941) 57 LQR 203.

[21] *Marten v Flight Refuelling Ltd* [1962] Ch 115; *Earl of Leicester v Wells-next-the-Sea UDC,* [1972] Ch 110, [1972] 3 All ER 77; *Wrotham Park Estate Co Ltd v Parkside Homes Ltd* [1974] 1 WLR 798, [1974] 2 All ER 321.

[22] Cheshire, p. 609; P & N, pp. 18–23. In *Griffiths v Band* (1974) 29 P & CR 243 at 246, GOULDING J, referred to "this somewhat muddy corner of legal history."

[23] *Reid v Bickerstaff* [1909] 2 Ch 305.

of the remaining hereditaments, and as the plaintiff was such an owner, the learned judge was right in the conclusion to which he came."

In *Re Selwyn's Conveyance* [1967] Ch 674, [1967] 1 All ER 339, GOFF J held that a covenant "for the protection of the adjoining or neighbouring land part of or lately part of the Selwyn Estate" was sufficient to annex the benefit to separate parts of the land.

In *Russell v Archdale,* [1964] Ch 38, [1962] 2 All ER 305[24] BUCKLEY J held that a restrictive covenant "to benefit and protect the vendor's adjoining and neighbouring land" was annexed to that land as a whole, but that the plaintiff, a subsequent purchaser of only part of that land, was not entitled to rely on the annexation. He said at p. 45: "The next question which was debated was whether this annexation was an annexation to the whole of the land referred to by the words 'adjoining and neighbouring land' or to each and every part of it, and in that connection I was referred by Mr. Arnold to the decision of the Court of Appeal in *Drake v Gray.* That was relied upon as authority for the proposition that where one finds annexation by general words such as 'for the benefit of the vendor's remaining land' or, such as we have in the present case, 'adjoining and neighbouring land', the proper interpretation is to construe that as a reference to each and every part of the land which falls within the description. . . .

In the course of his judgment, Romer LJ, said at p. 465: 'Most of the cases that have come before the court have been cases where a covenant has been entered into by a vendor for the benefit of, say, the AB estate for the time being. There, of course, no intention is shown that the benefit should enure for any particular part of the estate; but where one finds not "the land coloured yellow" or "the estate" or "the field named so-and-so" or anything of that kind, but "the lands retained by the vendor", it appears to me that there is a sufficient indication that the benefit of the covenant enures to every one of the lands retained by the vendor, and if a plaintiff in a subsequent action to enforce a covenant can say: "I am the owner of a piece of land that belonged to the vendor at the time of the conveyance", he is entitled to enforce the covenant. . . .'

No doubt every case of this kind, being one of construction, must be determined on the facts and the actual language used, but with the utmost respect to Romer LJ, I cannot see that the mere fact that the land intended to be benefited was described by such an expression as 'the land retained by the vendor' is sufficient to enable the court to come to the conclusion that the covenant is intended to benefit each and every part of that land. This observation of Romer LJ, was, I think, clearly obiter dictum, . . . and in my judgment that authority does not assist the plaintiffs to say that the benefit of this covenant is annexed to each and every part of what is described by the conveyance

---

[24] (1962) 78 LQR 334, 482 (R. E. M.); affd. CA (Lord DENNING MR, dissenting) *The Times,* 1 December 1962; where only the issue of acquiescence is discussed.

as 'the adjoining and neighbouring land of the vendor'. That being so, I think it must follow that the plaintiffs cannot, merely by reason of annexation of this covenant to the 'adjoining and neighbouring land of the vendor' in the conveyance of 1938 and the fact that they have acquired part only of that land, enforce the covenant."[1]

In *Federated Homes v Mill Lodge Properties Ltd* [1980] 1 WLR 594, [1980] 1 All ER 371 (p. 722, ante), BRIGHTMAN LJ said at p. 606:

"It was suggested by Mr. Price that, if this covenant ought to be read as enuring for the benefit of the retained land, it should be read as enuring only for the benefit of the retained land as a whole and not for the benefit of every part of it; with the apparent result that there is no annexation of the benefit to a part of the retained land when any severance takes place. He referred us to a passage in *In re Union of London and Smith's Bank Ltd's Conveyance* [1933] Ch 611, 628, which I do not think it is necessary for me to read.

The problem is alluded to in *Megarry and Wade, The Law of Real Property*, 4th edn., p. 763.

'In drafting restrictive covenants it is therefore desirable to annex them to the covenantee's land 'or any part or parts thereof.' An additional reason for using this form of words is that, if there is no indication to the contrary, the benefit may be held to be annexed only to the whole of the covenantee's land, so that it will not pass with portions of it disposed of separately. But even without such words the court may find that the covenant is intended to benefit any part of the retained land; and small indications may suffice, since the rule that presumes annexation to the whole only is arbitrary and inconvenient. In principle it conflicts with the rule for assignments, which allows a benefit annexed to the whole to be assigned with part, and it also conflicts with the corresponding rule for easements.'

I find the idea of the annexation of a covenant to the whole of the land but not to a part of it a difficult conception fully to grasp. I can understand that a covenantee may expressly or by necessary implication retain the benefit of a covenant wholly under his own control, so that the benefit will not pass unless the covenantee chooses to assign; but I would have thought, if the benefit of a covenant is, on a proper construction of a document, annexed to the land, prima facie it is annexed to every part thereof, unless the contrary clearly appears. It is difficult to see how this court can have reached its decision in *Williams v Unit Construction Co Ltd*, 19 Conveyancer 262, unless this is right. The covenant was, by inference, annexed to every part of the land and not merely to the whole, because it will be recalled that the

---

[1] Similarly in *Re Jeff's Transfer (No. 2)* [1966] 1 WLR 841, [1966] 1 All ER 937: ("for the benefit of the remainder of the Chorleywood Estate (Loudwater) belonging to the vendor"); *Stilwell v Blackman* [1968] Ch 508, [1967] 3 All ER 514: ("to benefit and protect the adjoining property of the vendor"). The Law Commission in Transfer of Land, Report on Restrictive Covenants (1967 Law Com No. 11), p. 15, recommends that the benefit of a land obligation (p. 777, post) should be annexed to each and every part unless a contrary intention is expressed. See also Victoria Property Law Act 1958, s. 79A.

plaintiff was a tenant of only one of the four houses which had the benefit of the covenant.

There is also this observation by Romer LJ in *Drake v Gray* [1936] Ch 451, 465. He was dealing with the enuring of the benefit of a restrictive covenant and he said:

[His Lordship quoted Romer LJ's dictum printed at page 287, ante, and continued]:

In the instant case the judge in the course of his judgment appears to have dismissed the notion that any individual plot-holder would be entitled, even by assignment, to have the benefit of the covenant that I have been considering. I express no view about that. I only say this, that I am not convinced that his conclusion on that point is correct. I say no more about it."

---

ii. BY EXPRESS ASSIGNMENT

If the benefit of a restrictive covenant is not annexed to the land of the covenantee, an assignee must show that the benefit passed to him by express assignment of the benefit at the time of the conveyance. Such express assignment will be necessary in fewer cases in the future if, on the authority of *Federated Homes Ltd v Mill Lodge Properties Ltd*,[2] annexation is held to be effected by section 78 of the Law of Property Act 1925. Cases requiring express assignment can, however, still arise; as where there is express provision to the effect that express assignment of the benefit of the covenant shall be required[3]; or where there is no identification in the conveyance of the land to be benefited[4]. Further, it may be possible to argue that the benefit of a covenant passed under the "general words" of section 62 of the Law of Property Act 1925 [5].

Preston and Newsom, *Restrictive Covenants Affecting Freehold Land* (6th edn. 1976) p. 33

"Where the defendant is the original covenantor, he is liable at law. Against him the original covenantee can succeed at common law in an ordinary action on the covenant. Further, a plaintiff who is the express assignee of the benefit of the covenant can succeed against the original covenantor in an action at law governed by the ordinary rules as to the assignment of a chose in action. But 'at law the benefit could not be assigned in pieces. It would have to be assigned as a whole or not at all.'[6] The plaintiff must therefore rely upon an equitable title even as against the original covenantor if the benefit of the covenant has been assigned "in pieces." And, more importantly, he must always rely on an equitable title against a defendant who is not the original covenantor (or his personal representative). For the burden of a covenant never runs at law and a successor of the covenantor is liable

---

[2] [1980] 1 WLR 594, [1980] 1 All ER 371, p. 722, ante.
[3] *Marquess of Zetland v Driver* [1937] Ch 651.
[4] *Newton Abbot Co-operative Society v Williamson and Treadgold Ltd* [1952] Ch 286, [1952] 1 All ER 279, p. 732, post. But see *Federated Homes Ltd v Mill Lodge Properties Ltd*, supra, at p. 604 per BRIGHTMAN LJ.
[5] P. 530, ante; p. 742, post; *Federated Homes Ltd v Mill Lodge Properties Ltd*, supra at p. 601.
[6] *Miles v Easter* [1933] Ch 611 at 630, per ROMER LJ.

in equity, under the rule in *Tulk v Moxhay*. Requiring the assistance of equity, against a defendant who is liable in equity only or because his own title depends upon equity, a plaintiff must therefore show that he is within the special rules laid down by equity for establishing whether a title by express assignment can be relied upon."

a. Contemporaneous with Conveyance

It has long been clear that it was possible in equity to assign expressly the benefit of a restrictive covenant on the sale of the land of the covenantee[7]. Such assignment must be contemporaneous with the conveyance; if once the covenant becomes separated from the land to be benefited, it ceases to be operative[8]. It was not, however, until 1952 that it was authoritatively held that the benefit would pass in this way[9]. And this decision has been criticised[10].

In *Re Union of London and Smith's Bank Ltd's Conveyance, Miles v Easter* [1933] Ch 611[11], ROMER LJ referred to *Renals v Cowlishaw* (1878) 9 ChD 125) and *Rogers v Hosegood* ([1900] 2 Ch 388; p. 719, ante) and said at p. 629: "In neither of these cases, therefore, did it become necessary for the court to inquire into the circumstances in which an express assignee of the benefit of a covenant that does not run with the land is entitled to enforce it. In the present case, however, it is necessary to do so, inasmuch as the defendants claim to be the express assignees of the benefit of the restrictive covenants contained in the deeds of 23 October 1908 and 11 May 1909.

Now it may be conceded that the benefit of a covenant entered into with the covenantee or his assigns is assignable. The use of the word 'assigns' indicates this: see Williams on Personal Property, 18th edn. p. 33. But it by no means follows that the assignee of a restrictive covenant affecting land of the covenantor is entitled to enforce it against an assign of that land. For the burden of the covenant did not run with the land at law, and is only enforceable against a purchaser with notice by reason of the equitable doctrine that is usually referred to as the rule in *Tulk v Moxhay*. It was open, therefore, to the Courts of Equity to prescribe the particular class of assignees of the covenant to whom they should concede the benefit of the rule. This they have done, and in doing so have included within the class persons to whom the benefit of the covenant could not have been assigned at law. For at

---

[7] *Renals v Cowlishaw* (1878) 9 ChD 125; *Ives v Brown* [1919] 2 Ch 314; *Lord Northbourne v Johnston & Son* [1922] 2 Ch 309; *Chambers v Randall* [1923] 1 Ch 149; *Re Union of London and Smith's Bank Ltd's Conveyance, Miles v Easter* [1933] Ch 611; *Re Rutherford's Conveyance* [1938] Ch 396, [1938] 1 All ER 495; (1948) 6 CLJ 339 (S. J. Bailey); (1952) 68 LQR 353 (Sir Lancelot Elphinstone). The assignment may be to a lessee; *South Eastern Rly Co v Associated Portland Cement Manufacturers* (1900) *Ltd* [1910] 1 Ch 12.

[8] *Chambers v Randall* (supra); *Re Union of London and Smith's Bank Ltd's Conveyance, Miles v Easter* (supra); cp. *Lord Northbourne v Johnston* (supra); *Newton Abbot Co-operative Society Ltd v Williamson and Treadgold Ltd* [1952] Ch 286, [1952] 1 All ER 279.

[9] *Newton Abbot*, etc. (supra).

[10] (1952) 68 LQR 353 (Sir Lancelot Elphinstone).

[11] (1933) 49 LQR 483 (H. A. Hollond).

law the benefit could not be assigned in pieces. It would have to be assigned as a whole or not at all. And yet in equity the right to enforce the covenant can in certain circumstances be assigned by the covenantee from time to time to one person after another. Who then are the assignees of the covenant that are entitled to enforce it? The answer to this question is to be found in several authorities which it now becomes necessary to consider.

[His Lordship referred to *Formby v Barker* ([1903] 2 Ch 539; p. 707, ante), *LCC v Allen* ([1914] 3 KB 642; p. 705, ante), and continued:)

It is plain, however, from these and other cases, and notably that of *Renals v Cowlishaw,* that if the restrictive covenant be taken not merely for some personal purpose or object of the vendor, but for the benefit of some other land of his in the sense that it would enable him to dispose of that land to greater advantage, the covenant, though not annexed to such land so as to run with any part of it, may be enforced against an assignee of the covenantor taking with notice, both by the covenantee and by persons to whom the benefit of such covenant has been assigned, subject however to certain conditions. In the first place, the 'other land' must be land that is capable of being benefited by the covenant — otherwise it would be impossible to infer that the object of the covenant was to enable the vendor to dispose of his land to greater advantage. In the next place, this land must be 'ascertainable' or 'certain', to use the words of Romer and Scrutton LJJ, respectively. For, although the Court will readily infer the intention to benefit the other land of the vendor where the existence and situation of such land are indicated in the conveyance or have been otherwise shown with reasonable certainty, it is impossible to do so from vague references in the conveyance or in other documents laid before the Court as to the existence of other lands of the vendor, the extent and situation of which are undefined. In the third place, the covenant cannot be enforced by the covenantee against an assign of the purchaser after the covenantee has parted with the whole of his land . . . "

NEWTON ABBOT CO-OPERATIVE SOCIETY LTD *v* WILLIAMSON AND TREADGOLD LTD
[1952] Ch 286, [1952] 1 All ER 279[12] (ChD, UPJOHN J)

In 1923, Mrs. Mardon, who was owner of premises known as Devonia, in Fore St., Bovey Tracey, on which she carried on business as an ironmonger, conveyed property on the other side of the street to a purchaser who covenanted not to use it for the business of an ironmonger. There was no indication in the conveyance of the land to be benefited, but Mrs. Mardon's address was given as Devonia.

In 1941, Mrs. Mardon died, having left Devonia in her will to her son Leonard Soper Mardon.

In 1947 the purchasers of the property opposite Devonia sold it to the defendants.

In 1948, Leonard Soper Mardon assigned the ironmongery business to Bovey Tracey Co-operative Society (which later amalgamated with

---

[12] (1952) 68 LQR 353 (Sir Lancelot Elphinstone).

the plaintiffs) together with the benefit of the restrictive covenant, and granted them a lease of Devonia for 21 years.

In 1950, the defendants began to expose articles of ironmongery for sale in breach of the restrictive covenant.

Held. The plaintiffs were entitled to an injunction. The covenant touched and concerned the land and had been validly assigned.

UPJOHN J: The sole issue before me is whether the plaintiffs are entitled to the benefit of the restrictive covenant, and, if so, whether they are entitled to enforce it against the defendants.

I will deal with the first point first. Mr. Binney on behalf of the plaintiffs submitted first that the benefit of the restrictive covenant was annexed to Devonia so as to pass with the assignment of Devonia in equity without any express mention in that subsequent assignment; in other words, that the covenant runs with the land. Alternatively, he said that the plaintiffs are the express assigns of the benefit of the covenant, and as such are entitled to enforce it. In this difficult branch of the law one thing in my judgment is clear, namely, that in order to annex the benefit of a restrictive covenant to land, so that it runs with the land without express assignment on a subsequent assignment of the land, the land for the benefit of which it is taken must be clearly identified in the conveyance creating the covenant.

[His Lordship referred on this point to *Renals v Cowlishaw* ((1878) 9 ChD 125; p. 721, ante), *Re Union of London and Smith's Bank Ltd's Conveyance, Miles v Easter* ([1933) Ch 611; p. 731, ante), and came to the conclusion that the land for the benefit of which the covenant was taken was not sufficiently identified by the conveyance to annex the benefit of it to the land.]

I turn then to his second submission, namely, that the plaintiffs are express assigns of the benefit of the restrictive covenant. Mr. Bowles, on behalf of the defendants, contends that, even if it be assumed that his submission (with which I shall deal later) that the covenant was not taken for the benefit of Devonia, but of the business carried on thereat, is wrong, and the covenant was taken by Mrs. Mardon for the benefit of Devonia to enable her to dispose of it to better advantage, yet there is no complete chain of assignments vesting the benefit in the plaintiffs. He says that there was never any assignment of the benefit of the covenant by the executors of Mrs. Mardon to Leonard Soper Mardon and therefore he was not in a position to assign the benefit of the covenant to the plaintiffs' predecessors in title. He relied on *Ives v Brown* ([1919] 2 Ch 314) and *Lord Northbourne v Johnston & Son* ([1922] 2 Ch 309).

In my judgment those authorities do not support his contention. The position as I see it was this: On the footing that the restrictive covenant was not annexed to the land so as to run with it, the benefit of the covenant is capable of passing by operation of law as well as by express assignment and formed part of Mrs. Mardon's personal estate on her death: see *Ives v Brown*.

It was not suggested that there was any implied assent to the assignment of the benefit of the covenant to the residuary legatee, but in my judgment, when her estate was duly wound up and administered, and this case has been argued before me on the footing that that happened many years ago, the benefit of the covenant was held by the executors as bare trustees for the residuary legatee, Leonard Soper Mardon, who was himself one of the executors. He therefore became entitled to the benefit of this restrictive covenant in equity and, in my judgment, he was entitled to assign the benefit in equity on an assignment of Devonia. No doubt had the covenant been assigned to him by the executors, he could also have assigned it at law. That this is the position is, in my judgment, made clear by the . . . judgment of Sargant J in *Lord Northbourne v Johnston & Son.*[13]. . .

The second main question was whether the defendants are liable to have the covenant enforced against them. This was Mr. Bowles' main defence in this action and he says that the restrictive covenant was not taken for the benefit of Devonia, and he puts his case in this way: First, he says that in any event this was not taken for the benefit of any land, but was a covenant with Mrs. Mardon personally, solely for the benefit of her business. Secondly, he says that in order that an express assign of the benefit may sue an assignee of the burden of the covenant there must be some reference in the conveyance creating that covenant to the land for the benefit of which it was taken. . . .

[His Lordship came to the conclusion that the covenant was taken for the benefit of Devonia, and continued:]

Mr. Bowles' second point was that, in order that the benefit of the covenant may be assignable, the land for which the benefit of the covenant is taken must in some way be referred to in the conveyance creating the covenant, and I was naturally pressed with the headnote in *Re Union of London and Smith's Bank Ltd's Conveyance, Miles ·v Easter* ([1933] Ch 611), which reads as follows: "Where on a sale otherwise than under a building scheme a restrictive covenant is taken, the benefit of which is not on the sale annexed to the land retained by the covenantee so as to run with it, an assign of the covenantee's retained land cannot enforce the covenant against an assign (taking with notice) of the covenantor unless he can show (i) that the covenant was taken for the benefit of ascertainable land of the covenantee capable of being benefited by the covenant, and (ii) that he (the covenantee's assign) is an express assign of the benefit of the covenant", and with the following passage in the judgment of Bennett J (at p. 625): "In my judgment, in order that an express assignee of a covenant restricting the user of land may be able to enforce that covenant against the owner of the land burdened with the covenant, he must be able to satisfy the court of two things. The first is that it was a covenant entered into for the benefit or protection of land owned by the covenantee at the date of the covenant. Otherwise it is a covenant in gross, and unenforceable except as between the parties to the covenant; see *Formby v Barker* ([1903] 2 Ch 539). Secondly, the assignee must be able to satisfy the court that the deed containing the

---

[13] See *Marten v Flight Refuelling Ltd* [1962] Ch at 140, [1961] 2 All ER 708, where WILBERFORCE J, relied upon SARGANT J's reasoning; *Earl of Leicester v Wells-next-the-Sea UDC* [1978] Ch 110. (special executors of settled land held to be bare trustees of benefit of restrictive covenant for beneficiary under S.L.A. 1925, s. 7 (1)).

covenant defines or contains something to define the property for the benefit of which the covenant was entered into: see James LJ in *Renals v Cowlishaw* ((1879) 11 ChD at 866).''

With all respect to the statement of the judge, I am unable to agree that where a person is suing as an assign of the benefit of the covenant there must necessarily be something in the deed containing the covenant to define the land for the benefit of which the covenant was entered into. In the first place, the passage in the judgment of James LJ in *Renals v Cowlishaw*, which I have already read, on which the judge relied, does not in my judgment support the statement of the law for which it was cited. In *Renals v Cowlishaw* there was no express assignment of the benefit of the restrictive covenant (see the statement of fact in the report in the court below); and when James LJ says that to enable an assign to take the benefit of restrictive covenants there must be something in the deed to define the property for the benefit of which they were entered into, he is, I think, dealing with the case where it is contended that the benefit of the covenant has been annexed to the land so as to run with the land. When he uses the word 'assign' he is using the word as meaning an assign of the land and not an assign of the benefit of the covenant. Secondly, the views expressed by Bennett J appear to me to be inconsistent with the views expressed in some of the earlier decisions. I do not propose to cite them, but I refer to the following observations on the law on this point, namely, the observations of Collins LJ, delivering the judgment of the Court of Appeal in *Rogers v Hosegood* ([1900] 2 Ch at 407), those of Vaughan Williams LJ in *Formby v Barker* ([1903] 2 Ch at 551); and to the observations of Cozens-Hardy MR in *Reid v Bickerstaff* ([1909] 2 Ch at 319, 325); and to the words of Buckley LJ in the same case. Finally, in *Re Union of London and Smith's Bank Ltd's Conveyance, Miles v Easter* ([1933] Ch at 628, 631), Romer LJ, reading the judgment of the Court of Appeal, having considered the cases where the benefit of the covenant is annexed to land so as to run without express mention, says: ''In all other cases the purchaser will not acquire the benefit of the covenant unless that benefit be expressly assigned to him — or to use the words of the Vice-Chancellor, 'it must appear that the benefit of the covenant was part of the subject-matter of the purchase'.''

[His Lordship then cited the paragraph from Romer LJ's judgment set out on p. 732, ante, and continued:]

In my judgment, therefore, the problem which I have to consider is this: First, when Mrs. Mardon took the covenant in 1923, did she retain other lands capable of being benefited by the covenant? The answer is plainly yes. Secondly, was such land "ascertainable" or "certain" in this sense that the existence and situation of the land must be indicated in the conveyance or otherwise shown with reasonable certainty?

Apart from the fact that Mrs. Mardon is described as of Devonia, there is nothing in the conveyance of 1923 to define the land for the benefit of which the restrictive covenant was taken, and I do not think that carries one very far; but, for the reasons I have given, I am, in my judgment, entitled to look at the attendant circumstances to see if the land to be benefited is shown "otherwise" with reasonable certainty. That is a question of fact and, on the admitted facts, bearing in mind the close juxtaposition of Devonia and the defendants' premises, in my view the only reasonable inference to draw from the circumstances at the time of the conveyance of 1923 was that Mrs. Mardon took the covenant restrictive of the user of the defendants' premises for the benefit of her own business of ironmonger and of her property Devonia where at all material times she was carrying on that business, which last-mentioned fact must have been apparent to the purchasers in 1923.

I should perhaps mention that at the date of her death, Mrs. Mardon owned other property in Fore Street, but counsel on neither side founded any argument on that circumstance.

It follows, therefore, in my judgment, that Mrs. Mardon could on any subsequent sale of her land Devonia, if she chose, as part of the transaction of sale, assign the benefit of the covenant so as to enable the purchaser from her and his assignees of the land and covenant to enforce it against an owner of the defendants' premises taking with notice, and her legatee, Leonard Soper Mardon, was in no worse position. I do not regard the fact that he assigned the covenant in the deed containing the assignment of the business as affecting the matter. I say nothing as to the position when the plaintiffs' lease expires so that their estate in Devonia comes to an end, nor whether Leonard Soper Mardon, having apparently assigned away the entire benefit of the covenant, will then be in any position further to enforce it.

Mr. Bowles took one further point. He submitted that a covenant restrictive of business could not be annexed to land, unless it was a covenant not to carry on a business so as to be a nuisance or annoyance to an adjoining occupier, but he cited no authority for that proposition and, in my judgment, it cannot be maintained: see *Nicoll v Fenning* ((1881) 19 ChD 258).

Accordingly, in my judgment, the plaintiffs are entitled to succeed in this action and to an injunction.

Marten v Flight Refuelling Ltd [1962] Ch 115, [1961] 2 All ER 696[14], raised again, inter alia, the questions (a) of the enforceability of the benefit of a covenant when the identity of the land to be benefited could be shown by the use of extrinsic evidence but was not defined in the conveyance itself; and (b) of the devolution of the benefit of a covenant through personal representatives.

In 1943 Mrs. Marten, the first plaintiff, was an infant tenant in tail of the Crichel estate, a large agricultural estate in Dorset of about 7,500 acres. In that year, the second plaintiffs, who were then holding the estate in trust for Mrs. Marten as special executors under the Settled Land Act 1925, conveyed to Harding in fee simple Crook Farm

---

[14] This is not a case involving annexation or express assignment. (1972) 36 Conv (NS) 20 (E. C. Ryder).

of some 562 acres of which 200 acres had been requisitioned by the Air Ministry for the establishment of an aerodrome. Harding covenanted with the vendors and their successors in title that no part of the land conveyed nor any building thereon should thereafter be used for any purposes other than agricultural purposes. This covenant was registered in 1943 under Land Charges Act 1925, section 10 (1)[15], as a land charge Class D (ii).

In 1947 the Air Ministry permitted the first defendants, Flight Refuelling Ltd, to occupy the aerodrome. In 1950 Mrs. Marten attained her majority and disentailed; the second plaintiffs assented to the vesting in her of the fee simple, but the assent did not mention the covenant. In 1958 the Air Ministry compulsorily purchased most of the land still occupied by Flight Refuelling Ltd from Harding's executors. The plaintiffs claimed a declaration that they were entitled to the benefit of the covenant and an injunction to restrain Flight Refuelling Ltd from using the land for industrial purposes.

WILBERFORCE J, held, inter alia, that the plaintiffs were entitled to the benefit of the covenant and to an injunction to restrain the company from undertaking industrial activities beyond those necessary for Air Ministry purposes.

He said at p. 129: "First, are the plaintiffs, or is one of them, entitled to the benefit of the restrictive covenant? This involves several subsidiary questions, namely (a) whether the covenant was entered into for the benefit of any land of the covenantee; (b) whether that land is sufficiently defined or ascertainable by permissible inference or evidence; (c) whether that land is, or was, capable of being benefited by the covenant; (d) whether, since the first plaintiff is not the express assignee of the covenant, the action can be brought by the second plaintiff or by the two plaintiffs jointly.

(a) and (b) ... An elaborate argument was addressed to me by the defendants to support a contention that the benefit of the covenant was not available to the plaintiffs. The conveyance, it was said, does not 'annex' the benefit of the covenant to any land so that it would pass automatically on a conveyance of the land to a purchaser. Further, it does not indicate that it was made for the benefit of any land, and even supposing that it was so made, it does not identify or provide any material upon which to identify what that land is.

It is, however, well established by the authorities that the benefit of restrictive covenants can pass to persons other than the original covenantee, even in the absence of annexation, provided that certain conditions are fulfilled. There is, however, dispute as to the nature of these conditions.

The defendants' contentions are, first, that there must appear from the terms of the deed itself an intention to benefit some land, and, secondly, that the precise land to be benefited must also be stated in the deed, or at least must be capable of ascertainment from the terms of the deed by evidence which is admissible in accordance with the normal rules of interpretation of documents. They rely principally on

---

[15] Now L.C.A. 1972, s. 2 (5).

Re Union of London and Smith's Bank Ltd's Conveyance, Miles v Easter ([1933] Ch 611), and submit that the decision of Upjohn J, in *Newton Abbot Co-operative Society Ltd v Williamson and Treadgold Ltd* ([1952] Ch 286, [1952] 1 All ER 279), which appears to admit parole evidence for the purpose of identifying the land to be benefited, goes too far.

[His Lordship then referred to *Re Union of London and Smith's Bank Ltd's Conveyance, Miles v Easter; Formby v Barker* ([1903] 2 Ch 539); *Lord Northbourne v Johnston & Son* ([1922] 2 Ch 309, and *Newton Abbot Co-operative Society Ltd v Williamson and Treadgold Ltd*, and, referring to the latter, continued:]

This decision was attacked by the Attorney-General in a lively argument, and I was invited not to follow it. Of course, it relates to its own special facts, and no doubt I could leave it on one side. But I see nothing in it contrary to the principles which appear to be securely laid down. Here were two shops in common ownership facing each other in the same street, one of them, Devonia, an ironmonger's shop. The shops opposite are sold with a covenant against carrying on an ironmonger's business. What could be more obvious than that the covenant was intended for the protection or benefit of the vendor's property Devonia? To have rejected such a conclusion would, I venture to think, have involved not only an injustice, but a departure from common sense. So far from declining the authority of this case, I welcome it as a useful guide. But it is only a guide, and I must ultimately reach my conclusion on the facts of the present case. . . .

On these facts I consider that I should come to the conclusion that the covenant was taken for the benefit of land of the vendors, that land being the Crichel estate. In doing so I do not, so it seems to me, go outside such surrounding or attendant circumstances as, in accordance with the authorities, it is legitimate for the court to take into account. A decision based on the mere wording of cl. 2 of the conveyance would, in my judgment be unduly narrow and indeed technical, and would go far to undermine the usefulness of the rule which equity courts have evolved that the benefit of restrictive covenants may be capable of passing to assigns of the 'dominant' land or of the covenant in cases other than those of annexation. I would add two observations: first, the rules in *Miles v Easter* properly relate to cases where the covenant is sought to be enforced by an assign from the original covenantee. In this case, however, the second plaintiff is the original covenantee and the first plaintiff is the person for whose benefit in equity the covenant was taken. To that important extent the plaintiffs' case is stronger than that of the defendant in *Miles v Easter*. Secondly, in holding that the covenant was for the benefit of the Crichel estate, I mean the Crichel estate as a whole, as a single agricultural estate which it was and is, and I express no opinion whether it enures for the benefit of each and every part, for example, if parts are separately sold off. That is not a question which arises in this case.

There remain certain specific arguments which were put forward, and I must shortly deal with them. . . .

It was said that unless the identity of the land to be benefited was clearly stated in, or directly ascertainable from, the conveyance, a purchaser would be placed in an impossible position: he would never know by whom the covenant could be enforced, or whether it was enforceable at all[16]. I am not impressed by this objection: the original covenantee is ascertainable from the document — and moreover appears on or can be ascertained from the land charges register[17]. In a case where the covenant is sought to be enforced by an assign from him, such assign must always prove his right to sue, whether by virtue of annexation, by devolution, by assignment of the benefit of the covenant. The plaintiff may also (as in *Tulk v Moxhay*) have to show that he retains property for whose benefit the covenant was imposed. These are matters which arise in all cases where restrictive covenants are sought to be enforced otherwise than as between the original parties, and I see no greater difficulty in dealing with them in cases such as the present. . . .

Question (c): Was the land capable of being benefited by the covenant? On this point, as on those last dealt with, the answer would appear to be simple. If an owner of land, on selling part of it, thinks fit to impose a restriction on user, and the restriction was imposed for the purpose of benefiting the land retained, the court would normally assume that it is capable of doing so. There might, of course, be exceptional cases where the covenant was on the face of it taken capriciously or not bona fide, but a covenant taken by the owner of an agricultural estate not to use a sold-off portion for other than agricultural purposes could hardly fall within either of these categories. As Sargant J said in *Lord Northbourne v Johnston & Son* ([1922] 2 Ch at 319): 'Benefit or detriment is often a question of opinion on which there may be the greatest divergence of view, and the greatest difficulty in arriving at a clear conclusion.' Why, indeed, should the court seek to substitute its own standard for those of the parties — and on what basis can it do so? However, much argument was devoted to this point, and evidence was called as to it. These I must consider.

First it was said that a mere examination of the figures showed that the covenant could not benefit the estate: the Crichel estate extends to some 7,500 acres, and it was asked how such a covenant could benefit the estate as a whole. In my view, there is no such manifest impossibility about this. I have already referred to the character of the estate, and I can well imagine that, for the owner of it, whether he wished to retain it in his family or to sell it as a whole, it might be of very real benefit to be able to preserve a former outlying portion from

---

[16] (1952) 68 LQR 353, 361.

[17] The position is rather more complex. Land charges are registered against the name of the estate owner whose estate is to be affected: that is against the name of the covenantor. A search will not reveal the name of the covenantee, nor a description of the land. The name and address of the original covenantee will be known to the Land Registry, for they would have been stated on the original application to register, and they may be ascertained by an application for an office copy of an entry in the register on Form K19, Land Charges Rules 1974. That will in most cases be sufficient to identify the benefited land; but often only with the assistance of extrinsic evidence.

development. This seems to me to be a question of fact to be determined on the evidence: and I note that when a similar argument was placed before the court in *Re Ballard's Conveyance* ([1937] Ch 473, [1937] 2 All ER 691), Clauson J, while accepting it in the absence of evidence, showed it to be his opinion that evidence could have been called. . . .

Question (d): Can the action be brought by the first plaintiffs or by the two plaintiffs jointly? I can deal with this point quite shortly. The second plaintiff is the original covenantee, and the first plaintiff is the person for whose benefit in equity the covenant was made. Taken together, the plaintiffs represent the whole legal and equitable interest in the covenant. The matter appears, therefore, to be completely covered by the judgment of Sargant J in *Lord Northbourne v Johnston & Son* the reasoning of which I adopt. So much was not really contested by the Attorney-General, who, however, reserved the right to challenge that judgment should this case go to a higher court."

(1968) 84 LQR at p. 29 (P. V. Baker)

"From the principles outlined above, and especially from the analogy of easements, we should expect the right to go along automatically with the benefited or dominant land, and, indeed, this happens where the benefit has been annexed by the original covenant[18]. There is, however, a complicating factor as not every restrictive covenant is initially annexed, and in these cases the covenantee has the option of annexing it to the land or allowing it to lapse. As it cannot exist as a separate piece of property like a profit in gross, there seems to be no justification in principle for requiring it to be passed by a succession of assignments parallel with the assignment of the benefited land, for this is still treating it as either a covenant which is only enforceable as such against the covenantor, or as existing in gross. If the original covenantor is still the owner of the burdened land, the benefit of the covenant could be assigned separately and then ultimately annexed, but if the burdened land has passed it is annexation or nothing, for it is a piece of property which is an adjunct of the benefited land. In other words, express assignment is delayed annexation. One puts together the deed containing the original covenant and the subsequent conveyance of the benefited land. The original covenant in these cases does not have to indicate the benefited land[19], but that deficiency is naturally supplied by the subsequent conveyance of it. Building schemes go still further since the annexation is effected by facts which are not necessarily or wholly indicated in the conveyance. . . .

The proposition that an express assignment of the benefit of covenant annexes it to the land so that it will thereafter pass to future owners without express assignment is supported by dicta in older

---

[18] *Rogers v Hosegood* [1900] 2 Ch 388; and see *Lawrence v South County Freeholds Ltd* [1939] Ch 656 at 680 ("a hidden treasure").
[19] *Newton Abbot Co-operative Society Ltd v Williamson and Treadgold Ltd* [1952] Ch 286, [1952] 1 All ER 279.

cases[20] and by some writers[1]. It is, however, repudiated by others, expressly[2] or by implication[3], and in one recent case it was assumed, though not decided, that a chain of assignments was necessary[4]. Until *Stilwell v Blackman*[5] there was no decision which was inconsistent with the proposition, but it must follow that if express assignment operates as a mode of annexation, it is necessarily excluded where annexation has already occurred. Nevertheless, as we have seen, it was decided that annexation did not preclude the passing of the benefit by express assignment.

To the learned judge it was 'a question of construction whether or not express assignment is excluded by annexation'. There was, he said, nothing to interfere with the ordinary principles of contract so that, for example, the covenant could in express terms provide that either annexation or express assignment should be the only method of passing the benefit, or 'since they do not operate against each other, and if there were any advantage in so doing, by both methods simultaneously'[6]. Reference was then made to the dicta in *Renals v Cowlishaw*[7] which supported the proposition that on express assignment the benefit became automatically annexed, but it was thought that these words were not directed to the question of the simultaneous application of both methods of passing the benefit, 'or, indeed, even to the recognition that this question arose'. Nor was it clear 'whether, if there were such automatic annexation, it is suggested that the annexation would be merely to the whole, or also to each and every part of the land passing to the express assignee of the covenant'. Ungoed-Thomas J expressed his final conclusion that 'there is no reason either in contract or in the relevant principles of equity why an express assignment of the benefit of a covenant with the passing of land should automatically operate exclusively, as an annexation of the covenant to the land (whether to the whole or to any part of it)'[8].

The reason, it is respectfully suggested, for such automatic annexation, is that when the burdened land passes from the covenantor, one leaves the realm of contract and enters that of property. The question then ceases to be exclusively a matter of what the original parties may or may not have agreed, but what incidents the law will allow. When one finds that the benefit of the covenant cannot exist by itself but only alongside the ownership of the benefited land, convenience suggests that it should be annexed to that land and not require a chain

---

[20] *Renals v Cowlishaw* (1878) 9 ChD 125 at 130, 131; affd. (1879) 11 ChD 866; *Rogers v Hosegood* [1900] 2 Ch 388 at 408; *Reid v Bickerstaff* [1909] 2 Ch 305 at 320.
[1] M & W, p. 768; M. Bowles [1962] JPL 234; S. J. Bailey (1938) 6 CLJ 339 at 360, 361.
[2] Preston and Newsom, p. 35, n. 28, relying on a dictum of ROMER LJ in *Re Union of London and Smiths' Bank Ltd's Conveyance* [1933] Ch 611 at 631.
[3] Cheshire, (10th edn., 1967) p. 546, relying on another dictum of ROMER LJ at p. 630 of the case last cited, but this was dealing with concurrent assignments of different parts of the benefited land by the original covenantee.
[4] *Re Pinewood Estate, Farnborough* [1958] Ch 280, criticised H. W. R. Wade, [1957] CLJ 146.
[5] [1968] Ch 508, [1967] 3 All ER 514.
[6] Ibid. at p. 525.
[7] See n. 20, supra.
[8] At p. 526.

of assignments parallel with the conveyances of the land. Further, if
the arguments in the earlier part of this article are accepted, the
assignment of the benefit of the covenant by the covenantee would
prima facie annex that benefit to each and every part of the land
comprised in that benefit."

b.   Law of Property Act 1925, section 62

(1971) 87 LQR at p. 570 (D. J. Hayton).

"It is true that the courts and writers have so far assumed that section
62 does not apply to assignable covenants but this is because no one
has yet argued that section 62 ought to apply, though Professor
Farrand[9] raises the question as a 'moot point' without discussing the
matter further. Indeed, in early cases where the need for express
assignments was first enunciated[10], the courts were concerned with
conveyances executed before the passing of section 62's precursor,
section 6 Conveyancing Act 1881, though such conveyances would
invariably contain some general words clause of the kind enacted in
section 6 and section 62. However, in those early days restrictive
covenants were still looked upon as contractual in nature instead of as
property interests as now. . . . Only in the one case has the point been
aired. In *Rogers v Hosegood* land before 1881 had been conveyed
together with 'all the rights easements or appurtenances belonging or
reputed to belong thereto'. Farwell J held that the covenants in
question had been annexed but that, if he had held otherwise and had
had to consider the 'general words' point, 'it may well be that the right
to sue thereon cannot be said to belong or be reputed to belong thereto;
but I express no final opinion on this point'[11]. It is submitted that, in
view of the much wider wording of section 62 and in view of the
[proprietary] nature of assignable covenants already emphasised, the
learned judge, if he now had the opportunity, would express a final
opinion in favour of the application of section 62."

iii.   SCHEME OF DEVELOPMENT[12]

The necessity to show either express annexation or express
assignment of the benefit of a restrictive covenant is avoided if the

---

[9] *Contract and Conveyance*, (2nd edn., 1973), p. 405.

[10] *Renals v Cowlishaw* (1878) 9 ChD 125; *Rogers v Hosegood* [1900] 2 Ch 388; *Reid v
Bickerstaff* [1909] 2 Ch 305 at 320, per COZENS-HARDY MR.

[11] Per FARWELL J in *Rogers v Hosegood* [1900] 2 Ch 388 at 398. See also *Federated
Homes Ltd v Mill Lodge Properties Ltd* [1980] 1 WLR 594, 601, [1980] 1 All ER 371.

[12] For the history of the development of the present doctrine, see: *Whatman v Gibson*
(1838) 9 Sim 196; *Coles v Sims* (1854) 5 De GM & G 1; *Sidney v Clarkson* (1865) 35
Beav 118; *Western v Macdermott* (1866) 2 Ch App 72; *Renals v Cowlishaw* (1878) 9
ChD 125; *Gaskin v Balls* (1879) 13 ChD 324; *Nottingham Patent Brick and Tile Co v
Butler* (1885) 15 QBD 261; on appeal (1886) 16 QBD 778; *Collins v Castle* (1887) 36
ChD 243; *Spicer v Martin* (1888) 14 App Cas 12; *Mackenzie v Childers* (1889) 43 ChD
265; *White v Bijou Mansions Ltd* [1938] Ch 351, [1938] 1 All ER 546. For recent
successful schemes see *Baxter v Four Oaks Properties Ltd* [1965] Ch 816, [1965] 1
All ER 906; *Re Dolphin's Conveyance* [1970] Ch 654, [1970] 2 All ER 664, p. 745, post;
Eagling v Gardner [1970] 2 All ER 838; *Brunner v Greenslade* [1971] Ch 993, [1970]
3 All ER 833; *Texaco Antilles Ltd v Kernochan* [1973] AC 609, [1973] 2 All ER 118.
This is in marked contrast to the usual fate of schemes during the previous four
decades. Preston and Newsom, pp. 53–55.

circumstances surrounding a series of sales indicate an intention that all the purchasers should be bound by restrictive covenants, and that each should be able to enforce them against the others. In such circumstances there is a Scheme of Development. There is created a sort of "local law"[13] among the purchasers, disregarding the ordinary rules of contract and covenants and permitting mutual enforcement. "The major theoretical difficulties", says MEGARRY J,[14] "based on the law of covenant seem to me to disappear when instead there is an equity created by circumstances which is independent of contractual obligation".

When does such a situation arise? It is difficult to answer with confidence. In the past 15 years, the emphasis has changed from a position in which specific requirements need to be observed to one in which there must be a defined area and "the existence of the common interest and the common intention actually expressed in the conveyances themselves"[15].

In *Elliston v Reacher* [1908] 2 Ch 374 PARKER J said at p. 384.

"I pass, therefore, to the consideration of the question whether the plaintiffs can enforce these restrictive covenants. In my judgment, in order to bring the principles of *Renals v Cowlishaw* ((1878) 9 ChD 125) and *Spicer v Martin* ((1888) 14 App Cas 12) into operation it must be proved (1) that both the plaintiffs and defendants derive title under a common vendor; (2) that previously to selling the lands to which the plaintiffs and defendants are respectively entitled, the vendor laid out his estate, or a defined portion thereof (including the lands purchased by the plaintiffs and defendants respectively), for sale in lots subject to restrictions intended to be imposed on all the lots, and which, though varying in details as to particular lots, are consistent and consistent only with some general scheme of development; (3) that these restrictions were intended by the common vendor to be and were for the benefit of all the lots intended to be sold, whether or not they were also intended to be and were for the benefit of other land retained by the vendor;[16] and (4) that both the plaintiffs and the defendants, or their predecessors in title, purchased their lots from the common vendor upon the footing that the restrictions subject to which the purchases were made were to enure for the benefit of the other lots included in the general scheme whether or not they were also to enure for the benefit of other lands retained by the vendors. If these four points be established, I think that the plaintiffs would in equity be entitled to enforce the restrictive covenants entered into by the defendants or their predecessors with the common vendor irrespective of the dates of the respective purchases. I may observe, with reference

---

[13] *Reid v Bickerstaff* [1909] 2 Ch 305 at 319; *Re Dolphin's Conveyance* [1970] Ch 654 at 663, [1970] 2 All ER 664, per STAMP J.

[14] *Brunner v Greenslade* [1971] Ch 993 at 1005; [1970] 3 All ER 833.

[15] *Re Dolphin's Conveyance* (supra) at p. 664; *Lund v Taylor* (1975) 31 P & CR 167 at 178.

[16] The reservation to the vendor of the right to sell land free from the restriction is of little force either for or against the existence of a building scheme; *Re Wembley Park Estate Co Ltd's Transfer* [1968] Ch 491 at 498, [1968] 1 All ER 457; *Eagling v Gardner* [1970] 2 All ER 838.

to the third point, that the vendor's object in imposing the restrictions must in general be gathered from all the circumstances of the case, including in particular the nature of the restrictions. If a general observance of the restrictions is in fact calculated to enhance the values of the several lots offered for sale, it is an easy inference that the vendor intended the restrictions to be for the benefit of all the lots, even though he might retain other land the value of which might be similarly enhanced, for a vendor may naturally be expected to aim at obtaining the highest possible price for his land. Further, if the first three points be established, the fourth point may readily be inferred, provided the purchasers have notice of the facts involved in the three first points, but if the purchaser purchases in ignorance of any material part of those facts, it would be difficult, if not impossible, to establish the fourth point. . . . .

It is, I think, enough to say, using Lord Macnaghten's words in *Spicer v Martin* ((1888) 14 App Cas 12), that where the four points I have mentioned are established, the community of interest imports in equity the reciprocity of obligation which is in fact contemplated by each at the time of his own purchase."

A further requirement was added in *Reid v Bickerstaff* [1909] 2 Ch 305, where COZENS- HARDY MR said at p. 319:
"In my opinion there must be a defined area within which the scheme is operative. Reciprocity is the foundation of the idea of a scheme. A purchaser of one parcel cannot be subject to an implied obligation to purchasers of an undefined and unknown area. He must know both the extent of his burden and the extent of his benefit. Not only must the area be defined, but the obligations to be imposed within that area must be defined. Those obligations need not be identical. For example, there may be houses of a certain value in one part and houses of a different value in another part. A building scheme is not created by the mere fact that the owner of an estate sells it in lots and takes varying covenants from various purchasers. There must be notice to the various purchasers of what I may venture to call the local law imposed by the vendors upon a definite area."[17]

In *Baxter v Four Oaks Properties Ltd* [1965] Ch 816, [1965] 1 All ER 906 there was no evidence that the common vendor "laid out the part of his estate . . . in plots before beginning to sell it off. He appeared to have sold plots, of the size which purchasers wished to take, to purchasers as they came along". CROSS J found sufficient evidence of an intention to create mutually binding covenants, although PARKER J's second requirement was not observed.

---

[17] See also BUCKLEY LJ at p. 323; *Torbay Hotel Ltd v Jenkins* [1927] 2 Ch 225 at 240, per CLAUSON J.

RE DOLPHIN'S CONVEYANCE
[1970] Ch 654, [1970] 2 All ER 664 (ChD, STAMP J)[18]

The Selly Hill Estate, of some 30 acres near Birmingham, became vested in fee simple in Ann and Mary Dolphin as tenants in common. In 1871 they sold off four parcels, and each purchaser entered into a restrictive covenant with them that only detached dwelling houses, each of at least one-quarter acre, should be built on the land. The vendors covenanted to procure similar covenants from subsequent purchasers of any other part of the estate. Ann Dolphin died in 1873, leaving by will her interest in the unsold part of the estate to her nephew, John Watts. In 1876 John became owner in fee simple in possession when Mary Dolphin made a deed of gift to him of her share. He then sold off the remainder of the estate in six parcels, in each case taking a restrictive covenant, and, except for the last parcel, giving a covenant to procure similar covenants from subsequent purchasers.

In 1969 part of the estate was purchased by Birmingham Corporation, whose predecessor in title had purchased part in 1871 from Ann and Mary, and part in 1877 from John. The Corporation wished to build in breach of the covenants, of which it had notice. It sought a declaration that the land was no longer subject to them, and argued that there was no building scheme, since there was no common vendor, and no lotted plan prior to the sales.

Held. There was a Scheme, and the covenants were binding.

STAMP J: As Cross J pointed out in the course of the judgment in *Baxter v Four Oaks Properties Ltd* [1965] Ch 816, [1965] 1 All ER 906, . . . the intention that the several purchasers from a common vendor shall have the benefit of the restrictive covenants imposed on each of them, may be evidenced by the existence of a deed of mutual covenant to which all the several purchasers are to be parties. That common intention may also be evidenced by, or inferred from, the circumstances attending the sales: the existence of what has often been referred to in the authorities as a building scheme. I have been referred to a considerable number of authorities where the court has had to consider whether there were, or were not, present in the particular case those facts from which a building scheme — and, therefore, the common intention to lay down a local law involving reciprocal rights and obligations between the several purchasers — could properly be inferred. In *Elliston v Reacher* [1908] 2 Ch 374, 384, Parker J laid down the necessary concomitants of such a scheme.

What has been argued before me is that here there is neither a deed of mutual covenant nor a building scheme. In the latter connection, it is pointed out that there was not a common vendor, for the parcels were sold off, first by the Dolphins and then by Watts. Nor, prior to the sales, had the vendors laid out the estate, or a defined portion of it, for sale in lots. Therefore, so it is urged, there were not present the factors which, on the authority of *Elliston v Reacher* [1908] 2 Ch 374, are necessary before one can find the existence of a building scheme.

[18] (1970) 86 LQR 445 (P.V.B.); 117 Sol Jo 798 (G. H. Newsom).

In my judgment, these submissions are not well-founded. To hold that only where you find the necessary concomitants of a building scheme or a deed of mutual covenant can you give effect to the common intention found in the conveyances themselves, would, in my judgment, be to ignore the wider principle on which the building scheme cases are founded and to fly in the face of other authority of which the clearest and most recent is *Baxter v Four Oaks Properties Ltd* [1965] Ch 816, [1965] 1 All ER 906. The building scheme cases stem, as I understand the law, from the wider rule that if there be found the common intention and the common interest referred to by Cross J at p. 825 in *Baxter v Four Oaks Properties Ltd* the court will give effect to it, and are but an extension and example of that rule. Hall VC remarked in his judgment in *Renals v Cowlishaw* (1878) 9 ChD 125, 129:

"This right exists not only where the several parties execute a mutual deed of covenant, but wherever a mutual contract can be sufficiently established. A purchaser may also be entitled to the benefit of a restrictive covenant entered into with his vendor by another or others where his vendor has contracted with him that he shall be the assign of it, that is, have the benefit of the covenant. And such contract need not be express, but may be collected from the transaction of sale and purchase."

That passage was quoted, with approval, by Lord Macnaghten in *Spicer v Martin* (1889) 14 App Cas 12, 24. (I ought perhaps to mention that the word "contract" in the last sentence I have quoted was substituted for the word "covenant" in the errata in the volume of the reports in which *Renals v Cowlishaw* is reported.) Moreover, where deeds of mutual covenant have fallen to be considered, effect has been given not to the deed of mutual covenant itself as such but to the intention evidenced by its existence. *Baxter v Four Oaks Properties Ltd* is such a case. As Parker J in *Elliston v Reacher* [1908] 2 Ch 374, 384, pointed out in a passage quoted by Cross J in *Baxter v Four Oaks Properties Ltd* the equity arising out of the establishment of the four points which he mentioned as the necessary concomitants of a building scheme has been sometimes explained by the implication of mutual contracts between the various purchasers and sometimes by the implication of a contract between each purchaser and the common vendor, that each purchaser is to have the benefit of all the covenants by the other purchasers, so that each purchaser is in equity an assign of the benefit of those covenants; but the implication of mutual contracts is not always a satisfactory explanation. Parker J in *Elliston v Reacher* [1908] 2 Ch 374, . . . points out that a prior purchaser may be dead or incapable of contracting at the time of a subsequent purchase, and that in any event it is unlikely that the prior and subsequent purchasers are ever brought into personal relationship, and yet the equity may exist betwen them.

There is not, therefore, in my judgment, a dichotomy between the cases where effect has been given to the common intention inferred from the existence of the concomitants of a building scheme and those where effect has been given to the intention evidenced by the existence of a deed of covenant. Each class of case, in my judgment, depends upon a wider principle. Here the equity, in my judgment, arises not by the effect of an implication derived from the existence of the four points specified by Parker J in *Elliston v Reacher* [1908] 2 Ch 374, 384, or by the implication derived from the existence of a deed of mutual covenant, but by the existence of the common interest and the common intention actually expressed in the conveyances themselves.

In *Nottingham Patent Brick and Tile Co v Butler* (1885) 15 QBD 261, 268, Wills J, in a passage which I find illuminating and which was referred to with approval in the Court of Appeal (1886) 16 QBD 778, put the matter thus: "The principle which appears to me to be deducible from the cases is that where the same vendor selling to several persons plots of land, parts of a larger property, exacts from each of them covenants imposing restrictions on the use of the plots sold without putting himself under any corresponding obligation, it is a question of fact whether the restrictions are merely matters of agreement between the vendor himself and his vendees, imposed for his own benefit and protection, or are meant by him and understood by the buyers to be for the common advantage of the several purchasers. If the restrictive covenants are simply for the benefit of the vendor, purchasers of other plots of land from the vendor cannot claim to take advantage of them. If they are meant for the common advantage of a set of purchasers, such purchasers and their assigns may enforce them inter se for their own benefit. Where, for instance, the purchasers from the common vendor have not known of the existence of the covenants, that is a strong, if not a conclusive, circumstance to shew that there was no intention that they should enure to their benefit. Such was the case in *Keates v Lyon* (1869) 4 Ch App 218; *Master v Hansard* (1876) 4 ChD 718; and *Renals v Cowlishaw* (1879) 11 ChD 866. But it is in all cases a question of intention at the time when the partition of the land took place, to be gathered, as every other question of fact, from any circumstances which can throw light upon what the intention was: *Renals v Cowlishaw* (1879) 11 ChD 866. One circumstance which has always been held to be cogent evidence of an intention that the covenants shall be for the common benefit of the purchasers is that the several lots have been laid out for sale as building lots, as in *Mann v Stephens* (1846) 15 Sim 377; *Western v Macdermott* (1866) 2 Ch App 72; *Coles v Sims* (1853) Kay 56, 5 De GM & G 1; or, as it has been sometimes said, that there has been 'a building scheme': *Renals v Cowlishaw* (1879) 11 ChD 866, 867."

I can approach the matter in another way. The conveyances of the several parts of the estate taking the form they do, and evidencing the same intention as is found in a deed of mutual covenant, I equate those conveyances with the deed of mutual covenant considered by Cross J, in *Baxter v Four Oaks Properties Ltd* [1965] Ch 816, [1965] 1 All ER 906 — the deed which he did not treat for the purposes of his judgment as itself bringing all the successive purchasers and persons claiming through them into contractual relations one with the other, but as showing the common intention. So equating them, I follow what I conceive to be the ratio decidendi of *Baxter v Four Oaks Properties*

Ltd and give effect to that intention by holding that the restrictive covenants are enforceable by the successors in title of each of the original covenantors against any of them who purchased with notice of those restrictions.

In *Lund v Taylor* (1975) 31 P & CR 167[19], the Court of Appeal (RUSSELL, STAMP LJJ and Sir John PENNYCUICK) held that no scheme of development could be inferred: STAMP LJ (delivering the judgment of the Court) said at p. 176:

"Because there was no extrinsic evidence, nor anything in his own conveyance to show a purchaser that there was a scheme relating to a defined area or that Tellings [the vendors], if they did, intended that stipulations should be imposed in respect of each part of that area, he could not on the authority of *Reid v Bickerstaff* [1909] 2 Ch 305 be subject to an implied obligation to the other purchasers. On this ground alone the action must in our opinion fail. Whatever scheme involving reciprocal rights and obligations Tellings may have sought to establish, the necessary evidence that the several purchasers intended to be bound by a scheme or local law under which they were to have reciprocal rights and obligations is lacking. The difficulties of the plaintiffs in this regard are perhaps emphasised when one observes that whatever inference you may draw from the conveyances there is nothing in them from which a purchaser could draw the inference that Tellings intended to confer on a purchaser a right to prevent Tellings from dealing as they thought fit — e.g. by the erection of a block of flats — with the unplotted part of the estate. . . . . .

Because it was submitted that in recent times the courts, in determining whether the necessary ingredients of a building scheme or local law are shown to have existed, have adopted what was called a more liberal approach than was formerly the case it is right that we should refer to the two cases relied upon in support of that submission. They are *Baxter v Four Oaks Properties Ltd* [1965] Ch 816 and *Re Dolphin's Conveyance* [1970] Ch 654. In both those cases it had been submitted that in order to establish a building scheme the requirements laid down by Parker J in *Elliston v Reacher* [1908] 2 Ch 374 must be satisfied. One of those requirements was, and we quote Parker J's judgment, that 'in order to bring the principles of *Renals v Cowlishaw* and *Spicer v Martin* into operation it must be proved . . . (2) that previously to selling the lands to which the plaintiffs and defendants are respectively entitled the vendor laid out his estate or a defined portion thereof (including the land purchased by the plaintiffs and defendants respectively) for sale in lots subject to restrictions intended to be imposed on all the lots. . . .

In his judgment in *Baxter v Four Oaks Properties Ltd* Cross J rejected the condition that the defined estate should have been laid out for sale in lots. He pointed out that *Elliston v Reacher* was not a case in

---

[19] *Harlow v Hartog* (1977) 245 Estates Gazette 140 (no scheme of development due to no estate plan).

which there was direct evidence afforded by the execution of a deed of mutual covenant that the parties intended a building scheme but *whether one could properly infer that intention in all the circumstances*. Cross J took the view, also adopted in *Re Dolphin's Conveyance,* that Mr. Justice Parker was not intending to lay down that the fact that the common vendor did not bind himself to sell off the defined area to which the local law was to apply in lots of any particular size but proposed to sell off parcels of various sizes according to the requirements of the various purchasers must, as a matter of law, preclude the court from giving effect to a clearly proved intention that the purchasers were to have rights *inter se* to enforce the provisions of the local law over the area.

In *Re Dolphin's Conveyance,* in which the *Baxter v Four Oaks* case was followed, the area over which the scheme or local law was to extend was specified and the intention that the purchasers were to have rights *inter se* to enforce the stipulations of the local law was, so the judge thought, expressed clearly in every conveyance. The stipulations which each purchaser covenanted to observe in the several conveyances were identical and the first and every subsequent conveyance by the vendor contained a covenant by him, in effect, to obtain a covenant from every other purchaser to observe them; a useless series of covenants except upon the basis that all could enforce them. It would, no doubt, have been better if the draftsman of the conveyances in that case had added the words 'to the intent that the covenants by the purchasers shall be mutually enforceable' and if a plan had been attached showing the area affected by the scheme; but the judge found a sufficient indication of that intention and a sufficient identification of that area.

No doubt the last mentioned two cases are authorities for the proposition that Mr. Justice Parker, in the well known passage of his judgment in *Ellison v Reacher,* did not intend to lay down that the fact that the common vendor did not bind himself to sell off the defined area to which the local law was to apply in lots of any particular size was fatal to the creation of a local law over that area, but rather that if the vendor has done so you have one of the necessary ingredients from which the creation of the local law may be inferred. And where you find that all those concerned — the vendor and the several purchasers — have by the effect of the documents they have executed evidenced the intention to create such a local law over a defined area those cases are authority for saying that the court may give effect to that intention. But we find nothing in those cases indicating that the conditions from which a "building scheme" may be inferred from the facts are any different than was formerly the case.

In the instant case the creation of a building scheme cannot for the reasons we have given be inferred; and there is absent from the deeds themselves that clear evidence of intention to create reciprocal rights and obligations over a defined area which was found in *Baxter v Four Oaks Properties Ltd* and in the *Dolphin's Conveyance* cases.

We allow the appeal.''

Preston and Newsom: *Restrictive Contracts Affecting Freehold Land*
(6th edn. 1976), pp. 52–55.

"If the scheme of local law is modern, the common vendor may be
called to give evidence of his own intention[20]. Or evidence may be given
by someone who was closely involved with the transactions of the
common vendor[1]. In the Lands Tribunal a common vendor has given
evidence himself on at least one occasion[2]. Where a scheme is old, there
may well be no documents at all except the formal conveyancing
instruments, and often only a few of them. The proportion of
conveyancing documents that survive varies enormously. In
Dolphin's case [1970] Ch 654, [1970] 2 All ER 664, almost all of
them had been found, though nothing else survived. In the *Wembley
Park* case [1968] Ch 491, [1968] 1 All ER 457, a great many conveyancing instruments were in evidence. In the *Texaco* case [1973] AC
609, [1973] All ER 118, where the estate was of some 500 lots, only
four conveyances were put in and one of them was of about 300 lots
expressed to be subject to no restrictions at all. Nevertheless the
scheme was upheld. On the other hand in *White v Bijou Mansions Ltd*
[1938] Ch 351, Lord Greene MR commented adversely on the fact that
only two conveyances were available, and the scheme was not upheld.
In *Baxter's* case [1965] Ch 816, [1965] 1 All ER 906, the intention of
mutuality was evidenced by a deed of mutual covenant.

In regard to the extrinsic evidence, where it survives, a lotted plan is
one of the ingredients from which the creation of a local law may be
inferred[3]. The same would no doubt be true of a set of particulars and
conditions of sale showing that all the lots were to be taken subject to
the relevant paragraphs of a set of standard stipulations. A print of a
common form of contract or of conveyance would point in the same
direction, though the mere fact that the conveyances are broadly in a
common form is not by itself enough[4]. The actual evidence in *Elliston v
Reacher* itself is always worth study if one has to consider a case in
which extrinsic evidence is going to be important. In *White v Bijou
Mansions Ltd* [1938] Ch 351, Lord Greene MR said that 'an auction
sale with provisions for each purchaser to give the same covenants is
strong evidence of the intention.'

To conclude this review of the principles underlying the doctrine of
schemes, two requirements are essential and are universally insisted
upon, *viz.* (i) that the area shall be defined; (ii) that the purchasers from
the person who creates the scheme shall purchase on the footing that
all purchasers shall be mutually bound by, and mutually entitled to
enforce, a defined set of restrictions (varying no doubt to some extent
as between lots). A common vendor is usual, but there may be cases in

---

[20] *Kelly v Battershell* [1949] 2 All ER 830 per COHEN LJ at p. 839.
[1] *Page v Kings Parade Properties Ltd* [1967] 20 P & CR 710; evidence was given by the
conveyancing managing clerk of the solicitors for the alleged common vendor.
[2] *Re Emery's Application* (1956) 8 P & CR 113; this evidence was accepted as a
substitute for a lotted plan.
[3] *Lund v Taylor* (1975) 31 P & CR 167.
[4] *Re Wembley Park Estate Co Ltd's Transfer* [1968] Ch 491, [1968] 1 All ER 457.

which the purpose of this requirement can be met by some other state of the title. A covenant is almost always necessary and so is a lotted map; but again the purposes which these requirements serve can perhaps be fulfilled in other ways. None of these elements is necessarily decisive in itself or even in combination if the scheme fails for want of either of the two essentials. . . . .

Elliston v Reacher appeared to have put the doctrine into something like a final shape, and during the next 60 years schemes were always discussed in terms of the judgment of Parker J in that case. But in retrospect it now seems clear that that judgment was treated too narrowly as defining what came to be known as the rule in *Elliston v Reacher*. This rule was applied with great precision. Thus in *Lawrence v South County Freeholds Ltd* [1939] Ch 656, Simonds J at p. 674 described the doctrine as 'this very artificial branch of the law,' and alleged schemes were held to fail in a remarkable number of cases[5]. Some of these decisions were indeed highly artificial and at least two of the cases (*Re Pinewood Estate, Farnborough* and *Page v Kings Parade Properties Ltd*) might very well be decided otherwise today. Between *Elliston v Reacher* in 1908 and *Baxter v Four Oaks Properties Ltd* [1965] Ch 816, in 1965 there appear to be only two reported cases in which schemes were upheld. One of them was *Bell v Norman C. Ashton Ltd* (1956) 7 P & CR 359 in 1956, a freehold case noticed above, and the other was a leasehold scheme in *Newman v Real Estate Debenture Corpn* [1940] 1 All ER 131. Of this last case Cohen LJ said in *Kelly v Battershell* [1949] 2 All ER 830 at 842 that it is 'the high water mark of cases where a scheme can be inferred.' Since *Baxter's* case, the courts have been prepared to approach the question of a scheme more broadly[6], appealing to *Renals v Cowlishaw* and *Spicer v Martin* rather than to *Elliston v Reacher*. Although the alleged schemes failed to be upheld in the *Wembley Park* case, and in *Lund v Taylor* (1975) 31 P & CR 167 these decisions were based on the fundamental ground that there was no defined area. In *Baxter's* case itself and also in *Dolphin's* case schemes were upheld notwithstanding the absence of lotting, and in the *Texaco* case notwithstanding a considerable scarcity of evidence. The doctrine of schemes, which had become very fragile through excessive reliance on *Elliston v Reacher*, has been given new vitality by the appeal to the principles of the earlier decisions. Nevertheless the limits to what can be enforced as a scheme are set by the two fundamental requirements upon which the court always insists.''

---

[5] See *Reid v Bickerstaff* [1909] 2 Ch 305; *Wille v St. John* [1910] 1 Ch 84, 325; *Browne v Flower* [1911] 1 Ch 219; *Torbay Hotel Ltd v Jenkins* [1927] 2 Ch 225; *Ridley v Lee* [1935] Ch 591; *White v Bijou Mansions Ltd* [1938] Ch 351; *Lawrence v South County Freeholds Ltd* [1939] Ch 656; *Re Pinewood Estate, Farnborough* [1958] Ch 280; *Page v Kings Parade Properties Ltd* (1967) 20 P & CR 710; *Re Wembley Park Estate Co Ltd's Transfer* [1968] Ch 491.

[6] But, curiously, in *Eagling v Gardner* (1970) 21 P & CR 723, decided six weeks after *Dolphin's* case, neither that case nor *Baxter's* case seems to have been cited, and the decision of the learned judge was founded entirely upon *Elliston v Reacher*.

QUESTIONS

1. Why have the strict technicalities which grew up in relation to restrictive covenants been relaxed in favour of a general rule based on the intention of the parties? *Re Dolphin's Conveyance* [1970] Ch 654, [1970] 2 All ER 664; *Brunner v Greenslade* [1971] Ch 993, [1970] 3 All ER 833; *Lund v Taylor* (1975) 31 P & CR 167; (1972 B) 31 CLJ 157 (H. W. R. Wade).

2. Are restrictive covenants in schemes of development registrable? (1928) 78 LJ 39 (J.M.L.); (1933) 77 Sol Jo 550: (1950) 20 Conv (NS) 370 (R.G. Rowley); *Emmet on Title* (17th edn. 1978), pp. 624–625; Farrand (2nd edn.), pp. 420–421: Barnsley, *Conveyancing Law and Practice* (1973), p. 340; Preston & Newsom pp. 57–58.

3. Which of the three views of the construction of LPA 1925, s. 78, as set out in the *Federated Homes* case at p. 604 (p. 724 ante), do you prefer? See the articles at p. 722 n4, and [1972 B] CLJ 151 (H.W.R. Wade).

C.   Third Party as Covenantee

LAW OF PROPERTY ACT 1925

56.   Persons taking who are not parties and as to indentures. — (1) A person may take an immediate or other interest in land or other property, or the benefit of any condition, right of entry, covenant or agreement over or respecting land or other property, although he may not be named as a party to the conveyance or other instrument.

The effect of this section, when it applies, is to make into a covenantee a person claiming the benefit of the covenant, even though he was not a party to the instrument in which the covenant was contained. The situation here is therefore different from those discussed under the previous heading. They dealt with situations in which the benefit of a covenant could pass on a conveyance to a purchaser of the land. Once, however, the benefit of a covenant is given to a person by section 56 (1), the benefit can then pass to his successors in title by annexation or assignment under the rules described above.

In *Beswick v Beswick* [1968] AC 58, [1967] 2 All ER 1197, Lord UPJOHN said, at p. 102: "Section 56 of the Law of Property Act 1925, has a long history behind it. Section 56 replaced section 5 of the Real Property Act 1845, which amended some very ancient law relating to indentures inter partes, so I shall start by stating the common law on the subject.

The rule was that a grantee or covenantee, though named as such in an indenture under seal expressed to be made inter partes, could not take an *immediate* interest as grantee nor the benefit of a covenant as covenantee unless named as a party to the indenture. This rule, as the authorities I shall quote show, applied not only to real estate but to personal grants and covenants.

But how narrow this rule was, but equally, how well understood, will also be shown by those authorities.

[His Lordship referred to *Scudamore v Vandenstene* (1587) 2 Co Inst

673; *Cooker v Child* (1673) 2 Lev 74; *Berkeley v Hardy* (1826) 5 B & C 355 and continued:]

In *Forster v Elvet Colliery Co Ltd* ([1908] 1 KB 629 at 639) Farwell LJ pointed out that the old rule of law still holds good that no one can sue on a covenant in an indenture who is not mentioned as a party to it, except so far as it had been altered by the Real Property Act 1845. Substituting a reference to section 56 for the Act of 1845 that statement, I suppose, is still true.

In 1844 Parliament abrogated this rule by section 11 of the Transfer of Property Act, 1844, which enacted:

> 'That it shall not be necessary in any case to have a deed indented; and that any person, not being a party to any deed, may take an immediate benefit under it in the same manner as he might under a deed poll.'

For whatever reason, this short workmanlike section, which plainly applied to all covenants whether relating to realty or personal grants or covenants, never had any operation, for it was repealed by the Real Property Act 1845, and replaced by section 5 of that Act in these terms:

> 'That, under an indenture, executed after 1 October 1845, an immediate estate or interest, in any tenements or hereditaments, and the benefit of a condition or covenant, respecting any tenements or hereditaments, may be taken, although the taker thereof be not named a party to the same indenture; . . .'

No one has ever suggested that that section was intended to do more than supplant the old common law rule relating to indentures inter partes in relation to realty.

Then came the great changes in the law of real property; the Law of Property Act 1922, and the Law of Property (Amendment) Act 1924. The researches of counsel have not revealed any amendment in those Acts to section 5 of the Act of 1845. The Law of Property Act 1925, was a consolidation Act consolidating those and many earlier Acts. It repealed section 5 of the Act of 1845 and replaced it by section 56 (1)."

Since a person who takes advantage of section 56 is treated as an original covenantee, it is essential that he should be in existence and identifiable at the time when the covenant was made; the section cannot be used to give the benefit of a covenant to future purchasers, for they could not be made covenantees[7]. Indeed, no enactment is needed to guard the interests of future purchasers, for they can obtain the benefit of existing covenants by virtue of the rules of annexation, or express assignment of the benefit of the covenant. The person who would suffer, apart from section 56 or the existence of a scheme of development, is the owner of adjoining land which needs protection from the covenant and which may have been sold to an earlier purchaser of the land sold off in plots by a common vendor.

Assume that X owns a piece of land, Blackacre, which he is selling off in plots, in circumstances which do not give rise to the existence of

---

[7] *Smith and Snipes Hall Farm Ltd v River Douglas Catchment Board* [1949] 2 KB 500, [1949] 2 All ER 179.

a scheme of development. Plot 1 is bought by A, who covenants, in terms appropriate to annex the benefit of the covenant to each and every part of the land retained by X, not to use the premises as a fish shop; plot 2 is bought by B who gives a similar covenant, and similarly plot 3 by C. B opens a fish shop. X of course can sue as covenantee; C will be able to sue as being the purchaser of land to which the benefit of the covenant is annexed; but A will not, for the benefit of B's covenant, being given later, was not annexed to the piece of land which he bought. Later purchasers, in other words, can sue earlier purchasers; earlier purchasers cannot sue later. Earlier purchasers can be given the right to sue by section 56. The safe way to do so is to draft the later covenants in such a way as to purport expressly to covenant with "A, his heirs and assigns, successors in title, owners for the time being of (plot 1) land adjoining the premises now sold." Some cases require that the benefit could only be taken by a person "to whom that ... instrument purports to grant something or with which (*sic*) some agreement or covenant is purported to be made[8]". It appears, however, that the rule is wider than this, and that a person can take the benefit if he is an existing person who, from the circumstances of the case, was clearly intended by the parties to be benefited or, in the case of a covenant which runs with the land, is an assignee of such a person. This will not, however, cover the ordinary case of the prior purchaser, unless there is an indication of an intention to benefit him. The application of section 56 to cases concerning "other property" is a matter beyond the scope of this work[9].

RE ECCLESIASTICAL COMMISSIONERS FOR ENGLAND'S CONVEYANCE
[1936] Ch 430 (ChD, LUXMOORE J)

An originating summons was brought under section 84 (2) Law of Property Act 1925[10], to decide whether West Heath House, in the ownership of the applicants, was bound by any, and if so, what, restrictive covenants. The applicants are successors in title of one Gotto who purchased in 1887 from the Ecclesiastical Commissioners giving the following covenant:

"The said Henry Gainsford Gotto doth hereby ... covenant with the said Ecclesiastical Commissioners and their successors" (in such a way as to annex the benefit of the covenant to the land retained by the vendor) "and also as a separate covenant with their assigns owners for the time being of land adjoining or adjacent to the said land hereby conveyed in manner following, that is to say:" A number of covenants follow.

---

[8] *White v Bijou Mansions Ltd* [1937] Ch 610, 625, [1937] 3 All ER 269; *affd.* [1938] Ch 351, [1938] 1 All ER 546, see p. 758, post; *Re Ecclesiastical Commissioners for England's Conveyance* [1936] Ch 430, infra.

[9] Cheshire and Fifoot, *Law of Contract* (9th edn.), pp. 442–445; Treitel, *Law of Contract* (5th edn.), pp. 492–495; *Beswick v Beswick* [1968] AC 58, [1967] 2 All ER 1197, esp. Lord PEARCE at pp. 93–94, and Lord UPJOHN at pp. 102–107; (1967) 30 MLR 687. (G. H. Treitel).

[10] See p. 767, post.

Some of the defendants were successors in title to land adjoining or adjacent to the applicants' house and which had been bought from the Ecclesiastical Commissioners before the conveyance of 1887. It was as to the position of these defendants that the main issue in the case arose.

Held. The owners of adjacent and adjoining lands and their successors in title were able to enforce the covenants although they or their predecessors in title were not parties to the conveyance of 1887.

LUXMOORE J: The questions to be determined are: (1) were any restrictions imposed on West Heath House before or by the conveyance of 21 April 1887; (2) were such restrictions imposed for the benefit of any, and what other hereditaments; and (3) who are the persons, if any, now entitled to the benefit of such restrictive covenants? It is not contended by any of the parties that West Heath House forms part of a larger estate which has been subjected to what is usually referred to as a building scheme, and it is quite plain that there is not sufficient evidence on which it could be argued with any hope of success that such a scheme existed. . . .

Having ascertained that restrictive covenants were imposed in respect of the West Heath House property and that the form of the covenants is such as to make the burden of them run with the land, it is necessary to consider whether they were imposed for the benefit of any and what other hereditaments. For it is well settled that, apart from any building scheme, restrictive covenants may be enforced if they are expressed in the original deed to be for the benefit of a particular parcel or particular parcels of land, either expressly mentioned or clearly identified in the deed containing the original covenants. It was argued on behalf of the applicants that the right to enforce such covenants is limited to the original covenantees and their successors in title — the right in the case of the successors in title being limited to those whose land was the property of the original covenantees at the date when the covenants were imposed. It was also argued that the right to enforce the covenants did not extend to any owners of land who were neither express assignees of the benefit of the covenants, nor successors in title of the original covenantees in respect of land acquired by such successors from the Ecclesiastical Commissioners subsequent to the date of the deed by which the covenants were imposed. I think these arguments failed to give due consideration to the provisions of section 5 of the Real Property Act, 1845, as repealed and re-enacted by section 56 of the Law of Property Act, 1925. Section 5 of the Act of 1845 provides that under an indenture, executed after 1 October 1845, the benefit of a condition or covenant respecting any tenements or hereditaments may be taken, although the taker thereof be not named as a party to the indenture. In the case of *Forster v Elvet Colliery Co Ltd* ([1908] 1 KB 629), it was held that the condition or covenant referred to in the section must, in order to be enforceable by a person not a party to the deed, be one the benefit of which runs with the land of the person seeking to enforce it. The actual decision was upheld in the House of Lords under the name *Dyson v Forster* ([1909] AC 98), but Lord Macnaghten expressed doubt whether the section ought to be so restricted. He refrained however from resolving the doubt, because he agreed with the view that the covenants in the particular case ran with the land and it was therefore unnecessary to do so.

The alteration which has been made in the verbiage of section 5 of the 1845 Act by section 56 of the 1925 Act, has not in my opinion affected the position so as to limit the right of a person not a party to the deed to enforce covenants affecting land to those which run with the land. The material words are as follows: "A person may take . . . the benefit of any condition . . . covenant or agreement . . . respecting land or other property, although he may not be named as a party to the conveyance or other instrument." It seems to me that the effect of these words is to enlarge the scope of the earlier words, for it extends the rights of a person not a party to a deed to covenants affecting every kind of property personal as well as real. So far as every species of personal property other than leasehold is concerned it is obvious that the covenants to be enforced cannot be restricted to those running with the property, for there are no such covenants. What it is necessary to consider is the true construction of the conveyance of 21 April 1887, in order to ascertain whether any persons, not parties thereto, are described therein as the covenantees, and whether such covenants are expressed to affect any and what hereditaments. To determine what is the true construction of that document it is necessary to consider the surrounding circumstances as they existed at the date when it was executed.

[His Lordship then examined the circumstances existing at the date of execution of the deed and concluded that the covenants were enforceable by the original covenantees, and persons deriving title under them; that the original covenantees need not have been parties to the conveyance of 1887; but that such persons could only enforce the covenant if they held land adjoining or adjacent to the applicants' house.]

WHITE *v* BIJOU MANSIONS LTD
[1937] Ch 610, [1937] 3 All ER 269, *affirmed* [1938] Ch 351; [1938] 1 All ER 546 (SIMONDS J, and CA, Sir Wilfrid GREENE MR, LUXMOORE and FARWELL JJ)

The owners of the Shaftesbury House Estate conveyed part of it in 1887 to James Israel Fellows. Fellows covenanted that he would build a dwelling house for a certain sum and would use it only as a private dwelling house or as a residence and place of practice of a medical man. The vendors covenanted that every building lease or future sale should include covenants from the lessee or purchaser with the builders imposing similar restrictions on the use of the land, though certain parts were to be permitted to be used as shops. The plaintiff was the successor in title to Fellows.

In 1890, a nearby plot was conveyed to Nicholson, who covenanted for himself, his heirs, executors, administrators and assigns with the intent to bind himself and his successors in title and the owner for the time being of the property thereby conveyed with the vendors, their heirs and assigns, that the piece of land thereby conveyed should be used for the purpose of a private dwelling house only. This plot was later conveyed to Miss Plumbly who, in 1935, leased it to two ladies for a term of 28 years; the lease contained a covenant that no part of the demised premises would be used for any purpose other than a private dwelling house or for private suites or flats. The lease was in due course assigned to the defendants who used the house for flatlets. The action was for an injunction to restrain a breach of covenant.

Held (by SIMONDS J, and the Court of Appeal). The plaintiff was not entitled to the benefit of the covenant given by Nicholson in the conveyance of 1890.

SIMONDS J (in the court of first instance): ... Then the question arises: Can the plaintiff here enforce that covenant? I turn to look at it once more. There are covenants entered into in the year 1890, the first with the Davidsons, the second with the Daws, and they are covenants which are not annexed to any particular parcel of land. They are covenants entered into four years after the plaintiff acquired the title to his land. They are covenants the benefit of which has not expressly or by implication, or in any manner whatsoever, been assigned to the plaintiff, and it appears to me to be quite impossible, apart from any building scheme or from the special statutory provision to which I shall presently refer, that the plaintiff can avail himself of this covenant and enforce it. There is here no question of a building scheme. ...

It remains to consider the only other ground on which, as it appears to me, Mr. Grant can possibly rest his case. He claims that he is entitled to enforce this covenant, entered into on 2 May 1890, on the ground that either under section 5 of the Real Property Act 1845, or under section 56 of the Law of Property Act 1925, that right is conferred on him. In the view which I take of both these sections it is unnecessary for me to consider whether he is in any way entitled to call in aid section 56 of the Act of 1925, with regard to covenants or agreements contained in a deed executed in 1890. It is necessary for me to say something about the earlier section before I come to consider the later section.

Section 5 of the Real Property Act 1845, which was, as its title suggests, an Act to amend the law of real property, was aimed at remedying certain mischiefs in the state of the common law as it then was. There was a highly technical and artifical rule that by an indenture, as distinguished from a deed poll, an immediate interest in land could not be granted in favour of a grantee unless that grantee was a party to the deed. That mischief this section was designed to remedy. Further, there was the defect, as it was supposed, in the common law, that a person could not take advantage of a covenant in a deed unless he was a party to the deed. Be it observed that the Act of

1845 dealt with real property. This section was confined to the case of an indenture, and of an immediate interest created by that indenture, for it was never the law that an estate in remainder could not be validly granted in favour of a grantee if he were not a party. Indeed the common form of settlement then for centuries in vogue had limited estates in remainder not only to persons not parties to the deed but to persons not yet in existence.

[His Lordship read section 5 and continued:] I think the important aspect of that section for my present purpose is this. It appears to me to be quite plain that the section has a limited operation. It is intended to confer a benefit only on those persons to whom the deed purports to grant an estate or interest or those persons with whom there purports to be a covenant or agreement. It is impossible, in my view, to regard this section as creating a benefit in favour of any persons who may like to avail themselves of it and say: "If we can take advantage of this it will be for our benefit." It seems to me clear that this section was intended merely to provide that A.B., the grantee under a deed, might take an immediate interest although he was not a party, and similarly that A.B., with whom the covenant was purported to be made by the deed, should be able to avail himself of it although he was not a party to the deed, and in the few cases which have arisen under this section since 1845 — and there appear to be very few — it will be found in every case where it has been applied that it has been in favour of a person who although not a party to the deed was a person to or with whom a grant or covenant purported to be made. That was the position under the Act of 1845.

I now turn to consider section 56 of the Act of 1925, which, it is said, however inaptly, takes the place of the earlier section. [His Lordship read subsection 1 and continued:] I think many difficulties may well arise on that section which do not fall to me to-day to solve. It appears to one at once that, so far as any other than an immediate interest in land is concerned the section is superfluous, because a person always could take another interest in land though not a party. It is at least a question how far such a provision is necessary at all in the case of personalty. Without deciding it, I should be disposed to think that equitable estates even in land were not subject to the old artificial rule and it is very doubtful if an interest in personalty was ever so subject. However that may be, for the purposes of the present case I think I am only concerned with one aspect of this question. Just as under section 5 of the Act of 1845 only that person could call it in aid who, although not a party, yet was a grantee or covenantee, so under section 56 of this Act only that person can call it in aid who, although not named as a party to the conveyance or other instrument, is yet a person to whom that conveyance or other instrument purports to grant some thing or with which [sic] some agreement or covenant is purported to be made. To give it any other meaning appears to me to open the door to claims or assertion of rights which cannot have been contemplated by the Legislature, for if that be not the limitation which must be imposed on this section, it appears to me that there is no limit and it will be open to anybody to come into court and say: "Here is a covenant which if enforced will redound to my advantage, therefore I claim the benefit of the section. I claim that this covenant or condition is one which should be enforced in my favour because it is for my benefit, whether intended for my benefit or not intended for my benefit would not appear to matter." I cannot give to the section any such meaning as that. I interpret it as a section which can be called in aid only by a person in whose favour the grant purports to be made or with whom the covenant or agreement purports to be made[11]. If that is so, whether the plaintiff's claim arises under the earlier or the later Act, he cannot sue on it in this Court because he is not a person who, under the deed of 1890, can point to any grant or any covenant purported to be made to or with him. That is the construction which I place on section 56, with the result that the plaintiff's claim must fail.

In the Court of Appeal, where SIMONDS J's decision was upheld, Sir Wilfrid GREENE MR said at p. 365: "Whatever else section 56 may mean, it is, I think, confined to cases where the person seeking to take advantage of it is a person within the benefit of the covenant in question, if I may use that phrase. The mere fact that somebody comes along and says: "It would be useful to me if I could enforce that covenant' does not make him a person entitled to enforce it under section 56. Before he can enforce it he must be a person who falls within the scope and benefit of the covenant according to the true construction of the document in question."

In *Stromdale and Ball Ltd v Burden* [1952] Ch 223, [1952] 1 All ER 59, the defendant, Mrs Burden, was under-lessee of a house of three storeys at 40 Romford Road, Stratford for an unexpired term of 45 years, the bottom floor of which was used as a café. In 1946, she sold the goodwill of the café business to two persons and granted to them a sub-lease of the ground floor. In 1948, the tenants arranged to sell their business to the plaintiff company. They obtained the consent of the defendant to the assignment of their lease in a deed dated March 1948 to which the defendant, the tenants, and Charles William Stromdale and Stanley Ball (directors of the plaintiff company) were parties. The company was not a party. The deed provided inter alia that the company should have an option to purchase the unexpired term of years in the premises held by the defendant.

In June 1948, the tenants assigned the residue of their lease to the plaintiff company, but the assignment contained no reference to the option.

---

[11] Similarly per CROSSMAN J in *Re Foster* [1938] 3 All ER 357 at 365.

In August 1948, the plaintiff company gave notice of intention to exercise the option, and in December 1949, brought this action for specific performance.

DANCKWERTS J held that the plaintiff company, although not a party to the instrument granting the option, could enforce it under section 56 (1) Law of Property Act 1925, and said, at p. 233: "Mr. Brightman argues . . . that section 56 of the Law of Property Act, 1925, enables the plaintiff company to take such an interest in land as is created by an option to purchase though not a party to the document conferring the option. In support of this argument, he referred me to certain decisions in which the provisions of the section were considered. In *White v Bijou Mansions Ltd* ([1937] Ch 610, [1937] 3 All ER 269)[12] a case concerned with covenants restricting the use of land, Simonds J, referring to section 5 of the Real Property Act 1845, after saying that the section had a limited operation, said: 'It is intended to confer a benefit only on those persons to whom the deed purports to grant an estate or interest or those persons with whom there purports to be a covenant or agreement', and he went on to say that the section did not create a benefit in favour of any persons who might like to avail themselves of it. With regard to section 56 of the Law of Property Act 1925, Simonds J said: [His Lordship quoted the four sentences set out on p. 758, ante from 'It appears to one at once that . . .' to '. . . is purported to be made'.: and continued:]

In the same case, in the Court of Appeal, Sir Wilfrid Greene MR said: 'Whatever else section 56 may mean, it is, I think, confined to cases where the person seeking to take advantage of it is a person within the benefit of the covenant in question, if I may use that phrase.'

It seems to me that those statements of the limited effect of section 56 of the Law of Property Act 1925, do none the less exactly cover the situation of the plaintiff company in the present case. I have not overlooked the decision of Crossman J in *Re Foster*[13] expressly declining to treat section 56 as creating such an enormous change in the law as to enable an agreement by A with B to pay money to C to be enforced by C. But it seems to me that in the present case the intention of clause 4 of the deed of licence is to enable the person therein named, the plaintiff company, and no one else, to obtain the leasehold interest of the defendant in No. 40 Romford Road. In the language of Simonds J, the plaintiff company is a person to whom the instrument purports to grant some thing or with which some agreement or covenant is purported to be made. Section 56 provides that a person may take an immediate or other interest in land or the benefit of any covenant or agreement over or respecting land, although he may not be named as a party to the instrument. It is difficult to see what the intention of clause 4 of the deed of licence was if it was not to confer on the plaintiff

---

[12] See p. 756, ante.
[13] (1938) 159 LT 279.

company an interest in No. 40 Romford Road and to give to the plaintiff company the benefit of the covenant or agreement conferring an option to acquire the defendant's leasehold interest. The question decided in *Woodall v Clifton* ([1905] 2 Ch 257), namely, whether an option to acquire the reversion in fee simple on a leasehold term ran with the leasehold term in the hands of an assignee of the reversion or of the term, seems to me to be a different matter. In the present case, for the purposes of section 56, the 'land' is No. 40 Romford Road, and an option to purchase a leasehold interest in this land seems to me to create an interest in that land and to be an agreement respecting that land, and so to be within the precise words of the section. I do not understand why the words 'agreement respecting land' should not be given their plain meaning. An option to purchase land is an agreement respecting land. Accordingly, I reach the conclusion that the provisions of section 56 of the Law of Property Act 1925, enable the plaintiff company to enforce the option in the present case. . . ."

In *Drive Yourself Hire Co (London) Ltd v Strutt* [1954] 1 QB 250, [1953] 2 All ER 1475, DENNING LJ, said, obiter at p. 271: "Mr. Montague Waters argued, however, that section 56 must be limited to persons 'with whom some agreement or covenant is purported to be made', relying on the observations of Simonds J in *White v Bijou Mansions Ltd* ([1937] Ch 610, [1937] 3 All ER 269)[14]. If the covenant had been formally expressed to be 'with' the superior landlord, it would, he said, have been enforceable by the superior landlord, although he was not a party: but as it was not so expressed, it was not enforceable. But, as Somervell LJ pointed out in the course of the argument, that may be too narrow an interpretation to place on the words used by Simonds J. Enforceability does not depend on the form of the obligation, but on the substance of it. A covenant is for this purpose, sufficiently made 'with' a person if it is, on the face of it, made directly for his benefit in such circumstances that it was intended to be enforceable by him. In support of this view, I would refer to the recent case of *Stromdale and Ball v Burden*, where Danckwerts J, as one ground of his judgment, held that an option to purchase was enforceable by a company as an 'agreement respecting land', although the company was not a party to the instrument and the agreement was not expressed in terms to be 'with' the company."[15]

The question arises again here, whether a covenant, the benefit of which is given to the plaintiff under section 56, is annexed to the plaintiff's land. It is annexed if the covenantor purports to covenant separately with the plaintiff using language appropriate for

---

[14] See also p. 756, ante.
[15] See also *Re Nesawood Properties' Ltd and Boltmore Properties' Ltd Application* [1975] JPL 733.

annexation, as in *Re Ecclesiastical Commissioners for England's Conveyance*[16]; or if section 78 of the Law of Property Act 1925 is held to apply[16a]. Where there is no "separate covenant", there appears to be no authority. The section allows the plaintiff to take the benefit of the covenant between other parties, and presumably the question of annexation to the plaintiff's land will turn upon the same factors as that of annexation to the land of the covenantee.

IV.   Declaration, Discharge and Modification[17]

A.   The Position Apart from Statute

i.   CHANGE IN CHARACTER OF NEIGHBOURHOOD. NON-ENFORCEMENT

CHATSWORTH ESTATES CO *v* FEWELL[18]
[1931] 1 Ch 224 (ChD, FARWELL J)

The predecessors in title of the plaintiffs, owners of Compton Place, Eastbourne, had sold land to the predecessors in title of the defendant subject to various covenants, of which the defendant had notice when he purchased, one of which was that he would not use the land "otherwise than as a private dwelling house". The land was on the sea front at Eastbourne, and various owners of adjoining land, which had also been purchased subject to the same covenant from the predecessors in title of the plaintiffs, had, with their consent, used the land for a school, for flats, and in three cases where the circumstances were exceptional for boarding houses. The defendant opened a guest house called Bella Vista; his attention was drawn to the covenant, and he was given an opportunity to apply under section 84 of the Law of Property Act 1925 for the modification of the covenant. He did nothing and this action was for an injunction and damages. The defendant admitted the breach and contended that the covenants were not enforceable for two reasons:

   (i) by reason of the change in the general character of the neighbourhood, whereby the object of those covenants had completely disappeared.

   (ii) by reason of the fact that this change had been brought about by the acts and omissions of the plaintiffs and their predecessors in title.

Held. The plaintiffs were entitled to an injunction.

FARWELL J: Nothing can be said against the defendant's conduct of his establishment except that it is a breach of covenant. That being so ought I to refuse the plaintiffs relief?

The defendant's first ground of defence is that there has been such a complete change in the character of the neighbourhood, apart from the plaintiffs' acts or omissions, that the covenants are now

---

[16] [1936] Ch 430. See p. 754, ante.
[16a] *Federated Homes Ltd v Mill Lodge Properties Ltd* [1980] 1 WLR 594, [1980] 1 All ER 371, p. 722, ante.
[17] Cheshire, pp. 616–621; M & W, pp. 772–775; MM, pp. 377–379; Preston and Newsom, pp. 149 et seq.
[18] (1948) 92 Sol Jo 570.

unenforceable. But to succeed on that ground the defendant must show that there has been so complete a change in the character of the neighbourhood that there is no longer any value left in the covenants at all. A man who has covenants for the protection of his property cannot be deprived of his rights thereunder merely by the acts or omissions of other persons unless those acts or omissions bring about such a state of affairs as to render the covenants valueless, so that an action to enforce them would be unmeritorious, not bona fide at all, and merely brought for some ulterior purposes. It is quite impossible here to say that there has been so complete a change in the character of this neighbourhood as to render the covenants valueless to the plaintiffs. Whether right or wrong the plaintiffs are bringing this action bona fide to protect their property, and it is hopeless to say that the change in the character of the neighbourhood is so complete that it would be useless for me to give them any relief.

The defendant really relied on the acts and omissions of the plaintiffs and their predecessors as a bar to equitable relief. Now the plaintiffs are not unduly insistent on the observance of these covenants in this sense, that they do not conduct inquisitorial examinations into their neighbours' lives, and do not make it their business to find out very carefully exactly what is being done, unless the matter is brought to their notice, either by complaints of other inhabitants, or by seeing some board or advertisement. I cannot think that plaintiffs lose their rights merely because they treat their neighbours with consideration. They are doing what they think sufficient to preserve the character of the neighbourhood. Whether they do enough is another matter, but I am quite satisfied that they are not intending, by their acts or omissions, to permit this area to be turned into anything other than a mainly residential area. There is no doubt however that they have permitted breaches of covenant in several cases where houses have been turned into flats, they have permitted at least four houses to be carried on as boarding-houses or hotels, and they have not prevented — in some cases because they did not know of them — some half a dozen other houses being used as boarding houses or guest houses.

There are still however a very large number of private dwelling houses in the area, and I am satisfied that while the use of Bella Vista as a guest house or boarding house may not at the moment cause any actual damage to Compton Place or its owners, there is a prospect of damage in the future if the defendant is allowed to continue to use Bella Vista in that way, because it might well lead to many other houses being so used which would undoubtedly damnify the owners of Compton Place, especially if they develop the park and grounds as intended. In that way it will certainly be detrimental to the plaintiffs to permit Bella Vista to be used as a guest house. But whether they are entitled to relief depends on the exact effect of their past acts and omissions.

Now, as stated in many authorities, the principle upon which this equitable doctrine rests is that the plaintiffs are not entitled to relief if it would be inequitable to the defendant to grant it. In some of the cases it is said that the plaintiffs by their acts and omissions have impliedly waived performance of the covenants. In other cases it is said that the plaintiffs, having acquiesced in past breaches, cannot now enforce the covenants. It is in all cases a question of degree. It is in many ways analogous to the doctrine of estoppel, and I think it is a fair test to treat it in that way and ask, "Have the plaintiffs by their acts and omissions represented to the defendant that the covenants are no longer enforceable and that he is therefore entitled to use his house as a guest house?"[19]

ii.   UNITY OF SEISIN

In *Texaco Antilles Ltd v Kernochan* [1973] AC 609, [1973] 2 All ER 118, Lord CROSS OF CHELSEA said, at p. 624:

"Their Lordships now turn to the 'unity of seisin' point which was the main ground upon which the appellants founded their contention that the restrictions were not binding on them. As stated above from 12 January 1942 until 12 November 1951, Chapmans Ltd owned both the lots now owned by the respondents and also the lots now owned by the appellants. As soon as the two sets of lots came into the same hands it became impossible for any action to enforce the covenants to be brought by the owner of one set against the owner of the other since he was the same person and that fact, so the argument runs, put an end to the restrictions so far as concerned the relations of the two sets of lots inter se. . . .

The point of law which arises for consideration is therefore whether in a case where there is nothing in the conveyance putting an end to the unity of seisin or in the surrounding circumstances to indicate that the restrictions in the scheme are no longer to apply as between the owners of the lots previously in common ownership the fact that they have been in common ownership puts an end to the restrictions so far as concerns the relations of subsequent owners for the time being of that part of the estate inter se so that if the common owner of those lots wished them to apply after the severance he would have to reimpose them as fresh restrictions under a sub-scheme relating to them. It would their Lordships think be somewhat unfortunate if this was the law. . . . It is no doubt true that if the restrictions in question exist simply for the mutual benefit of two adjoining properties and both those properties are bought by one man the restrictions will automatically come to an end[20] and will not revive on a subsequent severance unless the common owner then recreates them. But their

---

[19] See also *Westripp v Baldock* [1939] 1 All ER 279; and *Shaw v Applegate* [1977] 1 WLR 970; [1978] 1 All ER 123, where an injunction was refused against the original covenantor on grounds of acquiescence, but damages were awarded. BUCKLEY LJ said, at p. 978: "The real test, I think, must be whether upon the facts of the particular case, the situation has become such that it would be dishonest or unconscionable for the plaintiff, or the person having the right sought to be enforced, to continue to seek to enforce it."

[20] *Re Tiltwood, Sussex* [1978] Ch 269, [1978] 2 All ER 1091.

Lordships cannot see that it follows from this that if a number of people agree that the area covered by all their properties shall be subject to a 'local law' the provisions of which shall be enforceable by any owner for the time being of any part against any other owner and the whole area has never at any time come into common ownership an action by one owner of a part against another owner of a part must fail if it can be shown that both parts were either at the inception of the scheme or at any time subsequently in common ownership. The view which their Lordships favour is supported by dicta of Sir H. H. Cozens-Hardy MR in *Elliston v Reacher* [1908] 2 Ch 665, 673 and of Simonds J in *Lawrence v South County Freeholds Ltd* [1939] Ch 656, 677–683, [1939] 2 All ER 503, but at the time when this case was heard by the Court of Appeal there was no decision on the point. Subsequently, however, in *Brunner v Greenslade* [1971] Ch 993, [1970] 3 All ER 833 which raised the point, Megarry J followed those dicta. The appellants submitted that his decision was wrong but in their Lordships' view it was right."

B.   Law of Property Act 1925, section 84[1]

Under section 84 (2) the court may be asked to declare whether land is affected by a restrictive covenant, and, under section 84 (1) the Lands Tribunal has power in its discretion to modify or discharge such a covenant. Section 84 was substantially amended by Law of Property Act 1969, section 28, extending the powers of the Lands Tribunal to cover a situation where a restrictive covenant which prevents some reasonable use of land confers no substantial benefit on anyone or is contrary to the public interest. Compensation may be ordered in some cases. The section is printed as amended, and the alterations shown in italic.

LAW OF PROPERTY ACT 1925

84.   Power to discharge or modify restrictive covenants affecting land.

(1) The *Lands Tribunal* shall (without prejudice to any concurrent jurisdiction of the court) have power from time to time, on the application of any person interested in any freehold land affected by any restriction arising under covenant[2] or otherwise as to the user thereof

---

[1] See also Housing Act 1957, s. 165; *Josephine Trust Ltd v Champagne* [1963] 2 QB 160, [1962] 3 All ER 136; TCPA 1971, s. 127; Local Government Act 1972, ss. 120 (3), 124 (2). Applications made under the section are noted in Current Law under the heading, "Real Property and Conveyancing", and in the Journal of Planning and Environment Law. Some are reported in P & CR and the Estates Gazette. Condensed reports of all applications appear in Lands Tribunal Cases, published annually since 1974. For a detailed commentary, see Preston and Newsom, Chap. 7; (1974) JPL 72, 130; (1975) JPL 644; (1976) JPL 407; (1979) JPL 64 (G. H. Newsom).

[2] The covenant may be personal; *Shepherd Homes Ltd v Sandham (No. 2)* [1971] 1 WLR 1062, [1971] 2 All ER 1267.

or the building thereon, by order wholly or partially to discharge or modify any such restriction on being satisfied —

    (a) that by reason of changes in the character of the property or the neighbourhood[3] or other circumstances of the case which the *Lands Tribunal* may deem material, the restriction ought to be deemed obsolete; or

    (aa) that (*in a case falling within subsection (1A) below*) the continued existence thereof would impede *some* reasonable user of the land for public or private purposes or, as the case may be, would unless modified so impede such user; or

    (b) that the persons of full age and capacity for the time being or from time to time entitled to the benefit of the restriction, whether in respect of estates in fee simple or any lesser estates or interests in the property to which the benefit of the restriction is annexed, have agreed, either expressly or by implication[4], by their acts or omissions, to the same being discharged or modified; or

    (c) that the proposed discharge or modification will not injure the persons entitled to the benefit of the restriction;

and an order discharging or modifying a restriction under this subsection may direct the applicant to pay to any person entitled to the benefit of the restriction such sum by way of consideration[5] as the Tribunal may think it just to award under one, but not both, of the following heads, that is to say, either —

    (i) *a sum to make up for any loss or disadvantage suffered by that person in consequence of the discharge or modification; or*

    (ii) *a sum to make up for any effect which the restriction had, at the time when it was imposed, in reducing the consideration then received for the land affected by it.*

    (1A) *Subsection (1) (aa) above authorises the discharge or modification of a restriction by reference to its impeding some reasonable user of land in any case in which the Lands Tribunal is satisfied that the restriction, in impeding that user, either —*

    (a) *does not secure to persons entitled to the benefit of it any practical benefits of substantial value or advantage to them; or*

    (b) *is contrary to the public interest;*

and that money will be an adequate compensation for the loss or disadvantage (if any) which any such person will suffer from the discharge or modification.

---

[3] *Keith v Texaco Ltd* (1977) 34 P & CR 249 (coming of oil industry to Aberdeenshire).

[4] See *Memvale Securities Ltd's Application* (1975), 223 Estates Gazette 689; *Re Fettishaw's Application (No. 2)* (1973) 27 P & CR 292.

[5] In *SJC Construction Co Ltd v Sutton London Borough Council* (1975) 29 P & CR 322, STEPHENSON LJ said, arguendo, that "consideration" was probably a mis-print for "compensation". Preston and Newsom, p. 209.

(1B) *In determining whether a case is one falling within subsection (1A) above, and in determining whether (in any such case or otherwise) a restriction ought to be discharged or modified, the Lands Tribunal shall take into account the development plan and any declared or ascertainable pattern for the grant or refusal of planning permissions in the relevant areas, as well as the period at which and context in which the restriction was created or imposed and any other material circumstances.*

(1C) *It is hereby declared that the power conferred by this section to modify a restriction includes power to add such further provisions restricting the user of or the building on the land affected as appear to the Lands Tribunal to be reasonable in view of the relaxation of the existing provisions, and as may be accepted by the applicant; and the Lands Tribunal may accordingly refuse to modify a restriction without some such addition*[6].

(2) The court shall have power on the application of any person interested —

(a) to declare whether or not in any particular case any freehold land is, *or would in any given event be*, affected by a restriction imposed by any instrument; or

(b) to declare what, upon the true construction of any instrument purporting to impose a restriction, is the nature and extent of the restriction thereby imposed and whether the same is, *or would in any given event be*, enforceable and if so by whom.

(3) The *Lands Tribunal* shall, before making any order under this section, direct such enquiries, if any, to be made of any *government department or* local authority, and such notices, if any, whether by way of advertisement or otherwise, to be given to such of the persons who appear to be entitled to the benefit of the restriction intended to be discharged, modified, or dealt with as, having regard to any enquiries, notices, or other proceedings previously made, given or taken, the *Lands Tribunal* may think fit.

(3A) *On an application to the Lands Tribunal under this section the Lands Tribunal shall give any necessary directions as to the persons who are or are not to be admitted (as appearing to be entitled to the benefit of the restriction) to oppose the application, and no appeal shall lie against any such direction; but rules under the Lands Tribunal Act 1949 shall make provision*[7] *whereby, in cases in which there arises on such an application (whether or not in connection with the admission of persons to oppose) any such question as is referred to in subsection (2) (a) or (b) of this section, the proceedings on the application can and, if the rules so provide, shall be suspended to enable the decision of the court to be obtained on that question by an application under that*

---

[6] *Re Patten Ltd's Application* (1975) 31 P & CR 180; *Re Dransfield's Application* (1975) 31 P & CR 192; *Re Kershaw's Application* (1975) 31 P & CR 187; *Re Banks Application* (1976) 33 P & CR 138.

[7] Lands Tribunal Rules 1975 (S.I. 1975, No. 299); Lands Tribunal (Amendment) Rules 1977 (S.I. 1977 No. 1820).

subsection, or by means of a case stated by the Lands Tribunal, or otherwise, as may be provided by those rules or by rules of court.

(5) Any order made under this section shall be binding on all persons, whether ascertained or of full age or capacity or not, then entitled or thereafter capable of becoming entitled to the benefit of any restriction, which is thereby discharged, modified or dealt with, and whether such persons are parties to the proceedings or have been served with notice or not.

(8) This section applies whether the land affected by the restrictions is registered or not, but, in the case of registered land, the Land Registrar shall give effect on the register to any order under this section *in accordance with the Land Registration Act 1925.*

(9) Where any proceedings by action or otherwise are taken to enforce a restrictive covenant, any person against whom the proceedings are taken, may in such proceedings apply to the court for an order giving leave to apply to the *Lands Tribunal* under this section, and staying the proceedings in the meantime.

(12) Where a term of more than forty years is created in land (whether before or after the commencement of this Act) this section shall, after the expiration of twenty-five years of the term, apply to restrictions affecting such leasehold land in like manner as it would have applied had the land been freehold:

Provided that this subsection shall not apply to mining leases.

In *Ridley v Taylor*, [1965] 1 WLR 611, [1965] 2 All ER 51, HARMAN LJ said at p. 617:

"Section 84 (1) of the Law of Property Act 1925, primarily applies to restrictions on freehold land, but by subsection (12), as amended by the Landlord and Tenant Act 1954, is made applicable to restrictions affecting leasehold land where a term of more than 40 years is created by the lease of which more than 25 years have expired. It seems to me that it should be more difficult to persuade the court to exercise its discretion in leasehold than in freehold cases. In the latter the court is relaxing in favour of a freeholder's own land restrictions entered into for the benefit of persons owning other land. In the former the land in question is the property of the covenantee who is prima facie entitled to preserve the character of his reversion. Section 84 cases usually arise between the assigns of both the benefit and the burden of the covenant, and one may suppose that the section was designed with a view to cases within the doctrine of *Tulk v Moxhay*, but there is nothing in the language of the section to limit the power of the court to a case where the lessee is not himself bound by contract, and I do not feel able to say that such a covenant cannot be modified under the section, although it seems to me that the court should be slow to relieve an applicant of covenants which he himself has entered into. Were it otherwise, it would be easy to avoid the effect of the section by an assignment. It is to be observed that what is to be discharged or modified is not the covenant, but any restriction under the covenant, and it was suggested that this would leave direct contractual liability untouched. This would produce an extraordinary result in a case where the restriction was modified in favour of an assign if the covenantee could still sue the original covenantor in damages on his contractual liability although he had parted with all interest in the property. I cannot but think that the covenant must, where an order is made, be treated in all respects as modified or discharged."

(1979) 129 NLJ 523 (H. W. Wilkinson)
"In *Re Bass Ltd's Application* (1973) 26 P & CR 156, the Tribunal (J S Daniel QC) accepted the submission of counsel, Graham Eyre QC, that the questions which properly arose [under subsection (1) (*aa*)] were:
1. Is the proposed user reasonable?
2. Do the covenants impede that user?
3. Does impeding the proposed user secure practical benefits to the objectors?
4. If yes, are those benefits of substantial value or advantage?
5. Is impeding the proposed user contrary to the public interest?
6. If no, would money be an adequate compensation?
7. If yes, would money be an adequate compensation?

In considering questions 3 to 7 inclusive, regard must be had to the planning context, by subsection (1B).

The questions will be discussed in the order of formulation.

1. *Is the proposed user reasonable?*
In the *Bass* case (1973) the applicants sought the modification of a covenant in order to allow them to use some of their land for the loading and unloading of 228 articulated lorries daily — a 'trunker park'. There had been objections from over 200 nearby house owners. The Tribunal considered that the purpose of the restriction was to make a '*cordon sanitaire* of residential buildings masking any new industrial development'. The applicants already had planning permission for the development and the Tribunal said that 'planning permissions are very persuasive in this connection' though it must not be thought that the question of reasonable user 'could always be concluded in the affirmative by the production of a planning permission'. Partly because of the need for businesses in the area to be provided with communications it was held that the proposed user was reasonable.

The first hurdle is not usually difficult for an applicant to surmount. It is not easy for an objector to establish that there is anything unreasonable about a wish to build houses or flats or to extend a legitimate business enterprise. The requirement of reasonableness was satisfied in all the following cases (though not all the applications eventually succeeded):

Re John Twiname Ltd's Application (1972) 23 P & CR 413; covenant imposed in 1924 not to build within 200 feet of a mansion house, The Towers, which was now four habitations and had two pairs of semi-detached houses in its grounds. A proposal to build three pairs of semis and three detached houses within 200 feet of the house was held to be reasonable.

Re Beardsley's Application (1972) 25 P & CR 233; covenant imposed in 1922 forbade the building of more than two private residences on the site. A proposed development of 12 flats, each with a garage, was held to be reasonable.

Re Carter's Application (1973) 25 P & CR 542; infilling with a second house of conventional design in keeping with the other houses on the site held to be reasonable although there was a covenant against putting more than one dwelling house on the plot.

Re Osborn's and Easton's Application (1978) 38 P & CR 251; restrictions were imposed on two sites in 1913 to ensure that not more than one house was put on to each plot. A proposal to erect two blocks of flats to make 20 flats on one and 12 on the other was held reasonable.

2.   *Do the covenants impede that user?*

If the applicant did not consider that the covenant impeded or was likely to impede his proposed development he would not make the application under section 84 (1) and if the objector did not feel that the covenant impeded the user he would not object. An affirmative answer to question 2 will almost invariably follow an affirmative answer to question 1. If there is doubt about whether any land is affected by a restriction, or about the nature and extent of the restriction the appropriate procedure is to apply for construction of the restriction, under section 84 (2).

3.   *Does impeding the proposed user secure practical benefits to the objectors?*

The following decisions may help to give meaning to the phrase 'practical benefits'. The statute is silent on the matter.

(a) **Loss of privacy and view**

A proposed block of flats would have had a 'devastating effect' on the amenities and value of a house as the house's principal rooms would face it and be overlooked by it, *Re Mercian Housing Society's Application* (1971) 23 P & CR 116.

Gardens of existing houses would be overlooked by two proposed houses. One garden could be screened to some extent by a hawthorn hedge but as the Tribunal said, a hawthorn is a poor substitute for a covenant, *Re Gossip's Application* (1925) 25 P & CR 215[8].

(b) **Increase in density**

Covenants allowed one house per acre, the proposal was to put 32 houses onto four acres. It was held that this would be alien to the

---

[8] See also *Re Banks Application* (1976) 33 P & CR 138 ("direct view of the sea is of immense value").

character of the area, 'it is not merely the arithmetic of the density which matters, but the general effect on the amenity of the area', *Re Collins, Application* (1974) 30 P & CR 527.

A proposal to build ten houses on backland where covenants would allow none was refused. It would otherwise result in objectors finding 'dumped virtually on their back doors a group of houses with no apparent visual relationship with their own properties', *Re Patten Ltd's Application* (1975) 31 P & CR 180.

(c) Other loss of amenity

A proposed block of 12 flats would deprive the objectors of space, quiet, light and some sunlight, *Re Ward's Construction (Medway) Ltd's Application* (1973) 25 P & CR 223; another proposal would deprive objectors of 'peace and quiet and the feeling of openness which the restriction gave them', *Re Davies' Application* (1971) 25 P & CR 115. Both applications failed[9].

A local authority which had granted planning permission for six flats in a two-storey block objected validly that the block would injure the view from an old people's dwelling which they proposed to erect on the dominant land, *Re SJC Construction Co Ltd's Application* (1974) 28 P & CR 200.

Increased traffic, noise, fumes, vibration, dirt and the risk of accidents were important factors against the applicants in *Re Bass* (1973).

(d) Loss of value

Loss of amenity will often cause loss of value but the fact that it does not is not a reason for holding that the covenant does not secure a practical advantage. In *Re Collins* (1974) it was not disputed that the proposed development would not reduce the market value of existing houses. Nevertheless it was accepted as important that the objectors regarded the restrictions as having substantial advantage, some having bought their houses in reliance on them. Indeed in *Re Munday's Application* (1954) 7 P & CR 130 (a claim to declare a covenant obsolete) it was likely that a successful application would increase the value of the objectors' property by giving it a potential commercial user. The claim failed however as it was clear that the personal tastes of the objectors would be adversely affected if the covenant was lifted.

(e) "Thin end of the wedge" argument

It can be a relevant consideration that the proposal, though not particularly harmful in itself, must be rejected in case it gives rise to similar proposals which would succeed because the first had done so, and which would cumulatively be disadvantageous. In *Re Gossip* (1972) the applicant had converted two houses into flats in breach of covenant and now wished to build two further houses in their gardens.

---

[9] *Re Ballamy's Application* [1977] JPL 456 ("enjoyment of evening sunshine in the sun-lounge").

He argued that there had already been some breaches of covenant by other house-owners by conversions of single houses into flats but the Tribunal considered that these breaches had been minimal whereas a modification might be the "thin end of the wedge" for a considerable change in the amenities and character of the neighbourhood. The recent case of *Re Osborn* (1979) illustrates this consideration along with several others. The applicants wished to erect two three-storey blocks of flats on a large estate of eight-bedroomed houses. Sixty-three owners of such houses objected. It was held that if the applications were granted it would set an undesirable precedent for other developments on the estate, particularly as there was much profit in such developments. Other important considerations were that the building would be out of place in a high value, low density, single house estate; that the flats would be visually injurious there; and that the traffic noise generated by the greater numbers of people would be injurious.

The validity of the "thin end of the wedge" argument is not universally accepted. In *Re Forgacs' Application* (1976) 32 P & CR 464, Mr. J H Emlyn-Jones FRICS in his judgment quoted what he said in *Re Gaffney's Application* (1974), 35 P & CR 440 to the effect that if a modification is in itself unlikely to cause injury it should not be refused on the ground that later applications might do so. They should each be looked at on the merits when they arise and should then be rejected if need be.

4. *Are the benefits secured by the restrictions of substantial value or advantage to the objectors?*
The use of the words 'value or advantage' in harness was said by the Tribunal in *Re Bass* (1973) to indicate that pecuniary values are not the only things to be considered in this context and *Re Collins* (1974) and *Re Munday* (1954) support this. However, the benefits secured must be substantial. In *Re Dransfield's Application* (1975) 31 P & CR 192 the objector, in seeking to uphold a covenant made by the applicant himself only 20 years earlier, claimed that the proposed house would obstruct the view from the rear windows of his house and from the first floor terrace where he frequently entertained guests. It was held that the restriction which prevented building did not secure a substantial benefit to him and that £1,000 was adequate compensation in money terms[10].

5. *Is it contrary to the public interest to impede the proposed user?*
In *Re Collins* (1974) the Tribunal said that for an application to succeed on the ground of public interest 'it must be shown that that interest is so important and immediate as to justify the serious interference with private rights and the sanctity of contract.' Applications based on this ground seem to have a high rate of failure. We will examine three of the lines of approach which have been used.

---

[10] On the meaning of "substantial" see *Re Gaffney's Application* (1974) 35 P & CR 440.

(a) Shortage of accommodation

In *Re New Ideal Homes Ltd's Application* [1978] JPL 632 a covenant linked with planning permission allowed 79 houses to be built on a plot of land. The applicants asked for the covenant to be modified only four years after they had entered into it, to permit 150 houses to be built there. They claimed that the 1973/4 property collapse has made it uneconomic to build at such a low density and that the covenant was against the public interest in preventing them from satisfying the great need for housing locally. The Tribunal held that the restriction was not against the public interest merely because there was a housing need but modified it, on payment of compensation, because it did not secure practical benefits of substantial value to the objecting local authority.

Similarly in *Re Osborn* (1979) the Tribunal held that although it was government policy to encourage high density development, that did not mean that all low density development was against the public interest and that it ought to be replaced by high density development. In *Re Beardsley* (1972) an acute shortage of building land in a given area was held not of itself to prove that a restriction was contrary to the public interest, the question was to be considered in a wider context, having regard especially to the planning considerations mentioned in section 84 (1B).

(b) Existence of planning permission

It has been argued in several cases that where the local planning authority has granted planning permission a restriction which prevents the development from proceeding must be contrary to the public interest. That argument was firmly dealt with in *Re Bass* (1973) where the Tribunal said, 'a planning permission only says, in effect, that a proposal will be allowed; it implies perhaps that such a proposal will not be a bad thing but it does not necessarily imply that it will be positively a good thing and in the public interest, and that failure of the proposal to materialise would be positively bad. Many planning permissions have got through by the skin of their teeth'.

The Tribunal will resist attempts to turn the proceedings into a planning enquiry, by the introduction of miscellaneous documents concerning the planning of the vicinity or of wider areas. In *Re Collins* (1974) it refused to consider any documents save those which had been published, subjected to public enquiry and approved by the Minister, such as the approved town map or development plan.

(c) Economic advantages

In *Re Bass* (1973) it was said that the company had a need to expand its trunker park because mergers and rationalisations within the company required it to reorganise its distribution system. The Tribunal said that this was not an irrelevant factor but that it must be set against other questions, such as amenity, 'the proposition that this operation is in the public interest is strange indeed unless the public interest is to be equated to the economic benefits to this particular part of the beer trade'.

A case where the public interest argument succeeded was *Re S J C Construction Co Ltd* (1975). Here £47,000 worth of building work on flats had been done with planning permission from the local authority when the same authority issued a writ to enforce restrictive covenants which would have prevented the building of the flats. Modifications of the covenant to permit them to be built was allowed because: planning permission existed, the adverse effect on the dominant land would not be serious, there was a scarcity of building land in the area, the work already done would otherwise have been wasted, the applicants had gone ahead in good faith, and substantial compensation would be paid by them.

6 and 7.   *Would money be an adequate compensation to the objector?* It was emphasised by Lord Evershed MR in *Ghey and Galton's Application* [1957] 2 QB 650 that section 84 does not enable the court to expropriate objectors merely because an applicant may have put forward a worthy enterprise (in that case a proposal to turn a large house into a convalescent home). When modification is allowed money, in some cases coupled with a restriction on the development, must be capable of being an adequate compensation.

In *Re Carter* (1973) views of the sea from four dominant houses would have been impaired by a proposed bungalow. Sums of £200, £200 and £100 were awarded to three owners but nothing to the fourth as his loss was too small to be compensated. In addition an offer by the applicant to excavate so as to make the bungalow roof 2½ feet lower than originally intended was accepted and was made a condition of the modification order. *Re Banks Application* (1976) 33 P & CR 138 is a similar case but there compensation of £2,000 was ordered to be paid to each objector before the development was begun. In *Re Patten Ltd's Application* (1975) 31 P & CR 180 a proposed development of ten houses which would have caused overcrowding was allowed on payment of up to £750 compensation to objectors and the reduction of the number of houses to seven.

It might be thought that all compensation payments must in the nature of things be modest because large awards would indicate that the application should have been refused. This is not necessarily so. In *Re New Ideal Homes* (1978) an agreed sum of £51,000 was awarded, representing the reduction in purchase money which had been allowed because of the covenant when it was imposed. By section 84 (1) the Tribunal can award compensation either (a) for the loss or disadvantage suffered from the discharge or modification or (b) for making up for any effect the restriction had when it was imposed in reducing the consideration then received for the burdened land. In the *SJC Construction* case (1975) compensation was awarded so as to share the development value of the burdened land equally between the applicant and the objector. This decision purported to follow in principle *Wrotham Park Estate Co v Parkside Homes Ltd* (1973) 27 P & CR 296 where the compensation was calculated by taking 5 per cent of the profit made by the developer who had broken a layout covenant.

The basis of the award in the *SJC* case was upheld on appeal at (1975) 29 P & CR 322."

Preston and Newsom: *Restrictive Covenants Affecting Freehold Land* (6th edn. 1976), pp. v-vi.

"Enough of the decisions of the Lands Tribunal upon section 84 of the Law of Property Act 1925, as amended by the Law of Property Act 1969, have now appeared in the *Property and Compensation Reports* to show how the new rules are being applied. The Tribunal has made energetic and effective use of the new subsection (3A), which enables it to decide whether or not a given objector is entitled to the benefit of the relevant restriction, and, if he is not, to strike him out of the proceedings for modification of the restriction. Thus it has proved in a good many cases that no objector is entitled to be heard by the Tribunal, and the desired modification is then usually made with the minimum of delay, formality and expense. This change has been a great gain, since it has reduced the opportunities for obstruction by persons having no title to intervene. The Tribunal has also decided a number of cases at the substantive hearing, *i.e.* between the applicant and objectors who have been either proved or admitted to be entitled to the benefit of the restriction. The Tribunal takes great care to ensure that a proper case is made out, under the amended section, before interfering with the rights of such objectors. There has been no flood of modifications, though they have been made in a small number of cases in which they could not have been made under the old law. In a few of them, the Tribunal has awarded relatively small sums to the objectors by way of compensation. The new subsection allows the Tribunal, on the ground of public interest, to modify a restriction even where the result would be to cause substantial damage to objectors who are entitled to the benefit of the restriction. In a single exceptional case[11] that provision has been applied, and very substantial compensation was then awarded. The public interest provision has been invoked in many cases, but, with this one exception, always without success. The Tribunal has made it clear that the mere fact that the project proposed by the applicant has received planning permission is not enough. The most that the planning permission shows is that the proposals are not against the public interest, and perhaps also that they are reasonable within the meaning of paragraph (*aa*) of section 84 (1). This is by no means the same thing as finding that the unmodified restriction, in impeding them, operates against the public interest, which is the requirement of subsection (1A). The lesson of the decisions so far reported is that it is now slightly less difficult than it was before 1970 to persuade the Tribunal

---

[11] *Re SJC Construction Co Ltd's Application* (1974) 28 P & CR 200. An appeal to the Court of Appeal about the quantum of compensation failed: (1975) 29 P & CR 322.

to modify a restriction, but that it is still not at all easy to do so. Both before and after 1970, my own experience has been that I have never appeared for an objector who has lost, nor for an applicant who has won, except after forcing or persuading all the objectors to withdraw."

V.   Registered Land[12]

A restrictive covenant is a minor interest; and if it is to be enforceable against a purchaser of the burdened land, it needs to be protected as such[13]. Even if noted on the register, it will of course bind land only if it is of a character which would enable it to do so apart from the notice; noting does not add to its efficacy[14], but only prevents a diminution of its efficacy in relation to purchasers. The noting of the benefit of a covenant involves the further difficulty that it is often difficult to determine the extent to which the covenant runs with the land. The Registrar rightly regards the determination of such issues as not within his task.

"A note is made in the proprietorship register of the existence of positive covenants, and a copy of them is sewn up in the land or charge certificate, when they are created after the date of first registration. This procedure has been adopted, not because of any legal obligation, but because the Chief Land Registrar appreciates that when positive covenants are contained in a transfer which is filed in the registry they tend to be overlooked, or their exact nature forgotten, so that a vendor's solicitor might omit to take an indemnity covenant from the purchaser on a transfer of the land."[15]

LAND REGISTRATION ACT 1925

40. Creation and discharge of restrictive covenants. — (3) Entries shall be made on the register in the prescribed manner of all obligations and reservations imposed by the proprietor, of the release or waiver of any obligation or reservation, and of all obligations and reservations acquired by him for the benefit of the registered estate.

LAND REGISTRATION RULES 1925

78. Power for Registrar to decline to enter improper forms. — If it appears to the Registrar that any instrument or entry proposed to be entered or made in the register . . ., being a condition, does not run with the land, or is not capable of being legally annexed thereto, or of

---

[12] Cheshire, pp. 621–623; M & W, pp. 1068–1069; MM, p. 522; Farrand (2nd edn.), pp. 374–375, 427–429; Ruoff and Roper, pp. 715–720; Registered Land Practice Notes 1972, pp. 25–29, as amended: (1974) LS Gaz 395.
[13] See p. 125, ante.
[14] *Cator v Newton and Bates* [1940] 1 KB 415.
[15] Ruoff, pp. 116–117.

affecting assigns by registration of a notice or other entry, . . . he may decline to enter the same in the register, either absolutely or subject only to such modifications therein as he shall approve . . .

LAND REGISTRATION ACT 1925

50. Notices of restrictive covenants. — (1) Any person entitled to the benefit of a restrictive covenant or agreement (not being a covenant or agreement made between a lessor and lessee)[16] with respect to the building on or other user of registered land may apply to the registrar to enter notice thereof on the register, . . .; and where any such covenant or agreement appears to exist at the time of first registration, notice thereof shall be entered on the register. In the case of registered land the notice aforesaid shall take the place of registration as a land charge[17].

(2) When such a notice is entered the proprietor of the land and the persons deriving title under him (except incumbrancers or other persons who at the time when the notice is entered may not be bound by the covenant or agreement) shall be deemed to be affected with notice of the covenant or agreement as being an incumbrance on the land[18].

LAND REGISTRATION RULES 1925

212. Entry and discharge of restrictive covenants. — Restrictive covenants created under section 40, or noted against a title under section 50 of the Act, shall be entered in the Charges Register, in the method directed by section 50, and any release, waiver, discharge, or modification shall be noted on the register in such manner as the Registrar may direct.

VI. Law Commission Report on Restrictive Covenants (1967. Law Com No. 11)

The Law Commission recommends basic changes in the law in a series of 12 Propositions. Their proposals are specifically confined to restrictive covenants, but, in paragraph 30 of the Report, they say:

"The substance of our proposals is applicable in principle . . . to positive as well as to restrictive obligations, subject to any necessary modifications, and we consider that a common code could and should be devised from the Wilberforce recommendations and these Propositions."

---

[16] *Newman v Real Estate Debenture Corpn Ltd and Flower Decorations Ltd* [1940] 1 All ER 131.
[17] But, if the restrictive covenant was protected under L.C.A. 1972 before first registration, it will become unenforceable if no notice is entered on first registration; *Freer v Unwins Ltd* [1976] Ch 288, [1976] 1 All ER 634.
[18] *White v Bijou Mansions Ltd* [1937] Ch 610, [1937] 3 All ER 269 (lessee deemed to have notice of restrictive covenants entered on lessor's freehold registered title, even though he has no right to see it). For unregistered land, see p. 412, ante.

Paragraph 27 states the outline and scope of the Propositions:

"Briefly stated, these Propositions recommend the creation of a new interest in land called a Land Obligation, which will be available to regulate matters now dealt with by covenants as to user. Land Obligations will be capable of creation in respect of freehold or leasehold interests in land, but will not apply to rights between lessor and lessee in respect of the demised land. They will be imposed on specified land for the benefit of other specified land so that the burden and benefit will run automatically with the land until released, modified, discharged, or, for example, in the case of an obligation affecting a leasehold interest, brought to an end by effluxion of time: and they will be enforceable only by and against the persons currently concerned with the land as owners of interests in it or occupiers of it. They will thus in nature and attributes be more akin to easements than to covenants."

The Propositions "are intended to apply only to obligations entered into after a day to be appointed for the purposes of the new legislation (para. 34), and 'pre-appointed day' restrictive covenants should be left to take effect in accordance with the existing law" (para. 35).

The Law Commission is preparing a report on the reform of Positive and Restrictive Covenants, as the first of a series of reports on rights appurtenant to land. (Law Com No. 92, 13th Annual Report 1977–1978, para. 2.30).

13. Planning and Compulsory Purchase[1]

I. Planning by Covenant

It has been seen that it is possible for landowners to effect a measure of control over the development of land by selling or leasing land subject to covenants as to user[2]. Such private control can only have a limited effect. It can only be effective where a landowner is in control of a considerable area of undeveloped land, and has the foresight to devise a suitable system of obligations at a time when a demand for the development of that land is beginning to be felt — when that land

---

[1] Cheshire, 937–981; M & W, 1086–1108; MM, 532–543. See Heap, *Outline of Planning Law* (7th edn., 1978); Telling, *Planning Law and Procedure* (5th Edn., 1977); Davies, *Law of Compulsory Purchase and Compensation* (3rd edn., 1978); McCauslan, *Land, Law and Planning* (1975).

[2] Chap. 12, ante. See also Leasehold Reform Act 1967, which makes provision for schemes to replace the obligations resting on leaseholders who exercise their right of enfranchisement under the Act. The objects are to "maintain adequate standards of appearance and amenity, and regulate redevelopment in the area", which are essentially those of planning control. Such schemes are enforced by a system of charges, not covenants; the "landlord for the time being" (the previous landlord, a successor, or a local authority, or other body entrusted with the duty) has "the same powers and remedies under the Law of Property Act 1925 and otherwise as if he were a mortgagee by deed having power of sale and leasing and appointing a receiver." (s. 19.).

is "ripe for development". It also requires constant vigilance and determination to enforce the covenants over an indefinite period of time at the discretion of a succession of private owners who are not in any way responsible to the public, legally or politically, for ensuring that the policy is carried out or even that the controls actually imposed are desirable. And so, in spite of the many excellent schemes of residential development carried out under freehold and leasehold covenants in the more spacious suburbs of many large and small towns, including seaside resorts, spas and "garden cities",[3] a system of public control of the use and development of land had to be introduced. But planning control does not supersede control by private land covenants. The two systems co-exist.

II.   The Public Planning System

A.   Authorities[4]

A Minister of Town and Country Planning was first appointed in 1943, and his duties have now been inherited in substance by the Secretary of State for the Environment[5]. Local planning authorities administer the system of planning control in detail.

TOWN AND COUNTRY PLANNING ACT 1971

1.   Local planning authorities. — (1) Subject to the provisions of this section, the council of a county is the county planning authority for the county, and the council of a district is the district planning authority for the district. . . .[6]

(2A) References in this Act to a local planning authority shall, except as respects Greater London and the National Parks, be construed as references to a county planning authority and a district planning authority. . . .[7]

The new system of county and district planning authorities does away with the need for delegation of powers from county to district councils, except in Greater London. But this does not affect the general power of local planning authorities to delegate routine duties to their officers[8].

---

[3] See Burke, *Towns in the Making* (1971). For meaning of "development", see p. 783, post.
[4] Heap, pp. 31–37; Pl. Enc. 2: 2560–2071, 3702–3709.
[5] Secretary of State for the Environment Order (S.I. 1970 No. 1681).
[6] See *A-G v Taff-Ely Borough Council* (1979) 250 Estates Gazette 757.
[7] Inserted by the Local Government Act 1972, s. 182 (1). For the distribution of planning functions, see Sch. 16. For National Parks, see s. 182 (4)–(6). For London, see T.C.P.A. 1971, Sch. 3; and T.C.P. (Local Planning Authorities in Greater London) Regulations 1978 (S.I. 1978 No. 602).
[8] T.C.P.A. 1971, s. 4. Sch. 2 confers a wide power to set up committees; and s. 276 gives wide default powers to the Secretary of State. See Sch. 1 for joint planning boards.

B. Development Plans[9]

Development must normally conform with development plans made (after a survey) and constantly reviewed by local planning authorities. The system which formerly operated under the Town and Country Planning Act 1962 is being replaced by a new system introduced by the Town and Country Planning Act 1968. The object is to reduce delay and inflexibility in plans by making it unnecessary for the Secretary of State to approve (in normal cases) detailed or "local" plans as distinct from generalised "structure plans". The earlier system of plans has been "frozen", but the new system is only coming in gradually[10].

TOWN AND COUNTRY PLANNING ACT 1971

7. Preparation of structure plans. — (1) The local planning authority shall, within such period from the commencement of this section within their area as the Secretary of State may direct, . . . prepare and submit to him for his approval a structure plan for their area complying with the provisions of subsection (3) of this section.

(3) The structure plan for any area shall be a written statement —

(a) formulating the local planning authority's policy and general proposals in respect of the development and other use of land in that area (including measures for the improvement of the physical environment and the management of traffic);

(b) stating the relationship of those proposals to general proposals for the development and other use of land in neighbouring areas which may be expected to affect that area; and

(c) containing such other matters as may be prescribed or as the Secretary of State may in any particular case direct.

(5) A local planning authority's general proposals under this section with respect to land in their area shall indicate any part of that area (in this Act referred to as an "action area") which they have selected for the commencement during a prescribed period of comprehensive treatment, in accordance with a local plan prepared for the selected area as a whole, by development, redevelopment or improvement of the whole or part of the area selected, or partly by one and partly by another method, and the nature of the treatment selected[11].

(6) A structure plan for any area shall contain or be accompanied by such diagrams, illustrations and descriptive matter as the local planning authority think appropriate. . .

---

[9] Heap, pp. 38–81. Pl. Enc. 2: 2572–2607, 3689, 3704.

[10] For progress see (1974) J.P.L., pp. 501–503. For plans in London, see T.C.P.A. 1971, Sch. 4, and T.C.P. (Development Plans for Greater London) Regulations 1966 (S.I. 1966, No. 48, as amended by S.I. 1975 No. 1680).

[11] This often involves acquisition of land "for planning purposes" — see p. 845, post.

LOCAL GOVERNMENT ACT 1972

183. Discharge of functions of planning authorities. — (1) The functions of a local planning authority under sections 6 to 10 of the Town and Country Planning Act 1971 (surveys and structure plans) shall be exercisable by the county planning authority and references in those sections to a local planning authority shall be construed accordingly.

TOWN AND COUNTRY PLANNING ACT 1971

10C.[12] **Development plan schemes.** — (1) The functions of a local planning authority of preparing local plans under section 11 of this Act shall, subject to the following provisions of this section, be exercisable by the district planning authority.

(2) Subject to regulations under this section, it shall be the duty of the county planning authority in consultation with the district planning authorities to make, and thereafter to keep under review and amend, if they think fit, a scheme (to be known as a development plan scheme) for the preparation of local plans . . . and —

   (a) the scheme shall designate the local planning authority or authorities (whether county or district) by whom local plans are to be prepared for any such area . . . ; and
   (b) references in those sections to a local planning authority shall be construed accordingly.

   11. Preparation of local plans. — (2)[13] Where a structure plan for the area of a county planning authority has been approved by the Secretary of State, the local planning authority to whom it falls to prepare a local plan for any part of that area. . ., if they consider it desirable and they have not already done so, shall prepare one or more local plans for . . . the area.

   (3) A local plan shall consist of a map and a written statement and shall —

   (a) formulate in such detail as the authority think appropriate the authority's proposals for the development and other use of land in that part of their area or for any description of development or other use of such land (including in either case such measures as the authority think fit for the improvement of the physical environment and the management of traffic); and
   (b) contain such matters as may be prescribed or as the Secretary of State may in any particular case direct.

   (4) Different local plans may be prepared for different purposes for the same part of any area.

   (5) A local plan for any area shall contain, or be accompanied by, such diagrams, illustrations and descriptive matter as the local

---

[12] Inserted by Local Government Act 1972, s. 183 (2).
[13] Substituted by the Local Government Act 1972, Sch. 16, para. 1.

planning authority think appropriate for the purpose of explaining or illustrating the proposals in the plan . . .

(6) Where an area is indicated as an action area in a structure plan which has been approved by the Secretary of State, the local planning authority shall (if they have not already done so), as soon as practicable after the approval of the plan, prepare a local plan for that area.

Other provisions deal with publicity and the hearing of objections before plans formally come into effect, and alterations to and withdrawal of plans, after they have come into effect. There will normally be a public local inquiry into objections to a local plan, but an "examination in public" (into selected objections only) of a structure plan[14].

III.   The Meaning of "Development"

A.   The General Concept[15]

The concept of development is fundamental to planning law.

TOWN AND COUNTRY PLANNING ACT 1971

22.   Meaning of "development" and "new development".[16] — (1) In this Act, except where the context otherwise requires, "development", subject to the following provisions of this section, means the carrying out of building, engineering, mining or other operations in, on, over or under land, or the making of any material change in the use of any buildings or other land.

(2) The following operations or uses of land shall not be taken for the purposes of this Act to involve development of the land, that is to say:—

(a)   the carrying out of works for the maintenance, improvement or other alteration of any building, being works which affect only the interior of the building or which do not materially affect the external appearance of the building and (in either case) are not works for making good war damage or works begun after 5th December 1968 for the alteration of a building by providing additional space therein below ground;

(b)   the carrying out by a local highway[17] authority of any works required for the maintenance or improvement of a road, being works carried out on land within the boundaries of the road;

(c)   the carrying out by a local authority or statutory undertakers of any works for the purpose of inspecting, repairing or

---

[14] T.C.P.A., 1971, ss. 8–10, 12–21; T.C.P. (Amendment) Act 1972, ss. 1–4; T.C.P. (Structure and Local Plans) Regulations 1974 (S.I. 1974, No. 1486).

[15] Heap, pp. 82–100; Pl. Enc. 2: 2608–2620, 3: 685–686.

[16] For "new development" (T.C.P.A. 1971, ss. 22 (5)) see p. 856, post.

[17] For highways, see T.C.P.A. 1971, Part X.

renewing any sewers, mains, pipes, cables or other apparatus, including the breaking open of any street or other land for that purpose;

(d) the use of any buildings or other land within the curtilage of a dwellinghouse for any purpose incidental to the enjoyment of the dwellinghouse as such;

(e) the use of any land for the purposes of agriculture or forestry (including afforestation) and the use for any of those purposes of any building occupied together with land so used;

(f) in the case of buildings or other land which are used for a purpose of any class specified in an order made by the Secretary of State under this section, the use thereof for any other purpose of the same class.

(3) For the avoidance of doubt it is hereby declared that for the purposes of this section —

(a) the use as two or more separate dwellinghouses of any building previously used as a single dwellinghouse involves a material change in the use of the building and of each part thereof which is so used . . .

THE TOWN AND COUNTRY PLANNING (USE CLASSES) ORDER 1972[18]

2. Interpretation. — (1) The Interpretation Act 1889[19] shall apply to the interpretation of this order as it applies to the interpretation of an Act of Parliament.

(2) In this order —

"the Act" means the Town and Country Planning Act 1971;

"shop" means a building used for the carrying on of any retail trade or retail business wherein the primary purpose is the selling of goods by retail, and includes a building used for the purposes of a hairdresser, undertaker, travel agency, ticket agency or post office or for the reception of goods to be washed, cleaned or repaired, or for any other purpose appropriate to a shopping area, but does not include a building used as a funfair, amusement arcade, pin-table saloon, garage, launderette, petrol filling station, office, betting office, hotel, restaurant, snackbar or cafe or premises licensed for the sale of intoxicating liquors for consumption on the premises;

"office" includes a bank, and premises occupied by an estate agency, building society or employment agency, or (for office purposes only) for the business of car hire or driving instruction, but does not include a post office or betting office;

"post office" does not include any building used primarily for the sorting or preparation for delivery of mail or for the purposes of Post Office administration;

---

[18] S.I. 1972, No. 1385, made under T.C.P.A. 1971, s. 22 (2) (f), supra.
[19] Now Interpretation Act 1978.

"betting office" means any building in respect of which there is for the time being in force a betting office licence pursuant to the provisions of the Betting and Gaming Act 1960;

"launderette" includes any building used for the purpose of washing or cleaning clothes or fabrics in coin-operated machines;

"industrial building" means a building (other than a building in or adjacent to and belonging to a quarry or mine and other than a shop) used for the carrying on of any process[20] for or incidental to any of the following purposes, namely:—

(a) the making of any article or of part of any article, or

(b) the altering, repairing, ornamenting, finishing, cleaning, washing, packing or canning, or adapting for sale, or breaking up or demolition of any article, or

(c) without prejudice to the foregoing paragraphs, the getting, dressing or treatment of minerals,

being a process carried on in the course of trade or business other than agriculture, and for the purposes of this definition the expression "article" means an article of any description, including a ship or vessel;

"light industrial building" means an industrial building (not being a special industrial building) in which the processes carried on or the machinery installed are such as could be carried on or installed in any residential area without detriment to the amenity of that area by reason of noise, vibration, smell, fumes, smoke, soot, ash, dust or grit;

"general industrial building" means an industrial building other than a light industrial building or a special industrial building;

"special industrial building" means an industrial building used for one or more of the purposes specified in class V, VI, VII, VIII and IX referred to in the schedule to this order;

"motor vehicle" means any motor vehicle for the purposes of the Road Traffic Act 1960.

(3) References in this order to a building may, except where otherwise provided, include references to land occupied therewith and used for the same purposes.

3. **Use Classes.** — (1) Where a building or other land is used for a purpose of any class specified in the Schedule to this order, the use of such building or other land for any other purpose of the same class shall not be deemed for the purpose of the Act to involve development of the land[1].

---

[20] It is immaterial whether the process is carried on commercially or not: *Rael-Brook Ltd v Minister of Housing and Local Government* [1967] 2 QB 65, [1967] 1 All ER 262.

[1] Thus a change of use within a "use class" is not "material". Yet it can be validly prohibited by a condition in a planning permission, because the applicant can choose whether or not to accept a planning permission on those terms. See *Kingston-upon-Thames Royal London Borough Council v Secretary of State for the Environment* [1973] 1 WLR 1549, [1974] 1 All ER 193.

(2) Where a group of contiguous or adjacent buildings used as parts of a single undertaking includes industrial buildings used for purposes falling within two or more of the classes specified in the Schedule to this order as classes III to IX inclusive, those particular two or more classes may, in relation to that group of buildings, and so long as the area occupied in that group by either general or special industrial buildings is not substantially increased thereby, be treated as a single class for the purposes of this order[2].

(3) A use which is ordinarily incidental to and included in any use specified in the Schedule to this order is not excluded from that use as an incident thereto merely by reason of its specification in the said Schedule as a separate use.

SCHEDULE

Class I. — Use as a shop for any purpose except as:—
  (i) a shop for the sale of hot food;
  (ii) a tripe shop;
  (iii) a shop for the sale of pet animals or birds;
  (iv) a cats-meat shop;
  (v) a shop for the sale of motor vehicles.

Class II. — Use as an office for any purpose.

Class III. — Use as a light industrial building for any purpose.

Class IV. — Use as a general industrial building for any purpose.

Classes V–IX. — [Special industrial uses, listed in considerable detail in five separate use classes, and referred to as Special Industrial Groups A–E. The details are omitted here for reasons of space.]

Class X. — Use as a wholesale warehouse or repository for any purpose.

Class XI. — Use as a boarding or guest house, or an hotel providing sleeping accommodation.

Class XII. — Use as a residential or boarding school or a residential college.

Class XIII. — Use as a building for public worship or religious instruction or for the social or recreational activities of the religious body using the building.

Class XIV. — Use as a home or institution providing for the boarding, care and maintenance of children, old people or persons under disability, a convalescent home, a nursing home, a sanatorium or a hospital.

Class XV. — Use (other than residentially) as a health centre, a school treatment centre, a clinic, a creche, a day nursery or a dispensary, or use as a consulting room or surgery unattached to the residence of the consultant or practitioner.

---

[2] These are examples of planning units with multiple uses: see p. 792, post.

Class XVI. — Use as an art gallery (other than for business purposes), a museum, a public library or reading room, a public hall or an exhibition hall.

Class XVII. — Use as a theatre, cinema, music hall or concert hall.

Class XVIII. — Use as a dance hall, skating rink, swimming bath, Turkish or other vapour or foam bath or as a gymnasium or sports hall.

———————

It follows from this that land may be "developed" whether its physical state is altered by "operations" (building, engineering, etc.) or not; but, if not, the use of it must be subject to a "material" change. Often there is both an "operation" and a material change of use, as when a house is built on land hitherto used for farming. Yet every case has to be considered, according to its circumstances, as a question of fact and degree.

B. Operations[3]

CHESHIRE COUNTY COUNCIL *v* WOODWARD
[1962] 2 QB 126, [1962] 1 All ER 517 (Div Ct, Lord PARKER CJ, ASHWORTH and MACKENNA JJ)

The Cheshire County Council served an enforcement notice[4] on Woodward, requiring him to remove a large hopper and conveyor which he had installed in his coal-merchant's yard. The Minister of Housing and Local Government quashed the notice, holding that in the circumstances their installation did not involve development. The County Council appealed to the High Court[5] on the ground that, in so holding, the Minister had erred in law.

Held. There was no development, and the enforcement notice was lawfully quashed.

LORD PARKER CJ: Mr. Glover . . . has contended that the Minister was wrong in law — and this . . . can only be an appeal on a point of law — in holding that because the hopper does not rest of its own weight on the ground or is not attached to the ground, but is on four wheels, and because the conveyor is on wheels, for that reason and that reason alone the erection thereof cannot have been an operation constituting development.

The sections in question are not altogether easy to construe. Section 12 (2)[6], which defines "development", does so by reference to two matters, first, a change in use of the land, and secondly, quite regardless of the change of use, whether there has been a "carrying out

———————

[3] Heap, pp. 85–86; Pl. Enc. 2: 2611.
[4] For enforcement procedure, see pp. 811–816, post.
[5] For the jurisdiction of the courts, see pp. 805–806, post.
[6] T.C.P.A. 1947, now T.C.P.A. 1971, s. 22 (2).

of building, engineering, mining or other operations in, on, over or under land". I feel that the concept behind that definition is two-fold, first, in regard to change of use, one takes the land as it is and ascertains if it has been put to a different use, and secondly, and this is quite regardless of use, one has to ascertain whether the land itself has been changed by certain operations. . . .

Having got that far, the next question is: what sort of operations, in the case of an operation in or on the land, can be said to change the physical characteristics of the land. I do not think that there is any one test. The mere fact that something is erected in the course of a building operation which is affixed to the land does not determine the matter. Equally, as it seems to me, the mere fact that it can be moved and is not affixed does not determine the matter. It seems to me that the position is really rather analogous to the problems with which one is faced in dealing with fixtures when deciding what fixtures pass with the freehold. . . .

Here, as it seems to me, the inspector who reported and whose report has been accepted by the Minister, has considered the whole of the circumstances. . . .

On the face of it, therefore, he has not treated the mere fact that these two bits of equipment were on wheels as conclusive, nor has he treated it as conclusive that neither of them were affixed to or attached to the land. He has looked at the whole matter and said that in all the circumstances the installation did not involve development. In those circumstances, I for my part find it quite impossible to say that the Minister, who accepted that finding and recommendation, erred in law. . . .

Having come to the conclusion that it is impossible to say that the Minister erred in law, I would dismiss the appeal[7].

C.　"Material" Changes of Use[8]

EAST BARNET URBAN DISTRICT COUNCIL *v* BRITISH TRANSPORT COMMISSION

[1962] 2 QB 484, [1961] 3 All ER 878 (Div Ct, Lord PARKER CJ, ASHWORTH and VEALE JJ)

The appellants granted permission, expiring in 1958, to Vauxhall Motors, Ltd. to use land, owned by the British Transport Commission, as a transit depot for the handling and storage of crated motor vehicles. Part of this land had previously been used by coal merchants

---

[7] The construction of a permanent open-air model village has been treated as a "building operation"; *Buckinghamshire County Council v Callingham* [1952] 2 QB 515, [1952] 1 All ER 1166. Demolition was held to be an "operation" in *Coleshill and District Investment Co Ltd v Minister of Housing and Local Government* [1969] 1 WLR 746, [1969] 2 All ER 525; but that was a partial demolition, affecting the appearance of the buildings remaining on the site. The additional control afforded to buildings of special interest (see pp. 819–822, post) goes on the footing that demolition *cannot* be controlled as "development".

[8] Heap, pp. 87–89, Pl. Enc. 2: 2612–2614.

as a coal depot (the parts coloured pink and green on the map) and part had been vacant (coloured yellow). When Vauxhalls continued such use after 1958, the appellants served an enforcement notice on them and on the British Transport Commission, claiming that there had been a material change of use of this land. The justices quashed the enforcement notice.

Held. The change of use was not material and the enforcement notice was invalid.

LORD PARKER CJ: It seems clear to me that ... what is really to be considered is the character of the use of the land, not the particular purpose of a particular occupier. Some support for that is to be found in *Guildford R D C v Fortescue* ([1959] 2 QB 112, [1959] 2 All ER 111). In that case the justices had found that there had been no material change, albeit there had been an intensification of user in that case by an increase from 8 to 27 caravans. The court, while recognising that the intensification might be of such a nature as to amount to a change of use, felt unable in that case to interfere with the finding of the justices. ... Again, in *Marshall v Nottingham Corpn* ([1960] 1 WLR 707, [1960] 1 All ER 659, Glyn-Jones J, had to consider the question, not on a case stated, but on a trial, whether there had been a change of use and he deals with the sort of considerations which may arise in this way: "The mere fact that a dealer in the course of his business begins to deal in goods in which he had not dealt before does not necessarily involve a change, still less a material change, in his use of the land or premises where the business is carried on. ... This question, as I understand it, is one of fact and degree to be answered upon the evidence in this case: and my answer is that the plaintiff's company has not made a material change in the use of the land." It is to be observed that Glyn-Jones J, thought that the matter was one of fact and degree. For my part, I entirely accept that. ...

So far as the pink and light green area shown on the plan is concerned, it is land alongside a busy main line railway with sidings and had been used for storing coal which had been brought there by rail and would be taken away by rail. Assuming that any change in use, if it be a change, had been effected by the British Transport Commission themselves and not by Vauxhall's, it could not, I should have thought, be said that merely by changing the storage from coal to oil, if they were converting locomotives to diesel oil, there was a use for a different purpose. The mere fact that the commodity changes does not necessarily mean that the land is being used for a different purpose nor is there any relevance in the fact that the purpose for which the land is used is effected by other hands, in this case by Vauxhall's. Again, it can make no difference that the new commodity is not owned by the British Transport Commission. None of these considerations makes it necessary to say that the land is being used for a different purpose. ...

The intensification of an existing use may, as a question of fact and degree, sometimes constitute a material change.

In *Birmingham Corporation v Minister of Housing and Local Government and Habib Ullah* [1964] 1 QB 178, [1963] 3 All ER 668, houses, each previously let for occupation by a single family, were let with several families in each house. The Minister rejected the appellants' claim that there had been a material change of use. The Divisional Court allowed their appeal.

Lord PARKER CJ said at p. 190: "In my judgment the Minister erred in law in saying that because these houses remained residential or remained dwelling-houses in which people dwelt there could not be a material change of use. Whether there has been in any of the cases a material change of use is a matter of degree and fact, and, therefore, one for the Minister. . . ."

D. The Planning Unit

It is important to take a realistic view of the *unit* of property in relation to which the question of development control is to be considered in any particular case.

WOOD *v* SECRETARY OF STATE FOR THE ENVIRONMENT
[1973] 1 WLR 707, [1973] 2 All ER 404 (Div Ct, Lord WIDGERY CJ, CUSACK and CROOM-JOHNSON JJ)

Since before July 1948, parts of a farm had been used for selling agricultural produce. About 1968 by virtue of deemed planning permission[9] a conservatory was built on to the farmhouse. It was used mainly for selling, at a higher intensity than in other parts of the holding. In September 1972 an enforcement notice was served on the occupier alleging a material change of use and requiring her to discontinue the use as a shop. The occupier appealed to the Secretary of State who, after an inquiry, amended the enforcement notice to refer only to the conservatory but upheld the notice as amended.

Held (allowing the occupier's appeal). The permitted uses of the conservatory were the same as those of the farmhouse; and that, accordingly, the Secretary of State had erred in treating the conservatory in isolation as a planning unit separate from the farmhouse.

LORD WIDGERY CJ: . . . the Secretary of State has considered it right to treat the conservatory as though it were a separate unit. He has looked at it in isolation, and, looking at it in isolation, I have no doubt that he has correctly assessed the position in this way: that he finds that the conservatory was used primarily for selling and can quite properly in isolation be given the description of a retail shop. Accordingly, he has amended the enforcement notices so as drastically to reduce their effect, indeed, so as to exclude from their operation the

---

[9] P. 793, post (granted by virtue of the General Development Order).

entirety of this holding except for the conservatory, and the conservatory remains in the enforcement notice on the basis that it is a retail shop, and, as things stand, the appellant is required to discontinue the use of the conservatory as a retail shop.

The question for us is whether in reaching that conclusion the Secretary of State was right in law. I would approach this problem first of all by assuming that the conservatory had not been a later addition but had been a part of the original house when it was built. If that were the situation, it would seem to me abundantly clear that unless there are very special circumstances not shown in the documents before us it would not be proper to regard the conservatory as a separate planning unit, that is to say, separate from the building as a whole. . . .

The first case to which we have been referred is *Brooks v Gloucestershire County Council* (1967) 66 LGR 386. . . . The interesting thing about that case in my judgment is that it does support the view that in that somewhat similar problem to the present the proper approach was not to ask whether one room had become a shop and another room a restaurant but to ask oneself whether the building as a whole had suffered a material change of use. . . .

. . . There was a further decision of this court in *Burdle v Secretary of State for the Environment* [1972] 1 WLR 1207, [1972] 3 All ER 240. In that case Bridge J . . . [said]: "It may be a useful working rule to assume that the unit of occupation is the appropriate planning unit, unless and until some smaller unit can be recognised as the site of activities which amount in substance to a separate use both physically and functionally." That authority seems to me to support the view, which I would think to be right without such assistance, that it can rarely if ever be right to dissect a single dwelling house and regard one room in isolation as being an appropriate planning unit for present purposes.

Then the question arises: does it make any difference that this conservatory was not an original part of the house but was added later? Does that in any way justify the conclusion to treat it in isolation as a separate planning unit? The position with regard to new buildings is now covered by section 33 (2) of the Town and Country Planning Act 1971, which provides:

"Where planning permission is granted for the erection of a building, the grant of permission may specify the purposes for which the building may be used; and if no purpose is so specified, the permission shall be construed as including permission to use the building for the purpose for which it is designed."

Mr. Rich argues that this conservatory was erected under deemed planning permission derived from the Town and Country Planning General Development Order 1963, that that permission was possible only because it was a dwelling house which was being extended and improved and, therefore, under section 33 (2) of the Act of 1971 the only permitted use of this new part of the building, namely, the conservatory, is for residential purposes. The argument is attractive, and no doubt section 33 applies strictly in accordance with its terms in the more common example of a case where a new separate building is erected, but it seems to me that one must have regard to the fact that where an addition is made to a building under the General Development Order that addition is part of the original building. It is permitted only because it is an extension to or addition to the original building, and it seems to me that it would be almost unarguable that it did not take upon itself the characteristic of the orginal building in all respects, and I think that that is so.

Accordingly, it seems to me that the permitted uses in the conservatory here are the same as the permitted uses in the house, and, since it has been found that since 1948 the uses in the house have included the sale of imported horticultural produce, well, so does the conservatory. . . . I would therefore allow the appeal and send the case back to the Secretary of State for him to reconsider it in the light of the court's opinion.

There may, therefore, be multiple uses of a "unit" of land, sometimes with a separate area for each[10], sometimes with predominant and ancillary uses[11], sometimes with seasonal changes.

WEBBER *v* MINISTER OF HOUSING AND LOCAL GOVERNMENT
[1968] 1 WLR 29, [1967] 3 All ER 981 (CA; Lord DENNING MR, DIPLOCK and EDMUND DAVIES, LJJ)

LORD DENNING MR: The owner is a farmer at Axe Farm, Axmouth, near Seaton. He has a four-acre field. Since April 1960, this field has been used extensively for camping in the summer season between Easter and the end of September. The campers bring caravans, tents and Dormobiles to the field, but they are removed at the end of the summer. In the winter months the field has been used for grazing cattle, except on Saturdays, when it is used as a football pitch. It is also used on occasion for flower shows and other local events, but not frequently.

On September 3 1965, the Devon County Council, who are the local planning authority, served on the owner an enforcement notice requiring him to remove caravans, tents and Dormobiles within 28 days. He appealed. The Minister dismissed his appeal, and the Divisional Court upheld the Minister's decision[12]. He now appeals, with leave, to this court. . . . The "normal use" of a piece of land is to

---

[10] *Hartnell v Minister of Housing and Local Government* [1965] AC 1134, [1965] 1 All ER 490; *De Mulder v Secretary of State for the Environment* [1974] QB 792, [1974] 1 All ER 776.

[11] *Vickers-Armstrong v Central Land Board* (1957), 9 P & CR 33; *Mansi v Elstree RDC* (1964), 16 P & CR 153; and see p. 786, n. 2, ante.

[12] (1967) 65 L.G.R. 332.

be found by looking at its use from year to year over a considerable period. If you were to ask the owner: "What do you normally use this field for?" he would reply: "In the summer months for camping and in the winter months for grazing." In short, for two purposes. So long as he continues that normal use from year to year, there is no material change of use. . . .

By way of contrast from the "normal use", there is the "occasional use" of a piece of land. This arises when it is used on occasions for a purpose other than its normal use, such as for a football match, a flower show or a fete. So long as these do not amount to more than 28 days in the year, the occupier is covered by article 3 of the Town and Country Planning General Development Order 1963[13]. . . .

Applying these considerations to the present case, it is plain on the facts that ever since 1960 the normal use of this four-acre field has been a seasonal use, camping during the summer and grazing during the winter. That normal use continued for more than four years. The enforcement notice in September 1965 came too late. . . .

I would only add that if the normal use is abandoned for a time, a resumption of it afterwards would need planning permission[14].

IV. Planning Permissions

A. Automatic Permissions[15]

TOWN AND COUNTRY PLANNING ACT 1971

24. Development orders. — (1) The Secretary of State shall by order (in this Act referred to as a "development order") provide for the granting of planning permission.

(2) A development order may either —
  (a) itself grant planning permission for development specified in the order, or for development of any class so specified; or
  (b) in respect of development for which planning permission is not granted by the order itself, provide for the granting of planning permission by the local planning authority (or, in the cases hereinafter provided, by the Secretary of State) on an application in that behalf made to the local planning authority in accordance with the provisions of the order.

Under section 24 of the Town and Country Planning Act 1971 the Secretary of State has made general and special development orders giving automatic permission for various kinds of development. The only order which need to be noticed here is the Town and Country

---

[13] Now T.C.P. General Development Order 1977 (S.I. 1977 No. 289).
[14] See *Hartley v Minister of Housing and Local Government* [1970] 1 QB 413, [1969] 3 All ER 1658.
[15] Heap, 101-111. Pl. Enc. 2: 2628-2631.

Planning General Development Order 1977 (the "G.D.O")[16], which among other things lists 23 classes of permitted development, subject to various qualifications[17]. But article 4 of the Order empowers the Secretary of State to direct, or consent to, a withdrawal of the automatic permission in general or specific cases, *without* giving any owner affected a chance to object[18].

Other articles in the G.D.O. prescribe in detail the procedure to be followed in regard to making specific planning applications.

B.   Specific Permissions[19]

TOWN AND COUNTRY PLANNING ACT 1971

23. **Development requiring planning permission.** — (1) Subject to the provisions of this section[20], planning permission is required for the carrying out of any development of land.

29. **Determination of applications.** — (1) ... where an application is made to a local planning authority for planning permission, that authority, in dealing with the application, shall have regard to the provisions of the development plan, so far as material to the application[1] and to any other material considerations, and —

    (*a*) ... may grant planning permission, either unconditionally or subject to such conditions as they think fit; or

    (*b*) may refuse planning permission[2].

Section 23 of the 1971 Act dispenses with the need for any planning permission at all in certain special cases; and permission is "deemed" to be granted in certain other special cases[3].

Sections 25–28 of the Act of 1971, and provisions in the G.D.O. of 1973, govern the procedure for making planning applications.

---

[16] S.I. 1977 No. 289. The G.D.O. is of immense practical importance, but too detailed to reproduce here.

[17] Article 3 and Sch. 1.

[18] Owners affected are entitled to compensation, as of right, for consequent loss of development value, etc., on the footing of a revocation of permission, if after G.D.O. permission is withdrawn they apply for a specific planning permission and meet with a refusal, or a permission subject to burdensome conditions: T.C.P.A. 1971, s. 165. For compensation on revocation see p. 855, post. And see *Cole v Somerset County Council* [1957] 1 QB 23, [1956] 3 All ER 531.

[19] Heap, pp. 112–124; Pl. Enc. 2: 2621–2627, 2632–2673.

[20] These provisions are too specialised to be considered in this chapter. Many relate to uses dating back to 1948, when T.C.P.A. 1947 came into effect. See *LTSS Print and Supply Services v Hackney London Borough Council* [1976] QB 663, [1976] 1 All ER 311.

[1] See *Enfield London Borough Council v Secretary of State for the Environment* (1974) 233 Estates Gazette 53.

[2] On the implications of this, see T.C.P.A. 1971, s. 289, and *Westminster Bank Ltd v Minister of Housing and Local Government* [1971] AC 508, [1970] 1 All ER 734. Adverse planning decisions *may* justify serving a purchase notice, or claiming compensation; see p. 847–849 and 855–857, post.

[3] See T.C.P.A. 1971, ss. 40, 64, 270. See also Parts XI (statutory undertakers) and XIV (Crown land; minerals; other special cases).

Permissions normally "enure for the benefit of the land", and may be retrospective[4].

There is no obligation to carry out development authorised by a planning permission. But if it is carried out, there can be no continuation of, or reversion to, any use of the land which is inconsistent with what is authorised. Any further change (including a reversion to a previous use) will, if material, constitute fresh development.

PETTICOAT LANE RENTALS LTD *v* SECRETARY OF STATE FOR THE ENVIRONMENT
[1971] 1 WLR 1112, [1971] 2 All ER 793 (Div Ct, Lord PARKER CJ, WIDGERY LJ and BRIDGE J)

A cleared bomb-site in London was let out for daily use by market traders with stalls. Planning permission was then given for redevelopment, in the form of a commercial building erected on the site on pillars so that the ground area was open on all sides, and the permission stated that this area was for use as parking and loading space and "market trading on Sundays". Market traders used the ground area on weekdays. An enforcement notice was served requiring the discontinuance of the weekday trading, and was upheld on appeal. On further appeal to the Divisional Court:

Held. Trading on weekdays was not an authorised use.

WIDGERY LJ: . . . Where, as here, one has a clear area of land subsequently developed by the erection of a building over the whole of that land . . . in my judgment one gets an entirely new planning unit created by the new building. The land as such is merged in that new building and a new planning unit with no planning history is achieved. That new planning unit, the new building, starts with a nil use, that is to say, immediately after it was completed it was used for nothing, and thereafter any use to which it is put is a change of use, and if that use is not authorised by the planning permission, it is a use which can be restrained by planning control. As in *Prossor's* case, (1968) 67 LGR 109, it seems to me to make no difference whether the old use sought to be restored was expressly extinguished by the new planning permission, or whether it was merely omitted from the terms of grant in that permission. The fact that it is not authorised means that it is something which necessarily can be controlled because it is a change of use from the nil use which follows the erection of a new planning unit.

Mr. Rich has strenuously argued that notwithstanding the doctrine in *Prossor's* case and the considerations to which I have referred, the ground floor should retain in some way the existing use to which the old building site had been put. He also seeks to obtain some assistance from the fact that the ground floor in the present case is not enclosed. With the realism which his argument showed he realised that it would be very difficult to argue that with an enclosed ground floor the pre-

---

[4] T.C.P.A. 1971, ss. 33, 32.

development use of the open space had survived, but he says that as the ground floor is not enclosed, as it is therefore still an open space in one sense, then those pre-development uses survive. I can see no substance in that argument at all. Whether the ground floor is enclosed or not enclosed, it is part of the new building. The new building embraces the land and accordingly it is a new entity; the conclusion is that to which I have referred. I would therefore dismiss the appeal.

A change in the terms of a planning permission before the authorised development takes place would amount to a fresh planning permission, needing to be granted by the authority, or by its officer duly authorised by lawful delegation of power to act, in the same manner as the first permission. But if a change in the terms of a permission is no more than a trivial variation this is treated as being within the terms of the permission itself; and it is lawful for local planning authorities to empower their officers to decide when any such proposed variation is trivial.

In *Lever (Finance) Ltd v Westminster (City) London Borough Council* [1971] 1 QB 222, [1970] 2 All ER 496, the architect thought it desirable to make alterations in the detailed siting of houses about to be built by virtue of a planning permission granted by the defendants. The planning officer responsible, on being asked whether the alterations were "material", replied that they were not. The work therefore went ahead. Later the defendants notified the plaintiffs that the development in its altered form was not authorised by them; whereupon the plaintiffs issued a writ claiming a declaration that they were entitled to carry out the altered development project. The plaintiffs succeeded at first instance and again on appeal.

Lord DENNING MR said, at p. 230: "In my opinion a planning permission covers work which is specified in the detailed plans and any immaterial variation therein. . . . It is obvious that, as the developer proceeds with the work, there will necessarily be variations from time to time. Things may arise which were not foreseen. It should not be necessary for the developers to go back to the planning authority for every immaterial variation. The permission covers every variation which is not material. But then the question arises: Who is to decide whether a variation is material or not? In practice it has been the planning officer. This is a sensible practice and I think we should affirm it. If the planning officer tells the developer that a proposed variation is not material, and the developer acts on it, then the planning authority cannot go back on it."[5]

---

[5] See also *Norfolk County Council v Secretary of State for the Environment* [1973] 1 WLR 1400, [1973] 3 All ER 673; *Western Fish Products v Penwith District Council* (1979) 38 P & CR 7.

C. Time Limits and Outline Permissions[6]

A normal requirement in planning permissions is that development must begin within a stated time. This is now regulated by statute, which pays special attention to "outline" permissions. Article 5 of the G.D.O. gives discretion[7] to the local planning authority to grant an application for "outline" permission, if the development comprises building. This is a decision in principle, leaving details ("reserved matters") to be dealt with in subsequent applications.

TOWN AND COUNTRY PLANNING ACT 1971

41. Limit of duration of planning permission. — (1) Subject to the provisions of this section, every planning permission granted or deemed to be granted shall be granted or, as the case may be, be deemed to be granted, subject to the condition that the development to which it relates must be begun not later than the expiration of —

(*a*) five years beginning with the date on which the permission is granted or, as the case may be, deemed to be granted; or

(*b*) such other period (whether longer or shorter) beginning with the said date as the authority concerned with the terms of the planning permission may direct, being a period which the authority considers appropriate having regard to the provisions of the development plan and to any other material considerations.

(2) If planning permission is granted without the condition required by subsection (1) of this section, it shall be deemed to have been granted subject to the condition that the development to which it relates must be begun not later than the expiration of five years beginning with the date of the grant. . . .

42. Outline planning permission. — (1) In this section and section 41 of this Act "outline planning permission" means planning permission granted, in accordance with the provisions of a development order, with the reservation for subsequent approval by the local planning authority or the Secretary of State of matters (referred to in this section as "reserved matters") not particularised in the application.

(2) Subject to the provisions of this section, where outline planning permission is granted for development consisting in or including the carrying out of building or other operations, it shall be granted subject to conditions to the following effect —

(*a*) that, in the case of any reserved matter, application for approval must be made not later than the expiration of three years beginning with the date of the grant of outline planning permission; and

---

[6] Heap, pp. 124–136, Pl. Enc. 2: 2692–2704, 3: 869.
[7] Subject to a right of appeal to the Secretary of State.

(b) that the development to which the permission relates must be begun not later than whichever is the later of the following dates —

    (i) the expiration of five years from the date of the grant of outline planning permission; or

    (ii) the expiration of two years from the final approval of the reserved matters or, in the case of approval on different dates, the final approval of the last such matter to be approved.

(3) If outline planning permission is granted without the conditions required by subsection (2) of this section, it shall be deemed to have been granted subject to those conditions.

(4) The authority concerned with the terms of an outline planning permission may, in applying subsection (2) of this section, substitute, or direct that there be substituted, for the periods of three years, five years or two years referred to in that subsection such other periods respectively (whether longer or shorter) as they consider appropriate.

(5) The said authority may, in applying the said subsection, specify, or direct that there be specified, separate periods under paragraph (a) of the subsection in relation to separate parts of the development to which the planning permission relates; and, if they do so, the condition required by paragraph (b) of the subsection shall then be framed correspondingly by reference to those parts, instead of by reference to the development as a whole.

(6) In considering whether to exercise their powers under subsections (4) and (5) of this section, the said authority shall have regard to the provisions of the development plan and to any other material considerations.

44. Termination of planning permission by reference to time limit. — (1) The following provisions of this section shall have effect where, by virtue of section 41 or 42 of this Act, a planning permission is subject to a condition that the development to which the permission relates must be begun before the expiration of a particular period and that development has been begun within that period but the period has elapsed without the development having been completed.

(2) If the local planning authority are of opinion that the development will not be completed within a reasonable period, they may serve a notice (in this section referred to as a "completion notice") stating that the planning permission will cease to have effect at the expiration of a further period specified in the notice, being a period of not less than twelve months after the notice takes effect[8].

Thus, subject to express substitution by a planning authority of different periods, there is, in normal planning permissions, a standard

---

[8] A completion notice must be confirmed by the Secretary of State who may extend the period stated in it and must first grant a hearing if required; sub-ss. (3), (4).

five-year dead-line for beginning development, but in the case of "outline" permissions there is to be a standard three-year dead-line for seeking approval for all "reserved matters" (i.e. permission in detail) followed by a standard two-year dead-line for beginning development after final approval, or alternatively an *overall* dead-line of five years, whichever is longer[9]. And where these conditions apply, local planning authorities have a further power to serve a "completion notice", subject to Ministerial confirmation, requiring development to be completed within a specified period of not less than a year[10].

HERON CORPORATION LTD *v* MANCHESTER CITY COUNCIL
[1978] 1 WLR 937, [1978] 3 All ER 1240 (CA, Lord DENNING MR, ORR and BRIDGE LJJ)

Developers obtained "outline" permission for a complex urban redevelopment project, and then submitted details of the "reserved matters". At that point certain existing buildings on the site became "listed" under section 54 of the 1971 Act (p. 819 post).

LORD DENNING MR: The developers were thus faced with a problem. They had to revise their development plans so as to retain the listed buildings within the new complex of buildings there. It meant altering the layout and the phasing. . . . Faced with this new problem, the developers made a fresh layout and a fresh phasing. The various offices, shops, hotel, and so forth, were placed in different positions from the original layout: and the phasing was different.

Having got this fresh plan prepared, the developers in August 1975 applied for approval of the first phase of it. They were very anxious to retain their original grant of outline planning permission — for reasons which I will explain later — but they wanted to alter the details. So they applied under this heading for "Approval of reserved matters following grant of outline permission." . . . At the same time the developers appended to this application a plan showing the amended site layout and the new anticipated phasing of development.

The council did not give their approval to this change of plan. . . . Their main point was that the original grant of outline planning permission did not cover this new application. The council said that the developers ought to apply for a new grant of outline planning permission. . . . Faced with these objections, the developers on 26 March 1976 took out an originating summons seeking a declaration in effect that this application for approval of reserved matters was a valid application: and that it was not necessary for them to apply

---

[9] For difficulties over an "outline" permission before the statute, see *Kent County Council v Kingsway Investments (Kent) Ltd* [1971] AC 72, [1970] 1 All ER 70, p. 803, post.

[10] Conditions or rather "limitations" may prescribe when a change of use must itself end, or works be removed; these are temporary planning permissions and they are the exception rather than the rule: T.C.P.A. 1971, s. 30.

afresh for a new grant of outline planning permission. On 30 July 1976, Sir Douglas Frank Q.C. decided in favour of the developers. The council appeal to this court.

I said earlier that the developers wished to retain their original grant of outline planning permission: and did not wish to have to apply for a new outline planning permission. So they deliberately confined their application to "approval of reserved matters." There were good reasons for this: an application for outline planning permission is in law an "application for planning permission." It has to comply with all the requirements of the Town and Country Planning General Development Order . . . and in particular article 5 which requires it to be on a special form and accompanied by all the plans and drawings: and in accordance with the notices under the Act, and the various consultations. Whereas an application for "approval of reserved matters" need only be in writing under article 6 and without all the various notices and consultations. But apart from these there are often important consequences following on a grant of outline planning permission. Once granted, an outline permission is a valuable commodity which is annexed to the land. It runs with the land from purchaser to purchaser and enhances its value considerably. Often enough contracts of sale are concluded only subject to planning permission being granted. Everyone realises that it is of great worth. The date of the grant is also very important: because less tax may be payable on a grant before 1974 than after it. So it may be very important for a developer to keep his original grant rather than have to apply for a new one.

By contrast the "reserved matters" are matters of detail which are reserved for subsequent consideration by the planning authority. In particular the planning authority, when it grants outline permission, makes it subject to various conditions such as that detailed plans have to be submitted for approval, and the work is not to be begun until approval has been granted. The matters so reserved by the conditions are called "reserved matters" and are recognised by section 42 of the Act of 1971. That section sets a time limit for an application for approval. It is three years from the date when outline planning permission was given. But the approval, once given, relates back to the original grant of outline planning permission: so that the effective date of the grant is still the date of the outline, and not the date of the subsequent approval. . . . I see no reason why the application for approval of the reserved matter should cover the whole site. When a big development is in progress — when it is done in stages or phases — an application can be made for approval of the plan for each part or phase in time, without the developer committing himself to the details of a later stage or phase.

I must, however, add this word of warning. When an application is made for approval of a reserved matter, the application must be within the ambit of the outline planning permission and must be in accordance with the conditions annexed to the outline permission.

There is no provision whereby the applicant can, at his own instance, modify the permission. Only the planning authority can do it under section 45 of the Act. If the applicant desires to depart in any significant respect from the outline permission or the conditions annexed to it, he must apply for a new planning permission. . . . A developer is not required to complete every part of the permitted work: unless there is a special condition to that effect.

Lastly it was suggested that the original layout and phasing could not be varied by an application for approval of reserved matters: and that it could only be done by a new application for planning permission. I cannot agree. The original permission made it clear that the layout and phasing were for subsequent approval and could be altered phase by phase.

I find myself therefore in agreement with the declarations made by Sir Douglas Frank Q.C. . . . It seems to me, therefore, that the developers in August 1975 made a perfectly good application for approval of reserved matters, and it is for the council to consider the application on its planning merits. If refused, the developers can of course appeal to the Secretary of State. As I say, there is nothing wrong or invalid in the application. I would therefore dismiss the appeal.

D. Planning Conditions[11]

Conditions imposed by planning authorities must be reasonable and must be imposed for proper planning purposes, both in principle *and* in detail; if not, they are *ultra vires* and consequently invalid. Subject to this the authorities have complete discretion in deciding what conditions to impose[12].

In *Pyx Granite Co Ltd v Minister of Housing and Local Government* [1958] 1 QB 554, [1958] 1 All ER 625 the company was granted planning permission to quarry in the Malvern Hills, subject to conditions as to the tidiness of the site and the times at which crushing and screening could be operated. The Court of Appeal held[13] that these conditions were valid. Lord DENNING said at p. 572: "The principles to be applied are not, I think, in doubt. Although the planning authorities are given very wide powers to impose 'such conditions as they think fit'[14], nevertheless the law says that those conditions, to be valid, must fairly and reasonably relate to the permitted development. The planning authority are not at liberty to use their powers for an ulterior object, however desirable that object may seem to them to be in the public interest. If they mistake or misuse their powers, however bona fide, the court can interfere by declaration and injunction."

---

[11] Heap, pp. 130–136; Pl. Enc. 2: 2646–2662.
[12] T.C.P.A. 1971, s. 29 (1) (*a*); see p. 794, ante.
[13] Reversed on other grounds in the House of Lords [1960] AC 260.
[14] T.C.P.A. 1947, s. 14 (1), now T.C.P.A. 1971, s. 29 (1) (*a*).

In *Fawcett Properties Ltd v Buckingham County Council* [1961] AC 636, [1960] 3 All ER 503, the county council had given planning permission to a farmer for the erection of two cottages for farm workers in the green belt. Permission was subject to condition that they should be occupied by members of the agricultural population. The cottages were subsequently purchased by the appellant who challenged the validity of the condition. The House of Lords upheld it. Lord DENNING said, at p. 679: "[The best view is to put] planning conditions on much the same footing as by-laws made by a local authority, to which they are so closely akin. Indeed, I see no difference in principle between them. As with by-laws so with planning conditions. The courts can declare them void for unreasonableness but they must remember that they are made by a public representative body in the public interest. When planning conditions are made, as here, so as to maintain the green belt against those who would invade it, they ought to be supported if possible. And credit ought to be given to those who have to administer them, that they will be reasonably administered: see *Kruse v Johnson*, [1898] 2 QB 91, 99.

Such being the tests, how does this condition measure up to them? Mr. Megarry contended that the condition was totally unrelated to any legitimate planning considerations. He put forward the wide proposition that the statute gives the planning authority power to say in what *way* property is to be used: but no power to say by what *persons* it is to be used. I cannot subscribe to this proposition for a moment. I should have thought that a planning authority could very reasonably impose a condition that cottages were to be reserved for farm-workers and not let to city dwellers: for this would help to preserve the green belt. . . . It seems to me that the condition fairly and reasonably relates to the permitted development. Its effect is to ensure that the cottages will be occupied by persons who will help to maintain the normal life and character of this part of the green belt and not by outsiders to use as a dormitory. The cottages are for farm-workers or for men who work at the smithy shoeing horses, at the mill grinding the corn, or at the saw mills cutting up wood; or in modern times at the milk depot bottling the milk or at the repair shop mending the tractors; and so forth. They are not for people who go up and down to London every day."

If a condition is invalidated, does the permission survive without the condition; or is the permission also invalidated? This question is essentially one of planning policy, and for that reason it would be more in accordance with the rationale of the legislation for the courts to remit the case to the planning authority. But in fact they have taken to deciding this question. In reality it is artificial to separate conditions from permissions, except for the purposes of testing their validity. It is the project of development as a whole which needs to be considered in each case, in order to decide as a question of policy whether its implementation is desirable in the public interest; and the making of policy decisions, if intra vires, is within the competence of the appropriate planning authorities, not of the courts.

KENT COUNTY COUNCIL *v* KINGSWAY INVESTMENTS (KENT) LTD
[1971] AC 72, [1970] 1 All ER 70 (HL, Lords REID, MORRIS OF BORTH-Y-GEST, GUEST, UPJOHN and DONOVAN)

In 1952 Kent County Council granted outline planning permission to the plaintiffs to develop 365 acres, subject to a condition by which the permission would expire after the end of three years[15], unless within that time detailed plans had been submitted to and approved by them. The plaintiffs sought a declaration that the condition was unreasonable and void[16] and that the permission of 1952 still subsisted, freed from the condition.

Held. (Lords REID and UPJOHN dissenting). The condition was valid. Even if the condition had been invalid, the development would be unauthorised, for the permission could not stand without it[17].

LORD MORRIS OF BORTH-Y-GEST: The General Development Order, 1950[18] . . . makes provision . . . for appeal to the Minister. It would not be sensible to hold that though there is provision for appeal any success that an appeal might seem to yield would all be illusory and in vain . . . As a matter of common sense and to bring about an effective result I would consider that development could be commenced if in spite of a refusal of approval by the local planning authority the Minister held on appeal that there should not have been a refusal. This is not a matter of filling in gaps in legislative provisions. It is merely a matter of ensuring that each of two provisions is to have rational effect . . . I consider, therefore, in agreement with the result reached by Lord Denning MR, that [the condition] was not void. . . .

I turn . . . to consider whether, on the basis (contrary to my view) that [the condition] was void, the permissions nevertheless subsist . . . There might be cases where permission is granted and where some conditions, perhaps unimportant or perhaps incidental, are merely superimposed. In such cases if the conditions are held to be void the permission might be held to endure just as a tree might survive with one or two of its branches pruned or lopped off. It will be otherwise if some condition is seen to be a part, so to speak, of the structure of the permission so that if the condition is hewn away the permission falls

---

[15] Eventually extended to ten years.

[16] Chiefly on the supposed ground that, by causing the outline permission to terminate automatically, it would unwarrantably preclude the Minister (now the Secretary of State) from deciding any appeal on detailed plans which might have come before him.

[17] The developers thus failed in their contention that they had an effective planning permission. They had succeeded in the Court of Appeal (Lord DENNING dissenting) where it was held that the condition was void but "severable", thus leaving the permission intact without the condition.

[18] Now S.I. 1977, No. 289. See p. 794, ante.

away with it ... I agree with the learned judge[19] and with Lord Denning MR ... that if [the condition] is void it cannot be deleted so as to leave the permission ... still subsisting[20].

E.   "Called In" Applications and Appeals[1]

TOWN AND COUNTRY PLANNING ACT 1971

35.   Reference of applications to Secretary of State. — (1) The Secretary of State may give directions requiring applications for planning permission, or for the approval of any local planning authority required under a development order, to be referred to him instead of being dealt with by local planning authorities.

(5) Before determining an application referred to him under this section, other than an application for planning permission referred to a Planning Inquiry Commission under section 48 of this Act[2], the Secretary of State shall, if either the applicant or the local planning authority so desire, afford to each of them an opportunity of appearing before, and being heard by, a person appointed by the Secretary of State for the purpose.

36.   Appeals against planning decisions. — (1) Where an application is made to a local planning authority for planning permission to develop land, or for any approval of that authority required under a development order, and that permission or approval is refused by that authority or is granted by them subject to conditions, the applicant, if he is aggrieved by their decision, may by notice under this section appeal to the Secretary of State.

(2) Any notice under this section shall be served within such time (not being less than twenty-eight days from the date of notification of the decision to which it relates) and in such manner as may be prescribed by a development order[3].

(3) Where an appeal is brought under this section from a decision of a local planning authority, the Secretary of State, subject to the following provisions of this section, may allow or dismiss the appeal, or may reverse or vary any part of the decision of the local planning authority, whether the appeal relates to that part thereof or not, and may deal with the application as if it had been made to him in the first instance.

---

[19] LYELL J.

[20] See *Pyx Granite Co Ltd v Minister of Housing and Local Government* [1958] 1 QB 554, [1958] 1 All ER 625; *Hall & Co Ltd v Shoreham U.D.C.* [1964] 1 WLR 240, [1964] 1 All ER 1; and *Allnatt London Properties v Middlesex County Council* (1964), 15 P & CR 288. In *Hall & Co Ltd v Shoreham UDC*, it was made clear, by WILLMER LJ, in the Court of Appeal, that a planning condition must be considered both *in principle* and *in detail.* In that case the contested conditions were acceptable in principle, but were held to be unreasonable and void in respect of their detailed terms. But see p. 785, n. 1, ante.

[1] Heap, pp. 136-145, 234-248; Pl. Enc. 2: 2674-2685, 3349-3352.

[2] Planning Inquiry Commissions, comprising 3-5 members, may be set up to deal with projects involving matters of national or regional importance (e.g. a third London airport) or unfamiliar technical or scientific considerations.

[3] G.D.O. (S.I. 1977, No. 289) Art, 20. The time limit for appeals is 6 months.

(4) Before determining an appeal under this section, other than an appeal referred to a Planning Inquiry Commission under section 48 of this Act, the Secretary of State shall, if either the applicant or the local planning authority so desire, afford to each of them an opportunity of appearing before, and being heard by, a person appointed by the Secretary of State for the purpose.

245. Proceedings for questioning validity of . . . orders, decisions and directions. — (1) If any person —

(a) is aggrieved by any order to which this section applies and desires to question the validity of that order, on the grounds that the order is not within the powers of this Act, or that any of the relevant requirements have not been complied with in relation to that order; or

(b) is aggrieved by any action on the part of the Secretary of State to which this section applies and desires to question the validity of that action, on the grounds that the action is not within the powers of this Act, or that any of the relevant requirements have not been complied with in relation to that action,

he may, within six weeks from the date on which the order is confirmed or the action is taken, as the case may be, make an application to the High Court under this section.

(2) Without prejudice to subsection (1) of this section, if the authority directly concerned with any order to which this section applies, or with any action on the part of the Secretary of State to which this section applies, desire to question the validity of that order or action on any of the grounds mentioned in subsection (1) of this section, the authority may, within six weeeks from the date on which the order is confirmed or the action is taken, as the case may be, make an application to the High Court under this section.

(3) This section applies to any such order as is mentioned in subsection (2) of section 242 of this Act and to any such action on the part of the Secretary of State as is mentioned in subsection (3) of that section[4].

(4) On any application under this section the High Court —

(a) may by interim order suspend the operation of the order or action, the validity whereof is questioned by the application, until the final determination of the proceedings;

(b) if satisfied that the order or action in question is not within the powers of this Act, or that the interests of the applicant have been substantially prejudiced by a failure to comply with any of the relevant requirements in relation thereto, may quash that order or action:

---

[4] Section 242 forbids legal proceedings in respect of structure plans and of various orders, decisions (including appeals) and directions, except as provided by s. 245 and other provisions of Part XII of the Act. This covers, inter alia, decisions under ss. 35–36.

Provided that paragraph (*a*) of this subsection shall not apply to applications questioning the validity of tree preservation orders.

The restrictions upon the right of access to the courts[5], which are contained in these provisions, must be understood on the footing that the decision appealed from is inherently *valid.* The right to challenge a decision on the ground that is *invalid,* and a *nullity,* is unrestricted. This distinction appears in many aspects of administrative law[6].

Time limits (normally two months) are imposed on local planning authorities; if they fail to give a decision in due time, an appeal lies as if from a refusal[7].

Hearings of appeals by way of public local inquiry before an inspector are part of the normal procedure, and are governed by statutory regulations[8] and by the rules of natural justice[9]. In addition, the Secretary of State is now empowered in some cases to authorise inspectors not only to conduct inquiries but to decide the appeals themselves instead of making a report to guide him in reaching the necessary decisions[10]. The "calling in" procedure, though it normally only occurs in cases of special concern, includes applications comprising "reserved matters" after "outline" permission[11].

F. Revocation and Discontinuance[12]

TOWN AND COUNTRY PLANNING ACT 1971

45. Power to revoke or modify planning permission. — (1) If it appears to the local planning authority, having regard to the development plan and to any other material considerations, that it is expedient to revoke or modify any permission to develop land granted

---

[5] It should be noted that an adjoining owner has no *locus standi to* complain that a grant of permission is ultra vires: *Gregory v Camden London Borough Council* [1966] 1 WLR 899, [1966] 2 All ER 196.

[6] See *Anisminic Ltd v Foreign Compensation Commission* [1969] 2 AC 147, [1969] 1 All ER 208, Moreover there is much more freedom to challenge the legality of decisions of *local* planning authorities, as district from the Secretary of State, in the courts. For example a declaration may be sought: per Lord PARKER CJ, in *Edgware-bury Park Investments Ltd v Minister of Housing and Local Government* [1963] 2 QB 408 at 417, [1963] 1 All ER 124; and where other remedies are less convenient certiorari may be granted (*R v Hillingdon London Borough Council* [1974] QB 720, [1974] 2 All ER 643).

[7] T.C.P.A. 1971, s. 37; and G.D.O. Article 7 (6).

[8] See TCP (Inquiries Procedure) Rules 1974 (S.I. 1974 No. 419).

[9] It is important not to confuse issues of law and issues of fact with issues of policy. Genuine policy decisions which are *intra vires* cannot be challenged in court (see *Lord Luke of Pavenham v Minister of Housing and Local Government* [1968] 1 QB 172, [1967] 2 All ER 1066, in which an issue of policy had been confused with an issue of fact). But there must be a proper exercise of discretion (see *Stringer v Minister of Housing and Local Government* [1970] 1 WLR 1281, [1971] 1 All ER 65).

[10] See T.C.P.A. 1971, s. 36 (8) and Sch. 9 and T.C.P. (Determination of appeals by appointed persons) (Prescribed Classes) Regulations 1972 (S.I. 1972 No. 1652) as amended by S.I. 1977 Nos. 477 and 1939.

[11] T.C.P.A. 1971, s. 35 (1). For "outline" permission, see p. 797–801, ante.

[12] Heap, pp. 145–146, 230–231; Pl. Enc. 2:2705–2709, 2722–2726.

on an application made under this Part of this Act[13], the authority, subject to the following provisions of this section, may by order revoke or modify the permission to such extent as (having regard to those matters) they consider expedient.

(2) Except as provided in section 46 of this Act[14], an order under this section shall not take effect unless it is confirmed by the Secretary of State; and the Secretary of State may confirm any such order submitted to him either without modification or subject to such modifications as he considers expedient.

51. Orders requiring discontinuance of use or alteration or removal of buildings or works. — (1) If it appears to a local planning authority that it is expedient in the interests of the proper planning of their area (including the interests of amenity), regard being had to the development plan and to any other material considerations —

(*a*) that any use of land should be discontinued, or that any conditions should be imposed on the continuance of a use of land; or

(*b*) that any buildings or work should be altered or removed.

the local planning authority may by order require the discontinuance of that use, or impose such conditions as may be specified in the order on the continuance thereof, or require such steps as may be so specified to be taken for the alteration or removal of the buildings or works, as the case may be.

(4) An order under this section shall not take effect unless it is confirmed by the Secretary of State, either without modification or subject to such modifications as he considers expedient.

In each of these cases a hearing must be given to objections. In default of compliance with a discontinuance order under section 51 the authority concerned may enter and do the work themselves, and criminal penalties may also be imposed[15]. But authorities must pay full compensation for loss occasioned by these orders, even if made by the Secretary of State under his default powers[16].

G. Agreements and Determinations[17]

TOWN AND COUNTRY PLANNING ACT 1971

52. Agreements regulating development or use of land. — (1) A local planning authority may enter into an agreement with any person interested in land in their area for the purpose of restricting or regulating the development or use of the land, either permanently or during such period as may be prescribed by the agreement: and any

---

[13] Part III.
[14] Section 46 refers to uncontested orders where no loss is caused and consequently there is no ground for claiming compensation.
[15] T.C.P.A. 1971, s. 108.
[16] See pp. 855–856, post, and T.C.P.A. 1971, s. 276.
[17] Heap, pp. 99–100, 149; Pl. Enc. 2: 2727–2732, 3357–3360.

such agreement may contain such incidental and consequential provisions (including provisions of a financial character) as appear to the local planning authority to be necessary or expedient for the purposes of the agreement.

(2) An agreement made under this section with any person interested in land may be enforced by the local planning authority against persons deriving title under that person in respect of that land, as if the local planning authority were possessed of adjacent land and as if the agreement had been expressed to be made for the benefit of such land.

53. Applications to determine whether planning permission required. — (1) If any person who proposes to carry out any operations on land, or to make any change in the use of land, wishes to have it determined whether the carrying out of those operations, or the making of that change, would constitute or involve development of the land, and, if so, whether an application for planning permission in respect thereof is required under this Part of this Act, having regard to the provisions of the development order, he may, either as part of an application for planning permission, or without any such application, apply to the local planning authority to determine that question.

247.   Appeals to High Court against decisions under s. 53. — (1) If, in the case of any decision to which this section applies, the person who made the application to which the decision relates, or the local planning authority, is dissatisfied with the decision in point of law, that person or the local planning authority (as the case may be) may, according as rules of court may provide, either appeal against the decision to the High Court or require the Secretary of State to state and sign a case for the opinion of the High Court.

(2) This section applies to any decision of the Secretary of State —

(a) on an application under section 53 of this Act which is referred to the Secretary of State under the provisions of section 35 of this Act as applied by that section[18]: or

(b) on an appeal from a decision of the local planning authority under section 53 of this Act, being an appeal brought under the provisions of section 36 of this Act as so applied[19].

Section 52 allows the question of future use and development of land to be agreed on a general basis and not merely in relation to a particular project as when a planning application is submitted. An agreement may be enforced as if it were a restrictive covenant without the need for a benefit to be annexed to land[20].

---

[18] See p. 804, ante.
[19] See pp. 804–805, ante.
[20] See *LCC v Allen* [1914] 3 KB 642, p. 705, ante; *Beaconsfield District Council v Gams* (1974) 234 Estates Gazette 749. The Housing Act 1974 s. 126 now empowers local planning authorities to make planning agreements having the force of *positive* covenants of which the burden runs with the land affected.

In addition to enabling applicants to discover whether proposed acts on land are "development", and whether an application is necessary[1], section 53 also enables the Secretary of State to "call in" any such application, and provides for appeals to the Secretary of State. His decisions are themselves subject to the right of appeal under section 247.

H. Control of Industrial and Office Development[2]

TOWN AND COUNTRY PLANNING ACT 1971

66. Meaning of "industrial building". — (1) In this Part of this Act "industrial building" means a building used or designed for use —

    (*a*) for the carrying on of any process for or incidental to any of the following purposes, that is to say —

        (i) the making of any article or of part of any article; or

        (ii) the altering, repairing, ornamenting, finishing, cleaning, washing, freezing, packing or canning, or adapting for sale, or breaking up or demolition, of any article; or

        (iii) without prejudice to the preceding sub-paragraphs, the getting, dressing or preparation for sale of minerals or the extraction or preparation for sale of oil or brine;

    (*b*) for the carrying on of scientific research,

being a process or research carried on in the course of a trade or business.

    67. Industrial development certificates. — (1) Subject to the provisions of this section and of section 68 of this Act, an application to the local planning authority for permission to develop land by —

    (*a*) the erection thereon of an industrial building of one of the prescribed classes; or

    (*b*) a change of use whereby premises, not being an industrial building of one of the prescribed classes, will become such an industrial building.

shall be of no effect unless a certificate (in this Act referred to as an "industrial development certificate") is issued under this section by the Secretary of State, certifying that the development in question can be carried out consistently with the proper distribution of industry, and a copy of the certificate is furnished to the local planning authority together with the application.

    (3) In considering whether any development for which an industrial development certificate is applied for can be carried out consistently with the proper distribution of industry, the Secretary of State shall

---

[1] Procedure under s. 53, was discussed in *Wells v Minister of Housing and Local Government* [1967] 1 WLR 1000, [1967] 2 All ER 1041. No special formality is necessary; see *English Speaking Union of the Commonwealth v City of Westminster London Borough Council* (1973), 26 P & CR 575.

[2] Heap, pp. 174–196; Pl. Enc. 2: 2774–2838. The term "Secretary of State" in relation to control of industrial and office development means the Secretary of State for Trade and Industry.

have particular regard to the need for providing appropriate employment in development areas.

(7) In this section —

"the prescribed classes" means such classes or descriptions of industrial buildings as may be prescribed by regulations made for the purposes of this section by the Secretary of State;

"development area" means any area for the time being specified as such under section 15 of the Industrial Development Act 1966, and subsection (6) of that section (which provides for references to a development area in certain provisions to have effect as if certain localities outside that area were included therein) shall apply to any such reference in this section;

68. Exemption of certain classes of development. — (1) Notwithstanding anything in section 67 of this Act, but subject to section 69 of this Act, an industrial development certificate shall not be required if the industrial floor space to be created by the development in question (in this section referred to as "the proposed development"), together with any other industrial floor space created or to be created by any related development, does not exceed 5,000 square feet, excluding, where an industrial development certificate has been issued in respect of any related development, any floor space created or to be created by that development or by development carried out, or for which planning permission has been granted, before the issue of that certificate.

(3) In this section "industrial floor space" means floor space comprised in an industrial building or industrial buildings of any of the prescribed classes.

69. Power to vary exemption limit as to industrial floor space. — (1) The Secretary of State may by order direct that subsection (1) of section 68 of this Act shall be amended by substituting, for the number of square feet specified in the subsection as originally enacted or as previously amended under this subsection, such number of square feet as may be specified in the order being not less than 1,000 square feet[3].

Office development was also subject to additional control by "office development permits" in London and surrounding areas. But this was terminated on 6 August 1979 by the Control of Office Development (Cessation) Order 1979[4].

The Secretary of State may issue industrial development certificates subject to restrictions (on the mode of applying for planning permission) or to conditions (governing the development itself[5]). The statutes

---

[3] As from 7 August 1979, the T.C.P. (Industrial Development Certificates: Exemption) Order 1979 (S.I. 1979 No. 839) sets the exemption limit at 50,000 square feet in England, Wales and Scotland generally. See also the T.C.P. (Industrial Development Certificates) Regulations 1979 (S.I. 1979 No. 838) which specify areas where control has been withdrawn; these are "assisted areas" subject to economic depression.

[4] S.I. 1979 No. 908.

[5] T.C.P.A. 1971, s. 70. See also s. 72 (*planning* compensation if I.D.C. is refused).

contain no provision for any right of appeal against or compensation for these restrictions. Nor has there been much litigation over the control of such development[6].

V.   Breach of Planning Control[7]

A.   Enforcement Notices and Stop Notices

TOWN AND COUNTRY PLANNING ACT 1971

87.   Power to serve enforcement notice. — (1) Where it appears to the local planning authority that there has been a breach of planning control after the end of 1963, . . . the authority, if they consider it expedient to do so having regard to the provisions of the development plan and to any other material considerations, may serve a notice under this section (in this Act referred to as an "enforcement notice") requiring the breach to be remedied.

(2) There is a breach of planning control if development has been carried out, whether before or after the commencement of this Act, without the grant of planning permission required in that behalf in accordance with Part III of the Act of 1962 or Part III of this Act, or if any conditions or limitations subject to which planning permission was granted have not been complied with.

(3) Where an enforcement notice relates to a breach of planning control consisting in —

(a) the carrying out without planning permission of building, engineering, mining or other operations in, on, over or under land; or

(b) the failure to comply with any condition or limitation which relates to the carrying out of such operations and subject to which planning permission was granted for the development of that land; or

(c) the making without planning permission of a change of use of any building to use as a single dwelling-house,

it may be served only within the period of four years from the date of the breach.

(4) An enforcement notice shall be served on the owner and on the occupier[8] of the land to which it relates and on any other person having an interest in that land, being an interest which in the opinion of the authority is materially affected by the notice.

(6) An enforcement notice shall specify —

(a) the matters alleged to constitute a breach of planning control;

---

[6] But see *Stanger v Hendon Borough Council* [1948] 1 KB 571, where the Court of Appeal held that residential premises were being used as an "industrial building" because a consulting engineer set up in them a laboratory for testing building materials.

[7] Heap, pp. 212–233, Pl. Enc. 2: 2839–2894.

[8] Notices to owner and occupier must take effect at the same time and therefore (allegedly) be served at the same time: *Bambury v Hounslow London Borough Council* [1966] 2 QB 204, [1966] 2 All ER 532. A caravan dweller can be an "occupier"; *Stevens v Bromley London Borough Council* [1972] Ch 400, [1972] 1 All ER 712.

(b) the steps required by the authority to be taken in order to remedy the breach, that is to say steps for the purpose of restoring the land to its condition before the development took place[9] or (according to the particular circumstances of the breach) of securing compliance with the conditions or limitations subject to which planning permission was granted; and

(c) the period for compliance with the notice, that is to say the period (beginning with the date when the notice takes effect) within which those steps are required to be taken.

(7) The steps which may be required by an enforcement notice to be taken include the demolition or alteration of any buildings or works, the discontinuance of any use of land, or the carrying out on land of any building or other operations.

(8) Subject to section 88 of this Act[10], an enforcement notice shall take effect at the end of such period, not being less than twenty-eight days after the service of the notice, as may be specified in the notice.

(9) The local planning authority may withdraw an enforcement notice (without prejudice to their power to serve another) at any time before it takes effect; and, if they do so, they shall forthwith give notice of the withdrawal to every person who was served with the notice.

1.   Stop notices

90.[11] — (1) Where in respect of any land the local planning authority —

(a) have served an enforcement notice requiring a breach of planning control to be remedied; but

(b) consider it expedient to prevent, before the expiry of the period allowed for compliance with the notice, the carrying out of any activity which is, or is included in, a matter alleged by the notice to constitute the breach,

then, subject to the following provisions of this section, they may at any time before the notice takes effect serve a further notice (in this Act referred to as a 'stop notice') referring to, and having annexed to it a copy of, the enforcement notice and prohibiting the carrying out of that activity on the land, or any part of it specified in the stop notice.

(2) A stop notice shall not prohibit —

(a) the use of any building as a dwelling house, or

(b) the use of land as the site for a caravan occupied by any person as his only or main residence (and for this purpose 'caravan' has the same meaning as it has for the purposes of Part I of the Caravan Sites and Control of Development Act 1960), or

---

[9] It is not necessary to the validity of a notice for it to require the re-erection of structures, the removal of which was part of the wrongful development; *Iddenden v Secretary of State for the Environment* [1972] 1 WLR 1433, [1972] 3 All ER 722.

[10] See p. 814, post.

[11] As amended by T.C.P. (Amendment) Act 1977 s. 1.

(c) the taking of any steps specified in the enforcement notice as required to be taken in order to remedy the breach of planning control;

and where the period during which an activity has been carried out on land (whether continuously or otherwise) began more than twelve months earlier, a stop notice shall not prohibit the carrying out of that activity on that land unless it is, or is incidental to, building, engineering, mining or other operations or the deposit of refuse or waste materials.

(3) A stop notice shall not take effect (and so cannot be contravened) until such date as it may specify, being a date not earlier than three nor later than twenty-eight days from the day on which it is first served on any person.

(4) A stop notice shall cease to have effect when —

(a) the enforcement notice is withdrawn or quashed, or

(b) the period allowed for compliance with the enforcement notice expires, or

(c) notice of the withdrawal of the stop notice is first served under subsection (6) of this section;

and a stop notice shall also cease to have effect if or to the extent that the activities prohibited by it cease, on a variation of the enforcement notice, to be included in the matters alleged by the enforcement notice to constitute a breach of planning control.

(5) A stop notice may be served by the local planning authority on any person who appears to them to have an interest in the land or to be engaged in any activity prohibited by the notice; and where a stop notice has been served in respect of any land, the authority may display there a notice (in this section referred to as a 'site notice') stating that a stop notice has been served and that any person contravening it may be prosecuted for an offence under this section, giving the date when the stop notice takes effect and indicating its requirements.

(6) The local planning authority may at any time withdraw a stop notice (without prejudice to their power to serve another) by serving notice to that effect on persons served with the stop notice and, if a site notice was displayed in respect of the stop notice, displaying a notice of the withdrawal in place of the site notice.

An enforcement notice will be suspended while it is contested. A stop notice is appropriate where the planning authority fears that a developer will contest an enforcement notice, and press on with an unauthorized development in the hope of presenting a fait accompli which the authority may be reluctant to reverse. But the authority serving a stop notice may in some circumstances incur liability to pay compensation[12].

---

[12] T.C.P.A. 1971, s. 177, as amended by T.C.P. (Amendment) Act 1977 s. 2.

B.   Enforcement Appeals and Sanctions

TOWN AND COUNTRY PLANNING ACT 1971

88.   Appeal against enforcement notice. — (1) A person on whom an enforcement notice is served, or any other person having an interest in the land may, at any time within the period specified in the notice as the period at the end of which it is to take effect[13], appeal to the Secretary of State against the notice on any of the following grounds[14] —

   (a) that planning permission ought to be granted for the development to which the notice relates or, as the case may be, that a condition or limitation alleged in the enforcement notice not to have been complied with ought to be discharged;

   (b) that the matters alleged in the notice do not constitute a breach of planning control;

   (c) in the case of a notice which, by virtue of section 87 (3) of this Act, may be served only within the period of four years from the date of the breach of planning control to which the notice relates, that that period has elapsed at the date of service[15];

   (d) in the case of a notice not falling within paragraph (c) of this subsection, that the breach of planning control alleged by the notice occurred before the beginning of 1964;

   (e) that the enforcement notice was not served as required by section 87 (4) of this Act;

   (f) that the steps required by the notice to be taken exceed what is necessary to remedy any breach of planning control;

   (g) that the specified period for compliance with the notice falls short of what should reasonably be allowed.

(2) An appeal under this section shall be made by notice in writing to the Secretary of State, which shall indicate the grounds of the appeal and state the facts on which it is based; and on any such appeal the Secretary of State shall, if either the appellant or the local planning authority so desire, afford to each of them an opportunity of appearing before, and being heard by, a person appointed by the Secretary of State for the purpose.

(3) Where an appeal is brought under this section, the enforcement notice shall be of no effect pending the final determination or the withdrawal of the appeal.

(4) On an appeal under this section —

   (a) the Secretary of State may correct any informality, defect or error in the enforcement notice if he is satisfied that the informality, defect or error is not material;

---

[13] See *Howard v Secretary of State for the Environment* [1975] QB 235, [1974] 1 All ER 644; *Button v Jenkins* [1975] 3 All ER 585.

[14] Before the Caravan Sites and Control of Development Act 1960, appeal lay to the justices. It still does for caravan site licences and waste land notices; see pp. 823–826, post.

[15] For s. 87, see pp. 811–812, ante.

(*b*) in a case where it would otherwise be a ground for determining the appeal in favour of the appellant that a person required by section 87 (4) of this Act to be served with the notice was not served, the Secretary of State may disregard that fact if neither the appellant nor that person has been substantially prejudiced by the failure to serve him.

(5) On the determination of an appeal under this section, the Secretary of State shall give directions for giving effect to his determination, including, where appropriate, directions for quashing the enforcement notice or for varying the terms of the notice in favour of the appellant. . . .

93. Enforcement notice to have effect against subsequent development. — (1) Compliance with an enforcement notice, whether in respect of —

(*a*) the demolition or alteration of any buildings or works; or

(*b*) the discontinuance of any use of land,

or in respect of any other requirements contained in the enforcement notice, shall not discharge the enforcement notice.

246. Appeals to High Court relating to enforcement notices and similar notices. — (1) Where the Secretary of State gives a decision in proceedings on an appeal under Part V of this Act against —

(*a*) an enforcement notice;

(*b*) a listed building enforcement notice[16]; or

(*c*) a notice under section 103[17] of this Act,

the appellant or the local planning authority or any person (other than the appellant) on whom the notice was served may, according as rules of court may provide, either appeal to the High Court against the decision on a point of law or require the Secretary of State to state and sign a case for the opinion of the High Court.

———

Planning authorities may, in default of compliance with an enforcement notice, carry out themselves the works specified[18]. Criminal penalties are also prescribed[19].

It is also possible to apply to a local planning authority for an "established use certificate". This is intended to serve as conclusive proof, in the event of an enforcement appeal, that specified uses of land are authorised[20], but it is not of universal application.

---

[16] See p. 821, post.
[17] Enforcing the replacement of trees; see p. 818, post.
[18] T.C.P.A. 1971, s. 91.
[19] T.C.P.A. 1971, s. 89. See also s. 243 (restrictions on recourse to courts). If the statutory sanctions are ineffective, an injunction may be granted; *A-G v Bastow* [1957] 1 QB 514 [1957] 1 All ER 497; *A-G v Morris* (1973) 227 Estates Gazette 991.
[20] T.C.P.A. 1971, ss. 94, 95. Appeal against a refusal to grant a certificate unconditionally lies to the Secretary of State, who may alternatively "call in" an application.

Many leading cases on planning law which reach the courts arise out of enforcement notices. The courts have usually tended to interpret them very strictly, for example in regard to specifying time limits[1], and also to the strict technical accuracy of complaints which they contain. But purely technical points should not interfere with proper enforcement.

In *Miller-Mead v Minister of Housing and Local Government* [1963] 2 QB 196, [1963] 1 All ER 459, a landowner contested the legality of an enforcement notice on the ground that a recital therein contained an inaccuracy. Lord DENNING MR said, at p. 221: "The Minister has power . . . to correct any informality, defect or error in the enforcement notice if he is satisfied that the informality, defect or error is not a material one[2]. This seems to me to be wider than the 'slip rule'. I think that it gives the Minister a power to amend, which is similar to the power of the court to amend an indictment. He can correct errors so long as, having regard to the merits of the case, the correction can be made without injustice. No formality, defect or error is a material one unless it is such as to produce injustice. Applied to misrecitals, it means this: if the misrecital goes to the substance of the matter, then the notice may be quashed. But if the misrecital does not go to the substance of the matter and can be amended without injustice, it should be amended rather than that the notice should be quashed or declared a nullity. In this way the legislature has disposed of the proposition that there must be 'a strict and rigid adherence to formalities'."

VI.   Preservation of Amenity

A.   The General Concept

"Amenity" is second only in importance to "development" as a basic concept in planning law. Whereas "development" refers to physical acts and changes on land, however, "amenity" refers to the effect of the state of the land on people. The question is:—how far can that effect be made or kept pleasurable? In fact, the control of development and the safeguarding of amenity are two sides of the same coin, and planning authorities, in shaping their policies, must keep both concepts constantly in harmony.

Any aspect of land use may include questions of amenity. Planning law concentrates upon five main aspects.

---

[1] *Burgess v Jarvis and Sevenoaks RDC* [1952] 2 QB 41, [1952] 1 All ER 592. But see *Howard v Secretary of State for the Environment* [1975] QB 235, [1974] 1 All ER 644.
[2] See now T.C.P.A. 1971, s. 88 (4) (a), p. 814, ante.

B.   Trees[3]

TOWN AND COUNTRY PLANNING ACT 1971

59. Planning permission to include appropriate provision for preservation and planting of trees. — It shall be the duty of the local planning authority —

(*a*) to ensure, whenever it is appropriate, that in granting planning permission for any development adequate provision is made, by the imposition of conditions, for the preservation or planting of trees; and

(*b*) to make such orders under section 60 of this Act as appear to the authority to be necessary in connection with the grant of such permission, whether for giving effect to such conditions or otherwise.

60.   Tree preservation orders. — (1) If it appears to a local planning authority that it is expedient in the interests of amenity to make provision for the preservation of trees or woodlands in their area, they may for that purpose make an order (in this Act referred to as a "tree preservation order") with respect to such trees, groups of trees or woodlands as may be specified in the order; and, in particular, provision may be made by any such order —

(*a*) for prohibiting (subject to any exemptions for which provision may be made by the other) the cutting down, topping, lopping or wilful destruction of trees except with the consent of the local planning authority, and for enabling that authority to give their consent subject to conditions[4];

(*b*) for securing the replanting, in such manner as may be prescribed by or under the order, of any part of a woodland area which is felled in the course of forestry operations permitted by or under the order;

(*c*) for applying, in relation to any consent under the order, and to applications for such consent, any of the provisions of this Act falling within subsection (2)[5] of this section, subject to such adaptations and modifications as may be specified in the order.

(4) Except as provided under subsection (5) (*c*) of this section and in section 61 of this Act[6], a tree preservation order shall not take effect until it is confirmed by the Secretary of State, and the Secretary of State may confirm any such order either without modification or subject to such modification or subject to such modifications as he considers expedient.

---

[3] Heap, pp. 197–201, 231–232; Pl. Enc. 2: 2753–2763, 2909–2912.

[4] The Town and Country Amenities Act 1974, s. 8, inserts a new provision, s. 61A, in T.C.P.A. 1971. This states that "... any person who, in relation to [any tree in a conservation area ... in respect of which no tree preservation order is for the time being in force], does any act which might by virtue of section 60 (1) (*a*) above be prohibited by a tree preservation order shall be guilty of an offence". See below for conservation areas (p. 819).

[5] Dealing with procedure for planning applications, and with purchase notices (see p. 847, post). But the prescribed form of T.P.O. omits purchase notices.

[6] Dealing with unopposed and provisional T.P.O.s respectively.

(5) Provision may be made by regulations[7] under this Act with respect to the form of tree preservation orders, and the procedure to be followed in connection with the submission and confirmation of such orders; . . .

(6) Without prejudice to any other exemptions for which provision may be made by a tree preservation order, no such order shall apply to the cutting down, topping or lopping of trees which are dying or dead or have become dangerous, or the cutting down, topping or lopping of any trees in compliance with any obligations imposed by or under an Act of Parliament or so far as may be necessary for the prevention or abatement of a nuisance.

Tree preservation orders are in effect special ad hoc extensions of planning control, and it is important not to confuse the procedure for making them with the procedure for obtaining consents under them when made. They can be worded so as to apply to future trees to be planted in accordance with a planning condition of the kind referred to above in section 59 (*a*) of the 1971 Act[8]. The Act also makes provision for replacement of protected trees, enforcement notices and appeals, and criminal penalties for wrongful interference[9].

BARNET LONDON BOROUGH COUNCIL *v* EASTERN ELECTRICITY BOARD
[1973] 1 WLR 430, [1973] 2 All ER 319 (Div Ct, Lord WIDGERY CJ, EVELEIGH and MAY JJ)

The defendants, who excavated a trench in and near a highway, damaged and severed the roots of trees which were the subject of a tree preservation order. The local authority felled and replaced the trees, and preferred informations against the defendants for wilful destruction of them in contravention of the order. The defendants submitted that the damage could not amount to wilful destruction of the trees.

Held. The trees were "destroyed" because the injury was such that it was no longer worth preserving them as an amenity.

MAY J: The question which arises for decision in this case, therefore, is the proper construction of the words "wilful destruction" in the relevant tree preservation order. . . . Before a tree can be said to be destroyed we feel that it must have been rendered useless — but rendered useless as what? This last inquiry raises immediately the

---

[7] T.C.P. (Tree Preservation Order) Regulations 1969 (S.I. 1969, No. 17, as amended by S.I. 1975 No. 148).

[8] T.C.P.A. 1971, s. 60 (3).

[9] T.C.P.A. 1971, ss. 102, 103 extended by the Town and Country Amenities Act 1974, s. 10. See also ss. 174–175 (compensation); *Kent County Council v Batchelor* (1976) 33 P & CR 185.

question of the purpose for which the use of the tree may or may not continue to exist. Consequently in our judgment one must bear in mind in this case that the underlying purpose of the relevant legislation is the preservation of trees and woodlands as amenities, as living creatures providing pleasure, protection and shade; it is their use as such that is sought to be preserved, and a tree the subject of a tree preservation order is destroyed in the present context when as a result of that which is done to it, it ceases to have any use as amenity, as something worth preserving. For example, if a person intentionally inflicts on a tree so radical an injury that in all the circumstances any reasonably competent forester would in consequence decide that it ought to be felled, then in our opinion that person wilfully destroys the tree within the meaning of that word in the relevant legislation and order.

Further, having regard to the way in which the trees are identified and described in Schedule I to the order and to the annexed map, and indeed to general considerations as to what is or is not an amenity, we think that one of the relevant circumstances which a forester could or should take into account in deciding whether a given injured tree should be felled is its situation: a tree adjoining a highway, for instance, needs greater stability and more vigorous life than a similar tree in a country field and the former may thus, by reason of its position alone, be destroyed in contravention of the order by a lesser injury than would be needed to destroy the latter.

C. Buildings of Special Interest[10]
TOWN AND COUNTRY PLANNING ACT 1971

277. Designation of conservation areas.[11] — (1) Every local planning authority shall from time to time determine which parts of their area are areas of special architectural or historic interest the character or appearance of which it is desirable to preserve or enhance, and shall designate such areas as conservation areas.

(8) Where any area is for the time being designated as a conservation area, special attention shall be paid to the desirability of preserving or enhancing its character or appearance in the exercise, with respect to any buildings or other land in that area, of any powers under this Act, Part I of the Historic Buildings and Ancient Monuments Act 1953 or the Local Authorities (Historic Buildings) Act 1962.

54. Lists of buildings of special architectural or historic interest. — (1) For the purposes of this Act and with a view to the guidance of local planning authorities in the performance of their

---

[10] Heap, pp. 201–209, 231. Pl. Enc. 2: 2733–2752, 2895–2908, 3441–3442.
[11] Section 277 is in an amended form substituted by the Town and Country Amenities Act 1974, s. 1 (which also enacts s. 277B, requiring local planning authorities to "formulate and publish . . . proposals for the preservation and enhancement of . . . conservation areas").

functions under this Act in relation to buildings of special architectural or historic interest, the Secretary of State shall compile lists of such buildings, or approve, with or without modifications, such lists compiled by other persons or bodies of persons, and may amend any list so compiled or approved.

(2) In considering whether to include a building in a list compiled or approved under this section, the Secretary of State may take into account not only the building itself but also —

    (*a*) any respect in which its exterior contributes to the architectural or historic interest of any group of buildings of which it forms part; and

    (*b*) the desirability of preserving, on the ground of its architectural or historic interest, any feature of the building consisting of a man-made object or structure fixed to the building or forming part of the land and comprised within the curtilage of the building.

(3) Before compiling or approving, with or without modifications, any list under this section, or amending any list thereunder the Secretary of State shall consult with such persons or bodies of persons as appear to him appropriate as having special knowledge of, or interest in, buildings of architectural or historic interest.

(8) The Secretary of State shall keep available for public inspection, free of charge at reasonable hours and at a convenient place, copies of all lists and amendments of lists compiled, approved or made by him under this section; and every authority with whose clerk copies of any list or amendments are deposited under this section shall similarly keep available copies of so much of any such list or amendment as relates to buildings within their area.

(9) In this Act "listed building" means a building which is for the time being included in a list compiled or approved by the Secretary of State under this section; and, for the purposes of the provisions of this Act relating to listed buildings and building preservation notices, any object or structure fixed to a building, or forming part of the land and comprised within the curtilage of a building, shall be treated as part of the building.

55. Control of works for demolition, alteration or extension of listed buildings. — (1) Subject to this Part[12] of this Act, if a person executes or causes to be executed any works for the demolition of a listed building or for its alteration or extension in any manner which would affect its character as a building of special architectural or historic interest, and the works are not authorised under this Part of this Act, he shall be guilty of an offence.

(2) Works for the demolition of a listed building, or for its alteration or extension, are authorised under this Part of this Act only if —

    (*a*) the local planning authority or the Secretary of State have granted written consent (in this Act referred to as "listed

---

[12] Part IV (ss. 54–86).

building consent") for the execution of the works and the works are executed in accordance with the terms of the consent and of any conditions attached to the consent under section 56 of this Act[13]; and

(b) in the case of demolition, notice of the proposal to execute the works has been given to the Royal Commission and thereafter either —

(i) for a period of at least one month following the grant of listed building consent, and before the commencement of the works, reasonable access to the building has been made available to members or officers of the Commission for the purpose of recording it; or

(ii) the Commission have, by their Secretary or other officer of theirs with authority to act on the Commission's behalf for the purposes of this section, stated in writing that they have completed their recording of the building or that they do not wish to record it.

(3) In subsection (2) of this section "the Royal Commission" means, in relation to England, the Royal Commission on Historical Monuments (England) and, in relation to Wales, the Royal Commission on Ancient and Historical Monuments (Wales and Monmouthshire) . . .

Section 55 goes on to provide that contravention of "listed building" control is a criminal offence. Provision is also made for "listed building" enforcement notices[14] and purchase notices[15], and also for compensation[16] and compulsory purchase[17]. But a compulsory purchase order cannot be made unless the owner has first been given notice to put the listed building into proper repair and has failed to comply[18]. Any building not listed may be given temporary protection

---

[13] Conditions in listed building consents may refer to such matters as "preservation of particular features of the building" and "use of original materials so far as practicable". Detailed procedure is provided for in T.C.P.A. 1971, Sch. 11, T.C.P. (Listed Buildings and Buildings in Conservation Areas) Regulations 1972 (S.I. 1972, No. 1362, amended by S.I. 1974, No. 1336) and T.C.P. (Listed Buildings and Buildings in Conservation Areas) Regulations 1977 (S.I. 1977 No. 228).

[14] T.C.P.A. 1971, ss. 96-101. S. 101 is re-enacted in a substituted form by the Town and Country Amenities Act 1974, s. 5, and now empowers a local authority to carry out urgent repair works to unoccupied listed buildings, or other buildings in a conservation area if the Secretary of State so directs, after giving 7 days' notice to the occupier.

[15] An owner may serve a purchase notice after a decision which renders land "incapable of reasonably beneficial use"; T.C.P.A. 1971, s. 190; for purchase notices, see p. 847, post.

[16] T.C.P.A. 1971, ss. 171-172.

[17] T.C.P.A. 1971, ss. 114-117 "Minimum compensation", excluding any element of value reflecting the possibility of making any alterations, is payable if an owner has deliberately allowed a "listed building" to become ruinous.

[18] T.C.P.A. 1971, s. 115. Compliance earns a right of appeal to the justices (s. 114 (6)).

by means of a "building preservation notice" while the local planning authority request the Secretary of State to consider listing it[19].

Churches (but not parsonages)[20] and ancient monuments[1] are excluded from these provisions. Each local authority and local planning authority keeps a copy of the listed buildings in its area. "Conservation areas" are in effect areas especially rich in listed (or listable) buildings; and the duty of local planning authorities in respect of them may be expressed under three heads; (i) evolving a specific policy for safeguarding each area; (ii) publicising planning applications within each area; (iii) consulting preservation societies and other interested bodies as appropriate. Where buildings in a conservation area are listable but not listed, the local planning authority may make a direction subject to confirmation by the Secretary of State, applying listed building control to such listable buildings as may be specified, for the purpose of preserving them from demolition[2].

D.   Advertisements[3]

TOWN AND COUNTRY PLANNING ACT 1971

22.   Meaning of "development" . . .[4]

(4) Without prejudice to any regulations made under the provisions of this Act relating to the control of advertisements, the use for the display of advertisements of any external part of a building which is not normally used for that purpose shall be treated for the purposes of this section as involving a material change in the use of that part of the building.

63.   Control of advertisements. — (1) Subject to the provisions of this section, provision shall be made by regulations under this Act for restricting or regulating the display of advertisements so far as appears to the Secretary of State to be expedient in the interests of amenity or public safety[5].

---

[19] T.C.P.A. 1971, ss. 58, 175. See *Maltglade Ltd v St. Albans RDC* [1972] 1 WLR 1230, [1972] 3 All ER 129.

[20] On the question of whether the fact that a church ceases to be used for regular worship will automatically subject it to "listed building" control; see *A-G v Howard United Reformed Church Trustees, Bedford* [1976] AC 363; [1976] 2 All ER 337.

[1] See the Ancient Monuments and Archaeological Areas Act 1979.

[2] T.C.P. (Amendment) Act 1972, s. 8 and Sch. 2. The Town and Country Amenities Act 1974, s. 1, has inserted a new provision in T.C.P.A. 1971, s. 277A, which requires the consent of the local planning authority or the Secretary of State before demolition of any building in a conservation area which is not yet listed and is not exempt under T.C.P.A. 1971, s. 58 or by the Secretary of State's specific direction. Section 4 of the 1974 Act requires "the setting of a listed building" to be taken into account whenever any planning application is being considered which may affect such a building.

[3] Heap, pp. 153-162, 232-233; Pl. Enc. 2: 2609, 2764-2771.

[4] See p. 783, ante.

[5] But not censorship. See T.C.P. (Control of Advertisements) Regulations 1969 (S.I. 1969, No. 1532, as amended by S.I. 1975 No. 898). For payment of compensation in special cases, see T.C.P.A. 1971, s. 176. The Town and Country Amenities Act 1974, s. 3, now requires special provision to be made in the regulations for conservation areas and other areas which "require special protection on grounds of amenity".

64. Application for planning permission not needed for advertisements complying with regulations. — Where the display of advertisements in accordance with regulations made under section 63 of this Act involves development of land, planning permission for that development shall be deemed to be granted by virtue of this section, and no application shall be necessary in that behalf under Part III of this Act.

The details of the system of advertisement control must be sought in the regulations. There is a system of consents for advertisements; and, in many cases consent is "deemed" to be granted, under the regulations, for the general run of routine, modest-sized advertisements, within specified limits; though "areas of special control" may be declared, in which express consents are only available for specified kinds of advertisement. Contravention of the regulations is a criminal offence[6].

E. Caravan Sites[7]

CARAVAN SITES AND CONTROL OF DEVELOPMENT ACT 1960

1. Prohibition of use of land as caravan site without site licence. — (1) Subject to the provisions of this Part of this Act, no occupier of land shall after the commencement of this Act cause or permit any part of the land to be used as a caravan site unless he is the holder of a site licence (that is to say, a licence under this Part of this Act authorising the use of land as a caravan site) for the time being in force as respects the land so used.

(2) If the occupier of any land contravenes subsection (1) of this section he shall be guilty of an offence. . . .

(3) In this Part of this Act the expression "occupier" means, in relation to any land, the person who, by virtue of an estate or interest therein held by him, is entitled to possession thereof or would be so entitled but for the rights of any other person under any licence granted in respect of the land:

Provided that where land amounting to not more than four hundred square yards in area is let under a tenancy entered into with a view to the use of the land as a caravan site, the expression "occupier" means in relation to that land the person who would be entitled to possession of the land but for the rights of any person under that tenancy.

(4) In this Part of this Act the expression "caravan site" means land on which a caravan is stationed for the purposes of human habitation and land which is used in conjunction with land on which a caravan is so stationed.

---

[6] T.C.P.A. 1971, s. 109. See *John v Reveille Newspapers Ltd* (1955) 5 P & CR 95.
[7] Heap, pp. 163-173, Pl. Enc. 2: 1153-1232, 2355. The term "caravan" includes twin-unit caravans (see the Caravan Sites Act 1968, s. 13). And see the Mobile Homes Act 1975; *Taylor v Calvert* [1978] 1 WLR 899, [1978] 3 All ER 630.

3.   Issue of site licences by local authorities. — (1) An application for the issue of a site licence in respect of any land may be made by the occupier thereof to the local authority in whose area the land is situated.

The conditions contained in a site licence are more important than the granting of the licence, because the licence (obtained from the *local* authority) normally follows automatically upon a planning permission (obtained from the local *planning* authority) and lasts as long as that permission[8]. The conditions may be imposed for certain specified purposes[9], which pertain more to public health than to planning. Terms which have no connection with these purposes will almost certainly be "ultra vires"[10].

Appeal against site licence conditions, or against a decision or refusal to vary them, lies to a magistrates' court, on the ground that they are "unduly burdensome"[11]. There are various categories of exemption from control, such as use in the garden of a house, or occasional and intermittent use, and also use for seasonal and temporary workers, and circus and fairground showmen[12].

ESDELL CARAVAN PARKS LTD *v* HEMEL HEMPSTEAD
RURAL DISTRICT COUNCIL
[1966] 1 QB 895, [1965] 3 All ER 737 (CA, Lord DENNING MR,
HARMAN and WINN LJJ)

In 1960 Mrs. Edy owned a field which was an "existing site" within the Caravan Sites and Control of Development Act 1960, section 13; so that no *planning permission* was needed.

In 1961 the defendants issued a site licence, with a restriction that the maximum number of caravans should be 24.

In 1962 Mrs. Edy leased the field for 21 years to the plaintiff, who intended to develop it for 78 good-class modern caravans. When the defendants cancelled the licence and issued a new one to the plaintiff with the same restriction to 24 caravans, the plaintiff appealed to the magistrates' court claiming that this condition was unduly burdensome.

It was decided that the increase to 78 was undesirable because the field was in the Green Belt, and a new caravan site would not have been allowed (item 1); and also because it would upset the social balance between villagers and caravan dwellers (item k), cause difficulties for schools (item m), shoppers (item n), transport (items o

---

[8] See p. 795, ante. Both authorities will now normally be the district council.
[9] Set out in Caravan Sites and Control of Development Act, 1960, s. 5.
[10] See *Mixnam's Properties v Chertsey UDC* [1965] AC 735, [1964] 2 All ER 627.
[11] Caravan Sites and Control of Development Act 1960, ss. 7, 8. The Minister has issued Model Standards for Caravan Sites (Circular, No. 42/60), and the nearer the conditions of a site licence approach those standards, the more likely they are to be upheld.
[12] Caravan Sites and Control of Development Act 1960, Sch. 1.

and p), and impair amenities of neighbours (item q). The Divisional Court reversed the justices. On appeal by the defendant to the Court of Appeal.

Held (1) the condition was not unduly burdensome;
  (2) the justices were entitled to have regard to all the factors except that of the Green Belt; and
  (3) the case must be remitted to the justices for reconsideration.

LORD DENNING MR: There are two authorities which have power to control caravan sites. On the one hand, there is the planning authority. . . . On the other hand, there is the site authority. . . . The planning authority ought to direct their attention to matters in *outline*, leaving the site authority to deal with all matters of *detail*. Thus the planning authority should ask themselves this broad question: Ought this field to be used as a caravan site at all? If "Yes," they should grant planning permission for it, without going into details as to number of caravans and the like, or imposing any conditions in that regard. Once planning permission is given, or deemed to be given, the site authority should deal with the details. They should say how many caravans should be permitted; whether they should be residential caravans or holiday caravans; or the like. They must have regard to the model standards but are not bound by them. They can impose whatever conditions they think necessary or desirable in relation to the use of the site as a caravan site, so long as they are not unduly burdensome. But they must not impose conditions which have no relation to the use of the site: see *Mixnam's Properties Ltd v Chertsey UDC* ([1965] AC 735, [1964] 2 All ER 627) and the *Pyx Granite case (Pyx Granite Co Ltd v Ministry of Housing and Local Government* [1958] 1 QB 554 at 572, [1958] 1 All ER 625). . . .

I do not think it is possible to separate the various considerations into two distinct groups whereby each must be either a "planning consideration" or a "site consideration". No such distinction is drawn in the statutes. It cannot be defined. It is devoid of reality and of certainty. Many considerations relate both to planning and to site. . . . In all these matters there is a large overlap, where a condition can properly be based both on planning considerations and also on site considerations. In so far as it can be used on site considerations, it is clearly good, even though it might also be based on planning considerations.

In my opinion, therefore, the magistrates . . . were entitled to have regard to the effect which too many caravans might have in upsetting the social balance between village people and caravan dwellers (item (k)), in causing overcrowding of the schools (item (m)), and giving rise to shopping difficulties (item (n)), and transport problems (items (p) and (o)) and impairing amenities of neighbours (item (q)).

I do not think the magistrates were entitled to have regard to the fact that, *under the Green Belt provisions,* an application for a new caravan site on this field would be refused (item (1)). The magistrates were bound to accept the fact that there was an existing right to use this site as a caravan site, even though it was in the Green Belt. There was "deemed permission" for it. That was solely a planning consideration for the planning authority and not a site consideration for the site authority. It was "outline" and not "detail".

F.   Waste Land and Dumping[13]

TOWN AND COUNTRY PLANNING ACT 1971

65.   Proper maintenance of waste land. — (1) If it appears to a local planning authority that the amenity of any part of their area, or of any adjoining area, is seriously injured by the condition of any garden, vacant site or other open land[14] in their area, . . . the authority may serve on the owner and occupier of the land a notice requiring such steps for abating the injury as may be specified in the notice to be taken within such period as may be so specified.

(2) Subject to the provisions of Part V[15] of this Act, a notice under this section shall take effect at the end of such period (not being less than twenty-eight days after the service thereof) as may be specified in the notice.

Appeal lies to a magistrates' court, with a further appeal to the Crown Court[16], but the authority may, in default of compliance, do the specified works themselves at the defaulter's expense[17]. Further powers of control over dumping of refuse and abandonment of vehicles are given to local authorities (as such) by Part III of the Civic Amenities Act 1967.

VII.   Compulsory Purchase of Land

A.   Compulsory Purchase Orders[18]

ACQUISITION OF LAND (AUTHORISATION PROCEDURE) ACT 1946

1.   Procedure for compulsory purchase of land by local authorities, and by the Minister of Transport for highway purposes. — (1) The authorisation of any compulsory purchase of land —

(a) by a local authority where, apart from this Act, power to authorise the authority to purchase land compulsorily is

---

[13] Heap, pp. 209–211, 231, Pl. Enc. 2: 2772–2773, 2913–2921.

[14] An enclosed yard with scattered huts was held to be outside the scope of these words in *Stephens v Cuckfield RDC*, [1962] 2 QB 373, [1960] 2 All ER 716. The "condition" of the land includes the use to which it is put, such as a scrap dump; *Britt v Buckinghamshire County Council* [1964] 1 QB 77, [1963] 2 All ER 175.

[15] Dealing with enforcement procedure.

[16] T.C.P.A. 1971, ss. 105, 106.

[17] T.C.P.A. 1971, s. 107, Continuance or aggravation of the injury to amenity after the notice takes effect is a criminal offence (s. 104).

[18] Heap, pp. 280–282; Davies, pp. 26–65; Comp. Enc. 2: 427–480.

conferred by or under any enactment contained in a public general Act and in force immediately before the commencement of this Act[19]. . .

(*b*) by the Minister of Transport;

shall, subject to the provisions of this . . . section, be conferred by an order (in this Act referred to as a "compulsory purchase order") in accordance with the provisions of the First Schedule to this Act. . . .

There must always be a special or enabling Act, usually, but not necessarily, a public general Act, authorising specified bodies to acquire land for specified purposes by compulsion if necessary and, if so, by means of the procedure laid down in the Act of 1946. A few Acts prescribe a procedure of their own, but there is, even so, very little difference in detail[20]. Nearly all post-1946 statutes apply the standard procedure for making compulsory purchase orders, whatever the nature of the acquiring body[1]. The significance of the "C.P.O." procedure[2] is that it earmarks *particular* land for a purpose for which the special Act confers authority to acquire land *in general terms*[3].

B. Acquisition Procedure[4]

COMPULSORY PURCHASE ACT 1965

4. Time limit. — The powers of the acquiring authority for the compulsory purchase of the land[5] shall not be exercised after the expiration of three years from the date on which the compulsory purchase order becomes operative.

5. Notice to treat, . . . — (1) When the acquiring authority require to purchase any of the land subject to compulsory purchase, they shall

---

[19] Other than certain statutes specified in sub-s. (4).

[20] E.g. Part III of the Housing Act 1957, dealing with slum clearance.

[1] I.e. local authority, government department, or public corporation.

[2] The essence of the procedure is, first, the making of the C.P.O. in draft; second, publicity; third, a public inquiry into objections, and fourth, ultimate confirmation (modified or unmodified) or refusal to confirm, by whichever Minister or Secretary of State is appropriate. Publicity includes notification in newspapers, and also the service of notices upon owners, lessees and occupiers of the land included in the C.P.O. (but not persons enjoying easements or other servitudes over the land; *Grimley v Minister of Housing and Local Government* [1971] 2 QB 96, [1971] 2 All ER 431).

[3] There is a right of appeal to the High Court within 6 weeks on limited points of law only; Acquisition of Land (Authorisation Procedure) Act 1946 (1st Sched.). Inquiries are governed by the Compulsory Purchase by Public Authorities (Inquiries Procedure) Rules 1976 (S.I. 1976 No. 746), and the Compulsory Purchase by Ministers (Inquiries Procedure) Rules 1967 (S.I. 1967 No. 720). See the Compulsory Purchase of Land Regulations 1976 (S.I. 1976 No. 300) for procedure in general. See also *Fairmount Investments Ltd v Secretary of State for the Environment* [1976] 1 WLR 1255, [1976] 2 All ER 865, *R v Secretary of State for the Environment, ex parte Ostler* [1977] QB 122, [1976] 3 All ER 90.

[4] Davies, pp. 66–110; Comp. Enc. 2: 1528–1672; 2, 1811–1812; 2, 1857–1864.

[5] These powers do not authorise the compulsory creation (for acquiring authorities) of *new* rights in land, such as easements or leases, unless clear statutory authority exists for this; *Soumots Investments Ltd v Secretary of State for the Environment* [1979] AC 144, [1977] 2 All ER 385, p. 540, ante.

give notice (hereafter in this Act referred to as a "notice to treat") to all the persons interested in, or having power to sell and convey or release, the land, so far as known to the acquiring authority after making diligent inquiry[6].

20. Tenants at will, etc. — (1) If any of the land subject to compulsory purchase is in the possession of a person having no greater interest in the land than as tenant for a year or from year to year, and if that person is required to give up possession of any land so occupied by him before the expiration of his term or interest in the land, he shall be entitled to compensation for the value of his unexpired term or interest in the land, and for any just allowance which ought to be made to him by an incoming tenant, and for any loss or injury he may sustain.

TOWN AND COUNTRY PLANNING ACT 1968

30. Power of authorities possessing compulsory purchase powers to make general vesting declarations. — (1) Schedule 3 to this Act . . . shall have effect for the purpose of enabling any authority to whom this section applies to vest in themselves by a declaration land which they are authorised by a compulsory purchase order to acquire and with respect to the effect of such a declaration, the payment and recovery of sums in respect of compensation for the acquisition of land so vested and other matters connected therewith.

(2) This section applies to any Minister or local or other public authority authorised to acquire land by means of a compulsory purchase order, and any such authority is in the said Schedule 3 referred to as an acquiring authority.

The Town and Country Planning Act 1968, section 30 and Schedules 3 and 3A (the latter schedule having been added by the Land Commission (Dissolution) Act 1971) enact the "general vesting declaration" procedure, which authorities may use if they so state in their notice that a C.P.O. has been confirmed, or in a separate, later, notice. This new procedure combines in one step the two separate steps of the older procedure: notice to treat, followed by conveyance. It is provided that whatever consequences are stated in any Act to flow from the service of a notice to treat flow also from the making of a general vesting declaration.

Section 11 of the C.P.A. 1965 authorises an acquiring authority to enter on land after notice to treat[7], subject to service of a fourteen days' "notice of entry" on the occupier, on condition that interest is paid at a prescribed rate from entry until actual payment of

---

[6] Sub-s. (2) provides that the notice to treat "shall state that the acquiring authority are willing to treat for the purchase of the land. . . ." Disputes over compensation are dealt with under the Land Compensation Act 1961, s. 1; p. 844, post.

[7] See *Munton v Greater London Council* [1976] 1 WLR 649, [1976] 2 All ER 815.

compensation. Paragraph 8 of the 3rd Schedule to the 1968 Act makes a similar provision, but only where there is a short-term tenancy not covered by the vesting declaration. Tenants with yearly tenancies or lesser interests are not entitled to receive a notice to treat; the normal procedure therefore is for the acquiring authority on taking over the reversion to serve notice to quit[8]. Statutory security of tenure does not prevail against compulsory purchase[9].

Exceptions apart, freeholds and leaseholds, both legal and equitable[10], may be compulsorily acquired. It is assumed that easements, covenants and the like will not normally be interfered with, though compensation will be payable if they are[11]. The "land" authorised to be compulsorily acquired is normally defined to each authorising Act[12].

It should be noted that, whereas a C.P.O. makes lawful the compulsory purchase of specified land, such purchase is not in fact begun until there is a notice to treat or a general vesting declaration. But a long delay in completing the purchase may ultimately amount to an abandonment[13] of the notice to treat: consequently there can be no conveyance to the authority in such a case. Moreover the C.P.O. will be ineffective if the three-year time limit has expired.

In *Simpson's Motor Sales (London) Ltd v Hendon Corpn* [1964] AC 1088, [1963] 2 All ER 484, the respondents, under a compulsory purchase order, served a notice to treat in respect of the appellant's North Road site, which was required for council housing. They then reconsidered their proposals. The appellants, who had tried to persuade them to use the "Colindale" site instead, claimed that in the circumstances the respondents had abandoned their rights under the

---

[8] See *Newham London Borough Council v Benjamin* [1968] 1 WLR 694, [1968] 1 All ER 1195, in which the Court of Appeal held that such tenants are not entitled to have compensation assessed until "required to give up possession" (even if a notice to treat is in fact served on them) because C.P.A. 1965, s. 20, excludes them from the notice to treat procedure. What s. 20 is in fact alluding to is a *notice of entry*.

[9] See L. & T. Act 1954, s. 30 (1) (f), the Agricultural Holdings (Notices to Quit) Act 1977, ss. 2–3 and the Rent Act 1977, ss. 13–15.

[10] See *Oppenheimer v Minister of Transport* [1942] 1 KB 242, [1941] 3 All ER 485, in which the claimant was held to be entitled to compensation in respect of an option which he held over fields compulsorily purchased for a trunk road, i.e. a freehold in equity. Authorities often decide to take the freehold but not a leasehold subsisting in the land. Occasionally the reverse happens; see *London and Westcliff Properties Ltd v Minister of Housing and Local Government* [1961] 1 WLR 519, [1961] 1 All ER 610.

[11] Seemingly in cases of appropriation as well as acquisition: see *Dowty Boulton Paul Ltd v Wolverhampton Corpn (No. 2)* [1976] Ch 13, [1973] 2 All ER 491.

[12] See, for example, T.C.P.A. 1971, s. 290 (1). But, in relation to easements and other servitudes, acquisition of the *dominant* land normally includes the servitudes appurtenant to it, according to the ordinary principles of conveyancing; and acquisition of *servient* land either does not affect the servitudes over it, or else gives a right to compensation (for "injurious affection", see p. 840, post) if they are affected. And compulsory purchase in the form of a *newly created* easement or special right for the acquiring authority's benefit (e.g. a tunnel or a stratum of land; see *Pepys v London Transport Executive* [1975] 1 WLR 234, [1975] 1 All ER 748), instead of acquisition of ownership of the land as a whole, must be specifically authorised by the statute.

[13] *Grice v Dudley Corpn* [1958] Ch 329, [1957] 2 All ER 673.

compulsory purchase order. The House of Lords held that there had been no abandonment. Lord EVERSHED said at p. 1125: "It cannot, I think, be in doubt that in a case such as the present a local authority may abandon a right to purchase compulsorily land in respect of which a compulsory purchase order has been obtained: and that if such abandonment is accepted by the owner then the compulsory purchase order ceases to be effective. As is pointed out in one of the cases, the quasi-contractual relationship which the notice to treat has caused to come into existence is then determined. I also accept Mr. Megarry's contention that the private owner might not be willing to accept the abandonment but could proceed to enforce his claim under the notice to treat; and that in such event it would not be open to the local authority to rely upon their own wrongful act of abandonment to defeat the private owner's claim. But nothing of that kind occurred in the present case. . . . I cannot find in the incidents which occurred and the communications which passed between Simpsons and the corporation anything which could fairly amount to an abandonment by the corporation of their rights under the compulsory purchase order."

C.　Severance of Land[14]

An acquiring authority may decide, if necessary, upon a piecemeal acquisition of the land authorised to be taken, and may serve notice to treat on part of an owner's land. Taking part only is "severance". If portions of land are separated from other parts, or from convenient modes of access, in consequence of severance, the acquiring body may do "accommodation works" (such as bridges and tunnels) for the owner's benefit and so reduce his loss and hence his claim for severance compensation. But in some circumstances the owner has the right to object to severance and insist that the acquiring body shall take all of his land or none, even apparently if they are not authorised by the C.P.O. to take more than the part specified in the notice to treat. If the owner cannot or does not resist severance, he is entitled to compensation if the part that remains to him is depreciated in proportion to its size; this is known as "compensation for severance" and is referred to below in connection with compensation for depreciation[15].

COMPULSORY PURCHASE ACT 1965

8.　Other provisions as to divided land. — (1) No person shall be required to sell a part only —

    (*a*) of any house, building or manufactory, or
    (*b*) of a park or garden belonging to a house,

---

[14] Davies, pp. 111–118; Comp. Enc. 2: 1559–1563, 2568–2575.
[15] See p. 840, post.

if he is willing and able to sell the whole of the house, building, manufactory, park or garden, unless the Lands Tribunal[16] determines that —

    (i) in the case of a house, building or manufactory the part proposed to be acquired can be taken without material detriment to the house, building or manufactory, or

    (ii) in the case of a park or garden, the part proposed to be acquired can be taken without seriously affecting the amenity or convenience of the house,

and, if the Lands Tribunal so determine, the Lands Tribunal shall award compensation in respect or any loss due to the severance of the part proposed to be acquired, in addition to its value; and thereupon the party interested shall be required to sell to the acquiring authority that part of the house, building, manufactory, park or garden.

LAND COMPENSATION ACT 1973

58. Determination of material detriment where part of house etc. proposed for compulsory acquisition. — (1) In determining under section 8 (1) ... of the Compulsory Purchase Act 1965 ... whether —

    (a) part of a house, building or manufactory can be taken without material detriment or damage to the house, building or manufactory; or

    (b) part of a park or garden belonging to a house can be taken without seriously affecting the amenity or convenience of the house,

the Lands Tribunal shall take into account not only the effect of the severance but also the use to be made of the part proposed to be acquired and, in a case where the part is proposed to be acquired for works or other purposes extending to other land, the effect of the whole of the works and the use to be made of the other land.

53. Notice to treat in respect of part of agricultural land. — (1) Where an acquiring authority serve notice to treat in respect of any agricultural land on a person (whether in occupation or not) having a greater interest in the land than as tenant for a year or from year to year, and that person has such an interest in other agricultural land comprised in the same agricultural unit as that to which the notice relates, the person on whom the notice is served (hereafter referred to as "the claimant") may, within the period of two months beginning with the date of service of the notice to treat, serve on the acquiring authority a counter-notice —

    (a) claiming that the other land is not reasonably capable of being farmed, either by itself or in conjunction with other relevant land, as a separate agricultural unit; and

    (b) requiring the acquiring authority to purchase his interest in the whole of the other land.

---

[16] Set up by the Lands Tribunal Act 1949 (replacing Official Arbitrators).

54. Effect of counter-notice under section 53. — (1) If the acquiring authority do not within the period of two months beginning with the date of service of a counter-notice under section 53 above agree in writing to accept the counter-notice as valid, the claimant or the authority may, within two months after the end of that period, refer it to the Lands Tribunal; and on any such reference the Tribunal shall determine whether the claim in the counter-notice is justified and declare the counter-notice valid or invalid in accordance with its determination of that question.

55. Notice of entry in respect of part of agricultural holding. — (1) Where an acquiring authority serve notice of entry under section 11 (1) of the Compulsory Purchase Act 1965[17] on the person in occupation of an agricultural holding, being a person having no greater interest therein than as tenant for a year or from year to year, and the notice relates to part only of that holding, the person on whom the notice is served (hereafter referred to as "the claimant") may, within the period of two months beginning with the date of service of the notice of entry, serve on the acquiring authority a counter-notice —

    (a) claiming that the remainder of the holding is not reasonably capable of being farmed, either by itself or in conjunction with other relevant land, as a separate agricultural unit; and

    (b) electing to treat the notice of entry as a notice relating to the entire holding.

56. Effect of counter-notice under section 55. — (1) If the acquiring authority do not within the period of two months beginning with the date of service of a counter-notice under section 55 above agree in writing to accept the counter-notice as valid, the claimant or the authority may, within two months after the end of that period, refer it to the Lands Tribunal; and on any such reference the Tribunal shall determine whether the claim in the counter-notice is justified and declare the counter-notice valid or invalid in accordance with its determination of that question.

These "all or nothing" provisions are so worded that they will only avail a claimant in respect of a "house, building or manufactory", or a "park or garden belonging to a house", or agricultural land, as the case may be. The courts have allowed a wide meaning to the words "house" and "building"; while the Lands Tribunal has considered what is meant by "material detriment".

In *Ravenseft Properties Ltd v London Borough of Hillingdon* (1968) 20 P & CR 483, the Lands Tribunal had to decide whether the claimants could be required to sell part only of their property to the council of the London Borough of Hillingdon when they were willing and able to sell the whole.

---

[17] See p. 828, ante. "Holding" signifies the aggregate of farm land in a tenancy.

The sitting member of the Tribunal, J. S. Daniel Esq. QC, said, at p. 484: "The property in question is Old Bank House, High Street, Uxbridge — the cradle, I was told, of Barclays Bank. . . .

On 6 October 1967, the council served notice to treat in respect of part only of the property. . . .

On 24 October 1967, the claimants' solicitors wrote to the council a letter which was in effect a counter notice to the council's notice to treat. It was stated that the claimants were willing and able to sell the whole property, that the part proposed to be taken could not be taken without material detriment to Old Bank House, and that the claimants accordingly required the council to acquire the whole property. . . .

The weight of judicial opinion seems to me to be conclusively in favour of the view that the word 'house' extends to a building which is used for business purposes and should not be restricted to mere dwelling-houses.

I therefore find that Old Bank House is a 'house' for the purposes of section 8 of the Act of 1965. . . .

It is clearly not the intention of the section that whenever the detriment is measurable in terms of money the option should be inviolate, for the reference to compensation for severance would then be meaningless. It seems to me to be intended rather that the significance or materiality of the detriment should be considered and determined by reference to its nature and degree, and that at the end of the day the question should be whether it is reasonable to subject the owner against his will to a truncation of his property (with compensation) rather than make a clean sweep by taking the whole. . . . I am by no means satisfied that the part proposed to be acquired can be taken without material detriment being caused. Indeed I am satisfied of the opposite. For in my view there is quite clearly a material detriment resulting from the loss of the rear access, the garage and the garden. I have inspected Old Bank House and the curtilage and surroundings, but it hardly needed this for me to come into the conclusion that the taking of the whole of the rear portion transforms the property into something quite different from what it was before; and the change is wholly for the bad. . . .

My finding therefore is that the claimants' counter-notice was valid and should be upheld, with the result that they cannot be required to sell part only of the property in question."

D. Purchase Price Compensation[18]

Compensation should as far as possible be claimed on a once-for-all basis as a lump sum[19]. This includes purchase price compensation, and

---

[18] Heap, pp. 285–293; Davies, pp. 136–177; Comp. Enc. 2: 1058–1148.

[19] "A person seeking to obtain compensation under these Acts of Parliament must once and for all make one claim for all damages which can be reasonably foreseen"; per ERLE CJ in *Chamberlain v West End of London and Crystal Palace Rly Co* (1863) 2 B & S 617.

compensation for other loss. Purchase price compensation is to be the "market value" of the freehold or leasehold being acquired[20].

If a leasehold is a statutorily protected farm or business tenancy, that protection must be taken into account when it is valued; and correspondingly the landlord's interest must be valued as being in reversion to a protected tenancy[1].

LAND COMPENSATION ACT 1961

5. Rules for assessing compensation. — Compensation in respect of any compulsory acquisition shall be assessed in accordance with the following rules:

(1) No allowance shall be made on account of the acquisition being compulsory:

(2) The value of land shall, subject as hereinafter provided, be taken to be the amount which the land if sold in the open market by a willing seller might be expected to realise[2]:

(5) Where land is, and but for the compulsory acquisition would continue to be, devoted to a purpose of such a nature that there is no general demand or market for land for that purpose, the compensation may, if the Lands Tribunal is satisfied that reinstatement in some other place is bona fide intended, be assessed on the basis of the reasonable cost of equivalent reinstatement[3]:

(6) The provisions of rule (2) shall not affect the assessment of compensation for disturbance or any other matter not directly based on the value of land:

and the following provisions of this Part of this Act shall have effect with respect to the assessment.

9. Disregard of depreciation due to prospect of acquisition by authority possessing compulsory powers. — No account shall be taken of any depreciation of the value of the relevant interest which is attributable to the fact that ... the relevant land is, or is likely, to be acquired by an authority possessing compulsory purchase powers[4].

---

[20] See *Pointe Gourde Quarrying and Transport Co Ltd v Sub-Intendent of Crown Lands* [1947] AC 565; *Lambe v Secretary of State for War* [1955] 2 QB 612, [1955] 2 All ER 386; *Wilson v Liverpool Corpn* [1971] 1 WLR 302, [1971] 1 All ER 628.

[1] Land Compensation Act 1973, ss. 47, 48. See also s. 59 (farm tenants served with *notice to quit* by acquiring authority may choose to leave as if expropriated under C.P.A. 1965, s. 20; see p. 828, ante). Ss. 47–48 will benefit acquiring bodies rather than tenants.

[2] See *Pointe Gourde Quarrying and Transport Co Ltd v Sub-Intendent of Crown Lands* [1947] AC 565, *Jelson Ltd v Blaby District Council* [1977] 1 WLR 1020, [1978] 1 All ER 548; *Melwood Units Pty Ltd v Commissioner of Main Roads* [1979] AC 426, [1979] 1 All ER 161; Land Compensation Act 1961, ss. 6–9.

[3] This is appropriate for properties that have no market value in their present state of development, such as churches and similar charities. See *Birmingham Corpn v West Midland Baptist (Trust) Association Inc.* [1970] AC 874, [1969] 3 All ER 172 and *Zoar Independent Church Trustees v Rochester Corpn* [1975] QB 246, [1974] 3 All ER 5. See also Land Compensation Act 1973, s. 45 (equivalent reinstatement of premises adapted for disabled persons). See also T.C.P.A. 1971, s. 116, as amended by Town and Country Amenities Act 1974, s. 6 (listed buildings).

[4] See also Land Compensation Act 1973, s. 50 (no reduction by virtue of rehousing).

14. Assumptions as to planning permission. — (1) For the purpose of assessing compensation in respect of any compulsory acquisition, such one or more of the assumptions mentioned in sections fifteen and sixteen of this Act as are applicable to the relevant land or any part thereof shall be made in ascertaining the value of the relevant interest.

(2) Any planning permission which is to be assumed in accordance with any of the provisions of those sections is in addition to any planning permission which may be in force at the date of service of the notice to treat.

The market value of land comprises two main elements: the existing use and the prospect of development[5]. The latter of these depends on what planning permissions are available for that land, or could reasonably be expected to be available but for the compulsory purchase. The assumptions as to planning permission referred to in the Land Compensation Act 1961[6] must be applied. What they amount to is that any prospect of development, had compulsory purchase not occurred, may be included as an element of market value if it would be reasonable to do so both on general grounds, broadly in accordance with the development plan, and in the circumstances of the land itself. A "certificate of appropriate alternative development"[7] from the local planning authority may be applied for if the development plan does not "zone" the area for lucrative development. But the underlying principle remains the "willing seller" rule in section 5 (2) of the 1961 Act (subject to a possible "set-off" in some cases: section 7).

PROVINCIAL PROPERTIES (LONDON) LTD *v* CATERHAM AND WARLINGHAM URBAN DISTRICT COUNCIL
[1972] 1 QB 453, [1972] 1 All ER 60 (CA, Lord DENNING MR, CAIRNS and ROSKILL LJJ)

LORD DENNING MR: At Whyteleafe in Surrey there is a high ridge of land which commands a lovely countryside. On it there used to be a large house called Bleak House, with grounds of some six acres. . . . The owners of Bleak House and its grounds were Provincial Properties

---

[5] The value of houses "unfit for habitation" under the Housing Act 1957, is normally restricted to that of the site alone. But see ss. 30, 31 of that Act: Land Compensation Act 1961, Sch. 2; and Housing Acts 1965 and 1969. See also Housing Act 1974 ss. 110–113 (listed buildings in slum clearance areas).

[6] Section 14, part of which is set out on this page, and ss. 15–16. It is assumed that permission exists for marginal or "existing use" development within T.C.P.A. 1971, 8th Sched., (see p. 856, post). But planning permission merely *liberates* development value, it does not *create* it. Only the market does that: see *Viscount Camrose v Basingstoke Corpns* [1966] 1 WLR 1100, [1966] 3 All ER 161 (p. 837, post) and a similar Court of Appeal decision in *Myers v Milton Keynes Development Corpn* [1974] 1 WLR 696, [1974] 2 All ER 1096. Permission is assumed for the authority's own project.

[7] Land Compensation Act 1961, ss. 17–22. Section 18 gives to the owner or to the authority a right of appeal to the Secretary of State whose decision may be challenged by the standard procedure of appealing within six weeks to the High Court on limited points of law only: s. 21. (See the *Jelson* case, p. 848, n. 20, post.).

(London) Ltd. They applied for planning permission to build houses there. They got permission for a portion of the six acres, but not for the whole. . . . At the very top of the ridge there was a stretch of land of only two-thirds of an acre. It had been part of the grounds of Bleak House, and zoned accordingly for residential purposes. The owners applied for planning permission to put up three houses on that small two-thirds of an acre. On 11 May 1966, the council rejected it. Thereupon the owners served a notice requiring the local council to purchase the land compulsorily. . . . On 9 December 1966, [the Minister] confirmed the purchase notice. Accordingly, the local council were deemed to have served a notice to treat on the owners in respect of the land, so as compulsorily to acquire it as at that date: section 133 of the Act of 1962[8].

So the question is: What is the compensation to be paid for this little piece of land? It is two-thirds of an acre at the top of the hill. It is zoned for residential purposes, but it is agreed on all hands that in no circumstances will planning permission ever be granted for it. It is also agreed that, if planning permission could be expected for it, the value would be £10,500. (I assume that is three plots for three houses at £3,500 a plot.) But if planning permission could not be expected for it, the value would only be £500. (I assume that is agricultural value, plus "hope" value.) So the owners claim £10,500. The acquiring authority say £500. . . .

The question depends on the true interpretation of the Land Compensation Act 1961. Section 16 (2)[9] says:

"If the relevant land or any part thereof (not being land subject to comprehensive development) consists or forms part of an area shown in the current development plan as an area allocated primarily for a use specified in the plan in relation to that area, it shall be assumed that planning permission would be granted, in respect of the relevant land or that part thereof, as the case may be, for any development which — (*a*) is development for the purposes of that use of the relevant land or that part thereof, and (*b*) is development for which planning permission might reasonably have been expected to be granted in respect of the relevant land or that part thereof, as the case may be."

Applying that section here, the opening words are clearly satisfied. The current development plan was the Surrey Development Plan. The relevant land was this two-thirds of an acre. It was part of an area which was shown in the current development plan as allocated primarily for residential use. That was a use specified in the plan in relation to the area. Then the section goes on: ". . . it shall be assumed that planning permission would be granted, . . . for any development which — (*a*) is development for the purposes of that use . . ." — that is,

---

[8] Now T.C.P.A. 1971, s. 186. Strictly speaking, the reference of a purchase notice to the Minister (now the Secretary of State) is not an "appeal"; the claimant is not then required to take action, because the duty to transmit the notice arises automatically.
[9] See p. 835, n. 9, ante.

in this case will be granted for any development which is residential. There the important conjunction is "and" — "and (*b*) is development for which planning permission might reasonably have been expected to be granted. . . ." It is quite plain that paragraph (*a*) is satisfied for residential development, but that paragraph (*b*) is not satisfied. On all the evidence planning permission could not reasonably be expected to be granted for this little two-thirds of an acre. It would be refused. So one of the assumptions does not exist. You cannot assume that planning permission would have been granted. No houses would be permitted on this piece of land. . . .

If planning permission could not reasonably be expected, then compensation is to be assessed accordingly. The owner gets its value without planning permission, that is, usually as agricultural land, not as building land. . . .

I would, therefore, allow the appeal and say the proper compensation is £500, and not £10,500.

Prospective development value on top of existing use value depends on genuine market demand as well as likelihood of planning permission. If the former is absent (which is perhaps unusual) the latter is insufficient on its own, and vice versa.

VISCOUNT CAMROSE *v* BASINGSTOKE CORPORATION
[1966] 1 WLR 1100, [1966] 3 All ER 161 (CA, LORD DENNING MR, DAVIES and RUSSELL LJJ)

LORD DENNING MR: In 1952 some of our great cities were congested and overpopulated. In order to relieve the congestion, Parliament passed the Town Development Act 1952. The overspill was to be siphoned off to the smaller towns. These towns were to expand so as to receive the influx. They were given compulsory powers to acquire land for the purpose. Basingstoke was one of the towns selected to receive an influx from London. . . . A goodly portion of the land they required, namely, 550 acres, was owned by the Viscount Camrose and the Hon. Michael Berry. The Basingstoke Council agreed to buy this land. The price was to be the sum which would have been payable if it had been compulsorily acquired. Mr. Hobbs, a member of the Lands Tribunal, sat to fix the price. . . .

Out of the 550 acres, the council are taking 383 acres for residential purposes. One hundred and fifty acres are near to the present town. Mr. Hobbs fixed their value at £291,400. But 233 acres are much further away. Mr. Hobbs fixed their value at £95,000. The landowners accept the figure for the 150 acres; but not the figure for the 233 acres. . . .

They say that, in putting the value at £400 an acre, the tribunal treated the 233 acres as agricultural land, ignoring the fact that it is to be valued on the footing that it has planning permission. I cannot accept this criticism. Even though the 233 acres are assumed to have planning permission, it does not follow that there would be a demand for it. It is not planning permission by itself which increases value. It is planning permission coupled with demand. The tribunal thought that the demand for these 233 acres was so far distant as to warrant only a "hope" of development, and valued them accordingly. I see nothing wrong with this method of calculation.

E.   Depreciation and Disturbance[10]

COMPULSORY PURCHASE ACT 1965

7.   Measure of compensation in case of severance. — In assessing the compensation to be paid by the acquiring authority under this Act regard shall be had not only to the value of the land to be purchased by the acquiring authority, but also to the damage, if any, to be sustained by the owner of the land by reason of the severing of the land purchased from the other land of the owner, or otherwise injuriously affecting that other land by the exercise of the powers conferred by this or the special Act.

10.   Further provision as to compensation for injurious affection. — (1) If any person claims compensation in respect of any land, or any interest in land, which has been taken for or injuriously affected by the execution of the works, and for which the acquiring authority have not made satisfaction under the provisions of this Act, or of the special Act, any dispute arising in relation to the compensation shall be referred to and determined by the Lands Tribunal.

(2) This section shall be construed as affording in all cases a right to compensation for injurious affection to land which is the same as the right which section 68 of the Lands Clauses Consolidation Act, 1845, has been construed as affording[14] in cases where the amount claimed exceeds fifty pounds.

LAND COMPENSATION ACT 1973

44.   Compensation for injurious affection. — (1) Where land is acquired or taken from any person for the purpose of works which are to be situated partly on that land and partly elsewhere, compensation for injurious affection of land retained by that person shall be assessed by reference to the whole of the works and not only the part situated on the land acquired or taken from him.

---

[10] Davies, pp. 178–233. Comp. Enc. 2: 1547–1558, 1567–1578, 2551, 2463–2467, 2520–2539.

[11] Injurious affection where no land has been taken from the claimant: see p. 840, post.

1. Right to compensation. — (1) Where the value of an interest in land is depreciated by physical factors caused by the use of public works, then, if —

(a) the interest qualifies for compensation under this Part of this Act; and

(b) the person entitled to the interest makes a claim within the time limited by and otherwise in accordance with this Part of this Act,

compensation for that depreciation shall, subject to the provisions of this Part of this Act, be payable by the responsible authority to the person making the claim (hereafter referred to as "the claimant").

(2) The physical factors mentioned in subsection (1) above are noise, vibration, smell, fumes, smoke and artificial lighting and the discharge on to the land in respect of which the claim is made of any solid or liquid substance.

(3) The public works mentioned in subsection (1) above are —

(a) any highway;

(b) any aerodrome; and

(c) any works or land (not beng a highway or aerodrome) provided or used in the exercise of statutory powers.

(4) The responsible authority mentioned in subsection (1) above is, in relation to a highway, the appropriate highway authority and, in relation to other public works, the person managing those works.

(6) Compensation shall not be payable under this Part of this Act in respect of the physical factors caused by the use of any public works other than a highway unless immunity from actions for nuisance in respect of that use is conferred (whether expressly or by implication) by an enactment relating to those works or, in the case of an aerodrome and physical factors caused by aircraft, the aerodrome is one to which section 41 (2) of the Civil Aviation Act 1949 (immunity from actions for nuisance) for the time being applies.

(8) Compensation shall not be payable under this Part of this Act on any claim unless the relevant date in relation to the claim falls on or after 17th October 1969.

(9) Subject to section 9[12] below, "the relevant date" in this Part of this Act means —

(a) in relation to a claim in respect of a highway, the date on which it was first open to public traffic;

(b) in relation to a claim in respect of other public works, the date on which they were first used after completion.

---

[12] S. 9 empowers the making of further claims when public works are extended or otherwise altered at a later date. Other sections which should be noticed are s. 3, which prescribes the "claim period" (between 1 and 3 years after the works come into use); s. 5, which excludes most development value from the compensation; s. 6, which imposes a set-off if the claimant *benefits* from the works; and s. 7, which prohibits claims not exceeding £50.

2. Interests qualifying for compensation. — (1) An interest qualifies for compensation under this Part of this Act if it was acquired by the claimant before the relevant date in relation to the claim and the requirements of subsection (2) or, as the case may be, subsection (3) below are satisfied on the date on which notice of the claim for compensation in respect of that interest is served.

(2) If and so far as the interest is in land which is a dwelling, the said requirements are —

    (*a*) that the interest is an owner's interest; and

    (*b*) where the interest carries the right to occupy the land, that the land is occupied by the claimant in right of that interest as his residence.

(3) If and so far as the interest is not in such land as aforesaid, the said requirements are —

    (*a*) that the interest is that of an owner-occupier; and

    (*b*) that the land is or forms part of either —

        (i) a hereditament the annual value of which does not exceed the prescribed amount[13]; or

        (ii) an agricultural unit.

(4) In this section "owner's interest" in relation to any land, means the legal fee simple therein or a tenancy thereof granted or extended for a term of years certain of which, on the date of service of the notice of claim in respect thereof, not less than three years remain unexpired.

(5) In this section "owner-occupier", in relation to land in a hereditament, means a person who occupies the whole or a substantial part of the land in right of an owner's interest therein and, in relation to land in an agricultural unit, means a person who occupies the whole of that unit and is entitled, while so occupying it, to an owner's interest in the whole or any part of that land.

Included in the lump sum of compensation for reasonably foreseeable loss are other items beyond the purchase price. Any land *retained* by the owner after the compulsory purchase of the land *taken* may be "injuriously affected" — i.e. depreciated — by (*a*) "severance" (*pro rata* reduction in its value) or (*b*) what is done on the land taken[14]. "Disturbance" (loss and expenses through having to move and obtain new premises), and "any other matter" (such as the cost of preparing a compensation claim) may also be included; but these do not arise from land depreciation and are considered separately below.

"Injurious affection" of land *may* entitle its owner to compensation even if no land has been taken from him, but only for land depreciation (not trade or other loss) caused by the carrying out, by an acquiring authority, of works on nearby land and not by the subsequent use of

---

[13] The same as for blight notices: see p. 850, n. 4 post.
[14] "Severance", "injurious affection" and "disturbance" are nowhere defined. Their meaning is made apparent by context and usage.

those works, and only if the cause of loss would be actionable at common law[15].

Part I of the Land Compensation Act 1973 gives an additional, independent, right of compensation for land depreciation where no land has been taken, in cases where it is the subsequent use which causes the loss, in the form of "physical factors" as listed in section 1 (2). It is clear that the nature of "injurious affection" is broadly (but not precisely) the same as that of privately actionable nuisance, and that compensation for it is necessary in so far as public bodies are immune from liability in nuisance, or allegedly so.

The courts have held that disturbance compensation, which covers items of expenditure caused by "the fact of having to vacate the premises"[16], may be included, as of right, in any claim by an *owner-occupier*. It habitually covers such matters as loss of goodwill[17] and business profits[18], and the cost of removal and of acquiring other premises — even expenditure on an abortive purchase, provided it was bona fide. Extra expense on dearer property is to be "value for money" and not compensatable[19]. Expenses incurred in preparing a claim are compensatable as well[20], but under the residuary head of "any other matter[1], and not as disturbance. It should be noted that disturbance compensation is not consistent with a claim for purchase price compensation which includes prospective development value, because the vendor would sell willingly to obtain the latter and meet the cost of disturbance himself; the vendor is merely entitled to the higher of two amounts: existing use value with disturbance, or full development value without.

In *Harvey v Crawley Development Corporation* [1957] 1 QB 485, [1957] 1 All ER 504, the Court of Appeal held that the expenses involved in obtaining another house as a replacement for that compulsorily acquired were properly included in a claim for disturbance. DENNING LJ said, at p. 492:

"Mrs. Harvey is entitled to 'compensation for disturbance', which . . . includes all damage directly consequent on the taking of the house under statutory powers. The question is whether these costs of £241 10s. 1d. come within that head.

---

[15] Most of the law in this area has evolved through decided cases. See, for example, *Holt v Gas Light and Coke Co* (1872) LR 7 QB 728; *Duke of Buccleuch v Metropolitan Board of Works* (1872) LR 5 HL 418; *Hammersmith and City Rly Co v Brand* (1869) LR 4 HL 171; *Metropolitan Board of Works v McCarthy* (1874) LR 7 HL 243; *Ricket v Metropolitan Rly Co* (1867) LR 2 HL 175; *Re Simeon and Isle of Wight R.D.C.* [1937] Ch 525, [1937] 3 All ER 149; *Argyle Motors (Birkenhead) Ltd v Birkenhead Corpn* [1975] AC 99, [1974] 1 All ER 201.

[16] Per DAVIES LJ, in *Lee v Minister of Transport* [1966] 1 QB 111, [1965] 2 All ER 986.

[17] On this, see *Bailey v Derby Corpn* [1965] 1 WLR 213, [1965] 1 All ER 443, and Land Compensation Act 1973, s. 46.

[18] On the question of taxation, see *Stoke on Trent City Council v Wood, Mitchell & Co Ltd* [1979] 2 All ER 65.

[19] *Harvey v Crawley Development Corpn* [1957] 1 QB 485, [1957] 1 All ER 504. Items claimed must be reasonable and not too remote; per ROMER LJ, in that case.

[20] *LCC v Tobin* [1959] 1 WLR 354, [1959] 1 All ER 649.

[1] Land Compensation Act 1961, s. 5, rule (6). See p. 834, ante.

I would like to say at the outset that the sum of £4,148 1s. which Mrs. Harvey has already received does not include anything in respect of these costs of £241 10s 1d. to which she has been put in getting another house. If you sell your house for £4,000, you can put the £4,000 into the bank and keep it. If you buy another house for £4,000, you can take the money out of the bank to pay for it, and you have your value of £4,000 in the shape of the new house. But you have to find the costs from some other pocket. . . .

Mrs. Harvey gets compensation for having to move out her furniture and put in into the new house: she gets compensation for having to alter the curtains and carpets and remake them to fit the new windows and floors. Take business premises where fixtures and fittings have to be moved; or where there is loss of business through being turned out; or loss of goodwill. All that loss and expense is the proper subject of 'compensation for disturbance' in addition to the open market value of the land. . . .

These illustrations show that the owner only recovers costs of the present kind in a case where a house is occupied by an owner living there who is forced out and reasonably finds a house elsewhere in which to live. If he pays a higher price for the new house, he would not get compensation on that account, because he would be presumed to have got value for his money: but he does get the costs which he has to pay a surveyor and lawyer to get it. It seems to me that the costs are then the subject of compensation under the heading of 'disturbance' as specified in rule (6)."

HORN v SUNDERLAND CORPORATION
[1941] 2 KB 26, [1941] 1 All ER 480 (CA, GREENE MR SCOTT and GODDARD LJJ)

Sunderland Corporation served a notice to treat on Horn, as owner of Springwell Farm. Horn claimed, in addition to compensation assessed at £22,700 for the full development value as building land, compensation for disturbance in respect of its existing use as agricultural land.

Held. (GODDARD LJ dissenting). The true loss to be compensated would be either development value or existing use value plus disturbance, whichever was the greater; but not both.

GREENE MR: The truth of the matter is that . . . the sum to be ascertained is in essence one sum, namely, the proper price or compensation payable in all the circumstances of the case. If those circumstances are such as to make it impossible for the owner to claim that he has suffered damage through disturbance for which he ought to be compensated, then he is not entitled to have the price or compensation for his land increased by an addition for disturbance even if he has in fact been disturbed. . . .

In the present case the respondent was occupying for farming purposes land which had a value far higher than that of agricultural land. In other words, he was putting the land to a use which, economically speaking, was not its best use, a thing which he was, of course, perfectly entitled to do. The result of the compulsory purchase will be to give him a sum equal to the true economic value of the land as building land, and he thus will realize from the land a sum which never could have been realized on the basis of agricultural user. Now he is claiming that the land from which he is being expropriated is for the purpose of valuation to be treated as building land and for the purpose of disturbance as agricultural land, and he says that the sum properly payable to him for the loss of his land is (*a*) its value as building land plus (*b*) a sum for disturbance of his farming business. It appears to me that, subject to a qualification which I will mention later, these claims are inconsistent with one another. . . .

In *Mizen Bros v Mitcham UDC* (1929) 19th July (unreported) the same point as that which arises here was decided in favour of the acquiring authority by a Divisional Court consisting of Lord Hewart CJ, and Avory and Branson JJ. We have been furnished with a transcript of the argument and the judgment. There was no reasoned judgment, but the considerations which influenced the members of the Court sufficiently appear from their interlocutory observations. In that case the land was used as a market garden and was in a high state of cultivation. It had erected on it greenhouses and other trade fixtures. The value of the land (including greenhouses and fixtures) as market garden land did not exceed £12,000, but the land was ripe for immediate development for building and on that basis was valued by the arbitrator at £17,280, a sum which could only be realized if vacant possession were given, the seller being at liberty to remove the greenhouses, etc. and plants and crops. The arbitrator assessed the value of tenant right, fixtures, and disturbances (assuming that the owners were entitled to claim it) at £4,640, a sum which, when added to the valuation of £12,000 on a market garden basis, fell short of the value assessed on a building basis. The question submitted by the arbitrator for the opinion of the Court was:

"whether the claimants are entitled to receive compensation in respect of the greenhouses and other trade fixtures, forced sale or removal of crops and plants, and compensation for disturbance and loss of business, in addition to the amount which the land, if sold in the open market by a willing seller to a willing buyer with vacant possession, might be expected to realize."

This question the Court answered in the negative, and, in my opinion, rightly so. . . .

From what I have said, it will appear (and this is the qualification which I have mentioned) that, in my opinion, the respondent is disentitled to an award for disturbance only if the sum of £22,700 equals or exceeds the value of the land based on the hypothesis that it will be used only for farming purposes, plus whatever value should be attributed to the minerals, plus the loss by disturbance. To the extent (if at all) that the sum of these figures exceeds the sum of £22,700, compensation should be awarded.

In cases where a short-term tenant is not expropriated but dispossessed at common law by an acquiring authority compulsorily purchasing only the reversion, disturbance cannot be claimed because there is no compulsory purchase compensation claim in which to include it[2]. The authority obtains possession as *landlord*; and landlords do not pay disturbance to their departing tenants (although they may be liable under statute to make certain analogous payments to business and farm tenants who are dispossessed). Statutory provision for the payment of disturbance as of right[3] has now partially filled this gap[4].

F.   Assessment of Compensation[5]

LAND COMPENSATION ACT 1961

1.   Tribunal for assessing compensation in respect of land compulsorily acquired. — Where by or under any statute (whether passed before or after the passing of this Act) land is authorised to be acquired compulsorily, any question of disputed compensation and, where any part of the land to be acquired is subject to a lease which comprises land not acquired, any question as to the apportionment of the rent payable under the lease, shall be referred to the Lands Tribunal and shall be determined by the Tribunal in accordance with the following provisions of this Act.

An appeal lies, by way of case stated, on points of law only, to the Court of Appeal, and must be made within six weeks of the decision of the Lands Tribunal[6]. Where acquiring authorities serve notice of entry and take possession before payment of compensation, interest is payable on the compensation awarded[7]. Compensation should be assessed at the date, not of the notice to treat, but of the assessment

---

[2] The same applies to licensees. See *DHN Food Distributors Ltd v Tower Hamlets London Borough Council* [1976] 1 WLR 852, [1976] 3 All ER 462.

[3] See Part III of the Land Compensation Act 1973. Displaced residents may claim "home loss payments" (ss. 29–33); displaced farmers with terms of 3 years or longer may claim "farm loss payments" (ss. 34–6); displaced occupants of land other than farm land may, if not entitled to normal compensation, claim "disturbance payments" (ss. 37–8). See *R v Corby District Council, ex parte McLean* [1975] 1 WLR 735; [1975] 2 All ER 568.

[4] See also Land Compensation Act 1973, ss. 39–43, concerning the rehousing of displaced residents.

[5] Davies, pp. 121–135; Comp. Enc. 2: 738–757; 2, 1048–1057. Note that, under Land Compensation Act 1973, s. 52, if the acquiring authority take possession before payment they may be required by the claimant to pay in advance of completion 90% of the amount as agreed or estimated.

[6] Lands Tribunal Act 1949, s. 3 (4); Rules of Supreme Court (Revision) 1965, Sch. 1, Order 61. This is not, of course, confined to compulsory purchase disputes.

[7] C.P.A. 1965, s. 11; Land Compensation Act 1961, s. 32. See also Land Compensation Act 1973, s. 63. The authority must always pay the conveyancing costs (C.P.A. 1965, s. 23).

itself, (or of taking possession, if earlier) or of the beginning of reinstatement[8].

VIII. Compulsory Purchase in Planning

A. Planning Purposes and Community Land[9]

The Community Land Act 1975 brought into effect an elaborate system of land acquisition by local authorities in addition to the powers conferred on them by other statutes. The object of the Act was to ensure that land required for "relevant development" — i.e. development on any appreciable scale — should first be acquired by local authorities and then developed either by them or by private developers acquiring it from them. But in consequence of the change of government in 1979 the Act of 1975 is due to be repealed.

TOWN AND COUNTRY PLANNING ACT 1971

112. Compulsory acquisition of land in connection with development and for other planning purposes. — (1) The Secretary of State may authorise a local authority to whom this section applies to acquire compulsorily any land within their area if he is satisfied —

(a) that the land is required in order to secure the treatment as a whole, by development, redevelopment or improvement, or partly by one and partly by another method, of the land or of any area in which the land is situated; or

(b) that it is expedient in the public interest that the land should be held together with land so required; or

(c) that the land is required for development or redevelopment, or both, as a whole for the purpose of providing for the relocation of population or industry or the replacement of open space in the course of the redevelopment or improvement, or both, of another area as a whole; or

(d) that it is expedient to acquire the land immediately for a purpose which it is necessary to achieve in the interests of the proper planning of an area in which the land is situated.

(4) The Acquisition of Land (Authorisation Procedure) Act 1946 shall apply to the compulsory acquisition of land under this section and accordingly shall have effect as if this section had been in force immediately before the commencement of that Act.

(5) The local authorities to whom this section applies are the councils of counties and . . . districts, the Greater London Council and the councils of London boroughs.

---

[8] *Birmingham Corpn v West Midland Baptist (Trust) Association Inc.* [1970] AC 874, [1969] 3 All ER 172. For leaseholds, see *Holloway v Dover Corpn* [1960] 1 WLR 604, [1960] 2 All ER 193 (including the effect of statutory protection of tenure) and *Blamires v Bradford Corpn* [1964] Ch 585, [1964] 2 All ER 603 (equitable lease for life).
[9] Heap, pp. 282-284, 294-299; Davies, pp. 237-267; Comp. Enc. 2: 2003-2074.

122. Appropriation of land held for planning purposes. — (1) Where any land has been acquired or appropriated by a local authority for planning purposes and is for the time being held by the authority for the purposes for which it was so acquired or appropriated, the authority . . . may appropriate the land for any purpose for which they are or may be authorised in any capacity to acquire land by virtue of or under any enactment not contained in this Part of this Act[10].

123. Disposal of land held for planning purposes. — (1) Where any land has been acquired or appropriated by a local authority for planning purposes, and is for the time being held by the authority for the purposes for which it was so acquired or appropriated, the authority may dispose of the land to such person, in such manner and subject to such conditions as may appear to them to be expedient. . . .

124. Development of land held for planning purposes. — (1) The functions of a local authority shall include power for the authority, notwithstanding any limitation imposed by law on the capacity of the authority by virtue of its constitution, to erect, construct or carry out any building or work on any land to which this section applies, not being a building or work for the erection, construction or carrying out of which, whether by that local authority or by any other person, statutory power exists by virtue of, or could be conferred under, an alternative enactment.

(2) This section applies to any land which has been acquired or appropriated by a local authority for planning purposes and is for the time being held by the authority for the purposes for which it was so acquired or appropriated.

Land may also be acquired by agreement[11]. "Planning purposes" is not defined. In practice it usually refers to urban redevelopment or "urban renewal", otherwise known as "positive" planning[12]. But if authorities want to carry out development themselves instead of disposing of land to private developers, the consent of the Secretary of State is needed.

---

[10] Part VI, (ss. 112–133). For a general power to appropriate, see Local Government Act 1972, s. 122.

[11] T.C.P.A. 1971, s. 119.

[12] In a wider sense other bodies can be regarded as empowered to acquire land for planning purposes; for example development corporations and the Commission for the New Towns (under the New Towns Act 1965), local authorities (under the Town Development Act 1952) and the Countryside Commission and local authorities (under the Countryside Act 1968). There is also the question of acquisition of listed buildings (T.C.P.A. 1971, ss. 114–117; p. 821, n. 17, ante); while Part II of the Land Compensation Act 1973 gives authorities power to acquire land to avoid or mitigate "adverse effects" of public works on it or on adjoining properties.

B. Purchase Notices[13]

The procedure under these notices amounts to "compulsory purchase in reverse", that is to say, at the instance of the vendor and not of the acquiring authority. No C.P.O. is needed. Compensation is payable as for an ordinary compulsory purchase.

TOWN AND COUNTRY PLANNING ACT 1971

180. Purchase notice on refusal or conditional grant of planning permission. — (1) Where, on an application for planning permission to develop any land, permission is refused or is granted subject to conditions, then if any owner of the land claims —

(a) that the land has become incapable of reasonably beneficial use in its existing state; and

(b) in a case where planning permission was granted subject to conditions, that the land cannot be rendered capable of reasonably beneficial use by the carrying out of the permitted development in accordance with those conditions; and

(c) in any case, that the land cannot be rendered capable of reasonably beneficial use by the carrying out of any other development for which planning permission has been granted or for which the local planning authority or the Secretary of State has undertaken to grant planning permission,

he may, within the time and in the manner prescribed by regulations under this Act, serve on the council of the London borough or ... district in which the land is situated a notice requiring that council to purchase his interest in the land in accordance with the following provisions of this Part of this Act[14].

(7) A notice under this section, or under any other provision[15] of this Part of this Act to which this subsection is applied, is in this Act referred to as a "purchase notice".

181. Action by council on whom purchase notice is served — (1) The council on whom a purchase notice is served under section 180 of this Act shall, before the end of the period of three months beginning with the date of service of that notice, serve on the owner by whom the purchase notice was served a notice stating either —

(a) that the council are willing to comply with the purchase notice; or

(b) that another local authority or statutory undertakers specified in the notice under this subsection have agreed to comply with it in their place; or

(c) that, for reasons specified in the notice under this subsection, the council are not willing to comply with the purchase notice and have not found any other local authority or statutory

---

[13] Heap, pp. 143, 264–269; Davies, pp. 268–277; Comp. Enc. 2: 2122–2158.

[14] Part IX. See ss. 72, 191 for industrial development and s. 185 for office development.

[15] See ss. 188–191 (revocation, discontinuance, listed buildings, trees, advertisements).

undertakers who will agree to comply with it in their place, and they have transmitted a copy of the purchase notice to the Secretary of State, on a date specified in the notice under this subsection, together with a statement of the reasons so specified.

(2) Where the council on whom a purchase notice is served by an owner have served on him a notice in accordance with subsection (1) (a) or (b) of this section, the council, or the other local authority or statutory undertakers specified in the notice, as the case may be, shall be deemed to be authorised to acquire the interest of the owner compulsorily in accordance with the relevant provisions, and to have served a notice to treat in respect thereof on the date of service of the notice under that subsection.

(4) In this section "the relevant provisions" means the provisions of Part VI[16] of this Act or, in the case of statutory undertakers, any statutory provision (however expressed) under which they have power, or may be authorised, to purchase land compulsorily for the purposes of their undertaking.

For a purchase notice to take effect after rejection by the local authority it has to be confirmed by the Secretary of State. But he must not do so merely because the land would otherwise be less valuable, since this applies to nearly all cases of planning refusals: in effect the land must be virtually useless as a result of the adverse decision[17].

In *R v Minister of Housing and Local Government, ex parte Chichester RDC* [1960] 1 WLR 587, [1960] 2 All ER 407, the Minister had upheld a purchase notice which was served upon a local authority after an adverse planning decision, on the ground that the land had become of substantially less use and value to the owner. The purchase notice was quashed in the Divisional Court.

Lord PARKER CJ, said, at p. 589: "The fact that the land is less useful, to use a comprehensive term, in its present state than if developed is clearly not the test. The Minister continues: 'The Minister therefore accepts his inspector's view that the land in its existing state and with the benefit of the temporary planning permissions that have been granted is of substantially less use and value to its owner than it would be if planning permission had been granted (without limitation as to time) for the rebuilding of the buildings which stood on the land

---

[16] Relating to acquisition of land "for planning purposes"; see p. 846, ante.
[17] The claimant is *entitled* to have his purchase notice confirmed if his land is indeed rendered "incapable of reasonably beneficial use" by a refusal of planning permission; unless it was expressly or impliedly agreed, as a condition of receiving a *previous* planning permission, that the land in question *should for amenity reasons remain undeveloped,* (T.C.P.A. 1971, s. 184). For recent cases in which compensation principles were considered in relation to a purchase notice, see *Margate Corpn v Devotwill Investments Ltd* [1970] 3 All ER 864; *Jelson Ltd v Minister of Housing and Local Government* [1970] 1 QB 243, [1969] 3 All ER 147; *Provincial Properties (London) Ltd v Caterham and Warlingham UDC* [1972] 1 QB 453, [1972] 1 All ER 60; p. 835, ante.

on the appointed day, or which formerly stood there and have been demolished since 7 January 1937. He is accordingly satisfied that the conditions specified in ... the Act are fulfilled.' In my judgment that passage discloses an error of law in this speaking order. It is not, as I have said, a question of whether the land is of less use or substantially less use in its present state than if developed, and it is a non-sequitur to say that because it is of substantially less use than if developed, therefore the conditions specified ... are fulfilled. . . . I am satisfied that the ground, and the only ground, stated by the Minister, is not a valid ground at all and accordingly in my judgment this decision will have to be quashed."

C. Blight Notices[18]

Blight notice procedure, too, amounts to "compulsory purchase in reverse" and, as with purchase notices, no C.P.O. is needed and compensation follows the normal rules. But whereas purchase notices arise from adverse planning *decisions,* blight notices arise from adverse planning *proposals.*

TOWN AND COUNTRY PLANNING ACT 1971

192. Scope of these provisions.[19] — (1) The provisions of sections 193 to 207 of this Act shall have effect in relation to land which —

(a) is land indicated in a structure plan in force for the district in which it is situated either as land which may be required for the purposes of any functions of a government department, local authority or statutory undertakers, or of the National Coal Board, or as land which may be included in an action area[20]; or

(b) is land allocated for the purposes of any such functions by a local plan in force for the district or is land defined in such a plan as the site of proposed development for the purposes of any such functions; or

(c) is land indicated in a development plan (otherwise than by being dealt with in a manner mentioned in the preceding paragraphs) as land on which a highway is proposed to be constructed or land to be included in a highway as proposed to be improved or altered; or

(d) is land on or adjacent to the line of a highway proposed to be constructed, improved or altered, as indicated in an order or scheme which has come into operation under the provisions of Part II of the Highways Act 1959 relating to trunk roads or special roads or as indicated in an order which has come into operation under section 1 of the Highways Act 1971, being land in relation to which a power of compulsory acquisition conferred by any of the provisions of Part X of the said Act of

---

[18] Heap, pp. 269–279; Davies, pp. 278–291; Comp. Enc. 2: 2159–2209, 2587–2604.
[19] Now extended by the Land Compensation Act 1973 (see p. 851, post).
[20] See T.C.P.A. 1971, s. 7: p. 781, ante.

1959 or Part III of the said Act of 1971 (including a power compulsorily to acquire any right by virtue of section 47 of the said Act of 1971) may become exercisable, as being land required for purposes of construction, improvement or alteration as indicated in the order or scheme; or

(e) is land shown on plans approved by a resolution of a local highway authority as land comprised in the site of a highway as proposed to be constructed, improved or altered by that authority; or

(f) is land on which the Secretary of State proposes to provide a trunk road or a special road and has given to the local planning authority written notice of his intention to provide the road, together with maps or plans sufficient to identify the proposed route of the road; or

(g) is land in the case of which —

(i) there is in force a compulsory purchase order made by a highway authority in the exercise of highway land acquisition powers and providing, by virtue of section 47 of the Highways Act 1971, for the acquisition of a right or rights over that land; and

(ii) the highway authority have power to serve, but have not served, notice to treat in respect of the right or rights;

(h) is land indicated by information published in pursuance of section 31 of the Housing Act 1969 as land which a local authority propose to acquire in the exercise of their powers under Part II of that Act (general improvement areas); or

(i) is land authorised by a special enactment to be compulsorily acquired, or land falling within the limits of deviation within which powers of compulsory acquisition conferred by a special enactment are exercisable; or

(j) is land in respect of which a compulsory purchase order is in force, where the appropriate authority have power to serve, but have not served, notice to treat in respect of the land.

(3) Interests qualifying for protection under these provisions are either —

(a) interests in hereditaments or parts of hereditaments; or

(b) interests in agricultural units or parts of agricultural units.

(4) An interest in the whole or part of a hereditament shall be taken to be an interest qualifying for protection under these provisions if, on the date of service of a notice under section 193 of this Act in respect thereof, either —

(a) the annual value of the hereditament does not exceed such amount as may be prescribed for the purposes of this paragraph by an order made by the Secretary of State[1], and the

---

[1] £2,250; Town and Country Planning (Limit of Annual Value) Order 1973. (S.I. 1973 No. 425) which was made after the rating revaluation of that year. For the meaning of "owner-occupier" and "owner's interest", see T.C.P.A. 1971, s. 203, and p. 853, post.

interest in question is the interest of an owner occupier of the hereditament; or

(b) in a case not falling within the preceding paragraph, the interest in question is the interest of a resident owner occupier of the hereditament.

(5) An interest in the whole or part of an agricultural unit shall be taken to be an interest qualifying for protection under these provisions if on the date of service of a notice under section 193 of this Act in respect thereof, it is the interest of an owner occupier of the unit.

(6) In this section and in the said sections 193 to 207 "these provisions" means the provisions of this section and of those sections, "the specified descriptions" means the descriptions contained in subsection (1) (a) to (j) of this section and "blight notice" means a notice served under section 193 or 201 of this Act.

193. Power to serve blight notice.[2] — (1) Where the whole or part of a hereditament or agricultural unit is comprised in land of any of the specified descriptions, and a person claims that —

(a) he is entitled to an interest in that hereditament or unit; and

(b) the interest is one which qualifies for protection under these provisions; and

(c) he has made reasonable endeavours to sell that interest; and

(d) in consequence of the fact that the hereditament or unit or a part of it was, or was likely to be, comprised in land of any of the specified descriptions, he has been unable to sell that interest except at a price substantially lower than that for which it might reasonably have been expected to sell if no part of the hereditament or unit were, or were likely to be, comprised in such land,

he may serve on the appropriate authority a notice in the prescribed form requiring that authority to purchase that interest to the extent specified in, and otherwise in accordance with, these provisions.

The Land Compensation Act 1973, sections 68–76, has increased (in great detail) the scope of the "specified descriptions". These new provisions are chiefly concerned with making it possible to serve a blight notice at an earlier stage in the proceedings which foreshadow the official acquisition or use of the "blighted" land, for example while proposals are still being considered in draft before formal approval is given. But they also include additional categories of situation, for example slum clearance.

A "blight notice" is served on the prospective acquiring authority as such, not the local authority as such. The authority may object by means of a counter notice within two months, denying that the situation is within the "specified description", or that the interest of

----

[2] Section 193 was amended by the Land Compensation Act 1973, s. 77, and is set out here in its amended form. See also s. 79 of that Act (farms partially blighted).

the claimant is that of an owner occupier (or owner occupier's mortgagee, if entitled to exercise his power of sale) "qualifying for protection", or that genuinely unsuccessful efforts to sell on the open market have been made, or that they in fact intend to acquire any or all of the land.[3] If the claimant wishes to persist he may within a further two months refer the matter to the Lands Tribunal.[4] It should be noted that land is not defined or allocated in a development plan for the functions of some public body, and does not therefore come within one of the "specified descriptions", merely because it is "zoned" in such a plan for development which might be undertaken by some public body or by private developers.

BOLTON CORPORATION *v* OWEN
[1962] 1 QB 470, [1962] 1 All ER 101 (CA, Lord EVERSHED MR, WILLMER and DANCKWERTS LJJ)

The development plan showed the claimant's house as "within an area scheduled for residential development". The claimant argued that this brought his house within the "specified descriptions" as being required for the purpose of the housing authority.

Held. The residential development for which the area was "zoned" might be private or public. The land in question was not necessarily allocated for the functions of a public body, and the claim failed.

WILLMER LJ: The sole issue in this case . . . is whether the claimant is right in his contention that his house falls within [the specified descriptions] . . . By his decision, which was annexed to the case stated, together with the written statement and relevant maps comprised in the development plan, the member of the Lands Tribunal concluded that the appellants had not satisfied him that their objection to the claimant's notice was well founded, and he, therefore, declared that the notice was a valid notice. In this respect the member of the tribunal undoubtedly fell into error, as he himself recognised when he came to state the case; for the burden of proof was not upon the appellants to satisfy him that their objection was well founded. It is agreed that in the circumstances of this case . . . unless it is shown to the satisfaction of the tribunal that the objection is not well founded, the tribunal shall uphold the objection . . .

On this ground alone it seems to me that the appellants are entitled to succeed on this appeal, and that the decision of the Lands Tribunal cannot stand. But . . . I think it right to express my view, as briefly as I can, upon the question of principle which has been debated before us. . . .

The claimant's case is based upon the fact that the appellants, in addition to being the planning authority, are also the housing

---

[3] T.C.P.A. 1971, s. 194.
[4] The burden of proof is on the authority if they deny that they intend to acquire the land; otherwise the burden is on the claimant: T.C.P.A. 1971, s. 195. If they succeed on the ground of having no intention to acquire, their compulsory purchase powers over the land in question lapse; T.C.P.A. 1971, s. 199.

authority within the Housing Act 1957. Consequently, it is said, the claimant's house, being within an area scheduled for residential redevelopment, comes within the description of land allocated for the purposes of the functions of the appellants as such housing authority. The written statement, in relation to the redevelopment areas specified, is silent as to who is to carry out the redevelopment, i.e., whether it is to be done by the appellants or by private enterprise. But the member of the tribunal was invited to draw, and did draw, the inference that an area such as No. 6, within which the claimant's house is to be found, could as a matter of practical politics only be redeveloped by the local authority exercising its functions as such. . . .

It might be otherwise if the area in question was allocated by the development plan specifically for housing development by the appellants in pursuance of their powers under the Housing Act. But here the development plan is silent as to how the proposed development is to be carried out, and makes no reference to the powers and duties of the appellants under the Housing Act. In the absence of any such specific reference, I do not think it was permissible for the member of the Lands Tribunal to speculate upon the probability or otherwise of the area in question being cleared and redeveloped by the appellants in the exercise of their functions as housing authority, rather than by private enterprise.

In these circumstances I do not think that the claimant has discharged the burden of showing that the area within which his house falls is land allocated by the development plan for the purposes of the functions of the appellants as local authority.

An "owner occupier" must be a freeholder or a leaseholder with three years to run, having been in occupation either in whole or in part for at least six months before making the claim, or for at least six months before leaving the premises unoccupied for not longer than twelve months before making his claim[5].

IX. Betterment

A. Taxation of Development Value[6]

"Development value" must be distinguished from the "existing use value" of land and also from the actual cost of development. The price of land after it has been developed will represent an aggregation of all three items[7]. Development value depends on genuine suitability and

---

[5] T.C.P.A. 1971, s. 203. Section 201 gives a mortgagee a further period of 6 months in which to serve a notice.

[6] Davies, pp. 295–321; Enc. of Land Development: passim.

[7] "Betterment" in its modern sense of "development value" differs from its older sense of *increase in both the existing use value and the prospective development value of land due to public improvement of other land nearby;* see the Final Report of the Expert Committee on Compensation and Betterment 1942. Cmd. 6386 (the Uthwatt Committee).

market demand for development, plus planning permission. The argument goes that, unlike existing use value or *actual* development, an owner has not paid for it, but (in a sense) the community has. Two questions arise: *First:* Should there be compensation for loss of "betterment" by reason of planning control? *Second:* Should "betterment" be retained by owners who do have the benefit of it, or should all or any of it go to the community? The first question is dealt with by the law on planning compensation, the second by taxation of betterment, and the answers ought to be consistent.

DEVELOPMENT LAND TAX ACT 1976

1. **Development land tax.** — (1) A tax, to be called development land tax, shall be charged in accordance with the provisions of this Act in respect of the realisation of the development value of land in the United Kingdom.

(2) Subject to the provisions of this Act, a person shall be chargeable to development land tax on the realised development value, determined in accordance with this Act, which accrues to him on the disposal by him on or after the appointed day of an interest in land in the United Kingdom, and shall be so chargeable whether or not he is resident (for purposes of income tax or otherwise) in the United Kingdom.

2. **Deemed disposals at start of material development.** — (1) Immediately before a project of material development is begun on any land, every major interest then subsisting in that land shall be deemed for the purposes of this Act to be disposed of for a consideration equal to its market value at that time and to be immediately reacquired at that value.

(2) Part I of Schedule 1 to this Act shall have effect for determining what is a project of material development[8].

The rate of tax on "realised development value" was first set at 80%, subject to various exceptions. With the change of government in 1979 this has been reduced to 60%, and the first £50,000 of "realised development value" in each current financial year will be exempt.

Elaborate calculations are prescribed in order to ascertain what part, if any, of an actual or deemed disposal price constitutes "realised development value" in a particular case. As explained above (p. 835 ante), development value refers to the prospect of development, and is that part of the market value of land, if any, which relates to its prospective development as distinct from its existing use.

---

[8] "Material development" means development outside (a) the classes prescribed by the General Development Order (p. 794, ante) and (b) certain similar categories contained in Sch. 4, Part II, of the 1976 Act itself. The beginning of a project of "material development" is deemed to be a disposal of the land where the development takes place, because it is at that moment that an owner realises development value if he has decided to develop the land himself instead of selling it. But he realises that value as *land value* and not as money. The "appointed day" was 1 August 1976.

Development value is "realised" when it makes its first appearance in a disposal price. Thus if W sells a field to X, for farming use only, at a price of £1,000, and X then re-sells to Y for a price of £20,000, the additional sum of £19,000 (leaving aside inflation and other factors) will be attributable to market demand for prospective development, probably as a building plot, and will be an element of value "realised" at that point as "development value". If Y then re-sells to Z for £20,000, Y will recoup the "development value"; but it was X, not Y, who "realised" it and should be taxed in respect of it. It is, so to speak, a "windfall" received by X and no-one else.

Three calculations may be applied to the disposal price: "Base A", "Base B" and "Base C". Whichever of these produces the highest amount of "base value" is deducted from the net disposal price in each case. The remainder, if any, is the "realised development value". In general terms, public bodies and charities are exempt from the tax. Public bodies which *pay* a disposal price to a vendor will themselves deduct the tax, if any, from the price before paying it.

B. Planning Compensation[9]

TOWN AND COUNTRY PLANNING ACT 1971

164. Compensation where planning permission revoked or modified. — (1) Where planning permission is revoked or modified by an order under section 45 of this Act . . . then if, on a claim made to the local planning authority within the time and in the manner prescribed by regulations under this Act, it is shown that a person interested in the land —

(a) has incurred expenditure in carrying out work which is rendered abortive by the revocation or modification: or

(b) has otherwise sustained loss or damage which is directly attributable to the revocation or modification.

the local planning authority shall pay to that person compensation in respect of that expenditure, loss or damage.

(2) For the purposes of this section, any expenditure incurred in the preparation of plans for the purpose of any work, or upon other similar matters preparatory thereto, shall be taken to be included in the expenditure incurred in carrying out that work.

(4) In calculating, for the purposes of this section, the amount of any loss or damage consisting of depreciation of the value of an interest in land, it shall be assumed that planning permission would be granted for development of the land of any class specified in Schedule 8 to this Act[10].

---

[9] Heap, pp. 249–263; Davies, pp. 322–358 Pl. Enc. 2: 3005–3140.

[10] There is a similar right to compensation for discontinuance orders (T.C.P.A. 1971, s. 170) extending also to the net cost of works involved. See *Blow v Norfolk County Council* [1967] 1 WLR 1280, [1966] 3 All ER 579. Compensation is also payable in some cases in respect of tree preservation, listed building preservation, stop notices, pedestrian precincts and advertisements (T.C.P.A. 1971, ss. 171–177, 212); see *Bollans v Surrey County Council* (1969), 20 P & CR 745 (trees). See also T.C.P.A. 1971, s. 165 (p. 794, ante).

169.   Compensation for planning decisions restricting development other than new development. — (1) The provisions of this section shall have effect where, on an application for planning permission to carry out development of any class specified in Part II of Schedule 8 to this Act, the Secretary of State, either on appeal or on the reference of the application to him for determination, refuses the permission or grants it subject to conditions.

(2) If, on a claim made to the local planning authority within the time and in the manner prescribed by regulations under this Act, it is shown that the value of the interest of any person in the land is less than it would have been if the permission had been granted, or had been granted unconditionally, as the case may be, the local planning authority shall pay to that person compensation of an amount equal to the difference.

(8) No compensation shall be payable under this section in respect of an interest in land in respect of which a purchase notice is served.

Full compensation for loss is allowed as of right where an *existing* right to development value is lost by reason of revocation, modification or discontinuance, but *not* where a refusal to grant unconditional planning permission prevents the right from being obtained at the outset. Even in the latter case, however, full compensation is allowed as of right in *certain* cases (on a decision of the Secretary of State, not of a local planning authority) where the development restricted is not "new" or substantial, but merely marginal to "existing use". Development of the latter type is specified in T.C.P.A. 1971, Schedule 8[11]. Full compensation is payable by local planning authorities, under Part VIII of the 1971 Act (sections 164–179), in these various cases.

It may be noted that development within Parts I and II of the Eighth Schedule of the Town and Country Planning Act 1971 is assumed to be permitted when assessing compensation for compulsory purchase[12], but that *planning* compensation is only payable where development within Part II, not Part I, is restricted. The only remedy for the latter is to serve a purchase notice.

But compensation is payable in some cases even for refusal at the outset to grant an unconditional planning permission for "new development". It is payable only to the extent that a special asset known as the "unexpended balance of established development value" (the "U.X.B.") attaches to the claimant's interest in the land; though, even where this is so, there are many cases where the right is

---

[11] See also, s. 278 and Sch. 18. "New development" is defined in T.C.P.A. 1971, s. 22 (5), as "any development *other than* development of a class specified in Part I or Part II of Sch. 8 to this Act."

[12] Land Compensation Act 1961, s. 15. See p. 835, n. 9, ante. Schedule 8, which cannot be reproduced here for reasons of space, is of great importance, though in the sphere of compensation and not otherwise.

excluded[13]. It is payable by the Secretary of State (as distinct from the varieties of planning compensation already discussed, which are payable by *local* planning authorities) under Part VII of the Act (sections 134–163).

The "unexpended balance" represents an established claim to loss of development value under the Town and Country Planning Act 1947, adjusted and converted into an asset attached to the land by virtue of the Town and Country Planning Act 1954. It comes to an end as a result of realising development value by the receipt of planning or compulsory purchase compensation, or by the carrying out of "new" development[14]. If "U.X.B." compensation over £20 is paid, a notice must be registered as a local land charge. If permission is then granted for certain substantial kinds of development, that compensation will have to be repaid before development begins[15].

Disputes over compensation go to the Lands Tribunal[16]

TOWN AND COUNTRY PLANNING ACT 1971

146. General provision as to right to compensation. — Subject to the provisions of this Part of this Act[17], a person shall be entitled to compensation under this Part of this Act in respect of a planning decision whereby planning permission for the carrying out of new development of land is refused, or is granted subject to conditions, if —

(a) at the time of the decision he is entitled to an interest in any land to which the decision relates which has an unexpended balance of established development value; and

(b) the value of that interest, or, in the case of an interest extending to other land, the value of that interest in so far as it subsists in such land as is referred to in the preceding paragraph, is depreciated by the decision.

152. General provisions as to amount of compensation. — (1) Where a person is entitled to compensation under this Part of this Act in respect of depreciation by a planning decision of the value of an interest in land, the amount of the compensation, subject to the following provisions of this section, shall be whichever is the lesser of the following amounts, that is to say —

(a) the amount by which the value of that interest ... is depreciated by the decision; and

(b) the amount of the unexpended balance of established development value, immediately before the decision, of ... the land in which the interest subsists. ...

---

[13] T.C.P.A. 1971, ss. 147–149.

[14] T.C.P.A. 1971, ss. 134–145.

[15] T.C.P.A. 1971, ss. 158–161. See also ss. 166–168, and *Ministry of Housing and Local Government v Sharp* [1970] 2 QB 223, [1970] 1 All ER 1009.

[16] T.C.P.A. 1971, ss. 156, 179 (relating respectively to Parts VII and VIII of the Act).

[17] Part VII. And see T.C.P. (Compensation and Certificates) Regulations 1974 (S.I. 1974 No. 1242).

X.   New Planning Legislation

The Local Government, Planning and Land (No. 2) Bill currently before Parliament (March 1980) contains a number of clauses the purpose of which is to modify existing law on planning and compulsory purchase. They do not make many radical changes but deal rather with a variety of particular matters, the chief of which are as follows.

Parts XI and XII of the Bill repeal most of the Community Land Act 1975, but retain in being the Land Authority for Wales which will continue to exercise the function of acquiring land for disposal to developers in circumstances where it is likely that development could not otherwise be carried out. Certain incidental modifications in planning and compulsory purchase procedures are preserved, relating (for example) to certificates of appropriate alternative development and acquisition of land by the Crown.

Part IX amends planning law by reducing the part played by county councils in particular planning procedures, by allowing local plans to be adopted in advance of the corresponding structure plans, and by introducing a system of charging fees for planning applications. Certain changes in the control of amenity are introduced. Tree preservation orders are to be confirmed in future by local planning authorities. The Secretary of State will be empowered to certify that he does not propose to "list" any specified building, in which case he is debarred from doing so for five years; and he may make "repair grant agreements" towards meeting the cost of repairing buildings of special architectural or historic interest in conservation areas which are included in a special "town scheme."

Part X will empower the Secretary of State to compile a register of land held by public bodies which is "not sufficiently used" and order the sale of such land. Part XIV will empower him to continue "community land" policies in a modified form by directing local authorities to make assessments of land in their area which is suitable and available for housing development. It also makes provision for payment of grants towards the cost of reclaiming derelict land; and it modifies in detail the procedures for control of acquisition, appropriation and disposal of land by public authorities including the Crown.

Part XIII abolishes the rule that claims for compensation for depreciation of land by public works, under Part I of the Land Compensation Act 1973, must be made within two years of the "first claim date" (which is one year after the works first came into public use). It also abolishes the rule that "home loss payments" must be claimed within six months of displacement from a dwelling.

Parts XV and XVI amend the law relating to new towns, and introduce a new concept — "urban development" areas and corporations. These will resemble new towns and their development corporations, and their functions will comprise and assembly, planning, housing and the encouragement of industry. They will have planning and building control and also housing functions, and will share the grant and loan powers conferred on district councils by the Inner Urban Areas Act 1978 for encouraging commercial and industrial enterprise.

XI. Purchasers and Planning

It is often said that conveyancers nowadays need to spend more time investigating the planning aspects of land transactions than the pure conveyancing aspects. It will be apparent from reading this chapter why that should be so.

A purchaser's solicitor should normally, as a matter of course, apply for an official search of the relevant local land charges registers[18], which will disclose any restrictive orders of a public nature which affect the property[19]. In addition, there are the local lists of buildings of special interest, and also registers of planning applications and applications for consent to display advertisements, which are all available for public inspection and should be inspected if the circumstances warrant it[20].

---

[18] The County Council and the District Council for the area will each maintain such a register. See, generally, the Local Land Charges Rules, 1977 (S.I. 1977 No. 848); p. 46, ante.

[19] Planning examples are revocation and discontinuance orders, planning agreements, tree preservation orders, notices of compulsory purchase orders if vesting declarations are to be made, enforcement notices, planning compensation notices, and lists of buildings of special architectural or historic interest.

[20] T.C.P.A. 1971, ss. 34, 54; T.C.P. (Control of Advertisements) Regulations 1969, reg. 31. (S.I. 1969, No. 1532, as amended by S.I. 1975 No. 898).

Index